W9-AYQ-424

Designing Experiments and Analyzing Data

A Model Comparison Perspective

Designing Experiments and Analyzing Data

A Model Comparison Perspective

Scott E. Maxwell
University of Notre Dame

Harold D. Delaney
University of New Mexico

LAWRENCE ERLBAUM ASSOCIATES, PUBLISHERS
Mahwah, New Jersey   London

Acknowledgments

Excerpts on pp. 19, 20, from Kuhn, Thomas S., *The Structure of Scientific Revolutions*, Second Edition, pp. viii, 10, 102, 170-1, 206-7. Reprinted by permission of The University of Chicago Press.

Excerpts on pp. 7, 61 from Einstein, Albert, "Physics and Reality," *Journal of the Franklin Institute*, Copyright 1936, Volume 221, pp. 351-2. Reprinted with permission from Pergamon Press, Inc.

SAS is a registered trademark of SAS Institute Inc., Cary, North Carolina; BMDP is a registered trademark of BMDP Statistical Software, Inc. Los Angeles, California; SPSS-X is a registered trademark of SPSS Inc., Chicago, Illinois.

Originally published in 1990.

Lawrence Erlbaum Associates, Inc., Publishers
10 Industrial Avenue
Mahwah, New Jersey 07430

Library of Congress Cataloging-in-Publication Data
Maxwell, Scott E.
    Design experiments and analyzing data : a model comparison
  perspective / Scott E. Maxwell, Harold D. Delaney.
        p.   cm.
      Bibliography: p.
      Includes index.
      ISBN 0-8058-3706-X
      1. Experimental design. I. Delaney, Harold D. II. Title
      QA279.M384   1989
      519.5'3–dc20   89-34423

Books published by Lawrence Erlbaum Associates are printed on acid-free paper, and their bindings are chosen for strength and durability.

Printed in the United States of America

10 9 8 7 6 5 4 3 2 1

To our parents, and
To Katy, Melissa, Clifford
Nancy, Ben, Sarah, and Jesse

Contents

Preface

This book is written to serve as either a textbook or a reference book on the topic of designing experiments and analyzing experimental data. Our particular concern is with the methodology appropriate in the behavioral sciences. We believe that the model comparison perspective we introduce early in the book offers significant advantages over the traditional variance partitioning approach usually used to teach analysis of variance. Instead of presenting each experimental design in terms of a set of computational formulas to be used only for that design, the model comparison approach allows us to present a few basic formulas that can be applied with the same underlying logic to every experimental design. Our approach establishes an integrative theme that shows how the various designs we present are related to one another. In fact, the underlying logic can be applied directly to more complex data-analytic methodologies such as the structural equation modeling technique known as LISREL. Thus, our approach provides both a conceptual framework for understanding experimental design and a strong foundation for readers who decide to pursue more advanced topics at a later date.

Our emphasis throughout the book is conceptual, with an emphasis on understanding the logical underpinnings of design and analysis. We present definitional instead of computational formulas, relying on statistical packages to perform actual computations on a computer. The emphasis on definitional formulas allows us to concentrate on the meaning of what is being computed instead of worrying exclusively about how to perform the calculation. Nevertheless, we recognize the importance of doing hand calculations on occasion to better understand what it is that is being computed. Thus, we have included a number of exercises at the end of each chapter that give the reader the opportunity to calculate quantities by hand on small data sets. We have also included many thought questions, which are intended to develop a deeper understanding of the subject and to help the reader draw out logical connections in the materials. Finally, realistic data sets at the end of each chapter allow the reader to experience an analysis of data from each design in its entirety. Solutions to numerous selected (starred) exercises are provided at the back of the book. Answers for the remaining exercises are available in a supplementary solutions manual for instructors who adopt the book for classroom use.

The model comparison approach allows us to cover certain topics that are often omitted in experimental design texts. For example, we are able to introduce the multivariate approach to repeated measures as a straightforward generalization of the approach used for between-subjects designs. Similarly, the analysis of non-orthogonal designs (that is, designs with unequal cell sizes) fits nicely into our approach. Further, not only is the presentation of the standard analysis of covariance facilitated by the model comparison perspective, but we are also able to consider models that allow for heterogeneity of regression across conditions.

Despite the inclusion of such advanced topics, the necessary background for the book is minimal. We assume that readers will have had one undergraduate statistics course, and no mathematics beyond high school algebra is required.

The organization of the book allows it to be used in many different ways. Depending on the reader's or instructor's interests, chapters can be covered in various sequences or even omitted.

Part I (Chapters 1 and 2) explains the logic of experimental design and the role of randomization in the conduct of behavioral research. This introduction to the interface between experimental design and the philosophy of science establishes a broader context for understanding statistics. Although Part I is not required for understanding statistical issues in the remaining chapters of the book, it does help the reader see the "big picture."

Part II provides the foundation for the book. Chapter 3 introduces the concept of comparing full and restricted models. Most of the formulas used throughout the book are introduced in Chapters 3 and 4. Although most readers will want to follow these two chapters by reading at least Chapters 5, 7, and 8 in Part II, it would be possible to go straight to Chapters 13 and 14 on the multivariate approach to repeated measures if an advanced reader were interested only in that topic. Chapter 9, on Analysis of Covariance, is written in such a way that it can be read either immediately following Chapter 8 or deferred until after Part III.

Part III describes design and analysis principles for within-subjects designs (that is, repeated measures designs). These chapters are written to provide maximum flexibility in choosing an approach to the topic. In our own one-semester experimental design courses, we find it necessary to omit one of the four chapters on repeated measures. Covering only Chapters 11, 13, and 14 introduces the univariate approach to repeated measures but covers the multivariate approach in greater depth. Alternatively, covering only Chapters 11, 12, and 13 emphasizes the univariate approach. If time permits, one could cover all four chapters in the order they appear or follow the sequence 11, 13, 12, 14 to introduce both approaches to analyzing a simple repeated measures design before proceeding to more complicated designs. On the other hand, advanced readers might skip Chapters 11 and 12 entirely and read only Chapters 13 and 14. Although the difficulty level of Chapters 13 and 14 also permits less advanced readers to follow this strategy, they would probably need to familiarize themselves with the mixed-model approach at some point, given its continued application in behavioral research today.

Finally, Part IV presents robust alternatives to the methods given in Chapters 3 through 14. These can be introduced in either of two ways. First, Chapter 15 obviously can be read after all the other chapters. Second, because the sections of Chapter 15 parallel the sequence of topics in Chapters 3 through 14, it is also possible to cover each alternative in Chapter 15 after the more standard approach in the earlier chapter. Readers can select only a subset of these topics if they so desire.

We have taken several steps throughout the book to increase the readability of equations. First, the most important equations are numbered consecutively in each chapter as they are introduced. Second, if the same equation is repeated at a later point within the chapter, we use its original equation number followed by the designation "repeated," both to remind the reader that this equation has been introduced and to facilitate finding the point where it was first presented. Third, cross-references to equations in other chapters are indicated by including the chapter number followed by a period in front of the equation number. For example, a reference in Chapter 5 to Equation 4.35 refers to Equation 35 in Chapter 4. However, within Chapter 4 this equation is referred to simply as Equation 35. Finally, we have frequently provided tables that summarize important equations for a particular design or a specific concept, not only to make equations easier to find, but also to facilitate direct comparisons of the equations to enhance understanding of their differences and similarities.

Although only two names appear on the cover of this book, the number of individuals who contributed either directly or indirectly to its development defies accurate estimation. Because the preface is required to be shorter than the body of the text, we have to be selective in our acknowledgments. The advantages of the model comparison approach were first introduced to us by Elliot Cramer when we were graduate students at the University of North Carolina at Chapel Hill. We, however, are the ones to be blamed for the fact that it took us more than a dozen years to explore these advantages in depth and to present them in the current volume. We are obviously responsible as well for any deficiencies that remain in the book despite our best efforts to eliminate them. Much of the philosophy underlying our approach, though, can be traced to Elliot and our other mentors at the L. L. Thurstone Psychometric Lab (Mark Appelbaum, John Carroll, Lyle Jones, and Tom Wallsten). More recently we have benefited from insightful comments from many current and former students and teaching assistants who have used the book in manuscript form. We would particularly like to thank David Francis of the University of Houston for suggestions based on his experiences using earlier drafts of the book. We are also indebted to the University of Notre Dame and the University of New Mexico for providing us with sabbatical leaves to work on the book, and to the University of Edinburgh Psychology Department for accomodating one of us (H.D.D.) while on sabbatical. The encouragement of our colleagues must be mentioned, especially that of David Cole, George Howard, Steve Gangestad, Tim Goldsmith, Dick Harris, Bill Miller, and John Oller. The excellent secretarial support provided by Edie Hawley, Edna Mutchler, Judy Spiro, Pauline Wright, and Mary Hungate was also indispensable.

Similarly, Ken King, psychology editor at Wadsworth, has shown remarkable patience in understanding how we seemed to miss almost every deadline. We would also like to thank Michael Oates and Donna Linden for their excellent editorial help. Reviewers who provided many worthwhile suggestions for improving the text were James E. Carlson, Auburn University at Montgomery; James Jaccard, State University of New York at Albany; Willard Larkin, University of Maryland, College Park; K. J. Levy, State University of New York at Buffalo; Marjorie Marlin, University of Missouri, Columbia; Ralph G. O'Brien, University of Tennessee; Edward R. Stearns, California State University, Fullerton; Rand Wilcox, University of Southern California; and Jon Williams, Kenyon College.

Finally, and most importantly, we thank our families for providing us with the warmth, love, and understanding that have helped us not just to complete projects such as this but also to appreciate what is most important in life. Most critical are the roles played by Katy Brissey Maxwell and Nancy Hurst Delaney who, among many other things, made it possible in the midst of busy family and professional lives for us to invest the tremendous amount of time required to complete the book. Our parents, Lylton and Ruth Maxwell and Hugh and Lee Delaney, and our children, Melissa and Clifford Maxwell and Ben, Sarah, and Jesse Delaney, have also enriched our lives in ways we cannot begin to express. It is to our families that we dedicate this book.

Designing Experiments and Analyzing Data

A Model Comparison Perspective

Part One

Conceptual Bases of Experimental Design and Analysis

Man, being the servant and interpreter of Nature, can do and understand so much, and so much only, as he has observed, in fact or in thought, of the course of Nature. ... Human knowledge and human power meet in one; for where the course is not known, the effect cannot be produced. Nature, to be commanded, must be obeyed.

FRANCIS BACON, *NOVUM ORGANUM*, 1620

1   The Logic of Experimental Design

METHODS OF EXPERIMENTAL DESIGN and data analysis derive their value from the contributions they make to the more general enterprise of science. To appreciate what design and analysis can and cannot do for you, it is necessary to understand something of the logic of science. Although we will not attempt to provide a comprehensive introduction to the philosophy of science, we feel it is necessary to present some of the difficulties involved in attempting to draw valid inferences from experimental data regarding the truth of a given scientific explanation of a particular phenomenon.

We begin with a discussion of the traditional view of science and mention some of the difficulties inherent in this view. Next, we consider various responses that have been offered to the critique of the traditional view. Finally, we discuss distinctions that can be made among different types of validity and enumerate some specific types of threats to drawing valid inferences from data.

THE TRADITIONAL VIEW OF SCIENCE

Many trace the origins of modern science to the British statesman and philosopher Sir Francis Bacon (1561–1626). The context in which Bacon was writing was that of a culture that for over 1800 years had been held in the grips of an Aristotelian, rationalistic approach to obtaining knowledge. Although Aristotle had considered induction, the "predominant mode of his logic was deduction, and its ideal was the syllogism" (Durant & Durant, 1961, p. 174). Bacon recognized the stagnation that had resulted in science because of this stress on deduction rather than observation and because the ultimate appeal in scientific questions was to the authority of "the Philosopher," Aristotle. Bacon's complaint was thus not so much against the ancients as with their disciples, particularly the Scholastic philosophers of the late Middle Ages (Robinson, 1981, p. 209). Bacon's *Novum Organum* (1620/1928a) proposed that this old method be replaced with a new organ or system based on the inductive study of nature itself. In short, what Bacon immodestly attempted was to "commence a total reconstruction of sciences, [practical] arts, and all human knowledge, raised upon the proper foundations" (Bacon, 1620/1928b, p. 4). The critical element in this foundation was the method of experimentation. Thus, a deliberate manipulation of variables was to replace the "noting and naming" kind of empiricism that had characterized the Aristotelian approach when it did lower itself to observation (Robinson, 1981, p. 212).

The character of Bacon's reconstruction, however, was to have positive *and* negative consequences for the conception of science that predominated for the next three centuries. The Baconian ideal for science was as follows: At the start of their research, experimenters were to remove from their thinking all the "'idols' or time-honored illusions and fallacies, born of [their] personal idiosyncrasies of judgment or the traditional beliefs and dogmas of [their] group" (Durant & Durant, 1961, p. 175). Thus, in the Baconian view, scientific observations were to be made in a purely objective fashion by individuals having no loyalties to any hypotheses or beliefs that would cause them to be blind to any portion of the empirical evidence. The correct conclusions and explanatory principles would then emerge from the evidence relatively automatically and without the particular philosophical presuppositions of the experimenter playing any part. Thus, the "course of Nature" could be clearly observed if the experimenter would only look at Nature as it is. Nature, as it were, unambiguously dictated the adoption of true theories. The whole process of science, it was thought, could be purely objective, empirical, and rational.

Although this view of science may still be present in popular thought, and perhaps even be perpetuated by the treatment of the scientific method given by introductory texts in the sciences, it has undeniable flaws. Instead of personal judgment playing no role in science, it is critical to the whole process. Whether one considers the data collection, data analysis, or interpretation phases of a study, the process is not purely objective and rule-governed. First, the scientist's preexisting ideas about what is interesting and relevant undeniably guide decisions about what data are to be collected. For example, if one is studying the effects of drug treatments on recovery of function following brain injury, one has decided in advance that the drugs present in the bloodstream may be a relevant factor and one has likely also decided that the day of the week on which the drug treatment is administered is likely *not* a relevant factor. Data cannot be collected without some preexisting ideas about what may be relevant because it is those decisions that determine the variables to be manipulated or assessed in a particular experimental design. There are no logical formulas telling the scientist which particular variables must be examined in a given study.

Similarly, the patterns observed in a set of data are influenced by the ideas the investigator brings to the research. To be sure, a great deal can be said about what methods of analysis are most appropriate to aid in this pattern-detection process for a particular experimental design. In fact, much of this book is devoted to just that. However, both experiments in cognitive psychology and examples from the history of science suggest that to a large extent what one sees is determined by what one expects to see (see Kuhn, 1970, especially Chapter VI). Although statistical analysis can objectify to some extent the process of looking for patterns in data, statistical methods, as Koch (1981) and others have pointed out, even when correctly applied do not assure that the most appropriate ways of organizing the data will be found. For example, in a simple four-group experimental design, there are, at least in theory, an infinite number of comparisons of the four group means that could be tested for significance. Thus, even assuming that the most appropriate data had been collected, it is entirely possible that a researcher might fail to examine the most illuminating comparison. Admittedly, this problem of correctly perceiving at least approximately what the patterns in your data are is less serious than that of collecting the relevant data in the first place or that of what one makes of the pattern once it is discerned. Nonetheless, there are no absolutely foolproof strategies for analyzing data.

The final step in the inductive process is the most troublesome. Once data relevant to a question are collected and their basic pattern noted, how should the finding be explained? Put bluntly, "there is no *rigorous logical* procedure which accounts for the birth of theories or of the novel concepts and connections which new theories often involve. There is no 'logic of discovery'" (Ratzsch, 1986, p. 23). As many a doctoral candidate knows from painful experience after puzzling over a set of unanticipated results, data sometimes do not clearly suggest any theory, much less dictate the "correct" one.

RESPONSES TO THE CRITICISMS OF THE IDEA OF PURE SCIENCE

Over the years, the pendulum has swung back and forth regarding the validity and implications of this critique of the allegedly pure objectivity, rationality, and empiricism of science. We consider various kinds of responses to these criticisms. First, it is virtually universally acknowledged that certain *assumptions* must be made to do science at all. Next, we consider three major alternatives that have figured prominently in the shaping of *philosophy of science* in the twentieth century. Although there have been attempts to revise and maintain some form of the traditional view of science well into the current century, there is now wide agreement that the criticisms were more sound than the most influential revision of the traditional view. In the course of this discussion, we indicate our views on these various perspectives on philosophy of science and point out certain of the inherent limitations of science.

Assumptions

All rational argument must begin with certain assumptions, whether one is engaged in philosophical, scientific, or competitive debating. Although these assumptions are typically only implicitly present in the practice of scientific activities, there are some basic principles essential to science that are not subject to empirical test but that must be presupposed for science to make sense. Following Underwood (1957, pp. 3–6), we consider two assumptions to be most fundamental: the lawfulness of nature and finite causation.

Lawfulness of Nature. Although possibly itself a corollary of a more basic philosophical assumption, the assumption that the events of nature display a certain lawfulness is a presupposition clearly required by science. This is the belief that nature, despite its obvious complexity, is not entirely chaotic: regularities and principles in the outworking of natural events exist and wait to be discovered. Thus, on this assumption, an activity like science, which has as its goal the cataloging and understanding of such regularities, is conceivable.

There are a number of facets or corollaries to the principle of the lawfulness of nature that can be distinguished. First, at least since the ancient Greeks, there has been agreement on the assumption that *nature is understandable*, although not necessarily on the methods for how that understanding should be achieved. In our era, with the growing appreciation of the vastness of the universe and the complexities and indeterminacies at the subatomic level, the belief that we can understand is recognized as not a trivial assumption. At the same time, the undeniable successes of science in prediction and control of natural events provide ample evidence of the fruitfulness of the assumption and, in some sense, are more impressive in light of current knowledge. As Einstein said, the most incomprehensible thing about the universe is that it is comprehensible[1] (Einstein, 1936, p. 351; see Koch, 1981, p. 265).

A second facet of the general belief in the lawfulness of nature is that *nature is uniform*—that is, processes and patterns observed on only a limited scale will hold universally. This is obviously required in sciences like astronomy if statements are to be made on the basis of current observations about the characteristics of a star thousands of years ago. However, the validity of the assumption is questionable at least in certain areas of the behavioral sciences. Two dimensions of the problem can be distinguished. First, relationships observed in the psychology of the 1990s may not be true of the psychology of the 1930s or 2030s. For example, the social psychology of attitudes in some sense must change as societal attitudes change. Rape, for instance, was regarded as a more serious crime than homicide in the 1920s but as a much less serious crime than homicide in the 1960s (Coombs, 1967). One possible way out of the apparent bind this places one in is to theorize at a more abstract level. Rather than attempting to predict attitudes toward the likely suitability for employment of a rapist some time after a crime, one might instead theorize about the possible suitability for future employment of someone who had committed a crime of a specified level of perceived seriousness and allow which crime occupied that level to vary over time. Although one can offer such abstract theories, it is an empirical question as to whether the relationship will be constant over time when the particular crime occupying a given level of seriousness is changing.

A second dimension of the presupposition of the uniformity of nature that must be considered in the behavioral sciences pertains to the homogeneity of experimental material (subjects, people) being investigated. Although a chemist might safely assume that one hydrogen atom will behave essentially the same as another when placed in a given experimental situation, it is not at all clear that the people studied by a psychologist can be expected to display the same sort of uniformity. Admittedly, there are areas of psychology—for example, the study of vision—where there is sufficient uniformity across individuals in the processes at work that the situation approaches that in the physical sciences. In fact, studies with very small numbers of subjects are common in the perception area. However, generally it is the case that individual differences among people are sufficiently pronounced that they must be reckoned with explicitly. This variability is, indeed, a large part of the need for behavioral scientists to be trained in the areas of experimental design and statistics.

These areas focus on methods for accommodating to this sort of variability. We deal with the logic of this accommodation at numerous points, particularly in our discussion of external validity in this chapter and randomization in the next. In addition, Chapter 9 on concomitant variables is devoted in its entirety to methods for incorporating variables assessing individual differences among subjects into one's design and analysis.

A third facet of the assumption of the lawfulness of nature is the *principle of causality*. One definition of this principle, which was suggested by Underwood, is that "every natural event (phenomenon) is assumed to have a cause, and if that causal situation could be exactly reinstituted, the event would be duplicated" (Underwood, 1957, p. 4). At the time Underwood was writing, there was fair agreement regarding causality in science as a deterministic, mechanistic process. The past 30 years, however, have seen the emergence of a variety of views regarding what it means to say that one event causes another and, equally important, regarding how we can acquire knowledge about causal relationships. As Cook and Campbell have written, "the epistemology of causation, and of the scientific method more generally, is at present in a productive state of near chaos" (Cook & Campbell, 1979, p. 10).

Cook and Campbell admirably characterize the evolution of thinking in the philosophy of science about causality (1979, Chapter 1). We can devote space here to only the briefest of summaries of that problem. Through most of its first 100 years as an experimental discipline, the view of causation offered by the Scottish empiricist philosopher David Hume (1711–1776) has heavily influenced psychology. Hume argued that the inference of a causal relationship between unobservables is never justified logically. Even in the case of one billiard ball striking another, one does not observe one ball causing another to move. Rather, one simply observes a correlation between the ball being struck and its moving. Thus, for Hume, correlation is all we can know about causality. These eighteenth-century ideas, filtered through the nineteenth-century positivism of Auguste Comte (1798–1857), pushed twentieth-century psychology toward an empiricist monism, a hesitancy to propose causal relationships between hypothetical constructs. Rather, the search was for functional relationships between observables or, only slightly less modestly, between theoretical terms, each of which was operationally defined by one particular measurement instrument or set of operations in a given study. Thus, Boring in 1923 would define intelligence as what an intelligence test measures. Science was to give us sure knowledge of relationships that had been rigorously confirmed by empirical observation.

These views of causality have been found to be lacking on a number of counts. First, as every elementary statistics text reiterates, causation is now regarded as something different from mere correlation. This point must be stressed again here because we will be describing relationships in this text with statistical models that can be used for either correlational or causal relationships. This is potentially confusing, particularly because we follow the convention of referring to certain terms in the models as "effects." At times these effects will be the magnitude of the change an independent variable causes in the dependent variable; at other times, the effect is better thought of as simply a measure of the strength of the correlational relationship between two measures. The strength of the support for the interpretation of a relationship as causal, then, hinges not on the statistical model used but on the nature of the design employed. For example, in a correlational study, one of the variables may be dichotomous, such as high or low anxiety, rather than continuous. That one could carry out a *t* test of the difference in depression between high- and low-anxiety groups, rather than computing a correlation between depression and anxiety, does *not* mean that you have a more secure basis for inferring causality than if you had simply computed the correlation. If the design of the study were such that anxiety was a measured trait of individuals rather than a variable independently manipulated by the experimenter, then *that* limits the strength of the inference rather than the kind of statistic computed.

Second, using a single measurement device as definitional of one's construct entails a variety of difficulties, not least of which is that meters (or measures) sometimes are broken (invalid). We have more to say about construct validity later. For now, we simply note that in the behavioral sciences "one-variable, 'pure' measuring instruments are an impossibility. *All* measures involve many known theoretical variables, many as yet unknown ones, and many unproved presumptions" (Cook & Campbell, 1979, p. 14).

Finally, whereas early empiricist philosophers required causes and effects to occur in "constant conjunction"—that is, the cause was necessary and sufficient for the effect—current views are again more modest. The evidence supporting behavioral "laws" is typically probabilistic. If 90 of 100 patients in a treatment group, as opposed to 20 of 100 in the control group, were to be cured according to some criterion, the reaction is to conclude that the treatment caused a very large effect, *instead* of reasoning that, because the treatment was not sufficient for 10 subjects, it should not be regarded as the cause of the effect.

Most scientists, particularly those in the physical sciences, are generally realists, that is, they see themselves as pursuing theoretical truth about hidden but real mechanisms whose properties and relationships explain observable phenomena. Thus, the realist physicist would not merely say, as the positivist would, that a balloon shrinks as a function of time. Rather, he or she would proceed to say that the leakage of gas molecules caused the observed shrinkage. This is an assertion that not just a causal relationship was constructed in the physicist's mind but that a causal relationship really exists among entities outside of any human mind. Thus, in the realist view, theoretical assertions "have objective contents which can be either right or wrong" (Cook & Campbell, 1979, p. 29).

Others have wanted to include under their concept of cause, at least in sciences studying people, human volition. For example, Collingwood (1940) suggested "that which is 'caused' is the free and deliberate act of a conscious and responsible agent, and 'causing' him to do it means affording him a motive for doing it" (p. 285). This is the kind of attribution for the cause of action presupposed throughout most of the history of Western civilization but is now only a minority viewpoint in modern psychology, although still the prevailing view in other disciplines such as history and law. However, Howard and Conway (1986) and others argue that work in experimental psychology can proceed from this framework as well.

Thus, we see that a variety of views are possible about the kind of causal relationships that may be discovered through experimentation: the relationship may be probabilistic or not, the relationship may or may not be regarded as referring to real entities, and the role of the participant (subject) may or may not be regarded as that of an active agent. This last point makes clear that the assumption of the lawfulness of nature does not commit one to a position of philosophical determinism as a personal philosophy of life (Eacker, 1972). However, to presume the principle of causality is to adopt a methodological determinism. That is, to do science is to adopt determinism as a working assumption in the lab. In the remainder of the text, we discuss algebraic models of dependent variables that embody this assumption that the data to be analyzed are determined, within statistical limits, to take on certain values. You are assuming, in effect, that determinism is a sufficiently close approximation to the truth that the consistencies in your data will be discernible through the cloud of random variation (see Meehl, 1970b).

It should perhaps be noted, before we leave the discussion of causality, that in any situation there are a variety of levels at which one could conduct a causal analysis. Both nature and science are stratified, and properties of entities at one level cannot, in general, be reduced to constellations of properties of entities at a lower level. For example, simple table salt (NaCl) possesses properties that are different from either the properties of sodium (Na) or chloride (Cl) (see Manicas & Secord, 1983). To cite another simple example, consider the question of what causes a room to suddenly become dark. One could focus on what causes the light in the room to stop glowing, giving an explanation at the level of physics by talking about what happens in terms of electric currents when the switch controlling the bulb is turned off. A detailed, or even an exhaustive, account of this event at the level of physics would not do away with the need for a psychological explanation of why a person flipped off the switch (see Cook & Campbell, 1979, p. 15). Psychologists are often quick to argue against the fallacy of reductionism when it is hinted that psychology might some day be reduced to physics or, perhaps, biology. However, the same argument applies with equal force to the limitations of the causal relationships that behavioral scientists can hope to discover through empirical investigation. For example, a detailed, or even an exhaustive, psychological account of how someone came to hold a particular belief says nothing about the philosophical question of whether such a belief is true.

Having considered the assumption of the lawfulness of nature in some detail, we now consider a second fundamental assumption of science.

Finite Causation.   Science not only presupposes that there are natural causes of events but also that these causes are finite in number and discoverable. Science is predicated on the belief that generality of some sort is possible; that is, it is not necessary to replicate the essentially infinite number of elements operating when an effect is initially observed in order to have a cause sufficient for producing the effect again.

Those readers who have previously studied the analysis of variance may find it meaningful to think of this principle as equivalent to saying "the highest-order interactions are not always significant." Because any scientific investigation must be carried out at a particular time and place, it is necessarily impossible to recreate exactly the state of affairs operating then and there. Rather, if science is to be possible, one must assume that the effect of a factor does not depend on the levels of all the other variables present when that effect is observed.

A corollary of the assumption of finite causation has a profound effect on how we carry out the model comparisons that are the focus of this book. This corollary is the bias toward simplicity. It is a preference we consistently maintain, in test after test, until the facts in a given situation overrule this bias.

Many scientists, particularly physicists, stress the importance of a strong belief in the ultimate simplicity of scientific laws. As Gardner points out, "this was especially true of Albert Einstein. 'Our experience,' he wrote, 'justifies us in believing that nature is the realization of the simplest conceivable mathematical ideas'" (Gardner, 1979, pp. 169–170; see Einstein, 1950, p. 64). However, as physiological psychologists studying the brain know only too well, there is also an enormous complexity to living systems that at least obscures if not makes questionable the appropriateness of simple models. And, indeed, the same may be true in some sense in all areas of science. Simple first approximations are over time qualified and elaborated: Newton's ideas and equations about gravity were modified by Einstein; Gall's phrenology was replaced by Flourens's views of both the unity and diversification of function of different portions of the brain.

Thus, we take as our guiding principle that set forward for the scientist by Alfred North Whitehead: "Seek simplicity and distrust it." Or again, Whitehead suggests that the goal of science "is to seek the simplest explanation of complex facts" while attempting to avoid the error of concluding nature is simpler than it really is (Whitehead, 1957).

Admittedly, the principle of parsimony is easier to give lip service to than to apply. The question of how to measure the simplicity of a theory is by no means an easy one. Fortunately, within mathematics and statistics the problem is somewhat more tractable, particularly if you restrict your attention to models of a particular form. We adopt the strategy in this text of restricting our attention to various special cases of the general linear model. Although this statistical model can subsume a great variety of different types of analyses, it takes a fundamentally simple view of nature in that such models assume the effects of various causal factors simply cumulate or are added together in determining a final outcome. In addition, the relative simplicity of two competing models in a given situation may be easily described by noting how many more terms are included in the more complex model. We begin developing these ideas in much greater practical detail in Chapter 3.

Modern Philosophy of Science

Having now considered two fundamental assumptions of science, we continue with our discussion of responses to the critique of the traditional view of science by considering four alternative philosophies of science. We begin this by considering an attempt to revise and maintain the traditional view that has played a particularly important role in the history of psychology.

Positivism. In our discussion of the principle of causality as an aspect of the assumption of the lawfulness of nature, we have already alluded to the influence of Humean empiricism and nineteenth-century positivism on twentieth-century psychology. This influence has been so dominant over the first three-quarters of this century that something more must be said about the principal tenets of this approach and the opposing movements that over the past 25 years have continued to grow in strength to the point of overtaking this view.

This view was crystallized by "the Vienna Circle," a group of philosophers, scientists, and mathematicians in Vienna who early in the twentieth century set forth a view of science known as logical positivism. Rudolph Carnap and Herbert Feigl were two of the principal figures in the movement, with Carl Hempel and A. J. Ayer also being among those whose writings heavily influenced psychology. Their logical positivism represented a wedding of Comte's positivism with the logicism of Whitehead and Russell's *Principia Mathematica*.

The aim of Auguste Comte's positive philosophy was to advance the study of society beyond a theological or metaphysical stage, in which explanations for phenomena were sought at the level of supernatural volition or abstract forces, to a "positive" stage. The stage was conceived to be positive in two distinct senses. First, all knowledge in the positive stage would be based on the positive (that is, certain, sure) methods of the physical sciences. Rather than seeking a cause or an essence, one is content with a law or empirical generalization. Second, Comte expected that the philosophical unity that would be effected by basing all knowledge on one method would result in a religion of humanity uniting all men and women (Morley, 1955).

The logical positivists combined this positivism with the logicism of Bertrand Russell's mathematical philosophy (Russell, 1919a). Logicism maintains that mathematics is logic. "All pure mathematics deals exclusively with concepts definable in terms of a very small number of fundamental concepts, and . . . all its propositions are deducible from a very small number of logical principles" (Russell, 1937, p. xv). Thus, all propositions in mathematics can be viewed as the result of applying truth functions to interpret various combinations of elementary or atomic propositions—that is, one determines the implications of the fundamental propositions according to a set of strictly logical rules. The meaning or content of the elementary propositions plays no role in the decision about whether a particular molecular proposition constructed out of elementary propositions by means of operators is true or false. Thus, like logic, mathematics fundamentally "is concerned solely with syntax, i.e., with formal relations between symbols in accordance with precise rules" (Brown, 1977, p. 21).

The modern logical positivism, which has played such a dominant role in the way academic psychologists have thought about their field, is a form of positivism that takes such symbolic logic as its primary analytic tool. This is seen in the central doctrine of logical positivism, known as the Verifiability Criterion of Meaning. According to this criterion, a proposition is meaningful "if and only if it can be empirically verified, i.e., if and only if there is an empirical method for deciding if it is true or false" (Brown, 1977, p. 21). (The only exception to this rule is the allowance for analytical propositions, which are propositions that assert semantic identities or which are true just in virtue of the terms involved, for example, "all bachelors are unmarried.") Thus, scientific terms that could not be defined strictly and completely in terms of sensory observations were regarded as literally meaningless. Any meaningful statement must reduce then to elementary propositions that can literally be seen to be true or false in direct observation. The bias against statistical tests and in favor of black-or-white, present-or-absent judgment of relationships in data was only one practical outworking of this philosophical view.

The goal of the logical positivists was then to subsume the rationale and practice of science under logic. The central difficulty preventing this was that scientific laws are typically stated as universal propositions that cannot be conclusively verified by any number of observations. One cannot show, for example, that all infants babble simply by observing some critical number of babbling babies. In addition, there are a number of paradoxes of confirmation about which no consensus was ever achieved as to how they should be resolved (Brown, 1977, Chapter 2). Hempel's "paradox of the ravens" illustrates the most famous of these. (Hempel, 1945). As Wesley Salmon succinctly summarized in *Scientific American*,

> If all ravens are black, surely non-black things must be non-ravens. The generalizations are logically equivalent, so that any evidence that confirms one must tend to confirm the other. Hence the observation of a green vase seems to confirm the hypothesis that all ravens are black. Even a black raven finds it strange (Salmon, 1973, p. 75).

Such paradoxes were especially troublesome to a philosophical school of thought that had taken the purely formal analysis of science as its task, attempting to emulate Whitehead and Russell's elegant symbolic logic approach that had worked so well in mathematics.

Although the dilemmas raised because the contrapositive of an assertion is logically equivalent to the original assertion [that is, (raven → black) ↔ (nonblack → nonraven)] may not seem relevant to how actual scientific theories come to be accepted, this is typical of the logical positivist approach. Having adopted symbolic logic as the primary tool for the analysis of science, then proposition forms and their manipulation became the major topic of discussion. The complete lack of detailed analysis of major scientific theories or research efforts is thus understandable but unfortunate. When psychologists adopted a positivistic approach as the model of rigorous research in the physical sciences, they were in fact adopting a method that bore virtually no relation to the way physicists actually approached research.

The most serious failing of logical positivism, however, was the failure of its foundational principle of the Verifiability Criterion of Meaning. A number of difficulties are inherent in this principle (Ratzsch, 1986, p. 37ff.), but the most critical ones include the following: First, as we have seen in our discussion of the assumptions of science, some of the basic principles needed for science to make sense are not empirically testable. One cannot prove that events have natural causes, but without such assumptions, scientific research is pointless.

Second, attempts such as operationism to adhere to the criterion resulted in major difficulties. The operationist thesis, so compatible with behaviorist approaches, was originally proposed by P. W. Bridgman: "In general, we mean by any concept nothing more than a set of operations; the concept is synonymous with the corresponding set of operations" (Bridgman, 1927, p. 5). However, this was taken to mean that if someone's height, much less their intelligence, were to be measured by two different sets of operations, these are not two different ways of measuring height but are definitional of different concepts, which should be denoted by different terms (see the articles in the 1945 Symposium on Operationism published in *Psychological Review*, especially Bridgman, 1945, p. 247). Obviously, rather than achieving the goal of parsimony, such an approach to meaning results in a proliferation of theoretical concepts and, in some sense, "surrender of the goal of systematizing large bodies of experience by means of a few fundamental concepts" (Brown, 1977, p. 40). Finally, the Verifiability Criterion of Meaning undercuts itself. The criterion itself is neither empirically testable nor obviously analytic. Thus, either it is itself meaningless, or meaningfulness does not depend on being empirically testable—that is, it is either meaningless or false.

Thus, positivism failed in its attempts to subsume science under formal logic, did not allow the presuppositions necessary for doing science, prevented the use of generally applicable theoretical terms, and was based on a criterion of meaning that was ultimately incoherent. Unfortunately, it is still the philosophy of science guiding the research efforts of some behavioral scientists.

Popper.   An alternative perspective, which we believe holds considerably more promise for appropriately conceptualizing science, is provided by Karl Popper's falsificationism (Popper, 1968) and subsequent revisions thereof (Lakatos, 1978; Newton-Smith, 1981). These ideas have received increasing attention of late in the literature on methodology for the behavioral sciences (see Cook & Campbell, 1979, p. 20ff.; Dar, 1987; Gholson & Barker, 1985; Serlin & Lapsley, 1985). Popper's central thesis is that deductive knowledge is logically possible. In contrast to the "confirmationist" approach of the logical positivists, Popperians believe progress occurs by falsifying theories. Although this may seem counterintuitive, it rests on the logic of the compelling nature of deductive as opposed to inductive arguments.

What might *seem* more plausible is to build up support for a theory by observing that the predictions of the theory are confirmed. The logic of the seemingly more plausible confirmationist approach may be expressed in the following syllogism:

Syllogism of Confirmation

If theory T is true, then the data will follow the predicted pattern P.

The data follow predicted pattern P.

Therefore, theory T is true.

This should be regarded as an invalid argument but perhaps not as a useless one. The error of thinking that data prove a theory is an example of the logical fallacy known as "affirming the consequent." The first assertion in the syllogism states that T is sufficient for P. Although such if-then statements are frequently misunderstood to mean that T is necessary for P (see Dawes, 1975), that does not follow. This is illustrated in the Venn diagram in Figure 1.1(a). As with any Venn diagram, it is necessary to view the terms of interest, in this case theory T and data pattern P, as

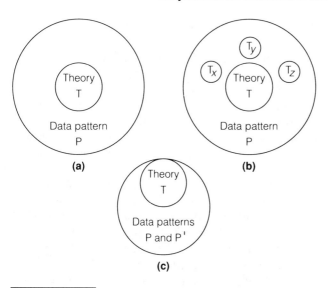

FIGURE 1.1   Venn diagrams illustrating that theory T is sufficient for determining data pattern P [see **(a)**], but that data pattern P is not sufficient for concluding theory T is correct [see **(b)**]. The Venn diagram in **(c)** is discussed later in this section of the text.

sets which are represented in the diagram as circles. This allows one to see visually the critical difference between a theory's being a sufficient explanation for a data pattern and its being necessarily correct. That theory T is sufficient for pattern P is represented by T being a subset of P. However, in principle at least, there are a number of other theories that also could explain the data, as illustrated by the presence of theories T_x, T_y, and T_z in Figure 1.1(b). Just being "in" pattern P does not imply that a point will be "in" theory T, that is, theory T is not necessarily true. In fact, the history of science provides ample support for what has been termed the *pessimistic induction*: "Any theory will be discovered to be false within, say 200 years of being propounded" (Newton-Smith, 1981, p. 14).

Popper's point, however, is that *rejection* of a theory as opposed to confirmation may, under certain assumptions, be done in a deductively rigorous manner. The syllogism now is:

Syllogism of Falsification

If theory T is true, then the data will follow the predicted pattern P.

The data do *not* follow predicted pattern P.

Therefore, theory T is false.

The logical point is that while the converse of an assertion is *not* equivalent to the assertion, the contrapositive, as we saw in the paradox of the ravens, *is*. That is, in symbols $(T \rightarrow P) \not\rightarrow (P \rightarrow T)$, but $(T \rightarrow P) \leftrightarrow (\text{not } P \rightarrow \text{not } T)$. In terms of Figure 1.1, if a point is in P, that does not mean it is in T, but if it is outside P, it is certainly outside T. Thus, although one cannot prove theories correct, one can, by this logic, prove them false.

While this example hopefully makes the validity of the syllogism of falsification clear, it is important to discuss some of the assumptions implicit in the argument and to raise briefly some of the concerns voiced by critics of Popper's philosophy, particularly as it applies to the behavioral sciences. First, consider the first line of the falsification syllogism. The one assumption pertinent to this, about which there is agreement, is that it is possible to derive predictions from theories. Confirmationists assume this as well. Naturally, theories differ in how well they achieve the desiderata of good theories regarding predictions—that is, they differ in how easily empirical predictions may be derived and in the range and specificity of these predictions. Unfortunately, psychological theories, particularly in recent years, tend to be very restricted in scope. And, unlike physics, the predictions that psychological theories do make are typically of a nonspecific form ("the groups will differ") rather than being point predictions ("the light rays will bend by x degrees as they go past the sun") (see Meehl, 1967, 1986). But whether specific or nonspecific, as long as it is assumed that a rather confident judgment can be made—for example, via a statistical test—about whether the results of an experiment are in accord with the predictions, the thrust of the argument maintains its force.

More troublesome than the lack of specificity or generality of the predictions of psychological theories is that the predictions not only depend on the core ideas of the theory but also on a set of additional hypotheses. These often have to do with the particular way in which the theoretical constructs of interest are implemented in a given study and may actually be more suspect than the theory itself. The difficulties this presents are well illustrated by a hypothetical research problem described by Paul Meehl:

> ...[I]n social science the auxiliaries A and the initial and boundary conditions of the system C are frequently as problematic as the theory T itself. *Example:* Suppose that a personologist or social psychologist wants to investigate the effect of social fear on visual perception. He attempts to mobilize anxiety in a sample of adolescent males, chosen by their scores on the Social Introversion (Si) scale of the Minnesota Multiphasic Personality Inventory (MMPI), by employing a research assistant who is a raving beauty, instructing her to wear Chanel No. 5, and adopt a mixed seductive and castrative manner toward the subjects. An interpretation of a negative empirical result leaves us wondering whether the main substantive theory of interest concerning social fear and visual perception has been falsified, or whether only the auxiliary theories that the Si scale is valid for social introversion and that attractive but hostile female experimenters elicit social fear in introverted young males have been falsified. Or perhaps even the particular conditions were not met; that is, she did not consistently act the way she was instructed to or the MMPI protocols were misscored (Meehl, 1978, p. 819).

We consider such difficulties further when we discuss construct validity later in this chapter.

Turning now to the second line of the falsification syllogism, much also could be said about caveats. For one thing, some philosophers of science, including Popper, have philosophical reservations about whether one can know with certainty that a predicted pattern has not been obtained because that knowledge is to be obtained via the fallible, inductive method of empirical observation (see Newton-Smith, 1981, Chapter III). More to the point for our purposes is the way in which empirical data are to be classified as conforming to one pattern or another. Assuming one's theory predicts that the pattern of the data will be that people in general will perform differently in the treatment and control conditions, how does one decide on the basis of a sample of data what is true of the population? That, of course, is the task of inferential statistics and is the sort of question to which the bulk of this book is addressed. First, we show in Chapter 2 how one may rigorously derive probability statements for very simple situations under the assumption that there is no treatment effect. If the probability is sufficiently small, the hypothesis of no difference is rejected. If the probability fails to reach a conventional level of significance, one might conclude the alternative hypothesis is false. (More on this in a moment.) Second, we show beginning in Chapter 3 how to formulate such questions for more complicated experiments using standard parametric tests. In sum, because total conformity with the exact null hypotheses of the social and behavioral sciences (or, for that matter, with the exact point predictions sometimes used—for example, in some areas of physics) is never achieved, inferential statistics serves the function of helping scientists to classify data patterns as being either confirmed predictions, falsified predictions, or, in some cases, ambiguous outcomes.

A final disclaimer is that Popper acknowledges that, in actual scientific practice, singular discordant facts alone rarely do or should falsify theories. Hence, in practice, as hinted at above, a failure to obtain a predicted data pattern may not *really* lead to a rejection or abandonment of the alternative hypothesis the investigator wanted to support. In all too many behavioral science studies, the lack of statistical power is a quite plausible explanation for failure to obtain predicted results. And, such statistical reasons for failure to obtain predicted results are only the beginning. Because of the existence of the other explanations we have considered (for example, "some auxiliary theory is wrong"), which are typically less painful to a theorist than rejection of the principal theory, in practice a combination of multiple discordant facts *and* a more viable alternative theory is usually required for the refutation of a theoretical conjecture (see Cook & Campbell, 1979, p. 22ff.).

We pause here to underscore some of the limitations of science that have emerged from our consideration of Popper and then highlight some of the general utility of his ideas. Regarding science's limitations, we have seen that not only is there no possibility of proving any scientific theory with logical certainty but also there is no possibility of falsifying one with logical certainty. That there are no proven theories is a well-known consequence of the limits of inductive logic. Such difficulties are also inherent to some extent in even the simplest empirical generalization (the generalization is not logically compelled, for reasons including the fact that you cannot be certain what the data pattern is because of limited data and potential future counterexamples to the current pattern and that any application of the generalization requires reliance on principles like uniformity). In short, "the data do not drive us inevitably to correct theories, and even if they did or even if we hit on the correct theory in some other way, we could not prove its correctness conclusively" (Ratzsch, 1986, p. 79). Further, theories cannot be proven false because of the possibility of explaining away purported refutations via challenges based on the fallibility of statistical evidence or of the auxiliary hypotheses relied on in testing the theory. In addition, there is the practical concern that despite the existence of discordant facts the theory may be the best available.

On the positive side of the ledger, Popper's ideas have much to offer both practically and philosophically. Working within the limitations of science, the practical problem for the scientist is how to eliminate explanations other than the theory of interest. We can see the utility of the Popperian conceptual framework in Figure 1.1. The careful experimenter proceeds, in essence, by trying to make the shaded area as small as possible, thereby refuting the rival theories. We mentioned previously that the syllogism of confirmation, though invalid, was not useless. The way in which rival hypotheses are eliminated is essentially by confirming the predictions of one's theory in more and more situations. Figure 1.1(c) illustrates this. The outer circle now represents the intersection or joint occurrence of obtaining the predicted data P and also predicted data P′. For example, if a positive result had been obtained in Meehl's hypothetical experiment, the interpretation that social fear was the causal variable would be strengthened considerably by confirming replications in which the construct was implemented in different ways. On the basis of only the experiment outlined by Meehl, a plausible rival explanation of a positive result might be that it was sexual arousal rather than social fear that had influenced the young males' visual perception. Confirming studies implementing social fear in radically different ways—for example, fear of embarrassment in the setting of a group of other males or anxiety over having to give a public speech, if these made sense in one's theory—would refute the sexual arousal hypothesis.

Indeed, part of the art of experimental design has to do with devising control conditions for which the theory of interest would make a different prediction than would a plausible rival hypothesis. (For example, the rival: "The deficit is due simply to the operation not the brain area destroyed" is discounted by showing no deficit in a sham surgery condition.) If the rival hypothesis is false, part of the credo of science is that with sufficient investigation it will be ultimately discovered. As Kepler wrote regarding rivals to the Copernican hypothesis that made some correct predictions,

> And just as in the proverb liars are cautioned to remember what they have said, so here false hypotheses which together produce the truth by chance, do not, in the course of a demonstration in which they have been applied to many different matters, retain this habit of yielding the truth, but betray themselves (Kepler, 1601).

Although in principle an infinite number of alternative hypotheses always remain, it is of little concern if no *plausible* ones can be specified. We return to this discussion of how rival hypotheses can be eliminated in the final section of this chapter.

Regarding other, more philosophical considerations, for Popper the aim of science is truth. However, given that he concurs with Hume's critique of induction, Popper cannot claim to know the truth of a scientific hypothesis. Thus, the reachable goal for science in the real world is to be that of a closer approximation to the truth, or in Popper's terms, a higher degree of *verisimilitude*. The method of achieving this is basically a rational one, via the logically valid refutation of alternative conjectures about the explanation of a given phenomenon. While the details of the definition of the goal of verisimilitude and the logic of the method are still evolving (see Popper, 1976; Meehl, 1978; Newton-Smith, 1981), we find ourselves in basic agreement with a neo-Popperian perspective, both in terms of ontology and of epistemology. However, we postpone further discussion of this until we have briefly acknowledged some of the other major positions in contemporary philosophy of science.

Kuhn. Thomas Kuhn, perhaps the best known contemporary philosopher of science, is perceived by some as maintaining a position in *The Structure of Scientific Revolutions* (1970) that places him philosophically at the opposite pole from Karl Popper. Whereas Popper has insisted that science is to be understood logically, Kuhn has maintained that science should be interpreted psychologically (Robinson, 1981, p. 24) or sociologically. Given Kuhn's emphasis on the history of science for clues about how science should be conceptualized, perhaps it is appropriate to mention a bit of his personal history. Once a doctoral student in theoretical physics, Kuhn left the field to carry out work in the history and philosophy of science. Spending 1958–1959 at the Center for Advanced Studies in the Behavioral Sciences helped crystallize his views. His major work is based on the history of the *physical sciences*. Others (for example, Gholson & Barker, 1985; see also Gutting, 1980) have, however, applied Kuhn's views to psychology in particular.

Kuhn's basic idea is that psychological and sociological factors are the real determinants of change in allegiance to a theory of the world and in some sense actually help determine the characteristics of the physical world that is being modeled. The notion is quasi-Kantian in that characteristics of the human mind, or at least of the minds of individual scientists, determine in part what will be observed.

Once we have described four of Kuhn's key ideas—paradigms, normal science, anomalies, and scientific revolutions—we will point out two criticisms commonly made of his philosophy of science.

Paradigms for Kuhn are "universally recognized scientific achievements that for a time provide model problems and solutions to a community of practitioners" (Kuhn, 1970, p. viii). Examples include Newton's *Principia* and Lavoisier's *Chemistry*, "works that served for a time implicitly to define the legitimate problems and methods of a research field" (1970, p. 10). The period devoted to solving the unresolved puzzles within an area following publication of such landmark works as these is what constitutes *normal science*. Inevitably, such periods of normal science turn up *anomalies*, or data that do not fit perfectly within the paradigm (1970, Chapter VI). Although such anomalies may emerge slowly because of the difficulties in perceiving them shared by investigators working within the Weltanschaung of a given paradigm, eventually a sufficient number of anomalies are documented to bring the scientific community to a crisis state (1970, Chapter VII). The resolution of the crisis eventually may require a shift to a new paradigm. If so, the transition to the new paradigm is a cataclysmic event. Although some may view the new paradigm as simply subsuming the old, according to Kuhn the transition— for example, from "geocentrism to heliocentrism, from phlogiston to oxygen, or from corpuscles to waves...from Newtonian to Einsteinian mechanics"—necessitated a "*revolutionary* reorientation," a conceptual transformation that is "decisively destructive of a previously established paradigm" (1970, p. 102).

Although his contributions have been immensely useful in stressing the historical development of science and certain of the psychological determinants of the behavior of scientists, there are, from our perspective, two major, related difficulties with Kuhn's philosophy. Kuhn, it should be noted, has attempted to rebut such criticisms [see especially points 5 and 6 in the Postscript added to *The Structure of Scientific Revolutions* (1970, pp. 198–207)]; however, in our view he has not done so successfully. First, paradigm shifts in Kuhn's system do not occur because of the objective superiority of one paradigm over the other. In fact, such cannot be demonstrated because, for Kuhn, paradigms are incommensurable. Thus, attempts for proponents of different paradigms to talk to each other result in communication breakdowns (Kuhn, 1970, p. 201). Although this view is perhaps not quite consensus formation via mob psychology, as Lakatos (1978) characterized it, it certainly implies that scientific change is not rational (see Manicas & Secord, 1983; Suppe, 1977). We are too committed to the real effects of psychological variables to be so rash as to assume that all scientific change is rational with regard to the goals of science. In fact, we readily acknowledge not only the role of psychological factors but also the presence of a fair amount of fraud in science (see Broad & Wade, 1982). However, we believe that these are best understood as deviations from a basically rational model (see Newton-Smith, 1981, pp. 5–13, 148ff.).

Second, we share with many a concern regarding what appears to be Kuhn's relativism. The reading of his work by a number of critics is that Kuhn maintains that there is no fixed reality of nature for science to attempt to more accurately describe. For example, he writes "we may...have to relinquish the notion, explicit or implicit, that changes of paradigm carry scientists and those who learn from them closer and closer to the truth.... The developmental process described in this essay has been a process of evolution *from* primitive beginnings—a process whose successive stages are characterized by an increasingly detailed and refined understanding of nature. But nothing that has been or will be said makes it a process of evolution *toward* anything" (Kuhn, 1970, pp. 170–171).

Kuhn elaborates on this in his Postscript:

> One often hears that successive theories grow ever closer to, or approximate more and more closely to, the truth. Apparently generalizations like that refer not to the puzzle-solutions and the concrete predictions derived from a theory but rather to its ontology, to the match, that is, between the entities with which the theory populates nature and what is "really there."
>
> Perhaps there is some other way of salvaging the notion of "truth" for application to whole theories, but this one will not do. There is, I think, no theory-independent way to reconstruct phrases like "really there"; the notion of a match between the ontology of a theory and its "real" counterpart in nature now seems to me illusive in principle (Kuhn, 1970, p. 206).

Perhaps it is the case, as the pessimistic induction suggests, that all theories constructed in this world are false. But it seems clear that some are less false than others. Does it not make sense to say that the earth revolves around the sun is a closer approximation to the truth of how things really are than to assert that the sun revolves around the earth or that the sun is made of blue cheese? Is it not reasonable to believe that the population mean score on the Wechsler Adult Intelligence Scale is really closer to 100 than to 70 or 130? In Kuhn's system, there is no standard to allow such judgments. We concur with Popper (1972) and Newton-Smith (1981, pp. 34–37, 102–124) that this relativism about the nature of the world is unreasonable. From our perspective, although certainly what is taken to be true varies from one theory to the next, the phenomenon being modeled at any point exists independently of the theory, and its reality is not immediately transformed by what you or I think.

This distinction is critical to the schools of philosophy of science that have risen to prominence over the last two decades. The pendulum has now swung from Kuhn's relativistic construal of reality to a realist position.

Realism. Although there are a multitude of different realist positions in the philosophy of science, certain core elements of realism can be identified (Fine, 1987, p. 359ff.). First, realism holds that a definite world exists, a world populated by entities with particular properties, powers, and relations and "the way the world is" is largely independent of the observer (Harré & Madden, 1975). Second, realist positions maintain that it is possible to obtain a substantial amount of accurate, relatively observer-independent information about the world, including information about structures and relations among entities as well as what may be more superficially observed. Third, the aim of science is to achieve such knowledge. Fourth, as we touched on in our earlier discussion of causality, realist positions maintain that scientific propositions are true or false by virtue of their correspondence or lack or correspondence with the way the world is, independently of ourselves (Newton-Smith, 1981, pp. 28–29). Finally, realist positions tend to be optimistic in their view of science by claiming that the historically generated sequence of theories of a mature science reflect an improvement in terms of the degree of approximation to the truth (Newton-Smith, 1981, p. 39).

These tenets of realism can be more clearly understood by contrasting these positions with alternative views. Although there have been philosophers in previous centuries, e.g., Berkeley (1685–1753), and in modern times, e.g., Russell (1950), who have questioned whether the belief in the existence of the physical world was logically justified, not surprisingly most find arguments for the existence of the world compelling (Russell's argument and rebuttals thereof are helpfully juxtaposed by Oller, 1989). As Einstein tells it, the questioning of the existence of the world is the sort of logical bind one gets oneself into by following Humean skepticism to its logical conclusion (Einstein, 1944, pp. 279–291). Hume correctly saw that our ideas about causal connections, for example, are not logically necessitated by our empirical experience. However, Russell and others extended this skepticism to any knowledge or perception we might have of the physical world. Russell's point is that, assuming causality exists (even though we can't know it does), our perception represents the end of a causal chain. Trying to reconstruct what "outside" caused that perception is a hazardous process. Even seeing an object such as a tree, if physics is correct, is a complicated, indirect affair. The light reaching the eye comes ultimately from the sun, not the tree, yet you do not say you are seeing the sun. Thus,

Russell concludes that "from what we have been saying it is clear that the relation of a percept to the physical object which is supposed to be perceived is vague, approximate and somewhat indefinite. There is no *precise* sense in which we can be said to perceive physical objects" (Russell, 1950, p. 206). And, not only do we not know the true character of the tree we think we are seeing but also "the colored surfaces which we see cease to exist when we shut our eyes" (Russell, 1914, p. 64). Here, in effect, Russell throws the baby out with the bathwater. The flaw in Russell's argument was forcefully pointed out by Dewey (1916). Dewey's compelling line of reasoning is that Russell's questioning is based on the analysis of perception as the end of a causal chain; however, this presupposes that there is an external object that is initiating the chain, regardless of how poorly its nature may be perceived.

Moving to a consideration of the other tenets of realism, the emphasis on accurate information about the world and the view that scientific theories come to more closely approximate a true description of the world clearly contrasts with relativistic accounts of science that see it as not moving toward anything. In fact, one early realist, C. S. Peirce, developed an influential view of truth and reality that hinges on there being a goal toward which scientific investigations of a question must tend (see Oller, 1989, p. 53ff.). Peirce wrote

> The question therefore is, how is true belief (or belief in the real) distinguished from false belief (or belief in fiction). ... The ideas of truth and falsehood, in their full development, appertain exclusively to the scientific method of settling opinion. ... All followers of science are fully persuaded that the processes of investigation, if only pushed far enough, will give one certain solution to every question to which it can be applied. ... The opinion which is fated to be ultimately agreed to by all who investigate, is what we mean by the truth and the object represented in this opinion is the real. ... Our perversity and that of others may indefinitely postpone the settlement of opinion; it might even conceivably cause an arbitrary proposition to be universally accepted as long as the human race should last. Yet even that would not change the nature of the belief, which alone could be the result of investigation, that true opinion must be the one which they would ultimately come to (Peirce, 1878, pp. 298–300).

Thus, in Peirce's view, for any particular scientific question that has clear meaning, there was one certain solution that would be obtained if only scientific investigation could be carried far enough. This view of science is essentially the same as Einstein's, who likened the process of formulating a scientific theory to the task facing

> a man engaged in solving a well designed word puzzle. He may, it is true, propose any word as the solution; but, there is only *one* word which really solves the puzzle in all its forms. It is an outcome of faith that nature—as she is perceptible to our five senses— takes the character of such a well formulated puzzle (Einstein, 1950, p. 64).

Scientific realism may also be contrasted with instrumentalist views. Instrumentalists argue that scientific theories are not intended to be literally true but are simply convenient summaries or calculational rules for deriving predictions. This distinction is illustrated particularly well by the preface that Osiander added to Copernicus's *The Revolutions of the Heavenly Spheres:*

> It is the duty of the astronomer to compose the history of the celestial motions through careful and skillful observation. Then turning to the causes of these motions or hy-

potheses about them, he must conceive and devise, since he cannot in any way attain to the true causes, such hypotheses as, being assumed, enable the motions to be calculated correctly from the principles of geometry, for the future as well as the past. The present author [Copernicus] has performed both these duties excellently. For these hypotheses need not be true nor even probable; if they provide a calculus consistent with the observations that alone is sufficient (Rosen, 1959, pp. 24–25).

Osiander recognized the distinction between factual description and a convenient formula for making predictions and is suggesting that whether the theory correctly describes reality is irrelevant. That is the instrumentalist point of view. On the other hand, many scientists, particularly in the physical sciences, tend to regard their theories as descriptions of real entities. This was the case for Copernicus and Kepler regarding the heliocentric theory and more recently for Bohr and Thomson regarding the electron. Besides the inherent plausibility of the realist viewpoint, the greater *explanatory power* of the realist perspective is a major argument offered in support of realism. Such explanatory power is perhaps most impressive when reference to a single set of entities allows predictions across different domains or allows predictions of phenomena that have never been observed but that subsequently are confirmed.

Some additional comments must be made about realism at this point, particularly as it relates to the behavioral sciences. First, scientific realism is not something that is an all-or-nothing matter. One might be a realist with regard to certain scientific theories and not with regard to others. Indeed, some have attempted to specify the criteria by which theories should be judged, or at least have been judged historically, as deserving a realistic interpretation (Gardner, 1987; Gingerich, 1973). Within psychology a realistic interpretation might be given to a brain mechanism that you hypothesize is damaged on the basis of the poor memory performance of a brain-injured patient. However, the states in a mathematical model of memory such as working memory may be viewed instrumentally, as simply convenient fictions or metaphors that allow estimation of the probability of recall of a particular item.

A second comment is that realists tend to be emergentists and to stress the existence of various levels of reality. Nature is viewed as stratified, with the higher levels possessing new entities with powers and properties that cannot be adequately explained by the lower levels (Bhaskar, 1982, especially Sections 2.5 and 3.3). "From the point of view of emergence, we cannot reduce personality and mind to biological processes or reduce life to physical and chemical processes without loss or damage to the unity and special qualities of the entity with which we began" (Titus, 1964, p. 250). Thus, psychology from the realist perspective is not in danger of losing its field of study to ardent sociobiologists any more than biologists would lose their object of inquiry if organic life could be produced by certain physical and chemical manipulations in the laboratory. Neither people nor other living things would cease to be real, no matter what the scientific development. Elements of lower orders are just as real, no more or less, than the comprehensive entities formed out of them. Both charged particles and thunderstorms, single cells and single adults exist and have powers and relations with other entities at their appropriate levels of analysis.

Because of the many varieties of realism—for example, critical realism (Cook & Campbell, 1979), metaphysical realism (Popper, 1972), transcendental realism

(Bhaskar, 1975)—and because our concern regarding philosophy of science is less with ontology than with epistemological method, we do not attempt to summarize the realist approach further. The interested reader is referred to the article by Manicas and Secord (1983) for a useful summary and references to the literature.

Summary. As is perhaps already clear, our own perspective is to hold to a realist position ontologically and a temperate rationalist position epistemologically of the neo-Popperian variety. The perspective is realist because it assumes phenomena and processes exist outside of our experience and that theories can be true or false, and among false theories, false to a greater or lesser extent depending on the degree of correspondence between the theory and the reality. Naturally, however, our knowledge of this reality is limited by the nature of induction—thus, it behooves us to be critical of the strength of our inferences about the nature of that reality (see Cook & Campbell, 1979).

We endorse a rational model as the ideal for how science should proceed. Given the progress associated with the method, there is reason to think that the methodology of science has in general resulted in choices between competing theories primarily on the strength of the supporting evidence. However, our rationalism is temperate in that we recognize that there is no set of completely specifiable rules defining the scientific method that can guarantee success and that weight should be given to empirically based inductive arguments even though they do not logically compel belief (see Newton-Smith, 1981, especially p. 268ff.).

We believe the statistical methods that are the primary subject matter of this book are consistent with this perspective and more compatible with this perspective than with some others. For example, thinking it is meaningful to attempt to detect a difference between fixed-population means seems inconsistent with a relativistic perspective. Similarly, using statistical methods rather than relying on one's ability to make immediate judgments about particular facts seems inconsistent with a logical positivist approach. In fact, one can view the primary role of statistical analysis as an efficient means for summarizing evidence (see Rosenthal & Rubin, 1985): Rather than being a royal road to a positively certain scientific conclusion, inferential statistics is a method for accomplishing a more modest but nonetheless critical goal, namely, quantifying the evidence or uncertainty relevant to a particular statistical conclusion. Doing this well is certainly not all there is to science, which is part of what we are trying to make clear, but it is a first step in a process that must be viewed from a broader perspective. Because there is no cookbook methodology that can take you from a data summary to a correct theory, it behooves the would-be scientist to think through the philosophical position from which the evidence of particular studies is to be viewed. Doing so provides you with a framework within which to decide if the evidence available permits you to draw conclusions that you are willing to defend publicly. That the result of a statistical test is only one, albeit important, consideration in this process of reaching substantive conclusions and making generalizations is something we attempt to underscore further in the remainder of this chapter.

THREATS TO THE VALIDITY OF INFERENCES FROM EXPERIMENTS

Having reviewed the perils of drawing inductive inferences at a philosophical level, we now turn to a consideration of threats to the validity of inferences at a more practical level. The classic treatment of the topic of how things can go wrong in attempting to make inferences from experiments was provided in the monograph by Campbell and Stanley (1963). Generations of graduate students around the country memorized their "threats to validity." A more modern version of their volume addressing many of the same issues is the book by Cook and Campbell (1979). Judd and Kenny (1981) and Krathwohl (1985) have provided very useful and readable discussions of these validity notions of Campbell and his associates. Cronbach's (1982) book also provides a wealth of insights into problems of making valid inferences, but like Cook and Campbell (1979), it presumes a considerable amount of knowledge on the part of the reader. [For a brief summary of the various validity typologies, see Mark (1986)].

For our part, we begin the consideration of the practical problems of drawing valid inferences by distinguishing among the principal types of validity discussed in this literature. Then, we suggest a way for thinking in general about threats to validity and for attempting to avoid such pitfalls.

Types of Validity

When a clinician reads an article in a journal about a test of a new procedure and then contemplates applying it in his or her own practice, a whole series of logical steps must all be correct for this to be an appropriate application of the finding. [Krathwohl (1985) offers the apt analogy of links in a chain for these steps.] In short, a problem could arise because the conclusion or design of the initial study was flawed or because the extrapolation to a new situation is inappropriate. Campbell and Stanley (1963) referred to these potential problems as threats to internal and external validity, respectively. Cook and Campbell (1979) subsequently suggested that actually four types should be distinguished: statistical conclusion validity, internal validity, construct validity, and external validity. We discuss each in turn, but first a word or two by way of general introduction.

Validity means essentially truth or correctness, a correspondence between a proposition describing how things work in the world and how they really work (see Russell, 1919b; Campbell, 1986, p. 73). Naturally, we never know with certainty if our interpretations are valid, but we try to proceed with the design and analysis of our research in such a way to make the case for our conclusions as plausible and compelling as possible.

The propositions or interpretations that abound in the discussion and conclusion sections of behavioral science articles are about how things work in general. Modal experiments involve particular people manifesting the effects of particular treatments on particular measures at a particular time and place. Modal conclusions involve few, if any, of these particulars. Most pervasively, the people (or patients, children, rats, classes, or, most generally, units of analysis) are viewed as a sample from a larger population of interest. The conclusions are about the population. The venerable tradition of hypothesis testing, which this volume endorses, is built on this foundational assumption: One unit of analysis will differ from another. The variability among units, however, provides the yardstick for making the statistical judgment of whether a difference in group means is "real."

What Cook and Campbell (1979), Cronbach (1982), and Campbell (1986) have eloquently pointed out is that the other components out of which experiments are built, most important the treatments and the measures, should also be viewed as representative of larger domains, in somewhat the same way that subjects are. A multifaceted treatment program for problem drinkers could have involved the same facets with different emphases (for example, more or less time with the therapist) or different facets not represented initially (for example, counseling for family members and close friends) and yet still be regarded as illustrating the theoretical concept of interest, controlled drinking. (In Chapter 10, we discuss statistical procedures that assume the treatments in a study are merely representative of other treatments of that type that could have been employed.)

Turning now to the third component of experiments—namely, measures—it is perhaps easier because of the familiarity of the concepts of "measurement error" and "validity of tests," to think of the measures, instead of the treatments, used in experiments as fallible representatives of a domain. Setting up a computer program to enter the 118 variables collected at intake for a study of the treatment of problem drinkers (as one of the authors has just done) makes it all too clear that alternative measures—for example, of drinking behavior—are available in abundance. Finally, regarding the component of the setting in which experiments take place, our comments about the uniformity of nature underscore what every historian or traveler knows but that writers of discussion sections sometimes ignore: What is true about behavior for one time and place may not be universally true. In sum, an idea to remember as you read about the various types of validity is how they relate to the question of whether a component of a study—such as the units, treatments, measures, or setting—truly reflects the domain of theoretical interest.

Statistical Conclusion Validity.   One of the ways in which a study might be an insecure base from which to extrapolate is that the conclusion reached by that study about a statistical hypothesis it tested might be wrong. As you likely learned in your first course in statistics, there are two types of errors or ways in which this can happen: Type I errors, or false positives—that is, concluding there is a relationship between two variables when there in fact is none—and Type II errors, or false negatives—that is, failing to detect a relationship that in fact exists in the population. Because the nominal alpha level or probability of a Type I error is fairly well established by convention within a discipline—for example, at .05—the critical issue in statistical conclusion validity is power. The power of a test is its sensitivity or ability to detect relationships that exist in the population, and so it is the complement of a Type II error. In conventional terms, power is the probability of rejecting the null hypothesis when it is false and equals 1 minus the probability of a Type II error.

As Cohen (1977) has stressed, one of the most pervasive threats to the validity of the statistical conclusions reached in the behavioral sciences is low power. It is critical in planning experiments and evaluating results to consider the likelihood that a given design would detect an effect of a given size in the population. As we discuss in detail beginning in Chapter 3, there are a variety of ways of estimating how strong the relationship is between the independent variable and the dependent variable and using this to compute a numerical value of the power of a study. Our concern here, however, is with why statistical conclusions are often incorrect; several reasons can be enumerated.

Studies typically have low power because sample sizes used are too small for the situation. Because the number required depends on the specifics of the research problem, one cannot specify in general a minimum number of subjects to have per condition. However, although other steps can be taken, increasing the number of participants is the simplest solution, conceptually at least, to the problem of low power.

Another important reason for low power is the use of an unreliable dependent variable. Reliability, of course, has to do with consistency and accuracy. Scores on variables are assumed to result from a combination of systematic or true score variation and random error variation. For example, your score on a multiple-choice quiz is determined in part by what you know and in part by other factors such as your motivation and your luck in guessing answers you don't know. Variables are unreliable, in a psychometric sense, when the random error variation component is large relative to the true score variation component (see Judd & Kenny, 1981, p. 111ff., for a clear introduction to the idea of reliability).

We acknowledge, as Nicewander and Price (1983) have stressed, that there are cases where the less reliable of two possible dependent variables can lead to greater power, for example, because a larger treatment effect on that variable may more than offset its lower reliability. However, other things being equal, the lower the reliability of a dependent measure is, the less sensitive it will be in detecting treatment effects. Solving problems of unreliability is not easy, in part because there is always the possibility that altering a test in an attempt to make it more reliable might change what it is measuring as well as its precision of measurement. However, the rule of thumb, as every standard psychometrics text makes clear (e.g., Nunnally, 1978) is that increasing the length of tests increases their reliability. The longer the quiz, the less likely you can pass simply by guessing.

Other reasons why unexplained variability in the dependent variable and hence the probability of a Type II error may be unacceptably high include implementing the treatment in slightly different ways from one subject to the next and failure to include in your model of performance for the situation important explanatory variables. Typically, in behavioral science studies, who the participant happens to be is a more important determinant of how he or she performs on the experimental task than the treatment to which the person is assigned. Thus, including a measure of the relevant individual differences among participants in your statistical model or experimentally controlling for such differences can often greatly increase your power (Chapters 9 and 11–14 discuss methods for dealing with such individual differences).

The primary cause of Type I error rates being inflated over the nominal or stated level is that the investigator has performed multiple tests of the same general hypothesis. Statistical methods exist for adjusting for the number of tests you are performing and are considered at various points in this text (see, for example, Chapter 5 on multiple comparisons). Violations of statistical assumptions can also affect Type I and Type II error rates, which we discuss at the end of Chapter 3.

Internal Validity. Statistical tests allow one to make conclusions about whether the mean of the dependent variable (typically referred to as variable Y) is the same in different treatment populations. If the statistical conclusion is that the means are different, one can then move to the question of what caused the difference, with one of the candidates being the independent variable (call it variable X) as it was implemented in the study. The issue of internal validity is, Is there a causal relationship between variable X and variable Y, regardless of what X and Y are theoretically supposed to represent? If variable X is a *true* independent variable and the statistical conclusion is valid, then internal validity is to a large extent assured (appropriate caveats follow). By a true independent variable, we mean one for which the experimenter can and does independently determine the level of the variable that each subject will experience—that is, assignment to conditions is carried out independently of any other characteristic of the subject or of other variables under investigation. Internal validity is, however, a serious issue in quasi-experimental designs where this condition is not met. Most commonly the problem is using intact groups of subjects. For example, in an educational psychology study, one might select the fifth-grade class in one school to receive an experimental curriculum and use the fifth-grade class from another school as a control group. Any differences observed on a common posttest might be attributed to preexisting differences between students in the two schools rather than your educational treatment. This threat to internal validity is termed *selection bias* because subjects were selected from different intact groups. Perhaps less obvious is the case where an attribute of the subjects is investigated as one of the factors in an experiment. Assume that depressed and nondepressed groups of subjects were formed by scores on an instrument like the Beck Depression Inventory; then, it is observed that the depressed group performs significantly worse on a memory task. One might like to claim that the difference in memory performance was due to the difference in level of depression; however, one encounters the same logical difficulty here as in the study with intact classrooms. Depressed subjects may differ from nondepressed subjects in many ways besides depression that are relevant to performance on the memory task.

Internal validity threats are typically thus "third" variable problems. Another variable besides X and Y may be responsible for either an apparent relationship or an apparent lack of a relationship between X and Y.

Other threats to internal validity include mortality (the problem that arises when possibly different types of people drop out of various conditions of a study) and a number of other issues that arise when subjects are assessed repeatedly over time.[2] This latter class of threats includes possible maturation of participants over time and "history," that is, events taking place between a pretest and posttest in addition to the treatment. Finally, other threats to the internal validity of a study occur when there is the possibility of communication during the course of a study among subjects from different treatment conditions. Thus, the mixture of effects of portions of different treatments that subjects functionally receive, filtered through their talkative friends, can be quite different from the single treatment they were nominally supposed to receive. This type of threat can be a particularly serious problem in long-term studies such as those comparing alternative treatment programs for clinical populations. For example, a waiting list control group may be demoralized by learning that others are receiving effective treatments while they are receiving nothing. Further, in a variety of other areas of psychology where studies tend to involve brief treatment interventions but where different people may participate over the course of an academic semester, the character of a treatment can be affected greatly by dissemination of information over time. Students who learn from previous participants the nature of the deception involved in the critical condition of a social psychology study may experience a considerably different condition than naive subjects would experience. These participants may well perform differently than those in other conditions, but the cause may have more to do with the possibly distorted information they received from their peers than the nominal treatment to which they were assigned.

Estimating the internal validity of a study is largely a thought problem in which you attempt to systematically think through the plausibility of various threats relevant to your situation.[3] On occasion, one can anticipate a given threat and gather information in the course of a study relevant to it. For example, questionnaires or other attempts to measure the exact nature of the treatment and control conditions experienced by subjects may be useful in determining whether extraexperimental factors differentially affected subjects in different conditions. Similarly, in the case of subject mortality, measures of the characteristics of individuals dropping out can be analyzed in an attempt to assess the strength of the threat of a selection bias.

Finally, a term from Campbell (1986) is useful for distinguishing internal validity from the other types remaining to be considered. Campbell suggests it might be clearer to call internal validity "local molar (pragmatic, atheoretical) causal validity" (p. 69). Although a complex phrase, this focuses attention on points deserving of emphasis. The concern of internal validity is causal in that you are asking what was responsible for the change in the dependent variable. The view of causes is molar—that is, at the level of a treatment package, or viewing the treatment condition as a complex hodgepodge of all that went on in that part of the study—thus emphasizing that the question is *not* what the "active ingredient" of the treatment is. Rather, the concern is pragmatic, atheoretical—did the treatment for whatever reason cause a change, did it work? Finally, the concern is local: did it work here? In internal validity, one is not concerned with generalization.

Construct Validity.   The issue regarding construct validity is, Given there is a valid causal relationship, is the interpretation of the constructs involved in that relationship correct? Construct validity pertains to both causes and effects. That is, the question for both the independent and dependent variables as implemented in the study is, Can I generalize from this one set of operations to a referent construct? What one investigator labels as construct A causing a change in construct C, another may interpret as an effect of construct B on construct C, or of construct A on construct D, or even of B on D. Showing a person photographs of a dying person may arouse what one investigator interprets as death anxiety and another interprets as compassion. Threats to construct validity are a pervasive and difficult problem in psychological research. We have implicitly addressed this issue earlier in this chapter in commenting on the meaning of theoretical terms. Since Cronbach and Meehl's (1955) seminal paper on construct validity in the area of assessment, something approaching a general consensus has been achieved that the specification of constructs in psychology is limited by the richness, generality, and precision of our theories. Given the current state of psychological theorizing, it is understandable why a minority continue to argue for strategies such as adopting a strict operationalism or attempting to avoid theorizing altogether. However, the potential for greater explanatory power offered by theoretical constructs places most investigators in the position of having to meet the problem of construct validity head on rather than sidestepping it by abandoning theoretical constructs.

The basic problem in construct validity is the possibility "that the operations which are meant to represent a particular cause or effect construct can be construed in terms of more than one construct, each of which is stated at the same level of reduction" (Cook & Campbell, 1979, p. 59). The qualifier regarding the level of reduction refers to the fact that alternative explanations of a phenomenon can be made at different levels of analysis and that sort of multiplicity of explanation does not threaten construct validity. This is most clearly true across disciplines. One's support for a political position could be explained at either a sociological level or by invoking a psychological analysis, for example, of attitude formation. Similarly, showing there is a physiological correlate of some behavior does not mean the behavioral phenomenon is to be understood as nothing but the outworking of physiological causes.

Some examples of specific types of artifacts serve to illustrate the confounding that can threaten construct validity. (*Confounding* means the inadvertent manipulation or assessment of other theoretically relevant variables besides the variable the investigator intended to study.) For example, a famous series of studies begun at the Western Electric plant at Hawthorne, Illinois, in 1927 investigated the effects of various changes in the physical environment on the productivity of workers in the plant (Roethlisberger & Dickson, 1939). When the brightness of the lights above a group of workers was increased, their performance improved. However, it was found that when the lighting for another selected group of workers was darkened somewhat, *their* performance also improved. In fact, it seemed that no matter what small change was made in the working environment of a group of workers, the result was an increase in their productivity. Although the investigators initially viewed the independent-variable construct merely as changes in level of illumination, that performance seemed to be affected similarly for the groups of workers being studied regardless of which feature of the physical environment was manipulated led eventually to the conclusion that other constructs were being manipulated as well. The "Hawthorne effect" eventually came to be identified with the effect of psychological variables such as the perception of concern by management over working conditions or, more generally, the effects of awareness that one is participating in a research study.

Another example of a threat to construct validity is the experimenter-bias effect demonstrated by Rosenthal (1976). This effect involves the impact of the researcher's expectancies and in particular the transmission of that expectancy to the subject in such a way that performance on the dependent variable is affected. Thus, when the experimenter is not blind to the hypothesis under investigation, the role of experimenter bias must be considered as well as the nominal treatment variable in helping to determine the magnitude of the differences between groups.

Two major pitfalls to avoid to minimize threats to construct validity can be cited: inadequate preoperational explication of the construct and mono-operation bias, or using only one set of operations to implement the construct (Cook & Campbell, 1979, p. 64ff.). First, regarding explication, the question is, What are the essential features of the construct for your theoretical purposes? For example, if you wish to study social support, does your conceptual definition include the perceptions and feelings of the recipient of the support or simply the actions of the provider of the support? Explicating a construct involves consideration not only of the construct you want to assess but also the other similar constructs from which you hope to distinguish your construct (see Campbell & Fiske, 1959; Judd & Kenny, 1981). Second, regarding mono-operation bias, using only a single dependent variable to assess a psychological construct typically runs the risk of both under-representing the construct and containing irrelevancies. For example, anxiety is typically regarded as a multidimensional construct subsuming behavioral, cognitive, and physiological components. Because measures of these dimensions will be much less than perfectly correlated, if one's concern is with anxiety in general, then using only a single measure is likely to be misleading.

External Validity. The final type of validity we consider refers to the stability across other contexts of the causal relationship observed in a given study. The issue in external validity is, Can I generalize this finding across populations, or settings, or time? As mentioned in our discussion of the uniformity of nature, this is more of an issue in psychology than in the physical sciences.

A central concern with regard to external validity is typically the heterogeneity and representativeness of the sample of people participating in the study. Unfortunately, most research in the human sciences is carried out using the sample of subjects that happens to be conveniently available at the time. Thus, there is no assurance that the sample is representative of the initial target population, not to mention some other population to which another researcher may want to generalize. In Chapter 2, we consider one perspective on analyzing data from convenience samples, which, unlike most statistical procedures, does not rely on the assumption of random sampling from a population.

For now it is sufficient to note that the concern with external validity is that the effects of a treatment observed in a particular study may not consistently be obtained. For example, one of the authors found that a classroom demonstration of a mnemonic technique that had repeatedly shown the mnemonic method superior to a control condition in a sophomore-level class actually resulted in worse performance than the control group in a class of students taking a remedial instruction course. Freshmen had been assigned to take the remedial course in part on the basis of their poor reading comprehension and apparently failed to understand the somewhat complicated written instructions given to the students in the mnemonic condition.

One partial solution to the problem of external validity is, where possible, to take steps to assure that the study will use a heterogeneous group of persons, settings, and times. Note that this is at odds with one of the recommendations we made regarding statistical conclusion validity. In fact, what is good for the precision of a study, such as standardizing conditions and working with a homogeneous sample of subjects, is often detrimental to the generality of the findings. The other side of the coin is that although heterogeneity makes it more difficult to obtain statistically significant findings, once they are obtained it allows generalization of these findings with greater confidence to other situations. In the absence of such heterogeneity or with a lack of observations with the people, settings, or times to which you wish to apply a finding, your generalization must rest on your ideas of what is theoretically important about these differences from the initial study (Campbell, 1986).

Conceptualizing and Controlling for Threats to Validity

As discussed by Campbell (1969), a helpful way to think about most of the artifacts that we have considered is in terms of incomplete designs or of designs having more factors than originally planned. For example, consider a two-group study where a selection bias was operating. Because the two treatment groups involved in essence subjects from two different populations, one could view the groups as but two of the four possible combinations of treatment and population. Similarly, when a treatment is delivered, there are often some incidental aspects of the experience that are not an inherent part of the treatment but that are not present in the control condition. These instrumental incidentals may be termed the *vehicle* used to deliver the treatment. Once again, a two-group study might be thought of as just two of the four possible combinations: the "pure" treatment being present or absent combined with the vehicle being present or absent (Figure 1.2).

In the case of such confoundings, a more valid experimental design may be achieved by using two groups that differ along only one dimension, namely, that of the treatment factor. In the case of selection bias, this obviously would mean sampling subjects from only one population. In the case of vehicle factor, one conceivably could either expand the control group to include the irrelevant details that were previously unique to the experimental group or "purify" the experimental group by eliminating the distinguishing but unnecessary incidental aspects of the treatment (Figure 1.3). Both options may not be available in practice. For example, in a physiological study involving ablation of a portion of the motor cortex of a rat, the surgical procedure of opening the skull may be a part of the ablation treatment that cannot practically be eliminated. In such a case, the appropriate controls are

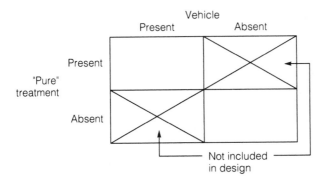

FIGURE 1.2 Original design.

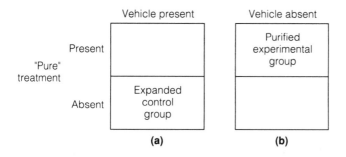

FIGURE 1.3 Preferred designs.

not untreated animals but an expanded control group: animals who go through a sham surgery involving the same anesthetic, opening of the skull, and so on but who do not experience any brain damage.

Regarding the issues having to do with increasing the generality of one's findings, viewing simple designs as portions of potentially larger designs is again a useful strategy. One might expand a two-group design, for example, by using all combinations of the treatment factor and a factor having levels corresponding to subpopulations of interest (Figures 1.4 and 1.5). If in your psychology of college sophomores, summer school students behave differently on your experimental task than regular academic year students, include both types to buttress the generality of your conclusions.

Finally, with regard to both construct validity and external validity, the key principle for protecting against threats to validity is *heteromethod replication* (Campbell, 1969, p. 365ff.). Replication of findings is, of course, a desirable way of demonstrating the reliability of the effects of an independent variable on a dependent variable. Operationism would suggest that one should carry out the details of the original design in exactly the same fashion as was done initially. The point we are making, however, is that construct and external validity are strengthened if the details of procedure deemed theoretically irrelevant are varied from one replication to the next. (In Chapter 3, we cover how statistical tests may be carried out to

F I G U R E **1. 4** Original design.

F I G U R E **1. 5** Expanded design.

determine if the effects in one study are replicated in another.) Campbell (1969, p. 366) even goes so far as to entertain the idea that every Ph.D. dissertation in the behavioral sciences be required to implement the treatment in at least two different ways and measure the effects of the treatment using two different methods. Although methodologically a good suggestion for assuring construct and external validity, Campbell rejects this idea as likely being too discouraging in practice because he speculates "full confirmation would almost never be found" (1969, p. 366).

Whether simple or complex, experimental designs require statistical methods for summarizing and interpreting data. And it is toward the development and explication of those methods that we move in subsequent chapters.

E X E R C I S E S

*1. Cite three flaws in the Baconian view that science can proceed in a purely objective manner.

2. a. Are there research areas in psychology where the assumption of the uniformity of nature regarding experimental material is not troublesome? That is, in what kinds of research is it the case that between-subject differences are so inconsequential that they can be ignored?

b. In other situations, although how one person responds may be drastically different from another, there are still arguments in favor of doing "single-subject" research. Cite an example of such a situation and suggest certain of the arguments in favor of such a strategy.

*3. Regarding the necessity of philosophical assumptions, much of twentieth-century psychology has been dominated by an empiricist, materialist monism, that is, the view that matter is all that exists and the only way one can come to know is by empirical observation. Some have even suggested that this position is necessitated by empirical findings. In what sense does attempting to prove materialism via empirical methods beg the question?

4. How might one assess the simplicity of a particular mathematical model?

5. Cite an example of what Meehl terms an auxiliary theory that must be relied on to carry out a test of a particular content theory of interest.

6. Explain why, in Popper's view, falsification of theories is critical for advancing science. Why are theories not rejected immediately upon failure to obtain predicted results?

7. Assume a study finds that children who watch more violent television programs are more violent themselves in a playground situation than children who report watching less violent television. Does this imply that watching television violence causes violent behavior? What other explanations are possible in this situation? How could the inference of the alleged causal relationship be strengthened?

8. Regarding statistical conclusion validity, sample size, as noted in the text, is a critical variable. Complete the following:
   a. Increasing sample size _____ the power of a test.
      increases   decreases   does not affect
   b. Increasing sample size _____ the probability of a Type II error.
      increases   decreases   does not affect
   c. Increasing sample size _____ the probability of a Type I error.
      increases   decreases   does not affect

*9. A learning theorist asserts, "If frustration theory is correct, then partially reinforced animals will persist longer in responding during extinction than will continuously reinforced animals." What is the contrapositive of this assertion?

*10. A national study involving a sample of more than two thousand individuals included a comparison of the performance of public and Catholic high school seniors on a mathematics achievement test. (Summary data are reported by Wolfle, L. M. (1987). "Enduring cognitive effects of public and private schools." *Educational Researcher*, *16*(4), 5–11.) The statistics on the mathematics test for the two groups of students were as follows:

	High School	
	Public	*Catholic*
Mean	12.13	15.13
SD	7.44	6.52

Would you conclude from such data that Catholic high schools are doing a more effective job in educating students in mathematics? What additional information could make this explanation of the difference in mean scores more or less compelling?

2 Introduction to the Fisher Tradition

DISCUSSION OF POTENTIAL THREATS to the validity of an experiment and issues relating to philosophy of science may at first blush seem unrelated to statistics. And, in fact, some presentations of statistics may border on numerology—whereby certain rituals performed with a set of numbers are thought to produce meaningful conclusions, with the only responsibility for thought by the investigator being the need to avoid errors in the calculations. This nonthinking attitude is perhaps made more prevalent by the ready availability of computers and statistical software. For all their advantages in terms of computational speed and accuracy, these conveniences may mislead some into thinking that, because calculations are no longer an issue, there is nothing more to statistics than learning the syntax for your software. It thus becomes easier to avoid facing squarely the central issue: How do I defend my answers to the scientific questions of interest in this situation?

However, statistical decisions, appropriately conceived, are essentially organized arguments. This is perhaps most obvious when the derivations of the statistical tests themselves are carried out in a mathematically rigorous fashion. (Although the point of the argument might be totally obscure to all but the most initiated, that it is a highly structured deductive argument is clear enough.) Thus, in a book on linear models, one could begin from first principles and proceed to prove the theorems necessary for use of the F tests and the associated probability tables. That is the approach taken in mathematical statistics texts [see, for example, one of the standard sources such as the book by Freund and Walpole (1980), by Hogg and Craig (1978), or by Mood, Graybill, and Boes (1974)]. It is, of course, possible to derive the theory without showing that it has any practical utility for analyzing data, although certain texts attempt to handle both (e.g., Graybill, 1976). However, rigorous treatment of linear models requires mastery of calculus at a level that not many students of the behavioral sciences have achieved. This fortunately does not preclude acquiring a thorough understanding of how statistics in general and linear models in particular can be used effectively in behavioral science research.

The view of statistics as a kind of rational argument was one that the prime mover in the area, Sir Ronald A. Fisher (1890–1962), heartily endorsed. In fact, Fisher reportedly was dismayed that by the end of his life statistics was being taught "essentially as mathematics" with an overelaborate notation apparently designed to make it appear difficult (Cochran, 1967, p. 1461). Fisher, on the other hand, saw statistics as being much more closely related to the experimental sciences in which the methods actually were to be used. He developed new methods in response to the practical needs he saw in serving as a consultant to researchers in various departments related to the biological sciences. A major portion of Fisher's contributions to mathematical statistics and to the design and analysis of experiments came early in his career when he was chief statistician at the Rothamsted Agricultural Station. Fisher, who later served as Galton Professor at the University of London and as Professor of Genetics at the University of Cambridge, was responsible for laying the foundations for a substantial part of the modern discipline of statistics.

Certainly the development and dissemination of the analysis of variance and the F test named for him were directly due to Fisher. His writings, which span half a century, provide masterful insights into the process of designing and interpreting experiments. His *Design of Experiments* (1935/1971) in particular can be read with great profit, regardless of mathematical background, and illustrates very effectively the close link that should exist between logical analysis and computations. It is the purpose of this chapter to provide a brief introduction to the kind of statistical reasoning that characterizes the tradition that Fisher set in motion.

We begin by examining one of the most fundamental ideas in statistics. A critical ingredient in any statistical test is determining the probability, assuming the operation of only chance factors, of obtaining a more extreme result than that indicated by the observed value of the test statistic. For example, in carrying out a one-sample z test manually in an elementary statistics course, one of the final steps is to translate the observed value of z into a probability. The probability being sought, which is called a p value, is the probability of obtaining a z score more extreme than that observed. Whenever the test statistic follows a continuous distribution like the z, t, or F, any treatment of this problem that goes deeper than "you look it up in the table" requires use of rather messy mathematical derivations. Fortunately, the same kind of argument can be developed in detail quite easily if inferences are based on a discrete probabilistic analysis of a situation rather than by making reference to a continuous distribution. Thus, we illustrate the development of a statistical test by using an example relying on a discrete probability distribution.[1] First, however, let us consider why any probability distribution is an appropriate tool for interpreting experiments.

INTERPRETATION AND ITS REASONED BASIS

What Fisher hoped to provide was an integrated methodology of experimental design and statistical procedures that together would satisfy "all logical requirements of the complete process of adding to knowledge by experimentation" (Fisher, 1935/1971, p. 3). Thus, Fisher was a firm believer in the idea that inductive inferences, although uncertain, could be made rigorously, with the nature and degree of uncertainty itself being specified. Probability distributions were used in this specification of uncertainty. However, as we have indicated, in Fisher's view statistics was not a rarefied mathematical exercise. Rather, it was part and parcel of experimentation, which in turn was viewed not merely as the concern of laboratory scientists but as the prototypical avenue by which people learn from experience. Given this, Fisher felt that an understanding of scientific inference was the appropriate concern of any intelligent person.

Experiments, Fisher wrote, "are only experience carefully planned in advance and designed to form a secure basis of new knowledge" (1935/1971, p. 8). The goal is to design experiments in such a way that the inferences drawn are fully justified and are logically compelled by the data. This does not mean that the particular conceptual interpretation you put on the statistical conclusion is correct. Your theoretical explanation for why a particular effect should be observed in the population is quite different from the statistical conclusion itself. Admittedly, the substantive interpretation is more problematic in the behavioral sciences than in the agricultural sciences where the experimental manipulation (for example, application of kinds of fertilizer) is itself the treatment of substantive interest rather than being only a plausible representation of a theoretical construct (Chow, 1988, p. 107). However, the details of the preliminary argument from sample observations to general statistical conclusions about the effectiveness of the experimental manipulation had not been worked out prior to Fisher's time. His key insight, which solved the problem of making valid statistical inferences, was that of randomization. In this way, one is assured that no uncontrolled factor would bias the results of the statistical test. The details of how this works out in practice are illustrated in subsequent sections.

For the moment, it is sufficient to note that the abstract random process and its associated probabilities are merely the mathematical counterparts of the use of randomization in the concrete experimental situation. Thus, in any true experiment, there will be points in the procedure when the laws of chance are explicitly introduced and are in sole control of what is to be done. For example, one might flip a coin to determine what treatment a particular subject will receive. The probability distribution used in the statistical test makes sense only because of the use of random assignment in the conduct of the experiment. By doing so, one assures that, if the null hypothesis of no difference between treatments is correct, the results of the experiment will be determined entirely by the laws of chance (Fisher, 1935/1971, p. 17). One might imagine, for example, a wide variety of factors that would determine how a particular phobic might respond on a posttest of performance in the feared situation after receiving one of an assortment of treatments. Assuming the treatments have no effect, any number of factors—such as the individual's conditioning history, reaction to the experiment, or indigestion from a hurried lunch—might in some way affect performance. If, in the most extreme view, the particular posttest performance of each individual who could take part in your experiment was thought to be completely determined from the outset by a number of, for your purposes, irrelevant factors, the random assignment to treatment conditions assures that in the long run these will balance out. That is, randomization implies that the population means in the various treatments will, under these conditions, be exactly equal and that even the form of the distribution of scores in the various conditions will be the same.

We will now see how this simple idea of control of irrelevant factors by randomization works out in a situation that can be described by a discrete probability distribution. Thus, we will be able to derive (by using only simple counting rules) the entire probability distribution that can be used as the basis for a statistical test.

A DISCRETE PROBABILITY EXAMPLE

Fisher introduced the principles of experimentation in his *Design of Experiments* (1935/1971) with an appropriately British example that has been repeatedly used to illustrate the power of randomization and the logic of hypothesis testing (see, for example, Kempthorne, 1952, pp. 14–17, 120–134). We simply quote the original description of the problem:

> A lady declares that by tasting a cup of tea made with milk she can discriminate whether the milk or the tea infusion was first added to the cup. We will consider the problem of designing an experiment by means of which this assertion can be tested (Fisher, 1935/1971, p. 11).

(Those enamored with single-subject experimentation might be bemused to note that the principles of group experimentation were originally introduced with an N-of-1 design.) If you try to come up with an exemplary design appropriate for this particular problem, your first thought might be of the variety of possible disturbing factors over which you would like to exert experimental control. That is, you may begin by asking what factors could influence her judgment and how could these be held constant across conditions so that the only difference between the two kinds of cups is whether the milk or tea was added first. For example, variation in the temperature of the tea might be an important clue so you might carefully measure the temperature of the mixture in each cup to attempt to assure they were equally hot when they were served. Numerous other factors could also influence her judgment, and some of these may be susceptible to experimental control. The type of cup used, the strength of the tea, the use of sugar, the amount of milk added are only illustrative of the myriad potential differences that might occur among the cups to be used in the experiment. The logic of experimentation up until the time of Fisher dictated that to have a valid experiment here all the cups to be used "must be exactly alike," except for the independent variable being manipulated. Fisher rejected this dictum on two grounds. First, he argued that it was logically impossible to achieve, both in the example and in experimentation in general. The cups will inevitably differ to some degree in their smoothness, the strength of the tea and the temperature would change slightly over the time between preparation of the first and last cups, and the amounts of milk or sugar added would not be exactly equal, to mention only a few problems in the present example. Second, Fisher argued that, even if it were conceivable to achieve "exact likeness" or more realistically "imperceptible difference" on various dimensions of the stimuli, it would in practice be too expensive to attempt. Although one could, with a sufficient investment of time and money, reduce the irrelevant differences between conditions to a specified criterion on any dimension, the question of whether it is worth the effort must be raised in any actual experiment. The foremost concern with this and other attempts at experimental control is to arrive at an appropriate test of the hypothesis of interest. Fisher argued that, because the validity of the experiment could be assured by the use of randomization, it was not the best use of inevitably limited resources to attempt to achieve exact equality of stimuli on all dimensions. Most causes of fluctuation in subjects' performance "*ought* to be deliberately ignored" (1935/1971, p. 19).

Consider now how one might carry out and analyze an experiment to test our British lady's claim. The difficulty with asking for a single judgment, of course, is that she might well correctly classify it just by guessing. How many cups then would be needed to constitute a sufficient test? The answer naturally depends on how the experiment is designed, as well as the criterion adopted for how strong the evidence must be in order to be considered compelling.

One suggestion might be that the experiment be carried out by mixing eight cups of tea, four with the milk added to the cup first (milk-first, or MF, cups) and four with the tea added first (tea-first, or TF, cups), and presenting them for classification by the subject in random order. Is this a sufficient number of judgments to request?

> In considering the appropriateness of any proposed experimental design, it is always needful to forecast all possible results of the experiment, and to have decided without ambiguity what interpretation shall be placed upon each one of them. Further, we must know by what argument this interpretation is to be sustained (Fisher, 1935/1971 p. 12).

Thus, Fisher's advice translated into the current vernacular might be "if you can't analyze an experiment, don't run it." To prescribe the analysis of the suggested design, we must consider what the possible results of the experiment are and the likelihood of the occurrence of each. To be appropriate, the analysis must correspond exactly to what actually went on in the experiment.[2] Assume the subject is told that the set of eight cups consists of four MF and four TF cups. The measure that indicates how compelling the evidence could be is the probability of a perfect performance occurring by chance alone. If this probability is sufficiently small, say less than 1 chance in 20, we conclude it is implausible that the lady has no discrimination ability. There are, of course, many ways of dividing the set of eight cups into two groups of four each, with the subject thinking that one group consists of MF cups and the other group TF cups. However, if the subject cannot discriminate at all between the two kinds of cups, each of the possible divisions into two groups would be equally likely.

Thus, the probability of a correct performance occurring by chance alone could be expressed simply as the proportion of the possible divisions of the cups that are correct:

$$\text{Pr (being correct by chance)} = \frac{\text{Number of divisions that are exactly correct}}{\text{Total number of possible divisions}} \quad (1)$$

Naturally, only one division would match exactly the actual breakdown into MF and TF cups, which means the numerator of the above fraction would be 1. So the only problem is to determine the total number of ways of splitting up eight things into two groups of four each. Actually, we can solve this by determining only the number of ways the subject could select a particular set of four cups as being the MF cups; because once four are chosen as being of one kind, the other four have to be put into the other category. Formulating the solution in terms of a sequence of decisions is easiest. Any one of the eight cups could be the first to be classified as an MF cup. For each of the eight possible ways of making this first decision, there are seven cups from which to choose the second cup to be classified as an MF cup. Given the 8 × 7, or 56, ways of making the first two decisions, there are six ways of choosing the third MF cup. Finally, for each of these 8 × 7 × 6 orderings of three cups, there would be five possible ways of selecting the fourth cup to be assigned to the MF category. Thus, there are 8 × 7 × 6 × 5, or 1680, ways of choosing four cups out of eight in a particular order. However, each set of four particular cups would appear $4 \times 3 \times 2 \times 1$, or 24, times in a listing of the 1680 orderings because any set of four objects could be ordered in 24 ways. We aren't concerned with the particular sequence in which the cups in a set of four were selected, only with *which* set was selected. Thus, we can find the number of distinct sets of cups by dividing the number of orderings, 1680, by the number of ways, 24, that each distinct set could be ordered. In summary,

$$\text{Total number of possible divisions} = \frac{8 \times 7 \times 6 \times 5}{4 \times 3 \times 2 \times 1} = \frac{1680}{24} = 70 \qquad (2)$$

Those who have studied what is known as counting rules, or "permutations and combinations" will recognize the above solution as the number of combinations of eight things taken four at a time, which may be denoted $_8C_4$. In general, if one is selecting r objects from a larger set n, by the reasoning followed above, we write

$$_nC_r = \frac{n(n-1)(n-2)\cdots(n-r+1)}{r(r-1)(r-2)\cdots 1} = \frac{n!}{r!(n-r)!} \qquad (3)$$

The solution here, of there being 70 distinct combinations or sets of four cups which could possibly be designated as MF cups, is critical to the interpretation of the experiment. Following Equation 1, because only 1 of these 70 possible answers is correct, the probability of the lady being exactly right by chance alone is 1/70. Because this is less than the 1/20, or .05, probability we adopted as our criterion for being so unlikely as to be convincing, if the lady were to correctly classify all the cups we would have a sufficient basis for rejecting the null hypothesis of no discrimination ability.

Notice that in essence we have formulated a statistical test of our null hypothesis, and instead of looking up a p value for an outcome of our experiment in a table, we have derived that value ourselves. Because the experiment involved discrete events rather than scores on a continuous variable, we were able to simply use the definition of probability and a counting rule, which we also developed "from scratch" for our situation, to determine a probability that could be used to judge the statistical significance of one possible outcome of our experiment.

Although no mean feat, we admittedly have not yet considered "all possible results of the experiment," deciding "without ambiguity what interpretation shall be placed on each one." One plausible outcome is that the lady might get most of the classifications correct but fall short of perfect performance. In the current situation, this would necessarily mean that three of the four MF cups would be correctly classified. Note that, because the subject's response is to consist of putting four cups into each category, misclassifying one MF cup necessarily means that one TF cup was inappropriately thought to be a MF cup. Note also that the decision about which TF cup is misclassified can be made apart from the decision about which MF cup is misclassified. Each decision may be thought of as a combinatorial problem: How many ways can one choose three things out of four? How many ways can one be selected out of four? Thus, the number of ways of making one error with each grouping of cups is

Number of ways of making one error of each kind

$$= {_4}C_3 \cdot {_4}C_1 = \frac{4!}{3!\,1!} \cdot \frac{4!}{1!\,3!} = 4 \cdot 4 = 16 \qquad (4)$$

It may seem surprising that there are as many as 16 ways to arrive at three out of four correctly classified MF cups: However, any one of the four could be the one to be left out, and for each of these any one of four wrong cups could be put in its place.

Making use again of the definition of the probability of an event as the number of ways that event could occur over the total number of outcomes possible, we can determine the probability of this near-perfect performance arising by chance. The numerator is what was just determined, and the denominator is again the number of possible divisions of eight objects into two sets of four each, which we previously (Equation 2) determined to be 70:

$$\text{Pr (three MF and one TF classified as MF)} = \frac{{_4}C_3 \cdot {_4}C_1}{{_8}C_4} = \frac{4 \cdot 4}{70} = \frac{16}{70} \qquad (5)$$

The fact that this probability of 16/70, or .23, is considerably greater than our criterion of .05 puts us in a position to interpret not only this outcome but all other possible outcomes of the experiment as well. Even though three out of four right represents the next best thing to perfect performance, the performance that good or better could arise $(16 + 1)/70 = .24$, or nearly one-quarter of the time, when the subject had no ability to discriminate between the cups, would mean it would not be good enough to convince us of her claim. And, because all other possible outcomes would be less compelling, they would also be interpreted as providing insufficient evidence to make us believe that the lady could determine which were the MF cups.

Let us now underscore the major point of what we have developed in this section. Although we have not made reference to any continuous distribution, we have developed from first principles a statistical test appropriate for use in the interpretation of a particular experiment. The test is in fact a more generally useful one and is known in the literature as Fisher's exact test (see Hays, 1981, p. 552).

It perhaps should be mentioned that Fisher's exact test, besides illustrating how one can determine the probability of an outcome of an experiment, can be viewed as the forerunner of a host of other statistical procedures. Recent years have seen the rapid development of such techniques for categorical data analysis. These are particularly useful in those research areas—for example, some types of public health or sociological research—where all variables under investigation are categorical. A number of good introductions to such methods are now available (see, for example, Bishop, Fienberg, & Holland, 1975).

Although these methods have some use in the behavioral sciences, it is much more common for the dependent variable in experiments to be quantitative instead of qualitative. Thus, we continue our introduction to the Fisher tradition by considering another example from his writing that makes use of a quantitative dependent variable. Again, however, no reference to a theoretical population distribution is required.

RANDOMIZATION TEST

Assume that a developmental psychologist is interested in whether brief training can improve performance of two-year-old children on a test of mental abilities. The test selected is the Mental Scale of the Bayley Scales of Infant Development, which yields a mental age in months. To increase the sensitivity of the experiment, the psychologist decides to recruit sets of twins and randomly assigns one member of each pair to the treatment condition. The treatment consists simply of watching a videotape of another child attempting to perform tasks similar to those making up the Bayley Mental Scale. The other member of each pair plays in a waiting area as a time-filling activity while the first is viewing the videotape. Then, both children are individually given the Bayley by a tester who is blind to their assigned conditions. One set of twins takes part in the experiment each day, Monday through Friday, and the experiment extends over a two-week period. Table 2.1 shows the data for the study in the middle columns.

Given the well-known correlations between twins' mental abilities, it would be expected that there would be some relationship between the mental ability scores for the two twins from the same family, although the correlation will be considerably lower at age two than at age eighteen. (Behavior of any two-year-old is notoriously variable from one time to another; thus, substantial changes in even a single child's test performance across testing sessions are common.) The measure of treatment

T A B L E **2. 1** Scores on Bayley Mental Scale (in Months) for 10 Pairs of Twins

Twin Pair	Condition		Difference
	Treatment	*Control*	*(Treatment − Control)*
Week 1 data			
1	28	32	−4
2	31	25	6
3	25	15	10
4	23	25	−2
5	28	16	12
Sum for Week 1	**135**	**113**	**22**
Week 2 data			
6	26	30	−4
7	36	24	12
8	23	13	10
9	23	25	−2
10	24	16	8
Sum for Week 2	**132**	**108**	**24**
Sum for two weeks	**267**	**221**	**46**
Mean for two weeks	**26.7**	**22.1**	**4.6**

effectiveness that would commonly be used then in such a study is simply the difference between the score of the child in the treatment condition and that of his or her twin in the control condition. These are shown on the right side of Table 2.1.

A t test would typically be performed to make an inference about the mean of these differences in the population. For this particular data set, some hesitation might arise because the sample distribution is U-shaped[3] rather than the bell-shaped distribution that would be expected if the assumption made by the t test of a normal population were correct. The t test might in practice be used despite this (see the discussion of assumptions at the end of Chapter 3). However, it is not necessary to make any assumptions about the form of the population distribution in order to carry out certain tests of interest here. In fact, one can use all the quantitative information available in the sample data in testing what Fisher referred to as "the wider hypothesis" (1935/1971, p. 43) that the two groups of scores are samples from the same, possibly nonnormal population.

The test of this more general hypothesis is based simply on the implications of the fact that subjects were randomly assigned to conditions. Hence, the test is referred to as a *randomization test*. The logic is as follows: If the null hypothesis is correct, then subjects' scores in the experiment are determined by factors other than what treatment they were assigned (that is, the treatment did *not* influence subjects' scores). In fact, one may consider the score for each subject to be predetermined prior to the random assignment to conditions. Thus, the difference between any two siblings' scores would have been the same in absolute value regardless of the assignment to conditions. For example, under the null hypothesis one subject in Pair one was going to receive a score of 28 and the other a score of 32; the random assignment then simply determined that the higher-scoring subject would be in the control condition here so that the difference of "treatment minus control" would be -4 instead of $+4$. Because a random assignment was made independently for each of the 10 pairs, 10 binary decisions were in effect made as to whether a predetermined difference would have a plus or minus sign attached to it. Thus, there were 2^{10} possible combinations of signed differences that could have occurred with these subjects, and the sum of the signed differences could be used to indicate the apparent benefit (or harm) of the treatment for each combination. The distribution of these 2^{10} sums is the basis for our test. The sum of the differences actually observed, including the four negative differences, was 46. A randomization test is carried out simply by determining how many of the 2^{10} combinations of signed differences would have totals equal to or exceeding the observed total of 46. Because under the null hypothesis each of these 2^{10} combinations is equally likely, the proportion of them having sums at least as great as the observed sum provides directly the probability to use in assessing the significance of the observed sum.

In effect, one is constructing the distribution of values of a test statistic (the sum of the differences) over all possible reassignments of subjects to conditions. Determining where the observed total falls in this distribution is comparable to what is done whenever one consults a table in a parametric test to determine the significance of an observed value of a test statistic. However, now the distribution is based directly on the scores actually observed rather than on some assumed theoretical distribution.

TABLE 2.2 Possible Sums of Differences Resulting from Reassignments of First-Week Cases

Assignment

	1	2	3	4	5	6	7	8	9	10	11	12	13	14	15	16
	12	12	12	12	12	12	12	12	12	12	12	12	12	12	12	12
	10	10	10	10	10	10	10	10	-10	-10	-10	-10	-10	-10	-10	-10
	6	6	6	6	-6	-6	-6	-6	6	6	6	6	-6	-6	-6	-6
	4	4	-4	-4	4	4	-4	-4	4	4	-4	-4	4	4	-4	-4
	2	-2	2	-2	2	-2	2	-2	2	-2	2	-2	2	-2	2	-2
Sum	**34**	**30**	**26**	**22**	**22**	**18**	**14**	**10**	**14**	**10**	**6**	**2**	**2**	**-2**	**-6**	**-10**

Assignment*

	17	18	19	20	21	22	23	24	25	26	27	28	29	30	31	32
	-12	-12	-12	-12	-12	-12	-12	-12	-12	-12	-12	-12	-12	-12	-12	-12
	10	10	10	10	10	10	10	10	-10	-10	-10	-10	-10	-10	-10	-10
	6	6	6	6	-6	-6	-6	-6	6	6	6	6	-6	-6	-6	-6
	4	4	-4	-4	4	4	-4	-4	4	4	-4	-4	4	4	-4	-4
	2	-2	2	-2	2	-2	2	-2	2	-2	2	-2	2	-2	2	-2
Sum	**10**	**6**	**2**	**-2**	**-2**	**-6**	**-10**	**-14**	**-10**	**-14**	**-18**	**-22**	**-22**	**-26**	**-30**	**-34**

*Note that assignments 17–32 are the same as assignments 1–16 except that 12 is assigned a negative sign rather than a positive sign, and so each sum is 24 less than the sum for the corresponding assignment above.

That one uses all the quantitative information in the sample and gets a statistical test without needing to make any distributional assumptions makes an attractive combination. There are disadvantages, however. A major one, which essentially prevented use of randomization tests until recent years in all but the smallest data sets, is the large number of computations required. To completely determine the distribution of possible totals for even the set of 10 differences in Table 2.1 would require examining $2^{10} = 1024$ sets of data. We summarize the results of this process below but illustrate the computations for the smaller data set consisting only of the five scores from week 1.

With five scores, there are $2^5 = 32$ possible assignments of positive and negative signs to the individual scores. Table 2.2 lists the scores in rank order of their absolute value at the top left. Then, 15 other sets, including progressively more minus signs, are listed along with the sum for each. The sums for the remaining 16 sets are immediately determined by realizing that when the largest number of 12 is assigned a negative rather than a positive sign the sum would be reduced by 24.

If the first week constituted the entire experiment, these 32 sums would allow us to determine the significance of the observed total Bayley difference for the first week of 22 $(= -4 + 6 + 10 - 2 + 12$, see Table 2.1). Figure 2.1 shows a grouped, relative frequency histogram for the possible sums, with the shaded portion on the right indicating the sums greater than or equal to the observed sum of 22. (An ungrouped histogram, although still perfectly symmetrical, appears somewhat less regular.) Thus, the probability of a total at least as large as and in the same direction as that observed would be $5/32 (= 3/32 + 2/32)$, or .16, which would not be sufficiently small for us to claim significance.

The same procedure could be followed for the entire set of 10 scores. Rather than listing the 1024 combinations of scores or displaying the distribution of totals, the information needed to perform a test of significance can be summarized by

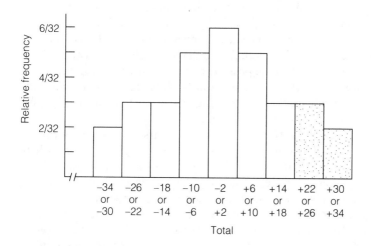

F I G U R E **2.1** Distribution of possible totals of difference scores using data from Week 1.

T A B L E **2. 3**   Number of Combinations of Signed Differences with Sums Equal to or Greater Than the Observed Sum

Number of Negative Values	Total Number of Combinations	Number of Combinations with		
		Sum > 46	*Sum = 46*	*Sum < 46*
0	1	1		
1	10	8	2	
2	45	12	6	27
3	120	5	5	110
4	210		1	209
5	252			252
6	210			210
7	120			120
8	45			45
9	10			10
10	1			1
Totals	**1024**	**26**	**14**	**984**

indicating the number of totals greater than or equal to the observed sum of 46. Fortunately, it is clear that if five or more numbers were assigned negative signs, the total would necessarily be less than 46. Table 2.3 shows the breakdown for the other possible combinations.

We now have the needed information to address the question with which we began this section: Does brief training improve the performance of two-year-olds on a test of mental abilities? Under the null hypothesis that the scores from the subjects receiving training and those not receiving training represent correlated samples from two populations having identical population distributions, the random assignment to conditions has allowed us to generate a distribution of possible totals of 10 scores based on the data actually observed. As shown in Table 2.3, we find that only 40 of 1024, or .039, of the possible combinations of signed differences result in totals as large or larger than that actually observed. Thus, we conclude that we have significant evidence that our training has resulted in improved performance among the children tested in the experiment.

Two points about this conclusion are noteworthy. First, we have performed a one-tailed test. A one-tailed test might be warranted in an applied setting where one is only interested in the treatment if it helps performance. If a two-tailed test had been performed, a different conclusion would have been reached. To see this, we make use of the symmetry of the distributions used in randomization tests (every combination of signed differences is matched by one in which every sign is reversed, so every positive total has a corresponding negative total of the same absolute value). Thus, there would be exactly 40 cases totaling −46 or less. This yields a combined probability of 80/1024, or .078, of observing a total as extreme or more extreme in either direction than that observed; hence, we would fail to reject the null hypothesis in favor of a *nondirectional alternative hypothesis.*

Second, it should be pointed out that the hypothesis tested by the randomization test is not identical to that tested by the *t* test. The hypothesis in the *t* test concerns the population mean of a continuous random variable. The hypothesis in the randomization test concerns the presumption that each of the observed difference scores could have been preceded by a positive or negative sign with equal likelihood. The *p* value yielded by performing a *t* test would be exact only if the theoretical distribution prescribed by its density formula were perfectly matched by the actual distribution of the test statistic given the current population, which it certainly will not be here. However, in part because of the factors summarized by the central limit theorem (discussed in the next section), the *p* value in the table generally will be a very good approximation to the exact *p* value even with nonnormal data such as we have in the current example. Similarly, the *p* value in the randomization test is the exact probability only for the distribution arising from hypothetical reassignments of the particular cases used in the study (Edgington, 1966, 1980). However, the closeness of the correspondence between the *p* value yielded by the randomization test and that yielded by the *t* test can be demonstrated mathematically under certain conditions (Pitman, 1937).

We can illustrate this correspondence in the current example as well. If we perform a *t* test of the hypothesis that the mean difference score in the population is 0, we obtain a *t* value of 2.14 with 9 degrees of freedom. This observed *t* value is exceeded by .031 of the theoretical *t* distribution, which compares rather closely with the .039 we obtained from our randomization test above. The correspondence is even closer if, as Fisher suggested (1935/1971, p. 46), we correct the *t* test for the discontinuous nature of our data.[4] Hence, with only 10 cases, the difference between the probabilities yielded by the two tests is on the order of 1 in 1000. In fact, one may view the *t* test and the randomization test as very close approximations to one another. Deciding to reject the hypothesis of the randomization test is tantamount to deciding to reject the hypothesis of the *t* test.

TOWARD TESTS BASED ON DISTRIBUTIONAL ASSUMPTIONS

Although this chapter may in some ways seem an aside in the development of analysis of variance procedures, in actuality it is a fundamental and necessary step. First, we have seen the possibility of empirically deriving our own significance levels for particular data-analysis situations. This is a useful conceptual development to provide an analogy for what follows, where we will be assuming normal distribution methods. Second, and perhaps more important, the close correspondence between the results of randomization and normal theory–based tests provides a justification for using the normal theory methods. This justification applies in two important respects, each of which we discuss in turn. First, it provides a rationale for use of normal theory methods regardless of whether subjects are in fact randomly *sampled* from a population. Secondly, it is relevant to the justification of use of normal theory methods regardless of the actual shape of the distribution of the variable under investigation.

Statistical Tests with Convenience Samples

The vast majority of psychological research uses subject pools that can be conveniently obtained rather than actually selecting subjects via a random sampling procedure from the population to which the experimenter hopes to generalize. Subjects may be those people at your university who were in Psychology 101 and disposed to volunteer to participate in your experiment, or they may be clients who happened to come to the clinic or hospital at the time your study was in progress. In no sense do these individuals constitute a simple random sample from the population to which you would like to generalize, for example, the population of all adults or all mental health clinic clients in the United States.

If your goal is to provide normative information that could be used in classifying individuals—for example, as being in the top 15 percent of all college freshmen on a reading comprehension test—then a sample that is obtained exclusively from the local area is of little help. You have no assurance that the local students have the same distribution of reading comprehension scores as the entire population. Although one can compute standard errors of the sample statistics and perhaps maintain that they are accurate for the hypothetical population of students for which the local students could be viewed as a random sample, they do not inform you of what you probably want to know—for example, how far is the local mean from the national mean, or how much error is probable in the estimate of the score on the test that would cut off the top 15 percent of the population of all college freshmen? Such misinterpretations by psychologists of the standard errors of statistics from nonrandom samples have been soundly criticized by statisticians (see Freedman, Pisani, & Purves, 1978, pp. 350–351, p. A–56).

The situation is somewhat, although not entirely, different with between-group comparisons based on a convenience sample where subjects have been randomly assigned to conditions. A randomization test could always be carried out in this situation and is a perfectly valid approach. The *p* value yielded by such a test, as we have seen, refers to where the observed test statistic would fall in the distribution obtained by hypothetical redistributions of subjects to conditions. Because the *p* value for a *t* test or *F* test is very close to that yielded by the randomization test and because the randomization test results are cumbersome to compute for any but the smallest data sets,[5] one may compute the more standard *t* or *F* test and interpret the inference as applying either to possible reassignments of the currently available subjects or to an imaginary population for which these subjects might be thought to be a random sample. The generalization to a real population or to people in general that is likely of interest is then made on *nonstatistical* grounds. Thus, behavioral scientists in general must make use of whatever theoretical knowledge they possess about the stability of the phenomena under investigation across subpopulations in order to make accurate, externally valid assertions about the generality of their findings.

The Assumption of Normality

The F tests that are the primary focus in the following chapters assume that the population distribution of the dependent variable in each group is normal in form. Because the dependent-variable distribution is never exactly normal in form, the distribution of the test statistic is only approximately correct, although generally the approximation to the theoretical F or the exact randomization test is good. Thus, the F tests that follow can actually be viewed as approximations to the exact randomization tests that could be carried out. The closeness of this approximation has been demonstrated both theoretically (Wald & Wolfowitz, 1944) and by numerical examples (Kempthorne, 1952, pp. 128–132; Pitman, 1937).

Approximations are expected to be better the closer the data are to being exactly normally distributed. Fortunately, there are good reasons for expecting the data in many behavioral science applications to be normally distributed.

First, bell-shaped data have repeatedly been observed empirically. Researchers have been noting for over 150 years that data are often normally distributed. Although the normal curve was derived as early as 1733 by Abraham De Moivre as the limit of the binomial distribution (Stigler, 1986, pp. 70–77), it was not until the work of Laplace, Guass, and Legendre in the early 1800s that the more general importance of the distribution was recognized. Many of the early applications of statistics were in astronomy, and it was an astronomer, F. W. Bessel, who in 1818 published the first comparison of an empirical distribution with the normal. [Bessel is known in the history of psychology for initiating the scientific study of individual differences by developing "the personal equation" describing interastronomer differences (Boring, 1950).] From a catalog of 60,000 individual observations of stars by the British Astronomer Royal James Bradley, Bessel examined in detail a group of 300 observations of the positions of a few selected stars. These data allowed an empirical check on the adequacy of the normal curve as a theory of the distribution of errors. The observations were records of Bradley's judgments of the instant when a star crossed the center line of a specially equipped telescope. The error of each observation could be assessed; Table 2.4 portrays a grouped frequency distribution of the absolute value of the errors in tenths of a second. Bessel calculated the number of errors expected to fall in each interval by using an approximation of the proportion of the normal distribution in that interval. In short, the fit was good. For example, the standard deviation for these data was roughly .2 seconds, and thus approximately two-thirds of the cases (that is, 200 of the 300 observations) were expected to fall within 1 standard deviation of the mean (that is, absolute values of errors less than .2), and in fact they did (see Stigler, 1986, p. 202ff.).

Within psychology, Francis Galton did pioneering work to determine the fit of the normal distribution to distributions of human abilities and characteristics. At

T A B L E **2. 4** Bessel's Comparison of the Distribution of the Absolute Values of Errors with the Normal Distribution for 300 Astronomical Observations

Range (in Seconds)	Frequency of Errors	
	Observed	*Estimated (Based on Normal Distribution)*
0.0–0.1	114	107
0.1–0.2	84	87
0.2–0.3	53	57
0.3–0.4	24	30
0.4–0.5	14	13
0.5–0.6	6	5
0.6–0.7	3	1
0.7–0.8	1	0
0.8–0.9	1	0

his Anthropometric Laboratory outside London in the late 1800s, Galton amassed data showing how both physical (for example, height) and mental (for example, examination scores) characteristics could be fit reasonably well with a normal curve (Stigler, 1986, Chapter 8). More recently, there are many areas of psychology in which large-scale studies indicate that commonly used dependent variables follow a normal distribution quite closely. We cite two examples to illustrate the point.

One of the most frequently used measures in current human experimental psychology is that of reaction time. Reaction time is used, for example, in a chronometric approach to cognitive psychology to assess the effects of manipulations such as priming (presenting a cue word immediately before a trial) on the mean time it takes to detect the presentation of a target word. Although over repeated trials a single individual's reaction time tends to follow a positively skewed distribution (more on this in a moment), it has been known for many years that *across* individuals the distribution of individual's average reaction time conforms very closely to the normal distribution. Figure 2.2 presents data originally reported by Fessard (1926) and cited by Woodworth and Schlosberg (1954, p. 37). Fessard measured the reaction time to sound for each of a group of 1000 men who were applicants for jobs as machinists in Paris. Each man was measured on 30 trials, and the mean of these was used in determining the frequencies shown in the figure. A few extreme cases (35 of 1000) were excluded by Fessard (1926, p. 218) from the table reporting his data. Although the correspondence between the data as plotted and the normal distribution is quite close, the complete data may have provided an even better fit because of the long tails of the normal distribution. Nonetheless, allowing for sampling variability, the data as presented correspond about as closely as one could hope to the theoretical normal distribution.

A second empirical example of normally distributed data in psychology is provided by scores on the MMPI. Figure 2.3 shows the distribution of scores of 699

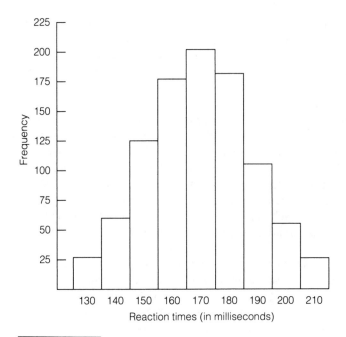

F I G U R E 2. 2 Group frequency distribution of simple reaction times.

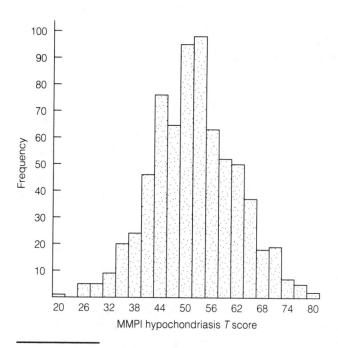

F I G U R E 2. 3 MMPI hypochondriasis scores.

Minnesotans on the Hypochondriasis scale of the MMPI, as reported by McKinley and Hathaway (1956). The respondents, originally described in Hathaway and McKinley (1940), were individuals who were not ill but who accompanied relatives or friends to the University of Minnesota Hospital. Again, a distribution that corresponds quite closely to a theoretical normal distribution is yielded by these test scores from "Minnesota normals."

These are but two examples of a finding repeated over and over. Measures of aptitude, personality, memory, and motor skill performance are often approximately normally distributed. In part this has to do with the global level at which constructs within the behavioral sciences are typically assessed. In a sense, the further the analysis of a phenomenon into its basic, elementary components has been carried, the less likely the data are to follow a normal distribution. Within some areas of physiological psychology, this is the case. The interest may, for example, be simply in the occurrence or nonoccurrence of a discrete event: Did the neuron fire?

Perhaps the most extensively modeled nonnormal, *continuous* processes are temporal ones. Mathematical psychologists have theorized in detail about the specific nonnormal form of, for instance, the distribution of simple reaction times *within an individual* to repeated presentations of a tone or the distribution of interresponse times in the recordings of a single nerve fiber (see McGill, 1963). However, most areas of psychology have not progressed to having theories about the form of distributions. Nor do we have many valid binary measures of elementary processes. Instead, most often the dependent variable is a composite of a number of measures, for example, the total of the responses to 40 items on a questionnaire. Although the questionnaire may be of interest because it is thought to indicate the presence or absence of a particular psychological state such as clinical depression, the distribution of the observed variable probably will not be such that it can be indicated by the frequency of two particular scores on the scale (for example 0 and 40). Rather, its distribution will be importantly determined by the fact that the score on the questionnaire is the sum of the responses to 40 different items, which are far from all being perfectly correlated. Because it is not unusual for the dependent variable in a behavioral science study to be of this composite nature, a remarkable theorem can give a reasonable basis for expecting your data in many situations to follow a bell-shaped curve.

This theorem, arguably the most important in statistics, is the *central limit theorem*. In its simplest form, the theorem states that the sum of a large number of independent random variables is approximately normally distributed. What is remarkable about the result is that there are almost no constraints placed on the individual distributions of the original random variables. Some could be discrete, others continuous; some could be U-shaped, some skewed, some flat; some could have large variances, some small; and still their sum would be normally distributed.

This theorem can be relied on in two ways in constructing an argument for why broad classes of behavioral science data might be expected to be normally distributed[6] (Bailey, 1971, p. 199ff.). First, theory may suggest that numerous independent factors are the causes of a particular phenomenon. For example, the keenness of an individual's vision may be viewed as the product of a series of partial causes, most of which are related to genetic background although some environmental factors such as quality of diet or amount of eyestrain experienced might also be posited in a particular theoretical account. If these various partial causes occur independently in nature and summate to determine the quality of an individual's vision, then the central limit theorem tells us that the distribution of visual acuity over individuals will follow a bell-shaped distribution.

A second way in which the central limit theorem could be used to justify the expectation of a normal distribution is through conceptualizing behavioral observations for various individuals as being the result of a distribution of errors around one true value. This approach fits nicely with the way in which we express statistical models in the next chapter. Instead of there being a distribution of true values across individuals as a result of specified causes, now there is assumed to be one true value around which individuals vary for unspecified reasons. To continue with another perceptual example, assume individuals are being asked to reproduce a line segment of a given length that they are shown briefly. Then, we might say that $Y_i = \tau + \varepsilon_i$, where Y_i is the measured length of the line drawn by individual i, τ is the true length of the line, and ε_i is the error term for individual i. Each of these ε_i scores may be viewed as each being a composite of a number of factors that cause the measured line length for an individual to depart from the true length. These would include both errors of measurement in recording the length of the line the subject draws and the momentary fluctuations in the individual that affect the perception of the length of the presented line and the exact length of the line the individual produces. This latter category might include the effects of slight changes in the point where the eyes are fixated at the time of exposure, fluctuations in attention, and variations in the hosts of neural processes involved in programming a response and muscular actions required to execute it. If each of these small factors independently contributes to the composite error score for each of the individuals performing the task, then the central limit theorem shows that the composite error scores, and hence the observed Y scores, will be normally distributed. (This view of errors as themselves being composites, and hence approximately normally distributed according to the central limit theorem, was first conceived by Laplace in 1810 and played a major role in the development of inferential statistics (Stigler, 1986, p. 143).)

Either or both of these factors may be at work to make the data in any particular study tend toward a normal distribution. Admittedly, at times the approximation to the normal may be rather gross. For instance, a single error factor may be so large that when it occurs it swamps the value of the composite error for a subset of the data. In the line-length task, a slip of the hand might result in the line drawn by an individual being considerably longer than the true length, yet the distribution of lengths across individuals still may have a single mode near the median of the distribution and thus be a rough approximation to the normal, even though somewhat skewed. Again, some of the causal factors, in the first account, or the error components, in the second account, may not be independent of each other. Yet if there are a number of independent components, the resultant distribution may be approximately bell-shaped.

Besides the empirical and conceptual reasons for expecting data to be normally distributed, in the historical development of statistics it was the case that assuming normality made it easier to solve some difficult mathematical problems. This increased tractability no doubt contributed to the rise to prominence of statistical methods based on the normal distribution. For example, working independently, Gauss in 1809 showed that a particular estimation problem could be solved if errors were assumed to be normally distributed, and Laplace's central limit theorem of 1810 provided good reasons for expecting normal distributions to occur. As Stephen Stigler tells the story in his excellent book on the history of statistics, "the remarkable circumstance that the curve that led to the simplest analysis also had such an attractive rationale was conceptually liberating" (1986, p. 145). The result was a synthesis of ideas and a development of techniques representing "one of the major success stories in the history of science" (1986, p. 158).

We have now argued that behavioral data frequently can be expected to be approximately normally distributed. We have also argued that normal-theory-based tests are close approximations to randomization tests regardless of the shape of the distribution. A final argument for the use of normal-theory-based procedures that concerns the robustness of those tests to violations of their assumptions is reserved until the end of Chapter 3, by which point we will have discussed the statistical assumptions made in linear model tests.

Recent years have seen a profusion of so-called robust or sturdy statistical procedures, which are offered as an alternative to normal theory procedures. We will consider some of these in the final chapter. However, for reasons such as those we have discussed regarding the reasonableness of the normal distribution assumption and the hard fact of a historical context in which normal-theory-based procedures have been dominant (Huberty, 1987), statistical methods based on the general linear model assuming normally distributed data are expected to continue as the most important analytic methods in the behavioral sciences. It is to a discussion of those methods that we now turn.

E X E R C I S E S

1. True or False: The observed value of a test statistic and hence the observed p value depends on the data collected in a study.

2. True or False: If a p value indicates the results of a study are highly statistically significant, the null hypothesis cannot be true.

3. True or False: Other things being equal the smaller the p value, the stronger the evidence against the null hypothesis.

4. True or False: The p value in a randomization test can be 0.

*5. True or False: The p value associated with the observed value of a test statistic is the probability the results are due to chance.

6. Assume a cognitive psychologist is planning an experiment involving brief presentations of letter strings that satisfy certain constraints. There are 14 such letter strings that satisfy the constraints but only 6 can be used in a particular paradigm.
   a. How many combinations of 6 letter strings can be chosen from the set of 14?

    b. Given that 6 letter strings have been selected, in how many different sequences could they conceivably be presented?

*7. Assume a staff member at the local state mental hospital who has been doing intake interviews for years claims that he can tell on the basis of his interviews whom the psychiatrists will judge to be sufficiently healthy to release from the hospital within the first week and whom the psychiatrists will require to stay longer than a week. As a young clinical intern at the hospital who is taken with actuarial as opposed to intuitive predictions, you are eager to prove the staff member wrong. You bet him that he will perform no differently than could be explained by chance (with alpha of .05, two-tailed) in his predictions about the next dozen patients. He agrees to the bet on the condition you first provide him information at the end of the week about how many of the dozen patients were released so that he will know how many such patients to name. With this figure, he thinks he can determine who the released patients were, just on the basis of his earlier interview (he has no subsequent contact with the patients). To your surprise, he correctly names five of the six patients released early. Do you owe him any money? Would it have made any difference if he had named five of six early-release patients out of a set of 15 intake interviews rather than 12? Support your answers.

8. A police officer in an urban police department alleges that minorities are being discriminated against in promotion decisions. As evidence is offered the difference in promotion rates in 1984. In that year, among those eligible for promotion to the rank of sergeant, 20 officers, including 7 members of minority groups, passed an objective exam to qualify them for consideration by the review board. The number of officers that can be promoted is determined by the number of vacancies at the higher rank, and in 1984, there were 10 vacancies at the rank of sergeant that needed to be filled. Eight of the 13 nonminority officers were promoted, for a promotion rate of 61.5 percent, whereas only 2 of the 7 minority officers were promoted for a promotion rate of 28.5 percent. If one assumes that the decisions about whom to promote were made independently of minority status, what is the probability that the discrepancy between proportions being promoted would be at least this different by chance alone, given the total number of officers under consideration and the total number of promotions possible?

*9. Biological changes that result from psychological manipulations, although typically not well understood, have captured attention in many areas such as health psychology. One early study examined the effects of the social environment on the anatomy of the brain in an effort to find evidence for the kind of changes in the brain as a result of experience demanded by learning theories. The experiments are described in Bennett, E. L, Diamond, M. C., Krech, D., & Rosenzweig, M. R. (1964). "Chemical and anatomical plasticity of the brain" *Science 146*, 610–619, and some of the raw data are presented in Freedman et al. (1978, p. 452). Pairs of male rats from a litter were used as subjects, with one member of each litter being chosen at random to be reared with other rats in an enriched environment, complete with playthings and novel areas to explore on a regular basis, whereas another member of the litter was randomly selected to be reared in isolation in a relatively deprived environment. Both groups were permitted to consume as much as they wanted of the same kinds of food and drink. After a month, the deprived environment animals were heavier and had heavier brains overall. Of critical interest though was the size of the cortex, or gray matter portion, of the brain in the two groups. The experiment was replicated a number of times. However, in the current exercise, we will be considering the data from only one of the replications (labeled Experiment 3 in Freedman et al., 1978, p. 452). The weights of the cortex (in milligrams) for the pairs of experimental (enriched) and control (deprived) subjects are shown in the table that follows:

Experiment #3

Experimental	Control
690	668
701	667
685	647
751	693
647	635
647	644
720	665
718	689
718	642
696	673
658	675
680	641

Test for the effect of the treatment in this experiment by doing a randomization test. That is, perform a test of the hypothesis that the sum of the difference scores is no different than you would expect if the + and − signs had been assigned with probability .5 to the absolute values of the obtained difference scores. Although a large number of rerandomizations are possible with 12 pairs of subjects, the randomization test can be carried out with even less computation than a t test here by thinking a bit about the possibilities. To carry out the test, you need to answer the following questions:

a. What is the observed sum of differences here?

b. How many assignments of signs to differences are possible?

c. What proportion of these would result in a sum at least as large in absolute value as that observed? To answer this question, use the following approach:

  (1) What is the largest possible positive sum that could be achieved, given the observed absolute values of the differences?

  (2) By considering how much this largest sum would be reduced by changing one or two of the signs of the absolute differences from positive to negative, determine which assignments of signs to differences would result in sums between (or equal to) the maximal sum and the observed sum.

  (3) Considering the symmetry of the distribution of sums resulting from rerandomizations, what is the total number of sums as extreme or more extreme, either positive or negative, as the observed sum?

*10. In 1876 Charles Darwin reported the results of a series of experiments on "The Effects of Cross- and Self-Fertilisation in the Vegetable Kingdom." The description of his experiment and the table of data for this problem are based on Fisher's discussion of "A Historical Experiment on Growth Rate" (Fisher, 1935/1971, Chapter III). The experimental method adopted by Darwin was to pit each self-fertilized plant against a cross-fertilized one under conditions that were as similar as possible for the two plants. Darwin emphasized this similarity by indicating "my crossed and self-fertilised plants ... were of exactly the same age, were subjected from first to last to the same conditions, and were descended from the same parents." One of the ways Darwin used to equalize conditions for the two members of a pair was to plant them in the same pot. The dependent measure was the height of the plant. (Darwin did not specify when this was

T A B L E **2. 5** Zea Mays (Young Plants)

	As Recorded by Mr. Darwin			Arranged in Order of Magnitude				
				In Separate Pots		In a Single Series		
Column I	II	III	IV	V	VI	VII	VIII
	Crossed	Self-Fertilized	Crossed	Self-Fertilized	Crossed	Self-Fertilized	Difference
	Inches	Inches	Inches	Inches	Inches	Inches	Inches
Pot I	$23\frac{4}{8}$	$17\frac{3}{8}$	$23\frac{4}{8}$	$20\frac{3}{8}$	$23\frac{4}{8}$	$20\frac{3}{8}$	$-3\frac{1}{8}$
	12	$20\frac{3}{8}$	21	20	$23\frac{2}{8}$	20	$-3\frac{2}{8}$
	21	20	12	$17\frac{3}{8}$	23	20	-3
Pot II	22	20	22	20	$22\frac{1}{8}$	$18\frac{5}{8}$	$-3\frac{4}{8}$
	$19\frac{1}{8}$	$18\frac{3}{8}$	$21\frac{4}{8}$	$18\frac{5}{8}$	$22\frac{1}{8}$	$18\frac{5}{8}$	$-3\frac{4}{8}$
	$21\frac{4}{8}$	$18\frac{5}{8}$	$19\frac{1}{8}$	$18\frac{3}{8}$	22	$18\frac{3}{8}$	$-3\frac{5}{8}$
Pot III	$22\frac{1}{8}$	$18\frac{5}{8}$	$23\frac{2}{8}$	$18\frac{5}{8}$	$21\frac{5}{8}$	18	$-3\frac{5}{8}$
	$20\frac{3}{8}$	$15\frac{2}{8}$	$22\frac{1}{8}$	18	$21\frac{4}{8}$	18	$-3\frac{4}{8}$
	$18\frac{2}{8}$	$16\frac{4}{8}$	$21\frac{5}{8}$	$16\frac{4}{8}$	21	18	-3
	$21\frac{5}{8}$	18	$20\frac{3}{8}$	$16\frac{2}{8}$	21	$17\frac{3}{8}$	$-3\frac{5}{8}$
	$23\frac{2}{8}$	$16\frac{2}{8}$	$18\frac{2}{8}$	$15\frac{2}{8}$	$20\frac{3}{8}$	$16\frac{4}{8}$	$-3\frac{7}{8}$
Pot IV	21	18	23	18	$19\frac{1}{8}$	$16\frac{2}{8}$	$-2\frac{7}{8}$
	$22\frac{1}{8}$	$12\frac{6}{8}$	$22\frac{1}{8}$	18	$18\frac{2}{8}$	$15\frac{4}{8}$	$-2\frac{6}{8}$
	23	$15\frac{4}{8}$	21	$15\frac{4}{8}$	12	$15\frac{2}{8}$	$+3\frac{2}{8}$
	12	18	12	$12\frac{6}{8}$	12	$12\frac{6}{8}$	$+0\frac{6}{8}$

measured, other than to say that all plants were of the same age when their height was measured.) Although sample sizes were relatively small, Darwin indicated in his report that the experiment required 11 years to complete. To be certain that his analysis of these valuable data was correct, Darwin requested and obtained statistical consulting from his half-cousin Francis Galton. Darwin's data and Galton's rearrangements of the data are shown in Table 2.5 on page 59. Darwin's paired data are shown in Columns II and III, where you see that varying numbers of pairs of plants were put in each pot. For example, there were three pairs in Pot I, five pairs in Pot III, and so on. Galton complained that the data had no "*prima facie* appearance of regularity." He attempted to rectify this problem by arranging the data by rank ordering according to heights, first within pots in Columns IV and V, and then collapsing across pots in Columns VI and VII. Galton's differences between the reordered lists are shown in Column VIII.

a. Criticize Darwin's experimental design.
b. Perform appropriate analyses of these data.
  (1) Begin simply. Determine how many of the within-pair differences in heights in the original data of Columns II and III favor cross-fertilization. If the cross-fertilization had no effect, how many differences would you expect on the average out of 15 to favor the cross-fertilized member of a pair? Is the observed number of differences favoring cross-fertilization significantly different from what you would expect by chance?
  (2) Perform the simplest possible parametric statistical test appropriate for analyzing Darwin's data. How does the p value for this test compare to that in part (1)? Why is the difference between the p values in this case in the direction it is?
  (3) What assumptions are required for your analyses in parts (1) and (2)?
  (4) One could, and Fisher in fact did, carry out a randomization test on these data. What assumptions does that test require and what hypothesis would it test here?
c. Criticize Galton's analysis. How differently would the strength of the evidence have appeared if the data in Columns VI and VII had been used for analysis rather than that in Columns II and III?

Part Two

Model Comparisons for Between-Subjects Designs

The aim of science is, on the one hand, a comprehension as complete as possible ... and, on the other hand, the accomplishment of this aim by the use of a minimum of primary concepts and relations.

ALBERT EINSTEIN, *PHYSICS AND REALITY*, 1936

3 Introduction to Model Comparisons: One-Way Between-Subjects Designs

THE BASIC PURPOSE OF analysis of variance (ANOVA) is to assist the researcher in formulating a linear model that is appropriate for describing the data obtained in a study. The most appropriate model is one that is as simple as possible but that still provides an adequate description of the data. Although the simplicity and adequacy of a particular model could be evaluated on an absolute basis, typically models are judged on a relative basis by comparisons with other possible models. This notion of searching for a simple yet adequate model is pervasive. It informs not only all applications of ANOVA but also many other kinds of hypothesis testing.

We begin our discussion of ANOVA and linear models by approaching the problem from a purely descriptive point of view. We define a *model* in this context, as we will develop below, as simply an algebraic statement of how the scores on the dependent variable arose. *Linear* is used in the sense of *linear combination*, that is, the models portray the dependent variable as being the result of the additive combination of various effects. We estimate the unknowns in each model in such a way that the model appears as adequate as possible, that is, the error of the model is minimized given a particular set of data. Statistical tests can then be developed as a comparison of the minimal errors associated with two competing models. To perform a hypothesis test is essentially to ask if a more complex model results in a substantially better fit to the data than does a simpler model.

To give an overview of the direction our discussion will take, we first present the rationale and form of the general linear model. In the remainder of the chapter, our discussion proceeds from the simplest case of this general linear model to more and more complex forms. We consider a one-group situation, a two-group situation, and then situations involving three or more groups of subjects. To ensure that the model-comparison approach is clear, we begin with experimental designs that are one or two steps simpler than those considered in typical ANOVA texts. Besides easing the introduction to linear models, this will illustrate the generality of the linear models approach.

When considering the situation involving a single population, typically the primary question to answer is, Is the mean of the population equal to a particular value? Naturally, any attempt to answer such a question involves estimating the population mean for the dependent variable on the basis of a sample of data. After analyzing this situation descriptively, we develop an intuitively reasonable test statistic and relate this to a statistical test with which you are probably already familiar.

In the two-group situation, our approach is similar, and our concern is to use the model-comparison procedure to address the question, Are the two population means equal? In other designs involving three or more populations, which is the simplest case in which most researchers would use ANOVA, the question simply generalizes to, Are all the population means the same?

Thus, our tactic is to consider first the general form of linear models and then one-sample tests, two-sample tests, and several-sample tests as special cases of the general approach. Once the general approach has been introduced for the tests in these different situations, we discuss other topics including methods for characterizing the effects observed in a study and the assumptions underlying the tests.

In each case considered in this chapter, we assume that the samples represent independent groups of participants and that these groups differ along a single dimension or factor. Hence, the experimental designs under consideration here are termed *one-way between-subject designs*. Once you understand the linear model approach in these simple situations, extensions to multiple-factor designs or topics such as regression or analysis of covariance should come relatively easily.

THE GENERAL LINEAR MODEL

The basic assumption underlying all models considered in this book is that any phenomenon is affected by multiple factors. Although our assumption of finite causation postulates that the number of factors causing any event is not infinitely large (hence, causes can be replicated and science is possible), we also must realistically acknowledge that many factors enter into why a particular subject obtains a particular score on any dependent variable that is likely to be of interest in behavioral science research. In any one research project, we can only hope to manipulate or measure a small number of the likely causal factors of any event. The remainder we either fail to recognize, or recognize but do not account for in our model. Thus at the simplest level, the basic structure of our models of data is as follows:

observed value   sum of effects   sum of effects
on dependent   = of "allowed-for" + of other
variable   factors   factors

We "allow for" the effect of a factor by explicitly incorporating a term into our statistical model for that factor. The other factors can be dealt with in one of two ways. First, variables that we know are important but that are not the immediate concern of our research can be held constant. We can thus "control for" the effect of age by selecting all subjects from the same age range or the effect of the location in which an experiment is run by using the same laboratory room for all subjects. Unrecognized factors such as certain common historical events could also conceivably be constant across all subjects in a sample. Second, we can allow certain other factors to vary across subjects. This may arise because we explicitly decide that it is not desirable to control for a particular factor. For example, characteristics of a person's skin may influence galvanic skin response (GSR) readings in a psychophysiological study but be too expensive in time and resources to independently measure. Or, intelligence may be recognized as an important factor in performance on a problem-solving task, but we may choose not to select subjects on the basis of intelligence so as to increase the generality of our findings. Furthermore, variation occurs without our knowledge in a host of factors besides those we allow for in our model. Most obviously, the previous history of individual subjects is for the most part beyond our knowledge. Other factors such as minor differences in environmental conditions vary from subject to subject and may influence performance in some way. The effects of all these other varying factors will be lumped together in our statistical model in an error or residual term that will be allowed to assume a unique value for each subject.

Thus, we can refine slightly the structure of our model to distinguish between other factors that are held constant and those that vary randomly over subjects:

$$
\begin{array}{lllll}
\text{observed value} & \text{effect of} & \text{sum of effects} & \text{randomly} \\
\text{on dependent} & = \text{constant} + \text{of allowed-for} + \text{varying} \\
\text{variable} & \text{factors} & \text{factors} & \text{other factors}
\end{array}
$$

To give a concrete example, there are obviously any number of factors exerting an influence on an individual child's performance on a particular IQ test. In one research project, we might be interested in concentrating on assessment of how various parental characteristics such as socioeconomic status (SES), parents' IQ, and time spent with the child are related to their child's IQ score. Thus, our model might be

$$
\begin{array}{ll}
\text{each child's IQ score} = & \text{a baseline IQ score} + \text{the effect of parents' SES} \\
& + \text{the effect of parents' IQ} \\
& + \text{the effect of amount of time spent with parents} \\
& + \text{the effect of other factors}
\end{array}
$$

As you can see, it quickly becomes cumbersome, even for just three specific factors, to write out the labels for each in an equation. Some sort of shorthand is obviously needed.

We follow the convention of using Y to denote the dependent variable and using Xs for the various "accounted-for" factors. We can then translate the verbal equation into a more typical algebraic form:

$$
Y_i = \beta_0 X_{0_i} + \beta_1 X_{1_i} + \beta_2 X_{2_i} + \beta_3 X_{3_i} + \varepsilon_i
$$

Here, Y_i represents the score of individual i on the dependent variable, and the Xs provide information about the level of individual i on the factors for which we are allowing. The βs are unknowns that we must estimate. Each β indicates something of the relationship between a particular X factor and the dependent variable. (Frequently, as noted in Chapter 1, [p. 8], we refer to these unknowns as *effect parameters*. However, whether one's interpretation should be that of a causal rather than a correlational relationship hinges on one's theory of the process. One's ability to persuade others of the causal nature of the relationship often hinges on the design of the study—for example, whether the experimenter independently determined the level of a factor experienced by a particular individual.)

The first unknown parameter and X variable listed in the model typically play the special role of reflecting the effect of the *constant factors*, that is, those factors that are common to all subjects. Thus, X_0 is usually simply a 1 for every individual, indicating that 1 times the constant is part of the equation for each individual; the constant β_0 is usually the mean of the population from which we are sampling (cf.

the following section). The final term in the equation also plays a special role. Epsilon (ε)—that is, the "e" of the Greek alphabet—designates *error*, or the *randomly varying other factors*, with ε_i being the error for individual i. In a sense, ε_i is a *nonvariable* because it simply takes up whatever "slack" is left in Y after you predict as well as you can with the X variables. However, this term, which makes up the difference between the predictions and reality, is a very important component of the model because it is the magnitude of these errors that will be the means by which we assess the adequacy of each model.[1]

The only change we must make to arrive at a very general form of the above model is to allow for some arbitrarily large number of factors in the model. If we say that p is the number of factors, then we have

$$Y_i = \beta_0 X_{0_i} + \beta_1 X_{1_i} + \beta_2 X_{2_i} + \beta_3 X_{3_i} + \cdots + \beta_p X_{p_i} + \varepsilon_i \qquad (1)$$

All univariate (single dependent measure) tests we consider in this text can be viewed as comparisons of various special cases of this general linear model.

ONE-GROUP SITUATION

Basics of Models

Consider the case where there is just a single group of scores that result from a particular study. For example, we might use the IQ score from the WISC-R as a dependent measure but not know anything that would allow different predictions to be made for the different individuals within the group. In such a situation, we clearly cannot be allowing for the variation of any factors across groups—there's just one group. Thus, if we eliminate allowed-for factors from our model, we are left with just the effect of constant factors and the effects of factors that randomly vary from one subject to the next. Such a random-variation model is typically expressed

$$Y_i = \mu + \varepsilon_i \qquad (2)$$

That is, our model postulates that variable Y has some unknown typical value in the population and that deviations from this typical value are due to random, uncontrolled factors. ε_i denotes this random error and is the sole source of variance in the Y scores. The typical value of Y in the population is usually denoted by the Greek letter *mu* (μ) and is generally unknown, although we might have some a priori ideas about its value.

We could just as well have used some other symbol such as β_0 for this typical value. We could also make explicit that this value is to be used as a prediction for *every* subject by saying that it is to be multiplied by 1 for every subject. You can see, then, that this random-variation model could be expressed more explicitly as a special case of the general linear model (see Equation 1):

$$Y_i = \beta_0 X_{0_i} + \varepsilon_i \qquad (3)$$

where $X_0 = 1$ for every subject.

However, to use μ and presume it is clear that our model implies a prediction equation for each subject is more common. Thus, we could view Equation 2 as being a shorthand for a set of n equations, where n is the number of subjects in our group. That is,

$$Y_1 = \mu + \varepsilon_1$$
$$Y_2 = \mu + \varepsilon_2$$
$$\vdots$$
$$Y_n = \mu + \varepsilon_n$$

(4)

The Y scores are values we observe for our sample, but μ and the n values of ε_i are unknown. From a pragmatic viewpoint, we typically are much more interested in finding the most appropriate value of μ than in determining the exact error for each subject. However, technically we have n equations in $n + 1$ unknowns (even if one unknown is of more interest than the others). This means that there are any number of possible values of μ and ε_i that we could use and still satisfy the equations. To obtain a unique solution for the unknowns in the equations in (4), we must impose some additional constraint or, in the terminology used by statisticians, "side condition."

To see what might be a reasonable constraint or criterion to adopt to estimate the unknowns in any model, we might view the model as a prediction equation. Generally, in prediction you want to make your guesses as close to the observed values as possible. The εs then could be viewed as the errors of prediction for each subject, which would be estimated by e_i, the difference between the observed value and your predicted value of μ. That is,

$$e_i = \hat{\varepsilon}_i = Y_i - \hat{\mu}$$

(5)

(We follow the convention of using a caret over a symbol—which here you read, e.g., "mu hat"—to indicate a predicted or estimated value.) Because your model constrains you to guess the same value for every score in your sample, you obviously will be wrong generally. However, you likely would want to choose your predicted value so that on the average your errors would balance out—that is, you might like the expected value of $Y_i - \hat{\mu}$ to be zero. In addition, you would probably not want systematic large positive errors simply to be canceled out by systematic large negative errors, but would think it more desirable if your errors in general, irrespective of sign, were small. Thus, you might hit upon using squared errors, $(Y_i - \hat{\mu})^2$, to indicate the lack of accuracy of your predictions, because squaring is a mathematically convenient way of ignoring the sign and emphasizes the importance of large errors. Simply specifying that we want the sum or average of these squared deviations to be as small as possible is sufficient to obtain a unique solution to the equations in (4). What's more, we use this simple desideratum any time we want to estimate parameters in *any* linear model. Choosing parameter estimates to minimize squared errors of prediction is known as the *least-squares criterion*. Least-squares estimates possess a number of desirable statistical properties such as always being unbiased. In addition, they are *minimum variance unbiased linear estimators*, which means that over replications of a study the least-squares estimates of the population parameter would be more efficient (have less variability) than would any other estimator that also is a linear combination of the observations in the sample. Incidentally, note that this holds whether ε_i is normally distributed or not. However, if normality holds, several important statistical results follow; the most important is that we can legitimately do standard statistical tests and justifiably consult statistical tables to determine the probability that the results of a study would have arisen, presuming only chance variation is operating.

In the one-group situation, the least-squares criterion implies that we should choose the estimate of the mean in such a way that we minimize the sum of squared errors; that is, we choose $\hat{\mu}$ to minimize

$$\sum_{i=1}^{n} e_i^2 = \sum_{i=1}^{n} (Y_i - \hat{\mu})^2 \tag{6}$$

You may well recall from a previous statistics course that the sample mean $\bar{Y}$ has the property that the sum of squared deviations from it is smaller than around any other value. This is proven in the following section. (The material in the paragraph that follows requires somewhat more use of mathematical arguments than does most of the text. Such sections marked Optional can be skipped on initial reading of the chapter, without loss of continuity.)

O P T I O N A L

Proof That $\bar{Y}$ Is the Least-Squares Estimate of μ. We can easily demonstrate algebraically that Y is the least-squares estimate of μ, and doing so has the additional pedagogical value of illustrating a little mathematical trick that will be repeatedly useful in seeing the relationship between different sums of squared errors. The algebraic proof is as follows: Assume that we want to use some constant value C, possibly different from $\bar{Y}$, as our estimate of μ. Then, our sum of squared errors would be

$$\sum_{i=1}^{n} e_i^2 = \sum_{i=1}^{n} (Y_i - C)^2 \tag{7}$$

Clearly, we would not change the expression on the right if we were to add a zero to it. The "trick" is that a very useful form of zero to add in is $-\bar{Y} + \bar{Y}$. This lets us see the relationship between these squared errors and something with which we are already familiar. Adding in $-\bar{Y} + \bar{Y}$, grouping terms and expanding, we have

$$\sum(Y_i - C)^2 = \sum(Y_i - \bar{Y} + \bar{Y} - C)^2 = \sum[(Y_i - \bar{Y}) + (\bar{Y} - C)]^2 \tag{8}$$

$$= \sum[(Y_i - \bar{Y})^2 + 2(Y_i - \bar{Y})(\bar{Y} - C) + (\bar{Y} - C)^2] \tag{9}$$

$$= \sum(Y_i - \bar{Y})^2 + \sum 2(Y_i - \bar{Y})(\bar{Y} - C) + \sum(\bar{Y} - C)^2 \tag{10}$$

When we factor out constants, note that the cross-product term—that is, the second summation in Equation 10—becomes $2(\bar{Y} - C)\sum(Y_i - \bar{Y})$, which equals 0 because $\sum(Y_i - \bar{Y}) = 0$. Further, you may recognize the term on the left in Equation 10 as the numerator of the familiar definitional formula for the unbiased sample variance s^2. That is,

$$s^2 = [\sum(Y_i - \bar{Y})^2]/(n - 1) \tag{11}$$

so

$$\sum(Y_i - \bar{Y})^2 = (n - 1)s^2 \tag{12}$$

Making this substitution for the term on the left in Equation 10 and dropping the middle term, we have

$$\sum(Y_i - C)^2 = (n - 1)s^2 + \sum(\bar{Y} - C)^2 \tag{13}$$

Because the term on the right is a constant value and adding up n such values is equivalent to multiplying the value by n, we see that the sum of squared deviations from C can be expressed as a function of two squared quantities:

$$\sum(Y_i - C)^2 = (n - 1)s^2 + n(\bar{Y} - C)^2 \tag{14}$$

Because on the right we have the sum of two squared quantities, we know neither can be negative and that $\sum(Y_i - C)^2$ must be at least as large as $(n - 1)s^2$. Further, $\sum(Y_i - C)^2$ will be a minimum when $n(\bar{Y} - C)^2$ is zero, which can only occur if $C = \bar{Y}$. Thus, we have proven that the way to minimize our errors of prediction—that is, the way to satisfy the least-squares criterion—is to use the sample mean as our estimate of the unknown parameter in our model.

Adopting $\bar{Y}$ as the best estimate of the parameter μ—that is, as the best value for $\hat{\mu}$—virtually completes the estimation problem: once $\hat{\mu}$ is determined, we can get the values of the errors associated with individual subjects immediately because $e_i = Y_i - \hat{\mu}$. Further, a very important by-product of using the least-squares criterion to estimate parameters is that it yields a measure of the adequacy of the model that is as fair as possible. That is, we know the sum of squared errors of prediction

$$\sum_{i=1}^{n} e_i^2 = \sum_{i=1}^{n} (Y_i - \bar{Y})^2$$

is as small as it could be for this model.

Naturally, other models for this one-group situation are also possible. One might be interested in how well a specific a priori value might do as an estimate of the observed scores. For example, we may wonder if it is plausible to model the IQ of a group of hyperactive children with the value of 100, which we know is representative of the population of all children. The appropriate model for such a supposition might be written

$$Y_i = \mu_0 + \varepsilon_i \tag{15}$$

where μ_0 is understood to be some *prespecified* constant value. This means that the values of e_i for this model are determined without any parameter estimation; that is, in this case,

$$e_i = \varepsilon_i = Y_i - \mu_0 \tag{16}$$

Thus, the total error (that is, the sum of squared errors) made by a model incorporating the restriction that $\mu = \mu_0$ is $\sum(Y_i - \mu_0)^2$. Typically, imposing such a restriction results in increased error relative to a model that is not so constrained. Examining the error associated with the current, restricted model allows us to see just what the increase in error will be. In fact, using the same technique that worked in proving $\bar{Y}$ was the least-squares estimator of μ—that is, adding and subtracting $\bar{Y}$—it can easily be shown[2] that

$$\sum(Y_i - \mu_0)^2 = \sum(Y_i - \bar{Y})^2 + n(\bar{Y} - \mu_0)^2 \tag{17}$$

When we compare this with the minimal error made with our unrestricted model $\sum(Y_i - \bar{Y})^2$, we see the magnitude of the increase in error associated with going to the restricted model is simply $n(\bar{Y} - \mu_0)^2$. This makes sense because it should depend on how far $\bar{Y}$ is from our hypothesized value of μ_0.

The question that logically follows is, How much must the error be increased for us to consider our supposition (hypothesis) to be false? Because the increase in error we just developed is in squared Y units, it is difficult to evaluate directly. However, an intuitively reasonable relative measure of its magnitude is achieved by looking at the proportional increase in error—that is, how large the increase is relative to the best we can do with the unconstrained model:

$$\text{proportional increase in error} = \frac{\text{increase in error}}{\text{minimal error}} \tag{18}$$

Development of the General Form of the Test Statistic

In the following paragraphs, we develop this idea of proportional increase in error into a test statistic. Our development does not proceed in the way the test statistic would be introduced in a mathematical statistics text. However, our goal is like the mathematician's in that we strive for generality, not just the solution to a single problem. We develop the test statistic rationally, not mathematically, as a reasonable index of the relative adequacy yet simplicity of two competing models. But, instead of developing things in a way that would work only in a one-sample situation, we introduce a method that works in essentially all cases we consider in this book. Doing so takes a few more lines than developing a test for only one sample. However, in so doing we are providing a perspective and a general procedure that together serve as a unifying theme for the book.

To carry out our development more succinctly, consider the following terminology. We call the unconstrained model the *full model* because it is "full" of parameters, with the number of parameters in the full model frequently equaling the number of groups in the design. In the full model for the one-group case, we have one unknown parameter μ, which is to be estimated on the basis of the data. The general method used to arrive at a second model is to place restrictions on the parameters of the first model. The restrictions are essentially our null hypothesis and serve to delete some of the parameters from the set used by the full model. We call the resultant constrained model simply the *restricted model*. In the one-group case, the restricted model does not require the estimation of any parameters. Although that is not usually the case in other designs, it is true that the restricted model always involves the estimation of fewer parameters than does the full model. Thus, we have the following models, least-squares estimates and errors, in the one-group case:

Model		**Least-Squares Estimates**	**Errors**
Full:	$Y_i = \mu + \varepsilon_{i_F}$	$\hat{\mu} = \bar{Y}$	$\sum e_{i_F}^2 = \sum (Y_i - \bar{Y})^2$
Restricted:	$Y_i = \mu_0 + \varepsilon_{i_R}$	No parameters estimated	$\sum e_{i_R}^2 = \sum (Y_i - \mu_0)^2$

We use E_F to designate the sum of squared errors $\sum e_{i_F}^2$ in the full model, and E_R to designate the analogous quantity $\sum e_{i_R}^2$ for the restricted model.[3] Letting PIE stand for the proportional increase in error, we can express our verbal equation comparing the adequacy of the two models in algebraic form as

$$\text{PIE} = \frac{E_R - E_F}{E_F} \qquad (19)$$

Substituting, we have

$$\text{PIE} = \frac{\sum e_{i_R}^2 - \sum e_{i_F}^2}{\sum e_{i_F}^2}$$

$$= \frac{\sum (Y_i - \mu_0)^2 - \sum (Y_i - \bar{Y})^2}{\sum (Y_i - \bar{Y})^2}$$

and using Equation 17 to simplify the numerator, we obtain

$$\text{PIE} = \frac{n(\bar{Y} - \mu_0)^2}{\sum (Y_i - \bar{Y})^2} \qquad (20)$$

Hopefully, the final way PIE is expressed looks at least vaguely familiar. One of the first hypothesis tests you likely encountered in your first statistics course was a one-sample t test. Recall that the form of a one-sample t test assessing the null hypothesis $H_0 : \mu = \mu_0$ looks at the deviation of a sample mean from the hypothesized value relative to the standard error of the mean

$$t = \frac{\bar{Y} - \mu_0}{\hat{\sigma}_{\bar{Y}}} = \frac{\bar{Y} - \mu_0}{s/\sqrt{n}}$$

$$= \frac{\sqrt{n}(\bar{Y} - \mu_0)}{\sqrt{\sum (Y_i - \bar{Y})^2/(n-1)}} \qquad (21)$$

where $\hat{\sigma}_{\bar{Y}}$ is the standard error of the mean (that is, the standard deviation of the sampling distribution of $\bar{Y}$) and s is the square root of the unbiased sample variance. Note that if we were to square the form of the one-sample t given on the right in Equation 21, we would have something very much like our PIE. In fact, all we would have to do to change PIE into t^2 is to divide the denominator[4] of the PIE by $(n-1)$. (Note that we have said nothing about distributional assumptions; we are simply pointing out the similarity between how we would compute an intuitively reasonable statistic for comparing two models and the form of the test statistic for the one-sample t. We consider assumptions about the distribution of Y scores shortly.)

We began our discussion of the model-comparison approach by noting that we want models that are simple yet adequate. You may have wondered if we couldn't incorporate both of these aspects into a summary measure for comparing models. We must in fact do so. PIE simply compares the adequacy of the models (actually, in comparing errors of prediction, it does so by contrasting the inadequacy of the models), without regard to their complexity. To make PIE a more informative summary of the relative desirability of the models, we really want to take into account the simplicity of the models. We know in advance that our simpler, restricted model is necessarily less adequate than our full model (see Equation 17). Thus, intuitively, we would like our summary measure to indicate something like, Is the loss in adequacy *per additional unit of simplicity* large? But how could we assess the simplicity of a model?

The simplicity of a linear model is determined by the number of parameters: the fewer parameters, the simpler the model. As we illustrate momentarily, each parameter that we must estimate entails the loss of a degree of freedom. In fact, we define the degrees of freedom (df) resulting from using a particular equation as a model for an experiment as the number of independent observations in the study minus the number of independent parameters estimated. Thus, the df associated with a model can be used as our index of its simplicity. Given that, for a study having a fixed number of observations, the number of df associated with a model is inversely related to the number of parameters in the model, the df can be taken as a direct indicator of the model's simplicity: the more df, the simpler the model.

This allows us to construct a very useful summary measure for comparing models. The error of our more adequate model relative to its df gives us a basis for evaluating the size of the increase in error entailed by adopting a simpler model relative to the corresponding increase in df. We can easily incorporate this consideration of the models' simplicity into our measure of the proportional increase in error.

Specifically, we need only to divide the denominator and numerator of PIE in Equation 19 by the degrees of freedom of the model(s) involved in each. That is, in the denominator we divide the error of the full model (E_F) by the degrees of freedom of the full model (df_F), and in the numerator we divide the difference between the error of the restricted model and the error of the full model $(E_R - E_F)$ by the difference in the degrees of freedom associated with the two models $(df_R - df_F)$. This yields a revised measure, which we denote by F, of the relative adequacy yet simplicity of the two models:

$$F = \frac{(E_R - E_F)/(df_R - df_F)}{E_F/df_F} \tag{22}$$

This simple comparison measure is in fact extremely useful and general. We can use it for carrying out all the hypothesis tests we will need for the various special cases of the general linear model we will consider. All tests in ANOVA, analysis of covariance, bivariate regression, and multiple regression can be computed using this formula. The models being compared may differ widely from one of these situations to the next, but our method of comparing them can always be the same.

If there is no difference between the two models' descriptive accuracy except for the additional free parameter(s) in the full model, then the numerator (the increase in error per additional degree of freedom associated with using the simpler, restricted model) would be expected to be approximately the same as the denominator (the baseline indication of error per degree of freedom). Thus, values of F near 1 would indicate no essential difference in the accuracy of the models, and the simpler model would be preferred on grounds of parsimony. However, if the increase in error associated with using the simpler model is larger than would be expected given the difference in parameters, then larger F values result, and we tend to reject the simpler model as inadequate.

For the two models we are considering for a design involving only one group of subjects, we can determine the degrees of freedom to use in our general formula quite easily. In the full model, we are estimating just one parameter, μ; thus, if we have n independent observations in our sample, the degrees of freedom associated with the full model is $n - 1$. In the restricted model, we do not have to estimate any parameters in this particular case; thus, $df_R = n$. When we subtract df_F from df_R, the number of subjects "drops out," and the difference is only the difference in the numbers of parameters estimated by the two models. Thus, for the one-group situation we have

$$F = \frac{(E_R - E_F)/(df_R - df_F)}{E_F/df_F}$$

$$= \frac{n(\bar{Y} - \mu_0)^2/[n - (n - 1)]}{\sum(Y_i - \bar{Y})^2/(n - 1)} = t^2 \tag{23}$$

To make this intuitively developed descriptive statistic useful for inferential purposes (i.e., hypothesis testing), we only need to assume that the individual errors have certain characteristics. Specifically, if we assume the error terms ε_i in our models are independently distributed as normal random variables with zero mean and variance σ^2, then it can be shown that the F in our general formula does in fact follow a theoretical F distribution with $df_R - df_F$ and df_F degrees of freedom.

Numerical Example

Assume that you work in the research office of a large school system. For the last several years, the mean score on the WISC-R, which is administered to all elementary school children in your district, has been holding fairly steady at about 98. A parent of a hyperactive child in one of your special education programs maintains that the hyperactive children in the district are actually brighter than this average. To investigate this assertion, you randomly select the files of six hyperactive children and examine their WISC-R scores. Table 3.1 shows these scores.

The unconstrained, or full, model does not make any a priori judgments about the mean IQ of hyperactive children. Rather, the estimate of μ is chosen so that $E_F = \sum e_{i_F}^2$ is minimized for this set of data. As we know, the sample mean, which

T A B L E **3. 1** Hyperactive Children's WISC-R Scores

Full-Model Analysis

IQ Scores Y_i	Prediction Equations	Parameter Term $\hat{\mu}$	Error Scores $e_{i_F} = Y_i - \hat{\mu}$	Squared Errors $e_{i_F}^2$
96	$= \hat{\mu} + e_1$	104	-8	64
102	$= \hat{\mu} + e_2$	104	-2	4
104	$= \hat{\mu} + e_3$	104	0	0
104	$= \hat{\mu} + e_4$	104	0	0
108	$= \hat{\mu} + e_5$	104	$+4$	16
110	$= \hat{\mu} + e_6$	104	$+6$	36

$\sum = 624$

$\bar{Y} = 104$

$\sum = 0$

$E_F = 120$

Restricted-Model Analysis

IQ Scores Y_i	Prediction Equations	Parameter Term μ_0	Error Scores $e_{i_R} = Y_i - \mu_0$	Squared Errors $e_{i_R}^2$
96	$= \mu_0 + e_1$	98	-2	4
102	$= \mu_0 + e_2$	98	4	16
104	$= \mu_0 + e_3$	98	6	36
104	$= \mu_0 + e_4$	98	6	36
108	$= \mu_0 + e_5$	98	10	100
110	$= \mu_0 + e_6$	98	12	144

$E_R = 336$

$$F = \frac{(E_R - E_F)/(df_R - df_F)}{E_F/df_F} = \frac{(336 - 120)/(6 - 5)}{120/5} = \frac{216}{24} = 9$$

$$t = \frac{\bar{Y} - \mu_0}{\hat{\sigma}_{\bar{Y}}} = \frac{\bar{Y} - \mu_0}{s/\sqrt{n}} = \frac{\bar{Y} - \mu_0}{\sqrt{\frac{\sum(Y - \bar{Y})^2}{n - 1}}\Big/\sqrt{n}} = \frac{104 - 98}{\sqrt{\frac{120}{5}}\Big/\sqrt{6}} = \frac{6}{\sqrt{\frac{24}{6}}} = 3$$

here equals $624/6 = 104$, minimizes this sum of squared errors. Computing the deviations from this estimated population mean, we note that they sum to zero. This is, of course, always going to be the case because

$$\sum e_{i_F} = \sum(Y_i - \bar{Y}) = \sum(Y - \sum Y/N)$$
$$= \sum Y - \sum(\sum Y/N) = \sum Y - N(\sum Y/N)$$
$$= \sum Y - \sum Y = 0$$

We square each of these error scores and sum to obtain what we will use as our index of the inadequacy of the model, that is, $E_F = 120$.

The degrees of freedom, which is the number of data values you would be free to choose once all parameter estimates have been specified, reflects the model's simplicity, as we have indicated. For example, in the full model, once the sample mean is determined to be 104, you could choose five of the data values to be whatever you like, but the sixth must be the value that would bring the total to 624 so that the mean of the six scores will in fact be 104, that is, $Y_6 = 6(104) - \sum_{i=1}^{5} Y_i$. As indicated in Table 3.1, the df for our full model is 5—that is, the number of independent observations in the sample (6) minus the number of parameters estimated (1, which here is μ). In general, the degrees of freedom associated with a model for a particular set of data is the total number of independent observations minus the number of parameters to be estimated in that model.

The analysis for the restricted model proceeds similarly. However, in this simplest case, there are no parameters to estimate, the average of the population having been hypothesized to be exactly 98. Thus, the error scores associated with this model can be computed directly by subtracting 98 from each score. When these error scores are squared and summed, we get a total error ($E_R = 336$) that is considerably larger than that associated with the full model ($E_F = 120$). Recall that the restricted model will always have as great or greater summed errors than that associated with the full model. In fact, as shown (see Equations 17 and 20), the increase in error here depends simply on how far $\bar{Y}$ is from μ_0, that is,

$$
\begin{aligned}
E_R - E_F &= n(\bar{Y} - \mu_0)^2 \\
&= 6(104 - 98)^2 = 6(6)^2 = 6(36) = 216 \\
&= 336 - 120
\end{aligned}
\tag{24}
$$

Finally, the degrees of freedom for the restricted model is simply equal to the number of observations—that is, 6—because no parameters had to be estimated.

Dividing our error summary measures by the corresponding degrees of freedom, as shown in our basic equation for the F near the bottom of Table 3.1, we obtain the values of the numerator and denominator of our test statistic. The value of 24 in the denominator is the squared error per degree of freedom for our full model (often referred to as mean square error). The value of 216 in the numerator is the increase in error per additional degree of freedom gained by adopting the restricted model. Computing their ratio, we get a value of 9 for F, which can be viewed, as we have indicated, at a descriptive level as an "adequacy yet simplicity" score. Its value here indicates that the additional error of the simpler restricted model per its additional degree of freedom is nine times larger than we would expect it to be on the basis of the error of the full model per degree of freedom. That is, the restricted model is considerably worse per extra degree of freedom in describing the data than is the full model relative to its degrees of freedom. Thus, intuitively it would seem that the restricted model should be rejected. We need, however, a statistical criterion for judging how large the F is.

To determine if the probability of obtaining an F this extreme is sufficiently small to justify rejecting the restricted model, we can consult the tabled values of the F distribution shown in Appendix Table A.2. To obtain a critical F value from the table, we consult the column corresponding to the degrees of freedom from the numerator of our test statistic—that is, $df_R - df_F$—and the main row of the table corresponding to the denominator degrees of freedom, that is, df_F. The third factor to be considered is the α level, that is, the probability of obtaining an F value larger than the tabled value, assuming that the restricted model is in fact correct. Critical F values are provided for six different α levels, namely .25, .10, .05, .025, .01, and .001, on six adjacent rows of the table for each denominator df. When the observed F value of 9 is compared against the tabled values of the F distribution with numerator and denominator degrees of freedom of $df_R - df_F = 1$ and $df_F = 5$, respectively, we find it exceeds the critical value of 6.61 for $\alpha = .05$. The conclusion would then be that there is significant reason to doubt that the population of hyperactive children has the same mean IQ as the other students in your district. The parent who brought the matter to your attention apparently was correct.

Relationship of Models and Hypotheses

As may be clear, the two models being compared are the embodiments of two competing hypotheses. The full model corresponds to the alternative hypothesis, and the restricted model to the null hypothesis. In the full model and the alternative hypothesis, the population parameter is not constrained to equal any particular value. The restricted model is obtained from the full model by imposing the restriction on its parameters stated in the null hypothesis. As indicated below, restricting the μ in the full model to a particular value μ_0, such as 98, yields the restricted model:

Hypothesis	**Model**	
$H_1 : \mu \neq \mu_0$	Full: $Y_i = \mu + \varepsilon_i$	(25)
$H_0 : \mu = \mu_0$	Restricted: $Y_i = \mu_0 + \varepsilon_i$	(26)

TWO-GROUP SITUATION

Development in Terms of Models

Designs involving a single group are rare in psychology and for good reason. Although it might be the case that there is one condition or treatment you are interested in, to evaluate that condition alone in an absolute sense in a compelling way is difficult. You may want to show that biofeedback is an effective way of reducing anxiety associated with public speaking. Trying the treatment with a group of volunteers and showing that after treatment their anxiety regarding public speaking was in the normal range would, of course, not constitute proof of the effectiveness of the biofeedback: their anxiety scores may have been normal to begin with. Selecting individuals for participation because they were very anxious about public speaking may seem like the obvious solution; but with only one group, improvement after biofeedback training could be attributed to regression toward the mean or to any of a number of other potential confounding variables (Campbell & Stanley, 1963; also see Chapter 1). Thus, using at least one comparison group is expected practice in psychological research. The model-comparison approach we developed for the one-group case can easily be extended for analysis of two-group designs.

We extend our statistical analysis to help us decide again between two alternative conceptions of the world. These competing viewpoints could be described verbally, or in terms of statistical hypotheses, or in terms of models of how the data arose. The question to be addressed is typically, Is there evidence that the two groups differ? Thus, we want to compare a view that says the groups differ with one that says they do not. These views would correspond, respectively, to a statistical hypothesis that the population means of the two groups differ and to a hypothesis that they are equal. A model embodying the first hypothesis (which is the hypothesis you usually want to find evidence to support) would indicate that each score equals the population mean *for its group* plus some random error. A model embodying the second hypothesis would differ only in that it would use a single parameter for the population mean because it is to embody the restriction that the two groups are drawn from the same population. We can express these hypotheses and models in symbols:

Hypothesis	**Model**
Alternative hypothesis: $\mu_1 \neq \mu_2$	Full model: $Y_{ij} = \mu_j + \varepsilon_{ij_F}$ (27)
Null hypothesis: $\mu_1 = \mu_2 = \mu$	Restricted model: $Y_{ij} = \mu + \varepsilon_{ij_R}$ (28)

Here, μ_1 and μ_2 are, of course, the population means of groups 1 and 2; more generally, we use μ_j to denote the population mean of the jth group. Note that the scores on the dependent variable Y now have two subscripts i and j: the j designates groups and here takes on the values 1 and 2; the i, as before, indicates the individuals within a group. We allow the number of subjects in groups 1 and 2, designated n_1 and n_2, respectively, to differ. Thus, the ranges of the subscripts can be indicated succinctly as $j = 1, 2$ and $i = 1, 2, 3, \ldots, n_j$. Like the one-group case, the error score for each individual ε_{ij} indicates how much the dependent-variable score deviates from the parameter value. The errors for the simpler, restricted model are again larger in general than those for the full model, and the subscripts R and F are used when necessary to distinguish between them.

We see the generality of the model-comparison approach when we raise the question of how to decide between these two competing accounts of the data. The question in terms of model comparisons is, Will a restricted model involving fewer parameters be a significantly less adequate representation of the data than a full model with a parameter for each group? This is the kind of question we address repeatedly in this book, and the method of resolving the trade-off between simplicity and adequacy is in terms of the general form of our F test, that is, $F = [(E_R - E_F)/(df_R - df_F)]/(E_F/df_F)$, where E_R and E_F are, as before, the sums of squared errors and df_R and df_F are the degrees of freedom associated with the two models.

Once again we want to determine the errors associated with a model so that each model is placed in the best possible light. Using the least-squares criterion, as we have seen, not only gives us parameter estimates that are in many ways optimal but also yields a measure of the model's adequacy, as we have defined it, that makes the model appear as adequate as possible. Let us work through the steps for determining the least-squares estimates of the parameters for the models, beginning with the restricted model.

A comparison of the restricted model in the two-group case, with the full model for the one-group situation (see Equations 28 and 25), reveals that they both involve using a single parameter to model the data. This suggests that the solution to the least squares–estimation problem should be the same, and in fact it is. That is, when one parameter estimate is to be used as the guess or prediction for all observations, the sum of squared errors is minimized when the mean of all observations is used as the estimate. Expressing this with symbols, the error associated with the restricted model for the two-group situation is

$$E_R = \sum_j \sum_i e_{ij_R}^2 = \sum_j \sum_i (Y_{ij} - \hat{\mu})^2 \qquad (29)$$

Following the identical reasoning to that employed in the one-group case, it is easily shown that E_R is minimized when

$$\hat{\mu} = \sum_j \sum_i Y_{ij}/N \qquad (30)$$

that is, when $\hat{\mu}$ is set equal to the grand mean of all observations, which we denote $\bar{Y}$. For the full model, the estimation problem appears more complicated because there are now two parameters to be estimated. However, the problem can be translated into a form where the same kind of solution can be used. Specifically, in the full model, we wish to minimize

$$E_F = \sum_j \sum_i e_{ij_F}^2 = \sum_{j=1}^{2} \sum_i (Y_{ij} - \hat{\mu}_j)^2 \qquad (31)$$

Because there are only two groups, we can express E_F simply as the sum of the total squared errors in group 1 and the total squared errors in group 2:

$$E_F = \sum_i (Y_{i1} - \hat{\mu}_1)^2 + \sum_i (Y_{i2} - \hat{\mu}_2)^2 \qquad (32)$$

Because each of the two terms on the right side of the equation is the sum of a set of squared numbers, each term must be positive, and the way in which E_F can be minimized is to minimize each of these separately. Thus, we have two minimization problems, but each is identical to the problem we addressed in the one-group case, namely, what number for a single group of scores results in the sum of squared deviations from that number being as small as possible? The answer, you will recall, is to use the mean of the observed scores in whatever group is being considered. Thus, the least-squares estimate of the population mean for each group is the sample mean for that group. That is, $\hat{\mu}_1 = (\sum_i Y_{i1})/n_1 = \bar{Y}_1$, and $\hat{\mu}_2 = (\sum_i Y_{i2})/n_2 = \bar{Y}_2$.

We now see how these measures of the adequacy of our two competing models for the two-group situation combine when they are entered into our general form of the F test:

$$F = \frac{(E_R - E_F)/(df_R - df_F)}{E_F/df_F} \qquad (22, \text{repeated})$$

Noting that $df_R = N - 1$ because we estimate a single parameter in the restricted model and $df_F = N - 2$ because we estimate a population mean for each of the two groups in the full model, we see that $df_R - df_F = (N - 1) - (N - 2) = 2 - 1 = 1$, thus obtaining

$$F = \frac{(\sum\sum e^2_{ij_R} - \sum\sum e^2_{ij_F})/1}{\sum\sum e^2_{ij_F}/(N - 2)} \tag{33}$$

$$= \frac{\sum_j\sum_i(Y_{ij} - \bar{Y})^2 - \sum_j\sum_i(Y_{ij} - \bar{Y}_j)^2}{\sum_j\sum_i(Y_{ij} - \bar{Y}_j)^2/(N - 2)} \tag{34}$$

It turns out that E_R, the term on the left in the numerator in Equation 34, can be expressed[5] as the total of two quantities: (1) the sum of the squared deviations of the scores within a group from their group mean $\sum_j\sum_i(Y_{ij} - \bar{Y}_j)^2$, and (2) the sum of squared deviations of the group means from the grand mean $\sum_j\sum_i(\bar{Y}_j - \bar{Y})^2$. Because the former of these two quantities is how E_F is defined here, the difference between E_R and E_F used in the numerator of our test may be expressed as just the latter of these quantities, that is,

$$E_R - E_F = \left[\sum_j\sum_i(Y_{ij} - \bar{Y}_j)^2 + \sum_j\sum_i(\bar{Y}_j - \bar{Y})^2\right] - \sum_j\sum_i(Y_{ij} - \bar{Y}_j)^2$$

$$= \sum_j\sum_i(\bar{Y}_j - \bar{Y})^2 \tag{35}$$

And, because how much the group mean deviates from the grand mean is a constant for all subjects within a group, we have

$$E_R - E_F = \sum_j n_j(\bar{Y}_j - \bar{Y})^2 \tag{36}$$

Thus, the general form of our F test for the two-group situation reduces to

$$F = \frac{\sum_j n_j(\bar{Y}_j - \bar{Y})^2}{\sum_j\sum_i(Y_{ij} - \bar{Y}_j)^2/(N - 2)} \tag{37}$$

Alternative Development and Identification with Traditional Terminology

Traditionally within psychology, statistics texts have presented F tests in ANOVA not as a method for comparing models but as a measure of the degree to which the data depart from what would be expected if chance alone were operating. This traditional approach can also be characterized by focusing on the question, Is the variability between groups greater than that expected on the basis of the within-group variability? That is, one asks if the variability among the group means is greater than would be expected given the variability observed among the individual scores within each of the groups.

The logic here is that if all scores in both groups were simply randomly selected from a single population of scores, the sample means of the two groups would still almost certainly differ because of sampling variability. Just how much the means would be expected to differ would depend on the variability of the population. This in turn can be estimated by either of the sample variances observed or, better, by a pooled estimate or weighted average of the two variances. If we use s_j^2 to denote the unbiased sample variance of the jth group of scores, that is,

$$s_j^2 = \frac{\sum_i (Y_{ij} - \bar{Y}_j)^2}{n_j - 1} \tag{38}$$

then the pooled estimate of the population variance σ^2, based on these within-group sample variances, can be expressed as

$$\text{estimated } \sigma^2 = \frac{(n_1 - 1)s_1^2 + (n_2 - 1)s_2^2}{n_1 + n_2 - 2} \tag{39}$$

The numerator in Equation 39 is typically expressed for computational convenience in terms of the raw scores, with the contribution of the jth group to this numerator being

$$(n_j - 1)s_j^2 = \sum_i (Y_{ij} - \bar{Y}_j)^2 \tag{40}$$

Hence, we see that the numerator consists of a sum of squared deviations from the group means; thus, the numerator is denoted *sum of squares within groups* or SS_{Within}. When the division by $n_1 + n_2 - 2$ is carried out, one obtains something like a mean or average squared deviation, and so the estimate of the population variance is denoted *mean square within* (MS_{Within}):

$$MS_{\text{Within}} = \frac{\sum_j \sum_i (Y_{ij} - \bar{Y}_j)^2}{\sum_j (n_j - 1)} \tag{41}$$

If the null hypothesis that all scores are drawn from the same population is true, then the variability between the sample means could be used to derive a separate estimate of population variance. This would provide a variance estimate that, under certain assumptions, is independent of the within-group variance MS_{Within}. Each sample mean, of course, has more stability than the individual scores in the sample. In fact, one of the most important results in statistics is the statement of just how much less variable means are than the scores on which they are based. Recall that the relationship depends solely on the number of scores on which the mean is based with the variance of sample means $\sigma_{\bar{Y}}^2$ equaling σ_Y^2/n. The variance of the distribution of sample means $\sigma_{\bar{Y}}^2$ can be estimated by the variability of the observed sample means, even when there are only two means present. When there are just two groups with the same number of subjects in each group, an unbiased estimate of the variance of the sampling distribution would be

$$\text{estimated } \sigma_{\bar{Y}}^2 = \left[\sum_{j=1}^{2} (\bar{Y}_j - \bar{Y})^2 \right] \Big/ (2 - 1) \tag{42}$$

That is, divide the squared deviations of the group means from the grand mean by the number of groups minus 1. To obtain an estimate of the population variance from this estimated variance of means we only need to multiply by n so that it will be on the appropriate scale:

$$\text{estimated } \sigma^2 = n \sum_{j=1}^{2} (\bar{Y}_j - \bar{Y})^2 / 1 \qquad (43)$$

This estimate is also an average squared deviation, but its magnitude is determined solely by the difference between the group means rather than by the variability within a group. Hence, the numerator is denoted SS_{Between}, and the variance estimate is denoted MS_{Between}. Here SS_{Between} and MS_{Between} happen to be the same because there are only two groups (in which case the denominator of MS_{Between}, as shown in Equation 43, is 1). When there are more than two groups, MS_{Between} and SS_{Between} differ.

We can generalize these estimates, based on group differences, somewhat. First, if there are unequal numbers of observations in the groups, then the deviation for a group is weighted by the number in the group, that is,

$$SS_{\text{Between}} = \sum_j n_j(\bar{Y}_j - \bar{Y})^2 \qquad (44)$$

Note that here $\bar{Y}$ is still the grand mean—that is, the mean of all the observations, *not* the mean of the group means. Second, if there were more than two groups, then the divisor to convert this from a sum of squares to a mean square would be greater than 1. If we designate the number of groups as a, then we can write a general form for MS_{Between} as

$$MS_{\text{Between}} = \left[\sum_{j=1}^{a} n_j(\bar{Y}_j - \bar{Y})^2 \right] \bigg/ (a - 1) \qquad (45)$$

The situation with more than two groups is developed more fully from a model-comparison perspective in a subsequent section.

Thus, we have two separate estimates of population variance. MS_{Within} is an unbiased estimate regardless of the presence of treatment effects or systematic differences between the groups. MS_{Between} is an unbiased estimate of σ^2 only if there are no treatment effects. When systematic differences between the groups exist along with the random variability among individuals, MS_{Between} tends to be larger than σ^2 and hence larger than MS_{Within}. The ratio of these two variance estimates then is used in the traditional approach to construct a test statistic, that is,

$$F = \frac{MS_{\text{Between}}}{MS_{\text{Within}}} \qquad (46)$$

Now we are ready to identify these mean squares with the measures of error associated with models on which we will be focusing. The minimal error—that is, E_F the error associated with our full model—is the squared deviations of the scores around their group means and hence can be identified with SS_{Within}. The difference in the errors associated with our two models—that is, $E_R - E_F$—depends on how much the group means vary around the grand mean and hence can be identified with SS_{Between}. The error associated with our restricted model, we have seen, is the total of SS_{Within} and SS_{Between} (see the discussion of Equations 34 and 35). Thus, E_R

here[6] is identified with what is traditionally called SS_{Total}. (Rather than spelling out "Within" and "Between" in the subscripts of these sums of squares, we economize our notation by referring to them as SS_W and SS_B and similarly denote the mean squares MS_W and MS_B.)

Tests of Replication

Up to now, we have assumed that the only comparison of interest in the two-group case is that between a cell mean model and a grand mean model. That is, we have compared the full model of

$$Y_{ij} = \mu_j + \varepsilon_{ij} \qquad \text{(27, repeated)}$$

with the model obtained when we impose the restriction that $\mu_1 = \mu_2 = \mu$. However, this is certainly not the only restriction on the means that would be possible. Occasionally, you can make a more specific statement of the results you expect to obtain. This is most often true when your study is replicating previous research that has provided detailed information about the phenomena under investigation. As long as you can express your expectation as a restriction on the values of a linear combination of the parameters of the full model, the same general form of our F test allows you to carry out a comparison of the resulting models.

For example, you may wish to impose a restriction similar to that used in the one-group case in which you specify the exact value of one or both of the population means present in the full model. To extend the numerical example involving the hyperactive-children data, we might hypothesize that a population of hyperactive children and a population of nonhyperactive children would both have a mean IQ of 98, that is,

$$\mu_1 = \mu_2 = 98 \qquad (47)$$

In this case, our restricted model would simply be

$$Y_{ij} = 98 + \varepsilon_{ij} \qquad (48)$$

Thus, no parameters need to be estimated, and hence the degrees of freedom associated with the model would be $n_1 + n_2$.

As a second example, one may wish to specify numerical values for the population means in your restriction but allow them to differ between the two groups. This also would arise in situations where you are replicating previous research. Perhaps you carried out an extensive study of hyperactive children in one school year and found the mean IQ of all identified hyperactive children was 106, whereas that of the remaining children was 98. If two years later you wondered if the values had remained the same and wanted to make a judgment on the basis of a sample of the cases, you could specify these exact values as your null hypothesis or restriction. That is, your restricted model would be

$$Y_{i1} = 106 + \varepsilon_{i1}$$
$$Y_{i2} = 98 + \varepsilon_{i2} \qquad (49)$$

Once again, no parameters must be estimated, and so $df_R = n_1 + n_2$. As with any model, the sum of squared deviations from the specified parameter values could be used as a measure of the adequacy of this model and compared with that associated with the full model.

In general, if we let c_j stand for the constant specified in such a restriction, we could write our restricted model

$$Y_{i1} = c_1 + \varepsilon_{i1}$$

$$Y_{i2} = c_2 + \varepsilon_{i2}$$

or equivalently,

$$Y_{ij} = c_j + \varepsilon_{ij}$$

The error term used as a measure of the adequacy of such a model would then be

$$E_R = \sum_j \sum_i e_{ij_R}^2 = \sum_j \sum_i (Y_{ij} - c_j)^2 \tag{50}$$

As a third example, you may wish to specify only that the *difference* between groups is equal to some specified value. Thus, if the hyperactive-group mean had been estimated at 106 and the normal-group mean at 98, you might test the hypothesis with a new sample that the hyperactive mean would be 8 points higher than the normal mean. This would allow for the operation of factors such as changing demographic characteristics of the population being sampled, which might cause the IQ scores to generally increase or decrease. The null hypothesis could still be stated easily as $\mu_1 - \mu_2 = 8$. It is a bit awkward to state the restricted model in this case, but thinking through the formulation of the model illustrates again the flexibility of the model-comparison approach. We do not wish in this case to place any constraints on the grand mean, yet we wish to specify the magnitude of the between-group difference at 8 points. We can accomplish this by specifying that the hyperactive-group mean will be 4 points above the grand mean and that the normal-group mean will be 4 points below the grand mean, that is,

$$Y_{i1} = \mu + 4 + \varepsilon_{i1}$$

$$Y_{i2} = \mu - 4 + \varepsilon_{i2} \tag{51}$$

Arriving at a least-squares estimate of μ in this context is a slightly different problem than we have encountered previously. However, we can solve the problem by translating it into a form we have considered. By subtracting 4 from both sides of the equation for the Y_{i1} scores and adding 4 to both sides of the equation for the Y_{i2} scores in Equation 51, we obtain

$$Y_{i1} - 4 = \mu + \varepsilon_{i1}$$

$$Y_{i2} + 4 = \mu + \varepsilon_{i2} \tag{52}$$

This is now essentially the same estimation problem that we used to introduce the least-squares criterion in the one-sample case. There we showed that the least-squares estimate of μ is the mean of all scores on the left side of the equations, which here would imply taking the mean of a set of transformed scores, with the scores from group 1 being 4 less than those observed and the scores in group 2 being 4 greater than those observed. In the equal-n case, these transformations cancel each other, and the estimate of μ would be the same as in a conventional restricted model. In the unequal-n case, the procedure described would generally result in a somewhat different estimate of the grand mean, with the effect that the predictions for the larger group are closer to the mean for that group than is the case for the smaller group. In any event, the errors of prediction are generally different for this restricted model than for a conventional model. In this case, we have

$$E_R = \sum_i (Y_{i1} - 4 - \hat{\mu})^2 + \sum_i (Y_{i2} + 4 - \hat{\mu})^2 \tag{53}$$

where $\hat{\mu}$ is the mean of the transformed scores, as described above.

This test, like the others considered in this chapter, assumes that the population variances of the different groups are equal. We discuss this assumption in more detail in the section "Statistical Assumptions" and present procedures there for testing the assumption. In the case where it is concluded that the variances are heterogeneous, refer to Wilcox (1985) for an alternative procedure for determining if the difference between two-group means differ by more than a specified constant. Additional techniques for imposing constraints on combinations of parameter values are considered in following chapters.

THE GENERAL CASE OF ONE-WAY DESIGNS

Formulation in Terms of Models

The consideration of the general case of ANOVA where we have an arbitrarily large number of groups can now be done rather easily because it is little different from the model comparisons we carried out in the two-group case. Of course, psychological experiments typically involve more than two groups. Most theoretical and empirical questions of interest involve the use of multiple treatment groups and may require multiple control groups as well. We subsequently consider cases where the several groups in a study arise from the "crossing" of different factors; for example, we may want to investigate the effects of instructions to compete or cooperate in a game situation for both males and females. If all combinations of gender of subject and type of instructions are represented in our experiment, those factors are said to be crossed. (If males were to be given only competitive instructions and females only cooperative, the factors would be said to be confounded rather than crossed, and the effects of the two factors could not be disentangled.) For now, we proceed as if each of the groups is uniquely of interest rather than being one of the groups that results from simultaneously crossing *factors* that are of more interest than any one group. However, we can anticipate later developments somewhat by noting here that all crossed factorial designs may in fact be viewed as special cases of the one-factor or one-way design with which we are now concerned.

Whatever the groups represent, we can designate them as different levels of a single factor. For example, in a behavior modification study investigating different methods of helping people stop smoking, a researcher might compare a condition using aversive conditioning with one involving positive reinforcement for not smoking. These might be compared with two control conditions: one group is told to try to stop smoking using whatever methods they think best, and the other group is a "waiting list" control, that is, during the actual experiment they are told that they are on a waiting list for treatment but they do not receive treatment until after the actual study is over. Although we can designate a group by a particular number—for example, group 1, group 2, group 3, and so on—the numbers, of course, do not rank the groups but simply name them. Thus, we might say we have a single factor here of "Smoking Condition" with four levels.

In general, to designate a factor by a single capital letter and the number of levels of the factor by the corresponding lowercase letter is frequently convenient. Hence, the general case of one-factor ANOVA might be designated by saying "factor A was manipulated," or "we had a groups in our study." The models being compared in an overall test of factor A are essentially identical to the two-group case, that is,

$$\text{Full model: } Y_{ij} = \mu_j + \varepsilon_{ij_F} \tag{54}$$

$$\text{Restricted model: } Y_{ij} = \mu + \varepsilon_{ij_R} \tag{55}$$

with the only difference being that now the subscript j, which designates groups, can take on more than two values, with a being its maximal value—that is, $j = 1$, $2, 3, \ldots, a$. Once again the least-squares estimate of μ_j would be the sample mean of observations in the jth group, and the least-squares estimate of μ would be the mean of all scores observed in the study. Using these as our "guesses" of the observations in the two models, we can compute error scores for each individual, as we have done before, and compare the sum of squared errors to compare the adequacy of the two models. We would then substitute these into our general form of the F test:

$$F = \frac{(E_R - E_F)/(df_R - df_F)}{E_F/df_F} \tag{22, repeated}$$

$$= \frac{\left(\sum\sum e_{ij_R}^2 - \sum\sum e_{ij_F}^2\right)\Big/(df_R - df_F)}{\sum\sum e_{ij_F}^2/df_F}$$

$$= \frac{\left[\sum_j\sum_i(Y_{ij} - \bar{Y})^2 - \sum_j\sum_i(Y_{ij} - \bar{Y}_j)^2\right]\Big/(df_R - df_F)}{\sum_j\sum_i(Y_{ij} - \bar{Y}_j)^2/df_F}$$

The difference between E_R and E_F can be expressed more simply. Following the identical logic to that used in the two-sample case (see the development of Equation 35) we again have

$$E_R - E_F = \sum_{j=1}^{a}\sum_i(\bar{Y}_j - \bar{Y})^2 \tag{56}$$

with the only difference from the previous case being that we are now summing over

a groups instead of two groups. As usual, because the term being summed in Equation 56 is a constant with respect to the summation over individuals within a group, we can simply multiply the constant by the number of individuals in that group:

$$E_R - E_F = \sum_{j=1}^{a} n_j(\bar{Y}_j - \bar{Y})^2 \tag{57}$$

In the special case where there are equal numbers of subjects per group, n would also be a constant with respect to the summation over j, and so we could factor it out to obtain

$$E_R - E_F = n \sum_{j=1}^{a} (\bar{Y}_j - \bar{Y})^2 \tag{58}$$

Regarding degrees of freedom, because in our restricted model we are estimating only one parameter just as we did in the two-group case, $df_R = N - 1$. In the full model, we are estimating as many parameters as we have groups; thus, in the general case of a groups, $df_F = N - a$. The degrees of freedom for the numerator of the test can be written quite simply as $a - 1$ because the total number of subjects drops out in computing the difference:

$$df_R - df_F = (N - 1) - (N - a) = N - 1 - N + a = a - 1 \tag{59}$$

The difference in degrees of freedom is thus just the difference in the number of parameters estimated by the two models. This is generally true. In the case of one-way ANOVA, this means $df_R - df_F$ is one less than the number of groups. Thus, the general form of our F test for the a-group situation reduces to

$$F = \frac{\sum_j n_j(\bar{Y}_j - \bar{Y})^2/(a - 1)}{\sum_j \sum_i (Y_{ij} - \bar{Y}_j)^2/(N - a)} \tag{60}$$

We can use this form of our F test to carry out the ANOVA for any one-way design.

Before proceeding to a numerical example, let us make two comments about developments to this point. First, regarding E_F, although the link between the within-group standard deviations and the denominator of the F statistic was noted in our discussion of the two-group case (see the development of Equation 41), it is useful to underscore this link here. In general, in one-way ANOVA, E_F can be determined by computing the sum of within-group variances, each weighted by its denominator, that is, by the number of subjects in that group less one. In symbols we have

$$E_F = \sum_j (n_j - 1)s_j^2 \tag{61}$$

In the equal-n case, notice that we can factor out $(n - 1)$:

$$E_F = (n - 1)\sum_j s_j^2 \tag{62}$$

and thus the denominator of the F statistic can be expressed very simply as the average within-group variance:

TABLE **3.2** Comparison of the Difference in Sum of Squared Errors for Various Designs

Situation	Predictions		Difference in Adequacy of Models (i.e., $E_R - E_F$)
	Full Model	*Restricted Model*	
One-group case	$\bar{Y}$	μ_0	$\sum\limits_{i=1}^{n} (\bar{Y} - \mu_0)^2$
Two-group case	$\bar{Y}_j$	$\bar{Y}$	$\sum\limits_{j=1}^{2} \sum\limits_{i=1}^{n_j} (\bar{Y}_j - \bar{Y})^2$
a-group case	$\bar{Y}_j$	$\bar{Y}$	$\sum\limits_{j=1}^{a} \sum\limits_{i=1}^{n_j} (\bar{Y}_j - \bar{Y})^2$
In general	$\hat{Y}_F$	$\hat{Y}_R$	$\sum\limits_{\text{all obs}} (\hat{Y}_F - \hat{Y}_R)^2$

$$\frac{E_F}{df_F} = \frac{(n-1)\sum s_j^2}{N-a} = \frac{(n-1)\sum s_j^2}{a(n-1)} = \frac{\sum s_j^2}{a} \tag{63}$$

This is a useful approach to take to computing E_F when standard deviations are available, for example, when reanalyzing data from articles reporting means and standard deviations or when analyzing your own data with a calculator having a single-key standard deviation.

Second, a general pattern can be seen in the special cases of the general linear model we have considered. All model comparisons involve assessing the difference in the adequacy of two models. In the major special cases of one-way ANOVA treated in this chapter—namely, the one-group case, the two-group case, and the *a*-group case—we began by determining the best estimates of the models' parameters, then used these to predict the observed values of the dependent variable. When we compared the errors of prediction for the two models under consideration to compute a value for the numerator of our tests, in each case all terms involving the individual *Y* scores have dropped out of our summaries. In fact, as shown in Table 3.2, we can express the difference in the adequacy of the models solely in terms of the differences in the two models' predictions. Indeed, this is true not only in one-way ANOVA but in factorial ANOVA, analysis of covariance and regression. The sum-of-squares term for the numerator of the *F* test can always be written, as shown at the bottom of Table 3.2, simply as the sum over all observations in the study of the squared difference in the predictions of the two models, that is,

$$E_R - E_F = \sum_{\text{all obs}} (\hat{Y}_F - \hat{Y}_R)^2 \tag{64}$$

Numerical Example

Although different mood states have, of course, always been of interest to clinicians, recent years have seen a profusion of studies attempting to manipulate

TABLE **3. 3** Global Affect Ratings
from Mood-Induction Study

Assigned Condition		
Pleasant	*Neutral*	*Unpleasant*
6	5	3
5	4	3
4	4	4
7	3	4
7	4	4
5	3	3
5	4	1
7	4	2
7	4	2
7	5	4
$\bar{Y}_j$ 6.000	4.000	3.000
s_j 1.155	0.667	1.054

mood states in controlled laboratory studies. In such induced-mood research, participants typically are randomly assigned to one of three groups: a depressed-mood induction, a neutral-mood induction, or an elated-mood induction. One recent study (Pruitt, 1988) used selected videoclips from several movies and public television programs as the mood-induction treatments. After viewing the video for her assigned condition, each participant was asked to indicate her mood on various scales. In addition, each subject was herself videotaped, and her facial expressions of emotion were rated on a scale of 1 to 7 (1 indicating sad; 4, neutral; and 7, happy) by an assistant who viewed the videotapes but was kept "blind" regarding the subjects' assigned conditions. Table 3.3 shows representative data[7] of these Global Affect Ratings for 10 observations per group, along with the means and standard deviations for the groups.

As had been predicted, the mean Global Affect Rating is highest in the pleasant condition, intermediate in the neutral condition, and lowest in the unpleasant. We need to carry out a statistical test to substantiate a claim that these differences in sample means are indicative of real differences in the population rather than reflecting sampling variability. Thus, we wish to compare the models shown in Equations 54 and 55:

$$\text{Full model: } Y_{ij} = \mu_j + \varepsilon_{ij_F} \qquad \text{(54, repeated)}$$

$$\text{Restricted model: } Y_{ij} = \mu + \varepsilon_{ij_R} \qquad \text{(55, repeated)}$$

To compute the value in this situation of our general form of the F statistic

$$F = \frac{(E_R - E_F)/(df_R - df_F)}{E_F/df_F} \qquad \text{(22, repeated)}$$

we begin by computing E_F, that is, the sum of squared errors for the full model or the sum of squared deviations of the observations from their group means:

$$E_F = \sum\sum e_{ij_F}^2 = \sum_j\sum_i (Y_{ij} - \bar{Y}_j)^2 \tag{65}$$

As shown in Table 3.4, this involves computing an error score for each subject by subtracting the group mean from the observed score, for example, $e_{11} = Y_{11} - \bar{Y}_1 = 6 - 6 = 0$. When each is squared and summed within each group, we obtain values of 12, 4, and 10 for the pleasant, neutral, and unpleasant conditions, respectively. Thus, E_F, or what would traditionally be denoted SS_W, is 26.

To compute the numerator of our F, we can use the form of $E_R - E_F$ shown in Equation 58 to determine how much more error our restricted model would make:

$$E_R - E_F = n\sum_{j=1}^{a}(\bar{Y}_j - \bar{Y})^2 \tag{58, repeated}$$

As shown in Table 3.4, this sum of squared deviations of group means around the grand mean, weighted by number per group, is 46.67. This value of $E_R - E_F$ is traditionally called SS_B.

TABLE 3.4 Computations for One-Way ANOVA on Mood-Induction Data

			Condition					
Pleasant			Neutral			Unpleasant		
Y_{i1}	e_{i1}	e_{i1}^2	Y_{i2}	e_{i2}	e_{i2}^2	Y_{i3}	e_{i3}	e_{i3}^2
6	0	0	5	1	1	3	0	0
5	−1	1	4	0	0	3	0	0
4	−2	4	4	0	0	4	1	1
7	1	1	3	−1	1	4	1	1
7	1	1	4	0	0	4	1	1
5	−1	1	3	−1	1	3	0	0
5	−1	1	4	0	0	1	−2	4
7	1	1	4	0	0	2	−1	1
7	1	1	4	0	0	2	−1	1
7	1	1	5	1	1	4	1	1

$\bar{Y}_1 = 6$ $\qquad$ $\sum = 12$ $\quad$ $\bar{Y}_2 = 4$ $\qquad$ $\sum = 4$ $\quad$ $\bar{Y}_3 = 3$ $\qquad$ $\sum = 10$

$$\bar{Y} = 4.333$$

$E_F = \sum\sum e_{ij}^2 = \sum\sum(Y_{ij} - \bar{Y}_j)^2 = 12 + 4 + 10 = 26 \,(= SS_W)$

$E_R - E_F = n\sum_j(\bar{Y}_j - \bar{Y})^2 = 10[(6 - 4.333)^2 + (4 - 4.333)^2 + (3 - 4.333)^2]$

$\qquad = 10[2.778 + 0.111 + 1.778] = 46.67 \,(= SS_B)$

$df_F = N - a = 30 - 3 = 27 \,(= df_W)$

$df_R - df_F = (N - 1) - (N - a) = a - 1 = 3 - 1 = 2 \,(= df_B)$

$F = \dfrac{(E_R - E_F)/(df_R - df_F)}{E_F/df_F} = \dfrac{46.67/2}{26/27} = \dfrac{23.33}{.963} = 24.23, p < .001$

The values of our degree-of-freedom terms are as usual dependent on the number of observations and the number of parameters estimated in each model. The degrees of freedom for the denominator of our test statistic is the total number of observations in the study, 30, less the number of parameters estimated in the full model, 3. This df_F of 27 is traditionally denoted df_W. The degrees of freedom for the numerator is simply the number of groups less 1, or 2. This $df_R - df_F$ is traditionally denoted df_B.

We are now ready to combine the values we have computed to determine the value of our test statistic. As shown at the bottom of Table 3.4, the numerator of our F, traditionally denoted MS_B, is 23.33, and the denominator of our F, traditionally denoted MS_W is .963. Note that we could have computed this denominator directly from the within-group standard deviations of Table 3.3 by using Equation 63:

$$\frac{E_F}{df_F} \underset{}{\overset{}{=}} \frac{\sum s_j^2}{a} \qquad\qquad (63, \text{repeated})$$

$$= \frac{(1.155)^2 + (0.667)^2 + (1.054)^2}{3}$$

$$= \frac{1.334 + 0.444 + 1.111}{3}$$

$$= \frac{2.890}{3} = .963$$

Combining our values of MS_B and MS_W, we obtain an F value of 24.23. Consulting Appendix Table A.2, we note that there is not an entry for denominator df of 27. In such a case, we would use the entries for the closest *smaller* value of denominator degrees of freedom. This means using the critical value for an F with 2 and 26 degrees of freedom, which is 9.12 for $p = .001$. Naturally, for most actual analyses, you will likely be using a computer program that will yield exact p values for your particular degrees of freedom. In any case, the obtained F of 24.23 is highly significant. In a report of this analysis, this would be indicated as $F(2, 27) = 24.23$, $p < .001$. Thus, we would conclude that the restricted model should be rejected. We do have statistical grounds for arguing that the mood-induction treatments would produce different population means on the Global Affect Rating Scale.

A Model in Terms of Effects

Models can be written in different ways. Up to now, we have employed cell mean or μ_j models. Our full models have had one parameter for each cell of the design, with the parameter being the population mean for that condition. Although this type of model works well in the one-way case, it proves unwieldy in the case of factorial designs; thus, in later chapters, we generally use a different approach that makes it easier to talk about the effects of the factors under investigation. To anticipate those developments, we introduce here a full model in terms of effects or an α_j model. Note that α_j (read "alpha sub j") is here being used as a parameter in a model and as such is totally unrelated to the use of α as a symbol for the probability of a Type I error.

We present the effects model for the general one-way situation where a treatment conditions or groups are being compared. The full model for this situation can be written

$$Y_{ij} = \mu + \alpha_j + \varepsilon_{ij} \tag{66}$$

where, as before, Y_{ij} and ε_{ij} are, respectively, the observed score and error of the model for the ith subject in the jth group. The unknown parameters are now μ, which represents a grand mean term common to all observations and the a α_js—that is, $\alpha_1, \alpha_2, \alpha_3, \ldots, \alpha_a$, each of which represents the effect of a particular treatment condition. We will be combining these $a + 1$ parameters to arrive at predictions for each of the a groups. Because we have more parameters than predictions, we must impose some additional constraint to arrive at unique estimates of the parameters. Simply requiring the effect parameters to sum to zero is the constraint that results in the parameters having the desired interpretation. This condition that the parameters are required to meet, namely,

$$\sum_{j=1}^{a} \alpha_j = 0 \tag{67}$$

is what is termed a *side condition* (see discussion of Equation 4), a technical constraint adopted to get a desired unique solution to an estimation problem. This is in contrast to a restriction with substantive meaning like our null hypotheses.

As you know, deviations from a mean sum to zero, and it is as deviations from a mean that our effect parameters are defined. This can be seen easily by comparing the effects full model with the cell mean model:

$$Y_{ij} = \mu + \alpha_j + \varepsilon_{ij} \tag{66, repeated}$$

$$Y_{ij} = \mu_j + \varepsilon_{ij} \tag{54, repeated}$$

The grand mean term plus the effect parameter of Equation 66 is equivalent to the cell mean parameter of Equation 54, that is,

$$\mu + \alpha_j = \mu_j \tag{68}$$

Subtracting μ from both sides of Equation 68, we have

$$\alpha_j = \mu_j - \mu \tag{69}$$

Thus, the effect of a particular treatment is defined here as the extent to which the population mean for that condition departs from the grand mean term. Further, the constraint in Equation 67 that the effects sum to zero can be stated in terms of the deviations of Equation 69, that is,

$$\sum_{j=1}^{a} (\mu_j - \mu) = 0 \tag{70}$$

which, when one solves for μ, implies that the grand mean term in the effects model is just the mean of treatment population means, that is,

TABLE 3.5 Population Means and Effect
Parameters for Four Treatments

Condition	Mean μ_j	Effect α_j
1. Educational program	32	+9
2. Standard abstinence program	20	−3
3. Antabuse therapy	18	−5
4. Controlled drinking	22	−1
Mean of means μ	**23**	

$$\mu = \frac{\sum\limits_{j=1}^{a} \mu_j}{a} \tag{71}$$

To illustrate, assume that the population means were for four treatments for alcohol abuse. The dependent variable is number of drinks per week, which is assessed one year after the end of treatment. Assume that the population means for the four treatments are as shown in Table 3.5. The mean of the treatment-population means, which here is 23 drinks per week, serves as the value of μ in Equation 66 for this domain and is the baseline against which the effects of the treatments are evaluated. For example, the effect of treatment 3, Antabuse therapy, was to lower the mean 5 drinks per week below this baseline, that is, $\alpha_3 = \mu_3 - \mu = 18 - 23 = -5$.

Parameter Estimates. As usual, we estimate the parameters of our model to minimize the squared errors of prediction. For the effects model, the predictions are

$$\hat{Y}_{ij} = \hat{\mu} + \hat{\alpha}_j$$

which means that the least-squares estimates of μ and α_j are arrived at by minimizing

$$\sum_j \sum_i e_{ij_F}^2 = \sum_j \sum_i (Y_{ij} - \hat{Y}_{ij})^2 = \sum_j \sum_i [Y_{ij} - (\hat{\mu} + \hat{\alpha}_j)]^2 \tag{72}$$

Because we have enough free parameters to have a different prediction for each cell (i.e., for each group), it should not be surprising that the way to minimize these squared errors of prediction is to choose our parameters in such a way that they combine to equal the observed cell means, that is,

$$\hat{Y}_{ij} = \bar{Y}_j = \hat{\mu} + \hat{\alpha}_j \tag{73}$$

Because the effects are required to sum to zero across groups, adding these predictions over the a groups indicates that the least-squares estimate of μ is the average of the observed cell means, that is,

$$\hat{\mu} = \frac{\sum\limits_{j=1}^{a} \bar{Y}_j}{a} \tag{74}$$

We designate this sample mean $\bar{Y}_u$, that is,

$$\bar{Y}_u = \frac{\sum_j \bar{Y}_j}{a} \tag{75}$$

to indicate it is a grand mean computed as an unweighted average of the group means. In cases where the same number of subjects is observed in each group, this mean of the means $\bar{Y}_u$ equals the conventional grand mean of all the observations $\bar{Y}$. In the case where there are different numbers of observations per group, these values can differ.[8] From the viewpoint of the restricted model, each subject, regardless of his or her group assignment, is sampled from one and the same population and thus should contribute equally to the estimate of the population's mean. However, in the full model, the logic is that there are as many populations as there are groups, each with its own mean. Thus the "grand mean" is more reasonably thought of as a mean of the different group means. Substituting this value into Equation 73 and solving for $\hat{\alpha}_j$ yields

$$\hat{\alpha}_j = \bar{Y}_j - \bar{Y}_u \tag{76}$$

Notice that these least-squares estimates of μ and α_j indicated in Equations 74 and 76 are equivalent to the definitions in Equations 71 and 69, respectively, with sample means substituted for population means.

Computation of the Test Statistic.   The observed F value for a model comparison involving a model stated in terms of effects is identical to that for a model comparison using the equivalent cell means model. For a one-way ANOVA, the models to be compared using an effects approach are

$$\text{Full model: } Y_{ij} = \mu + \alpha_j + \varepsilon_{ij} \qquad \text{(66, repeated)}$$

$$\text{Restricted model: } Y_{ij} = \mu + \varepsilon_{ij} \qquad \text{(55, repeated)}$$

The predictions of the full model, as shown in Equation 73, are the observed group means, just as was true for the cell means full model of Equation 54. The restricted models are identical in the effects and cell means cases; thus, the predictions are, of course, identical, namely, the grand mean of all observations. The degrees of freedom associated with this common restricted model are $N - 1$.

The one point of possible confusion concerns degrees of freedom of the full effects model. Although as written in Equation 66, this model appears to require $a + 1$ parameters (a αs and 1 μ); implicit in the model is the side condition that the sum of the α_js is zero. This implies that one of these parameters could be eliminated. For example, we could say that an arbitrarily chosen one of the αs—for example, the final one—is equal to the negative of the sum of the remaining αs:

$$\alpha_a = -\sum_{j=1}^{a-1} \alpha_j \tag{77}$$

Thus, in reality there are a parameters in our full model, one μ parameter, and $a - 1$ *independent* α_js. Because all terms making up the general form of our F statistic—namely, E_R, E_F, df_R, and df_F—are the same in the effects and cell mean cases, the observed Fs must be the same.

Further, in the case where there are an equal number of observations in each group, the sum of squares, $E_R - E_F$, for the numerator of our F test can be expressed simply in terms of the estimated effect parameters. In particular, this difference in errors for our two models is just the sum over all observations of the estimated effects squared, that is,

$$E_R - E_F = \sum_{j=1}^{a} \sum_{i=1}^{n} \hat{\alpha}_j^2 \qquad (78)$$

Because the estimated effect is the same for all individuals within a group, we can replace the summation over i by a multiplier of n:

$$E_R - E_F = n \sum_{j=1}^{a} \hat{\alpha}_j^2 \qquad (79)$$

For example, if the means shown in Table 3.5 were sample means and estimated effects from a study based on 10 observations per cell, we could compute $E_R - E_F$ directly from the estimated effects:

$$\begin{aligned} E_R - E_F &= 10[9^2 + (-3)^2 + (-5)^2 + (-1)^2] \\ &= 10(81 + 9 + 25 + 1) = 10(116) \\ &= 1160 \end{aligned}$$

In the unequal-n case, we still use the general principle that the difference in the models' adequacy can be stated in terms of the difference in their predictions:

$$E_R - E_F = \sum_{\text{all obs}} (\hat{Y}_F - \hat{Y}_R)^2 \qquad \text{(64, repeated)}$$

Because the predictions of the effects full model are the group means (see Equation 73), this can be written in terms of means in exactly the same way as in the cell mean model:

$$E_R - E_F = \sum_{j=1}^{a} n_j (\bar{Y}_j - \bar{Y})^2 \qquad \text{(57, repeated)}$$

Having now developed our model-comparison procedure using parameters reflecting the effects of the treatments, we now turn to alternative ways of characterizing the strength of effects of the treatments being investigated.

ON TESTS OF SIGNIFICANCE AND MEASURES OF EFFECT

Up to this point, we have more or less presumed that conducting a test of significance was the most meaningful quantitative summarization one could make of the results of an experiment. We must now explicitly consider this presumption and discuss some alternative approaches to summarizing results.

Statistical hypothesis testing has not been without its critics (cf. Morrison & Henkel, 1970). Some of the criticisms offered have been as mundane as asserting that aspects of the approach are not well understood by some of its users. The prime example cited is the misunderstanding of a test's p value as the probability that the results were due to chance. That is, some researchers (and textbook writers!) occasionally have made the mistake of saying that the p value is the probability that the null hypothesis is true, given the obtained data. Instead, as we have tried to make clear by our development of p values through the discrete probability examples in Chapter 2, the p value is the probability of obtaining a test statistic as extreme or more extreme than that observed, given that the null hypothesis (or restricted model) is assumed to be true. Granted, chance *is* involved, but that is in the sampling variability inherent in obtaining data from only a sample. However, a p value from a test is always a conditional probability of data given the null hypothesis, not a conditional probability of the null hypothesis being true given the data. We believe that the appropriate response to a misunderstanding of p values is simply to try to prevent such misunderstanding in the future, not to question the statistical testing methodology.

Several other more forceful criticisms of hypothesis testing have been advanced as well. (These have been helpfully reviewed and responded to by Chow, 1988.) The major difficulty, in the eyes of some, is the role played by the size of the sample in determining the outcome of a test. As we develop more explicitly below, other things being equal, the magnitude of a test statistic is directly related to the size of the sample. Thus, a treatment and a control condition could result in means differing by the same amount in each of two studies, yet the effect could be declared "highly significant" in one while not approaching significance in the other, simply because the first study included more participants. Given the fact that the number of participants in a study is arbitrary, it is reasonable to ask whether something does not need to be done to prevent this arbitrariness from affecting the directions in which significance tests push science.

Indeed, some have argued that the process is necessarily arbitrary because the null hypothesis is never true (Bakan, 1966). That is, the restriction that certain population parameters be exactly equal will virtually never be satisfied, so the only question in doing a significance test is whether the investigator invested enough effort recruiting subjects to detect the particular inequality.

A somewhat different line of attack is to fault significance tests for diverting attention from other questions. For example, significance testing conventionally has focused on whether the p value meets the accepted probability of a Type I error, while virtually ignoring the probability of a Type II error or conversely the power of the test (cf. Cohen, 1977).

As Chow (1988) points out, these concerns regarding sample size and effect size have to do with the role of statistical analyses in scientific investigations. Our view, which we developed in Chapter 1, is that experiments involve imperfect embodiments of independent-variable and dependent-variable constructs. Nonetheless, experiments shed light on the plausibility of explanatory theories by providing a basis for choosing between two alternative assertions. The assertions concern whether the data follow the pattern predicted by the theory, such as "the mean in the experimental group will be higher than in the control" (see the discussion of the syllogisms of confirmation and falsification in Chapter 1). In fact, it is the significance test that permits the decision of whether the data conform to the predicted pattern. Thus, the accept–reject logic of hypothesis testing fits well with the theory–corroboration view of experimentation (cf. Chow, 1988).

Of course, experiments serve other purposes besides theory testing. Generally, the empirical question itself is of interest apart from the question of why the effect occurs. In certain applied research such as evaluation of clinical or educational treatments, the empirical questions of which treatment is most effective and by how much are in fact of primary interest. Particularly if decisions are to be made on the basis of an experiment about whether it would be cost effective to implement a particular program, to have an estimate of the magnitude of the effect is critical. Thus, in many applied contexts, we would concur with those who argue for the need for estimates of effect size in addition to hypothesis tests. In theory-testing areas, these magnitude-of-effect estimates may be of less interest because the implemented treatment is only indirectly related to the theoretical mechanism of interest. Your theory may concern how different personalities respond to anxiety about death. Yet the lack of dramatic changes in indicators of anxiety you observe in a laboratory study can be viewed as saying more about your auxiliary theory that showing death-related slides induces death anxiety than it says about your substantive theory itself. You realize your treatment is not a pure form of the construct of interest, even if your theory is correct; thus, the magnitude of the effect of your operationalization is less important than the question of whether you have statistical evidence indicating the theory is a viable one.

The "sample-size problem" relates to the validity of these statistical conclusions. However, from our viewpoint, that smaller and smaller differences can be detected with larger and larger samples is not so much a problem as the way it should be. As more members of each population are sampled, it makes sense that your estimate of each mean should be more precise and that your ability to discriminate among differing means increases. The only problem really is that investigators may fail to take advantage of the available procedures for determining the appropriate sample size for their studies. We consider these procedures for power analysis in the final section of the chapter, and, these procedures in turn depend on your being able to characterize the magnitude of effect that it is meaningful to detect. Thus, because of their role in indicating what you expect to happen in a study as well as their more obvious utility in describing what actually did happen, we turn now to a discussion of measures of effects.

MEASURES OF EFFECT

As we have suggested above, the numerical value of a test statistic is determined as much by the number of participants in the study as it is by any absolute measure of the size of the treatment effect. In particular, the two factors multiply together to determine the test statistic:

$$\text{Test statistic} = \text{Size of effect} \times \text{Size of study} \qquad (80)$$

The size-of-study term is some function of the number of participants and will often be a degrees-of-freedom term. The size-of-effect term can be expressed in different ways in different contexts. Rosenthal (1987, pp. 106–107) presents several forms of the general equation shown in Equation 80 for χ^2, z, independent-groups t, dependent-groups t, and F tests. We illustrate first the size-of-effect term with our general form of the F test. Recall that we began the development of the F test in the one-sample case by using the proportional increase in error, which was defined as follows:

$$\text{proportional increase in error} = \frac{\text{increase in error}}{\text{minimal error}} = \frac{E_R - E_F}{E_F} \qquad (81)$$

Using this measure of how much more adequate the full model is as a size-of-effect index, we express our F in the form of Equation 80 as follows:

$$F = \frac{E_R - E_F}{E_F} \times \frac{df_F}{df_R - df_F} \qquad (82)$$

This form of the F underscores the general principle that one can get larger test statistics either by increasing the effect size or by increasing the study size.

There are a number of different ways of assessing effects. Yeaton and Sechrest (1981) make a useful distinction between two broad categories of such measures: those that measure effect size and those that measure association strength. Measuring effect size involves examining differences between means. Measuring association strength, on the other hand, involves examining proportions of variance and is perhaps most easily described using the terminology of correlational research. One perspective on the distinction between these kinds of measures is that "a difference between means shows directly how much effect a treatment has; a measure of association shows the dependability or uniformity with which it can be produced" (Yeaton & Sechrest, 1981, p. 766). The proportional increase in error of our F test would be considered an association measure. Although association measures are closely related to test statistics, often the simpler, more direct effect-size measures are more useful in interpreting and applying results. We consider such effect-size measures first.

Measures of Effect Size

Mean Difference.   The simplest measure of the treatment effect is the difference between means. Such a simple measure is most appropriate whenever there are only two groups under study. The treatment effect in the population then could be described simply as $\mu_1 - \mu_2$. The difference between the sample means $\bar{Y}_1 - \bar{Y}_2$ is an unbiased estimate of the population difference. One advantage of this effect measure is that it is on the same, meaningful scale as the dependent variable.

For example, Gastorf (1980) found a $\bar{Y}_1 - \bar{Y}_2$ difference of 3.85 minutes in a comparison of when students who scored high on a scale of Type A behavior arrived for an appointment as opposed to the later-arriving, low scorers on the scale. As Yeaton and Sechrest (1981) point out, this sort of effect measure can easily be translated in a meaningful way into applied settings. A difference of 3.85 minutes in arrival time is of a magnitude that, for a firm employing 1000 workers at $10 an hour, would translate into $150,000 of additional work per year, assuming the difference manifested itself only once daily.

When there are more than two conditions in a one-way design, then there are, of course, multiple mean differences that may be considered. Often the range of means is used as the best single indicator of the size of the treatment effect. For example, using the data from the mood-induction study presented in Table 3.3— where the means for the pleasant, neutral and unpleasant conditions were 6, 4 and 3, respectively—we could easily compute the difference between the largest and smallest means, $\bar{Y}_{max} - \bar{Y}_{min}$:

$$\bar{Y}_{max} - \bar{Y}_{min} = 6 - 3 = 3$$

Thus, the effect of receiving a pleasant-mood induction as opposed to an unpleasant-mood induction amounted to a difference of 3 points on the 7-point Global Affect Rating Scale. Chapter 5 considers various ways of testing differences between pairs of means chosen like these to reflect the range of effects present in a study.

Estimated Effect Parameters. An alternative solution when there are more than two groups is to describe the effects in terms of the estimates of the α_j parameters in the full model written in terms of effects:

$$Y_{ij} = \mu + \alpha_j + \varepsilon_{ij} \qquad \text{(66, repeated)}$$

As you know, these effect parameters are defined as deviations of the treatment means from the mean of the treatment means. They are then smaller on the average than the pairwise differences between means we considered in the previous section. For example, in the mood-induction study, the mean of the treatment means was 4.333, resulting in estimated effects of $+1.667$, $-.333$ and -1.333 for the pleasant, neutral, and unpleasant conditions, respectively. Thus, the neutral condition is seen to be somewhat more like the unpleasant treatment than the pleasant treatment in that its effect is to lower the Global Affect Rating .333 units below the grand mean of the study.

If a single measure of treatment effect is desired, the standard deviation of the α_j parameters could be used to indicate how far, on the scale of the dependent variable, the typical treatment causes its mean to deviate from the grand mean. In fact, we use this measure in developing a standardized measure of effect size in our discussion of power at the end of the chapter.

The Standardized Difference Between Means. The measures of effect size considered thus far have the advantage of being expressed in the units of the dependent variable. That is also their weakness. In most areas of the behavioral sciences, there is not a single universally accepted dependent variable. Even within a fairly restricted domain and approach such as depression as assessed by the individual's self-report, there typically are various measures being used in different research laboratories and clinics across the country. As a result, to compare effect sizes across measures, it is necessary to transform them to a common scale. In fact, part of the motivation for developing standardized measures of effects was to permit their use in quantitative research integration studies or metaanalyses, as suggested by Glass (1976). The goal then is to have a standard scale for effects like the z-score scale, and the solution is achieved in the same way as with z scores, that is, divide by the standard deviation so that differences can be expressed in standard deviation units. Following Cohen (1977, p. 20) we denote this standardized difference between two population means as d:

$$d = (\mu_1 - \mu_2)/\sigma_\varepsilon \qquad (83)$$

where σ_ε is the common within-group population standard deviation. We can estimate this standardized effect measure by substituting sample statistics for the corresponding population parameters, and we denote this estimate $\hat{d}$:

$$\hat{d} = (\bar{Y}_1 - \bar{Y}_2)/S \qquad (84)$$

where following Hedges (1981, p. 110) S is the pooled within-group standard deviation estimate. That is, S^2 is the weighted average of the sample within-group variances:

$$S^2 = \frac{\sum(n_j - 1)s_j^2}{\sum(n_j - 1)} \qquad (85)$$

We first encountered such pooled variance estimates in the two-group case (see Equation 39). As we pointed out there, we can express such within-group variances estimates either in terms of the full model's sum of squared error or in terms of traditional terminology, that is,

$$S^2 = \frac{E_F}{df_F} = \frac{SS_W}{df_W} = MS_W \qquad (86)$$

For the mood-induction data in Table 3.3, we found the average variance to be .963 (see bottom of Table 3.4, p. 90), implying $S = .981$. With this as the metric, we can say that the pleasant condition resulted in a mean Global Affect Rating that was 2 standard deviations higher than that in the neutral condition: $\hat{d} = (\bar{Y}_1 - \bar{Y}_2)/S = (6 - 4)/.981 = 2.038$.

Hedges (1981) determined the mathematical distribution of $\hat{d}$ values[9] and extended this work in several subsequent publications (see, e.g., Hedges, 1982, 1983). The use of a standardized effect-size measure in research integration is illustrated by Smith and Glass's (1977) review of psychotherapy outcome studies and Rosenthal and Rubin's (1978) discussion of interpersonal expectancy effects—for example, the effect of teachers' expectations on students' gains in intellectual performance.

Like the previous measures we have considered, standardized differences can be adapted for use as summary measures when there are more than two treatment conditions. Most simply, one can use the standardized difference between the largest and smallest means as the overall summary of the magnitude of effects in an a-group study. Again following Cohen (1977), we denote the standardized difference that is large enough to span the range of means d. This is estimated by the standardized range of sample means:

$$\hat{d} = (\bar{Y}_{max} - \bar{Y}_{min})/S \tag{87}$$

For the mood-induction study, we would have $\hat{d} = (6 - 3)/.981 = 3.058$. This is an unusually large effect.

We employ d in the final section of the chapter as part of a simplifying strategy for approximating the power of a study. In addition, a multiple of d proves useful in follow-up tests after an a-group ANOVA (see the discussion of the studentized range in Chapter 5).

There is a second way of adapting standardized differences for a-group studies, besides ignoring all but the two most extreme means. As we just mentioned in "Estimated Effect Parameters," one could use the standard deviation of the group means as an indicator of the typical effect and divide *that* by the within-group standard deviation to get an overall standardized effect. Because the conditions included in a study are regarded as all that are of interest, we can treat the a levels as the population of levels of interest and define

$$\sigma_m = \sqrt{\frac{\sum(\mu_j - \mu)^2}{a}} = \sqrt{\frac{\sum \alpha_j^2}{a}} \tag{88}$$

Then a standardized treatment standard deviation, which Cohen (1977, p. 274) denotes f, would be

$$f = \frac{\sigma_m}{\sigma_\varepsilon}. \tag{89}$$

This particular summary measure figures prominently in our upcoming discussion of power.

Measures of Association Strength

Describing and understanding relationships constitute a major goal of scientific activity. As discussed in Chapter 1, causal relationships are of special interest. The clearest example of a causal relationship is one where the cause is necessary and sufficient for the effect to occur. Unfortunately, in the behavioral sciences, we have few examples of such infallible, deterministic relationships. Rather, most phenomena of interest are only probabilistically related to the causes to which we have access. Further, the causes that we can manipulate or control in an experiment may only be a small subset of the determinants of the scores on the dependent variable. It is easy to lose sight of this, however, if one focuses exclusively on hypothesis testing. Computing a measure of the association strength between your independent variable and dependent variable often provides a safeguard against overestimating the importance of a statistically significant result.

Measures of association strength can be thought of as proportions. The goal is to indicate, on a 0-to-1 scale, how much of the variability in the dependent variable is associated with the variation in the independent-variable levels.

Our models' perspective allows us to arrive at such a proportion immediately in terms of the measures of inadequacy of our two models. The proportion is to indicate how much knowledge of group membership improves prediction of the dependent variable. That is, we want to express the reduction in error that results from adding group membership parameters to our model as a proportion of the error we would make without them in the model. This proportionate reduction in error (PRE) measure is most commonly designated R^2:

$$R^2 = \frac{E_R - E_F}{E_R} \tag{90}$$

where the restricted model is a grand mean model and the full model is a cell means model, as in Equations 55 and 54, respectively. This ratio is a descriptive statistic indicating the proportion of variability in the observed data that is accounted for by the treatments. R^2 is very commonly used in the context of multiple regression, which we develop in the extension to this chapter, to indicate directly a model's adequacy in accounting for the data. As we develop there, R^2 is the square of the correlation between observed scores and predicted scores. It is sometimes denoted $\hat{\eta}^2$ (lowercase Greek *eta*, hat, squared) (Maxwell, Camp, & Arvey, 1981, p. 527).

There is no question of the legitimacy of R^2 as a descriptive index for sample data (cf. Hays, 1981, p. 349). Because of its clear interpretation and the fact that, unlike a test statistic, it does not tend to increase with sample size, R^2 has much to recommend it as a useful supplement to the p value of a test. However, other measures of association, most notably $\hat{\omega}^2$ (lowercase Greek *omega*, hat, squared), are available; their rationale and advantages relative to R^2 merit consideration. One can argue, as Hays (1981, p. 290) does, that what is of most interest is the proportion of variance in the population that would be accounted for by the treatments. If this is granted, then characteristics of R^2 as an estimator must be considered. In this regard, recall that the numerator of R^2 depends on the variability among the group means:

$$E_R - E_F = \sum_j \sum_i (\bar{Y}_j - \bar{Y})^2 \tag{see 56}$$

However, even if the population-group means were identical, the sample means will almost certainly differ from each other. Thus, although in the population the treatments may account for no variance, R^2 would nonetheless be expected to be greater than zero because of this sampling variability in the observed means. This positive bias of R^2, or tendency to systematically overestimate the population proportion, in fact is present whether the population-treatment means are equal or not. It turns out that the extent of positive bias of R^2 can be estimated and is a decreasing function of sample size.

The other measures of association like $\hat{\omega}^2$ attempt to correct for this positive bias by shrinking the numerator in Equation 90. Thus, the formula for $\hat{\omega}^2$ for an a-group one-way ANOVA can be written

$$\hat{\omega}^2 = \frac{(E_R - E_F) - (a - 1)(E_F/df_F)}{E_R + (E_F/df_F)} \tag{91}$$

or in terms of the traditional ANOVA notation in which $\hat{\omega}^2$ is typically described:

$$\hat{\omega}^2 = \frac{SS_B - (a - 1)MS_W}{SS_{Total} + MS_W} \tag{92}$$

Although it is clear from comparing Equations 90 and 91 that $\hat{\omega}^2$ is smaller than R^2, it is not obvious how much less. For all practical purposes, the amount of shrinkage of R^2 can be estimated using some early work by Wherry (1931). Wherry showed that the proportion of unexplained variability in the population is actually larger than $1 - R^2$ by a factor of approximately df_R/df_F. From this we can estimate the adjusted (or shrunken) R^2, which we denote $\tilde{R}^2$, as follows:

$$\tilde{R}^2 = 1 - \frac{df_R}{df_F}(1 - R^2) = 1 - \frac{N-1}{N-a}(1 - R^2) \tag{93}$$

Maxwell et al. (1981) review work showing that the value of $\tilde{R}^2$ is typically within .02 of $\hat{\omega}^2$.

We illustrate numerically how these association-strength measures compare using the mood-induction data in Table 3.4 (p. 90). From the values of $E_R = 72.67$, $E_F = 26$, $df_R = 29$, and $df_F = 27$, we can easily compute the value of R^2 from Equation 90

$$R^2 = \frac{E_R - E_F}{E_R} = \frac{72.67 - 26.00}{72.67} = \frac{46.67}{72.67} = .642$$

the value of $\hat{\omega}^2$ from Equation 91

$$\hat{\omega}^2 = \frac{(E_R - E_F) - (a - 1)(E_F/df_F)}{E_R + (E_F/df_F)}$$

$$= \frac{(72.67 - 26.00) - (2)(26/27)}{72.67 + 26/27} = \frac{46.67 - 1.926}{72.67 + .963} = .608$$

and the value of $\tilde{R}^2$ from Equation 93

$$\tilde{R}^2 = 1 - \frac{N-1}{N-a}(1 - R^2) = 1 - \frac{29}{27}(1 - .642)$$

$$= 1 - 1.074(.358) = 1 - .384 = .616$$

In this case, the mood-induction treatments appear to account for over 60 percent of the variability in the population as well as the sample. Although the differences among the three association-strength measures are small here, R^2 can be considerably larger than $\hat{\omega}^2$ or $\tilde{R}^2$ if the sample sizes are small, especially when $1 - R^2$ is relatively large. In fact, $\hat{\omega}^2$ and $\tilde{R}^2$ can yield values that are less than zero, in which case the estimated population proportion would be set equal to zero.

Evaluation of Measures. Measures of association strength provide an additional perspective on the amount of control your treatment manipulation has over the dependent variable. Like the measures of effect size, association measures cannot be made to look impressive simply by running more subjects. But unlike the effect size indices, association measures are assessed on a bounded, unitless metric (that is, a 0-to-1 scale); further, they clearly reflect how much variability remains unaccounted for, besides reflecting the treatment effects.

However, despite these advantages, association measures have been criticized on a variety of fronts (e.g., Abelson, 1985; O'Grady, 1982; Rosenthal & Rubin, 1982; Yeaton & Sechrest, 1981). First, the measures are borrowed from correlational research and are less appropriate for an experimental situation where certain fixed levels of an independent variable are investigated (Glass & Hakstian, 1969). As O'Grady (1982, p. 771ff.) notes, the number and choice of levels of the factor under investigation are decided on by the experimenter and can greatly influence the PRE measures. Including only extreme groups in a study of an individual difference variable would tend to exaggerate the PRE. On the other hand, failing to include an untreated control group in a clinical study comparing reasonably effective treatments might greatly reduce PRE but would not alter the actual causal powers of the treatments.

Thus, the arbitrary-choice-of-levels problem relates to the more general difficulty of attempting to infer the importance of a factor as a cause of an outcome from a PRE measure. The conventional wisdom is that correlations that indicate a factor accounts for, say, 10 percent or less of the variability in an outcome are of trivial importance practically or theoretically. For example, this was the rationale of Rimland (1979) in suggesting that a review of 400 psychotherapy outcome studies showing such an effect sounded the "death knell" for psychotherapy. Similarly, the Type A effect on arrival time mentioned previously was noted by Strahan (1981) as corresponding to an R^2 of about .02.

In fact, if one pursues research in the human sciences, one is forced in many areas to proceed by the cumulation of knowledge based on effects of this magnitude. The most important reason for this is that the effects of interest—for example, psychological adjustment—are determined by a large number of factors. In addition, the measure of the construct of interest may be of low reliability or validity. These points have been illustrated in a compelling fashion by authors who have cited effects of factors recognized to be important despite their low PREs. For example, Rosenthal (1987, p. 115) notes that a placebo-controlled study of propranolol was halted by the National Heart, Lung, and Blood Institute because "the results were so favorable to the treatment that it would be unethical" to withhold the treatment from the placebo-controlled patients. The effect of the drug was to increase survival rate of patients by 4 percent, a statistically significant effect in a study of 2108 patients. The compelling argument to make the drug available to all patients is hardly offset by the fact that it accounted for only 0.2 percent of the variance in the treatment outcome (living or dying). Many psychological variables of interest may have as many potential causes as living or dying, thus limiting correlations to similarly low levels as in the propranolol study. What is more, our constructs are generally measured with much lower reliability or validity than the outcome variable in that study, which further limits the strength and interpretability of the effects that can be observed. Such psychometric issues regarding association measures have been helpfully reviewed by O'Grady (1982).

A final difficulty with the measures of explained variability is the nature of the scale. The benefit of having a 0-to-1 scale is achieved at the cost of working from ratios of squared units. The practical implications of a value on such a scale are not as immediately obvious as one on the scale of the dependent variable. The squaring tends further to make the indices take on values close to zero, which can result in effects being dismissed as trivial. An alternative measure, which can alleviate these difficulties in certain situations, is discussed in the next section.

With these caveats in mind, PRE measures can be a useful adjunct to a test of significance. Because the population is typically of more interest than the sample and because the bias in the sample R^2 can be substantial if N is, say, less than 30, some type of adjusted R^2 is preferred for general use. The $\hat{\omega}^2$ measure satisfies this and seems to be the most widely used PRE measure. Further, general algorithms have been developed to calculate $\hat{\omega}^2$ in complex designs. Thus, we recommend $\hat{\omega}^2$ for inferential purposes.

Alternative Representations of Effects

Various other tabular, numerical, and graphical methods have been suggested for communicating information about treatment effects. We describe some of these briefly and refer the reader to other sources for more detailed treatments.

Binomial Effect Size Display (BESD). Rosenthal and Rubin (1982) suggest the BESD as a simple summary of results that would be easier to understand than the proportion-of-variance measures. In a sense, the measure represents a compromise: like the measures of effect size, it uses the dependent-variable scale (albeit in dichotomized form); like the measures of association, it is based on a measure of relationship (albeit R instead of R^2).

The BESD presents results in a 2×2 table. Table 3.6 shows an example. The virtual doubling of the success rate as the result of the experimental treatment is one most would agree is substantial, particularly if the outcome categories corresponded to "alive" and "dead." Surprisingly, the effect shown is one where the treatment condition accounts for 10 percent of the variance. In fact, simply taking the difference in success rates here immediately gives the value of R—that is, $R = .66 - .34 = .32$—which when squared yields the proportion of variance accounted for, for example, $R^2 = (.32)^2 = .10$.

The limitations on the method are that you can only consider two conditions and two possible outcomes. Because most outcomes of behavioral interventions are continuous variables, it is necessary to artificially dichotomize the scores on the dependent variable—for example, those above or below the overall median—to create a BESD. Rosenthal and Rubin (1982, p. 168) have suggestions on refinements

T A B L E **3.6** A Binomial Effect Size Display

		Outcome		
		Success	*Failure*	
Condition	*Treatment*	66	34	100
	Control	34	66	100
		100	100	200

of the display, which depend on the form of the dependent-variable distribution and the value of R. However, technicalities aside, in many applied settings such a comparison of success rates may be the most meaningful supplement to the hypothesis test for communicating clearly the treatment effect.

Confidence Intervals.   Thus far in our discussion of measures of effect, we have used the sample mean in a condition as the indicator of the population mean. Although $\bar{Y}_j$ is always an unbiased estimator of μ_j, it is important to remember that as an estimator $\bar{Y}_j$ can also be characterized by its variance. That the variance of a sample mean $\sigma^2_{\bar{Y}_j}$ is directly related to the variance of the population and inversely related to the number of scores in the sample is one of the most fundamental ideas in statistics, that is,

$$\sigma^2_{\bar{Y}_j} = \sigma^2_\varepsilon / n_j \tag{94}$$

This population variance in turn may be estimated by $s^2_{\bar{Y}_j}$, the value obtained by substituting our observed value of mean square error E_F/df_F for σ^2_ε; that is,

$$s^2_{\bar{Y}_j} = (E_F/df_F)/n_j \tag{95}$$

A useful way of characterizing the imprecision in your estimate of the sample mean is to use the standard error of the mean, that is, the square root of the quantity in Equation 95 to construct a confidence interval for the population mean. Under the standard ANOVA assumptions, this interval is the one centered around $\bar{Y}_j$ and having as its limits the quantities

$$\bar{Y}_j \pm \sqrt{F_{1,df_F}}\, s_{\bar{Y}_j} \tag{96}$$

where F_{1,df_F} is the critical value from Appendix Table A.2 for the α level corresponding to the desired degree of confidence $(1 - \alpha) \times 100$. For example, if the critical values for $\alpha = .05$ were to be used, the interpretation of the confidence interval is that if repeated samples of size n_j were observed under treatment j and such a confidence interval were constructed for each sample, 95 percent of them would contain the true value of μ_j.

Indicators of the variability of the estimates of the difference between combinations of means are considered in Chapters 4–6. These often are of as much interest as the variability of the individual means.

Graphical Methods.   Plots of data are, of course, useful in helping you and others gain an understanding of the trends in your data. Rough, hand-drawn plots showing the individual data points in each condition may bring to your attention differences in variability across conditions or the occurrence of individual aberrant scores. (Statistical methods for testing for heterogeneity of variance are considered in the following section.) Final plots in the published reports of findings typically show only the means in the various conditions. The informativeness of these plots can be increased by adding a vertical line going through the point corresponding to the group mean to points 1 standard error above and below the mean.

Recent years have seen the development of a number of graphical methods (e.g., Tukey, 1977; Cleveland, 1985), which can be used to supplement standard plots of means. Most newer methods involve plotting medians or other percentiles. For example, Tukey's box graph includes five horizontal lines for each group corresponding to the 10th, 25th, 50th, 75th, and 90th percentiles for that group. Refer to the book by Cleveland (1985, pp. 129ff.) for details.

As is perhaps obvious from the wide-ranging discussion of ways of characterizing effects, the methods available are not nearly as standardized as the methods of testing for significance. But the message you have hopefully received is that, whether through graphs, tables, or numerical methods, measures of effect can carry useful information over and above that contained in the p value of the test.

STATISTICAL ASSUMPTIONS

The F test for comparing two models is a very flexible procedure, in that it can be used in a wide variety of circumstances. However, for the expression

$$F_{obs} = \frac{(E_R - E_F)/(df_R - df_F)}{E_F/df_F}$$

to follow an F distribution, certain assumptions must be met. If these assumptions fail to hold for one's data, it is conceivable that the use of the F table in Appendix A.2 is inappropriate. For example, suppose that an experiment is conducted comparing three groups of 6 subjects each (18 subjects in all). Inspection of the F table shows that the critical F value here is 3.68 for an α level of .05. In other words, the observed F value (F_{obs}) exceeds 3.68 only 5 percent of the time (in the long run) if the null hypothesis is true. Using the value of 3.68 as a critical value thus ensures that we will make a Type I error only 5 percent of the time.

However, the assurance that F_{obs} exceeds 3.68 5 percent of the time depends on a set of statistical assumptions. Without these assumptions, F_{obs} can exceed 3.68 either more or less than 5 percent of the time, in which case our statistical analysis may produce either too many or too few Type I errors.

Three assumptions must be met for F_{obs} to follow an F distribution:

1. The population distribution of scores on the dependent variable (Y) must be normal within each group. In other words, if an entire population of scores were obtained in a particular condition, it is assumed that those scores would be normally distributed.

2. The population variances of scores on Y must be equal for all a groups. In symbols, $\sigma_1^2 = \sigma_2^2 = \cdots = \sigma_a^2$, where σ_j^2 represents the variance of Y scores for group j, and $j = 1, 2, \ldots, a$.

3. The scores must be statistically independent of each other. More is said about this assumption later.

These assumptions are often stated in terms of the errors (εs) of the ANOVA model instead of in terms of Y. In fact, these two formulations are identical for our model because the Y scores are independent and normal and equally variable within groups if and only if the error components in the model are themselves normal, equally variable, and independent of each other.

Implications for Expected Values

These assumptions imply certain things about what population value is being estimated by the numerator and denominator of our test statistic. Beginning with the denominator, as we have noted (see Equation 63), E_F/df_F is an average of the sample variances for the groups in the design. Within any given group j, the sample variance, s_j^2 computed by dividing the sum of squared deviations from the group mean by $n-1$, is an unbiased estimator of the population variance for that group σ_j^2 and hence of the population variance of the errors σ_ε^2. Using $\mathcal{E}$ to indicate expected value (see Hays, 1981, p. 625ff.), we can write this as

$$\mathcal{E}(s_j^2) = \sigma_\varepsilon^2 \tag{97}$$

This in turn implies that the average of the sample variances in the denominator of our test is also an unbiased estimator of population error variance, that is,

$$\mathcal{E}\left[\frac{E_F}{df_F}\right] = \mathcal{E}\left[\frac{\sum_j (n_j - 1)s_j^2}{\sum_j (n_j - 1)}\right]$$

$$= \frac{\sum_j (n_j - 1)\mathcal{E}(s_j^2)}{\sum_j (n_j - 1)}$$

$$= \frac{\sum_j (n_j - 1)\sigma_\varepsilon^2}{\sum_j (n_j - 1)} = \sigma_\varepsilon^2 \tag{98}$$

Under our assumptions, it is the case that E_F/df_F or MS_W is an unbiased estimator of population error variance regardless of whether the null hypothesis of equal population means is true or false.

On the other hand, the numerator of our test statistic estimates one value when the null hypothesis is true and other values when it is false. In particular, it can be shown (e.g., Kirk, 1982, pp. 66–69) that the expected value of MS_B, the numerator of the F, is

$$\mathcal{E}\left[\frac{E_R - E_F}{df_R - df_F}\right] = \sigma_\varepsilon^2 + \frac{\sum_j n_j \alpha_j^2}{a - 1} \tag{99}$$

That is, when the hypothesis that all the treatment effects are zero is exactly true, the numerator of the F estimates only population error variance. Otherwise, the numerator is estimating some larger value, with the particular value depending on just how large the treatment effects are.

Under our assumption that the groups of scores represent samples from a normal population distribution, the numerator and denominator of our test statistic are statistically independent. And, if the null hypothesis is true, their ratio is distributed as an F under our assumptions of normality, homogeneity of variance, and independence.

Robustness of ANOVA

In many ANOVA applications, these assumptions are reasonably well satisfied. For example, the normal distribution is frequently a good model for much behavioral data. As discussed in Chapter 2, both theoretical suggestions (cf. Hays, 1981, pp. 214–215) and empirical experience suggest that data will often at least closely approximate normality. Also, the assumption of homogeneous (equal) variances is often plausible because different treatments may be expected to affect the mean level of response but not the variability. Whether the independence-of-errors assumption is met is determined largely by the experimental design employed, as will be seen later.

Even if a researcher's data are not perfectly normally distributed, they may be close enough to normal (e.g., unimodal, symmetric, most scores centrally located, few scores at the extremes) that there would seem to be little cause for concern. Of course, in the real world, this question inevitably arises: How close is close enough? Statisticians have conducted a number of studies to answer this question for ANOVA. These studies allow us to characterize the robustness of ANOVA (*robustness* is the term used to denote the extent to which a statistical method produces correct results even when its assumptions fail to hold).

We will simply summarize findings concerning the robustness of ANOVA. References that provide additional details are cited where relevant. We will discuss robustness to violations of each of the three previously mentioned assumptions in turn.

1. ANOVA is generally robust to violations of the normality assumption, in that even when data are nonnormal, the actual Type I error rate is usually close to the nominal (i.e., desired) value. For example, even if the data in our study comparing three groups of six subjects are not normally distributed, the percentage of observed F values exceeding 3.68 is still very close to 5 percent. Thus, many researchers do not regard lack of normality as a serious impediment to the use of ANOVA.

Two additional points should be considered. First, robustness is not really "either/or" but rather is a matter of degree. As data get farther from normality, the actual Type I error rate tends to get farther from the nominal value. It is possible mathematically for data to deviate so wildly from normality that the actual Type I error rate is rather different from the nominal value (e.g., an actual rate of .10 when the nominal level is .05), but it is questionable how often such data occur in practice (see Bradley, 1978, and Glass, Peckham, & Sanders, 1972, for conflicting views). Second, most studies of robustness have focused on Type I error instead of Type II error (or power). The evidence that is available suggests that ANOVA is also generally robust in terms of power to violations of normality (Glass, Peckham, & Sanders, 1972). When normality and the other assumptions hold, ANOVA is the most powerful test of the omnibus null hypothesis, that is, the null hypothesis that

$\mu_1 = \mu_2 = \cdots = \mu_a$. Although its power is relatively unaffected by violations of normality, the power of alternate approaches (e.g., nonparametric methods) changes considerably under nonnormality. As a consequence, some of these alternate approaches may be more powerful than ANOVA when normality fails to hold (Blair, 1981). Chapter 15 presents approaches that might be preferable in such a situation.

2. ANOVA is generally robust to moderate violations of homogeneity of variance as long as the sample sizes in each group are equal to each other and are not unreasonably small (e.g., less than five per group). However, when ns are unequal, even moderate heterogeneity of variance can produce actual Type I error rates considerably different from the nominal value. When the groups with smaller population variances have larger samples, the pooled estimate of population variance in the denominator of the F tends to be smaller than it would be in the equal-n case, with the result that the actual Type I error rate will be greater than .05. For example, when variances are in the ratio of 1:1:3 and corresponding sample sizes are 7, 5, and 3, the actual probability of a Type I error is .11 instead of the nominal value of .05 (Scheffé, 1959). If the sample sizes were even more unbalanced, the departure would be even more pronounced. Sample sizes of 9, 5, and 1 (in that order), for example, would produce an actual Type I error rate of .17 when the variances are in the 1:1:3 ratio (Scheffé, 1959). On the other hand, when the groups with smaller population variances are represented by smaller samples, the pooled variance estimate tends to be larger than it would be in the equal-n case, and the actual Type I error rate is less than .05. For example, when variances are in the ratio of 1:1:3 and corresponding sample sizes are 1, 5, and 9, the actual probability of a Type I error is .013 instead of the nominal value of .05 (Scheffé, 1959). Although a lower probability of making a Type I error might not sound so bad, it is in fact a serious problem because it implies an increase in the probability of a Type II error. In other words, the price to be paid here for a conservative test is a decrease in power.

When sample sizes are equal, heterogeneity of variance must be more pronounced to produce a substantial distortion in the probability of a Type I error, but it can still occur. For example, Wilcox (1987a) reviews studies showing that in a four-group case with 12 observations in each group when the variances are in the ratio of 1:1:1:16 the probability of a Type I error is .101 instead of the nominal value of .05. When sample sizes are larger, the effect of unequal variances is reduced.

When sample sizes are unequal and population variances are heterogeneous, the standard F test of this chapter is inappropriate. Nonparametric approaches such as the Kruskal-Wallis test (described in Chapter 15) are sometimes recommended when variances are heterogeneous. However, parametric modifications are generally preferable to the Kruskal-Wallis test in this situation. Chapter 15 presents two parametric modifications, the Brown-Forsythe F^* and Welch's W, either of which is preferable to the standard F test when sample sizes are unequal and variances are heterogeneous. It should be noted that these approaches are preferable only when *population* variances are unequal. Procedures for testing this hypothesis are described later in this chapter.

3. ANOVA is *not* robust to violations of the independence-of-errors assumption. The actual probability of a Type I error may depart dramatically from the

nominal level when errors are correlated. As stated earlier, the reasonableness of this assumption depends primarily on the design employed. The meaning of this assumption can perhaps best be understood by considering a couple of examples where the assumption is not met. First, suppose that a researcher wants to test whether relaxation training lowers subjects' blood pressure. To answer this question, the researcher measures pretest blood pressure on a group of 15 subjects, exposes them to relaxation training, and then obtains posttest readings on these subjects. Thus, 30 scores in all are obtained, 2 from each subject. However, these 30 scores are not all independent of each other because only 15 subjects were tested. It is highly likely that a subject with a high pretest reading will also have a high posttest reading, so that pretest and posttest scores will be correlated. Such an occurrence violates the independence-of-scores (errors) assumption. Chapters 11–14 describe procedures for analyzing such data, which represent a repeated measures (or within-subjects) design.

In between-subjects designs, such as those we have been considering in this chapter, what violations of the assumption of independent errors would mean is somewhat more difficult to understand. As Kenny and Judd (1986) suggest, instead of thinking of the assumption in terms of a correlation between variables, one should think of the assumption in terms of the conditional probability of one observation given another observation. For example, suppose that an educational psychologist wants to compare a structured classroom environment versus an open classroom for teaching arithmetic to second-grade children. One class of 30 children is randomly assigned to the structured condition, and a second class of 30 children is assigned to the open condition. The researcher reports that an ANOVA on posttest arithmetic knowledge reveals a statistically significant group difference, $F(1, 58) = 6.83$. Once again, the independence assumption has likely been violated because children influence each other within the classroom setting. As Glass and Stanley (1970) point out, one unruly child in one of the classrooms may lower the scores of all children in that classroom. Thus, even if the instructional treatment being manipulated had no effect, observing a particular score of one child in a classroom could alter the conditional probability of observing particular scores from other children in the classroom. One alternative that avoids this problem is to regard the experimental design of such a study as a nested design. As Chapter 10 shows, when such an approach is taken, it is imperative to assign several classrooms (not just one) to each of the treatment conditions being compared.

Tests of Normality and Homogeneity of Variance

A number of procedures have been developed for assessing the adequacy of the normality and homogeneity-of-variance assumptions in ANOVA. Gross violations of normality can be detected easily through graphical procedures, especially with large samples. Useful references are Chambers, Cleveland, Kleiner, and Tukey (1983) and Iman and Conover (1983). Statistical tests for assessing normality are also available. Both BMDP and SPSS-X provide procedures for tests of skewness and kurtosis because standard errors of both statistics are reported. SAS performs the Shapiro–Wilk test when sample size is 50 or less and a modified Kolmogorov–Smirnov test when sample size is greater than 50.

All three major statistical packages (BMDP, SAS, and SPSS-X) also provide tests of the homogeneity-of-variance assumption. Available tests are the Bartlett–Box F, Hartley's F_{max}, and Cochran's C. Unfortunately, all three tests are extremely sensitive to the normality assumption (O'Brien, 1981). Thus, if the data are nonnormal, results of these three tests can be quite misleading. O'Brien describes an alternate procedure for testing homogeneity of variance that is robust to violations of normality. For a one-way design, the steps of this procedure are as follows:

1. For each group, compute the sample mean $\bar{Y}_j$ and the unbiased sample variance:

$$s_j^2 = \sum_i (Y_{ij} - \bar{Y}_j)^2/(n_j - 1)$$

2. For each observation Y_{ij}, compute a transformed score,

$$r_{ij} = \frac{(n_j - 1.5)n_j(Y_{ij} - \bar{Y}_j)^2 - .5s_j^2(n_j - 1)}{(n_j - 1)(n_j - 2)}$$

3. Verify that for each group the mean of r is equal to the variance of the original Y scores, that is, $\bar{r}_j = s_j^2$.

4. Perform an ANOVA using r as the dependent variable. When sample sizes are very unbalanced [the largest sample size $\max(n_j)$ is four or more times larger than the smallest $\min(n_j)$], O'Brien recommends that a Welch-type ANOVA be used. Not only is this procedure robust, but it also generalizes easily to factorial designs.

Transformations

When data are nonnormal and/or variances are unequal, it is often possible to transform the data so that the new scores display normality and equality of variances. For example, when data are positively skewed, either a square root or a logarithmic transformation often produces data that are more nearly normal; in some circumstances, the same transformation also achieves equality of variances. Emerson and Stoto (1983) is a useful reference for choosing a transformation to better satisfy statistical assumptions.

However, there are potential disadvantages to transforming one's data. Primary among these is that interpretation of results may be less clear. For example, most individuals find it difficult to understand the mean value of the square root of their original scores. Also, in general, the null hypothesis that groups have the same mean on Y does not imply and is not implied by the null hypothesis that group means on a transformed variable are equal. As Games (1983, p. 382) says, "the use of curvilinear transformations in data analysis is a rather complex topic that involves philosophy of science considerations as well as statistical considerations." Readers contemplating a transformation of their data should examine the spirited exchange between Levine and Dunlap (1982, 1983) and Games (1983, 1984).

POWER OF THE *F* TEST: ONE-WAY ANOVA

As noted in Chapter 1, the power of a test is its sensitivity in detecting real differences between groups. That is, power, denoted $1 - \beta$, is defined as the probability of rejecting the null hypothesis (or the restricted model) given that it is false (or given that the full model is the correct description of the data). Power analyses are useful for determining how sensitive a particular experimental design is. Most often such analyses are performed to determine the sample size required to give an experiment adequate power.

Besides the assumptions about the independence, variability, and normality of the scores in various groups, to determine the power of the *F* test one must also specify the magnitude of the treatment effects in the population. In the preceding section, we considered those statistical assumptions that are necessary for the observed *F* statistic to have the distributional shape presumed by the probability values indicated in a conventional *F* table. It bears repeating that it is also necessary for the null hypothesis to be true for the observed *F* to have this distribution over replications. If the statistical assumptions are met, but the null hypothesis is false, the test statistic follows what is termed a *noncentral F* distribution. Such a distribution depends not only on the typical degrees of freedom associated with a central *F* but also on a noncentrality parameter indicating the magnitude of the difference among the population means relative to the within-group population variance.

Because the noncentrality parameter also depends on the sample size, which is typically what you are doing a power analysis to determine, it is easier to begin thinking about the magnitude of the expected effect using an alternative measure. Most useful perhaps is f, one of the standardized measures of effect size, which we introduced previously:

$$f = \sigma_m/\sigma_\varepsilon \qquad (89, \text{ repeated})$$

Recall that σ_ε is the square root of the population within-cell error variance and that σ_m can be viewed as the standard deviation of the population means for the various groups in your design, or equivalently as the standard deviation of the effect parameters:

$$\sigma_m = \sqrt{\frac{\sum(\mu_j - \mu)^2}{a}} = \sqrt{\frac{\sum \alpha_j^2}{a}} \qquad (88, \text{ repeated})$$

Here μ is the mean of the population means, that is, $\mu = (\sum_j \mu_j)/a$. If you have data from the literature or from pilot work, these can be used to provide estimates of σ_ε and μ_j. If such data are not available, one can utilize a suggestion of Cohen (1977, Chapter 8) that a "small" effect size be defined as $f = .10$, a "medium" effect size as $f = .25$, and a "large" effect size as $f = .40$. Thus, for a medium effect size, the standard deviation of the population means would be one-quarter of the within-group standard deviation. In a two-group study, because the standard deviation of two population means is just half the difference between them, this definition of medium effect size would imply that the expected value of the difference between the means in your study would be half of the expected within-group standard deviation.

Cohen (1977, pp. 289–354) provides tables that allow you to read off the power for particular combinations of the degrees of freedom of the numerator of your test ($df_R - df_F$), the Type I error rate (α), the effect-size parameter (f) and the number of subjects per group. With four factors varying, it perhaps should not be surprising that the tables require 66 pages.

Some simplifying strategy is clearly needed. The one most often used is to summarize the information about the noncentral F distribution in a series of charts (such as those found in Appendix Table A.11) and, if necessary, use "visual interpolation" between lines on the graphs to approximate the power for your situation. The information required to read a power value from these charts is

1. The numerator degrees of freedom for your test—that is, $df_R - df_F$—denoted df_{num} in the charts

2. The Type I error rate α

3. The denominator degrees of freedom df_F, denoted df_{denom}

4. An effect-size parameter ϕ, which reflects the sample size and the magnitude of the effects

The effect size parameter ϕ (lowercase Greek *phi*) is the following simple transformation of f:

$$\phi = f\sqrt{n} \tag{100}$$

where n is the number of subjects per group. Note that you must use a value of n to determine both ϕ and df_F. Thus, if you are planning a study, a power analysis proceeds in a trial-and-error fashion where you test out different values of n.

For example, assume that you are planning a reaction time study involving three groups. Pilot research and data from the literature suggest that the means in your three groups might be 400, 450, and 500 with a within-group standard deviation of 100. Thus, substituting these values in the formula defining σ_m (Equation 88), we obtain

$$\sigma_m = \sqrt{\frac{(400 - 450)^2 + (450 - 450)^2 + (500 - 450)^2}{3}}$$

$$= \sqrt{\frac{2500 + 0 + 2500}{3}} = \sqrt{\frac{5000}{3}} = \sqrt{1666.66} = 40.82$$

This means that f here is in the large range:

$$f = \frac{\sigma_m}{\sigma_\varepsilon} = \frac{40.82}{100} = .4082$$

Suppose that you want to have power of .8 for $\alpha = .05$, so that if the population parameters are as you hope, four times out of five your study will allow you to declare your results significant. Your might hope that you can get by with only 10 subjects per group. This would mean a total N of 30, and hence the values required to enter the charts would be

$$df_{num} = df_R - df_F = (N - 1) - (N - a) = a - 1 = 3 - 1 = 2$$
$$df_{denom} = df_F = N - a = 30 - 3 = 27$$

and,

$$\phi = f\sqrt{n} = .4082\sqrt{10} = 1.29$$

From the chart for $df_{num} = 2$, following the curve for $df_{denom} = 30$ (the closest value to 27), we find the power for our parameter values by determining the height of the curve directly above the point on the horizontal axis that seems to approximate a ϕ value of 1.29 for $\alpha = .05$. Thus, the power here is approximately .45, which is unacceptably small. Thus, we might next try 25 subjects per group. This would change df_{denom} to 72, and ϕ would be $.4082\sqrt{25} = .4082(5) = 2.041$. Following the curve for $df_{denom} = 60$ to our value of ϕ suggests a power of .87, which is more than we required. Eventually, we could iterate to $n = 21$, yielding $df_{denom} = 60$ and $\phi = 1.8706$ and a power of essentially .8.

A second strategy that simplifies things still further is to define the effect size simply in terms of the number of standard deviations between the largest and smallest population means anticipated. Recall that we designated this measure of effect size d (see Equations 83 and 87):

$$d = \frac{\mu_{max} - \mu_{min}}{\sigma_\varepsilon}$$

Table 3.7, which is similar to tables published by Bratcher, Moran, and Zimmer (1970), allows one to read directly the sample size required for detecting an effect for various values of d. The price paid for this simplicity is that the anticipated value of all other means except the two most extreme means does not affect the value of d. In fact, the tables are computed by presuming that all other means except the two extremes are exactly equal to the grand mean μ. If this is not the case, somewhat greater power will result than is indicated by the table. The relationship between f and d, as Cohen (1977) notes, depends on what the particular pattern of means is, but in most cases d is between two and four times as large as f.

For our particular data, the "other" (nonextreme) mean was exactly at the grand mean (450), so the results of Table 3.7 are exact for our case. One enters the table with a desired value of power $(1 - \beta)$, a standardized effect size d, and the number of groups a. For our hypothesized data

$$d = \frac{\mu_{max} - \mu_{min}}{\sigma_\varepsilon} = \frac{500 - 400}{100} = 1.0$$

Reading from the column labeled 1.00 from the section of the table for power $= .80$, we find the entry for the row for $a = 3$ indicates the required n for $\alpha = .05$ to be 21, the same value we determined earlier by use of the charts.

We have now completed the introduction of the model-comparison approach to one-way ANOVA. As we have indicated, an advantage of this approach is that the logic of searching for an adequate yet simple model is the same for all other applications of the general linear model that we will consider. In fact, in a sense it

TABLE 3.7 Minimum Sample Size per Group Needed to Achieve Specified Levels of Power with $\alpha = .05$

| Number of Levels | Power = 1 − β = .50 | | d | | | |
a	0.25	0.50	0.75	1.00	1.25	1.50
2	124	32	15	9	7	5
3	160	41	19	11	8	6
4	186	48	22	13	9	7
5	207	53	24	14	10	7
6	225	57	26	15	10	8

| Number of Levels | Power = 1 − β = .80 | | d | | | |
a	0.25	0.50	0.75	1.00	1.25	1.50
2	253	64	29	17	12	9
3	310	79	36	21	14	10
4	350	89	40	23	15	11
5	383	97	44	25	17	12
6	412	104	47	27	18	13

| Number of Levels | Power = 1 − β = .95 | | d | | | |
a	0.25	0.50	0.75	1.00	1.25	1.50
2	417	105	48	27	18	13
3	496	125	56	32	21	15
4	551	139	63	36	23	17
5	596	150	67	39	25	18
6	634	160	72	41	27	19

is the case that in terms of between-groups designs we have already covered the most complex design we need to consider because all other designs can be considered as special cases of the one-way design. However, to appreciate the sense in which this is true and to develop the follow-up tests that are likely of interest in multiple-group designs, we must develop methods that allow particular combinations of means of interest to be tested. We will apply the model-comparison approach to these issues of testing specific contrasts of interest in the chapters that follow.

EXERCISES

1. The full model is _____ than the restricted model.
   a. simpler   b. less simple

2. The full model corresponds to the _____ hypothesis.
   a. null   b. alternative

3. True or False: The restricted model is a special case of the full model.

4. True or False: For a fixed total N, the simpler the model, the greater the degrees of freedom.

*5. True or False: When the null hypothesis is true, MS_B estimates the variance of the sampling distribution of sample means.

6. True or False: The sum of squared errors for the restricted model (E_R) is always less than the sum of squared errors for the full model (E_F).

*7. True or False: The sum of squared errors associated with the restricted model E_R is always SS_{Total}.

*8. Gauss said, "The estimation of a magnitude using an observation [that is] subject to a larger or smaller error can be compared not inappropriately to a game of chance in which one can only lose and never win and in which each possible error corresponds to a loss." (See LeCam, L., & Neyman, J. (1965). *Bayes-Bernoulli-Laplace Seminar.* New York: Springer, p. viii.) What "loss function" is employed in the solution of the estimation problems in this book?

9. Assume that a psychologist has performed a study to compare four different treatments for alleviating agoraphobia. Three subjects have been randomly assigned to each of four types of therapy: rational-emotive (R-E), psychoanalytic (P), client-centered (C-C), and behavioral (B). The following posttest scores were obtained on a fear scale, where higher scores indicate worse phobia:

R-E	P	C-C	B
2	10	4	8
4	12	6	10
6	14	8	12

   a. Carry out the model comparison necessary to test whether there is a statistically significant difference between the means of the four groups. State the models, estimate their parameters, calculate the predicted scores and errors for each individual subject, compute the summary measures E_R and E_F, and finally determine the value of F and its significance.

   b. Calculate the t value for comparing each pair of means. You should have six such t values. Note that with equal n

   $$t = \frac{\bar{Y}_1 - \bar{Y}_2}{\sqrt{\dfrac{s_1^2 + s_2^2}{n}}}$$

   HINT: There is a peculiar relationship among the four s_j^2 values for these data. This should simplify your task considerably.

   c. Square each of the t values you calculated in part b. Do you see any relationship between these six t^2 values and the F value you calculated in part a?

*10. As described in the Chapter 2 exercises, an important series of studies by Bennett et al. (1964) attempted to find evidence for changes in the brain as a result of experience. Posttreatment weights of the cortex of animals reared in an enriched environment or in a deprived environment are shown below for three replications of the study done at different times of year. Cortex weights (in milligrams) for experimental and control animals are as follows:

Experiment 1		Experiment 2		Experiment 3	
Experimental	Control	Experimental	Control	Experimental	Control
688	655	707	669	690	668
655	623	740	650	701	667
668	652	745	651	685	647
660	654	652	627	751	693
679	655	649	656	647	635
663	646	676	642	647	644
664	600	699	698	720	665
647	640	696	648	718	689
694	605	712	676	718	642
633	635	708	657	696	673
653	642	749	692	658	675
676	661	691	618	680	641

(Raw data are adapted from those reported in Freedman et al., 1978, p. 452.)

Twelve pairs of rats served as subjects in each study, with one member of each pair being randomly assigned to the enriched environment and the other to the deprived environment. The two scores on the same row above for a given experiment came from two male rats taken from the same litter. The experimental hypothesis was that, even though both groups were permitted to feed freely, animals reared in the more stimulating environment would develop heavier cortexes. In Chapter 2 you were asked to test this hypothesis using a randomization test. Now a series of parametric analyses are requested.

First Analysis, Experiment 2 Data Only
a. How many independent observations are there in Experiment 2?
b. What full model should be used to describe these independent observations?
c. What constraint on this model is it of interest to test? What restricted model incorporates this constraint?
d. What is the sum of squared errors associated with the full model? With the restricted model?
e. Carry out the statistical test comparing these two models.
f. What is your conclusion?

Second Analysis, Data from Experiments 1, 2, and 3
g. Now use the data from all three experiments. Assume that you are interested in whether the three experiments revealed the same advantage for the experimental animals within sampling error regardless of the time of year when the experiment was run. State the models appropriate for testing this hypothesis and carry out the analysis, again providing parameter estimates and sums of squared errors for your models as well as stating your conclusion.

*11. Again using the data from the previous problem, reanalyze the data from Experiment 2 under a different set of assumptions about what went on. Assume that the treatment and control subjects all came from different litters so that there was no pairing of observations.
a. Under this assumption, state the models that are likely of interest and carry out

the test comparing these two models, stating the estimated parameter values and sum of squared errors for each model.

b. How does the strength of the evidence against the restricted model in this analysis compare to that in your analysis in parts a–f of Exercise 10?

*12. For the Experiment 2 data analyzed as a two independent-groups design as in Exercise 11, characterize the magnitude of the effect in the following ways:

a. As a standardized difference between means, $\hat{d}$.

b. By computing the following measures of the proportional reduction in error: R^2 and $\hat{\omega}^2$.

13. For your master's thesis you are doing a study that in part replicates previous research. You plan to use three groups and expect the means on the dependent variable to be 55, 67, and 79. On the basis of previous research, you have evidence that leads you to expect the population within-group variance to be about 3600. How many subjects will be required per cell to achieve a power of .80 with $\alpha = .05$?

*14. Assume that you are planning a study and that you are at the point of trying to determine how many subjects will be needed for your four-group design. You decide that all groups will have the same number of subjects. Assume the following group means of 21, 24, 30, and 45 are the actual population means instead of sample statistics. Under this hypothesis and assuming the population within-group standard deviation is 20, how many subjects would be needed per group in order to have a power of .8 in a one-way ANOVA with $\alpha = .05$?

15. Suppose that we are planning a study to compare three treatments for depression. Group 1 subjects will receive weekly therapy sessions using client-centered therapy. Group 2 subjects will also receive client-centered therapy but will only be seen every two weeks. Group 3 subjects will serve as a waiting list control group. Posttest assessment will occur three months into the study. The dependent measure will be the CES-D, the Center for Epidemiology Studies' Depression Scale.

a. Our best guess as to the likely magnitude of group differences is reflected in the following population means: $\mu_1 = 15$, $\mu_2 = 18$, and $\mu_3 = 24$. We expect the population standard deviation (within-groups) to be around 10. Naturally, we will set α at .05. What is the *total* number of subjects we should include in our study, assuming equal n per group in order to have a power of .8?

b. Suppose that our estimate of the population standard deviation in part a is too small. Specifically, assume that the true value is 14 instead of 10. Because we planned our study using the value of 10, the number of subjects we use is still the number you found in part a. If we use this many subjects, but in fact 14 is the true standard deviation, what will be the actual value of our power?

16. Throughout this book, we make extensive use of the principle of least squares. In this chapter, we have proven mathematically that the sample mean $\bar{Y}$ is the least-squares estimator of a population mean μ. This exercise explores this fact in additional detail from an empirical (as opposed to mathematical) perspective.

a. Suppose we have a sample of five scores: 43, 56, 47, 61, and 43. Calculate the sum of squared deviations from the mean for these five scores. Also, calculate the sum of squared deviations from the median for the five scores. Which is less? Will this always be true? Why or why not?

b. Suppose that we were to choose our estimator not to minimize the sum of squared errors, but instead to minimize the sum of the absolute values of the errors. Calculate the sum of absolute deviations from the mean and from the median. Which is less? Do you think this will always be true? Why or why not?

17. You are planning a large-scale replication of a study of a treatment for problem drinkers that previously has been shown in a different location to be significantly more effective than a control condition. You begin by conducting a pilot study with five subjects per group. Your results for this pilot study are shown below, where the dependent variable is the estimated number of days of problem drinking per year after treatment.

Group	
Treatment	**Control**
41	214
23	199
20	194
16	189
0	174

a. The previous researchers had found means of 12 and 174 on this dependent variable for their implementations of the treatment and control conditions, respectively. Conduct a test of whether your pilot results replicate this previous research, by comparing a model that allows for different population means in the two conditions with one that assumes means of 12 and 174.

b. Alternatively, you could have simply asked the question of whether the *difference* between your means was significantly different from the 162-point difference obtained by the previous investigators. Perform the test comparing the models relevant to this question.

c. What do you conclude on the basis of the results of the tests in parts a and b?

Extension   Regression

Most readers have encountered simple linear regression and correlation in a previous statistics course. These techniques as well as multiple regression can also be subsumed under the general linear model. Several books are now available that focus on the use of multiple regression in the behavioral sciences, with the most popular being Pedhazur (1982) and Cohen and Cohen (1983). Particularly when one considers the many alternative approaches to regression currently available, such as ridge regression (for references and a critique see Rozeboom, 1979), that we cannot hope to cover the field in depth is obvious. Nonetheless, we present here a brief overview for several reasons. Perhaps most important is our desire to make clear that ANOVA and regression are intimately related. Thus, to illustrate this, at the end of this extension we show how a one-way design could be analyzed as a multiple-regression problem. Second, the notion of correlated predictor variables in multiple regression can be used as a very effective tool in helping one understand some of the complexities of nonorthogonal ANOVA and analysis of covariance, which we encounter later in this volume.

Review of Simple Linear Regression

The basic idea of regression is prediction, with the simplest case being that of predicting one continuous variable from another. One of the first uses of the method was by Galton for predicting heights of sons from heights of fathers (Stigler, 1986). In that context, it was concluded that sons of men of a particular height would have an average height only about half as far from the mean as the fathers. Thus, the best prediction on the average for a son was to *regress* back toward the mean a fraction of the distance his father's height was from the mean.

The prediction equation in simple linear regression is often written as

$$\hat{Y}_i = a + bX_i \tag{E.1}$$

or perhaps as

$$\hat{Y}_i = \bar{Y} + b(X_i - \bar{X}) \tag{E.2}$$

where b refers to the slope of the line and a is the intercept. These are, of course, just special cases of prediction equations derived from the general linear model presented at the beginning of Chapter 3, that is,

$$Y_i = \beta_0 X_{0_i} + \beta_1 X_{1_i} + \beta_2 X_{2_i} + \cdots + \beta_p X_{p_i} + \varepsilon_1 \tag{E.3}$$

In simple linear regression, X_0 would be 1 for every subject, and because there is only one predictor variable X_1, it can be designated X, and the associated parameter can be designated β. Thus, we have

$$Y_i = \beta_0 + \beta X + \varepsilon_i \tag{E.4}$$

Optimal estimates of β_0 and β can be determined by using expressions that flow from the calculus solution to the problem of how to make the sum of squared errors as small as possible. The expressions for these least-squares estimates are

$$\hat{\beta}_0 = b_0 = \bar{Y} - b\bar{X} \tag{E.5}$$

and

$$\hat{\beta} = b = \frac{\sum(X - \bar{X})(Y - \bar{Y})}{\sum(X - \bar{X})^2} \tag{E.6}$$

If a lowercase letter is used to indicate the deviation from a mean, the slope estimate can be expressed particularly simply as

$$b = \frac{\sum xy}{\sum x^2} \tag{E.7}$$

Note that the least-squares estimates in Equations E.5 and E.6 imply that all regression lines must pass through the point $(\bar{X}, \bar{Y})$. This is clear in the form of the prediction equation given in Equation E.2 where the least-squares expression in terms of the slope has been substituted for the intercept. When an individual is at the mean of the predictor variable—that is, when $X_i = \bar{X}$—the least-squares estimate of Y is simply $\bar{Y}$.

Partitioning the Total Sum of Squares

Just as in the traditional approach to ANOVA, one can approach regression from the point of view of partitioning the total variability in the data. The development again begins by viewing the basic ingredient of the total variance formula, namely, the deviation of an individual score on the dependent variable from its mean, as the sum of two components. In regression the components are the deviation of the score from its predicted value and the deviation of the predicted value from the mean. In symbols this identity may be thought of as the result of adding $\hat{Y}_i - \hat{Y}_i$ to $Y_i - \bar{Y}$, that is,

$$Y_i - \bar{Y} = Y_i - \bar{Y} + \hat{Y}_i - \hat{Y}_i = (Y_i - \hat{Y}_i) + (\hat{Y}_i - \bar{Y}) \qquad (E.8)$$

When both the left- and right-hand sides of this equation are squared and summed, the cross-product term drops out of the expansion of the right-hand expression to yield the basic partitioning equation of regression analysis:

$$\sum_i (Y_i - \bar{Y})^2 = \sum_i (Y_i - \hat{Y}_i)^2 + \sum_i (\hat{Y}_i - \bar{Y})^2 \qquad (E.9)$$

The typical labels given these sums of squared deviations are

$$SS_{\text{Total}} = SS_{\text{Residual}} + SS_{\text{Regression}}$$

This analysis of total variance can also fruitfully be expressed in terms of proportions:

$$1 = \frac{SS_{\text{Residual}}}{SS_{\text{Total}}} + \frac{SS_{\text{Regression}}}{SS_{\text{Total}}} \qquad (E.10)$$

We have thus broken down the total sum of squares into two parts, one indicating the variability in Y that can be predicted by X and the other indicating the residual variability that is *not* predicted by the X variable. Recall that the proportion of variance in Y associated with X is one of the definitions of R^2, the square of the correlation between X and Y, or equivalently the square of the correlation between $\hat{Y}$ and Y.

Another perspective on the correlation coefficient is provided by its definition as the ratio of the covariance of two variables to the product of their standard deviations. In a sample, the statistic would be calculated as $r = s_{xy}/s_x s_y$, where s_{xy} is the sample covariance that would be computed by dividing the sum of cross-products of deviation scores (the numerator of the expressions below) by $N - 1$. Because the sample-size terms in the numerator and denominator cancel out, we can define r simply in terms of combinations of deviation scores:

$$r = \frac{\sum(X - \bar{X})(Y - \bar{Y})}{\sqrt{\sum(X - \bar{X})^2 \sum(Y - \bar{Y})^2}}$$

$$= \frac{\sum xy}{\sqrt{\sum x^2 \sum y^2}}. \tag{E.11}$$

Relationship to *F* Tests

Defining R^2 as the proportion of variance accounted for suggests an alternative method for viewing the inadequacy of a model. The SS_{Residual} associated with a model is simply the sum of squared errors of prediction that we have been using to indicate a model's inadequacy. This can be expressed simply in terms of R^2 because

$$1 = \frac{SS_{\text{Residual}}}{SS_{\text{Total}}} + R^2 \tag{E.12}$$

and

$$SS_{\text{Residual}} = (1 - R^2)SS_{\text{Total}} \tag{E.13}$$

Here, R^2 is the square of the correlation between the predictions of the model and the observed scores. In the case of two competing models, the sum-of-squares total would be the same for both models, and so it seems that one should be able to compare the adequacy of the models simply by comparing their R^2s. That this is the case can be seen simply by substituting expressions like those in Equation E.13 for the E_R and E_F terms in our familiar formula for an F test. That is, we use the fact that we can write

$$E_R = SS_{\text{Residual}_R} = (1 - R_R^2)SS_{\text{Total}}$$

and

$$E_F = SS_{\text{Residual}_F} = (1 - R_F^2)SS_{\text{Total}} \tag{E.14}$$

Substituting these into

$$F = \frac{(E_R - E_F)/(df_R - df_F)}{E_F/df_F}$$

yields

$$F = \frac{[(1 - R_R^2) - (1 - R_F^2)]SS_{\text{Total}}/(df_R - df_F)}{(1 - R_F^2)SS_{\text{Total}}/df_F}$$

Thus,

$$F = \frac{(1 - R_R^2) - (1 - R_F^2)/(df_R - df_F)}{(1 - R_F^2)/df_F} \tag{E.15}$$

This form of the F is essentially as general as our standard form.

Multiple Regression

Although the above development is perfectly general as a method of comparing models, the computation of the R^2s to be compared very quickly becomes quite tedious as the number of predictors increases. One exception is in the case of predictors that are mutually uncorrelated. With naturally occurring variables such as personality or aptitude measures, exactly zero correlations will, of course, virtually never occur. Nonetheless, such a case provides a useful point of departure for development of how R^2 is computed in more realistic situations.

With two uncorrelated predictors, the squared multiple correlation or the square of the correlation of the observed scores with the optimal linear combination of predictors is simply the sum of the squared correlations of the individual predictors with the dependent variable. That is, if we let $R_{Y \cdot 12}$ denote this multiple correlation and r_{Y1} and r_{Y2} denote the correlations of the dependent variable with the predictors X_1 and X_2, respectively, then we may assert that

$$R^2_{Y \cdot 12} = r^2_{Y1} + r^2_{Y2} \qquad \text{(E.16)}$$

in the special case where the correlation between the predictors r_{12} is zero. Thus, with uncorrelated predictors, each of which correlates, say, .5 with the criterion, the squared multiple correlation would be $R^2_{Y \cdot 12} = .5^2 + .5^2 = .25 + .25 = .50$. This relationship can be represented schematically by the Venn diagrams shown in Figure 3E.1. (It must be stressed, however, that unlike set relations, correlational relationships cannot always be represented accurately by such diagrams.)

In the case of correlated predictors, the proportion of variance in Y that is predicted by X_1 may overlap to a large extent with that predicted by X_2. Thus, frequently the situation can be represented by a diagram like that shown in Figure 3E.2. Now the predictive power of the two variables X_1 and X_2 is no longer equal to the sum of their separate measures of overlap with Y. Rather, as is illustrated in Figure 3E.2, the whole will typically be less than the sum of its parts, that is, $R^2_{Y \cdot 12}$ will typically be less than $r^2_{Y1} + r^2_{Y2}$.

How do we determine how much R^2 will increase as a result of adding X_2 to a model already containing X_1? What we would like to do is to isolate that part of X_2 that is unrelated to X_1 so that we would have a situation like that in Equation

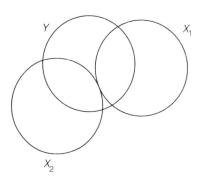

F I G U R E **3E. 1** Multiple regression with uncorrelated predictors.

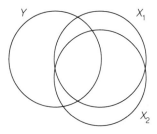

F I G U R E 3E. 2 Multiple regression with correlated predictors.

E.16, and then see how strongly that part of X_2 relates to Y. What is the part of X_2 that is unrelated to X_1? If X_2 is regressed on X_1, the predicted X_2 scores would summarize all information in X_2 that could be predicted by X_1, and the deviation scores $X_2 - \hat{X}_2$ would be that part of X_2 that does not relate to X_1. These deviation scores could then be used to predict Y and the resultant correlation used as in Equation E.16.

Such a correlation between X_2 and Y in which the variability in X_2 associated with X_1 has been removed is referred to as a *semipartial correlation* and is denoted $r_{Y(2 \cdot 1)}$. Fortunately, the value of this semipartial correlation can be expressed simply in terms of the simple correlations among the variables. Specifically,

$$r_{Y(2 \cdot 1)} = \frac{r_{Y2} - r_{Y1}r_{12}}{\sqrt{1 - r_{12}^2}}. \tag{E.17}$$

For example, if we again assume that $r_{Y1} = r_{Y2} = .5$ but that now $r_{12} = .8$, we would have

$$r_{Y(2 \cdot 1)} = \frac{.5 - (.5)(.8)}{\sqrt{1 - (.8)^2}} = \frac{.5 - .4}{\sqrt{1 - .64}} = \frac{.1}{\sqrt{.36}} = \frac{.1}{.6} = .1\overline{6}$$

Thus, the multiple correlation for a model, including both X_1 and X_2, would be $R_{Y \cdot 12}^2 = r_{Y1}^2 + r_{Y(2 \cdot 1)}^2 = (.5)^2 + (.16)^2 = .25 + .0256 = .2756$.

The same principle applies in more complicated multiple-regression situations as well. If all current predictors are partialed from each new predictor, the squared correlation of the resulting residual values with the criterion variable indicates how much of an increment in R^2 would result when the new predictor is added to the model. That is, in the general case of, say, p predictors, we have

$$R_{Y \cdot 123,\ldots,p}^2 = r_{Y1}^2 + r_{Y(2 \cdot 1)}^2 + r_{Y(3 \cdot 12)}^2 + r_{Y(4 \cdot 123)}^2 + \cdots + r_{Y(p \cdot 123,\ldots,p-1)}^2 \tag{E.18}$$

The degrees of freedom associated with a regression model, as with any model, is the number of independent observations minus the number of parameters estimated. If a model includes p predictor variables, as in Equation E.3, then you must estimate p slopes, $\beta_1, \beta_2, \beta_3, \ldots \beta_p$, and 1 intercept, β_0, for a total of $p + 1$ parameters. Thus, with N observations, you would have $N - (p + 1)$ or $N - p - 1$ degrees of freedom. For example, if there are $a - 1$ predictor variables besides the constant term, which is the case in the full model for an a-group ANOVA as we will develop in the next section, then the degrees of freedom would be $N - p - 1 = N - (a-1) - 1 = N - a$. On the other hand, if a model includes no predictor variables besides the constant, then the degrees of freedom would be $N - p - 1 = N - 0 - 1 = N - 1$.

Numerical Example

Consider the case of a one-way ANOVA design with four groups. To make it possible for the calculations to be done easily by hand, we use the simple data set shown in Table 3E.1. The full model in terms of effects for such a case would be

$$Y_{ij} = \mu + \alpha_j + \varepsilon_{ij} \qquad\qquad (3.66, \text{repeated})$$

where $j = 1, 2, 3, 4$. Imposing the typical side condition that $\sum \alpha_j = 0$ allows us to eliminate one of the αs. Following the convention of eliminating the parameter associated with the last group, we make use of the fact that $\alpha_4 = -\alpha_1 - \alpha_2 - \alpha_3$. Thus, we could express our model shown in Equation 3.66 in terms of the following four equations for our four groups:

$$Y_{i1} = \mu + \alpha_1 + \varepsilon_{i1}$$

$$Y_{i2} = \mu + \alpha_2 + \varepsilon_{i2}$$

$$Y_{i3} = \mu + \alpha_3 + \varepsilon_{i3}$$

$$Y_{i4} = \mu - \alpha_1 - \alpha_2 - \alpha_3 + \varepsilon_{i4}$$

In terms of the general regression model shown in Equation E.3, we would have four predictor variables, counting the constant or intercept. Thus, the μ, α_1, α_2, and α_3 parameters correspond to the regression coefficients (βs) to be estimated. Recall that regression coefficients are typically multiplied times the continuous predictor variables. Here, however, the only multipliers of the μ and α terms are *their* coefficients. For example, for subjects in group 1, we have $Y_{i1} = 1\mu + 1\alpha_1 + 0\alpha_2 + 0\alpha_3$, and for subjects in group 4, we have $Y_{i4} = 1\mu + -1\alpha_1 + -1\alpha_2 + -1\alpha_3$. These 1s, 0s and -1s simply indicate the combination of parameters appropriate for each cell. However, the set of coefficients associated with a given parameter across all subjects can be viewed as a variable. Such *indicator variables* are in fact the Xs that are used in treating an ANOVA data set as a multiple-regression problem.

The values of the Y variable and the indicator variables associated with α_1, α_2, and α_3 are shown in Table 3E.2. To carry out the test of the significance of the

T A B L E **3E. 1** Data to Illustrate
Regression Approach to ANOVA

Group			
1	2	3	4
11	13	15	17
13	15	17	19

T A B L E 3E. 2 Computations for Regression Approach to One-Way ANOVA

Variables and Cross-Products of Deviation Scores

Y	x_1	x_2	x_3	y	$x_1 y$	$x_2 y$	$x_3 y$	$x_1 x_2$	$x_1 x_3$	$x_2 x_3$	x_1^2	y^2
11	1	0	0	−4	−4	0	0	0	0	0	1	16
13	1	0	0	−2	−2	0	0	0	0	0	1	4
13	0	1	0	−2	0	−2	0	0	0	0	0	4
15	0	1	0	0	0	0	0	0	0	0	0	0
15	0	0	1	0	0	0	0	0	0	0	0	0
17	0	0	1	2	0	0	2	0	0	0	0	4
17	−1	−1	−1	2	−2	−2	−2	1	1	1	1	4
19	−1	−1	−1	4	−4	−4	−4	1	1	1	1	16
			Sum:	−12	−8	−4	2	2	2	2	4	48

Computation of Basic Correlations

$$r_{x_1 Y} = \frac{\sum x_1 y}{\sqrt{\sum x_1^2 \sum y^2}} = \frac{-12}{\sqrt{4 \cdot 48}} = \frac{-12}{13.856} = -.866 \qquad \text{NOTE: } \sum x_2^2 = \sum x_3^2 = \sum x_1^2 = 4$$

$$r_{x_2 Y} = \frac{-8}{13.856} = -.577 \qquad r_{x_3 Y} = \frac{-4}{13.856} = -.289$$

$$r_{x_1 x_2} = r_{x_1 x_3} = r_{x_2 x_3} = \frac{2}{\sqrt{4 \cdot 4}} = .5$$

Computation of Semipartial Correlations and R^2

$$R_{Y \cdot 123}^2 = r_{Y1}^2 + r_{Y(2 \cdot 1)}^2 + r_{Y(3 \cdot 12)}^2$$

$$r_{Y(2 \cdot 1)} = \frac{r_{Y2} - r_{Y1} r_{12}}{\sqrt{1 - r_{12}^2}} = \frac{-.577 - (-.866)(.5)}{\sqrt{1 - (.5)^2}} = \frac{-.144}{.866} = -.1\overline{66}$$

$$r_{Y(3 \cdot 12)} = \frac{r_{Y(3 \cdot 1)} - r_{Y(2 \cdot 1)} r_{23 \cdot 1}}{\sqrt{1 - r_{23 \cdot 1}^2}} = \frac{r_{Y(3 \cdot 1)} - r_{Y(2 \cdot 1)}(r_{3(2 \cdot 1)}/\sqrt{1 - r_{13}^2})}{\sqrt{1 - [r_{3(2 \cdot 1)}^2/(1 - r_{13}^2)]}}$$

$$r_{Y(3 \cdot 1)} = \frac{r_{Y3} - r_{Y1} r_{13}}{\sqrt{1 - r_{13}^2}} = \frac{-.289 - (-.866)(.5)}{\sqrt{1 - (.5)^2}} = \frac{.144}{.866} = .1\overline{66}$$

$$r_{3(2 \cdot 1)} = \frac{r_{23} - r_{13} r_{12}}{\sqrt{1 - r_{12}^2}} = \frac{.5 - (.5)(.5)}{\sqrt{1 - (.5)^2}} = \frac{.25}{.866} = .289$$

$$r_{Y(3 \cdot 12)} = \frac{.1\overline{66} - (-.1\overline{66})(.289/.866)}{\sqrt{1 - [(.289)^2/(1 - .5^2)]}} = \frac{.2\overline{22}}{\sqrt{.888}} = .236$$

$$R_{Y \cdot 123}^2 = (-.866)^2 + (-.1\overline{66})^2 + (.236)^2 = .750 + .028 + .0\overline{55} = .8\overline{33}$$

Test of Regression

$$F = \frac{(R_F^2 - R_R^2)/(df_R - df_F)}{(1 - R_F^2)/df_F} = \frac{R_{Y \cdot 123}^2 - R_{Y \cdot 0}^2}{(1 - R_{Y \cdot 123}^2)/4} = \frac{(.8\overline{33} - 0)/3}{(1 - .8\overline{33})/4} = \frac{.2\overline{77}}{.042} = 6.\overline{66}, \; p < .05$$

regression of Y on these indicator variables, we simply need to determine the R^2 associated with this model (see Equation E.15). (The comparison restricted model, in which all the α_js are presumed equal to zero, would predict a single constant value for each subject, and hence R_R^2 would be zero.) We illustrate the computation of the R^2 for the full model by starting with the squared correlation of Y with one of the predictors and successively incrementing this with squared semipartial correlations as indicated in Equation E.18.

To start we must compute the correlation between all possible pairs of variables, which we can do by multiplying deviation scores as indicated in Equation E.11. Computations of these correlations are shown in the top of Table 3E.2. We can use these correlations to compute the needed semipartial correlations and ultimately the R^2 for the model. Computations of these semipartial correlations are also shown in Table 3E.2; note that for ease of notation the predictor variables in this section of the table are denoted by a single numerical subscript, for example, r_{12} is used for $r_{X_1 X_2}$. Notice also that the formula for $r_{Y(3 \cdot 12)}$ is similar to that for $r_{Y(2 \cdot 1)}$, except that all the correlations used in computing the former have already been adjusted for X_1. Finally, the F test is computed in terms of R^2 at the bottom of the table.

The value of R^2 and hence of the F test can be confirmed here by performing the computations of the basic components of a standard ANOVA. We have already determined that $SS_{\text{Total}} = 48 \ (= E_R)$. The sum of squared deviations around the group means SS_W can be determined by inspection for this particularly simple data set to be equal to 8 times 1^2, or just 8 $(= E_F)$. Thus, SS_B, that is $E_R - E_F$, equals $48 - 8 = 40$. Because we formulated the regression model here to reflect the four-group design, the ratio of SS_B to SS_{Total} is identical to the ratio of $SS_{\text{Regression}}$ to SS_{Total}. And because we have defined the latter ratio as R^2, we have $R^2 = SS_B / SS_{\text{Total}} = 40/48 = .833$. As desired, this value checks with the value of R^2 we obtained by using semipartial correlations. Obviously, this ANOVA approach is much simpler computationally and hence would be used if you actually do the calculations by hand. Because real data are almost certainly analyzed by computer and because messy ANOVA data sets (nonorthogonal designs or multiple co-variates) do not lend themselves to such straightforward arithmetic, to be able to translate F tests into comparisons of multiple-regression models and of R^2s is important.

4   Individual Comparisons of Means

IN CHAPTER 3 YOU learned how to test a null hypothesis that all a groups have the same mean. A global test such as this one that is sensitive to any differences among the levels of the factor is often referred to as testing an *omnibus null hypothesis*. Although the importance of this methodology cannot be over-emphasized, it must also be recognized that it has certain limitations. Specifically, anytime a is three or greater and the null hypothesis is rejected, the precise inference to be made is unclear. For example, if a equals three, all that the statistical test has informed us at this point is that the statement $\mu_1 = \mu_2 = \mu_3$ is false. However, it is not necessarily true that all three means are different from each other. For example, one possible inference is that $\mu_1 = \mu_2$, but both μ_1 and μ_2 differ from μ_3. On the other hand, perhaps $\mu_2 = \mu_3$, but both differ from μ_1. Obviously, we need a way to decide which individual means do indeed differ from each other. The name given to this topic is *individual comparisons*.

For example, suppose that a researcher is interested in treatments to reduce hypertension. Consider a hypothetical study with four independent groups of subjects, each of whom is randomly assigned to one of the following treatments: drug therapy, biofeedback, dietary modification, and a treatment combining all aspects of the other treatments. For simplicity, suppose the dependent variable is a single blood pressure reading taken two weeks after the termination of treatment. In Chapter 3, you learned how to test an omnibus null hypothesis that all four treatments are equally effective. However, there are a number of other questions that might be addressed here, either in addition to or instead of the omnibus null hypothesis. For example, is there a difference in the effectiveness of drug therapy versus biofeedback? Drug therapy versus diet? Biofeedback versus diet? Is the combination treatment more effective than any of the individual treatments? Is it more effective than the average of the individual treatments? In this chapter, you will learn how to answer these questions and others like them.

To preview the next two chapters for you, we first show how to use a model-comparisons approach to test hypotheses concerning individual comparisons. Then a more traditional but mathematically equivalent approach to individual com-parisons is developed. Chapter 5 considers issues that arise when more than one individual comparison is performed in a single study. As we will see, in most studies, several comparisons are indeed tested, leading to the topic of multiple comparisons. The desire to test multiple comparisons can arise in either of two circumstances. First, there are occasions where a researcher may decide to test several specific comparisons either instead of or in addition to performing a test of the omnibus null hypothesis that all a population means are equal. Such an approach is called *planned comparisons* because the specific comparisons to be investigated are decided on at the beginning of the study. Second, on other occasions, the omnibus null hypothesis will be tested. If it is rejected, further data analyses are conducted to explore which groups contributed to the statistically significant result. This approach is called *post hoc comparisons* because the comparisons to be tested are decided on after having examined the data. The distinction between these two situations is described in detail in Chapter 5.

A MODEL COMPARISON APPROACH FOR TESTING INDIVIDUAL COMPARISONS

Relationship to Model Comparisons

Recall from Chapter 3 that we learned how to test the null hypothesis that all a groups in an a-group study have the same population mean. Symbolically, this corresponds to

$$H_0 : \mu_1 = \mu_2 = \cdots = \mu_a \tag{1}$$

Using the principle of model comparisons, we began with a full model

$$Y_{ij} = \mu_j + \varepsilon_{ij} \tag{2}$$

We obtained the restricted model from our null hypothesis that all μ_j parameters in fact equal a single value, which we denoted μ. Thus, our restricted model was given by

$$Y_{ij} = \mu + \varepsilon_{ij} \tag{3}$$

At this point, our purpose is to consider a different null hypothesis. Instead of testing that all a groups have the same mean, suppose that we simply want to test a null hypothesis that the population means of the first and second groups are equal, that is, our null hypothesis now is

$$H_0 : \mu_1 = \mu_2 \tag{4}$$

Once again we can use the principle of model comparisons to test this hypothesis. Our full model remains the same as our previous full model, namely,

$$Y_{ij} = \mu_j + \varepsilon_{ij} \tag{5}$$

According to H_0, however, this model is too complex. Instead, a restricted model where $\mu_1 = \mu_2$ provides a simpler but (according to H_0) just as adequate a description of scores on the dependent variable. It is difficult to represent this restricted model compactly with symbols. One solution is simply to write the restricted model as

$$Y_{ij} = \mu_j + \varepsilon_{ij} \tag{6}$$

where $\mu_1 = \mu_2$. However, for greater clarity, we might write

$$Y_{i1} = \mu^* + \varepsilon_{i1} \tag{7}$$

$$Y_{i2} = \mu^* + \varepsilon_{i2}$$

$$Y_{ij} = \mu_j + \varepsilon_{ij} \qquad j = 3, 4, \ldots, a$$

where μ^* represents the common population mean of the first and second groups. Notice that Equation 7 allows groups 3 through a to each have their own potentially unique population mean, but groups 1 and 2 are restricted to having equal population means.

Now that the full and restricted models have been identified, it is possible to perform a test of the null hypothesis by comparing the sums of squared errors of the two models as we did in Chapter 3. Finding the sum of squared errors for the full model here is easy because it is simply the full model of the previous chapter. As we saw there,

$$E_F = \sum_{j=1}^{a} \sum_{i=1}^{n_j} (Y_{ij} - \bar{Y}_j)^2 = SS_W \tag{8}$$

Finding the sum of squared errors for the restricted model here is similar to the process used in Chapter 3. As before, the principle of least squares is used. We now have $a - 1$ parameters to estimate in the restricted model: $\mu^*, \mu_3, \mu_4, \ldots, \mu_a$. You should realize that there are only $a - 1$ parameters to be estimated in the restricted model because the separate μ_1 and μ_2 parameters of the full model have been replaced by the single parameter μ^* in the restricted model. The only new wrinkle here is estimating μ^* because the least-squares estimates of μ_3 through μ_a are again the corresponding sample means, that is, $\bar{Y}_3$ through $\bar{Y}_a$, respectively. Intuitively, it seems reasonable that the estimate of μ^* should be based on the sample means of the first two groups. Indeed, with equal n, we will see momentarily that

$$\mu^* = (\bar{Y}_1 + \bar{Y}_2)/2$$

So, for example, if $\bar{Y}_1 = 6$ and $\bar{Y}_2 = 10$, our best single guess is that the common value of the population mean for groups 1 and 2 is 8. We now show algebraically that this intuitive reasoning is correct while we develop a more general formula that can be used when sample sizes are unequal.

The goal in estimating μ^* is to choose as an estimate whatever value minimizes the following expression:

$$\sum_{i=1}^{n_1} (Y_{i1} - \hat{\mu}^*)^2 + \sum_{i=1}^{n_2} (Y_{i2} - \hat{\mu}^*)^2 \tag{9}$$

which is the sum of squared errors for subjects in the first and second groups. However, this expression is equivalent to

$$\sum_{j=1}^{2} \sum_{i=1}^{n_j} (Y_{ij} - \hat{\mu}^*)^2 \tag{10}$$

Notice that in this expression we are summing over $n_1 + n_2$ individual scores. Although in fact these scores come from two distinct groups, the sum would be the same if we had a single group of $n_1 + n_2$ scores. We have already seen that the sample mean of a group provides the best (in a least-squares sense) estimate in this case. Thus, to minimize Equation 10, we should choose $\hat{\mu}^*$ equal to the sample mean of the $n_1 + n_2$ scores in the first and second groups. Symbolically,

$$\hat{\mu}^* = \sum_{j=1}^{2} \sum_{i=1}^{n_j} Y_{ij} \bigg/ (n_1 + n_2) \tag{11}$$

Equivalently, it can be shown that the estimate $\hat{\mu}^*$ is a weighted mean of $\bar{Y}_1$ and $\bar{Y}_2$:

$$\hat{\mu}^* = (n_1 \bar{Y}_1 + n_2 \bar{Y}_2)/(n_1 + n_2) \tag{12}$$

which in the special case of equal sample sizes ($n_1 = n_2$) simplifies to

$$\hat{\mu}^* = (\bar{Y}_1 + \bar{Y}_2)/2 \tag{13}$$

As we said earlier, this expression for estimating μ^* should make intuitive sense because according to the restricted model, $\mu_1 = \mu_2 = \mu^*$. If this is actually true, $\bar{Y}_1$ and $\bar{Y}_2$ differ from one another only because of sampling error, and the best estimate of the single population mean is obtained by averaging $\bar{Y}_1$ and $\bar{Y}_2$.

To test the null hypothesis that $\mu_1 = \mu_2$, it is necessary to find E_R. This turns out to be easy conceptually now that we know the least-squares parameter estimates for Equation 6 (or, equivalently, Equation 7). That it is also easy computationally becomes apparent shortly. If we let $\bar{Y}^*$ represent our estimate $\hat{\mu}^*$, we have

$$E_R = \sum_{j=1}^{2} \sum_{i=1}^{n_j} (Y_{ij} - \bar{Y}^*)^2 + \sum_{j=3}^{a} \sum_{i=1}^{n_j} (Y_{ij} - \bar{Y}_j)^2 \tag{14}$$

Recall that our real interest is in the increase in error brought about with the restricted model, $E_R - E_F$. To help make it easier to see what this difference equals, we can rewrite Equation 8 as

$$E_F = \sum_{j=1}^{2} \sum_{i=1}^{n_j} (Y_{ij} - \bar{Y}_j)^2 + \sum_{j=3}^{a} \sum_{i=1}^{n_j} (Y_{ij} - \bar{Y}_j)^2 \tag{15}$$

Now, by subtracting the terms in Equation 15 from those in Equation 14, we see that the difference $E_R - E_F$ equals

$$E_R - E_F = \sum_{j=1}^{2} \sum_{i=1}^{n_j} (Y_{ij} - \bar{Y}^*)^2 - \sum_{j=1}^{2} \sum_{i=1}^{n_j} (Y_{ij} - \bar{Y}_j)^2 \tag{16}$$

After some straightforward but tedious algebra, Equation 16 simplifies to

$$E_R - E_F = \frac{(\bar{Y}_1 - \bar{Y}_2)^2}{\left(\dfrac{1}{n_1} + \dfrac{1}{n_2}\right)}$$

$$= \frac{n_1 n_2}{n_1 + n_2}(\bar{Y}_1 - \bar{Y}_2)^2 \tag{17}$$

Thus, the increase in error is a function of the sample sizes and the magnitude of the difference between $\bar{Y}_1$ and $\bar{Y}_2$. Larger discrepancies between $\bar{Y}_1$ and $\bar{Y}_2$ suggest that μ_1 may not equal μ_2, as reflected by the larger increase in error. This should seem reasonable because in the long run the magnitude of the difference between $\bar{Y}_1$ and $\bar{Y}_2$ should reflect the magnitude of the difference between μ_1 and μ_2. Once again, the problem arises of "how large is large?" The answer is provided by the same form of the F statistic we encountered in Chapter 3:

$$F = \frac{(E_R - E_F)/(df_R - df_F)}{E_F/df_F} \tag{18}$$

The only term in this expression yet to be found for our problem is $df_R - df_F$. Recall that the degrees of freedom for a model equals the number of independent observations in the study minus the number of parameters estimated. In the current problem, a parameters were estimated in the full model, and $a - 1$ were estimated in the restricted model. Hence,

$$df_F = N - a \qquad (19)$$

so $df_F = df_W$, as in Chapter 3.

$$df_R = N - (a - 1) = N - a + 1 \qquad (20)$$

where N represents the total number of subjects in the study (summed over all groups). Subtracting Equation 19 from Equation 20 yields

$$df_R - df_F = 1 \qquad (21)$$

As demonstrated in Equation 21, an individual comparison has 1 degree of freedom associated with it, that is, the test of a single restriction on means involves 1 degree of freedom in the numerator. Finally, for testing the null hypothesis of $H_0 : \mu_1 = \mu_2$, we obtain the following test statistic by making the appropriate substitutions into Equation 18:

$$F = \frac{\dfrac{n_1 n_2}{n_1 + n_2}(\bar{Y}_1 - \bar{Y}_2)^2 \Big/ 1}{SS_W / df_W} \qquad (22)$$

which simplifies[1] to

$$F = \frac{n_1 n_2 (\bar{Y}_1 - \bar{Y}_2)^2}{(n_1 + n_2) MS_W} \qquad (23)$$

or in the case of equal n,

$$F = \frac{n(\bar{Y}_1 - \bar{Y}_2)^2}{2 MS_W} \qquad (24)$$

Numerical Example

It may be instructive here to consider a numerical example. Table 4.1 displays hypothetical data for four groups of subjects, corresponding to the four treatments

TABLE 4.1 Hypothetical Systolic Blood Pressure Data

	Drug Therapy	Biofeedback	Diet	Combination
	84	81	98	91
	95	84	95	78
	93	92	86	85
	104	101	87	80
		80	94	81
		108		
Mean ($\bar{Y}_j$)	94.0	91.0	92.0	83.0
Var (s_j^2)	67.3	132.0	27.5	26.5

for hypertension introduced at the beginning of the chapter. Specifically, we assume that a group of 24 mild hypertensives have been independently and randomly assigned to one of four treatments: drug therapy, biofeedback, dietary modification, and a treatment combining all aspects of the other treatments. The scores shown in Table 4.1 are systolic blood pressure readings for each subject taken two weeks after the termination of treatment.

T A B L E **4. 2** Illustrative Test of a Pairwise Comparison for Data in Table 4.1

Test of $H_0 : \mu_1 = \mu_2$

Approach of Equation 23

$$F = \frac{n_1 n_2 (\bar{Y}_1 - \bar{Y}_2)^2}{(n_1 + n_2) MS_W}$$

$$= \frac{(4)(6)(94 - 91)^2}{(4 + 6)(67.375)}$$

$$= 0.32$$

because

$$MS_W = \frac{\sum\limits_{j=1}^{a} (n_j - 1) s_j^2}{N - a}$$

$$= \frac{3(67.3) + 5(132.0) + 4(27.5) + 4(26.5)}{20 - 4}$$

$$= 67.375$$

Approach of Equation 18

$$F = \frac{(E_R - E_F)/(df_R - df_F)}{E_F/df_F}$$

$$E_F = \sum_{j=1}^{a} \sum_{i=1}^{n_j} (Y_{ij} - \bar{Y}_j)^2$$

$$= \sum_{i=1}^{n_1} (Y_{i1} - 94)^2 + \sum_{i=1}^{n_2} (Y_{i2} - 91)^2 + \sum_{i=1}^{n_3} (Y_{i3} - 92)^2 + \sum_{i=1}^{n_4} (Y_{i4} - 83)^2$$

$$= 1078.00$$

$$E_R = \sum_{i=1}^{n_1} (Y_{i1} - \bar{Y}^*)^2 + \sum_{i=1}^{n_2} (Y_{i2} - \bar{Y}^*)^2 + \sum_{i=1}^{n_3} (Y_{i3} - \bar{Y}_3)^2 + \sum_{i=1}^{n_4} (Y_{i4} - \bar{Y}_4)^2$$

$$= \sum_{i=1}^{n_1} (Y_{i1} - 92.2)^2 + \sum_{i=1}^{n_2} (Y_{i2} - 92.2)^2 + \sum_{i=1}^{n_3} (Y_{i3} - 92)^2 + \sum_{i=1}^{n_4} (Y_{i4} - 83)^2$$

$$= 214.96 + 668.64 + 110.00 + 106.00$$

$$= 1099.60$$

Then,

$$F = \frac{(1099.60 - 1078.00)/(17 - 16)}{1078.00/16} = 0.32$$

Two preliminary remarks must be made. First, we said that 24 subjects were assigned to treatment groups, but Table 4.1 shows scores for only 20 subjects. In general, we can proceed with a meaningful analysis of such data only if we can reasonably assume that the reasons for the missing subjects are unrelated to the treatments themselves, that is, the treatment did not cause these subjects to be missing. We act as if such an assumption is reasonable here. In fact, these hypothetical data were created with unequal sample sizes to illustrate the most general situation for testing comparisons. Second, we could use the principles of Chapter 3 to perform an omnibus test. If we were to do so, we would obtain an observed F value of 1.66 for these data, which is nonsignificant at the .05 level. However, we assume that our real interest is in testing contrasts among the groups. The relationship between contrasts and the omnibus test is discussed more fully in Chapter 5.

In an actual study, we would probably test several contrasts. However, to keep things simple, we illustrate a test for only one contrast. Specifically, we suppose that the hypothesis to be tested is whether there is a difference in the effectiveness of drug therapy and biofeedback.

Table 4.2 shows two equivalent ways to test this hypothesis. Although Equation 23 is easier to use in practice, the approach based on Equation 18 is also shown, primarily for pedagogical reasons. With either approach, the observed F value is 0.32, with 1 and 16 degrees of freedom. The observed value is less than the critical F value of 4.49 (see Appendix Table A.2) for $\alpha = .05$, so the difference between the means is nonsignificant at the .05 level. Thus, the hypothesis that drug therapy and biofeedback are equally effective cannot be rejected at the .05 level.

COMPLEX COMPARISONS

Models Perspective

The approach we have just developed is adequate for testing hypotheses of the form $H_0 : \mu_1 = \mu_2$. More generally, any hypothesis of the form

$$H_0 : \mu_l = \mu_m \tag{25}$$

where μ_l and μ_m are the population means of any two groups is said to involve a *pairwise comparison* because it involves an equality of only two groups' means. Equation 23 provides a computationally simple method for testing hypotheses of this form.

Although research questions often center on pairwise comparisons, there are occasions where hypotheses concern a difference involving more than two means. For example, in the hypothetical blood pressure study we have been discussing, one question we raised at the beginning of the chapter was whether the combination treatment is more effective than the average of the other three treatments. We could write the null hypothesis for this question as

$$H_0 : \tfrac{1}{3}(\mu_1 + \mu_2 + \mu_3) = \mu_4 \tag{26}$$

Notice that this null hypothesis does not necessarily stipulate that all four population means are equal to each other. For example, if $\mu_1 = 88$, $\mu_2 = 87$, $\mu_3 = 83$, and $\mu_4 = 86$, the null hypothesis would be true because the average of 88, 87, and 83 is 86. Also notice that, as Equation 26 shows, the null hypothesis being tested here involves more than two groups. Such a hypothesis involves a *complex comparison*.

When a complex comparison is to be tested, it is not at all intuitively obvious how least-squares estimates of parameters are obtained in the appropriate restricted model. In fact, it is difficult even to write down an appropriate expression for the restricted model, unless we simply say it is

$$Y_{ij} = \mu_j + \varepsilon_{ij} \tag{27}$$

where

$$\tfrac{1}{3}(\mu_1 + \mu_2 + \mu_3) = \mu_4$$

Given this formulation of the restricted model, the least-squares estimates are still not apparent.[2] Although it is possible to describe a procedure that yields the least-squares estimates, we instead take a different approach. The primary rationale for this approach is that we are typically not interested in the parameter estimates themselves, but rather we are interested in the difference between the sum of squared errors for the restricted and full models, $E_R - E_F$, just as we were when we tested pairwise comparisons. There is a general procedure for finding this difference for any contrast we might wish to test. In particular, a contrast such as that expressed by the null hypothesis of Equation 26 can be tested rather easily with the approach we now develop.

It is convenient to rewrite the hypothesis expressed in Equation 26 in the following manner:

$$H_0 : \tfrac{1}{3}\mu_1 + \tfrac{1}{3}\mu_2 + \tfrac{1}{3}\mu_3 - \mu_4 = 0 \tag{28}$$

The expression on the left-hand side of the equals sign—that is, $\tfrac{1}{3}\mu_1 + \tfrac{1}{3}\mu_2 + \tfrac{1}{3}\mu_3 - \mu_4$—is a linear combination of the group population means. In general, we might express a hypothesis concerning the means as

$$H_0 : c_1\mu_1 + c_2\mu_2 + c_3\mu_3 + c_4\mu_4 = 0 \tag{29}$$

where c_1, c_2, c_3, and c_4 are coefficients (or weights) chosen by the experimenter to test a hypothesis of substantive interest. Notice that Equation 28 is a special case of Equation 29 where $c_1 = 1/3$, $c_2 = 1/3$, $c_3 = 1/3$, and $c_4 = -1$. An expression of the form

$$c_1\mu_1 + c_2\mu_2 + c_3\mu_3 + c_4\mu_4 \tag{30}$$

is called a *contrast* or a *comparison* (the terms are used interchangeably). The general definition of a contrast is that it is a linear combination of population means in which the coefficients of the means add up to zero. In the general case of a groups, we can represent a contrast quite compactly with Σ notation as

$$\sum_{j=1}^{a} c_j\mu_j \tag{31}$$

Instead of writing this expression every time we refer to a contrast, it is conventional to use a lowercase Greek *psi*(ψ) to represent the numerical value of a contrast. In other words,

$$\psi = \sum_{j=1}^{a} c_j \mu_j \tag{32}$$

Several points need mentioning here. First, the general concept of a comparison as exemplified in Equation 32 is very powerful because this formulation permits a wide range of hypotheses to be tested. The primary reason for this tremendous flexibility is that a researcher is free to choose contrast coefficients (the c_j terms) in whatever manner that corresponds to the substantive hypothesis of interest. For example, we see in a moment that the general expression in Equation 33 enables us to test whether the combination hypertension treatment (group 4) is more effective than the average of the other three treatments. We will accomplish this by choosing c_1, c_2, and c_3 to equal 1/3, and c_4 to equal -1. Alternatively, as a second example, suppose that we want to test the difference between drug therapy and biofeedback, as we did earlier in the chapter. This null hypothesis could be written as

$$H_0 : \mu_1 - \mu_2 = 0$$

To test this hypothesis, then, we can choose coefficients as follows: $c_1 = 1, c_2 = -1$, $c_3 = 0$, and $c_4 = 0$. The resultant contrast ψ is given by

$$\psi = (1)\mu_1 + (-1)\mu_2 + (0)\mu_3 + (0)\mu_4 = \mu_1 - \mu_2$$

Thus, testing a null hypothesis that ψ as defined in this manner equals zero is equivalent to testing whether $\mu_1 = \mu_2$. The general point to be understood here is that by choosing c_j values appropriately, it is possible to define ψ to test any particular comparison, either pairwise or complex, that may be of interest. Second, realize that ψ is simply a number because it is a linear combination of the population means. For example, consider the following definition of ψ:

$$\psi = \tfrac{1}{3}\mu_1 + \tfrac{1}{3}\mu_2 + \tfrac{1}{3}\mu_3 - \mu_4$$

If $\mu_1 = 88$, $\mu_2 = 87$, $\mu_3 = 83$, and $\mu_4 = 86$, then $\psi = 0$. Notice here that the null hypothesis is true. On the other hand, if $\mu_1 = 88$, $\mu_2 = 87$, $\mu_3 = 83$, but $\mu_4 = 80$, then $\psi = -6$. In this case, the null hypothesis is false because the combination treatment is better than the average of the other treatments (remember that lower blood pressure readings are better—at least until they approach zero!). Admittedly, in actual research we do not know what number ψ represents because it is a population parameter, but nevertheless it is a number. Because we cannot know the population value of ψ, we must use sample data to estimate and test hypotheses about ψ. Third, as the previous example illustrates, ψ equals zero when the null hypothesis is true and is nonzero when it is false. For this reason, we can rewrite our null hypothesis as

$$H_0 : \psi = 0 \tag{33}$$

More formally, Equation 33 follows from substituting ψ from Equation 32 into Equation 29.[3] Fourth, the mathematics for forming F tests would work even if the coefficients did not sum to zero. However, we refer to the set of coefficients in this case as defining a particular linear combination rather than a contrast or comparison (e.g., $\mu_1 + \mu_2$ combines two means but does not contrast or compare their values with one another). Typically, linear combinations that are not contrasts do not address theoretically meaningful questions. Fifth, as we will again see later, we are usually interested in several different contrasts in one study. To avoid confusion, we often use subscripts for ψ; for example, we might have ψ_1, ψ_2, and ψ_3 in a particular study. Each ψ would have its own coefficients and would represent a hypothesis of interest to the experimenter. For example, with four groups, we might be interested in the following three contrasts:

$$\psi_1 = \mu_1 + \mu_2 - \mu_3 - \mu_4 \tag{34}$$

$$\psi_2 = \mu_1 - \mu_2$$

$$\psi_3 = \mu_3 - \mu_4$$

For the moment, we continue to focus our attention on testing a hypothesis about a particular contrast, say, ψ_1. (In Chapter 5, we consider issues that arise in testing more than one contrast.)

In general, our purpose is to develop a test of a null hypothesis of the form expressed in Equation 33, namely, $\psi = 0$. Once again, we use our expression for an F test:

$$F = \frac{(E_R - E_F)/(df_R - df_F)}{E_F/df_F} \tag{18, repeated}$$

However, Equation 18 can be simplified here because it is possible to develop a general expression for $E_R - E_F$ when testing a hypothesis that $\psi = 0$. It can be shown (see the extension at the end of the chapter) in this case that a general expression for the difference between the sum of squared errors of the restricted and full models is given by

$$E_R - E_F = (\hat{\psi})^2 \left/ \sum_{j=1}^{a} (c_j^2/n_j) \right. \tag{35}$$

where $\hat{\psi}$ is a sample estimate of the population parameter ψ. Because $E_R - E_F$ represents a difference in sum of squared errors associated with ψ, we often use $SS(\psi)$ to represent $E_R - E_F$ for a contrast, that is, $SS(\psi) = E_R - E_F$. Because $\bar{Y}_j$ is the least-squares estimate of μ_j, the least-squares estimate of ψ is obtained by simply replacing each population mean in Equation 32 by the corresponding sample mean. Thus,

$$\hat{\psi} = \sum_{j=1}^{a} c_j \bar{Y}_j \tag{36}$$

We will see throughout the book that Equation 35 is important. We will want to test contrasts for statistical significance in a variety of designs, and we will continually return to Equation 35 to find the sum of squares associated with the contrast of interest. For this reason, we digress momentarily to help you to develop an intuitive appreciation of the formula. From the numerator, we can see that the restricted model is inferior to the full model to the extent that $\hat{\psi}$ differs from zero (either positively or negatively). This makes sense because our null hypothesis is that ψ is zero. If ψ really is zero, $\hat{\psi}$ has a mean of zero and differs from zero only because of sampling error; however, if ψ is nonzero, $\hat{\psi}$ differs from zero both because of sampling error and because its mean is nonzero. Thus, $(\hat{\psi})^2$, and hence the difference in errors $E_R - E_F$, tends to be larger when the null hypothesis is false than when it is true. Also, notice that the n_j term appears in the denominator of the denominator. As a result, all other things being equal, larger sample sizes produce larger sums of squares, just as we would expect based on the discussion of power in Chapter 3. The final term in the formula is c_j. The intuitive justification for including the coefficients in the formula is that we can make $(\hat{\psi})^2$ as large or as small as we want by multiplying or dividing all of the c_j coefficients by a constant. To illustrate this point, consider two hypotheses that might be tested in a four-group study:

$$H_0 : \mu_1 + \mu_2 = \mu_3 + \mu_4$$

$$H_0 : .5(\mu_1 + \mu_2) = .5(\mu_3 + \mu_4)$$

These two hypotheses are logically equivalent because the .5 values on either side of the second hypothesis cancel one another. However, what happens if we translate these hypotheses into contrasts? We could define

$$\psi_1 = \mu_1 + \mu_2 - \mu_3 - \mu_4$$

for the first hypothesis, and

$$\psi_2 = .5\mu_1 + .5\mu_2 - .5\mu_3 - .5\mu_4$$

for the second. Now, suppose that we have obtained the following sample means based on 10 subjects in each group

$$\bar{Y}_1 = 10, \; \bar{Y}_2 = 12, \; \bar{Y}_3 = 10, \text{ and } \bar{Y}_4 = 8$$

Then, the sample value of ψ_1 equals

$$\hat{\psi}_1 = 1(10) + 1(12) - 1(10) - 1(8) = 4$$

The sample value of ψ_2 equals

$$\hat{\psi}_2 = .5(10) + .5(12) - .5(10) - .5(8) = 2$$

If we only considered the $\hat{\psi}$ values, we might mistakenly conclude that there is more evidence against the null hypothesis for the first contrast than for the second. However, the sum of squared coefficients $\sum_{j=1}^{a} c_j^2$ is also relevant because for ψ_1,

$$\sum_{j=1}^{a} c_j^2 = (1)^2 + (1)^2 + (-1)^2 + (-1)^2 = 4$$

whereas for ψ_2,

$$\sum_{j=1}^{a} c_j^2 = (.5)^2 + (.5)^2 + (-.5)^2 + (-.5)^2 = 1$$

Thus, $\sum_{j=1}^{a} c_j^2$ is four times larger for the first contrast than the second, just as $(\hat{\psi})^2$

is four times larger for the first contrast than the second. As a result, substituting the values for $(\hat{\psi})^2$, $\sum_{j=1}^{a} c_j^2$, and n_j into Equation 35 produces a value of 40 for the sum of squares, for both contrasts. Because the contrasts are logically equivalent, it is sensible that the two sums of squares should also be equivalent. The inclusion of the squared-coefficients term in the denominator of Equation 35 ensures that logically equivalent contrasts yield the same sum of squares, regardless of the absolute size of the coefficients.

The only remaining term in Equation 18 to be discussed is the difference in degrees of freedom, $df_R - df_F$. To find df_R, we must determine the number of independent parameters in the restricted model. Consider the null hypothesis of Equation 28 when $a = 4$:

$$H_0: \tfrac{1}{3}\mu_1 + \tfrac{1}{3}\mu_2 + \tfrac{1}{3}\mu_3 - \mu_4 = 0 \qquad \text{(28, repeated)}$$

The corresponding restricted model was

$$Y_{ij} = \mu_j + \varepsilon_{ij} \qquad \text{(27, repeated)}$$

where $1/3\mu_1 + 1/3\mu_2 + 1/3\mu_3 - \mu_4 = 0$. This model has four parameters when $a = 4$, but it only has three independent parameters because we know that the four parameters must obey the restriction that

$$\tfrac{1}{3}\mu_1 + \tfrac{1}{3}\mu_2 + \tfrac{1}{3}\mu_3 - \mu_4 = 0$$

For example, suppose that $\mu_1 = 88, \mu_2 = 87, \mu_3 = 83$. Then, according to the model, we know it should be true that $\mu_4 = 86$. Once the values of any three population means have been determined, the fourth is fixed. In the general case of a groups, there would be one restriction on the parameter values, implying that there would be $a - 1$ independent parameters. Thus, in the general case,

$$df_R - df_F = [N - (a - 1)] - (N - a)$$
$$= 1$$

Because E_F/df_F is MS_W, Equation 18 becomes

$$F = \frac{(\hat{\psi})^2}{MS_W \sum_{j=1}^{a} (c_j^2/n_j)} \qquad (37)$$

which may be used for testing any null hypothesis that can be expressed as

$$H_0: \psi = \sum_{j=1}^{a} c_j \mu_j = 0$$

Numerical Example

To illustrate calculations for testing a complex comparison, we return to the hypertension data shown in Table 4.1. Recall that Table 4.2 showed two equivalent approaches for testing a pairwise comparison, one based on Equation 23 and one based on Equation 18. Similarly, Table 4.3 shows two equivalent approaches for

T A B L E **4. 3** Illustrative Test of a Complex Comparison for Data in Table 4.1

$$\text{Test of } H_0 : 1/3(\mu_1 + \mu_2 + \mu_3) = \mu_4$$

Approach of Equation 37

$$F = \frac{(\hat{\psi})^2}{MS_W \sum_{j=1}^{a} (c_j^2/n_j)}$$

$$= \frac{[1/3(94 + 91 + 92) - 83]^2}{67.375\{[(1/3)^2/4] + [(1/3)^2/6] + [(1/3)^2/5] + [(-1)^2/5]\}}$$

$$= \frac{(92.33 - 83)^2}{67.375(0.2685)}$$

$$= 4.82$$

Approach of Equation 18

$$F = \frac{(E_R - E_F)/(df_R - df_F)}{E_F/df_F}$$

$$E_F = \sum(Y_{i1} - 94)^2 + \sum(Y_{i2} - 91)^2 + \sum(Y_{i3} - 92)^2 + \sum(Y_{i4} - 83)^2$$

$$= 1078.00$$

$$E_R = \sum(Y_{i1} - 91.103)^2 + \sum(Y_{i2} - 89.069)^2 + \sum(Y_{i3} - 89.683)^2 + \sum(Y_{i4} - 89.952)^2$$

$$= 235.57 + 682.37 + 136.84 + 347.65$$

$$= 1402.43$$

Then,

$$F = \frac{(1402.43 - 1078.00)/(17 - 16)}{1078.00/16} = 4.82$$

testing complex comparisons, one based on Equation 37 and one based on Equation 18. Notice that Equation 23 is not illustrated because it is appropriate only for pairwise comparisons.

For purposes of illustration, we continue to assume that we are interested in testing whether the combined treatment is more effective than the average of the other treatments. As the top half of Table 4.3 shows, the observed F value for this contrast is 4.82, which exceeds the critical F value of 4.49 for 1 and 16 degrees of freedom. Thus, we can assert that the combined treatment is in fact more effective than the average of the other treatments.

The bottom half of Table 4.3 shows the calculations using Equation 18. The primary reason for presenting these calculations is to demonstrate that they produce the same result as Equation 37. However, as should be obvious from comparing the two halves of Table 4.3, Equation 37 is much simpler, so it will be used in the remainder of the book, instead of going back to first principles of model comparisons using Equation 18. Nevertheless, it is important for you to see that Equation 37 is also based on a comparison of models.

In fact, the approach based on Equation 18 is even more tedious than the bottom half of Table 4.3 implies. The reason for this additional complication is that the least-squares estimates for the parameters in the restricted model are tedious to find. Given the restriction that ψ equals zero, the least-squares estimates of the parameters in the restricted model[4] are given by

$$\hat{\mu}_j = \bar{Y}_j - \left(\frac{1}{\sum\limits_{j=1}^{a} (c_j^2/n_j)} \right) \left(\frac{c_j}{n_j} \right) (\hat{\psi})$$

Thus, in our example, the parameter estimates subject to the constraint $1/3\mu_1 + 1/3\mu_2 + 1/3\mu_3 - 1\mu_4 = 0$ are given by

$$\hat{\mu}_1 = 94 - \left(\frac{1}{0.2685} \right) \left(\frac{1/3}{4} \right) (9.3333) = 91.103$$

$$\hat{\mu}_2 = 91 - \left(\frac{1}{0.2685} \right) \left(\frac{1/3}{6} \right) (9.3333) = 89.069$$

$$\hat{\mu}_3 = 92 - \left(\frac{1}{0.2685} \right) \left(\frac{1/3}{5} \right) (9.3333) = 89.683$$

$$\hat{\mu}_4 = 83 - \left(\frac{1}{0.2685} \right) \left(\frac{-1}{5} \right) (9.3333) = 89.952$$

Notice that as required by the constraint, $\frac{1}{3}\hat{\mu}_1 + \frac{1}{3}\hat{\mu}_2 + \frac{1}{3}\hat{\mu}_3 - \hat{\mu}_4 = 0$ because $\frac{1}{3}(91.103) + \frac{1}{3}(89.069) + \frac{1}{3}(89.683) - 89.952 = 0$ (within rounding error). Thus, by doing all this additional work, as Table 4.3 shows, we can use Equation 18 to duplicate the results of Equation 37.

One other point must be made here. Although in some situations a researcher may only be interested in pairwise comparisons, in many studies hypotheses involving complex comparisons will also be of interest. In particular, complex comparisons potentially reveal interesting features of the data that may be hidden from pairwise comparisons. For example, in the hypothetical hypertension data in Table 4.1, it turns out that none of the six pairwise differences between means is significant at the .05 level. However, we have just seen that a complex comparison is significant at the .05 level. If we had only tested pairwise comparisons, this finding would have gone undetected. On the other hand, it might be argued that if we test a large number of hypotheses, some will inevitably be statistically significant, even if every null hypothesis is true. This problem is discussed in detail in Chapter 5. The general point to understand here is that you should not always restrict your testing to pairwise comparisons. In some studies, complex comparisons should also be tested. In general, formulate comparisons that correspond to the hypotheses you want to test, remembering that the resultant contrasts may be either pairwise or complex.

THE *t*-TEST FORMULATION OF HYPOTHESIS TESTING FOR CONTRASTS

To summarize the chapter to this point, we have seen that testing hypotheses concerning contrasts can be thought of as a comparison of models. As in the last chapter, least squares is used to estimate parameters in full and restricted models. Then, the sums of squared errors of the two models are compared adjusting for degrees of freedom, yielding an F value. This F value is then compared to the table of the F distribution to determine whether the null hypothesis should be rejected.

Some textbooks do not present the test of a contrast as an F test, but rather as a *t* test. Although at first this may seem disconcerting, it should be remembered that the t is a special case of the F. Specifically, when the F has a single numerator degree of freedom, $t^2 = F$. Indeed, this relationship holds for testing a contrast because $df_R - df_F = 1$, so the F has 1 numerator degree of freedom.

Practical Implications

There are two practical implications here of the relationship between the t test and the F test. First, so far in our discussion of contrasts, we have implicitly been conducting two-tailed tests. However, we might very well want to conduct a one-tailed test in certain situations. For example, we might want to test

$$H_0 : \mu_1 \geq \mu_2 \qquad \text{versus} \qquad H_1 : \mu_1 < \mu_2$$

A one-tailed t test is straightforward because tables are readily available (see Appendix Table A.1). If $\alpha = .05$, instead of finding a critical value corresponding to an area of .025 in each tail, we find the critical value that has an area of .05 in the one relevant tail. If $\bar{Y}_1 < \bar{Y}_2$ and the resulting t value exceeds the critical t in absolute value, the null hypothesis is rejected at the .05 level. A one-tailed test can also be performed using F tables. Instead of using the critical F in the .05 table, the critical F is found in the .10 table, although the actual α is .05. If the direction of the difference corresponds to H_1 (here $\bar{Y}_1 < \bar{Y}_2$) and the F exceeds the .10 critical F, the null hypothesis is rejected at the .05 level, one-tailed. Thus, the first practical implication is that researchers can choose between one-tailed and two-tailed tests of contrasts, according to whichever provides a more appropriate test of their theory. Also, either a t test or an F test can be used to perform each type of hypothesis test. The second practical implication is that a t test for testing $H_0 : \mu_1 = \mu_2$ was already developed in Chapter 3. How are the procedures of this chapter different from those of Chapter 3, if they differ at all? First, in the Chapter 3 t test, there were only two groups, whereas in this chapter there are a groups. Hence, testing a contrast such as

$$\tfrac{1}{3}\mu_1 + \tfrac{1}{3}\mu_2 + \tfrac{1}{3}\mu_3 - \mu_4$$

requires the procedures of this chapter. However, what about $\mu_1 - \mu_2$? We could test $H_0 : \mu_1 = \mu_2$ using either the procedures of Chapter 3 or the procedures of this chapter. Although in either case we can perform either a t test or an F test, the results of the Chapter 3 test will be at least somewhat different from those of this chapter. If we compare Equation 17 of this chapter with the procedures of Chapter 3, we see that $E_R - E_F$ is the same for the two approaches. Also, with both approaches, $df_R - df_F = 1$. However, E_F and df_F are not the same in the two approaches. In Chapter 3, E_F was the sum of squared errors for the full model, which was based on the two groups of subjects being compared. However, in this chapter, E_F is based on all a groups, regardless of which groups are being compared in a particular contrast. The same difference exists for the degrees of freedom.

To ensure that this difference is clear, consider the numerical example of Table 4.1 once again. Suppose we want to test $H_0 : \mu_1 = \mu_2$ versus $H_1 : \mu_1 \neq \mu_2$. We saw earlier that using the procedures of this chapter the observed F is 0.32, with 1 and 16 degrees of freedom. However, if we were to use the approach of Chapter 3, the F would be 0.20 with 1 and 8 degrees of freedom. Naturally the question arises as to which approach is better. As it happens, the correct answer to this question is, It depends. Specifically, it depends on the validity of the homogeneity-of-variance assumption. The obvious difference between the two approaches is that in the numerical example the third and fourth groups contribute to E_F for the approach of this chapter but are completely irrelevant for the Chapter 3 approach. At this point, we must ask ourselves whether the third and fourth groups contain information pertinent to the comparison of the first two groups. At first blush, it would seem that if the goal is simply to compare groups 1 and 2, then groups 3 and 4 should be irrelevant. However, if the homogeneity-of-variance assumption is true, all four population variances are equal. Under this condition, E_F/df_F of Chapter 3 and E_F/df_F of this chapter both provide unbiased estimates of the common population variance. However, E_F/df_F of this chapter provides a more precise estimate because it is based on more observations than is E_F/df_F of Chapter 3.

The practical import is that, if the assumption is met, in the long run the average value of the F using the Chapter 3 approach will approximately equal the F of this chapter; however, the F of Chapter 3 will be more variable from sample to sample because it is based on fewer observations, as reflected by its lower denominator degrees of freedom. Inspection of the F table shows that as the denominator degrees of freedom decrease, the critical F required for significance increases. Thus, to obtain a significant result, the F from the Chapter 3 approach must be larger than the F of the approach of this chapter. For this reason, the method of this chapter is more powerful than the method of Chapter 3 when homogeneity of variance holds.

What if the homogeneity-of-variance assumption is not met? After the discussion of robustness of Chapter 3, it would not be surprising to learn that this assumption is not really important for testing contrasts. However, it turns out that the homogeneity assumption is in fact very important for testing contrasts. After some reflection, this should make intuitive sense. For example, if a contrast of the form $\mu_1 - \mu_2$ is tested when $a = 4$ and if the variances of the third and fourth groups are very different from those of the first and second groups, it seems reasonable that information from the third and fourth groups should be ignored. If we mistakenly assume homogeneity of variance, our resulting test may be either too liberal or too conservative. If the within-group population variance of the third and fourth groups is less than that of the first and second groups, MS_W underestimates the actual variability of $\bar{Y}_1 - \bar{Y}_2$. Because MS_W is in the denominator of the F, the observed F value in this situation is on the average larger than it should be; thus, the observed F exceeds the critical F more than 5 percent of the time, creating a liberal test. On the other hand, if the third and fourth groups have larger variances than the first and second groups, just the opposite occurs, and the test is conservative. Although an α level below .05 is not a problem in and of itself, here it is accompanied by lower power, lessening the ability to detect a true difference if one exists.

The problem of testing mean differences when variances are unequal has plagued statisticians for several decades. This problem is often referred to as the "Behrens–Fisher problem" because Behrens and Fisher studied the problem extensively in the 1930s. A number of alternate approaches have been proposed over the years. The approach described here is a generalization of a method derived independently by Welch (1938) and Satterthwaite (1946) as a solution to the Behrens–Fisher problem of testing the difference between two population means when population variances are unequal. The numerator term of the F remains the same as under the homogeneity assumption. However, in the denominator of (37) MS_W is replaced by

$$\text{denom} = \sum_{j=1}^{a} [(c_j^2/n_j)s_j^2] \Big/ \sum_{j=1}^{a} (c_j^2/n_j) \tag{38}$$

where s_j^2 is the unbiased variance estimate for the jth group. The observed test statistic, which is distributed approximately as an F variable, is obtained by dividing the expression in Equation 35 by the expression in Equation 38. This value is compared to a critical F whose numerator degrees of freedom equal 1 and whose denominator degrees of freedom are given by

$$df = \frac{\left(\sum_{j=1}^{a} c_j^2 s_j^2 \big/ n_j \right)^2}{\sum_{j=1}^{a} [(c_j^2 s_j^2/n_j)^2/(n_j - 1)]} \tag{39}$$

The important fact to realize here is that the denominator of the F test is a weighted mean of the sample variances s_j^2 of the a groups, whether the denominator is derived from Equation 38 or is based on MS_W. In other words, in either case, the denominator is of the general form

$$\text{denom} = \left(\sum_{j=1}^{a} w_j s_j^2 \right) \Big/ \sum_{j=1}^{a} w_j \tag{40}$$

However, the two possible denominators differ in the weights w_j to be used because one denominator does not assume homogeneity of variance, whereas the other does. As Equation 38 shows, the denominator when variances are not assumed to be equal is based on weights given by

$$w_j = c_j^2/n_j \tag{41}$$

We can understand the reason for these weights by considering the variance of $\hat{\psi}$. Because $\hat{\psi}$ is defined to be $\hat{\psi} = \sum_{j=1}^{a} c_j \bar{Y}_j$, the variance of $\hat{\psi}$ is given by

$$\text{Var}(\hat{\psi}) = \sum_{j=1}^{a} c_j^2 \text{Var}(\bar{Y}_j)$$

$$= \sum_{j=1}^{a} c_j^2 \sigma_j^2 / n_j$$

We can rewrite this as

$$\text{Var}(\hat{\psi}) = \sum_{j=1}^{a} (c_j^2/n_j)\sigma_j^2,$$

to get an expression that shows that weights of the form (c_j^2/n_j) should be applied to each variance, as claimed in Equation 41. However, because σ_j^2 is unknown, we must estimate it with s_j^2, yielding as an estimate of $\text{Var}(\hat{\psi})$:

$$\text{estimated}\quad \text{Var}(\hat{\psi}) = \sum_{j=1}^{a} (c_j^2/n_j)s_j^2 \tag{42}$$

Notice then that when we divide the numerator of the F (from Equation 35) by the denominator (from Equation 38), we obtain

$$F = \frac{(\hat{\psi})^2 \bigg/ \sum_{j=1}^{a} (c_j^2/n_j)}{\sum_{j=1}^{a} (c_j^2/n_j)s_j^2 \bigg/ \sum_{j=1}^{a} (c_j^2/n_j)}$$

which equals

$$F = \frac{(\hat{\psi})^2}{\sum_{j=1}^{a} (c_j^2/n_j)s_j^2}$$

However, we have just seen from Equation 42 that the denominator here is the estimated variance of $\hat{\psi}$. Thus, effectively, this F statistic is of the form

$$F = \frac{(\hat{\psi})^2}{\text{estimated Var}(\hat{\psi})} \tag{43}$$

where no assumption of equal variances has been made. Equation 43 shows explicitly that the denominator of the F statistic using Equation 38 is the estimated variance of the particular contrast being tested. Notice that each individual contrast is thus allowed to have its own particular variance, in keeping with the desire not to assume equal variances across groups. We encounter this separate variance approach for testing contrasts again when we discuss within-subject designs (i.e., repeated measures designs) in Chapters 11–14.

If we are willing to assume equal variances, the variance of the contrast can be written as $\text{Var}(\hat{\psi}) = \sum_{j=1}^{a} c_j^2 \sigma^2/n_j$. We can factor out σ^2, yielding $\text{Var}(\hat{\psi}) = \sigma^2 \sum_{j=1}^{a} c_j^2/n_j$. Now the problem is that we must estimate the common population variance σ^2. The best estimate is given by MS_W, which equals

$$MS_W = \sum_{j=1}^{a} (n_j - 1)s_j^2 \bigg/ \sum_{j=1}^{a} (n_j - 1)$$

Notice then that MS_W is a special case of Equation 40 where $w_j = n_j - 1$. Thus, both the pooled error term of MS_W and the separate error term of Equation 38 are based on estimating the variance of the contrast to be tested. They differ from one another in how they weight the sample variances of each group.

What are the practical implications of this difference in weighting? When the homogeneity-of-variance assumption is valid, both approaches provide an unbiased estimate of the variance of the contrast. However, the estimate using MS_W is somewhat more efficient, so tests based on MS_W are at least slightly more powerful than tests based on a separate error term. However, when population variances are unequal, only the separate variance approach provides an unbiased estimate of the variance of the contrast to be tested.[5] As a result, tests of contrasts based on MS_W can either be quite liberal or quite conservative, depending on whether MS_W underestimates or overestimates the variance of the particular contrast being tested. For some contrasts, the hypothesis test using MS_W as the error term may have a Type I-error rate badly in excess of .05, whereas for other contrasts, the test may be conservative and hence lack power to detect true mean differences.

Although the separate variance approach provides a tremendous improvement over the traditional one when variances are heterogeneous, it has received little attention to date for a number of reasons. First, in many experimental studies, the homogeneity-of-variance assumption is met reasonably well. Even if the population variances are not literally identical, they are close enough to one another that the traditional approach suffices. However, Wilcox (1987a), who surveyed educational research studies, and Fenstad (1983) argue that large discrepancies in variances are more common than most researchers realize. Second, these approaches are difficult and tedious to implement by hand, as should be obvious from Equation 39. Fortunately, SPSS ONEWAY computes the appropriate statistic, alleviating the need for hand calculations. SAS and BMDP also provide procedures that can be used in the special case of pairwise comparisons. Third, these procedures have been ignored because many researchers mistakenly believe that tests of contrasts are robust to violations of homogeneity of variance. It should be emphasized that, although the omnibus test tends to be robust when sample sizes are equal (as we discussed in Chapter 3 and discuss further in Chapter 15), in general tests of contrasts are *not* robust to heterogeneity even with equal n.

Numerical Example

Although testing contrasts without assuming homogeneity of variance is best done on the computer, we illustrate the calculations behind this approach by using the data in Table 4.1 once again. Recall that Table 4.2 illustrates a test of a pairwise comparison (group 1 versus group 2), and Table 4.3 illustrates a test of a complex comparison (group 4 versus the average of the other three groups). Both of these previous tests assumed homogeneity of variance, as illustrated by the use of MS_W as an error term.

Table 4.4 shows the result of testing each of these contrasts without assuming homogeneity of variance. The pairwise comparison remains nonsignificant, just as

Test of $H_0 : \mu_1 = \mu_2$

$$SS(\psi) = E_R - E_F = (\hat{\psi})^2 \Big/ \sum_{j=1}^{a} (c_j^2/n_j)$$

$$= (94 - 91)^2/[(1/4) + (1/6)]$$

$$= 21.6$$

$$\text{denom} = [(1/4)(67.3) + (1/6)(132.0)]/[(1/4) + (1/6)]$$

$$= 93.18$$

$$F = SS(\psi)/\text{denom}$$

$$= 0.23*$$

$$df = \frac{\{[(1)(67.3)/4] + [(1)(132.0)/6]\}^2}{\dfrac{[(1)(67.3)/4]^2}{3} + \dfrac{[(1)(132.0)/6]^2}{5}}$$

$$= \frac{(16.8 + 22.0)^2}{\dfrac{(16.8)^2}{3} + \dfrac{(22.0)^2}{5}}$$

$$= 7.9$$

Test of $H_0 : 1/3\mu_1 + 1/3\mu_2 + 1/3\mu_3 = \mu_4$

$$SS(\psi) = E_R - E_F = (\hat{\psi})^2 \Big/ \sum_{j=1}^{a} (c_j^2/n_j)$$

$$= [1/3(94 + 91 + 92) - 83]^2/\{[(1/3)^2/4] + [(1/3)^2/6] + [(1/3)^2/5] + [(-1)^2/5]\}$$

$$= 87.11/0.2685$$

$$= 324.44$$

$$\text{denom} = \{[(1/3)^2/4](67.3) + [(1/3)^2/6](132.0) + [(1/3)^2/5](27.5) + [(-1)^2/5](26.5)\}/$$
$$\{[(1/3)^2/4] + [(1/3)^2/6] + [(1/3)^2/5] + [(-1)^2/5]\}$$

$$= 10.225/0.2685$$

$$= 38.08$$

$$F = SS(\psi)/\text{denom}$$

$$= 8.52^\dagger$$

$$df = \frac{[((1/3)^2(67.3)/4) + ((1/3)^2(132.0)/6) + ((1/3)^2(27.5)/5) + ((-1)^2(26.5)/5)]^2}{\dfrac{[(1/3)^2(67.3)/4]^2}{3} + \dfrac{[(1/3)^2(132.0)/6]^2}{5} + \dfrac{[(1/3)^2(27.5)/5]^2}{4} + \dfrac{[(-1)^2(26.5)/5]^2}{4}}$$

$$= \frac{(1.87 + 2.44 + 0.61 + 5.30)^2}{\dfrac{(1.87)^2}{3} + \dfrac{(2.44)^2}{5} + \dfrac{(0.61)^2}{4} + \dfrac{(5.30)^2}{4}}$$

$$= \frac{104.45}{9.47}$$

$$= 11.0$$

*The p value for $F = 0.23$ with 1 and 7.9 degrees of freedom is .64.
†The p value for $F = 8.52$ with 1 and 11.0 degrees of freedom is .01.

it was when homogeneity was assumed (see Table 4.2). Both the observed F and the degrees of freedom for the denominator have decreased for this contrast. As Table 4.4 shows, the complex comparison is again statistically significant, as it was when homogeneity is assumed (see Table 4.3). Interestingly, the observed F value has increased appreciably, from 4.82 to 8.52. As a result, the p value has decreased from .04 to .01. How can this happen if the approach that does not assume homogeneity is more conservative? The answer is that this approach is not necessarily more conservative. The denominator from Equation 38 is smaller than MS_W for some contrasts and larger than MS_W for others. For the contrast of group 4 versus the other three groups, Equation 38 weights group 4 more heavily than each of the other three groups because its contrast coefficient is three times larger than the others. In these particular data, group 4 has a small variance (namely, $s_4^2 = 26.5$), so giving it a larger weight produces a smaller value for the denominator. The smaller number in the denominator yields a larger F value than is obtained with MS_W in the denominator. However, another contrast might show just the opposite pattern. The only sense in which the approach of Equation 38 is necessarily "conservative" is that the denominator degrees of freedom are less than with MS_W. This reflects the fact that when the homogeneity assumption is true, MS_W is a more efficient estimate of the population variance, so a lower critical value can be used. However, when homogeneity fails to hold, only the denominator of Equation 38 yields an accurate test.

TESTING MORE THAN ONE CONTRAST

In most studies, it is rarely the case that an investigator is interested in testing only a single contrast. Instead, there typically are several comparisons of interest. When this is true, a number of questions arise. For example, is there a limit to the number of contrasts that should be tested in a study? Is it permissible to perform multiple tests using an α level of .05 for each? Does it matter whether the contrasts were planned prior to conducting the study or were arrived at after inspecting the data? These and other questions are considered in this section and in Chapter 5.

How Many Contrasts Should Be Tested?

How many contrasts is it reasonable to test in a single study? There is no simple answer to this question because the "correct" number depends on substantive as well as statistical considerations. In some experiments, there may be only a few explicit questions of interest, so only a small number of contrasts will be tested. In other studies, the questions to be addressed may be broader in scope, necessitating the testing of many different contrasts. Thus, the number of contrasts that should be tested depends primarily on the nature of the research endeavor. Nevertheless, there are some statistical considerations that should be remembered when deciding how many contrasts to test. It is to these considerations that we now turn.

A natural place to begin is to consider from a purely mathematical standpoint the number of contrasts that might possibly be tested in a study. Let's consider the simplest case of $a = 3$ (why not $a = 2$?). There are three pairwise contrasts that might be tested:

$$\mu_1 - \mu_2, \quad \mu_1 - \mu_3, \quad \text{and} \quad \mu_2 - \mu_3$$

In addition, various complex comparisons could be tested. For example, possible candidates are

$$\tfrac{1}{2}(\mu_1 + \mu_2) - \mu_3$$
$$\tfrac{1}{2}(\mu_1 + \mu_3) - \mu_2$$
$$\tfrac{1}{2}(\mu_2 + \mu_3) - \mu_1$$

It might seem that this list exhausts the supply of possible contrasts, but this is far from true, at least mathematically. For example, some other possibilities are

$$\tfrac{1}{3}\mu_1 + \tfrac{2}{3}\mu_2 - \mu_3$$
$$\tfrac{4}{5}\mu_1 + \tfrac{1}{5}\mu_2 - \mu_3$$
$$\tfrac{1}{10}\mu_1 + \tfrac{9}{10}\mu_2 - \mu_3$$

and so forth. Some reflection should convince you that the "and so forth" goes on forever. Our only stipulation for a contrast is that the coefficients sum to zero, that is, $\sum c_j = 0$. Mathematically, there are an infinite number of contrasts that satisfy this rule, even when a is as low as 3. In fact, for $a \geq 3$, there are always infinitely many contrasts that might be tested. Of course, not all these tests may answer meaningful questions, but from a purely statistical perspective they are all possible to perform.

It might be suspected that with three groups, some of the information contained in the infinite number of contrasts is redundant, and indeed this is true. We use an example to consider the maximum number of contrasts that might be tested without introducing redundancy when $a = 3$. Suppose that an investigator expresses an interest in the following contrasts:

$$\psi_1 = \mu_1 - \mu_2 \tag{44}$$
$$\psi_2 = \mu_1 - \mu_3$$
$$\psi_3 = \tfrac{1}{2}(\mu_1 + \mu_2) - \mu_3$$

Are these three contrasts providing redundant information? We can see that the answer is Yes by realizing that $\psi_3 = \psi_2 - 1/2\psi_1$. In other words, the value of ψ_3 is completely determined if we already know the values of ψ_1 and ψ_2. In this sense, ψ_3 provides no new information over that contained in ψ_1 and ψ_2. Alternatively, we could say that ψ_1 is redundant with ψ_2 and ψ_3 because $\psi_1 = 2(\psi_2 - \psi_3)$. The basic point here is that once we know the values of any two of the contrasts, the third is determined precisely. It can be shown that in the general case of a groups, there can be no more than $a - 1$ contrasts without introducing redundancy. Indeed, this is one way of conceptualizing why it is that the omnibus test of mean differences between a groups has $a - 1$ numerator degrees of freedom; in a sense, there are $a - 1$ different ways in which the groups might differ.

Linear Independence of Contrasts

In the previous example, we say that the set of three contrasts ψ_1, ψ_2, and ψ_3 is linearly dependent because the set contains redundant information. More formally, a set of contrasts is linearly dependent if it is possible to express at least one member of the set as a linear combination of the other contrasts. Conversely, any set that is not linearly dependent is said to be linearly independent.[6] Notice that this is exactly what we did when we found that ψ_3 was equal to $\psi_2 - 1/2\psi_1$. The concept of linear dependence is important for using some statistical packages such as SPSS MANOVA, BMDP2V, and BMDP4V, for testing the significance of contrasts, because these programs require the user to create a set of $a - 1$ linearly independent contrasts, even if only a single contrast is to be tested. Unfortunately, that all sets of $a - 1$ contrasts are linearly independent is not true. Suppose the following three contrasts are to be tested when $a = 4$:

$$\psi_1 = \mu_1 - \mu_2, \quad \psi_2 = \mu_1 - \mu_3, \quad \text{and} \quad \psi_3 = \mu_2 - \mu_3$$

It is easily verified that $\psi_3 = \psi_2 - \psi_1$, so that the contrasts are linearly dependent, even though there are only three contrasts in the set. This illustration simply serves as a warning that determination of linear indepedence can be complicated, especially for large values of a. The most general procedure for assessing linear independence involves matrix algebra. The interested reader is referred to Kirk (1982) for more detail.

Let's return to our earlier example where $a = 3$. Our three contrasts were

$$\psi_1 = \mu_1 - \mu_2 \qquad \text{(44, repeated)}$$

$$\psi_2 = \mu_1 - \mu_3$$

$$\psi_3 = \tfrac{1}{2}(\mu_1 + \mu_2) - \mu_3$$

Suppose for the moment that we were to limit our tests to ψ_1 and ψ_2, that is, we would simply ignore ψ_3. The contrasts ψ_1 and ψ_2 are not redundant with one another because ψ_2 includes information about μ_3, which is not included in ψ_1. However, a careful examination of the coefficients for ψ_1 and ψ_2 suggests that, although the two contrasts are not completely redundant with one another, there is some overlap in the information they provide because in each case we are comparing the mean of group 1 with the mean of another group. The statistical term for such overlap is *nonorthogonality*. This means that the information in ψ_1 is correlated with the information in ψ_2.

Orthogonality of Contrasts

Two topics demand attention now: First, how can we assess whether two contrasts are orthogonal to one another? Second, what are the implications of orthogonality versus nonorthogonality? The determination of orthogonality is straightforward from the definition, which we now introduce. Suppose that we have two contrasts ψ_1 and ψ_2 such that

$$\psi_1 = \sum c_{1j}\mu_j \qquad \text{and} \qquad \psi_2 = \sum c_{2j}\mu_j$$

(Notice that the coefficients now have two subscripts. The first subscript indexes which contrast the coefficients are for, whereas the second subscript indexes the group. For example, c_{23} would be the coefficient for ψ_2 for the third group.) The two contrasts ψ_1 and ψ_2 are defined as orthogonal when sample sizes are equal if and only if their coefficients satisfy the following property:

$$\sum c_{1j}c_{2j} = 0 \tag{45}$$

When sample sizes are unequal, the orthogonality condition is that

$$\sum c_{1j}c_{2j}/n_j = 0 \tag{46}$$

To ensure understanding of Equation 45, consider the three contrasts of Equation 44. Earlier we argued intuitively that ψ_1 and ψ_2 were nonorthogonal. To see that this is true mathematically, let's apply the definition of Equation 45, assuming equal n. It is helpful first to write out the individual coefficients of each contrast. In this case, we have

$$c_{11} = 1 \qquad c_{12} = -1 \qquad c_{13} = 0$$
$$c_{21} = 1 \qquad c_{22} = 0 \qquad c_{23} = -1$$

According to Equation 45, we now must multiply the ψ_1 coefficients times the ψ_2 coefficients for each group and then sum the products. This yields $(1)(1) + (-1)(0) + (0)(-1) = 1$. The nonzero result means that the contrasts are nonorthogonal.

Consider a second example. Are ψ_1 and ψ_3 of Equation 44 orthogonal? Writing out the coefficients yields

$$c_{11} = 1 \qquad c_{12} = -1 \qquad c_{13} = 0$$
$$c_{31} = 1/2 \qquad c_{32} = 1/2 \qquad c_{33} = -1$$

Multiplying and adding the products results in $(1)(1/2) + (-1)(1/2) + (0)(-1) = 0$. Thus, ψ_1 and ψ_3 are orthogonal to one another.

In the general case of a groups, one might be interested in whether several contrasts considered together are orthogonal. A set of contrasts is orthogonal if and only if every pair of contrasts in the set is orthogonal to one another. Consider an example where $a = 4$, with equal n:

$$\psi_1 = \mu_1 - \mu_2$$
$$\psi_2 = \tfrac{1}{2}(\mu_1 + \mu_2) - \mu_3$$
$$\psi_3 = \tfrac{1}{3}(\mu_1 + \mu_2 + \mu_3) - \mu_4$$

Do these three contrasts form an orthogonal set? To answer this question, we must consider three pairs of contrasts: ψ_1 and ψ_2, ψ_1 and ψ_3, and ψ_2 and ψ_3. Using

Equation 45 shows that ψ_1 and ψ_2 are orthogonal, ψ_1 and ψ_3 are orthogonal, and ψ_2 and ψ_3 are orthogonal. Thus, the three contrasts form an orthogonal set because every pair of contrasts in the set is orthogonal to one another. Notice that it is meaningless to try to apply the condition of Equation 45 to all three contrasts simultaneously. Instead, Equation 45 considers only two contrasts at a time. To evaluate the orthogonality of a set, the equation is applied $C(C-1)/2$ times, where C is the number of contrasts in the set. [The expression $C(C-1)/2$ equals the number of distinct pairs of C objects.]

If a study has a groups, how many contrasts might be in an orthogonal set? It can be proven that there can be at most $a-1$ contrasts in an orthogonal set. In other words, any set with a or more contrasts is by mathematical necessity nonorthogonal. Note carefully that there are many (actually, infinitely many) possible sets of $a-1$ orthogonal contrasts. The limit of $a-1$ pertains to the number of contrasts in a set but says nothing about how many sets of orthogonal contrasts may exist. Recall that we encountered a limit of $a-1$ in our earlier discussion of linear independence. It turns out that orthogonal contrasts are by mathematical necessity linearly independent, so they also must obey this limit. In fact, orthogonal contrasts represent a special case of linear independence. With linearly independent contrasts, we argued that the information gained from the set is nonredundant. When the contrasts are orthogonal as well, the information contained in the contrasts has additional properties that we now consider.

What difference does it make whether contrasts are orthogonal to one another? The primary implication is that orthogonal contrasts provide nonoverlapping information about how the groups differ. More formally, when two contrasts ψ_1 and ψ_2 are orthogonal, the sample estimates (e.g., $\hat{\psi}_1$ and $\hat{\psi}_2$) are statistically independent of one another.[7] In other words, there is no relationship between $\hat{\psi}_1$ and $\hat{\psi}_2$, and in this sense, each provides unique information about group differences.

OPTIONAL

Example of Correlation Between Nonorthogonal Contrasts

We explore this idea more fully with an example using the contrasts of Equation 44. Suppose that unbeknown to us, $\mu_1 = \mu_2 = \mu_3 = 10$. In this case, it follows that $\psi_1 = \psi_2 = \psi_3 = 0$. Although the population means are equal for the three groups, the sample means, of course, vary from group to group and from replication to replication. According to our assumptions, the $\bar{Y}_j$ values are normally distributed across replications. For simplicity in this example, we assume that each $\bar{Y}_j$ can take on only three values: $\mu_j - 2$, μ_j, and $\mu_j + 2$. In effect, we are assuming that the error for a group mean is either -2, 0, or 2 in any sample. We also assume that these three values are equally likely. (Although this assumption for the error term is unrealistic, it makes the implications of orthogonality much easier to show than does the normality assumption.) According to our simple model, then, each $\bar{Y}_j$ is either 8, 10, or 12, and these three values occur equally often. What is the relationship between $\bar{Y}_1$, $\bar{Y}_2$, and $\bar{Y}_3$? They are independent of one another because the three

T A B L E **4.5** Orthogonality

$\bar{Y}_1$	$\bar{Y}_2$	$\bar{Y}_3$	$\hat{\psi}_1$	$\hat{\psi}_2$	$\hat{\psi}_3$
8	8	8	0	0	0
8	8	10	0	-2	-2
8	8	12	0	-4	-4
8	10	8	-2	0	1
8	10	10	-2	-2	-1
8	10	12	-2	-4	-3
8	12	8	-4	0	2
8	12	10	-4	-2	0
8	12	12	-4	-4	-2
10	8	8	2	2	1
10	8	10	2	0	-1
10	8	12	2	-2	-3
10	10	8	0	2	2
10	10	10	0	0	0
10	10	12	0	-2	-2
10	12	8	-2	2	3
10	12	10	-2	0	1
10	12	12	-2	-2	-1
12	8	8	4	4	2
12	8	10	4	2	0
12	8	12	4	0	-2
12	10	8	2	4	3
12	10	10	2	2	1
12	10	12	2	0	-1
12	12	8	0	4	4
12	12	10	0	2	2
12	12	12	0	0	0

groups of subjects are independent. This means, for example, that knowing $\bar{Y}_1 = 8$ says nothing about whether $\bar{Y}_2$ is 8, 10, or 12. The first three columns of Table 4.5 show the 27 possible combinations of $\bar{Y}_1$, $\bar{Y}_2$, and $\bar{Y}_3$ that can occur, given our assumptions. As a result of the independence between groups, each of these 27 combinations is equally likely to occur, that is, each has a probability of 1/27. The next three columns show for each combination of $\bar{Y}_j$ values the resulting values for $\hat{\psi}_1$, $\hat{\psi}_2$, and $\hat{\psi}_3$ where

$$\hat{\psi}_1 = \bar{Y}_1 - \bar{Y}_2$$
$$\hat{\psi}_2 = \bar{Y}_1 - \bar{Y}_3$$
$$\hat{\psi}_3 = \tfrac{1}{2}(\bar{Y}_1 + \bar{Y}_2) - \bar{Y}_3$$

The primary purpose for obtaining the values in Table 4.5 is to investigate the relationships among the different contrasts. Earlier we argued intuitively that ψ_1 and ψ_2 were related to one another. Specifically, it would seem reasonable that if

TABLE 4.6 Contingency Tables Illustrating Relationship of $\hat{\psi}_1$ to $\hat{\psi}_2$ and $\hat{\psi}_1$ to $\hat{\psi}_3$

	$\hat{\psi}_2$				
$\hat{\psi}_1$	−4	−2	0	2	4
4			1	1	1
2		1	2	2	1
0	1	2	3	2	1
−2	1	2	2	1	
−4	1	1	1		

	$\hat{\psi}_3$								
$\hat{\psi}_1$	−4	−3	−2	−1	0	1	2	3	4
4			1		1		1		
2		1		2		2		1	
0	1		2		3		2		1
−2		1		2		2		1	
−4			1		1		1		

$\hat{\psi}_1$ is large, then $\hat{\psi}_2$ would be large also because both involve comparing $\bar{Y}_1$ with another group. This possibility can be explored systematically by forming a contingency table relating the $\hat{\psi}_1$ and $\hat{\psi}_2$ values of Table 4.5. The top half of Table 4.6 is such a contingency table. Each entry in this table equals the number of times that a particular combination of $\hat{\psi}_1$ and $\hat{\psi}_2$ values occurs in Table 4.5. For example, the combination $\hat{\psi}_1 = 4$ and $\hat{\psi}_2 = 4$ occurs once in Table 4.5, while $\hat{\psi}_1 = 0 = \hat{\psi}_2 = 0$ occurs three times. The combination $\hat{\psi}_1 = 4$ and $\hat{\psi}_2 = -4$ never occurs. If we were to divide each entry in the contingency table by 27, the result would be a bivariate probability distribution, but this degree of formality is unnecessary for our purposes. Instead, the important point here is simply that $\hat{\psi}_1$ and $\hat{\psi}_2$ are correlated. Specifically, they are positively correlated because higher values of $\hat{\psi}_1$ tend to be associated with higher values of $\hat{\psi}_2$. Thus, samples where $\hat{\psi}_1$ exceeds zero have a systematic tendency to yield $\hat{\psi}_2$ values that are in excess of zero. Is this also true of ψ_1 and ψ_3? We saw earlier that according to the definition of orthogonality, ψ_1 and ψ_3 are orthogonal. The bottom half of Table 4.6 displays the contingency table for ψ_1 and ψ_3. Are $\hat{\psi}_1$ and $\hat{\psi}_3$ correlated? Can we predict $\hat{\psi}_3$ from $\hat{\psi}_1$ (or vice versa)? Suppose that $\hat{\psi}_1 = 4$. When $\hat{\psi}_1 = 4$, the best guess concerning $\hat{\psi}_3$ is zero, because zero is the mean value of $\hat{\psi}_3$ when $\hat{\psi}_1$ is four. Suppose that $\hat{\psi}_1 = 2$. The best guess for $\hat{\psi}_3$ is still zero. In fact, for any given value of $\hat{\psi}_1$, the best guess for $\hat{\psi}_3$ is zero. Knowledge of

$\hat{\psi}_1$ does not improve prediction of $\hat{\psi}_3$. Thus, $\hat{\psi}_1$ and $\hat{\psi}_3$ are uncorrelated. In this example, $\hat{\psi}_1$ and $\hat{\psi}_3$ are not statistically independent because the errors were distributed as -2, 0, and 2 instead of normally. With normally distributed errors, $\hat{\psi}_1$ and $\hat{\psi}_3$ would have been statistically independent as well as uncorrelated. Thus, orthogonal contrasts possess the beneficial property of being uncorrelated with one another.

Another Look at Nonorthogonal Contrasts: Venn Diagrams

Another property of orthogonal contrasts can best be illustrated by example. Consider the data for three groups in Table 4.7. It can easily be shown that the sum of squares for the test of the omnibus null hypothesis is given by $SS_B = 190$ for these data. Let's reconsider our three contrasts of Equation 44:

$$\psi_1 = \mu_1 - \mu_2$$
$$\psi_2 = \mu_1 - \mu_3$$
$$\psi_3 = \tfrac{1}{2}(\mu_1 + \mu_2) - \mu_3$$

We can test each contrast in turn by forming an appropriate restricted model and comparing its error sum of squares to the error sum of squares of the full model. After some computation, it turns out that

$$SS(\psi_1) = 2.5$$
$$SS(\psi_2) = 160.0$$
$$SS(\psi_3) = 187.5$$

Interestingly enough, the sum of $SS(\psi_1) + SS(\psi_3) = 190$, which was the between-

T A B L E **4. 7** Hypothetical Data for Three Groups

	1	2	3	
	12	10	6	
	10	8	2	
	11	12	3	
	9	14	4	
	13	6	0	
$\bar{Y}_j$	11	10	3	$\bar{Y} = 8$
$\sum_{i=1}^{n_j}(Y_{ij} - \bar{Y}_j)^2$	10	40	20	
$\sum_{i=1}^{n_j}(Y_{ij} - \bar{Y})^2$	55	60	145	

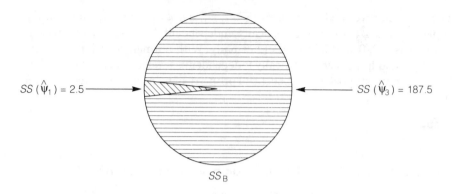

F I G U R E 4. 1   Venn diagram of relationship between $SS(\hat{\psi}_1)$, $SS(\hat{\psi}_2)$, and SS_B.

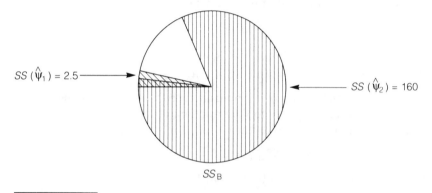

F I G U R E 4. 2   Venn diagram of relationship between $SS(\hat{\psi}_1)$, $SS(\hat{\psi}_2)$, and SS_B.

group sum of squares. As you might suspect, this occurrence is not accidental. Given three groups, two orthogonal contrasts partition the sum of squares between groups, that is, the sum of the sum of squares for the contrasts equals SS_B. More generally, for a groups, $a - 1$ orthogonal contrasts partition the between-group sum of squares. This fact provides another perspective on the unique information provided by each member of a set of orthogonal contrasts. If we decide to test ψ_1 and ψ_3 as given here, then we have completely accounted for all differences between the three groups. In this sense, ψ_1 and ψ_3 together extract all available information concerning group differences. Venn diagrams are sometimes used to depict this situation visually. Figure 4.1 shows how ψ_1 and ψ_3 together account for SS_B, which is represented by the entire circle. On the other hand, suppose we were to test ψ_1 and ψ_2. The sum of $SS(\psi_1)$ and $SS(\psi_2)$ fails to account for all of the between-group sum of squares because these two contrasts are nonorthogonal. Figure 4.2 shows that ψ_1 and ψ_2 overlap. At this point, you might think that the combination of ψ_1 and ψ_2 is inferior to ψ_1 and ψ_3 because 2.5 plus 160 is less than the 190 sum of 2.5 and 187.5. Consider, however, the possibility of testing ψ_2 and ψ_3 together. It would

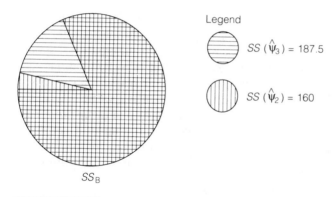

Legend

$SS\,(\hat{\psi}_3) = 187.5$

$SS\,(\hat{\psi}_2) = 160$

SS_B

F I G U R E 4. 3 Venn diagram of relationship between $SS(\hat{\psi}_2)$, $SS(\hat{\psi}_3)$, and SS_B.

seem that these two contrasts, which are nonorthogonal, somehow account for more of a difference between the groups than actually exists. That this is not true can be seen from Figure 4.3. Because ψ_2 and ψ_3 are nonorthogonal, there is substantial overlap in the areas they represent. Thus, they do not account for more between-group variability than exists. This illustrates an important principle: The sums of squares of nonorthogonal contrasts are not additive—for example, the sum of 160 and 187.5 has no meaning here. On the other hand, the sums of squares of orthogonal contrasts can be added to determine the magnitude of the sum of squares they jointly account for.

One additional point concerning orthogonality is of interest. Why is a contrast defined to have the restriction that the sum of its coefficients must equal zero, that is, $\sum_{j=1}^{a} c_j = 0$? The reason for this restriction is that it guarantees that the contrast will be orthogonal to the grand mean μ. Notice that μ is like a contrast in the sense that it is a linear combination of the population means. With equal n for a groups,

$$\mu = \sum_{j=1}^{a} \mu_j/a = \sum_{j=1}^{a} (1/a)\mu_j$$

Consider a general contrast of the form

$$\psi = \sum_{j=1}^{a} c_j\mu_j$$

Is ψ orthogonal to μ? Applying Equation 45 yields

$$(1/a)(c_1) + (1/a)(c_2) + \cdots + (1/a)(c_a)$$

as the sum of the products. Because $1/a$ is a common term, it can be factored out, resulting in

$$(1/a)(c_1 + c_2 + \cdots + c_a),$$

which equals $1/a \sum_{j=1}^{a} c_j$. This must equal zero for ψ to be orthogonal to μ, but we know $\sum_{j=1}^{a} c_j$ does equal zero, given the definition of a contrast. The $\sum_{j=1}^{a} c_j = 0$ condition also can be shown to apply for unequal n, given the more general definition of nonorthogonality. If we allowed contrasts where $\sum_{j=1}^{a} c_j$ was nonzero, such a contrast would not be orthogonal to μ. Why should a contrast be orthogonal to μ? Contrasts are supposed to represent differences between the groups and should thus be insensitive to the mean score averaged over all groups. By requiring that $\sum_{j=1}^{a} c_j = 0$, the information obtained from ψ is independent of the grand mean and hence reflects pure differences between the groups. If a contrast where $\sum_{j=1}^{a} c_j \neq 0$ were allowed, the information would reflect some combination of group differences and the size of the grand mean. For example, consider a four-group problem where the experimenter decides to test a linear combination of population means with coefficients given by $c_1 = 2, c_2 = -1, c_3 = 0$, and $c_4 = 0$. Then ψ can be written as

$$\psi = 2\mu_1 - \mu_2$$

However, we can re-express ψ as

$$\psi = (0.25 + 1.75)\mu_1 + (0.25 - 1.25)\mu_2 + (0.25 - 0.25)\mu_3 + (0.25 - 0.25)\mu_4$$

Rearranging terms yields

$$\psi = (0.25\,\mu_1 + 0.25\,\mu_2 + 0.25\,\mu_3 + 0.25\,\mu_4) + 1.75\,\mu_1 - 1.25\,\mu_2 - 0.25\,\mu_3 - 0.25\,\mu_4$$
$$= \mu + (1.75\,\mu_1 - 1.25\,\mu_2 - 0.25\,\mu_3 - 0.25\,\mu_4)$$

Thus, this linear combination equals the sum of the grand mean and a contrast whose coefficients do sum to zero. Although statistical statements about the population magnitude of this linear combination could be made, the meaning of the results would be uninterpretable.

From the previous discussion, it might seem that researchers who want to test several contrasts involving a groups should be certain that these contrasts form an orthogonal set. However, this viewpoint is overly restrictive. Although there are statistical advantages to forming contrasts in an orthogonal manner, an investigator might nevertheless decide to test contrasts that are nonorthogonal. The reason for such a decision is very simple—when the investigator contemplates all hypotheses of scientific interest, the corresponding contrasts may be nonorthogonal. To answer the questions of interest, these contrasts should be tested. At the same time, the investigator should be aware that he or she is not extracting information on group differences as efficiently as could be done with orthogonal contrasts. Further guidelines for choosing an appropriate set of contrasts to be tested are developed in the next chapter.

EXERCISES

*1. Write out the coefficients for contrasts to be used for testing each of the following hypotheses in a four group study.
   a. $H_0 : \mu_1 = \mu_2$
   b. $H_0 : \mu_1 = .5(\mu_2 + \mu_3)$
   c. $H_0 : \mu_2 = \mu_4$
   d. $H_0 : \mu_4 = 1/3(\mu_1 + \mu_2 + \mu_3)$

2. Which of the contrasts in Exercise 1 are pairwise? Which are complex?

*3. A psychologist collected data for three groups. The sample means are as follows: $\bar{Y}_1 = 12$, $\bar{Y}_2 = 10$, and $\bar{Y}_3 = 6$. The value of MS_W is 25, and there are 10 subjects in each group. The psychologist is interested in comparing the average of the group 1 and 2 means to the group 3 mean.

    a. The psychologist forms a contrast whose coefficients are given by .5, .5, and -1. Test this contrast for statistical significance.

    b. A colleague has suggested that it would be simpler to test a contrast with coefficients of 1, 1, and -2. Does this produce the same result as part a?

    c. What is the relationship between $(\hat{\psi})^2$ of part a and $(\hat{\psi})^2$ of part b? What is the relationship of $\sum_{j=1}^{a} c_j^2$ in part a to $\sum_{j=1}^{a} c_j^2$ in part b? Does this explain why the $\sum c_j^2$ term is needed in Equation 37? Justify your answer.

4. Yet another contrast that might be used in Exercise 3 is one with coefficients of -1, -1, and 2. How does the F value for this contrast compare with the F value obtained in Exercise 3? What general rule does this illustrate?

5. A psychologist conducted a study to compare several treatments for hyperactivity in children. Eleven subjects are randomly assigned to each condition, and the following data are obtained:

Group	Mean	Var(s^2)
Behavior therapy	12	11
Drug therapy	11	8
Placebo	7	12
Waiting list control	6	9

    a. Find the sum of squares for the comparison that contrasts the average of the two therapies with the average of placebo and waiting list.

    b. Test the comparison in part a for statistical significance.

6. A study was conducted to compare four approaches for alleviating agoraphobia: placebo, cognitive, behavioral, and cognitive plus behavioral. The researcher's hypothesis is that the "cognitive plus behavioral" approach will be the most effective of the four approaches. Can a contrast with coefficients of -1, -1, -1, and 3 be used to test this hypothesis? Why or why not?

*7. A graduate student designed her master's thesis study with three groups: a cognitive intervention, a behavioral intervention, and a control group. A total of 50 subjects are randomly assigned to groups: 20 to each intervention and 10 to the control group. The following data are obtained:

	Cognitive	Behavioral	Control
Sample size	20	20	10
Mean	6.0	4.0	3.8
S.D. (s)	3.2	2.9	3.3

    a. Is there a statistically significant difference between the means of the cognitive and the behavioral groups?

    b. Is there a statistically significant difference between the means of the cognitive and the control groups?

    c. Which pair of means is more different—cognitive and behavioral or cognitive and control? How can you reconcile this fact with your answers to parts a and b?

8. A psychologist is planning a three-group study in which he wants to test the following two comparisons: group 1 versus group 3 (ψ_1) and group 2 versus group 3 (ψ_2).

    Sixty subjects are available to participate in the study. His initial thought was to assign 20 subjects at random to each condition. However, after further thought, he has decided to assign twice as many subjects to the third group as to the first two groups because the third group is involved in both comparisons. (Notice that subjects will still be randomly assigned to conditions.) Is this a good idea? To explore the answer to this question, we must consider the variances of the two contrasts. Why the variances? Both sample size–allocation schemes will produce unbiased estimates of the population value ψ of the contrast in question. However, the two schemes will differ in the imprecision— that is, the variance—of the estimate. It can be shown that (assuming homogeneity of variance) the population variance of a contrast is given by $\sigma^2 \sum_{j=1}^{a} c_j^2/n_j$.

    a. Find an expression for the variance of $\hat{\psi}_1$ and $\hat{\psi}_2$ when 20 subjects are assigned to each treatment.

    b. Find an expression for the variance of $\hat{\psi}_1$ and $\hat{\psi}_2$ when 15 subjects are assigned to group 1, 15 to group 2, and 30 to group 3.

    c. Which method of allocating subjects to groups is better for testing ψ_1 and ψ_2 if homogeneity holds?

    d. Will any allocation scheme yield a smaller variance than the two schemes already proposed? Consider the possibility of assigning 18 subjects to group 1, 18 subjects to group 2, and 24 subjects to group 3. Find the variance of $\hat{\psi}_1$ and $\hat{\psi}_2$ and compare your answer to the answers you obtained in parts a and b.

    e. All other things being equal, variance is minimized by assigning an equal number of subjects to each group. How does this help explain why the 18, 18, 24 scheme results in a lower variance than does the 15, 15, 30 scheme?

9. I. B. Normal, a graduate student at Skew U., has conducted a study with four groups. The first three groups are treatment groups, and the fourth group is a control group. The following data are obtained:

Treatment 1	Treatment 2	Treatment 3	Control
9	7	5	4
8	8	7	5
7	7	6	2
10	4	7	7
5	5	4	5
9	5	7	7

    a. Normal's adviser says that the first question Normal should address is whether the mean of the treatment subjects differs from the mean of the control subjects. The adviser tells her to perform a t test comparing the 18 treatment subjects to the 6 control subjects. In other words, the adviser recommends that the three treatment groups be combined into one group, ignoring (for this analysis) the distinction among the three treatment groups. What did Normal find? (HINT: It will be helpful for parts c and d that follow if you analyze these data as a one-way ANOVA, using the principles discussed in Chapter 3.)

    b. Normal was rather disappointed with the result she obtained in part a. Being the obsessive type, she decided also to test a contrast whose coefficients were 1, 1, 1, and -3. What did she find?

    c. Why are the results to parts a and b different? After all, they both compare treatment subjects to control subjects. To see why the results differ, we look at the numerator and the denominator of the F statistic individually. How does the value of the sum of squares for the contrast in part b compare to the value of the sum of squares between groups in part a?

d. How does the value of the within-group sum of squares in part b compare to the value of the within-group sum of squares in part a? Notice that the within-group sum of squares in part b is based on four groups, whereas the within-group sum of squares in part a is based on only two groups. As a consequence, the full model in part b has four parameters to be estimated, whereas the full model in part a has only two parameters.

e. Verify that the following expressions provide the correct sums of squares (within rounding error) for the full models in parts a and b. For part a:

$$E_F = \sum(Y_{ij} - 6.67)^2 + \sum(Y_{ij} - 5)^2$$
$$\quad\quad\quad\text{Treatment}\quad\quad\quad\text{Control}$$
$$\quad\quad\quad\text{subjects}\quad\quad\quad\text{subjects}$$

For part b:

$$E_F = \sum(Y_{ij} - 8)^2 + \sum(Y_{ij} - 6)^2 + \sum(Y_{ij} - 6)^2 + \sum(Y_{ij} - 5)^2$$
$$\quad\quad\text{Group 1}\quad\quad\text{Group 2}\quad\quad\text{Group 3}\quad\quad\text{Group 4}$$

f. The between-group sum of squares for differences among the three treatment groups equals 16 for these data. How does this relate to the difference in the two approaches? Why?

g. Which approach do you think would generally be preferable—that of part a or part b? Why?

*10. The following data are obtained in a four-group study (to be done on computer or by hand).

	1	2	3	4
	3	7	9	11
	4	5	2	7
	5	6	5	11
	5	5	9	7
	3	7	5	4
Mean	4	6	6	8
Var(s^2)	1	1	9	9

This exercise asks you to compare the results of using MS_W to the results of using separate error terms when sample variances differ widely from one another.

a. Test a comparison of group 3 versus group 4, first using MS_W and then using a separate error term. How do the results compare?

b. Test a comparison of group 1 versus group 2, first using MS_W and then using a separate error term. How do the results compare? Do they support the common belief that the use of a separate error term is conservative? Explain your answer.

c. Test a comparison of the average of groups 1 and 2 versus the average of groups 3 and 4, first using MS_W and then using a separate error term. How do the results compare? In interpreting the relationship between the two approaches here, it is helpful to know that the test of an individual comparison is robust to violations of homogeneity of variance with equal n if and only if the absolute values of the coefficients for every group are equal to one another (see Note 5).

11. A psychologist designs a study with four independent groups. However, the number of subjects in each group is very unequal: $n_1 = 10$, $n_2 = 50$, $n_3 = 50$, and $n_4 = 10$. One specific comparison of interest is the contrast of groups 1 and 4. Believing that homogeneity of variance will hold here, he decides to use MS_W as the error term for

his comparison. However, his research assistant argues that even with homogeneity, the data in groups 2 and 3 should be completely ignored because groups 1 and 4 are so much smaller. In other words, the research assistant maintains that the large samples for groups 2 and 3 will make the observed F for comparing groups 1 and 4 much larger than it would be if a separate error term were used (i.e., an error term based just on groups 1 and 4). Thus, even with homogeneity, the test should be based only on the 10 subjects in group 1 and 10 subjects in group 4, to avoid an inflated F from the large sample in groups 2 and 3.

a. Would you expect the observed F to be larger using MS_W instead of a separate error term, if homogeneity holds? Why or why not? (HINT: How would you expect MS_W to compare to the error term given by Equation 38, if homogeneity holds?)

b. How will the critical F based on MS_W compare to the critical F based on a separate error term?

c. Which approach is preferable, if homogeneity holds?

12. Is the following set of contrasts among four groups (i.e., $a = 4$) orthogonal?

	1	2	3	4
ψ_1	1	−1	0	0
ψ_2	1	1	0	−2
ψ_3	1	1	−3	1
ψ_4	0	0	−1	1

Show your work or explain your answer.

13. In a six-group study, an investigator wants to test the following two comparisons:

$$\mu_1 + \mu_2 + \mu_3 - \mu_4 - \mu_5 - \mu_6 \quad \text{and} \quad \mu_1 + \mu_2 - 2\mu_3$$

Construct three additional comparisons that will yield an orthogonal set. Assume equal n.

Extension   Matrix Formulation

The concepts of Chapter 4 can be developed more compactly using matrix algebra. For the purpose of testing the statistical significance of a single contrast, the matrix approach offers little advantage over Equation 4.35. Nevertheless, the matrix algebra approach is presented here for two reasons. First, its flexibility and utility can be illustrated in a relatively straightforward context. Second, we will show that Equation 4.35, which we used to find the sum of squares attributable to a contrast, is in fact derived from the difference between the sums of squared errors of full and restricted models. We will continue to use Equation 4.35 in later chapters because, as the numerical example in Table 4.3 showed, it is much easier to use Equation 4.35 than to find E_R and E_F directly. A primary purpose of this extension is to show that using Equation 4.35 is equivalent to calculating E_R and E_F directly and then forming the difference $E_R - E_F$. Demonstrating this equivalence provides a formal justification for being able to use Equation 4.35 instead of calculating E_R and E_F for testing contrasts.

First, we consider the matrix representation of the null hypothesis to be tested. In scalar notation, the null hypothesis is $\sum_{j=1}^{a} c_j \mu_j = 0$. The a-group means can be represented as an $a \times 1$ vector $\boldsymbol{\mu}$ as follows:

$$\boldsymbol{\mu} = \begin{bmatrix} \mu_1 \\ \mu_2 \\ \vdots \\ \mu_a \end{bmatrix} \tag{E.1}$$

Similarly, the coefficients of the contrast can be represented as a $1 \times a$ vector $\mathbf{c}'$:

$$\mathbf{c}' = [c_1, c_2, \ldots, c_a] \tag{E.2}$$

If the $\boldsymbol{\mu}$ vector is premultiplied by the $\mathbf{c}$ vector, the result is

$$[c_1, c_2, \ldots, c_a] \begin{bmatrix} \mu_1 \\ \mu_2 \\ \vdots \\ \mu_a \end{bmatrix} = c_1 \mu_1 + c_2 \mu_2 + \cdots + c_a \mu_a$$

or

$$\mathbf{c}' \boldsymbol{\mu} = \sum_{j=1}^{a} c_j \mu_j \tag{E.3}$$

Thus, testing that $\sum_{j=1}^{a} c_j \mu_j = 0$ can be rewritten as testing that $\mathbf{c}' \boldsymbol{\mu} = 0$. In matrix notation, the null hypothesis to be tested is

$$H_0 : \mathbf{c}' \boldsymbol{\mu} = 0 \tag{E.4}$$

Next, we consider the matrix representation of the increase in sum of squared errors brought about by the restricted model. We will use $\mathbf{X}$ to represent the $N \times a$ design matrix, which depicts group membership for each subject. (A one in the jth column of the ith row of $\mathbf{X}$ indicates that the ith subject is a member of group j. All other entries are zero.) We will let $\hat{\boldsymbol{\beta}}$ be an $a \times 1$ vector of least-squares parameter estimates, that is, $\hat{\boldsymbol{\beta}}$ is simply a vector of the a sample–group means. Lunneborg and Abbott (1983, p. 198) show that the difference between the sums of squared errors of the restricted and full models can be written as

$$E_R - E_F = (\mathbf{c}' \hat{\boldsymbol{\beta}})'(\mathbf{c}'(\mathbf{X}'\mathbf{X})^{-1}\mathbf{c})^{-1}(\mathbf{c}' \hat{\boldsymbol{\beta}}) \tag{E.5}$$

Although this expression may seem rather imposing, it is actually simple to show that it is equivalent to the scalar expression given by Equation 4.35. Before considering the equivalence mathematically, we return to our earlier numerical example to discover how the matrices in Equation 5 combine in such a way to arrive at the same value as was obtained using Equation 4.35. The next section shows the step-by-step matrix manipulations for testing the null hypothesis

$$H_0 : \tfrac{1}{3}\mu_1 + \tfrac{1}{3}\mu_2 + \tfrac{1}{3}\mu_3 - \mu_4 = 0.$$

Matrix Approach to Numerical Example

Three matrices are involved in Equation 5: $\mathbf{c}$, $\hat{\boldsymbol{\beta}}$, and $\mathbf{X}$. The vector $\mathbf{c}$ is determined by the contrast to be tested. Here, our null hypothesis is

$$\tfrac{1}{3}\mu_1 + \tfrac{1}{3}\mu_2 + \tfrac{1}{3}\mu_3 - \mu_4 = 0,$$

so $\mathbf{c}' = [1/3 \quad 1/3 \quad 1/3 \quad -1]$. $\hat{\boldsymbol{\beta}}$ is a vector of sample means, which here equals

$$\hat{\boldsymbol{\beta}} = \begin{bmatrix} 94.0 \\ 91.0 \\ 92.0 \\ 83.0 \end{bmatrix}$$

$\mathbf{X}$ is the design matrix, which here is given by

$$\mathbf{X} = \begin{bmatrix} 1 & 0 & 0 & 0 \\ 1 & 0 & 0 & 0 \\ 1 & 0 & 0 & 0 \\ 1 & 0 & 0 & 0 \\ 0 & 1 & 0 & 0 \\ 0 & 1 & 0 & 0 \\ 0 & 1 & 0 & 0 \\ 0 & 1 & 0 & 0 \\ 0 & 1 & 0 & 0 \\ 0 & 1 & 0 & 0 \\ 0 & 0 & 1 & 0 \\ 0 & 0 & 1 & 0 \\ 0 & 0 & 1 & 0 \\ 0 & 0 & 1 & 0 \\ 0 & 0 & 1 & 0 \\ 0 & 0 & 0 & 1 \\ 0 & 0 & 0 & 1 \\ 0 & 0 & 0 & 1 \\ 0 & 0 & 0 & 1 \\ 0 & 0 & 0 & 1 \end{bmatrix}$$

Here, we must manipulate the matrices according to the instructions of Equation

5. First, we consider the product $\mathbf{c}'\hat{\boldsymbol{\beta}}$, which is obtained by multiplying $\mathbf{c}'$ times $\hat{\boldsymbol{\beta}}$. The result is simply $(1/3)(94.0) + (1/3)(91.0) + (1/3)(92.0) + (-1)(83.0) = 9.33$. When a row vector is multiplied by a column vector (in this order), the result is just a number (i.e., a scalar). In this case, the number is simply the value of $\hat{\psi}$. The first term on the right side of Equation 5 is $(\mathbf{c}'\hat{\boldsymbol{\beta}})'$, the transpose of $\mathbf{c}'\hat{\boldsymbol{\beta}}$. However, the transpose of a number is just the number itself. (To find the transpose of a matrix, the rows and columns are interchanged. If a number is conceptualized as a 1×1 matrix, interchanging its rows and columns has no effect; we are still left with the same 1×1 matrix. Thus, it is reasonable that the transpose of a number is still just the number.) Hence, $\mathbf{c}'\hat{\boldsymbol{\beta}}$ and $(\mathbf{c}'\hat{\boldsymbol{\beta}})'$ both equal $\hat{\psi}$.

Now we work with the inside expression of Equation 5, that is, $(\mathbf{c}'(\mathbf{X}'\mathbf{X})^{-1}\mathbf{c})^{-1}$. To find the result of these manipulations, we must begin within the inner parentheses and work toward the outside. Therefore, we should first find the product $\mathbf{X}'\mathbf{X}$. If the transpose of $\mathbf{X}$ is multiplied by $\mathbf{X}$, the result is

$$\mathbf{X}'\mathbf{X} = \begin{bmatrix} 4 & 0 & 0 & 0 \\ 0 & 6 & 0 & 0 \\ 0 & 0 & 5 & 0 \\ 0 & 0 & 0 & 5 \end{bmatrix}$$

a diagonal matrix of dimension 4×4 (or in general, $a \times a$). Notice that the diagonal entry in row j and column j equals the number of observations in group j. (In other words, the 4 in row 1 and column 1 means there were four observations in the first group, the 6 in row 2 column 2 means there were six observations in group 2, etc.). The next step is to find the inverse of $(\mathbf{X}'\mathbf{X})$. Fortunately, the inverse of a diagonal matrix is very easy to find—it is another diagonal matrix whose entries are the reciprocals of the original matrix. For our example, then,

$$(\mathbf{X}'\mathbf{X})^{-1} = \begin{bmatrix} 1/4 & 0 & 0 & 0 \\ 0 & 1/6 & 0 & 0 \\ 0 & 0 & 1/5 & 0 \\ 0 & 0 & 0 & 1/5 \end{bmatrix}$$

This matrix must now be premultiplied by $\mathbf{c}'$ and postmultiplied by $\mathbf{c}$. It does not matter whether we premultiply or postmultiply first, so arbitrarily let's premultiply. Then,

$$\mathbf{c}'(\mathbf{X}'\mathbf{X})^{-1} = \begin{bmatrix} 1/3 & 1/3 & 1/3 & -1 \end{bmatrix} \begin{bmatrix} 1/4 & 0 & 0 & 0 \\ 0 & 1/6 & 0 & 0 \\ 0 & 0 & 1/5 & 0 \\ 0 & 0 & 0 & 1/5 \end{bmatrix}$$

$$= \begin{bmatrix} 1/12 & 1/18 & 1/15 & -1/5 \end{bmatrix}$$

Notice that when a 1×4 vector multiplies a 4×4 matrix, the result is a 1×4

vector. Now

$$\mathbf{c}'(\mathbf{X}'\mathbf{X})^{-1}\mathbf{c} = [1/12 \quad 1/18 \quad 1/15 \quad -1/5] \begin{bmatrix} 1/3 \\ 1/3 \\ 1/3 \\ -1 \end{bmatrix}$$

$$= (1/12)(1/3) + (1/18)(1/3) + (1/15)(1/3) + (-1/5)(-1)$$

$$= .2685$$

We saw earlier that $.2685 = \sum_{j=1}^{a} (c_j^2/n_j)$ for our data. In matrix notation, the equivalent expression is $\mathbf{c}'(\mathbf{X}'\mathbf{X})^{-1}\mathbf{c}$ because $(\mathbf{X}'\mathbf{X})^{-1}$ represents $1/n_j$ in its diagonal elements. Equation 5 requires that the inverse of $\mathbf{c}'(\mathbf{X}'\mathbf{X})^{-1}\mathbf{c}$ be found, but the inverse of a number is simply its reciprocal. Thus, we have

$$E_R - E_F = (9.33)(1/.2685)(9.33) = 324.43$$

This figure agrees with the value we reported earlier in Table 4.3.

General Formulation

We have just seen that the matrix calculations of Equation 5 produce the same value of $E_R - E_F$ in our numerical example as we obtained using Equation 4.18. In fact, this equivalence holds for testing any contrast of parameters in a cell means model such as our full model

$$Y_{ij} = \mu_j + \varepsilon_{ij} \qquad \text{(4.2, repeated)}$$

As shown in Equation 5, the increase in sum of squared errors due to a restriction that $\sum_{j=1}^{a} c_j \mu_j = 0$ can be written as

$$E_R - E_F = (\mathbf{c}'\hat{\boldsymbol{\beta}})'(\mathbf{c}'(\mathbf{X}'\mathbf{X})^{-1}\mathbf{c})^{-1}(\mathbf{c}'\hat{\boldsymbol{\beta}}) \qquad \text{(E.5, repeated)}$$

where $\mathbf{c}$ is the vector of contrast coefficients, $\hat{\boldsymbol{\beta}}$ is the vector of sample means, and $\mathbf{X}$ is the design matrix. However, Equation 5 can be greatly simplified in this case. As we saw in the numerical example, the matrix $(\mathbf{X}'\mathbf{X})^{-1}$ is a diagonal matrix whose jth diagonal element is $1/n_j$. Pre- and postmultiplying by the vector of coefficients produces a scalar (i.e., a number) whose value equals $\sum_{j=1}^{a} (c_j^2/n_j)$. It then follows that

$$(\mathbf{c}'(\mathbf{X}'\mathbf{X})^{-1}\mathbf{c})^{-1} = 1 \bigg/ \sum_{j=1}^{a} (c_j^2/n_j) \qquad \text{(E.6)}$$

In addition, $\mathbf{c}'\hat{\boldsymbol{\beta}} = \sum c_j \bar{Y}_j$, so that

$$\mathbf{c}'\hat{\boldsymbol{\beta}} = \hat{\psi} \qquad \text{(E.7)}$$

Substituting Equations 6 and 7 into Equation 5 yields

$$E_R - E_F = (\hat{\psi})' \bigg(1 \bigg/ \sum_{j=1}^{a} c_j^2/n_j \bigg) (\hat{\psi}) \qquad \text{(E.8)}$$

Because all three terms in Equation 8 are numbers (instead of matrices), we can rearrange terms, so that

$$E_R - E_F = (\hat{\psi})^2 \left(1 \bigg/ \sum_{j=1}^{a} c_j^2/n_j \right)$$

$$= (\hat{\psi})^2 \bigg/ \sum_{j=1}^{a} (c_j^2/n_j)$$

However, this is exactly the same expression as Equation 4.35. Thus, Equations 4.35 and 5 are mathematically equivalent for testing a contrast of parameters in a cell means model. For this reason, we can rely on Equation 4.35 when we need to find the sum of squares attributable to a contrast.

5 Testing Several Contrasts: The Multiple-Comparisons Problem

IN CHAPTER 4 YOU learned how to test individual comparisons among means. You were also introduced to the concepts of linear independence and orthogonality. As these two concepts demonstrate, often several contrasts are tested on the same set of data. Linear independence and orthogonality concern the degree of overlap in information obtained from testing several contrasts among a groups. In this chapter, another issue that arises in testing several contrasts is considered.

MULTIPLE COMPARISONS

Experimentwise and Per-Comparison Error Rates

We begin by considering the example from the beginning of the previous chapter, where there are four treatments for hypertension to be compared. Suppose it was decided to test the following three contrasts:

$$\psi_1 = \mu_1 - \mu_2$$
$$\psi_2 = \tfrac{1}{2}(\mu_1 + \mu_2) - \mu_3$$
$$\psi_3 = \tfrac{1}{3}(\mu_1 + \mu_2 + \mu_3) - \mu_4$$

Assuming equal n, these three contrasts form an orthogonal set, as we verified near the end of Chapter 4. Suppose that each of these contrasts is tested using an α level of .05. If the four treatments are in fact equally effective, how likely are we to obtain at least one significant result in our study? In other words, how probable is it that we will make at least one Type I error? The answer is obviously a number greater than .05 because we are performing three different tests at the .05 level. At first glance, the answer might seem to be .05 × 3, or .15. Although .15 is a number we return to momentarily, it is not the answer to this question. Recall from probability theory that probabilities of events cannot be summed unless the events are mutually exclusive, that is, unless the occurrence of one event rules out the occurrence of another. This is not the case here because if the H_0 for ψ_1 is mistakenly rejected, the hypotheses for ψ_2 and ψ_3 might or might not be rejected. It turns out that for orthogonal contrasts, the binomial formula provides an answer to our question:

$$\Pr (\text{at least one Type I error}) = 1 - \Pr (\text{no Type I errors}) \qquad (1)$$
$$= 1 - (1 - \alpha)^C$$

where α is the alpha level for a single contrast and C is the number of contrasts tested. For our example, then, $\alpha = .05$ and $C = 3$. Substituting into Equation 1, we find that the probability of at least one Type I error in our study is .143.

Before we comment further on this number, several comments on Equation 1 are in order. First, the expression $1 - (1 - \alpha)^C$ is obtained from the binomial formula for the probability of at least one success in C trials, when the probability of a success on a single trial is α. It may be necessary to remind oneself that here a "success" is a Type I error. Second, Equation 1 is only appropriate when the C contrasts to be tested form an orthogonal set because the binomial requires an assumption that the C trials be statistically independent. This assumption is not met for nonorthogonal contrasts, so Equation 1 is inappropriate unless the contrasts are orthogonal. Third, strictly speaking, Equation 1 holds only for large n because although the $\hat{\psi}$ values of orthogonal contrasts are uncorrelated, the F tests all use the same denominator term—namely, MS_W, assuming homogeneity of variance. Thus, the F tests are not strictly independent. However, this is a technical point and need not concern us.

Let's return to our value of .143. Remember that this is the probability of committing at least one Type I error in the study. Is this a problem? After all, it seemed that our α level was .05, but now we are saying that our probability of a Type I error is almost three times as large as .05. To clarify this issue, it is helpful to develop some terminology. First, the *error rate per contrast* (α_{PC}), is the probability that a particular contrast will be falsely declared significant. In other words, if a contrast whose true population value is zero were to be tested over and over again in repeated studies, α_{PC} is the proportion of times that the contrast would be found to be statistically significant. Second, the *error rate per experiment* (ERPE) is the expected number of contrasts that will be falsely declared significant in a single experiment. Notice that ERPE is not a probability and in fact can exceed one under some circumstances. Third, the *experimentwise error rate* (α_{EW}) is the probability that one or more contrasts will be falsely declared significant in an experiment. In other words, if an experiment were to be conducted repeatedly, α_{EW} is the proportion of those experiments (in the long run) that would contain at least one Type I error. Fourth, in designs with more than one factor, it is necessary to define yet another error rate, called the *familywise error rate* (α_{FW}). As discussed in more detail in Chapter 7, in multifactor designs, significance tests involving different factors are usually regarded as constituting different families. For this reason, a single experiment may contain several families of tests, in which case α_{FW} and α_{EW} are different. However, in single-factor designs, which is all that we have discussed until now, α_{FW} and α_{EW} are identical, so we will wait until Chapter 7 to discuss familywise error rate.

The distinctions among these three types of error rates (i.e., α_{PC}, α_{EW}, and ERPE) can perhaps best be understood by returning to our example with four groups and three contrasts to be tested. In this example, α_{PC} is equal to .05 because each comparison was tested at an α level of .05. For any single comparison, there is a 5 percent chance of a Type I error. What is the value of ERPE? ERPE will equal .15 because the expected number of Type I errors per contrast is .05 and there are three contrasts tested in the experiment. In general, with C contrasts each tested at an α level of α_{PC}, ERPE equals $C\alpha_{PC}$. Finally, α_{EW} is the probability of at least one Type I error being made in the experiment. Earlier we found that this probability equals .143.

That there are three types of error rates and that each has a different numerical value here poses a problem. Even though the value of .05 is somewhat arbitrary, at least it provides an objective standard for making decisions in most disciplines that employ inferential statistics. So, suppose that we can agree that .05 is the standard we wish to use. The problem that immediately confronts us is, Which error rate should be .05? In our four-group example, α_{PC} was .05, but ERPE and α_{EW} exceeded .05. What if we were to have chosen either ERPE or α_{EW} to be .05? In this case, it turns out that α_{PC} must be less than .05 anytime more than a single contrast is tested in an experiment. Thus, when multiple contrasts are tested, it is impossible to achieve a .05 value for all three types of error. Instead, a decision must be made regarding which type of error is to be controlled at the 5 percent level.

Although this is an issue about which reasonable people may choose to differ, our preference is to control α_{EW} at .05. The basic argument in favor of this approach is that there must be an explicit control on the number of studies in the literature that contain Type I errors. By keeping α_{EW} at .05, the probability of a Type I error occurring anywhere in a given experiment is at most .05. (However, this does not necessarily mean that 5 percent of published findings represent Type I errors. See Greenwald, 1975, for an interesting discussion of this issue.) If, instead, α_{PC} were controlled at .05, studies with multiple contrasts would have a higher Type I–error rate than .05. In this situation, an experimenter could increase his or her chances of obtaining a statistically significant result simply by testing many contrasts. By choosing to set α_{EW} rather than α_{PC} at .05, this problem is avoided. Of course, it might be argued that the structure imposed by a single experiment is rather arbitrary. Miller (1981, pp. 31–32) provides a humorous discussion along these lines:

> Two extremes of behavior are open to anyone involved in statistical inference. A non-multiple comparisonist regards each separate statistical statement as a family, and does not give increased protection to any group of statements through group error rates. At the other extreme is the ultraconservative statistician who has just a single family consisting of every statistical statement he might make during his lifetime. If all statisticians operated in this latter fashion at the 5 percent level, then 95 percent of the world's statisticians would never falsely reject a null hypothesis, and 5 percent would be guilty of some sin against nullity. There are a few statisticians who would adhere to the first principle, but the author has never met one of the latter variety.

Why do you suppose Miller has never met such an ultraconservative statistician—after all, aren't statisticians stereotypically considered to be rather conservative? Suppose there was such a statistician somewhere. Further suppose he or she figures that the total number of statistical hypotheses he or she might test in a lifetime is 1000; this set of 1000 hypotheses then can be thought of as an "experiment" in terms of Type I error. Algebraic manipulation of Equation 1 shows that

$$\alpha_{PC} = 1 - \sqrt[c]{1 - \alpha_{EW}} \qquad (2)$$

for unrelated hypotheses. If for simplicity we assume the 1000 hypothesis tests are independent and that α_{EW} is to be kept at .05, Equation 2 tells us that α_{PC} must be set at .0000513, or essentially, .05 divided by 1000. If you remember that there is an inverse relationship between Type I and Type II errors it should be obvious that in lowering the α level from .05 to .00005, we are inevitably increasing the probability of a Type II error. In other words, if we decide to control α_{EW} rather than α_{PC} at .05, we must set α_{PC} at .00005. As a result, the power to detect real effects (differences) in the population is greatly diminished. The same effect occurs *anytime* we decide to control α_{EW} at .05, although the magnitude of the effect is much weaker when the number of hypotheses in the experiment is not so large. Indeed, in this sense, the decision about controlling α_{EW} or α_{PC} at .05 really involves a trade-off between Type I and Type II errors.

Overview of Techniques

The remainder of the chapter discusses a variety of techniques that have been developed to control α_{EW} at .05. To provide a structure for reading the rest of the chapter, we present a brief overview of the multiple-comparisons procedures we recommend. First, when a researcher plans to test a small number of contrasts based on theoretical hypotheses prior to data collection, a technique known as the Bonferroni adjustment is appropriate. Second, when all pairwise comparisons are of potential interest, Tukey (1953) developed a procedure to maintain α_{EW} at .05. Third, Scheffé's procedure can be used when an investigator decides to test complex comparisons suggested by the data. In other words, Scheffé's method permits "data snooping," so that even after having examined the data, multiple tests can be performed, and α_{EW} will be maintained at .05.

We first consider why it is important whether contrasts to be tested have been selected prior to or after having collected the data. Then we present the Bonferroni, Tukey, and Scheffé procedures. Besides describing the mechanics of how to perform each test, we also develop the logic behind each technique. This discussion of logical underpinnings is especially important because the literature is filled with many more multiple-comparisons procedures than just these three. As a result, you need to understand what it is that these three methods accomplish, which many competing methods do not. To further attain this goal, after presenting the three techniques we recommend, we also briefly discuss liabilities of some of the more popular competitors. Finally, we also present a flowchart (i.e., a decision tree) to help you decide which technique should be used in a particular situation.

Planned Versus Post Hoc Contrasts

As might be expected, controlling α_{EW} at .05 is considerably more difficult than simply deciding to use an α level of .05 for each contrast to be tested. The first step in our task distinguishes between planned and post hoc contrasts. A *planned contrast* is a contrast that the experimenter decided to test prior to any examination of the data. A *post hoc contrast*, on the other hand, is a contrast that the experimenter decided to test only after having observed some or all of the data; for this reason, it is often said that a post hoc contrast is a contrast suggested by the data.

Why is the distinction between planned and post hoc contrasts important? The importance can be illustrated by the following example. Suppose that a researcher obtains the following means in a four-group study: $\bar{Y}_1 = 50$, $\bar{Y}_2 = 44$, $\bar{Y}_3 = 52$, and

$\bar{Y}_4 = 60$. Consider the single contrast $\mu_2 - \mu_4$. There is an important difference between deciding in advance to compare groups 2 and 4 versus deciding after having looked at the data to compare these two groups. The difference can be exemplified most easily by supposing that unbeknown to the researcher all four population means are equal, that is,

$$\mu_1 = \mu_2 = \mu_3 = \mu_4 \tag{3}$$

If the comparison of groups 2 and 4 has been planned and $\alpha_{PC} = .05$ is used, then (in the long run) 5 out of every 100 times the experiment would be conducted, the contrast would be statistically significant, and a Type I error would have been committed. However, suppose that this contrast had not been planned. How would things change? Suppose that the study were repeated, yielding a different set of sample means: $\bar{Y}_1 = 46$, $\bar{Y}_2 = 57$, $\bar{Y}_3 = 49$, and $\bar{Y}_4 = 54$. From inspecting these data, it is doubtful that an experimenter would decide to compare groups 2 and 4. Instead, the data suggest this time that the comparison of groups 1 and 2 should be investigated. In other words, if the contrast to be tested is suggested by the data, it is only natural that the largest difference between means be tested because the usual goal of hypothesis testing is to obtain a statistically significant result. Suppose that a procedure was followed where this largest difference is always tested using an α level of .05 for the contrast. The result would be that the probability of committing a Type I error would greatly exceed .05, especially for large a. The crucial point is that $\bar{Y}_2 - \bar{Y}_4$ has a very different sampling distribution from $\bar{Y}_{max} - \bar{Y}_{min}$, where $\bar{Y}_{max}$ and $\bar{Y}_{min}$ are the largest and smallest sample means, respectively. The critical value of the F distribution that provides an α level of .05 for judging the significance of $\bar{Y}_2 - \bar{Y}_4$ is too small for judging the significance of $\bar{Y}_{max} - \bar{Y}_{min}$. The point of this discussion has simply been to convince you that it matters greatly whether a contrast is planned or has been selected post hoc. We now turn to a consideration of procedures for testing more than one planned comparison in a study. In the following section, we consider how to test post hoc contrasts, where such topics as the sampling distribution of $\bar{Y}_{max} - \bar{Y}_{min}$ become relevant.

MULTIPLE PLANNED COMPARISONS

We illustrate the use of multiple planned comparisons by an example. Consider a four-group study whose purpose is to investigate the effects of strategy training on a memory task for children of two age levels. Independent samples of six-year-olds and eight-year-olds are obtained. One-half of the children in each group are assigned to a strategy-training condition, while the other half receive no training and serve as a control group. The general question of interest concerns the effect of strategy training on mean level of memory task performance for the two age groups.

How should the investigator attempt to answer this question? If the investigator has not planned to compare specific groups prior to collecting data, a test of the omnibus null hypothesis for all four groups could be performed. If the test were nonsignificant, no further tests would be performed; if the test were significant, contrasts suggested by the data might be further tested. While this approach is entirely permissible, we defer discussion of it for the moment. Instead, we discuss an alternative approach whereby the investigator plans to test a number of specific hypotheses instead of the general omnibus hypothesis. For example, suppose that an investigator decides prior to obtaining data that he or she is interested in testing the following contrasts in our four-group study:

$$\psi_1 = \mu_{T6} - \mu_{C6}$$

$$\psi_2 = \mu_{T8} - \mu_{C8}$$

$$\psi_3 = \tfrac{1}{2}(\mu_{T6} + \mu_{C6}) - \tfrac{1}{2}(\mu_{T8} + \mu_{C8})$$

where the first subscript represents treatment (T) or control (C), and the second subscript represents the child's age group (six or eight). The first contrast equals the effect of training for six-year-olds, the second equals the effect for eight-year-olds, and the third equals an age effect averaged over condition. We should hasten to point out that we are not claiming these are the three "correct" contrasts to test. What is "correct" depends on the scientific questions the study is designed to answer. For our purposes, we assume that these three contrasts have been chosen to allow us to address the questions of scientific interest. Keep in mind, however, that a researcher with different goals might formulate a very different set of contrasts. Indeed, even the number of contrasts might be very different from three.

Assuming that these three contrasts have been chosen, how should the investigator proceed? The first step is to compute an F statistic for each contrast. This can be accomplished using any of the approaches described in Chapter 4. For example, if we are willing to assume homogeneity of variance, Equation 4.37 might be used:

$$F = \frac{(\hat{\psi})^2}{MS_W \sum_{j=1}^{a} (c_j^2 / n_j)} \qquad \text{(4.37, repeated)}$$

Suppose that we have done this calculation for our first contrast, and we obtained an F value equal to 4.23. Let's say there were 11 subjects per group, so this F value has associated with it 1 and 40 degrees of freedom. Can we reject the null hypothesis that the population value of the first contrast is zero? If we refer to an F table, the critical F for an α of .05 with 1 and 40 degrees of freedom is 4.08. The observed F exceeds the critical F, which would seem to imply a statistically significant result. However, recall our earlier distinction between α_{PC} and α_{EW}. The procedure that was just described used .05 for α_{PC}. However, earlier we demonstrated that if three orthogonal contrasts (with equal n) are each tested with an α of .05, then $\alpha_{EW} = .143$. In other words, if we test ψ_1, ψ_2, and ψ_3 using $\alpha_{PC} = .05$ for each, there is a 14.3 percent chance of committing at least one Type I error. This seems to defeat the primary purpose behind inferential statistics, namely, to avoid a declaration of a difference between groups (or a relationship between variables) where in fact none exists in the population.

Bonferroni Adjustment

Instead of letting α_{EW} be at the mercy of α_{PC}, it seems reasonable to work backward. In other words, it would be preferable to control α_{EW} at .05, but to accomplish this, α_{PC} would have to be lowered by some amount. The problem is to determine an appropriate value of α_{PC} to result in $\alpha_{EW} = .05$. It turns out that there is a remarkably simple and intuitive solution. In the general case of C hypotheses to be tested, set α_{PC} at .05/C. It can be proven mathematically that with this procedure, α_{EW} will be .05 or less. To use this approach in our current example, α_{PC} would be set equal to .05/3, or .0167. The critical F for $p = .0167$ with 1 and 40 degrees of freedom is 6.25, which is naturally somewhat larger than the value of 4.08 that we found for α_{PC} equal to .05. In fact, we would now judge our observed F of 4.23 to be nonsignificant because it fails to exceed the critical value of 6.25. In an actual study, the second and third contrasts would also be tested for significance. The use of α_{PC} values other than .05 can sometimes be awkward in practice because appropriate tables of the F distribution may be unavailable. There are two possible solutions to this problem. Appendix Table A.3 can be used to find critical values for an F distribution with 1 numerator degree of freedom and an α_{PC} equal to .05/C (two-tailed). Each row of the table represents a particular value for denominator degrees of freedom, and each column represents a value of C. It should be noted that the table only applies to F distributions with 1 numerator degree of freedom. This limitation poses no problem for testing a contrast because such a test has 1 degree of freedom in the numerator; however, there are other procedures similar to the method we discuss that involve more than 1 numerator degree of freedom. Table A.3 could not be used for this situation. Second, if a computer program analyzes your data and if the program provides a p value in the output, the Bonferroni adjustment is extremely easy to apply. All that must be done is to compare the p value from the printout with .05/C because .05/C is the per-comparison α level. The contrast is statistically significant if and only if the p value is below .05/C. Notice that this procedure works as well in the more general case where the numerator degrees of freedom exceed 1.

At this point, more detail for the rationale behind the .05/C adjustment must be provided. The procedure was first applied to the problem of multiple contrasts by Dunn (1961), so the Bonferroni adjustment is also known as Dunn's procedure. She based the procedure on an inequality derived by the Italian mathematician Bonferroni, who proved mathematically that

$$1 - (1 - \alpha)^C \le C\alpha \qquad (4)$$

for any value of C whenever $0 \le \alpha \le 1$. The practical importance of this inequality for us can be seen by realizing that the left-hand side of Equation 4 is identical to the expression in Equation 1. Thus, it is true that

$$\text{Pr (at least one Type I error)} \le C\,\alpha$$

whenever C orthogonal contrasts are each tested at the same α level (indicated simply by α). By setting $\alpha = .05/C$, it follows from Equation 4 that

$$\text{Pr (at least one Type I error)} \le .05 \qquad (5)$$

T A B L E **5. 1** Comparison of
$1 - [1 - (.05/C)]^C$ and .05 for
Orthogonal Contrasts

C	Actual Probability of at Least One Type I Error $1 - [1 - (.05/C)]^C$
1	.050000
2	.049375
3	.049171
4	.049070
5	.049010
⋮	⋮
10	.048889
⋮	⋮
20	.048830
⋮	⋮
50	.048794

Indeed, this is precisely what is done in the Bonferroni approach. Several comments are pertinent here. First, because Equation 4 is an inequality, it might happen that the actual probability of a Type I error is much less than .05 when the Bonferroni adjustment is used. However, for orthogonal contrasts and small values of α, the inequality is for all practical purposes an equality, as Table 5.1 shows. Thus, the adjustment does not result in a conservative test. Second, so far we have only considered orthogonal contrasts. Remember that $1 - (1 - \alpha)^C$ equals the probability of at least one Type I error only for orthogonal contrasts. It turns out that if the set of contrasts is nonorthogonal, the probability of at least one Type I error will always be less than $1 - (1 - \alpha)^C$. Thus, the Bonferroni procedure maintains α_{EW} at .05 for nonorthogonal and for orthogonal contrasts. However, the procedure is somewhat conservative for nonorthogonal contrasts.

A second way of viewing the rationale for the Bonferroni adjustment is in many ways simpler than the first perspective. Recall that in our discussion of error rates we defined the error rate per experiment ERPE to be the expected number of Type I errors in an experiment. If we perform C tests of significance, each at an α value of α_{PC}, then the expected number of Type I errors is simply

$$ERPE = C\, \alpha_{PC} \tag{6}$$

If we choose α_{PC} to equal .05/C, then obviously ERPE will equal .05. As a result, the expected number of Type I errors in an experiment will equal .05, regardless of the number of tests that are performed. What is the relationship between α_{EW} and ERPE? The former equals the proportion of experiments that have Type I errors, whereas the latter equals the number of Type I errors per experiment. In symbols,

$$\alpha_{EW} = \frac{\text{number of experiments with errors}}{\text{number of experiments}} \tag{7}$$

$$\text{ERPE} = \frac{\text{number of errors}}{\text{number of experiments}} \tag{8}$$

Obviously, α_{EW} and ERPE share the same denominator. However, the numerator for α_{EW} is less than or equal to the numerator for ERPE, for the same set of data, because the numerator of Equation 7 is at most 1 per experiment, whereas the numerator of Equation 8 is incremented by 1 or more whenever the numerator of Equation 7 is 1. Thus, it is true that $\alpha_{EW} \leq$ ERPE. We showed a moment ago that the Bonferroni approach yields a value of ERPE equal to .05. Because $\alpha_{EW} \leq$ ERPE, the Bonferroni procedure guarantees that $\alpha_{EW} \leq .05$.

Two other points are worth mentioning. First, in theory the α_{EW} of .05 need not be divided into C equal pieces of .05/C in the Bonferroni method. Instead, it is only necessary that the C α_{PC} values sum to .05. For example, an experimenter testing three contrasts might use α_{PC} values of .03, .01, and .01. This could be done if the first contrast was considered most important. Notice that the larger α value for it would increase the power for detecting an effect, if one exists. However, there is a catch that limits the value of such unequal splitting of α in practice—the choice about how to divide .05 must be made prior to any examination of data. Otherwise, the experimenter could capitalize on chance and obtain statistically significant findings too often. Second, you might wonder why we did not use Equation 2 to find the value of α_{PC} that would keep α_{EW} at .05:

$$\alpha_{PC} = 1 - \sqrt[C]{1 - \alpha_{EW}} \tag{2, repeated}$$

Although we derived this equation for C orthogonal contrasts, Sidak (1967) proved that an inequality similar to Bonferroni's holds in the general case of nonorthogonal or orthogonal contrasts. Specifically, if α_{PC} is set equal to $1 - \sqrt[C]{.95}$, then α_{EW} will be .05 or less. It turns out that Sidak's value of α_{PC} is always slightly higher than the Bonferroni value (for C > 1), so that the Sidak modification is more powerful than the Bonferroni approach. However, the difference in power is very small as long as α_{EW} is low. In addition, the Bonferroni α_{PC} is much easier to calculate. For these reasons, in practice the Bonferroni approach is usually preferable to Sidak's method (for more detail on the Sidak approach, see Kirk, 1982, or Holland and Copenhaver, 1988).

There is a final point regarding planned multiple comparisons that must be mentioned. The procedure we have described guarantees that α_{EW} will be .05 or less regardless of how many contrasts an experimenter plans. Thus, the overall probability of a Type I error being made somewhere in the experiment is the same as it would be if the researcher were to perform a test of the omnibus null hypothesis instead of planned comparisons. In this way, the chances of obtaining statistical significance in a study are not increased simply by performing multiple tests. At the same time, however, there is a penalty imposed on the investigator who plans a large number of contrasts because α_{PC} is set at .05/C. As C increases, it becomes more difficult to detect each individual true effect, all other things being equal. Although the experiment as a whole has an α level of .05, each individual hypothesis is tested at .05/C. It could be argued that this puts each hypothesis test at an unfair disadvantage. Indeed, some behavioral statisticians (e.g., Keppel, 1982; Kirk, 1982) used this line of reasoning for planned contrasts. With their approaches, α_{EW} is allowed to exceed .05 because they allow up to $a - 1$ contrasts to be tested with an α_{PC} level of .05. There is disagreement within this camp about whether the $a - 1$ contrasts must form an orthogonal set in order to set α_{PC} at .05. Although this general approach has some appeal, it nevertheless fails to control α_{EW} at .05. We prefer the Bonferroni approach because it accomplishes this goal.

Modification of the Bonferroni Approach with Unequal Variances

As we discussed in Chapter 4, using MS_W as an error term for testing contrasts is problematic when population variances are unequal. Just as heterogeneous variances affect α_{PC}, they also may affect α_{EW}. However, a rather straightforward solution is available. The Bonferroni procedure is easily modified by using Equations 4.38 and 4.39 when population variances are unequal. As we showed in Chapter 4, the resultant F statistic in this case is given by

$$F = \frac{(\hat{\psi})^2}{\sum_{j=1}^{a} (c_j^2/n_j)s_j^2} \tag{9}$$

and the denominator degrees of freedom equal

$$df = \frac{\left(\sum_{j=1}^{a} c_j^2 s_j^2/n_j\right)^2}{\sum_{j=1}^{a} (c_j^2 s_j^2/n_j)^2/(n_j - 1)} \tag{10}$$

As usual with the Bonferroni adjustment, the obtained p value is then compared to α_{EW}/C (usually .05/C) to assess the statistical significance of the contrast.

PAIRWISE COMPARISONS

Frequently, a researcher decides to consider only pairwise differences between groups. In other words, no complex comparisons will be tested. How can α_{EW} be controlled at .05 in this situation? One possible approach would be to use a Bonferroni adjustment. However, care must be taken in using the proper value of C. Most often, $C = a(a - 1)/2$ for testing pairwise comparisons. The reason is that with a levels of the factor, there are $a(a - 1)/2$ pairs of means that can be compared. Thus, when all pairwise comparisons might be tested, the α_{EW} value of .05 must be divided by $a(a - 1)/2$.

It is important to understand the connection between this section on pairwise comparisons and the previous discussion of planned comparisons. To solidify this connection, suppose that a researcher is conducting a four-group study and is interested for theoretical reasons in comparing the following pairs of means: μ_1 versus μ_2, μ_2 versus μ_3, and μ_3 versus μ_4. As long as these comparisons have been selected prior to collecting data, α_{EW} can be maintained at .05 by using an α_{PC} equal to .05/3. Thus, C = 3 in this situation, even though there are a total of six pairs of means; using C = 3 restricts the investigator to ignore the other three pairs of means, no matter how interesting such differences might appear after having collected data. For example, it would not be permissible to decide after examining data that μ_1 versus μ_4 should also be tested, and then redefine C to equal 4. Similarly, suppose that the investigator originally planned to test all pairwise comparisons, but after looking at data, decided not to test μ_1 versus μ_3 or μ_2 versus μ_4. Again, it would not be legitimate to define C = 4; instead the value of C must be set at 6.

Thus, when a specific subset of mean differences is chosen in advance of collecting data, C equals the number of comparisons in the subset. However, C must be set equal to $a(a - 1)/2$ if any of the following conditions apply:

1. All pairwise comparisons are to be tested.
2. The original intent was to test all pairwise comparisons, but after looking at the data, fewer comparisons are actually tested.
3. The original intent was to test a subset of all possible pairwise comparisons, but after looking at the data, one or more additional pairwise comparisons are also to be tested.

In any case, the Bonferroni adjustment can be used to control α_{EW} when performing pairwise comparisons. However, when one of the three conditions listed above applies, so that C must be set at $a(a - 1)/2$, the Bonferroni approach is usually not as powerful as other special-purpose techniques that have been developed specifically for testing all pairwise comparisons. The technique we generally recommend for testing pairwise comparisons in between-subjects designs was developed by Tukey (1953), and is referred to as Tukey's WSD (or, interchangeably, Tukey's HSD).[1] This technique generally is more powerful than the Bonferroni approach when $C = a(a - 1)/2$, and yet it allows a researcher to test all possible pairwise comparisons and still maintain the α_{EW} level at .05 (or any other desired level).

Tukey's WSD Procedure

Tukey's WSD procedure allows a researcher to perform tests of all possible pairwise comparisons in an experiment and still maintain the α_{EW} level at .05.[2] This control of α_{EW} is accomplished by adopting a critical value appropriate for testing the significance of that pair of means that is found post hoc to yield a larger F value than any other pair of means. To make things concrete, suppose that $a = 3$. In this situation, there are three pairwise comparisons that can be tested:

$$\psi_1 = \mu_1 - \mu_2$$
$$\psi_2 = \mu_1 - \mu_3$$
$$\psi_3 = \mu_2 - \mu_3$$

For the moment, we restrict ourselves to the case of equal n and homogeneity of variance. (Tukey made both of these assumptions in deriving his procedure; in a later section, we consider modifications when either condition is not satisfied.) To test the significance of the three contrasts, Equation 4.24 can be applied three times. With equal n, this yields

$$F_{\psi_1} = \frac{n(\bar{Y}_1 - \bar{Y}_2)^2}{2MS_W}$$

$$F_{\psi_2} = \frac{n(\bar{Y}_1 - \bar{Y}_3)^2}{2MS_W}$$

$$F_{\psi_3} = \frac{n(\bar{Y}_2 - \bar{Y}_3)^2}{2MS_W}$$

It is obvious from these three equations that the largest F value will be obtained for the pair of sample means whose values are most different from one another. In symbols,

$$F_{\text{pairwise maximum}} = \frac{n(\bar{Y}_{\text{max}} - \bar{Y}_{\text{min}})^2}{2MS_W}$$

(Notice that because the difference between means is squared, we could just as well subtract $\bar{Y}_{\text{max}}$ from $\bar{Y}_{\text{min}}$.) How can we achieve our goal of maintaining α_{EW} at .05? If we were to use a single critical value (which we will abbreviate as CV) against which to judge each contrast, there would be a statistically significant result in the experiment if and only if $F_{\text{pairwise maximum}} > CV$. Our goal is that the α_{EW} should be .05, so we need to determine how large CV must be so that $F_{\text{pairwise maximum}}$ will exceed it only 5 percent of the time when the null hypothesis is true. The appropriate value of CV can be found from the sampling distribution of $F_{\text{pairwise maximum}}$, which has been derived mathematically. Specifically, it can be shown that the expression $\sqrt{2F_{\text{pairwise maximum}}}$ has a "studentized range" distribution if all assumptions are met. It is traditional to represent the studentized range with the letter q, so we can write $q = \sqrt{2F_{\text{pairwise maximum}}}$. To obtain an α level of .05, the critical value CV is chosen to be that value in the right tail of the q distribution beyond which lies 5 percent of the area. Appendix Table A.4 presents critical values of the studentized range distribution for both $\alpha = .05$ and $\alpha = .01$. Before we examine this table, we summarize the mechanics of Tukey's procedure. To employ Tukey's method, an observed F is calculated in the usual way for each pairwise contrast. However, instead of comparing this observed F to a critical F value, we take the square root of $2F$ and compare this number to a critical q value. This procedure is repeated for each contrast to be tested.

   To illustrate Tukey's method, we return to the hypothetical data shown earlier in Table 4.7 and reproduced here as Table 5.2. We define the three pairwise comparisons as follows:

$$\psi_1 = \mu_1 - \mu_2$$
$$\psi_2 = \mu_1 - \mu_3$$
$$\psi_3 = \mu_2 - \mu_3$$

TABLE 5.2 Hypothetical Data for Three Groups

	Group			
	1	*2*	*3*	
	12	10	6	
	10	8	2	
	11	12	3	
	9	14	4	
	13	6	0	
$\bar{Y}_j$	11	10	3	$\bar{Y} = 8$
$\sum_{i=1}^{n_j} (Y_{ij} - \bar{Y}_j)^2$	10	40	20	
$\sum_{i=1}^{n_j} (Y_{ij} - \bar{Y})^2$	55	60	145	

By using Equation 4.24 for each contrast, it is easily verified that the observed F values for the three contrasts are 0.43, 27.43, and 21.00, respectively. The next step is to compare $\sqrt{2F}$ to q for each contrast. However, an equivalent and simpler approach is to compare F to $q^2/2$ for each contrast. This will be equivalent because $\sqrt{2F}$ exceeds q if and only if F exceeds $q^2/2$. It is simpler because we only need to transform the one q value from the table instead of transforming the three observed F values. Thus, the next step is to find the appropriate q value in appendix Table A.4. We must know three things to use the table. First is α_{EW}, for which we will use .05 (the table also includes $\alpha_{EW} = .01$). Second is degrees of freedom for the error term, that is, the degrees of freedom for the denominator of the observed F. The error term here is MS_W, which with $n = 5$ and $a = 3$ has 12 df associated with it. Third is the number of groups in the study, that is, a. The critical q is found by looking in the row that corresponds to the appropriate df and α_{EW} and the column that corresponds to a. The entry in the table for $df = 12$, $\alpha_{EW} = .05$, and $a = 3$ is $q = 3.77$. Now we must calculate $q^2/2$, which equals 7.11. Comparing each of the observed F values to 7.11, we learn that the second and third contrasts are statistically significant, whereas the first contrast is not.

As this example demonstrates, what makes Tukey's method different from the previously encountered methods for testing contrasts is the use of a different critical value. Instead of comparing an observed F to a critical F with an α level of .05 or .05/C, the observed F is compared to $q^2/2$. Notice, then, that the observed test statistic itself is unchanged—what has changed is the critical value for assessing significance. As mentioned earlier, this critical value is chosen to maintain α_{EW} at .05.

Table 5.3 illustrates how the use of $q^2/2$ controls α_{EW} at the desired value. The specific values in the table are for $df_{error} = 12$, but the general pattern would hold for other values as well. For the moment, we concentrate on the first two columns of critical values, which show that whenever $a \geq 3$, the critical value for Tukey's method is larger than the critical value that would be used if α_{PC} were set at .05. The

TABLE 5.3 Comparison of Corresponding Per-Comparison, Tukey, and Bonferroni Critical Values for Testing All Pairwise Comparisons with $df_{error} = 12$

Number of Groups	Critical Value		
	Per-Comparison	Tukey	Bonferroni
2	4.75	4.75	4.75
3	4.75	7.14	7.73
4	4.75	8.78	9.92
5	4.75	10.17	11.76
6	4.75	11.33	13.32

table also shows that the Tukey critical value increases dramatically as a increases. This is not surprising because the rationale for Tukey's approach is that $F_{pairwise\ maximum}$ exceeds the Tukey critical value only 5 percent of the time. As a increases, there are more pairs of groups to be contrasted, so that $F_{pairwise\ maximum}$ tends to be larger in the long run. (Of course, it is also true that in Table 5.3, the degrees of freedom for error is 12 regardless of a; as a increases, there are necessarily fewer subjects per group.) For this reason, the Tukey critical value is larger for higher values of a. In this way, α_{EW} is maintained at .05. A necessary consequence is that implicitly α_{PC} is less than .05 whenever $a > 2$ for Tukey's method.

This leads us to a comparison of the second and third columns of critical values. Suppose that an investigator plans to test all $a(a-1)/2$ pairwise contrasts in an a-group study. From our earlier discussion, it would seem that the Bonferroni adjustment could be applied, in which case the third column displays the appropriate critical values. In the four cases where $a > 2$, the Bonferroni critical value is larger than the Tukey critical value. The smaller critical value for Tukey's method illustrates the point made earlier that Tukey's WSD is more powerful than the Bonferroni procedure for testing all pairwise comparisons. Although both procedures are guaranteed to control α_{EW} at the desired level (as long as necessary statistical assumptions are met), Tukey's technique is preferable in between-subjects designs because it is more powerful. However, we will see in Chapter 13 that the Bonferroni approach may be preferable to Tukey's WSD in within-subjects designs because of the restrictive assumptions required by the WSD approach in such designs.

So far the presentation of Tukey's method has been restricted to the equal sample size, equal variance condition. We now discuss modifications that can be employed when either or both of these conditions fail to hold.

Modifications of Tukey's WSD

Consider an experiment where the sample sizes of the various groups are unequal, but homogeneity of variance is assumed. The recommended procedure to employ here was developed by Kramer (1956). Recall that we developed Tukey's procedure using Equation 4.24, which is a special case of Equation 4.23 to be used only when $n_1 = n_2$. Kramer's approach for unequal n is simply to compute the observed F using the general form of Equation 4.23 that allows for unequal n. In other words, the F is calculated in exactly the same way as it was calculated for planned contrasts with unequal n. As with Tukey's approach, the observed F for each contrast is compared to a critical value given by $q^2/2$, where q is found in Appendix Table A.4, using the appropriate α, a, and degrees of freedom for error.

When population variances are unequal, the situation is considerably more complicated. As we discussed in Chapter 4, procedures using Equation 4.23 are not robust to violations of homogeneity of variance, so neither Tukey's procedure nor the Kramer modification is appropriate when variances are heterogeneous. A number of modifications of these procedures, which involve different formulas for calculating an observed F value and for calculating a critical value, have been suggested. Our recommendation is based on a synthesis of findings reported in Games, Keselman, and Rogan (1981), Hochberg and Tamhane (1987), and Wilcox (1987b). When a researcher is unwilling to assume homogeneity of variance, the observed F statistic for comparing groups g and h should be calculated as

$$F = \frac{(\bar{Y}_g - \bar{Y}_h)^2}{\dfrac{s_g^2}{n_g} + \dfrac{s_h^2}{n_h}} \tag{11}$$

where the g and h subscripts refer to the two groups involved in the specific comparison. This expression for the F statistic is simply a special case of the more general formula developed in Chapter 4 for dealing with heterogeneity (also see Equation 5.9). Similarly, the appropriate degrees of freedom in this special case can be written as

$$df = \frac{(s_g^2/n_g + s_h^2/n_h)^2}{s_g^4/n_g^2(n_g - 1) + s_h^4/n_h^2(n_h - 1)} \tag{12}$$

Fortunately, current versions of widely distributed statistical packages calculate a t-statistic analog to Equations 11 and 12. In other words, they calculate the square root of the F in Equation 11; the degrees of freedom are the same for the F and the t statistics. For example, these values are obtained from the separate variance estimate calculations in SPSS-X T-TEST and SPSS-X ONEWAY, from the unequal variances calculation in SAS PROC TTEST, and the separate calculations in BMDP3D.

Once the observed t (or F) has been obtained, it must be compared to a critical value. Statisticians have proposed numerous critical values as possibilities here. Current evidence suggests that when sample sizes are small (i.e., fewer than 50 per group), a critical value suggested by Dunnett is most appropriate. For larger samples, a different critical value suggested by Games and Howell is better. Dunnett's procedure, which is called Dunnett's T3 (the T comes from a statistician named Tamhane, who developed the predecessor to T3), is based on the studentized maximum modulus distribution.[3] The observed t statistic is compared to a critical value V obtained from Appendix Table A.5. (Alternatively, F can be compared to

V squared.) The columns of Table A.5. correspond to the number of groups,[4] and the rows correspond to degrees of freedom calculated from Equation 12. When the observed t exceeds the critical V, the contrast is statistically significant.

For larger samples, we recommend a procedure suggested by Games and Howell (1976). To use their procedure, the observed t statistic is compared to $q/\sqrt{2}$ (or equivalently, F is compared to $q^2/2$), where the degrees of freedom for the studentized range again come from Equation 12. If the observed t exceeds $q/\sqrt{2}$, the contrast is statistically significant. The reason Dunnett's T3 is recommended instead of the Games–Howell procedure for smaller sample sizes is that Dunnett (1980) found that the Games–Howell approach becomes slightly liberal (i.e., α_{EW} is slightly above .05) when sample sizes are small.

POST HOC COMPLEX COMPARISONS

The previous section provides a method for maintaining α_{EW} at .05 when all pairwise contrasts are tested. Now the Scheffé method is introduced to maintain α_{EW} at .05 when at least some of the contrasts to be tested are complex and suggested by the data. Although in many situations the data may suggest that a researcher compare all pairs of groups, there are times when other comparisons may also be of interest, as we saw in the hypertension example of Chapter 4. To consider another such example, suppose that the effects of different dosage levels of a drug on some aspect of behavior are being investigated. A researcher might conduct a three-group study, where the groups are defined by the dosage level they receive, say 1 mL, 2 mL, or 3 mL. Assume that on examination of the data, the intermediate dosage seems to be most effective. Then, one contrast of interest might be

$$\psi_1 = \tfrac{1}{2}(\mu_1 + \mu_3) - \mu_2$$

to see whether the average of the effects of 1 and 3 mL equals the effect of 2 mL. Suppose that the researcher also wants to test the three pairwise contrasts

$$\psi_2 = \mu_1 - \mu_2$$

$$\psi_3 = \mu_1 - \mu_3$$

$$\psi_4 = \mu_2 - \mu_3$$

Although it would be possible to use the Bonferroni approach if these are planned contrasts, we assume for the moment that they have instead been formed post hoc. After developing an appropriate technique for testing these contrasts post hoc, we return to the planned versus post hoc distinction.

If these four contrasts are to be tested post hoc, neither the Bonferroni nor the Tukey method is appropriate. The Bonferroni method is not applicable because these particular contrasts were not selected prior to examining the data. Thus, it would be incorrect to set C equal to 4 and use the Bonferroni adjustment with $\alpha_{PC} = .05/4$. Tukey's method is not applicable either: not all the contrasts are pairwise because ψ_1 involves three groups. We now turn to Scheffé's approach for a method that allows all four contrasts to be tested post hoc and yet keep α_{EW} at .05.

Our presentation of the logic underlying Scheffé's method is similar to the presentation of the rationale for Tukey's method. Recall that for Tukey's approach, we considered the sampling distribution of $F_{pairwise\ maximum}$. Now, however, we do not want to restrict ourselves to only pairwise contrasts. The logic of Scheffé's method is to consider the sampling distribution of $F_{maximum}$, which represents the largest possible F value for any contrast in the data, either pairwise or complex. Although finding this distribution would seem to be an extremely difficult task, it actually becomes rather easy with a few additional facts at our disposal.

Proof That $SS_{max} = SS_B$

We detour momentarily to develop these facts. Recall that we are interested in finding the sampling distribution of $F_{maximum}$. Notice that the contrast that produces the largest F value is whatever contrast yields the largest sum of squares because the F value is simply the sum of squares divided by mean square within, that is,

$$F_\psi = SS_\psi / MS_W.$$

It then follows that

$$F_{maximum} = SS_{max}/MS_W \tag{13}$$

where SS_{max} is the sum of squares of the contrast with the largest sum of squares. We now show that for any set of data, SS_{max} equals the between groups sum of squares SS_B.

First, we must convince you that the sum of squares for a contrast must always be less than or equal to the between group sum of squares, that is,

$$SS_\psi \leq SS_B \tag{14}$$

This must be true because of the models on which these sums of squares are based. To see why, consider the following three models:

$$\text{I} \qquad Y_{ij} = \mu_j + \varepsilon_{ij}$$

$$\text{II} \qquad Y_{ij} = \mu_j + \varepsilon_{ij} \qquad \text{where } \sum c_j \mu_j = 0, \text{ and}$$

$$\text{III} \qquad Y_{ij} = \mu + \varepsilon_{ij}$$

The between-group sum of squares is defined to be the difference between the sum of squared errors of Models III and I:

$$SS_B = E_{III} - E_I \tag{15}$$

Similarly, the sum of squares for a contrast equals the difference between the sum of squared errors of Models II and I:

$$SS_\psi = E_{II} - E_I \tag{16}$$

The crucial point here is that the sum of squared errors of Model III has to be at least as large as the sum of squared errors of Model II:

$$E_{II} \le E_{III} \tag{17}$$

Equation 17 is necessarily true because Model III is a more restricted model than Model II.[5] If we subtract E_I from both sides of Equation 17, the result is

$$E_{II} - E_I \le E_{III} - E_I \tag{18}$$

However, from Equation 15,

$$SS_B = E_{III} - E_I \tag{15, repeated}$$

and from Equation 16,

$$SS_\psi = E_{II} - E_I \tag{16, repeated}$$

Substituting these expressions into Equation 18 yields

$$SS_\psi \le SS_B \tag{14, repeated}$$

which is what we were seeking to prove. Thus, it follows that no contrast can have a sum of squares larger than the between-group sum of squares, implying that

$$SS_{max} \le SS_B \tag{19}$$

The final step in this argument is to show that it is always possible (after obtaining the data) to find a contrast whose sum of squares will equal SS_B. This is accomplished by defining contrast coefficients to be equal to (or proportional to) the weighted deviations of each group mean from the grand mean, where the weights for the deviations are given by the sample sizes of the groups. In other words, the contrast whose sum of squares equals SS_B has coefficients of the form

$$c_j = n_j(\bar{Y}_j - \bar{Y}) \tag{20}$$

For any sample data, the contrast whose coefficients are defined as in Equation 20 will have a sum of squares equal to SS_B.[6] This contrast is then necessarily the contrast with the largest possible sum of squares because we saw earlier from Equation 19 that

$$SS_{max} \le SS_B \tag{19, repeated}$$

However, as proved in Footnote 6, there is always a contrast whose sum of squares equals SS_B. Combining these two facts allows us to amend Equation 19. We can now say that

$$SS_{max} = SS_B \tag{21}$$

Earlier, we argued that

$$F_{maximum} = SS_{max}/MS_W \tag{13, repeated}$$

Substituting Equation 21 into Equation 13 yields

$$F_{maximum} = SS_B/MS_W \tag{22}$$

Thus, for a given set of data, the largest F value for a contrast always equals SS_B/MS_W.

Remember that the task at hand was to find the sampling distribution of $F_{maximum}$. This is made simple now that we know $F_{maximum} = SS_B/MS_W$ because we can rewrite this as

$$F_{maximum} = (a - 1)MS_B/MS_W \tag{23}$$

because $SS_B = (a - 1)MS_B$. However, if all necessary assumptions are met, MS_B/MS_W is distributed as an F variable with $a - 1$ and $N - a$ degrees of freedom under the null hypothesis. It follows that $F_{maximum}$ is simply distributed as $(a - 1)$ times such an F variable. Therefore, even if the omnibus null hypothesis is true, so every contrast has a population value of zero, $F_{maximum}$ exceeds

$$(a - 1)F_{.05;a-1,N-a} \tag{24}$$

only 5 percent of the time. By using $(a - 1)F_{.05;a-1,N-a}$ as a critical value against which to judge the significance of a contrast, we guarantee ourselves of maintaining α_{EW} at .05, regardless of how many contrasts we test, even after having looked at the data. (Of course, as always, the necessary assumptions must be met in order for the actual α level to equal the nominal value.) Notice that once again in order to use the Scheffé method, the observed F value is calculated from Equation 4.37 (or one of its equivalent forms). What distinguishes this method from the other multiple-comparisons procedures is the use of Equation 24 for the critical value.

A nice feature of Scheffé's method is that it has a direct correspondence to the test of the omnibus null hypothesis. Remember that the omnibus null hypothesis will be rejected if and only if

$$MS_B/MS_W > F_{.05;a-1,N-a} \tag{25}$$

Suppose that we were to test the contrast corresponding to $F_{maximum}$ with Scheffé's approach. Recall that $F_{maximum} = (a - 1)MS_B/MS_W$. The critical value for Scheffé is $(a - 1)F_{.05;a-1,N-a}$.

This contrast is judged to be statistically significant if and only if its observed F value exceeds the Scheffé critical value, that is, if and only if

$$F_{maximum} > (a - 1)F_{.05;a-1,N-a} \tag{26}$$

However, from Equation 23,

$$F_{maximum} = (a - 1)MS_B/MS_W \tag{23, repeated}$$

Substituting this result into Equation 26, we see that the contrast is significant if and only if

$$(a - 1)MS_B/MS_W > (a - 1)F_{.05;a-1,N-a}$$

However, we can cancel the $(a - 1)$ terms, implying that the contrast is significant if and only if

$$MS_B/MS_W > F_{.05;a-1,N-a}$$

However, this repeats Equation 25, which is the condition under which the omnibus null hypothesis is rejected. Thus, the maximum contrast is statistically significant by Scheffé's method if and only if the omnibus null hypothesis is rejected.

Thus, if the omnibus null hypothesis is rejected, at least one contrast exists that is significant by Scheffé's method (namely, the contrast corresponding to $F_{maximum}$). Conversely, if the omnibus null hypothesis is not rejected, it is impossible to find a significant contrast using Scheffé's method. All this should seem eminently reasonable. After all, if we declare the means to be different from one another, we should be able to specify how they are different. On the other hand, if we declare them to be the same, it makes no sense to turn around and say how they are different. Although this is indeed reasonable, not all multiple-comparison procedures share this property. For example, with Tukey's method, inconsistencies can occur. It is possible to reject the omnibus null hypothesis and yet reject none of the pairwise differences. The opposite can also occur—it is possible to reject one or more of the pairwise contrasts although the omnibus null hypothesis cannot be rejected.

Comparison of Scheffé to Bonferroni and Tukey

Scheffé's method is very useful in that it allows the researcher to test literally any contrast that may be suggested by the data. Because the critical value is based on the sampling distribution of $F_{maximum}$, all possible contrasts could be tested for an experiment, and α_{EW} would still be maintained at .05. As we have noted before, the number of contrasts that may be tested is infinite. Although many of these may have little or no scientific meaning, they can all be tested for significance with Scheffé's method. On the other hand, what if we are really interested in testing just a few of these contrasts? In this situation, the Scheffé method is typically quite conservative, in that the actual α_{EW} for the few contrasts we actually test may be considerably less than the .05 that would result from testing all possible contrasts. Indeed, this points out the advantage of planned contrasts. If the experimenter plans the contrasts prior to the study and if the number of contrasts to be tested is relatively small, the Bonferroni critical value will be less than the Scheffé critical value, so the Bonferroni approach will be more powerful. Table 5.4 illustrates this point where $a = 4$ and $df_{error} = 30$. From the table, we can see that as many as eight planned comparisons could be tested and still use a lower critical value with the Bonferroni than with the Scheffé. Only an investigator who might be interested in more than eight contrasts among the four groups would find the Scheffé method superior.

Table 5.5 provides a more complete view of the choice between Bonferroni and Scheffé. Each entry in the table is the maximum number of contrasts that could be planned and still have the Bonferroni critical value less than the Scheffé. The entries are a function of a and df_{error}. Notice that the entry for $a = 4$ and $df_{error} = 30$ is 8, agreeing with Table 5.4. This table is useful for helping decide whether you should perform planned contrasts or use the Scheffé method for testing your contrasts post hoc. If the number of contrasts you might conceivably test is less than or equal to the number in Table 5.5 for your values of a and df_{error}, the Bonferroni approach is better. On the other hand, if you might test more contrasts than the number in the table, Scheffé's method is better, even if all the contrasts are planned. In the face of this discussion of how the Bonferroni and Scheffé techniques compare, do not forget Tukey's method.

TABLE 5.4 Comparison of
Bonferroni and Scheffé Critical
Values for $a = 4$ and $df_{error} = 30$

C	Bonferroni	Scheffé
	$F_{.05/C; 1, 30}$	$3F_{.05; 3, 30}$
1	4.17	8.76
2	5.57	8.76
3	6.45	8.76
4	7.08	8.76
5	7.56	8.76
6	8.01	8.76
7	8.35	8.76
8	8.64	8.76
9	8.94	8.76
10	9.18	8.76

TABLE 5.5 Maximum Number of Contrasts That Should Be
Tested in a Study with the Bonferroni Approach

	Number of Groups							
df_{error}	3	4	5	6	7	8	9	10
5	2	4	8	12	17	24	31	40
6	2	5	9	14	21	30	41	55
7	2	5	10	16	25	37	52	71
8	2	6	11	18	29	44	64	89
9	2	6	12	20	33	51	75	107
10	2	6	12	22	37	58	87	127
12	3	7	13	25	43	70	110	166
14	3	7	14	28	49	82	132	205
16	3	7	15	30	54	93	153	243
18	3	7	16	32	58	103	173	281
20	3	7	17	33	63	112	191	316
30	3	8	18	39	78	147	267	470
40	3	8	20	43	87	170	320	586
50	3	8	20	45	94	187	360	674
60	3	8	21	47	98	199	390	743
70	3	9	21	48	102	209	414	799
80	3	9	21	49	105	217	433	844
90	3	9	22	50	107	223	449	882
100	3	9	22	50	109	228	462	913
110	3	9	22	51	111	232	473	941
120	3	9	22	51	112	236	483	964

We saw earlier that Tukey's method is generally superior to the Bonferroni for testing all pairwise contrasts. The Scheffé is even less appropriate. Notice that almost all values in Table 5.5 exceed $a(a - 1)/2$ (the number of pairwise contrasts), indicating that the Bonferroni is almost always better than the Scheffé for this number of contrasts. But we have already seen that Tukey is superior to Bonferroni here; Tukey is also superior to Scheffé for this purpose. Thus, using Scheffé's method to test pairwise comparisons sacrifices power. Scheffé's method should not be used unless at least one of the comparisons to be tested is complex.

Modifications of Scheffé's Method

When population variances are unequal, it may be desirable to use a separate variances modification of Scheffé's method for testing comparisons. Such a modification was proposed by Brown and Forsythe (1974). Several simulation studies have suggested that their modification successfully controls α_{EW} when variances are heterogeneous.[7]

The Brown–Forsythe procedure is based on the same F statistic we have repeatedly seen previously when a separate variances approach is taken. Specifically, an observed F is calculated as

$$F = \frac{(\hat{\psi})^2}{\sum_{j=1}^{a} (c_j^2/n_j)s_j^2} \qquad \text{(9, repeated)}$$

The denominator degrees of freedom are given by

$$df = \frac{\left(\sum_{j=1}^{a} c_j^2 s_j^2/n_j\right)^2}{\sum_{j=1}^{a} (c_j^2 s_j^2/n_j)^2/(n_j - 1)} \qquad \text{(10, repeated)}$$

The observed F from Equation 9 is compared to a critical F equal to $(a - 1)F_{.05;a-1,df}$.

Notice that this is the same critical F as used in Scheffé's method (see Equation 24), except that the denominator degrees of freedom are given by Equation 10 instead of simply being equal to $N - a$.

OTHER MULTIPLE-COMPARISON PROCEDURES

Although the Bonferroni, Tukey, and Scheffé multiple-comparison procedures are probably the most widely used and most generally appropriate techniques, they are far from the only ones that have been developed. Without making any attempt to be exhaustive, we introduce three other techniques. The first, Dunnett's procedure, is particularly useful when one of the groups in a study is a control group.

The second and third methods, Fisher's LSD and the Newman–Keuls procedure, are presented because they appear frequently in the behavioral sciences literature. However, we argue against their use because they may not maintain control of the α_{EW} level. Nevertheless, we present both of these methods in some detail, so that you can understand our objection to them and thus evaluate their appropriateness when you encounter them in the literature.

Dunnett's Procedure

In some studies, the primary tests of interest may involve comparing one of the groups with each of the other $a - 1$ groups individually. For example, a researcher might plan to compare each of $a - 1$ different treatments with a control group. Although the Bonferroni procedure could be used, Dunnett (1955) developed a test that is more powerful in this situation, which is often referred to as "many-one" testing because many groups are each compared to one other group. (Do *not* confuse this procedure with Dunnett's T3, which is an entirely different procedure we presented earlier for performing pairwise comparisons with unequal variances.) There is no change in the calculation of the observed F test statistic for Dunnett's procedure. As in the methods previously encountered, however, the critical value is altered to maintain the α_{EW} level at .05. Appendix Tables A.6 and A.7 provide the necessary critical values for two-tailed and one-tailed tests, respectively. The columns of the table correspond to the number of groups, including the control group. The entry in the table must be squared to establish a critical value for the F statistic. In other words, the entries in the table are critical t values against which to judge an observed t statistic.

Fisher's LSD (Protected *t*)

Another approach to multiple comparisons was developed by Fisher (1935) and is known as Fisher's Least Significant Difference (LSD) method or, equivalently, as the protected *t*-test method. Although this technique was developed nearly 20 years earlier than the other multiple-comparison methods described in this chapter, it is still in use today, partly because of its simplicity. The test proceeds in two stages. First, the omnibus null hypothesis is tested. If it is not rejected, no further tests are performed; if it is rejected, the process continues to the second stage. At this stage, individual contrasts among the groups are tested using an α_{PC} level of .05 for each contrast. Traditionally, only pairwise contrasts are tested in the second step (Fisher developed the procedure for this purpose), but as Keppel (1982) points out, the logic of the procedure does not rule out complex comparisons as well in the second stage. The LSD has another advantage besides its simplicity—the critical values at the second stage are less than those for the Bonferroni, Tukey, or Scheffé methods. This is true because the LSD uses an α_{PC} of .05, whereas the others use an α_{EW} of .05. The implication is that the LSD has more power to detect true differences. You may be thinking that this is an unfair comparison, however, because the objective of a multiple-comparisons procedure is to control α_{EW} at .05.

We now consider whether the LSD succeeds in maintaining α_{EW} at .05. The basic logic behind the LSD is that, because it requires a statistically significant omnibus F value, in only 5 of every 100 studies (in the long run) will the process mistakenly lead to stage 2 when in fact all the population means are equal. Even if the second stage were to always produce a statistically significant result, only 5 percent of the time would a Type I error be committed because the omnibus test of stage 1 protects tests performed in the second stage. It seems that by requiring the omnibus test to be significant before testing individual contrasts, the goal of maintaining α_{EW} at .05 is accomplished. Indeed, the reasoning to this point is valid. As long as all a population means are equal (i.e., the complete null hypothesis is true), α_{EW} is held at .05 by the LSD. However, suppose that some but not all of the null hypothesis is true. For example, with $a = 11$, it might happen that the first 10 groups all have identical population means. The eleventh treatment, however, has been included in the study because prior evidence suggests it to be very different from the first 10. If the eleventh group is different enough from the first 10, the omnibus null hypothesis will be rejected with a probability approaching 1.0 for a large enough sample size. Conceivably, then, the second stage of the LSD will be reached with a high probability. Now, however, the LSD offers no further protection for contrasts among the first 10 groups. In other words, there is no protection for that part of the complete null hypothesis that is true. If all pairwise contrasts among the 10 truly identical groups are performed, the probability of at least one significant result using $\alpha_{PC} = .05$ is approximately .60. Thus, in 60 of every 100 such experiments (in the long run), a Type I error would be committed. Thus, the LSD fails to maintain α_{EW} at .05, except in the special case where the entire null hypothesis is true. None of the other approaches (Bonferroni, Tukey, Scheffé, Dunnett) suffer from this limitation—they all maintain α_{EW} at .05 under all circumstances as long as the basic ANOVA assumptions are satisfied. Indeed, as mentioned earlier, Tukey's method is referred to as the Wholly Significant Difference (WSD) precisely because the whole set of pairwise contrasts is protected at .05 with his approach.

Newman–Keuls Procedure

Several other methods have been developed that in many ways represent a compromise between the LSD and Tukey's approach for testing pairwise comparisons. Two of the most widely used compromises are the Newman–Keuls and the Duncan procedures. Both are referred to as multiple-range tests or layered methods because they involve testing ranges between groups in a layered fashion. The exact procedure for the Newman–Keuls approach is illustrated in an example.

Suppose that in a four-group study with seven subjects per group, the following means have been obtained:

$$\bar{Y}_1 = 16.0 \qquad \bar{Y}_2 = 22.0 \qquad \bar{Y}_3 = 10.0 \qquad \bar{Y}_4 = 14.5$$

We will also suppose that MS_W has been calculated and equals 28.0. The first step in the Newman–Keuls method is to rank order the groups according to the sample means. For our data, we have

$$\bar{Y}_3 = 10.0 \qquad \bar{Y}_4 = 14.5 \qquad \bar{Y}_1 = 16.0 \qquad \bar{Y}_2 = 22.0$$

ranking the groups from low to high (an ordering from high to low would also work). Observed F statistics are calculated as before from Equation 4.23 for each pairwise contrast. Again, what distinguishes the Newman–Keuls from other methods is the choice of critical value. The critical value to be used here for a contrast depends on how many "steps" separate the two groups being compared. For example, groups 2 and 3 are defined to be separated by four steps; groups 2 and 4 by three steps; and groups 2 and 1 by two steps. In general, if the rank of one group is R_1 and the rank of another is R_2, then the number of steps separating them is defined as

$$|R_1 - R_2| + 1.$$

The number of steps separating any two groups in an a-group study thus ranges from 2 to a. Traditional notation uses r to represent the number of steps between two groups. The Newman–Keuls critical value against which the observed F statistic is to be compared is given by

$$q^2(\alpha, r, df_{\text{error}})/2$$

where α is the alpha level (usually .05), r is the number of steps between the groups, and df_{error} is the degrees of freedom for error. The letter q again refers to the studentized range distribution, whose critical values are given in Appendix Table A.4. For the data set being analyzed, the relevant q values are

$$q(.05, 2, 24) = 2.92$$

$$q(.05, 3, 24) = 3.53$$

$$q(.05, 4, 24) = 3.90$$

The Newman–Keuls method requires that the mean differences be compared to the critical values in a specific order. The procedure is simplified by constructing a table of differences between the group means, where the groups have been rank ordered (see Table 5.6 for the data under study here). Each entry in the matrix equals the difference between the mean of the group in the column and the mean of the group in the row. (Only the top half of the matrix must be calculated because the matrix would be symmetric, that is, the numbers in the lower half would be identical in absolute value to the numbers in the top half.) The first difference to be tested for significance is the one in the extreme upper right corner, that is, the difference of 12.0 between groups 2 and 3. Instead of using Equation 23 to compare

$$F = \frac{n(\bar{Y}_2 - \bar{Y}_3)^2}{2MS_{\text{w}}}$$

versus $q^2/2$, it is simpler and equivalent to compare $\bar{Y}_2 - \bar{Y}_3$ versus

$$q(.05, r, 24)\sqrt{MS_{\text{w}}/n}$$

Because $r = 4$ here, $\bar{Y}_2 - \bar{Y}_3$ would have to exceed $(3.90)\sqrt{28/7} = 7.80$ to be significant. The observed difference is larger than the critical value, so we conclude that

TABLE **5.6** Differences Between
Ordered Means for Newman–Keuls
Method

	$\bar{Y}_3$	$\bar{Y}_4$	$\bar{Y}_1$	$\bar{Y}_2$
$\bar{Y}_3 = 10.0$	—	4.5	6.0	12.0
$\bar{Y}_4 = 14.5$		—	1.5	7.5
$\bar{Y}_1 = 16.0$			—	6.0
$\bar{Y}_2 = 22.0$				—

$\mu_2 \neq \mu_3$. If the result of this test had been nonsignificant, no further tests would be performed (if the smallest and largest means cannot be declared different, it would make no sense to declare less discrepant means to be different). However, because the test was significant, we move to the left in this same row and test the difference between groups 1 and 3. They are separated by three steps, so the critical value for $\bar{Y}_1 - \bar{Y}_3$ is $(3.53)\sqrt{28/7} = 7.06$. The observed difference is smaller than this critical difference, so groups 1 and 3 are not significantly different. Because this result is nonsignificant, no further tests are performed in this row. Also, no further tests are performed in the column headed by $\bar{Y}_1$ because the remaining differences (in this case, just 1.5) must be smaller than 6.0. We now move to the right-most column of the second row. Groups 2 and 4 are separated by three steps, yielding a critical value of 7.06, which 7.5 exceeds. Thus, groups 2 and 4 are significantly different. The difference of 1.5 for groups 1 and 4 is not tested because the difference of 6.0 for groups 1 and 3 was already found to be nonsignificant. Instead, the difference of 6.0 for groups 1 and 2 is tested. The critical difference for 2 steps is $(2.92)(2) = 5.84$, which 6.0 exceeds, so groups 1 and 2 are significantly different. The final conclusion, then, for these data is that the mean of group 2 is significantly different from the means of the other groups. No other difference is significant with the Newman–Keuls method. What if Tukey's method had been used for these data? The critical difference for all the pairwise contrasts would have been the same, namely, 7.80. The only significant difference would have been between groups 2 and 3. This illustrates a general principle—the Newman–Keuls approach is more powerful than Tukey's. However, this advantage is illusory in that the two approaches do not attempt to control α level in the same way. To explore the difference further, it is necessary to briefly consider the logic of the Newman–Keuls approach.

Recall that the critical value of the Tukey method was based on the sampling distribution of $F_{\text{pairwise maximum}}$. This maximum F occurs for the two most discrepant groups—that is, the groups that are a steps apart—so Tukey's method uses the distribution of F when $r = a$ to find a critical value against which to test all contrasts. The basic logic of the Newman–Keuls procedure is that using $r = a$ is unduly conservative when the actual number of steps separating the groups is less than a. For example, if $a = 4$, but the groups being compared are only two steps apart, a smaller critical value than $q(.05, 4, 24)$ might seem appropriate. While this may seem intuitively appealing, the consequence of using this smaller critical value is that α

is not explicitly controlled at either the per-comparison or experimentwise level. Instead, α is controlled for each set of means that are a steps apart. To clarify this idea, consider our numerical example with $a = 4$ and $\alpha = .05$. The first test involved a comparison of the most discrepant groups, so $r = 4$. The basis of $\alpha = .05$ is that given all four groups, a critical value was chosen to insure that $\bar{Y}_{maximum} - \bar{Y}_{minimum}$ would be significant only 5 percent of the time. Next, two tests were performed with $r = 3$ and $\alpha = .05$. In each case, the critical value was chosen so that $\bar{Y}_{max} - \bar{Y}_{min}$ would be significant only 5 percent of the time with three groups. As long as the complete null hypothesis is true, the Newman–Keuls approach maintains α_{EW} at .05. However, when some but not all of the means are equal, α_{EW} can exceed .05 with the Newman–Keuls. To demonstrate how this can happen, suppose $a = 10$ and that the population means are equal in pairs, so that

$$\mu_1 = \mu_2 < \mu_3 = \mu_4 < \mu_5 = \mu_6 < \mu_7 = \mu_8 < \mu_9 = \mu_{10}$$

If the differences between unequal means are large and the sample size is relatively large, it should happen that all differences for which $r \geq 3$ will be significant because they all represent true differences in the population. Thus, nine tests where $r = 2$ will be performed. For four of these (μ_2 versus μ_3, μ_4 versus μ_5, μ_6 versus μ_7, μ_8 versus μ_9), the null hypothesis is false, so there is no need to consider Type I errors. However, the other five tests (μ_1 versus μ_2, μ_3 versus μ_4, μ_5 versus μ_6, μ_7 versus μ_8, μ_9 versus μ_{10}) represent true null hypotheses, each of which will be tested at $\alpha = .05$. The resulting α_{EW} is $1 - (1 - .05)^5 = .23$, from Equation 1 (notice that these contrasts are orthogonal). Thus, in this situation, the Newman–Keuls method fails to maintain α_{EW} level at .05.

The Newman–Keuls procedure is not the only layered, or multiple-range, method. Duncan's New Multiple Range Test, mentioned earlier, is based on logic very similar to the Newman–Keuls. It differs only in that instead of using the same α level for each set of ordered means, the α level for means separated by r steps is set at $1 - (1 - \alpha)^{r-1}$. It can be seen that the resulting α level for a set increases as r increases. As a result, α_{EW} can be even higher for Duncan's method than for Newman–Keuls.

SIMULTANEOUS CONFIDENCE INTERVALS

Although the primary focus of this chapter has been on hypothesis testing, the concept of multiple comparisons is also relevant for confidence intervals. Consider an example with $a = 3$, where the goal is to form three 95 percent confidence intervals, one for each pairwise difference between means, that is, $\mu_1 - \mu_2$, $\mu_1 - \mu_3$, and $\mu_2 - \mu_3$. Because more than one interval is being formed, the 95 percent figure could take on either of two meanings. First, the confidence level might be 95 percent for each interval considered individually. In other words, for a single pairwise difference, 95 percent of such intervals would contain the true difference. Second, the 95 percent figure might pertain to the entire collection of intervals, in which case it is referred to as a 95 percent simultaneous confidence interval. In other words, 95 percent of the time that three (in this case) such intervals were constructed, *all three* would contain the true difference. A 95 percent confidence interval for a single contrast is directly analogous to a hypothesis test where $\alpha_{PC} = .05$, whereas a 95 percent simultaneous confidence interval is directly analogous to a collection of hypothesis tests where $\alpha_{EW} = .05$.

Simultaneous confidence intervals can be constructed using either the Bonferroni, Tukey, Scheffé, or Dunnett procedures. Another disadvantage of the LSD, Newman–Keuls, and Duncan methods is that they are restricted to hypothesis testing because of their stagewise or layered approaches; thus, they cannot be used for confidence intervals. The formation of simultaneous confidence intervals for any of the other four methods follows the same basic formula. To form a confidence interval for a contrast ψ, under the assumption of homogeneity, the interval is given by

$$\hat{\psi} \pm w \sqrt{MS_W \sum_{j=1}^{a} (c_j^2/n_j)}$$

where w depends upon the multiple comparison procedure employed.

$w = \sqrt{F(.05/C, 1, df_{error})}$ for Bonferroni

$w = q(.05, a, df_{error})/\sqrt{2}$ for Tukey

$w = \sqrt{(a-1)F(.05, a-1, df_{error})}$ for Scheffé

$w = D(.05, a, df_{error})$ for Dunnett

For all four procedures, there is a direct correspondence between the confidence interval and the hypothesis test. The null hypothesis is rejected if and only if the simultaneous confidence interval fails to contain the hypothesized value of ψ (which in almost all applications is zero). Thus, proper interpretation of a simultaneous confidence interval conveys the information contained in a hypothesis test for each of these four multiple-comparison procedures. However, a simultaneous confidence interval is often more informative than the corresponding hypothesis test because the interval shows both the magnitude of the difference and the precision with which the magnitude is estimated.

CHOOSING AN APPROPRIATE PROCEDURE

The practical implication of this chapter is that we have recommended four multiple-comparisons procedures for general use: Bonferroni, Tukey, Scheffé, and Dunnett. Figure 5.1 is a flowchart (i.e., a decision tree) that is intended to provide a general guideline for choosing from among these four procedures in a particular situation. We should stress the phrase "general guideline" here; it is important that you understand the principles we have presented in the chapter so that you can use

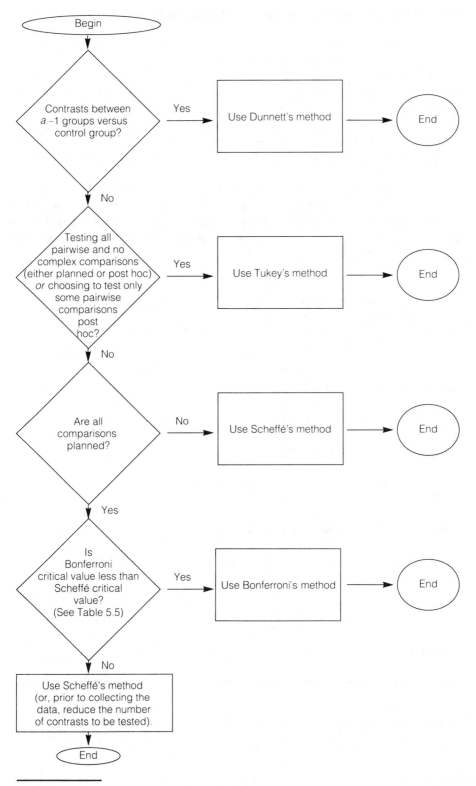

FIGURE 5.1 General guideline for choosing a multiple-comparisons procedure.

this flowchart as an aid to choosing a technique without being at the complete mercy of a set of mechanical rules to follow blindly.

We would be remiss if we did not take a moment to explain where the omnibus test of Chapter 3 fits into this framework. In particular, it is important that you understand that the omnibus test is not a prerequisite for either the Bonferroni or Tukey procedures. Instead, the Bonferroni and Tukey methods should be viewed as substitutes for the omnibus test because they control α_{EW} at the desired level all by themselves. Requiring a significant omnibus test before proceeding to perform Bonferroni or Tukey analyses, as is sometimes done, only serves to lower α_{EW} below the desired level (Bernhardson, 1975) and hence inappropriately decreases power.

The proper role of the omnibus test is that it should be viewed as a precursor to Scheffé's method. As discussed earlier, if the omnibus test is significant, there is at least one contrast that will be significant with Scheffé's method, namely, a contrast whose coefficients are given by

T A B L E **5. 7** Test Statistics and Critical Values for Multiple-Comparisons Procedures

	Test Statistic	Critical Value
Assuming Homogeneity of Variance		
Bonferroni	$(\hat{\psi})^2 \left/ \left[MS_W \sum_{j=1}^{a} (c_j^2/n_j) \right] \right.$	$F_{.05/C; 1, N-a}$
Tukey	$\dfrac{n_g n_h (\bar{Y}_g - \bar{Y}_h)^2}{(n_g + n_h) MS_W}$	$(q_{.05; a, N-a})^2/2$
Scheffé	$(\hat{\psi})^2 \left/ \left[MS_W \sum_{j=1}^{a} (c_j^2/n_j) \right] \right.$	$(a-1)F_{.05; a-1, N-a}$
*Without Assuming Homogeneity of Variance**		
Bonferroni	$(\hat{\psi})^2 \left/ \left[\sum_{j=1}^{a} (c_j^2/n_j)s_j^2 \right] \right.$	$F_{.05/C; 1, df}$
Tukey	$\dfrac{(\bar{Y}_g - \bar{Y}_h)^2}{\dfrac{s_g^2}{n_g} + \dfrac{s_h^2}{n_h}}$	large n: $(q_{.05; a, df})^2/2$ small n: $V_{.05; a, df}^2$
Scheffé	$(\hat{\psi})^2 \left/ \left[\sum_{j=1}^{a} (c_j^2/n_j)s_j^2 \right] \right.$	$(a-1)F_{.05; a-1, df}$

*For all procedures, $df = \dfrac{\left(\sum\limits_{j=1}^{a} c_j^2 s_j^2/n_j \right)^2}{\sum\limits_{j=1}^{a} (c_j^2 s_j^2/n_j)^2/(n_j - 1)}$

$$c_j = n_j(\bar{Y}_j - \bar{Y}) \qquad\qquad \text{(20, repeated)}$$

Thus, a significant omnibus test is a signal that it is worthwhile to search for significant contrasts. On the other hand, if the omnibus test is nonsignificant, searching for any significant contrast is pointless because none exists. Thus, the omnibus test serves a very definite purpose, but it does so only when neither the Bonferroni nor Tukey procedures are appropriate for addressing an investigator's questions.

As further assistance, Tables 5.7 and 5.8 summarize the procedural details for the Bonferroni, Tukey, and Scheffé procedures. Table 5.7 provides formulas for hypothesis testing, and Table 5.8 provides formulas for forming simultaneous confidence intervals. Both tables provide procedures to use when homogeneity of variance is assumed as well as when it is not. Although the entries in the tables assume that α_{EW} has been set at .05, other values of α_{EW} could be substituted for .05.

In closing, we should mention that research on multiple-comparisons procedures is very active in the field of statistics. Readers who are interested in more details are advised to consult Hochberg and Tamhane (1987) or Wilcox (1987a, 1987b).

T A B L E 5. 8 Formulas for Forming Simultaneous Confidence Intervals

---

Assuming Homogeneity of Variance

Bonferroni $\quad \hat{\psi} \pm \sqrt{F_{.05/C;1,N-a}} \sqrt{MS_{\text{W}} \sum_{j=1}^{a} (c_j^2/n_j)}$

Tukey $\quad (\bar{Y}_g - \bar{Y}_h) \pm (q_{.05;a,N-a}/\sqrt{2}) \sqrt{MS_{\text{W}}\left(\dfrac{1}{n_g} + \dfrac{1}{n_h}\right)}$

Scheffé $\quad \hat{\psi} \pm \sqrt{(a-1)F_{.05;a-1,N-a}} \sqrt{MS_{\text{W}} \sum_{j=1}^{a}(c_j^2/n_j)}$

Without Assuming Homogeneity of Variance*

Bonferroni $\quad \hat{\psi} \pm \sqrt{F_{.05/C;1,df}} \sqrt{\sum_{j=1}^{a} [(c_j^2/n_j)s_j^2]}$

Tukey $\quad$ large n: $(\bar{Y}_g - \bar{Y}_h) \pm (q_{.05;a,df}/\sqrt{2})\sqrt{(s_g^2/n_g) + (s_h^2/n_h)}$

$\qquad\qquad$ small n: $(\bar{Y}_g - \bar{Y}_h) \pm V_{.05;a,df}\sqrt{(s_g^2/n_g) + (s_h^2/n_h)}$

Scheffé $\quad \hat{\psi} \pm \sqrt{(a-1)F_{.05;a-1,df}} \sqrt{\sum_{j=1}^{a} [(c_j^2/n_j)s_j^2]}$

---

* For all procedures, $df = \dfrac{\left(\sum_{j=1}^{a} c_j^2 s_j^2/n_j\right)^2}{\sum_{j=1}^{a} (c_j^2 s_j^2/n_j)^2/(n_j - 1)}$

EXERCISES

1. An investigator decides to test the following four contrasts in a five-group study:

	1	2	3	4	5
ψ_1	1	-1	0	0	0
ψ_2	0	0	1	-1	0
ψ_3	1	1	-1	-1	0
ψ_4	1	1	1	1	-4

Find the α_{EW} level if each contrast is tested with an α_{PC} level of .05.

*2. A researcher has conducted a five-group study. She plans to test the following pairwise comparisons: μ_1 versus μ_2, μ_2 versus μ_3, and μ_4 versus μ_5.
   a. What multiple comparisons procedure should be used to maintain the α_{EW} level at .05?
   b. What will the critical F value be for each contrast, if there are 13 subjects per group?
   c. Suppose that after looking at the data, the researcher decides to replace the comparison of μ_2 versus μ_3 with a comparison of μ_3 versus μ_4. What multiple-comparisons procedure should be used to maintain the α_{EW} level at .05?
   d. What will the critical F value be in part c if there are 13 subjects per group?
   e. What implications does the difference in critical values you found in parts b and d have for revising planned comparisons after having examined the data?

*3. The following summary data are obtained in a four-group study, with 25 subjects per group:

$$\bar{Y}_1 = 52 \qquad \bar{Y}_2 = 46 \qquad \bar{Y}_3 = 51 \qquad \bar{Y}_4 = 54$$
$$s_1^2 = 96 \qquad s_2^2 = 112 \qquad s_3^2 = 94 \qquad s_4^2 = 98$$

The experimenter decides after examining the data to compare the means of groups 2 and 4. He finds that the mean difference is nonsignificant using Scheffé's method.
   a. Is he correct that this mean difference cannot be declared significant using Scheffé's method? (You can assume homogeneity of variance.)
   b. Is there a better method available for testing this contrast that will maintain α_{EW} at .05 although the contrast was chosen post hoc? If so, can the contrast be declared significant with this method?

4. A graduate student conducts a study with eight independent groups. After obtaining a significant overall F, she decides to compare only the group with the largest sample mean versus the group with the smallest sample mean using the Newman–Keuls procedure. The result is significant at the .05 level. However, her adviser argues that she should have used Tukey's WSD because it controls α_{EW} at 05. The adviser argues that with the Tukey approach, the result may not be significant. What do you think of this argument? Why?

*5. This problem asks you to reconsider the data from Exercise 10 in Chapter 4. The data are given here once again:

	1	2	3	4
	3	7	9	11
	4	5	2	7
	5	6	5	11
	5	5	9	7
	3	7	5	4
Mean	4	6	6	8
Var (s^2)	1	1	9	9

We assume that all pairwise comparisons are to be tested and that α_{EW} is to be maintained at .05. Although all comparisons are of potential interest, this exercise only requires you to consider two specific comparisons: group 1 versus group 2 and group 3 versus group 4.

a. Test the difference in the means of groups 3 and 4, first using MS_W as the error term and then using a separate error term. How do the results compare?
b. Test the difference in the means of groups 1 and 2, first using MS_W as the error term and then using a separate error term. How do the results compare?
c. Which error term do you think is more appropriate here? Why?

This problem uses the same data as Exercise 5. However, we assume here that the goal now is to form confidence intervals instead of testing hypotheses. Assume that a confidence interval is to be formed for each pairwise comparison, but as in Exercise 5, this exercise only requires you to consider two specific comparisons: group 1 versus group 2 and group 3 versus group 4.

a. Form a 95 percent simultaneous confidence interval for $\mu_3 - \mu_4$, first using MS_W as the error term and then using a separate error term. How do the results compare?
b. Form a 95 percent simultaneous confidence interval for $\mu_1 - \mu_2$, first using MS_W as the error term and then using a separate error term. How do the results compare?
c. Based on the respective confidence intervals, which error term do you think is more appropriate here? Why?

A graduate student has conducted a four-group study in which he tested the following three planned comparisons:

	1	2	3	4
ψ_1	1	−1	0	0
ψ_2	.5	.5	−1	0
ψ_3	1/3	1/3	1/3	−1

The sums of squares for the three comparisons are 75, 175, and 125, respectively. The value of MS_W equals 25, and there were 11 subjects in each group. The student's adviser wonders whether the omnibus F test of $H_0: \mu_1 = \mu_2 = \mu_3 = \mu_4$ would be statistically significant for these data. Can you help her?

a. Is it possible to perform the test of the omnibus null hypothesis from the available information? If so, is the test significant? If it is not possible, explain why not.
b. Find the observed F value for each of the planned comparisons tested by the student. Which, if any, are statistically significant with an α_{EW} level of .05?

   c. What relationship, if any, is there between the single observed F value of part a and the three observed F values of part b?

8. A researcher has conducted an experiment with six independent groups of 12 subjects each. Although the omnibus F test was nonsignificant, he decided to use Scheffé's method of multiple comparisons. His calculations revealed that the average of the first three groups was significantly different from that of the last three. How would you interpret his findings?

9. A graduate student has designed a study in which she will have four independent groups of seven subjects each. Parts a–h ask you to decide which multiple-comparisons procedure (MCP) should be used to achieve maximal power while maintaining experimentwise α at .05. For each part, tell which MCP she should use and *briefly* justify your answer.
   a. The student plans to test all pairwise comparisons.
   b. The student decides after having looked at the data to test all pairwise comparisons.
   c. The student plans to test only 4 pairwise comparisons.
   d. The student decides after having looked at the data to test only 4 pairwise comparisons.
   e. The student plans to test 7 planned comparisons.
   f. The student decides after having looked at the data to test 7 specific comparisons.
   g. The student plans to test 20 planned comparisons. (HINT: The critical t value for $\alpha_{PC} = .05/20$ is 3.376.)
   h. The student decides after having looked at the data to test 20 specific comparisons.

10. The following data were obtained in a four-group study:

	1	2	3	4
	6	6	3	5
	5	9	7	3
	7	9	6	1
	5	4	3	4
	3	5	4	3
	4	6	7	5
Mean	5.0	6.5	5.0	3.5
Var (s^2)	2.0	4.3	3.6	2.3

   a. Are the four group means significantly different from each other?
   b. Suppose all pairwise comparisons were investigated. If the α_{FW} level is maintained at .05, is the difference between the means of groups 2 and 4 significant? (You can assume homogeneity of variance).
   c. How can you explain the results of parts a and b? What general pattern of means is most likely to produce this type of result?
   d. What does this example imply about the necessity of obtaining a statistically significant omnibus test before using Tukey's WSD method to test all pairwise comparisons?

*11. A professor has obtained the following data for a three-group between-subjects design:

Group	Mean	SD(s)
1	10	10.00
2	10	14.00
3	22	12.41

There were 11 subjects per group (i.e., 33 subjects in all).

a. The professor claims that he can reject the omnibus null hypothesis. Do you agree? Show your work.

b. Having allegedly found the three groups to be somewhat different, the professor uses Tukey's WSD method to test all pairwise comparisons. He claims that no differences were significant. Do you agree? Show your work.

c. On the basis of the results found in parts a and b, the professor argues that the omnibus test is misleading. He concludes that he cannot state that there are any differences among these three groups. Do you agree? Why or why not?

12. A graduate student used a four-group between-subject design for her thesis. She had $n = 11$ subjects per group. Her sample means are $\bar{Y}_1 = 12$, $\bar{Y}_2 = 13$, $\bar{Y}_3 = 20$, and $\bar{Y}_4 = 19$. The value of MS_W was 55.

a. Should she reject an omnibus null hypothesis that $\mu_1 = \mu_2 = \mu_3 = \mu_4$? Show your work.

b. Based on her answer to part a, she decides to investigate which groups are different. She decides to test all pairwise differences, assuming homogeneity of variance and using an appropriate method for controlling familywise error rate. Does she obtain any significant differences? Why or why not?

c. Her adviser asks her to compare the average of groups 1 and 2 with the average of groups 3 and 4, again controlling for familywise error rate. She argues in light of part b that testing the complex comparison here is fruitless because tests of complex comparisons are more conservative then tests of pairwise comparisons. Is she correct? Show your work or explain your answer.

d. She has shown the results of parts a–c to her adviser, who is thoroughly confused. He argues that according to the results she claims to have obtained, she has shown that $12(\bar{Y}_1)$ and $20(\bar{Y}_3)$ are not significantly different, but that 12.5 and 19.5 are, which is obviously absurd. Is his argument correct?

13. In an experiment with five independent groups (five subjects per group), the omnibus F value observed is 3.00, just barely significant at the .05 level. Noticing that the sample means are $\bar{Y}_1 = 10$, $\bar{Y}_2 = 10$, $\bar{Y}_3 = 15$, $\bar{Y}_4 = 20$, and $\bar{Y}_5 = 30$, it is decided to test the following post hoc comparison: $\psi = -7\mu_1 - 7\mu_2 - 2\mu_3 + 3\mu_4 + 13\mu_5$.

a. Find SS for this comparison. Show your work.

b. What will the observed F value for this comparison be? Why?

c. Will the result in part b be significant using Scheffé's method? Why or why not?

d. What is the value of MS_W here?

14. Dr. S. Q. Skew performed an experiment involving four treatment groups with 16 subjects per group. His research assistant performed one MANOVA run on the data, but it did not answer all of Skew's questions. So far, Skew knows from this analysis that $SS_B = 864$ and $SS_W = 4320$. He also knows that the observed F for the pairwise comparison of groups 1 and 2 is equal to 1.000 and that the observed F for the pairwise comparison of groups 3 and 4 is only 0.111 (i.e., literally 1/9). Because neither of these is significant, Skew wants to compare the average of the first two groups versus the average of the last two groups. Unfortunately, unbeknown to Skew, his

assistant has lost the data! Knowing that you are a statistical whiz, the assistant comes to you desperate for help. Your task is to test this third comparison for significance. Show your work. Also, assume that Skew chose this contrast after having examined the data.

15. The following data are from a completely randomized (between-subjects) design:

1	2	3
48	59	68
54	46	62
47	49	53
54	63	59
62	38	67
57	58	71

Five psychologists analyze this data set individually, each with different goals in mind. Your task is to duplicate the results obtained by each.

a. Psychologist 1 formulates three planned comparisons of interest: group 1 versus 2, 1 versus 3, and 2 versus 3. Perform these planned comparisons, assuming homogeneity of variance.

b. Psychologist 2 has no a priori comparisons, so she first performs the omnibus test. Following this, all pairwise comparisons are tested for significance, assuming homogeneity of variance. Once again, provide observed and critical values.

c. Psychologist 3 differs from 2 only in that he decides not to assume homogeneity of variance for testing the comparison (don't worry about this assumption for the omnibus test). Once again, provide observed and critical values.

d. Psychologist 4 differs from 2 only in that she decides post hoc to test not only all pairwise comparisons but also the average of groups 1 and 2 versus group 3. Like 2, she assumes homogeneity. Once again, provide observed and critical values.

e. Psychologist 5 performs the same tests as 4. However, 5 has planned to conduct these particular tests prior to examining the data. Homogeneity is assumed.

f. Finally, write a brief explanation (one to two paragraphs) of why the various psychologists did not all arrive at the same conclusions regarding group differences. You need not specify one approach as "best," but you should explain the patterns of findings *for these data*. Also you need not discuss *all* findings in relationship to one another; instead, focus your attention on differences that emerge, and the reasons for such differences.

6 Trend Analysis

207

IN THE EXAMPLES CONSIDERED in Chapters 4 and 5, the factor was qualitative in the sense that the different groups that constituted the factor differed from each other in quality and not just in quantity. For example, at the beginning of Chapter 4, we discussed a study that compared four treatments for hypertension: drug therapy, biofeedback, dietary modification, and a combination. Although we could assign the numbers 1, 2, 3, and 4 to the four treatments, it is not at all clear which treatment should be assigned a 1, which a 2, and so forth. In other words, we cannot describe the treatments in terms of differences in magnitude of a single quantity. In this sense, we might say that the treatment levels form a nominal scale. We have simply formed four groups, which serve to classify subjects.

QUANTITATIVE FACTORS

Let's now consider a different experiment. Suppose young children are given a fixed length of time to study a list of words to be memorized. One group of children is allowed one minute to study the list, another group gets two minutes, a third group gets three minutes, and a fourth group gets four minutes. The distinction among the groups in this study can be described in a purely quantitative manner, unlike the groups in the hypertension study. As a result, we say that we have a *quantitative factor* in the memory study.

What difference does it make whether we have a quantitative factor? As we will see shortly, up to a point it does not matter because we still typically want to compare group means by testing contrasts, just as we did in Chapters 4 and 5. However, we consider quantitative factors to be a separate topic here because the particular contrast coefficients we will choose (i.e., the c_j terms) will usually be different for quantitative factors than for qualitative factors.

Testing contrasts of levels of a quantitative factor is often referred to as *trend analysis*. Another term that is frequently used to describe this form of analysis is the *method of orthogonal polynomials*. The meaning behind these terms will become clear as we develop the underlying concepts. For the moment, to keep things in perspective, it is important to remember that what we are about to discuss simply involves testing contrasts. What we will develop is a special case of what we've already developed in Chapter 4. Indeed, the only really new idea to be presented here can be thought of as finding a method for choosing appropriate contrast coefficients to test the hypotheses we are interested in.

Before we jump into the statistical aspects of trend analysis, it may be helpful to say a bit more about when trend analysis might be used. Trend analysis is almost invariably used anytime the factor under investigation is quantitative. A moment's reflection should convince you that psychologists and other behavioral scientists are often interested in the effects of quantitative factors. Examples of quantitative factors whose effects behavioral scientists might examine are amount of study time in a memory task, number of hours of food deprivation, number of hours of sleep, number of reinforcements, frequency of reinforcements, drug dosage, and age. We should also stress that this chapter is concerned only with trend analysis in between-subject designs, that is, designs where each level of the factor consists of different groups of subjects. Beginning with Chapter 11, we consider within-subject designs, where each subject is observed at every level of the factor. As we will see later in the book, trend analysis is also useful for studying quantitative factors in within-subject designs. Thus, the concepts we develop now are useful later in the book as well, although some of the specific formulas in the two designs are different from one another.

STATISTICAL TREATMENT OF TREND ANALYSIS

To motivate the statistical treatment of trend analysis, consider the data shown in Table 6.1. These data are intended to represent recall scores of 24 children assigned to one of four experimental conditions. Each child is allowed a fixed period of time to study a list of 12 words. Six of the children are randomly assigned to a condition where they are given one minute to study the words, a second group is given two minutes, a third group is given three minutes, and the fourth group is given four minutes. The dependent variable is the number of words the child recalls after a brief interference task.

How should the data of Table 6.1 be analyzed? Although we could certainly apply the ANOVA techniques of Chaper 3 to these data, these techniques would not take advantage of the quantitative nature of the experimental manipulation. To capitalize on the quantitative nature of the factor, we instead consider the data from the standpoint of regression, which was touched upon briefly in the extension of

T A B L E **6. 1**   Hypothetical Memory Data

	Study Time			
	1 Minute	*2 Minutes*	*3 Minutes*	*4 Minutes*
	2	6	6	11
	3	8	8	10
	1	5	10	7
	2	3	5	9
	0	7	10	8
	4	7	9	9
Mean	**2**	**6**	**8**	**9**

Chapter 3. We will shortly see that even from a regression perspective, trend analysis of quantitative factors becomes a matter of testing contrasts of group means.

To understand the motivation behind trend analysis, it is helpful to examine a visual representation of the data of Table 6.1. Figure 6.1 shows a scatterplot of recall scores plotted as a function of study time. This figure strongly suggests that recall improves with increases in study time, just as we would expect in an experiment of this sort. To formalize this intuition, we might develop a model that specifies that recall is a linear function of study time. As discussed in the extension of Chapter 3, the equation for a straight line consists of an intercept and a slope. If we let Y_{ij} represent the recall score for individual i in group j and if we let X_{ij} be that same individual's level of study time, an appropriate model is given by

$$Y_{ij} = \beta_0 + \beta_1 X_{ij} + \varepsilon_{ij} \tag{1}$$

where β_0 is the population intercept of the straight line, β_1 is the population slope, and ε_{ij} is an error term. We can immediately simplify this equation by dropping the i subscript from the X_{ij} term because every individual in group j has the same score on X. For example, in our recall study, $X_{i1} = 1$ for all i because every subject's X score in group 1 is one minute. Thus, we can simply say that $X_1 = 1$. Rewriting Equation 1 in this fashion results in

$$Y_{ij} = \beta_0 + \beta_1 X_j + \varepsilon_{ij} \tag{2}$$

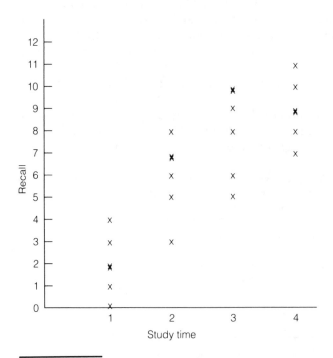

F I G U R E 6. 1   Scatterplot of recall scores as a function of study time.

The Slope Parameter

As usual, the task is to estimate parameters and test hypotheses concerning these parameters in our model. In our situation, we are primarily interested in the slope parameter (β_1) because it reflects the extent to which X is linearly related to Y. As shown in most elementary statistics textbooks, the general formula for the least-squares estimate of the slope parameter is given by

$$\hat{\beta}_1 = \left[\sum_{j=1}^{a} \sum_{i=1}^{n_j} (X_{ij} - \bar{X})(Y_{ij} - \bar{Y}) \right] \Bigg/ \sum_{j=1}^{a} \sum_{i=1}^{n_j} (X_{ij} - \bar{X})^2 \qquad (3)$$

where $\bar{X}$ and $\bar{Y}$ are the sample means of X and Y, respectively, averaged across all subjects in the study regardless of group.

Equation 3 can be simplified through several steps. First, as we saw before, X_{ij} can be replaced by X_j. This substitution results in

$$\hat{\beta}_1 = \left[\sum_{j=1}^{a} \sum_{i=1}^{n_j} (X_j - \bar{X})(Y_{ij} - \bar{Y}) \right] \Bigg/ \sum_{j=1}^{a} \sum_{i=1}^{n_j} (X_j - \bar{X})^2$$

Second, to simplify the notation, we represent $X_j - \bar{X}$ as c_j. Notice then that c_j simply is a deviation score on the X variable (i.e., it represents distance from the mean in either a positive or a negative direction). The reason we have chosen c_j as the symbol for this deviation score will become apparent momentarily. With this substitution, the equation simplifies to

$$\hat{\beta}_1 = \left[\sum_{j=1}^{a} \sum_{i=1}^{n_j} c_j(Y_{ij} - \bar{Y}) \right] \Bigg/ \sum_{j=1}^{a} \sum_{i=1}^{n_j} c_j^2$$

Third, the c_j term can be moved outside the summation over i because c_j is a constant for every i. This yields

$$\hat{\beta}_1 = \left[\sum_{j=1}^{a} c_j \sum_{i=1}^{n_j} (Y_{ij} - \bar{Y}) \right] \Bigg/ \sum_{j=1}^{a} n_j c_j^2$$

After some additional algebraic manipulation,[1] the numerator of Equation 3 ultimately simplifies to $\sum_{j=1}^{a} c_j n_j \bar{Y}_j$. Making this substitution yields

$$\hat{\beta}_1 = \sum_{j=1}^{a} c_j n_j \bar{Y}_j \Bigg/ \sum_{j=1}^{a} n_j c_j^2 \qquad (4)$$

Equation 4 thus provides the formula for estimating the slope relating X and Y. Although applying Equation 4 is relatively straightforward, the conceptual implications of the equation are much clearer if we make a simplifying assumption that each group has the same number of subjects. In other words, we assume that there are the same number of subjects at each level of X, in which case $n_1 = n_2 = \cdots = n_a$, so that n_j can be replaced with just n. Substituting n for n_j in Equation 4 yields

$$\hat{\beta}_1 = \sum_{j=1}^{a} c_j n \bar{Y}_j \Bigg/ \sum_{j=1}^{a} n c_j^2$$

We can factor out the n term in both the numerator and the denominator, leaving

$$\hat{\beta}_1 = \sum_{j=1}^{a} c_j \bar{Y}_j \bigg/ \sum_{j=1}^{a} c_j^2 \tag{5}$$

Several points about Equation 5 must be made here. First, notice that the estimated slope $\hat{\beta}_1$ depends only on the sample means $\bar{Y}_j$ and not on the values of the individual Y_{ij} data points. Thus, the extent to which we estimate X and Y to be linearly related depends in some manner on how the $\bar{Y}_j$ values relate to X. Second, notice that the term $\sum_{j=1}^{a} c_j \bar{Y}_j$ is simply a sample contrast, as shown in Equation 4.36. We typically require that the contrast coefficients sum to zero, that is, $\sum_{j=1}^{a} c_j = 0$. This condition will be met for trend analysis because $\sum_{j=1}^{a} c_j = \sum_{j=1}^{a} (X_j - \bar{X}) = 0$ as long as we have equal n. In fact, using our earlier notation for contrasts, we could write

$$\hat{\psi}_{\text{linear}} = \sum_{j=1}^{a} c_j \bar{Y}_j \tag{6}$$

so that

$$\hat{\beta}_1 = \hat{\psi}_{\text{linear}} \bigg/ \sum_{j=1}^{a} c_j^2 \tag{7}$$

The estimated regression slope simply equals the sample value of the linear contrast divided by the sum of squared c_j values. Thus, the slope can be found by forming a contrast, just as we discussed throughout Chapter 4. Third, as always, the defining characteristic of the contrast comes from the coefficients used to form the contrast. In other words, the slope of a linear trend can be found by forming a contrast of the group means on $\bar{Y}_j$, where the coefficients take on a special form, namely,

$$c_j = X_j - \bar{X} \tag{8}$$

as long as we have equal n. With unequal n, the same idea applies, but the formulas become more complicated as we will see later in the chapter.

Numerical Example

How can we apply what we have done so far to our numerical example? From Equation 7, the estimated slope for our data is

$$\hat{\beta}_1 = \hat{\psi}_{\text{linear}} \bigg/ \sum_{j=1}^{a} c_j^2 \qquad \text{(7, repeated)}$$

where

$$\hat{\psi}_{\text{linear}} = \sum_{j=1}^{a} c_j \bar{Y}_j \qquad \text{(6, repeated)}$$

Table 6.1 shows that $\bar{Y}_1 = 2$, $\bar{Y}_2 = 6$, $\bar{Y}_3 = 8$, and $\bar{Y}_4 = 9$ for our data. The contrast coefficients are defined to be

$$c_j = X_j - \bar{X} \qquad \text{(8, repeated)}$$

For our data, $X_1 = 1$, $X_2 = 2$, $X_3 = 3$, and $X_4 = 4$. Thus, the mean X is $\bar{X} = 2.5$.

The corresponding contrast coefficients are $c_1 = -1.5$, $c_2 = -0.5$, $c_3 = 0.5$, and $c_4 = 1.5$. Applying these four coefficients to the four $\bar{Y}_j$ values according to Equation 6 yields

$$\hat{\psi}_{linear} = -1.5(2) - 0.5(6) + 0.5(8) + 1.5(9)$$
$$= 11.5$$

To find the estimated slope, we must also calculate $\sum_{j=1}^{a} c_j^2$, the sum of squared coefficients. Here we have

$$\sum_{j=1}^{a} c_j^2 = (-1.5)^2 + (-0.5)^2 + (0.5)^2 + (1.5)^2$$
$$= 5.0$$

Then, from Equation 7, the estimated slope is given by

$$\hat{\beta}_1 = \hat{\psi}_{linear} \bigg/ \sum_{j=1}^{a} c_j^2$$
$$= 11.5/5.0$$
$$= 2.3$$

What meaning can be attached to this value of 2.3? The interpretation here would be that when we fit a linear trend to the data, we estimate that every

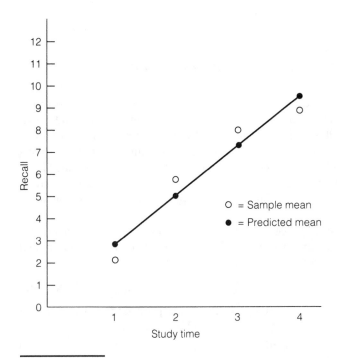

additional minute of study time translates into an average gain of 2.3 additional words recalled. To fully appreciate this statement, it is helpful to once again see a graphical depiction of the data. The open circles in Figure 6.2 show the sample mean recall score $\bar{Y}_j$ for each level X_j of study time. The closed circles are the predicted means obtained from the linear trend. The straight line is obtained from the previously determined slope value $\hat{\beta}_1 = 2.3$ and from the intercept, whose least-squares estimate is found from the following equation:

$$\hat{\beta}_0 = \bar{Y} - \hat{\beta}_1 \bar{X}$$

For our data, the estimated intercept is

$$\hat{\beta}_0 = 6.25 - (2.3)(2.5)$$
$$= 0.50$$

Thus, the equation of the straight line shown in Figure 6.2 is

$$\hat{Y}_{ij} = 0.50 + 2.3X_j$$

Although this straight line fits the sample means reasonably well, the fit is not perfect in the sense that the sample means do not lie perfectly on the straight line. As we will see later, this "imperfection" could either reflect some nonlinear trend in the data, or it might simply reflect sampling error. Also, the estimated slope could have been negative, in which case the straight line would have sloped downward (when moving from left to right) instead of upward.

HYPOTHESIS TEST OF SLOPE PARAMETER

So far we have learned how to estimate the slope coefficient for a linear trend. We have seen that this slope depends solely on the sample means and that it can be formulated in terms of a contrast. The second major topic to consider here is hypothesis testing. Is the estimated slope coefficient statistically significantly different from zero? For example, in our memory study, we estimated the slope coefficient to equal 2.3. While this value suggests that recall improves with increases in study time, we cannot rule out the possibility that the population value of the slope coefficient is zero.

To address this possibility, we must perform a hypothesis test. As usual, we operationalize our test as a comparison of full and restricted models. The full model here is given by our earlier straight-line model for the data:

$$\text{Full:} \qquad Y_{ij} = \beta_0 + \beta_1 X_j + \varepsilon_{ij} \qquad \text{(2, repeated)}$$

The null hypothesis to be tested is that $\beta_1 = 0$, so an appropriate restricted model is given by

$$\text{Restricted:} \qquad Y_{ij} = \beta_0 + \varepsilon_{ij} \qquad (9)$$

As usual, to compare these two models, we must find the sum of squared errors for each model. It can be shown[2] that for simple linear regression models such as these,

$$E_R = \sum_{j=1}^{a} \sum_{i=1}^{n_j} (Y_{ij} - \bar{Y})^2$$

and

$$E_F = \sum_{j=1}^{a} \sum_{i=1}^{n_j} (Y_{ij} - \bar{Y})^2 - \left[\hat{\beta}_1^2 \sum_{j=1}^{a} \sum_{i=1}^{n_j} (X_{ij} - \bar{X})^2 \right]$$

Of particular interest is the difference in the sum of squared errors of the two models, that is, $E_R - E_F$. Simple subtraction shows that

$$E_R - E_F = \hat{\beta}_1^2 \sum_{j=1}^{a} \sum_{i=1}^{n_j} (X_{ij} - \bar{X})^2$$

We can now simplify this expression somewhat in our problem. First, recall that X_{ij} can be replaced by X_j because every subject's X score is the same within a group. This substitution yields

$$E_R - E_F = \hat{\beta}_1^2 \sum_{j=1}^{a} \sum_{i=1}^{n_j} (X_j - \bar{X})^2$$

Second, from Equation 8, $c_j = X_j - \bar{X}$. Incorporating this substitution gives us

$$E_R - E_F = \hat{\beta}_1^2 \sum_{j=1}^{a} \sum_{i=1}^{n_j} c_j^2$$

Third, c_j^2 is a constant within each group, so we can bring it outside the summation over i (individuals). For simplicity, we continue to assume equal n, in which case we now have

$$E_R - E_F = n\hat{\beta}_1^2 \sum_{j=1}^{a} c_j^2 \tag{10}$$

because

$$\sum_{j=1}^{a} \left(\sum_{i=1}^{n} c_j^2 \right) = \sum_{j=1}^{a} n c_j^2 = n \sum_{j=1}^{a} c_j^2$$

Although our equation for $E_R - E_F$ is now fairly straightforward, it still does not look familiar. However, we now show that in fact it is equivalent to an equation we developed in Chapter 4. To approach this more familiar form, we saw in Equation 7 that

$$\hat{\beta}_1 = \hat{\psi}_{\text{linear}} \left/ \sum_{j=1}^{a} c_j^2 \right. \tag{7, repeated}$$

Substituting this expression for $\hat{\beta}_1$ into Equation 10 produces

$$E_R - E_F = n(\hat{\psi}_{\text{linear}})^2 \left(\sum_{j=1}^{a} c_j^2 \right) \left/ \left(\sum_{j=1}^{a} c_j^2 \right)^2 \right.$$

which reduces to

$$E_R - E_F = n(\hat{\psi}_{linear})^2 \Big/ \sum_{j=1}^{a} c_j^2 \tag{11}$$

However, Equation 11 is just the formula for the sum of squares of a contrast, with equal n. Thus, the difference in the sum of squared errors for the full and restricted models simply equals the sum of squares of the linear contrast:

$$E_R - E_F = SS_{\psi_{linear}}$$

An F test can then be performed by dividing the sum of squares due to the contrast by mean square within, as in Chapters 4 and 5:

$$F = SS_\psi/MS_W.$$

An appropriate critical value is found as usual. If the observed F exceeds the critical F, the null hypothesis $\beta_1 = 0$ is rejected, and there is a statistically significant linear trend in the data. Of course, consistent with the discussion in Chapter 5, we need to distinguish between α_{PC} and α_{EW} if we perform multiple tests of comparisons instead of just testing the linear trend.

Numerical Example

To make the discussion less abstract, let's return to the memory-study data of Table 6.1. We saw previously that the least-squares estimate of the slope coefficient is $\hat{\beta}_1 = 2.3$. Can we infer that the population slope β_1 is nonzero? To answer this question, we must test the significance of the contrast corresponding to the linear trend. According to Equation 8, the coefficients for this contrast are given by

$$c_j = X_j - \bar{X} \tag{8, repeated}$$

which as we saw earlier implies $c_1 = -1.5$, $c_2 = -0.5$, $c_3 = 0.5$, and $c_4 = 1.5$ for our data. All that must be done to calculate an observed F statistic is to find the values of SS_ψ and MS_W. From Equation 11, the sum of squares for the contrast is given by

$$SS_\psi = n(\hat{\psi}_{linear})^2 \Big/ \sum_{j=1}^{a} c_j^2 \tag{11, repeated}$$

In our example, $n = 6$ and $\sum_{j=1}^{a} c_j^2 = 5$. Recall that $\hat{\psi} = \sum_{j=1}^{a} c_j \bar{Y}_j$, so that

$$\hat{\psi}_{linear} = (-1.5)(2) + (-0.5)(6) + (0.5)(8) + (1.5)(9)$$
$$= 11.5$$

Substituting these values into Equation 11 yields

$$SS_\psi = 6(11.5)^2/5 = 158.7$$

Thus, the sum of squares attributable to the linear trend is 158.7 for these data. To obtain an observed F value, we must divide SS_ψ by MS_W. It is easily verified that $MS_W = 2.9$ for these data. As a result, the F statistic for the linear trend equals

$$F = 158.7/2.9 = 54.72,$$

which is statistically significant beyond the .001 level. Thus, we can assert that there is a linear trend in the population. In this example, increases in study time lead to increased recall.

Two further interpretational points deserve mention here. First, the alert reader may have noticed that the last sentence of the previous paragraph made it sound as if a claim was being made that increases in study time *cause* increases in recall. Because subjects were randomly assigned to study conditions, a causal inference is in fact legitimate here. Some readers might object that we cannot infer causation because we have tested a regression slope, which is equivalent to testing a correlation, and everyone knows that correlation does not imply causation. Half of this argument is correct. We did test a regression slope, which is equivalent to testing a correlation coefficient. However, as we discussed in Chapter 1, the legitimacy of a causal inference is determined not by how we analyze the data (e.g., regression versus ANOVA), but instead by the design of the study. The presence of random assignment permits a causal inference to be made here, although the question of *why* study time increases recall is left open to debate. Second, the meaning of a significant linear trend is sometimes misunderstood by researchers. To consider this issue, reconsider the plots shown earlier in Figures 6.1 and 6.2. The existence of a significant linear trend means that if a straight line is fit to either set of data (i.e., either Figure 6.1 or Figure 6.2), that straight line has a nonzero slope. In other words, there is a general tendency for Y to either decrease on average or increase on average as a function of X. The important point to realize here is that the presence of a significant linear trend says absolutely nothing about the possible presence of nonlinear trends. Some researchers mistakenly believe that finding a significant linear trend implies that the relationship between Y and X is strictly linear. However, it is entirely possible for the same data to exhibit both linear and nonlinear trends. Indeed, the plot of sample means in Figure 6.2 suggests such a possibility for the recall data.

Although recall increases as study time increases, there is some indication that an extra minute of study time may not always produce the same average increase in recall. For example, increasing study time from one minute to two minutes in this sample resulted in an average improvement of four words (see Table 6.1). However, increasing study time from three minutes to four minutes resulted in an average improvement of only one word. This pattern suggests the possibility of a nonlinear trend because a strictly linear trend would imply that the change in recall produced by increasing study time one minute should always be the same, in our case 2.3 words. Alternatively, the discrepancies from this value of 2.3 may simply reflect sampling error.[3] In other words, with only six subjects per group, we would not expect sample differences in recall to be exactly the same for every one-minute change in study time. Not surprisingly, there is a way we can resolve this question of whether the pattern obtained here reflects true nonlinearity or just sampling error.

TESTING FOR NONLINEARITY

The test for nonlinearity is often referred to as a test for *deviations* (or *departures*) *from linearity*. This phrase holds the key for understanding how to test for nonlinearity. For simplicity, we assume equal n throughout our discussion. At the end of the chapter, we briefly discuss the additional complexities that arise with unequal n.

Recall that the model for a linear trend was given by

$$Y_{ij} = \beta_0 + \beta_1 X_j + \varepsilon_{ij} \qquad \text{(2, repeated)}$$

Nonlinear relationships between X and Y can be incorporated into the model by including powers of X (e.g., X squared, X cubed, etc.) on the right-hand side of the equation. For example, we might have a model of the form

$$Y_{ij} = \beta_0 + \beta_1 X_j + \beta_2 X_j^2 + \beta_3 X_j^3 + \varepsilon_{ij}$$

This equation raises a question of how many powers of X should be included, that is, should we stop with X^3, or should we go on to X^4, X^5, and so on? The answer is that with a levels of the factor (i.e., with a values of X), we can include at most terms up to and including X^{a-1} (i.e., X raised to the $a-1$ power) in the model. To understand why, consider the simple case where $a = 2$—that is, we have only two groups of subjects. According to the above rule, we can include only X to the first power in the model. Thus, the model would be

$$Y_{ij} = \beta_0 + \beta_1 X_j$$

The reason for this is that with only two groups, there are only two group means we are trying to explain, and the relationship between these two means and X can always be explained with a straight line because a straight line can always be drawn between any two points. For this reason, terms of the form X^2, X^3, and so on are not needed. The same logic holds for values of a above 2 as well. For example, when $a = 3$, the model allowing for all possible nonlinear trends would be

$$Y_{ij} = \beta_0 + \beta_1 X_j + \beta_2 X_j^2$$

It turns out that with X and X^2 in the model, any three values for the means of Y can be fit perfectly with this model. Terms such as X^3, X^4, and so forth would simply be redundant (i.e., linearly dependent—see Chapter 4). Thus, a general model allowing for nonlinear trends with a levels of the factor includes all powers of X up to and including X to the $a-1$ power. The model then has the general form

$$Y_{ij} = \beta_0 + \beta_1 X_j + \beta_2 X_j^2 + \cdots + \beta_{a-1} X_j^{a-1} + \varepsilon_{ij} \qquad (12)$$

Departures from linearity are represented by X^2, X^3, and so forth. Thus, to test these departures for significance, we state a null hypothesis that

$$\beta_2 = \beta_3 = \cdots = \beta_{a-1} = 0$$

In other words, the hypothesis to be tested is that in the population all trends other than the linear trend are zero. This null hypothesis implies a restricted model of the form

$$Y_{ij} = \beta_0 + \beta_1 X_j + \varepsilon_{ij} \qquad \text{(2, repeated)}$$

which is simply the linear trend model with which we have already been working. As usual, the task is to compare these two models by finding the sum of squared errors and degrees of freedom for each model. Because we have already encountered the restricted model of Equation 2, we begin with it. We claimed earlier that the sum of squared errors for this model is given by

$$E_R = \sum_{j=1}^{a} \sum_{i=1}^{n} (Y_{ij} - \bar{Y})^2 - \left[\hat{\beta}_1^2 \sum_{j=1}^{a} \sum_{i=1}^{n} (X_{ij} - \bar{X})^2 \right]$$

We can simplify this expression in two ways. First, the term $\sum_{j=1}^{a} \sum_{i=1}^{n} (Y_{ij} - \bar{Y})^2$ equals what we referred to in Chapter 3 as SS_{total}. Second, we saw earlier in this chapter that

$$\hat{\beta}_1^2 \sum_{j=1}^{a} \sum_{i=1}^{n} (X_{ij} - \bar{X})^2 = SS_{linear}$$

Making these two substitutions,

$$E_R = SS_{total} - SS_{linear} \tag{13}$$

The degrees of freedom for the restricted model are straightforward because there are two parameters to be estimated (β_0 and β_1). Thus

$$df_R = N - 2 \tag{14}$$

where N is total sample size.

Next, let's turn our attention to the full model of Equation 12:

$$Y_{ij} = \beta_0 + \beta_1 X_j + \beta_2 X_j^2 + \cdots + \beta_{a-1} X_j^{a-1} + \varepsilon_{ij} \tag{12, repeated}$$

The degrees of freedom for this model are again straightforward because in general there are a parameters to be estimated. Thus,

$$df_F = N - a \tag{15}$$

To understand the sum of squared errors of this model, remember why we stopped adding powers of X at $a - 1$. Including powers up to this point guarantees that the resulting trend passes through the mean value of Y for each group. In other words, the predicted value of Y at each value of X is the mean value of Y for the group of subjects at that particular value of X. As a result, the predicted score on Y for individual i in group j is $\bar{Y}_j$, the mean Y score for all subjects in that group. Thus, for the full model of Equation 12,

$$\hat{Y}_{ij}(F) = \bar{Y}_j$$

where $\hat{Y}_{ij}(F)$ indicates the predicted score from the full model for subject i in group j. The sum of squared errors for the model is then given by

$$E_F = \sum_{j=1}^{a} \sum_{i=1}^{n} [Y_{ij} - \hat{Y}_{ij}(F)]^2$$

which is equivalent to

$$E_F = \sum_{j=1}^{a} \sum_{i=1}^{n} (Y_{ij} - \bar{Y}_j)^2$$

However, the term $\sum_{j=1}^{a} \sum_{i=1}^{n} (Y_{ij} - \bar{Y}_j)^2$ is simply the within-group sum of squares, so we can write

$$E_F = SS_W \tag{16}$$

Indeed, it turns out to be the case that the full model here, that is,

$$Y_{ij} = \beta_0 + \beta_1 X_j + \beta_2 X_j^2 + \cdots + \beta_{a-1} X_j^{a-1} + \varepsilon_{ij} \tag{12, repeated}$$

is equivalent to the full cell means model we have previously encountered:

$$Y_{ij} = \mu_j + \varepsilon_{ij}$$

Although the two full models obviously look very different, they both have a parameters, and both allow for a separate predicted Y score for each group. As a result, the two full models are mathematically equivalent.

We are now ready to compare the full and restricted models with our usual F statistic:

$$F = \frac{(E_R - E_F)/(df_R - df_F)}{E_F/df_F}$$

Substituting from Equations 13, 16, 14, and 15 for E_R, E_F, df_R, and df_F, respectively, yields

$$F = \frac{(SS_{total} - SS_{linear} - SS_W)/[(N - 2) - (N - a)]}{SS_W/(N - a)}$$

All three components of this expression can be simplified. First, consider $SS_{total} - SS_{linear} - SS_W$. From Chapter 3, $SS_{total} = SS_B + SS_W$, so substituting this expression for SS_{total} results in $SS_B + SS_W - SS_{linear} - SS_W$, which is obviously just $SS_B - SS_{linear}$. Similarly, $(N - 2) - (N - a)$ simplifies to $a - 2$. Finally, the ratio $SS_W/(N - a)$ is just MS_W. Putting the simplified components back together again yields

$$F = \frac{(SS_B - SS_{linear})/(a - 2)}{MS_W} \tag{17}$$

Equation 17 thus provides a formula for testing the statistical significance of nonlinear trends.

Numerical Example

To see an example of this test, reconsider the data in Table 6.1. Earlier in the chapter, we found that for these data $SS_{linear} = 158.7$ and $MS_W = 2.9$. From principles and formulas of Chapter 3, it is easily verified that $SS_B = 172.5$ for these data. Substituting these values along with $a = 4$ into Equation 17 yields

$$F = \frac{(172.5 - 158.7)/(4 - 2)}{2.9} = 2.38$$

which with 2 and 20 degrees of freedom is not significant at the .05 level. Thus, the results of this test suggest that the possible nonlinearity observed in Figure 6.2 for these data may simply reflect sampling error. Notice that as always we should not assert that the null hypothesis is true. We have not proved that the nonlinear trends here are zero; instead, we lack sufficient evidence to declare them to be nonzero.

We have just seen the procedure for testing departures from linearity. Although this test is frequently appropriate to address a researcher's questions, at times an alternate strategy is better. Instead of performing one test for *any* departures from linearity, it may be more informative to test for specific forms of departure. To understand this distinction, recall the null hypothesis we formulated for testing departure from linearity. In the full model

$$Y_{ij} = \beta_0 + \beta_1 X_j + \beta_2 X_j^2 + \cdots + \beta_{a-1} X_j^{a-1} + \varepsilon_{ij} \qquad (12, \text{repeated})$$

we tested a null hypothesis of the form

$$H_0 : \beta_2 = \beta_3 = \cdots = \beta_{a-1} = 0$$

Notice that the null hypothesis stipulates that each and every one of these $a - 2$ parameters equals zero, which is why the F statistic has $a - 2$ numerator degrees of freedom. In some situations, however, we may be interested in performing separate tests on one or more of these $a - 2$ parameters, much as we performed a separate test on β_1 to test the linear trend.

TESTING INDIVIDUAL HIGHER-ORDER TRENDS

Just as the test of the linear trend can be conceptualized as a test of a contrast, tests of the other β parameters (which are said to reflect higher-order trends) can also be formulated in terms of contrasts. There are two issues to consider here. First, what sort of trend do these individual β parameters represent? That is, what meaning can be attached to those individual parameters? Second, how are appropriate contrast coefficients found for testing the significance of these parameters?

To understand the meaning of the individual β parameters, consider a specific case with four groups, so that $a = 4$. In this case, the full model can be written as

$$Y_{ij} = \beta_0 + \beta_1 X_j + \beta_2 X_j^2 + \beta_3 X_j^3 + \varepsilon_{ij}$$

Figure 6.3(a–c) shows the types of trends represented by each individual β parameter. Figure 6.3(a) shows that the role of β_1 is to account for any straight line relationship between X and Y. As X increases, Y systematically increases also (assuming that the slope of the line is positive; otherwise, Y systematically decreases). Notice that the X variable here is raised to the first power and that there are no (i.e., zero) changes in the direction of the trend. In other words, X to the first power produces a trend with zero bends. Figure 6.3(b) shows that the inclusion of X^2 in the model allows Y to systematically decrease as X moves away (either higher or lower) from some central point on the x-axis. This pattern is called a *quadratic trend*. Figure 6.3(b) corresponds to a plot where the sign of β_2 is negative; if β_2 were positive, the trend would be reversed, and Y would systematically increase as X moves away from the central point. Notice that when X is raised to the second power, there is one change of direction (i.e., bend) in the curve. Figure 6.3(c) shows that the inclusion of X^3 in the model allows Y to first increase, then decrease, and then increase again as X increases. This pattern is called a *cubic trend*. Once again, if the sign of β_3 were reversed, the plot would be reversed as well (i.e., it would be flipped over about a horizontal line). Notice that when X is raised to the third power, there are two changes of direction (i.e., bends) in the curve. Regardless of the value of a, this same pattern occurs. Namely, if X is raised to some power P, the curve associated with X^P has $P - 1$ bends in it.

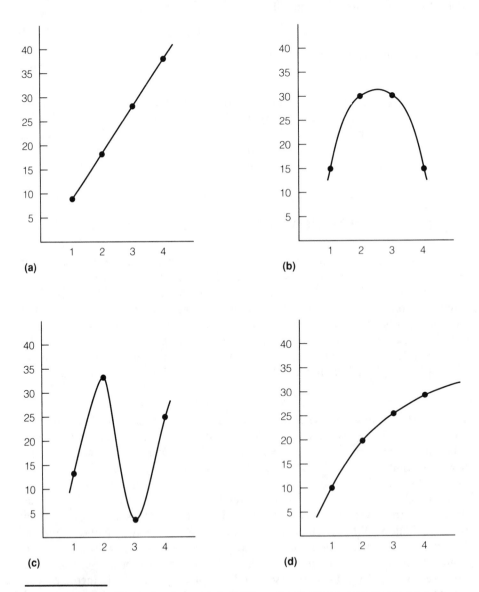

F I G U R E **6. 3**   Plots of various trends: (a) linear trend, (b) quadratic trend, (c) cubic trend, and (d) linear and quadratic trends.

Figure 6.3(d) serves as a reminder that in an actual study, the pattern of means may very well reflect a combination of two or more of the pure forms shown in Figure 6.3(a–c). Although the means in Figure 6.3(d) tend to increase as X increases, the increases themselves are becoming smaller. Such a negatively accelerated curve is fairly common in the behavioral sciences and reflects a model with both linear and quadratic components. Because such combinations of trends are possible, it is usually necessary to test higher-order trends regardless of whether the linear trend is statistically significant. We will return to this issue after we discuss the choice of appropriate contrast coefficients.

Contrast Coefficients for Higher-Order Trends

Now that we have considered the form that higher-order trends take on, it is necessary to consider how to test these trends as contrasts. In other words, we need to determine appropriate contrast coefficients for testing each trend. Recall that we have already shown that with equal n, the appropriate contrast coefficients for testing the linear trend are given by

$$c_j = X_j - \bar{X}$$

Although we could go through similar steps to find the appropriate coefficients for testing higher-order trends (e.g., quadratic, cubic, etc.), we will not do so because the steps would be tedious. In addition, many statistical packages calculate the appropriate coefficients and conduct the corresponding significance tests automatically. Thus, what is important is that the concepts underlying trend analysis be understood, as opposed to being able to derive contrast coefficients.

Although calculations are usually best left to the computer, it is helpful to present higher-order trend coefficients to better understand the meaning of the trends. Appendix Table A.10 presents contrast coefficients for performing trend analysis whenever two conditions are met. First, equal spacing of the X variable is assumed. Equal spacing implies that the numerical difference between adjacent values of X is a constant. For example, X values of 7, 12, 17, 22, and 27 would be equally spaced because the difference between adjacent values is always 5. On the other hand, a developmental psychologist who compared children of ages 12 months, 13 months, 15 months, 18 months, and 22 months would have unequally spaced values. A researcher might choose to use such unequal spacing if theoretical considerations implied the possibility of rapid change in the months shortly after month 12, followed by less rapid change in later months (see Keppel, 1982, p. 132, for a good discussion of this issue). Many statistical packages automatically generate appropriate coefficients even when values are unequally spaced. Second, Table A.10 assumes that sample sizes are equal in every group. Whether these coefficients are also appropriate with unequal n is subject to debate, as we discuss at the end of the chapter.

To understand Table A.10, let's consider the four-group case in some detail. According to the table, the appropriate contrast coefficients for testing the linear trend are given by values of -3, -1, 1, and 3 for groups 1, 2, 3, and 4, respectively. Are these the same coefficients that we developed in the four-group case earlier in the chapter? No, they are not, because in the word-recall study described earlier, we used contrast coefficients of -1.5, -0.5, 0.5, and 1.5 for the four groups, based on $X_j - \bar{X}$. However, these two sets of coefficients are proportional to one another because we can multiply each recall-study coefficient by two to obtain the coefficients shown in Table A.10. As we saw in Chapter 4, multiplying all coefficients of a contrast by a constant does not change the sum of squares attributable to the contrast. As a result, the observed F value for the contrast also remains the same. Thus, the tabled values of -3, -1, 1, and 3 are consistent with the values of -1.5, -0.5, 0.5, and 1.5 that we used earlier.

According to Table A.10, the coefficients for testing a quadratic trend among four groups are equal to 1, -1, -1, and 1. In what sense do these coefficients test a quadratic trend? Instead of attempting to provide a mathematical answer, reconsider Figure 6.3(a–c). What happens if we apply these coefficients to the means shown in Figure 6.3(a)? The resultant contrast has a value of zero, implying no quadratic trend, which is just what we would expect for means that perfectly fit a straight line. Similarly, applying the coefficients to the means shown in Figure 6.3(c) also yields a value of zero because these means correspond to a pure cubic trend. However, applying the coefficients to the means of Figure 6.3(b) produces a nonzero value because these data show a quadratic trend. Similarly, the cubic trend coefficients shown in Table A.10 yield a contrast whose value equals zero for Figure 6.3(a and b) but which is nonzero for Figure 6.3(c). Thus, the coefficients shown in Table A.10 provide an appropriate set of values for testing the pure forms of trend shown in Figure 6.3(a–c).

Another perspective on higher-order trends can be gained by plotting the coefficients themselves on the y-axis, with the corresponding X values on the x-axis. If we do this, we discover that the resultant plot looks exactly like the type of trend those coefficients are designed to detect. Thus, the coefficients for a linear trend form a straight line when we plot them. Similarly, the coefficients for a quadratic trend form a U shape like that shown in Figure 6.3(b),[4] and the coefficients for a cubic trend display two bends, as in Figure 6.3(c). As you might guess, this equivalence of plots is not a coincidence, but instead results from a fact we developed in Chapter 5. We showed in Chapter 5 that the sum of squares for a contrast equals the entire between-group sum of squares if we define the coefficients to equal weighted deviations from the grand mean, that is,

$$c_j = n_j(\bar{Y}_j - \bar{Y}) \qquad (5.20)$$

With equal n as we are assuming here, a contrast completely accounts for between-group differences if its coefficients match the pattern of mean differences. As we have seen, this is exactly what the trend coefficients accomplish.

One other property of the contrasts defined in Appendix Table A.10 should be mentioned. Assuming equal n, as we are here, it is fairly easy to show that the contrasts defined by these coefficients form an orthogonal set. In other words, for a particular number of groups, trend components are orthogonal to each other, with equal n. As a result, sums of squares attributable to individual trends can be added together. The implications of this orthogonality can be discussed most easily in the context of our numerical example, to which we now turn.

Numerical Example

We now illustrate testing higher-order trends individually in our numerical example. Although we have already tested the linear trend, we include that test here as well, for the sake of completeness and to show results in terms of the coefficients from Appendix Table A.10.

Table 6.2 shows intermediate calculations used to find the sum of squares attributable to each contrast. As always (with equal n), each sum of squares is found from

$$SS_\psi = \frac{n(\hat{\psi})^2}{\sum\limits_{j=1}^{a} c_j^2}$$

Recall that in this example, $n = 6$. All other quantities needed in the calculation are shown in Table 6.2.

Table 6.3 presents the ANOVA table for these data. The first line of the table shows the between-group sum of squares for the data. The corresponding F test is the test of the omnibus null hypothesis that all four group population means are equal, as we discussed in Chapter 3. Consistent with the discussion in Chapter 5, the omnibus test need not necessarily be performed when testing trends because we

T A B L E **6. 2** Intermediate Calculations for Sum of Squares for Each Trend Component

	Group						
	1	*2*	*3*	*4*			
Mean	2	6	8	9			
	Contrast Coefficients				$\hat{\psi}$	$\sum\limits_{j=1}^{a} c_j^2$	SS
	1	*2*	*3*	*4*			
Linear	−3	−1	1	3	23	20	158.7
Quadratic	1	−1	−1	1	−3	4	13.5
Cubic	−1	3	−3	1	1	20	0.3

T A B L E **6. 3** ANOVA Table for Recall Data of Table 6.1

Source	SS		df		MS	F	p
Between	172.5		3		57.5	19.83	.001
Linear		158.7		1	158.7	54.72	.001
Deviation from linearity		13.8		2	6.9	2.38	.118
Quadratic			13.5	1	13.5	4.66	.043
Cubic			0.3	1	0.3	0.10	.751
Within	58.0		20		2.9		

may have planned to test these trends prior to collecting the data; it is presented here primarily to show how it relates to the tests of individual trends. The second line of Table 6.3 shows the results for the linear trend, which as we have already seen is highly statistically significant. The third line presents the sum of squares and corresponding test for departure from linearity. As we have seen, the test is not significant at the .05 level. Notice that as exemplified by Equation 17 earlier in the chapter

$$SS_{\text{deviation from linearity}} = SS_B - SS_{\text{linear}}$$

or equivalently,

$$SS_B = SS_{\text{linear}} + SS_{\text{deviation from linearity}} \tag{18}$$

With equal n, the between-group sum of squares can be partitioned into two additive components: linear and nonlinear. The fourth line of Table 6.3 shows the results for the quadratic trend. When tested individually with $\alpha_{PC} = .05$, this trend is significant. We discuss the apparent inconsistency between this result and the nonsignificant result for departure from linearity momentarily. First, however, notice that the fifth line of Table 6.3 presents the results for the cubic trend, which is nonsignificant for these data. Notice also that with equal n the sum of squares attributable to non-linearity can be partitioned into two additive components:

$$SS_{\text{deviation from linearity}} = SS_{\text{quadratic}} + SS_{\text{cubic}} \tag{19}$$

If there were more than four groups, the SS_{cubic} term would instead be

$$SS_{\text{deviation from quadratic}}$$

which would represent the sum of squares attributable to trends above the quadratic model, that is, a model that includes linear and quadratic components. Substituting the right-hand side of Equation 19 for $SS_{\text{deviation from linearity}}$ into Equation 18 yields

$$SS_B = SS_{\text{linear}} + SS_{\text{quadratic}} + SS_{\text{cubic}}$$

Thus, when $a = 4$ and sample sizes are equal, the three trend contrasts completely account for the variation among the groups. This relationship holds because the trend contrasts form an orthogonal set as long as sample sizes are equal.

Let's now return to the apparent discrepancy between the significant quadratic trend and the nonsignificant deviation from linearity. How can we assert that the β_2 parameter is nonzero and at the same time fail to reject a hypothesis that both β_2 and β_3 are zero? After all, if β_2 is nonzero, then it cannot be true that both β_2 and β_3 are zero. Equation 19 is helpful for understanding this apparent dilemma:

$$SS_{\text{deviation from linearity}} = SS_{\text{quadratic}} + SS_{\text{cubic}} \tag{19, repeated}$$

The F test for deviation from linearity equals

$$F = \frac{(SS_{\text{quadratic}} + SS_{\text{cubic}})/2}{MS_W} \tag{20}$$

while the F statistic for the quadratic trend by itself equals

$$F = \frac{SS_{\text{quadratic}}}{MS_W} \tag{21}$$

When SS_{cubic} is small, as in this example, the F statistic of Equation 21 may be nearly twice as large as the F statistic of Equation 20. This reflects the fact that the test of the quadratic trend by itself is more powerful than the test of deviation from linearity if the population quadratic trend is nonzero but the population cubic trend is zero.

What does this imply about which tests shown in Table 6.3 should be performed and interpreted? In most behavioral studies, trends beyond quadratic are largely uninterpretable. For this reason, one strategy is to test the linear trend separately, the quadratic trend separately, and then to perform a combined test of all remaining trends (i.e., cubic, quartic, etc.). This last test is usually not directly interpreted, except insofar as it indicates whether linear and quadratic components are adequate to explain between-group differences. A slightly different strategy can be employed if theory dictates that any differences between groups should be linear in nature. In this situation, the linear trend can be tested by itself, and all remaining trends are tested together as the departure from linearity. As in our numerical example, these two strategies do not always reach the same conclusion. Which is more appropriate is dictated primarily by theoretical considerations.

FURTHER EXAMINATION OF NONLINEAR TRENDS

Now, it may be helpful to further examine our numerical example in order to gain a better understanding of nonlinear trends, especially how both linear and nonlinear trends might exist in the same data. As shown in Figure 6.1, there is a systematic tendency in these data for Y (number of words recalled) to increase as X (study time) increases. This tendency explains why the linear trend is significant, as shown in Figure 6.2.

To understand the meaning of the quadratic trend here, it is helpful to remove the effects of the linear trend from the data. To do this, we must first describe the linear trend. This can be done in either of two ways. First, earlier in the chapter we derived the equation of the best-fitting straight line for these data:

$$\hat{Y}_{ij} = 0.50 + 2.3X_j$$

Notice from this equation that all subjects in group 1 (i.e., $X_1 = 1$) are predicted by the linear trend model to have a recall score of 2.8, subjects in group 2 are predicted to have a score of 5.1, and so forth. Alternatively, we can arrive at these same predicted values by using the following equation:

$$\hat{Y}_{ij} = \bar{Y} + \left[\hat{\psi}_{linear} \bigg/ \sum_{j=1}^{a} c_{j(linear)}^2 \right] c_{j(linear)} \tag{22}$$

where the $c_{j(linear)}$ coefficients come from Appendix Table A.10. For our data, $\hat{\psi}_{linear} = 23$ and $\sum_{j=1}^{a} c_{j(linear)}^2 = 20$ from earlier calculations shown in Table 6.2. Also, $\bar{Y} = 6.25$. Substituting these values into Equation 22 yields

$$\hat{Y}_{ij} = 6.25 + (23/20)c_{j(\text{linear})}$$

To get predicted scores, $c_{j(\text{linear})}$ values from Appendix Table A.10 are simply substituted into the equation. For our data, the following values are obtained: $\hat{Y}_{i1} = 2.8$, $\hat{Y}_{i2} = 5.1$, $\hat{Y}_{i3} = 7.4$, and $\hat{Y}_{i4} = 9.7$. It is easily verified that these predicted scores are identical to those obtained from using the equation of the best-fitting straight line,

$$\hat{Y}_{ij} = 0.50 + 2.3X_j$$

Regardless of which way we obtain predicted scores, we can now look at the errors of the linear trend model. Figure 6.4 shows this error for each of the 24 subjects in the study. Even more useful is Figure 6.5, which shows the mean error for each group. In other words, the mean error in group 1 is −0.8 because the predicted score for every subject in this group is 2.8, but in fact the actual sample mean for subjects in this group is only 2.0. Notice also that the values plotted in Figure 6.5 correspond to the differences between the actual means and the predicted means shown earlier in Figure 6.2.

The plots in Figures 6.4 and 6.5 display the data with the linear trend removed. If the only true trend in the data is linear, there should be no apparent pattern to the data in Figures 6.4 and 6.5. In fact, however, as seen most clearly in Figure 6.5, these data bear a strong resemblance to the quadratic curve shown in Figure 6.3(b).

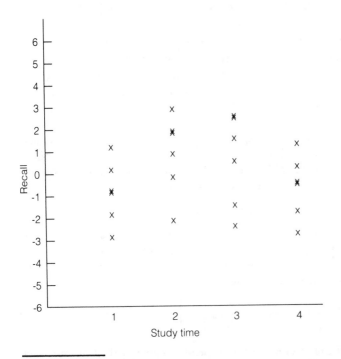

F I G U R E 6. 4 Scatterplot of Figure 6.1 data with linear trend removed.

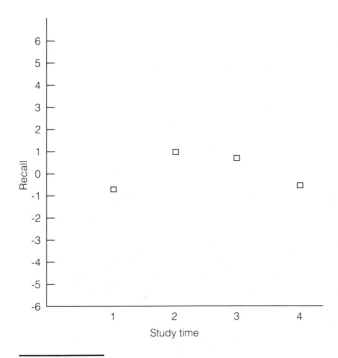

FIGURE 6.5 Plot of sample means with linear trend removed.

The plot of the data strongly suggests that the linear trend is not sufficient by itself to fully describe the data. This visual impression is consistent with the statistically significant effect of the quadratic trend shown earlier in Table 6.3.

What sort of curve is produced when both linear and quadratic trends are included in the model? Remember that with only the linear trend in the model, predicted scores of the model could be found from Equation 22:

$$\hat{Y}_{ij} = \bar{Y} + \left[\hat{\psi}_{\text{linear}} \middle/ \sum_{j=1}^{a} c_{j(\text{linear})}^2 \right] c_{j(\text{linear})} \qquad \text{(22, repeated)}$$

A similar equation can be used when the quadratic trend is added to the model:

$$\hat{Y}_{ij} = \bar{Y} + \left[\hat{\psi}_{\text{linear}} \middle/ \sum_{j=1}^{a} c_{j(\text{linear})}^2 \right] c_{j(\text{linear})}$$

$$+ \left[\hat{\psi}_{\text{quadratic}} \middle/ \sum_{j=1}^{a} c_{j(\text{quadratic})}^2 \right] c_{j(\text{quadratic})} \qquad \text{(23)}$$

where once again $c_{j(\text{linear})}$ and $c_{j(\text{quadratic})}$ coefficients can be found in Appendix Table A.10. For our data, $\bar{Y} = 6.25$, $\hat{\psi}_{\text{linear}} = 23$, $\sum_{j=1}^{a} c_{j(\text{linear})}^2 = 20$, $\hat{\psi}_{\text{quadratic}} = -3$, and $\sum_{j=1}^{a} c_{j(\text{quadratic})}^2 = 4$ (see Table 6.2). Substituting these values into Equation 23 yields

$$\hat{Y}_{ij} = 6.25 + 1.15c_{j(\text{linear})} - 0.75c_{j(\text{quadratic})}$$

As before, to get predicted scores, $c_{j(\text{linear})}$ and $c_{j(\text{quadratic})}$ values from Appendix Table A.10 are substituted into the equation. The following predicted scores are obtained for each group:

Group 1: $\quad \hat{Y}_{i1} = 6.25 + 1.15(-3) - 0.75(1) = 2.05$

Group 2: $\quad \hat{Y}_{i2} = 6.25 + 1.15(-1) - 0.75(-1) = 5.85$

Group 3: $\quad \hat{Y}_{i3} = 6.25 + 1.15(1) - 0.75(-1) = 8.15$

Group 4: $\quad \hat{Y}_{i4} = 6.25 + 1.15(3) - 0.75(1) = 8.95$

Notice that the inclusion of the quadratic term increases the predicted scores for groups 2 and 3 but decreases the predicted scores for groups 1 and 4, which is exactly what Figure 6.5 suggests needs to be done.

Figure 6.6 shows the actual sample means and the predicted means obtained from the quadratic model of Equation 23, that is, the model that includes both linear and quadratic trends. It seems clear from comparing Figure 6.2 for the linear trend model to Figure 6.6 for the quadratic model that the quadratic model fits the data better. Once again, the graphs confirm the statistically significant quadratic trend as shown in Table 6.3.

Just as we looked at errors of the linear trend model, we can also look at the

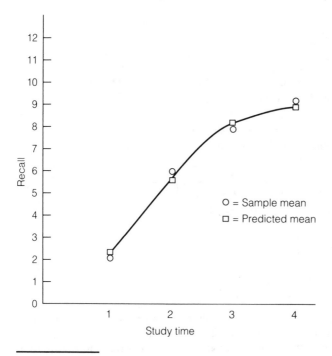

FIGURE 6.6 Plot of sample means and estimated means from quadratic model.

errors of the quadratic trend model. Figure 6.7 shows this error for each of the 24 subjects in the study, and Figure 6.8 shows the mean error for each group. Two things must be said about Figure 6.8. First, and most important, the means in Figure 6.8 all hover close to zero. Unless the within-group variance is very small (and we can tell from Figure 6.7 that it is not), this suggests that the remaining variation in sample means is likely to be random rather than systematic. Once again, this visual impression is corroborated by the statistical test of the cubic trend, which as we saw in Table 6.3 was nonsignificant. Second, the obsessive–compulsives among you may have noticed that although the means in Figure 6.8 hover around zero, it is nevertheless true that the pattern of these means fits the pattern of means shown in Figure 6.3(c) for a cubic trend. Doesn't this similarity suggest that there is in fact a cubic trend to the data, regardless of what the significance test might say? The answer is No, it does not, because the only pattern that the means can possibly display is one like Figure 6.3(c) (or its negative), once the linear and quadratic trends have been removed. After their removal, the only source of between-group variance remaining must be cubic because, as we saw earlier with four groups and equal n,

$$SS_B = SS_{linear} + SS_{quadratic} + SS_{cubic}$$

The important question, however, is the extent to which SS_{cubic} is "large." As suggested by Figure 6.7, the cubic trend for these data is nonsignificant.

Although we have decided that the cubic trend is unnecessary for these data, it

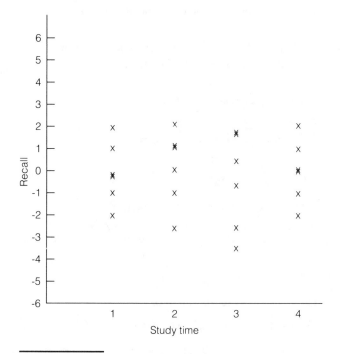

F I G U R E 6.7 Scatterplot of Figure 6.1 data with linear and quadratic trends removed.

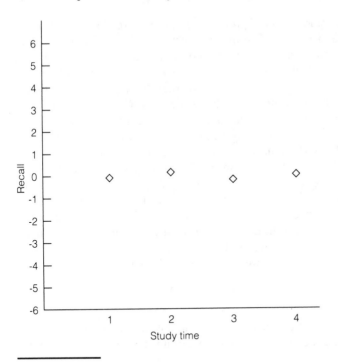

FIGURE 6.8 Plot of sample means with linear and quadratic trends removed.

is instructive to see what would happen if we were to add the cubic trend component to our model. Predicted scores can be found from the following equation:

$$\hat{Y}_{ij} = \bar{Y} + \left[\hat{\psi}_{\text{linear}} \Big/ \sum_{j=1}^{a} c^2_{j(\text{linear})} \right] c_{j(\text{linear})}$$

$$+ \left[\hat{\psi}_{\text{quadratic}} \Big/ \sum_{j=1}^{a} c^2_{j(\text{quadratic})} \right] c_{j(\text{quadratic})}$$

$$+ \left[\hat{\psi}_{\text{cubic}} \Big/ \sum_{j=1}^{a} c^2_{j(\text{cubic})} \right] c_{j(\text{cubic})} \tag{24}$$

where, as before contrast coefficients are obtained from appendix Table A.10. For our data, $\bar{Y} = 6.25$, $\hat{\psi}_{\text{linear}} = 23$, $\sum_{j=1}^{a} c^2_{j(\text{linear})} = 20$, $\hat{\psi}_{\text{quadratic}} = -3$, $\sum_{j=1}^{a} c^2_{j(\text{quadratic})} = 4$, $\hat{\psi}_{\text{cubic}} = 1$, and $\sum_{j=1}^{a} c^2_{j(\text{cubic})} = 20$ (see Table 6.2). Substituting these values into Equation 24 yields

$$\hat{Y}_{ij} = 6.25 + 1.15c_{j(\text{linear})} - 0.75c_{j(\text{quadratic})} + 0.05c_{j(\text{cubic})}$$

As a result, the following predicted scores are obtained for each group:

Group 1: $\hat{Y}_{i1} = 6.25 + 1.15(-3) - 0.75(1) + 0.05(-1) = 2.00$

Group 2: $\hat{Y}_{i2} = 6.25 + 1.15(-1) - 0.75(-1) + 0.05(3) = 6.00$

Group 3: $\hat{Y}_{i3} = 6.25 + 1.15(1) - 0.75(-1) + 0.05(-3) = 8.00$

Group 4: $\hat{Y}_{i4} = 6.25 + 1.15(3) - 0.75(1) + 0.05(1) = 9.00$

The predicted means of 2, 6, 8, and 9 are literally identical to the observed sample means. Thus, the inclusion of the cubic trend has resulted in a model that completely accounts for all between-group variation. Although at first glance this may seem impressive, it is in fact a mathematical necessity of the trend-analysis model. As we discussed previously, with a groups, it is always the case that a model with $a - 1$ trend components completely explains the between-group variance, and as a consequence, predicted means equal actual sample means. The important practical point to be understood in the numerical example is that as Figure 6.6 shows, the quadratic trend model provides a very close fit to the sample means. As a consequence, there is no evidence for needing to include the cubic trend in the model.

TREND ANALYSIS WITH UNEQUAL SAMPLE SIZES

Trend analysis becomes more complicated when sample sizes are unequal. In essence, the reason for the additional complication is that the contrasts defined by the trend coefficients of Appendix Table A.10 are no longer orthogonal when sample sizes are unequal. As a result, trend components as defined by these coefficients no longer partition the between-group sum of squares additively. We do not attempt to deal with all the implications of this added complexity. Instead, we briefly present two alternate strategies for dealing with unequal n.

The first approach involves a hierarchical approach to model comparisons. With this approach, individual trend components are added to the model in successive steps, in a prespecified theoretical order. The first component to enter the model is the linear trend. The two models to be compared are thus defined to be

$$\text{I} \qquad Y_{ij} = \beta_0 + \varepsilon_{ij}$$

$$\text{II} \qquad Y_{ij} = \beta_0 + \beta_1 X_j + \varepsilon_{ij}$$

The sum of squares attributable to the linear trend then equals $E_\text{I} - E_\text{II}$. Second, a quadratic term is added to Model II, yielding

$$\text{III} \qquad Y_{ij} = \beta_0 + \beta_1 X_j + \beta_2 X_j^2 + \varepsilon_{ij}$$

The sum of squares attributable to the quadratic trend then equals $E_\text{II} - E_\text{III}$. Additional terms are added to the model in this fashion until all possible terms have been entered.

The second approach simply continues to use the contrast coefficients of Appendix Table A.10 despite the fact that sample sizes are unequal. The sum of squares attributable to any particular trend is given by

$$SS_\psi = (\hat{\psi})^2 \left/ \sum_{j=1}^{a} (c_j^2/n_j) \right.$$

Which of these two approaches is preferable? Fortunately, with equal n, the two approaches yield identical results, so no choice is necessary. With unequal n, however, the two approaches do not necessarily lead to the same conclusion. To make the choice more difficult, sometimes one approach is better, and at other times the other approach is better. To understand this dilemma, it is helpful to compare contrast coefficients. It can be shown that the hierarchical approach is equivalent to testing contrasts whose coefficients are influenced by the sample size of each group. For example, the contrast coefficients for testing the linear trend with the hierarchical approach can be shown to equal

$$c_j = n_j(X_j - \bar{X}_{\text{w}}) \tag{25}$$

where $\bar{X}_{\text{w}}$ is the weighted sample mean of the X values. The second approach, on the other hand, is often called an unweighted approach because it continues to use unweighted contrast coefficients of the form

$$c_j = X_j - \bar{X}_{\text{U}} \tag{26}$$

where $\bar{X}_{\text{U}}$ is the unweighted sample mean of the X values.[5] Notice that the coefficients of Equation 26 differ from those of Equation 25 in that groups implicitly receive equal weights of 1.0 instead of weights dependent on sample size.

Which approach is better—weighted or unweighted coefficients? The answer is, It depends. For example, if the only true trend in the population is linear, then the weighted coefficients of Equation 25 are superior because the test of the linear trend will be more powerful than the test using unweighted coefficients. The hierarchical approach also produces additive sums of squares, unlike the unweighted approach. However, if there are in fact nonlinear trends in the population, the weighted coefficients of Equation 25 may result in a biased estimate of the true population slope coefficient. For this reason, a linear trend deemed to be statistically significant by the weighted coefficients may in fact be reflective of a true quadratic trend in the population means. The linear trend for the population means may very well be zero. Exercise 11 at the end of the chapter explores this point in more detail. Because the use of weighted coefficients potentially leads to bias, our general recommendation is to continue to use unweighted coefficients, as shown in Appendix Table A.10 for equally spaced intervals of X. However, when there are strong theoretical reasons to believe that the only true population trend is linear, the use of weighted coefficients may be justified. Perhaps most important is simply to be aware of the distinction and to know which type of coefficient your favorite statistical package uses. With most packages, either type of coefficient can be used, although to do so may require overriding certain default values built into the program. In addition, you might be reassured to know that the distinction between weighted and unweighted means is discussed in greater detail in Chapter 7, when we discuss two-way ANOVA with unequal sample sizes.

CONCLUDING COMMENTS

We conclude the presentation of trend analysis with brief mention of four miscellaneous points. First, we introduced trend analysis as a valuable tool for studying group differences whenever the defining characteristic of groups is quantitative. Hale (1977), in an article directed primarily toward developmental psychologists, argues persuasively that many psychologists tend to underutilize trend analysis. He describes potential benefits of the trend-analysis approach, particularly when the form of the trend is expected to be monotonic. Second, researchers using trend analysis must be careful to avoid extrapolating beyond the data. Statistical inferences regarding trends pertain only to the values of X (the factor) actually used in the study. For example, suppose a four-group study with X values of 1, 2, 3, and 4 yields a linear trend of the form

$$Y_{ij} = 0.50 + 2.3X_j$$

It is inappropriate to use this equation to predict that if X were equal to 10, the mean Y value would be 23.50. Even if the trend appears to be purely linear throughout the range from 1 to 4, there is no guarantee that the trend would remain linear beyond X values of 4. Third, interpolation must also be used carefully and thoughtfully. For example, in the four-group study, it may be reasonable to predict that if X were equal to 3.5, the mean value of Y would be 8.55. However, such a prediction requires some theoretical justification because there are no data that can directly be used to predict Y when X is between 3 and 4. However, in many practical situations, interpolation, unlike extrapolation, is probably reasonably well justified. Fourth, there is a whole host of techniques available for curve fitting beyond the use of orthogonal polynomial trends. Although trend analysis is typically the methodology of choice for analyzing data with quantitative factors, theoretical considerations sometimes suggest other methodologies. The interested reader is referred to Lewis's (1960) classic book on curve fitting.

EXERCISES

1. Appendix Table A.10 shows that the trend coefficients for four equally spaced levels of a quantitative factor are given by

	Level			
	1	2	3	4
Linear	-3	-1	1	3
Quadratic	1	-1	-1	1
Cubic	-1	3	-3	1

   Show that the contrasts defined by these coefficients form an orthogonal set with equal n.

*2. The plot in Figure 6.3(a) represents a pure linear trend for four groups. The purpose of this exercise is to verify that the figure does in fact reflect a pure form. Assume $n = 10$ subjects per group throughout. The means shown in Figure 6.3(a) are $\bar{Y}_1 = 10$, $\bar{Y}_2 = 20$, $\bar{Y}_3 = 30$, and $\bar{Y}_4 = 40$.
   a. Find the sum of squares for the linear trend.
   b. Find the sum of squares for the quadratic trend.
   c. Find the sum of squares for the cubic trend.
   d. Does Figure 6.3(a) reflect a pure linear trend?

3. The plot in Figure 6.3(b) represents a pure quadratic trend for four groups. The purpose of this exercise is to verify that the figure does in fact reflect a pure form. Assume $n = 10$ subjects per group throughout. The means shown in Figure 6.3(b) are $\bar{Y}_1 = 15$, $\bar{Y}_2 = 30$, $\bar{Y}_3 = 30$, and $\bar{Y}_4 = 15$.
   a. Find the sum of squares for the linear trend.
   b. Find the sum of squares for the quadratic trend.
   c. Find the sum of squares for the cubic trend.
   d. Does Figure 6.3(b) reflect a pure quadratic trend?

4. The plot in Figure 6.3(c) represents a pure cubic trend for four groups. The purpose of this exercise is to verify that the figure does in fact reflect a pure form. Assume $n = 10$ subjects per group throughout. The means shown in Figure 6.3(c) are $\bar{Y}_1 = 15$, $\bar{Y}_2 = 35$, $\bar{Y}_3 = 5$, and $\bar{Y}_4 = 25$.
   a. Find the sum of squares for the linear trend.
   b. Find the sum of squares for the quadratic trend.
   c. Find the sum of squares for the cubic trend.
   d. Does Figure 6.3(c) reflect a pure cubic trend?

*5. An investigator conducted a five-group study where the groups represent equally spaced levels of a quantitative factor. Data are obtained for 15 subjects in each group. The following sample means are obtained: $\bar{Y}_1 = 80$, $\bar{Y}_2 = 83$, $\bar{Y}_3 = 87$, $\bar{Y}_4 = 89$, and $\bar{Y}_5 = 91$. The value of mean square within (MS_W) equals 150.
   a. Assume that the investigator has planned to test only the linear trend. Is the trend statistically significant at the .05 level?
   b. Is the omnibus test of group differences statistically significant? In other words, can the null hypothesis $H_0 : \mu_1 = \mu_2 = \mu_3 = \mu_4 = \mu_5$ be rejected?
   c. Why is the observed F value so much larger for the linear trend than for the omnibus test? (HINT: Compare SS_{linear} to SS_B for these data. If SS_{linear} equals SS_B, how would the respective F values compare?)
   d. What are the implications of your answer to part c for the potential benefits of testing a planned linear trend instead of testing the omnibus null hypothesis?
   e. Is it legitimate to claim a planned linear trend as statistically significant if the omnibus test for the data is nonsignificant?

6. We saw that the estimated slope parameter for the data in Table 6.1 is $\hat{\beta}_1 = 2.3$. However, slopes between adjacent levels of the factor differ appreciably from 2.3. In particular, the slope of the line connecting the one-minute and two-minute means is 4, the slope from two minutes to three minutes is 2, and the slope from three minutes to four minutes is 1. Verify the statement made in Note 3 that the slope $\hat{\beta}_1$ is a weighted average of these individual slopes. Specifically, show that the value of $\hat{\beta}_1$ here equals $\hat{\beta}_1 = .3d_1 + .4d_2 + .3d_3$, where $d_1 = \bar{Y}_2 - \bar{Y}_1$, $d_2 = \bar{Y}_3 - \bar{Y}_2$, and $d_3 = \bar{Y}_4 - \bar{Y}_3$.

7. A graduate student used a three-group study employing equally spaced levels of a quantitative factor for her thesis. Her theory suggests that the relationship between her factor and her dependent variable should be linear. She obtains the following data ($n = 10$ per group): $\bar{Y}_1 = 10$, $\bar{Y}_2 = 50$, and $\bar{Y}_3 = 30$. Her test of the linear trend yields an F value of 10.0, which is significant at the .01 level. Does this finding support her theory? Why or why not?

*8. A developmental psychologist is interested in the extent to which childrens' memory for facts improves as children get older. Ten children each of ages 4, 7, and 10 are randomly selected to participate in the study. The three-group means on the dependent measure of accuracy are 5.5, 7.7, and 10.2. To estimate the slope parameter, the psychologist finds linear trend coefficients of -1, 0, and 1 for three groups from Appendix Table A.10. Equation 7 is used to find the estimated slope. Specifically, $\hat{\psi} = 4.7$ and $\sum_{j=1}^{a} c_j^2 = 2$, so the estimated slope appears to be $\hat{\beta}_1 = 4.7/2 = 2.35$. However, this seems to imply an average increase of 2.35 units on the dependent measure for every increase of 1 year in age. Thus, we might expect 10-year-olds to outperform 4-year-olds by approximately 14.10 units (note that 14.10 equals the product of 6 and 2.35). In fact, however, 10-year-olds outperform 4-year-olds by only 4.7 units in the study. Is the psychologist's estimated slope of 2.35 accurate? Why or why not?

9. An interesting question to developmental psychologists is whether children's generosity (or altruism) steadily increases with age. The following study is modeled after an experiment reported in Zarbatany, L., Hartmann, D. P., & Gelfand, D. M. (1985). "Why does children's generosity increase with age: Susceptibility to experimenter influence or altruism?" *Child Development, 56,* 746–756. First-, third-, and fifth-grade children were allowed to select from among four alternatives what they would do if a fixed amount of money were donated to their school. A separate group of children of similar ages was used to create a generosity scale, using a paired-comparisons format. (Interestingly, in the actual study, the experimenters also used a scale with rational weights and obtained different results for the two weighting schemes.) Consider the following data, where each score represents the rating of the child's chosen alternative on the generosity scale:

First Graders	Third Graders	Fifth Graders
0	2	3
1	1	2
0	3	3
2	0	1
0	0	2
1	2	0
3	0	3
2	1	1
2	0	1
1	1	2
3	1	3
0	2	0
2	1	2
2	2	1
1	0	3

a. Suppose that the experimenter plans to test both the linear and the quadratic trends. Perform these tests for these data.

b. Plot the predicted means based on a linear trend model, that is, a model without a quadratic component. How do these means compare to the actual sample means?

c. Plot the predicted means based on a model that includes both linear and quadratic trend components. How do these means compare to the actual sample means? Why?

*10. A physiological psychologist is interested in the differential effects of four dosage levels of a particular drug on the ability of rats to learn how to find their way through a maze. The dependent variable for each animal is the mean number of incorrect turns made over five trials after exposure to the drug and an initial acquaintance with the maze. The following data are obtained:

	Level		
1	2	3	4
6.6	4.8	3.4	4.2
7.2	5.0	3.6	4.8
5.0	3.8	3.8	5.0
6.2	4.2	3.2	4.6
5.8	4.4	3.2	5.2

Assume that the levels of drug dosage are equally spaced in units of size 1 (as in 1, 2, 3, 4), throughout the remainder of the problem.

a. Starting with the coefficients shown in Appendix Table A.10, modify them as required by Equations 7 and 8 to obtain an estimated slope parameter.

b. Using standard procedures for testing the statistical significance of a contrast, test the linear trend for significance.

c. Use the regression routine of a statistical package to regress number of errors Y on drug dosage X. What is the least-squares estimate of the slope parameter? How does this value compare with the answer you obtained in part a? (To be done by computer.)

d. As part of the output you obtained in part c, you should have a significance test of the slope parameter. Depending on the specific program, the test statistic should be either $t = -2.70$, or equivalently, $F = 7.28$. How does this value compare to the F value you calculated in part b?

e. To explore why the answers to parts b and d are different, we first consider the difference between the sum of squared errors of the full and restricted models of the two approaches. Is this value (i.e., the numerator sum of squares) identical in the two approaches?

f. Now consider the denominator of the F statistic in the two approaches. Is the error sum of squares identical in the two approaches? What about the degrees of freedom of the error term (i.e., the degrees of freedom of the denominator)?

g. The reason the error sums of squares of the two approaches are different is because the error term is based on a different full model in the two approaches. In the regression analysis of part d, the error term is based on a full model of the form $Y_{ij} = \beta_0 + \beta_1 X_{ij} + \varepsilon_{ij}$. However, the error term of the contrast approach of part b is based on a cell means model of the form: $Y_{ij} = \mu_j + \varepsilon_{ij}$. Why is the sum of squared errors larger for the error term of the regression approach than for the error term used to test the contrast? (HINT: What role do the nonlinear trends play in the difference between these two models, that is, the models on which the error terms are based?)

h. Based on your answer to part g, which approach do you think would generally be preferable for testing a linear trend? Why?

11. Two different methods are presented in the chapter for testing trends with unequal n. This exercise explores how these methods differ. Consider a four-group study where the groups represent equally spaced levels of a quantitative factor. Assume that the following data have been obtained:

$$n_1 = 30 \qquad n_2 = 30 \qquad n_3 = 5 \qquad n_4 = 5$$
$$\bar{Y}_1 = 2 \qquad \bar{Y}_2 = 4 \qquad \bar{Y}_3 = 4 \qquad \bar{Y}_4 = 2$$

Further assume that mean square within $(MS_W) = 2$.

a. One approach described in the text is a hierarchical approach. Find the contrast coefficients for testing the statistical significance of the linear trend for these data using this approach.

b. Based on the coefficients of part a, test the linear trend for statistical significance.

c. The other approach described in the text is an unweighted approach. What are the contrast coefficients for the linear trend using this approach?

d. Based on the coefficients of part c, test the linear trend for statistical significance.

e. Plot the sample means obtained here as a function of the level of the quantitative factor. Which plot of those shown in Figure 6.3 does your plot most resemble? Does your plot suggest the existence of a linear trend?

f. Which approach, hierarchical or unweighted, seems preferable here? Why?

g. Explain why the linear trend is significant here with the hierarchical approach.

12. A question currently being studied by developmental psychologists is how parent–infant play changes as infants get older. The following study is modeled after an experiment reported in Power, T. G. (1985) "Mother– and father–infant play: A developmental analysis." *Child Development, 56,* 1514–1524. Parents of 16 children at each of three ages (7, 10, and 13 months) were videotaped during toy-play interactions with their infants. Raters judged the number of seconds over a 10-minute period during which parents encouraged different types of infant play. One dependent variable of interest was the proportion of time parents encouraged pretend play in their children. Suppose that the following data were obtained:

7-month-olds	10-month-olds	13-month-olds
.02	.15	.09
.01	.11	.03
.07	.22	.18
.04	.05	.12
.01	.09	.18
.09	.05	.43
.05	.15	.24
.06	.11	.40
.05	.14	.02
.01	.21	.19
.04	.06	.15
.03	.12	.07
.02	.11	.45
.02	.19	.20
.13	.12	.49
.06	.04	.19

a. Suppose that the experimenter plans to test both the linear and the quadratic trends. Perform these tests for these data.

b. Plot the predicted means based on a linear trend model, that is, a model without a quadratic component. How do these means compare to the actual sample means?

c. Plot the predicted means based on a model that includes both linear trend and quadratic trend components. How do these means compare to the actual sample means? Why?

d. When the dependent measure is a proportion, as it is here, it is sometimes recommended to transform the dependent variable before performing the analysis. The particular transformation usually recommended is an inverse sine transformation that defines a new dependent variable Y' in terms of the original variable Y as follows:

$$Y' = 2 \arcsin(\sqrt{Y})$$

Perform the trend tests of part a using Y' as the dependent variable. (HINT: This transformation is straightforward to apply using many statistical packages. For example, both SAS and SPSS-X have SQRT and ARSIN functions to perform the necessary transformation.)

7   Two-Way Between-Subjects Factorial Designs

So far we have seen how to compare the means of *a* groups of individuals. This chapter continues this theme but in a more general context. We now consider designs where the groups are defined by two or more factors (independent variables). For example, suppose that a psychologist wants to evaluate the effectiveness of biofeedback and drug therapy for treating hypertension, that is, for lowering blood pressure. The psychologist might design a study with four groups: both biofeedback training and drug therapy, biofeedback but no drug therapy, drug therapy but no biofeedback, neither biofeedback nor drug therapy. We will see later in this chapter that such a design provides efficient tests of the individual effects of biofeedback and drug therapy as well as the effect of the two in combination. As before, each subject selected to participate in the study would be assigned to one of the four groups, ideally at random.

THE 2 × 2 DESIGN

To explore this design and analysis in detail, consider the hypothetical data of Table 7.1. As usual in our data sets, the number of subjects is kept small to minimize the computational burden. For the sake of discussion, we assume that the scores in the table represent systolic blood pressure readings taken at the end of the treatment period. Based on what we have learned so far, we might analyze these data either of two ways. First, we might perform an omnibus test to compare all four groups. Table 7.2 shows the ANOVA table that would result from this approach. There is a statistically significant difference among the four groups, but, of course, the omnibus test does not reveal which specific groups are different.

TABLE 7.1 Blood Pressure Data for 2 × 2 Factorial Design

	Group			
	1: Biofeedback and Drug	2: Biofeedback Alone	3: Drug Alone	4: Neither
	158	188	186	185
	163	183	191	190
	173	198	196	195
	178	178	181	200
	168	193	176	180
Mean	168	188	186	190
s	7.9057	7.9057	7.9057	7.9057

TABLE 7.2   ANOVA for Data in Table 7.1

Source	SS	df	MS	F	p
Between	1540.00	3	513.33	8.21	.002
Within	1000.00	16	62.50		
Total	**2540.00**	19			

Second, instead of performing the omnibus test, we might have decided to test planned comparisons. Naturally, the comparisons of most interest should assess the effectiveness of biofeedback and of drug therapy. There are several reasonable ways in which we might define such contrasts, but for the moment we will only consider one. To evaluate the biofeedback effect, notice that groups 1 and 2 received biofeedback training, while groups 3 and 4 did not. Thus, a contrast we could form to test the biofeedback effect would have coefficients of 1, 1, −1, and −1. Similarly, the effect of drug therapy could be tested by a contrast with coefficients of 1, −1, 1, and −1.

If we apply Chapter 4 principles to the data of Table 7.1, we find that the sum of squares attributable to the biofeedback contrast is 500, while that for drug therapy is 720. The respective F values, obtained by dividing each sum of squares by MS_W (which equals 62.50, from Table 7.2), are 8.00 and 11.52. Both are statistically significant if we use an α_{PC} level of .05 (more on this later in the chapter). Thus, our two tests suggest that both biofeedback and drug therapy have an effect.

At this point, there is a question we should ponder. Have the tests we performed completely explained the differences among our four groups? To answer this question, we can compare SS_B in Table 7.2 with the sum of squares associated with each of our contrasts. From Table 7.2 we see that the between-group sum of squares is 1540 for our data; the sums of squares for our two contrasts are 500 and 720. Can we say here that the two contrasts together account for a sum of squares equal to 500 + 720 = 1220? Recall from Chapter 4 that sum of squares for contrasts are additive if the contrasts are orthogonal. Indeed, our biofeedback and drug therapy contrasts are orthogonal, as we can see from applying Equation 4.45:

$$(1)(1) + (1)(-1) + (-1)(1) + (-1)(-1) = 0$$

For future reference, notice that this formula requires equal n, which we have here. Thus, so far with two contrasts, we have accounted for a sum of squares of 1220. However, this means that we have failed to account for a sum of squares equal to 320 (i.e., 1540 − 1220). Notice that although we have used two contrasts and hence 2 degrees of freedom to examine group differences, with four groups we have 3 degrees of freedom in all for assessing group differences. Thus, there is 1 degree of freedom yet to be examined.

It can be shown that there is only one contrast orthogonal to the two we have formed so far and that its coefficients are 1, −1, −1, and 1 (of course, coefficients of −1, 1, 1, and −1 would also work, as would .5, −.5, −.5, and .5, but these are all really the same contrast).[1] Indeed, if we calculate the sum of squares for this contrast, it equals 320, as it must. The corresponding F value is 5.12, which is significant at the .05 level. Thus, this contrast has detected a significant effect. But what does this effect mean?

Before answering this question, recall the meaning of our other two contrasts. One of these tested the effectiveness of biofeedback, whereas the other tested the effectiveness of drug therapy. However, if we look carefully at the contrasts, a more specific interpretation emerges. The first contrast compared the difference between the means of the two groups that received biofeedback versus the two groups that did not. However, notice that there were two groups in each case because one-half of the groups received drug therapy whereas the other half did not. In other words, the first contrast averages over the drug condition. As a result, it tests the *average effect* of biofeedback by comparing group means with biofeedback versus those without, giving equal weight to groups receiving drug therapy as those not receiving it. Notice that the second contrast similarly tests an average effect of drug therapy. These average effects are referred to as *main effects*, that is, the effect that each factor has in the main or on the average.

The Concept of Interaction

Thus, our first two contrasts tested main effects, the average effect of biofeedback and drug therapy, respectively. The possibility remains, however, that the biofeedback effect in the presence of drug therapy is different from the average effect of biofeedback. Indeed, this is precisely what the third contrast tests. This test is referred to as an *interaction test*. To say that an interaction exists in our data means that the biofeedback effect in the presence of drug therapy is different from the average effect of biofeedback.

This can be clarified by looking at the means shown in Table 7.3. The four group means are arranged in a 2 × 2 table, where the two rows represent the presence or absence of drug therapy and the two columns represent the presence or absence of biofeedback. The average of each row (called the row marginal mean because it's placed at the margin of the table) and of each column (the column marginal mean) is also presented, as is the grand mean (the average of all the scores). What have we tested with our three planned comparisons? The first comparison combined the means of 168 and 188 in the first column and compared them to the means of 186 and 190 in the second column. This is equivalent to testing the difference between

TABLE 7.3 Factorial Arrangement of Means from Table 7.1

		Biofeedback		
		Present	*Absent*	**Average**
Drug Therapy	*Present*	168	186	**177**
	Absent	188	190	**189**
	Average	**178**	**188**	**183**

178 and 188, the two column marginal means. When we average over the rows, do the two columns differ? As previously stated, this tests the average effect of biofeedback. Similarly, the second contrast tested the difference between 177 and 189, the two row marginal means.

The third contrast, the test of the interaction, is more complicated. Remember that it tests whether the biofeedback effect in the presence of drug therapy is the same as the average effect of biofeedback. Here, the biofeedback effect in the presence of drug therapy is to lower blood pressure 18 points (186 − 168). The average effect, however, is to lower blood pressure only 10 points (188 − 178). The F value of 5.12 was statistically significant at the .05 level for these data, implying that the effect of 18 is discernibly different from the average effect of 10. Thus, biofeedback has a larger effect in the presence of drug therapy than it has on the average. There is yet one other way of viewing this test. Notice that the average effect of 10 is the average of 18, the biofeedback effect in the presence of drug therapy, and 2, the biofeedback effect in the absence of drug therapy. We are claiming that the effect of 18 is significantly different from the average of the 18 itself and 2. But this simply amounts to saying that the effect of 18 is significantly different from the effect of 2. That is, a significant interaction here means that the biofeedback effect in the presence of drug therapy is significantly different from the biofeedback effect in the absence of drug therapy. In terms of the means in Table 7.3, the difference between columns 1 and 2 is *not* the same in row 1 as in row 2.

Additional Perspectives on the Interaction

So far, we have only considered whether the biofeedback effect is the same in the presence of drug therapy as in the absence of drug therapy. However, it may be just as interesting to determine whether the drug therapy effect is the same in the presence of biofeedback as in the absence of biofeedback. Table 7.3 shows that the magnitude of the drug therapy effect is 20 in the presence of biofeedback but only 4 in its absence. The difference in effectiveness is thus 16, the same difference that was found for biofeedback. That the same number resulted for both differences is not a coincidence—instead, it is a mathematical necessity. We can see why first algebraically and then geometrically. Recall that the coefficients of the interaction contrast were 1, −1, −1, and 1. Thus, this contrast tests the following null hypothesis:

$$H_0 : \mu_{\text{drug \& biofeedback}} - \mu_{\text{drug}} - \mu_{\text{biofeedback}} + \mu_{\text{neither}} = 0 \qquad (1)$$

We can rewrite this expression in either of two ways. First, the equation is equivalent to

$$H_0 : \mu_{\text{drug \& biofeedback}} - \mu_{\text{drug}} = \mu_{\text{biofeedback}} - \mu_{\text{neither}} \qquad (2)$$

This statement, if true, implies that the biofeedback effect in the presence of drug therapy equals the biofeedback effect in the absence of drug therapy. Alternatively, the equation can be written as

$$H_0 : \mu_{\text{drug \& biofeedback}} - \mu_{\text{biofeedback}} = \mu_{\text{drug}} - \mu_{\text{neither}} \qquad (3)$$

which asks whether the drug therapy effect in the presence of biofeedback equals the drug therapy effect in the absence of biofeedback.

Because all three equations are equivalent mathematically, they are in fact all testing the same null hypothesis. Thus, the interaction test addresses the question of whether the effect of one factor is the same for each level of the other factor. If the answer is Yes for one factor, it must also be Yes for the other factor as well.

The meaning of an interaction is often clarified by a graphical display (the geometric approach mentioned earlier). Figure 7.1 presents pictorial representations of the group means of Table 7.3. Figure 7.1(a) shows clearly that biofeedback lowers blood pressure an average of 18 units when drug therapy is present but only 2 units when drug therapy is absent. Recall that the significant interaction here means that the 18 and 2 are significantly different from one another. Geometrically, this implies that the two lines shown in Figure 7.1(a) depart significantly from parallelism. If the lines were parallel, the vertical distance between them would be the same at every level of drug therapy. However, in these data, the distances are unequal, and the lines are not parallel. This provides another way of conceptualizing the significance test for interaction. If the group means are plotted as in Figure 7.1(a), is there a significant departure from parallelism? In other words, is there evidence "beyond a reasonable doubt" that lines connecting population means would also not be parallel?

Notice that Figure 7.1(b) simply reverses the roles of biofeedback and drug therapy. Once again, the lines are not parallel because the same four means are plotted as in Figure 7.1(a). Although Figure 7.1(b) is mathematically redundant with Figure 7.1(a), it is often useful visually to draw both figures because the biofeedback effect is visually highlighted in Figure 7.1(a), while the drug therapy effect is clearer in Figure 7.1(b). In addition, an interaction that is disordinal in one figure (meaning that the lines cross one another besides not being parallel) may not be disordinal

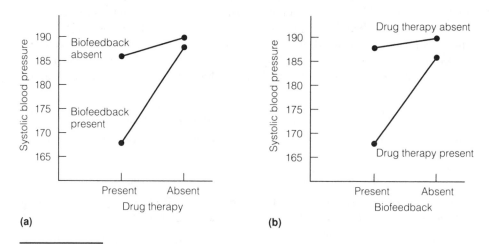

FIGURE 7.1   Geometric depiction of group means shown in Table 7.3.

in the other figure (meaning that although the lines may not be parallel, they do not cross).[2]

The concept of an interaction is extremely important in statistics and represents the most novel idea in this chapter. For this reason, at the risk of beating a dead horse, yet one more perspective is provided on the meaning of an interaction. It is sometimes said that if two factors interact, their effects are not additive. What does it mean to test whether two factors combine in an additive manner? To answer this question, reconsider Equation 1:

$$H_0 : \mu_{\text{drug \& biofeedback}} - \mu_{\text{drug}} - \mu_{\text{biofeedback}} + \mu_{\text{neither}} = 0 \quad (1, \text{repeated})$$

This can be rewritten as

$$H_0 : \mu_{\text{drug \& biofeedback}} = \mu_{\text{drug}} + \mu_{\text{biofeedback}} - \mu_{\text{neither}}$$

If we subtract a μ_{neither} term from both sides of the equation, we obtain

$$H_0 : \mu_{\text{drug \& biofeedback}} - \mu_{\text{neither}} = \mu_{\text{drug}} + \mu_{\text{biofeedback}} - \mu_{\text{neither}} - \mu_{\text{neither}}$$

Rearranging terms on the right-hand side yields

$$H_0 : \mu_{\text{drug \& biofeedback}} - \mu_{\text{neither}} = (\mu_{\text{drug}} - \mu_{\text{neither}}) + (\mu_{\text{biofeedback}} - \mu_{\text{neither}}) \quad (4)$$

The left-hand side of the equation represents the combined effect of the two factors, that is, how the combination of both differs from the absence of both. On the right-hand side, the first term represents the drug therapy effect in isolation, that is, in the absence of biofeedback. Similarly, the second term represents the biofeedback effect in isolation. Thus, the null hypothesis states that the combined effect of drug therapy and biofeedback equals the sum of their separate effects individually. In other words, the hypothesis states that the effect of combining drug therapy and biofeedback equals the sum of their individual effects, so the two individual effects literally add together to produce the combined effect. Because Equation 4 is mathematically equivalent to Equation 1, the null hypothesis of Equation 4 expresses a statement that the two factors do not interact. Thus, the lack of an interaction corresponds to an additive effect, whereas the presence of an interaction implies a nonadditive effect.

A MODEL COMPARISON APPROACH TO THE GENERAL TWO-FACTOR DESIGN

In the previous section, we performed three hypothesis tests in our two-factor design: drug therapy main effect, biofeedback main effect, and interaction. In this section, we see how these three tests can be conceptualized in terms of model comparisons. Our earlier example was restricted to a 2 × 2 design, where each factor had only two levels. In general, however, each factor may have two or more levels. For ease of discussion, we refer to the two factors as A and B, where in general A has a levels and B has b levels. For example, A might be presence or absence of biofeedback (so $a = 2$), and B might represent three types of drug therapy (so $b = 3$) for treating hypertension.

The full model in the general situation of an $a \times b$ design can be written in either of two equivalent ways. First, the model can be written as

$$Y_{ijk} = \mu_{jk} + \varepsilon_{ijk} \qquad (5)$$

where Y_{ijk} represents the score on the dependent variable of the ith subject at level j of the A factor and level k of the B factor, μ_{jk} is the population mean of Y for level j of A and level k of B, and ε_{ijk} is an error term associated with the ith subject at level j of A and level k of B. Notice that the value of the j subscript ranges from 1 to a, the value of the k subscript ranges from 1 to b, and the value of i ranges from 1 to n_{jk}, where n_{jk} is the number of subjects in the jk cell (i.e., the jth level of A and kth level of B). The model is often referred to as a cell means model because just like the full model for the one-way design in Chapter 3, it states that any subject's score is dependent only on the cell of the design in which the subject resides and an error component. Indeed, mathematically this full model for the two-way design is no different from the full model we developed earlier for the one-way design. In particular, we will see later that the least-squares parameter estimates and error sum of squares can be found using the same logic as before.

Alternate Form of Full Model

Although this form of the full model is perfectly valid mathematically, it is often convenient[3] to rewrite it in the following form:

$$Y_{ijk} = \mu + \alpha_j + \beta_k + (\alpha\beta)_{jk} + \varepsilon_{ijk} \qquad (6)$$

where μ represents a grand mean term common to all observations, α_j is the effect of the jth level of A, β_k is the effect of the kth level of B, and $(\alpha\beta)_{jk}$ is the interaction effect of level j of A and level k of B in combination with one another. We have chosen to represent this effect with the combination of α and β instead of with some other single Greek letter because the effect represents the interaction of A and B.[4] However, as we will see momentarily, $(\alpha\beta)_{11}$ (we have arbitrarily picked row 1 and column 1 as an example) is a single parameter, and as a consequence $(\alpha\beta)_{11}$ ultimately equals some number, just as α_1 (for example) did in one-way designs. It is particularly important that you realize that $(\alpha\beta)_{jk}$ does *not* mean the product of multiplying α_j by β_k. Although $(\alpha\beta)_{jk}$ is related to α_j and β_k in a way that we will soon see, the relationship is not multiplicative.

To understand the meaning of an *effect*, it is helpful to return to the concept of a *marginal mean*. The idea of a sample marginal mean was introduced in the discussion of Table 7.3; the focus now is on the notion of a population marginal mean. Consider the hypothetical 3×4 design shown in Table 7.4. Each cell entry represents a population mean (in an actual study, we obviously would not know precise values of population means, but here we assume that population values are known, for pedagogical purposes). *Population marginal means* (PMM) are defined for each row, for each column, and for rows and columns combined in the following

T A B L E **7. 4** Population Means in a 3 × 4 Design

		B				Marginal Means
		1	2	3	4	
	1	10	15	20	11	14
A	2	15	10	5	14	11
	3	8	5	14	5	8
Marginal Means		11	10	13	10	11

manner. The PMM for the jth row (i.e., jth level of A) is

$$\mu_{j.} = \sum_{k=1}^{b} \mu_{jk}/b \tag{7}$$

which tells us to sum the cell means across columns in row j and then divide by the number of columns. The period following the j in $\mu_{j.}$ is a reminder that we have averaged over the second subscript k, which represents columns. For the means of Table 7.4, then we would have

$$\mu_{1.} = (10 + 15 + 20 + 11)/4 = 14$$
$$\mu_{2.} = (15 + 10 + 5 + 14)/4 = 11$$
$$\mu_{3.} = (8 + 5 + 14 + 5)/4 = 8$$

These numbers simply tell us that the mean score in the first row is 14, the mean in the second row is 11, and so on. It should be noted that the mean here is an unweighted mean, in that each column is weighted equally. (We will return to the importance of weights later in the chapter.) The PMM for the kth column is defined as

$$\mu_{.k} = \sum_{j=1}^{a} \mu_{jk}/a \tag{8}$$

For the data in Table 7.4, then, the column means are given by $\mu_{.1} = 11$, $\mu_{.2} = 10$, $\mu_{.3} = 13$, and $\mu_{.4} = 10$. Finally, the population grand mean is defined as

$$\mu_{..} = \sum_{j=1}^{a} \sum_{k=1}^{b} \mu_{jk}/ab \tag{9}$$

which equals 11 for the data in Table 7.4. Notice that $\mu_{..}$ is simply the unweighted mean of all individual cell means in the population.

We are now finally ready to define the effects in the full model as represented by Equation 6:

$$Y_{ijk} = \mu + \alpha_j + \beta_k + (\alpha\beta)_{jk} + \varepsilon_{ijk} \tag{6, repeated}$$

First, μ in Equation 6 is simply the $\mu_{..}$ term defined in Equation 9. Second, α_j is defined as

$$\alpha_j = \mu_{j.} - \mu_{..} \tag{10}$$

which represents the difference between the marginal mean in row j and the grand mean. For example, for the data in Table 7.4, α_1 would equal 3, α_2 would equal 0, and α_3 would equal -3. On the average, the effect of row 1 is to raise scores 3 points, the second row has no effect, and the third row lowers scores 3 points.[5] Third, β_k is defined as

$$\beta_k = \mu_{.k} - \mu_{..} \tag{11}$$

which represents the difference between the marginal mean in column k and the grand mean. For example, for the data in Table 7.4, $\beta_1 = 0$, $\beta_2 = -1$, $\beta_3 = 2$, and $\beta_4 = -1$. Finally, the $(\alpha\beta)_{jk}$ terms are defined by

$$(\alpha\beta)_{jk} = \mu_{jk} - (\mu_{..} + \alpha_j + \beta_k) \tag{12}$$

which represents the difference between a cell mean and the additive effect of the two factors. In other words, the $(\alpha\beta)_{jk}$ parameters reflect the extent to which the cell means fail to conform to an additive pattern. Notice that there is one $(\alpha\beta)_{jk}$ parameter for each cell in the design. To be certain that Equation 12 is clear, let's find the value of $(\alpha\beta)_{11}$ for the data in Table 7.4. From the equation,

$$(\alpha\beta)_{11} = \mu_{11} - (\mu_{..} + \alpha_1 + \beta_1)$$

We saw earlier that for these data, $\mu_{..} = 11$, $\alpha_1 = 3$, and $\beta_1 = 0$. Thus,

$$(\alpha\beta)_{11} = 10 - (11 + 3 + 0) = -4$$

The nonzero value for $(\alpha\beta)_{11}$ indicates an interactive (i.e., nonadditive) effect for this cell. If the effects of A and B were strictly additive, the population mean in the (1,1) cell would be 14, because row 1 raises scores 3 units on the average and column 1 has no effect on the average, so together the mean should be 3 points above 11, or 14. The fact that the population mean is actually 10 reflects that the particular combination of A_1 and B_1 lowers scores, contrary to their average effects separately. Applying Equation 12 to all 12 of the cells of Table 7.4 shows that

$(\alpha\beta)_{11} = -4$	$(\alpha\beta)_{12} = 2$	$(\alpha\beta)_{13} = 4$	$(\alpha\beta)_{14} = -2$
$(\alpha\beta)_{21} = 4$	$(\alpha\beta)_{22} = 0$	$(\alpha\beta)_{23} = -8$	$(\alpha\beta)_{24} = 4$
$(\alpha\beta)_{31} = 0$	$(\alpha\beta)_{32} = -2$	$(\alpha\beta)_{33} = 4$	$(\alpha\beta)_{34} = -2$

Equations 9–12 are important for two reasons. First, they provide formal definitions of the A main effect, B main effect, and interaction parameters. It is important to understand what these parameters mean because we formulate hypothesis tests in terms of these parameters. Second, the algebraic expressions we have developed are helpful for developing least-squares parameter estimates and corresponding sum of squared errors of various models.

We have now discussed in some detail two forms of the full model for a two-way design. Before we introduce a restricted model and subsequent hypothesis testing, we first compare the two different forms of the full model. Recall that the first form was

$$Y_{ijk} = \mu_{jk} + \varepsilon_{ijk} \tag{5, repeated}$$

and the second form was

$$Y_{ijk} = \mu + \alpha_j + \beta_k + (\alpha\beta)_{jk} + \varepsilon_{ijk} \qquad \text{(6, repeated)}$$

We now demonstrate that these two forms are mathematically equivalent. Remember that the interaction parameters $(\alpha\beta)_{jk}$ of Equation 6 were defined as

$$(\alpha\beta)_{jk} = \mu_{jk} - (\mu_{..} + \alpha_j + \beta_k) \qquad \text{(12, repeated)}$$

Making this substitution into Equation 6 and remembering that $\mu_{..} = \mu$, we obtain

$$Y_{ijk} = \mu_{jk} + \varepsilon_{ijk}$$

which of course is exactly the same as Equation 5. How can these two forms be equivalent, when they look so different? After all, they do not even appear to have the same number of parameters. The model in Equation 5 has ab parameters, whereas the model in Equation 6 has $1 + a + b + ab$ parameters. However, it turns out that the parameters in the Equation 6 model are not all independent. For example, it can be shown algebraically that $\sum_{j=1}^{a} \alpha_j = 0$, given the definition of each α_j in Equation 10.[6] For the data in Table 7.4, the α_j parameters add to zero (as they must) because $\alpha_1 = 3$, $\alpha_2 = 0$, and $\alpha_3 = -3$. If the effect of row 1 is $+3$ and the effect of row 2 is 0, then the effect of row 3 must be -3 because the effects are all defined relative to the grand mean and the average of the row means must be the grand mean. Hence, there are only two independent α_j parameters for these data; once we know any two values, the third is completely determined. Similarly, it turns out that as a consequence of our definitions of β_k and $(\alpha\beta)_{jk}$ that they possess the following properties:

$$\sum_{k=1}^{b} \beta_k = 0$$

$$\sum_{j=1}^{a} (\alpha\beta)_{jk} = 0 \qquad \text{for each value of } k$$

$$\sum_{k=1}^{b} (\alpha\beta)_{jk} = 0 \qquad \text{for each value of } j$$

As a consequence of these constraints, the model of Equation 6 has $1 + (a - 1) + (b - 1) + (a - 1)(b - 1)$ independent parameters. However, multiplying the terms of this expression and performing the necessary subtraction shows that the number of independent parameters is simply ab, the same as Equation 5. Thus, the models of Equations 5 and 6 are indeed equivalent.

Comparison of Models for Hypothesis Testing

We are now ready to consider tests of hypotheses in terms of model comparisons in the $a \times b$ factorial design. As we have seen earlier in this chapter, there are three null hypotheses to be tested. Each of these null hypotheses leads to a restricted model, which then is compared to the full model.

In each case, to test a hypothesis, we use our usual F test for comparing two models, namely,

$$F = \frac{(E_R - E_F)/(df_R - df_F)}{E_F/df_F}$$

The primary challenge is finding E_F and E_R, the error sum of squares for the full and restricted models. Notice that the specific form of the restricted model depends on the hypothesis being tested (A main effect, B main effect, or AB interaction). The full model, on the other hand, is the same for every hypothesis. Because the full model remains the same, it is easiest to consider its error sum of squares first.

The error sum of squares for the full model (E_F) can be found most easily by writing the full model in the form of Equation 5:

$$Y_{ijk} = \mu_{jk} + \varepsilon_{ijk}$$

Recall that E_F is given by

$$E_F = \sum_{\substack{\text{all} \\ \text{obs}}} [Y_{ijk} - \hat{Y}_{ijk}(F)]^2$$

where $\hat{Y}_{ijk}(F)$ is a subject's predicted score when the parameters of the model are estimated using least squares. The parameters of the full model are simply the population means of each cell. Least-squares estimates these population means by their respective sample means, so that

$$\hat{Y}_{ijk}(F) = \bar{Y}_{jk} \tag{13}$$

Thus,

$$E_F = \sum_{\substack{\text{all} \\ \text{obs}}} (Y_{ijk} - \bar{Y}_{jk})^2 \tag{14}$$

which we have previously seen as the within-cell (or within-group) sum of squares in the single-factor design. As in the one-way design, we can represent E_F as SS_W. As before, E_F simply measures the magnitude of variation within cells, that is, the extent to which scores within a group differ from each other. Also keep in mind that when we divide E_F by df_F, the resultant ratio is simply MS_W.

Although E_F can be found most easily by writing the full model in the form of Equation 5, it can also be found by writing it in the form of Equation 6. We also present the least-squares estimation of parameters for the Equation 6 model because this form of the model translates more easily to restricted models. The least-squares estimates can be found simply by substituting sample means for the corresponding population means in Equations 9–12.[7] Thus,

$$\hat{\mu} = \bar{Y}_{..} = \sum_{j=1}^{a} \sum_{k=1}^{b} \bar{Y}_{jk}/ab \tag{15}$$

$$\hat{\alpha}_j = \bar{Y}_{j.} - \bar{Y}_{..} \tag{16}$$

$$\hat{\beta}_k = \bar{Y}_{.k} - \bar{Y}_{..} \tag{17}$$

$$\widehat{\alpha\beta}_{jk} = \bar{Y}_{jk} - (\bar{Y}_{..} + \bar{Y}_{j.} - \bar{Y}_{..} + \bar{Y}_{.k} - \bar{Y}_{..})$$

$$= \bar{Y}_{jk} - \bar{Y}_{j.} - \bar{Y}_{.k} + \bar{Y}_{..} \tag{18}$$

In case it's not clear, $\bar{Y}_{j.}$ is the sample mean of all scores at the jth level of A. (We will consider alternate meanings of $\bar{Y}_{j.}$ with unequal n later in the chapter.) Similarly, $\bar{Y}_{.k}$ is the sample mean of all scores at the kth level of B. With this formulation, a predicted score from the full model is given by

$$\hat{Y}_{ijk}(F) = \hat{\mu} + \hat{\alpha}_j + \hat{\beta}_k + \widehat{\alpha\beta}_{jk} \tag{19}$$

Substituting for $\hat{\mu}$, $\hat{\alpha}_j$, $\hat{\beta}_k$, and $\widehat{\alpha\beta}_{jk}$ from Equations 15–18 yields $\hat{Y}_{ijk}(F) = \bar{Y}_{jk}$, the same as Equation 13. This simply underscores the equivalence of the models of Equations 5 and 6.

Next, we must consider the restricted model to be compared with the full model. Recall that the restricted model depends on the null hypothesis to be tested. First, consider the null hypothesis that the A main effect is zero in the population. We can conceptualize the implications of this hypothesis by considering the full model written according to Equation 6.

$$\text{Full:} \qquad Y_{ijk} = \mu + \alpha_j + \beta_k + (\alpha\beta)_{jk} + \varepsilon_{ijk}$$

According to the null hypothesis, all the marginal means of the levels of the A factor are equal to one another, that is, the effect of each and every level of the A factor is zero. Symbolically, the null hypothesis can be written as

$$H_0 : \alpha_1 = \alpha_2 = \cdots = \alpha_a = 0 \tag{20}$$

This null hypothesis then leads to the following restricted model:

$$Y_{ijk} = \mu + \beta_k + (\alpha\beta)_{jk} + \varepsilon_{ijk} \tag{21}$$

The error sum of squares of this restricted model (E_R) can be found by once again using least squares to estimate the parameters of the model. With equal n per cell (as we are assuming here), parameter estimates for μ, β_k, and $(\alpha\beta)_{jk}$ are once again obtained from Equations 15, 17, and 18, just as they were in the full model. The omission of the α_j parameters does not change the estimates of the other parameters because the effects are orthogonal to one another with equal n (this orthogonality was demonstrated earlier in the chapter in the case of the 2×2 design). Notice that a predicted score from the restricted model is give by

$$\hat{Y}_{ijk}(R) = \hat{\mu} + \hat{\beta}_k + \widehat{(\alpha\beta)}_{jk} \tag{22}$$

Substituting for $\hat{\mu}$, $\hat{\beta}_k$, and $\widehat{\alpha\beta}_{jk}$ from Equations 15, 17, and 18 yields

$$\hat{Y}_{ijk}(R) = \bar{Y}_{jk} - \hat{\alpha}_j \tag{23}$$

where $\hat{\alpha}_j = \bar{Y}_{j.} - \bar{Y}_{..}$.

Before formally finding E_R, it is instructive to compare Equations 13 and 23 for the predicted scores from the full and restricted models, respectively. To the extent that the α_j parameters differ from zero, the predicted scores of the full model are superior to those of the restricted model—that is, they are closer to the actual scores (when the error in prediction is squared). This must be true because the sample means minimize the sum of squared deviations.

What is the formula for the error sum of squares E_R of the model given by Equation 21? As usual,

$$E_R = \sum_{k=1}^{b} \sum_{j=1}^{a} \sum_{i=1}^{n} [Y_{ijk} - \hat{Y}_{ijk}(R)]^2$$

When $\bar{Y}_{jk} - \hat{\alpha}_j$ is substituted for $\hat{Y}_{ijk}(R)$, simple algebra reveals that E_R can be written as

$$E_R = E_F + nb \sum_{j=1}^{a} (\bar{Y}_{j.} - \bar{Y}_{..})^2 \tag{24}$$

where n is the number of observations per cell and b is the number of levels of the B factor. Obviously, then, the difference in the error sum of squares of the full and restricted models equals

$$E_R - E_F = nb \sum_{j=1}^{a} (\bar{Y}_{j.} - \bar{Y}_{..})^2 \tag{25}$$

Before finishing the necessary details of the F test, several comments are in order concerning Equation 25. First, the numerical value obtained for $E_R - E_F$ here is referred to as the sum of squares attributable to the A main effect and is usually written as SS_A. Second, notice that this sum of squares is a measure of the extent to which the sample marginal means of A differ from the grand mean. In other words, it reflects the degree to which some levels of A have higher mean scores than other levels of A, averaging across the B factor. Third, it is interesting to compare Equation 25 with the expression we obtained in Chapter 3 (see Equation 3.58) for $E_R - E_F$ in the single-factor design, which (for equal n) was given by

$$E_R - E_F = n \sum_{j=1}^{a} (\bar{Y}_j - \bar{Y})^2 \tag{26}$$

Although Equations 25 and 26 look rather different, there is in fact an underlying equivalence. The equivalence can be seen most clearly by realizing that Equations 25 and 26 are actually both special cases of a formula we presented earlier in Chapter 3:

$$E_R - E_F = \sum_{j=1}^{a} \sum_{i=1}^{n} \hat{\alpha}_j^2 \tag{3.78, repeated}$$

which can be written more generally as

$$E_R - E_F = \sum_{\text{all obs}} \hat{\alpha}_j^2$$

In both the one-way design and the factorial design (with equal n), $\hat{\alpha}_j$ is given by

$$\hat{\alpha}_j = \bar{Y}_j - \bar{Y}$$

In the factorial design, then

$$E_R - E_F = \sum_{\text{all obs}} (\bar{Y}_j - \bar{Y})^2$$

To sum over all observations, we must sum over rows, columns, and subjects within cells, so that

$$E_R - E_F = \sum_{j=1}^{a} \sum_{k=1}^{b} \sum_{i=1}^{n} (\bar{Y}_j - \bar{Y})^2$$

However, the squared deviation term $(\bar{Y}_j - \bar{Y})^2$ is a constant within a cell and within a row, so that we can write

$$E_R - E_F = \sum_{j=1}^{a} \sum_{k=1}^{b} n(\bar{Y}_j - \bar{Y})^2$$

$$= \sum_{j=1}^{a} nb(\bar{Y}_j - \bar{Y})^2$$

$$= nb \sum_{j=1}^{a} (\bar{Y}_j - \bar{Y})^2$$

which is equivalent to Equation 25. In the one-way design, the difference in sum of squared errors is also given by

$$E_R - E_F = \sum_{\text{all obs}} (\bar{Y}_j - \bar{Y})^2$$

However, to sum over all observations, we must sum over groups and subjects within groups, so that

$$E_R - E_F = \sum_{j=1}^{a} \sum_{i=1}^{n} (\bar{Y}_j - \bar{Y})^2$$

As before, the squared deviation term is a constant for every subject within a group, so

$$E_R - E_F = \sum_{j=1}^{a} n(\bar{Y}_j - \bar{Y})^2$$

$$= n \sum_{j=1}^{a} (\bar{Y}_j - \bar{Y})^2$$

in agreement with Equation 26. As a result of this equivalence, in equal n designs, the sum of squares due to A in the factorial design exactly equals the sum of squares due to A in a single-factor design when the data are analyzed as if the B factor never existed. This should seem reasonable: Remember that the sum of squares due to A—that is, the A main effect—considers only the marginal means of A because the calculations average over the B factor. (Exercise 5 at the end of the chapter asks you to demonstrate this empirically on the numerical example presented in Table 7.5.)

We are now ready to finalize the details of the F test for the main effect of the A factor. Recall that the formula for the F statistic is given by

$$F = \frac{(E_R - E_F)/(df_R - df_F)}{E_F/df_F}$$

We have derived formulas for E_F (Equation 14) and $E_R - E_F$ (Equation 25). All that remains is to find df_R and df_F, the degrees of freedom of the two models. Remember that the degrees of freedom for a model equals the total number of observations (subjects) minus the number of independent parameters in the model. We saw earlier that the full model (Equation 5 or 6) has ab independent parameters. The restricted model (Equation 21) is the same as the full model except that the α_j parameters have been omitted. Although there are a levels of A, there are only $a - 1$ independent α_j

parameters because, as we saw earlier, the sum of the α_j parameters is constrained to equal zero. Thus, with a total of nab subjects in the design,

$$df_F = nab - ab$$
$$= ab(n - 1) \tag{27}$$

and

$$df_R - df_F = a - 1 \tag{28}$$

Substituting Equations 14, 25, 27, and 28 into the formula for the F statistic yields

$$F = \frac{nb \sum\limits_{j=1}^{a} (\bar{Y}_{j.} - \bar{Y}_{..})^2/(a - 1)}{\sum\limits_{j=1}^{a} \sum\limits_{k=1}^{b} \sum\limits_{i=1}^{n} (Y_{ijk} - \bar{Y}_{jk})^2/ab(n - 1)} \tag{29}$$

The observed F value obtained from Equation 29 is compared to a critical F value with $a - 1$ numerator degrees of freedom and $ab(n - 1)$ denominator degrees of freedom. If the observed F exceeds the critical F, there is a statistically significant main effect for the A factor.

Although it may be tempting to heave a sigh of relief at this point, we must remind you that we have only accomplished one-third of our task. The B main effect and the AB interaction remain to be tested. However, the underlying logic for these tests is the same as for the A main effect. For this reason, instead of presenting the derivation of E_F and E_R in detail, we can consider these tests much more rapidly. This is especially true because the full model remains the same for all three hypothesis tests.

The restricted model to be used in testing the B main effect is given by

$$Y_{ijk} = \mu + \alpha_j + (\alpha\beta)_{jk} + \varepsilon_{ijk} \tag{30}$$

If we were to follow the same steps as we did for the A main effect, we would find that the F statistic for testing the B main effect is given by

$$F = \frac{na \sum\limits_{k=1}^{b} (\bar{Y}_{.k} - \bar{Y}_{..})^2/(b - 1)}{\sum\limits_{j=1}^{a} \sum\limits_{k=1}^{b} \sum\limits_{i=1}^{n} (Y_{ijk} - \bar{Y}_{jk})^2/ab(n - 1)} \tag{31}$$

The observed F value is compared to a critical F value with $b - 1$ numerator degrees of freedom and $ab(n - 1)$ denominator degrees of freedom. Notice that Equation 31 for testing the B main effect bears a strong resemblance to Equation 29, which provides the F statistic for testing the A main effect. The denominators of the two equations are identical because they both equal MS_W. The numerator of Equation 31 has the same basic form as the numerator of Equation 29, but Equation 31 is based on differences among the marginal means of the B factor, instead of the A factor.

Finally, the restricted model to be used in testing the AB interaction is given by

$$Y_{ijk} = \mu + \alpha_j + \beta_k + \varepsilon_{ijk} \tag{32}$$

Predicted scores from the restricted model equal

$$\hat{Y}_{ijk}(R) = \bar{Y}_{..} + (\bar{Y}_{j.} - \bar{Y}_{..}) + (\bar{Y}_{.k} - \bar{Y}_{..}) = \bar{Y}_{j.} + \bar{Y}_{.k} - \bar{Y}_{..}$$

It can then be shown that the difference in the sum of squared errors of the restricted and full models is given by

$$E_R - E_F = n \sum_{j=1}^{a} \sum_{k=1}^{b} (\bar{Y}_{jk} - \bar{Y}_{j.} - \bar{Y}_{.k} + \bar{Y}_{..})^2 \tag{33}$$

Equation 33 provides what is referred to as *the interaction sum of squares* because its magnitude reflects the extent to which the A and B effects are nonadditive. The sum of squares for the interaction is also a special case of the general formula we developed in Chapter 3 for $E_R - E_F$, just as we found earlier for the main effects sums of squares. Specifically, by substituting $\widehat{\alpha\beta}_{jk}$ from Equation 18 into Equation 33, we can see that

$$SS_{AB} = E_R - E_F$$

$$= n \sum_{j=1}^{a} \sum_{k=1}^{b} (\widehat{\alpha\beta})_{jk}^2$$

$$= \sum_{\text{all obs}} (\text{estimated parameter})^2$$

To find the expression for the F statistic to test the interaction for statistical significance, we must find $df_R - df_F$. The restricted model has $a + b - 1$ independent parameters; recall that the full model has ab parameters. Thus,

$$df_R - df_F = ab - (a + b - 1),$$

which after some algebraic manipulation can be shown to be equal to

$$df_R - df_F = (a - 1)(b - 1) \tag{34}$$

Thus, the F statistic for testing the interaction equals

$$F = \frac{n \sum_{j=1}^{a} \sum_{k=1}^{b} (\bar{Y}_{jk} - \bar{Y}_{j.} - \bar{Y}_{.k} + \bar{Y}_{..})^2 / (a-1)(b-1)}{\sum_{j=1}^{a} \sum_{k=1}^{b} \sum_{i=1}^{n} (Y_{ijk} - \bar{Y}_{jk})^2 / ab(n-1)} \tag{35}$$

This observed F is compared to a critical F with $(a - 1)(b - 1)$ numerator degrees of freedom and $ab(n - 1)$ denominator degrees of freedom.

Numerical Example

Instead of proceeding with further theory development, it would probably be helpful to consider a numerical example at this point. Table 7.5 presents hypothetical data from a study investigating the effects of biofeedback and drug therapy on hypertension. We (arbitrarily) refer to the presence or absence of biofeedback as factor A and to the type of drug as factor B. Hence, we have a 2 × 3 design. Also notice that $n = 5$, that is, there are five subjects in each cell of the design. (Power

T A B L E **7.5** Blood Pressure Data for 2 × 3 Design

	Biofeedback and Drug X	Biofeedback and Drug Y	Biofeedback and Drug Z	Drug X Alone	Drug Y Alone	Drug Z Alone
	170	186	180	173	189	202
	175	194	187	194	194	228
	165	201	199	197	217	190
	180	215	170	190	206	206
	160	219	204	176	199	224
Mean	170	203	188	186	201	210
s	7.91	13.91	13.84	10.84	10.93	15.81

T A B L E **7.6** Cell Means and Marginal Means for Table 7.5 Data

		B (Drug)			
		1 (X)	2 (Y)	3 (Z)	Marginal Means
A (Biofeedback)	1 (Present)	170	203	188	187
	2 (Absent)	186	201	210	199
	Marginal Means	178	202	199	193

considerations might dictate a larger n, but only five will be used here to simplify computations.)

Table 7.6 shows the cell means for these data displayed in a 2 × 3 form. We have (arbitrarily) chosen to display the A factor in terms of rows and the B factor in terms of columns. The table also shows the sample marginal means for these data.

Table 7.7 shows the full model and the three restricted models to be compared, as well as the error sum of squares of each model. The bottom third of Table 7.7 presents an ANOVA table for these data. This type of table is often used for summarizing results in a journal article and is the type of table produced by most statistical packages. This table shows that both main effects are significant but that the interaction is nonsignificant at the .05 level. The meaning of these tests is best understood by referring to the means shown in Table 7.6. The significant A main effect implies that biofeedback has a nonzero effect, averaging over type of drug. Specifically, the marginal mean of 187 is significantly different from the mean of 199. Similarly, the significant B main effect implies that the marginal means of drugs X, Y, and Z are not all equal to each other. Notice that this does not mean that they are *all* different, but rather that there is a difference somewhere. The precise location of the difference remains to be found, using contrasts as in the single-factor design. The nonsignificant interaction implies that (within sampling error) the biofeedback effect is the same for every drug, which is equivalent to saying that

TABLE **7.7**   Analysis of Table 7.5 Data

Models Underlying Hypothesis Tests

F: $Y_{ijk} = \mu + \alpha_j + \beta_k + (\alpha\beta)_{jk} + \varepsilon_{ijk}$
$R1$: $Y_{ijk} = \mu + \beta_k + (\alpha\beta)_{jk} + \varepsilon_{ijk}$
$R2$: $Y_{ijk} = \mu + \alpha_j + (\alpha\beta)_{jk} + \varepsilon_{ijk}$
$R3$: $Y_{ijk} = \mu + \alpha_j + \beta_k + \varepsilon_{ijk}$

Error Sum of Squares for Models

$$E_F = 3738$$
$$E_{R1} = 4818$$
$$E_{R2} = 7158$$
$$E_{R3} = 4518$$

ANOVA Table

Source	SS	df	MS	F	p
A	1080	1	1080.00	6.93	.014
B	3420	2	1710.00	10.98	.001
AB	780	2	390.00	2.50	.101
Within cells	3738	24	155.75		

differences among the drugs are the same in the presence of biofeedback as in its absence. As usual, however, we cannot claim to have proved that the null hypothesis is true. In other words, we cannot be certain that the effects of biofeedback and drug are really additive. Instead, there may be a true interaction in the population, which we had little power to detect with only five subjects per cell.

Familywise Control of Alpha Level

The careful reader may have noticed that we have performed three statistical tests on our data (one each for the A main effect, the B main effect, and the interaction), and yet we seem to have forgotten Chapter 5 because we have said nothing about preventing the inflation of Type I errors when multiple tests are performed. The reason for our lack of attention to this potential problem until now is that, although three tests are being performed in the experiment, these tests are conceptualized as each constituting a separate family of tests. In other words, we regard questions of the A main effect (biofeedback in our example) as representing one family of questions to be addressed. The α level is held at .05 for this family. Questions of the drug main effect and the interaction are considered separately because they represent conceptually distinct questions. Recall that in Chapter 5 we briefly distinguished between α_{EW}, experimentwise α level, and α_{FW}, familywise α level. In the factorial design, each type of major effect (A, B, and AB) is defined to represent a family, and traditional practice is to control α_{FW} at .05.[8] Thus, although the α level for the experiment as a whole (the α_{EW} level) is allowed to exceed .05, the α_{FW} rate is set at .05 for each of the three families under consideration.

FOLLOW-UP TESTS

Further Investigation of Main Effects

Let's return to the data shown in Table 7.5. As we saw in Table 7.7, both main effects are significant. However, the precise meaning of the drug main effect is unclear because we do not know which specific column marginal means are different from each other. As in Chapter 4, we can address this question by forming contrasts of the means. (Notice that we do not need to worry about contrasts for the A main effect in our numerical example—why not?) Indeed, contrasts are formed and tested in exactly the same manner as in the one-way design. The sum of squares for a contrast of the levels of the B factor is given by

$$SS_\psi = na(\hat{\psi})^2 \bigg/ \sum_{k=1}^{b} c_k^2 \tag{36}$$

where $\hat{\psi}$ is the sample value of the contrast. The na term appears in the numerator because each B marginal mean is based on n times a observations. Similarly, if we wanted to contrast marginal means of the A factor, the sum of squares would be

$$SS_\psi = nb(\hat{\psi})^2 \bigg/ \sum_{j=1}^{a} c_j^2 \tag{37}$$

In either case, the contrast would be tested for statistical significance by calculating an observed F value:

$$F = SS_\psi / MS_W \tag{38}$$

The critical value against which to compare this observed F would depend on the same decisions as discussed in Chapter 5 on multiple-comparisons procedures. In other words, the critical value might be obtained through either the Bonferroni, Tukey, or Scheffé methods, keeping in mind that the number of levels potentially being compared equals the number of levels for that factor.

To see an example of testing contrasts, reconsider the sample means in Table 7.6. So far, we know that the drug main effect is statistically significant, implying that the population means of drugs X, Y, and Z are not all equal to each other. Let's suppose we have decided to compare drug X versus drug Y. From Table 7.6, we can see that the corresponding marginal means are 178 and 202. Formally, we can represent the test of their difference as a comparison of population marginal means (as defined earlier in Equation 8):

$$\psi = 1\mu_{.1} - 1\mu_{.2} + 0\mu_{.3}$$

The population value of the contrast is estimated with $\hat{\psi}$:

$$\hat{\psi} = 1\bar{Y}_{.1} - 1\bar{Y}_{.2} + 0\bar{Y}_{.3}$$

which for these data corresponds to

$$\hat{\psi} = 1(178) - 1(202) + 0(199)$$

so that $\hat{\psi}$ equals -24. Substituting this value along with $n = 5$, $a = 2$, and $\sum_{k=1}^{b} c_k^2 = 2$ into Equation 36 yields

$$SS_\psi = 5(2)(-24)^2/2 = 2880$$

As shown in Equation 38, the observed F value is obtained by dividing the sum of squares for the contrast by the value of mean square within, which equals 155.75 for these data. Thus, for our contrast, the observed F equals

$$F = 2880/155.75 = 18.49$$

Because we are testing a pairwise comparison, we should use Tukey's WSD to control α_{FW}, unless this contrast is one of a small number we planned prior to collecting the data. As in the one-way design (see Table 5.7), the observed F must be compared to a critical value of the form $(q_{.05,b,df_{error}})^2/2$. Notice that we have used b instead of a to subscript q here because we are comparing marginal means of the B factor. With this in mind, we have here that $b = 3$, and $df_{error} = 24$, so from appendix Table A.4, the critical q value is 3.53. Thus, the critical value against which we should compare the observed F equals 6.23 (i.e., 3.53 squared and then divided by 2). The observed value exceeds the critical value, so we can conclude that the marginal means of drugs X and Y are significantly different from one another. Remember, as we pointed out at the end of Chapter 5, if our interest lies solely in pairwise comparisons, in fact the B main-effect test need not be performed because Tukey's WSD by itself controls α_{FW}. Nevertheless, the main-effect test might be reported because it provides a context for the pairwise comparisons and because most behavioral researchers traditionally do report main-effect tests in this situaton.

OPTIONAL

Marginal Mean Comparisons Without Homogeneity Assumption. It is often helpful in working with contrasts of marginal means to realize that in effect the factorial design is reduced to a one-way design when marginal means are being examined. Thus, the same principles we developed there also apply here. This conceptualization is especially helpful if we are concerned about possible violations of homogeneity of variance. For example, suppose that we want to test the difference between drug X and drug Y, just as we did in the preceding section, except now we are unwilling to assume homogeneity of variance. We can express the contrast in terms of the six cell means as

$$\psi = .5\mu_{11} + .5\mu_{21} - .5\mu_{12} - .5\mu_{22} + 0\mu_{13} + 0\mu_{23}$$

For our data, $\hat{\psi}$ is given by

$$\begin{aligned}
\hat{\psi} &= .5\bar{Y}_{11} + .5\bar{Y}_{21} - .5\bar{Y}_{12} - .5\bar{Y}_{22} \\
&= .5(170) + .5(186) - .5(203) - .5(201) \\
&= -24
\end{aligned}$$

The corresponding sum of squares for the contrast can be found from Equation 4.35:

$$SS_\psi = E_R - E_F = (\hat{\psi})^2 \Bigg/ \sum_{j=1}^{ab} (c_j^2/n_j) \qquad \text{(see 4.35)}$$

Where the j subscript ranges from 1 to the number of cells in the original factorial design. For these data, the sum of squares equals

$$SS_\psi = (-24)^2/(.25/5) + (.25/5) + (.25/5) + (.25/5) = 2880$$

Notice that this is precisely the value we obtained when we used Equation 36 (of this chapter) to calculate the sum of squares directly from the marginal means. As in the one-way design, the only difference that emerges, if we are unwilling to assume homogeneity, is that we do not use MS_W as the error term. Instead, the separate variance approach uses an error term of the form

$$\text{denom} = \left(\sum_{j=1}^{ab} (c_j^2/n_j)s_j^2 \right) \Bigg/ \sum_{j=1}^{ab} (c_j^2/n_j) \qquad \text{(see 4.38)}$$

In our example, the appropriate error term equals

$$\text{denom} = \frac{(.25/5)(62.5) + (.25/5)(117.5) + (.25/5)(193.5) + (.25/5)(119.5)}{(.25/5) + (.25/5) + (.25/5) + (.25/5)}$$

$$= 123.25$$

The resultant F value is thus given by $F = 2880/123.25 = 23.37$. Assuming that we wish to use Tukey's WSD to control α_{FW},[9] from Table 5.7, we can see that the appropriate critical value equals $(q_{.05,b,df})^2/2$, where

$$df = \frac{\left(\sum_{j=1}^{ab} c_j^2 s_j^2/n_j \right)^2}{\sum_{j=1}^{ab} [(c_j^2 s_j^2/n_j)^2/(n_j - 1)]} \qquad \text{(see 4.39)}$$

For our data, it turns out that $df = 14$, or just over half the degrees of freedom we had when we assumed homogeneity. From Appendix Table A.4, the critical q value is 3.70 (remember that $b = 3$, even though there are six individual cell means). The critical value for the F is then 6.84 (i.e., 3.70 squared and then divided by 2). As happened when we assumed homogeneity, the observed F exceeds the critical value, so we can conclude that there is a difference in the population marginal means of drug X and drug Y.

Further Investigation of an Interaction—Simple Effects

If a statistically significant interaction had occurred in the data shown in Table 7.5, we probably would have wanted to interpret the data differently. Specifically, the interpretation of the main effects is changed when an interaction is found because an interaction implies that the effects of a factor are not consistent across

TABLE 7.8   Additional Observations for Table 7.5 Data

Biofeedback and Drug X	Biofeedback and Drug Y	Biofeedback and Drug Z	Drug X Alone	Drug Y Alone	Drug Z Alone
158	209	194	198	195	204

TABLE 7.9   Cell Means and Marginal Means Based on Six Observations per Cell

	1 (X)	2 (Y)	3 (Z)	Marginal Means
1 (Present)	168	204	189	187
2 (Absent)	188	200	209	199
Marginal Means	**178**	**202**	**199**	**193**

the levels of another factor. Although the marginal mean still reflects an average, the average itself may be misleading because the interaction is a signal that the individual effects are significantly different from the average effect.[10] For this reason, it is usually more meaningful to test the significance of these individual effects of a factor at each level of the other factor separately rather than test the main effect.

To discuss this argument further, reconsider the data of Table 7.5. Suppose that there were in fact six subjects per group: the five per group already shown in Table 7.5 plus one additional observation per group, shown in Table 7.8. The cell means based on all six scores per group are shown in Table 7.9. Performing our usual three tests of significance for these data reveals that all three effects are significant: for the A main effect, $F = 9.49$, $p = .0046$; for the B main effect, $F = 15.02$, $p = .0001$; and for the AB interaction, $F = 4.22$, $p = .0237$. Even in the presence of a significant interaction, the significant main effects imply that marginal means are significantly different from one another. For example, the two marginal means for A, which equal 187 and 199 in the sample, are significantly different. Average blood pressure readings are lower in the presence of biofeedback than in its absence. On the average, the difference is estimated to be 12 points. However, is this 12 points an accurate indication of the effect under each of the three drugs? No, it is not. Why not?— because of the significant interaction, which means that the 20-point difference under drug X, the −4-point difference under drug Y, and the 20-point difference under drug Z are *not* all the same. Notice that the mean of these effects (20, −4, and 20) is indeed 12, the difference in the marginal means. However, we can be certain (at the .05 level) that the sample values of 20, −4, and 20 do not all come from the same population. Using one number (i.e., 12 for these data) to estimate a single population effect in this situation is usually misleading.

A reasonable alternative to interpreting the marginal mean difference of 12 is to interpret the individual effects whose average is 12. In other words, we need to consider each of the three effects individually. Is there a biofeedback effect for drug X? For drug Y? For drug Z? These effects are referred to as *simple effects*. Tests of simple effects of A proceed by examining the effect of A at a fixed level of B. In our example, there are three simple effects tests of A: A at B_1 (drug X), A at B_2 (drug Y), and A at B_3 (drug Z). Similarly, there are two simple effects tests of B: B at A_1 (biofeedback present) and B at A_2 (biofeedback absent). Notice that in each case we have reduced the two-factor design to a one-factor design. For this reason, we can test the significance of a simple effect by treating the data as if they came from a single-factor design. For example, consider the effect of A at B_1. Are the sample means of 168 and 188 significantly different from one another? We can calculate a sum of squares for this effect using the same formula we used in the single-factor design:

$$SS_{\text{effect}} = n \sum_{j=1}^{a} (\bar{Y}_j - \bar{Y})^2 \tag{39}$$

For our data, $n = 6$, $\bar{Y}_1 = 168$, $\bar{Y}_2 = 188$, and $\bar{Y} = 178$. Performing the arithmetic yields $SS = 1200$ for the A within B_1 effect. Because we are comparing two means, the degree of freedom for the effect is just 1 (in general, $df =$ number of groups $- 1$). If we are willing to assume homogeneity of variance, E_F/df_F (which is simply MS_W) continues to be an appropriate error term. Hence, we can obtain an observed F value from

$$F = \frac{SS_{\text{effect}}/df_{\text{effect}}}{MS_W} = \frac{1200/1}{136.6} = 8.78$$

The p value associated with this F for 1 and 30 degrees of freedom is .0060, indicating a statistically significant biofeedback effect with drug X. Similar calculations for the other two drugs show $F = 0.35$ ($p = .5644$) for drug Y and $F = 8.78$ ($p = .0060$) for drug Z. Thus, biofeedback has a significant effect when used together with drug X or drug Z but not with drug Y.

Just as we have tested the biofeedback effect within each type of drug, we can also test the drug effect within each level of the biofeedback factor. For example, consider the effect of B (drug) at A_1 (biofeedback present). Are the sample means of 168, 204, and 189 significantly different from each other? Using Equation 39, we find that $SS = 3924$ for the B-within-A_1 effect. Because we are comparing three means, this effect has two degrees of freedom. The F for this effect thus equals

$$F = \frac{SS_{\text{effect}}/df_{\text{effect}}}{MS_W} = \frac{3924/2}{136.6} = 14.36$$

which has an associated p value of .0001. Thus, the three drugs are significantly different from each other in the presence of biofeedback. It turns out that the drugs also differ in the absence of biofeedback; the observed F value is 4.88, $p = .0145$. In both cases, we must keep in mind that we have not necessarily shown that all three drugs are different; instead, we have only shown that they are not all the same. To determine which specific drugs are different, we would need to test comparisons just as we did in the single-factor design. In factorial designs, such comparisons are usually referred to as *cell mean comparisons* because we are literally comparing means of individual cells to one another. For example, suppose we want to compare drugs Y and Z in the presence of biofeedback. Are the sample means of 189 and 204 significantly different from one another? To answer this question, we must find the sum of squares associated with the relevant contrast. Recall that (with equal n) the SS for a contrast is given by

$$SS_\psi = n(\hat\psi)^2 \Bigg/ \sum_{j=1}^{a} c_j^2$$

For our data, $n = 6$, $\hat\psi = -15$, and $\sum_{j=1}^{a} c_j^2 = 2$, so the SS for the contrast equals 675. The corresponding degree of freedom equals 1 because we are testing a single contrast. Thus, the observed F value is given by

$$F = \frac{SS_{contrast}/df_{contrast}}{MS_W} = \frac{675/1}{136.6} = 4.94,$$

which has a p value of .0320. With an α_{PC} of .05, this would be significant. However, if we are to be consistent with the principles we developed in Chapter 5 for the one-way design, we should use an appropriate multiple-comparisons procedure to control the familywise error rate.

Consideration of Type I Error Rate in Testing Simple Effects. When simple effects tests are performed in an attempt to interpret the meaning of a significant interaction, it is inevitable that multiple significance tests will be conducted. If each test is conducted with $\alpha = .05$, the overall Type I error rate may be considerably greater than .05. Some researchers maintain that this inflation should not be regarded as problematic because they will conduct these tests only if the interaction is significant, which will happen only 5 percent of the time if in fact there is no interaction. Although this logic holds if there is literally no interaction in the population, it fails when the interaction null hypothesis is partially true. Indeed, the problem with this logic is the same as the problem with the logic of Fisher's LSD (the protected t test) discussed in Chapter 5.

Even if it is agreed that it is inappropriate to conduct every test at $\alpha = .05$, there can still be legitimate disagreement over what constitutes a family (see Keppel, 1982, and Kirk, 1982, for two examples). The approach advocated here is to consider all tests regarding differences among rows (biofeedback, in our example) as one family and all tests regarding differences among columns (drugs, in our example) as a second family. The goal is to maintain α at .05 for each family. We can accomplish this goal in the following manner. First, consider tests of row effects—that is, tests of the A factor, which in our example is biofeedback. We will conduct three tests of biofeedback, one for each level of drugs. The familywise α can be maintained at .05 by performing each of these tests at an α level of .05/3. In general, we would use an α level of .05/b for each test. Second, consider tests of the B factor. By the same logic, using an α level of .05/a for each test would maintain the α_{FW} at .05.

In addition, if a simple effects test yields a significant result, it typically is necessary to test comparisons of individual cell means unless the factor in question has only two levels (in which case the precise nature of the difference is already identified). Again the α level can be maintained by using the principles of Chapter

5. However, it must be kept in mind that the α level for the simple effects test that preceded the cell means comparison was not .05 but instead $.05/b$ for simple effects tests of A and $.05/a$ for simple effects tests of B. Thus, it is this smaller α level that should be used in performing subsequent multiple comparisons. It should be noted that this can create practical difficulties because it necessitates finding Tukey and Scheffé critical values for α levels other than .05 or .01. This problem can be circumvented by using the computer. As of this writing, SAS ANOVA and SAS GLM both allow specification of any value between 0 and 1 for the α level with Tukey's or Scheffé's method.

Figure 7.2 is a flowchart that summarizes approaches to understanding effects either in the presence or the absence of an interaction. It should be stressed that the flowchart is meant to be used only as a guideline—not as a rigid structure that must always be obeyed. In particular, when enough theoretical background is available, a researcher may plan certain tests to be performed that deviate from the flowchart. Also, it may not be of theoretical interest to test both simple effects of A within B and of B within A when a significant interaction is found. Other exceptions to the flowchart undoubtedly could be uncovered as well. Data analysis should not follow a formula but instead should correspond to theoretical questions; nevertheless, the flowchart is a useful guide toward appropriate analyses as long as it is not interpreted too strictly.

Error Term for Testing Simple Effects.   Throughout the previous discussion it was implicitly assumed that the denominator (error term) to be used for testing simple effects would be mean square within. Is this a reasonable error term? To answer this question, consider our numerical example. One simple effects test we performed was the test of drug (B) differences in the presence of biofeedback (i.e., within the first level of A). We calculated a sum of squares for this effect as if we had a one-way design with three groups. Not surprisingly, data from the three groups that did not receive biofeedback have no influence on the sum of squares for B within A_1. However, data from these three groups do influence the value for MS_W because MS_W is simply the average variance within each of the six cells in the design. Should data from the biofeedback-absent groups be included in the error term, if we want to compare only the differences among the biofeedback-present groups? It depends. If the homogeneity of variance assumption is met, using MS_W as the error term for all tests is appropriate. Statistical power is maximized because the estimate of the population error variance is most efficient when all relevant data are combined to form the estimate.

On the other hand, if variances are heterogeneous, using MS_W for testing all effects may be quite misleading. Some tests will be too liberal while others will be too conservative. When heterogeneity of variance is suspected, we thus recommend that MS_W not be used as the error term. Instead, the error term should be based only on the groups actually being compared. For example, if we are testing the simple effect of B at A_1, the error term could be based only on the three biofeedback-present groups. In this case, the analysis is literally a one-way ANOVA with three groups. Procedures for performing an omnibus ANOVA without assuming homogeneity of variance will be discussed in Chapter 15. As before, tests of comparisons

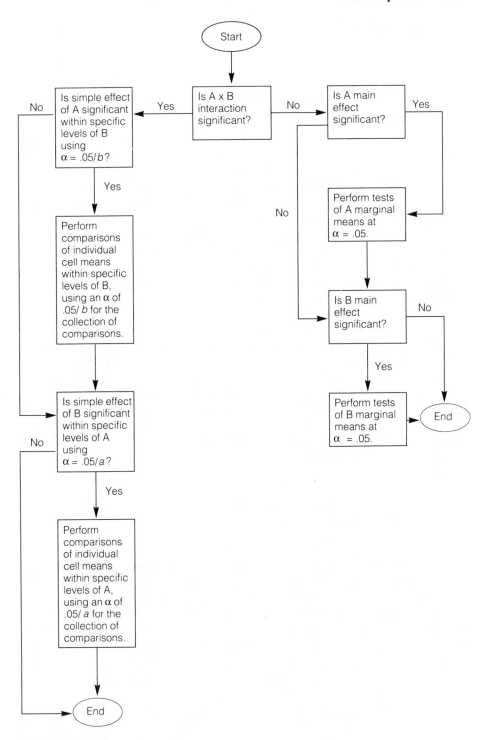

FIGURE 7.2 General guideline for analyzing effects in a two-factor design.

can be performed without assuming homogeneity by using appropriate procedures from Chapters 4 and 5.

An Alternative Method for Investigating an Interaction— Interaction Contrasts

Most researchers follow up a significant interaction by testing simple effects. However, there is an alternative approach, which some behavioral statisticians (e.g., Levin & Marascuilo, 1972) recommend. To introduce this approach, remember how we interpret the meaning of a main effect, which we designate as the A effect for convenience. When the factor has more than two levels, we form comparisons of the marginal means. The comparisons are called *subeffects* because each comparison represents one specific way in which the means might differ. Each comparison has 1 degree of freedom, whereas the effect as a whole has degrees of freedom equal to $a - 1$. How might we interpret an interaction in a similar manner? Recall that the interaction as a whole has $(a - 1)(b - 1)$ degrees of freedom. We could again form single degree-of-freedom comparisons to investigate which subeffects are contributing to the overall example.

Consider our earlier numerical example, with the cell means shown in Table 7.9. Recall that we obtained a significant interaction, implying that the biofeedback effect is not the same for every drug. Does this imply that the biofeedback effect is different for *all* three drugs? No, as we can easily tell just by "eyeballing" these artificial data. The biofeedback effect in the sample is 20 for *both* drug X and drug Z. The effect appears to be different for drug Y. We could test a null hypothesis that the biofeedback effect for drug Y is different from that for X or Z. For example, suppose we wanted to compare the biofeedback effect for Y to that for X. The null hypothesis could be written formally as:

$$H_0 : \mu_{12} - \mu_{22} = \mu_{11} - \mu_{21}$$

where the cells are labeled to correspond to the rows and columns shown in Table 7.9. We could rewrite this as

$$H_0 : \mu_{12} - \mu_{22} - \mu_{11} + \mu_{21} = 0$$

which has the form of a comparison. Using principles from Chapter 4, the sum of squares for this comparison equals 864, which corresponds to an F value of 6.33 (using MS_W as the error term). If we were to use an α level of .05 for this test, the result would be significant. If this comparison has been chosen post hoc, however, we can maintain our α_{FW} at .05 by using a Scheffé critical value given by $(a - 1)(b - 1)F_{.05,(a-1)(b-1),N-ab}$. For our example, the appropriate Scheffé critical value would equal $(2 - 1)(3 - 1)F_{.05,(2-1)(3-1),36-6}$, which is $2F_{.05,2,30} = 2(3.32) = 6.64$. Thus, if we have indeed chosen this comparison post hoc, we canot assert it to be significant.

The lack of a significant comparison here might seem puzzling because the interaction as a whole was significant. It turns out, however, that we have not identified the optimal subeffect, which here contrasts the biofeedback effect for drug

Y with the average of the biofeedback effects for drugs X and Z. You should verify that this subeffect produces a sum of squares of 1152, which corresponds to an F value of 8.43, which is significant even with the Scheffé critical value. Kirk (1982, pp. 378–379) presents formulas for determining the coefficients of the optimal subeffect, that is, the particular interaction contrast that maximally accounts for the entire interaction sum of squares.

Two other comments are pertinent here. First, Levin and Marascuilo (1972) argue that interaction contrasts rather than simple effects should be used to interpret a significant interaction because the simple effects are *not* subeffects of the interaction. Games (1973), on the other hand, argues that the simple effects tests more often answer the theoretical questions raised by most researchers. The interested reader is referred to Marascuilo and Levin (1976), which includes references to both sides of the debate. Second, yet one other method of interpreting an interaction is to test several interaction contrasts simultaneously. Such tests are called *partial interaction tests*. The interested reader is referred to Boik (1979), Keppel (1982), or Kirk (1982) for details.

STATISTICAL POWER

Researchers should, of course, be concerned about the statistical power of their studies. As in the one-way design, it is possible to determine power if α level, sample size, and effect size are known. A general formula for the ϕ value of an effect in a fixed-effects design (which is all that we will consider until Chapter 10) can be written as

$$\phi_{\text{effect}} = \sqrt{\left[\sum_{\text{all obs}} (\text{effect parameter})^2\right] \bigg/ (df_{\text{effect}} + 1)\sigma_\varepsilon^2}$$

The numerator of this expression requires some additional explanation. Notice that it is very similar to the general formula we have seen for the sum of squares due to an effect:

$$SS_{\text{effect}} = \sum_{\text{all obs}} (\text{estimated parameter})^2$$

The only difference is that the numerator of ϕ is based on the parameter value itself, as opposed to an estimate. Table 7.10 provides a specific expression for the numerator for all three effects (A, B, and A by B) in the two-way design, as well as for df_{effect}. The ϕ value for an effect is referred to power charts as in the one-way design to determine power.

An important implication of the formula for ϕ is that whenever $a > 2$ and $b > 2$, the power for testing an interaction of a particular effect size is less than the power for testing a main effect of that same effect size. As a consequence, larger samples (i.e., more subjects per cell) are typically required for having sufficient power to test interactions. Consider, for example, a 3×4 design (A has 3 levels; B has 4 levels).

T A B L E **7. 10** Explanation of ϕ^2 in an A × B Factorial Design

Effect	Numerator Expression	df_{effect}
A	$nb \sum_{j=1}^{a} \alpha_j^2$	$a - 1$
B	$na \sum_{k=1}^{b} \beta_k^2$	$b - 1$
A × B	$n \sum_{j=1}^{a} \sum_{k=1}^{b} [(\alpha\beta)_{jk}]^2$	$(a - 1)(b - 1)$

It can be shown that to achieve a power of .8 for detecting an A main effect of "medium" size as defined by Cohen (1977), a study should use 14 subjects per cell, or 168 subjects in all. However, to achieve a power of .8 for detecting an A × B interaction of "medium" size requires 20 subjects per cell, or 240 subjects in all, more than a 40 percent increase in sample size. The intuitive explanation for this discrepancy is that the A main-effect test is based on the A marginal means, which themselves are based on nb observations, which in this specific design equals $4n$. However, the interaction test is based on individual cell means and hence requires more subjects per cell to achieve the same power, all other things being equal.

ADVANTAGES OF FACTORIAL DESIGNS

Continuing the theme of our numerical example, suppose that we were interested in the effectiveness of various treatments for hypertension. Specifically, we wonder whether biofeedback reduces blood pressure, and we are also interested in comparing drugs X, Y, and Z. Would it be better to conduct a 2 × 3 factorial study or to perform two separate single-factor studies?

The most obvious advantage of the factorial design is that it enables us to test the existence of an interaction. With two single-factor studies, we could never learn that differences between drugs might differ depending on the presence or absence of biofeedback. In particular, stop and think about the single-factor study to compare the three drugs. This study most likely would be conducted in the absence of biofeedback, so in effect we are performing what would be a simple effects test in the factorial design. However, the simple effects test may convey only one-half of the relevant ways in which drugs differ. In summary, it may be of theoretical interest to discover an interaction, which implies the necessity of a factorial design.

What if an interaction is not expected? Is there still any advantage to the factorial design? Yes, because the factorial design enables greater generalizability. If our hypertension study is conducted as a factorial design and there is no interaction, we can conclude that drug differences are the same in the presence of biofeed-back as in its absence. (However, an alternate explanation, especially with small sample sizes, is that the power to detect an interaction was inadequate. Even with sufficient power, one should really conclude that any differences that may exist are so small that we can regard them as nonexistent for all practical purposes because we should not literally accept the null hypothesis.) In other words, we can generalize drug effects across two levels of the biofeedback factor. If we had instead conducted a single-factor study, we could not assess the extent of generalizability.

So far we have seen that a factorial design may be preferable to a series of single-factor studies because we can test interaction effects and we can assess generalizability (notice that these two advantages are really opposite perspectives on one advantage). However, don't factorial designs require larger sample sizes? Let's consider two hypothetical psychologists: Dr. Single and Dr. Multiple. Dr. Single decides to conduct two single-factor studies. The first study investigates the relative effectiveness of drugs X, Y, and Z. Thirty subjects are assigned at random to each of the three drugs. In the second study, biofeedback is compared to a control. Forty-five subjects are assigned at random to each of the two groups. In the two studies combined, Dr. Single has used 180 subjects. Dr. Multiple conducts a 2 × 3 factorial study investigating the effect of biofeedback and drug effects simultane-ously. Fifteen subjects are assigned at random to each of the six groups. Of course, Dr. Multiple can test an interaction that Dr. Single cannot, but how else will their tests be different? Both will test whether biofeedback has an effect. Dr. Single's comparison involves 45 subjects in each group. But so does Dr. Multiple's because there were 15 subjects at each level of drug, implying that 45 subjects received biofeedback whereas 45 others did not. Both investigators will also test for drug differences. By the same logic, both Dr. Single and Dr. Multiple will have exposed 30 subjects to each type of drug. Thus, it should be the case that Dr. Multiple's statistical power for assessing biofeedback and drug effects should be equivalent to Dr. Single's. Does this mean that Dr. Single's and Dr. Multiple's approaches are equally good in how efficiently subjects are used? Recall that Dr. Single used 180 subjects in all. However, Dr. Multiple used a total of 6 × 15 = 90 subjects. Dr. Multiple's factorial design produced the same power with half as many subjects as Dr. Single's two separate studies! The implicaton is that the factorial design uses subjects more efficiently than would a series of single-factor studies.[11]

Does this mean that researchers should strive to design studies with as many factors as they can imagine? This issue and problems in analyzing designs with three or more factors are considered in Chapter 8. Before proceeding, however, there is one other topic to be covered in the two-factor design.

NONORTHOGONAL DESIGNS

So far in this chapter, we have only considered designs where there are the same number of subjects in each cell in the design. Although this condition is *not* an assumption of the model, it simplifies calculations of sums of squares. This section considers designs where this condition is not met. However, we assume throughout that the factors are completely crossed, that is, there are no missing cells. For discussion of designs with missing cells, see Searle (1987). When the number of observations (subjects) varies from cell to cell, the design is said to be *nonorthogonal* (or, *unbalanced*).

This use of the term *nonorthogonal* appears to be at odds with the meaning we developed in Chapter 4. In fact, however, the usage here is entirely consistent. Unequal-n factorial designs are said to be nonorthogonal because contrasts representing the A main effect, B main effect, and A by B interaction are no longer orthogonal with unequal n. Recall that one of the first things we did at the beginning of this chapter was to show that the biofeedback main-effect contrast was orthogonal to the drug therapy main-effect contrast in our 2×2 design. The respective contrast coefficients were 1, 1, -1, and -1 for biofeedback and 1, -1, 1, and -1 for drug therapy. We saw that these two contrasts are orthogonal by applying Equation 4.45: $(1)(1) + (1)(-1) + (-1)(1) + (-1)(-1)$, which equals zero, the condition for orthogonality. However, with unequal n, the test for orthogonality is given by

$$\frac{(1)(1)}{n_{11}} + \frac{(1)(-1)}{n_{21}} + \frac{(-1)(1)}{n_{12}} + \frac{(-1)(-1)}{n_{22}}$$

This expression equals zero if and only if

$$\frac{1}{n_{11}} + \frac{1}{n_{22}} = \frac{1}{n_{21}} + \frac{1}{n_{12}}$$

Although unequal cell sizes might obey this requirement (e.g., 10 subjects in both cells of row 1 and 8 subjects in both cells of row 2), in general they do not. Thus, unequal cell sizes typically yield nonorthogonal effects. As we saw in Chapter 4, sums of squares of nonorthogonal contrasts are not additive, which leads to complications in data analysis.

One sign of the increased difficulty in analyzing data from nonorthogonal designs is that the proper analysis method is still the source of some controversy. Our approach essentially consists of providing an understanding of the logic behind the various approaches that we believe are most often preferable. However, at the outset, we should state that we agree with Herr and Gaebelein's (1978) statement that different approaches may be optimal in different situations.

Design Considerations

Before considering issues of analysis, it is important to discuss reasons that a nonorthogonal design may have arisen. It is useful to distinguish designs involving classification factors from designs involving experimental factors. As an example of the former, we might randomly sample the employees of a business organization and classify each individual according to gender and level of educational attainment (e.g., college graduates versus noncollege graduates). There is no reason in general to believe that the number of individuals who would be placed in each cell of the

2×2 design would be equal. Thus, when the factors of the design are classificatory in nature, it typically is the case that a nonorthogonal design occurs.

On the other hand, the factors may represent experimental variables, where the experimenter assigns subjects to specific cells of the design. In such a situation, the experimenter usually assigns an equal number of subjects to each cell. (This assignment process typically maximizes robustness and power as well as simplifying the analysis.) However, the number of subjects on whom data are obtained may be reduced because of subject attrition. If data are not obtained for all subjects, the resulting design is likely to be nonorthogonal because the number of subjects with missing data will likely vary from cell to cell.

Relationship Between Design and Analysis

The analysis methods to be presented do not necessarily yield meaningful answers when cell sizes are unequal. Whether any of the analysis methods yield meaningful information depends on *why* the design is nonorthogonal. If the factors are classification factors, the methods to be presented do yield meaningful data as long as subjects are randomly sampled from the population of interest. If the factors are experimental factors, the picture is less clear. The analysis methods yield meaningful information only if it can be assumed that the reasons for subject attrition are independent of the treatments. In other words, it is necessary to assume that the treatments are not differentially responsible for subjects failing to complete the study. This assumption may be unrealistic, especially if some treatments are more aversive or more rewarding than others. If the treatments have indeed differentially affected subject attrition, none of the analysis methods presented here yields meaningful answers. When treatments have such differential effects, the subjects for whom scores are available in one cell are systematically different from those with scores in another cell. *Any* comparison of scores is likely to confound true treatment effects with preexisting differences between subjects because there is a "selection bias" here that threatens internal validity, as discussed in Chapter 1. On the other hand, if the treatments have *not* differentially caused subject attrition, then within each cell, the subjects for whom data are available are for all practical purposes a random sample of the original random sample. In this case, groups of subjects are not systematically different except insofar as the treatments truly have different effects, so analysis can proceed unambiguously.

In summary, the analysis methods to be represented are appropriate in either of two situations. First, the factors may be classification factors, where unequal cell sizes reflect true differences in population sizes. Second, the factors may be experimental factors, where the treatments have not differentially caused subject attrition.

Analysis of the 2×2 Nonorthogonal Design

Just as we did for the equal-n case, we begin with the 2×2 design because the concepts are easier to grasp in this simpler case. Once the concepts have been developed for the 2×2 design, we consider a general two-factor design where both factors may have more than two levels.

T A B L E **7. 11** Hypothetical Salary Data (in Thousands) for Female and Male Employees

	Females		**Males**	
	College Degree	No College Degree	College Degree	No College Degree
	24	15	25	19
	26	17	29	18
	25	20	27	21
	24	16		20
	27			21
	24			22
	27			19
	23			
Mean	**25**	**17**	**27**	**20**

To illustrate the 2 × 2 design, we examine data from a hypothetical organization that has been accused of salary discrimination against female employees. Specifically, the allegation is that newly hired females are underpaid relative to newly hired males. Table 7.11 presents hypothetical data for 12 females and 10 males who have just been hired by the organization. The mean salary for the 12 females is $22,333 while the mean for the 10 males is $22,100. These numbers would certainly seem to argue that females have not been discriminated against because not only does the small difference of $233 turn out to be statistically nonsignificant,[12] but its direction favors females. If anything, females seem slightly overpaid, although their "advantage" is within the bounds of sampling error. However, Table 7.11 contains information about an additional characteristic of employees, namely, whether they received a college degree. It is obvious from glancing at the table that a majority of the new female employees are college graduates, while a majority of the males are not. How should this affect our interpretation that there is no discrimination?

To begin to address this question, notice that we can conceptualize these data in terms of a 2 × 2 design, where one factor is the employee's gender and the other factor is the employee's educational attainment.[13] It is immediately apparent that this design is nonorthogonal because there is an unequal number of observations in the four cells.

Test of the Interaction

Our substantive interest here is primarily in the gender main effect, although the gender by education interaction may also help us understand the nature of any possible discrimination in pay. Because it may be difficult to interpret the main effect if the interaction is significant, we first consider how to test the interaction in a 2 × 2 nonorthogonal design. Recall from the beginning of the chapter that the interaction in a 2×2 design can be tested via a contrast with coefficients of 1, -1, -1, and 1 for the $(1, 1), (1, 2), (2, 1)$ and $(2, 2)$ cells, respectively. Further, recall that the sum of squares for a contrast is given by

$$SS_\psi = (\hat{\psi})^2 \Big/ \sum_{j=1}^{a} c_j^2/n_j \qquad \text{(4.35, repeated)}$$

where $\hat{\psi}$ is the value of the contrast, c_j is the contrast coefficient for group j, and n_j is the sample size for group j. In our specific problem, we can simplify this formula by noting that

$$\hat{\psi} = \bar{Y}_{11} - \bar{Y}_{12} - \bar{Y}_{21} + \bar{Y}_{22}$$

and

$$c_1^2 = c_2^2 = c_3^2 = c_4^2 = 1$$

Making these substitutions yields

$$SS_{AB} = (\bar{Y}_{11} - \bar{Y}_{12} - \bar{Y}_{21} + \bar{Y}_{22})^2/(1/n_{11} + 1/n_{12} + 1/n_{21} + 1/n_{22})$$

which can be rewritten as

$$SS_{AB} = \tilde{n}(\bar{Y}_{11} - \bar{Y}_{12} - \bar{Y}_{21} + \bar{Y}_{22})^2/4 \qquad (40)$$

where $\tilde{n}$ denotes the harmonic mean of n_{11}, n_{12}, n_{21}, and n_{22}.

Three points deserve mention here. First, because the harmonic mean is probably unfamiliar, we take a moment to explain it briefly. The harmonic mean of a set of numbers is an average value, similar to the usual arithmetic mean. In general, the harmonic mean of a set of scores $X_1, X_2, \ldots, X_a$ is defined to be

$$\tilde{X} = a \Big/ \left[\sum_{j=1}^{a} (1/X_j) \right]$$

Thus, the harmonic mean of the four cell sizes $n_{11}, n_1, n_{21},$ and n_{22} is

$$\tilde{n} = 4/(1/n_{11} + 1/n_{12} + 1/n_{21} + 1/n_{22})$$

For our data, the harmonic mean of the cell sizes equals

$$\tilde{n} = 4/(1/8 + 1/4 + 1/3 + 1/7) = 4.699$$

Notice that this value is close to, but somewhat less than, the arithmetic mean of the cell sizes, which equals 5.5. The reason the harmonic mean appears in the formula instead of the arithmetic mean is that the variance of each cell mean is proportional to the reciprocal of the number of subjects in that cell.[14] Second, notice the similarity to the formula for SS_{AB} in the 2×2 design with equal n, in which case SS_{AB} is given by

$$SS_{AB} = n(\bar{Y}_{11} - \bar{Y}_{12} - \bar{Y}_{21} + \bar{Y}_{22})^2/4$$

Thus, with unequal n, the only complication in the formula is that an average cell size (specifically, the harmonic mean) is used instead of the single cell size common to all cells in the equal-n design. Third, it turns out that this modification is restricted

TABLE 7.12 Sample Means for Salary Data in Table 7.11

		Educational Level (B)	
		College Degree	No College Degree
Sex (A)	Female	$n_{11} = 8$ $\bar{Y}_{11} = 25$	$n_{12} = 4$ $\bar{Y}_{12} = 17$
	Male	$n_{21} = 3$ $\bar{Y}_{21} = 27$	$n_{22} = 7$ $\bar{Y}_{22} = 20$

to designs where all factors have only two levels. When some factors have more than two levels, we will see later that additional complications arise because the sum of squares for effects cannot be calculated as the sum of squares of a single contrast.

The interaction sum of squares for the data in Table 7.11 can be calculated as

$$SS_{AB} = 4.699(25 - 17 - 27 + 20)^2/4$$

Performing the necessary arithmetic yields $SS_{AB} = 1.1748$. The interaction can be tested for significance as usual by dividing the interaction mean square by the mean square within. The mean square within is calculated for unequal n in exactly the same manner as it was calculated for equal n. For the data in Table 7.11, this yields $MS_W = 2.7778$, so the F value for the interaction is 0.4229. This value is non-significant at the .05 level, so there is no evidence that gender and education interact. Thus, the difference between female and male salaries is the same for those with a college degree as for those without, at least within sampling error.

We can now consider whether this consistent gender difference is a true difference or whether it is within sampling error of zero. To do this, we need to consider the main effect of gender. As we learned at the beginning of this chapter, a main effect involves a comparison of marginal means, averaging across the other factor. To help conceptualize the marginal means for our data, consider Table 7.12, which shows the four cell means of Table 7.11 arranged in a 2 × 2 design.

Unweighted Marginal Means and Type III Sum of Squares

To find the marginal mean for females, we should average the two cell means in the first row, that is, 25 and 17. An obvious solution would be to add 25 and 17 and divide by 2, yielding a marginal mean of 21. Following the same logic for males would produce a marginal mean of 23.5. Notice that we have calculated the marginal mean in each case by taking an unweighted average of the relevant cell means. For this reason, the marginal means we have calculated are referred to as *unweighted marginal means*. We will see momentarily that this is indeed a reasonable method for calculating a marginal mean, but there are two other reasonable possibilities as well. Before considering these other possibilities, let's see how we can test whether the difference between the two unweighted marginal means is statistically significant.

When the factor in question has two levels (as in our example), the test of a difference between unweighted marginal means can be accomplished easily because once again the difference can be stated in terms of a single comparison. The difference in A marginal means (where A represents gender, the row factor in Table 7.12) can be represented as a contrast with coefficients of .5, .5, −.5, and −.5, for the (1, 1), (1, 2), (2, 1), and (2, 2) cells, respectively.[15] Once again, the usual formula for the sum of squares of a contrast applies:

$$SS_\psi = (\hat{\psi})^2 \Big/ \sum_{j=1}^{a} c_j^2/n_j \qquad \text{(4.35, repeated)}$$

In our specific case, the formula becomes

$$SS_\psi = (.5\bar{Y}_{11} + .5\bar{Y}_{12} - .5\bar{Y}_{21} - .5\bar{Y}_{22})^2/(1/4n_{11} + 1/4n_{12} + 1/4n_{21} + 1/4n_{22})$$

Rearranging terms yields

$$SS_\psi = \tilde{n}(.5\bar{Y}_{11} + .5\bar{Y}_{12} - .5\bar{Y}_{21} - .5\bar{Y}_{22})^2$$

If we let $\bar{Y}_{1.(U)}$ and $\bar{Y}_{2.(U)}$ represent the unweighted sample marginal means, the formula simplifies yet further to

$$SS_\psi = \tilde{n}(\bar{Y}_{1.(U)} - \bar{Y}_{2.(U)})^2$$

Finally, the sum of squares for the difference between unweighted marginal means is often called the *Type III sum of squares* (remember that there are two other ways of defining marginal means yet to be discussed). Thus, we can write the sum of squares as

$$\text{Type III} \qquad SS_A = \tilde{n}(\bar{Y}_{1.(U)} - \bar{Y}_{2.(U)})^2 \qquad \text{(41)}$$

when the A factor has two levels. We should emphasize again that this formula is restricted to a two-level factor; additional complications arise when the factor has three or more levels.

At this point, let's calculate the Type III sum of squares due to A for our data. Substituting $\tilde{n} = 4.699$ (as before for testing the interaction), $\bar{Y}_{1.(U)} = 21.0$, and $\bar{Y}_{2.(U)} = 23.5$ yields a sum of squares equal to 29.3706. Dividing by the MS_W value of 2.7778 produces an F value of 10.5734, which has an associated p value of .0044. Thus, we can say that females' and males' unweighted marginal means are significantly different at the .05 level. Further note that the female mean is the smaller of the two, by $2500.

Unweighted Versus Weighted Marginal Means

This result appears to contradict the earlier statement that females are paid more than males, although the earlier difference was nonsignificant. Specifically, we stated earlier that females were favored by $233. Now we seem to be saying that males are favored by $2500. Which is correct? As we will see, both differences are numerically correct, but they address different questions.

The $2500 difference in favor of males occurred when we compared a female salary of $21,000 versus a male salary of $23,500. The $2500 difference is literally an average (unweighted) of the $2000 difference for college graduates and the $3000 difference for nongraduates (refer to Table 7.12 to see where the figures $2000 and $3000 come from). Thus, if we compare an average female to an average male—both of whom have the same educational level—the mean difference in their salary is $2500. Recall that the nonsignificant interaction told us that the $2000 difference for graduates is not significantly different from the $3000 difference for nongraduates, so in this sense the $2500 difference can be regarded as a correct estimate within sampling error both for graduates and nongraduates. The most important point to realize here is that the difference between the rows is being calculated within each column, and then an unweighted average is calculated across the columns.

The $233 difference in favor of females was arrived at in a rather different manner. This value is the difference between the mean of $22,333 for the 12 females and the mean of $22,100 for the 10 males. Notice that these means were calculated ignoring educational level. In effect, what we have done here is to calculate a *weighted marginal mean*, where the weights are a function of the number of observations at each educational level. For example, the female marginal mean of $22,333 was obtained from $(8/12)(25,000) + (4/12)(17,000)$. Similarly, the weighted marginal mean for males was obtained from $(3/10)(27,000) + (7/10)(20,000)$. The unweighted marginal means were calculated as $(1/2)(25,000) + (1/2)(17,000)$ for females and $(1/2)(27,000) + (1/2)(20,000)$ for males. The reason that the weighted mean for females ($22,333) is greater than the unweighted mean for females ($21,000) is because a majority of the females in the sample have a college degree and employees with such a degree tend to be paid more than those without. The same logic explains why the weighted mean for males ($22,100) is less than the unweighted mean for males ($23,500). Thus, it is because a greater proportion of females than males have college degrees in this sample that for weighted means, females are paid more than males (although the difference is nonsignificant), but for unweighted means, females are paid less than males.

It is important to emphasize that testing differences in weighted marginal means answers a different question from testing differences in unweighted marginal means. When we test differences in weighted marginal means, we are testing whether the rows (for example) have different means irrespective of any association between the rows and columns. In our example, the 12 females are paid slightly more than the 10 males on the average, as reflected by the weighted marginal means. (Again, the difference is nonsignificant.) This is an entirely correct statement, but it may or may not answer the question in which we are interested. In particular, differences in the weighted marginal means do *not* tell us whether females and males of similar educational attainment tend to be paid equally. This question can be answered by comparing unweighted marginal means. For our data, females are paid significantly less than males of the same educational level. To summarize for our data, females are paid slightly more than males on the whole, but once we take educational level into account (i.e., allow for the effects of educational level on salary), females are significantly underpaid. In this sense, although females are paid slightly more than males overall, their apparent advantage is significantly less than it should be, given their average superior educational level in this sample.

Three further points merit attention here regarding weighted and unweighted means. First, notice that the distinction was unnecessary in an equal-n design, because the weights used to calculate weighted means would all be equal to one another. As a result, in an equal-n design, weighted and unweighted means are identical to one another. Second, although we may be tempted to conclude in our example that females are indeed being discriminated against, in fact we should also consider other qualifications that might differentiate the females from the males in this sample. For example, years of work experience might be an important factor, which potentially could either favor the females in the sample (increasing the actual discrimination) or the males (decreasing the actual discrimination). Third, although we stated earlier in the discussion that the difference between the weighted marginal means of $22,333 for females and $22,100 for males is nonsignificant, we did not provide the computational details. Once again, when the factor has two levels, the sum of squares for the difference between weighted marginal means can be calculated as the sum of squares for a contrast. In general, the coefficients for testing the difference in weighted row marginal means are given by n_{11}/n_{1+}, n_{12}/n_{1+}, $-n_{21}/n_{2+}$, and $-n_{22}/n_{2+}$, where n_{1+} and n_{2+} are the total number of subjects in rows 1 and 2, respectively. For our data, the resulting coefficients are $8/12$, $4/12$, $-3/10$, and $-7/10$. Applying the usual formula for the sum of squares due to a contrast (Equation 4.35) yields a value of 0.2970. Dividing this value by the MS_W of 2.7778 yields an F value of 0.1069, which is nonsignificant at the .05 level.

The sum of squares for the difference in row marginal means is called a *Type I sum of squares*, where effects due to row have been included in the model but effects due to column have not.[16] This terminology is discussed more fully momentarily, when we consider nonorthogonal designs beyond the 2×2.

Type II Sum of Squares

At this point, we have discussed two different types of sums of squares—Type I and Type III. Not surprisingly, there is also a Type II sum of squares.[17] Before introducing Type II sum of squares, it is relevant to reconsider the question addressed by Type III sum of squares, which you should recall was used to test differences in unweighted marginal means. The difference in unweighted row marginal means averages differences between the rows within each column, giving equal weight to the columns. To understand the rationale for Type II sum of squares, consider a situation where there is no interaction of rows and columns in the population and there are more observations in the first column than in the second column. The lack of an interaction implies that the difference between the population mean in row 1 versus row 2 is the same in both columns. Thus, the quantities $\bar{Y}_{11} - \bar{Y}_{21}$ and $\bar{Y}_{12} - \bar{Y}_{22}$ are both estimates of the same population parameter. If there are more observations in the first column than in the second column, $\bar{Y}_{11} - \bar{Y}_{21}$ will probably be a better estimate than $\bar{Y}_{12} - \bar{Y}_{22}$. The rationale behind Type II sum of squares is to give the better estimate more weight than the other estimate. Notice that the Type III sum of squares does not capitalize on the opportunity in this situation because its value is based on a difference where $\bar{Y}_{12} - \bar{Y}_{22}$ receives the same weight as $\bar{Y}_{11} - \bar{Y}_{21}$.

It can be shown that in this situation the optimal weights are $n_{11}n_{21}/n_{+1}$ for $\bar{Y}_{11} - \bar{Y}_{21}$ and $n_{12}n_{22}/n_{+2}$ for $\bar{Y}_{12} - \bar{Y}_{22}$.[18] Once again, when the factor has two levels, the test can be performed by testing the significance of a contrast. The contrast coefficients are given by $n_{11}n_{21}/n_{+1}$ (for the 11 cell), $n_{12}n_{22}/n_{+2}$ (for the 12 cell), $-n_{11}n_{21}/n_{+1}$ (for the 21 cell), and $-n_{12}n_{22}/n_{+2}$ (for the 22 cell). For our data, the contrast coefficients are given by 2.1818, 2.5455, -2.1818, and -2.5455. Alternatively, we can divide each weight by 4.7273 (the sum of 2.1818 and 2.5455) to obtain units comparable to the original metric, in which case the weights are 0.4615, 0.5385, -0.4615, and -0.5385. Notice that the gender difference for nongraduates receives a little more weight than the gender difference for graduates. The reason is that a difference between means based on samples of size 4 and 7 is less variable than a difference based on samples of size 3 and 8 (the harmonic mean of 4 and 7 is larger than the harmonic mean of 3 and 8; see Note 14). For our data, the difference in marginal means equals .4615(27,000 $-$ 25,000) + .5385(20,000 $-$ 17,000), which equals $2538.50, only slightly larger than the $2500 difference in unweighted marginal means. Application of Equation 4.35 yields a Type II sum of squares of 30.4615, which corresponds to an F value of 10.9662 and a p value of .0039. Thus, for our data, the Type II and Type III sum of squares yield very similar conclusions. Although this is quite often the case, particularly if the interaction is nonexistent, in other circumstances substantial differences can occur. We will return to comparing these two approaches after we have considered the general $a \times b$ nonorthogonal design.

Summary of Three Types of Sum of Squares

Table 7.13 summarizes the differences between the coefficients of Type I, Type II, and Type III sums of squares for the row main effect in a 2 $\times$ 2 design. Table 7.14 presents the corresponding hypothesis being tested by each type of sum of square. As we emphasized earlier, this table shows clearly that the three types of sums of squares are generally answering different questions. However, there are three special circumstances where some of the hypotheses (and also the sums of squares) converge. First, if $n_{11} = n_{12}$ and $n_{21} = n_{22}$, all three types test the same hypothesis, and all three yield identical sums of squares. Second, if $n_{11} = n_{21}$ and

T A B L E 7. 13 Contrast Coefficients for the A (Row) Main Effect in a 2 $\times$ 2 Design

			Cell	
	11	*12*	*21*	*22*
Type I SS*	n_{11}/n_{1+}	n_{12}/n_{1+}	$-n_{21}/n_{2+}$	$-n_{22}/n_{2+}$
Type II SS[†]	$n_{11}n_{21}/n_{+1}$	$n_{12}n_{22}/n_{+2}$	$-n_{11}n_{21}/n_{+1}$	$-n_{12}n_{22}/n_{+2}$
Type III SS	1/2	1/2	$-1/2$	$-1/2$

*The A factor is entered into the model first.
[†] These coefficients are not on the same scale as the original metric, which can be preserved by dividing each coefficient shown here by $\frac{1}{2}(\tilde{n}_{.1} + \tilde{n}_{.2})$, where $\tilde{n}_{.1}$ and $\tilde{n}_{.2}$ are the harmonic means of the cell sizes in the first and second columns, respectively.

TABLE **7. 14**   Hypotheses Tested by Three Types of Sums of
Squares for A Main Effect in a 2×2 Design

General Expression

Type I   SS* $H_0 : \dfrac{1}{n_{1+}}(n_{11}\mu_{11} + n_{12}\mu_{12}) = \dfrac{1}{n_{2+}}(n_{21}\mu_{21} + n_{22}\mu_{22})$

Type II   SS† $H_0 : \dfrac{1}{(\tilde{n}_{.1} + \tilde{n}_{.2})}(\tilde{n}_{.1}\mu_{11} + \tilde{n}_{.2}\mu_{12}) = \dfrac{1}{(\tilde{n}_{.1} + \tilde{n}_{.2})}(\tilde{n}_{.1}\mu_{21} + \tilde{n}_{.2}\mu_{22})$

Type III   SS $H_0 : 1/2(\mu_{11} + \mu_{12}) = 1/2(\mu_{21} + \mu_{22})$

Specific Expression for Table 7.11 Data

Type I $H_0 : .6667\mu_{11} + .3333\mu_{12} = .3000\mu_{21} + .7000\mu_{22}$

Type II $H_0 : .4615\mu_{11} + .5385\mu_{12} = .4615\mu_{21} + .5385\mu_{22}$

Type III $H_0 : .5000\mu_{11} + .5000\mu_{12} = .5000\mu_{21} + .5000\mu_{22}$

*The A factor is entered into the model first
†$\tilde{n}_{.1}$ and $\tilde{n}_{.2}$ are the harmonic means of the cell sizes in the first and second columns, respectively.

$n_{12} = n_{22}$, Types I and II are the same, but Type III is different. Third, if the population interaction is zero (so $\mu_{11} - \mu_{21}$ equals $\mu_{12} - \mu_{22}$), Types II and III test the same hypothesis, but their sums of squares are still generally somewhat different. We have more to say about which Type is "best" after we discuss the general $a \times b$ design.

Although our discussion has focused on the row main effect, obviously the same logic applies to the column main effect because it is arbitrary which factor is represented as rows and which as columns to begin with. Also, notice that the different types of sums of squares were not discussed for the interaction because the interaction is a test of cell mean differences instead of marginal mean differences. Thus, the various approaches to "averaging" across the other factor are not an issue for testing the interaction.

ANALYSIS OF THE GENERAL $a \times b$ NONORTHOGONAL DESIGN

The concepts we developed in the 2×2 design are also applicable in the general $a \times b$ design. For example, there is still a distinction among Type I, Type II, and Type III sum of squares for a main effect. Although the concepts remain the same, the necessary calculations become considerably more difficult because the sum of squares for an effect cannot be obtained from a single contrast when the effect has more than 1 degree of freedom.

To consider the $a \times b$ design, we return to our model-comparisons strategy. In the process, we see how the various types of sums of squares we initially encountered in the 2 × 2 design can be conceptualized in terms of model comparisons.

You may remember that earlier in the chapter we presented a flowchart (Figure 7.2) to be used as a guideline for analyzing effects in a two-factor design. Although this flowchart was presented in the context of equal-n designs, it is also applicable for unequal-n designs. According to the flowchart, the first step in analyzing two-way designs is generally to test the interaction.

Test of the Interaction

The test of the interaction in the general $a \times b$ design with unequal n involves the same full and restricted models as in the equal-n design:

$$\text{Full:} \qquad Y_{ijk} = \mu + \alpha_j + \beta_k + (\alpha\beta)_{jk} + \varepsilon_{ijk} \qquad \text{(6, repeated)}$$

$$\text{Restricted:} \qquad Y_{ijk} = \mu + \alpha_j + \beta_k + \varepsilon_{ijk} \qquad \text{(32, repeated)}$$

Least-squares estimates of the parameters of the full model are easy to obtain, even with unequal n, because as we saw earlier in the chapter, this model is a cell means model. As a consequence, the sum of squared errors for the full model is given by

$$E_{\text{F}} = \sum_{k=1}^{b} \sum_{j=1}^{a} \sum_{i=1}^{n_j} (Y_{ijk} - \bar{Y}_{jk})^2$$

$$= SS_{\text{W}} \qquad (42)$$

where SS_{W} denotes the within-group sum of squares. Unfortunately, there is no correspondingly simple expression for the sum of squared errors of the restricted model because formulas for the least-squares estimates of its parameters have no simple form without resorting to matrix algebra (Searle, 1987, p. 102). As a consequence, there is no simple expression for the interaction sum of squares, SS_{AB}, which equals $E_{\text{R}} - E_{\text{F}}$, the difference in the sum of squared errors of the restricted and full models.[19] Thus, for all practical purposes, computations must be performed on a computer, except in the 2 × 2 design. However, what is important for our purposes is to realize that the test of the A × B interaction is based on comparing the same models in the unequal-n design as in the equal-n design. Although calculations are much more formidable with unequal n, the meaning of the test does not change because the interaction parameters continue to have the same meaning that we developed at some length at the beginning of the chapter. It is also important to realize that there is a single numerical value for the interaction sum of squares—that is, the Type I, Type II, and Type III sums of squares are all equal to each other for the interaction.[20]

According to the flowchart in Figure 7.2, if the interaction is statistically significant, we would typically perform simple-effect tests. These tests are relatively straightforward to conduct, even with unequal n because the sum of squares for a simple effect is based on a single level of the other factor. As a result, the sum of squares can be calculated using appropriate formulas from Chapter 3 for a one-way design. The presence of unequal cell sizes presents no special problems here because there is no need to average over levels of another factor.

Test of Unweighted Marginal Means

If the interaction is not significant, the next step would typically involve testing main effects. We arbitrarily focus on the A main effect (at the end of this section, we present comparable formulas for B). With equal n, we found the sum of squares due to A by comparing the following pair of models:

$$\text{Full:} \qquad Y_{ijk} = \mu + \alpha_j + \beta_k + (\alpha\beta)_{jk} + \varepsilon_{ijk} \qquad \text{(6, repeated)}$$

$$\text{Restricted:} \qquad Y_{ijk} = \mu + \beta_k + (\alpha\beta)_{jk} + \varepsilon_{ijk} \qquad \text{(21, repeated)}$$

These same two models can also be compared with unequal n. It can be shown that the null hypothesis being tested here is of the form

$$H_0 : \mu_{1.(U)} = \mu_{2.(U)} = \cdots = \mu_{a.(U)} \qquad (43)$$

where $\mu_{1.(U)}$ is the unweighted marginal means of row 1, $\mu_{2.(U)}$ is the unweighted marginal mean of row 2, and so forth. Notice that the unweighted marginal mean for row j would be defined as

$$\mu_{j.(U)} = \sum_{k=1}^{b} \mu_{jk}/b$$

The important point to realize here is that comparing Equations 6 and 21 with unequal n provides a test of whether unweighted row marginal means are equal to one another. As usual, the test is performed by finding the difference in the sum of squared errors of the two models, that is, $E_R - E_F$. Searle (1987, p. 90) shows[21] that this difference equals

$$E_R - E_F = \sum_{j=1}^{a} b\tilde{n}_{j.}(\bar{Y}_{j.(U)} - \bar{Y}_{G(A)})^2 \qquad (44)$$

where

$$b = \text{number of levels of the B factor}$$

$$\tilde{n}_{j.} = b \bigg/ \sum_{k=1}^{b} (1/n_{jk})$$

$$\bar{Y}_{j.(U)} = \sum_{k=1}^{b} \bar{Y}_{jk}/b$$

and

$$\bar{Y}_{G(A)} = \sum_{j=1}^{a} \tilde{n}_{j.} \bar{Y}_{j.(U)} \bigg/ \sum_{j=1}^{a} \tilde{n}_{j.}$$

To make Equation 44 more understandable, it might help to compare it to Equation 25, which provided the formula for SS_A with equal n:

$$E_R - E_F = nb \sum_{j=1}^{a} (\bar{Y}_{j.} - \bar{Y}_{..})^2 \qquad \text{(25, repeated)}$$

It will be helpful to move the nb term in Equation 25 inside the summation and to place b before n, in which case we have (for equal n):

$$E_R - E_F = \sum_{j=1}^{a} bn(\bar{Y}_{j.} - \bar{Y}_{..})^2 \qquad (45)$$

Notice that each term in Equation 45 for equal n has a corresponding term in Equation 44 for unequal n. However, some of the specific terms differ. In particular, the cell size n in Equation 45 has been replaced by $\tilde{n}_{j.}$ in Equation 44. The $\tilde{n}_{j.}$ term is the harmonic mean of the cell sizes in row j. As such, it equals the "effective" cell size (see Note 14, referred to earlier, for more detail) for cells in the jth row. In this sense, the $\tilde{n}_{j.}$ term reflects sample size in Equation 44, just as n does in Equation 45. Also, the marginal mean $\bar{Y}_{j.}$ in Equation 45 is written as $\bar{Y}_{j.(U)}$ in Equation 44 because with unequal n we must distinguish between weighted and unweighted marginal means. Finally, $\bar{Y}_{G(A)}$ in Equation 44 is a grand mean similar to $\bar{Y}_{..}$ in Equation 45. However, $\bar{Y}_{G(A)}$ is calculated as a weighted average of the row marginal means, with the weights given by the "effective" sample sizes of the rows. Thus, although Equation 44 is somewhat more tedious to calculate than is Equation 45, in many respects, their underlying rationales are the same.

Recall that when we tested a null hypothesis of equality among unweighted means in the 2×2 unequal-n design, we referred to the corresponding sum of squares as Type III (see Table 7.14, for a reminder). The same terminology is used in the general $a \times b$ design. Thus, we can say that the Type III sum of squares for the A main effect is obtained when we compare models of the form

Full: $Y_{ijk} = \mu + \alpha_j + \beta_k + (\alpha\beta)_{jk} + \varepsilon_{ijk}$ (6, repeated)

Restricted: $Y_{ijk} = \mu + \beta_k + (\alpha\beta)_{jk} + \varepsilon_{ijk}$ (21, repeated)

Because Equation 44 provides the formula for the difference in the sums of squared errors of these two models, it follows that the Type III sum of squares for the A main effect can be written as

Type III $SS_A = \sum_{j=1}^{a} b\tilde{n}_{j.}(\bar{Y}_{j.(U)} - \bar{Y}_{G(A)})^2$ (46)

where all terms are defined just as they were in Equation 44. As a final point, notice that the Type III sum of squares is obtained by allowing for all of the other effects in the model. In other words, both the restricted and the full models allow for the possibility of a B main effect as well as an A by B interaction. In a sense, then, B and A by B effects are "controlled for" when the Type III sum of squares is used to test the A main effect.

Test of Marginal Means in an Additive Model

Notice, however, that Figure 7.2 generally recommends testing (and interpreting) main effects only when the interaction is nonsignificant. It might be argued that if the interaction is nonsignificant, the interaction parameters can be (or even should be) dropped from our model. The resultant full model would be an additive model and could be written as

$$\text{Full:} \qquad Y_{ijk} = \mu + \alpha_j + \beta_k + \varepsilon_{ijk} \qquad \text{(32, repeated)}$$

In fact, as we saw earlier, the additive model of Equation 32 is the restricted model for the interaction test; a nonsignificant F test implies that this restricted model is not significantly worse at explaining our data than is the model that also includes interaction parameters. By the principle of parsimony, as discussed in Chapter 1, we might then prefer to consider the additive model of Equation 32 as a new full model.

From this perspective, we can test the A main effect by testing a null hypothesis that all of the α_j parameters in the full model of Equation 32 equal zero. Thus, we need to compare the following pair of models:

$$\text{Full:} \qquad Y_{ijk} = \mu + \alpha_j + \beta_k + \varepsilon_{ijk} \qquad \text{(32, repeated)}$$

$$\text{Restricted:} \qquad Y_{ijk} = \mu + \beta_k + \varepsilon_{ijk} \qquad \text{(47)}$$

The resultant difference in the sums of squared errors of the full and the restricted models produces the Type II sum of squares for the A main effect. Unfortunately, there is no simple expression for the Type II sum of squares in the $a \times b$ design. It is possible, however, to write a general expression for the hypothesis being tested by the Type II sum of squares for A in the general $a \times b$ design:

$$\text{H}_0 : \sum_{k=1}^{b} [n_{jk} - (n_{jk}^2/n_{+k})]\mu_{jk} = \sum_{j \neq j'} \sum_{k=1}^{b} (n_{jk} n_{j'k}/n_{+k})\mu_{jk}' \qquad \text{(48)}$$

where $j = 1, 2, \ldots, a - 1$. Comparing this null hypothesis to the null hypothesis for the Type III sum of squares (see Equation 43) makes it clear that interpreting Type II sums of squares may be much less straightforward than interpreting Type III sums of squares. However, just as we showed earlier in the 2×2 design, it turns out here as well that the Type II sum of squares for A can be conceptualized as testing the more straightforward hypothesis of Equation 43 if there is no interaction in the population. This lack of interaction is consistent with our decision to drop the $(\alpha\beta)_{jk}$ parameters from our model, in the first place. When the population interaction is truly zero, omitting the $(\alpha\beta)_{jk}$ parameters increases power, so Type II sums of squares are preferable to Type III sums of squares. However, when the population interaction is not zero, the decision to omit $(\alpha\beta)_{jk}$ parameters is incorrect, and Type II sums of squares are considerably more difficult to interpret than are Type III sums of squares. Of course, the real problem here is that we never know with absolute certainty whether there is an interaction in the *population*, even after we have tested the interaction in our sample. We discuss this issue in more detail at the end of the chapter.

Test of Weighted Marginal Means

Remember that we began our consideration of the A main effect by comparing two models, both of which allowed for both B and A by B effects. The resultant comparison produced the Type III SS for A. Then we compared two models both of which allowed for B, but not for A by B. The resultant comparison produced the Type II SS for A. Suppose that we were to omit not just the interaction parameters but also the B main-effect parameters from our model. Our models would then be

$$\text{Full:}\qquad Y_{ijk} = \mu + \alpha_j + \varepsilon_{ijk}$$

$$\text{Restricted:}\qquad Y_{ijk} = \mu + \varepsilon_{ijk}$$

Not surprisingly, the difference in the sums of squared errors of these two models equals the Type I sum of squares for A (when A is entered first in the hierarchical sequence). By ignoring B and A by B effects, the Type I sum of squares attributes any differences among rows to the A factor, irrespective of potential column effects (i.e., any effects involving the B factor). Recall that this phenomenon was illustrated in our numerical example of the 2×2 design, where the Type I sum of squares ignored the effects of educational level and thus attributed any difference between females' and males' average salaries to the gender factor itself. By ignoring possible B and A by B effects, the Type I sum of squares for A is testing a null hypothesis that the weighted marginal means for all rows are equal to one another. We can write this in symbols as

$$H_0 : (1/n_{1+}) \sum_{k=1}^{b} n_{1k}\mu_{1k} = (1/n_{2+}) \sum_{k=1}^{b} n_{2k}\mu_{2k} = \cdots = (1/n_{a+}) \sum_{k=1}^{b} n_{ak}\mu_{ak} \qquad (49)$$

If we use $\bar{Y}_{j.(\text{W})}$ to represent the weighted sample mean for row j (where the weights applied to $\bar{Y}_{jk}$ equal n_{jk}/n_{j+}), the Type I sum of squares for A can be written as

$$\text{Type I } SS_A = \sum_{j=1}^{a} n_{j+}(\bar{Y}_{j.(\text{W})} - \bar{Y}_{..(\text{W})})^2 \qquad (50)$$

where $\bar{Y}_{..(\text{W})}$ is defined as

$$\bar{Y}_{..(\text{W})} = \sum_{j=1}^{a} n_{j+} \bar{Y}_{j.(\text{W})} \Big/ \sum_{j=1}^{a} n_{j+}$$

Summary of Types of Sum of Squares

At this point, it probably is helpful to summarize what we have learned about the nonorthogonal $a \times b$ design. First, the sum of squares for the interaction is unambiguous because it does not involve averaging over any of the cells in the design. Second, there are three possible ways to test a main effect. In particular, we could test the A main effect by any of the following:

1. Ignoring both B and A by B (Type I)
2. Allowing for B, but ignoring A by B (Type II)
3. Allowing for possible B and A by B effects (Type III)

The most important thing to understand here is that with unequal n, these three approaches generally test different hypotheses. Thus, the investigator's responsibility is to clearly formulate a hypothesis and choose the corresponding type of sum of squares. We will say more about this choice shortly. Third, Tables 7.15–7.18

T A B L E 7.15 Type III Sums of Squares

A Main Effect

Models	Null Hypothesis	Sum of Squares
Full: $Y_{ijk} = \mu + \alpha_j + \beta_k + (\alpha\beta)_{jk} + \varepsilon_{ijk}$ Restricted: $Y_{ijk} = \mu + \beta_k + (\alpha\beta)_{jk} + \varepsilon_{ijk}$	$H_0: \mu_{1.(U)} = \mu_{2.(U)} = \cdots = \mu_{a.(U)}$	$SS_A = \sum_{j=1}^{a} b\tilde{n}_{j.}(\bar{Y}_{j.(U)} - \bar{Y}_{G(A)})^2$

B Main Effect

Models	Null Hypothesis	Sum of Squares
Full: $Y_{ijk} = \mu + \alpha_j + \beta_k + (\alpha\beta)_{jk} + \varepsilon_{ijk}$ Restricted: $Y_{ijk} = \mu + \alpha_j + (\alpha\beta)_{jk} + \varepsilon_{ijk}$	$H_0: \mu_{.1(U)} = \mu_{.2(U)} = \cdots = \mu_{.b(U)}$	$SS_B = \sum_{k=1}^{b} a\tilde{n}_{.k}(\bar{Y}_{.k(U)} - \bar{Y}_{G(B)})^2$

T A B L E 7.16 Type II Sum of Squares

A Main Effect

Models	Null Hypothesis	Sum of Squares
Full: $Y_{ijk} = \mu + \alpha_j + \beta_k + \varepsilon_{ijk}$ Restricted: $Y_{ijk} = \mu + \beta_k + \varepsilon_{ijk}$	$H_0: \sum_{k=1}^{b} [n_{jk} - (n_{jk}^2/n_{+k})]\mu_{jk} = \sum_{j'\neq j}^{} \sum_{k=1}^{b} (n_{jk} n_{j'k}/n_{+k})\mu_{j'k}$ where $j = 1, 2, \ldots, a - 1$	No simple expression (see text and Note 19)

B Main Effect

Models	Null Hypothesis	Sum of Squares
Full: $Y_{ijk} = \mu + \alpha_j + \beta_k + \varepsilon_{ijk}$ Restricted: $Y_{ijk} = \mu + \alpha_j + \varepsilon_{ijk}$	$H_0: \sum_{j=1}^{a} [n_{jk} - (n_{jk}^2/n_{j+})]\mu_{jk} = \sum_{k'\neq k}^{} \sum_{j=1}^{a} (n_{jk} n_{jk'}/n_{j+})\mu_{jk'}$ where $k = 1, 2, \ldots, b - 1$	No simple expression (see text and Note 19)

TABLE 7.17 Type I Sum of Squares—A Entered First

A Main Effect

Models
Full: $Y_{ijk} = \mu + \alpha_j + \varepsilon_{ijk}$
Restricted: $Y_{ijk} = \mu + \varepsilon_{ijk}$

Null Hypothesis
$$H_0: (1/n_{1+})\sum_{k=1}^{b} n_{1k}\mu_{1k} = (1/n_{2+})\sum_{k=1}^{b} n_{2k}\mu_{2k} = \cdots = (1/n_{a+})\sum_{k=1}^{b} n_{ak}\mu_{ak}$$

Sum of Squares
$$SS_A = \sum_{j=1}^{a} n_{j+}(\bar{Y}_{j.(W)} - \bar{Y}_{..(W)})^2$$

B Main Effect

Models
Full: $Y_{ijk} = \mu + \alpha_j + \beta_k + \varepsilon_{ijk}$
Restricted: $Y_{ijk} = \mu + \alpha_j + \varepsilon_{ijk}$

Null Hypothesis
Same as H_0 for Type II SS for B (see Table 7.16)

Sum of Squares
Same as Type II SS for B (see Table 7.16)

TABLE 7.18 Type I Sum of Squares—B Entered First

A Main Effect

Models
Full: $Y_{ijk} = \mu + \alpha_j + \beta_k + \varepsilon_{ijk}$
Restricted: $Y_{ijk} = \mu + \beta_k + \varepsilon_{ijk}$

Null Hypothesis
Same as H_0 for Type II SS for A (see Table 7.16)

Sum of Squares
Same as Type II SS for A (see Table 7.16)

B Main Effect

Models
Full: $Y_{ijk} = \mu + \beta_k + \varepsilon_{ijk}$
Restricted: $Y_{ijk} = \mu + \varepsilon_{ijk}$

Null Hypothesis
$$H_0: (1/n_{+1})\sum_{j=1}^{a} n_{j1}\mu_{j1} = (1/n_{+2})\sum_{j=1}^{a} n_{j2}\mu_{j2} = \cdots = (1/n_{+b})\sum_{j=1}^{a} n_{jb}\mu_{jb}$$

Sum of Squares
$$SS_B = \sum_{k=1}^{b} n_{+k}(\bar{Y}_{k(W)} - \bar{Y}_{..(W)})^2$$

summarize these approaches by presenting in each case the models being compared, the hypotheses being tested, and the sums of squares for both the A main effect and the B main effect. Although our theoretical development focuses exclusively on the A main effect, as these tables show, corresponding formulas are obtained for the B main effect simply by interchanging rows and columns. Also, notice that two versions of Type I sums of squares are presented because in the hierarchical approach either A effects or B effects can enter the model first. In other words, model building can either first include α_j parameters, and then add β_k parameters at a second step, or vice versa. Fourth, we should mention that it is conventional to use mean square within as the error term for all of these model comparisons. Thus, in all cases, an F statistic is formed as

$$ F = \frac{SS_{\text{effect}}/df_{\text{effect}}}{MS_{\text{W}}} $$

Which Type of Sum of Squares Is Best?

In an equal-n design, Type I, Type II, and Type III sums of squares are all identical. The reason is that the A, B, and AB factors are orthogonal to each other in an equal-n design. Thus, with equal n, when testing A (for example), it does not matter whether B parameters are included in the model. However, in an unequal-n design, the factors are typically correlated. The three Types of sum of squares usually are at least somewhat different in this situation. Which one should be used? This is a complicated question, which has been debated extensively in the psychological statistics literature. Not surprisingly, the correct answer is, It depends.

Type I sums of squares are usually not appropriate because the test of differences in weighted marginal means obviously depends on cell sizes. Such an approach is meaningful only if the cell sizes themselves are thought to represent population sizes, as they may when the factors in question are classificatory rather than experimental. In this situaton, Type I sums of squares are meaningful, but even here it must be kept in mind that the other factor is being ignored. Thus, in our salary data example, it may be of interest to discover that females are paid slightly more than males and that the difference is nonsignificant. However, this result must be interpreted extremely carefully because it ignores any effects of educational level. Howell and McConaughy (1982) provide additional examples of situations where differences in weighted marginal means may be informative. However, the crucial point is that tests based on Type I sum of squares ignore the effects of the other factor in the design, which usually defeats the purpose behind including multiple factors.

Type II and Type III sums of squares are based on differences within the levels of the other factor, unlike Type I sum of squares. Thus, they are usually more appropriate than Type I sum of squares for interpreting a main effect. Which of these two is better—Type II or Type III? As stated earlier, it depends on whether the interaction is zero in the population. If it is, the Type II approach is more powerful because stable differences are weighted more heavily than unstable differences. If the interaction is nonzero, the Type III approach is preferable because it is more easily interpreted. To see why, let's return to our hypothetical salary data. The

Type III sum of squares always provides a test of unweighted marginal means. In our example, this corresponds to averaging the gender difference in salaries for college graduates with the difference for nongraduates. The important point is that we are giving the same weight to the difference we observe for graduates as to the weight we observe for nongraduates. Thus, the "average" is easy to interpret. However, the Type II approach is estimating .4615 times the difference for graduates plus .5385 times the difference for nongraduates. If the two differences are the same, this weighted average is easily interpreted because it simply equals the constant difference that exists for both graduates and nongraduates. Of course, the two differences are the same in the population if and only if the interaction is zero in the population. On the other hand, if there is an interaction in the population, whatever difference exists for nongraduates is receiving more weight than the difference for graduates. This complicates interpretation, especially because the differential weights are entirely a function of the cell sizes, which may be unequal for reasons we are not interested in interpreting. However, as Tables 7.14 and 7.16 show, the cell sizes influence not only the F test but also the null hypothesis being tested with Type II sum of squares if there is an interaction in the population.

What should we do? One approach would be to test the interaction. If it is nonsignificant, we could proceed with Type II sum of squares. However, we would have to concern ourselves here with the probability that we have made a "Type II error."[22] That is, the interaction might be nonzero in the population, but our statistical test failed to detect its presence. Because of this difficulty, our general recommendation is to test marginal means based on Type III sum of squares. However, it should be recognized that some researchers prefer Type II sum of squares, particularly in situations where there are strong theoretical reasons to suspect the lack of an interaction and the empirical test of the interaction results in a p value substantially above .05 (e.g., above .20 or .25). As implied earlier, there is a long history of debate on this topic. The interested reader is referred to Cramer and Appelbaum (1980); Herr and Gaebelein (1978); and Overall, Spiegel, and Cohen (1975); and the references they cite for further information.

To end this discussion on a less controversial note, we mention two further approaches to handling nonorthogonal data, neither of which is recommended. First, earlier textbooks often recommended an "unweighted means analysis." In this approach, equal-n formulas are used to calculate sums of squares, except that n (the sample size assumed to be equal for each cell) is replaced by the harmonic mean of the cell sizes. Although this approach is simple to implement, the resulting mean squares do not generally have chi-square distributions, so dividing them by MS_W results in distributions that are only approximately F distributions. The one situation where the resulting ratios have exact F distributions is when every factor has two levels. In this special case, unweighted means analysis produces Type III sums of squares. Otherwise, the results are only approximate, so this method should be avoided. Its primary appeal was ease of calculation, but with the advent of statistical packages to perform calculations on computers, computational simplicity is no longer relevant. Nevertheless, you need to be aware that some statistical packages (see Dallal, 1988) may still use an unweighted means analysis for nonorthogonal designs because this type of analysis is easier to write for the author of the program.

Second, some researchers when faced with unequal n randomly delete observations from all but the smallest cell to achieve equal n. Such an approach obviously lowers power and may tempt researchers to delete a few observations nonrandomly if they fail to conform to expectations. Better yet, why not delete observations randomly but try the randomization process repeatedly until the "erroneous" observations have been "randomly" selected for deletion! This is obviously inappropriate and would create a bias making any statistical analysis uninterpretable.

In summary, least-squares analysis performed by comparing models provides appropriate hypothesis tests for factorial designs, both in equal n- and unequal n-conditions. However, the choice of models to be compared in unequal-n designs is complicated because there are three potentially reasonable ways of calculating a marginal mean.

A Note on Statistical Packages for Analyzing Nonorthogonal Designs

Once we have decided which type of sum of squares is appropriate for testing hypotheses in which we are interested, we still have to worry about performing the actual calculations. Although even with unequal n we may be able to calculate sums of squares for main effects by hand (see Tables 7.14–7.18), the only practical way to calculate the interaction sum of squares with unequal n is with a computer (except in the case of a 2×2 design). Of course, using a computer is no guarantee of accuracy. For example, a decade or so ago, the ANOVA program of one widely distributed statistical package would sometimes report that the interaction sum of squares was negative in nonorthogonal designs. The program, as computers are wont to do, was unconcerned with this impossible result and proceeded to report a negative F value as well. The problem was that the computational algorithm used by the programmer was appropriate only for equal-n designs.

One way to avoid this problem is to use a multiple-regression program. Although multiple regression is an extremely flexible methodology worthy of intensive study, most regression programs are clumsy for actually performing ANOVA. In any event, all major mainframe statistical packages include programs that analyze data from nonorthogonal factorial designs. As of this writing, particular programs with this capability are ANOVA and MANOVA in SPSS-X, PROC GLM in SAS, and P4V in BMDP. However, the default type of sum of squares varies from program to program, sometimes even within the same package. For example, the default sums of squares in SPSS-X ANOVA are Type II, whereas those in SPSS-X MANOVA are Type III. In all three packages, it is possible to override default specifications to obtain other types of sums of squares that may be more appropriate for the hypotheses you want to test. The most important point here is that in a nonorthogonal design, you cannot necessarily assume that the statistical package you are using is really testing the hypothesis you want to test. Such a failure is especially likely if you are using a microcomputer program that your advisor or a colleague stumbled upon with unknown origins (see Dallal, 1988). If you cannot tell from reading the manual what type(s) of sums of squares the program computes, it is probably wise to run some test data (where you already know what the answers are supposed to be) through the program. To facilitate this process and to put all our abstract theoretical developments into practice, we conclude our presentation of nonorthogonal designs with a numerical example.

Numerical Example

Suppose that a clinical psychologist is interested in comparing the relative effectiveness of three forms of psychotherapy for alleviating depression. Fifteen subjects are randomly assigned to each of three treatment groups: cognitive-behavioral, Rogerian, and assertiveness training. The Depression Scale of the MMPI serves as the dependent variable. A one-way ANOVA of the data yields an observed F value of 2.35, which fails to exceed the critical F value of 3.23 for 2 and 40 degrees of freedom (the actual denominator degrees of freedom equal 42, but the critical F is based on 40 df because 42 df are not included in Appendix Table A.2). As a result, the null hypothesis cannot be rejected, so insufficient evidence of differential effectiveness has been found.

However, it occurs to the psychologist that subjects were classified according to the severity of their depression as either mild, moderate, or severe. What would happen if a severity factor were incorporated into the design, along with type of therapy? Table 7.19 shows hypothetical MMPI scores for 45 subjects, each of whom

T A B L E **7.19** MMPI Depression Scale Scores

		Degree of Severity (B)		
		Mild	*Moderate*	*Severe*
	Cognitive-Behavioral	41	51	45
		43	43	55
		50	53	56
			54	60
			46	58
				62
				62
	Rogerian	56	58	59
		47	54	55
Type of Therapy (A)		45	49	68
		46	61	63
		49	52	
			62	
	Assertiveness Training	43	59	55
		56	46	69
		48	58	63
		46	54	56
		47		62
				67

is placed in one cell of a 3×3 design. One factor (A, the row factor) is type of therapy. The other factor (B, the column factor) is degree of severity.

We must make three comments before embarking on the analysis of these data. First, as Table 7.19 shows, we are faced with a nonorthogonal design because cell sizes are unequal (they range from 3 to 7). Such an imbalance is not surprising, even though subjects have been randomly assigned to groups. Although random assignment guarantees that in the long run one-third of the individuals at each severity level would be assigned to each treatment, with a total of only 45 subjects, some departure from strict equality would inevitably occur due to sampling error. Second, if we were to totally ignore the severity factor and analyze these data with a one-way ANOVA, we would obtain an observed F value of 2.35, which, as we already discussed, is nonsignificant. Third, an analysis of these data, which includes severity level as a second factor, may provide a more powerful test of the treatment effect than the one-way ANOVA. This use of a second factor is called *post hoc blocking*. We will have much more to say about blocking in Chapter 9. For the moment, we simply say that in some circumstances, post hoc blocking provides an appropriate method for increasing power.[23]

We are now ready to consider the analysis of the data shown in 7.19. To facilitate interpretations of the data, Table 7.20 presents cell sizes, cell means, and marginal means. The cell sizes and cell means follow naturally from Table 7.19, but some explanation of the marginal means is probably required. The Type I marginal means (labeled as I in the table) are the weighted marginal means for the levels of the factor if that factor is entered first in the model. As such, they are sample estimates of the population marginal means being tested when the sum of squares for a main effect is calculated while ignoring both the other main effect and the interaction (see Table 7.17, for a reminder). For example, the Type I sum of squares

T A B L E **7. 20** Cell Sizes, Cell Means, and Marginal Means for Table 7.19 Data

		Degree of Severity (B)			
		Mild	Moderate	Severe	Marginal Means
	Cognitive-Behavioral	$n_{11} = 3$ $\bar{Y}_{11} = 44.67$	$n_{12} = 5$ $\bar{Y}_{12} = 49.40$	$n_{13} = 7$ $\bar{Y}_{13} = 56.86$	I: 51.93 II: 50.18 III: 50.31
Type of Therapy (A)	Rogerian	$n_{21} = 5$ $\bar{Y}_{21} = 48.60$	$n_{22} = 6$ $\bar{Y}_{22} = 56.00$	$n_{23} = 4$ $\bar{Y}_{23} = 61.25$	I: 54.93 II: 55.39 III: 55.28
	Assertiveness Training	$n_{31} = 5$ $\bar{Y}_{31} = 48.00$	$n_{32} = 4$ $\bar{Y}_{32} = 54.25$	$n_{33} = 6$ $\bar{Y}_{33} = 62.00$	I: 55.27 II: 54.81 III: 54.75
	Marginal Means	I: 47.46 II: 46.96 III: 47.09	I: 53.33 II: 53.29 III: 53.22	I: 59.71 II: 60.13 III: 60.04	

for A is based on comparing weighted marginal means of the form

$$\bar{Y}_{j.(W)} = \sum_{k=1}^{b} n_{jk} \bar{Y}_{jk}/n_{j+}$$

Thus, the "Type I" marginal mean for the first row in our data equals

$$\bar{Y}_{1.(W)} = [3(44.67) + 5(49.40) + 7(56.86)]/15 = 51.93$$

The "Type II" marginal means, like the Type II sum of squares, have no simple form. Thus, for all practical purposes, they must be calculated by computer.[24] The "Type III" marginal means are simply unweighted means, averaging over the other factor. For example, the "Type III" marginal mean for row j is of the form

$$\bar{Y}_{j.(U)} = \sum_{k=1}^{b} \bar{Y}_{jk}/b$$

Thus, the "Type III" marginal mean for the first row in our data equals

$$\bar{Y}_{1.(U)} = (44.67 + 49.40 + 56.86)/3 = 50.31$$

It is important to remember that none of these marginal means are "right" or "wrong"; instead, as we discussed earlier, they address different hypotheses.

What does an ANOVA of these data reveal? First, the interaction of treatment and degree of severity is nonsignificant ($SS_{A \times B} = 14.19$, $F = 0.13$, $p = .97$). Thus, we have some justification for interpreting main-effect tests. As discussed in the previous section, our general recommendation is to report and interpret Type III sums of squares. In any event, we would normally only report whichever type corresponds to the hypotheses of interest. However, for pedagogical purposes, we report all three types here.

Table 7.21 presents all three possible tests of both the A main effect and the B main effect. Of particular interest is the fact that the A main effect is statistically significant for both Type III and Type II sums of squares. Notice that both F values here (3.67 for Type III and 4.27 for Type II) are appreciably larger than the F value of 2.35 we obtained in the one-way ANOVA where severity level was entirely ignored. As we discuss in more detail in Chapter 9, the primary reason for the larger F values in the two-way design is that the error term (MS_W) is smaller because individual differences in MMPI scores that are attributable to severity level no longer contribute to the error term, as they did in the one-way design. The reduction in error is substantial here because, as Table 7.21 shows, the effect of severity level on MMPI depression score is highly significant for these data.

At this point, we illustrate the calculations of Type III and Type I sums of squares using the formulas we presented earlier in the chapter. We focus our attention on the therapy main effect because it is the effect of primary interest. Similar steps could be undertaken for the severity main effect.

The Type III sum of squares for the A main effect was presented earlier in Equation 46:

$$\text{Type III} \qquad SS_A = \sum_{j=1}^{a} b\tilde{n}_{j.}(\bar{Y}_{j.(U)} - \bar{Y}_{G(A)})^2 \qquad \text{(46, repeated)}$$

The first step in using this formula is to calculate the "effective" cell size $\tilde{n}_{j.}$ for

T A B L E **7. 21**   Main Effect Tests for Table 7.19 Data

	Sum of Squares	F	p
A Main Effect			
Type III	204.76	3.67	.04
(allowing for B and AB)			
Type II	238.48	4.27	.02
(allowing for B, but ignoring AB)			
Type I—B entered first	238.48	4.27	.02
(allowing for B, but ignoring AB)			
Type I—A entered first	101.11	1.81	.18
(ignoring B and AB)			
B Main Effect			
Type III	1181.11	21.15	<.01
(allowing for A and AB)			
Type II	1253.19	22.44	<.01
(allowing for A, but ignoring AB)			
Type I—A entered first	1253.19	22.44	<.01
(allowing for A, but ignoring AB)			
Type I—B entered first	1115.82	19.98	<.01
(ignoring A and AB)			

each row, where

$$\tilde{n}_{j.} = b \left/ \sum_{k=1}^{b} (1/n_{jk}) \right.$$

For our data,

$$\tilde{n}_{1.} = 3/(1/3 + 1/5 + 1/7) = 4.4366$$

$$\tilde{n}_{2.} = 3/(1/5 + 1/6 + 1/4) = 4.8649$$

$$\tilde{n}_{3.} = 3/(1/5 + 1/4 + 1/6) = 4.8649$$

Although we have already calculated the unweighted marginal means for each row, we repeat the calculations here and report results to four decimal places to reduce rounding error in subsequent calculations:

$$\bar{Y}_{1.(U)} = (44.6667 + 49.4000 + 56.8571)/3 = 50.3079$$

$$\bar{Y}_{2.(U)} = (48.6000 + 56.0000 + 61.2500)/3 = 55.2833$$

$$\bar{Y}_{3.(U)} = (48.0000 + 54.2500 + 62.0000)/3 = 54.7500$$

Next, we can calculate $\bar{Y}_{G(A)}$ from the following formula:

$$\bar{Y}_{G(A)} = \sum_{j=1}^{a} \tilde{n}_{j.} \bar{Y}_{j.(U)} \left/ \sum_{j=1}^{a} \tilde{n}_{j.} \right.$$

$$= (4.4366)(50.3079) + (4.8649)(55.2833)$$

$$+ \frac{(4.8649)(54.7500)}{(4.4366 + 4.8649 + 4.8649)}$$

$$= 53.5420$$

Now that we have completed intermediate calculations, we can substitute appropriate values into Equation 46:

$$\text{Type III } SS_A = (3)(4.4366)(50.3079 - 53.5420)^2$$
$$+ (3)(4.8649)(55.2833 - 53.5420)^2$$
$$+ (3)(4.8649)(54.7500 - 53.5420)^2$$
$$= 204.76$$

in agreement with the value shown in Table 7.21.

Although Type I sums of squares are often of little interest, for the sake of completeness, we also illustrate the Type I sum of squares for the therapy main effect. From Equation 50,

$$\text{Type I } SS_A = \sum_{j=1}^{a} n_{j+}(\bar{Y}_{j.(W)} - \bar{Y}_{..(W)})^2 \qquad \text{(50, repeated)}$$

For the Table 7.19 data,

$$n_{1+} = 3 + 5 + 7 = 15$$

$$n_{2+} = 5 + 6 + 4 = 15$$

$$n_{3+} = 5 + 4 + 6 = 15$$

$$\bar{Y}_{1.(W)} = [3(44.6667) + 5(49.4000) + 7(56.8571)]/15 = 51.9333$$

$$\bar{Y}_{2.(W)} = [5(48.6000) + 6(56.0000) + 4(61.2500)]/15 = 54.9333$$

$$\bar{Y}_{3.(W)} = [5(48.0000) + 4(54.2500) + 6(62.0000)]/15 = 55.2667$$

$$\bar{Y}_{..(W)} = [15(51.9333) + 15(54.9333) + 15(55.2667)]/(15 + 15 + 15) = 54.0444$$

Substituting these values into Equation 50, we have

$$\text{Type I } SS_A = 15(51.9333 - 54.0444)^2 + 15(54.9333 - 54.0444)^2$$
$$+ 15(55.2667 - 54.0444)^2$$
$$= 101.11$$

once again in agreement with the value shown in Table 7.21.

Final Remarks

In closing, it is undoubtedly obvious now that unequal cell sizes tremendously complicate the analysis of factorial designs. Indeed, Appelbaum and Cramer (1974, p. 335) state that "the nonorthogonal multifactor analysis of variance is perhaps the most misunderstood analytic technique available to the behavioral scientist, save factor analysis." As if the complications we have already described are not bad enough, we feel compelled to mention yet another potential problem. As you might anticipate from our discussion of the effects of heterogeneity of variance in earlier chapters, unequal population variance can create substantial problems in non-orthogonal factorial designs (see Milligan, Wong, and Thompson, 1987, for further details). Some readers may be tempted to conclude from all of the discussion that the best lesson to be learned here is never to have unequal-n designs. Although we agree that equal-*n* designs are strongly preferable whenever possible, there are nevertheless some circumstances where unequal-*n* designs are inevitable. The message on nonorthogonal designs we would like for you to come away with is twofold. First, think carefully about precisely what null hypotheses you want to test. Second, choose an appropriate method for testing your hypotheses.

EXERCISES

*1. Consider the following sets of population means in a 3 × 3 two-way design. For each set of means, your task involves answering four questions: (1) Find the values of α_1, α_2, and α_3. (2) Find the values of β_1, β_2, and β_3. (3) Find the value of each interaction parameter $\alpha\beta_{jk}$. (4) Which effects (A, B, or A by B) are nonzero in the population?

a.

		B		
		1	*2*	*3*
	1	10	10	10
A	*2*	12	12	12
	3	17	17	17

b.

		B		
		1	*2*	*3*
	1	10	15	20
A	*2*	10	15	20
	3	10	15	20

c.

		B		
		1	*2*	*3*
	1	26	22	21
A	*2*	23	19	18
	3	17	13	12

d.

		B		
		1	*2*	*3*
	1	26	23	20
A	*2*	18	19	23
	3	13	15	14

e.

		B		
		1	*2*	*3*
	1	26	22	21
A	*2*	25	17	18
	3	15	15	12

2. Consider the following hypothetical population means in a 2 × 2 design:

		B	
		1	*2*
A	*1*	10	8
	2	12	18

    a. Plot the cell means in a manner similar to that shown in Figure 7.1 (a and b), using levels of A on the horizontal axis.

    b. Based on the figure you have drawn in part a, is there an interaction in the population? If so, is the interaction ordinal or disordinal?

    c. Repeat part a, but this time use levels of B on the horizontal axis of the figure.

    d. Based on the figure you have drawn in part c, is there an interaction in the population? If so, is the interaction ordinal or disordinal?

    e. Which main-effect test do you think would be less misleading for this population? Why?

3. A graduate student conducted a two-factor design to investigate children's learning performance. One factor was form of practice, either massed or spaced. The second factor was presence or absence of feedback to the children. The following cell means were obtained:

		Feedback	
		Present	*Absent*
Practice	*Massed*	62	47
	Spaced	75	68

There are 15 subjects per cell, and $MS_W = 400$.

    a. The student claims that the difference between massed and spaced practice is smaller when feedback is present than when it is absent. Do you agree?

    b. A friend of the student's claims that the effect of feedback is weaker when practice is spaced than when it is massed. Do you agree?

    c. Are the effects of feedback and type of practice additive in this situation?

*4. The following sample means were obtained in an equal-n design with eight subjects per cell:

		B		
		1	*2*	*3*
	1	8	10	15
A	*2*	9	14	10
	3	13	9	11

    a. Find $\hat{\alpha}_j$ for each row (i.e., for each value of j).

    b. Based on your answer to part a, calculate SS_A.

    c. Find $\hat{\beta}_k$ for each column (i.e., for each value of k).

    d. Based on your answer to part c, calculate SS_B.

    e. Find $\widehat{\alpha\beta}_{jk}$ for each cell (i.e., for each pair of j and k values).

    f. Based on your answer to part e, calculate SS_{AB}.

*5. The purpose of this exercise is to compare the meaning of a main effect in a two-way design to the comparable omnibus effect in a one-way design. Consider the data shown in Table 7.5 for a 2×3 design.

a. Find the sum of squares for the biofeedback main effect using Equation 25:

$$SS_A = E_R - E_F = nb \sum_{j=1}^{a} (\bar{Y}_{j.} - \bar{Y}_{..})^2$$

b. Suppose that the drug factor was not included in the design, so that the design was conceptualized as a single-factor design. Specifically, 15 subjects are in the biofeedback-present condition, and 15 subjects are in the biofeedback-absent condition. Find the sum of squares for biofeedback in this one-way design using Equation 26:

$$SS_A = E_R - E_F = n \sum_{j=1}^{a} (\bar{Y}_j - \bar{Y})^2$$

c. How do your answers to parts a and b compare to one another? What implication does this have for interpreting a main effect in an equal-n two-way design?

6. A counseling psychologist is interested in three types of therapy for modifying snake phobia. However, she does not believe that one type is necessarily best for everyone; instead, the best type may depend upon degree (i.e., severity) of phobia. Undergraduate students enrolled in an introductory psychology course are given the Fear Schedule Survey (FSS) to screen out subjects showing no fear of snakes. Those displaying some degree of phobia are classified as either mildly, moderately, or severely phobic on the basis of the FSS. One-third of subjects within each level of severity are then assigned to a treatment condition: either systematic desensitization, implosive therapy, or insight therapy. The following data are obtained, using the Behavioral Avoidance Test (higher scores are better):

Desensitization			Implosion			Insight		
Mild	*Moderate*	*Severe*	*Mild*	*Moderate*	*Severe*	*Mild*	*Moderate*	*Severe*
14	15	12	10	12	10	8	9	6
17	11	10	16	14	3	10	6	10
10	12	10	19	10	6	12	7	8
13	10	9	20	11	8	14	12	9
12	9	11	19	13	2	11	11	7

Your task is to analyze these data, to answer any questions you believe would be of theoretical interest. Don't feel compelled to perform an analysis just because it would be possible statistically. Longer is not necessarily better! On the other hand, you probably will not want to stop after testing only main effects and the interaction.

You should describe your findings in a manner consistent with the results section of an APA journal. If it seems appropriate, you may want to briefly justify your choice of α level, error term, and so on, but do not let this discussion overshadow what the results mean. Also, you may not want to focus exclusively on significance tests—descriptive statistics may also be useful.

7. A psychologist is interested in evaluating the effectiveness of behavioral treatments for hypertension. Specifically, he is interested in comparing a cognitive therapy to a form of relaxation therapy. He also is interested in the effects of diet. A subject pool of 120 subjects is available to him. He is debating between two different designs. The first design would involve randomly assigning 40 subjects to each of three conditions:

cognitive, relaxation, and relaxation plus diet. The second design would involve randomly assigning 30 subjects to each of four conditions: cognitive, relaxation, relaxation plus diet, and cognitive plus diet.

a. Which, if either, design will allow the psychologist to assess whether the difference between the psychological approaches (cognitive and relaxation) interacts with diet?

b. The psychologist is leaning toward the first design because he believes that it will provide a more powerful test of the difference between the cognitive and relaxation approaches than would the second design. Do you agree? Why or why not?

*8. A commonly heard rule of thumb for choosing sample size is "10 subjects per cell of the design." The purpose of this exercise is to determine the magnitude of statistical power that results from following this rule of thumb for various designs.

We assume throughout that we are interested in the power associated with a large effect size, as defined by Cohen (1977). It can be shown that the value of ϕ for a large effect size in a one-way design is given by

$$\phi = .40\sqrt{n},$$

where n is the number of subjects per group. For factorial designs, this formula generalizes to

$$\phi = .40\sqrt{\frac{df_F}{df_R - df_F + 1} + 1}$$

or equivalently,

$$\phi = .40\sqrt{\frac{df_{denominator}}{df_{effect} + 1} + 1}$$

where df_{effect} and $df_{denominator}$ are the numerator and denominator degrees of freedom, respectively, for the F test. Use the Pearson–Hartley power charts (appendix Table A.11) to calculate the power of detecting a large effect for each of the following designs, assuming 10 subjects per cell.

a. Omnibus effect in a one-way design with two groups
b. Omnibus effect in a one-way design with five groups
c. Main effect in a 2 × 2 design
d. Interaction effect in a 2 × 2 design
e. Main effect in a 3 × 3 design
f. Interaction effect in a 3 × 3 design
g. It is often recommended that the power of a test to be performed be at least .8. For which of the above effects is the power this high for detecting a large effect with 10 subjects per cell?
h. In light of your answers to parts a through g, what is your reaction to the general utility of the "10 subjects per cell" rule?

9. A clinical psychologist is interested in comparing three types of therapy for modifying snake phobia. However, she does not believe that one type is necessarily best for everyone; instead, the best type may depend upon degree (i.e., severity) of phobia. Undergraduate students enrolled in an introductory psychology course are given the Fear Schedule Survey (FSS) to screen out subjects showing no fear of snakes. Those displaying some degree of phobia are classified as either mildly or severely phobic on the basis of the FSS. One-third of subjects within each level of severity are then

randomly assigned to a treatment condition: either systematic desensitization, implosive therapy, or insight therapy. The following data are obtained, using the Behavioral Avoidance Test (higher scores indicate less phobia):

Desensitization		Implosion		Insight	
Mild	*Severe*	*Mild*	*Severe*	*Mild*	*Severe*
16	16	14	13	15	15
13	10	16	7	15	10
12	11	17	3	12	11
15	12	15	10	14	7
11	6	13	4	13	5
12	8	17	2	11	12
14	14	15	4	11	6
13	12	16	9	12	8

a. Test the main effects and interaction. Which effects, if any, are statistically significant?

b. Test the simple effect of therapy within each level of severity, using a pooled error term. Are there statistically significant therapy effects at either level of severity?

c. Continue part b by performing pairwise tests of therapy differences within each level of severity, again using a pooled error term. Maintain the α_{FW} level at .05 within each level of severity.

d. Test the simple effect of therapy within each level of severity, as in part b, but this time use a separate error term specific to the particular level of severity. How do your results compare to the results you obtained in part b? If the results are different, explain why.

e. Perform pairwise tests of therapy difference within each level of severity, as in part c, but this time use a separate error term specific to the particular contrast. As before, maintain the α_{FW} level at .05 within each level of severity. How do your results compare to the results you obtained in part c? If the results are different, explain why.

10. A graduate student obtained the following sample means in an equal-n 3×2 factorial design:

		B	
		1	*2*
	1	11	13
A	*2*	8	12
	3	5	11

He performed an ANOVA on these data, but his six-year old daughter spilled sulphuric acid on a portion of the ANOVA table. What remains is the following:

Source	SS	df	MS	F
A				
B				
A × B	44			
Within	1620	60		

Knowing that you are a statistics whiz, the graduate student asks you (in the questions below) to fill in the remainder of his table.
a. Find the value of SS_A.
b. Find the value of SS_B.
c. Fill in the missing degree of freedom entries in the table.
d. Calculate the mean square for each source in the table.
e. Calculate the F value for each effect. Which effects are significant at the .05 level?
f. The graduate student claims that the interaction is nonsignificant here. Because he is primarily interested in the A main effect, he decides to reanalyze the data as a one-way design with three groups, simply ignoring B. What will he find? Show your work.

*11. A clinical psychologist conducted a study to compare two forms of therapy. Ten females and 10 males were randomly assigned to each form of therapy (i.e., each cell contains 10 subjects). The following sample means are obtained:

	Females	Males
Therapy A	60	40
Therapy B	80	60

Mean square within for these data equals 800. The psychologist presented these data to four different graduate students and asked each to analyze the data and report back to her. As it turned out, each student analyzed the data somewhat differently. Your task is to reproduce each of these analyses, which are described in parts a–d below.
a. Student 1 compared the two therapies within each sex, that is, separate analyses were performed for females and males. The pooled MS_W was used as the error term for each analysis.
b. Student 2 used the same approach as student 1, but used a separate error term for each sex. Assume that $MS_W = 800$ for the females and that $MS_W = 800$ for the males. (We would expect MS_W for females to equal MS_W for males in the long run if homogeneity of variance holds. In an actual study, however, MS_W for females would inevitably be somewhat different from MS_W for males, if for no other reason than sampling error. We have chosen to act as if there were no sampling error here to make the difference between the approaches of student 1 and student 2 clearer, when homogeneity is met.)
c. Student 3 tested the two main effects and the interaction in the 2 × 2 design. Is the difference between the therapies statistically significant?
d. Student 4 ignored the gender factor altogether and simply performed a t test comparing the 20 subjects who received therapy A to the 20 subjects who received therapy B.
e. Which of the four approaches do you think is best for these data?

12. The theoretical importance of a statistically significant interaction is sometimes

difficult to interpret because the nature of the interaction may depend on the scale of the dependent variable. In particular, a significant interaction may become nonsignificant when a monotonic transformation is performed on the dependent variable. This exercise illustrates how this apparent inconsistency can occur. For further reading, see Busemeyer (1980). A cognitive psychologist measured subjects' reaction times in identifying a stimulus in a 2×2 design. The data are as follows:

A_1		A_2	
B_1	B_2	B_1	B_2
340	508	635	608
503	535	540	745
375	468	551	1022
456	592	648	982
413	580	592	822
402	524	568	783
426	546	623	755
434	516	574	851

a. Test the statistical significance of the two-way interaction for these data.
b. Because reaction times are often positively skewed, it is common (as discussed in Chapter 3) to perform a logarithmic transformation of the dependent variable. Test the interaction using the log of reaction time as the dependent variable.
c. Another possibility here is to analyze each subject's speed of response. Speed is inversely proportional to reaction time, so speed of response can be operationalized as the reciprocal of reaction time. In other words, speed can be defined as Speed = 1/Reaction time. Test the interaction using speed as the dependent variable.
d. How do the results of a–c compare? Can it clearly be stated that A and B interact in this study?

13. In Chapter 6 (Exercise 12), we introduced a study investigating how parent–infant play changes as infants get older. The current exercise expands on the earlier exercise by introducing a second factor into the design. Whereas the Chapter 6 exercise studied proportion of pretend play as a function of the child's age, the current exercise investigates the same hypothetical data as a function of the child's gender as well as age. Consider the following hypothetical data:

7-Month-Olds		10-Month-Olds		13-Month-Olds	
Girls	Boys	Girls	Boys	Girls	Boys
.02	.05	.15	.14	.09	.02
.01	.01	.11	.21	.03	.19
.07	.04	.22	.06	.18	.15
.04	.03	.05	.12	.12	.07
.01	.02	.09	.11	.18	.45
.09	.02	.05	.19	.43	.20
.05	.13	.15	.12	.24	.49
.06	.06	.11	.04	.40	.19

a. Test the significance of the age main effect, the gender main effect, and the age-by-gender interaction.
b. Based on your answer to part a, what follow-up tests should be performed here? Should cell means or marginal means be compared?
c. Test the significance of the linear and quadratic trends of the marginal means for age.
d. Suppose that it was deemed important to compare all pairs of the age marginal means. Test all of these pairwise comparisons and maintain the α_{FW} level at .05.

14. Manuck, Kaplan, Adams, and Clarkson report a series of studies investigating behavioral influences on coronary artery disease in monkeys. In one study, they examined the effects of a psychosocial manipulation (periodic group reorganization) on the development of atherosclerosis in animals of dominant or subordinate social status (Manuck, S. B., Kaplan, J. R., Adams, M. R., & Clarkson, T. B. (1988) "Studies of psychosocial influences on coronary artery atherogenesis in cynomolgus monkeys." *Health Psychology*, 7, 113–124). In one condition ("unstable"), animals are redistributed every one to three months into new social groups. In the other condition ("stable"), animals remain in the same social group throughout the course of the investigation. The following data are modeled after data reported by Manuck and colleagues:

	Stable		Unstable	
	Social Status		*Social Status*	
Dominant	*Subordinate*	*Dominant*	*Subordinate*	
.23	.34	.54	.39	
.17	.62	.68	.23	
.26	.54	.70	.27	
.32	.30	.76	.49	
.41	.51	.58	.53	
.38	.44	.87	.42	
.49	.41	.81	.34	

Social Condition

The above scores reflect coronary intimal area measurements (in mm^2); higher scores indicate greater disease.

a. Test the significance of the condition main effect, the status main effect, and the condition-by-status interaction.
b. Based on your answer to part a, what follow-up tests should be performed here? Should cell means or marginal means be compared?
c. Test the simple effect of condition within each level of status, maintaining α_{FW} at .05 for condition effects.
d. Test the simple effect of status within each level of condition, maintaining α_{FW} at .05 for status effects.
e. Test the difference between the dominant unstable cell and the average of the other three cells. What percentage of the between cells sum of squares does this contrast account for?

15. Brehm reports the results of a study investigating the extent to which children diminish or enhance the attractiveness of objects taken away from them (Brehm, S. S. (1981) "Psychological reactance and the attractiveness of unobtainable objects: Sex differences

in children's responses to an elimination of freedom." *Sex Roles, 7,* 937–949). Half of female and male elementary school children were led to believe that they would be asked to choose between two objects; the other half were told that they would receive one of two objects, but were not led to believe that they would be asked to make a choice between the objects. After each subject ranked the attractiveness of 10 objects, each subject was given his or her third-ranked object and denied his or her fourth-ranked object. Subjects were then asked to rerank the attractiveness of the 10 objects. One dependent variable of interest was the new rank of the denied object, which was initially ranked fourth for each subject. The following data are modeled after the data reported by Brehm (higher scores indicate less attractiveness on reranking):

Females		Males	
Choice	*No Choice*	*Choice*	*No Choice*
4	5	4	5
3	3	3	4
6	4	3	4
4	4	5	6
7	3	6	3
5	2	4	7
4	5	4	6
5	3	5	5
5	6	3	6

a. Test the significance of the gender main effect, the choice-condition main effect, and the gender-by-choice-condition interaction.
b. Based on your answer to part a, what follow-up tests should be performed here? Should cell means or marginal means be compared?
c. Test the simple effect of gender within each choice condition. Perform each test at an α level of .05.
d. Is there a choice-condition effect for females? For males? Answer each question using an α level of .05.

*16. For your master's thesis, you undertake a correlational study of personality types, environmental stress, and blood pressure. Twenty subjects are selected who are Type As and twenty who are Type Bs. Each subject's environment is classified as either high stress or low stress. (In reality, it might be preferable to regard stress as a continuous variable. We describe such an approach in Chapter 9, which covers analysis of covariance models.) Mean blood pressure and sample sizes for the four cells of the design are shown below.

		Stress	
		High	*Low*
	A	170	150
		$n = 14$	$n = 6$
Type	B	140	120
		$n = 6$	$n = 14$

    a. If you want to separate out the stress effects from the personality-type effects, what kind of marginal means should you use? What are their numerical values here?

    b. Is the estimated magnitude of the mean blood pressure difference between personality types greater, different, or smaller when the effect of stress is taken into account than when it is not?

17. The psychology department at a hypothetical university has been accused of underpaying female faculty members. The following data represent salary (in thousands of dollars) for every assistant professor and associate professor in the department:

Assistant Professors		Associate Professors	
Females	*Males*	*Females*	*Males*
23	29	32	33
26	28	30	30
25	30	34	39
28	34	33	37
32			38
27			41
			38
			35

    a. Is the interaction of gender and rank (i.e., assistant versus associate) statistically significant? What does this result imply about the advisability of interpreting main effects?

    b. Write each of the null hypotheses for the gender main effect using Type I, Type II, and Type III sums of squares. Which of these hypotheses is (are) most pertinent to the question of possible sex discrimination? Why?

    c. Test the gender main effect null hypotheses associated with Type I, Type II, and Type III sums of squares.

    d. Form a 95 percent confidence interval for the contrast corresponding to the Type I sum of squares main effect for gender.

    e. Form a 95 percent confidence interval for the contrast corresponding to the Type II sum of squares main effect for gender. Be certain to use coefficients that preserve the original metric.

    f. Form a 95 percent confidence interval for the contrast corresponding to the Type III sum of squares main effect for gender.

    g. How do the confidence intervals of parts d–f compare to each other? What do they suggest about the extent to which females are underpaid?

    h. Can you conclude beyond a reasonable doubt that the department is discriminating? Why or why not? (HINT: Can you unequivocally conclude that gender is a *cause* of pay in this department?)

18. During the 1980s, findings from the National Assessment of Educational Progress (NAEP) have shown that the size of average achievement differences between white and black students has been steadily decreasing. In Jones, L. V. (1984) "White-black achievement differences: The narrowing gap." *American Psychologist, 39*, 1207–1213, national data are reported suggesting that some of the existing difference between blacks'

and whites' average mathematics achievement test scores may be due to differences in enrollment patterns in high school math courses. The following hypothetical data are modeled after the data reported by Jones (1984). Suppose that a group of high school seniors who have taken 0, 1, 2, or 3 high school math courses have received the following scores on a standardized math achievement test:

	Blacks				Whites		
	Number of Courses				Number of Courses		
0	*1*	*2*	*3*	*0*	*1*	*2*	*3*
45	51	61	71	42	61	63	77
34	59	73	82	51	48	68	68
51	53	55	70	39	46	78	79
54	49	77		55	63	60	66
40	60				55	73	85
46	65						80
	59						

a. Find the mean achievement test score for all black students, irrespective of number of courses. Find the comparable mean for white students. How large is the difference between the means?
b. Find the unweighted marginal mean for black students in the two-way design. Find the comparable mean for white students. How large is the difference between the means?
c. Why is the difference in part b much smaller than the difference in part a?
d. Test the significance of the race main effect allowing for a "number-of-courses" main effect and a "number of courses" by race interaction.

*19. A clinical psychologist conducted a study comparing cognitive-behavioral therapy (CBT) and client-centered therapy (CCT). Subjects were randomly assigned to a therapy condition. The psychologist is also interested in gender differences, so gender is included as a second factor in the design. However, the resultant cell sizes are somewhat unequal (reflecting sampling error and/or attrition, presumed to be random here). The following cell sizes and cell means are obtained:

	Females	Males
CBT	$n_{11} = 6$ $\bar{Y}_{11} = 52$	$n_{12} = 4$ $\bar{Y}_{12} = 46$
CCT	$n_{21} = 8$ $\bar{Y}_{21} = 48$	$n_{22} = 5$ $\bar{Y}_{22} = 42$

Notice that the mean score for CBT is 4 points higher than the mean for CCT, both for females and for males. Thus, our single best estimate is that CBT is 4 points better than CCT. However, it may be important to know the margin of error in this estimate. The precision of the estimate is revealed by forming a confidence interval.

We suppose throughout the remainder of this problem that mean square within $(MS_W) = 19$.

a. From Table 7.13, we can see that the Type III sum of squares for the therapy main effect here is based on a contrast of the form

$$\psi = .5\mu_{11} + .5\mu_{12} - .5\mu_{21} - .5\mu_{22}$$

Form a 95 percent confidence interval for ψ. Explain in one sentence what this interval means.

b. From Table 7.13, we can see that the Type II sum of squares for the therapy main effect is based on a contrast of the form

$$\psi = (n_{11}n_{21}/n_{+1})\mu_{11} + (n_{12}n_{22}/n_{+2})\mu_{12}$$
$$- (n_{11}n_{21}/n_{+1})\mu_{21} - (n_{12}n_{22}/n_{+2})\mu_{22}$$

Form a 95 percent confidence interval for the corresponding contrast that preserves the original metric of the dependent variable.

c. Which contrast can be estimated more precisely—the one corresponding to Type III sum of squares or the one corresponding to Type II sum of squares? What does this result suggest about which type of sum of square is preferable when there is no true interaction (notice in these data that there is literally no interaction even in the sample).

d. Some investigators would take an entirely different approach here. Instead of dealing with the nonorthogonal design, observations might be randomly deleted to produce four subjects in each cell. Although the subsequent analysis is undoubtedly simpler, is there a cost associated with this approach? To answer this question, we again consider the precision of our estimated treatment effect. Suppose that after subjects are randomly deleted, the data are as follows:

	Females	Males
CBT	$n_{11} = 4$ $\bar{Y}_{11} = 52$	$n_{12} = 4$ $\bar{Y}_{12} = 46$
CCT	$n_{21} = 4$ $\bar{Y}_{21} = 48$	$n_{22} = 4$ $\bar{Y}_{22} = 42$
	$MS_W = 19$	

Notice that the cell means and MS_W are unchanged from their previous values, which is what we would expect *in the long run* when observations are randomly deleted. The therapy main effect is represented by the following contrast:

$$\psi = .5\mu_{11} + .5\mu_{12} - .5\mu_{21} - .5\mu_{22}$$

Find a 95 percent confidence interval for this contrast.

e. How does the confidence interval you found in part d compare to the intervals you found in parts a and b? What does this result imply about the wisdom of randomly deleting observations to obtain an equal-n design?

8   Higher-Order Between-Subjects Factorial Designs

IN CHAPTER 7, WE extended the presentation of one-way designs in Chapter 3 to designs with two factors. In this chapter, we extend our presentation further, by considering designs with more than two factors. We focus the great majority of our attention on designs with three factors because once you understand the extension from two to three factors, generalizations to designs with even more factors should be relatively straightforward.

We saw in Chapter 7 that consideration of factorial designs introduces the concept of interaction. With the addition of a third factor, we can generalize the concept of an interaction because it may happen that all three factors interact. Alternatively, one or more pairs of the factors might interact, although the three factors together do not. The primary purpose of this chapter is to explore these various ways in which factors can interact with one another. Once we have developed the concepts, we consider their implications for analyzing data from higher-order factorial designs.

THE 2 × 2 × 2 DESIGN

We begin our discussion of three-way (i.e., three-factor) designs by restricting ourselves to the case where each factor has only two levels, in which case we have a 2 × 2 × 2 design. The reason we begin with this design is that the concepts we need to develop are easier to illustrate when each factor has only two levels. Once we have introduced concepts in the 2 × 2 × 2 design, we will consider more general $a \times b \times c$ designs. We should also mention that we only consider equal-n designs until the end of the chapter, at which time we discuss the additional issues that arise in nonorthogonal designs.

To make our discussion more concrete, we continue with one of the examples we introduced in Chapter 7. Specifically, suppose that a psychologist wants to examine the effectiveness of various therapies for treating hypertension. In Chapter 7, we considered a 2 × 2 design; each factor (biofeedback training and drug therapy) had two levels because each form of therapy was either present or absent in the treatment combination presented to a particular subject. We now add a third factor, diet therapy, to the design. Specifically, we suppose that one-half of all subjects receive individualized dietary plans, which they are to follow, while the remaining subjects receive no dietary instructions. We further suppose that subjects have been randomly and independently assigned to each of the eight possible combinations of biofeedback, drug therapy, and diet therapy.

At this point, we could consider how to obtain F tests for analyzing sample data. However, we defer this topic until we reach the general $a \times b \times c$ design because the F tests for a three-way design follow exactly the same logic as F tests for a two-way design. The new feature of the three-way design involves the meaning of the effects being tested, which can be made clearest through population means instead of sample data. For this reason, we consider hypothetical population means that might occur in our hypertension study. Table 8.1 presents eight population means, one for each cell of the 2 × 2 × 2 design. Our interest here is to describe what effects exist in the population. Be certain you understand that tests of statistical significance are irrelevant here because we are pretending that we have population data. Thus, any nonzero effect is a true effect because these population means are not affected by sampling error. Also, the discussion for the moment is restricted to equal-n designs, so we need not concern ourselves with differences between weighted and unweighted means.

Recall from Chapter 7 that in a two-way factorial design there are three effects of interest: an A main effect, a B main effect, and an A × B interaction. Not surprisingly, there are additional effects in a three-way design. If we label the third factor as C, the seven effects in a three-way design are an A main effect, a B main effect, a C main effect, an A × B interaction, an A × C interaction, a B × C interaction, and an A × B × C interaction. At this point, we need to consider the meaning of each of these effects. We begin with the main effects, then the two-way interactions, and finally the three-way interaction.

The Meaning of Main Effects

We saw in Chapter 7 that a main effect in a two-way design involves averaging over the levels of the other factor. For example, the A main effect compares levels of A after we have averaged over levels of B. In a three-way design, the A main effect compares levels of A after averaging over levels of both B and C. In general, the main effect for a factor in any factorial design involves comparing the levels of that factor after having averaged over all other factors in the design. To consider this point in detail, consider the data in Table 8.1. We designate the biofeedback factor as A, the drug factor as B, and the diet factor as C. To determine whether a nonzero A main effect exists in the population, it is necessary to average over levels of B and C. The resultant marginal mean when biofeedback is present is given by

$$(180 + 200 + 170 + 185)/4$$

T A B L E **8. 1** Hypothetical Population Means for a 2 × 2 × 2 Hypertension Study

	Diet Absent		Diet Present	
	Biofeedback Present	Biofeedback Absent	Biofeedback Present	Biofeedback Absent
Drug Present	180	205	170	190
Drug Absent	200	210	185	190

which equals 183.75 for our data. Similarly, the marginal mean for the biofeedback-absent condition is given by

$$(205 + 210 + 190 + 190)/4$$

which equals 198.75. The fact that these two marginal means are different implies the existence of a nonzero biofeedback main effect in the population. What this means is that the mean blood pressure score is different when biofeedback is present than when it is absent, when we average across the four combinations of drug and diet as well as across subjects.

The B and C main effects are found in exactly the same manner. Specifically, the B effect is found by averaging over levels of A and C, whereas the C effect is found by averaging over levels of A and B. Following the same logic used for A, you should be able to convince yourself that the main effects for B and C are also both nonzero in the population. (Exercises 3 and 4 at the end of the chapter ask the reader to perform the relevant calculations.)

The Meaning of Two-Way Interactions

Next, we consider the three different two-way interactions: A × B, A × C, and B × C. Let's begin with the A × B interaction. We just saw that the main effect for a factor is found by first averaging over all other factors in the design and then comparing the resultant marginal means. The concept of a two-way interaction in a higher-order factorial design (i.e., a design with three or more factors) follows the same general logic in that it is necessary to average over the factor(s) not involved in the interaction effect. For example, the A × B interaction averages over the levels of C. The result is a two-way table of population means, which is shown in Table 8.2 for our data. Each cell mean in this table is the average of two of the original cell means from Table 8.1. For example, the value of 175.0 in Table 8.2 is simply the average of 180.0 and 170.0, the means for diet absent and diet present, respectively, when both biofeedback and drug therapy are present.

We can determine whether an A × B interaction exists in these population data directly from Table 8.2. Recall that an A × B interaction in the two-way design meant that the A effect differed at different levels of B. The meaning of an A × B interaction is precisely the same in a three-way design, except that we must first average across levels of C, as we have already done in Table 8.2. From the table, we can see that the effect of a drug is 17.5 when biofeedback is present, but the effect

T A B L E **8. 2** Population Means for Biofeedback and Drug Factors Averaging Across Levels of Diet

	Biofeedback Present	Biofeedback Absent
Drug Present	175.0	197.5
Drug Absent	192.5	200.0

TABLE **8.3** Population Means for
Drug and Diet Factors Averaging
Across Biofeedback

	Diet Absent	Diet Present
Drug Present	192.5	180.0
Drug Absent	205.0	187.5

TABLE **8.4** Population Means for Biofeedback
and Diet Factors Averaging Across Levels of
Drug Factor

	Diet Absent	Diet Present
Biofeedback Present	190.0	177.5
Biofeedback Absent	207.5	190.0

of a drug is only 2.5 when biofeedback is absent. Thus, the magnitude of the drug effect differs at different levels of biofeedback, implying an interaction. Thus, there is a two-way drug × biofeedback interaction in this population. Tables 8.3 and 8.4 show the population means used to assess the drug × diet and biofeedback × diet interactions, respectively. By the same logic used in examining Table 8.2, Tables 8.3 and 8.4 show that there are also nonzero drug × diet and biofeedback × diet interactions in this population.

The major point to be made so far is that the logic of main effects and two-way interactions in a three-way design is basically the same as in a two-way design. The only difference is that there is an additional factor to average across in the three-way design. This brings us to the one new type of effect in a three-way design, namely, the three-way interaction.

The Meaning of the Three-Way Interaction

Before considering the meaning of a three-way interaction, let's review the meaning of a two-way interaction in a two-way design. An A × B interaction in a two-way design-means that the A effect differs at different levels of B, or equivalently, that the B effect differs at different levels of A. How could we extend this logic to apply to an A × B × C interaction in a three-way design? An A × B × C interaction means that the two-way A × B effect differs at different levels of C, just as an A × B interaction means that the A effect differs at different levels of B.

To better understand the meaning of a three-way interaction, let's return to our hypothetical population data. To assess the existence of a drug × biofeedback × diet interaction, we must consider whether the drug × biofeedback interaction is the same when the diet is absent as when it is present. Table 8.5 presents two sets

TABLE 8.5 Population Means for Drug and Biofeedback Combinations, Separately by Diet

	Diet Absent		Diet Present	
	Biofeedback Present	Biofeedback Absent	Biofeedback Present	Biofeedback Absent
Drug Present	180	205	170	190
Drug Absent	200	210	185	190
Drug Effect	20	5	15	0
Difference in Drug Effect	15		15	

of drug and biofeedback means, first when the diet is absent and second when the diet is present. The 2 × 2 table when the diet is absent shows that the drug effect is 20 when biofeedback is present, but the drug effect when biofeedback is absent is only 5. Thus, there is a two-way drug × biofeedback interaction when the diet is absent because the drug effect is 15 units larger when biofeedback is present than when it is absent. Let's now consider the 2 × 2 table of population means when the diet is present. This table shows that the drug effect is 15 when biofeedback is present, but the drug effect when biofeedback is absent is 0. Thus, there is a two-way drug × biofeedback interaction when the diet is present because the drug effect is 15 units larger when biofeedback is present than when it is absent. Notice that this difference of 15 units for the drug effect is the same when the diet is present as when the diet is absent. This equality implies that the two-way drug × biofeedback interaction is the same at both levels of the diet factor. Because the magnitude of the two-way interaction is the same at every level of the third factor, there is no three-way interaction in this population. In other words, the null hypothesis of no three-way interaction is true for these data.

So far, we have conceptualized the three-way drug × biofeedback × diet interaction in terms of the consistency of the magnitude of the drug × biofeedback interaction at the various levels of diet. It turns out that there are two other conceptualizations that are mathematically equivalent to this one. First, we could consider the consistency of the magnitude of the two-way drug × diet interaction at the various levels of the biofeedback factor. Table 8.6 shows the population means of Table 8.1 from this perspective. We can see from Table 8.6 that the difference in the drug effect for the diet absent versus present conditions is 5 units when biofeedback is present. However, the difference in the drug effect for diet absent versus present is also 5 units when biofeedback is absent. Thus, the magnitude of the drug × diet interaction is the same at both levels of the biofeedback factor, implying that the three-way interaction is zero. Alternatively, Table 8.6 also shows that the difference in the diet effect when the drug is present versus absent is 5 units, both when biofeedback is present and when it is absent. This equality also simply affirms that the two-way drug × diet interaction is the same at both levels of biofeedback.

T A B L E **8. 6** Population Means for Drug and Diet Combinations, Separately by Levels of Biofeedback

	Biofeedback Present			
	Diet Absent	*Diet Present*	*Diet Effect*	*Difference in Diet Effect*
Drug Present	180	170	10	
Drug Absent	200	185	15	5
Drug Effect	20	5		
Difference in Drug Effect		5		

	Biofeedback Absent			
	Diet Absent	*Diet Present*	*Diet Effect*	*Difference in Diet Effect*
Drug Present	205	190	15	
Drug Absent	210	190	20	5
Drug Effect	5	0		
Difference in Drug Effect		5		

Thus, we reach the same conclusion by examining the consistency of the two-way drug × diet interactions at each level of biofeedback as we did by examining the consistency of the two-way drug × biofeedback interactions at each level of the diet factor. Second, yet another equivalent conceptualization is to consider the consistency of the two-way biofeedback × diet interactions at each level of the drug factor. Instead of presenting a table of cell means to represent this conceptualization, we leave this as an exercise for the reader. Specifically, Exercise 5 at the end of the chapter asks whether the biofeedback × diet interaction is consistent at both levels of the drug factor for the data in Table 8.1.

Graphical Depiction

As we saw in the two-way design (Chapter 7), yet another way of viewing main effects and interactions is to graph cell means. Figure 8.1 provides a graphical depiction of the population means given earlier in Table 8.1. Figure 8.1(a) plots cell means for biofeedback and drug combinations when the diet is absent. Figure 8.1(b) presents corresponding cell means when the diet is present. This figure reveals a number of important aspects of the data. First, if we were to consider main effects here (thereby averaging over all other factors), blood pressure values are lower when biofeedback is present than when it is absent. The same holds true for drug and diet as well. Thus, all three factors have a nonzero main effect for these population data. However, we must qualify interpretations of main effects due to the presence of interactions. In particular, we can tell from the plot in Figure 8.1(a) that biofeedback and drug interact when the diet is absent because the lines shown in the figure are not parallel. As we saw earlier in Table 8.5 when the diet is absent, the drug effect is 15 points larger when biofeedback is present than when it is absent. The plot in Figure 8.1(b) shows that biofeedback and drug also interact when the diet is present. A three-way interaction is determined by whether the two-way biofeedback by drug interaction is the same when the diet is absent as when the diet is present. Using Figure 8.1 to decide this question requires some clarification. Although the plot in Figure 8.1(a) is not identical to the plot in Figure 8.1(b) (even moving the plots upward or downward), there is nevertheless an underlying equivalence. The form of nonparallelism is the same in both cases because the extent to which the biofeed-back effect is larger when the drug is present than when the drug is absent is 15 in both plots (i.e., $25 - 10 = 20 - 5$). Thus, Figure 8.1 implies the lack of a three-way interaction for these population data.

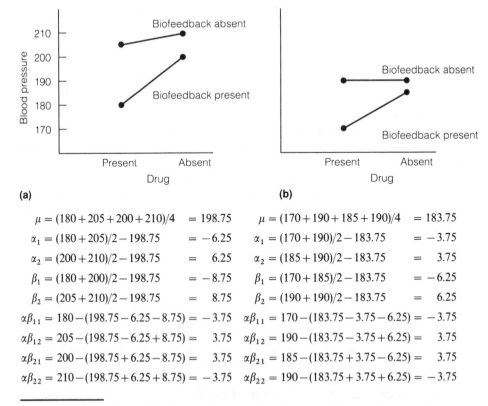

$$\mu = (180 + 205 + 200 + 210)/4 = 198.75 \qquad \mu = (170 + 190 + 185 + 190)/4 = 183.75$$

$$\alpha_1 = (180 + 205)/2 - 198.75 = -6.25 \qquad \alpha_1 = (170 + 190)/2 - 183.75 = -3.75$$

$$\alpha_2 = (200 + 210)/2 - 198.75 = 6.25 \qquad \alpha_2 = (185 + 190)/2 - 183.75 = 3.75$$

$$\beta_1 = (180 + 200)/2 - 198.75 = -8.75 \qquad \beta_1 = (170 + 185)/2 - 183.75 = -6.25$$

$$\beta_2 = (205 + 210)/2 - 198.75 = 8.75 \qquad \beta_2 = (190 + 190)/2 - 183.75 = 6.25$$

$$\alpha\beta_{11} = 180 - (198.75 - 6.25 - 8.75) = -3.75 \qquad \alpha\beta_{11} = 170 - (183.75 - 3.75 - 6.25) = -3.75$$

$$\alpha\beta_{12} = 205 - (198.75 - 6.25 + 8.75) = 3.75 \qquad \alpha\beta_{12} = 190 - (183.75 - 3.75 + 6.25) = 3.75$$

$$\alpha\beta_{21} = 200 - (198.75 + 6.25 - 8.75) = 3.75 \qquad \alpha\beta_{21} = 185 - (183.75 + 3.75 - 6.25) = 3.75$$

$$\alpha\beta_{22} = 210 - (198.75 + 6.25 + 8.75) = -3.75 \qquad \alpha\beta_{22} = 190 - (183.75 + 3.75 + 6.25) = -3.75$$

F I G U R E 8. 1 Plots of Table 8.1 cell means as a function of diet condition: (a) diet absent and (b) diet present.

T A B L E **8. 7** Alternate Population Means for Drug and Biofeedback
Combinations, Separately by Diet

	Diet Absent		Diet Present	
	Biofeedback Present	*Biofeedback Absent*	*Biofeedback Present*	*Biofeedback Absent*
Drug Present	180	205	175	190
Drug Absent	200	210	185	190
Drug Effect	20	5	10	0
Difference in Drug Effect		15		10

The correspondence between the two plots is formalized in the calculations of parameter values shown underneath each plot. The parameters shown here are not the parameters of the three-way full model, but instead are the parameters corresponding to two separate two-way full models, one when the diet is absent and one when the diet is present. As such, the values have been calculated using Equations 7.9–7.12. What is important for our purposes is to notice that each $\alpha\beta$ parameter has the same value when the diet is absent as when the diet is present. Formally, this implies that the biofeedback × drug interaction when the diet is absent is equivalent to the biofeedback × drug interaction when the diet is present. Thus, there is no three-way interaction in these data. Finally, we should add that, just as we saw in Chapter 7 for the two-way design, there is more than one way to plot the cell means in a three-way design. For example, we might plot means for biofeedback absent in Figure 8.1(a) and means for biofeedback present in Figure 8.1(b), with the diet present versus absent on the *x*-axis. Some effects are easier to see with certain plots than with others, so how we decide to plot the data should be determined largely by which effects we want to feature most clearly.

Notice that the null hypothesis for the three-way interaction requires that the magnitude of the two-way A × B effect at C_1 (the first level of C) must exactly equal the magnitude of the two-way effect at all other levels of C. To illustrate this point, consider the population means shown in Table 8.7. These data show a different possible configuration of population means that might exist in our hypothetical study. Specifically, the only change from Table 8.5 is that the mean blood pressure when drug, biofeedback, and diet are all present is now presumed to be 175 instead of 170 as in Table 8.5. Naturally, the difference in the drug effect is still 15 when the diet is absent. However, the difference in the drug effect when the diet is present is now only 10 units because the drug effect when biofeedback and diet are present is 10 in Table 8.7. For these population means, there is a nonzero three-way drug × biofeedback × diet interaction. The reason is that, as we have seen, the magnitude of the drug × biofeedback interaction is not the same when the diet is present as when it is absent. Although it is true for both levels of diet that the drug is more effective when biofeedback is present than when it is absent, the exact magnitude of the difference in the drug effect is not the same when the diet is present as when it is absent. Specifically, for the data of Table 8.7, there is a stronger 2-way drug × biofeedback interaction when the diet is absent than when the diet is present. This inequality implies the existence of a three-way drug × biofeedback × diet interaction for the population means shown in Table 8.7.

Summary of Meaning of Effects

It may be helpful at this point to summarize the meaning of effects in a three-way design. Table 8.8 describes the meaning of the three main effects, the three two-way interactions, and the single three-way interaction in an A × B × C design. It is important to understand that the seven effects described in Table 8.8 are logically independent of each other. In other words, the presence or absence of any particular effect in the population has no particular implications for the presence or absence of any other effect. In other words, any possible combination of the seven

T A B L E **8. 8** Meaning of Effects in a Three-Way A × B × C Design

	Meaning
Main Effects	
A	Comparison of marginal means of A factor, averaging over levels of B and C
B	Comparison of marginal means of B factor, averaging over levels of A and C
C	Comparison of marginal means of C factor, averaging over levels of A and B
Two-Way Interactions	
A × B	Examines whether the A effect is the same at every level of B, averaging over levels of C (equivalently, examines whether the B effect is the same at every level of A, averaging over levels of C)
A × C	Examines whether the A effect is the same at every level of C, averaging over levels of B (equivalently, examines whether the C effect is the same at every level of A, averaging over levels of B)
B × C	Examines whether the B effect is the same at every level of C, averaging over levels of A (equivalently, examines whether the C effect is the same at every level of B, averaging over levels of A)
Three-Way Interaction	
A × B × C	Examines whether the two-way A × B interaction is the same at every level of C (equivalently, examines whether the two-way A × C interaction is the same at every level of B; equivalently, examines whether the two-way B × C interaction is the same at every level of A)

effects can conceivably exist in a population. However, as in the two-way design, our interpretation of certain effects may be colored by the presence or absence of other effects in our data. For example, we might refrain from interpreting a statistically significant A main effect if we also obtain a significant A × B interaction. We deal further with such interpretational issues later in the chapter.

Although our discussion to this point has been limited to the special case of a 2 × 2 × 2 design, it turns out that the concepts generalize directly to the more general A × B × C design. For example, the meaning of effects depicted in Table 8.8 is equally appropriate for the A × B × C design. The only difference is that in the 2 × 2 × 2 design each effect accounts for only 1 degree of freedom, whereas in the A × B × C design, effects generally account for more than 1 degree of freedom.

THE GENERAL A × B × C DESIGN

We examine the general case of an A × B × C design using model comparisons. For the moment, we restrict ourselves to the situation where the number of subjects is the same in each cell of the design. Later in the chapter, we consider the additional complications that arise with unequal n.

The Full Model

As in the two-factor design, the full model for the three-factor design can be written in either of two equivalent ways. First, the full model can be written as

$$Y_{ijkl} = \mu_{jkl} + \varepsilon_{ijkl} \tag{1}$$

where Y_{ijkl} represents the score on the dependent variable of the ith subject at the jth level of A, the kth level of B, and the lth level of C; μ_{jkl} is the population cell mean of Y for level j of A, level k of B, and level l of C; and ε_{ijkl} is an error term associated with the ith subject at level j of A, level k of B, and level l of C. Notice that the value of the i subscript ranges from 1 to n, the value of j ranges from 1 to a, the value of k ranges from 1 to b, and the value of l ranges from 1 to c. Thus, the full model reflects an attempt to understand the score of all n subjects within every cell of the A × B × C design. Further, notice that this full model is a cell means model because, like the full models we have considered in previous chapters, it states that any subject's score is dependent only on the cell of the design the subject appears in plus an error component.

Although the form of the full model given in Equation 1 is perfectly valid, it is convenient to rewrite it in another form, just as we did for the one-way and two-way designs of Chapters 3 and 7, respectively. This alternate form of the full model is given by

$$Y_{ijkl} = \mu + \alpha_j + \beta_k + \gamma_l + (\alpha\beta)_{jk} + (\alpha\gamma)_{jl} + (\beta\gamma)_{kl} + (\alpha\beta\gamma)_{jkl} + \varepsilon_{ijkl} \tag{2}$$

T A B L E **8.9**   Algebraic Expressions for Parameters in a Full
Model of Three-Way A × B × C Design

Parameter		Expression
μ	$=$	$\sum\limits_{j=1}^{a} \sum\limits_{k=1}^{b} \sum\limits_{l=1}^{c} \mu_{jkl}/abc$
α_j	$=$	$\mu_{j..} - \mu$
β_k	$=$	$\mu_{.k.} - \mu$
γ_l	$=$	$\mu_{..l} - \mu$
$(\alpha\beta)_{jk}$	$=$	$\mu_{jk.} - (\mu + \alpha_j + \beta_k)$
$(\alpha\gamma)_{jl}$	$=$	$\mu_{j.l} - (\mu + \alpha_j + \gamma_l)$
$(\beta\gamma)_{kl}$	$=$	$\mu_{.kl} - (\mu + \beta_k + \gamma_l)$
$(\alpha\beta\gamma)_{jkl}$	$=$	$\mu_{jkl} - [\mu + \alpha_j + \beta_k + \gamma_l + (\alpha\beta)_{jk} + (\alpha\gamma)_{jl} + (\beta\gamma)_{kl}]$

where Y_{ijkl} represents the score on the dependent variable of the ith subject at the jth level of A, the kth level of B, and the lth level of C; μ is the grand mean parameter; α_j is the effect associated with the jth level of A; β_k is the effect associated with the kth level of B; γ_l is the effect associated with the lth level of C; $(\alpha\beta)_{jk}$ is the effect of the interaction of the jth level of A and the kth level of B; $(\alpha\gamma)_{jl}$ is the effect of the interaction of the jth level of A and the lth level of C; $(\beta\gamma)_{kl}$ is the effect of the interaction of the kth level of B and the lth level of C; $(\alpha\beta\gamma)_{jkl}$ is the effect of the three-way interaction of the jth level of A, the kth level of B, and the lth level of C; and ε_{ijkl} is the error for the ith subject at level j of A, level k of B, and level l of C.

The meaning of the parameters in the full model of Equation 2 is very similar to the meaning of parameters in the two-way design of Chapter 7. (For a review, see Equations 7.6–7.12.) Table 8.9 shows the algebraic representation of these population parameters for the model in Equation 2. It may be helpful to compare the algebraic representation of parameters in Table 8.9 to the verbal representation of effects shown earlier in Table 8.8 because these two tables are essentially two different ways of conveying the same information.

As shown in Tables 8.8 and 8.9 as well as in Equation 2, there are seven effects in the full model, each of which we are typically interested in testing. In other words, there are seven different null hypotheses we may want to test. Each of these null hypotheses leads to a restricted model, that is, a restricted version of the full model depicted in Equation 2. We use our usual F test to compare the full and restricted models to one another:

$$F = \frac{(E_R - E_F)/(df_R - df_F)}{E_F/df_F} \tag{3}$$

As this point, we have two tasks confronting us. First, we must identify a restricted model for each null hypothesis we wish to test. Second, we must calculate the sum of squared errors and degrees of freedom for both the full and the restricted models.

Formulation of Restricted Models

The task of identifying appropriate restricted models turns out to be trivial. To test one of the seven null hypotheses of interest, a restricted model is formed simply by omitting from the full model those parameters that equal zero according to the null hypothesis. For example, suppose that we want to test the A main effect. If the null hypothesis is true that there is no A main effect in the population, then every α_j parameter in the full model equals zero. Thus, a restricted model for testing the A main effect is obtained by omitting the α_j parameters from the full model, in which case we are left with a model of the form

$$Y_{ijkl} = \mu + \beta_k + \gamma_l + (\alpha\beta)_{jk} + (\alpha\gamma)_{jl} + (\beta\gamma)_{kl} + (\alpha\beta\gamma)_{jkl} + \varepsilon_{ijkl}$$

Table 8.10 shows the restricted models used to test each of the seven null hypotheses of interest. Notice that each of these restricted models has omitted the parameters of one effect, namely the effect to be tested.

The second task is to compute the sum of squared errors and degrees of freedom for the full model and for the seven models shown in Table 8.10. The sum of squared errors for the full model (E_F) can as usual be found most easily by expressing the full model in the form of Equation 1:

$$Y_{ijkl} = \mu_{jkl} + \varepsilon_{ijkl} \qquad \text{(1, repeated)}$$

As in the other designs we have considered, E_F is defined to be

$$E_F = \sum_{j=1}^{a} \sum_{k=1}^{b} \sum_{l=1}^{c} \sum_{i=1}^{n} [Y_{ijkl} - \hat{Y}_{ijkl}(F)]^2$$

where $\hat{Y}_{ijkl}(F)$ is a subject's predicted score when the parameters of the model are estimated using least squares. Notice that the full model has as many parameters as there are cells in the design, namely $a \times b \times c$. In fact, each parameter is simply the population mean of a cell. Not surprisingly, the least-squares estimate of a population mean is as before the corresponding sample mean. Thus, the full model predicts a subject's score to be the sample mean of that subject's cell. In terms of

T A B L E **8. 10** Restricted Models for Testing Main Effects, Two-Way Interactions, and Three-Way Interaction in a Three-Way A × B × C Design

Effect to Be Tested	Restricted Model
A	$Y_{ijkl} = \mu + \beta_k + \gamma_l + (\alpha\beta)_{jk} + (\alpha\gamma)_{jl} + (\beta\gamma)_{kl} + (\alpha\beta\gamma)_{jkl} + \varepsilon_{ijkl}$
B	$Y_{ijkl} = \mu + \alpha_j + \gamma_l + (\alpha\beta)_{jk} + (\alpha\gamma)_{jl} + (\beta\gamma)_{kl} + (\alpha\beta\gamma)_{jkl} + \varepsilon_{ijkl}$
C	$Y_{ijkl} = \mu + \alpha_j + \beta_k + (\alpha\beta)_{jk} + (\alpha\gamma)_{jl} + (\beta\gamma)_{kl} + (\alpha\beta\gamma)_{jkl} + \varepsilon_{ijkl}$
A × B	$Y_{ijkl} = \mu + \alpha_j + \beta_k + \gamma_l + (\alpha\gamma)_{jl} + (\beta\gamma)_{kl} + (\alpha\beta\gamma)_{jkl} + \varepsilon_{ijkl}$
A × C	$Y_{ijkl} = \mu + \alpha_j + \beta_k + \gamma_l + (\alpha\beta)_{jk} + (\beta\gamma)_{kl} + (\alpha\beta\gamma)_{jkl} + \varepsilon_{ijkl}$
B × C	$Y_{ijkl} = \mu + \alpha_j + \beta_k + \gamma_l + (\alpha\beta)_{jk} + (\alpha\gamma)_{jl} + (\alpha\beta\gamma)_{jkl} + \varepsilon_{ijkl}$
A × B × C	$Y_{ijkl} = \mu + \alpha_j + \beta_k + \gamma_l + (\alpha\beta)_{jk} + (\alpha\gamma)_{jl} + (\beta\gamma)_{kl} + \varepsilon_{ijkl}$

symbols, this implies that

$$\hat{Y}_{ijkl}(F) = \bar{Y}_{jkl}$$

Thus, the sum of squared errors is given by

$$E_F = \sum_{j=1}^{a} \sum_{k=1}^{b} \sum_{l=1}^{c} \sum_{i=1}^{n} (Y_{ijkl} - \bar{Y}_{jkl})^2 \tag{4}$$

which is the within-cell sum of squares. Thus, E_F is an index of the extent to which scores vary within each cell in the design.

To obtain the degrees of freedom of the full model, we must calculate the number of independent parameters included in the model. We just saw that there is one parameter for each cell in the design, so there are abc independent parameters in the model.[1] As in earlier chapters, the ratio E_F/df_F, which forms the denominator of the F statistic, is referred to as the mean square within and is often written as MS_W. As in previous designs, MS_W is simply an average within-group variance. Specifically, it can be shown that in the three-way design with equal n, MS_W is given by

$$MS_W = \sum_{j=1}^{a} \sum_{k=1}^{b} \sum_{l=1}^{c} s_{jkl}^2 / abc \tag{5}$$

where s_{jkl}^2 is the variance of scores within the cell represented by the jkl combination of A, B, and C. Thus, the error term for testing an effect in the three-way design simply reflects an average within-group variance.

To complete the F test for an effect, we must consider E_R and df_R, the sum of squared errors and degrees of freedom for the relevant restricted model. Although it is useful conceptually to realize that the sum of squared errors for a restricted model can be calculated by using least squares to estimate the parameters of the model and then finding the squared error for each subject, there is a simpler approach in practice. It turns out that after some tedious algebra similar to that demonstrated for the two-way design in Chapter 7, it is possible to write general expressions for the sums of squares attributable to each effect in the three-way design.

Table 8.11 shows two equivalent expressions for the sum of squares of each of the seven effects to be tested. The general expressions demonstrate that the sum of squares for any effect equals the sum of squared parameter estimates for that effect in the full model, where the sum is computed across all $abcn$ observations. That this is true should come as no surprise because we have previously seen the same relationship in Chapter 3 for the one-way design and in Chapter 7 for the two-way design. The specific expressions show the sum of squares for each effect in terms of sample means instead of estimated parameters. However, the general and specific expressions for an effect are equivalent because parameter estimates are simply a function of sample means. For example, consider the A main effect. Its general expression is given by

$$SS_A = \sum_{j=1}^{a} \sum_{k=1}^{b} \sum_{l=1}^{c} \sum_{i=1}^{n} \hat{\alpha}_j^2 \tag{6}$$

T A B L E 8. 11 Sum of Squares and Degrees of Freedom for Each Effect in Three-Way Between-Subject Design

Effect	General Expression for SS	Specific Expression for SS	df
A	$\sum_{j=1}^{a}\sum_{k=1}^{b}\sum_{l=1}^{c}\sum_{i=1}^{n}\hat{\alpha}_j^2$	$bcn\sum_{j=1}^{a}(\bar{Y}_{j..}-\bar{Y}_{...})^2$	$a-1$
B	$\sum_{j=1}^{a}\sum_{k=1}^{b}\sum_{l=1}^{c}\sum_{i=1}^{n}\hat{\beta}_k^2$	$acn\sum_{k=1}^{b}(\bar{Y}_{.k.}-\bar{Y}_{...})^2$	$b-1$
C	$\sum_{j=1}^{a}\sum_{k=1}^{b}\sum_{l=1}^{c}\sum_{i=1}^{n}\hat{\gamma}_l^2$	$abn\sum_{l=1}^{c}(\bar{Y}_{..l}-\bar{Y}_{...})^2$	$c-1$
A × B	$\sum_{j=1}^{a}\sum_{k=1}^{b}\sum_{l=1}^{c}\sum_{i=1}^{n}(\widehat{\alpha\beta})_{jk}^2$	$cn\sum_{j=1}^{a}\sum_{k=1}^{b}(\bar{Y}_{jk.}-\bar{Y}_{j..}-\bar{Y}_{.k.}+\bar{Y}_{...})^2$	$(a-1)(b-1)$
A × C	$\sum_{j=1}^{a}\sum_{k=1}^{b}\sum_{l=1}^{c}\sum_{i=1}^{n}(\widehat{\alpha\gamma})_{jl}^2$	$bn\sum_{j=1}^{a}\sum_{l=1}^{c}(\bar{Y}_{j.l}-\bar{Y}_{j..}-\bar{Y}_{..l}+\bar{Y}_{...})^2$	$(a-1)(c-1)$
B × C	$\sum_{j=1}^{a}\sum_{k=1}^{b}\sum_{l=1}^{c}\sum_{i=1}^{n}(\widehat{\beta\gamma})_{kl}^2$	$an\sum_{k=1}^{b}\sum_{l=1}^{c}(\bar{Y}_{.kl}-\bar{Y}_{.k.}-\bar{Y}_{..l}+\bar{Y}_{...})^2$	$(b-1)(c-1)$
A × B × C	$\sum_{j=1}^{a}\sum_{k=1}^{b}\sum_{l=1}^{c}\sum_{i=1}^{n}(\widehat{\alpha\beta\gamma})_{jkl}^2$	$n\sum_{j=1}^{a}\sum_{k=1}^{b}\sum_{l=1}^{c}(\bar{Y}_{jkl}-\bar{Y}_{jk.}-\bar{Y}_{j.l}-\bar{Y}_{.kl}+\bar{Y}_{j..}+\bar{Y}_{.k.}+\bar{Y}_{..l}-\bar{Y}_{...})^2$	$(a-1)(b-1)(c-1)$

Where does the specific expression come from? We know from Table 8.9 that the population α_j effect is defined as

$$\alpha_j = \mu_{j..} - \mu \tag{7}$$

The estimated α_j effect is obtained by estimating the population means on the right-hand side of Equation 7 by their respective sample means, which leads to

$$\hat{\alpha}_j = \bar{Y}_{j..} - \bar{Y}_{...}$$

(Estimated parameter values for the other effects shown in Table 8.11 are similarly obtained by estimating population values in Table 8.9 with corresponding sample means.) Thus, Equation 6 is equivalent to

$$SS_A = \sum_{j=1}^{a} \sum_{k=1}^{b} \sum_{l=1}^{c} \sum_{i=1}^{n} (\bar{Y}_{j..} - \bar{Y}_{...})^2 \tag{8}$$

Because $(\bar{Y}_{j..} - \bar{Y}_{...})^2$ does not contain an i, k, or l subscript, it is a constant for all levels of i (subjects), k (the B factor), and l (the C factor). We know that there are n subjects, b levels of B, and c levels of C, so that Equation 8 can be written as

$$SS_A = bcn \sum_{j=1}^{a} (\bar{Y}_{j..} - \bar{Y}_{...})^2$$

which is the specific expression for the sum of squares due to the A main effect, as shown in Table 8.11. The same type of relationship holds for the other effects listed in the table.

Table 8.11 also shows the degrees of freedom associated with each effect, which equals the number of independent parameters omitted from the full model. For example, as Table 8.10 shows, in order to test the A main effect, the α_j parameters were omitted from the full model. Although there are a such parameters (i.e., there is an α_j value for each of the a levels of A), only $a - 1$ of these parameters are independent. Thus, the difference in the number of independent parameters in the full and restricted models equals $a - 1$. In terms of symbols,

$$df_R - df_F = a - 1$$

From Table 8.11 and Equation 5, it is possible to test any of the seven null hypotheses of interest. Our usual F statistic is given by

$$F = \frac{(E_R - E_F)/(df_R - df_F)}{E_F/df_F} \tag{3, repeated}$$

From Table 8.11, for testing any effect, the difference in the error sum of squares of the restricted and full models is

$$E_R - E_F = SS_{effect}$$

Similarly,

$$df_R - df_F = df_{effect}$$

We also know that the ratio of SS_{effect} divided by df_{effect} is simply the mean square for the effect:

$$MS_{\text{effect}} = SS_{\text{effect}}/df_{\text{effect}}$$

Finally, from Equation 5, we know that the ratio of E_F divided by df_F for the full model being used here is mean square within:

$$MS_W = E_F/df_F$$

Substituting these expressions into Equation 3 yields

$$F = MS_{\text{effect}}/MS_W$$

The observed F can be compared to a critical F with df_{effect} numerator degrees of freedom and $N - abc$ denominator degrees of freedom to assess its statistical significance.

NUMERICAL EXAMPLE

At this point, it will probably be helpful to consider a numerical example for the general three-way $a \times b \times c$ design. This example builds from the hypertension example used in Chapter 7 for the two-way design. Table 8.12 presents hypothetical data from a study investigating the effects of biofeedback, drug therapy, and diet therapy on hypertension. For purposes of comparison, the data for the diet-absent condition in Table 8.12 are identical to the data shown in Tables 7.5 and 7.8 to illustrate a two-way design; thus, the data for the current example differ only in that data have been added for the diet-present condition. We (arbitrarily) refer to the

T A B L E **8. 12** Blood Pressure Data

Biofeedback and Drug X	Biofeedback and Drug Y	Biofeedback and Drug Z	Drug X Alone	Drug Y Alone	Drug Z Alone
Diet Absent					
170	186	180	173	189	202
175	194	187	194	194	228
165	201	199	197	217	190
180	215	170	190	206	206
160	219	204	176	199	224
158	209	194	198	195	204
Diet Present					
161	164	162	164	171	205
173	166	184	190	173	199
157	159	183	169	196	170
152	182	156	164	199	160
181	187	180	176	180	179
190	174	173	175	203	179

T A B L E **8. 13**   Cell Means for Data Shown in Table 8.12

		Diet Absent			
		Drug X	*Drug Y*	*Drug Z*	**Marginal Means**
Biofeedback	*Present*	168	204	189	187
	Absent	188	200	209	199
	Marginal Means	178	202	199	193

		Diet Present			
		Drug X	*Drug Y*	*Drug Z*	**Marginal Means**
Biofeedback	*Present*	169	172	173	171.33
	Absent	173	187	182	180.67
	Marginal Means	171	179.5	177.5	176

T A B L E **8. 14**   ANOVA Table for Data Shown in Table 8.12

Source	SS	df	MS	F	p
A (biofeedback)	2048	1	2048.0	13.07	<.001
B (drug)	3675	2	1837.5	11.73	<.001
C (diet)	5202	1	5202.0	33.20	<.001
A × B	259	2	129.5	0.83	.44
A × C	32	1	32.0	0.20	.65
B × C	903	2	451.5	2.88	.06
A × B × C	1075	2	537.5	3.43	.04
Within cells	9400	60	156.7		

presence or absence of biofeedback as factor A, to the type of drug as factor B, and to the presence or absence of diet as factor C. Thus, we have a 2 × 3 × 2 design. As in Chapter 7, $n = 6$, that is, there are only six subjects per cell. As before, power considerations would typically dictate a larger sample size, but we work with $n = 6$ to make computations more manageable.

Table 8.13 shows the cell means for these data, displayed as two 2 × 3 tables, one for diet absent and one for diet present. The table also shows some but not all marginal means for these data. For example, the marginal mean for biofeedback and Drug X averaging over diet would be 168.5 (the mean of 168 and 169), but this value is not shown in the table. We will see momentarily that the marginal means that are in fact shown in the table are the ones in which we are most interested for this particular study.

Table 8.14 shows the ANOVA table for these data. From this table, we can see that all three main effects are highly statistically significant. None of the three two-way interactions are statistically significant at the .05 level, although the drug × diet interaction just misses .05. Because none of the two-way interactions are significant, it might seem that the main effects can be interpreted unambiguously. In fact, however, it is necessary to consider not only the two-way interactions but also the three-way interaction. Table 8.14 shows that the biofeedback × drug × diet interaction is statistically significant at the .05 level for these data.

Implications of Three-Way Interaction

What are the implications of a statistically significant three-way interaction? First, as we have discussed earlier in the chapter, the significant three-way interaction implies that two-way interactions cannot be interpreted unambiguously. To see why, let's consider the biofeedback × drug interaction. We know from Table 8.14 that this interaction (A × B) does not even approach significance at the .05 level. However, the fact that the three-way interaction is significant implies that the biofeedback × drug interaction when the diet is absent is significantly different from the biofeedback × drug interaction when the diet is present. As a result, instead of interpreting the average biofeedback × drug interaction effect, we should interpret two individual biofeedback × drug interaction effects, one for each level of the diet. Although the average biofeedback × drug interaction is nonsignificant, it is entirely possible that either or both of the individual biofeedback × drug interaction effects within the two levels of the diet factor are statistically significant. We will have more to say about performing such tests momentarily. The important point for now is that we should generally not attempt to interpret two-way interactions when the three-way interaction is statistically significant.

The second implication of a significant three-way interaction is that we should generally not interpret main effects either. To see why this is so, let's consider the drug main effect. Because the three-way interaction is significant, the biofeedback × drug interaction is not the same when the diet is absent as when it is present. However, this implies that the biofeedback × drug interaction cannot be null both when the diet is absent and when it is present, or else it would then be the same for both. In other words, there is a biofeedback × drug interaction either when the diet is absent, when it is present, or both.[2] However, the existence of a nonzero two-way interaction for at least one level of the diet factor implies that the effect of drugs varies as a function of the level of biofeedback, for that level of the diet factor. Thus, the effect of drugs is not consistent and generally cannot be interpreted unambiguously.

In general, then, a significant three-way interaction implies that the effect of one factor is not consistent at all combinations of the other two factors. Thus, for example, it may be misleading to conclude on the basis of the significant drug main effect shown in Table 8.14 that the difference between the three drugs included in this study can be interpreted on the basis of their marginal means. For the sake of illustration, if we were to attempt to make such an interpretation, we would calculate the marginal means for drugs X, Y, and Z, averaging over biofeedback and diet. From Table 8.13, we can see that the appropriate values of these marginal means are 174.5 for drug X, 190.75 for drug Y, and 188.25 for drug Z. Remembering that lower blood pressure values are better, we would probably conclude that drug X is better than either drug Y or drug Z. Of course, we would want to verify our impression by conducting a formal test of a contrast. However, the point we are trying to make here concerns the meaning of such a statement. Although it would be correct that drug X truly does have a lower mean than drugs Y or Z for these data, such a statement is true only if we average across both biofeedback and diet. However, we will see momentarily that in fact there is not a significant drug effect at all when the diet is present. In addition, there is a biofeedback × drug interaction when the diet is absent, implying that the differences between drugs X, Y, and Z vary as a function of presence or absence of biofeedback when the diet is absent. As a result, although it may be true that drug X is the most effective drug of these three drugs on the average, it may be much more important to realize that its superiority is not at all consistent across different levels of diet and biofeedback. In general, it is important to remember that main effects represent effects that are averaged over all other factors in the design, as we showed earlier in Table 8.8. However, a statistically significant three-way interaction is a signal that these average effects are not consistent and thus are not representative of the effects at individual levels of the other factors. As a result, when a significant three-way interaction is obtained, it is generally preferable to consider effects within such individual levels of other factors instead of interpreting the main effects themselves.

General Guideline for Analyzing Effects

How should we proceed with the interpretation of the data in our hypothetical study? Figure 8.2 presents a flowchart, which serves as a general guideline for analyzing effects in a three-way design. We orient the discussion of data analysis in our hypothetical example around this flowchart. Three cautions should be mentioned before proceeding. First, as with the flowcharts we have seen in previous chapters, this flowchart also is intended to be used only as a guideline. For example, the flowchart does not include the possibility of performing certain planned comparisons instead of omnibus tests. Nevertheless, the flowchart is a useful guide as long as it is used flexibly. Second, not all parts of the flowchart are self-explanatory. At several points, it will be necessary to expand on or clarify the figure. Thus, it is important to read and understand the following pages of text. Third, the flowchart provides no assistance for choosing an error term or for defining a family when considering Type I error rates. The logic underlying these issues is the same as it was in Chapter 7 for the two-way design. In the following analysis, we use MS_W as the error term for all tests, and we use $\alpha = .05$ for each test until we consider comparisons of cell means. We have made these choices not necessarily because they are "correct," but quite frankly because they simplify the presentation and allow the reader to concentrate on understanding the necessary steps to analyze data from a three-way design.

With these cautions in mind, we can now consider the analysis of our data, using Figure 8.2 as a guideline. According to Figure 8.2, we must begin by ascertaining whether the three-way interaction is statistically significant. From Table 8.14, we can see that A × B × C is significant at the .05 level, so the answer to the question in the flowchart is Yes. Thus, we branch to the left in the flowchart.

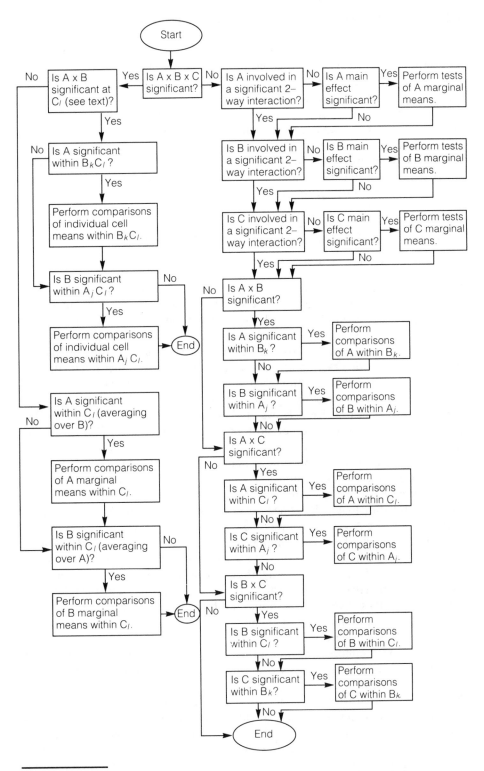

FIGURE 8.2 General guideline for analyzing effects in a three-factor design.

Because the three-way $A \times B \times C$ interaction was significant, the next step is to determine whether $A \times B$ is significant at C_l. Before attempting to answer this question, we must understand what is being asked. As we saw earlier in the chapter, a significant three-way interaction implies that the two-way interaction is not the same at every level of the third factor. Thus, the flowchart suggests that we test the two-way $A \times B$ interaction separately at each individual level of C (recall that C_l refers to level l of factor C).

At this point, we must discuss an important issue that is not revealed in the flowchart. From a statistical standpoint, a significant three-way interaction can be viewed from any of three perspectives:

1. The $A \times B$ interaction is different at individual levels of C.
2. The $A \times C$ interaction is different at individual levels of B.
3. The $B \times C$ interaction is different at individual levels of A.

These three perspectives are equivalent and thus equally valid statistically. However, in most research situations, one of these three perspectives is more interesting than the other two. In our example, we assume that the investigator is most interested in examining the biofeedback $\times$ drug interaction separately for each level of the diet factor. From a statistical perspective, we could also investigate the biofeedback $\times$ diet interaction for each drug and the drug $\times$ diet interaction for both levels of biofeedback. Although it would be legitimate to perform all three tests, we will only test biofeedback $\times$ drug at each level of the diet factor. We would also suggest that in practice it is usually best not to perform all three tests, but instead to test only the question of most interest and importance. There are essentially two reasons not to perform all three tests. First, attempting to describe all three tests may become overbearing, in light of the potential follow-up tests to be conducted. The number of potential tests can be appreciated most easily by referring again to Figure 8.2 and realizing that the left-hand side of the figure only shows tests corresponding to $A \times B$ at one level of C. If we test not only $A \times B$ at multiple levels of C, but also $A \times C$ at all levels of B, and $B \times C$ at all levels of A, the resultant number of tests may be overwhelming. Second, the three tests ($A \times B$ within C, $A \times C$ within B, and $B \times C$ within A) are somewhat redundant because they all involve $SS_{A \times B \times C}$. Stated another way, the contrasts underlying these various tests are not orthogonal to each other, which can additionally complicate the interpretation. Although these two reasons should not be viewed as prohibiting the testing of all three effects, in most situations one of the effects stands out for theoretical reasons as the single effect to be tested.

Thus, in our example, we will test the biofeedback $\times$ drug interaction at each level of the diet factor, that is, $A \times B$ within C_l. Such a test is often called a *simple interaction test* because it pertains to a single level of one factor (viz., C), much like the *simple effects test* we encountered in Chapter 7. Be sure to understand that we will test the $A \times B$ interaction here at each and every level of C. In other words, although we will test $A \times B$ at an individual level of C, we will conduct the test not only for C_1 but also for C_2, because C has two levels in our example. In general, there would be as many "simple $A \times B$ interaction tests" as there were levels of C

T A B L E **8. 15** Simple Interaction Tests Performed According to Guidelines of Figure 8.2

Source	SS	df	MS	F	p
A × B w C$_1$ (biofeedback × drug for diet absent)	1152	2	576.0	3.68	.03
A × B w C$_2$ (biofeedback × drug for diet present)	182	2	91.0	0.58	.57
Within cells	9400	60	156.7		

in the design. We should also mention that the sums of squares for these effects can be found by regarding the data as a two-way design and using the computational formulas of Chapter 7. For example, to find $SS_{A \times BwC_1}$, the A × B interaction sum of squares at the first level of C, we could literally ignore the data from the other levels of C. The resultant design would be a two-way A × B design and could be analyzed accordingly. As usual, careful thought should be given concerning whether the error term for testing this effect should also ignore data from the other levels of C (if heterogeneity of variance is suspected) or should incorporate data from all subjects (under the assumption of homogeneity of variance).

Table 8.15 shows the results of testing biofeedback × drug at each level of the diet factor. From the table, it is clear that there is a significant (at the .05 level) biofeedback × drug interaction when the diet is absent but not when it is present. Notice that such a discrepancy is consistent with, although not required by, the significant three-way effect we had already observed. Because A × B is significant at C$_1$ (diet absent) but nonsignificant at C$_2$ (diet present), the next test to be performed is different for the two levels of the diet factor. Before actually performing the tests, however, it is helpful to realize that conceptually we have two two-way designs here, one when the diet is absent and one when the diet is present. Because A and B interact when the diet is absent but not when it is present, the subsequent tests to be performed will not be the same for the two levels of the diet factor.

Let's first consider what further tests should be performed when the diet is absent. So far we know that biofeedback and drug interact when the diet is absent. Thus, the effect of biofeedback is not the same for every drug; similarly, the differences among drugs are not the same when biofeedback is present as when it is absent. For this reason, we must test the effect of biofeedback at each individual level of the drug factor, and the drug effect at each level of biofeedback.[3] On the one hand, we have tests of A at each level of B; on the other hand, we have tests of B at each level of A. However, throughout these tests, we are restricting our attention to the diet-absent condition, so that all tests are performed at the first level of C. As a result, the tests of A are of the form A within B$_1$C$_1$, A within B$_2$C$_1$, and A within B$_3$C$_1$. The two tests of B are B within A$_1$C$_1$, and B within A$_2$C$_1$. Notice that in each case, we effectively have a one-way design, so that the sum of squares for any

TABLE 8.16   Simple, Simple Main Effects When Diet Is Absent

Source	SS	df	MS	F	p
AwB_1C_1 (biofeedback for drug X when diet is absent)	1200	1	1200.0	7.66	.007
AwB_2C_1 (biofeedback for drug Y when diet is absent)	48	1	48.0	0.31	.589
AwB_3C_1 (biofeedback for drug Z when diet is absent)	1200	1	1200.0	7.66	.007
BwA_1C_1 (drugs for biofeedback present when diet is absent)	3924	2	1962.0	12.52	<.001
BwA_2C_1 (drugs for biofeedback absent when diet is absent)	1332	2	666.0	4.25	.018
Within cells	9400	60	156.7		

of these effects can be found using formulas from Chapter 3. The results of these tests, which are commonly called *simple, simple main effects* because we are fixing the levels of two other factors, are shown in Table 8.16. We can see from this table that in the absence of the diet, biofeedback has an effect when combined with drug X or drug Z but not drug Y. In addition, when the diet is absent, there is a significant difference among the drugs whether biofeedback is present or absent. At this point, you may want to refer back to the cell means shown in Table 8.13 to better understand these results. Table 8.16 tells us that, for the diet-absent condition, column differences are significant within the first row (biofeedback present) and within the second row (biofeedback absent) and that row differences are significant within the first column (drug X) and the third column (drug Z) but not the second column (drug Y).

According to the flowchart, we now should perform comparisons of individual cell means within B_1C_1 and within B_3C_1 because A within B_1C_1 and A within B_3C_1 are both significant. In general, the idea here is that when the A simple, simple main effect is significant, we must compare the individual levels of A to determine which levels are different from each other. However, in our example, A has only two levels, so such comparisons are unnecessary. When the simple, simple main effect of A is significant in our example, it must be the case that mean blood pressure is different when biofeedback is present than when it is absent.

The drug factor, on the other hand, has three levels. Thus, we do need to perform comparisons of individual cell means, both within A_1C_1 and within A_2C_1, to understand the nature of drug differences. These comparisons can be of any form

TABLE **8. 17**   Individual Cell Mean Comparisons When Diet Is Absent

Source	SS	df	MS	F
X vs. YwA_1C_1 (drug X vs. drug Y when biofeedback is present and diet is absent)	3888	1	3888.0	24.82
X vs. ZwA_1C_1 (drug X vs. drug Z when biofeedback is present and diet is absent)	1323	1	1323.0	8.44
Y vs. ZwA_1C_1 (drug Y vs. drug Z when biofeedback is present and diet is absent)	675	1	675.0	4.31
X vs. YwA_2C_1 (drug X vs. drug Y when biofeedback is absent and diet is absent)	432	1	432.0	2.76
X vs. ZwA_2C_1 (drug X vs. drug Z when biofeedback is absent and diet is absent)	1323	1	1323.0	8.44
Y vs. ZwA_2C_1 (drug Y vs. drug Z when biofeedback is absent and diet is absent)	243	1	243.0	1.55
Within cells	9400	60	156.7	

discussed in Chapter 4, with an appropriate adjustment to the critical value as discussed in Chapter 5. For illustrative purposes, we suppose that pairwise comparisons are of interest here.[4] Table 8.17 shows the results of performing pairwise comparisons of cell means (as shown earlier in Table 8.13) to our data. We define a family to be a particular combination of A and C. To keep the α_{FW} at .05, Tukey's WSD can be used. The critical q from Appendix Table A.4 is 3.40 for $\alpha = .05$, $df = 60$, and three means. To be statistically significant, an observed F must exceed $q^2/2$, which equals 5.78 here. Three of the observed F values in Table 8.17 exceed this value, and thus the corresponding comparisons are statistically significant. For our data, when diet is absent, drug X differs significantly from drug Y as well as drug Z when biofeedback is present, and drug X differs significantly from drug Z when biofeedback is absent.

We have obtained a thorough analysis of the effects of biofeedback and drugs when the diet is absent. However, the analysis when the diet is present is still stranded near the top of the flowchart! The last analysis we performed for the diet-present condition showed that the biofeedback × drug interaction is non-significant for diet present (see Table 8.15). Because these two factors do not interact when the diet is present, we can interpret their main effects unambiguously, within the second level of the diet factor. As a result, we do not follow the same strategy as we did for the diet-absent condition, where simple, simple main effects were tested.

T A B L E **8.18** Simple Main-Effect Tests When Diet Is Present

Source	SS	df	MS	F	p
AwC_2 (biofeedback when diet is present)	784	1	784.0	5.00	.027
BwC_2 (drugs when diet is present)	474	2	237.0	1.51	.227
Within cells	9400	60	156.7		

Instead, as Figure 8.2 shows, we test the A (biofeedback) effect within C_2 (diet present) by averaging over levels of B (drug). Similarly, we will test the B (drug) effect within C_2 (diet present) by averaging over levels of A (biofeedback).

We first test the A (biofeedback) effect within the second level of the diet factor (i.e., within C_2, diet present). Table 8.18 shows that this effect is significant at the .05 level. In general, as the flowchart shows, we would next perform comparisons of A marginal means within C_2. However, because A has only two levels in our example, further comparisons are unnecessary. We already know which specific means are different—the marginal mean of 171.33 for biofeedback present is significantly different from the marginal mean of 180.67 for biofeedback absent when the diet is present (see Table 8.13 to understand from where these values come).

The second test to be performed is a test of B within C_2, that is, the drug effect when the diet is present. As Table 8.18 shows, this effect is nonsignificant. Thus, further investigation of specific differences among the three drugs is unwarranted. The marginal means of 171, 179.5, and 177.5 (see Table 8.13) are not significantly different from each other, so there is no evidence of differential effectiveness of the three drugs when the diet is present.

Summary of Results

At this point, it may be helpful to summarize what we have discovered about our data. Table 8.19 repeats the means shown earlier in Table 8.13. However, Table 8.19 also includes superscripts (small letters $a–g$) to designate which means are significantly different from one another and which are not. Means that are in the same row or column as each other but do not share a superscript in common are significantly different from each other. Means that are in the same row or column as each other and that do share a superscript in common are not significantly different from each other. Differences between means that are in different rows and different columns have not been tested, so their superscripts cannot be compared.

To see what all of this means, look at Table 8.19. We'll begin with the diet-present condition because findings here are less complicated. The first thing to notice is that superscripts are associated with the marginal means instead of the cell means. The reason is that biofeedback and drug did not interact when the diet is present, so we can unambiguously interpret marginal means. Next, notice that the super-

T A B L E **8. 19** Cell Means for Hypothetical Data

		Diet Absent			
		Drug X	Drug Y	Drug Z	**Marginal Means**
Biofeedback	Present	168^a	204^{be}	189^b	**187**
	Absent	188^c	200^{cde}	209^d	**199**
		178	202	199	**193**

		Diet Present			
		Drug X	Drug Y	Drug Z	**Marginal Means**
Biofeedback	Present	169	172	173	171.33^f
	Absent	173	187	182	180.67^g
		171^h	179.5^h	177.5^h	**176**

script for the biofeedback-present marginal mean is f, while the superscript for the biofeedback-absent marginal mean is g. The fact that the two superscripts are different signifies that the two marginal means are significantly different, that is, there is a statistically significant biofeedback effect in the diet-present condition (see Table 8.18). Next, consider the column marginal means. The fact that all three superscripts here are h implies that these means are not significantly different from each other (recall from Table 8.18 that the drug effect when the diet is present is nonsignificant). Finally, be certain you understand that comparing superscripts of row marginal means to superscripts of column marginal means has no meaning because we never performed such tests. Thus, do not be misled into thinking that the row 1 marginal mean (171.33) is significantly different from the column 1 marginal mean (171). Such a test could be performed, in which case we could incorporate it into our subscripts; however, in the great majority of cases, only comparisons within a row or within a column are interpretable. For this reason, the notational system adopted here is meaningful only for comparisons within a row or within a column.

The situation is more complicated when the diet is absent. First, notice that the superscripts here are associated with individual cell means, not marginal means, as they were in the diet-present condition. The reason is that biofeedback and drug were found to interact when the diet is absent. Thus, we interpret row differences within each column and column differences within each row. Let's start with the row differences. Table 8.19 shows that there is a significant biofeedback effect for drug X (a and c are different) and for drug Z (b and d are different) but not for drug Y (be and cde share the e superscript in common). What about the column differences? Within the first row, drug X differs from both drug Y and drug Z, but drugs Y and Z do not differ from one another. Within the second row, drug X differs from drug Z (c and d are different). However, drug Y is not significantly different from either drug X (c and cde share c in common) or drug Z (d and cde share d in common). As in the diet-present condition, comparing superscripts of means that differ in both their row and their column is not meaningful. For example, the values of 189 and 188 have different superscripts (*b* and *c*, respectively), but they obviously would not be different from one another if we were to test them. However, the notational system simply reflects the fact that such differences have not been tested and typically would not be interpretable or interesting. Also notice that it is meaningless here to compare means when the diet is absent to means where the diet is present because we performed tests within each level of the diet factor individually. This does not mean that such tests could not be performed, but rather that they were judged not to be interesting in the context of this study.

Graphical Depiction of Data

A table like that given in Table 8.19 is certainly not the only way in which data analyses from a three-way design might be summarized. For example, an alternative might be to plot the cell means, as shown in Figure 8.3. This plot aids understanding of the statistically significant results we have obtained for these data. For example, the plot shows clearly that the three-way interaction we obtained can be conceptualized as due to the existence of a strong biofeedback × drug interaction when the diet is absent, but little or no such interaction when the diet is present. Notice that this interpretation is consistent with the *F* tests reported earlier in Table 8.15. The figure is also consistent with Table 8.19. For example, the figure and the table together imply that when the diet is present, biofeedback has an effect, but there are

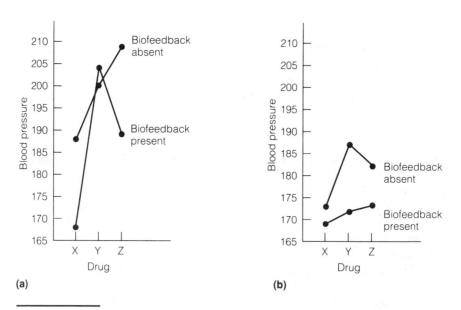

FIGURE 8.3 Plot of Table 8.13 cell means as a function of diet condition: (a) diet absent and (b) diet present.

no significant differences among the drugs. On the other hand, when the diet is absent, biofeedback has an effect only for drugs X and Z. In addition, when the diet is absent, drugs X and Z differ both when biofeedback is present and when it is absent; drugs X and Y differ only when biofeedback is present; and, drugs Y and Z do not differ in either case. As usual, remember that the plot could have been constructed differently, if we wanted to emphasize different effects. The most important point to be made here is that our interpretation should ultimately hinge not only on the F and p values of Tables 8.14–8.18 but also on the cell means themselves, which, after all, are what the F and p values are derived from.

Other Questions of Potential Interest

We do not want to leave the impression that the analyses we have presented exhaust the range of questions we might address with these data. For example, from a clinical perspective, the microscopic analyses reported here may not have directly addressed a fundamental question, namely, what combination of therapies is most effective. Should biofeedback, drug, and diet therapies all be combined into one package? The main-effects tests reported earlier in Table 8.14 would seem to suggest that they should be combined because all three factors had highly significant main effects. In particular, Table 8.20 shows the marginal means associated with each main effect. For example, the value of 179.17 for biofeedback present is the (unweighted) average of the six cell means from Table 8.13 when biofeedback is present. Also shown in Table 8.20 is the deviation from the grand mean (which equals 184.50) for each effect. As shown earlier in Tables 8.9 and 8.11, these deviations are estimates of the effect parameters associated with each main effect. For example, $\hat{\alpha}_1 = -5.33$, which implies that the effect of biofeedback averaged over all conditions is to lower blood pressure 5.33 units relative to the grand mean. Similarly, drug X lowers blood pressure by 10.00 units, and the diet lowers blood pressure by 8.50 units. We might then expect that biofeedback, drug X, and diet in combination would lower blood pressure by 23.83 units (notice that 23.83 is the sum of 5.33, 10.00, and 8.50). Such a reduction from the grand mean (184.50) would produce a mean of 160.67.

TABLE **8. 20** Marginal Means for Main Effects

	Marginal Mean	Deviation from Grand Mean
Biofeedback present	$\bar{Y}_{1..} = 179.17$	-5.33
Biofeedback absent	$\bar{Y}_{2..} = 189.83$	5.33
Drug X	$\bar{Y}_{.1.} = 174.50$	-10.00
Drug Y	$\bar{Y}_{.2.} = 190.75$	6.25
Drug Z	$\bar{Y}_{.3.} = 188.25$	3.75
Diet present	$\bar{Y}_{..1} = 176.00$	-8.50
Diet absent	$\bar{Y}_{..2} = 193.00$	8.50

However, as we have seen (in Tables 8.13 and 8.19 and in Figure 8.3), the actual mean for this condition is 169, considerably higher than we might have thought. What has gone wrong here? The reason these two values do not agree is that the value of 160.67 was obtained based on the assumption that the three factors combine additively. However, we know that in fact there are significant interactions for these data. The value of 160.67 was based on the assumption that μ_{112} would equal the sum of $\mu_{...}$, α_1, β_1, and γ_2, but this happens only if the factors do not interact. In general, the equation for μ_{112} comes from Equation 2 earlier in the chapter, and is given by

$$\mu_{112} = \mu_{...} + \alpha_1 + \beta_1 + \gamma_2 + (\alpha\beta)_{11} + (\alpha\gamma)_{12} + (\beta\gamma)_{12} + (\alpha\beta\gamma)_{112}$$

Of course, with sample data, we can only estimate these parameters, in which case we can write the equation as

$$\bar{Y}_{112} = \bar{Y}_{...} + \hat{\alpha}_1 + \hat{\beta}_1 + \hat{\gamma}_2 + \widehat{(\alpha\beta)}_{11} + \widehat{(\alpha\gamma)}_{12} + \widehat{(\beta\gamma)}_{12} + \widehat{(\alpha\beta\gamma)}_{112} \qquad (9)$$

Expressions for these parameter estimates follow directly from the formulas shown in Tables 8.9 and 8.11. For our data, we have already seen that $\bar{Y}_{112} = 169$, $\bar{Y}_{...} = 184.5$, $\hat{\alpha}_1 = -5.33$, $\hat{\beta}_1 = -10.00$, and $\hat{\gamma}_2 = -8.50$. After some tedious calculations[5] based on the formulas in Tables 8.9 and 8.11, it can be shown that for our data, $\widehat{(\alpha\beta)}_{11} = -0.67$, $\widehat{(\alpha\gamma)}_{12} = 0.67$, $\widehat{(\beta\gamma)}_{12} = 5.00$ and $\widehat{(\alpha\beta\gamma)}_{112} = 3.33$. Substituting these values into Equation 9, we find that

$$169 = 184.50 + (-5.33) + (-10.00) + (-8.50) + (-0.67) + (0.67)$$
$$+ (5.00) + (3.33),$$

which is in fact an equality, as it must be. The point of this equation is to illustrate why the combination of the biofeedback, drug X, and diet is less effective than might be expected based on their average effects. The parameter estimates we have calculated show that two influences are primarily responsible here. First, the combination of drug X and the diet is 5 points less effective at lowering blood pressure than the average effect of each would suggest. For this reason, it might be said that drug X and the diet interact antagonistically with one another. (If the whole were better than the sum of its parts, we could say that we have a *synergistic interaction*.) Second, the combination of all three therapies is 3.33 points less effective than their joint (pairwise) effects would suggest.

The previous discussion suggests that it might be wise not to combine drug X and the diet in the same package. Indeed, if we combine drug X and biofeedback without the diet, the cell mean is 168, the lowest mean of all (realize, however, that this mean is not statistically significantly lower than all other means). Alternatively, we might combine the diet and either drug Y or Z with biofeedback, and the resultant sample mean is only slightly higher. An ultimate clinical decision would necessarily depend on additional factors such as possible side effects, costs, problems of compliance, and so forth. Nevertheless, it is important to realize that treatments in combination may behave differently from what would be expected on the basis of their separate effects. As pointed out in Chapter 7, the primary advantage of factorial designs is their ability to detect such patterns.

Tests to Be Performed When the Three-Way Interaction Is Nonsignificant

Although it may seem incredible, we have not yet finished Figure 8.2. In fact, in a sense we are only half-finished! The reason is that so far we have only considered what happens when the three-way interaction is statistically significant. Now we must consider what tests to perform when the three-way interaction is nonsignificant.

In the absence of a three-way interaction, all two-way interactions can be interpreted unambiguously. The reason is that the magnitude of each two-way interaction is consistent (within sampling error) at the various levels of the third factor. As a result, we need not consider all three factors simultaneously but instead can focus on pairs of factors. In effect, we have a two-way design. However, there is an additional complication because we essentially have three different two-way designs: A × B, A × C, and B × C. For this reason, the right-hand side of the flowchart in Figure 8.2 looks very much like Figure 7.2 in triplicate. For example, whereas we had only one two-way interaction to test in the two-way design of Chapter 7, we now have three two-way interactions to test in the three-way design. Nevertheless, the right-hand side of Figure 8.2 for the three-way design follows basically the same logic as did the flowchart in Chapter 7. The primary conceptual difference involves testing of main effects.

When are tests of main effects unambiguous? From Figure 8.2, we can see that a main-effect test is interpreted only when the factor in question is involved in no significant two-way interaction *and* the three-way interaction is nonsignificant. For example, if A × B, A × C, and A × B × C are all nonsignificant, the effect of A is consistent at all combinations of B and C, so the A main effect is unambiguous. However, if any interaction involving A is significant, the effect of A is not the same for every combination of B and C, in which case the main effect of A may be misleading.

It may be helpful to explicitly compare the conditions under which a main effect is generally interpreted in the three-way design to those where a main effect would be interpreted in a two-way design. To make the example more concrete, we continue to consider the A main effect. In the two-way design, the A main effect is usually interpreted if and only if the A × B interaction is nonsignificant. Similarly, in the three-way design, the A main effect is usually interpreted if and only if the A × B, the A × C, and the A × B × C interactions are all nonsignificant. Thus, in both designs, the A main effect is interpreted if and only if the A factor interacts with no other effects in the design. In contrast, when A does interact with another factor, in both designs the effect of A is typically examined within individual levels of the other factor.

As Figure 8.2 shows, when significant two-way interactions occur, they are interpreted just as they were in the two-way design. For example, suppose that the A × B interaction is statistically significant. According to the figure, tests of A within B and of B within A would be performed next. Two points need to be made here. First, there is no requirement that both types of tests be performed. For example, as we mentioned in Chapter 7, for theoretical reasons only tests of B within A might be of interest in a particular situation. Second, when A × B is statistically significant, the flowchart says to test A within B_k. You should realize that this generally implies that A would be tested within each and every level of B. In other words, the k subscript in B_k simply refers to an arbitrary level of the B factor.

Figure 8.2 should prove useful as a guideline for interpreting effects in a three-factor design. However, as we mentioned when we introduced the flowchart, it is by no means a complete solution to all data-analysis problems in a three-way design. For example, the flowchart provides no assistance in deciding whether to use a pooled error term such as MS_W for all tests or to use separate error terms. It also provides no assistance in defining a family and choosing an appropriate procedure for maintaining the α_{FW} level at a desired level. The flowchart also assumes that interactions will be followed up by tests of simple effects; however, as we saw in Chapter 7, there are circumstances where interaction contrasts may be more informative than simple effects. That you understand the logic of the principles that underly the flowchart is important. If you not only can use the flowchart but also understand its logic, you need not be a slave to the flowchart. Instead, when exceptions occur in your studies, you can recognize them and act accordingly. Finally, the logic underlying this flowchart also holds for designs with four or more factors. If you understand the principles used to create Figure 8.2, generalizing them to designs with four or more factors should be reasonably straightforward.

NONORTHOGONAL DESIGNS

So far in this chapter we have restricted ourselves to equal-n designs. After the discussion of nonorthogonal two-way designs in Chapter 7, it should not surprise you to learn that additional complications arise in the three-way design as well when cell sizes are unequal.

As in the two-way design, it is extremely important prior to analyzing the data to understand why cell sizes are unequal. Because the issues are the same in a three-way design as in a two-way design, we refer you back to Chapter 7 instead of repeating the discussion here.

In terms of analysis, the same general issues are pertinent in the three-way design as were pertinent in the two-way design. In particular, it is once again true that there are different weights that can be applied when one or more factors are averaged over. As a result, there are again Type I, Type II, and Type III sums of squares. As we pointed out in Chapter 7, Type I sums of squares are generally of little interest, so we restrict our attention here to Type II and Type III sums of squares.

Recall that in the two-way design, the test of the A × B interaction yielded the same value for Type II and Type III sums of squares. The reason for this equivalence was that the A × B interaction in the two-way design did not average over any other factors. However, two-way interactions in three-way designs do average over another factor. For example, the A × B interaction in a three-way design averages over levels of C (as we saw earlier in Table 8.8). Thus, in a nonorthogonal three-way design, both two-way interactions *and* main effects yield different values for Type II and Type III sums of squares. However, the A × B × C interaction in a three-way interaction does not average over any other factors, and as a consequence, Type II and Type III sums of squares for A × B × C are identical, even in a nonorthogonal design. In general, then, Type II and Type III sums of squares of the highest-order interaction (i.e., the interaction of all factors in the design) are identical to each other. However, tests of lower-order interactions (i.e., interactions that do not involve all factors) and tests of main effects differ, depending on whether these tests are based on Type II or Type III sums of squares.

The procedure for obtaining the Type III sum of squares for an effect is straightforward when conceptualized in terms of model comparisons. Regardless of the effect to be tested, the full model for Type III sum of squares is the same full model that we worked with earlier in the chapter, namely, a model that includes all possible effects:

$$Y_{ijkl} = \mu + \alpha_j + \beta_k + \gamma_l + (\alpha\beta)_{jk} + (\alpha\gamma)_{jl} + (\beta\gamma)_{kl} + (\alpha\beta\gamma)_{jkl} + \varepsilon_{ijkl} \quad (2, \text{repeated})$$

The restricted model simply omits the parameters associated with the effect to be tested. Thus, the restricted models have the same form as those shown earlier in Table 8.10. The only complication that arises in nonorthogonal designs is that the actual calculation of sums of squares is more complicated than with equal *n*. In particular, the formulas shown in Table 8.11 are not appropriate in nonorthogonal designs. As in the two-way design, a comparison of models based on Type III sums of squares is a test of unweighted means. In other words, all levels of the factor(s) being averaged over are weighted equally.

The Type II sum of squares for an effect can also be found through model comparisons. However, here even the full model omits parameters of a higher order than the effect being tested if the parameters include the effect being tested. To understand what this means, we will look at tests for each of three effects based on Type II sum of squares: the three-way A × B × C interaction, a two-way interaction (A × B), and a main effect (A). First, let's consider the three-way interaction. To decide what the full model should be, we must deal with the "order" of the effect to be tested, where order depends on the number of factors involved in the effect. For example, a main effect includes no other factors in the effect and is thus said to be of *order zero*. A two-way interaction is of the next highest order, namely *order one*. A three-way interaction is then referred to as a *second-order* interaction. In a three-way design, there is no higher-order effect than the three-way interaction. Thus, when testing the three-way interaction based on Type II sum of squares, there are no parameters of a higher order than the effect being tested to omit from the model. Hence, the full model is again of the form

$$Y_{ijkl} = \mu + \alpha_j + \beta_k + \gamma_l + (\alpha\beta)_{jk} + (\alpha\gamma)_{jl} + (\beta\gamma)_{kl} + (\alpha\beta\gamma)_{jkl} + \varepsilon_{ijkl} \quad (2, \text{repeated})$$

The restricted model is found by omitting the parameters associated with the effect being tested, namely, $(\alpha\beta\gamma)_{jkl}$. Thus, the restricted model is given by

$$Y_{ijkl} = \mu + \alpha_j + \beta_k + \gamma_l + (\alpha\beta)_{jk} + (\alpha\gamma)_{jl} + (\beta\gamma)_{kl} + \varepsilon_{ijkl}$$

which is the same as the restricted model for Type III sum of squares. Thus, Type II and Type III sums of squares are identical for testing the three-way $A \times B \times C$ interaction in a three-factor design.

How do we find the Type II sum of squares for a two-way interaction such as $A \times B$? Recall that a two-way interaction is a first-order interaction. Parameters associated with second-order effects are therefore omitted from the full model, if they include parameters associated with $A \times B$. The parameters for the second-order effect (i.e., $A \times B \times C$) are $(\alpha\beta\gamma)_{jkl}$, which includes both α and β, so these parameters are omitted from the full model. Thus, the full model for testing $A \times B$ (or $A \times C$, or $B \times C$, for that matter) is given by

$$Y_{ijkl} = \mu + \alpha_j + \beta_k + \gamma_l + (\alpha\beta)_{jk} + (\alpha\gamma)_{jl} + (\beta\gamma)_{kl} + \varepsilon_{ijkl}$$

The restricted model for testing the $A \times B$ interaction omits, in addition, the $(\alpha\beta)_{jk}$ parameters, yielding

$$Y_{ijkl} = \mu + \alpha_j + \beta_k + \gamma_l + (\alpha\gamma)_{jl} + (\beta\gamma)_{kl} + \varepsilon_{ijkl}$$

Notice that the Type II comparison is different from the Type III comparison in that both of the Type II models omit the $(\alpha\beta\gamma)_{jkl}$ parameters and thus assume that the $A \times B \times C$ interaction is zero in the population. As in the two-way design, when the interaction is indeed zero, leaving out the $(\alpha\beta\gamma)_{jkl}$ parameters in both models increases power; however, when the interaction is nonzero, a bias occurs.

Finally, we need to consider the Type II sum of squares for a main effect. We will use the A main effect as an example. The full model here must omit parameters for all higher-order effects that include α parameters. The higher-order effects here are $A \times B, A \times C, B \times C$, and $A \times B \times C$. The corresponding parameters are $(\alpha\beta)_{jk}$, $(\alpha\gamma)_{jl}, (\beta\gamma)_{kl}$, and $(\alpha\beta\gamma)_{jkl}$, respectively. All these parameters except for $(\beta\gamma)_{kl}$ contain α and are thus omitted from the full model; thus, the full model for testing the A main effect is given by

$$Y_{ijkl} = \mu + \alpha_j + \beta_k + \gamma_l + (\beta\gamma)_{kl} + \varepsilon_{ijkl}$$

The restricted model constrains each α_j to equal zero and is thus given by

$$Y_{ijkl} = \mu + \beta_k + \gamma_l + (\beta\gamma)_{kl} + \varepsilon_{ijkl}$$

Again, the Type II sum of squares is different from the Type III sum of squares in that the Type II sum of squares assumes certain effects to be zero. Specifically, for testing the A main effect, the Type II sum of squares approach assumes that the $A \times B, A \times C$, and $A \times B \times C$ effects are all zero in the population and hence omits them from both the full and the restricted models.[6] Notice that the effects that are omitted here are the ones that Figure 8.2 shows must be nonsignificant in order for the interpretation of the A main effect to be unambiguous. That is, the A effect is consistent at all combinations of B and C if and only if the $A \times B, A \times C$, and $A \times B \times C$ effects truly are zero in the population. The difference between Type II and Type III sums of squares is that the calculation of Type II sum of squares assumes that these higher-order effects are literally zero, based on a nonsignificant result in the sample. If the effects are indeed zero in the population, tests based on Type II sum of squares are more powerful than tests based on Type III sum of squares. However, if some of the effects are nonzero, tests based on Type III sum of squares are much more easily interpreted than tests based on Type II sum of squares. In this situation, both tests involve the average A effect (for example) at the $b \times c$ different combinations of the B and C factors. The Type III sum of squares test is easy to interpret because (as in the two-way design) it is based on an unweighted average of the $b \times c$ different A effects. Thus, even if there is in fact some interaction in the population that our interaction tests fail to detect, at least the A effect we are testing is an unweighted average of the various effects that A has at the different combinations of B and C. However, the Type II sum of squares in this situation weights these various effects unequally, where the weights are a complicated function of the cell sizes. Because the cell sizes are typically unequal for reasons we are not interested in, tests based on Type II sum of squares are generally uninterpretable if a true population interaction has gone undetected in the sample. As we said in Chapter 7, our general recommendation is to perform tests based on Type III sums of squares. However, some researchers prefer Type II sums of squares, particularly in situations where there are strong theoretical reasons to expect interactions to be zero and empirical tests of the interactions result in p values substantially above .05 (e.g., above .20 or .25).

HIGHER-ORDER DESIGNS

Although this chapter has not considered designs with more than three factors, the logic we have developed here extends in a straightforward manner to such designs. For example, suppose we obtain an $A \times B \times C \times D$ interaction in a four-way design. What would it mean? A four-way interaction would imply that each three-way interaction is different at the different levels of the fourth factor. For example, it would mean that the $A \times B \times C$ interaction is not the same at every level of D. As in two-way and three-way designs, there are other equivalent statements of this interaction as well. Here there are three other equivalent statements: $A \times B \times D$ is not the same at every level of C; $A \times C \times D$ is not the same at every level of B; $B \times C \times D$ is not the same at every level of A.

The same logic applies to a five-way interaction, a six-way interaction, or in fact to a n-way interaction, regardless of the value of n. However, a point comes when it is not terribly informative to say that the $A \times B \times C \times D$ interaction is not the same at every level of E. For this reason (and because of sample-size requirements), designs with many factors are uncommon in the behavioral sciences. Nevertheless, it is useful to know that the logic we have developed here generalizes to higher-order designs.

Two other pieces of information are useful when working with higher-order factorial designs. First, there is a simple formula for the total number of omnibus effects in any factorial design. By "omnibus effects," we mean main effects and interactions, but not such effects as simple effects or cell mean comparisons. Specifically, in a completely crossed factorial design (i.e., no missing cells) with F factors,

T A B L E **8. 21** Number of Effects of Each Order and Total Number of Omnibus Effects in a Completely Crossed Factorial Design

| Number of Factors | Main Effects | Two-Way Interactions | Number of | | | Total of Omnibus Effects |
			Three-Way Interactions	Four-Way Interactions	Five-Way Interactions	
2	2	1	—	—	—	3
3	3	3	1	—	—	7
4	4	6	4	1	—	15
5	5	10	10	5	1	31

the number of effects equals $2^F - 1$. For example, suppose that we have a two-way design, so that $F = 2$. Then the number of effects according to the formula is $2^2 - 1$; 2 raised to the second power is 4, and 4 minus 1 is 3, so there are three omnibus effects. Indeed, this is correct because the omnibus effects are A, B, and A × B. As a second example, suppose that we have a three-way design. Then the formula tells us that the number of omnibus effects is seven, which agrees with our finding earlier in the chapter (see Table 8.8).

Second, there is a formula for the number of effects of each "order" as well. Recall that main effects are of order zero, two-way interactions are of order one, and so forth. In a completely crossed factorial design with F factors, the number of effects of order R is given by

$$\frac{F!}{(R + 1)!(F - R - 1)!} \tag{10}$$

where the exclamation sign means factorial. To see how the formula works, consider a three-way design, so $F = 3$. We can find the number of main effects by substituting $F = 3$ and $R = 0$ into Equation 10, yielding

$$\frac{3!}{(0 + 1)!(3 - 0 - 1)!}$$

which equals 6/(1)(2), or 3. Indeed, we already knew that there are three main effects (i.e., effects of order zero) in a three-way design. Similarly, substituting $F = 3$ and $R = 1$ into Equation 10 also produces a value of 3, because there are three two-way interactions in a three-factor design. Finally, substituting $F = 3$ and $R = 2$ into Equation 10 produces a value of 1 because there is only one three-way interaction in a three-factor design. Table 8.21 provides additional examples of these two formulas for different values of F, that is, for different numbers of factors.

EXERCISES

1. True or False: A statistically significant three-way A × B × C interaction implies that none of the two-way interactions can be interpreted unambiguously.

2. True or False: Main effects in a three-factor design can be interpreted unambiguously even if there is a statistically significant three-way interaction as long as none of the two-way interactions are significant.

*3. Consider the hypothetical population cell means shown in Table 8.1. Assuming equal n, find the marginal mean for the drug-present condition. Also find the corresponding marginal mean for the drug-absent condition. Is there a drug main effect in the population?

4. Consider the hypothetical population cell means shown in Table 8.1. Assuming equal n, find the values of the marginal means to be compared to ascertain whether there is a main effect of diet. Is there a diet main effect in the population?

5. Consider the hypothetical population means shown in Table 8.1 for a $2 \times 2 \times 2$ design. Table 8.5 shows these population means for drug and biofeedback combinations, separately by diet. Similarly, Table 8.6 shows these same means for drug and diet combinations, separately by levels of biofeedback.
   a. Construct a table of these means for biofeedback and diet combinations, separately by drug.
   b. Does the table you constructed in part a demonstrate a three-way interaction in the population? How can you tell?
   c. Is the two-way biofeedback by diet interaction the same when the drug is present as when it is absent? Which effect addresses this question?

6. Under what conditions can the B main effect in a three-way $A \times B \times C$ design be interpreted unambiguously?

7. Figure 8.3 shows one way to plot the cell means of Table 8.13. However, there are five additional ways these data could be displayed because we could have separate plots for any of the three factors, and then either of the two remaining factors could be plotted on the x-axis. For example, we might choose to create one plot for the biofeedback-present condition and a second plot when biofeedback is absent. Further, we might choose to place level of diet on the x-axis.
   a. Draw this plot for the cell means shown in Table 8.13.
   b. What features of the data are highlighted more clearly by the plot in part a than by the plot in Figure 8.3?
   c. What features of the data are highlighted more clearly by the plot in Figure 8.3 than by the plot in part a?

*8. In a $2 \times 2 \times 2$ design, a contrast using the following coefficients is applied to the four cells at C_1, that is, at level 1 of factor C:

$$\begin{array}{cccc} A_1B_1 & A_1B_2 & A_2B_1 & A_2B_2 \\ \hline 1 & -1 & -1 & 1 \end{array}$$

The estimated value of ψ at C_1 is -8. The same coefficients applied to the four cell means at C_2 yields an estimated value of ψ at C_2 of $+8$. From this, which of the following is (or are) true?
   a. A contrast assessing the three-way interaction would have an estimated value of zero.
   b. There is some evidence of an AB interaction overall.
   c. There is some evidence of an ABC interaction.
   d. Tests of the simple two-way interactions of A and B at the two levels of C would be significant.

9. Consider the evidence for main effects and interactions indicated by the cell means shown in the plots and duplicated in the tables below. Assume equal n.

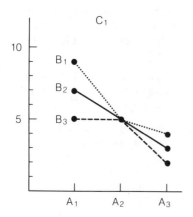 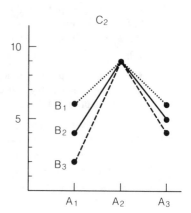

The matrices of cell means plotted above are as follows:

	C_1				C_2		
	A_1	A_2	A_3		A_1	A_2	A_3
B_1	9	5	4	B_1	6	9	6
B_2	7	5	3	B_2	4	9	5
B_3	5	5	2	B_3	2	9	4

a. For which of the effects listed below would the sum of squares be nonzero? In other words, there is some evidence present for which of the following effects?

    (1) A   (5) AC
    (2) B   (6) BC
    (3) C   (7) ABC
    (4) AB

b. Verbally describe any interactions you believe are present.

*10. Below are the cell means in a three-way factorial design. Assume that there are 10 subjects per cell and that $SS_W = 86{,}400$.

	C_1				C_2		
	B_1	B_2	B_3		B_1	B_2	B_3
A_1	45	55	65	A_1	40	40	70
A_2	55	75	65	A_2	20	30	40

a. Estimate the effect parameters for the main effects of factors A and B.
b. Perform tests of the main effects of factors A and B.

c. Plot the cell means shown above. Is there evidence for a three-way interaction in these data? Support your answer either with a verbal explanation or with numerical evidence.

*11. According to the text, there are three equivalent interpretations of a three-way interaction: (1) the A × B interaction varies as a function of C, (2) the A × C interaction varies as a function of B, and (3) the B × C interaction varies as a function of A. This exercise investigates why these three statements are identical. For simplicity, we restrict ourselves to a 2 × 2 × 2 design.

a. Write the coefficients for a contrast of the eight cell means that would compare A × B at C_1 to A × B at C_2. (HINT: The A × B at C_1 subeffect can be represented as a contrast of four cell means. Let's call this contrast ψ_{c1}. Similarly, the A × B at C_2 subeffect compares four other cell means and can be written as ψ_{c2}. Then the contrast comparing A × B at C_1 to A × B at C_2 is literally given by $\psi_{c1} - \psi_{c2}$, the difference between the contrasts for the subeffects.)

b. Write the coefficients for a contrast of the eight cell means that would compare A × C at B_1 to A × C at B_2.

c. Write the coefficients for a contrast of the eight cell means that would compare B × C at A_1 to B × C at A_2.

d. How do the contrast coefficients of parts a–c relate to each other? What does this imply about the three equivalent interpretations of a three-way interaction?

*12. A three-factor, between-subjects design, having two levels of factor A, three levels of factor B, and two levels of factor C, has been conceptualized as a one-way design with 12 groups. Assume that you want to use the "special contrasts" option in SPSS-X MANOVA to assess the following effects; A, B, C, AB, AC, BC, ABC. Assume that you enter the 12 groups in such a way that the first 6 groups are at level 1 of A, the last 6 are at level of 2 of A; within each of these sets of groups the first 2 are at level 2 of B, the next 2 at level 2 of B and the last 2 at level 3 of B; and, any two successive groups are at different levels of C. The first few lines of contrast coefficients are shown below with labels attached to indicate the effects to which they correspond:

												Effect
1	1	1	1	1	1	1	1	1	1	1	1/	
1	1	1	1	1	1	−1	−1	−1	−1	−1	−1/	A
1	1	0	0	−1	−1	1	1	0	0	−1	−1/	B
0	0	1	1	−1	−1	0	0	1	1	−1	−1/	
1	−1	1	−1	1	−1	1	−1	1	−1	1	−1/	C

a. Add the appropriate additional contrasts to the above that will allow all the desired effects to be tested. Indicate, for each contrast or set of contrasts, the label of the corresponding effect.

b. After completing your analysis you find that you have a significant three-way interaction. You are interested in assessing the simple AB interactions.
  (1) What contrasts would allow you to test AB at C_1 and AB at C_2?
  (2) What rows of the original set of contrasts in part a would these new contrasts replace?

13. Which effect(s) in a four-way A × B × C × D nonorthogonal design will have the same value for Type II sum of squares as for Type III sum of squares? Why?

14. Social psychologists during the 1970s and 1980s investigated the generality of the "overjustification effect," which refers to the effect of subjects' receiving greater extrinsic rewards than are justified by their level of effort or performance. The following description is modeled after one of the experiments reported by Crano, W. D., Gorenflo, D. W., and Shackelford, S. L. (1988) "Overjustification, assumed consensus, and attitude change: Further investigation of the incentive-aroused ambivalence hypothesis." *Journal of Personality and Social Psychology, 55,* 12–22. The focus of this study concerns students' attitudes toward a recent tuition increase at their university. Through a clever procedure, students were asked to read a prepared speech arguing against the increase but were led to believe that this request was unrelated to the study for which they had been recruited. Subjects were randomly assigned to a payment condition. Half of the subjects received a $5 payment, while the other half were not paid. After reading their speech, half of the subjects in each payment condition were asked to read a speech that presented arguments in favor of the increase; the other half of subjects received no such countercommunication. The dependent variable to be considered here is a general measure of attitude toward the tuition increase. Higher scores represent more positive attitudes. Finally, a third factor in the design was a subject's initial attitude toward the increase (neutral, negative, very negative) prior to participating in the study. Consider the following hypothetical (but realistic) cell means:

Countercommunication Present					
$5 Payment			$0 Payment		
Neutral	*Negative*	*Very Negative*	*Neutral*	*Negative*	*Very Negative*
33.1	31.6	29.3	25.1	23.3	21.1

Countercommunication Absent					
$5 Payment			$0 Payment		
Neutral	*Negative*	*Very Negative*	*Neutral*	*Negative*	*Very Negative*
30.7	29.3	26.9	26.8	25.3	23.3

Assume that there were 10 subjects per cell and that $MS_w = 23.3$.
  a. Test the statistical significance of the main effects, two-way interactions, and three-way interaction.
  b. Can the main effect of payment be interpreted unambiguously? If not, perform the relevant simple effects tests of payment.
  c. Can the main effect of countercommunication be interpreted unambiguously? If not, perform the relevant simple effects tests of countercommunication.

15. In the exercises for Chapters 6 and 7, we considered a study investigating how parent–infant play changes as infants grow older. This exercise uses the same data, but adds the parent's gender as a third factor. Specifically, mothers of four girls and of four boys at each of three ages (7, 10, and 13 months) were videotaped during toy-play interactions with their infants. An equal number of fathers from different families were also observed. The dependent variable to be considered here was the proportion

of time parents encouraged pretend play in their children. Suppose the following hypothetical data were obtained:

Mothers					
Girls			Boys		
7-Month-Olds	10-Month-Olds	13-Month-Olds	7-Month-Olds	10-Month-Olds	13-Month-Olds
.01	.09	.18	.02	.11	.45
.09	.05	.43	.02	.19	.20
.05	.15	.24	.13	.12	.49
.06	.11	.40	.06	.04	.19

Fathers					
Girls			Boys		
7-Month-Olds	10-Month-Olds	13-Month-Olds	7-Month-Olds	10-Month-Olds	13-Month-Olds
.02	.15	.09	.05	.14	.02
.01	.11	.03	.01	.21	.19
.07	.22	.18	.04	.06	.15
.04	.05	.12	.03	.12	.07

a. Test the statistical significance of the three main effects, the three two-way interactions, and the three-way interaction.
b. Plot the cell means in a manner similar to that shown in Figure 8.3. Specifically, draw one plot for girls and a second plot for boys. Place "Age" on the x-axis for each plot.
c. What effects appear to be present in your plots? Is the visual impression consistent with the results of the significance tests from part a?
d. What additional tests involving the factor of the child's sex should be performed, based on your results from part a? (HINT: You may want to consult Figure 8.2.)
e. According to the flowchart shown in Figure 8.2, what additional tests might be performed here of effects involving the parent's gender and the child's age?
f. Perform any and all appropriate tests of simple effects of parent's gender within levels of the child's age.
g. Perform any and all appropriate tests of simple effects of the child's age separately for mothers and fathers.
h. Test the linear trend of child's age, separately for mothers and fathers.
i. Summarize the nature of your findings for these data.

16. During the 1980s social psychologists renewed their investigation of how subjects are influenced by persuasive information. The following study is modeled after an experiment reported by DeBono, K. G., and Harnish, R. J. (1988) "Source expertise, source attractiveness, and the processing of persuasive information: A functional approach." *Journal of Personality and Social Psychology, 55*, 541–546. Subjects listened to a tape-recorded speech criticizing a university calendar picturing members of the pom-pom squad. All subjects listened to the same speaker, but subjects were randomly

assigned either to an expert condition, where they were led to believe that the speaker was a nationally known research psychologist, or to an attractive source condition, where they believed that the speaker was a leader in student government. Within each source condition, subjects were randomly assigned to hear one of two versions of the tape, one of which presented strong arguments and the other of which presented weak arguments. The dependent variable was a 7-point Likert scale item (1 = worthless, 7 = valuable) measuring how valuable they thought the calendar was. Finally, subjects were classified as either high or low self-monitoring based on their responses to the Self-Monitoring Scale. Consider the following hypothetical data:

High Self-Monitors

Strong Argument		Weak Argument	
Expert Source	Attractive Source	Expert Source	Attractive Source
4	4	3	5
3	4	5	5
4	2	3	7
5	3	2	5
2	5	6	6
5	3	4	4
4	2	4	3
6	3	3	5
3	4	5	6
4	3	3	7
5	2	2	7
4	4	3	6

Low Self-Monitors

Strong Argument		Weak Argument	
Expert Source	Attractive Source	Expert Source	Attractive Source
3	5	5	6
5	4	6	4
5	3	4	4
4	2	7	2
3	4	6	4
2	6	7	5
1	2	5	4
5	4	6	3
3	4	4	4
4	3	6	2
3	4	7	3
4	3	5	4

a. Test the statistical significance of the main effects, the two-way interactions, and the three-way interaction.

b. Is the effect of argument strength (i.e., weak versus strong) the same when it comes from an expert as from an attractive source?

c. Answer part b for high self-monitoring subjects only.

d. Answer part b for low self-monitoring subjects only.

e. How can you reconcile the answers you gave in parts c and d with your answer to part b?

f. Are high self-monitoring subjects influenced by argument strength (weak versus strong) if the argument comes from an attractive source?

g. Are high self-monitoring subjects influenced by argument strength if the argument comes from an expert source?

h. Are low self-monitoring subjects influenced by argument strength if the argument comes from an attractive source?

i. Are low self-monitoring subjects influenced by argument strength if the argument comes from an expert source?

j. Which of the following statements provides the most accurate description of the effect of argument strength for these data:

(1) Argument strength has an effect only if it is believed to come from an expert source.

(2) Argument strength has an effect only on high self-monitoring subjects who believe the source is an expert.

(3) Argument strength has an effect only on low self-monitoring subjects who believe the source is an expert or on high self-monitoring subjects who believe the source is attractive.

(4) Argument strength has an effect only on low self-monitoring subjects who believe the source is an expert.

17. A counseling psychologist is interested in comparing three types of therapy for modifying snake phobia. However, she does not believe that one type is necessarily best for everyone; instead, the best type may depend upon degree (i.e., severity) of phobia. Undergraduate students enrolled in an introductory psychology course are given the Fear Schedule Survey (FSS) to screen out subjects showing no fear of snakes. Those displaying some degree of phobia are classified as either mildly or severely phobic on the basis of the FSS. One-third of females and one-third of males within each level of severity are then randomly assigned to a treatment condition: either systematic desensitization, implosive therapy, or insight therapy. The following data are obtained, using the Behavioral Avoidance Test (higher scores indicate less phobia):

	Desensitization			Implosion			Insight		
	Mild	*Moderate*	*Severe*	*Mild*	*Moderate*	*Severe*	*Mild*	*Moderate*	*Severe*
Females	10	12	10	15	12	6	13	11	10
	12	9	11	12	10	7	9	7	6
	13	10	9	14	11	5	11	8	8
Males	16	11	12	17	14	10	16	10	11
	14	15	11	18	13	9	12	12	10
	17	13	13	16	12	11	14	14	9

Your task is to analyze these data, to answer any questions you believe would be of theoretical interest. Don't feel compelled to perform an analysis just because it would be possible statistically. Longer is not necessarily better! On the other hand, you probably will not want to stop after testing only main effects and the interaction.

You should describe your findings in a manner consistent with the results section of an APA journal. If it seems appropriate, you may want to briefly justify your choice of α level, error term, and so on, but do not let this discussion overshadow what the results mean. Also, you may not want to focus exclusively on significance tests—descriptive statistics may also be useful.

9   Designs with Concomitant Variables: ANCOVA and Blocking

353

THE PRIMARY GOAL OF the models approach to data analysis is to develop a model that is an adequate representation of the data. Up to now, we have approached this task using as explanatory or predictor variables only those variables that denote group membership. In most situations, such group-membership variables account for a relatively small proportion of the total variance in the dependent variable. The between-group sum of squares almost certainly will be less than half of the total sum of squares and frequently will be much smaller than the within-group sum of squares. This should not be surprising. Although the more extreme early behaviorists may have hoped that they could explain all the variance in behavior by their experimental manipulations, most researchers in the behavioral sciences today expect that preexisting differences among subjects will be at least as important a predictor of their scores on the dependent variable as any treatment variable. This chapter considers how best to make use of information you might obtain about the individual differences among subjects that are present at the beginning of your study.

These preexisting differences typically are not the principal focus of your investigation but might be information collected on your subjects besides the measures of specific interest to you. Hence, these variables might be labeled *concomitant variables*: ones that come along with the more central parts of the study. Alternatively, they may be called *covariates* because they typically are expected to covary, or correlate, with the dependent variable.

A correlation would most obviously be expected in the case where the concomitant variable represents the same conceptual measure as the dependent variable. For example, in a study of the effects of differing instructions on the amount of private speech a young child produces, one might measure the private speech each child produces before and after the experimental manipulation. There is great variation in how much different children talk to themselves; knowing how much each child tends to do this before the manipulation will likely correlate more highly with the postmeasure than will the treatment-group variables. Because the sensitivity of your statistical tests is directly dependent on the size of the explained variance for your study, to incorporate this continuous variable into your model is clearly desirable. As we tried to anticipate in our discussion in Chapter 3 and its extension on multiple regression, the X variables used as predictors in linear models can be either continuous or discrete variables. We will indicate the form of a model with both discrete and continuous variables shortly, but first some preliminary points must be made.

Although it is perhaps easiest to think of the concomitant variable as involving the same instrument or as being the same conceptual measure as the dependent variable, it is not necessary to do so. One could predict a child's private speech after instructions by his or her private speech before instructions, but one might also use a quite different variable such as chronological age or mental age as the concomitant variable. Variables that are on the same scale or expressed in the same units, for example, verbal IQ and performance IQ, are said to be *commensurate*. If one is to compute differences between measures, as is done in a matched-pairs *t* test, it is necessary that the variables be commensurate[1]. However, for most of the analyses considered in this chapter, the concomitant and the dependent variables are not required to be commensurate.

A second preliminary point concerns the need to distinguish between using the concomitant variable in the design of the study as opposed to the analysis. It is possible to use a concomitant variable in the design of the study but not in the analysis, in the analysis but not in the design, or in both the analysis and the design, though not all these options are necessarily desirable. The concomitant variable is used in the design of the study if it is used in the assignment of subjects to groups. The concomitant variable is used in the analysis if it is represented in the models employed in analyzing the data. The goal in part, then, may be to equate the groups either experimentally or statistically. To accomplish this "experimentally," one can form the treatment groups in such a way that they are "matched" on the concomitant variable, as long as the concomitant variable scores are available prior to the formation of the treatment groups. The sense in which the groups are matched and the specifics of how the matching can be carried out are described later in the section on blocking. Statistical equating of groups is accomplished by allowing for variation in the concomitant variable both within and between groups in analyzing data. Both experimental and statistical means of controlling for ancillary variables yield advantages.

A related point to the distinction between using the concomitant variable in design as opposed to analysis is the issue of whether the concomitant variable is to be treated as a continuous variable. When the concomitant variable is a continuous variable used to form the groups for the design, it is common practice to ignore at least some of the continuous information in the concomitant variable when the time comes to analyze the data. As we will argue subsequently in the chapter, to do so is to throw away information. Alternatively, the concomitant variable can be viewed as a continuous variable throughout. In this situation, the concomitant variable is viewed as varying along with the dependent variable. Thus, the concomitant variable would then be called a covariate, and the analysis method that takes into account the relationship between the covariate and the dependent variable is referred to as *analysis of covariance* (ANCOVA). In most ANCOVA studies, the covariate is not considered at the time of forming groups, although as we will see, there could be some advantages in doing so. Rather, ANCOVA is typically viewed as a method of analysis that statistically adjusts for differences on the concomitant variable by including it as a continuous predictor variable in the analysis.

In sum, ANCOVA, like ANOVA, refers to a comparison of models that are special cases of the general linear model. In one sense, the only new wrinkle in ANCOVA is that one of the predictors is a continuous variable. The conceptual problem of interpreting the meaning of an ANCOVA can be difficult, however, particularly in the case where one has not randomly assigned subjects to groups. Perhaps because of the logical difficulties of statistical adjustment, some have preferred to form groups or blocks of subjects that are relatively similar with respect to the covariate. Thus, the covariate in such a blocked design is transformed into an additional factor with discrete levels that is crossed with any other factors included in the design.

This chapter considers the approaches to handling concomitant variables that are represented by both ANCOVA and blocking. We begin with a consideration of analysis methods that treat the concomitant variable as a continuous variable. The primary data-analysis method of ANCOVA is compared with other related approaches of the analysis of change scores and the analysis of residuals. Next, we consider methods of analyzing blocked designs and include a discussion of issues that arise when the blocking is carried out after, rather than before, the study is run. Finally, we conclude with a comparison of ANCOVA and blocking approaches.

ANCOVA

The Logic of ANCOVA

The designs in which ANCOVA could be used arise with great regularity in psychological research. The minimal requirements, as far as the design is concerned, are that there be two or more groups and that you have information on some characteristic of your subjects besides the dependent variable. (There are a number of statistical assumptions that are required, of course, for the statistical tests to be valid; we will not concern ourselves with those for the moment.)

The logic of ANCOVA is to address the conditional question of Would the groups have been different on the postmeasure if they had been equivalent on the covariate? Thus, one wants to allow for the covariate in essentially the same way that the effects of confounded factors are allowed for in nonorthogonal ANOVA. Put differently, one wants to remove from the unexplained variability and from the treatment effect any variability that is associated with variability in the covariate.

Thus, including a covariate in your model affects your analysis in two ways. First, the within-group variability will be reduced by an amount dependent on the strength of the relationship between the dependent variable and the covariate. This reduction is often substantial, particularly when the covariate represents an earlier administration of the same instrument as the dependent variable. In fact, for the sum of squares associated with the covariate (sometimes referred to as the sum of squares regression) to be much larger than the sum of squares associated with the treatment effect is not unusual. Thus, the primary impact of entering the covariate into your model is typically a substantial reduction in the unexplained variance and hence a corresponding increase in the power of your analysis to detect treatment effects.

The second possible effect of including a covariate is the adjustment of the estimated magnitude of the treatment effect itself. How large this adjustment will be also can depend on how strongly related the dependent variable and the covariate are, but more important, the adjustment is affected by how different the experimental groups are on the covariate. If the observed group means on the covariate were all identical, there would be no effect of including a covariate in the model on the magnitude of the estimated treatment effect. In studies where subjects are randomly assigned to groups, there is reason to expect the group means on the covariate to be similar if not virtually identical; thus, the adjustment in the estimated magnitude of the treatment effect will also be correspondingly small. However, in nonrandomized studies or in studies using intact groups such as ethnic or cultural groups, the adjustment in the estimated treatment effect can be substantial. In fact, under certain conditions, which we illustrate shortly, the adjustment can be so dramatic that an effect that would be judged as a significant advantage of group A over group B by an ANOVA might be evaluated as a significant advantage of group B over group A by ANCOVA. This ability to compensate to some extent for preexisting differences among groups is why ANCOVA is often recommended as a means of addressing the threats to the internal validity that arise in studies with selection differences between groups (e.g., Cook & Campbell, 1979, Chapter 4). Nonetheless, using ANCOVA to equate groups should *not* be viewed as a substitute for randomization. Even if all the statistical assumptions made by ANCOVA were perfectly met, the equating accomplished by ANCOVA for intact groups is not in the same league as random assignment. When subjects are randomly assigned to groups, you are assured that in the long run—that is, over repeated applications of a study carried out in the same fashion—there will be no differences between the groups at the start of your study on *any* dimension. ANCOVA, at best, equates the groups on the dimension(s) represented by the particular covariate(s) included in the analysis. There is no assurance that the particular variables chosen represent all, or even the more important, dimensions along which the groups differ. Further, matching groups on one dimension might mean that you are creating differences along a second dimension.

For example, suppose that you want to look at differences between inner-city and suburban school children in their ability to use a particular cognitive strategy in their studying. You might think that it was important to control for potential differences in the IQs of the children so that you would be dealing with two groups of children at approximately the same mental level. This equating of the groups on IQ could be accomplished by forming your groups in such a way that each child in the suburban group would be matched with a child in the inner-city group having approximately the same IQ. As an alternative to such matching, the IQs of children could simply be included as a predictor in your model and an ANCOVA carried out. In either case, the logic of equating the groups is the same. The attempt is to arrive at a "fairer" comparison of inner-city and suburban children by using groups with equal IQs. However, as Meehl (1970a) points out, such systematic matching may result in systematic mismatching. Perhaps, inner-city children in general may have lower IQs but *equal* motivation to achieve when compared with suburban children; further, IQ and achievement motivation may be positively correlated within each group. By selecting samples of children having a mean IQ that is higher than average for inner-city children but lower than average for suburban children, one might have inadvertently assured that the subpopulations for which your groups represent random samples differ considerably in achievement motivation. That is, inner-city children with above-average IQs may represent a subpopulation of inner-city children who also have high motivation to achieve; conversely, your sample of suburban children who have IQs that are lower than that of suburban children in general may represent a subpopulation of low achievement–motivation suburbanites. The same charge could be leveled at an analysis that covaried IQ even though the groups represented random samples from the entire populations of inner-city and suburban children. The ANCOVA test for treatment effects can be thought of as an evaluation of the difference between the performance of inner-city and suburban children having IQs that are intermediate between the mean IQs for the two groups. Either method of controlling for IQ, matching or ANCOVA, can result in a comparison of subpopulations that differ from the intact populations in important ways that are relevant to performance on the experimental task.

In sum, although ANCOVA can be used in an effort to make more nearly comparable intact groups that differ in known ways, always remember that the adjustment may well introduce or exaggerate differences along some dimensions while it reduces the differences along other dimensions. The oft-quoted conclusion of Frederic Lord (1967) regarding this quandary bears repeating:

> With the data usually available for such studies, there is simply no logical or statistical procedure that can be counted on to make proper allowances for uncontrolled preexisting differences between groups. (p. 307)

On the other hand, in randomized studies there is virtually no other design and analysis alternative to ANCOVA that can be as widely and easily used to bring about a legitimate increase in the power of your tests.

Linear Models for ANCOVA

Recall that in Chapter 3 when we first introduced linear models, we indicated the general form of a linear model both verbally and using symbols. Using words, the structure of a linear model is

$$
\begin{array}{lcl}
\text{observed value} & & \text{sum of effects} \quad\quad \text{sum of effects}\\
\text{on dependent} & = & \text{of allowed-for} \; + \; \text{of other}\\
\text{variable} & & \text{factors} \quad\quad\quad\quad\; \text{factors}
\end{array}
$$

In symbols, we can say the same thing as follows:

$$ Y_i = \beta_0 X_{0_i} + \beta_1 X_{1_i} + \beta_2 X_{2_i} + \beta_3 X_{3_i} + \cdots + \beta_p X_{p_i} + \varepsilon_i $$

where Y_i is the score of individual i on the dependent variable, the βs are unknown parameters, and the X terms represent the factors being used to predict performance. Up to now, the X variables have always been either dummy variables indicating group membership or the coefficients for contrasts among selected groups. Thus, all our analyses have involved only discrete predictor variables.

One of the happy advantages of the model-comparison approach is that ANCOVA can be conceptualized as simply a change in form of one of the predictor variables from a discrete to a continuous variable. Older approaches to psychological statistics, which were built around schemes of hand calculations appropriate for desk calculators, frequently encountered real difficulty in trying to present

ANCOVA clearly because the computational formulas for ANCOVA are rather messy and hard to code in intuitively meaningful ways. It was easy for the student to miss the logic of ANCOVA by focusing on the calculations involved in following the computational formulas. In contrast, our approach, as usual, emphasizes the model comparison involved in ANCOVA.

To make things concrete, consider the following pre-post design. Assume that you are conducting a training program designed to assist people in losing weight. You solicit a group of volunteers, collect an initial weight measurement for each individual, and randomly assign subjects to either a treatment condition or a waiting-list control. At the end of the training program for the treatment group, you get another weight measurement for each subject. The research question of interest is whether the weight of the subjects receiving the treatment is lower when completing the treatment than the weight of subjects who also volunteered for the program but have not yet received it.

Clearly, in this situation, we would expect that within each group a person's initial weight would be positively correlated with his or her final weight. Thus, the test of the treatment effect could be made more sensitive by including the initial weight in the model.

The test of primary interest in ANCOVA is this test of the treatment effect. In a one-way design, the ANCOVA test of the treatment effect involves the comparison of the following models:

$$\text{Full:} \qquad Y_{ij} = \mu + \alpha_j + \beta X_{ij} + \varepsilon_{ij} \qquad\qquad (1)$$

$$\text{Restricted:} \qquad Y_{ij} = \mu + \beta X_{ij} + \varepsilon_{ij} \qquad\qquad (2)$$

where Y_{ij} is the score of the ith individual in the jth group on the dependent variable, μ is a "grand mean" parameter (but, as we will see, should be conceived as an intercept for a regression line, rather than an estimate of the mean of the Y scores), β is a population regression coefficient, X_{ij} is the score of the ith subject in the jth group on the concomitant variable,[2] and ε_{ij} is the error term for the same subject. As in the general case of one-way ANOVA, these models can be applied to any number of groups and to varying numbers of subjects per group; that is, $j = 1, 2, 3, \ldots, a$ and $i = 1, 2, 3, \ldots, n_j$. We will present the formulas as we proceed for this general case but will illustrate them using examples of the simplest case of two groups. In terms of the concrete example, X would be the individual's initial weight, Y would be final weight, and β would be directly related to the correlation between these two weights.

Parameter Estimates. We once again want to choose the estimates for the parameters of our models in such a way that the fit to the data is as close as possible. ANCOVA models have a major advantage over ANOVA models in attempting to fit the data in that ANCOVA models have the capability of making a different prediction for each individual subject rather than having to make the same prediction for all individuals within a group. This is the case because in ANCOVA the predictions are a function of the score on the covariate X_{ij}, which is uniquely determined for each individual.

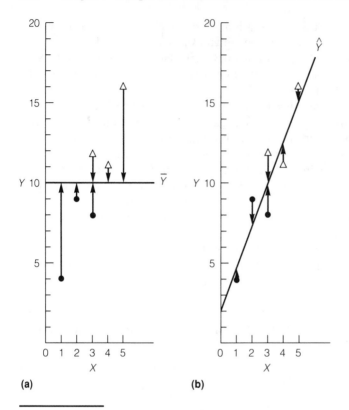

F I G U R E 9. 1   Comparison of errors in (a) ANOVA and (b) ANCOVA restricted models.

Figure 9.1 illustrates this advantage in minimizing errors in ANCOVA. Figure 9.1(a) is relevant to the restricted model for ANOVA, and Figure 9.1(b) is relevant to the restricted model for an ANCOVA of the same data. The data represented in each panel are the scores for six subjects.[3] (The numerical values are given in Table 9.1.) These subjects are divided into two groups of three subjects each, but for the moment we will ignore group membership. This corresponds to the way the data would be represented by the restricted models because they would not include a group-membership parameter.

The restricted model for a two-group ANOVA would make the same prediction for all subjects, namely, the grand mean. Thus, the predictions in this model are illustrated by a flat line at $\overline{Y}$, and the errors of prediction are the vertical distances of the data points from this flat line. Rather than picturing the data in a vertical column for each group, the data points are scattered horizontally across the graph with the location being determined by both the X and Y value. However, information on any covariate is ignored by the ANOVA models.

In ANCOVA, in both the restricted and the full models, the predictions are a function of the individuals' X scores. Thus, differential predictions are made for each X value, and in the current example, the predictions of the restricted model

TABLE **9.1** Data for
Comparison of ANOVA and
ANCOVA

Subject	Group	X	Y
1	1	1	4
2	1	2	9
3	1	3	8
4	2	3	12
5	2	4	11
6	2	5	16

would fall along the sloped line shown in Figure 9.1(b). Obviously, the magnitude of the errors, represented again by the length of the vertical lines from the data points to the prediction line, is much less in the ANCOVA case than in the ANOVA situation.

The price paid statistically for this increase in predictive accuracy is a relatively small one, namely, a degree of freedom is used to estimate the parameter indicating how steeply sloped the prediction line is. We now move to a consideration of how to estimate this parameter and the other parameters of our ANCOVA models.

Beginning with the ANCOVA restricted model,

$$\text{Restricted:} \qquad Y_{ij} = \mu + \beta X_{ij} + \varepsilon_{ij} \qquad (2, \text{repeated})$$

we must arrive at estimates for μ and β, which for the moment we designate $\hat{\mu}$ and $\hat{\beta}$. Thus, our prediction equation would be

$$\hat{Y}_{ij} = \hat{\mu} + \hat{\beta} X_{ij} \qquad (3)$$

$\hat{\mu}$ is then the value we would predict for Y when $X_{ij} = 0$, which, as can be seen in Figure 9.1(b), is where the line of predictions intersects the Y-axis. In ANCOVA $\hat{\mu}$ is not in general an estimate of the grand mean of the Y scores but is the Y intercept of a regression line. β, on the other hand, indicates how many units change in predicted Y scores there should be for each unit change in X. In the simple situation here, once the data are represented in a scatterplot, as in Figure 9.1(b), it is possible to arrive at quite reasonable estimates by inspection. For example, looking at the figure we see that as X increases 4 units, from 1 to 5, Y increases from 4 to 16, or 12 units. Thus, a line with such a slope going through the center of the scatterplot would appear to intersect the Y-axis at a Y value of 1 or 2. Although in realistic data-analysis situations you will likely have a computer doing calculations, it is a very good idea to plot your data, or at least a sample of it if the number of cases is large, to assure that the computer-generated parameter values make sense in light of what your inspection of the data tells you should be reasonable. Many graduate students have been embarrassed by writing theses based on computer-generated summary statistics, only later to learn that the results were nonsensical. Frequent pitfalls include giving the computer incorrect values as input, telling it to look in the wrong place for a particular variable, or, having entered everything correctly, reading off the wrong number from a terminal or printout. Although using a machine that does arithmetic perfectly would seem a foolproof method of analyzing data, the capacity of the human to foul up things is frequently astounding. Try to offset this to some extent by always plotting the raw data, preferably by hand, for any research study. Especially as the design or analysis becomes more complicated, such as when trying to interpret adjusted means in ANCOVA, a simple graph can prove invaluable in understanding why your computer output must be wrong, or preferably, why it does make perfect sense. In the explanations of ANCOVA that follow, we make extensive use of plots so that you can see what is happening at each step in the analysis.

The statistical criterion used to arrive at "optimal" estimates of the parameters in ANCOVA is, again, the least-squares criterion. In the restricted model, this means choosing the values of $\hat{\mu}$ and $\hat{\beta}$ in such a way that we minimize the sum of squared errors of our predictions:

$$E_R = \sum_j \sum_i e_{ij}^2 = \sum_j \sum_i (Y_{ij} - \hat{Y}_{ij})^2 = \sum_j \sum_i (Y_{ij} - \hat{\mu} - \hat{\beta} X_{ij})^2 \qquad (4)$$

Clearly E_R will change as a function of what we choose $\hat{\mu}$ and $\hat{\beta}$ to be, with the rate of change in E_R being indicated by what in calculus is called the derivative of the function with respect to $\hat{\mu}$ or $\hat{\beta}$. The only point at which the rate of change of this function will be zero is at its minimal value. Thus, the solution from calculus to this least-squares problem is to set equal to zero the derivatives of the last expression on the right above, and solve for $\hat{\mu}$ and $\hat{\beta}$. Taking derivatives with respect to $\hat{\mu}$ and $\hat{\beta}$ results in the following expressions, respectively, each of which is set equal to zero:

$$2\sum_j \sum_i (Y_{ij} - \hat{\mu} - \hat{\beta} X_{ij})(-1) = 0 \qquad (5)$$

$$2\sum_j \sum_i (Y_{ij} - \hat{\mu} - \hat{\beta} X_{ij})(-X_{ij}) = 0$$

These are referred to as the *normal equations*. Solving the first for $\hat{\mu}$ readily yields

$$\hat{\mu} = \bar{Y} - \hat{\beta} \bar{X} = a \qquad (6)$$

We might designate this estimate a, as indicated above, the symbol frequently used for the intercept in elementary statistical texts. When we substitute this into the second equation, a little algebraic manipulation yields the least-squares estimate of β:

$$\hat{\beta} = \frac{\sum_j \sum_i (X_{ij} - \bar{X})(Y_{ij} - \bar{Y})}{\sum_j \sum_i (X_{ij} - \bar{X})^2} = b_T \qquad (7)$$

As indicated above, we designate this estimated value b_T, because it is the slope when the total sample is treated as one group.

We can illustrate the use of these results by solving for the slope and intercept for the simple data set we have been examining in Figure 9.1 and Table 9.1. We begin with the formula for the slope because Equation 6 requires that we know the slope in order to compute the intercept. First, look closely at Equation 7 to see if you have encountered at least parts of it in different contexts. Note that the definitional formula that we will be applying has a numerator that is identical to the definitional formula for the correlation coefficient, r:

$$r = \frac{\sum_j \sum_i (X_{ij} - \bar{X})(Y_{ij} - \bar{Y})}{\sqrt{\sum_j \sum_i (X_{ij} - \bar{X})^2 \sum_j \sum_i (Y_{ij} - \bar{Y})^2}} \tag{8}$$

Of course, the correlation coefficient is unitless because the XY units in the numerator are canceled by those in the denominator. The regression coefficient however is in "Y over X" units, which is reasonable because a slope indicates how many units in Y the regression line rises or falls for a one-unit increase in X. Realize, however, this means that a regression coefficient of .1 in one study may indicate a stronger relationship than a regression coefficient of 1000 in another study if different variables are involved.

Returning to our numerical example, we first compute deviations from the mean for both X and Y. Then, the sum of the squared deviations in X is computed for the denominator of the slope formula and the sum of the cross-products of deviations is computed for the numerator, as shown in Table 9.2. Thus, the least-squares estimate of b_T is shown to be 2.6, which is slightly smaller than the value

TABLE 9.2 Calculation of Least-Squares Estimates of Slope and Intercept for the ANCOVA Restricted Model

X	$X - \bar{X}$	Y	$Y - \bar{Y}$	$(X - \bar{X})^2$	$(X - \bar{X})(Y - \bar{Y})$
1	−2	4	−6	4	12
2	−1	9	−1	1	1
3	0	8	−2	0	0
3	0	12	2	0	0
4	1	11	1	1	1
5	2	16	6	4	12
$\sum = 18$		$\sum = 60$		$\sum = 10$	$\sum = 26$
$\bar{X} = 3$		$\bar{Y} = 10$			

Using Equation 7 to compute the slope:

$$b_T = \frac{\sum_j \sum_i (X_{ij} - \bar{X})(Y_{ij} - \bar{Y})}{\sum_j \sum_i (X_{ij} - \bar{X})^2} = \frac{26}{10} = 2.6$$

Using Equation 6 to compute the intercept:

$$a = \bar{Y} - \hat{\beta}\bar{X} = \bar{Y} - b_T\bar{X} = 10 - 2.6(3) = 10 - 7.8 = 2.2$$

The resulting prediction equation:

$$\hat{Y}_{ij} = a + b_T X_{ij} = 2.2 + 2.6 X_{ij}$$

T A B L E 9. 3 Computation of Error Sum
of Squares Associated with the ANCOVA
Restricted Model

X	Y	$\hat{Y}$	$Y - \hat{Y}$	$(Y - \hat{Y})^2$
1	4	4.8	−.8	.64
2	9	7.4	1.6	2.56
3	8	10.0	−2.0	4.00
3	12	10.0	2.0	4.00
4	11	12.6	−1.6	2.56
5	16	15.2	.8	.64
				$\sum = 14.40 = E_R$

Predicted values for the ANCOVA restricted model are
calculated as follows:

$$\hat{Y}_{ij} = 2.2 + 2.6X_{ij}$$
$$\hat{Y}_{11} = 2.2 + 2.6(1) = 2.2 + 2.6 = 4.8$$
$$\hat{Y}_{21} = 2.2 + 2.6(2) = 2.2 + 5.2 = 7.4$$
$$\hat{Y}_{31} = 2.2 + 2.6(3) = 2.2 + 7.8 = 10.0$$
$$\hat{Y}_{12} = 2.2 + 2.6(3) = 2.2 + 7.8 = 10.0$$
$$\hat{Y}_{22} = 2.2 + 2.6(4) = 2.2 + 10.4 = 12.6$$
$$\hat{Y}_{32} = 2.2 + 2.6(5) = 2.2 + 13.0 = 15.2$$

we guessed by looking at the extreme values on X and Y. To obtain the least-squares
estimate of the intercept, we substitute the numerical value we just obtained for the
slope into Equation 6. This is done at the bottom of Table 9.2, where we have used
b_T rather than $\hat{\beta}$ to denote the estimated value of the slope and a rather than $\hat{\mu}$ to
denote the estimated intercept parameter. Thus, the prediction equation corre-
sponding to the ANCOVA restricted model is seen to be

$$\hat{Y}_{ij} = 2.2 + 2.6X_{ij} \tag{9}$$

and we can be certain that these numerical estimates of the slope and intercept
parameters result in a smaller sum of squared errors than any other estimates we
might try. The computation of the error sum of squares for this restricted model is
shown in Table 9.3. Note that the prediction equation given in Equation 9 is in fact
the equation for the regression line shown in Figure 9.1(b). Thus, the error sum of
squares of 14.40 computed in Table 9.3 corresponds to the sum of squared distances
of the observed data points from that line—that is, the sum of the squared lengths
of the arrows in Figure 9.1(b).

    Now let us move to a consideration of the parameters of the ANCOVA full
model:

$$\text{Full:} \qquad Y_{ij} = \mu + \alpha_j + \beta X_{ij} + \varepsilon_{ij} \tag{1, repeated}$$

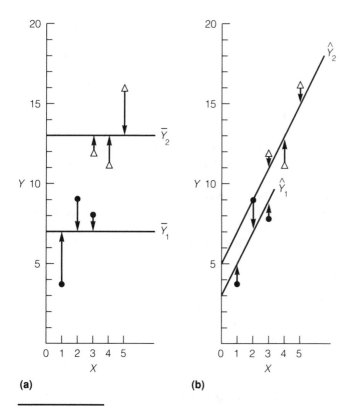

F I G U R E 9. 2   Comparison of errors in (a) ANOVA and (b) ANCOVA full models.

This model, like the restricted model, has a single slope parameter. However, the full model allows for an effect of the treatment variable. We can also use the simple data set of Table 9.1 to illustrate this model and the difference between it and a typical one-way ANOVA model. We assume now that the first three subjects were randomly assigned to treatment 1 and the next three subjects make up the group randomly assigned to treatment 2. The data are plotted in this fashion in Figure 9.2; Figure 9.2(a) indicates the predictions of the ANOVA full model, and Figure 9.2(b) indicates the predictions of the ANCOVA full model.

Looking first at Figure 9.2(a), the predictions of the ANOVA full model are represented by two flat lines, one at the sample mean for each group. The predictions of the ANCOVA full model, on the other hand, vary again as a function of the individual's score on the covariate X. Once again the predictions of the ANCOVA full model are closer to the data than those of the ANOVA model. In terms of the graphs, in ANCOVA one is free to tilt the prediction lines in whatever way necessary to best fit the data (as long as the lines for the two groups remain parallel), whereas in ANOVA the prediction lines must not only be parallel but also flat. Thus, the errors of prediction in the ANCOVA model can be no larger than those in ANOVA, and the ANCOVA errors will be smaller if there is any linear relationship between the covariate and the dependent variable. The magnitude of the ANCOVA errors, of course, are the values with the smallest sum of squares that result when the least-squares estimates of the slope and other parameters are inserted in the following:

$$E_F = \sum_j \sum_i e_{ij}^2 = \sum_j \sum_i (Y_{ij} - \hat{Y}_{ij})^2 = \sum_j \sum_i (Y_{ij} - \hat{\mu} - \hat{\alpha}_j - \hat{\beta} X_{ij})^2 \quad (10)$$

To determine just how steeply to slope the lines to minimize errors, one could view the problem initially as a question of how steep the slope should be in each group separately. In actual practice, we compute a single, pooled estimate of slope directly. However, here we first consider how to compute estimates of the slope separately for each group and how these separate estimates could be pooled to compute a pooled slope. Then, we present the definitional formula that would actually be used for computing the estimate of β in the ANCOVA full model. Considering the groups separately, the methods we developed above for determining the least-squares estimates for the restricted model could be applied to each group as if it were the total sample. In general, we could designate the slope for the jth group b_j. So in the two-group case, the slope in group 1 is b_1, and the slope in group 2 is b_2. Then we would have

$$b_1 = \frac{\sum_i (X_{i1} - \bar{X}_1)(Y_{i1} - \bar{Y}_1)}{\sum_i (X_{i1} - \bar{X}_1)^2}$$

$$b_2 = \frac{\sum_i (X_{i2} - \bar{X}_2)(Y_{i2} - \bar{Y}_2)}{\sum_i (X_{i2} - \bar{X}_2)^2} \quad (11)$$

Table 9.4 shows the computation of these slopes for the two separate groups. Here, the example was contrived so that $b_1 = b_2 = 2$.

Now the ANCOVA full model has a single slope parameter rather than a separate one for each group. Thus, at issue is how the separate slope estimates should be combined into a single, pooled estimate. Rather than establishing the results using calculus here, we simply state the definitional formulas and attempt to make them plausible by drawing comparisons to things you already know about pooled estimates and about simple regression. In the current data set, because a slope of 2 fits each of the two groups as well as possible, using 2 as the pooled estimate is the only reasonable choice. However, in real data sets there almost certainly will be some variation from one group to the next in the numerical estimate of the slope. The situation is similar to that in ANOVA where one has separate estimates of the population variance—namely, the observed variance within each group—and the problem is how to pool these estimates. The solution here, as in the within-group variance case, is to compute a weighted average of the individual group estimates. And, as in computation of mean square within (cf. Equations 3.61 and 3.63), the weight applied to each separate estimate is the denominator of the formula used to compute that estimate (i.e., $n_j - 1$ for mean square within and $\sum (X_{ij} - \bar{X}_j)^2$ here). Thus, in the two-group case the least-squares estimate of the pooled within-group estimate can be written as

$$\hat{\beta} = \frac{\sum_i (X_{i1} - \bar{X}_1)^2 b_1 + \sum_i (X_{i2} - \bar{X}_2)^2 b_2}{\sum_i (X_{i1} - \bar{X}_1)^2 + \sum_i (X_{i2} - \bar{X}_2)^2} = b_W \quad (12)$$

TABLE 9.4 Calculation of Least-Squares Estimates Relevant to the ANCOVA Full Model

X	$X - \bar{X}$	Y	$Y - \bar{Y}$	$(X - \bar{X})^2$	$(X - \bar{X})(Y - \bar{Y})$
Group 1					
1	−1	4	−3	1	3
2	0	9	2	0	0
3	1	8	1	1	1
$\sum = 6$		$\sum = 21$		$\sum = 2$	$\sum = 4$
$\bar{X}_1 = 2$		$\bar{Y}_1 = 7$			
Group 2					
3	−1	12	−1	1	1
4	0	11	−2	0	0
5	1	16	3	1	3
$\sum = 12$		$\sum = 39$		$\sum = 2$	$\sum = 4$
$\bar{X}_2 = 4$		$\bar{Y}_2 = 13$			

Computing the slope for each group separately:

$$b_1 = \frac{\sum(X_{i1} - \bar{X}_1)(Y_{i1} - \bar{Y}_1)}{\sum(X_{i1} - \bar{X}_1)^2} = \frac{4}{2} = 2$$

$$b_2 = \frac{\sum(X_{i2} - \bar{X}_2)(Y_{i2} - \bar{Y}_2)}{\sum(X_{i2} - \bar{X}_2)^2} = \frac{4}{2} = 2$$

Using Equation 12 to compute b_W from b_1 and b_2:

$$b_W = \frac{\sum(X_{i1} - \bar{X}_1)^2 b_1 + \sum(X_{i2} - \bar{X}_2)^2 b_2}{\sum(X_{i1} - \bar{X}_1)^2 + \sum(X_{i2} - \bar{X}_2)^2} = \frac{2 \cdot 2 + 2 \cdot 2}{2 + 2} = \frac{8}{4} = 2$$

More typically, Equation 13 would be used to compute b_W directly from the sum of squares and cross-products within groups:

$$b_W = \frac{\sum\sum(X_{ij} - \bar{X}_j)(Y_{ij} - \bar{Y}_j)}{\sum\sum(X_{ij} - \bar{X}_j)^2} = \frac{4 + 4}{2 + 2} = \frac{8}{4} = 2$$

Using Equations 16 and 17 to compute the intercepts:

$$a_1 = \bar{Y}_1 - b_W\bar{X}_1 = 7 - 2(2) = 7 - 4 = 3$$
$$a_2 = \bar{Y}_2 - b_W\bar{X}_2 = 13 - 2(4) = 13 - 8 = 5$$

The weight applied to each slope in the numerator in Equation 12 is inversely proportional to the variance of that slope estimate: the more stable the slope estimate derived for a particular group, the heavier it is weighted. The denominator, as in all weighted averages, is simply the sum of the weights. Also, on the right of Equation 12, we introduce the notation by which we refer to this average or pooled within-group slope, b_W.

Fortunately, as in the case of mean square within, rather than computing a parameter estimate separately for each group and then weighting each by the denominator used in computing the estimate, there is an easier way. We can simply add the numerators for all separate estimates (i.e., add the sums of cross-products of deviations from the group mean) and divide by the sum of the denominators of the separate estimates (i.e., by the sum of the sums of squared deviations around the group means). Using symbols to say the same thing (which is probably clearer here) we have

$$b_W = \frac{\sum_j \sum_i (X_{ij} - \bar{X}_j)(Y_{ij} - \bar{Y}_j)}{\sum_j \sum_i (X_{ij} - \bar{X}_j)^2} \tag{13}$$

Table 9.4 shows computations using this definitional formula for b_W, as well as using the weighted average of Equation 12.

We now must consider how to estimate the remaining parameters of the ANCOVA full model. Although it may be surprising, it is easiest to consider the estimates for μ and α at the same time. If we substitute estimates for the parameters in Equation 1, the prediction for the full model could be written

$$\hat{Y}_{ij} = \hat{\mu} + \hat{\alpha}_j + \hat{\beta} X_{ij} \tag{14}$$

In the case where $X = 0$, our predictions could be written

$$\hat{Y}_{ij} = \hat{\mu} + \hat{\alpha}_j \tag{15}$$

Thus, in terms of our hypothetical data set, $\hat{\mu} + \hat{\alpha}_1$ would be the Y value where the prediction line for group 1 intersects the Y-axis, and $\hat{\mu} + \hat{\alpha}_2$ would be the Y intercept for group 2. Analogous to the bivariate regression case, the prediction line for each group goes through the point corresponding to the mean value of X and the mean value of Y for that group. That is, the regression line for group 1 minimizes errors by being centered at the point $(\bar{X}_1, \bar{Y}_1)$ and decreases by b_W units for each unit decrease in X. Thus, in going from an X value of $\bar{X}_1$ to an X value of 0, the predicted value drops $b_W \bar{X}_1$ units down from $\bar{Y}_1$. In terms of parameter estimates, this means

$$\hat{\mu} + \hat{\alpha}_1 = \bar{Y}_1 - b_W \bar{X}_1 = a_1 \tag{16}$$

So, as in the restricted model, we can arrive at an estimate of the intercept quite readily once the value of the slope is known, and we denote this intercept by an a, now adding a subscript to designate group number. In the second group in the example, then, we would have

$$\hat{\mu} + \hat{\alpha}_2 = \bar{Y}_2 - b_W \bar{X}_2 = a_2 \tag{17}$$

or in general

$$\hat{\mu} + \hat{\alpha}_j = \bar{Y}_j - b_W \bar{X}_j = a_j \tag{18}$$

The bottom of Table 9.4 shows computations for the intercepts of our two-group example.

Comparison of Models.   Now we are ready to carry out the model comparison to determine if the ANCOVA full model is a significantly better description of the

TABLE **9.5** Calculation of the Error Sum of
Squares for the ANCOVA Full Model

X	Y	$\hat{Y}$	$Y - \hat{Y}$	$(Y - \hat{Y})^2$
Group 1				
1	4	5	−1	1
2	9	7	2	4
3	8	9	−1	1
				$\sum = 6$
Group 2				
3	12	11	1	1
4	11	13	−2	4
5	16	15	1	1
				$\sum = 6$

$$E_F = \sum_j \sum_i (Y_{ij} - \hat{Y}_{ij})^2 = 6 + 6 + 12$$

Predicted values for the ANCOVA full model are calculated as follows:

$$Y_{ij} = a_j + b_W X_{ij}$$

Group 1:

$$\hat{Y}_{i1} = a_1 + b_W X_{i1}$$
$$\hat{Y}_{11} = 3 + 2(1) = 3 + 2 = 5$$
$$\hat{Y}_{21} = 3 + 2(2) = 3 + 4 = 7$$
$$\hat{Y}_{31} = 3 + 2(3) = 3 + 6 = 9$$

Group 2:

$$\hat{Y}_{i2} = a_2 + b_W X_{i2}$$
$$\hat{Y}_{12} = 5 + 2(3) = 5 + 6 = 11$$
$$\hat{Y}_{22} = 5 + 2(4) = 5 + 8 = 13$$
$$\hat{Y}_{32} = 5 + 2(5) = 5 + 10 = 15$$

data than is the ANCOVA restricted model. The form of our F test, of course, is
the same general form that we have encountered repeatedly in this book, that is,

$$F = \frac{(E_R - E_F)/(df_R - df_F)}{E_F/df_F}$$

We computed the error sum of squares for the restricted model in Table 9.3.
Computation of the corresponding quantity for the full model is carried out in Table
9.5. Thus, the comparison of the adequacy of the model including parameters for
a group effect with the model without group parameters boils down here to a

comparison of a value of E_F of 12.0 and a value of E_R of 14.4. Naturally, the difference in the simplicity of the models must also be considered. The restricted model for this two-group situation involves the computation of one slope and one intercept parameter. In general, this will be the case for one-way ANCOVA designs. Thus, we will have

$$df_R = N - 2 \tag{19}$$

in general, which here means that $df_R = 6 - 2 = 4$. For the full model we will have a different intercept for each group, plus a common slope parameter, so the degrees of freedom will in general depend on a, the number of groups in the design. That is, we will be estimating $a + 1$ parameters, so

$$df_F = N - (a + 1) = N - a - 1 \tag{20}$$

This implies that the ANCOVA test of the treatment effect in an a-group case involves an F having $(a - 1)$ and $(N - a - 1)$ degrees of freedom:

$$F = \frac{(E_R - E_F)/[(N-2)-(N-a-1)]}{E_F/(N-a-1)} = \frac{(E_R - E_F)/(a-1)}{E_F/(N-a-1)} \tag{21}$$

in general. In our simple two-group case then, $df_F = 6 - 2 - 1 = 3$. Thus, the F test for the group effect, allowing for the covariate, has $4 - 3 = 1$ and 3 degrees of

T A B L E **9.6** Computations for ANOVA
of Two-Group Data

X	Y	$Y - \bar{Y}_j$	$(Y - \bar{Y}_j)^2$
Group 1			
1	4	-3	9
2	9	2	4
3	8	1	1
	$\sum = 21$		$\sum = 14$
	$\bar{Y}_1 = 7$		
Group 2			
3	12	-1	1
4	11	-2	4
5	16	3	9
	$\sum = 39$		$\sum = 14$
	$\bar{Y}_2 = 13$		

$$E_F = \sum_j \sum_i (Y_{ij} - \bar{Y}_j)^2 = 14 + 14 = 28$$

$$E_R - E_F = \sum_j n(\bar{Y}_j - \bar{Y})^2 = 3(7-10)^2 + 3(13-10)^2 = 2 \cdot 3 \cdot 3^2 = 54$$

$$F = \frac{(E_R - E_F)/(df_R - df_F)}{E_F/df_F} = \frac{54/1}{28/4} = 7.714$$

freedom and is computed as follows:

$$F = \frac{(14.4 - 12)/(4 - 3)}{12/3} = \frac{2.4/1}{4} = .6 \qquad (22)$$

which clearly is nonsignificant. Thus, we conclude that the model including the X scores but not the group effect adequately accounts for the data.

How does this compare with the result that would have been achieved had we carried out an ANOVA of these data to test for the group effect? Table 9.6 shows computation of the ANOVA, which ignores the covariate. If the covariate had not been considered, we would have concluded that there was a significant group effect because the observed F of 7.714 is larger than the tabled value of 7.71. How can this occur given the greater power that we expect when we use ANCOVA? We address this question in the next section.

Two Consequences of Using ANCOVA

Recall that including a covariate in the model results in two consequences: First, the sum of squares of the errors in your models is decreased; second, the sum of squares for the group effect—that is, the difference between E_R and E_F—is adjusted. Because appreciating these two consequences is the essence of understanding ANCOVA, we consider them now in some detail in the context of our numerical example. We can examine both of these effects explicitly here by comparing the ANCOVA and ANOVA sums of squares.

Test of Regression. The first consequence is seen by a comparison of the ANCOVA full model with the ANOVA full model, that is,

$$Y_{ij} = \mu + \alpha_j + \beta X_{ij} + \varepsilon_{ij} \qquad \text{(1, repeated)}$$

and

$$Y_{ij} = \mu + \alpha_j + \varepsilon_{ij} \qquad (23)$$

In fact, the latter could be viewed as a special case of the former where the slope is restricted to zero. That means that the sum of squared errors for the models can be compared in an F test. The test is typically referred to as the *test of regression* because it reflects the strength of the regression of Y on X. For the current data, the test of regression would yield

$$F = \frac{(28 - 12)/1}{12/3} = \frac{16}{4} = 4$$

which is not close to the critical value for $\alpha = .05$ of 10.1. However, although because of the very few degrees of freedom available in this sample data set this result is not significant, the sum of squared errors has been reduced to less than half of its initial value (i.e., from 28 to 12) by the addition of the covariate. Thus, in fact, smaller effects could be detected by ANCOVA here rather than by ANOVA.

Estimated Conditional Means.   However, the particular numerical estimate of the magnitude of the group effect in ANCOVA typically is somewhat different than in ANOVA. This is the second consequence of using ANCOVA. In the ANOVA test of the group effect (see Table 9.6), the addition of the group parameter to the model resulted in a reduction of 54 in the sum of squared errors in the restricted model. In the ANCOVA test of the group effect (see Equation 22), on the other hand, adding in the group effect resulted in a reduction of only 2.4 in the sum of squared errors in the restricted model. We can refer to the plots of these data as a way of understanding these results. The plots for the restricted and full models were shown in Figures 9.1 and 9.2, respectively. For ease of comparison, Figure 9.3(a) presents these predictions again for the ANOVA models, and Figure 9.3(b) presents these predictions again for the ANCOVA models. In terms of these plots, the reduction in sum of squares associated with the group effect—that is, the numerator sum of squares for the F test—is related to the distance between the lines in the plot. For ANOVA, the sum of squares for the effect is directly related to the distance between the two lines representing the predictions of the full model. The difference between these lines of six units corresponds of course to the difference between the

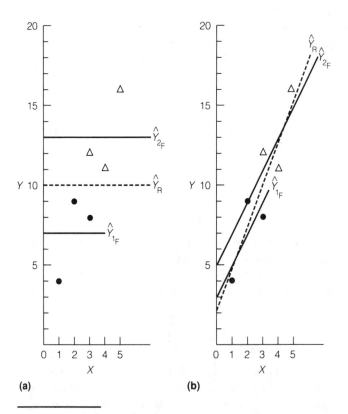

FIGURE 9.3   The difference between the predictions of the full and restricted models for both (a) ANOVA and (b) ANCOVA.

two sample means of 13 and 7. For ANCOVA, the prediction lines for the two groups are clearly much closer together. The ANCOVA–full model predictions can be similar in the two groups but still fit the data well because of the prediction lines' steep slope, which reflects the strong regression of Y on X.

To describe the situation somewhat more precisely, the sum of squares for an effect will in general depend on the extent to which the predictions of the full model depart from those of the restricted model. In terms of the plots, the critical feature is how far the predictions made by the full model for the six observations deviate from the corresponding predictions made by the restricted model. That is, how far are the solid lines from the dashed line? In terms of symbols, it can be shown that the numerator sum of squares can be expressed simply in terms of the difference between $\hat{Y}_F$ and $\hat{Y}_R$. As noted in Chapter 3 (see p. 88), it is the case that

$$E_R - E_F = \sum_{\text{all obs}} (\hat{Y}_F - \hat{Y}_R)^2 \tag{24}$$

where the subscript "all obs" just means that the summation is over all observations. Here, because of the steep regression line in the entire sample, the predictions of the restricted model $\hat{Y}_R$ are quite close to those for the full model $\hat{Y}_F$.

Perhaps the clearest perspective on the reduced sum of squares for the group effect in ANCOVA as opposed to ANOVA is provided by returning to the conditional question asked by ANCOVA. ANCOVA asks, What would the group effect have been *if* the two groups had been at the same mean value on the covariate? Answering this involves examination of the predicted Y values at a particular point on the X scale—namely, at $\bar{X}$, the grand mean across all observations on the covariate. These predicted values are typically called *adjusted means* and are the estimates according to the full model of the expected values on Y for the various groups when $X = \bar{X}$. Because the prediction equation for the full model is

$$\hat{Y}_j = a_j + b_W X_{ij} \tag{25}$$

we could use our numerical values for a_j and b_W and set X_{ij} equal to $\bar{X}$ to get the appropriate predicted values. However, the difference from the observed means is made somewhat clearer if we express $\hat{Y}_F$ in terms of $\bar{Y}_j$. Recall that $a_j = \bar{Y}_j - b_W \bar{X}_j$ (see Equation 18). Substituting this for a_j in Equation 25 and factoring b_W, we obtain

$$\hat{Y}_j = \bar{Y}_j - b_W \bar{X}_j + b_W X_{ij} = \bar{Y}_j - b_W(\bar{X}_j - X_{ij}) \tag{26}$$

Thus, to obtain the predicted value of $\hat{Y}$ at the grand mean on the covariate, we let X_{ij} equal $\bar{X}$ in Equation 26. This gives us the following expression for obtaining "adjusted" means, $\bar{Y}_j'$—that is, the mean Y scores we would have expected to observe in the study, assuming the correctness of our model, if the groups had been equivalent on the covariate

$$\bar{Y}_j' = \bar{Y}_j - b_W(\bar{X}_j - \bar{X}) \tag{27}$$

Although we follow here the convention of calling this an adjusted mean, it should be stressed that this is simply an estimate of a particular conditional mean. That is, $\bar{Y}_j'$ is the estimate of the mean of the Y scores in group j for those subjects who meet the condition of having an X score equal to $\bar{X}$. We could estimate other means as well, for any other X value of interest. However, because in most research projects only one overall indicator of the performance in a treatment condition is of interest, the estimated conditional mean for $X = \bar{X}$ is denoted *the* adjusted mean. The adjustment in the mean of Y to take into account the deviation of the group's covariate mean from the grand covariate mean is comparable to what happens in nonorthogonal ANOVA when we allow for the effects of other factors (see Chapter 7). Here, we are examining the group effect by estimating the marginal means after removing any variability that could be accounted for by variability among the group means on X.

In the particular numerical example we have been working on, the adjustment for the covariate would change the mean in group 1 from 7 to 9. In group 2, the adjusted mean would be 11 as opposed to the observed value of 13. Figure 9.4 shows the simple computations and the relationship between the observed and adjusted means. (The group means are taken from our original computations for the full model in Table 9.4.) Notice carefully the way in which the predicted Y value (or adjusted mean) differs from the observed mean $\bar{Y}_j$ as a function of the relationship between the observed group mean on X, $\bar{X}_j$, and the grand mean on X. For example,

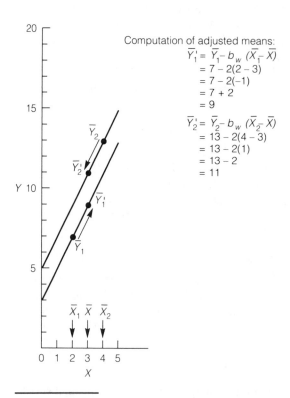

$$\bar{Y}_1' = \bar{Y}_1 - b_w (\bar{X}_1 - \bar{X})$$
$$= 7 - 2(2 - 3)$$
$$= 7 - 2(-1)$$
$$= 7 + 2$$
$$= 9$$

$$\bar{Y}_2' = \bar{Y}_2 - b_w (\bar{X}_2 - \bar{X})$$
$$= 13 - 2(4 - 3)$$
$$= 13 - 2(1)$$
$$= 13 - 2$$
$$= 11$$

F I G U R E 9. 4 Portrayal and computation of adjusted means as predicted Y scores at the point where the covariate score is $\bar{X}$.

in group 1, the mean X score of 2 is below the grand mean X score of 3. Because there is a positive relationship between X and Y, we would expect that, if group 1 in general had higher X scores, their mean Y score would also have been higher. The slope of the regression line, of course, indicates how much higher we should expect the Y score to be for each unit increase in X. In fact, the "adjustment" process can be thought of quite simply but correctly as sliding the mean Y score up or down the regression line as necessary so that you are directly above the grand mean on X. In group 2, because the observed mean on X was higher than the grand mean and the slope of the line was positive, our predicted Y value for the point $X = \bar{X}$ is *lower* than $\bar{Y}_2$. This sliding of the expected Y values up or down the regression lines is represented in the figure by the arrows.

In this particular case then, the second consequence of ANCOVA was to reduce substantially the numerator sum of squares in the F test. Because the numerator sum of squares could be affected in different ways, it is important to put this in perspective.

It should be clear from Figure 9.4 that, as we anticipated in our discussion of the logic of ANCOVA, two factors affect how the means will be adjusted: (1) the differences between the group means on the covariate and (2) the slope of the regression lines. In fact, there is a multiplicative relationship between these factors, as shown in the computations in the figure, whereby $\bar{X}_j - \bar{X}$ is multiplied by b_W. Thus, if either of these two factors is zero in the population, the adjusted means tend to be very similar to the unadjusted means, and hence the ANCOVA numerator sum of squares would typically be quite similar to the ANOVA numerator sum of squares. In any study where the covariate is assessed prior to the assignment to groups and then subjects are assigned *at random* to treatment conditions, we would expect the group means on the covariate to be rather similar. Because this typically happens in laboratory experiments and in analog clinical studies, using ANCOVA in these situations produces numerator sums of squares that are little different from those that would be obtained in ANOVA. In particular, the difference between the adjusted means has the same expected value as the difference between the unadjusted means over replications of the experiment with different subjects.

Examples of Adjusted Effects. The current numerical example is actually more representative of what might happen in a nonrandomized study or quasi-experiment, for example, where intact groups are employed. In such a case, adjusted effects can be considerably different than unadjusted effects. Figure 9.5 illustrates several possibilities. In each case, we designate the group that has the higher conditional mean on Y as group 2. For example, group 2 might be a treatment that is thought to produce some benefit on the outcome measure relative to the group 1 (control) condition. The question is, How do you adjust your estimate of the treatment-control difference for the preexisting differences on the concomitant variable X? We illustrate different examples of adjustments where the outcome and covariate are positively correlated within groups [Figure 9.5(a, c, and e)] and where the outcome and covariate are negatively correlated within groups [Figure 9.5(b, d, and f)]. In each case, the dependent-variable Y is taken as a direct indicator of how positive the outcome is. Figure 9.5(a) illustrates an outcome like that in the

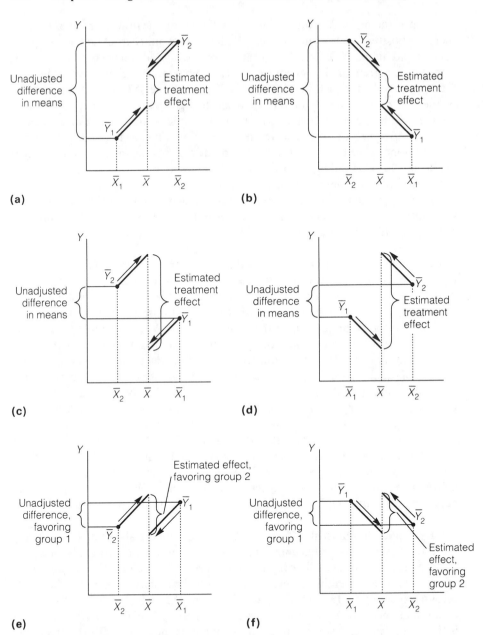

FIGURE 9.5 Some possible relationships between unadjusted and adjusted estimates of treatment effect: (a and b) An apparent treatment benefit due primarily to preexisting differences; (c and d) estimate of treatment effect increased by adjusting for preexisting differences; (e and f) an apparent harmful effect of treatment seen as benefit by adjusting for preexisting differences.

simple numerical examples we have been considering. This is perhaps the most common result of using ANCOVA in quasi-experiments where one is attempting to control for a specific threat to internal validity. For example, in an aggressive treatment program for problem drinkers, a larger number of individuals may drop out than from an untreated control group. Comparing those completing treatment with the control group may show a large apparent treatment benefit. A partial control for this differential mortality might be accomplished by covarying a pre-measure of compliance that indicated who was likely to complete treatment. Assuming that the mean compliance of those completing treatment $(\bar{X}_2)$ is higher than that of the untreated controls $(\bar{X}_1)$ and that compliance is positively related to outcome (as indicated by the positive slopes of the within-group regression lines), the adjusted estimate of the treatment effect could be considerably smaller than the unadjusted difference in means, as in Figure 9.5(a). Figure 9.5(b) shows the same type of effect but for a covariate that is negatively related to outcome. In this example, X might be an indicator of the pretreatment severity of the individual's drinking problem.

Figure 9.5 (c, d, e, and f) illustrate situations where a more favorable picture of the treatment effect is given by adjusting for a covariate. Figure 9.5(c) illustrates a case where, although there is a positive relationship between the covariate and the dependent variable within each group, the group with the higher observed mean on the dependent variable actually started with the lower covariate mean. Thus, the treatment effect, reflected in the advantage of $\bar{Y}_2$ over $\bar{Y}_1$, means that the treatment received by group 2 has more than made up for an initial deficit. This would be the ideal outcome in many social programs such as Headstart. There the children selected for special treatment would frequently be lower on some predictor variable such as socioeconomic status (SES) that would be positively related to a dependent variable such as reading achievement at the end of the first grade. If such a group actually achieved a higher score on the dependent variable, the initial deficit would make the benefit of the treatment all the more impressive. If the two groups had been at the same level on the covariate initially, it is plausible to expect that the treatment group's advantage would have been even larger. This in fact would be the implication of covarying SES for the estimated treatment effect, as is illustrated by the adjusted means (the points above $\bar{X}$) in Figure 9.5(c). The same result is shown in Figure 9.5(d) for a covariate, such as number of hours per week spent watching television, that is negatively related to outcome.

If the groups are sufficiently disparate on the covariate and sufficiently close on the unadjusted Y means, even though the group with the higher covariate mean is ahead of the other group on the unadjusted dependent measure, our best guess of the expected results if both groups had been at $\bar{X}$ might be that the group with the lower mean on Y might have had a significant advantage. This situation is illustrated in Figure 9.5(e), and an analogous situation for a negative covariate–dependent variable relationship is shown in Figure 9.5(f). For example, Headstart children might score lower on reading achievement at the end of the first grade than children who were included in the program; however, if children had all been at the same SES level (or had been subjected to the same number of hours of television viewing), then Headstart might have shown a significant benefit. ANCOVA with its adjusted means provides some evidence relevant to such conditional assertions.[4]

Summary.   To summarize, the primary statistical effect of including a covariate in your model in randomized experiments is typically to bring about a substantial reduction in the unaccounted-for variance. This means you will have greater power for the detection of treatment effects. A secondary effect in randomized experiments is that the estimated magnitude of the treatment effect itself can be different in ANCOVA than in ANOVA. In nonrandomized studies, on the other hand, this effect of adjusting the treatment effect may be much more important than the reduction in within-group error because of large differences across groups on the covariate. The adjusted treatment means are appropriately thought of as estimates based on the full model of the mean performance that would have been obtained in each treatment group if it had comprised a subpopulation of subjects with a covariate score of $\bar{X}$. Such predictions could actually be made for any X score, either graphically by reading off the Y values on the regression lines directly above that X score or numerically by setting X_{ij} in Equation 26 to the X score of interest. The variability of these estimated Y scores depends on exactly where the X value of interest is. Consideration of the details concerning estimating such variability and of more complex ANCOVA models is postponed until we have dealt with the assumptions underlying the statistical tests in ANCOVA.

Assumptions in ANCOVA

For the statistical tests we have described to be valid, the following minimal assumptions must be met concerning the elements of the ANCOVA model:

$$Y_{ij} = \mu + \alpha_j + \beta X_{ij} + \varepsilon_{ij} \qquad \text{(1, repeated)}$$

1. In the population, the error scores ε_{ij} must be independently and normally distributed.
2. In the population, the error scores ε_{ij} must have an expected value of zero and a constant variance.

Basic Implications.   Several aspects of these mathematical assumptions are not obvious. Some of these can be explicitly tested; other aspects lend themselves only to logical analysis. We will discuss various components of these assumptions in turn. First, because in the model

$$Y_{ij} = \mu + \alpha_j + \beta X_{ij} + \varepsilon_{ij} \qquad \text{(1, repeated)}$$

all the terms on the right-hand side of the equation are assumed to be fixed (more on this in a moment) except for the error term, if ε_{ij} is normally distributed, then the conditional Y scores must be normally distributed. By "conditional Y scores," we mean the subpopulation of Y scores at a particular combination of values of α_j and X_{ij}. This is illustrated in Figure 9.6 in which the probability distribution of Y is sketched in for selected values of X, separately for each group.

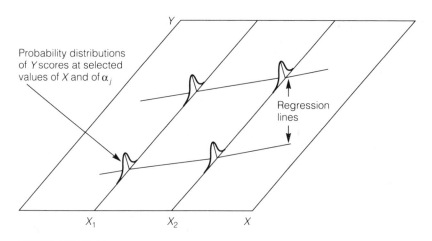

Probability distributions
of *Y* scores at selected
values of *X* and of α_j

Regression
lines

X_1 X_2 X

FIGURE **9.6**   Conditional Y probability distributions.

Second, the relationship between Y and X is presumed to be linear. The assumption that the errors have an expected value of zero implies that the expected value of Y may be written as

$$\mathscr{E}(Y_{ij}) = \mathscr{E}(\mu + \alpha_j + \beta X_{ij} + \varepsilon_{ij}) = \mu + \alpha_j + \beta X_{ij} + \mathscr{E}(\varepsilon_{ij})$$

$$= \mu + \alpha_j + \beta X_{ij} \qquad (28)$$

Thus, the conditional mean of Y is a linear function of X within each group. Tests and generalizations of this feature of the model are considered briefly later in the chapter.

Third, implicit in the statement of the model is the presumption that the separate within-group regression lines have the same slope. For the standard ANCOVA linear model to be appropriate for a data-analysis situation, the slopes of the regression lines in the different groups should be equal within sampling error. In the chapter extension, we consider the issue of possible heterogeneity of regression in detail, including how to test for heterogeneity and how to alter your analysis if heterogeneity appears to be present.

Fourth, the fact that the covariate values are assumed to be fixed does *not* mean that the values of the covariate were decided upon before the experiment was run. Rather, the assumption is that statistical inferences will be made about the characteristics of the population of hypothetical replications having the same distribution of covariate scores. Thus, statistical inferences can technically be made only to the Y values expected at the particular X values included in the study, which is conventional in regression. The question of whether the covariate is fixed or random is a logical one to be answered not only by consideration of how the values were obtained, but also by consideration of what inferences are of interest (see Rogosa, 1980, p. 308). Because the values of the covariate are often obtained in the same manner as the dependent variable—for example, by administrating the same paper-and-pencil test pre and post—some authors have recommended that the covariate be regarded as a random effect (cf. Huitema, 1980, pp. 86, 121). (We discuss random effects in Chapter 10.) In terms of how the standard ANCOVA test of the treatment effect is carried out, it does not matter whether the covariate is regarded as fixed or random (Scheffé, 1959, p. 196). Typically, investigators have been content to make their statistical inferences to the levels of X included in the study and make any extrapolations to other levels on nonstatistical grounds.

Lack of Independence of Treatment and Covariate. Although not technically a requirement, there are other conditions that when met make the interpretation of an ANCOVA much more straightforward. The basic desideratum is that the covariate and the treatment be statistically independent. The issue is similar to the desire for orthogonality in factorial designs. When two factors are orthogonal, one can interpret tests of one factor without regard to the other. In a one-way ANCOVA, the covariate can be viewed as a second factor. If the covariate and the treatment are not statistically independent, allowing for the covariate in your model will as a rule alter the magnitude of the estimated treatment effect, just as the test for one of two nonorthogonal factors is different when you allow for the other rather than ignore it.

There are two opposite and rather extreme views regarding the role of the independence conditions. As with most extreme views, the best course is to avoid both extremes. One extreme position is to expect ANCOVA to serve as a panacea for problems of nonindependence. The other extreme view is to shun the use of ANCOVA altogether if the groups differ in their mean X scores. Keep each of these positions in mind as we mention how to test for independence and discuss how lack of independence can arise.

How to Test for Lack of Independence. Because the treatment variable is discrete and the covariate is a continuous variable, one can test for the primary implication of the independence of the two—namely, equal means on the covariate across groups—quite simply by performing an ANOVA using the covariate as the dependent variable. Significant dependence is indicated by the rejection of the null hypothesis in this test.

How Lack of Independence Can Arise. At least four different situations could result in a rejection of the null hypothesis of no relationship between the treatment variable and the covariate. Because interpretations and further methods of analysis differ across the various situations, it is important to distinguish among them. The situations are presented in the order of increasing difficulty of interpretation.

Case 1: One might have carefully collected scores on the covariate prior to the start of the experiment and randomly assigned subjects to treatment conditions only to find when you begin your data analysis that the treatment groups differ "significantly" on the covariate. This might be termed a *fluke random assignment*. And, in fact, you know that the decision indicated by the ANOVA of the covariate represents a Type I error because, over hypothetical replications of the random-assignment procedure, you are assured that the mean covariate scores will be equal across groups. This will be true whether the replications of the random-assignment process are conceptualized as involving the same set of X scores as those used in your study, just assigned to different conditions (the situation presumed by a randomization test), or whether the replications are conceptualized as involving new random samples of X scores from a larger population (the situation presumed by an ANOVA of X). However, despite this, the problem remains of how to carry out and interpret your ANCOVA on the collected data because the typical ANCOVA involves making inferences to replications involving new Y scores but the *identical distribution of* X *scores*. Thus, an ANOVA of X is potentially helpful, despite the fact that you know random assignment assures you the null hypothesis it tests is true; a significant ANOVA alerts you to the fact that the ANCOVA will involve assessing the conditional means on the dependent variable at a point considerably far away from at least certain of the group means on X. Because the precision of your estimation of an adjusted mean diminishes the farther away the group mean on the covariate is from the grand mean on the covariate, the power of your test of the treatment effect might be considerably less than it would have been had you happened to get a "better" random assignment. Such "bad" random assignments will, of course, turn up with no less nor greater regularity than their prescribed .05 probability, given the simple random-assignment procedure is correctly followed. The best solution to this problem is to avoid it entirely by using an assignment procedure that assures equal means on X, not just in the long run but in your particular study. The advantages of such stratified random assignment have been demonstrated by Maxwell, Delaney, and Dill (1984) and are discussed in greater detail in a subsequent section comparing ANCOVA and blocking. Given this modified type of random assignment was not used and you find yourself with markedly different group means on X despite simple random assignment, what can be done?

Certainly, you should not feel that your experiment is thereby rendered uninterpretable, and in particular you should not feel that the ANCOVA has hindered your scientific progress. As an ultimate fallback, one could perform a simple ANOVA of your dependent variable. The ANOVA F test is, of course, derived by taking into account that the random process by which groups are formed will sometimes produce groups that are dissimilar and thus is perfectly valid regardless of the distribution of values on the covariate. Collecting information on the covariate allows you to lessen the chance of making an erroneous statistical decision, which one would be more likely to commit by using an ANOVA. Thus, although an ANOVA would be valid here, an ANCOVA would be preferred. The reason for preferring ANCOVA, besides the usual one of increased power through reduced error, is that it can adjust for the bad hand dealt you by the random assignment.

It is critical here to note that the differences between groups on the covariate scores are being assumed to have arisen despite the fact that, for all values of X, subjects had an equal probability of being in each one of the treatments. Perhaps it is worth noting that certain procedures used to recruit subjects for psychology experiments do not meet this criterion, despite the fact that the reason for the relationship between the treatment conditions and the covariate may not be obvious at all to the experimenter. For example, suppose that in a human-learning experiment you recruit subjects for different treatment conditions by posting a sign-up sheet for each that bears only the name of the experiment and the time the session is to be run. If you find that the GPA scores you were planning to use as a covariate differ significantly across the treatment conditions, you cannot be assured that the covariance adjustment will be adequate. It may well be that, for whatever reason, experimental sessions at different times may attract students who differ in their GPAs and possibly other characteristics. Allowing subjects to distribute themselves across experimental conditions, even though they have minimal information about the conditions, does not constitute random assignment. If the subjects have distributed themselves across the conditions, your experiment would fall into the fourth cause of nonindependence of treatment and covariate discussed later. But if you controlled the assignment to conditions in such a way that subjects had an equal probability of being placed in each treatment condition regardless of their X score, ANCOVA can be used knowing that the adjusted estimate of the treatment effect is unbiased regardless of how nonrandom any particular instance of random assignment might appear (see Rubin, 1977).

Case 2: A second situation in which lack of independence between the covariate and the treatment can arise is in using *biased assignment procedure*. This refers to the situation "where the covariate is used as a measure of the extent to which subjects 'need' some kind of treatment" (Huitema, 1980, p. 140). For example, subjects with a phobia score above a certain value may be assigned to a phobia-treatment condition and those with a lower score would be assigned to a different condition such as a waiting-list control. As long as the phobia score is the sole basis of assigning subjects to the treatment conditions, ANCOVA can be used without hesitation to perform a test of the adjusted treatment effect. This yields an unbiased test and an estimated treatment effect that is independent of the difference on the pretest regardless of whether the covariate contains measurement error (Rubin, 1977). Readers are cautioned, however, that implementations of the biased assignment study that permit no overlap between groups in the X scores represented rely heavily on model assumptions, for example, homogeneity of regression (cf. Weisberg, 1979, p. 1153). Rather than having groups that do not overlap in X scores, one could have the probability of assignment to a treatment condition changing as a function of their X score (cf. Huitema, 1980, p. 141). For example, one could divide subjects into thirds on the basis of their X scores, with the lowest third being assigned to the treatment, the highest third being assigned to the control condition, and the middle third being randomly divided between the two conditions. Thus, the probability of assignment to treatment would be 0, 1, or $\frac{1}{2}$.

Case 3: A third, more problematic situation occurs when the *treatment affects the covariate*. This only occurs, of course, when the covariate is assessed after the onset of treatment. In some cases, it may seem a trivial matter whether the questionnaire that will be used to collect information to be used as a covariate is passed out to subjects before or after the instruction sheet that constitutes the different "treatment" conditions. However, to avoid ambiguity, it is best if at all possible to assess the subjects' covariate scores prior to any differential treatment of subjects taking place. The basic concern is that if the treatments differentially affect the covariate scores, then an ANCOVA of the dependent variable, which equates the groups on the covariate, would in fact remove from the treatment sum of squares part of the treatment effect that you really want included. Suppose that an investigator wants to determine the relative effectiveness of two strategies for coping with pain. Instruction and practice in a single strategy are given in each of 10 sessions, with the dependent measure being the number of seconds the subject tolerated an increasingly painful stimulus. Perhaps the investigator suspects, reasonably enough, that there are individual differences in pain tolerance and attempts to predict variation in the dependent measure by an assessment of pain tolerance taken at the end of the first session. Using such a measure as a covariate in an attempt to maximize the chances of detecting a treatment effect on the dependent variable would be misguided. Presuming the treatments do produce differential effects, that these effects may at least begin to emerge by the end of a single session is altogether reasonable. To covary the first session's pain tolerance is to ask the conditional question, How different would the expected scores on the dependent measure be if the groups were at the same point on the covariate? But the two groups may already differ at the end of the first session because of the treatment effect. If so, it is quite possible that the major effect of covarying session 1 tolerance would not be a reduction in residual error, but a reduction in the treatment sum of squares by removing part of the effect of interest.

As is often the case, such a usage of ANCOVA would be inappropriate not because the technique produced the wrong answer but because it was used to answer the wrong question, or more accurately, the question ANCOVA addresses was not understood and hence its answer was misinterpreted. ANCOVA could, however, shed some light here on a question that would be of interest. That is, one might wonder if the treatment produced an effect in session 10 over and above what would be predicted on the basis of the effect present at session 1.

This use of ANCOVA also can frequently be capitalized on to see if a particular variable should be ruled out as a potential mediator of a treatment effect on another variable. A fairly standard example (cf. Myers, 1979, p. 430) of this is an investigation of teaching methods where one method produces higher scores on a common examination but also results in students studying more. It may be of interest then to pursue the question, Can the effect on examination scores be accounted for by the difference in time spent studying? If a significant treatment effect on examination scores is still observed when study time is covaried, then one can conclude that the study-time differences are not responsible for the exam-score differences. Note, however, that the converse is not true. That is, if the test of treatment effects were no longer significant when study time was adjusted for, it does not mean that the study-time differences caused the exam-score differences. The different teaching methods may have affected a third variable that was responsible for both the study-time and the exam-score effects. One teaching method may have so captured the students' attention that they picked up more information in the initial teaching session and spent more time studying on their own.

To conclude this consideration of the impact of having the treatment affect the covariate, if one's purpose is, as is usually the case in experimental studies, to simply increase the precision of your analysis of the treatment effect on the dependent variable, then one should avoid using as a covariate a variable that has, or even could have, been affected by the treatment. If, on the other hand, one's purpose is to explore whether a particular variable served to mediate the treatment's effects on the dependent variable, then ANCOVA can be used with caution. Part of the need for caution concerns the potential for committing errors of the general form of "correlation implies causation." Another cause for caution is that the adjusted effect must be interpreted by making inferences about whether the treatment effect can be accounted for (do *not* read "caused by") the covariate *as measured in the experiment.* As Huitema (1980, p. 108) stresses, frequently investigators' real interest is in the construct (e.g., time spent on task) that is only fallibly measured by the covariate (e.g., time a student reports having studied). Conclusions regarding such underlying constructs, whatever the outcome of the ANCOVA, must be made at least partially on nonstatistical grounds.

Case 4: A fourth and final cause of lack of independence between the covariate and the treatment is that the study is not a true experiment but a quasi-experiment— that is, subjects are *not randomly assigned* to treatment conditions. This situation poses the most difficult interpretation problems of all. As we previously considered at length in our discussion of the logic of ANCOVA, there is no way of knowing that the differences on the covariate are the only important ones between groups when differential selection factors are operating.

Although certainly not an equivalent of random assignment, ANCOVA can be helpful nonetheless, and its use could still be recommended though interpretations of the results of the analysis must be made very cautiously. Modifications of ANCOVA to deal with measurement error in the covariate may also be required in the nonequivalent-group case. Consider the extremely complicated problem of differences across racial groups in measured IQ. For example, Jensen (1980, p. 44) reports the difference between black and white students' tested IQ to be approximately 15 points. Despite the wide variation of opinion among psychologists about the validity of a single IQ score for measuring intelligence and despite the even greater controversy concerning the cause of differences between racial groups in tested IQ, a reasonable consensus could be obtained for the proposition that a nontrivial proportion of the variation in IQ of young adults is related to variation in their home environments. Clearly, this is a question that does not lend itself to experimental control because one cannot ethically carry out the required manipulation. ANCOVA can be used to shed some light on how much of an adjustment in the group differences would be called for. However, to recall our earlier remarks about the correlation–causation fallacy, there is no way of knowing whether experimentally controlling home environments at a standard level would produce (cause) a reduction in the group means of the amount suggested by an ANCOVA. To make the example more concrete, a measure of socio-economic status (SES) might be used as an indicator of the characteristics of the home environment, which would be relevant to predicting tested IQ. However, two factors besides the correlation-does-not-imply-causation problem virtually assure that a typical ANCOVA would *not* make exactly the correct adjustment. Both are related to the assumption that the covariate is measured without error. First, the measurement of SES is itself a difficult problem, and it is practically assured that some measurement error would perturb the results—for example, a parent's occupation may be erroneously reported or inappropriately scored as an indicator of SES. We consider how to adjust for measurement error in the next section. Second, the SES measure is of interest as an indicator itself of the underlying construct, quality of home environment. Thus, even if a perfectly reliable measure of SES were obtained, the construct of interest would still be measured imperfectly. Families at the same SES level, for example, might have home environments that differ considerably in features relevant to the measured IQs of children from those homes.

A further problem in using ANCOVA with intact groups, besides that raised by having a fallible covariate, is the possibility that the question addressed by ANCOVA concerns a population of subjects that does not exist. For example, assume that a developmental psychologist conducts a study of the effectiveness of a cognitive-training strategy with a covariate assessing the developmental level of the child. Perhaps the covariate is the numerical score on an assessment procedure designed to assess whether the child is at the stage of concrete processing or at the stage of formal operations. It may actually be the case that the data display all the characteristics implied by the statistical assumptions listed earlier. However, if Piaget is right and the assessment procedure is a valid measure of the developmental stages he hypothesized, the distribution of scores on the covariate should be bi-modal. In fact, there should be no subjects midway between the concrete operations mean and the formal operations mean, but that is in effect the point to which ANCOVA is extrapolating to make the treatment comparison. One might still reason in this situation that the *test* of the constant treatment effect is of interest, because if the ANCOVA model is correct, this would be appropriate for concrete operations and formal operations subjects. However, the typical *adjusted means*, which are estimated at the grand mean on the covariate, would likely not be of interest because no such subject exists.

A relatively large literature exists that is devoted to the problems of modeling and interpreting nonequivalent group studies. Readers are referred to the papers by Meehl (1971), Overall and Woodward (1977), Reichardt (1979), and Weisberg (1979) for their helpful discussion of the problem and references to additional literature.

Summary Regarding Lack of Independence of Treatment and Covariate. Certainly we have seen that ANCOVA cannot blithely be applied with the expectation that an appropriate correction for the lack of independence of the treatment and covariate will always be made. Nonetheless, it is also clear that ANCOVA can be used to address data-analysis questions of interest in each of the four cases we have considered. Certainly, Keppel's view that "if there is any possibility that the treatments may have affected the scores on the control variable, the analysis of covariance is inappropriate" (1982, p. 503) represents an extreme view that would preclude fruitful and legitimate uses of ANCOVA. However, the difficulties of interpretation can be great; particularly in nonequivalent group studies, ambiguities are virtually assured. However, as Huitema argues, to condemn ANCOVA because of these ambiguities is inappropriate: "ANCOVA is innocent; measurement error and nonequivalent group studies are culpable" (Huitema, 1980, p. 115).

Measurement Error in Covariate. What is the consequence of employing such a fallible "covariate"? If the study employed random assignment, the major effect is simply that the power of the ANCOVA test would be somewhat less than it would have been with a perfectly reliable covariate, but still the power with ANCOVA would likely be greater than that with an ANOVA ignoring the covariate. With a nonrandomized study, on the other hand, the problem is considerably more serious than a slight loss of power. In an intact group study such as the study of racial differences in IQ the point of using ANCOVA was an attempt to adjust for differences across groups on the covariate. As we have seen—for example, in Figure 9.4—the magnitude of the adjustment in the treatment means depends on how far apart the groups are on the covariate. In fact, if $\mu_{YW} - \mu_{YB}$ is the difference between the mean IQs of whites and blacks in the population and $\mu_{XW} - \mu_{XB}$ is the corresponding difference between the two racial groups in quality of home environment relevant to performance on the IQ test, we can then express the difference in the adjusted mean IQ quite simply.

First, however, we must introduce a bit of notation. Let

$$\frac{\sigma^2_{\text{true } X}}{\sigma^2_X}$$

be the proportion of the variation in the observed X scores corresponding to variation in the construct of interest. Let $\beta_{\text{true } X}$ be the population regression coefficient appropriate for predicting the IQ scores from the true values of the covariate construct, and let $\beta_{\text{fallible } X}$ be the population regression coefficient being estimated when the fallible measure is used as the covariate. Then, measurement error causes a reduction in the slope as follows:

$$\beta_{\text{fallible } X} = \beta_{\text{true } X} \left(\frac{\sigma^2_{\text{true } X}}{\sigma^2_X} \right) \tag{29}$$

Thus, whereas we would like to estimate the adjusted population effect

$$\mu_{YW} - \mu_{YB} - \beta_{\text{true } X}(\mu_{XW} - \mu_{XB})$$

with a fallible covariate, we are actually estimating the following adjusted effect:

$$\mu_{YW} - \mu_{YB} - \beta_{\text{true } X} \left(\frac{\sigma^2_{\text{true } X}}{\sigma^2_X} \right)(\mu_{XW} - \mu_{XB}) \tag{30}$$

Because

$$\frac{\sigma^2_{\text{true } X}}{\sigma^2_X}$$

is always less than 1 unless X is a perfect measure, ANCOVA represents an underadjustment for preexisting differences in the mean values on X. Depending on the pattern of means, this underadjustment can either produce significant ANCOVA F tests when the true adjusted effect is zero or result in failure to detect treatment effects present in the true adjusted effects.

Figure 9.7 illustrates the former situation for our race-differences-in-intelligence example. Assume that the tested IQ for whites in the population is 108 and for

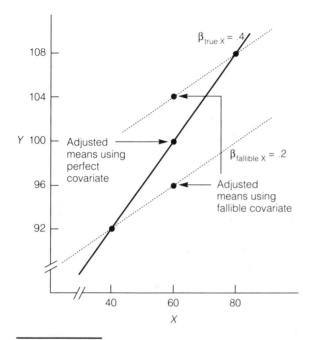

FIGURE 9.7 Underadjustment resulting from using a fallible covariate in a nonequivalent-group study.

blacks it is 92. Further assume that the corresponding means on the measure of home environments are 40 for blacks and 80 for whites. Finally, assume that with a perfect measure of home environments that the regression slope would be .4, but that the proportion of true score variance in our fallible measure is only .5. Whereas a correct adjustment would result in identical mean IQ scores for blacks and whites, using a fallible covariate means here that the observed difference between group means was reduced only half as much as it should have been.

A number of corrections for measurement error in the covariate have been proposed. The basic requirement over and above those for a standard ANCOVA is that you have an estimate of the reliability of the covariate. The interested reader is referred to Huitema (1980, Chapter 14) for references and a computational example of one of the procedures.

Comparisons Among Adjusted Group Means

Tests of specific contrasts among the adjusted group means can be developed by considering their variances. Recall the adjusted mean of the jth group, adjusting for the departure of the group's covariate mean from the grand covariate mean, is

$$\bar{Y}_j' = \bar{Y}_j - b_W(\bar{X}_j - \bar{X}) \qquad (27, \text{repeated})$$

In a randomized study, this adjusted mean estimates the population mean of the

jth group, which we denote μ_j. As we develop in the chapter extension, the variance of this estimator is

$$\sigma^2_{\bar{Y}_j} = \sigma^2_\varepsilon \left[\frac{1}{n_j} + \frac{(\bar{X}_j - \bar{X})^2}{\sum_j \sum_i (X_{ij} - \bar{X}_j)^2} \right] \tag{31}$$

We can estimate this simply by substituting for σ^2_ε the observed mean square error for our full model (see Equation 1) and denote this estimator $s^2_{\bar{Y}_j}$:

$$s^2_{\bar{Y}_j} = \frac{E_F}{df_F} \left[\frac{1}{n_j} + \frac{(\bar{X}_j - \bar{X})^2}{\sum_j \sum_i (X_{ij} - \bar{X}_j)^2} \right] \tag{32}$$

When the overall test of the treatment effect is significant in a one-way ANCOVA involving three or more groups, it may be of interest to perform tests of specific pairwise differences between groups. The contrast or difference between adjusted means in two selected groups—say, groups l and m—can be expressed as

$$\hat{\psi} = \bar{Y}'_l - \bar{Y}'_m = \bar{Y}_l - b_W(\bar{X}_l - \bar{X}) - [\bar{Y}_m - b_W(\bar{X}_m - \bar{X})]$$
$$= \bar{Y}_l - \bar{Y}_m - b_W(\bar{X}_l - \bar{X}_m) \tag{33}$$

This estimates the difference between the population means μ_l and μ_m and has variance

$$\sigma^2_{\bar{Y}'_l - \bar{Y}'_m} = \sigma^2_\varepsilon \left[\frac{1}{n_l} + \frac{1}{n_m} + \frac{(\bar{X}_l - \bar{X}_m)^2}{\sum_j \sum_i (X_{ij} - \bar{X}_j)^2} \right] \tag{34}$$

Again, this variance can be estimated simply by substituting our observed mean square for σ^2_ε:

$$s^2_{\bar{Y}'_l - \bar{Y}'_m} = \frac{E_F}{df_F} \left[\frac{1}{n_l} + \frac{1}{n_m} + \frac{(\bar{X}_l - \bar{X}_m)^2}{\sum_j \sum_i (X_{ij} - \bar{X}_j)^2} \right] \tag{35}$$

Under the standard ANCOVA assumptions, the ratio of the square of the estimated contrast value in Equation 33 to its variance is distributed as an F with 1 and $N - a - 1$ degrees of freedom:

$$F = \frac{(\bar{Y}'_l - \bar{Y}'_m)^2}{s^2_{\bar{Y}'_l - \bar{Y}'_m}} \tag{36}$$

(This type of ratio of a squared contrast value to its variance is one of the ways tests of contrasts were developed in Chapter 4. If you need a review, see the discussion of Equation 4.43.)

If C such planned pairwise comparisons among adjusted means are conducted, then as usual a Bonferroni adjustment to control the overall α at .05 could be accomplished by requiring the F in Equation 36 to be significant at α/C.

Just like multiple comparisons in one-way ANOVA discussed in Chapter 5, if all possible pairwise comparisons between means are of interest or if the pairs to be tested are decided on after examining the data, then tests should be carried out by making reference to a studentized range distribution. This can be done in the ANCOVA situation in one of two ways, depending on what is assumed about the concomitant variable. If the X variable is regarded as fixed, as in the one-way ANOVA case, a Tukey test can be performed by comparing the F value computed for each pairwise test using Equation 36 against $q^2/2$, where q is the value in Appendix Table A.4 at the desired α for a groups and $N - a - 1$ denominator degrees of freedom. If, on the other hand, the covariate is regarded as a random effect, then the same F value would be compared against a slightly different critical value from the *generalized studentized–range distribution* (Bryant & Paulson, 1976). The critical value is q_{BP}^2, where the value of q_{BP}, the generalized studentized range, is read from Table A.8. Generally, q_{BP} will be slightly (less than 5 percent) larger than the q critical value for the same α level, number of means, and error df.

When tests of complex comparisons involving multiple treatment means are desired, generalizations of the above expressions for the estimated value and variance of pairwise contrasts can be used. The estimated contrast value in general is just the linear combination of adjusted means of interest:

$$\hat{\psi} = \sum_j c_j \bar{Y}_j' \tag{37}$$

which can be expressed in terms of the observed group means on X and Y:

$$\hat{\psi} = \sum_j c_j [\bar{Y}_j - b_W(\bar{X}_j - \bar{X})] = \sum_j c_j \bar{Y}_j - b_W \sum_j c_j \bar{X}_j \tag{38}$$

The estimated variance of such a contrast can be written (cf. Cochran, 1957; Neter, Wasserman, & Kutner, 1985, p. 873)

$$s_{\hat{\psi}}^2 = \frac{E_F}{df_F} \left[\sum_j \frac{c_j^2}{n_j} + \frac{\left(\sum_j c_j \bar{X}_j\right)^2}{\sum_j \sum_i (X_{ij} - \bar{X}_j)^2} \right] \tag{39}$$

Then, the test statistic

$$F = \frac{\hat{\psi}^2}{s_{\hat{\psi}}^2} \tag{40}$$

is distributed as an F with 1 and $N - a - 1$ degrees of freedom. If multiple complex comparisons are being tested, each may be evaluated either using the Bonferroni method, if the contrasts are planned, or against a Scheffé critical value, if the contrasts are post hoc. The Scheffé critical value for an a-group study would be $(a - 1)F_{(a-1),(N-a-1)}$.

Generalizations of the ANCOVA Model

The basic ANCOVA model we have been discussing throughout the chapter

$$\text{Full:} \qquad Y_{ij} = \mu + \alpha_j + \beta X_{ij} + \varepsilon_{ij} \tag{1, repeated}$$

can be easily generalized to encompass different relationships and variables. We mention some possible extensions here but do not go into computational details. The logic of the analyses as a way of accommodating to individual differences remains the same. However, the computations are such that you will amost certainly want to use a computer program for the analyses discussed in this section. Fortunately, SAS, SPSS-X, and BMDP can easily be used to carry out such analyses.

Multiple Covariates.   The ANCOVA model can readily accommodate more than a single predictor. Denoting a second concomitant variable as Z and subscripting the slopes to indicate the associated predictor variable, we would have the full model:

$$Y_{ij} = \mu + \alpha_j + \beta_X X_{ij} + \beta_Z Z_{ij} + \varepsilon_{ij} \tag{41}$$

As we noted in our discussion of multiple regression in the Chapter 3 extension, the increase in the adequacy of the model resulting from adding variable Z depends not only on the relationship between Z and Y but also on that between Z and X. Thus, other things being equal, variable Z would contribute more to the predictive accuracy of the model if it were relatively unrelated to X. Although it is the case that adding more covariates almost certainly increases the model's R^2, one rapidly reaches the point of diminishing returns. Because the estimate of the parameters in a model depends on the other terms being estimated, including additional covariates can actually make the estimates of the treatment effects of primary interest less precise. This is particularly true when the study involves relatively few subjects. Most behavioral science studies are sufficiently small that two or three covariates will be the upper limit.

Adjusted means for the model in Equation 41, of course, depend on the group mean on Z as well as X. Specifically,

$$\bar{Y}'_j = \bar{Y}_j - b_{w_x}(\bar{X}_j - \bar{X}) - b_{w_z}(\bar{Z}_j - \bar{Z}) \tag{42}$$

Kirk (1982, p. 737) provides further computational details.

Nonlinear Relationships.   The linear (that is, straight line) relationship between X and Y, which we have noted is assumed by the basic ANCOVA model (see our discussion of Equation 28), is not a necessary part of covariance analysis (Neter et al., 1985, p. 851). The general linear model is linear in the parameters, not in the X–Y relationship. That is, the prediction represents some linear (that is, additive) combination or weighted sum of parameter estimates, but, as we noted in Chapter 6, the weights may be such that the relation between X and Y is curvilinear. A tremendous variety of curve forms could be modeled by including combinations of various powers of X in the model. However, in most behavioral science research, the linear relationship between Y and X accounts for the vast majority of the variability in Y that is associated with X. If, for theoretical reasons or because of trends you note in scatterplots of your data, you suspect a nonlinear relationship between the dependent variable and covariate, then this should be examined in your modeling. You may allow for a quadratic relationship simply by including X^2 as well as X in your model, that is,

$$Y_{ij} = \mu + \alpha_j + \beta_L X_{ij} + \beta_Q X_{ij}^2 + \varepsilon_{ij} \tag{43}$$

where we have added subscripts L and Q to our βs to indicate linear and quadratic trends, respectively. In fact, a test for linearity[5] can be carried out by comparing the model in Equation 43 with the basic ANCOVA model in Equation 1. If the test indicates that X^2 significantly enhances adequacy, then it can be retained in your model for testing other effects and contrasts of interest.

Multifactor Studies. To this point, we have considered ANCOVA only for single-factor designs. Naturally, ANCOVA can be used in designs involving more than a single factor. For example, we could generalize our basic ANCOVA model having effect parameters α_j and slope parameter β to include the effects γ_k of another factor, say factor C:

$$Y_{ijk} = \mu + \alpha_j + \gamma_k + \alpha\gamma_{jk} + \beta X_{ijk} + \varepsilon_{ijk} \tag{44}$$

where $j = 1, 2, \ldots, a$ levels of factor A, $k = 1, 2, \ldots, c$ levels of factor C, and $i = 1, 2, \ldots, n_{jk}$ subjects in cell jk. Now, besides the adjusted cell means, one will likely be interested in the adjusted marginal means. The adjusted cell means, A marginals and C marginals are, respectively,

$$\bar{Y}'_{jk} = \bar{Y}_{jk} - b_{\mathrm{W}}(\bar{X}_{jk} - \bar{X}_{..})$$
$$\bar{Y}'_{j.} = \bar{Y}_{j.} - b_{\mathrm{W}}(\bar{X}_{j.} - \bar{X}_{..})$$
$$\bar{Y}'_{.k} = \bar{Y}_{.k} - b_{\mathrm{W}}(\bar{X}_{.k} - \bar{X}_{..}) \tag{45}$$

Kirk (182, p. 743ff.) or Neter, Wasserman, and Kutner (1985, p. 873ff.) provide computational details.

ALTERNATE METHODS OF ANALYZING DESIGNS WITH CONCOMITANT VARIABLES

There are numerous alternative methods of analyzing designs with concomitant variables. None are as flexible or as generally useful as the ANCOVA procedures we have discussed. However, because of their widespread use in the literature and the fact that some of the methods are preferred over ANCOVA in certain situations, we consider three alternatives, albeit briefly. The three methods are the ANOVA of residuals, the analysis of gain scores, and blocking.

ANOVA of Residuals

ANCOVA is sometimes presented as being strictly equivalent to first regressing the dependent variable on the concomitant variable, then computing a set of residual scores by subtracting the estimates yielded by the regression equation from the observed scores, and finally performing an ANOVA of these residual scores. Although intuitively appealing, it has been shown by Maxwell, Delaney, and Manheimer (1985) that the two methods are not equivalent. Performing an ANOVA of a single set of residuals results in a model comparison in which the parameter estimates used in one of the models are not least-squares estimates for that model. This results in the test statistic not being appropriately distributed. Thus, despite the fact that the method has been used in the literature, performing an ANOVA of a set of residuals is an analysis strategy that should be avoided.

Gain Scores

Earlier in the chapter, we noted that in ANCOVA the dependent variable and the covariate need not be commensurate. In those cases where they are, an analysis of gain scores may be of interest either instead of, or more likely in addition to, an ANCOVA. ANCOVA is, of course, designed for making comparisons across groups. The unique advantage of analyzing gain scores is that it allows one to ask the question, Was there significant change from pretreatment to posttreatment? This question frequently is of interest in applied situations. For example, if a variety of clinical treatments are being compared for their effectiveness in helping a group of clients, one is almost certain to be interested in whether there was significant evidence for improvement overall. ANCOVA is not suited for addressing such questions. Assuming that one has commensurate variables, such as a pretest and posttest on the same clinical instrument, then the question of whether there has been significant change from pretest to posttest is answered by performing what is essentially a matched-pairs t test of the data. The denominator of the test differs somewhat from a matched-pairs t because the error term is based on within-group deviations rather than deviations around the grand mean.

If X_{ij} is the score on the pretest and Y_{ij} the score on the posttest, one would compute a difference score for each subject, $D_{ij} = Y_{ij} - X_{ij}$. The test for a significant gain would correspond to a comparison of the following models:

$$\text{Full:} \quad D_{ij} = \mu + \varepsilon_{ij} \tag{46}$$

$$\text{Restricted:} \quad D_{ij} = 0 + \varepsilon_{ij}$$

However, the denominator of the test would use the conventional error term for a between-subjects ANOVA on the difference scores, that is, the sum of squared errors associated with the fullest possible model;

$$D_{ij} = \mu_j + \varepsilon_{ij} \tag{47}$$

One could also carry out a test of whether the mean gain scores differ across groups—that is, a standard one-way ANOVA using D_{ij} as the dependent variable. However, an ANCOVA of the posttest scores typically would be preferred. Both an ANOVA of gain scores and an ANCOVA would address the same general question, Allowing for preexisting differences, are there differences between groups on the posttest? The distinction between the methods has to do with how the adjustment for initial differences is made. We could write the models being compared in an ANOVA of gain scores:

$$\text{Full:} \quad Y_{ij} = \mu + \alpha_j + X_{ij} + \varepsilon_{ij} \tag{48}$$

$$\text{Restricted:} \quad Y_{ij} = \mu + X_{ij} + \varepsilon_{ij}$$

These are identical to the models used in ANCOVA, except that the slope of regression of the postscores on the prescores has been constrained to be 1 in both the full and the restricted models. Because the relationship between the postscores and prescores is almost certainly not perfect, the error scores in these models in general are larger than those in the corresponding ANCOVA models where the slope estimates can be chosen to minimize error. The result of this in randomized studies is that an ANCOVA typically is more powerful than an ANOVA of gain scores.

It should be stressed here that, although the same general question is being addressed, quite different conclusions might be reached by the two methods in the same study, particularly in nonrandomized studies. When subjects are randomly assigned to conditions, the expected magnitude of the treatment effects will be the same in the two analyses. However, because of smaller errors in ANCOVA, it is possible that an ANOVA of gains might miss the significance level needed for you to reject the hypothesis that all groups gained the same amount; yet, at the same time, an ANCOVA might result in the conclusion that the groups differ significantly in their posttest scores, even though there may be no differences between groups on the pretest.

The converse is also possible, though more rare. Because an ANOVA of gains requires the estimation of one less parameter, the critical F value needed for significance is slightly less than that in ANCOVA. If the true slope is in fact very close to 1, the ANOVA of gains could conceivably lead to a larger F than an ANCOVA, particularly if the study involved a very small number of subjects. These anomalies, of course, only illustrate the point that statistical decisions are not black-and-white and that, in the case of marginal evidence for an effect, the conclusion drawn depends on the particular procedure used and the criterion adopted for claiming significance. Nonetheless, with randomized studies, the two methods are in general, if not exact, agreement.

This is not the case with intact group studies. A famous example of this point was offered by Frederic Lord and has come to be known as Lord's paradox. The hypothetical example concerned the interest of a large university "in investigating the effects on the students of the diet provided in the university dining halls and any sex difference in these effects" (Lord, 1967, p. 304). Assume that weights are available for both male and female students eating in the dining halls at the beginning and end of an academic year. Thus, one could perform either an ANOVA of gain scores or an ANCOVA with gender as the between-groups factor. In Lord's example, the mean weight for the group of women students at the end of the year was identical to that at the beginning. Although some individual women had gotten heavier and some lost weight, the overall distribution of weights was unchanged over the course of the year. The same was true for men. This situation is represented by the scatterplots in Figure 9.8.

An analysis of the gain scores that could be computed here would indicate that there was no change overall and that there was no evidence of a gender difference in amount of change because the mean gain score in each group was zero. But when an ANCOVA is performed on these data, one obtains a highly significant group effect. The apparent discrepancy between these two analyses constitutes the paradox.

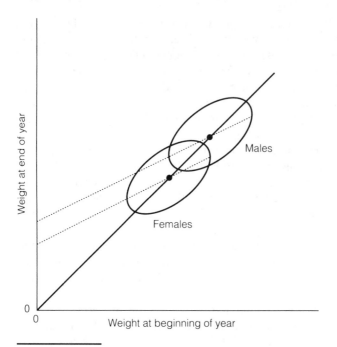

F I G U R E   9. 8   Scatterplots of initial and final weights for male and female students (after Lord, 1967).

The paradox is fairly easily resolved, however, in the light of our previous discussions of the logic of ANCOVA (see the beginning of this chapter) and of the use of ANCOVA with intact groups (see "Lack of Independence of Treatment and Covariate"). ANCOVA gives a different answer than an ANOVA of gains here because it is addressing a different specific question. Remember the conditional nature of the question being addressed, which is sometimes expressed, If the groups were equivalent on the premeasure, would we expect there to be a difference on the postmeasure? Here we could phrase the question, For subpopulations of males and females having identical pretest weights—say, at the grand mean weight for the two sexes combined—would a difference in mean weight at the end of the year be expected? For example, if the mean weight of females is 120 pounds and that of males is 160, the grand mean, assuming equal numbers of males and females, is 140 pounds. Males weighing 140 pounds are lighter than the average male and some regression back toward the mean of the whole population of males would be expected over the course of the year. Females weighing 140 similarly would be unusually far above the mean weight for females and would be expected as a group to show some regression downward over the academic year.

The same point is illustrated graphically by the within-group regression lines, which are the dashed lines in Figure 9.8. ANCOVA is asking whether there is any vertical separation between these lines, and clearly there is. In terms of the adjusted means, which would lie on these lines, the adjusted mean for males is higher than that for females. The fly in the ointment, which hopefully can now be seen clearly, is that these adjusted means (or the question addressed by ANCOVA) are not of interest in this situation. We are not interested in whether those males and females who start the year weighing the same will weigh the same at the end of the year. Rather, we want to know the change in females as a group and in males as a group, whatever their initial weights happen to be. When the conditional question asked by ANCOVA is not of interest, as may frequently be the case in intact group studies, then the ANOVA of gain scores is to be preferred. The choice between the two analyses will have to be made in quasi-experiments after careful consideration of the goals of the analysis.

Blocking

A method of handling concomitant variables that is relatively common in some research areas is that of blocking. Subjects are first sorted into groups or blocks that are relatively homogeneous as far as scores on the concomitant variable are concerned, and then treatments are randomly assigned within each block. The method involves treating the concomitant variable explicitly as a factor having certain discrete levels in the analysis. For example, if the motor skills of an elderly population were being studied by comparing the performance of different groups of subjects on a variety of tasks, the groups might be subdivided into various age categories, for example, 60–69 years, 70–79 years, and 80 and above. Thus, instead of having a single-factor design with a covariate of age, one would employ a two-way ANOVA with the factors of task and age.

Such randomized block designs were inherited by psychology from agricultural experimentation where the blocking variable frequently was a discrete variable. For example, cattle from each of various farms might be randomly assigned to one of two diets. The farms then could be used as a blocking factor. (There are some additional complications for the analysis that arise in such a study because farms might be viewed a random factor. This is discussed in Chapter 10.)

In psychology, on the other hand, the individual difference variables most commonly used do not take on discrete values naturally but must be artificially grouped for purposes of analysis. Whenever one treats a continuous variable like age as a discrete variable, one is throwing away information, and one might suspect there would be a cost in terms of a drop in the precision in the analysis. In fact, there is.

On the other hand, it should be noted that blocking typically implies not only an analysis method but also a method of assigning subjects to conditions in the first place. There are various methods by which the blocks can be formed. These methods attempt to achieve one of two goals. That is, the blocks are formed either (1) so that equal segments of the range of the concomitant variable are included in each block or (2) so that equal proportions of the population fall into each block. The most commonly used method is a variation of the latter procedure. If there are to be b blocks of subjects and a treatments, typically the total number of subjects used in the experiment would be selected to be a multiple of the number of treatment–block combinations,—for example, *a b n*—so that there could be an equal number of subjects per cell. Subjects are first ranked according to their scores on the concomitant variable X. The *a n* subjects with the highest scores on X would be block 1, the *an* subjects with the next highest scores on X would be block 2, and so on. Within each block, subjects would be randomly assigned to conditions subject to the constraint that there be *n* subjects from that block placed in each treatment.

This restricted randomization method assures that the means of the concomitant variable in the different treatment conditions are very similar. This should be obvious because the assignment method assures that equal numbers of subjects from each portion of the X distribution are included in each treatment condition, so the distribution of X is similar across treatments. This fact has favorable implications for the sensitivity of the analysis. The general principle at work, of course, is that of experimental control: the less the influence of random variation, the more apparent a treatment effect of a fixed magnitude becomes. The specifics of how this works here can be seen more clearly by considering what the result would be of forming treatment groups by using a randomized block–assignment procedure and then doing an ANCOVA (which is the procedure we recommend). Recall from our expressions of the error of an adjusted mean (see Equations 31 and 32) that the sensitivity of our analysis is greater the closer the group mean of the covariate is to the grand covariate mean. Because the randomized block–assignment procedures assure that the covariate means are virtually identical across treatments, the adjusted means are less variable and the analysis more sensitive.

With the assignment procedure we have discussed, the typical randomized block analysis is a straightforward two-way ANOVA. The fullest possible model would be

$$Y_{ijk} = \mu + \alpha_j + \beta_k + \alpha\beta_{jk} + \varepsilon_{ijk} \tag{49}$$

where α_j refers as usual to the effect of treatment j, β_k is the effect associated with the kth block of subjects, $\alpha\beta_{jk}$ is the treatment × block–interaction effect associated with cell jk, and ε_{ijk} is the population error score for the ith individual in cell jk. Such a design would usually have equal n, so that all effects would be orthogonal.

An example serves to illustrate how the randomized block analysis compares to an ANCOVA. Assume that three blocks of elderly subjects, with six subjects per block, are formed according to age, as mentioned above. That is, equal numbers of participants from those in their sixties, seventies, and eighties are assigned to three task conditions assessing motor control. The dependent variable is a count of the number of errors made in performing the task. Table 9.7 presents a hypothetical data set[6] showing the ages (X) and error scores (Y), along with a summary table giving cell and marginal means. While the ages range from 60–87, the stratified assignment procedure results in the means on the covariate all being within one year of each other. With simple random assignment, on the other hand, we would have expected the range of means on the covariate to be more than four times as large.

A randomized block analysis would treat this design as a 3 × 3, two-way ANOVA. The source table for this analysis is shown in the upper portion of Table 9.8. The most striking thing about this summary of the results is the very large effect

T A B L E **9. 7** Data Illustrating a Randomized Block Design

		Task (Factor A)					
		1		*2*		*3*	
		X	Y	X	Y	X	Y
	1	60	14	62	10	63	19
		69	24	66	16	67	25
Block (Factor B)	2	74	16	71	22	73	30
		76	26	78	30	76	36
	3	82	36	83	41	86	44
		85	40	87	47	87	50

Cell and Marginal Means Task

		1		*2*		*3*		*Marginals*	
		X	Y	X	Y	X	Y	X	Y
Block	1	64.5	19	64.0	13	65.0	22	64.50	18.00
	2	75.0	21	74.5	26	74.5	33	74.67	26.67
	3	83.5	38	85.0	44	86.5	47	85.00	43.00
Marginals		74.33	26.00	74.50	27.67	75.33	34.00	74.72	29.22

T A B L E **9. 8** Alternative Analyses of Data in Table 9.7

Source Table for Randomized Block Analysis

Source	SS	df	MS	F	p
Task (factor A)	213.78	2	106.89	4.18	.052
Blocks (factor B)	1933.78	2	966.89	37.83	.001
Task × blocks (AB)	99.55	4	24.89	.97	.469
Error	230.00	9	25.56		

Source Table for ANOVA

Source	SS	df	MS	F	p
Task	213.78	2	106.89	0.71	.512
Error	2263.33	15	150.89		

Source Table for ANCOVA

Source	SS	df	MS	F	p
Task	152.04	2	76.02	5.25	.020
Within-cell regression	2060.45	1	2060.45	142.20	.001
Error	202.88	14	14.49		

of the blocking factor, which here reflects the deterioration of motor control with advancing age. On occasion, the test of the blocking factor is not mentioned in journal article reports of analyses because the effect is obviously expected, as it would be here. However, its importance in increasing the sensitivity of the analysis is clear when one compares the test of the task effect with that in a conventional one-way ANOVA where information about the age of the subjects is ignored (see middle part of Table 9.8). Although the sum of squares associated with the task effect is identical in the two analyses, the F is less than 1 in a one-way ANOVA but approaches significance in the randomized block analysis when the block main effect and the blocks × task interaction have been removed from the error term. Notice that the sums of squares for blocks, task × blocks, and error in the randomized block analysis add up exactly to the sum of squares for error in the one-way ANOVA (1933.78 + 99.55 + 230.00 = 2263.33).

Thus, the randomized block analysis represents a substantial improvement over the one-way analysis in terms of sensitivity. However the question remains of how the randomized block analysis compares to an ANCOVA. The source table for the ANCOVA is provided at the bottom of Table 9.8.

Although the ANCOVA source table is similar to that for the randomized block analysis, there are differences, and these illustrate the distinctions between the two methods. There are three principal points to be noted.

1. The conventional ANCOVA allows for only the *linear* relationship between the dependent and the concomitant variables, whereas the typical randomized block analysis allows for all possible trends. This means that the direct effect of the concomitant variable will have 1 degree of freedom associated with it in ANCOVA but $b - 1$ degrees of freedom in randomized blocks, where b = the number of blocks. In most applications in the behavioral sciences, this proves to be a disadvantage for the randomized block analysis because the linear trend accounts for the lion's share of the explainable variance. Because the sums of squares associated with the concomitant variable typically are about the same in the two analyses, allowing for two, three, or four trends makes the mean square associated with the concomitant variable in the randomized block analysis one-half, one-third, or one-quarter that in the ANCOVA. With 3 blocks of subjects, as in the current example, the randomized block analysis allows for linear and quadratic trends, and the mean square of 966.87 associated with age is approximately half of the comparable value of 2060.45 in the ANCOVA results.

2. ANCOVA *makes use of all the quantitative information* in the covariate, whereas the randomized block analysis typically ignores information. Although subjects were grouped into blocks according to age, it is clear from Table 9.7 that there is some heterogeneity of ages remaining within blocks and this is predictive of the number of errors made. Thus, although only a linear trend is allowed for, more variability in the dependent variable can be predicted by the concomitant variable in ANCOVA (notice the larger sum of squares, 2060.45 versus 1933.78, in Table 9.8) because of using exact ages rather than decades.

The greater sensitivity of ANCOVA to quantitative information shows up in another way as well, namely, by adjusting for the variation among the group means on the covariate. The randomized block analysis, on the other hand, is carried out as if the concomitant variable and the task factors were orthogonal. Although the decades of ages are equally represented in each task group, there is some variation among the mean ages for the groups, as seen at the bottom of Table 9.7. Notice also that just as there is a positive relationship between age and errors in each task condition, the group means on the dependent variable have the same rank order as the covariate group means. Thus, when allowance is made for this, the sum of squares for tasks is reduced, here from 213.78 to 152.04. [If the rationale for this is not immediately obvious, reference back to the similar situation in Figures 9.4 and 9.5(a) and the related discussion should clarify things quickly.] The bottom line, as far as use of quantitative information is concerned, is that ANCOVA presents a more accurate picture of the data, both in terms of within-group and between-group adjustments for the exact value of the covariate.

3. Interaction tests can be carried out either using a covariance or a blocking analysis, but ANCOVA interaction tests consume fewer degrees of freedom and permit inferences to be made about the treatment effect at any point on the X dimension. The loss of degrees of freedom in blocking analyses can become critical in designs employing relatively few subjects, such as this one. This is particularly true if there is a large number of cells in the design even without the blocking factor or if there is a large number of blocks, because the degrees of freedom available for error is equal to the total number of subjects minus the product of these numbers. (For example, with 18 subjects, three task conditions and three blocks, the degrees of freedom for error is $18 - (3 \times 3) = 9$. If there had been five task conditions, adding a blocking factor with three levels would have required estimation of 15 parameters, so only three degrees of freedom would be available for error.) Thus, in multifactor designs, to add a blocking factor with as many levels as one would like may be impossible. If a covariance approach is adopted, on the other hand, the greatest number of parameters required (i.e., allowing for an interaction or heterogeneity of regression) is just twice that which would be needed if the con- comitant variable were ignored, rather than b times the same quantity as in the blocking approach. As we develop in the chapter extension, 2 parameters are required for each cell in the ANCOVA approach when the test of heterogeneity is carried out. However, in this particular example as one might have expected on the basis of the task × block interaction, there is little evidence for heterogeneity of regression. When the test of heterogeneity of regression is carried out here, one obtains $F(2, 12) = 1.75$, $p > .2$, with the residual error in the full model that allows for a different slope in each cell being $E_F = 157.07$. Because the model assum- ing homogeneous slopes results in only slightly more error, the conventional ANCOVA, as shown at the bottom of Table 9.8, can be used to carry out the test of the task effect, which is presumably of most interest in this situation.

This comparison of the ANCOVA and blocking tests of the task factor is not atypical. The greater sensitivity to within-group variation on the concomitant variable and the fact that fewer degrees of freedom are consumed by other effects permits ANCOVA to achieve a smaller mean square error and a larger F value for the test of the task factor. Here, the test is significant at the $\alpha = .05$ level in ANCOVA but just misses significance ($p = .052$) in the block analysis. Although varying significance across the two tests obtains only for marginal effects, the greater sensitivity of ANCOVA over blocked analyses for the same data is a very general result (see Maxwell, Delaney, & Dill, 1984).

Conclusions Regarding Blocking. Although randomized block analyses address similar questions to ANCOVA and result in greater power than designs ignoring concomitant variables, they generally should be avoided in favor of ANCOVA approaches. However, whenever data on the concomitant variable can be obtained prior to assignment to conditions, it is advantageous to use a randomized block procedure for the formation of groups. Although groups are formed by this restricted randomization procedure, ANCOVA should be used for the analysis in general because of its greater sensitivity to intragroup and intergroup variations on the covariate. Its use of fewer degrees of freedom is also frequently an important advantage. When the concomitant variable is not available in advance, ANCOVA can still be used (remembering the previous discussion about the relationship between the treatment and the covariate). Attempts to perform post hoc blocking can encounter such difficulties as having a nonorthogonal design or a design with missing cells when no subjects from a particular block are represented in a treatment.

There are exceptions when a randomized block analysis might be preferred. One would occur in the admittedly unusual situation where the relationship between the concomitant variable and the dependent variable was expected to be nonlinear but of unknown form. (If the form of the relationship could be specified, the correct term, for example, X^2 for quadratic or X^3 for cubic trends, could be included, as we have noted, as a covariate in the analysis in addition to X.) A second situation calling for a blocking analysis would be when types of subjects are identified on the basis of profiles that contain some variables for some subjects and different variables for others. Problem drinkers might be those who report drinking over a specified amount, who are reported by a significant other as having behavioral problems resulting from drinking, or who have a physical condition threatened by their drinking. If categories of subjects are identified but cannot be ordered, then obviously ANCOVA could not be used, but we would normally tend to think of this design as simply including an additional factor with discrete levels rather than including a concomitant variable.

EXERCISES

1. In a one-way design with a premeasure, one could test for treatment effects either by using an ANOVA (i.e., ignoring the premeasure) or an ANCOVA. What is the conceptual difference in the question addressed by ANCOVA as opposed to ANOVA?

*2. What do you look for in a covariate? That is, in thinking about the design of a study, what characteristics of a variable would make it a promising covariate? Why?

3. Assume that the covariate in a two-group study is correlated negatively within groups with the dependent variable and that the mean of the covariate is higher in the treatment group than the control. Further assume that the unadjusted mean on the dependent variable in the treatment group is higher than that in the control group. Will the difference between the ANCOVA adjusted means on the dependent variable be greater or less than the difference between the unadjusted means on the dependent variable? Why?

*4. Consider the following simple set of data for a two-group study, where prescores and postscores are available for each of five subjects in each of the groups.

Group C		Group T	
Pre	*Post*	*Pre*	*Post*
1	5	5	14
3	8	7	17
3	7	7	16
1	2	5	11
2	3	6	12

a. In an ANCOVA test of the difference between the groups' postscores adjusting for the prescores, what models are being compared?

b. Plot the data. As you might suspect on the basis of your plot, an ANOVA of the postscores ignoring the prescores is highly significant, $F(1, 8) = 31.15$. On the basis of your plot, attempt to "intuit" the approximate results of the ANCOVA test of the group effect. That is, would the ANCOVA F be larger or smaller than that for the ANOVA test? Why?

c. Considering only group C, determine the regression equation for predicting postscores from prescores. Do the same for group T. What do your results imply the estimated parameter values for your full model in part a will be?

d. Using the results of part c, determine the score that the full model would predict for each subject. Use these to determine the errors of prediction and E_F.

e. Determine the sum of squared errors associated with the restricted model. Some intermediate results that you could use to determine this value easily are that the sum of squares total for the postscores is 254.5 and the correlation between prescores and postscores obtained when all 10 pairs of scores are treated as being in one group is .95905.

f. Using the results of parts d and e, perform the ANCOVA test of the treatment effect and state your conclusion.

5. An experimenter hoped to increase the precision of his experiment by obtaining information on subjects that could be used as a covariate in an ANCOVA. Because it was inconvenient to collect this information at the start of the experiment, he did so at the completion of the experimental session for each subject, just before debriefing subjects. He had 20 subjects available for a single-factor experiment with four treatment conditions. Subjects were randomly assigned to conditions with the restriction of equal sample sizes in each group. Once all the data were in hand, the experimenter performed three analyses: one being the planned ANCOVA, one an ANOVA of the dependent variable, and one an ANOVA of scores on the covariate. Results are on the next page.

ANCOVA Analyses

Source	SS	df	MS	F
A (adj)	18.65	3	6.22	<1
Within (adj)	128.12	15	8.54	

ANOVA of Dependent Variable

Source	SS	df	MS	F
A	112.15	3	37.38	4.05*
Within	147.60	16	9.22	

ANOVA of Covariate Scores

Source	SS	df	MS	F
A	27.40	3	9.13	6.01†
Within	24.40	16	1.52	

$*p < .05$
$†p < .01$

a. One test that is not reported is the test of within-group regression of the dependent variable on the covariate. If it is possible to perform such a test given the information above, carry out and interpret this test of regression that would normally be performed as a part of the ANCOVA. In any case, specify the models being compared in such a test.

b. Based on the experimental design and the above analyses, how do you interpret the results of the ANCOVA? Is ANCOVA appropriate here?

6. You perform an experiment comparing two methods for teaching a particular arithmetic skill. All students participating are randomly assigned to one of the two conditions. Prior to administering the treatments to your two groups of subjects, you have each subject take a pretest that results in scores that are generally in the middle of the range of possible scores on the test. However, on the posttest (which is a parallel form of the pretest), you observe something of a ceiling effect in both groups. You are contemplating whether to perform an analysis of gain scores or an ANCOVA. Which should you use? Why?

7. It is sometimes stated that ANCOVA requires the treatment and covariate to be independent. Some psychologists further state that if they are not independent, then ANCOVA should not be used. Do you agree? Briefly justify your answer.

8. A graduate student is planning a study to investigate the effectiveness of the "keyword" method (a mnemonic strategy) for increasing subjects' ability to remember. A total of 30 subjects will be used; specifically, 15 will be randomly assigned to her treatment group and 15 to her control group. Her adviser recommends that she block on IQ and then randomly assign to treatments within her blocks.

a. Is this a good idea? Why or why not?

b. Let's suppose that she does block on IQ and has five IQ blocks. Her adviser says that because the blocking factor is of no intrinsic interest (i.e., it simply assures that the groups are comparable), she can simply perform a one-way between-subjects ANOVA to test her treatment effect. Is this good advice? Why or why not?

c. A fellow graduate student has suggested that she analyze her data as a 2×5 factorial design. Is this approach better than her adviser's? Why or why not?

    d. Are there any other approaches besides her adviser's or the fellow student's that she should consider? Briefly justify your answer.

*9. The primary statistical advantage of including a pretest in a randomized design is to decrease error variance. Suppose we let σ_ε^2 represent the error variance in a posttest-only design. It can be shown that in a randomized design where the pretest and posttest have equal variances (often a reasonable assumption), the error variances for ANCOVA and a gain score analysis are

$$\sigma_{\varepsilon(\text{ANCOVA})}^2 = \sigma_\varepsilon^2(1 - \rho^2)$$

$$\sigma_{\varepsilon(\text{gains})}^2 = \sigma_\varepsilon^2 2(1 - \rho)$$

where ρ is the population correlation within groups between the pretest and the posttest. A graduate student is planning a randomized study where he anticipates that

$$\mu_1 = 10, \quad \mu_2 = 20, \quad \mu_3 = 30$$

and $\sigma_\varepsilon = 20$ (these figures correspond to a large effect size). He plans to use 10 subjects per group.

Find the power the student will have with each approach (posttest only, ANCOVA, and gain scores) in each of the following situations (assuming $\alpha = .05$, and equal variances for the pretest and posttest):

a. $\rho = 0$

b. $\rho = .3$

c. $\rho = .5$

d. $\rho = .7$

e. What overall conclusion(s) do you draw here?

(HINT: You will need to calculate ϕ, as we discussed back in Chapter 3. Recall

$$\phi = \frac{\sqrt{\sum \alpha_j^2 / a}}{\sigma_\varepsilon / \sqrt{n}}$$

where σ_ε is to be understood as referring to the error standard deviation of the approach being used.)

Extension Heterogeneity of Regression

As we have noted, the specification of the traditional ANCOVA model is such that all the separate within-group slopes are presumed to be equal. Of course, it is quite possible that at this point our model is incorrect to a greater or lesser extent. Some textbook authors have treated homogeneity of regression as if it were the most critical statistical assumption in ANCOVA. For example, Kirk (1982, p. 733) speaks of the assumption of homogeneity of regression as "this key assumption." Cohen and Cohen in a similar vein refer to the "crucial [ANCOVA] assumption of equal covariate regression coefficients" (1983, p. 319, but see also fn. 7, p. 320, and p. 381). However, the excellent work of Rogosa (1980) has demonstrated the reasonableness of tests of an overall treatment effect in certain situations involving heterogeneous regression slopes. Rogosa proposes that ANCOVA can be used but advises that in general one should be using ANCOVA models that allow for heterogeneous regressions. This is because even moderate heterogeneity results in the standard ANCOVA F statistic being inappropriately distributed. We consider Rogosa's suggested procedures after we detail how a test for heterogeneity of regression could be carried out.

Test for Heterogeneity of Regression

As usual, the test involves the comparison of two models with one model being a special case of the other. At issue is whether a model that allows for not only different intercepts but also different slopes across the groups will have significantly less error than a model that constrains the slopes to be equal. Thus, the restricted model for the test of heterogeneity of regression is identical to the full model used in the ANCOVA test of treatment effects. The full model differs only in that the slope parameter is subscripted to indicate that it takes on a different value in each group. That is, we compare

$$\text{Full:}\quad Y_{ij} = \mu + \alpha_j + \beta_j X_{ij} + \varepsilon_{ij} \tag{E.1}$$

$$\text{Restricted:}\quad Y_{ij} = \mu + \alpha_j + \beta X_{ij} + \varepsilon_{ij} \tag{E.2}$$

The estimates of the parameters in the restricted model are, of course, the same here as when this model was considered previously:

$$\hat{\beta} = b_{\mathrm{w}} = \frac{\sum_j \sum_i (X_{ij} - \bar{X}_j)(Y_{ij} - \bar{Y}_j)}{\sum_j \sum_i (X_{ij} - \bar{X}_j)^2} \tag{9.13, repeated}$$

$$\hat{\mu} + \hat{\alpha}_j = a_j = \bar{Y}_j - b_{\mathrm{w}} \bar{X}_j \tag{9.18, repeated}$$

Likewise in the full model, the slope estimate for each group separately is just the sum of cross-products for that group over the sum of squared deviations on the covariate:

$$\hat{\beta}_j = b_j = \frac{\sum_i (X_{ij} - \bar{X}_j)(Y_{ij} - \bar{Y}_j)}{\sum_i (X_{ij} - \bar{X}_j)^2} \tag{E.3}$$

Thus, in each group, the regression line intersects the mean for that group (i.e., the point $\bar{X}_j$, $\bar{Y}_j$), but it slopes somewhat differently in each group. In any group j, the regression line is at a height of $\bar{Y}_j$ when it is $\bar{X}_j$ units away from the origin along the horizontal axis. Thus the intercept for the jth group is $b_j \times \bar{X}_j$ units below the mean for that group. That is, in the *full model* here, we have

$$\hat{\mu} + \hat{\alpha}_j = a_j = \bar{Y}_j - b_j \bar{X}_j \qquad (E.4)$$

A comparison of these two models, of course, involves a comparison of their sum of squared errors. Thus, once more we need to examine $E_R - E_F$. For the test of homogeneity of regression, we have

$$E_R - E_F = \sum_j \sum_i (Y_{ij} - \hat{Y}_{ij_R})^2 - \sum_j \sum_i (Y_{ij} - \hat{Y}_{ij_F})^2 \qquad (E.5)$$

Now, we can write our prediction equations in deviation score form:

$$\hat{Y}_{ij_R} = \bar{Y}_j + b_W(X_{ij} - \bar{X}_j) \text{ and } \hat{Y}_{ij_F} = \bar{Y}_j + b_j(X_{ij} - \bar{X}_j)$$

Thus, the increase in error resulting from assuming homogeneous slopes can be written

$$E_R - E_F = \sum_j \sum_i [Y_{ij} - \bar{Y}_j - b_W(X_{ij} - \bar{X}_j)]^2 - \sum_j \sum_i [Y_{ij} - \bar{Y}_j - b_j(X_{ij} - \bar{X}_j)]^2 \quad (E.6)$$

It turns out[1] that this difference in errors can be written very simply here:

$$E_R - E_F = \sum_j (b_j - b_W)^2 \sum_i (X_{ij} - \bar{X}_j)^2 \qquad (E.7)$$

That is, the differences of the individual slopes from their weighted average b_W are squared, weighted by the denominators of the individual slopes and summed across groups. (This corresponds exactly to the form of SS_B in ANOVA, where the differences of the individual group means from their weighted average $\bar{Y}$ are squared, weighted by the denominators of the expressions for the cell means n and summed across groups.)

The test of this difference in the adequacy of the two models would as always follow our general form for the F test, with the degrees of freedom in the numerator being the difference in the number of parameters required by the two models. In the full model here, we would be estimating a intercepts and a slopes; whereas in the restricted model, we require a intercepts and a single slope. Thus, the numerator will have $[N - (a + 1)] - [N - 2a]$, or $a - 1$, degrees of freedom.

We can now write the general form of our test of homogeneity of regression for the one-way ANCOVA as follows:

$$F = \frac{(E_R - E_F)/(df_R - df_F)}{E_F/df_F}$$

$$= \frac{\sum_j (b_j - b_W)^2 \sum_i (X_{ij} - \bar{X}_j)^2 / (a - 1)}{\sum_j \sum_i [Y_{ij} - \bar{Y}_j - b_j(X_{ij} - \bar{X}_j)]^2 / (N - 2a)} \qquad (E.8)$$

We can illustrate this test with the simple two-group numerical example we have been using up to this point in the chapter, after making some minor modifications in the data so that they will reflect some heterogeneity of regression. Table 9E.1 shows the modified data. The data were altered in such a way that the means in both groups are the same as in the original example, as is the pooled within-group slope. However, now the slope in group 2 is considerably steeper than that in group 1. Table 9E.2 shows the computations for the pooled slope and intercepts in the

TABLE **9 E. 1** Hypothetical
Data to Illustrate Heterogeneity
of Regression

Subject	Group	X	Y
1	1	1	5
2	1	2	9
3	1	3	7
4	2	3	11
5	2	4	11
6	2	5	17

typical ANCOVA model. Those for the ANCOVA model modified to allow for heterogeneity of regression, which we might refer to as the ANCOHET model, are in Table 9E.3. Figure 9E.1 shows the data together with the prediction lines.

Using the individual error scores computed in the tables, we can obtain the values of E_R and E_F and use the general form of the F test to carry out the test of heterogeneity of regression. From Table 9E.2 we have $E_R = \sum_j \sum_i (Y_{ij} - \hat{Y}_{ij_R})^2 = 8 + 8 = 16$, and from Table 9E.3 we have $E_F = \sum_j \sum_i (Y_{ij} - \hat{Y}_{ij_F})^2 = 6 + 6 = 12$. Thus, we have

$$F = \frac{(E_R - E_F)/(df_R - df_F)}{(E_F/df_F)} = \frac{(16 - 12)/(3 - 2)}{12/2} = \frac{4/1}{6} = .667,$$

which obviously is not significant. The interested reader will, of course, want to confirm that $E_R - E_F$ here could be obtained by the formula shown in Equation E.7 for the sum of squares for heterogeneity of regression:

$$E_R - E_F = \sum_j (b_j - b_W)^2 \sum_i (X_{ij} - \bar{X}_j)^2 = (1 - 2)^2 2 + (3 - 2)^2 2 = 2 + 2 = 4$$

Naturally, a difference in slopes across groups as striking as that shown in Figure 9E.1 will typically be detected as significant in a real study. Here, of course, the example was constructed so that the calculations could readily be followed without even a calculator. However, this means that there is virtually no power to detect an effect because of the very small number of cases. The main point of the example is simply to illustrate how to calculate the test, but it also raises the issue of what should be done when you have reason to suspect, either on the basis of a scatterplot like that in Figure 9E.1 or on the basis of a test, that there is some evidence for heterogeneity of regression in the population.

Accommodating Heterogeneity of Regression

Fortunately, a range of techniques exist for effectively modeling this situation. Unfortunately, they have not been widely used because of misconceptions about the meaningfulness of inferences about treatment effects in the presence of hetero-

TABLE 9 E.2 Solution for the Model Assuming Homogeneous Slopes

	X	$X - \bar{X}_j$	Y	$Y - \bar{Y}_j$	$(X - \bar{X}_j)^2$	$(X - \bar{X}_j)(Y - \bar{Y}_j)$	$\hat{Y}_R$	$Y - \hat{Y}_R$	$(Y - \hat{Y}_R)^2$
Group 1									
	1	-1	5	-2	1	2	5	0	0
	2	0	9	2	0	0	7	2	4
	3	1	7	0	1	0	9	-2	4
	$\sum = 6$		$\sum = 21$		$\sum = 2$	$\sum = 2$			$\sum = 8$
	$\bar{X}_1 = 2$		$\bar{Y}_1 = 7$						
Group 2									
	3	-1	11	-2	1	2	11	0	0
	4	0	11	-2	0	0	13	-2	4
	5	1	17	4	1	4	15	2	4
	$\sum = 12$		$\sum = 39$		$\sum = 2$	$\sum = 6$			$\sum = 8$
	$\bar{X}_2 = 4$		$\bar{Y}_2 = 13$						

$$b_W = \frac{\sum_j \sum_i (X_{ij} - \bar{X}_j)(Y_{ij} - \bar{Y}_j)}{\sum_j \sum_i (X_{ij} - \bar{X}_j)^2} = \frac{2 + 6}{2 + 2} = \frac{8}{4} = 2$$

$$a_1 = \bar{Y}_1 - b_W \bar{X}_1 = 7 - 2(2) = 3$$

$$a_2 = \bar{Y}_2 - b_W \bar{X}_2 = 12 - 2(4) = 5$$

$$\hat{Y}_{i1_R} = 3 + 2X_{i1}$$

$$\hat{Y}_{i2_R} = 5 + 2X_{i2}$$

TABLE 9 E.3 Solution for the Model Allowing for Heterogeneous Slopes

X	$X - \bar{X}_j$	Y	$Y - \bar{Y}_j$	$(X - \bar{X}_j)^2$	$(X - \bar{X}_j)(Y - \bar{Y}_j)$	$\hat{Y}_F$	$Y - \hat{Y}_F$	$(Y - \hat{Y}_F)^2$
Group 1								
1	-1	5	-2	1	2	6	-1	1
2	0	9	2	0	0	7	2	4
3	1	7	0	1	0	8	-1	1
$\sum = 6$		$\sum = 21$		$\sum = 2$	$\sum = 2$			$\sum = 6$
$\bar{X}_1 = 2$		$\bar{Y}_1 = 7$						
Group 2								
3	-1	11	-2	1	2	10	1	1
4	0	11	-2	0	0	13	-2	4
5	1	17	4	1	4	16	1	1
$\sum = 12$		$\sum = 39$		$\sum = 2$	$\sum = 6$			$\sum = 6$
$\bar{X}_2 = 4$		$\bar{Y}_2 = 13$						

$$b_1 = \frac{\sum_i (X_{i1} - \bar{X}_1)(Y_{i1} - \bar{Y}_1)}{\sum_i (X_{i1} - \bar{X}_1)^2} = \frac{2}{2} = 1 \qquad b_2 = \frac{\sum_i (X_{i2} - \bar{X}_2)(Y_{i2} - \bar{Y}_2)}{\sum_i (X_{i2} - \bar{X}_2)^2} = \frac{6}{2} = 3$$

$$a_1 = \bar{Y}_1 - b_1 \bar{X}_1 = 7 - 1(2) = 5 \qquad a_2 = \bar{Y}_2 - b_2 \bar{X}_2 = 13 - 3(4) = 1$$

$$\hat{Y}_{i1_F} = 5 + 1X_{i1}$$

$$\hat{Y}_{i2_F} = 1 + 3X_{i2}$$

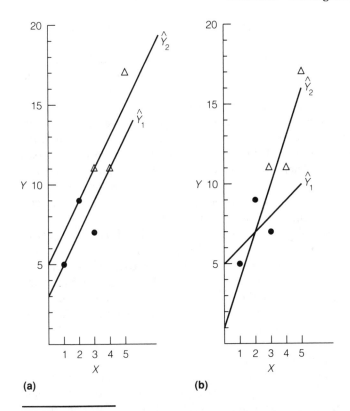

FIGURE 9E. 1 Comparison of the predictions of the (a) ANCOVA model assuming homogeneous slopes with those of the (b) ANCOHET model that allows for heterogeneity of regression.

geneity of regression and because of the dearth of packaged programs to perform the analyses and of textbook treatments of how such analyses should be interpreted. We move now to a consideration of these techniques based on the ANCOHET model.

An analogy may help to introduce the techniques. In two-way ANOVA, the interest is more often in the main effects of the factors than in their interaction. Nonetheless, we used an error term based on a model that incorporated an interaction parameter so that we would have an unbiased estimate of population variance regardless of the correctness of any decision about the significance of any particular effect. Even more to the point, when evidence for an interaction is obtained, the analysis does not stop, but one usually proceeds to tests of simple main effects. The same strategy can be applied effectively in ANCOVA allowing for heterogeneous slopes.

Rogosa (1980) shows that if there is heterogeneity of regression in the population the typical ANCOVA test of treatment effects will not be appropriately distributed. An alternative procedure in the presence of mild to moderate heterogeneity is to compute the adjusted treatment sum of squares as in a typical ANCOVA but to use as an error term the error associated with the ANCOHET model, just as would be done in ANOVA when the interaction was nonsignificant. (How to make decisions about the extent of heterogeneity is discussed below.) This provides an appropriately distributed test of the hypothesis that there are no treatment effects, at the cost of only $a - 1$ degrees of freedom for error.

To characterize the treatment effect more completely, it is desirable with moderate to pronounced heterogeneity to assess the treatment effect as a function of the value of the covariate. The need for this should be obvious from considering a plot like that in Figure 9E.1(b). There, for low X values, the predicted Y scores in treatment 1 are higher than those in treatment 2, whereas the reverse is true for individuals with high X scores. If the traditional ANCOVA model were exactly right, of course, the vertical distance between the population regression lines would be a constant for all values of X. When there is reason to believe this is not the case, one would like to estimate the magnitude of the treatment effect as a function of X and have a way of assessing its significance. Our basic tack is to develop an estimate of the treatment effect somewhat like we did with the difference between adjusted means—that is, the difference between the predicted scores for different conditions at a given value of X—and then derive the variability of this estimated difference. A ratio of the square of the estimated effect to its variance estimate can then be used as a statistical test.

The basic problem involves the estimation of the vertical distance between regression lines. Because this is difficult to envision, let us begin our consideration of this problem by referring to the simple regression situation involving a single group with one predictor and one dependent variable. Besides deriving estimates of the dependent variable in this case using a simple regression equation, we can also relatively easily derive estimates of the variability of our predictions. The variability in the predictions themselves can be illustrated by considering what might happen over repeated samples where the X values remain fixed across samples. Figure 9E.2 displays the regression lines that might result for three samples of Y values.

Two points about the variability of estimated Y values are suggested by the plot. First, the farther the particular X value is from $\bar{X}$, the more the predicted Y values vary across repeated samplings. Second, the variation in the predicted Y values is the result of two features of the regression line: the height of the line generally and its slope.

We can see these results more rigorously by considering a deviation form of the regression equation. Let X_p be the particular X value at which we wish to estimate Y and let the corresponding predicted value $\hat{Y}_p$ be the estimated mean of the conditional probability distribution. Then, in the simple (i.e., two-variable) regression situation, as we developed in the Chapter 3 extension (see Equation 3E.2), we can write

$$\hat{Y}_p = \bar{Y} + b(X_p - \bar{X}) \tag{E.9}$$

Under the assumption that the X values are fixed and that the errors are normally distributed in the population, the variability of $\hat{Y}_p$ can be shown[2] to be decom-

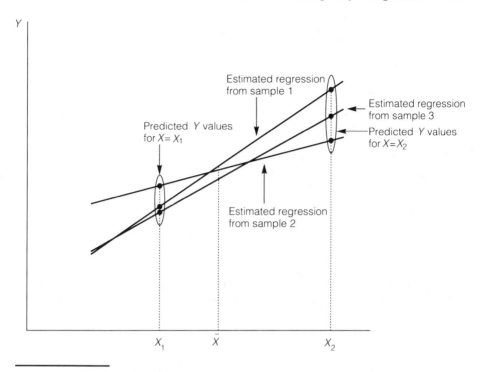

F I G U R E **9E. 2** Sampling variability in regression lines.

posable into the following two components:

$$\sigma^2_{\hat{Y}_p} = \sigma^2_{\bar{Y}} + (X_p - \bar{X})^2 \sigma^2_b \qquad (E.10)$$

The first component, the variability of $\bar{Y}$, should by now be quite familiar, that is, $\sigma^2_{\bar{Y}} = \sigma^2/n$. However, we now have the magnitude of the estimate of error depending on the X value as well as the variability in Y. That is, because β is not known but is estimated by a statistic, we expect our slope estimates to vary somewhat from sample to sample as illustrated in Figure 9E.2. How much difference the error in b makes gets larger and larger as X_p moves farther away from $\bar{X}$. This is illustrated in Figure 9E.3.

The variance of our slope statistic itself can be derived fairly easily once we rewrite the definitional formula for the slope in a convenient form, namely,

$$b = \sum k_i Y_i \qquad (E.11)$$

where the k_i are simple functions[3] of the X values:

$$k_i = \frac{X_i - \bar{X}}{\sum(X_i - \bar{X})^2} \qquad (E.12)$$

Now, because the variance of a linear combination of independent random variables is simply the sum of the original variances, each weighted by the square of the original weight, we immediately have the following expression for σ^2_b, the variance

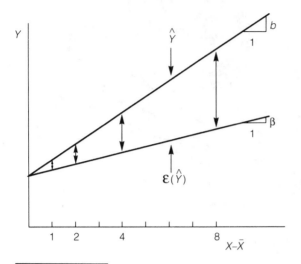

FIGURE 9E. 3 When doubling the extent to which X deviates from $\bar{X}$, the extent to which the estimated conditional mean deviates from the true conditional mean also doubles.

of the slope estimate b:

$$\sigma_b^2 = \mathrm{Var}(b) = \mathrm{Var}(\sum k_i Y_i) = \sum k_i^2 \, \mathrm{Var}(Y_i) \tag{E.13}$$

where Var is to be read as "the variance of" the expression that follows within parentheses. Making use of the fact that the variances of Y_i are constant and equal to σ^2, then substituting for k_i we obtain

$$\sigma_b^2 = \sigma^2 \sum k_i^2 = \sigma^2 \sum \left[\frac{X_i - \bar{X}}{\sum (X_i - \bar{X})^2} \right]^2$$

$$= \sigma^2 \frac{\sum (X_i - \bar{X})^2}{[\sum (X_i - \bar{X})^2]^2} = \sigma^2 \frac{1}{\sum (X_i - \bar{X})^2} \tag{E.14}$$

We are now ready to substitute our results back into Equation E.10 to obtain the final form of the variability of our estimated conditional mean $\hat{Y}_p$:

$$\sigma_{\hat{Y}_p}^2 = \frac{\sigma^2}{n} + (X_p - \bar{X})^2 \frac{\sigma^2}{\sum (X_i - \bar{X})^2}$$

$$= \sigma^2 \left[\frac{1}{n} + \frac{(X_p - \bar{X})^2}{\sum (X_i - \bar{X})^2} \right] \tag{E.15}$$

Thus, we have derived the variance of the estimated mean Y score for a particular X score X_p in simple regression, and we have shown that it will be more variable than the sample mean Y score, and increasingly so as X_p departs more from $\bar{X}$, just as was illustrated by Figures 9E.2 and 9E.3.

A similar, but somewhat different result obtains in ANCOVA. The similarity concerns the variance of the estimated mean Y score for a particular X score in a particular group. For $X = X_p$ and group j, we have

$$\hat{Y}_{p_j} = \hat{\mu} + \hat{\alpha}_j + \hat{\beta}X_p = \bar{Y}_j - b_W\bar{X}_j + b_WX_p = \bar{Y}_j + b_W(X_p - \bar{X}_j) \qquad \text{(E.16)}$$

Thus, as in the simple-regression situation, the variance of our estimated conditional mean Y score increases as X_p departs from $\bar{X}_j$:

$$\sigma^2_{\hat{Y}_{p_j}} = \text{Var}(\bar{Y}_j) + \text{Var}[b_W(X_p - \bar{X}_j)] = \frac{\sigma^2}{n_j} + (X_p - \bar{X}_j)^2\,\text{Var}(b_W)$$

$$= \sigma^2 \left[\frac{1}{n_j} + \frac{(X_p - \bar{X}_j)^2}{\sum_j\sum_i (X_{ij} - \bar{X}_j)^2} \right] \qquad \text{(E.17)}$$

(The intermediate steps of the derivation follow along the same lines as those for Equation E.15.) However, in ANCOVA interest centers on the predicted scores at the grand mean on X (i.e., the adjusted Y means) and in the vertical distance between them. Letting $X_p = \bar{X}$ in Equation E.16 results in the standard equation for the adjusted means:

$$\hat{Y}_j = \bar{Y}_j + b_W(\bar{X} - \bar{X}_j) = \bar{Y}_j - b_W(\bar{X}_j - \bar{X}) \qquad \text{(9.27, repeated)}$$

Thus, the square of the standard error of this adjusted mean, following Equation E.17, is

$$\sigma^2_{\hat{Y}_j} = \sigma^2 \left[\frac{1}{n_j} + \frac{(\bar{X}_j - \bar{X})^2}{\sum_j\sum_i (X_{ij} - \bar{X}_j)^2} \right] \qquad \text{(E.18)}$$

In one-way designs, the contrasts that are most often of interest are pairwise comparisons between groups. Because interpretation of a treatment effect is considerably more complicated in the case of heterogeneous regressions, where the magnitude of the difference between groups changes continuously as a function of the covariate, it is even more likely that contrasts will focus on only two groups at a time. Thus, for these reasons and for simplicity of development in what immediately follows, we consider only the two-group case. After the tests for this situation have been developed, we will suggest a strategy for the general a-group situation. With only two groups, under the assumption of homogeneous slopes, we would be most interested in the difference between the two adjusted means:

$$\hat{Y}_1 - \hat{Y}_2 = \bar{Y}_1 - b_W(\bar{X}_1 - \bar{X}) - [\bar{Y}_2 - b_W(\bar{X}_2 - \bar{X})]$$

$$= (\bar{Y}_1 - \bar{Y}_2) - b_W(\bar{X}_1 - \bar{X}_2) \qquad \text{(E.19)}$$

Notice that, although the comparison is a comparison of the estimated Y means at $\bar{X}$, $\bar{X}$ does not appear in the final form of Equation E.19. Further, this would be true regardless of the particular value X_p at which we might compute the difference between our estimates of the conditional Y means. Thus, it perhaps should not be surprising that, although it is unlike the simple regression situation, the standard error of this estimated treatment effect does not depend on the value of X at which we estimate it. That is, when homogeneous slopes are assumed, the precision of our estimate of the treatment effect is "maintained for all values of X" (Rogosa, 1980, p. 311), with the variance of our estimate in Equation E19 being

$$\sigma^2_{\hat{Y}_1 - \hat{Y}_2} = \sigma^2 \left[\frac{1}{n_1} + \frac{1}{n_2} + \frac{(\bar{X}_1 - \bar{X}_2)^2}{\sum_j \sum_i (X_{ij} - \bar{X}_j)^2} \right] \tag{E.20}$$

This variance expression is like those for the conditional mean (in Equation E.15) and for the adjusted mean (in Equation E.18) in that there is a component for the variability of the mean estimates and another component for the variability of the slope estimate. Because we now have two independent group means, the variance of their difference is the sum of the variances of each mean separately. For the slope estimate, its variance is simply multiplied by the square of the coefficient $(\bar{X}_1 - \bar{X}_2)$ shown in Equation E.19. We can estimate this variance by replacing σ^2 in Equation E.20 by the mean square error associated with our traditional ANCOVA full model. Denote this mean square error s^2. Thus, $(N - 3)s^2$ would be equal to the residual sum of squares associated with the model using a common, pooled estimate of the slope.

We are now finally ready to return to the problem of estimating the vertical distance between two nonparallel regression lines and determining the variability of that estimate. These results build on those we have just presented for the simple regression situation and for ANCOVA with homogeneous slopes. Recall that our prediction equation for the ANCOHET model can be written (see Equations E.1, E.3, and E.4):

$$\hat{Y}_{ij} = a_j + b_j X_{ij} \tag{E.21}$$

Thus, if we substitute for X_{ij} some particular value of the covariate—say, X_p—the difference in estimated conditional means for the two groups would be

$$\hat{Y}_{p1} - \hat{Y}_{p2} = a_1 + b_1 X_p - (a_2 + b_2 X_p)$$
$$= a_1 - a_2 + (b_1 - b_2) X_p \tag{E.22}$$

An alternative way of writing this estimated difference, in which we substitute the expressions for our estimated values of the intercepts, makes it easier to understand the variance estimate. That is, we can write the vertical distance between the two regression lines:

$$\hat{Y}_{p1} - \hat{Y}_{p2} = (\bar{Y}_1 - b_1 \bar{X}_1) - (\bar{Y}_2 - b_2 \bar{X}_2) + (b_1 - b_2) X_p$$
$$= \bar{Y}_1 - \bar{Y}_2 + b_1 (X_p - \bar{X}_1) - b_2 (X_p - \bar{X}_2) \tag{E.23}$$

To determine the variability of this estimate, we must consider not only the sampling error of the Y group means but also both the variance of our estimate of b_1, which equals $\sigma^2 / \sum_i (X_{i1} - \bar{X}_1)^2$, and the variance of our estimate of b_2, $\sigma^2 / \sum_i (X_{i2} - \bar{X}_2)^2$. Thus, similar to Equation E.20, but now allowing for heterogeneous slopes, the variability of our estimate of the vertical distance between the lines can be written:

$$\sigma^2_{\hat{Y}_{p1} - \hat{Y}_{p2}} = \sigma^2 \left[\frac{1}{n_1} + \frac{1}{n_2} + \frac{(X_p - \bar{X}_1)^2}{\sum_i (X_{i1} - \bar{X}_1)^2} + \frac{(X_p - \bar{X}_2)^2}{\sum_i (X_{i2} - \bar{X}_2)^2} \right] \tag{E.24}$$

A comparison with the variance of the estimate of a single mean in regression (Equation E.15) or ANCOVA (Equation E.17) shows that the variance of the distance between two regression lines is simply the sum of the variances of conditional means estimated by each. We can estimate this variance, and thereby move toward carrying out a test of the significance of the difference between the regression lines at any arbitrary value of X, by simply replacing σ^2 in Equation E.24 by the mean square error associated with the model allowing for heterogeneous slopes, which we denote s_{het}^2. In the two-group situation where we estimate a slope and an intercept for each group, our model would have $N - 4$ degrees of freedom. Thus, a test of the significance of the difference between the two lines—that is, of the treatment effect at an X value X_p—would be carried out as a simple t test with $N - 4$ degrees of freedom. That is,

$$t = \frac{\hat{Y}_{p1} - \hat{Y}_{p2} - 0}{\hat{\sigma}_{\hat{Y}_{p1} - \hat{Y}_{p2}}} \tag{E.25}$$

where the denominator is

$$\hat{\sigma}_{\hat{Y}_{p1} - \hat{Y}_{p2}} = s_{\text{het}} \left[\frac{1}{n_1} + \frac{1}{n_2} + \frac{(X_p - \bar{X}_1)^2}{\sum_i (X_{i1} - \bar{X}_1)^2} + \frac{(X_p - \bar{X}_2)^2}{\sum_i (X_{i2} - \bar{X}_2)^2} \right]^{1/2} \tag{E.26}$$

with s_{het} being the square root of s_{het}^2, which, as we suggested previously, is the error E_F for the ANCOHET model (Equation E.1) divided by $N - 4$.

As can be seen in the expression for the estimated standard error above (Equation E.26), the precision of our estimate of the treatment effect decreases the farther the particular point X_p at which we are evaluating it is from the group means of the covariate. This is similar to what we saw in the simple regression situation (Equation E.15 and Figure 9E.3). On the other hand, if X_p is chosen near the center of the distribution of X scores, the accuracy of our estimation of the treatment effect increases. In fact, it turns out that the accuracy is greatest at a point corresponding to a weighted average of the group means on the covariate (with the weight for each mean being the sum of squares on the covariate in the other group). This point is referred to in the literature as the center of accuracy, denoted C_a. Surprisingly, the vertical distance between the two nonparallel regression lines at the center of accuracy corresponds exactly to the estimate of the difference between adjusted means in a typical ANCOVA assuming a common slope. Thus, one can interpret the difference between adjusted means in ANCOVA as the treatment effect for an "average" individual—that is, an individual whose X score is roughly at the center of the distribution of X scores—regardless of whether the regressions are parallel. The difference between the ANCOHET and the ANCOVA tests of this difference is in the error term. The ANCOVA test is perfectly valid only if the assumption of parallelism is exactly met. The ANCOHET test is actually more like the tests commonly employed in factorial ANOVA in that it is valid regardless of whether there is an interaction in the population (nonparallelism). The form of the error term for the ANCOHET test of the treatment effect at the center of accuracy reduces to

$$\hat{\sigma}_{\hat{Y}_{C_a 1} - \hat{Y}_{C_a 2}} = s_{\text{het}} \left[\frac{1}{n_1} + \frac{1}{n_2} + \frac{(\bar{X}_1 - \bar{X}_2)^2}{\sum_j \sum_i (X_{ij} - \bar{X}_j)^2} \right]^{1/2} \tag{E.27}$$

Let us pause at this point to underscore what the methodology we have now introduced allows us to do. The test of heterogeneity of regression (Equation E.8) permits an initial assessment of the need for allowing for varying slopes. Certainly, if this test is significant, we would proceed in the analysis making use of an ANCOHET model. And, we may well want to use an ANCOHET model even if the test for heterogeneity of regression is not significant—either because the test approached significance or because we have reason to suspect heterogeneity on other grounds. The formulas presented in Equations E21–E27 make it possible to perform what may be thought of as tests of simple main effects. These tests can be made at any point of interest on the X dimension. In the absence of practical reasons for preferring other points, the treatment effect would typically be evaluated at the center of accuracy, a point in between the group means on the covariate where our estimate of the treatment effect can be made with the greatest accuracy. The calculations for carrying out such a test for the simple data set presented in Tables 9E.1–9E.3 are illustrated in Table 9E.4.

As shown in the table, the test of the treatment effect in the center of the distribution, allowing for heterogeneous slopes, is nonsignificant. Three points regarding the computations are noteworthy. First, if one compares this test with a standard ANCOVA test, the results turn out to be quite similar. The ANCOVA test yields $F(1, 3) = 0.45$, or $t(3) = \sqrt{(0.45)} = .67$, as opposed to the ANCOHET test result of $t(2) = -.63$. Here, our estimate of population error variance s_{het}^2 in the ANCOHET model is actually larger than the corresponding estimate s^2 in the ANCOVA model (6 versus 5.33). This is so because, with the extremely small n in the current situation, the reduction in error sum of squares resulting from allowing for heterogeneous slopes is more than offset by the loss of a single degree of freedom. Because this will generally not be true and because in a pragmatic if not in a conceptual sense the only difference between the two tests is in the estimate of error variance, the ANCOHET test of the treatment effect at the center of accuracy will typically yield larger F values than the corresponding ANCOVA test.

Second, it is worth confirming, as we indicated would be the case above, that the difference between the ANCOVA adjusted means is exactly equal to the vertical difference between the nonparallel regression lines at the center of accuracy. This is particularly easy to do here because of the location of the center of accuracy in this artificial data set. Because the sums of squares around the covariate group means are identical for the two groups (both equal 2), when these are used as weights to compute the weighted average of the group means that defines the center of accuracy, the resulting value is simply the grand mean on the covariate. The estimated Y values for the nonparallel regression lines corresponding to this $\bar{X}$ value of 3 can be read easily off the plot in Figure 9E.1(b) or the computed $\hat{Y}$ values shown in Table 9E.3. There we determine that in group 1 the estimated Y value at $X = 3$ is 8, whereas in group 2 a Y value of 10 is estimated. Although these are different from the corresponding ANCOVA adjusted means of 9 and 11, respectively, the point is that the treatment effect indicated by the difference between the two adjusted means is identical to the treatment effect in the ANCOHET model at the center of accuracy, that is, $9 - 11 = 8 - 10 = -2$.

Third, and finally, we must stress that the significance test just performed is appropriate for the case where you want to examine the treatment effect only at a

TABLE 9E.4 Test of Treatment Effect at the Center of Accuracy

Means*		ANCOHET Model Estimates*		ANCOVA Model Estimates*	
$\bar{X}_1 = 2$	$\bar{Y}_1 = 7$	$b_1 = 1$	$a_1 = 5$	$b_W = 2$	$a_1 = 3$
$\bar{X}_2 = 4$	$\bar{Y}_2 = 13$	$b_2 = 3$	$a_2 = 1$		$a_2 = 5$
		$E_F = 12$	$df_F = 2$	$E_R = 16$	$df_R = 3$

Computation of Adjusted Treatment Effect in ANCOVA

$$\text{Adjusted means: } \bar{Y}'_j = \bar{Y}_j - b_W(\bar{X}_j - \bar{X}) \qquad \text{(9.27, repeated)}$$

For group 1: $\bar{Y}'_1 = 7 - 2(2 - 3) = 7 - 2(-1) = 7 + 2 = 9$

For group 2: $\bar{Y}'_2 = 13 - 2(4 - 3) = 13 - 2(1) = 13 - 2 = 11$

Difference between adjusted means: $\bar{Y}'_1 - \bar{Y}'_2 = 9 - 11 = -2$

Computation of Standard Error of the Estimate of the Treatment Effect at the Center of Accuracy

$$\hat{\sigma}_{\hat{Y}_{C_a1} - \hat{Y}_{C_a2}} = s_{\text{het}} \left[\frac{1}{n_1} + \frac{1}{n_2} + \frac{(\bar{X}_1 - \bar{X}_2)^2}{\sum_j \sum_i (X_{ij} - \bar{X}_j)^2} \right]^{1/2} \qquad \text{(E.27, repeated)}$$

$$s_{\text{het}}^2 = \frac{E_F}{df_F} = \frac{\sum_j \sum_i (Y_{ij} - \hat{Y}_{ij_F})^2}{N - 4} = \frac{6 + 6}{6 - 4} = \frac{12}{2} = 6 \qquad \text{(from Table 9E.3)}$$

$$\sum_j \sum_i (X_{ij} - \bar{X}_j)^2 = 2 + 2 = 4$$

$$\hat{\sigma}_{\hat{Y}_{C_a1} - \hat{Y}_{C_a2}} = \sqrt{6} \left[\frac{1}{3} + \frac{1}{3} + \frac{(2-4)^2}{4} \right]^{1/2} = \sqrt{6} \left[\frac{2}{3} + \frac{4}{4} \right]^{1/2} = \sqrt{6} \cdot \sqrt{5/3} = \sqrt{30/3} = \sqrt{10}$$

Test of Treatment Effect at Center of Accuracy

$$t = \frac{\hat{Y}_{C_a1} - \hat{Y}_{C_a2}}{\hat{\sigma}_{\hat{Y}_{C_a1} - \hat{Y}_{C_a2}}} = \frac{\bar{Y}'_1 - \bar{Y}'_2}{(10)^{1/2}} = \frac{-2}{3.16} = -0.63, \text{ nonsignificant}$$

*Previous results computed in Tables 9E.1–9E.3.

single prespecified point on the X dimension. If you want to investigate the treatment effect at multiple points on the X dimension, which you would be prone to do when the covariate is itself a factor of interest rather than just a "nuisance" variable to be statistically controlled, then some modification of these procedures is needed. These are detailed in the next section.

Simultaneous Tests. The reason for needing simultaneous tests is essentially the same as that discussed in Chapter 5 when we introduced multiple-comparison procedures. When performing multiple tests or when performing tests after examining the data, possibility of Type I error increases unless adjustments are made in the tests. The concern in the earlier chapters was because of the variety of contrasts that could be examined in multiple-group studies, but here the concern is with the large number of points on the X dimension at which the treatment effect could be investigated.

Potthoff (1964) extends a procedure known as the Johnson–Neyman technique to handle the problem of controlling α despite the large number of possible X values at which tests could be made. His solution makes use of the Working–Hotelling procedure for establishing confidence bounds around a regression line (see Neter, Wasserman, & Kutner, 1985, p. 154ff.). The solution is in practice a simple one and is similar to the Scheffé procedure for multiple comparisons in that the only difference from the test developed previously is that a multiple of a value taken from a standard F table is used as the critical value for your test. That is, the square of the observed t value computed using Equation E.25 would be compared not against an F with 1 and $N - 4$ degrees of freedom but against a somewhat larger critical value. We might, following Neter, Wasserman, and Kutner (1985, p. 154), refer to this critical value as W^2 where for any desired α

$$W^2 = 2F(2, N - 4) \tag{E.28}$$

This critical value can be used to test the significance of the treatment effect at any number of X values, and the probability of a Type I error being made anywhere in the set of tests will not be more than the nominal α level used in selecting the F value. In fact, a common approach to summarizing the results of such tests is to determine regions of significance. That is, one could specify the portion(s) of the X-axis at which the treatment effect was significantly different from zero. This information can be most useful in clinical, educational, or other applied settings where the instrument being used as a covariate in one study is being explored to determine within what ranges of scores assignment to one treatment rather than another would be expected to produce a difference. Such information could be used in planning how future assignment to treatment or instructional options could be carried out to maximize expected outcomes. See Rogosa (1980, 1981) for additional details on regions of significance.

If there are more than two groups in the study and you wish to do multiple pairwise comparisons, the procedures we have developed can be used simply by using a Bonferroni procedure to determine the α level for the selection of a critical value of F and hence for W^2 in Equation E.28. Thus, with five contrasts by using $.05/5 = .01$ as the α level for choosing the F in Equation E.28, you can control α_{EW} for the tests at .05.

Summary Regarding Heterogeneity of Regression.   We have now developed how to test for heterogeneity of regression; how to carry out a summary test of the treatment effect at a single, preselected X value, which will be valid whether or not there is heterogeneity of regression; and, finally, how to determine at any and all X values of interest whether the treatment effect is significant there. What remains to be done is to specify a set of guidelines indicating when these procedures should be used.

As noted previously, texts frequently treat homogeneity of regression as a necessary assumption for use of ANCOVA. Guidelines regarding the use of ANCOVA in the face of heterogeneity of regression have been drawn from Monte Carlo studies such as those reported and discussed in Glass, Peckham, and Sanders (1972) and Hamilton (1976, 1977). These can now be viewed in a somewhat different light given Rogosa's (1980) analytical results.

It is quite possible to argue that the effects of heterogeneity of regression when present will typically be small and in a conservative direction so that one can proceed with a typical ANCOVA without much uneasiness even when you suspect heterogeneity of regression. However, our recommendation is that one should have a bias for using the ANCOHET procedures. The only disadvantage of ANCOHET would be a potential for a slight loss in power if the regressions were perfectly parallel, whereas the advantages are substantial—the possibility of a much more thorough description of your data in those cases where the treatment effect depends on X.

Admittedly, there will be times when a complete conditional analysis will not be of interest—for example, differential assignment to conditions in the future may not be practical even if you know how treatment effectiveness varies as a function of X. Nonetheless, as we have shown, ANCOHET could be used to provide a single, overall test of the treatment effect. Such an ANCOHET test is recommended in this situation because (1) given that some evidence for heterogeneity is virtually assured, the overall ANCOHET test will be more powerful than the corresponding ANCOVA test of treatment effect; and (2) the models being used in the test are being made sufficiently flexible to represent any population heterogeneity of regression at a very small cost, that is, slight reduction in the denominator degrees of freedom of the test.

In practical terms, one might carry out an ANCOHET analysis if any of a set of preliminary conditions were met. First, if one has reason to expect heterogeneity on the basis of theory or previous empirical work, then use the ANCOHET approach. Second, if heterogeneity is not anticipated but a test for heterogeneity approaches significance—say, $p < .2$—then use the ANCOHET approach.

Once one has opted for the ANCOHET approach, the question arises as to whether to test for the treatment effect at a single point or use the simultaneous test procedures to allow for tests to be carried out at several points on the X dimension. Certainly, if the regression lines intersect within the range of X values observed in the study, a simultaneous analysis would be called for. Otherwise, if there is practical or theoretical interest in the treatment effect for various subpopulations identified by X scores, then one would want to carry out the simultaneous analysis. If neither of these conditions are met, then a single overall ANCOHET test of the treatment effect would suffice.

The practical cost of following these recommendations is merely that a few hand calculations may be required because the major computer packages at the moment do not have routines for testing the significance of the treatment effect at arbitrary points on X. Nonetheless, as we have shown in Table 9E.4, the required tests can be carried out as a simple t test. The predicted Y scores are readily computed as an option in one of the standard computer routines. The standard error used in the denominator of the test can be computed, following Equation E.27 as illustrated in Table 9E.4, with a hand calculator in a few minutes once the within-group regressions have been computed and an ANOVA on the covariate has been performed so that the means and within-group sum of squares for X are known.

10   Designs with Random or Nested Factors

421

DESIGNS WITH RANDOM FACTORS

Introduction to Random Effects

TO THIS POINT, WE have considered models appropriate for the situation where all factors have levels selected because of the interest of the investigator in *those* particular levels. Such factors are said to be *fixed* because the same, fixed levels would be included in replications of the study. If one were interested in comparing the relative effectiveness of behavior modification and psychoanalytic approaches to treating agoraphobia, then only experiments containing implementations of these two particular approaches would be relevant to the question of interest.

In other experimental situations, the levels included in any one test of a factor are arbitrary, and the concern is with generalizing not to the effects of a few particular levels of a factor but to a population of levels that the selected levels merely represent. For example, if one wonders about the effects of different high school math teachers in a school district on the math achievement scores of students in their classes, it might not be feasible to include all the math teachers in a study. However, if you randomly select a small group of teachers to participate in your study, you would like to make inferences to the effects of the whole population of teachers in the district, just as you want to make inferences to a population of subjects even though you can only randomly sample a small group for inclusion in your study.

Factors having randomly selected levels are, naturally enough, termed *random factors*, and the statistical models appropriate for analyzing experiments based on such factors are termed *random-effects models*. If an experiment contains both random and fixed factors, a *mixed model* is appropriate. The terms involved in the linear model appear the same in all these cases. For example, in a two-factor design, the linear model could be written

$$Y_{ijk} = \mu + \alpha_j + \beta_k + (\alpha\beta)_{jk} + \varepsilon_{ijk}$$

regardless of whether the design involved only fixed effects, only random effects, or a combination of fixed and random effects. However, the assumptions made about the terms in the linear model would differ, and consequently the way the ANOVA should be carried out would also differ across these three cases.

Recall that in the fixed-effects case we only have to make a few assumptions about the errors ε_{ijk} in our model in order to get a "valid" F. In particular, we assume that the errors are normally and independently distributed, with each having an expectation of zero and a variance of σ_ε^2, over hypothetical replications of the experiment. Implicitly, we also assume that the levels of the factors are fixed, so that if replications of the experiment are carried out, the same levels of the factors are used. Thus, the values of the effect parameters applicable to the study are the same for each replication. Although, of course, we typically don't know the "true" effect of a factor for the population, we do assume that what we are seeing in any one experiment is that true effect on each individual, perturbed only by random error.

One implication of these assumptions in the fixed-effects case is that the variability observed in our dependent variable is due only to the random errors in individual scores. That is, $\sigma_Y^2 = \sigma_\varepsilon^2$ because in the prediction equation (linear model) only ε_{ijk} is a random variable. Further, because the variability in the Y scores is due solely to the variability of the error component of our equation, estimates of σ_Y^2 like MS_A or MS_B, under the null hypothesis, depend only on σ_ε^2. In the random-effects case, such mean squares reflect other components of variability as well, namely, the variability introduced by including different randomly selected levels of the factors in each replication of the experiment.

In the random-effects case (sometimes referred to as a *variance-components* case), we assume that the levels of a factor included in the experiment are drawn at random from a population of levels. Frequently, it is appropriate to view such independent variables as being not so much "manipulated" as "sampled". Thus, one may sample classrooms, therapists, dosage levels of a drug, or possible orderings of stimuli presented in a study. To examine the effects of such factors, the appropriate model assumes that the corresponding effect parameters in the model—for example, α_js—randomly vary as well as the ε_{ijk}s. As always, our statistical model must reflect the realities of the experimental situation in order for our analysis to be valid.

However, there will be at times an element of choice, or at least room for debate, in how one defines the "realities of the experimental situation." Perhaps most commonly in psychology, the issue of whether a factor should be a random factor is debatable because the levels of that factor represent a convenience sample rather than a true random sample from some population of levels. For example, in a clinical outcome study, you might employ a number of clinical psychologists as therapists to administer various treatment modalities. You then would typically want to know whether therapists differ in effectiveness in this situation. The particular therapists included in the study would in all likelihood be those friends or colleagues that you could conveniently get to participate, rather than a sample drawn at random from a large population of therapists.

How you analyze your data in such a situation depends in part at least on what questions are of interest. As one alternative, you may wonder if the effectiveness of your treatments varies across this particular set of therapists. In that case, therapists would be treated as a fixed factor, and your inferences would be to the population of hypothetical replications involving the same therapists but different clients. On the other hand, your interest may be in whether these treatments would vary in their impact on clients across therapists in general. In that case, therapists should be treated as a random factor. Then, one's inferences would be to the set of hypothetical replications involving different clients on each replication *and* different therapists.

Although one can always offer logical arguments to support extrapolations beyond the particular levels of a factor included in a study, this latter procedure allows such arguments to be buttressed to some extent by statistical evidence. That is, the hypothesis tested in a random-effects design concerns the effects of a population of therapists rather than just those included in the study. The population, however, is often purely hypothetical in that it is, for example, that set of therapists for which the actual therapists in the study represent a simple random sample. Thus, the inference from the results to any real population would still necessarily be made to some extent on nonstatistical grounds. Keeping this in mind, we now present the procedures for testing hypotheses regarding the effects of a population of potential levels of a factor, starting first with the single-factor case and then generalizing to two-factor and mixed designs.

One-Factor Case

Model. Chapter 3 introduced a model for one-way designs in terms of the population means of the a groups. We now use a very similar full model to introduce a one-way random-effects analysis:

$$Y_{ij} = \mu_j + \varepsilon_{ij} \tag{1}$$

where $i = 1, 2, 3, \ldots, n_j$ and $j = 1, 2, 3, \ldots, a$. The terms of the model are the same as in the fixed-effects case (cf. Equation 3.54) but we assume some of the terms have different characteristics. The error scores are still presumed to be normally distributed in the population with mean zero and variance σ_ε^2. However, now we assume that the μ_j, rather than being fixed from one replication to the next, are also independent, random variables with mean zero and variance σ_α^2. The α subscript is used because variation in the μ_j reflects the effect of factor A. Finally, the μ_j and the ε_{ij} are assumed to be independent.

The distinction between the two kinds of variability in this model is made clear by portraying them graphically and illustrating their meaning in concrete examples. The μ_j will be sampled from one normal distribution, which will have a mean of μ and a standard deviation of σ_α, as shown at the top of Figure 10.1. In the figure, three values of μ_j are indicated, corresponding to three conditions that might conceivably be selected. Each of these values in turn corresponds to the mean of a distribution of Y values. The variances of the three distributions of Y values shown in the lower part of the figure are all assumed to be equal to each other but will in general be different from the value of σ_α^2.

For example, to continue the illustration of therapists as defining the levels of the random factor, the director of a clinic in a large psychology department might wonder how much of the variability in the general severity index his graduate trainees give clients on intake is due to which trainee is doing the rating rather than variability among clients. The μ_j term then is the mean of the general severity rating that would be obtained if the jth clinical graduate student were to evaluate everyone in the population of potential clients, σ_ε is the standard deviation of the ratings given by this trainee, μ is the mean of all such means for the population of graduate trainees, and σ_α is the standard deviation of the trainees' individual means around μ.

One area of psychology in which random-effects models are used with some

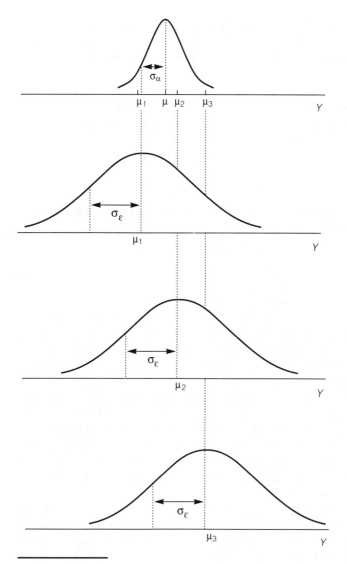

FIGURE 10. 1   Representation of a full model for a one-way random-effects design.

regularity is the area of psycholinguistics (cf. Clark, 1973; Forster & Dickinson, 1976; Wike & Church, 1976). One difficulty in that area is that there are a vast number of ways to select words and combine them to illustrate a particular linguistic form. Thus, such "materials" factors are often treated as a random effect. For example, in a study of prose comprehension, of the host of paragraphs that would meet the constraints of a particular study such as length and structure, you might select three for use in your study. Using reading time as the dependent variable, the mean reading time of all possible subjects on a particular passage corresponds to

μ_j in the model. The variability of all potential subjects' reading times on a given passage is assumed to be σ_ε^2 for each passage, whereas the variability among all the means for the various passages that might have been included in the study is σ_α^2.

Model Comparisons. In the one-factor mixed-model design, the test of interest, as in the fixed-effects case, asks whether constraining the means of all levels of the factor to be the same significantly increases the lack of fit of the model. Thus, to test factor A, we compare the following models:

$$\text{Full:} \qquad Y_{ij} = \mu_j + \varepsilon_{ij}$$

$$\text{Restricted:} \qquad Y_{ij} = \mu + \varepsilon_{ij} \tag{2}$$

The hypotheses corresponding to these models are expressed somewhat differently than in the fixed-effects case, namely,

$$H_1 : \sigma_\alpha^2 > 0$$

$$H_0 : \sigma_\alpha^2 = 0 \tag{3}$$

Although the null hypothesis again implies that all the group means are equal and the alternative hypothesis allows for them to vary, as was true in the fixed-effects case, the use of σ^2s instead of μs represents more than just a change in notation. Now one's inferences will be not just regarding the effects of those levels included in the study but regarding the effects of the whole population of levels of the factor from which the selected levels were sampled.

Despite this difference in the nature of the hypotheses, the test for a one-factor design is carried out in exactly the same way as we did in the fixed-effects case. However, there are differences in the expected value of various terms in the analysis. As we will see shortly, although these do not affect the analysis in the one-way case, such differences in expected values imply the presence of a random factor will typically alter the way the analysis is carried out in more complicated designs.

Expected Values. The expected values of the terms in the F test depend in part on the expected value and variance of the Y scores. Because of the assumptions made about the means and independence of the μ_j and ε_{ij} terms, the expected value and variance of the Y scores, respectively, are

$$\mathcal{E}(Y_{ij}) = \mu \tag{4}$$

$$\text{Var}(Y_{ij}) = \sigma_\alpha^2 + \sigma_\varepsilon^2 \tag{5}$$

As was true in the fixed-effect case, the error scores computed in the least-squares solution for the full model are simply the deviations from the cell means. Thus, the variance estimate derived from these deviation scores is an unbiased estimate of the population variance of the ε_{ij}. That is,

$$\mathcal{E}(E_F/df_F) = \mathcal{E}(MS_W) = \sigma_\varepsilon^2 \tag{6}$$

regardless of whether the null hypothesis is true or false.

The critical expected value in designs involving random factors is that of the numerator of the typical F test, that is, $\mathscr{E}[(E_R - E_F)/(df_R - df_F)]$. In the case of an equal-n design,[1] this expected mean square for the A effect can be written

$$\mathscr{E}(MS_A) = \mathscr{E}[(E_R - E_F)/(df_R - df_F)] = \sigma_\varepsilon^2 + n\sigma_\alpha^2 \qquad (7)$$

Note the relationship between the expected values of the numerator and denominator of the F. Under the null hypothesis, $\sigma_\alpha^2 = 0$ and $\mathscr{E}(MS_A) = \mathscr{E}(MS_W)$. To the extent σ_α^2 is nonzero, the numerator tends to reflect this and be greater than the denominator. Thus, numerator and denominator manifest the desired relation of the numerator's expected mean square having only one additional term over those in the denominator, and that additional term corresponding to the effect being tested.

Two-Factor Case

Expected Mean Squares.   When we move to designs involving two independent variables, all three conceivable variations on the presence of random factors are possible. That is, if neither factor is random, we have the fixed-effects case; if both are random, it is a random-effects case; and if only one factor is random, the design is said to be mixed.

With such multiple-factor designs, a somewhat counterintuitive result occurs in the impact of the random factor on the expected mean square for the various effects. Specifically, the presence of a random factor causes the term for the interaction of that factor with the other factor in the design to appear in the expression for the expected mean square for the main effect of the *other* factor. Let us see something of how this may occur by considering a simple numerical example.

To expand on the clinical graduate student example introduced earlier in the chapter, assume that each of the trainees is asked to do multiple-therapy sessions, some taking a behavioral approach, some taking a psychodynamic approach, and some taking a Rogerian approach. After each session, a faculty supervisor rates the effectiveness of the session on a seven-point scale.

Let us assume that the situation is such that some student therapists earn higher ratings with one clinical modality than another but that overall there are no differences in the average abilities of the student therapists, nor in the average effectiveness of the various approaches to therapy. To illustrate what we should expect the numerator of the F tests for main effects to equal, consider the means in Table 10.1 to be the population mean ratings for the 18 clinical trainees in a particular program. Each student has a rating for each of the three therapy modes under consideration, reflecting his or her *true* effectiveness with that method. Note that we are bypassing the error component that would cause variability in individual scores. The numbers presented are to be interpreted as population means, for example, the mean rating that would be obtained if a particular trainee were to use a particular method with all the potential clients. Although we, of course, would not know these values in practice and although the means in the table are clearly more patterned than one would expect in reality, such a set of means illustrates the difficulty that the presence of a random factor introduces into the analysis of

TABLE **10.1** Example of the Effects of an Interaction in the Population Between a Random Factor and a Fixed Factor

I. Population Means for Three Therapy Modes and for the Entire Population of Trainees

| | | | | | | | | | Clinical Trainee | | | | | | | | | | |
Therapy Mode	a	b	c	d	e	f	g	h	i	j	k	l	m	n	o	p	q	r	Mean
Psychodynamic	7	6	5	7	6	5	4	4	4	1	2	3	4	4	4	1	2	3	4
Behavioral	4	4	4	1	2	3	7	6	5	7	6	5	1	2	3	4	4	4	4
Rogerian	1	2	3	4	4	4	1	2	3	4	4	4	7	6	5	7	6	5	4
Mean	4	4	4	4	4	4	4	4	4	4	4	4	4	4	4	4	4	4	4

II. Population Means for Three Therapy Modes and for a Sample of Trainees

| | Clinical Trainee | | | |
Therapy Mode	g	k	r	Mean
Psychodynamic	4	2	3	3.00
Behavioral	7	6	4	5.67
Rogerian	1	4	5	3.33
Mean	4	4	4	4.00

factorial designs. The numbers are arranged so that, as indicated by the marginal means, the 18 trainees all have the same average effectiveness scores and the means achieved under the three therapy modes are identical as well. Thus, in the population there is no main effect of either the factor of clinical trainee or therapy mode.

Will this be the case if we randomly sample levels of the clinical trainee factor rather than including all 18 graduate students? Results will differ depending on which trainees are selected. If we were to select students g, k, and r, for example, to serve as the "levels" of the random factor of clinical trainee, the marginal means for the trainees would still be identical, but the marginal means for the fixed factor of therapy mode would differ. That is, there appears to be a main effect of therapy mode. As shown in the lower part of Table 10.1, this particular set of students would make the behavioral approach appear most effective, the Rogerian approach somewhat worse than average, and the psychodynamic approach worst of all.

The reason for this apparent difference across levels of therapy mode when in fact there are no differences overall in the population is, of course, that clinical trainee and therapy mode interact. What the numerical example shows is that the presence of an interaction between a random and a fixed factor does not affect the main effect of the random factor, but it can cause the variability among the means for the fixed factor to increase. Thus, a model comparison assessing the effect of restricting the parameter corresponding to the fixed-effects factor to be zero may suggest that this leads to an increase in error in describing the data when in fact it would not if *all* levels of the random factor had been included in the study. This

T A B L E **10. 2** Expected Values of Numerators of the Test Statistic for
Individual Effects in Various Two-Factor Crossed Designs*

	Design		
Effect	Fixed Effects (Factors A and B both fixed)	Mixed (Factor A fixed, Factor B random)	Random Effects (Factors A and B both random)
A	$\sigma_\varepsilon^2 + bn\theta_\alpha^2$	$\sigma_\varepsilon^2 + n\sigma_{\alpha\beta}^2 + bn\theta_\alpha^2$	$\sigma_\varepsilon^2 + n\sigma_{\alpha\beta}^2 + bn\sigma_\alpha^2$
B	$\sigma_\varepsilon^2 + an\theta_\beta^2$	$\sigma_\varepsilon^2 + an\sigma_\beta^2$	$\sigma_\varepsilon^2 + n\sigma_{\alpha\beta}^2 + an\sigma_\beta^2$
AB	$\sigma_\varepsilon^2 + n\theta_{\alpha\beta}^2$	$\sigma_\varepsilon^2 + n\sigma_{\alpha\beta}^2$	$\sigma_\varepsilon^2 + n\sigma_{\alpha\beta}^2$

* Results are for a design with a levels of factor A, b levels of factor B, and n subjects per cell. Symbols are explained in the text. Values given above are expectations of the form $\mathscr{E}(MS_{\text{effect}}) = \mathscr{E}[(E_R - E_F)/(df_R - df_F)]$, where the restricted model in each case is arrived at by imposing the restriction on the full model that all effect parameters associated with a particular effect are zero.

implies that our typical F test would have a positive bias in testing this effect. That is, the numerator would reflect components other than just error and the effect being tested. The test statistic we have employed previously could be expressed here verbally as the ratio of the following components:

$$\text{"Standard" test for therapy mode} = \frac{\text{Variability due to subjects, therapy mode} \times \text{clinical trainee, and therapy mode}}{\text{Variability due to subjects}}$$

Because we want our test statistic to have a numerator that differs from the denominator only as a result of the effect of the factor being tested, some adjustment of our test statistics is required.

The precise adjustment needed can be seen by examining the expected value of the mean square for each effect, that is, the expected value of the difference in sums of squared errors for the models being compared over the difference in the number of parameters in the two models. These expected values are shown for three types of equal-n, two-factor designs in Table 10.2. For all designs, note that the mean square within—that is, E_F divided by df_F—will have an expected value of σ_ε^2.

Model Comparisons. The model comparisons involved are the usual ones for a particular effect, regardless of the type of design. For example, the mean square for factor A is derived from a comparison of models:

$$\text{Full:} \qquad Y_{ijk} = \mu + \alpha_j + \beta_k + (\alpha\beta)_{jk} + \varepsilon_{ijk}$$

$$\text{Restricted:} \qquad Y_{ijk} = \mu + \beta_k + (\alpha\beta)_{jk} + \varepsilon_{ijk} \tag{8}$$

In the equal-n case, we have

$$E_R - E_F = SS_A = \sum_j \sum_k \sum_i e_{ijk,R}^2 - \sum_j \sum_k \sum_i e_{ijk,F}^2$$

$$= \sum_j \sum_k \sum_i \hat\alpha_j^2$$

$$= bn \sum_j \hat\alpha_j^2 = bn \sum_j (\bar{Y}_{j.} - \bar{Y}_{..})^2 \tag{9}$$

Dividing by the number of independent α_j parameters yields

$$(E_R - E_F)/(df_R - df_F) = \frac{SS_A}{df_A} = MS_A = bn\frac{\sum_j \hat{\alpha}_j^2}{a-1} \tag{10}$$

The expected value of this mean square, however, will differ depending on the type of design.

In the fixed-effects case, the expected mean square will be simply the sum of two components, one reflecting the within-cell error variance and the other the extent to which the population marginal means at different levels of factor A differ from each other. That is,

$$\mathscr{E}(MS_A) = \mathscr{E}\left(\frac{bn\sum_j \hat{\alpha}_j^2}{a-1}\right) = \sigma_\varepsilon^2 + bn\frac{\sum_j \alpha_j^2}{a-1} \tag{11}$$

Because the quantities $\alpha_j = \mu_j - \mu$ represent the entire set of population mean deviations, dividing the sum of their squares by $a - 1$ does not actually yield a variance. Thus, rather than denoting it by a σ^2, we need to use a different symbol, and the conventional one, as shown in Table 10.2, is θ^2 (Greek letter *theta*, squared). The value of θ^2 for an effect is defined as the sum of the squared population parameter values for that particular effect divided by the degrees of freedom for the effect. Thus we have

$$\theta_\alpha^2 = \frac{\sum_j \alpha_j^2}{a-1} \qquad \theta_\beta^2 = \frac{\sum_k \beta_k^2}{b-1} \qquad \theta_{\alpha\beta}^2 = \frac{\sum_j \sum_k (\alpha\beta)_{jk}^2}{(a-1)(b-1)} \tag{12}$$

The expected values for the other designs shown in Table 10.2 also deserve comment. The mixed design corresponds to our example, with therapy mode being the fixed factor A and clinical trainee the random factor B. As our numerical example suggests, the mean square for the main effect of the random factor reflects only random error and variability among the various levels of the factor in the population. Note that the interaction effect of a fixed factor and a random factor is a random effect because the particular interaction parameters included in a study will depend on which levels of factor B were randomly selected. Perhaps of most interest in the mixed-design case is the expected mean square for the fixed-effect factor. As is also suggested by our numerical example, $\mathscr{E}(MS_A)$ for this design reflects not only random error associated with individual scores and the magnitude of the effect of factor A in the population θ_α^2 but also the interaction of the two factors in the population.

The situation is similar in the random-effects design. However, because the "other" factor is a random factor regardless of which main effect is being considered, the expected mean square for each main effect includes the interaction of that factor with the other.

Selection of Error Terms.   For the fixed-effects design, the appropriate error term or denominator of the test statistic for all effects is, of course, E_F/df_F or MS_W. Mean square within is the correct denominator term because each of the effects in the fixed-effects design differs from MS_W in expected value only by one component,

TABLE **10. 3** Error Terms for Tests of Specific Effects in Different Types of
Completely Crossed Two-Factor Designs*

Design					
Fixed Effects (Factors A and B both fixed)		*Mixed (Factor A fixed, Factor B random)*		*Random Effects (Factors A and B both random)*	
Effect	Error Term	Effect	Error Term	Effect	Error Term
A	MS_W	A	MS_{AB}	A	MS_{AB}
B	MS_W	B	MS_W	B	MS_{AB}
AB	MS_W	AB	MS_W	AB	MS_W

*$MS_W = E_F/df_F$, and $MS_{AB} = (E_R - E_F)/(df_R - df_F)$, where the restricted model imposes the restriction on the null model that all $(\alpha\beta)_{jk} = 0$.

namely, that for the effect under consideration. This is true also for the interaction effect in the mixed- and random-effects two-factor design. Thus, MS_W can be used as the denominator in tests of the AB effect for these designs as well.

However, if we were to use MS_W in the test of the main effect of the fixed factor in the mixed design, we would *not* really be testing simply the main effect of the fixed factor. Rather, we would actually be performing a test of whether there was evidence for a main effect of the fixed factor *or* an interaction. This would be true also for each of the main effects in the random-effects design. Fortunately, we can meet the criterion of having an error term that differs in expected value only by the component associated with the effect being tested by using the mean square for the interaction as the error term in such cases. Table 10.3 shows the error terms for all effects in the different types of two-factor designs we have been considering.

We can summarize rather succinctly the source of the difficulty for the analysis posed by the presence of a random factor and the nature of the solution outlined above. The difficulty is that the expected value of the mean square—that is, the expected value of $(E_R - E_F)/(df_R - df_F)$—for an effect will include, besides error variance, not only a component for the population magnitude of that effect but also a component reflecting the magnitude of the interaction of that effect with any random factor.

The solution is to choose an error term that is appropriate for the particular effect being considered. The rules for how to determine such an error term can be stated fairly simply as well, not only for two-factor designs but also for any completely crossed, between-subjects factorial design. Specifically, two rules determine the exact error term for an effect:

1. If there are no random factors in the design or if the effect being tested contains all random factors, then use $MS_W = E_F/df_F$ as the error term.

2. Otherwise, use as the error term the interaction with a random factor of the effect being tested. That is, use as the error term $MS_{interaction} = (E_R - E_F)/(df_R - df_F)$, where the restriction imposed on the fullest model is that these

interaction parameters are zero. If there is more than one random factor besides any included in the current effect, no exact test is possible.

The flowchart in Figure 10.2 summarizes these rules.

Several comments are in order at this point. First, it appears from Figure 10.2 that you can reach a dead end where there is no acceptable error term. This rarely occurs. Note in this regard that, as long as there is *only* one random factor among

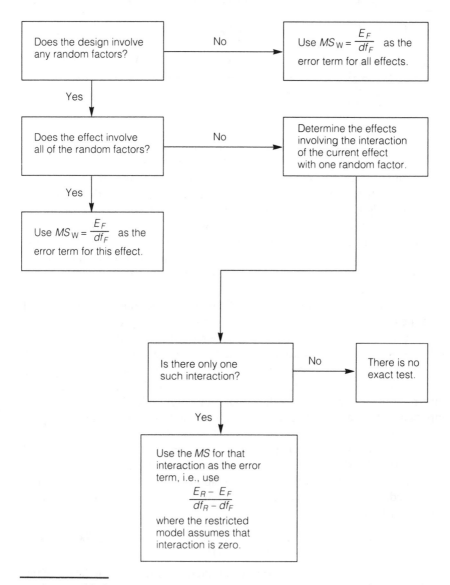

FIGURE 10. 2   Flowchart to assist in the selection of appropriate denominator terms for tests of effects in completely crossed factorial designs.

those factors crossed with each other in a factorial design, then there is always an exact test. Because use of random independent variables is relatively unusual in the behavioral sciences, for a single experiment to involve multiple random factors is very unusual.

Second, random factors are often not of interest in themselves but are included merely as control factors. The random-factor levels may represent different materials such as different prose passages in a human memory experiment, which are not at all the main focus of the experiment. Thus, a common, and perfectly legitimate approach to analyzing the data in such a situation is to do a preliminary analysis of the random control factors, particularly to determine if the control factor interacts with any other factors in the experiment. If it does not, then one can ignore this factor entirely in subsequent analyses. Following this strategy frequently allows one to sidestep the problem of multiple random factors not permitting exact tests of certain effects. The primary cost entailed in such a strategy is that the mean square error associated with the full model may be slightly larger than it might have been because the variability due to the random factor will not have been removed. This is likely to appear a negligible cost compared to the benefit of being able to carry out exact tests of the effects of interest. Further, the degrees of freedom in the denominator of the F ratio are generally much smaller when an interaction with a random factor is used as the error term instead of mean square within. If the number of levels of the random factor is small, the critical value for the F required to declare significance may be quite large. This is a consideration that might motivate one to perform such a preliminary analysis of the random factor; if there is little evidence for its importance—for example, all effects involving this factor yielding $p > .2$—drop the factor from the final analysis in order to have tests of the effects of primary interest based on more degrees of freedom.

Third, if one concludes that multiple random factors must be retained either because of their inherent interest or because of the presence of evidence for their interacting with other factors, it is possible to construct quasi-F ratios in those cases where there is not an exact test available. The logic in such a case is to take a combination of mean squares for various effects, adding some and subtracting others, so that the linear combination will have the desired expected value. The resulting test statistic will only approximately follow an F distribution. The interested reader is referred to Chapter 12 for a brief introduction to quasi-F ratios, or to Myers (1979, p. 191ff.) or Kirk (1982, p. 394ff.) for more detailed treatments.

DESIGNS WITH NESTED FACTORS

Introduction to Nested Factors

We have opted to discuss random and nested factors in a single chapter. Although they are conceptually distinct, in practice they occur together very often. The conceptual distinctions can be stated simply. Whereas the basic idea of a

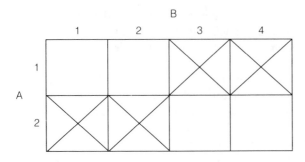

F I G U R E **10. 3** A simple nested design. Note that factor B is nested within levels of factor A. An ✕ in a cell indicates that no observations are available for that cell.

random factor has to do with how the levels of a factor are selected, the essential idea of a nested factor has to do with how the levels of multiple factors are combined. And, whereas the basic implication of having a random factor in a design has to do with what error term is appropriate for testing individual effects, the essential implication of having a nested factor in a design has to do with what effects it even makes sense to try to test and interpret in the first place.

A factor is said to be nested within a second factor if each level of the first factor occurs in conjunction with only one level of the second factor. Note that nesting in general is not a symmetrical arrangement. Figure 10.3 illustrates a design in which factor B is nested within levels of factor A. Whereas level 1 of factor B occurs in conjunction with only level 1 of factor A, level 1 of factor A occurs in conjunction with both levels 1 and 2 of factor B. As the figure suggests, one way of thinking about nested designs is that they are designs with missing cells.

A factor can also be nested within multiple factors instead of a single factor. A factor is said to be nested within a combination of other factors if each of its levels occurs in conjunction with only one combination of levels of the other factors. Figure 10.4 presents the simplest example of this type of design. Factors A and B each have two levels and are crossed with each other so that all possible combinations of levels of these two factors are represented. Factor C is nested within these combinations of levels of factors A and B. Note that there are eight different levels of factor C. If C were to be crossed with A and B, there would be $2 \times 2 \times 8$, or 32, cells in the design. Yet, because of the nesting, we have observations only in eight cells.

That we do not have as many cells as we would in a completely crossed factorial implies that we do not have as many between-cell degrees of freedom and hence that we cannot carry out all the conventional tests of main effects and interactions. Recall that our fullest possible model in terms of means would have one parameter for each of the eight nonvacant cells. Thus, seven independent contrasts, or restrictions, on these eight parameters could be tested. But the conventional test in a

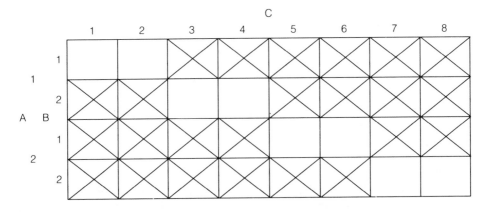

F I G U R E 10. 4 Nesting within a combination of factors. Note that factor C is nested within combinations of levels of factors A and B, or briefly, within A and B. An ✕ in a cell again indicates the cell is missing.

three-way design of, say, the main effect of a factor C with eight levels would itself require seven restrictions which would not leave any available for testing for the effects involving factors A or B.

To determine which effects it makes most sense to test, we return to the simple nested design shown in Figure 10.3 and point out some of the assumptions we will be making about the nested factor. As indicated at the beginning of the chapter, in the behavioral sciences, random factors are sometimes included in a design as a crossed rather than a nested factor. However, if a nested factor *is* included in a design, it is typically a random factor. Thus, we begin our discussion with the analysis of a two-factor nested design where the nested factor is random. Second, although it is not necessary that the number of levels of the nested factor be held constant across levels of the other factor, we assume that this is the case in order to simplify the discussion of the analysis.

Some reflection on the design shown in Figure 10.3 should convince you that certain of the effects that would be tested in a crossed design cannot be evaluated here. Consider first the interaction between factors A and B. An interaction is indicated by the extent to which the difference between levels 1 and 2 of A at one particular level of factor B is different from that at another selected level of factor B. However, because levels 1 and 2 of factor A do not both occur at *any* level of B, there is obviously no way in this design to determine the extent to which the difference between them changes across B. A similar statement can be made about the consistency of differences between two levels of the nested factor B. Although multiple levels of B occur at one level of A so that one can compute the difference in their effects at that level of A, levels of B occur in conjunction with only one level of A, so there is nothing to which this difference can be compared. Note that we are not saying that there is no interaction in the population; there may well be. Rather, the assertion is just that we cannot determine whether there is an interaction with this design.

Consider next the main effect of the nested factor. At first glance, it might appear that this may be tested because we could obtain a marginal mean for each level of B and use these to test the restriction that the corresponding population means are all equal. Although such a restriction could be tested, the test would not be simply one of the main effect of B. In the nested design of Figure 10.3, the "marginal" means for B are simply the cell means, because there is only one cell per level of B. And, the difference between the two cells at a_1 and the two cells at a_2 will be affected by any effect of factor A.

What then is interpretable? Although the overall main effect of B cannot be assessed, the simple main effect of this nested factor can be assessed within each level of factor A. Tests of these simple main effects could be carried out separately, essentially as one-way ANOVAs. However, more often one is equally interested in all the effects that could be attributed to B, and thus a single test of the pooled simple effects of the nested factor is performed. (We present an example of such a test shortly.) Thus, the question being asked is, Is there an effect of factor B at level 1 of A *or* at level 2 of A?

Now consider the effect of the fixed, non-nested factor, factor A. If factor B is random, the population means for the cells within a given level of A will vary over replications to the extent that there are simple effects of factor B. Therefore, even if there were no variability at all among the subjects within a cell nor any effect of factor A, we would nonetheless expect the mean of all observations within a particular level of A to vary from one replication to the next because of sampling a different set of levels of B to include in that replication. This is very similar to what characterizes the main effect of the fixed factor in a mixed crossed design—it can be tested but one must take into account in the test the fact that the presence of the random factor may influence the apparent effect of the fixed factor. Because the mean square for the fixed, non-nested factor here reflects both population error variance and the effect of the nested random factor, as well as the true effect in the population of the fixed factor, the appropriate error term is the mean square for the simple effects of the random factor because it reflects both of the first two components but not the effect to be tested.

To summarize, in a design where a random factor is nested within the levels of a fixed factor, the main effect of the random factor and its interaction with the fixed factor cannot be tested. However, the simple main effects of the random factor can be tested, and the main effect of the fixed factor can be tested by selection of the appropriate denominator term for the test. In general, in designs involving nested random factors, their effects intrude on the expected mean squares of the factors within which they are nested. Table 10.4 shows the specific expected mean squares for such two-factor designs.

This last point about the impact of nested random factors is one that we have not discussed explicitly in prior chapters. However, it has been implicit in all the F tests we considered in previous chapters. Although it would have been unnecessarily cumbersome to develop tests in this way initially, it is useful now to note that in all of our between-subjects designs we have implicitly been dealing with a random

T A B L E **10. 4** Expected Values of Numerators of the Test Statistic for Effects in Two-Factor Designs Involving a Random Nested Factor (Factor B Is Nested Within Levels of Factor A)*

Effect	Design	
	Mixed (Factor A fixed, Factor B random)	Random Effects (Factors A and B both random)
A	$\sigma_\varepsilon^2 + n\sigma_\beta^2 + bn\theta_\alpha^2$	$\sigma_\varepsilon^2 + n\sigma_\beta^2 + bn\sigma_\alpha^2$
B/A	$\sigma_\varepsilon^2 + n\sigma_\beta^2$	$\sigma_\varepsilon^2 + n\sigma_\beta^2$

* Results are for a design with a levels of factor A, b different levels of factor B at each level of A, and n subjects per cell. Values given above are expectations of the form $\mathscr{E}(MS_{\text{effect}}) = \mathscr{E}[(E_R - E_F)/(df_R - df_F)]$, where the restricted model in each case is arrived at by imposing the restriction on the full model that all effect parameters associated with a particular effect are zero.

nested factor of subjects. The sampling error resulting from randomly sampling and/or assigning subjects for the groups in a between-subjects design contributed to the variability among the group means. The σ_ε^2 component in the expected mean squares for the effects in a fixed-effects design (see Table 10.2) is there because of a random factor of subjects nested within each of these effects. Some authors—for example, Keppel (1982)—emphasize this by referring to the within-groups source of variance not as error variance but as, for example, S/AB, where the slash notation, which we employ as well, indicates that the factor to the left of the slash—in this case, subjects—is nested within combinations of levels of the factors to the right, here factors A and B.

One way of schematically representing nested factors that is a useful heuristic for determining the influence of a nested factor on the other effects in the design is the hierarchical diagram shown in Figure 10.5. Figure 10.5(a) shows how what we have treated as a basic two-way crossed design would be represented if subjects were to be treated explicitly as a factor. Nesting is indicated by the fact that the subscripts designating particular subjects are different as one moves from one combination of levels of A and B to another. Although perhaps totally explicit, this seems an unnecessarily complex way of representing a basic 2 × 2 design. Thus, we will not treat subjects explicitly as a factor until we are forced to do so in Chapter 11. Figure 10.5(b) presents the hierarchical structure of a basic two-factor nested design, where again the levels of the nested factor are subsumed under the levels of the factor within which it is nested. The variability induced by the nested factor here being a random factor is transmitted upward to all higher levels of the hierarchy, in something of the same fashion that the shaking of the foundations of a physical structure is felt at all higher levels of the structure. This is true both in the upside-down tree structure of Figure 10.5(a), where explicit variability among subjects causes variability among the means of the basic A × B design, and in Figure 10.5(b), where which levels of factor B are selected at a particular level of factor A will contribute to the variability of the marginal A means over replications.

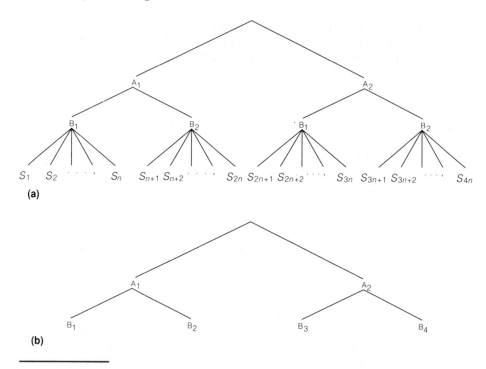

(a)

(b)

F I G U R E   10. 5   Using hierarchical diagrams to represent nested factors. (a) Treating subjects explicitly as a factor nested within combinations of levels of two crossed factors. (b) Factor B nested within levels of factor A. The factor of subjects, which is nested within combinations of levels of A and B, is suppressed.

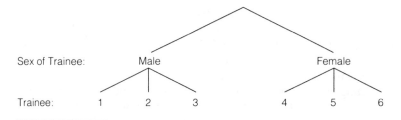

F I G U R E   10. 6   Hierarchical structure of clinical trainee example.

Example

We can expand slightly on the student therapist example of the random-effects section to illustrate a nested design. Assume that the director of the clinic decides to test for a difference across genders in the general severity ratings that graduate students assign to clients. If three male and three female clinical students are randomly selected to participate and each is randomly assigned four clients with whom to do an intake interview, then we would have a design of the form shown in Figure 10.6 and might obtain data like that shown in Table 10.5. We discuss the analysis of these data as we introduce the relevant model comparisons.

TABLE 10.5 Data and Analyses for Clinical Trainee Example

I. General Severity Ratings

	Male j=1									Female j=2								
	Trainee 1 k=1			Trainee 2 k=2			Trainee 3 k=3			Trainee 4 k=1			Trainee 5 k=2			Trainee 6 k=3		
i	Cl	Rating		Cl	Rating		Cl	Rating		Cl	Rating		Cl	Rating		Cl	Rating	
1	a	49	1	e	42	1	i	42	1	m	54	1	q	44	1	u	57
2	b	40	2	f	48	2	j	46	2	n	60	2	r	54	2	v	62
3	c	31	3	g	52	3	k	50	3	o	64	3	s	54	3	w	66
4	d	40	4	h	58	4	l	54	4	p	70	4	t	64	4	x	71
$\bar{Y}_{jk}$:		40			50			48			62			54			64
$\bar{Y}_{j.}$:		162			46									60			
$\sum_i (Y_{ijk} - \bar{Y}_{jk})^2$:		162			136			80			136			200			106

II. Test of Simple Effects of Trainee

$$E_F = 162 + 136 + 80 + 136 + 200 + 106 = 820 = SS_W$$

$$E_R - E_F = \sum_{\text{allobs}} (\hat{Y}_{jk_F} - \hat{Y}_{jk_R})^2 = \sum_j \sum_k \sum_i (\bar{Y}_{jk} - \bar{Y}_{j.})^2$$

$$= 4[(40-46)^2 + (50-46)^2 + (48-46)^2 + (62-60)^2 + (54-60)^2 + (64-60)^2]$$

$$= 4(112) = 448 = SS_{B/A}$$

$$F = \frac{(E_R - E_F)/(df_R - df_F)}{E_F/df_F} = \frac{448/4}{820/(24-6)} = \frac{112}{820/18} = \frac{112}{45.56} = 2.45, \ n.s.$$

(continued)

T A B L E **10.5** (Continued)
III. Test of a Main Effect of Gender of Trainee

$$E_R - E_F = \sum_j \sum_k \sum_i (\bar{Y}_{j.} - \bar{Y})^2 = bn \sum_j (\bar{Y}_{j.} - \bar{Y})^2 = 3 \cdot 4[(46 - 53)^2 + (60 - 53)^2]$$

$$= 12(49 + 49) = 1176$$

$$F = \frac{(E_R - E_F)/(df_R - df_F)}{SS_{B/A}/df_{B/A}} = \frac{1176/1}{448/4} = \frac{1176}{112} = 10.5, p < .05.$$

Models and Tests

For this nested design, we write our full model in terms of cell means in the same way as we did for a two-way crossed design:

$$\text{Full:} \qquad Y_{ijk} = \mu_{jk} + \varepsilon_{ijk} \qquad (13)$$

where $j = 1, 2, \ldots, a$ designates levels of factor A; $k = 1, 2, \ldots, b$ designates levels of factor B nested within a level of A; and, in the case of an equal-n design, $i = 1, 2, \ldots, n$ designates subjects in the jkth cell. Note that now k is like the i subscript in that it refers to a particular level within a given nest of levels. As indicated in Table 10.5, level $k = 2$ of the trainee factor refers to a different trainee when $j = 1$ (males) than when $j = 2$ (females).

To test the effect of the nested factor, we simply impose the restrictions that the means within given levels of the other factor are equal. Thus, in our example, we have

$$\mu_{11} = \mu_{12} = \mu_{13}$$
$$\mu_{21} = \mu_{22} = \mu_{23} \qquad (14)$$

These restrictions imply four independent contrasts in the cell means. Although sums of squares might be obtained for these individual contrasts via the methods of Chapters 4 and 5, we are generally interested in the omnibus test in which all effects of the nested factor are tested simultaneously. We can achieve this result by comparing the full model with a restricted model of the form

$$\text{Restricted:} \qquad Y_{ijk} = \mu_{j.} + \varepsilon_{ijk} \qquad (15)$$

where

$$\mu_{j.} = \frac{\sum\limits_{k} \mu_{jk}}{b}$$

Least-squares estimates are the usual cell means for our full model and are the marginal means at levels of A for this particular restricted model, that is, $\hat{\mu}_{jk} = \bar{Y}_{jk}$ and $\hat{\mu}_{j.} = \bar{Y}_{j.}$. Thus, we obtain the values for E_F and $E_R - E_F$ shown in Table 10.5 for the test of the simple effects of Trainee. The observed F value is compared against a critical value of $F(4, 18) = 2.93$ and thus is nonsignificant at $\alpha = .05$.

The test of the main effect of gender is a test of the restriction that the marginal mean for males is different from that for females, $\mu_{1.} = \mu_{2.}$. We wish to determine the increase in error resulting from imposing such a restriction on the full model. As was indicated in Chapter 7, in an equal-n design, this increase in error is exactly equivalent to that observed in the comparison of two simpler models, namely, one that allows only for this main effect and one that includes only the grand mean. These may be expressed as follows:

$$\text{Full:} \qquad Y_{ijk} = \mu_{j.} + \varepsilon_{ijk}$$
$$\text{Restricted:} \qquad Y_{ijk} = \mu + \varepsilon_{ijk} \qquad (16)$$

Least-squares estimates of these parameters are, of course, the marginal and grand means in the sample data, that is, $\hat{\mu}_{j.} = \bar{Y}_{j.}$ and $\hat{\mu} = \bar{Y}$. The numerator of our test as usual is based on the difference in the errors of these two models over the difference in their degrees of freedom. As we argued above, however, to compare this against something other than mean square within is necessary. As Table 10.4 suggests, the mean square for the effect of the random nested factor has the exactly appropriate expected value to allow an isolation of the effect of the factor within which it is nested. Using the mean square for the nested factor as the denominator in the test of the main effect of the nonnested factor is illustrated at the bottom of Table 10.5. This means that the denominator term involves only 4 degrees of freedom; thus, the critical F required to claim significance at the .05 level is $F(1, 4) = 7.71$. In the present test, our observed F exceeds this value, and we would conclude, given the pattern of means, that female trainees give significantly higher severity ratings than do male trainees.

It may be disconcerting at first that the test of the fixed factor here is based on so few denominator degrees of freedom and that this will remain unaffected by the number of clients that each trainee rates. However, the question asked at this top level of the hierarchy is one appropriately answered by reference to the variability observed at the next highest level. That is, the question of whether male trainees rate differently from female trainees is appropriately answered by reference to the variability among trainees and by taking into consideration how many trainees were sampled.

Fixed-Effects Case

Although the nested factor is typically random, there is no necessity that it be so. For example, one might carry out a two-factor design, similar to what we have just discussed, in a clinic where there were only three male and three female psychologists involved in treatment delivery. If one's interest is simply in generalizing to the typical performance of *these* six individuals, then both the effect of therapist gender and the effect of therapist nested within gender would be treated as fixed. In this case, the expected mean square for the effect of both the nested and the nonnested factor would involve only within-cell error and a term reflecting the true effect in the population of that factor. Thus, as in the fixed-effects designs we considered in previous chapters, MS_W can be used as the denominator term for all effects, assuming homogeneity of variance.

Using Statistical Computer Programs to Analyze Nested Designs

You may have noted that it is possible to use the same notation for the levels of a nested design as we used with a crossed factor (see Equation 13). Although it is critical to keep the nesting in mind in deciding which effects to test and, when the nested factor is random, how these effects should be tested, at a superficial level there are similarities to a crossed design as long as the number of levels of the nested factor stays the same across all "nests." In particular, the total number of groups is then the product of the maximum values of the subscripts used to designate levels of the various factors in both crossed and nested designs.

A pragmatic implication of this fact is that one can specify the factors, whether nested or crossed, involved in a problem in the same way in the initial description of a design in most computer programs. For example, as of this writing, the first line of input for SPSS-X's MANOVA procedure could be

MANOVA Y BY THERAPY (1, 2), TRAINEE (1, 3)/

regardless of whether trainees were nested within or crossed with therapies. The nesting would affect only the list of which effects are to be tested. This is done on what SPSS-X designates a DESIGN statement, for example,

DESIGN = THERAPY VS 1, TRAINEE WITHIN THERAPY = 1 VS WITHIN/

Although perhaps confusing at first glance because WITHIN has two meanings on this line, the first indicating nesting and the second within-cell error, it is clearer once it is understood that VS is used to indicate the denominator term to be used in testing a particular effect.

SAS's PROC GLM also employs a structure that allows both kinds of factors to be listed in the same fashion initially (on a CLASS statement) and nesting to be indicated on the list of effects to be tested (the MODEL statement), although error terms for individual effects are specified elsewhere (on a TEST statement). In addition, SAS generates expected mean squares for effects if requested, either through the RANDOM statement in PROC GLM or through the separate NESTED or VARCOMP procedures.

The expected mean squares, however, are rarely of interest in themselves. Typically, they are of interest only as a means of determining what error term is appropriate as the denominator in the test of a particular effect. This step of consulting tables of expected mean squares, however, can be bypassed entirely in most cases where an exact test of an effect exists, by following a fairly simple set of rules for deciding on an error term. It is to such a set of decision rules that we now turn.

Selection of Error Terms When Nested Factors Are Present

The rules stated in the discussion of selection of error terms at the beginning of this chapter, when the concern was with crossed random factors, must be elaborated to accommodate designs involving nesting. The basic issue with nested designs, as we have seen, is that the variability induced by a random nested factor in a hierarchical design is transmitted up to all higher levels of the hierarchy. Previously we had said that, in mixed- or random-crossed designs, tests of effects not involving all random factors should use as a denominator term the interaction of that effect with a random factor, assuming there is only one such interaction effect. Now we must place "having a random factor nested under the effect to be tested" on a par with "having an interaction of the effect to be tested with a random factor." This is done in Figure 10.7, a flowchart to help one select the correct error term in nested designs.

In the case of nested designs involving only two factors, applying the rules is straightforward. Table 10.6 shows resulting denominator terms for the four possible

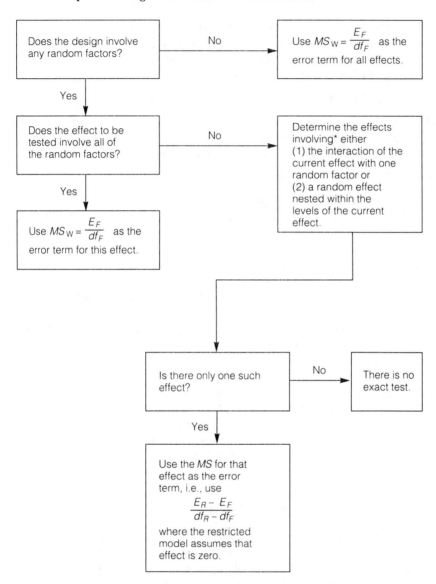

* See text for interpretation of these rules in designs that involve both nesting and more than two factors.

FIGURE 10.7 Flowchart to assist in the selection of appropriate denominator terms for tests of effects in crossed or nested designs.

TABLE **10. 6** Denominator Terms for Testing Effects in Two-Factor Nested Designs (Factor B is Nested Within Levels of Factor A)

		Design		
	Fixed Effects	*Mixed*		*Random Effects*
Effect	(Factors A and B both fixed)	(Factor A fixed, Factor B random)	(Factor A random, Factor B fixed)	(Factors A and B both random)
A	MS_W	$MS_{B/A}$	MS_W	$MS_{B/A}$
B/A	MS_W	MS_W	MS_W	MS_W

such designs. We consider these briefly in turn. In the fixed-effects case, MS_W is used because there are no random factors present. In the other three cases shown in Table 10.6, the answer to the first question in the flowchart of Figure 10.7 is Yes. The most typical case is where only the nested factor is random. In this case, in determining the error term for the A effect, the answer to the second question of whether the effect involves all random factors in the design is No, and following the rules presented in the flowchart, we determine that the B/A effect qualifies for consideration and eventually for selection as the denominator term. MS_W is used for testing B/A because that effect involves all the random factors.

The second mixed design of Table 10.6 in which the nested factor is fixed is the one most seldom encountered. For both A and B/A effects in this design, MS_W is used as the denominator term because there are no other random effects besides those involved in the specification of these effects. Note that, for purposes of this flowchart, a factor is said to be involved in the effect to be tested even if it appears to the right of the slash, that is, even if it is merely the factor within which the nesting is occurring. Thus, in this sense, B/A "involves" A, the random factor.

The final case, where both factors are random, results in selecting B/A as the denominator term for A because B/A is the one random effect nested within levels of the effect to be tested. (Recall that subjects are considered explicitly as a factor only in repeated measures designs where the subjects factor is crossed with other factors, as in Chapter 11 and 12.) In the case of the test of B/A, both random factors are involved in the effect. Thus, MS_W is once again the appropriate denominator term.

Complications That Arise in More Complex Designs

Regardless of the complexity of the design, the only contributors to the expected mean square of an effect besides the effect itself are random factors that interact with or are nested within the effect. Two caveats are offered, however, for how to determine whether a term is to be listed as a potential error term as a result of applying the rules in the box on the right of the flowchart in Figure 10.7 for determining potential error terms other than MS_W. These caveats will be stated briefly in the context of an abstract three-factor case and then illustrated in the context of some final variations on our repeatedly used therapist example. In working with such complex designs, to have a way of designating very briefly which of the factors are random rather than fixed is convenient. Thus, in the following discussion, we continue to designate factors by single letters but adopt the convention (cf. Keppel, 1982) of using lowercase letters to designate random factors and capitals to designate fixed factors.

First, regarding rule (1) in the flowchart, consider the case of a three-factor design in which c is a random factor nested in A but crossed with B. Then, in testing AB, Bc/A *would* be judged, for present purposes, an interaction of the effect to be tested with a random factor. Although Bc/A is not really an interaction of AB with c, the concern here is that some interaction with a random effect might intrude on the effect of interest. Here at each level of A, if there is an interaction in the population between B and c, which levels of c are sampled will affect the magnitude of the B marginal means at that level of A. And, because different levels of c are sampled for each level of A, the B means will be affected differentially across levels of A, thus contributing to the AB interaction.

Second, regarding rule 2, not all factors listed to the right of a slash are created equal. In particular, in considering the potential error terms to list, an additional *fixed factor* to the right of a slash can be ignored, but not extra *random factors*. For example, if random factor c is nested within combinations of factors A and B, in considering what potential error terms are for testing the A effect, one makes different decisions about the appropriateness of the nested effect of c depending on the characteristics of B, the other factor besides A within which it is nested. Note that there are only two ways that B can be related to A, either crossed with it or nested directly within the levels of A. In either case, when B is fixed, the c effect is the appropriate error term for testing A. (That is, the extra *capital* B to the right of the slash may be ignored in the application of rule 2: c/AB is regarded as a potential error term for testing A because it involves only one other *random* factor.) However, when this other factor is random (hence b), then b/A in the case of nesting, or Ab in the case of crossing, qualifies as the appropriate error term, not c/Ab. (That is, the additional lowercase b to the right of the slash is *not* ignored: c/Ab is not a potential error term for testing A because it involves two other random factors.) The reason for the asymmetry is that, although the B means in both cases reflect sampling variability in levels of c, only in the case where B is random as well does it contribute variability over and above this to the expected mean square for A. Thus, in designs that involve both nesting and more than two factors, rule 2 must be understood to mean: "Determine the effects involving a random effect nested within the levels of the current effect *or within combinations of levels of the current effect and of a fixed factor(s)*."

To illustrate these rules with some concrete variations on our previous examples, assume now that samples of therapists (factor t) are drawn randomly from various clinics in a study of the effectiveness of various treatment modalities (M). How to combine such factors in a design is not just an abstract point. Frequently, in applied clinical studies, it is a real concern whether therapists and sites should be crossed with or nested within treatment modalities. The issues are the familiar ones of construct and internal validity, and usually it is a matter of choosing your poison because there are no perfect solutions. For example, if in the interests of construct validity of your treatment modality implementation you want to use as the therapist for each modality someone who believes that modality to be the most effective approach, then therapists will necessarily be confounded with modalities, which threatens the internal validity of your study. A partial solution in this situation is to have multiple therapists nested within each modality and use, as we indicate below, variability among therapists within modalities as an error term for assessing the modality effect. On the other hand, you might think it better just to have each therapist provide all treatment modalities to avoid such confoundings of the differences between therapists with modalities. This may be better for internal validity, but now construct validity will likely be threatened because each therapist is plausibly biased toward a particular modality and the effectiveness of a modality may depend on the proportion of therapists you have in your sample who are biased toward that particular modality. As we indicate below, one would want in such a case to use an indicator of the extent to which a modality's effectiveness depended on the therapist administering it (i.e., the modality × therapist interaction) as the error term for assessing the modality effect. Although the substantive issues may be clear enough to dictate one design rather than another (e.g., in some situations potential carryover effects of delivering one treatment might preclude an individual from administering another fairly), the particular error term appropriate for testing the effect of most interest in a given design is also relevant. We consider several possible arrangements of the three factors of therapists, clinic, and modality in Table 10.7.

In the first design, the clinics (c) to be included in the study are sampled randomly as well as the therapists within the clinics. Assume also that the structure of this first design is such that equal numbers of therapists *from each clinic* are asked to employ each of the modalities. Thus, modalities would be crossed with clinics, and therapists would be nested within clinic–modality combinations. This structure can be indicated briefly by the notation $t/M \times c$. The sources to be tested in such a design are then M, c, Mc, and t/Mc. Assume that observations are collected on n clients for each therapist in the study. The error term for all effects other than modality is straightforwardly determined by the flowchart. However, in the test of factor M, t/Mc would *not* be considered a potential error term because of the extra factor c in the specification. Thus, Mc is the one effect that qualifies as a denominator term for testing M.

Next, consider what would happen if there were only three clinics to which you wish to generalize and you include them all in your study so that it can be regarded as a fixed factor. Then in the test of treatment modalities, t/MC would be the appropriate denominator term. Sources and corresponding denominator terms are listed in parts 1 and 2 of Table 10.7 for these two designs.

Finally, two other designs are shown in the table as well. The third design assumes that all therapists in a clinic will use the same modality and that each modality will be implemented in multiple clinics, with therapists and clinics both being randomly sampled and again n clients being observed per therapist. This means that not only are therapists nested within clinic–modality combinations, but

TABLE **10.7** Sources and Error
Terms for Various Three-Factor
Designs Involving Nested
Random Factors

Design	Source	Error Term
1. t/M × c	M	Mc
	c	t/Mc
	Mc	t/Mc
	t/Mc	Within
2. t/M × C	M	t/MC
	C	t/MC
	MC	t/MC
	t/MC	Within
3. t/c/M	M	c/M
	c/M	t/c/M
	t/c/M	Within
4. M × t/C	C	t/C
	t/C	None*
	M	Mt/C
	MC	Mt/C
	Mt/C	None*

*If multiple observations per cell were available,
then Within would be the error term.

that clinics are nested within modalities—a design structure we may denote t/c/M.
Note that in the case of the test of modalities, c/M is the error term of choice because
it reflects the random variation induced by clinics as well as that induced by the
random factor of therapists lower in the hierarchy. In terms of rule 2 in the flowchart,
t/c/M is excluded from consideration as an error term for factor M because its
designation includes more than one random effect. In the fourth design, therapists
are randomly sampled from each clinic, clinics are fixed, but now each therapist
employs all treatment modalities. We designate the structure of this design:
M × t/C. Assume in this last case that only one client serves in each therapist–
modality combination. You will see in the next two chapters that this yields a design
of essentially the same structure as a repeated measures design. We recommend that
the reader work through the decisions of the Figure 10.7 flowchart to see that the
indicated error terms do in fact follow from the structure of the design in the four
cases presented in Table 10.7.

EXERCISES

1. True or False: In a one-factor design, whether the factor is fixed or random does not
affect the way in which the test of that factor is carried out.

2. True or False: In a two-factor mixed design, the test of the effect of the fixed factor is carried out in the same way it would be in a fixed-effects design.

3. True or False: The numerator and denominator of the F statistic should have the same expected value if the null hypothesis is true.

4. True or False: When the null hypothesis is false, the expected values of the numerator and denominator of the F should differ only by the component associated with the effect being tested.

5. True or False: That some of the factors in a design are nested renders uninterpretable certain of the effects that normally would be tested if all of the factors in the design were completely crossed.

6. Explain intuitively why in a mixed design the presence in the population of an interaction between a random and a fixed factor inflates the estimate of the main effect of the fixed factor.

*7. Assume that a master's student plans to investigate the effectiveness of listening to different types of tape recordings as a way of helping children cope with the discomfort of dental procedures. In particular, she wants to see whether listening to children's music or to children's stories is more effective and whether any advantage that does occur is consistent across two procedures: teeth cleaning and filling cavities. There obviously are any number of tape recordings that could be used in the study. She selects three musical and three story tapes for investigation from published lists of children's tapes. She proposes to use a total of 60 children in her study and to randomly assign an equal number of children to each possible combination of a tape and a dental procedure.

   One of the student's master's thesis committee members says that he likes her basic design but he is concerned about the power of the test of the factor of kind of tape. He wants her to run twice as many subjects so that she will have more degrees of freedom in the denominator of her test of this effect; this in turn will result in her being able to claim significance at a lower critical value of F.

   a. Describe the design and the appropriate analysis:
      (1) Diagram the design and label the basic structure, specifying any nesting
      (2) List all testable effects and indicate for each whether it is fixed or random
      (3) For each testable effect, indicate its degrees of freedom and the appropriate error term and the degrees of freedom of the error term.
   b. On the basis of your answer to part a, suggest how the student should respond (in a positive, constructive manner, of course) to her master's thesis committee member.

8. A management consultant firm has developed a new method of conducting workshops, which they believe has a number of advantages over the already established procedure. They want to evaluate the relative effectiveness of the two methods. However, there is one problem: They offer workshops on a wide variety of topics (e.g., on-the-job training, productivity, selection, etc.) and don't want to expend a great deal of resources on the evaluation. Therefore, they decide to concentrate on their three most popular workshop categories (topics) and for each category conduct 4 workshops, 2 using the new method and 2 using the old method (resulting in a total of 12 separate workshops). Assume that 11 subjects participate in each workshop.

   a. Indicate the structure of the design; then for each effect, determine the appropriate error term. Indicate the degrees of freedom associated with each effect and error term.
   b. A critic observes that the critical value of the F test for the methods effect is so large that it will be difficult in this design to achieve significance. Do you agree? Why? If you do agree, what could be done to remedy the problem?

*9. A researcher is interested in comparing two different concept-formation tasks, one involving a disjunctive concept and the other involving a conjunctive concept, under two conditions of informative feedback—either immediate knowledge of results or knowledge of results that is delayed by 10 seconds. The researcher realizes that concept learning problems differ considerably from each other in difficulty, and so he decides to use a variety of problems selected from those used in previously published research in order to increase the external validity of his study. Four different problems are selected for use in conjunction with *each* of the two types of concept-formation tasks. Presented below are the mean numbers of errors made before reaching a performance criterion. Each cell mean is based on the performance of the two subjects randomly assigned to that condition.

	Mean Errors to Criterion					
	Disjunctive			**Conjunctive**		
	Feedback			*Feedback*		
	Immediate	*Delayed*			*Immediate*	*Delayed*
Problem 1	3	3	Problem 5		1	2
Problem 2	3	5	Problem 6		1	1
Problem 3	2	6	Problem 7		4	5
Problem 4	4	6	Problem 8		0	2

a. Describe the structure of the design, indicating whether factors are crossed or nested, fixed or random. If a factor is nested, indicate the factor(s) within which it is nested.

b. List the effects that can be tested in this design and the appropriate denominator error term for each.

c. Perform an ANOVA to test the effects you listed in part b. Assume that MS_W is 5.0.

*10. Dr. R. U. Normal has obtained data from 45 subjects to compare three methods of therapy: rational-emotive therapy (RET), client-centered therapy (CCT), and behavior modification (BMOD). Three therapists were employed; each therapist treated five clients with each method of therapy. Assume the following ratings of the effectiveness of the therapy were obtained.

		Therapist		
		1	*2*	*3*
	RET	40, 42, 36, 35, 37	40, 44, 46, 41, 39	36, 40, 41, 38, 45
Method	*CCT*	42, 39, 38, 44, 42	41, 45, 40, 48, 46	41, 39, 37, 44, 44
	BMOD	48, 44, 43, 48, 47	41, 40, 48, 47, 44	39, 44, 40, 44, 43

a. Dr. Normal analyzed these data as a one-way design, completely ignoring "therapist." What did he find?

b. Dr. I. M. Skewed analyzed these data as a two-way design, treating both factors as fixed. His primary interest was in the method main effect—was it statistically significant?

c. Dr. Kurtosis also analyzed these data as a two-way design, but she treated the "therapist" factor as random. What did she find? Was the method main effect statistically significant?

d. How do the sums of squares for the method main effect compare in parts a, b, and c?

e. How do the error terms for testing the method main effect compare in parts a, b, and c?

f. Does it seem sensible that Skewed and Kurtosis obtained different results? Why or why not?

11. In the examples of nested designs considered in the text, it was always the case that the number of levels per nest was the same throughout the design. Sometimes this condition will not be met. Consider the following design where factor B is nested within factor A, where as in the text an X indicates a missing cell.

Cell Means on Dependent Variable

		Factor B				
		1	2	3	4	5
Factor A	1	8	12	X	X	X
	2	X	X	16	20	24

Assuming that factor B is random and that there are 10 observations per cell with an overall MS_W of 40, perform tests by hand of the effect of factor B within A and the effect of factor A. (Although alternative approaches to the solution of this problem are possible, recall that any design can be considered to be a special case of a one-way design where the effects of interest can be assessed by contrasts. Because there are five groups here, you can assess the effects of interest using four orthogonal contrasts, one assessing the main effect of A and three assessing the simple effects of B.)

Part Three

Model Comparisons for Designs Involving Within-Subjects Factors

The method of pairing [a variation of a within-subjects design]
... illustrates well the way in which an appropriate experimental
design is able to reconcile two desiderata, which sometimes appear
in conflict. On the one hand we require the utmost uniformity in
the ... material, which is the subject of experiment, in order to
increase the sensitiveness of each individual observation, and, on
the other, we require to multiply observations so as to demonstrate
so far as possible the reliability and consistency of the results.

SIR RONALD A. FISHER, *DESIGN OF EXPERIMENTS*

11   One-Way Within-Subjects Designs: Univariate Approach

455

ALL THE DESIGNS WE have considered to this point share a common characteristic: there has been a single observed value of the dependent measure for each subject. As a consequence, to test the existence of a treatment effect, we have compared scores between different groups of subjects. For this reason, the designs we have encountered so far are often referred to as *between-subjects designs*.

In contrast, this chapter considers designs where two or more measures are obtained for each subject in the study. Thus, with this type of design, we can test the existence of a treatment effect by comparing the several different scores obtained within a group of subjects. Not surprisingly, a common name given to this type of design is *within-subjects designs*. Another term often used in the psychological literature to describe this design is a *repeated-measures design* because two or more measures are collected for each subject.

The repeated-measures design constitutes the second major building block of experimental design. Most designs used in psychology represent some combination of the repeated-measures design and the between-subjects design. Thus, this chapter is very important because it sets the stage for most of the more complex designs encountered in psychological research. These more complex designs will be discussed in Chapters 12 and 14.

PROTOTYPICAL WITHIN-SUBJECTS DESIGNS

Before considering the data analysis of within-subjects designs, we briefly introduce some typical situations where a repeated-measures design might arise. Specifically, three different types of situations lead to a repeated-measures design.

The first situation is where each subject or unit of analysis is observed in *a* different treatment conditions. The same behavioral measure would be used as the dependent variable in each condition. For example, suppose that a physiological psychologist is interested in the differential effects of two drugs. Drug A might be thought to increase aggressive behavior and drug B to decrease aggressive behavior. Perhaps the population in which the drugs are to be tested is pairs of rhesus monkeys, with a score giving the total number of aggressive behaviors by either monkey during an observation period being a single measure for the pair. (In this case, the pair is the unit of analysis.) Almost certainly there will be pronounced differences between pairs of monkeys in the amount of aggressive behavior that would be observed normally. To prevent these between-pair differences from inflating the error term used to assess the effects of the drugs, the investigator might employ a design in which each pair experienced both drugs. Half the pairs of subjects might both be given drug A and then be observed for the period of time the drug is expected to be active; later the same pairs of subjects would all receive drug B and again have their aggressive behavior observed. The other half of subjects would also experience both drugs but in a reverse order. Thus, the same measure of aggressive behavior would be taken twice for each unit. Such a repeated-measures design would allow an assessment of the effects of the drugs in which the differences across pairs in average level of aggressiveness would not influence the magnitude of the error estimate at all. This capability of achieving a more sensitive design by preventing individual differences from contributing to the error variance is typically the primary motivation for selecting a within-subjects design.

A second situation that produces a repeated-measures design occurs when scores on each of a different tests are collected for each subject. For example, scores on the MMPI Psychasthenia Scale and the MMPI Depression Scale might be obtained for a group of individuals. Repeated measures ANOVA could be used to test for a difference in the means of these two scales for the population from which this sample was drawn. In general, for the results of such a comparison to be meaningful, the two tests (or subtests) must be comparably scaled. In other words, the comparison of the two MMPI scales is meaningful because both scales were constructed so as to have a mean of 50 and a standard deviation of 10 in the norm group. On the other hand, a comparison of the MMPI Schizophrenia Scale and the WAIS (Wechsler Adult Intelligence Scale) for a group of subjects would be meaningless because the tests are not comparably scaled. Although there is nothing in the statistical machinery to prohibit such a comparison, the results would have no psychologically meaningful interpretation.

The third situation to be considered is that some aspect of a subject's behavior may be measured at two or more different times. For example, a developmental psychologist might be interested in how performance on a certain task changes with a child's age. The performance of a group of children might be measured every 6 months from the time a child is 18 months old until he or she is 36 months old. Notice that such a design implies a longitudinal study, as opposed to the cross-sectional study of the between-subjects design.

A few more words regarding terminology are appropriate here. First, some authors prefer to restrict "repeated measures" to the third situation, where the same individual is literally measured repeatedly across time. With this terminology, all three situations involve "within-subjects" designs, but only the third is characterized as repeated measures. Our preference is to consider any of the three possibilities to be repeated-measures designs. Second, situations such as the second, where a test scores are compared, are often referred to as "profile analysis," because a basic goal of the study is to assess the mean profile of subjects' scores on these tests. Finally, the repeated-measures design is closely related to the randomized-block design. In the general case of this design, na subjects are divided into n blocks of a subjects each. Subjects are then assigned (randomly, if possible) to the a treatment conditions within each block. When $a = 2$, the design is often called a *matched-pairs design*. The repeated-measures design can be conceptualized as a randomized-block design where within each block there are a replicates of the same subject.

ADVANTAGES OF WITHIN-SUBJECTS DESIGNS

At this point, we briefly mention two of the advantages of a within-subjects design. First, more information is obtained from each subject in a within-subjects design than in a between-subjects design. This is obviously true because in the within-subjects design, each subject contributes a scores, whereas in the between-subjects design, each subject contributes only one score on the dependent variable. As a result, the number of subjects needed to reach a certain level of statistical power is often much lower in within-subjects designs than in between-subjects designs. When the cost of obtaining subjects is high (in terms of money, time, or effort), the within-subjects design has a distinct advantage in this regard.

Second, as mentioned previously, because comparisons in the repeated-measures design are made within subjects, variability in individual differences between subjects is removed from the error term. In essence, each subject serves as his or her own control in the within-subjects design, reducing the extraneous error variance. The effect is very similar to that for ANCOVA in a randomized experiment. In both cases, the practical implication is that statistical power can be increased by using each subject as his or her own control.

We should hasten to add that the within-subjects design also possesses a number of potential disadvantages. A full discussion of the choice between repeated-measures and between-subjects designs is premature until procedures for analyzing repeated-measures data have been presented. Thus, we now turn to issues of data analysis. Once this presentation is complete, we will return to the issues involved in choosing between the two types of design.

ANALYSIS OF REPEATED-MEASURES DESIGNS WITH TWO LEVELS

The Problem of Correlated Errors

We begin the investigation of how to analyze repeated-measures designs by considering the simplest possible case, namely, the situation where there are only two levels of the repeated factor. Consider the data displayed in Table 11.1. (Ignore the column labeled e for the moment.) Six subjects have been observed under each of two treatment conditions, yielding 12 scores in all on the dependent variable. How might we determine whether the population mean for condition 1 differs from the population mean for condition 2?

First, consider the model we used in Chapter 3 for the one-way between-subjects design:

$$Y_{ij} = \mu + \alpha_j + \varepsilon_{ij} \tag{1}$$

where Y_{ij} is the score on the dependent variable for the ith subject in the jth condition, μ is the grand mean parameter, α_j is the effect associated with the jth

T A B L E **11. 1** Data for a Two-Level
Repeated-Measures Design

Subject	Treatment Condition	Y	e
1	1	8	0
	2	10	0
2	1	3	−5
	2	6	−4
3	1	12	4
	2	13	3
4	1	5	−3
	2	9	−1
5	1	7	−1
	2	8	−2
6	1	13	5
	2	14	4

T A B L E **11. 2** Pattern
of e_{ij} Values for Data in
Table 11.1

Subject	e_{i1}	e_{i2}
1	0	0
2	−5	−4
3	4	3
4	−3	−1
5	−1	−2
6	5	4

condition, and ε_{ij} is the error for the ith subject in the jth condition. It turns out that there is a special need here to focus on ε, the error term. Recall from Chapter 3 that the analog in the sample of the population value of ε_{ij} is given by

$$e_{ij} = Y_{ij} - \bar{Y}_j \tag{2}$$

for a one-way design, where the treatment condition means $\bar{Y}_1$ and $\bar{Y}_2$ are here 8 and 10, respectively. The last column of Table 11.1 displays the values of e_{ij} for these hypothetical data. Careful inspection of these error values shows a striking pattern. As can be seen more clearly from Table 11.2, subjects with positive errors (Y scores above the treatment-condition mean) for condition 1 also have positive errors (Y scores above the treatment-condition mean) for condition 2: the same is true of negative errors (scores below the mean). Specifically, the correlation between e_{i1} and

ε_{i2} can be shown to equal 0.96 here. Although it is conceivable that this correlation is a chance occurrence in the sample and unrepresentative of the population as a whole, it seems more plausible to conclude that a correlation exists in the population.[1] In other words, ε_{i1} and ε_{i2} are likely correlated because a subject who achieves a high score in one condition is also likely to achieve a relatively high score in the other condition. If ε_{i1} and ε_{i2} are indeed correlated, we have a problem. Remember from Chapter 3 that a basic ANOVA assumption is that errors must be independent from one another. However, correlation implies dependence, so this assumption is violated whenever ε_{i1} and ε_{i2} are correlated. Two further points should be made here. First, ε_{i1} and ε_{i2} are correlated in almost every repeated-measures study. For most behavioral phenomena, there are systematic individual differences between subjects, creating a correlation between the errors. Second, in general, ANOVA is not robust to violations of the independence assumption. For these reasons, we need to employ different data-analysis procedures for the within-subjects design than we used in the between-subjects design.

Reformulation of Model

There are several ways we might modify the model of Equation 1 to make it appropriate for a within-subjects design. We will illustrate the modification that is most straightforward for the special case of a two-level factor. We will see later that this modification also provides a foundation for the multivariate approach to be presented in Chapter 13.

Let's reexamine the model represented by Equation 1:

$$Y_{ij} = \mu + \alpha_j + \varepsilon_{ij} \qquad \text{(1, repeated)}$$

We could write this model in two parts as

$$Y_{i1} = \mu + \alpha_1 + \varepsilon_{i1} \qquad (3)$$

for treatment condition 1, and as

$$Y_{i2} = \mu + \alpha_2 + \varepsilon_{i2} \qquad (4)$$

for condition 2. Suppose that we were to subtract Equation 3 from 4. The result would be

$$Y_{i2} - Y_{i1} = \alpha_2 - \alpha_1 + \varepsilon_{i2} - \varepsilon_{i1} \qquad (5)$$

The following substitutions could now be made: D_i for $Y_{i2} - Y_{i1}$, μ for $\alpha_2 - \alpha_1$, and ε_i for $\varepsilon_{i2} - \varepsilon_{i1}$, yielding

$$D_i = \mu + \varepsilon_i \qquad (6)$$

as a new model for the data. D_i represents the difference between the scores obtained in the second and first conditions for the ith subject, μ represents the difference between the effects of the second and first conditions, and ε once again represents error. Notice that the original model of Equation 1 was based on two scores from each subject, whereas the model of Equation 6 requires only one score per subject.

As a consequence, each subject contributes only one observation of ε, removing the dependency among the errors in Equation 1.

The null hypothesis of Equation 1 was written

$$H_0 : \alpha_1 = \alpha_2 = 0 \tag{7}$$

Because μ is defined to be $\alpha_2 - \alpha_1$, the equivalent null hypothesis for Equation 6 is thus

$$H_0 : \mu = 0 \tag{8}$$

The corresponding restricted model is given by

$$D_i = 0 + \varepsilon_i \tag{9}$$

or just

$$D_i = \varepsilon_i \tag{10}$$

To test the null hypothesis, least-squares estimates can be obtained, and the sum of squared errors compared as before. The procedure is very simple, because the model in Equation 6 contains only one parameter and the model in Equation 9 (or, equivalently, Equation 10) has no parameters. In Equation 6, the least-squares estimate of μ is given by $\bar{D}$, so that

$$E_F = \sum_i (D_i - \bar{D})^2 \tag{11}$$

In Equation 9, each estimated score is zero, yielding

$$E_R = \sum_i (D_i - 0)^2 = \sum_i D_i^2 \tag{12}$$

The difference between E_R and E_F is easier to find if we first rewrite E_F as

$$E_F = (\sum D_i^2) - n\bar{D}^2 \tag{13}$$

Then,

$$E_R - E_F = n\bar{D}^2 \tag{14}$$

Recall from previous chapters that the expression for the F test statistic is in general given by

$$F = \frac{(E_R - E_F)/(df_R - df_F)}{E_F/df_F}$$

Making the appropriate substitutions for the problem at hand,

$$F = \frac{n\bar{D}^2/[n - (n - 1)]}{[(\sum D_i^2) - n\bar{D}^2]/(n - 1)} \tag{15}$$

which reduces to

$$F = \frac{n\bar{D}^2}{s_D^2} \tag{16}$$

where

$$s_D^2 = \frac{\sum D_i^2 - n\bar{D}^2}{n - 1} \qquad (17)$$

is the unbiased estimate of the population variance of the D scores. The observed F value must be compared to a critical F with 1 and $n - 1$ degrees of freedom. Because the F has a single numerator degree of freedom here, the test could also be written as a t test with $n - 1$ degrees of freedom. Specifically,

$$t = \frac{\sqrt{n}\bar{D}}{s_D} \qquad (18)$$

or as

$$t = \frac{\bar{D}}{s_D/\sqrt{n}} \qquad (19)$$

Equation 19 should look familiar because it is the formula for a dependent t test, as found in most behavioral statistics texts. Thus, with two levels of the repeated factor, the model-comparisons test reduces to the usual dependent t test. Table 11.3 shows step-by-step calculations for testing the null hypothesis for the data in Table 11.1.

T A B L E **11. 3**   Calculations for Data in Table 11.1

Subject	Y_1 = score in Condition 1	Y_2 = score in Condition 2	$D = Y_2 - Y_1$	D^2
1	8	10	2	4
2	3	6	3	9
3	12	13	1	1
4	5	9	4	16
5	7	8	1	1
6	13	14	1	1
			$\sum D = 12$	$\sum D^2 = 32$

$$E_F = \sum (D_i - \bar{D})^2$$
$$= (2 - 2)^2 + (3 - 2)^2 + (1 - 2)^2 + (4 - 2)^2 + (1 - 2)^2 + (1 - 2)^2$$
$$= 8$$

Alternatively: $E_F = (\sum D_i^2) - n\bar{D}^2 = 32 - 6(2)^2 = 32 - 24 = 8$

$$E_R = \sum D_i^2 = 32$$

$$F = \frac{(E_R - E_F)/(df_R - df_F)}{E_F/df_F} = \frac{(32 - 8)/(6 - 5)}{8/5} = 15.0$$

Alternatively: $F = \frac{n\bar{D}^2}{(\sum D_i^2 - n\bar{D}^2)/(n - 1)} = \frac{6(2)^2}{[32 - 6(2)^2]/(6 - 1)} = \frac{24}{8/5} = 15.0$

$F_{.05;1,5} = 6.61$, so H_0 is rejected at .05 level.

ANALYSIS OF WITHIN-SUBJECTS DESIGNS WITH MORE THAN TWO LEVELS

When the repeated factor consists of more than two levels (i.e., when $a > 2$), the analysis becomes considerably more complicated. Once again the model used previously for between-subjects designs is inappropriate here because errors typically will be correlated due to systematic individual differences. There are two very different approaches that can be taken to deal with this problem. The approach that we prefer is the multivariate approach and is discussed in detail in Chapters 13 and 14. In brief, the logic of this approach is based on the formation of D variables (i.e., difference scores), as we used for the two-level case. However, in the a-group case, we need to form $a - 1$ D variables. When $a = 2$, we only need one D variable, which makes the resulting analysis quite simple. More generally, with a levels, the analysis is somewhat more complicated.

Instead of presenting the multivariate approach now, we first present an alternate approach, which is more traditional in the psychological literature. This approach, called the *univariate* or *mixed-model approach*, requires a set of restrictive assumptions, which we discuss later in the chapter. Nevertheless, the approach is important for two reasons. First, it continues to be widely used in psychological research. That you are aware of the necessary assumptions is important, so that you can evaluate whether these assumptions have been violated in a particular application of this approach. Second, there are several modifications of this approach that attempt to circumvent the restrictive set of assumptions. For the moment, we simply say that these modifications appear to work reasonably well, so that they constitute a viable alternative to the multivariate approach in some situations.

TRADITIONAL UNIVARIATE (MIXED-MODEL) APPROACH

The traditional view of a repeated-measures design is to regard it as a two-factor design. Specifically, one factor represents the repeated condition (e.g., time, drug, subtest, etc.), while the second factor represents subjects. The rationale for this conceptualization can be understood by considering the data in Table 11.4. When the data are displayed this way, the design looks very much like other factorial designs we have already encountered.

Although the traditional analysis of repeated-measures data proceeds by treating the data in terms of this two-factor design, there are two ways in which the design differs from the typical factorial designs we have discussed previously. First, there is only one observation per cell of the design. Second, while treatment condition is usually a fixed factor, the subjects factor is a random factor because these particular subjects have been randomly selected from a larger population. Thus, the design is like the mixed designs of Chapter 10 in that there is one fixed factor and

TABLE **11.4** Data for a-Level
Repeated-Measures Design (with $a = 4$)

		Treatment Condition			
		1	*2*	*3*	*4*
	1	8	10	7	5
	2	9	9	8	6
	3	7	5	8	4
	4	9	6	5	7
Subject	*5*	8	7	7	6
	6	5	4	4	3
	7	7	6	5	4
	8	8	8	6	6
	9	9	8	6	5
	10	7	7	4	5

one random factor. It should now be obvious that the reason this method of analysis is often called the mixed-model approach is because with this conceptualization the effects do indeed follow a mixed model.

Comparison of Full and Restricted Models

An appropriate model for repeated-measures data is given by

$$Y_{ij} = \mu + \alpha_j + \pi_i + (\pi\alpha)_{ij} + \varepsilon_{ij} \tag{20}$$

where Y_{ij} is the score on the dependent variable for the ith subject in the jth condition, μ is the grand mean parameter, α_j is the effect associated with the jth condition, π_i is the effect associated with the ith subject, $(\pi\alpha)_{ij}$ is the effect of the interaction of the ith subject and the jth condition, and ε_{ij} is the error for the ith subject in the jth condition. Notice that the above model is identical to the model we used in Chapter 7 for a factorial design.[2] The hypothesis to be tested here is

$$H_0 : \alpha_1 = \alpha_2 = \cdots = \alpha_a = 0$$

so a restricted model is given by

$$Y_{ij} = \mu + \pi_i + (\pi\alpha)_{ij} + \varepsilon_{ij} \tag{21}$$

However, you should recall from our discussion of random-effects models in Chapter 10 that the proper denominator term of the F statistic (i.e., the error term) depends on whether the effect being tested is fixed or random. In our design, there is one fixed factor (condition) and one random factor (subjects). The effect being tested is fixed because it is the main effect of condition. According to Chapter 10, to test a fixed effect when there is one random factor in the model, the appropriate denominator term is obtained by restricting the interaction of the fixed and random factors to zero. This can be accomplished most easily[3] in our design by omitting the $(\pi\alpha)_{ij}$ interaction parameters from Equations 20 and 21; in this case, our models become

$$\text{Full model:}\quad Y_{ij} = \mu + \alpha_j + \pi_i + \varepsilon_{ij} \tag{22}$$

$$\text{Restricted model:}\quad Y_{ij} = \mu + \pi_i + \varepsilon_{ij} \tag{23}$$

At this point, an F test can be obtained from the usual formula:

$$F = \frac{(E_R - E_F)/(df_R - df_F)}{E_F/df_F}$$

A special word is needed for computing the degrees of freedom here. Suppose that n subjects are each observed under a repeated conditions, yielding na scores in all. Then, the degrees of freedom for the two models are

$$\begin{aligned}
df_F &= na - (\text{\# independent parameters}) \\
&= na - [1 + (a - 1) + (n - 1)] \\
&= na - n - a + 1 \\
&= (n - 1)(a - 1)
\end{aligned}$$

$$\begin{aligned}
df_R &= na - (\text{\# independent parameters}) \\
&= na - [1 + (n - 1)] \\
&= na - n \\
&= n(a - 1)
\end{aligned}$$

Notice then that

$$\begin{aligned}
df_R - df_F &= n(a - 1) - (n - 1)(a - 1) \\
&= [n - (n - 1)](a - 1) \\
&= a - 1
\end{aligned}$$

Estimation of Parameters: Numerical Example

To perform the F test, we must calculate E_R and E_F, which necessitates obtaining parameter estimates in each model. To see how parameter estimates are obtained, consider the data displayed in Table 11.5. The data show that 12 subjects have been observed in each of four conditions. To make the example easier to discuss, let's suppose that the 12 subjects are children who have been observed at 30, 36, 42, and 48 months of age. In each case, the dependent variable is the child's

TABLE **11.5** Hypothetical McCarthy Data for 12 Children

Subject	30	36	42	48	Marginal Mean
	Age (Months)				
1	108	96	110	122	**109**
2	103	117	127	133	**120**
3	96	107	106	107	**104**
4	84	85	92	99	**90**
5	118	125	125	116	**121**
6	110	107	96	91	**101**
7	129	128	123	128	**127**
8	90	84	101	113	**97**
9	84	104	100	88	**94**
10	96	100	103	105	**101**
11	105	114	105	112	**109**
12	113	117	132	130	**123**
Marginal Mean	**103**	**107**	**110**	**112**	**108**

age-normed general cognitive score on the McCarthy Scales of Children's Abilities. Although the test is normed so that the mean score will be independent of age for the general population, our 12 children may come from a population where cognitive abilities are either growing more rapidly or less rapidly than average. Indeed, this is the hypothesis our data will allow us to address.[4] In other words, although the sample means suggest that the children's cognitive abilities are growing, a significance test is needed if we want to rule out sampling error as a likely explanation for the observed differences.

The estimation of parameters in models 22 and 23 is actually very straightforward. Because there is an equal number of subjects in each treatment condition (i.e., the design is orthogonal), parameter estimates for Equation 22 are given by:

$$\hat{\mu} = \sum_{i=1}^{n} \sum_{j=1}^{a} Y_{ij}/na = \bar{Y}_{..}$$

$$\hat{\alpha}_j = \left(\sum_{i=1}^{n} Y_{ij}/n \right) - \bar{Y}_{..} = \bar{Y}_{.j} - \bar{Y}_{..}$$

$$\hat{\pi}_i = \left(\sum_{j=1}^{a} Y_{ij}/a \right) - \bar{Y}_{..} = \bar{Y}_{i.} - \bar{Y}_{..}$$

and for Equation 23 are given by:

$$\hat{\mu} = \sum_{i=1}^{n} \sum_{j=1}^{a} Y_{ij}/na = \bar{Y}_{..}$$

$$\hat{\pi}_i = \left(\sum_{j=1}^{a} Y_{ij}/a \right) - \bar{Y}_{..} = \bar{Y}_{i.} - \bar{Y}_{..}$$

Thus, the parameter estimates simply depend on the marginal means of the data.

In particular, notice that $\hat{\mu}$ is just the mean of all scores, whereas $\hat{\alpha}_j$ is the difference between the mean of condition j (averaged over subjects) and the grand mean, and $\hat{\pi}_i$ is the difference between the mean of subject i (averaged over conditions) and the grand mean.

To find the sum of squared errors of each model, we must consider $\hat{Y}_{ij}$, the predicted score for subject i in condition j. For the full model, we have

$$\hat{Y}_{ij} = \hat{\mu} + \hat{\alpha}_j + \hat{\pi}_i$$
$$= \bar{Y}_{..} + (\bar{Y}_{.j} - \bar{Y}_{..}) + (\bar{Y}_{i.} - \bar{Y}_{..})$$
$$= \bar{Y}_{.j} + \bar{Y}_{i.} - \bar{Y}_{..} \tag{24}$$

For the restricted model, the corresponding expression is

$$\hat{Y}_{ij} = \hat{\mu} + \hat{\pi}_i$$
$$= \bar{Y}_{..} + (\bar{Y}_{i.} - \bar{Y}_{..})$$
$$= \bar{Y}_{i.} \tag{25}$$

Let's pause for a moment to compare Equations 24 and 25. The difference between these equations, and hence the nature of the restriction being imposed, can be understood most easily by comparing Tables 11.6 and 11.7. Table 11.6 presents predicted scores from the full model (based on Equation 24) for the data of Table 11.5. Table 11.7 presents the corresponding scores for the restricted model (based on Equation 25). Table 11.6 shows that the full model allows for differences between both rows and columns. The restricted model, on the other hand, allows for differences between rows (i.e., subjects), but the columns of predicted scores are identical (see Table 11.7). Thus, the restricted model regards any differences between the columns (i.e., the conditions) in the actual data (Table 11.5) as simply being due to sampling error. However, to the extent that the columns do in fact differ from

T A B L E **11. 6** Predicted Scores from the Full Model for the Data of Table 11.5

Subject	Age (Months)			
	30	36	42	48
1	104	108	111	113
2	115	119	122	124
3	99	103	106	108
4	85	89	92	94
5	116	120	123	125
6	96	100	103	105
7	122	126	129	131
8	92	96	99	101
9	89	93	96	98
10	96	100	103	105
11	104	108	111	113
12	118	122	125	127

T A B L E **11. 7**   Predicted Scores from the
Restricted Model for the Data of Table 11.5

	Age (Months)			
Subject	*30*	*36*	*42*	*48*
1	109	109	109	109
2	120	120	120	120
3	104	104	104	104
4	90	90	90	90
5	121	121	121	121
6	101	101	101	101
7	127	127	127	127
8	97	97	97	97
9	94	94	94	94
10	101	101	101	101
11	109	109	109	109
12	123	123	123	123

one another, the full model will provide a better fit to the data than will the restricted model.

Once again, to perform a test of the null hypothesis, we must find the sum of squared errors for the two different models. In each case, then, we must calculate

$$\sum_{i=1}^{n} \sum_{j=1}^{a} (Y_{ij} - \hat{Y}_{ij})^2$$

where $\hat{Y}_{ij}$ is the predicted score from the particular model. In words, we need to square each discrepancy between an actual score and a predicted score and add up these squared discrepancies. Tables 11.8 and 11.9 show the calculations for our data. We now turn to a more general formulation of the sum of squared errors.

Making use of the predictions we developed in Equations 24 and 25, we see that the sum of squared errors for the full model equals

$$E_F = \sum_{i=1}^{n} \sum_{j=1}^{a} (Y_{ij} - \hat{Y}_{ij})^2$$

$$= \sum_{i=1}^{n} \sum_{j=1}^{a} [Y_{ij} - (\bar{Y}_{.j} + \bar{Y}_{i.} - \bar{Y}_{..})]^2$$

$$= \sum_{i=1}^{n} \sum_{j=1}^{a} (Y_{ij} - \bar{Y}_{.j} - \bar{Y}_{i.} + \bar{Y}_{..})^2$$

We have seen this formula earlier in a different context. Recall from Chapter 7 that this is the formula for the interaction sum of squares in a two-way factorial design. Thus, the sum of squared errors for the full model can be found simply by calculating the interaction sum of squares. Symbolically, we have

$$E_F = SS_{A \times S} \tag{26}$$

where $SS_{A \times S}$ represents the sum of squares due to the treatment by subject interaction.

TABLE **11.8** Discrepancies Between Actual Scores (Table 11.5) and Predicted Scores of the Full Model (Table 11.6)

	Age (Months)			
Subject	30	36	42	48
1	4	−12	−1	9
2	−12	−2	5	9
3	−3	4	0	−1
4	−1	−4	0	5
5	2	5	2	−9
6	14	7	−7	−14
7	7	2	−6	−3
8	−2	−12	2	12
9	−5	11	4	−10
10	0	0	0	0
11	1	6	−6	−1
12	−5	−5	7	3
$\sum_{i=1}^{12}(Y_{ij}-\hat{Y}_{ij})^2$	474	584	220	728

$$E_F = \sum_{j=1}^{4}\sum_{i=1}^{12}(Y_{ij}-\hat{Y}_{ij})^2 = 2006$$

TABLE **11.9** Discrepancies Between Actual Scores (Table 11.5) and Predicted Scores of the Restricted Model (Table 11.7)

	Age (Months)			
Subject	30	36	42	48
1	−1	−13	1	13
2	−17	−3	7	13
3	−8	3	2	3
4	−6	−5	2	9
5	−3	4	4	−5
6	9	6	−5	−10
7	2	1	−4	1
8	−7	−13	4	16
9	−10	10	6	−6
10	−5	−1	2	4
11	−4	5	−4	3
12	−10	−6	9	7
$\sum_{i=1}^{12}(Y_{ij}-\hat{Y}_{ij})^2$	774	596	268	920

$$E_R = \sum_{j=1}^{4}\sum_{i=1}^{12}(Y_{ij}-\hat{Y}_{ij})^2 = 2558$$

In a similar fashion, the sum of squared errors for the restricted model is given by

$$E_R = \sum_{i=1}^{n} \sum_{j=1}^{a} (Y_{ij} - \hat{Y}_{ij})^2 = \sum_{i=1}^{n} \sum_{j=1}^{a} (Y_{ij} - \bar{Y}_{i.})^2$$

This can be rewritten as

$$E_R = \sum_{i=1}^{n} \sum_{j=1}^{a} (Y_{ij} - \bar{Y}_{i.} - \bar{Y}_{.j} + \bar{Y}_{..} + \bar{Y}_{.j} - \bar{Y}_{..})^2$$

which after some tedious algebra reduces to

$$E_R = \sum_{i=1}^{n} \sum_{j=1}^{a} (Y_{ij} - \bar{Y}_{.j} - \bar{Y}_{i.} + \bar{Y}_{..})^2 + \sum_{j=1}^{a} n(\bar{Y}_{.j} - \bar{Y}_{..})^2$$

The first expression on the right-hand side of the equality is just $SS_{A \times S}$. The second expression is identical to what we encountered in Chapter 7 for the sum of squares for a main effect in a two-factor design, in this case, SS_A. Thus, we have

$$E_R = SS_{A \times S} + SS_A$$

Obviously, then

$$E_R - E_F = SS_A \qquad (27)$$

We can now obtain an F test from the general formula

$$F = \frac{(E_R - E_F)/(df_R - df_F)}{E_F/df_F}$$

which reduces to

$$F = \frac{SS_A/(a - 1)}{SS_{A \times S}/(n - 1)(a - 1)}$$

or

$$F = \frac{MS_A}{MS_{A \times S}} \qquad (28)$$

For the data in Table 11.5, we have $E_R = 2558$ (see Table 11.9) and $E_F = 2006$ (see Table 11.8); thus,

$$F = \frac{552/3}{2006/33} = 3.03$$

which for an F distribution with 3 and 33 degrees of freedom implies a p value of .042. Thus, we can reject the null hypothesis that the population means at all four ages are equal.

It might be helpful to consider the formula for the F statistic in Equation 28 more closely. Why should the ratio of MS_A to $MS_{A \times S}$ inform us about whether to reject the null hypothesis? First, this makes intuitive sense, because $MS_{A \times S}$ is an index of the extent to which the A effect varies from subject to subject. Large variability signifies that differences in means are less consistent across individuals. Thus, the ratio of MS_A to $MS_{A \times S}$ reflects the average magnitude of condition differences relative to the inconsistency of those differences. As a consequence, the observed F value will be large to the extent that there are consistent condition differences from subject to subject. Such consistency provides confidence that observed average differences can safely be generalized beyond the particular sample to the population. Inconsistent condition differences, on the other hand, create greater doubt about the nature of condition differences beyond the observed data. Second, this F test has the same form as the F test we developed in Chapter 10 for a mixed two-factor design. As Table 10.3 shows, when A is fixed and B is random, $MS_{A \times B}$ is the appropriate error term. In the repeated-measures design, the random factor is subjects, which we have designated by S, so $MS_{A \times S}$ is the proper error term for testing the A effect, as shown in Equation 28.

ASSUMPTIONS IN THE TRADITIONAL UNIVARIATE (MIXED-MODEL) APPROACH

To use the previous approach to analyze repeated-measures data, the data must meet a set of rather restrictive assumptions. Besides the usual assumptions of random sampling from the population, independence of subjects, and normality, there is a homogeneity assumption similar to that required in between-subjects designs. Specifically, for within-subjects designs, there is a *homogeneity of treatment-difference variances* assumption.[5] This means that if we take two treatment levels— say, l and m—and subtract scores for one level from scores for another level, the resulting score $Y_l - Y_m$ must have the same population variance for every pair of levels. The variance of the difference $Y_l - Y_m$ can be written as

$$\sigma^2_{Y_l - Y_m} = \sigma^2_{Y_l} + \sigma^2_{Y_m} - 2\text{Cov}(Y_l, Y_m) \tag{29}$$

$$= \sigma^2_{Y_l} + \sigma^2_{Y_m} - 2\rho_{lm}\sigma_{Y_l}\sigma_{Y_m} \tag{30}$$

where ρ_{lm} is the population correlation of scores in treatment level l with those in treatment level m.

Homogeneity, Sphericity, and Compound Symmetry

Huynh and Feldt (1970) and Rouanet and Lépine (1970) showed independently that the homogeneity of treatment-difference variances assumption is equivalent to assuming that the population covariance matrix has a certain form. This form, which is called *sphericity* (or interchangeably, *circularity*), can for all practical purposes only be defined with matrix algebra. For this reason, we instead discuss a special case of sphericity, which is known as *compound symmetry*. A covariance matrix is defined to possess compound symmetry if and only if all the variances are equal to each other and all the covariances are equal to each other. However, an equivalent property is that every measure must have the same variance and all correlations between any pair of measures must be equal. Symbolically, we can represent these two conditions as

$$\sigma_{Y_l}^2 = \sigma_{Y_m}^2 \tag{31}$$

for all l and m and

$$\rho_{lm} = \rho_{jk} \tag{32}$$

for all j, k, l, and m. For simplicity, when Equations 31 and 32 are true, we could use σ^2 to represent the common variance of every measure and use ρ to represent the common correlation between every pair of measures. What does compound symmetry imply about the variances of the differences between treatment levels? From Equation 30, we know that the general form of this variance is given by

$$\sigma_{Y_l - Y_m}^2 = \sigma_{Y_l}^2 + \sigma_{Y_m}^2 - 2\rho_{lm}\sigma_{Y_l}\sigma_{Y_m} \tag{30, repeated}$$

However, when compound symmetry holds, we can replace $\sigma_{Y_l}^2$ and $\sigma_{Y_m}^2$ with σ^2 (and, of course, σ_{Y_l} and σ_{Y_m} with σ) and ρ_{lm} with ρ. As a result we have

$$\sigma_{Y_l - Y_m}^2 = \sigma^2 + \sigma^2 - 2\rho\sigma\sigma = 2\sigma^2(1 - \rho).$$

Notice that the variance of the difference does not depend on the particular levels l and m. Thus, compound symmetry implies that the homogeneity of treatment-difference variances assumption is satisfied. Stated differently, compound symmetry is a sufficient condition for the validity of the mixed-model approach. However, strictly speaking, compound symmetry is technically not a necessary condition because compound symmetry is a special case of sphericity. As Figure 11.1 shows, matrices that satisfy compound symmetry are a subset of those that satisfy sphericity, and from a technical standpoint, sphericity is the assumption required

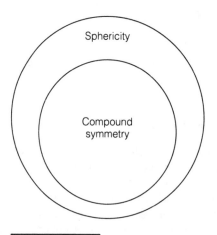

F I G U R E 11. 1 Relationship between compound symmetry and sphericity.

by the mixed-model approach. However, in practice there are only two related situations in which the distinction between sphericity and compound symmetry is of potential importance. First, when there are only two levels of the repeated factor, there is only one difference between levels, so Equation 30 is always satisfied. Thus, when $a = 2$, the sphericity assumption is always met. However, the population matrix does not necessarily possess compound symmetry because the variance of scores at level 1 may not equal the variance at level 2. Nevertheless, the mixed-model approach is always valid (at least in terms of the homogeneity assumption) when $a = 2$ because sphericity is guaranteed here. Second, we will see in Chapter 12 that sphericity can also be satisfied even when compound symmetry does not hold in designs with two or more repeated factors; this distinction is usually only important when at least one of the repeated factors has only two levels. In the single-factor design we are considering in this chapter, it would be highly unusual (although theoretically possible) to find a matrix that possesses sphericity but not compound symmetry unless $a = 2$. Thus, for all practical purposes, compound symmetry is a requirement for the mixed-model analysis method in a one-way repeated-measures design any time the repeated factor has more than two levels.

Numerical Example

To develop further understanding of these conditions, it might be helpful to reconsider the data displayed in Table 11.5. Although we obviously cannot compute population variances and correlations for these data, we can compute their sample counterparts. The sample variances (s^2) turn out to be 187.96 for the 30-month scores, 200.51 for the 36-month scores, 177.96 for the 42-month scores, and 217.86 for the 48-month scores. Informal inspection of these four sample variances suggests that the values are rather similar to each other and any differences between them might simply reflect sampling error. Instead of considering a formal test at this point, let's consider the correlations among the scores. Table 11.10 shows the six correlations among the four variables in the form of a 4×4 matrix. We can see that the values of the sample correlations vary substantially from each other. For example, scores at 36 and 48 months correlate only 0.466, whereas scores at 42 and 48 months

TABLE **11.10**   Correlations Between Measures on McCarthy Scores of Table 11.5

Age (Months)	Age (Months)			
	30	36	42	48
30	1.000	.795	.696	.599
36	.795	1.000	.760	.466
42	.696	.760	1.000	.853
48	.599	.466	.853	1.000

T A B L E **11. 11**   Variances of the
Difference Between Each Pair of
Levels for Table 11.5 Data*

$\text{Var}(Y_2 - Y_1) = 79.82$
$\text{Var}(Y_3 - Y_2) = 91.27$
$\text{Var}(Y_4 - Y_3) = 59.82$
$\text{Var}(Y_3 - Y_1) = 111.27$
$\text{Var}(Y_4 - Y_2) = 223.64$
$\text{Var}(Y_4 - Y_1) = 163.64$

* Y_1 = McCarthy score at 30 months,
Y_2 = McCarthy score at 36 months,
Y_3 = McCarthy score at 42 months, and
Y_4 = McCarthy score at 48 months.

correlate 0.853. In general, correlations are highest here for those pairs of measures that are closest together in time, a common finding in the behavioral literature. This pattern of roughly equal variances but substantially different correlations across levels of the within-subjects factor is perhaps the most common result in repeated-measures designs in the behavioral sciences. However, as Table 11.11 shows, this pattern of roughly equal variances but unequal correlations leads to differences in the variances of the differences between the various pairs of levels. Specifically, in accordance with Equation 30, the variance of the difference tends to be smallest when scores from the two levels are highly correlated and tends to be largest when the correlation is low. If this pattern holds in the population as well as in the sample, it represents a violation of the homogeneity of treatment-difference variances required for the validity of the traditional univariate approach to analyzing such designs.

Even though these sample correlations are unequal, such inequalities might simply reflect sampling error. Perhaps the corresponding population correlations are in fact equal to one another. More precisely, real interest centers on whether the required treatment–differences homogeneity assumption is met for the population. Mauchly's sphericity test is a procedure for testing the null hypothesis that the homogeneity condition holds in the population. However, we will not present the details of this test, because Keselman, Rogan, Mendoza, and Breen (1980) have shown that Mauchly's test has little value as a preliminary test prior to the test of mean differences. (Readers desiring more information on Mauchly's test should refer to Keselman et al., 1980, or to Kirk, 1982, p. 260).

After the discussion of robustness in between-subjects designs, a reasonable guess would be that Mauchly's test is of little value because the mixed-model approach is robust to violations of the homogeneity assumption. However, as McCall and Appelbaum (1973) and others have shown, the mixed-model approach is *not* robust to violations of homogeneity. When the assumption is false, the actual probability of a Type I error may be as high as .10 or .15 as compared to a nominal value of .05. Thus, the usual mixed-model ANOVA test is inappropriate unless the homogeneity condition is met.

ADJUSTED UNIVARIATE TESTS

When the homogeneity assumption is false, it is possible to perform an "adjusted test" of the equality of means. Box (1954) derived a measure denoted by ε which indexes how far a population covariance matrix departs from homogeneity. A matrix satisfying the homogeneity assumption always has an ε value of 1.0; any other matrix has an ε value between 0.0 and 1.0, where lower values indicate a more extreme departure from the assumption. He also showed that the ratio of MS_A to $MS_{A \times S}$ (our observed F) approximately follows an F distribution with adjusted degrees of freedom even when homogeneity is false. Specifically, the F distribution which $MS_A/MS_{A \times S}$ approximates has numerator degrees of freedom equal to $\varepsilon(a - 1)$ and denominator degrees of freedom equal to $\varepsilon(n - 1)(a - 1)$. If ε were known, it would be possible to calculate the observed F as $MS_A/MS_{A \times S}$ and compare it to a new critical F with appropriately adjusted degrees of freedom. However, this result is of limited practical value, because ε is an unknown population parameter. Fortunately, there is a practical alternative; in fact, there are three: the Geisser–Greenhouse lower-bound correction, Box's $\hat{\varepsilon}$ adjustment, and the Huynh–Feldt $\tilde{\varepsilon}$ adjustment. For each of these three approaches, we will briefly describe its underlying theory and then apply it to the data in Table 11.5.

Lower-Bound Adjustment

Geisser and Greenhouse (1958) showed that the lowest possible value for ε in an a-level design equals $1/(a - 1)$. For example, if $a = 2$, $\varepsilon = 1.0$ (Why?); if $a = 3$, ε can be no smaller than .50; if $a = 4$, ε can be no smaller than .33; etc. Geisser and Greenhouse recommended that a conservative test of the null hypothesis that all means are equal could be obtained by comparing $MS_A/MS_{A \times S}$ to a critical value with 1 and $n - 1$ degrees of freedom. Notice that their lower bound implies that

$$df_{num} = \varepsilon(a - 1) \geq \left(\frac{1}{a - 1}\right)(a - 1) = 1$$

$$df_{den} = \varepsilon(n - 1)(a - 1) \geq \left(\frac{1}{a - 1}\right)(n - 1)(a - 1) = n - 1 \tag{33}$$

In other words, their lower bound for ε together with Box's ε-adjusted degrees of freedom suggests that the smallest possible appropriate degrees of freedom equal 1 for the numerator and $n - 1$ for the denominator. Notice also that this procedure is conservative because smaller degrees of freedom correspond to a larger critical F value. In this sense, the Geisser–Greenhouse lower-bound approach suggests that no matter how badly the homogeneity assumption is violated, the largest possible critical F value needed is one with 1 and $n - 1$ degrees of freedom.

For the data in Table 11.5, the observed F value was 3.03. With the Geisser–Greenhouse lower-bound approach, this F should be compared to a critical value with 1 and 11 (i.e., $12 - 1$) degrees of freedom. The corresponding critical F is 4.84. Because the observed F is less than the critical F, the null hypothesis cannot be rejected with this approach.

$\hat{\varepsilon}$ Adjustment

Box's $\hat{\varepsilon}$ (pronounced "epsilon hat") approach provides a method for estimating the population value of ε on the basis of observed sample data. The value of $\hat{\varepsilon}$, like that of ε, is always between $1/(a - 1)$ and 1.0. Because the sample value is almost always above the theoretical lower bound, the $\hat{\varepsilon}$ adjustment is usually less severe than the Geisser–Greenhouse adjustment. Unfortunately, the calculation of $\hat{\varepsilon}$ is extremely tedious, as shown by its computational formula:

$$\hat{\varepsilon} = \frac{a^2(\bar{E}_{jj} - \bar{E}_{..})^2}{(a - 1)[(\sum\sum E_{jk}^2) - (2a\sum \bar{E}_{j.}^2) + (a^2\bar{E}_{..}^2)]}$$

where E_{jk} is the element in row j and column k of the sample covariance matrix, $\bar{E}_{jj}$ is the mean of the diagonal entries (variances) in the sample covariance matrix, $\bar{E}_{j.}$ is the mean of the entries in the jth row of the sample covariance matrix, and $\bar{E}_{..}$ is the mean of all entries in the sample covariance matrix. Fortunately, BMDP, SAS, and SPSS-X calculate $\hat{\varepsilon}$ as well as the corresponding adjusted degrees of freedom: $df_{num} = \hat{\varepsilon}(a - 1)$ and $df_{den} = \hat{\varepsilon}(n - 1)(a - 1)$. As of this writing, BMDP and SAS also provide a p value, but SPSS-X does not. We should also mention that all three packages describe the $\hat{\varepsilon}$-adjusted procedure as the Geisser–Greenhouse adjusted procedure, presumably because Geisser and Greenhouse extended the $\hat{\varepsilon}$ adjustment to more complicated designs.

For the data in Table 11.5, it turns out that the value of $\hat{\varepsilon}$ equals 0.61, indicating a marked departure from the homogeneity condition. Notice, however, that the .61 value still is substantially above the .33 theoretical minimum of the Geisser–Greenhouse approach. For $a = 4$, $n = 12$, and $\hat{\varepsilon} = 0.61$, the resulting degrees of freedom are 1.83 and 20.13. Finding the appropriate critical value is complicated by the presence of fractional degrees of freedom. One can either round downward (to 1 and 20 here), interpolate, or find the critical F for the fractional degrees of freedom using a computer program. Taking the latter course (using PROC BETAINV of SAS) shows that the appropriate critical F value is 3.59. Although this value is considerably less than the Geisser–Greenhouse critical value, it is still larger than the observed F of 3.03, so the null hypothesis cannot be rejected with the $\hat{\varepsilon}$ approach. Notice that with either BMDP or SAS there is no need to calculate the critical value because the p value itself is given.

Until the mid-1980s, the lower-bound correction was used much more frequently than the $\hat{\varepsilon}$ adjustment because the value of $\hat{\varepsilon}$ is so tedious to calculate. Now that statistical packages have incorporated calculations of $\hat{\varepsilon}$, the use of the $\hat{\varepsilon}$ adjustment is preferable to the lower-bound correction because the $\hat{\varepsilon}$ adjustment is less conservative. Numerous studies (e.g., Collier, Baker, Mandeville, & Hayes, 1967; Maxwell & Arvey, 1982) have found that the $\hat{\varepsilon}$ procedure properly controls Type I error and yet is more powerful than the lower-bound correction. Nevertheless, even the $\hat{\varepsilon}$ procedure tends to be somewhat conservative because $\hat{\varepsilon}$ tends to systematically underestimate ε, particularly when ε is close to 1.0. An intuitive explanation for this underestimation comes from the way in which $\hat{\varepsilon}$ is calculated. In particular, although it is certainly not obvious from the formula, it turns out that $\hat{\varepsilon}$ can equal 1.0 only if all sample treatment-difference variances are exactly equal to each other; otherwise,

$\hat{\varepsilon}$ is less than 1.0. However, if the homogeneity assumption is satisfied (so that $\varepsilon = 1.0$), it is the *population* treatment-difference variances that are all equal. Even in this situation, the *sample* treatment-difference variances will inevitably be somewhat different from each other, and $\hat{\varepsilon}$ will be less than 1.0. Thus, $\hat{\varepsilon}$ tends to overadjust the degrees of freedom by underestimating ε. Huynh and Feldt (1976) developed another estimate of ε in an attempt to correct the bias in $\hat{\varepsilon}$ for large values of ε.

$\tilde{\varepsilon}$ Adjustment

The Huynh–Feldt $\tilde{\varepsilon}$ procedure (pronounced "epsilon tilde") provides yet a third method of adjustment, which is similar to Box's $\hat{\varepsilon}$ approach in that the population value of ε is once again estimated from sample data. They derived $\tilde{\varepsilon}$ as the ratio of two unbiased estimators, but as they acknowledge, $\tilde{\varepsilon}$ itself is not unbiased. Whereas $\hat{\varepsilon}$ tends to underestimate ε, $\tilde{\varepsilon}$ tends to overestimate ε. In fact, $\tilde{\varepsilon}$ can be greater than 1.0; when this occurs, $\tilde{\varepsilon}$ is set equal to 1.0 because it is known that the population parameter ε can never be larger than 1.0. Once $\hat{\varepsilon}$ has been calculated, it is easy to find the value of $\tilde{\varepsilon}$. In a single-factor design, the relationship is given by

$$\tilde{\varepsilon} = \frac{n(a-1)\hat{\varepsilon} - 2}{(a-1)[n-1-(a-1)\hat{\varepsilon}]} \tag{34}$$

Once again, BMDP, SAS, and SPSS-X all are capable of calculating $\tilde{\varepsilon}$. It can be shown that $\tilde{\varepsilon} \geq \hat{\varepsilon}$ for any set of data, with equality holding only when $\hat{\varepsilon} = 1/(a-1)$. Thus, the degrees of freedom for the $\tilde{\varepsilon}$ procedure will always be at least as large as the degrees of freedom for the $\hat{\varepsilon}$ procedure. As a result, the critical F for $\tilde{\varepsilon}$ will typically be smaller than the critical F for $\hat{\varepsilon}$, leading to more rejections of the null hypothesis. While this implies an increase in power, it also implies an increase in the Type I error rate. We return to this point in a moment.

For the data in Table 11.5, the value of $\tilde{\varepsilon}$ is 0.72, which is larger than the $\hat{\varepsilon}$ value of 0.61, as it must be. The adjusted degrees of freedom for the Huynh–Feldt approach equal $\tilde{\varepsilon}(a-1)$ for the numerator and $\tilde{\varepsilon}(n-1)(a-1)$ for the denominator. For $a = 4, n = 12$, and $\tilde{\varepsilon} = 0.72$, the resulting degrees of freedom are 2.18 and 23.94. The corresponding critical F value is 3.31. Although this value is less than the critical F for both the Box and the Geisser–Greenhouse approaches, it is still larger than the observed F of 3.03, so the null hypothesis cannot be rejected with the $\tilde{\varepsilon}$ approach.

Summary of Four Mixed-Model Approaches

We have now seen four different ways to test the null hypothesis that all means are equal in a within-subjects design. Table 11.12 presents a summary of the four approaches, both in general and in the specific case of the Table 11.5 data. As Table 11.12 shows, all four of the mixed-model approaches use Equation 28 to obtain an observed F value:

$$F = \frac{MS_{A}}{MS_{A \times S}} \tag{28, repeated}$$

TABLE 11.12   Summary of Four Mixed-Model Approaches

| Approach | General Form | | | | Table 11.5 Data | | | |
| | Test Statistic | df for Critical F | | | Observed F Statistic | df for Critical F | | Critical F |
		Numerator	Denominator			Numerator	Denominator	
Unadjusted	$F = \dfrac{MS_A}{MS_{A \times s}}$	$a - 1$	$(a-1)(n-1)$		3.03	3	33	2.90
Huynh–Feldt $\tilde{\varepsilon}$	$F = \dfrac{MS_A}{MS_{A \times s}}$	$\tilde{\varepsilon}(a - 1)$	$\tilde{\varepsilon}(a-1)(n-1)$		3.03	2.18	23.94	3.31
Greenhouse–Geisser $\hat{\varepsilon}$ (Box's $\hat{\varepsilon}$)	$F = \dfrac{MS_A}{MS_{A \times s}}$	$\hat{\varepsilon}(a - 1)$	$\hat{\varepsilon}(a-1)(n-1)$		3.03	1.83	20.13	3.59
Greenhouse–Geisser lower-bound correction	$F = \dfrac{MS_A}{MS_{A \times s}}$	1	$n - 1$		3.03	1	11	4.84

The only difference among the methods concerns the degrees of freedom for the critical F value. As a result, for any set of data, the methods can be ranked in terms of the likelihood of rejecting the null hypothesis in the following order (from most to least likely): unadjusted, $\tilde{\varepsilon}$ adjusted, $\hat{\varepsilon}$ adjusted, and lower-bound adjusted.

How should a researcher choose which approach is best? We can make several general recommendations. First, we believe that the unadjusted mixed-model test should never be used because it is extremely sensitive to the sphericity assumption. As we mentioned earlier, the actual α level can be as high as .10 or .15 for a nominal α level of .05. For a nominal α level of .01, the actual α level can be as high as .06 (Keselman & Rogan, 1980), so even a "highly significant" result with a p value near .01 cannot necessarily be trusted. Despite our recommendation, which simply echoes many earlier recommendations, many behavioral researchers continue to employ the unadjusted test. For example, Vasey and Thayer (1987) found that more than 50 percent of within-subjects studies published in the 1984 and 1985 volumes of *Psychophysiology* reported only the unadjusted test. However, Jennings (1987) describes a new editorial policy begun by *Psychophysiology* in 1987 that requires that all papers with repeated-measures designs must either use one of the adjusted mixed-model tests or the multivariate approach to be described in Chapters 13 and 14. The recent implementation of adjusted tests in statistical packages is likely to hasten the demise of the unadjusted test, appropriately so in our opinion.

A second general conclusion is that the Greenhouse–Geisser lower-bound correction is overly conservative. This approach was quite useful before $\hat{\varepsilon}$ and $\tilde{\varepsilon}$ adjustments were available in statistical packages, but as we pointed out earlier, the $\hat{\varepsilon}$ adjustment is more powerful than the lower-bound correction and yet still maintains Type I error at or below the nominal value.

Thus, the two viable approaches listed in Table 11.12 are the $\tilde{\varepsilon}$-adjusted and $\hat{\varepsilon}$-adjusted methods. Our general recommendation is to use the $\hat{\varepsilon}$ adjustment because on occasion $\tilde{\varepsilon}$ can fail to properly control the Type I error rate. Fortunately, it can be shown from Equation 34 that for large n, the values of $\hat{\varepsilon}$ and $\tilde{\varepsilon}$ are virtually identical, so these two methods usually reach the same conclusion except for small sample sizes. When they do differ, $\hat{\varepsilon}$ is the safer choice because it avoids the potential liberal bias of $\tilde{\varepsilon}$.

Recall that earlier in the chapter we mentioned yet another approach for analyzing data from within-subjects designs—the multivariate approach. As Chapters 13 and 14 will show, there are some situations where the multivariate approach is preferable to any of the mixed-model approaches considered in this chapter. Chapters 13 and 14 discuss the relative advantages of the approaches in detail.

COMPARISONS AMONG INDIVIDUAL MEANS

Individual comparisons of means are usually of interest in within-subjects designs, just as they are in between-subjects designs. The traditional method of testing comparisons in a repeated-measures design involves using the same formula we used in the between-subjects design for finding the sum of squares due to the contrast:

$$E_R - E_F = \frac{(\hat{\psi})^2}{\sum \frac{c_j^2}{n_j}} \qquad \text{(4.35, repeated)}$$

Because we have equal n in the repeated-measures design, this formula can be rewritten as

$$SS_\psi = \frac{n(\hat{\psi})^2}{\sum c_j^2}$$

Then, in the traditional approach, a test statistic is obtained by dividing the sum of squares for the contrast by the interaction mean square:

$$F = \frac{SS_\psi}{MS_{A \times S}} \qquad (35)$$

Appropriate critical values to take into account other comparisons to be tested follow the same logic as we presented in Chapter 5 for between-subjects designs. In particular, Bonferroni's method would simply require comparing the p value corresponding to the F value from Equation 35 to .05/C. A critical value for Tukey's method would be

$$\frac{q_{.05; a, (a-1)(n-1)}^2}{2} \qquad (36)$$

whereas for Scheffé's method, the critical value would be

$$(a - 1)F_{.05; a-1, (a-1)(n-1)} \qquad (37)$$

Although Equations 35–37 constitute the traditional formulas for testing contrasts in repeated-measures designs, we believe that they should not be used because these traditional approaches depend strongly on the sphericity assumption. In fact, tests of comparisons are considerably more sensitive to violations of sphericity than is the main-effect test. Boik (1981) showed that even small departures from sphericity can lead to highly biased tests of comparisons. The problem arises because $MS_{A \times S}$ is an average error term, but the average value is too small for some contrasts and too large for others when sphericity fails to hold. When $MS_{A \times S}$ is too small for a specific contrast, Boik found that the actual error rate for that contrast can reach .70 or more for a nominal α level of .05. When $MS_{A \times S}$ is too large for a specific contrast, the power for testing that contrast can be near .05, even for a moderately strong effect. Thus, using $MS_{A \times S}$ as the error term for testing contrasts can have deleterious effects on both Type I error and power. In addition using $\hat{\varepsilon}$ or $\tilde{\varepsilon}$ adjustments here is not a satisfactory solution because they fail to address the lack of power problem.

Recall that we encountered a similar situation in Chapters 4 and 5 when we discussed tests of contrasts in between-subjects designs. We saw in these chapters that when the homogeneity of variance assumption is false, using MS_W as an error term for testing all contrasts cannot be recommended. The solution in the between-subjects design was to use a separate variance estimate approach, which allowed each contrast to have its own error term. It turns out that this same strategy can also be used in within-subjects designs. However, we defer a discussion of the separate variance estimate approach in within-subjects designs until Chapters 13 and 14. The reason for this organization of topics is that we will see that the separate variance estimate approach for testing contrasts is consistent with the multivariate approach for testing the condition main effect.

CONSIDERATIONS IN DESIGNING WITHIN-SUBJECTS EXPERIMENTS

As we pointed out at the beginning of the chapter, there are three types of repeated measures designs:

1. Subjects can be observed in different treatment conditions.

2. Scores on different tests (or scales) can be compared.

3. Subjects can be observed longitudinally across time.

The remainder of the chapter deals with the first type of design. In particular, we hope to achieve two goals. First, we discuss some further issues in properly designing this type of study. Second, we compare the relative merits of within-subjects and between-subjects designs for comparing the effects of different treatments.

Order Effects

We will orient our discussion around a hypothetical example we introduced at the beginning of the chapter. Suppose that a physiological psychologist wants to compare the effects of drugs A and B on aggressiveness in pairs of monkeys. Further suppose that the psychologist has decided to use a repeated-measures design, so that every pair of monkeys will be observed under the influence of both drug A and drug B.

How should the study be conducted? One possibility would be to administer drug A to every pair, observe the subsequent interactions for a period of time, and then administer drug B to every pair. However, such a design has poor internal validity (see Chapter 1) because it confounds potential drug differences with the possible effects of time. In other words, even if a significant difference between the drugs is obtained, the difference may not have occurred because the drugs truly have a differential effect on aggressiveness. A plausible rival hypothesis is that the monkeys were becoming more or less aggressive (whichever is consistent with the data) across time, independently of differential drug effects. Alternatively, a true difference between the drugs might fail to be detected because time effects might cancel out the real difference in the drugs.

An obvious solution to this problem is to *counterbalance* the order in which treatments are administered. To counterbalance, we administer drug A first to half of the monkeys and drug B first to the other half, where monkeys are randomly assigned to one half or the other. This type of design is known as a *crossover design* because midway through the study each subject crosses over to the other treatment condition. The logic behind the crossover design is that any main effect of order will be controlled for (although not eliminated). As a result, the crossover design possesses much stronger internal validity than does the design where order and treatment condition were confounded.

Differential Carryover Effects

However, even the crossover design is not immune to threats to validity. The greatest threat is the potential presence of a *differential carryover effect*. The general idea of a carryover effect is that the first treatment administered to a subject may continue to have an effect that carries over to the subject's behavior during the second treatment condition. For example, after pairs of monkeys have received drug A, the nature of their interaction may be altered as a result of drug A, even when we observe them after administering drug B. Carryover per se is not necessarily a problem; however, differential carryover is. Differential carryover occurs when the carryover effect of treatment condition 1 onto treatment condition 2 is different from the carryover effect of treatment condition 2 onto treatment condition 1. When drugs constitute the treatments, as in our example, this problem is usually handled by incorporating a "wash-out" period between the two drugs. With a long enough time interval between the two administrations, the hope is that any effects of the first drug will have disappeared by the time the second drug is administered.

Although this procedure may successfully eliminate differential carryover effects of drugs (see Fisher & Wallenstein, 1981, for further discussion), even a wash-out period may be insufficient to prevent differential carryover in some behavioral research. For example, suppose that a psychologist wants to investigate the effectiveness of teaching eight-year-old children a "chunking" strategy to improve free-recall performance. We further suppose that the strategy condition is to be compared to a control condition where no special instructions are given. If a repeated-measures design is used, free-recall performance of one-half of the subjects should first be assessed in the control condition, followed by strategy training, and then a second assessment of performance. The other half of subjects should first receive strategy training and assessment, followed by the control condition and a second assessment. However, there is a problem in this design. If the strategy training is effective, its effect will likely carry over into the second phase of performance, the control condition. However, when the control condition comes first, it will likely have a much smaller carryover effect. Because the two carryover effects are unequal, we have differential carryover. The specific problem can be understood by examining Table 11.13, which shows a set of means that might plausibly occur in this study. The subjects who receive the control instructions first show a 10-point improvement from strategy instruction. However, the subjects who receive strategy

TABLE **11.13** Plausible
Treatment Means for Strategy
Instruction Crossover Study

	Time	
Group	*1*	*2*
Control, then strategy	10	20
Strategy, then control	20	20

first show no effects of strategy whatsoever. As a result, our best guess (assuming equal *n*) would appear to be that strategy instructions cause a 5-point improvement in scores. However, a more plausible interpretation is that the treatment comparison is confounded by differential carryover and that in fact strategy instruction really improves scores by 10 points.[6] The important point is that the crossover design is a poor choice for answering the question of interest here.

What alternative design might be used instead? One possibility might be to let control precede strategy for all subjects. However, this design would be even worse because, as we have seen, treatment effects and order effects are completely confounded in this design. Another possibility might be to allow a long wash-out period. However, if the strategy instructions truly have the desired effect, there is likely to be some permanent change in the manner in which subjects approach such tasks in the future. Somewhat paradoxically then, if the treatment has the desired effect, no amount of wash-out time may be long enough to eliminate differential carryover. What are we to do then? Probably the best course of action here would be to abandon the within-subjects design entirely. As we discuss momentarily, some types of questions are simply much better suited to between-subjects designs, and questions involving comparisons of different strategies usually fall into this category.

Controlling for Order Effects with More Than Two Levels: Latin Square Designs

Controlling for main effects of order is fairly straightforward with two levels of the repeated factor. However, additional practical complications arise when the repeated factor has more than two levels. To understand why, suppose we want to compare four treatments in a within-subjects design. Following our previous discussion for two levels, to control for order main effects, we could randomly assign an equal number of subjects to each possible order of the four treatments. However, we would quickly discover that there are 24 possible orders of four treatments, so we need 24 subjects just to represent each order once. In fact, we would probably want to have several subjects per order, necessitating a considerably larger sample. In general, with *a* treatments to be compared, the number of possible orders is *a*! (*a* factorial). For example, when *a* is 3, there are 6 orders; when *a* is 4, there are 24 orders; when *a* is 5, there are 120 orders; and so forth. Thus, administering treatments in all possible orders may not be practical.

$4! = 24$

TABLE **11. 14** A Cyclic
Latin Square Design for
Four Treatments*

	Order			
Subject	*1*	*2*	*3*	*4*
1	A	B	C	D
2	B	C	D	A
3	C	D	A	B
4	D	A	B	C

* A, B, C, and D refer to the four treatment conditions.

There are basically two alternatives to using all possible orders. First, we can randomize the order of treatments for each individual subject. For example, suppose that we now want to compare the effects of four different drugs (A, B, C, and D) on aggressiveness in pairs of monkeys. With this approach, we would randomly choose an order for the first pair, then choose a random order for the second pair, and so forth. By randomizing the order of treatments individually for each subject, we are guaranteed that the order main effect will be controlled for in the long run, that is, the control is probabilistic rather than deterministic.

A second alternative provides a more deterministic control over the order main effect. Table 11.14 displays a possible arrangement for administering treatments. For example, one group of subjects receives the treatments in the order A, B, C, D; a second group receives them in the order B, C, D, A; and so forth. The important feature of this design is that each treatment appears exactly once in each possible order. For example, treatment A is first for group 1, second for group 4, third for group 3, and fourth for group 2. Such a design is called a *Latin square.* Its main benefit is that the main effect of order is controlled for because every treatment appears equally often in every order.

Many researchers who use Latin square designs seem to believe that the Latin square shown in Table 11.14 is the only Latin square for four treatment groups. If this were so, there would be a serious problem with Latin square designs. To understand the problem with this particular design, notice that treatment B always follows immediately after A, C always immediately follows B, D always immediately follows C, and A always immediately follows D. This systematic pattern makes this particular Latin square particularly susceptible to carryover effects.

The specific Latin square shown in Table 11.14 is called a *cyclic square*. A cyclic square of any size (not just 4 × 4) is obtained by first ordering the treatments alphabetically in row 1. Then, row 2 is formed by moving the first treatment in row 1 to the far right and by shifting all other treatments one position to the left. The same operation is then applied to successive rows. As we have seen, although the cyclic design is popular with many researchers, it is not a good design. Fortunately, there are other Latin squares to consider as alternatives.

Table 11.15 shows 3 additional Latin squares for the $a = 4$ design, as well as the

TABLE **11.15** Standard
Squares for Four Treatments

Square 1

Subject	Order			
	1	*2*	*3*	*4*
1	A	B	C	D
2	B	C	D	A
3	C	D	A	B
4	D	A	B	C

Square 2

Subject	Order			
	1	*2*	*3*	*4*
1	A	B	C	D
2	B	A	D	C
3	C	D	A	B
4	D	C	B	A

Square 3

Subject	Order			
	1	*2*	*3*	*4*
1	A	B	C	D
2	B	A	D	C
3	C	D	B	A
4	D	C	A	B

Square 4

Subject	Order			
	1	*2*	*3*	*4*
1	A	B	C	D
2	B	D	A	C
3	C	A	D	B
4	D	C	B	A

cyclic square of Table 11.14. Notice that in each square, each treatment appears exactly once in each order. Also notice that both the first row and first column of every square are in the order A, B, C, D. A square where the first row and first column are both in alphabetical order is called a *standard square*. As shown in Table 11.15, there are 4 standard squares for the $a = 4$ design.

Table 11.15 might seem to suggest that there are a total of 4 possible Latin squares to choose from when $a = 4$. In fact, there are 576 possible Latin squares when $a = 4$ because it is possible to rearrange the rows and columns of the squares shown in Table 11.15 and still have a Latin square.

How should one of these 576 squares be chosen? The first step is to randomly select one of the standard squares. Then rows and columns are randomly permuted producing a new Latin square. To understand this process, suppose that we have randomly chosen square 3. Next, to permute the rows, we must randomly order the numbers 1, 2, 3, and 4. Suppose that our random order is 3, 1, 4, 2. We then rewrite square 3 with row 3 at the top, then row 1, and so forth. Rewriting square 3 in this way yields

C	D	B	A
A	B	C	D
D	C	A	B
B	A	D	C

Finally, we select another random ordering of the numbers 1, 2, 3, and 4 to permute the columns. Suppose that this time our random ordering is 3, 4, 1, and 2. Rewriting the columns in this order produces

B	A	C	D
C	D	A	B
A	B	D	C
D	C	B	A

Notice that each treatment appears exactly once in each order, meeting the requirements of a Latin square. Further notice that this square improves upon the cyclic square of Table 11.14 in that treatment A no longer always precedes B, B no longer always precedes C, and so forth.

In actual research, there would typically be more than four subjects included in the study. When this is so, the square we have just produced should generally be used only for the first four subjects. A second group of four subjects would receive the treatments based on a separately randomly constructed square, as would a third group, and so forth. The use of separate random Latin squares strengthens the validity of the design. Such a design is called a *replicated Latin square design*. Notice that the design requires that the number of subjects must be a multiple of a.

An alternative to randomly constructing a square in the aforementioned manner is to use a *digram-balanced square*, which is a Latin square where each treatment immediately follows and immediately precedes each other treatment exactly once.[7] An example of such a square for $a = 4$ is

A	B	D	C
B	C	A	D
C	D	B	A
D	A	C	B

Rows of this square can be permuted, but columns cannot be. Digram-balanced squares can be constructed only when a is even; when a is odd, it is also necessary to construct and use a mirror image of the square. Further details are available in Cochran and Cox (1957), Fleiss (1986), Namboodiri (1972), and Wagenaar (1969).

Two further comments need to be made regarding Latin squares. First, the discussion of analyzing data from Latin squares has been conspicuous because of its absence. In some respects, this absence mirrors current practice, which is often to use a Latin square to design the study but to ignore it in data analysis. Such researchers simply use the procedures we developed earlier in the chapter for analyzing data from one-way within-subjects designs. However, as Fisher (1935, pp. 74–75) pointed out more than 50 years ago, and as Gaito (1961) echoed more than 25 years ago, the data analysis should match the design. The reason we have not discussed data analysis here is that the proper method of analysis depends on issues that will be discussed in Chapter 12. Thus, Chapter 12 will present data analysis for the Latin square design. Second, it is important to realize what the Latin square design does not control for. Although it does control for order main effects, it does not control for persistent differential carryover. Thus, when persistent differential carryover is anticipated, a between-subjects design is once again more appropriate.

RELATIVE ADVANTAGES OF BETWEEN-SUBJECTS AND WITHIN-SUBJECTS DESIGNS

At the beginning of the chapter, we briefly mentioned some advantages of within-subjects designs for comparing the effects of different treatment conditions. We will now summarize these advantages as well as possible disadvantages of the within-subjects design.

The first major potential advantage of the within-subjects design is that n subjects generate na data points. For example, if $a = 4$, 10 subjects produce 40 data points. A between-subjects design would require 40 subjects to yield 40 data points. When acquiring enough subjects for a study is difficult, as it often is in behavioral research, the need for fewer subjects in a within-subjects design can be a tremendous advantage. On the other hand, if subjects are readily available, but obtaining data in each condition takes a long time, a between-subjects design may actually be preferable.

The second major potential advantage of the within-subjects design is increased power to detect true treatment effects. Because differences between treatments are obtained by comparing scores within each subject, the influence of the subject main effect has been removed from the error term (see the full model of Equation 22). Thus, systematic individual differences do not contribute to the error term, as they do in between-subjects designs. In this regard, the within-subjects design is similar to the analysis of covariance, which we saw in Chapter 9 uses a covariate to control for individual differences between subjects and hence reduces the magnitude of the error term. It is important to understand that this power advantage for the within-subjects design over the between-subjects design (with no covariates) exists even when the within-subjects design includes n subjects and the between-subjects design includes na subjects. To the extent that systematic individual differences between subjects are large, $MS_{A \times S}$ in the within-subjects design will be less than MS_W in the between-subjects design, yielding more power for the within-subjects design. Vonesh (1983) compared the power of within-subjects and between-subjects designs for testing individual comparisons. Although his results are complicated by several factors, the general practical implication appears to be that the within-subjects approach is typically more powerful whenever the minimum correlation between measures is at least .25.

The primary potential disadvantage of the within-subjects design is differential carryover, which we have seen biases estimates of treatment effects. For this reason, certain types of independent variables are typically not manipulated in a within-subjects design. Examples of such variables would include strategy training, instructions involving deception, and types of psychotherapy. A common characteristic of these variables is that their effects are likely to persist over time. Although permanent effects do not necessarily lead to differential carryover, in most practical situations they will. Thus, within-subjects designs are usually most appropriate for studying independent variables whose effects are likely to be temporary.

Another issue that needs to be considered is that within-subjects and between-subjects designs may not be answering the same question, even when the manipulated variables appear to be the same. The reason they may differ is that in the within-subjects design, subjects experience each manipulation in the context of other manipulations. In the between-subjects design, each subject experiences only one manipulation. We are not trying to argue that either situation is better, simply that they are different. For further discussion of this issue, see Greenwald (1976), Grice (1966), Kazdin (1980), Poulton (1975), and Rothstein (1974).

We will make two final points in closing. First, do not forget that within-subjects designs are also useful for purposes other than comparing manipulated variables. In particular, one of the most frequent uses of within-subjects designs in the behavioral sciences is to study change over time. Second, within-subjects factors are often combined with between-subjects factors in the same design. These designs are discussed in Chapter 12 (mixed-model approach) and in Chapter 14 (multivariate approach).

E X E R C I S E S

1. Within-subjects designs and ANCOVA are similar in that they both attempt to achieve greater power by doing what?

2. Some experimental factors can be manipulated either between subjects or within subjects.
   a. What are the two principal advantages of using a within-subjects design?
   b. What weakness of within-subjects designs might cause an experimenter to decide against using them in certain areas of research even though conceivably they could be employed there?

*3. The following hypothetical data represent level of EEG activity in four locations of the brain among five subjects who were engaged in a mental arithmetic task. The question of interest is whether there is differential level of EEG activity across the four locations.

		Location		
Subject	*1*	*2*	*3*	*4*
1	3	6	4	5
2	4	7	4	8
3	2	1	1	3
4	4	5	1	5
5	7	6	5	9

a. Calculate predicted scores for the full model for these data.
b. Calculate discrepancies between the actual scores and the predicted scores of part a.
c. Calculate predicted scores for the restricted model for these data.
d. Calculate discrepancies between the actual scores and the predicted scores of part c.
e. Use the results of parts b and d to calculate an observed F value for these data. Is there a statistically significant difference among the locations, using an unadjusted test?
f. Would your answer to part e change if you used the Geisser–Greenhouse lower-bound correction?
g. How do the results of using the $\hat{\varepsilon}$ adjustment compare to the results you obtained in parts e and f?
h. How do the results of using the $\tilde{\varepsilon}$ adjustment compare to the results you obtained in parts e and f?

*4. Consider the data shown in Table 11.1 of the text.
a. Find SS_A and $SS_{A \times S}$ for these data.
b. Based on your answer to part a, calculate an observed F value for these data.
c. How does the F value you found in part b compare to the F value reported in Table 11.3 for testing $H_0 : \mu_D = 0$?
d. Is your answer to part c consistent with the assertion that Equation 16 is a special case of Equation 28?

*5. The following data have been collected from five individuals in a one-way within-subjects design with three levels:

	Treatment Condition		
Subject	*1*	*2*	*3*
1	10	12	14
2	2	5	5
3	5	6	10
4	12	15	18
5	16	17	18

   a. Calculate SS_A, SS_S, and $SS_{A \times S}$ for these data.

   b. Can you reject a null hypothesis that the population means of the three treatment conditions are equal to each other?

   c. Suppose that an investigator mistakenly analyzed these data as if they came from a between-subjects design. Find SS_A and SS_W for these data. How do these values compare to the values you calculated in part a?

   d. Could you reject a null hypothesis that the population means of the three treatment conditions are equal to each other if the data were analyzed as if they came from a between-subjects design?

   e. How do parts a–d demonstrate one of the major potential advantages of a within-subjects design?

*6. Consider the data of Table 11.5.

   a. Perform a one-way between-subjects ANOVA on an adjusted dependent variable defined as $Y_{ij} - \bar{Y}_{i.}$. In other words, subtract the row marginal mean from each score prior to performing the ANOVA.

   b. How does the F value you obtained in part a compare to the F value obtained from Equation 28 in the text?

   c. How do the answers to parts a and b help explain that a one-way within-subjects ANOVA is like a one-way between-subjects ANOVA where each subject serves as his or her own control?

7. True or False: In a one-way within-subjects design having two levels, the fact that the minimum value of ε is 1.0 indicates that the restrictive assumption of homogeneity of treatment-difference variances made by the univariate approach *cannot* be violated in such a design.

8. A psychologist has conducted a study involving one within-subjects factor with five levels. The test of the omnibus null hypothesis yields an F value of 4.43, with 4 numerator and 20 denominator degrees of freedom. When a colleague argues that the finding might be misleading if sphericity was violated, the psychologist argues that the finding was "robust" because of the very low p value ($p = .01$).

   a. Are you convinced by this argument, or might the low p value plausibly be a result of violating the sphericity assumption?

   b. Would your answer change if the psychologist had obtained an F value of 6.80? Why or why not?

*9. Find the theoretical minimum value of ε in each of the following situations:

   a. $n = 15, a = 3$

   b. $n = 12, a = 4$

   c. $n = 16, a = 5$

   d. $n = 10, a = 2$

10. Find the numerator and denominator degrees of freedom for the critical F using the Geisser–Greenhouse lower-bound correction in each of the following situations:

   a. $n = 15, a = 3$

   b. $n = 12, a = 4$

   c. $n = 16, a = 5$

   d. $n = 10, a = 2$

*11. Find the critical F value for the unadjusted mixed-model approach and the critical F value for the Geisser–Greenhouse lower-bound correction approach in each of the following situations:

   a. $n = 15, a = 3$

b. $n = 12, a = 4$
c. $n = 16, a = 5$
d. $n = 10, a = 2$

12. Explain in your own words why $\hat{\varepsilon}$ tends to underestimate ε when the sphericity assumption is valid in the population.

13. According to Table 11.11, the variance of the difference between 48- and 36-month McCarthy scores in the Table 11.5 data is much greater than the difference between 48- and 42-month scores.
    a. Calculate the change from 36 to 48 months for each subject.
    b. Calculate the variance of the scores you calculated in part a.
    c. Calculate the change from 42 to 48 months for each subject.
    d. Calculate the variance of the scores you calculated in part c.
    e. Is there more variability in change from 36 to 48 months than in change from 42 to 48 months? Does such a pattern seem plausible in actual data? Explain your answer.

14. Consider the following population covariance matrix:

$$\begin{bmatrix} 1.0 & 0.5 & 1.0 & 1.5 \\ 0.5 & 2.0 & 1.5 & 2.0 \\ 1.0 & 1.5 & 3.0 & 2.5 \\ 1.5 & 2.0 & 2.5 & 4.0 \end{bmatrix}$$

Each entry on the diagonal represents a population variance, whereas each off-diagonal element represents a covariance.
    a. Does this matrix possess compound symmetry? How can you tell?
    b. Is the homogeneity of treatment-difference variances assumption met for these data?
    c. How do your answers to parts a and b relate to the relationship between compound symmetry and sphericity shown in Figure 11.1?

15. An experimenter is planning to conduct a study using a repeated-measures design with four levels, which we label A, B, C, and D. A total of 20 subjects will be included in the study. To control for order effects, one group of 5 subjects will receive the treatments in the order A, B, C, D. A second group of 5 subjects will receive the treatments in the order B, C, D, A. A third group of 5 subjects will receive the treatments in the order C, D, A, B. The final group of 5 subjects will receive the treatments in the order D, A, B, C. Will the proposed design properly control order effects? Why or why not?

16. (To be done by computer.) A developmental psychologist is interested in the role of the sound of a mother's heartbeat in the growth of newborn babies. Fourteen babies were placed in a nursery where they were constantly exposed to a rhythmic heartbeat sound piped in over the PA system. Infants were weighed at the same time of day for four consecutive days, yielding the following data (weight is measured in ounces):

Subject	Day 1	Day 2	Day 3	Day 4
1	96	98	103	104
2	116	116	118	119
3	102	102	101	101
4	112	115	116	118
5	108	110	112	115

Subject	Day 1	Day 2	Day 3	Day 4
6	92	95	96	98
7	120	121	121	123
8	112	111	111	109
9	95	96	98	99
10	114	112	110	109
11	99	100	99	98
12	124	125	127	126
13	100	98	95	94
14	106	107	106	107

a. Test the omnibus null hypothesis that the population mean weight is the same for all four days, using the unadjusted mixed-model approach.
b. Would your answer to part a change if you were to use the $\hat{\varepsilon}$ adjustment? (HINT: After finding the answer to part a, you should be able to answer part b without having to calculate $\hat{\varepsilon}$.)
c. Would your answer to part a change if you were to use the $\tilde{\varepsilon}$ adjustment? (HINT: After finding the answer to part a, you should be able to answer part c without having to calculate $\tilde{\varepsilon}$.)
d. How do the results of parts a–c compare to each other?
e. Is this a good design for assessing the effects of a heartbeat sound on infants' growth? Why or why not? How could the internal validity of the design be strengthened?

17. Psychologists have become increasingly interested in the role of perceived control as it affects individuals' abilities to cope with stress. This exercise is modeled after Bandura, A., Taylor, C. B., Williams, L., Mefford, I. N., & Barchas, J. D. (1985) "Catecholamine secretion as a function of perceived coping self-efficacy." *Journal of Consulting and Clinical Psychology, 53*, 406–414. They hypothesized that perceived coping self-efficacy would mediate the effects of an environmental stressor on hormone secretions indicative of a physiological response to stress. Twelve individuals with phobic dread of spiders served as subjects. They each rated their perceived coping self-efficacy for 18 tasks requiring increasingly threatening interactions with a large spider. Three of the 18 tasks were individually selected for each subject, so as to have one strong, one medium, and one weak self-efficacy task for each subject. Subjects were then individually instructed to perform each of their 3 tasks, in a counterbalanced order. In reality, no subject was able to perform the weak perceived self-efficacy task. The dependent variable to be considered here, level of norepinephrine secretion, was one of several physiological measures obtained from each subject.

Consider the following (hypothetical) data, where higher scores are indicative of greater stress.

Subject	Strong	Medium	Weak
1	.38	.25	.20
2	.36	.41	.37
3	.16	.49	.43
4	.22	.26	.18
5	.17	.27	.24
6	.41	.48	.40
7	.34	.39	.22

Subject	Strong	Medium	Weak
8	.19	.25	.34
9	.25	.35	.30
10	.36	.40	.32
11	.24	.33	.29
12	.30	.35	.27

a. Does the mean level of norepinephrine differ according to the strength of perceived self-efficacy? Analyze the data using the unadjusted F test.
b. Would your answer to part a change if you used the Geisser–Greenhouse lower-bound adjusted test?
c. (To be done by computer.) What is the value of $\hat{\varepsilon}$ for these data? Does your answer to part a change with this procedure?
d. Suppose that it was decided post hoc to test two comparisons: strong versus weak and medium versus the average of strong and weak. Is either of these comparisons statistically significant?
e. Suppose strength of self-efficacy were conceptualized as a quantitative factor with equally spaced levels. How would you label the comparisons tested in part d?
f. It seems plausible that subjects might have experienced less stress if they had been allowed to begin with their strong self-efficacy task, then move to the medium task, and finally end with the weak task. Would this design have been preferable to the design which was actually used? Why or why not?

18. (To be done by computer.) Until the 1960s it was believed that infants had little or no pattern vision during the early weeks or even months of their lives. The following study is modeled after an experiment reported by Fantz, R. L. (1963) "Pattern vision in newborn infants." *Science, 140,* 296–297. Fourteen infants under 48 hours old were exposed to a series of targets, presented in a random sequence to each infant. Three of the targets contained black-and-white patterns: a schematic face, concentric circles, and a section of newspaper. The fourth target was an unpatterned white circle. A blue background was provided in all cases to contrast with the target. The dependent measure is the length of gaze (in seconds) of an infant at a particular target. The following (hypothetical) data were obtained:

Subject	Face	Circle	Newspaper	White
1	3.1	3.4	1.7	1.8
2	1.3	0.6	0.7	0.5
3	2.1	1.7	1.2	0.7
4	1.5	0.9	0.6	0.4
5	0.9	0.6	0.9	0.8
6	1.6	1.8	0.6	0.8
7	1.8	1.4	0.8	0.6
8	1.4	1.2	0.7	0.5
9	2.7	2.3	1.2	1.1
10	1.5	1.2	0.7	0.6
11	1.4	0.9	1.0	0.5
12	1.6	1.5	0.9	1.0
13	1.3	1.5	1.4	1.6
14	1.3	0.9	1.2	1.4

a. Test the omnibus null hypothesis for these data using the unadjusted mixed-model approach.
b. Test the same hypothesis using the $\hat{\varepsilon}$ adjustment.
c. Test the same hypothesis using the $\tilde{\varepsilon}$ adjustment.
d. How do the results of parts a–c compare to each other?

12   Higher-Order Designs with Within-Subjects Factors: Univariate Approach

THIS CHAPTER EXTENDS THE mixed-model methodology developed in Chapter 11 for one-way within-subjects designs to more complicated factorial designs. In this respect, this chapter is related to Chapter 11 just as Chapters 7 and 8 are related to Chapter 3 for between-subjects designs. We will see that the concepts developed in Chapters 7 and 8 for between-subjects factorial designs are applicable for within-subjects factorial designs as well. The only real difference is that the statistical tests must once again take into account the fact that the design involves a within-subjects factor.

There are two rather different ways in which the one-way within-subjects design of Chapter 11 can be generalized. First, there might be a second within-subjects factor included in the design. Although it is possible for one factor to be nested under the other, more frequently these two factors are crossed with one another. For this reason, we focus our attention almost exclusively on the design where the within-subjects factors are crossed. Second, besides a within-subjects factor, there might also be a between-subjects factor. In other words, one (or more) between-subjects factor could be crossed with one (or more) within-subjects factor in the same design.

We discuss these two types of designs separately, beginning with the design where both factors (or more generally, all factors) are within-subjects. At the outset, we should state that this chapter describes only the mixed-model approach to analyzing such designs. However, a set of restrictive assumptions similar to those discussed in Chapter 11 must be met for this approach to be valid. As in the one-way design, $\hat{\varepsilon}$- and $\tilde{\varepsilon}$-adjustment procedures can also be used in factorial designs when the assumptions of the unadjusted approach have not been met. Alternatively, the multivariate approach does not require these restrictive assumptions and thus needs no adjustments. Chapter 14 presents the multivariate approach for factorial within-subjects designs.

DESIGNS WITH TWO WITHIN-SUBJECTS FACTORS

To motivate the analysis of this type of design, we orient our discussion around a specific study where a two-way within-subjects design might be used. Suppose that a perceptual psychologist studying the visual system was interested in determining the extent to which interfering visual stimuli slow the ability to recognize letters. Subjects are brought into a laboratory and seated in front of a tachistoscope. Subjects are told that they will see either the letter T or the letter I displayed on the screen. In some trials, the letter will appear by itself, but in other trials, the target letter will be embedded in a group of other letters. This variation in the display

T A B L E **12. 1** Hypothetical Reaction Time Data for 2 × 3 Perceptual Experiment

	Noise Absent			Noise Present		
Subject	0° Angle	4° Angle	8° Angle	0° Angle	4° Angle	8° Angle
1	420	420	480	480	600	780
2	420	480	480	360	480	600
3	480	480	540	660	780	780
4	420	540	540	480	780	900
5	540	660	540	480	660	720
6	360	420	360	360	480	540
7	480	480	600	540	720	840
8	480	600	660	540	720	900
9	540	600	540	480	720	780
10	480	420	540	540	660	780
Mean	**462**	**510**	**528**	**492**	**660**	**762**

constitutes the first factor, which is referred to as "noise." The noise factor has two levels—absent and present. The other factor varied by the experimenter is where in the display the target letter appears. This factor, which is called "angle," has three levels. The target letter is either shown at the center of the screen (i.e., 0° off-center, where the subject has been instructed to fixate), 4° off-center, or 8° off-center (in each case, the deviation from the center varies randomly between left and right). Table 12.1 presents hypothetical data for 10 subjects. As usual, the sample size is kept small to make the calculations easier to follow. The dependent measure is reaction time (latency), measured in milliseconds (ms), required by a subject to identify the correct target letter. Notice that each subject has six scores, one for each combination of the 2 × 3 design. In an actual perceptual experiment, each of these six scores would itself be the mean score for that subject across a number of trials in the particular condition. Although "trials" could be used as a third within-subjects factor in such a situation, more typically trials are simply averaged over to obtain a more stable measure of the individual's performance in each condition.

Omnibus Tests

The questions to be addressed in this factorial design are exactly the same as those discussed in Chapter 7 for two-way between-subjects designs. In any two-way design, the initial questions typically of most interest are the significance of the two main effects and the interaction.[1] In other words, the effects to be tested are the same whether the factors are within or between subjects. However, the reason we cannot immediately finish the chapter here is that, although the effects are the same, the way in which they are tested changes. Thus, our attention throughout the chapter largely is focused on choosing an appropriate error term. We devote somewhat less attention to the rationale for the sequence of tests we choose to perform because the underlying logic is identical to that developed in Chapters 7 and 8 for the between-subjects design. If you feel the need for a reminder, we especially encourage you to look back at Figures 7.2 and 8.2, which present general guidelines for choosing tests to perform in two-way and three-way designs.

The three effects to be tested for the data of Table 12.1 are the main effect of angle (which we will designate as A), the main effect of noise (which we will designate B), and the interaction of angle and noise. To consider how we might test these effects, recall from Chapter 11 how we analyzed data from a design with only one within-subjects factor. The one-way design was analyzed as a two-factor design, with one factor representing the repeated condition and the second factor representing subjects. Exactly the same approach can be taken in the case of multiple within-subjects factors.

An appropriate full model for the two-way within-subjects design is given by

$$Y_{ijk} = \mu + \alpha_j + \beta_k + \pi_i + (\alpha\beta)_{jk} + (\alpha\pi)_{ji} + (\beta\pi)_{ki} + (\alpha\beta\pi)_{jki} + \varepsilon_{ijk} \qquad (1)$$

where Y_{ijk} is the score on the dependent variable for the ith subject at the jth level of A and kth level of B; μ is the grand mean parameter; α_j is the effect associated with the jth level of A; β_k is the effect associated with the kth level of B; π_i is the effect associated with the ith subject; $(\alpha\beta)_{jk}$ is the effect of the interaction of the jth level of A and the kth level of B; $(\alpha\pi)_{ji}$ is the effect of the interaction of the jth level of A and the ith subject; $(\beta\pi)_{ki}$ is the effect of the interaction of the kth level of B and the ith subject; $(\alpha\beta\pi)_{jki}$ is the effect of the three-way interaction of the jth level of A, the kth level of B, and ith subject; and ε_{ijk} is the error for the ith subject in the jth level of A and kth level of B. The above model is identical to the model we used in Chapter 8 for a three-way between-subjects design, except that now the third factor is "subject."

As shown in Equation 1, there are seven effects included in the full model for the two-way within-subjects design. Specifically, there are three main effects (A, B, and S), three two-way interactions (A × B, A × S, and B × S), and one three-way interaction (A × B × S). Recall that this agrees with our discussion in Chapter 8 of three-way between-subjects designs, where we stated that there were seven effects of potential interest.

The magnitude of each of these seven effects can be determined by comparing the full model of Equation 1 to a restricted model that omits the parameters associated with the effect in question. The resulting difference in sum of squared errors represents the sum of squares attributable to that particular effect. As usual with equal n, this difference can be obtained directly from the full model. The sum of squares attributable to an effect equals the sum of squared parameter estimates for that effect in the full model, where the sum is computed across all abn observations. Although it is useful conceptually to realize that these sums of squares can be calculated by using least squares to estimate parameters in the full and the restricted models, there is a simpler alternative in practice. After some tedious algebra similar to that demonstrated in Chapter 7 for the two-way between-subjects design, it is possible to write general expressions for the sum of squares attributable to each effect in the two-way within-subjects design. Table 12.2 shows these sums of squares and corresponding degrees of freedom. Examining Table 12.2 shows that the sum of squares and degrees of freedom for each effect are calculated in exactly

TABLE **12. 2** Sum of Squares and Degrees of Freedom for Each Effect in a Two-Way Within-Subjects Design

Effect	General Expression for SS	Specific Expression for SS	df
S	$\sum_{k=1}^{b}\sum_{j=1}^{a}\sum_{i=1}^{n}\hat{\pi}_i^2$	$ab\sum_{i=1}^{n}(\bar{Y}_{i..}-\bar{Y}_{...})^2$	$n-1$
A	$\sum_{k=1}^{b}\sum_{j=1}^{a}\sum_{i=1}^{n}\hat{\alpha}_j^2$	$bn\sum_{j=1}^{a}(\bar{Y}_{.j.}-\bar{Y}_{...})^2$	$a-1$
A × S	$\sum_{k=1}^{b}\sum_{j=1}^{a}\sum_{i=1}^{n}\widehat{(\alpha\pi)}_{ji}^2$	$b\sum_{j=1}^{a}\sum_{i=1}^{n}(\bar{Y}_{ij}-\bar{Y}_{i..}-\bar{Y}_{.j.}+\bar{Y}_{...})^2$	$(a-1)(n-1)$
B	$\sum_{k=1}^{b}\sum_{j=1}^{a}\sum_{i=1}^{n}\hat{\beta}_k^2$	$an\sum_{k=1}^{b}(\bar{Y}_{..k}-\bar{Y}_{...})^2$	$b-1$
B × S	$\sum_{k=1}^{b}\sum_{j=1}^{a}\sum_{i=1}^{n}\widehat{(\beta\pi)}_{ki}^2$	$a\sum_{k=1}^{b}\sum_{i=1}^{n}(\bar{Y}_{i.k}-\bar{Y}_{i..}-\bar{Y}_{..k}+\bar{Y}_{...})^2$	$(b-1)(n-1)$
A × B	$\sum_{k=1}^{b}\sum_{j=1}^{a}\sum_{i=1}^{n}\widehat{(\alpha\beta)}_{jk}^2$	$n\sum_{j=1}^{a}\sum_{k=1}^{b}(\bar{Y}_{.jk}-\bar{Y}_{.j.}-\bar{Y}_{..k}+\bar{Y}_{...})^2$	$(a-1)(b-1)$
A × B × S	$\sum_{k=1}^{b}\sum_{j=1}^{a}\sum_{i=1}^{n}\widehat{(\alpha\beta\pi)}_{jki}^2$	$\sum_{k=1}^{b}\sum_{j=1}^{a}\sum_{i=1}^{n}(Y_{ijk}-\bar{Y}_{ij.}-\bar{Y}_{i.k}-\bar{Y}_{.jk}+$ $\bar{Y}_{i..}+\bar{Y}_{.j.}+\bar{Y}_{..k}-\bar{Y}_{...})^2$	$(a-1)(b-1)(n-1)$

the same manner as for any other completely crossed three-way design.[2] As we will see shortly, the only distinguishing feature of the two-way within-subjects design is how error terms are chosen for testing these effects.

As stated earlier, we are interested in testing three effects in this two-way design: the A main effect, the B main effect, and the AB interaction. If this were not a within-subjects design and if all factors were fixed instead of random, mean square within (MS_W) could be used as an error term (i.e., denominator in the F statistic) for testing each effect. However, in the present design, a different error term is needed, just as it was in Chapters 10 and 11; indeed, there is not even a within-cell term that could be used in this design because there is only one observation per cell. As in the previous two chapters, the choice of an error term is dictated by the expected mean squares of the effects in the model.

Table 12.3 shows the expected mean square associated with each effect, where it is assumed that factors A and B are fixed but S is random. As usual, the error term for an effect should be chosen so that the expected mean square of the effect itself contains only one additional term over those in the denominator and that term should correspond to the effect being tested. Given Table 12.3, it is easy to choose appropriate error terms for the A, B, and AB effects. For example, the expected mean square for the A × S interaction differs from the expected mean square for the A main effect only in that the latter includes an additional term, namely, $nb\theta_\alpha^2$. However, this term reflects the A main effect itself and will be zero if the null hypothesis is true. Thus, the A × S interaction is an appropriate error term

TABLE 12.3 Expected Mean Squares for Each Effect in a Two-Way Within-Subjects Design*

Design	
Effect	$\mathscr{E}(MS_{effect})$
S	$\sigma_\varepsilon^2 + ab\sigma_\pi^2$
A	$\sigma_\varepsilon^2 + b\sigma_{\alpha\pi}^2 + nb\theta_\alpha^2$
A × S	$\sigma_\varepsilon^2 + b\sigma_{\alpha\pi}^2$
B	$\sigma_\varepsilon^2 + a\sigma_{\beta\pi}^2 + na\theta_\beta^2$
B × S	$\sigma_\varepsilon^2 + a\sigma_{\beta\pi}^2$
A × B	$\sigma_\varepsilon^2 + \sigma_{\alpha\beta\pi}^2 + n\theta_{\alpha\beta}^2$
A × B × S	$\sigma_\varepsilon^2 + \sigma_{\alpha\beta\pi}^2$

*Results are for a design with a levels of factor A, b levels of factor B, and n subjects. Factors A and B are assumed to be fixed.

for testing the A main effect. As a result, when the null hypothesis is true, the ratio

$$F = MS_A/MS_{A \times S} \qquad (2)$$

is distributed as an F statistic with $(a - 1)$ numerator and $(a - 1)(n - 1)$ denominator degrees of freedom (when requisite assumptions, to be discussed later, are met). Similarly, the B effect is tested by

$$F = MS_B/MS_{B \times S} \qquad (3)$$

and the AB effect is tested by

$$F = MS_{A \times B}/MS_{A \times B \times S} \qquad (4)$$

A general pattern should be apparent in Equations 2–4. In all three cases, the denominator of the F test is the interaction of subjects with the effect being tested. This pattern exemplifies a general rule that can be used in more complicated designs, as long as all factors are within-subjects and are considered to be fixed rather than random (of course, the subjects factor itself is considered to be random). The general rule in this case is that any effect can be tested by forming a ratio of the mean square of the effect divided by the mean square of the interaction between subjects and the effect:

$$F = MS_{effect}/MS_{effect \times S} \qquad (5)$$

In fact, this general rule follows from the principles developed for designs with random factors because the within-subjects factorial design is a special case of the designs considered in Chapter 10. That Equation 5 is consistent with Chapter 10 can be seen most easily by reconsidering Figure 10.2. According to Figure 10.2, when there is only one random factor in the design, the appropriate denominator term of the F statistic for testing any fixed effect is the interaction of the random factor and the fixed effect being tested. However, this is precisely the form of the F statistic shown in Equation 5.

As we pointed out in Chapter 11, Equation 5 also has a strong intuitive rationale. Recall that an interaction between two factors is an index of the extent to which a main effect of one factor is *not* consistent across levels of the other factor. Thus, $MS_{effect \times S}$ is an index of the extent to which the "effect" in question is inconsistent from one subject to another. Because $MS_{effect \times S}$ is in the denominator of the F statistic, larger values of $MS_{effect \times S}$ (i.e., less consistency of the effect from one subject to another) lead to smaller F values. Thus, the numerator of the F statistic of Equation 5 (i.e., MS_{effect}) is an index of the average size of the effect (i.e., averaging over subjects), whereas the denominator is an index of the inconsistency of the effect across subjects.

Numerical Example

At this point, it is appropriate to reconsider the data shown in Table 12.1. Table 12.4 shows the cell means and marginal means for these data. Table 12.5 presents the corresponding ANOVA table for these data. The sums of squares are obtained by applying the formulas of Table 12.2, and the appropriate error term for each effect is chosen in accordance with the principles discussed regarding Table 12.3. The p values of Table 12.5 show that both main effects and the interaction are statistically significant at the .05 level. As with the other designs we have considered previously, significant omnibus effects are typically pursued with further tests.

T A B L E **12. 4** Cell Means and Marginal Means for Table 12.1 Data

		Noise (B)		Marginal Means
		Absent	*Present*	
	0° *Angle*	462	492	477
Angle (A)	4° *Angle*	510	660	585
	8° *Angle*	528	762	645
	Marginal Means	**500**	**638**	**569**

T A B L E **12. 5** ANOVA Table for Data in Table 12.1

Source	SS	df	MS	F	p
A	289,920	2	144,960	40.72	.0001
A × S	64,080	18	3,560		
B	285,660	1	285,660	33.77	.0003
B × S	76,140	9	8,460		
A × B	105,120	2	52,560	45.31	.0001
A × B × S	20,880	18	1,160		

The nature of follow-up tests to be performed in the two-way within-subjects design is the same as in the two-way between-subjects design discussed in Chapter 7; as was true for the omnibus tests, the only difference is what source is used as the denominator of the F test.

Further Investigation of Main Effects

The meaning to be attached to significant effects in the two-way within-subjects design is the same as in the two-way between-subjects design. For example, consider the statistically significant main effects found for both A (angle) and B (noise) in our numerical example. The statistically significant main effect for A implies that the three marginal means for A whose sample values are 477, 585, and 645 (see Table 12.4) are not all equal to each other in the population.[3] Similarly, the statistically significant B effect implies that the population marginal mean for noise absent is different from the population marginal mean for noise present. Notice that no further tests are necessary for interpreting the noise effect because it has only two levels. However, specific comparisons would typically be performed on the angle factor, to better understand the precise nature of the angle main effect.

There are two different approaches for testing contrasts (either comparisons of marginal means, comparisons of cell means, or interaction contrasts) in the two-way within-subjects design, just as there have been in previous designs. As before, the distinction between the two approaches is whether to use a pooled error term or a separate error term for each contrast. To illustrate both approaches, we assume that we are testing a comparison involving marginal means of the A factor, which we will designate A_{comp}. An F statistic based on a pooled error term is given by

$$F = SS_{A_{comp}}/MS_{A \times S} \qquad (6)$$

Alternatively, the F ratio based on a separate error term is given by

$$F = SS_{A_{comp}}/MS_{A_{comp} \times S} \qquad (7)$$

Notice that Equations 6 and 7 both follow the basic logic of Equation 5. However, Equation 6 uses the same error term for testing every contrast of A marginal means, while Equation 7 uses a separate error term for each contrast.

To see how Equations 6 and 7 work in practice, let's return to the marginal means shown in Table 12.4. Because angle is a quantitative factor, we might want to perform a trend analysis, much as we discussed in Chapter 6 for between-subjects designs. Specifically, suppose we decide to test the quadratic trend for the angle marginal means. From appendix Table A.10, the contrast coefficients for a quadratic trend with three levels are 1, -2, and 1. In general, the sum of squares for a contrast of the A marginal means equals

$$SS_\psi = nb(\hat{\psi})^2 \Big/ \sum_{j=1}^{a} c_j^2 \qquad (8)$$

where $\hat{\psi}$ is the sample value of the contrast and c_j is the contrast coefficient for level j. Notice that b appears in Equation 8 because we are comparing A marginal means, each of which is based on nb individual scores. For our data,

$$\hat{\psi} = 477 - 2(585) + 645 = -48$$

Thus, the quadratic sum of squares equals

$$SS_\psi = (10)(2)(-48)^2/6 = 7680$$

The F value for the quadratic trend using Equation 6 is given by

$$F = 7680/3560 = 2.16$$

with 1 and 18 degrees of freedom. It turns out that $MS_{A_{comp} \times S} = 2880$ for the quadratic trend, so the F value for Equation 7 equals

$$F = 7680/2880 = 2.67$$

with 1 and 9 degrees of freedom. Thus, the quadratic trend for angle is nonsignificant, whether the error term of Equation 6 or Equation 7 is used. It should be stressed that it is possible in some circumstances for Equations 6 and 7 to yield very different results from one another.

We defer a complete theoretical comparison of the two tests until Chapters 13 and 14. However, we state now that the F statistic in Equation 6 is valid only when a homogeneity assumption like that discussed in Chapter 11 is met. Equation 7, on the other hand, uses a separate error term for each comparison, which makes the homogeneity assumption unnecessary. The distinction between Equations 6 and 7 should seem somewhat familiar because we discussed a similar problem for testing comparisons in between-subjects designs. In both types of designs, the use of pooled error terms (as in Equation 6) is not robust to violations of homogeneity assumptions. As a consequence, in most within-subjects designs, where the homogeneity assumption is likely to be violated, using Equation 7 is generally preferred to Equation 6. However, as we will see in the next chapter, the use of a separate error term as exemplified by Equation 7 is more compatible with the multivariate approach to repeated measures designs than the mixed-model approach. As we will discover in Chapter 13, a significant main effect when tested with the multivariate approach implies the existence of at least one contrast that would be declared significant by Equation 7 with a critical value chosen to maintain the α_{FW} level appropriately. Similarly, a nonsignificant multivariate A main effect implies that no such contrast exists. Because this one-to-one correspondence holds, the multivariate main-effect test is said to be "coherent" with the use of Equation 7 for tests of comparisons. However, the mixed-model omnibus test turns out to be coherent with Equation 6 but not with Equation 7. If the homogeneity assumption is met, this poses no problems because Equation 6 is appropriate when homogeneity holds. Equation 7 is also appropriate when homogeneity holds. However, F tests based on Equation 7 will be somewhat less powerful than those based on Equation 6 when the homogeneity assumption is met because of the larger denominator degrees of freedom with the pooled error term. If homogeneity is violated, the separate error term of Equation 7 is generally more appropriate, but its results are not necessarily consistent with the mixed-model main-effect test. Indeed, as we will discuss in Chapters 13 and 14, this is one of the primary reasons that we generally prefer the multivariate approach over the mixed-model approach to repeated measures.

Further Investigation of an Interaction—Simple Effects

As in between-subjects factorial designs, the most frequent method of interpreting a statistically significant interaction is to perform tests of simple effects. In our numerical example, we found a significant angle × noise interaction. To better understand this interaction, a logical next step would be to test the angle effect at each noise level individually, as well as to test the noise effect at each individual level of angle. Notice that in either case we have effectively reduced the two-factor design to a one-factor design. For this reason, we can find the numerator sum of squares for the F statistic by treating data as if they came from a single-factor design. For example, consider the effect of angle when noise is absent (i.e., the effect of A within B_1). As usual, in a one-way design, the sum of squares for an effect is given by

$$SS_{\text{effect}} = n \sum_{j=1}^{a} (\bar{Y}_j - \bar{Y}_.)^2$$

where $\bar{Y}_j$ indicates the means of the individual levels and $\bar{Y}_.$ is the grand mean of *these* means (notice that $\bar{Y}_.$ here is *not* the grand mean of all the means in the design, but only of the three means when noise is absent). For our data, the relevant means are shown in Table 12.4: $\bar{Y}_1 = 462$, $\bar{Y}_2 = 510$, $\bar{Y}_3 = 528$, and $\bar{Y}_. = 500$. Hence, the sum of squares due to angle when noise is absent is given by

$$SS_{\text{effect}} = 10[(462 - 500)^2 + (510 - 500)^2 + (528 - 500)^2] = 23,280$$

The question of an appropriate error term now arises. The logic of Equation 5 would suggest using the interaction of subjects and the A-within-B_1 effect as the error term, and indeed this is appropriate. However, it is simpler computationally and conceptually to realize that this interaction term is just the interaction of subjects and angle for the noise-absent data. In other words, this error term is literally identical to the mixed-model error term in the one-way design where angle is the only factor because scores under the noise-present condition are completely disregarded. For the data in Table 12.1, the error sum of squares equals 41,520. Taking a ratio of the corresponding mean squares results in

$$F = \frac{23,280/2}{41,520/18} = 5.05$$

which with 2 numerator and 18 denominator degrees of freedom corresponds to a p value of .018. To reiterate, this is exactly the same result that would be obtained from conducting a one-way within-subjects analysis of the angle effect for the data obtained in the noise-absent condition only. Because we have effectively performed a one-way mixed-model analysis, the assumptions required for the simple-effects test are the same as those discussed in Chapter 11. In particular, the homogeneity assumption discussed there is required, although ε adjustments (to be discussed later in this chapter) can be performed when the assumption is violated. Table 12.6 presents the F values, degrees of freedom, and p values for all the simple-effects tests that might be of interest for the data in Table 12.1. All the simple effects are significant at the .05 level, except for the effect of noise at an angle of zero degrees. As we discussed in Chapter 7 for the two-way design, some investigators might use

T A B L E **12. 6** Simple-Effects Tests for the Data in Table 12.1

Effect*	Numerator df	Denominator df	F	p
AwB_1	2	18	5.05	.018
AwB_2	2	18	77.02	.001
BwA_1	1	9	1.55	.244
BwA_2	1	9	19.74	.002
BwA_3	1	9	125.59	.001

* A = angle, B = noise

a Bonferroni adjustment to control the α_{FW} level for each effect. In this case, tests of A within B would need to be significant at the .05/b level (.025 in our example), and tests of B within A would need to be significant at the .05/a level (.017 in our example). In our particular data, the results are the same with the Bonferroni adjustment as without.

Notice that the effects of angle at a fixed level of noise have two numerator degrees of freedom (see Table 12.6) because the angle factor has three levels. As usual we would typically test specific comparisons of the angle factor, both for noise absent and for noise present, because both angle simple effects were statistically significant. As we have already stated, we defer detailed discussion of comparisons until Chapters 13 and 14. However, notice that comparisons conducted as a follow-up to a significant simple-effects test are in essence comparisons in a one-way within-subjects design. As a consequence, either Equation 6 or Equation 7 can be used, although as before Equation 7 is generally to be preferred because it requires fewer assumptions.

Interaction Contrasts

We should also mention that interaction contrasts provide an alternative method for investigating an interaction, just as they did in the between-subjects design. In a two-way within-subjects design, if the A factor has a levels and the B factor has b levels, the A × B interaction has $(a - 1)(b - 1)$ numerator degrees of freedom (see Table 12.2). The sum of squares for a given component in the within-subjects design is found in just the same manner as in the between-subjects design. Specifically, the component can be represented as a contrast among the ab means in the design. To illustrate this in some detail, suppose that we want to test whether the difference between reaction times for 0° and 8° angles is the same when noise is present as when noise is absent. From Table 12.4, we see that the mean difference in reaction time between 0° and 8° is 270 ms when noise is present but only 66 ms when noise is absent. The sum of squares attributable to this contrast can be calculated as

$$SS_\psi = n(\hat{\psi})^2 \bigg/ \sum_{j=1}^{ab} c_j^2 \qquad (9)$$

where $\hat{\psi}$ is the sample value of the contrast and c_j is the contrast coefficient for level j.[4] Notice that Equation 9 regards the data as coming from a one-way design with ab levels $[ab = (3)(2) = 6$ in our example] because we are no longer explicitly considering the factorial structure of the data in our calculations. For the data in Table 12.4, $\hat{\psi} = 204$ (i.e., $270 - 66$), $n = 10$, and $\sum_{j=1}^{ab} c_j^2 = 4$ (notice that the AB_{11} and AB_{32} cells receive weights of $+1$ and the AB_{31} and AB_{12} cells receive weights of -1, whereas the AB_{21} and AB_{22} cells receive weights of 0). Thus, the sum of squares for this interaction contrast equals 104,040.

Recall from Equations 6 and 7 that either of two error terms might be used to test a comparison of marginal means. A similar choice exists for testing the significance of an interaction contrast. An F test analogous to Equation 6 for testing an interaction contrast is

$$F = SS_{A_{comp} \times B_{comp}} / MS_{A \times B \times S} \tag{10}$$

whereas an F test analogous to Equation 7 is

$$F = SS_{A_{comp} \times B_{comp}} / MS_{A_{comp} \times B_{comp} \times S} \tag{11}$$

The same issues we discussed in comparing Equations 6 and 7 are also relevant for choosing between Equations 10 and 11. Consistent with our earlier preference for Equation 7, we generally prefer Equation 11 because it does not assume homogeneity. However, Equation 11, like Equation 7, is more compatible with the multivariate approach to be described in Chapters 13 and 14 than with the mixed-model approach of this chapter.

For the data in Table 12.1, Equations 10 and 11 yield very similar results. From Table 12.5, we know that $MS_{A \times B \times S}$ equals 1160 for these data; thus, using Equation 10 yields

$$F = 104,040/1160 = 89.69$$

with 1 and 18 degrees of freedom. It turns out that $MS_{A_{comp} \times B_{comp} \times S} = 1240$, so the F for Equation 11 equals

$$F = 104,040/1240 = 83.90$$

with 1 and 9 degrees of freedom. Obviously, this interaction contrast is highly significant regardless of which error term is used. Thus, the difference in reaction time between $0°$ and $8°$ angles is different when noise is present than when it is absent. Specifically, from the means in Table 12.4, we can see that the mean difference in reaction time between $0°$ and $8°$ angle conditions is larger when noise is present than when it is absent. Alternatively, an equivalent statement is that the noise effect is larger in the $8°$ angle condition than in the $0°$ angle condition.

Statistical Packages and Pooled Error Terms Versus Separate Error Terms

Although the differences in the F values we obtained with pooled and separate error terms were negligible, other effects in these data might show large differences between the two approaches. In general, the two approaches can lead to quite different conclusions. As we discussed at some length in Chapter 4 (and briefly in subsequent chapters), when homogeneity is violated, the pooled error term test is too liberal for some contrasts and too conservative for others. For this reason, we generally prefer the use of a separate error term, especially in within-subjects designs where homogeneity is likely to be violated. Unfortunately, when analyses are performed by statistical packages, insufficient documentation may be provided to ascertain which type of error term is being used. However, it is simple to determine which type has been used by examining denominator degrees of freedom. Tests of comparisons using a separate error term have $n - 1$ denominator degrees of freedom in within-subjects designs. On the other hand, tests based on Equation 6 would have $(a - 1)(n - 1)$ denominator degrees of freedom [or $(b - 1)(n - 1)$ df for the comparisons involving the B factor], and tests based on the pooled error term of Equation 10 would have $(a - 1)(b - 1)(n - 1)$ denominator degrees of freedom. Thus, the denominator degrees of freedom shown in the printout for the F test reveal which type of error term has been used.

Assumptions

The mixed-model approach to analyzing data from factorial within-subjects designs requires similar assumptions to those presented in Chapter 11 for one-way within-subjects designs. In particular, there is once again a homogeneity assumption that must be met if the mixed-model F tests are to be valid.

Recall from Chapter 11 that the homogeneity assumption is equivalent to a sphericity assumption for the covariance matrix. Although the assumption actually pertains to the covariance matrix, it is usually much easier to interpret correlations than covariances, so at times we will discuss the assumption in terms of correlations.

In the one-way design, the validity of the homogeneity assumption can be examined by considering an $a \times a$ covariance matrix, where a is the number of levels of the within-subjects factor. A similar approach is relevant when there are multiple within-subjects factors, except now there is a different matrix for each within-subjects effect. To clarify this point, consider the data of Table 12.1. If these data came from a one-way design with six levels, we would form a 6×6 covariance matrix to consider the extent to which the homogeneity assumption has been met. In fact, however, the data came from a 3×2 factorial design. As a consequence, we did not test a null hypothesis that all levels have the same population mean. Instead, we performed three omnibus tests: the A main effect, the B main effect, and the AB interaction. Because these three tests we perform in the factorial design are different from the tests we would have performed if the data came from a one-way design with six levels, the covariance matrices that must be examined for homogeneity are also different.

In fact, we need to consider a different covariance matrix for each effect to be tested. Thus, there will be one covariance matrix for the A main effect, a second for the B main effect, and a third for the AB interaction. The homogeneity assumption can be satisfied for any one of these matrices but not the others, so we must consider each one individually. It should also be noted that yet other matrices will be of

T A B L E **12. 7**   Mean Reaction Times for
Each Subject for Each Level of the Angle
Factor, Averaging over Noise

Subject	0° Angle	4° Angle	8° Angle
1	450	510	630
2	390	480	540
3	570	630	660
4	450	660	720
5	510	660	630
6	360	450	450
7	510	600	720
8	510	660	780
9	510	660	660
10	510	540	660
Mean	**477**	**585**	**645**

interest when other tests are performed, such as simple-effects tests. We will consider the relevant covariance matrices for each of the three omnibus tests to be performed.

To understand the nature of the covariance matrix corresponding to the A main effect, it is necessary to recall the meaning of the main effect. Remember that a main effect involves differences between marginal means, where these means have been calculated by averaging across any other factors in the design. For example, we saw in Table 12.4 that the A marginal means for our sample are 477, 585, and 645. One way to conceptualize the test of the A main effect is to regard not just the means but also the scores for the individual subjects as averaged over the other factors in the design. Table 12.7 presents such scores for the A effect for the data in Table 12.1. Notice that each score for a given subject is simply that subject's mean response time for that angle, where the mean is the average of the noise-absent and the noise-present scores. It can be shown that performing a one-way mixed-model ANOVA on the data in Table 12.7 yields an F value of 40.72, which is exactly the value we reported in Table 12.5 for the A main effect in the factorial design.[5] Because the F values are identical (as they always will be, for any data), they must require the same assumptions. However, we already know from Chapter 11 what assumptions are required for the F statistic calculated from the data in Table 12.7 to be valid. Specifically, the three levels of A shown in Table 12.7 must obey the homogeneity of treatment-difference variances assumption.

Table 12.8 presents the covariance matrix for the data shown in Table 12.7. To simplify interpretations, correlations between the variables are also shown and are discussed momentarily. Notice that the covariance matrix has three rows and three columns because the A factor in our design has three levels. We can see from Table 12.8 that the correlations between scores in different angle conditions are very similar to each other. On the other hand, the variances are rather different, with more variability in scores in the 8° condition than in the 0° condition. As we

T A B L E **12. 8** Covariances and Correlations Between
the Three Angle Scores Shown in Table 12.7*

	0° Angle	4° Angle	8° Angle
0° Angle	4090	.75	.72
4° Angle	3950	6850	.79
8° Angle	4350	6150	8850

*Variances appear on the diagonal, covariances appear below
the diagonal, and correlations appear above the diagonal.

T A B L E **12. 9** Mean Reaction Time for
Each Subject for Each Level of the Noise
Factor, Averaging over Angle

Subject	Noise Absent	Noise Present
1	440	620
2	460	480
3	500	740
4	500	720
5	580	620
6	380	460
7	520	700
8	580	720
9	560	660
10	480	660
Mean	**500**	**638**

discussed in Chapter 11, Mauchly's test of sphericity could be performed to ascertain
whether the homogeneity assumption has been met for the A main effect. However,
as pointed out in Chapter 11, it is generally preferable to modify the degrees of
freedom of the critical value with an ε-adjustment procedure, instead of performing
Mauchly's test. We consider ε adjustments after we discuss the homogeneity
assumption for the B main effect and the AB interaction.

As we stated earlier, a different covariance matrix is relevant for the B main
effect because the B effect averages over levels of A, whereas the A effect averages
over levels of B. Table 12.9 presents each subject's mean score for noise absent and
for noise present, where the mean is the average of the three angle scores at that
particular level of noise. Once again, a one-way mixed-model ANOVA on the data
of Table 12.9 yields an F value of 33.77, identical to the value reported in Table 12.5
for the B main effect in the factorial design. For this F statistic to be valid, the two
levels of B shown in Table 12.9 must obey the homogeneity of treatment-difference
variances assumption.

TABLE **12. 10**   Covariance Matrix and
Correlation Coefficient for the Two Noise Scores
Shown in Table 12.9*

	Noise Absent	Noise Present
Noise Absent	4088.89	.64
Noise Present	4000.00	9551.11

*Variances appear on the diagonal, the covariance appears
below the diagonal, and the correlation appears above the
diagonal.

Table 12.10 presents the covariance matrix and the correlation for the data
shown in Table 12.9. The matrix has two rows and two columns because the B
factor has two levels. It is important to realize that with only two levels of the factor,
there is only one correlation coefficient, so inequality of correlations is not a concern
here as it was for the A factor (which has three levels and hence three correlation
coefficients). Although Table 12.10 shows that scores are considerably more variable
when noise is present than when noise is absent, this disparity is also not of concern
when the factor has only two levels. The reason is that the assumption we discussed
in detail in Chapter 11 requires that the variance of the difference scores formed
from any two levels of the factor must be a constant. However, when the factor only
has two levels, there is only one such difference, so that the assumption is automatically met for any set of data. Thus, the F test presented for the B main effect
in Table 12.5 is necessarily valid because B has only two levels (as usual, we must
also assume normality, but this is a less important assumption for Type I error).
Notice that it is not necessary that scores at the two levels of B be equally variable
because the assumption pertains to difference scores formed from the two levels.
Although the mixed-model approach being discussed here generally produces a
different F value from the multivariate approach of Chapters 13 and 14, we will see
in Chapter 14 that the multivariate approach also yields an F value of 33.77 (with
1 and 9 degrees of freedom) for the B main effect for the data in Table 12.1.

Finally, yet a third covariance matrix is relevant for the AB interaction because
this effect does not average over either A or B. Instead, the interaction assesses
whether the B difference is the same at each level of A. Table 12.11 presents scores
that address this question. For each subject, a given score represents the noise effect
(i.e., reaction time when noise is present minus reaction time when noise is absent)
at a particular level of the angle factor. It can be shown that a one-way mixed-model
ANOVA on the data of Table 12.11 yields an F value of 45.31, identical to the value
reported in Table 12.5 for the AB interaction. For this F statistic to be valid, the
three levels of A shown in Table 12.11 must obey the homogeneity of treatment-
difference variances assumption. Be careful to notice that, although there were also
three levels of A in Table 12.7, the scores themselves are completely different, so the
homogeneity assumption might be met for one of the effects but not the other.

Table 12.12 presents covariances and correlations for the data shown in Table
12.11. We can see from Table 12.12 that both the correlations and the variances are

TABLE 12.11 Noise Effect on Reaction Time
for Each Subject at Each Level of Angle*

Subject	0° Angle	4° Angle	8° Angle
1	60	180	300
2	−60	0	120
3	180	300	240
4	60	240	360
5	−60	0	180
6	0	60	180
7	60	240	240
8	60	120	240
9	−60	120	240
10	60	240	240
Mean	30	150	234

* Each score is the difference between a subject's reaction time
when noise is present minus the reaction time when noise is
absent.

TABLE 12.12 Covariances and Correlations Between
the Three Angle Scores Shown in Table 12.11*

	0° Angle	4° Angle	8° Angle
0° Angle	5800	.86	.52
4° Angle	7000	11400	.71
8° Angle	2600	5000	4360

*Variances appear on the diagonal, covariances appear below
the diagonal, and correlations appear above the diagonal.

rather different from each other. Although once again Mauchly's test could be
performed, ε adjustments are generally preferable.

To this point, we have seen that the extent to which the homogeneity assumption has been met may differ from one effect to another. Before considering ε adjustments, we need to mention one other approach that is sometimes used to analyze data from factorial within-subjects designs. This approach uses the same error term to test all effects, unlike the approach we have presented (which uses $MS_{A \times S}$ to test A, $MS_{B \times S}$ to test B, and $MS_{A \times B \times S}$ to test AB). This error term is obtained as

$$MS_{error} = (SS_{A \times S} + SS_{B \times S} + SS_{A \times B \times S})/(df_{A \times S} + df_{B \times S} + df_{A \times B \times S}) \quad (12)$$

As Equation 12 shows, MS_{error} is a weighted average of $MS_{A \times S}$, $MS_{B \times S}$, and $MS_{A \times B \times S}$. For the data in Table 12.1, MS_{error} equals 3580. F ratios are calculated in this approach by using MS_{error} as the denominator for all tests. For our data, this approach yields $F = 40.49$ for the A main effects, $F = 79.79$ for the B main effect, and $F = 14.68$ for the AB interaction. Each of these F ratios would now have 45 denominator degrees of freedom, instead of the 9 or 18 associated with the approach presented in Table 12.5. Indeed, the only potential advantage of using MS_{error} for all tests is that the denominator degrees of freedom are increased, leading to a lower critical value and hence somewhat higher power. However, this potential advantage comes at a high cost because the required homogeneity assumption is now even stricter. For an F statistic formed from MS_{error} to be valid, the entire $ab \times ab$ (6×6 in our example) matrix must obey the homogeneity assumption. In essence, this implies that not only do the individual matrices of Tables 12.8, 12.10, and 12.12 possess homogeneity but also that $MS_{A \times S}$, $MS_{B \times S}$, and $MS_{A \times B \times S}$ differ from each other only due to sampling error. We believe that such a strong assumption is unlikely to be met in most applications and thus recommend against the general use of MS_{error} as an error term in factorial within-subjects designs.

Adjusted Univariate Tests

We presented three adjusted univariate test procedures in Chapter 11: the Geisser–Greenhouse lower-bound correction, Box's $\hat{\varepsilon}$ adjustment (also called the Geisser–Greenhouse $\hat{\varepsilon}$ adjustment), and the Huynh–Feldt $\tilde{\varepsilon}$ adjustment. All three approaches can also be used for factorial within-subjects designs. As in the one-way design, each involves an adjustment of the numerator and denominator degrees of freedom of the critical value against which the observed value is judged. Notice that the adjustment is applied only to the critical value; the observed value is not adjusted in any of the three approaches.

Each effect being tested in a factorial within-subjects design is subject to a different adjustment because, as we have seen, effects may differ in the extent to which the homogeneity assumption has been satisfied. In particular, for the data of Table 12.1, the adjustment for the A main effect is based on the covariance matrix in Table 12.8, the adjustment for the B main effect is based on the matrix in Table 12.10, and the adjustment for the interaction is based on the matrix in Table 12.12. As a consequence, there are three potentially different $\hat{\varepsilon}$ values and three potentially different $\tilde{\varepsilon}$ values.

As we discussed in Chapter 11, calculation of $\hat{\varepsilon}$ or $\tilde{\varepsilon}$ by hand is extremely tedious. Fortunately, all three major mainframe statistical packages (BMDP, SAS, and SPSS-X) now calculate both $\hat{\varepsilon}$ and $\tilde{\varepsilon}$ for factorial as well as one-way within-subjects designs. However, as of this writing, only BMDP and SAS provide corresponding p values. The computations of $\hat{\varepsilon}$ and $\tilde{\varepsilon}$ are based on the same formulas as we presented in Chapter 11 for the one-way design:

$$\hat{\varepsilon} = \frac{r^2(\bar{E}_{jj} - \bar{E}_{..})^2}{(r - 1)\left[\left(\sum_{k=1}^{r}\sum_{j=1}^{r} E_{jk}^2\right) - \left(2r\sum_{j=1}^{r}\bar{E}_{j.}^2\right) + (r^2\bar{E}_{..}^2)\right]}$$

$$\tilde{\varepsilon} = \frac{n(r - 1)\hat{\varepsilon} - 2}{(r - 1)[n - 1 - (r - 1)\hat{\varepsilon}]}$$

Three comments must be made here. First, E_{jk} is the element in row j and column k of the covariance matrix for the effect being tested. Notice that to use these formulas for our data, the correlations shown above the diagonal in Tables 12.8, 12.10, and 12.12 would need to be replaced by the corresponding covariances, which is simple to do because each matrix is symmetric (i.e., the element in row j and column k is identical to the element in row k and column j). Second, the r in these formulas indicates the number of rows of the covariance matrix. In Chapter 11, r was always equal to a, so we wrote the formula in terms of a. Now, however, r can assume different values for different effects. Third, we have presented these formulas not so much because we expect you to calculate $\hat{\varepsilon}$ and $\tilde{\varepsilon}$ by hand, but instead primarily to show you explicitly that the underlying logic behind $\hat{\varepsilon}$ and $\tilde{\varepsilon}$ adjustments in factorial within-subjects designs is identical to the logic we developed in Chapter 11 for the one-way design. The only real change here is that it is necessary to identify the covariance matrix that corresponds to the effect being tested.[6] For our purposes, it will suffice to report that the value of $\hat{\varepsilon}$ for the A main effect equals 0.96 as calculated from the covariance matrix in Table 12.8. The corresponding $\tilde{\varepsilon}$ value equals 1.21, but because this exceeds 1.00, it is shrunk back to 1.00. For the B main effect, $\hat{\varepsilon}$ can be calculated from the covariance matrix in Table 12.10 to equal 1.00. However, $\hat{\varepsilon}$ always equals 1.00 when the factor has only two levels because, as we have already seen, homogeneity is guaranteed to hold. Also $\tilde{\varepsilon}$ is set equal to 1.00 when the factor has only two levels, as B does. Finally, $\hat{\varepsilon}$ for the AB interaction equals 0.90 based on the covariance matrix in Table 12.12. The corresponding $\tilde{\varepsilon}$ value equals 1.11, which is again shrunk back to 1.00.

Table 12.13 summarizes the effects of the various adjustment procedures for the data in Table 12.1. The adjustments have little effect here for two reasons. First, the observed F values are quite large, so that there is substantial evidence that the effects being tested are nonzero. Second, the covariance matrices do not depart substantially from homogeneity. Even if they did, however, the results for the Geisser–Greenhouse lower-bound procedure in Table 12.13 show that all three effects are still easily statistically significant at the .05 level.

We must stress that the various procedures will not always agree as nicely as they do in Table 12.13. Particularly when some factors have many levels, results may diverge considerably because the theoretical minimum values for $\hat{\varepsilon}$ and $\tilde{\varepsilon}$ become very small as the number of levels increases.

It is also important to remember that $\hat{\varepsilon}$ and $\tilde{\varepsilon}$ values are different for different effects. For example, although ε necessarily equals 1.0 for a B main effect with two levels, ε could be as low as 0.5 for an A main effect with three levels, even in the same data set. Also, $\hat{\varepsilon}$ and $\tilde{\varepsilon}$ values must be calculated for other effects that might be tested, such as simple effects. For example, for the data in Table 12.1, it can be shown that the $\hat{\varepsilon}$ value for the simple effect of angle when noise is present equals 0.78. Notice that this value is considerably less than any of the values for the A main effect, the B main effect, or the AB interaction. Thus, it is usually necessary in factorial within-subjects designs to consider the extent to which homogeneity has been violated separately for every effect to be tested.

T A B L E **12. 13** Results of Applying Adjusted Univariate Procedures
to Data in Table 12.1

Effect	Procedure	Numerator df	Denominator df	Critical Value*	p Value
A	Unadjusted	2	18	3.55	.0001
	Huynh–Feldt $\tilde{\varepsilon}$	2	18	3.55	.0001
	Greenhouse–Geisser $\hat{\varepsilon}$ (Box's $\hat{\varepsilon}$)	1.92	17.31	3.62	.0001
	Geisser–Greenhouse lower-bound correction	1	9	5.12	.0001
B	Unadjusted	1	9	5.12	.0003
	Huynh–Feldt $\tilde{\varepsilon}$	1	9	5.12	.0003
	Greenhouse–Geisser $\hat{\varepsilon}$ (Box's $\hat{\varepsilon}$)	1	9	5.12	.0003
	Geisser–Greenhouse lower-bound correction	1	9	5.12	.0003
AB	Unadjusted	2	18	3.55	.0001
	Huynh–Feldt $\tilde{\varepsilon}$	2	18	3.55	.0001
	Greenhouse–Geisser $\hat{\varepsilon}$ (Box's $\hat{\varepsilon}$)	1.81	16.27	3.73	.0001
	Geisser–Greenhouse lower-bound correction	1	9	5.12	.0001

*Critical value for $\alpha = .05$.

Quasi-*F* Ratios

So far in this chapter, we have assumed that both A and B are fixed-effects factors. In some situations, however, it might make sense to regard one of the factors as random, as we discussed in Chapter 10. Although it would also be possible to have two random factors (in addition to subjects), such designs are very unusual in practice, so we restrict our attention to designs where one factor is fixed but the other is random. We consider two different types of within-subjects designs where one factor is fixed and the other is random. As usual, we continue to regard the subjects factor as random.

We begin consideration of the first type of design with an example. Suppose that a developmental psychologist is interested in comparing fathers' responsivity to infant cues when the mothers are present versus absent. Infants, mothers, and fathers are brought into a laboratory room designed to mimic a living room in the natural environment. For one-half of all families, all three family members are brought into the room initially. After a fixed period of time, the experimenter asks the mother to leave the room. For the other half of families, only the infant and father initially enter the room. After a fixed period of time, the mother also enters. While sequence effects might be of interest themselves in this study, they will be ignored for our purposes here.[7] A score for each father's responsivity to the infant is obtained from trained observers using a Likert Rating Scale (e.g., each father might be rated from 1 to 7 by each observer). Although there might be some advantages to having different observers (i.e., raters) in the different conditions, we assume here that the same observers are used in both conditions. Thus, the design is a two-way within-subjects factorial design, exactly like the design we have considered to this point. For example, we could let A represent the condition factor (mother present versus absent), let B represent the observer factor, and let S represent the subject (i.e., family) factor, in which case we have an A × B × S design.

Unlike our previous discussion of this design, however, we might regard B as a random effects factor because we would presumably want to generalize our results beyond the specific observers included in the study. As we noted in Chapter 10, some researchers would disagree, primarily because it is unlikely that our particular observers have been randomly sampled from some larger population of observers. In any event, we proceed as if observer were a random factor. Sums of squares and degrees of freedom can still be calculated as shown in Table 12.2. However, the expected mean squares shown in Table 12.3 are no longer correct because B is a random factor. Table 12.14 presents the expected mean squares for each effect when the B factor is random. These expected mean squares show that the ratio $MS_A/MS_{A \times S}$ is in general no longer an appropriate F statistic for testing the A main effect, that is, the effect of the mother being present or absent. Notice that, as we have seen before, it is the fixed effect whose test of significance is changed when the other factor is now regarded as random. It turns out that no single effect is an appropriate error term for testing A. Instead, we must resort to a quasi-F ratio of the form

$$F' = \frac{MS_A + MS_{A \times B \times S}}{MS_{A \times S} + MS_{A \times B}} \tag{13}$$

(The notation F' denotes a quasi-F.) The rationale for this ratio is that the expected value of the numerator now contains only one additional term $(nb\theta_\alpha^2)$ not contained in the expected value of the denominator. Because this term corresponds to the effect to be tested, the ratio is an appropriate statistic. However, the ratio is only approx-

T A B L E **12. 14** Expected Mean Squares
for Each Effect in a Two-Way Within-Subjects
Design When the B Factor Is Random

Effect	$\mathscr{E}(MS_{\text{effect}})$
S	$\sigma_\varepsilon^2 + \sigma_{\alpha\beta\pi}^2 + a\sigma_{\beta\pi}^2 + ab\sigma_\pi^2$
A	$\sigma_\varepsilon^2 + \sigma_{\alpha\beta\pi}^2 + n\sigma_{\alpha\beta}^2 + b\sigma_{\alpha\pi}^2 + nb\theta_\alpha^2$
A × S	$\sigma_\varepsilon^2 + \sigma_{\alpha\beta\pi}^2 + b\sigma_{\alpha\pi}^2$
B	$\sigma_\varepsilon^2 + a\sigma_{\beta\pi}^2 + na\sigma_\beta^2$
B × S	$\sigma_\varepsilon^2 + a\sigma_{\beta\pi}^2$
A × B	$\sigma_\varepsilon^2 + \sigma_{\alpha\beta\pi}^2 + n\sigma_{\alpha\beta}^2$
A × B × S	$\sigma_\varepsilon^2 + \sigma_{\alpha\beta\pi}^2$

imately distributed as an F, even when all assumptions hold. Also, calculation of degrees of freedom for a critical F value is very tedious. The interested reader is referred to Kirk (1982, p. 394ff.) or Myers (1979, p. 191ff.) for details. We should mention one other point regarding this design. The use of a quasi-F test here would necessitate having a large number of observers, if power to detect a meaningful A effect is to be adequate. It is much more typical in studies using observers (i.e., raters) to use a relatively small number of raters and to test the A effect by forming the ratio of MS_A to $MS_{A \times S}$ as if B were fixed. However, this approach can be defended even if B is random if there is sufficient theoretical rationale to believe that $\sigma_{\alpha\beta}^2$ equals zero because then under the null hypothesis $\mathscr{E}(MS_A)$ equals $\mathscr{E}(MS_{A \times S})$, even when B is random. In particular, if raters are sufficiently trained so that interrater agreement is very high, $\sigma_{\alpha\beta}^2$ will be zero or practically zero because it reflects the extent to which raters disagree (i.e., are inconsistent) across levels of A. Thus, sufficient training of raters may justify testing A as if B were fixed, even if the investigator wants to generalize findings across raters. Intuitively, if raters can be trained so well that they always agree with each other, then any results that are obtained with one rater would be obtained with other raters as well.[8]

We now consider a second type of within-subjects design where one factor is fixed and the other is random. Santa, Miller, and Shaw (1979) give an example of a social psychologist who is interested in the effects of gender bias in advertising. Subjects read and evaluate a set of job advertisements, one-third of which are biased for females, one-third of which are biased for males, and one-third of which are neutral. An experimenter would probably want to include several advertisements within each of these classes, to be certain that any effects claimed to be due to bias were not in fact really produced by other specific characteristics of the particular advertisements. This design differs from our previous design because advertisement is now nested under the bias factor instead of being crossed with it. When the advertisement factor is regarded as fixed, usual F tests are appropriate (provided other mixed-model assumptions have been met). However, when the factor is regarded as random, once again a quasi-F ratio is necessary. The interested reader is referred to Santa, Miller, and Shaw (1979) for additional information.

ONE WITHIN-SUBJECTS FACTOR AND ONE BETWEEN-SUBJECTS FACTOR IN THE SAME DESIGN

A second way in which the one-way design of Chapter 11 can be generalized is to have one within-subjects factor and one between-subjects factor. This type of design is common in the behavioral sciences because it provides a compromise between a design where all factors are within-subjects and one where all factors are between-subjects. Such a compromise often proves to be extremely useful because it offers the economy of subjects of the within-subjects design while it is less susceptible to problems of differential carryover or an excessive number of trials for each subject that might occur with a completely within-subjects design. This design is also naturally suited for studying different groups of subjects across time in a longitudinal fashion. Notice that the samples might be from naturally occurring populations such as females and males, or they might be the result of the experimenter's manipulation such as treatment and control. In any event, the important point for our purposes is that this design is used often in the behavioral sciences, so a thorough understanding of data analysis is essential.

To motivate the data analysis from this design, we consider a variation of the example we discussed earlier for the two-way within-subjects factorial design. Suppose that a perceptual psychologist is interested in age differences in task performance, where the task is similar to that described earlier. Specifically, the researcher is interested in determining whether older adults respond more slowly than do younger adults. Although age might be regarded as a continuous variable, we assume that the researcher is interested in comparing individuals who are approximately 20 years old with individuals who are at least 60. For example, young subjects might consist of college students, and older subjects might consist of college faculty over the age of 60.[9] To simplify the resultant design somewhat, we assume that the noise factor is no longer of interest but that the angle factor still is. Thus, the design to be used will have two factors—age and angle. Given the nature of these two factors, it seems natural for age to be between-subjects and angle to be within-subjects. To see why, let's consider two other alternatives, the first of which is for both factors to be between-subjects. The primary disadvantage of this design is that it would require many more subjects because each subject would contribute scores at only one level of angle. In most research settings, subjects are at a premium, so there is a distinct advantage to gathering as much data as would be meaningful from each subject.[10] The second alternative is for both factors to be within-subjects. However, it is impractical to use age as a within-subjects factor unless the age range to be studied is small (typically no more than a few months or at most a few years, as it might be for studying children, because developmental changes are usually most rapid at younger ages). In our perceptual example, the age difference of interest compares subjects who are approximately 20 years of age with subjects who are at least 60. It hardly seems practical to wait 40 years to see how the 20-year-olds develop. Thus, for practical reasons, age needs to be a between-subjects factor here. However, we said that angle should probably be a within-subjects factor, in which case we end up with a design where one factor is between-subjects and the other is within-subjects.

Before proceeding with our example, a word about terminology may be helpful. This type of design is often called a *split-plot design*, which is a holdover from its uses in agricultural research. The design is also sometimes called a *mixed design* because it mixes between-subjects and within-subjects factors. However, in the statistical literature, the term *mixed design* is usually used for any design that has both random- and fixed-effect factors, regardless of whether they are between-subjects or within-subjects.

As usual, to make our discussion of data analysis more concrete, we consider a set of hypothetical data. Table 12.15 presents data for 10 older subjects. Once again, the dependent measure is reaction time. Notice that each subject has three

T A B L E **12. 15** Reaction Time for Each Older
Subject for Each Level of the Angle Factor

Subject	0° Angle	4° Angle	8° Angle
1	420	570	690
2	600	720	810
3	450	540	690
4	630	660	780
5	420	570	780
6	600	780	870
7	630	690	870
8	480	570	720
9	690	750	900
10	510	690	810
Mean	**543**	**654**	**792**

scores, one for each level of the angle factor. We use the data presented in Table 12.7 to represent the reaction times of the young subjects. Notice that Table 12.7 presented data as a function of the angle factor alone because scores were averaged over the noise factor. Thus, we have data for 20 subjects in all—the 10 younger subjects whose scores are shown in Table 12.7 and the 10 older subjects whose scores are shown in Table 12.15.

Omnibus Tests

Notice that once again we have a two-factor design. As we discussed earlier, the effects to be tested are the same whether the factors are within- or between-subjects. Thus, we typically are interested in testing the two main effects and the interaction. The sums of squares for these effects are calculated just as for other two-way designs. However, the error terms to be used in significance tests must once again take into account whether the effect being tested is within- or between-subjects.

The three effects to be tested in our example are the main effect of age (which we designate as A), the main effect of angle (which we now designate as B, instead of A), and the interaction of age and angle. Because there is a within-subjects factor in the design (viz., angle), "subjects" are once again included as a factor in the design and as an effect in the full model for the data.

An Appropriate Full Model. An appropriate full model for this design is given by

$$Y_{ijk} = \mu + \alpha_j + \beta_k + \pi_{i(j)} + (\alpha\beta)_{jk} + (\beta\pi)_{ki(j)} + \varepsilon_{ijk} \tag{14}$$

where Y_{ijk} is the score on the dependent variable for the ith subject at the jth level of A and kth level of B, μ is the grand mean parameter, α_j is the effect associated with the jth level of A, β_k is the effect associated with the kth level of B, $\pi_{i(j)}$ is the effect associated with the ith subject in the jth level of A, $(\alpha\beta)_{jk}$ is the effect of the interaction of the jth level of A and the kth level of B, $(\beta\pi)_{ki(j)}$ is the effect of the interaction of the kth level of B and the ith subject in the jth level of A, and ε_{ijk} is the error for the ith subject in the jth level of A and kth level of B. The $i(j)$ notation indicates that subjects (indexed by i) are nested within levels of A (indexed by j).

How is this model different from the model we used for the two-way within-subjects factorial design, that is, the model where both factors (A and B) were within-subjects? That model was written as

$$Y_{ijk} = \mu + \alpha_j + \beta_k + \pi_i + (\alpha\beta)_{jk} + (\alpha\pi)_{ji} + (\beta\pi)_{ki} + (\alpha\beta\pi)_{jki} + \varepsilon_{ijk}$$
(1, repeated)

Comparing Equations 1 and 14 reveals a difference in the way that the subjects effect is represented. In Equation 1, subjects appears as an effect in four terms: π_i, $(\alpha\pi)_{ji}$, $(\beta\pi)_{ki}$, and $(\alpha\beta\pi)_{jki}$. However, in Equation 14, subjects appears as an effect in only two terms: $\pi_{i(j)}$ and $(\beta\pi)_{ki(j)}$.

To begin to understand why the models treat subjects differently, let's consider the $(\alpha\pi)_{ji}$ term of Equation 1. Remember that this term represents the interaction of subjects and the A factor and thus reflects the extent to which the A effect is different from one subject to another. There is no $(\alpha\pi)_{ji}$ term in Equation 14 because subjects are not crossed with the A factor in the split-plot design. Instead, each subject appears in only one level of A, so it is impossible with this design to ascertain the extent to which the A effect is different from one individual subject to another. For instance, in our specific example, we cannot determine the extent to which age and subject interact—that is, some subjects age differently from others—because each subject is either old or young. Because we have a cross-sectional rather than a longitudinal design, this issue cannot be addressed in our design. Statistically speaking, the subjects factor is nested under the age factor instead of being crossed with it. The $\pi_{i(j)}$ term in Equation 14 represents the nested effect of subjects within an age group. Recall from Chapter 10 that such a nested effect takes the place of a main effect and an interaction in a factorial design. This is exactly what has happened here because $\pi_{i(j)}$ in Equation 14 has taken the place of $\pi_i + (\alpha\pi)_{ji}$ in Equation 1. A similar argument shows that $(\beta\pi)_{ki(j)}$ in Equation 14 has taken the place of $(\beta\pi)_{ki} + (\alpha\beta\pi)_{jki}$ in Equation 1. To summarize, the model of Equation 14 differs from the model of Equation 1 because the subjects factor is no longer crossed with the A factor, the between-subjects factor. Instead, the subjects factor is nested under A. As a consequence, the single $\pi_{i(j)}$ term replaces the main effect and interaction terms that appeared in Equation 1. For this reason, there are now only five effects included in the full model for the split-plot design.

Before proceeding, be certain you understand why the $(\beta\pi)_{ki(j)}$ term *does* appear in the model although it represents the interaction of subjects with the B factor (angle in our example). The reason is that the subjects factor is completely crossed with the B factor; each subject has a score at each and every level of B, so it is possible to determine the extent to which the B effect varies from one subject to another. Thus, an interaction term of S and B appears in the model because these two factors are crossed, but an interaction term of S and A does not appear because S is nested under A instead of being crossed with A.

T A B L E **12. 16** Sums of Squares and Degrees of Freedom for Each Effect in a
Split-Plot Design

Effect	General Expression for SS	Specific Expression for SS	df
A	$\sum\limits_{k=1}^{b} \sum\limits_{j=1}^{a} \sum\limits_{i=1}^{n} \hat{\alpha}_j^2$	$bn \sum\limits_{j=1}^{a} (\bar{Y}_{.j.} - \bar{Y}_{...})^2$	$a-1$
S/A	$\sum\limits_{k=1}^{b} \sum\limits_{j=1}^{a} \sum\limits_{i=1}^{n} \hat{\pi}_{i(j)}^2$	$b \sum\limits_{j=1}^{a} \sum\limits_{i=1}^{n} (\bar{Y}_{ij.} - \bar{Y}_{.j.})^2$	$N-a$
B	$\sum\limits_{k=1}^{b} \sum\limits_{j=1}^{a} \sum\limits_{i=1}^{n} \hat{\beta}_k^2$	$an \sum\limits_{k=1}^{b} (\bar{Y}_{..k} - \bar{Y}_{...})^2$	$b-1$
A × B	$\sum\limits_{k=1}^{b} \sum\limits_{j=1}^{a} \sum\limits_{i=1}^{n} \widehat{(\alpha\beta)}_{jk}^2$	$n \sum\limits_{j=1}^{a} \sum\limits_{k=1}^{b} (\bar{Y}_{.jk} - \bar{Y}_{.j.} - \bar{Y}_{..k} + \bar{Y}_{...})^2$	$(a-1)(b-1)$
B × S/A	$\sum\limits_{k=1}^{b} \sum\limits_{j=1}^{a} \sum\limits_{i=1}^{n} \widehat{(\beta\pi)}_{ki(j)}^2$	$\sum\limits_{k=1}^{b} \sum\limits_{j=1}^{a} \sum\limits_{i=1}^{n} (Y_{ijk} - \bar{Y}_{ij.} - \bar{Y}_{.jk} + \bar{Y}_{.j.})^2$	$(N-a)(b-1)$

Restricted Models. The magnitude of each of the five effects in Equation 14
can be determined by comparing the full model of Equation 14 to a restricted model
that omits the parameters associated with the effect in question. The resulting
difference in sum of squared errors represents the sum of squares attributable to
that particular effect. Table 12.16 shows sums of squares and degrees of freedom for
each effect in the model. The S/A and B × S/A notation, which we introduced in
Chapter 10, serves as a reminder that the S effect is nested under A. Thus, the S/A
notation corresponds to the $\pi_{i(j)}$ effect term in Equation 14, whereas B × S/A
corresponds to the $(\beta\pi)_{ki(j)}$ term.

Comparing the specific expressions for sums of squares in Table 12.16 with
those for the two-way within-subjects design, shown in Table 12.2, is instructive.
Notice that the sums of squares for the three effects to be tested (i.e., A, B, and A × B)
are identical in the two cases. The differences occur in the remaining terms, which,
as we will see momentarily, are the error terms. For example, Table 12.16 shows
that $SS_{S/A}$ is calculated by squaring the difference between each subject's average
score (averaging over levels of B) and the average of all scores in that group,
summing these squared differences across groups, and multiplying the result by b,
the number of levels of B. This calculation is similar to that for SS_S in Table 12.2,
except that in the two-way within-subjects design, an average score can be calculated for each subject averaging over both A and B. Such a calculation is
impossible in the split-plot design because each subject appears at only one level of
A. Comparing Tables 12.16 and 12.2 also shows that the relationship between
$SS_{B \times S/A}$ and $SS_{B \times S}$ follows the same pattern as the aforementioned relationship
between $SS_{S/A}$ and SS_S.

Error Terms. Table 12.17 shows the expected mean square associated with
each effect, where it is assumed that factors A and B are fixed but S is random. From

TABLE **12.17** Expected
Mean Squares for Each Effect
in a Split-Plot Design*

Effect	$\mathcal{E}(MS_{effect})$
A	$\sigma_\varepsilon^2 + b\sigma_\pi^2 + nb\theta_\alpha^2$
S/A	$\sigma_\varepsilon^2 + b\sigma_\pi^2$
B	$\sigma_\varepsilon^2 + \sigma_{\beta\pi}^2 + na\theta_\beta^2$
A × B	$\sigma_\varepsilon^2 + \sigma_{\beta\pi}^2 + na\theta_{\alpha\beta}^2$
B × S/A	$\sigma_\varepsilon^2 + \sigma_{\beta\pi}^2$

*Results are for a design with a levels
of factor A, b levels of factor B, and n
subjects. Factors A and B are assumed
to be fixed.

the general principles we developed earlier for choosing an error term, it should be obvious how to test the A, B, and AB effects of interest here. The respective F tests are given by

$$F = MS_A/MS_{S/A} \tag{15}$$

$$F = MS_B/MS_{B \times S/A} \tag{16}$$

$$F = MS_{A \times B}/MS_{B \times S/A} \tag{17}$$

As usual, for these tests to be valid, statistical assumptions must be considered. We discuss this topic later in the chapter.

At this point, it may be helpful to develop an intuitive understanding of the error terms used in Equations 15–17. First, consider the F test of Equation 15 for the main effect of the between-subjects factor. Recall that a main effect represents a difference among marginal means, where all other factors in the design have been averaged over. For the data of Tables 12.7 and 12.15, we could calculate an average (i.e., mean) score for each subject, averaging over the three levels of angle. Notice that the resulting data fit a one-way between-subjects design; the within-subjects factor in the original design has been eliminated because we have averaged over it. Analyzing these data in a one-way between-subjects design would yield exactly the same F value as is obtained from Equation 15. We will see later in the chapter that this equivalence has important implications for the assumptions underlying the F test of the between-subjects main effect.

Second, consider the F test of the within-subjects main effect, shown in Equation 16. The error term used for this test, $MS_{B \times S/A}$, is very similar to the error term we developed earlier for designs where all factors are within-subjects. Recall that in the completely within-subjects design, an appropriate error term for testing any effect is given by $MS_{effect \times S}$, that is, the mean square interaction of the effect and subjects. In the split-plot design, $MS_{B \times S/A}$ is the mean square interaction of the B effect and subjects nested within A. How does $MS_{B \times S/A}$ relate to $MS_{\text{effect} \times S}$ of the completely within-subjects design? It can be shown that $MS_{B \times S/A}$ is a weighted average (i.e., a weighted mean) of the a different $MS_{B \times S}$ values that could be calculated at each separate level of A. Specifically, with two levels of A as in our example, it can be shown that

$$MS_{B \times S/A} = \frac{(n_1 - 1)MS_{B \times S/A_1} + (n_2 - 1)MS_{B \times S/A_2}}{(n_1 - 1) + (n_2 - 1)} \tag{18}$$

whereas in the general case of a levels of A, the equation is given by

$$MS_{B \times S/A} = \frac{\sum(n_j - 1)MS_{B \times S/A_j}}{\sum(n_j - 1)} \tag{19}$$

Equations 18 and 19 show that $MS_{B \times S/A}$ is a weighted average of the separate $MS_{B \times S/A_j}$ terms, with weights proportional to $n_j - 1$, the degrees of freedom for S/A_j. From Equations 18 and 19, you should be able to understand the rationale for using $MS_{B \times S/A}$ as an error term for testing the B main effect. In essence, we know from Chapter 11 that $MS_{B \times S/A_j}$ is an appropriate error term for testing B at the jth level of A (if homogeneity assumptions are met) because this is simply a one-way within-subjects design since we are ignoring all other levels of A. The rationale for averaging the separate $MS_{B \times S/A_j}$ terms across the levels of A is based on an assumption that separate $MS_{B \times S/A_j}$ values differ from one another only due to sampling error. As a result, it is important to notice that using $MS_{B \times S/A}$ as an error term is based on two logically distinct assumptions. The first assumption is that $MS_{B \times S/A_j}$ is an appropriate error term for level j of the A factor. The second assumption is that the a separate $MS_{B \times S/A_j}$ terms are all estimates of a single common population value. As we discuss later in the chapter, it is possible either for both assumptions to be met, or one but not the other, or for both to be violated. However, the basic point for the moment is that $MS_{B \times S/A}$ has the same meaning in a split-plot design as $MS_{\text{effect} \times S}$ has in completely within-subjects designs.

Third, we need to consider the F test for the interaction of the between- and within-subjects factors, shown in Equation 17. Notice that the error term for this test, $MS_{B \times S/A}$, is the same as the error term for the within-subjects main effect. Because we are testing the A $\times$ B interaction, the logic of the $MS_{\text{effect} \times S}$ error term might suggest $MS_{A \times B \times S}$ as an appropriate error term here. However, there is no A $\times$ B $\times$ S term in the split-plot design because A and S are not crossed. Instead, the appropriate error term is given by $MS_{B \times S/A}$, as shown in Equation 17. The error term for the A $\times$ B interaction is the same as the error term for the B main effect because we are still interested in the separate B effects at each level of A. However, as we saw in Chapter 7 when we first discussed interactions, instead of averaging these separate effects to obtain the B main effect, the A $\times$ B interaction compares these separate effects to each other. Nevertheless, in both cases the error term is the same. The most important point to notice here is that the interaction of the between-subjects factor with the within-subjects factor is analyzed using a within-subjects source of variance as an error term.

It should also be pointed out that the three F tests shown in Equations 15–17

T A B L E **12. 18**   Cell Means and Marginal Means for
Data of Tables 12.7 and 12.15

		Angle (Within-Subjects)			
		0°	4°	8°	
Age (Between-Subjects)	Young	477	585	645	**569**
	Old	543	654	792	**663**
		510	**619.5**	**718.5**	

T A B L E **12. 19**   ANOVA Table for Data in Tables 12.7 (Young
Subjects) and 12.15 (Old Subjects)

Source	SS	df	MS	F	p
A	132,540	1	132,540	7.28	.0147
S/A	327,900	18	18,217		
B	435,090	2	217,545	143.91	.0001
A × B	21,090	2	10,545	6.98	.0028
B × S/A	54,420	36	1,512		

are consistent with the principles we developed in Chapter 10. That this is true can be seen by reconsidering Figure 10.3.

Numerical Example.   Now that we have developed the omnibus tests for the split-plot design, let's reconsider the data of Tables 12.7 and 12.15. Table 12.18 displays the cell means and the marginal means for our data. Table 12.19 presents the corresponding ANOVA table. The sums of squares are obtained by applying the formulas of Table 12.16, and the appropriate error term is chosen according to Equations 15–17. The p values of Table 12.19 show that both main effects and the interaction are statistically significant at the .05 level. As in other designs, significant omnibus effects are typically pursued with further tests.

The nature of follow-up tests to be performed in the split-plot design is the same as in the two-way between-subjects design of Chapter 7 and the two-way within-subjects design discussed earlier in this chapter. In other words, the nature of the questions is the same as in the other two-way factorial designs. The only difference is once again what source is used as the denominator of the F test.

Further Investigation of Main Effects

Between-Subjects Factor.   The meaning of a main effect in a split-plot design is the same as in the other two-way factorial designs we have already discussed. For example, consider the statistically significant main effect we found for age, the between-subjects factor in our numerical example. As usual, the statistically significant A main effect implies that the two marginal means are different from one another in the population. From Table 12.18, the sample marginal mean for young subjects is 569 (notice that this is the mean of 477, 585, and 645 because we are averaging over B), and the sample marginal mean for old subjects is 663 (which is the mean of 543, 654, and 792). Thus, the p value of .0147 for the A main effect means that a difference as large as we observed in our sample (i.e., 569 versus 663) would occur in only 1.47 of every 100 experiments if the null hypothesis were true. For this reason, we can reject the null hypothesis at the .05 level. Because there are only two levels of A, it is unnecessary to perform further tests to ascertain which specific levels of A are different from one another. However, in cases where A has more than two levels and the A main effect is statistically significant, multiple-comparisons procedures would typically be used.

We already know how to use multiple-comparisons procedures for pursuing the meaning of a significant between-subjects main effect in a split-plot design. By performing the between-subjects main effect test, we are averaging over the within-subjects factor and effectively eliminating it from the design. As we discussed earlier, the between-subjects main effect F test in the split-plot design is identical to the F test that would occur if each subject's mean score were used as the dependent variable in a purely between-subjects design. The same relationship holds for individual comparisons as well, so that contrasts of the marginal means for the A factor can be tested simply by averaging each subject's scores across the within-subjects factor and performing between-subjects contrasts of the resulting scores. As a result, the principles developed in Chapters 4 and 5 apply with no modifications whatsoever to tests of the between-subjects marginal means in a split-plot design.

Within-Subjects Factor.   In our numerical example, we also obtained a statistically significant main effect for angle, the within-subjects factor. Because the angle factor has three levels, we might want to test comparisons among these levels, to better understand the nature of the angle main effect.[11] As we have seen in previous designs, there are two basic approaches for testing a within-subjects comparison in a split-plot design. One approach uses a pooled error term, whereas the other approach uses a separate error term for each contrast. Before seeing the formulas for the F tests of the two approaches, recall that in our notation B represents the within-subjects factor (angle in the numerical example) and A represents the between-subjects factor (age in the numerical example). The first approach for testing a within-subjects comparison in a split-plot design is to form an F ratio given by

$$F = SS_{B_{comp}}/MS_{B \times S/A} \tag{20}$$

The second approach forms the F ratio as

$$F = SS_{B_{comp}}/MS_{B_{comp} \times S/A} \tag{21}$$

Obviously, the only difference between these two approaches involves the choice of error term. Notice that the F test of Equation 20 uses the same error term for all contrasts, whereas the F test of Equation 21 uses a separate error term for each specific contrast. If you look back at Equations 6 and 7, you should see that Equation 20 is the split-plot equivalent of Equation 6 and Equation 21 is the split-plot equivalent of Equation 7. (Notice that Equations 6 and 7 test a comparison of A marginal means because A was a within-subjects factor in that design, whereas Equations 20 and 21 test a comparison of B marginal means because we have used B to represent the within-subjects factor in the split-plot design. However, Equations 6 and 7 could be rewritten by replacing A with B to make them look more like Equations 20 and 21.)

The choice between Equations 20 and 21 involves the same issues as the choice between Equations 6 and 7. Specifically, Equation 20 is valid only if a homogeneity assumption like that discussed in Chapter 11 is met. When the assumption is violated, using Equation 20 can be very misleading because the F test using a single common error term is not robust when homogeneity fails to hold. As a consequence, in most split-plot designs, where the homogeneity assumption is likely to be violated, using Equation 21 is generally preferred over Equation 20. However, Equation 21 turns out to be more compatible with the multivariate approach to repeated measures than the mixed-model approach. For this reason, we defer further consideration of the choice of error terms until Chapters 13 and 14.

To see how Equations 20 and 21 work in practice, let's test the quadratic trend for the marginal means of the angle factor. As shown in Table 12.18, the sample angle marginal means are 510, 619.5, and 718.5. The contrast coefficients for a quadratic trend among three levels are 1, -2, and 1 (see Appendix Table A.10). The sum of squares for the contrast equals

$$SS_{B_{comp}} = na(\hat{\psi})^2 \left/ \sum_{k=1}^{b} c_k^2 \right. \tag{22}$$

where $\hat{\psi}$ is the sample value of the contrast and c_k is the contrast coefficient for level k. Notice that a appears in Equation 22 because we are comparing B marginal means, each of which is based on na individual scores. (With unequal n, na would simply be replaced by N, the total number of subjects in the sample.) For our data,

$$\hat{\psi} = 510 - 2(619.5) + 718.5 = -10.5$$

Thus, the quadratic sum of squares equals

$$SS_{B_{quad}} = (10)(2)(-10.5)^2/6 = 367.5$$

The F value for the quadratic trend using Equation 20 is given by

$$F = 367.5/1512 = 0.24$$

with 1 and 36 degrees of freedom. It turns out that $MS_{B_{quad} \times S/A} = 1160.83$, so the F value using Equation 21 equals

$$F = 367.5/1160.83 = 0.32$$

with 1 and 18 degrees of freedom. For these data, the quadratic trend for angle is nonsignificant even with α_{PC} set at .05, whether the error term of Equation 20 or 21 is used. However, we should emphasize again that in many circumstances Equation 21 may yield a very different result from Equation 20.

Further Investigation of an Interaction—Simple Effects

As in other factorial designs, the most typical method of interpreting a statistically significant interaction in a split-plot design is to perform tests of simple effects. In our numerical example, we found a significant age $\times$ angle interaction, which might be pursued by testing the angle effect within each level of age, as well as testing the age effect within each level of angle. We need to discuss both types of simple-effects tests because in one case (angle within age) we effectively have a one-way within-subjects design; whereas in the other case (age within angle) we effectively have a one-way between-subjects design.

Within-Subjects Effects at a Fixed Level of Between-Subjects Factor.   We begin by considering the simple effect of angle (the within-subjects factor) at a fixed level of age (the between-subjects factor). For example, consider the effect of angle for young subjects. The question is, are the three sample means of 477 (for 0°), 585 (for 4°), and 645 (for 8°) shown in Table 12.18 significantly different from each other? Looking at the layout of these means in Table 12.18 should convince you that in effect we have a one-way within-subjects design because we are no longer considering the older subjects whose inclusion was responsible for the between-subjects factor. As usual, in a one-way design, the sum of squares for an effect is given by

$$SS_{effect} = n \sum_{j=1}^{a} (\bar{Y}_j - \bar{Y})^2$$

where $\bar{Y}_j$ indicates the means of the individual levels and $\bar{Y}$ is the grand mean of *these* means. For the sake of comparison, notice that in our original notation (see Table 12.16), the sum of squares for the effect of B at A_1 could be written as

$$SS_{B \text{ at } A_1} = n \sum_{k=1}^{b} (\bar{Y}_{.1k} - \bar{Y}_{.1.})^2$$

Substituting the sample means of 477, 585, and 645 together with $n = 10$ (because we are only using the data from young subjects) yields

$$SS_{B \text{ at } A_1} = 144{,}960$$

We must now consider the choice of an error term, that is, a denominator against which to test $SS_{B \text{ at } A_1}$. Recall that we calculated $SS_{B \text{ at } A_1}$ by realizing that in effect we have a one-way within-subjects design when we investigate the B effect at a fixed level of A. Following this logic, it would seem reasonable to use the same error term that would be used in a one-way within-subjects design, namely the mean square interaction of the effect with subjects (as usual, the validity of this error term rests on a homogeneity assumption to be discussed later). Because we are considering only young subjects, this interaction would be B × S for subjects at the A_1 level of the A factor. We previously designated this interaction as $MS_{B \times S/A_1}$ (you may want to refer back to Equation 18 for a reminder of this notation). For our data (in Table 12.7, for young subjects), the value of $MS_{B \times S/A_1}$ equals 1780. An F test for testing the effect of B at A_1 can be obtained from

$$F = MS_{B \text{ at } A_1}/MS_{B \times S/A_1} \tag{23}$$

Because $SS_{B \text{ at } A_1}$ equals 144,960 and B has three levels,

$$MS_{B \text{ at } A_1} = 144{,}960/2 = 72{,}480$$

Thus, the F value for the simple effect of angle for young subjects equals

$$F = 72{,}480/1780 = 40.72$$

which is significant at the .05 level (or at the .025 level, if we decided to divide α by the number of simple effects tests of the angle factor, which is one approach we discussed in Chapter 7).

We might now perform comparisons of the mean angle levels for young subjects, but before considering that possibility, we must consider an alternate error term that might be used instead of $MS_{B \times S/A_1}$. Recall from Equation 18 that $MS_{B \times S/A}$ is an average of $MS_{B \times S/A_1}$ and $MS_{B \times S/A_2}$ when A has two levels, as it does in our example. The assumption made in using $MS_{B \times S/A}$ as an error term for omnibus tests of B and A × B is that $MS_{B \times S/A_1}$ and $MS_{B \times S/A_2}$ differ from one another only because of sampling error. If this assumption is true, $MS_{B \times S/A}$ provides a better estimate of the common population variance than either $MS_{B \times S/A_1}$ or $MS_{B \times S/A_2}$ by themselves because $MS_{B \times S/A}$ is based on more subjects. The superiority of the estimate is translated into increased degrees of freedom, and as a result, increased statistical power. However, as we explained in our Chapter 7 discussion of simple-effects tests in factorial between-subjects designs, simple-effects tests are not robust to violations of this assumption. When the assumption is violated, simple-effects F tests tend to be too large for some levels of A and too small for others. Which error term should be preferred? With large samples (e.g., when the degrees of freedom for $MS_{B \times S/A_j}$ exceeds 50 as an arbitrary but reasonable guideline), using a separate error term of the form $MS_{B \times S/A_j}$ is preferable because the additional degrees of freedom afforded by $MS_{B \times S/A}$ will have literally almost no effect. However, with small samples, the choice is more difficult because the power advantage of using $MS_{B \times S/A}$ can be substantial if the assumption is met. Also, the assumption will often be true (or true for all practical purposes) in many behavioral applications, especially when the between-groups factor reflects a manipulation on the part of the experimenter rather than preexisting intact groups. As of this writing, the major mainframe statistical packages (e.g., BMDP, SAS, and SPSS-X) all use $MS_{B \times S/A}$ as the error term in their split-plot analysis of variance procedures. However, it is obviously simple (no pun intended) to use $MS_{B \times S/A_j}$ as the error term, by literally ignoring all other groups.[12] For our numerical example, the simple effect of angle for the young subjects remains statistically significant if we use $MS_{B \times S/A}$ as the error term because the F value we obtain equals 72,480/1512 = 47.95.

As we stated earlier, because the simple effect of angle is statistically significant for young subjects, we would typically test specific comparisons of the angle factor for young subjects. Notice that these comparisons are in effect comparisons in a one-way within-subjects design. As a consequence, an error term specific to that individual comparison (as in Equation 7) is generally preferred.

So far we have considered only one side of the possible simple-effects tests to be performed in a split-plot design, namely, the effect of the within-subjects factor at a fixed level of the between-subjects factor. In many research situations, however, we may be just as interested in the simple-effects test of the between-subjects factor at a fixed level of the within-subjects factor.

Between-Subjects Effects at a Fixed Level of Within-Subjects Factor. In our numerical example, we would almost certainly be interested in testing the age effect at each level of angle (assuming that we are interested in simple-effects tests in the first place). For example, let's consider the effect of age in the $0°$ angle condition. The question is, are the two sample means of 477 (for young subjects) and 543 (for old subjects) as shown in Table 12.18 significantly different from one another? Looking at the layout of means in Table 12.18 should convince you that for this question we in effect have a one-way between-subjects design because we are no longer considering multiple levels of angle, which was the within-subjects factor. The sum of squares for an effect in a one-way design is easy to calculate. If we let $\bar{Y}_1 = 477$ and $\bar{Y}_2 = 543$, then

$$SS_{\text{effect}} = \sum_{j=1}^{a} n_j(\bar{Y}_j - \bar{Y})^2$$

where n_j is the number of subjects on which $\bar{Y}_j$ is based and $\bar{Y}$ is the grand mean of *these* means. For the sake of completeness, notice that in our original notation (see Table 12.16), the sum of squares for the effect of A at B_1 could be written as

$$SS_{\text{A at B}_1} = \sum_{j=1}^{a} n_j(\bar{Y}_{j1} - \bar{Y}_{..1})^2$$

Substituting the sample means of 477 and 543 into either formula together with $n_1 = 10$, $n_2 = 10$, and a grand mean of 510 yields

$$SS_{\text{A at B}_1} = 21,780$$

Notice that because there are only two levels of A in our example, the degrees of freedom for the A effect (either the A main effect or the simple effect of A at a fixed level of B) equals 1. Hence,

$$MS_{\text{A at B}_1} = SS_{\text{A at B}_1}/1 = 21,780$$

As usual, we must now consider the choice of an appropriate error term. Recall that we calculated $SS_{\text{A at B}_1}$ by realizing that in effect we have a one-way between-subjects design when we investigate the A effect at a fixed level of B. Following this logic, it seems natural to use the same error term that would be used in a one-way between-subjects design, namely, MS_W. Because we are only considering scores in the 0° angle condition, we could designate this mean square within as $MS_{S/A \text{ at } B_1}$. (Notice that we might also write this term as $MS_{W \text{ at } B_1}$. However, the S/A notation is probably better because it reminds us that subjects are nested under A, the between-subjects factor.) It is easy to calculate $MS_{S/A \text{ at } B_1}$, the mean square within age groups for the 0° angle scores, using the formulas developed in Chapter 3 for a one-way between-subjects design. For our data,

$$MS_{S/A \text{ at } B_1} = 6890$$

Thus, the F value for the simple effect of A (age) at B_1 (0° angle) is given by

$$
\begin{aligned}
F &= MS_{A \text{ at } B_1}/MS_{S/A \text{ at } B_1} \\
&= 21{,}780/6890 \\
&= 3.16
\end{aligned}
\tag{24}
$$

In general, there are $a - 1$ numerator and $N - a$ denominator degrees of freedom associated with this F value. In our specific case, the degrees of freedom equal 1 and 18; the corresponding p value is .092, so the effect is nonsignificant even without any possible adjustments of the α level for tests of A that might also be performed at B_2 and B_3.

Once again there is an alternate error term that might be used here. Notice that in the approach we have developed so far, a separate error term is used for each simple-effects test of the between-subjects factor. Specifically, $MS_{S/A \text{ at } B_k}$ is used to test the simple effect of A at the kth level of B. However, an alternate procedure would be to use a pooled error term obtained from the average of all b $MS_{S/A \text{ at } B_k}$ separate error terms. The formula for this error term, which is traditionally referred to as $MSWCELL$ (which is not the same as $MS_{S/A}$), is

$$MSWCELL = \sum_{k=1}^{b} MS_{S/A \text{ at } B_k}/b \tag{25}$$

You may wonder why $MSWCELL$ is an unweighted average, unlike other pooled error terms, which have been weighted averages. In fact, $MSWCELL$ is a weighted average, but the weights are all equal because there must be the same number of subjects at each level of B. Thus, in this case (i.e., equal weights), the weighted average simplifies to an unweighted average. It can be shown that an equivalent computational form for $MSWCELL$ is given by[13]

$$MSWCELL = (SS_{S/A} + SS_{B \times S/A})/b(N - a) \tag{26}$$

which is usually more convenient than Equation 25 for calculating $MSWCELL$ in a split-plot design.

As usual, the potential advantage of $MSWCELL$ over $MS_{S/A \text{ at } B_k}$ is an increase in degrees of freedom, which implies a lower critical value and hence more power if the homogeneity assumption is met. However, when the assumption is violated, typically all simple-effects tests are biased, with some yielding F values that systematically tend to be too small and others yielding F values that systematically tend to be too large. As of this writing, the major mainframe statistical packages (BMDP, SAS, and SPSS-X) all use $MS_{S/A \text{ at } B_k}$ instead of $MSWCELL$ as the error term for testing simple effects of the between-subjects factor at a fixed level of the within-subjects factor.[14] At first glance, this seems inconsistent because all three packages use a pooled error term for testing effects of the within-subjects factor at a fixed level of the between-subjects factor. In neither case are the resulting tests with a pooled error term robust to violation of assumptions, so robustness cannot be the explanation for using a pooled error term for one test but a separate error term for the other. Instead, the rationale for this difference is that one assumption is often more likely to be violated than the other in behavioral research. We stated earlier that the various $MS_{B \times S/A_j}$ terms often estimate the same population variance, especially when the levels of A represent groups formed by the experimenter. Thus, a pooled error term is often justified for testing B effects within levels of A. For testing A effects within levels of B, the assumption required for a pooled error term is that the various $MS_{S/A \text{ at } B_k}$ terms all estimate the same population variance. Although this assumption is undoubtedly valid in some behavioral applications of the split-plot design, in many behavioral studies the assumption is likely to be false. It is especially likely that the assumption will fail to hold when the within-subjects factor is time, as it often is in split-plot designs, because scores often become more variable with the passage of time. In any event, the test using $MS_{S/A \text{ at } B_k}$ always requires fewer assumptions than the test using $MSWCELL$, so for this reason we tend to prefer it, unless the degrees of freedom for $MS_{S/A \text{ at } B_k}$ is small and there is a strong theoretical reason to believe that scores will be equally variable within groups (i.e., levels of A) for the different levels of the within-subjects factor (B).

In our particular data, the choice between $MS_{S/A \text{ at } B_1}$ and $MSWCELL$ as the error term for testing the age difference in the $0°$ angle condition turns out to make no practical difference. From Equation 26 and Table 12.19, $MSWCELL$ equals 7080 for our data. Using this error term for the age effect at $0°$ produces an F value of 3.08, which with 1 and 54 degrees of freedom is still nonsignificant at the .05 level.

In general, when statistically significant simple effects of A are found at a fixed level of B, further tests are performed to isolate the nature of the A effect. Of course, such tests are unnecessary when A has only two levels, as it does in our example. However, when A has three or more levels, specific comparisons can be tested by regarding the data as representing a one-way between-subjects design. Thus, the principles we developed in Chapters 4 and 5 can be applied in this situation.

Interaction Contrasts

As in other factorial designs, another approach to probing a statistically significant interaction is to test interaction contrasts. The sum of squares attributable to an interaction contrast can be found most easily by conceptualizing the contrast as a comparison among the ab means in the design. To illustrate this procedure in some detail, we make use of our numerical example.

Recall that earlier in the chapter we found that the quadratic trend for angle was nonsignificant for our data. However, this does not preclude the possibility that the quadratic trend for angle differs as a function of age. In other words, the quadratic trend for angle might be different for young subjects as compared to old subjects. Before proceeding, you may want to convince yourself that this is indeed possible in our data, despite the nonsignificant quadratic trend for angle. (HINT: Look at Table 12.18. Which means are involved in testing whether the quadratic trend differs as a function of age? Were the same means used in obtaining the nonsignificant quadratic trend for angle?) Recall that because the angle factor has three levels, the coefficients for the quadratic trend are 1, -2, and 1 (see appendix Table A.10). From Table 12.18, we can see that the value of the angle quadratic trend for young subjects equals -48. For old subjects, the value of the angle quadratic trend is 27. We want to test the difference between these two values, so the value of the contrast to be tested equals 75 (i.e., $27 - (-48)$). It should be noted that subtracting 27 from -48 and obtaining a value of -75 would ultimately yield the same sum of squares. Also, notice that in terms of the six cell means shown in Table 12.18, our interaction contrast has coefficients (reading across the rows, from left to right) of -1, 2, -1, 1, -2, and 1. Thus, we are giving negative weights to the contrast coefficients that were initially 1, -2, and 1 in the first row because what we are interested in is the value of the quadratic trend for old subjects minus the value of the quadratic trend for young subjects. We can then find the sum of squares for the interaction contrast from

$$SS_\psi = n(\hat{\psi})^2 \left/ \sum_{j=1}^{ab} c_j^2 \right.$$

where $\hat{\psi}$ is the sample value of the contrast and c_j is the contrast coefficient for cell j. Notice that j ranges from 1 to 6 in our example, and from 1 to ab in general, because we are simply conceptualizing the data in terms of six cell means at this point. For the data in Table 12.18, we have $\hat{\psi} = 75$, $n = 10$, and $\sum_{j=1}^{ab} c_j^2 = 12$ (recall that the six coefficients equaled -1, 2, -1, 1, -2, and 1). Thus, the sum of squares for the interaction contrast is given by

$$SS_\psi = 10(75)^2/12 = 4687.5$$

As usual, the next problem is determining an error term, and several possibilities arise. Because the interaction contrast represents 1 of the $(a-1)(b-1)$ degrees of freedom of the omnibus A × B interaction, one approach is to use the error term that was used for the interaction, namely $MS_{B \times S/A}$. The equation for this F test would be

$$F = SS_{A_{comp} \times B_{comp}} / MS_{B \times S/A} \tag{27}$$

For our data, this F test yields a value of $4687.5/1512 = 3.101$, with 1 and 54 degrees of freedom for the age difference in the angle quadratic trend. This F value would not allow us to reject the null hypothesis at the .05 level, even without a possible adjustment of the α level for any other contrasts we might also test.[15]

Using $MS_{B \times S/A}$, a pooled error term, for testing interaction contrasts has the usual pros and cons. If requisite assumptions are met, degrees of freedom are maximal, so power is somewhat higher than with a separate error term. However, the F test of Equation 27 is not robust to violations of homogeneity. In particular, two homogeneity assumptions are required, one across levels of A and the other across levels of B. The necessity of this assumption can perhaps be made clearest by realizing that in our 2×3 design, $MS_{B \times S/A}$ is an unweighted average of four components[16]:

$$MS_{B \times S/A} = (MS_{B_{linear} \times S/A_1} + MS_{B_{linear} \times S/A_2} + MS_{B_{quad} \times S/A_1} + MS_{B_{quad} \times S/A_2})/4 \quad (28)$$

In our example, the values of these four components turn out to be $MS_{B_{linear} \times S/A_1} = 2120.00$, $MS_{B_{linear} \times S/A_2} = 1605.00$, $MS_{B_{quad} \times S/A_1} = 1440.00$, and $MS_{B_{quad} \times S/A_2} = 881.67$. It is easily verified that the average of these four values is 1511.67, which has been rounded off to 1512 throughout the chapter for simplicity.

It might be argued that, because we are testing only the quadratic trend of angle, our error term should be based on this specific component of the angle effect. Because the interaction contrast involves both A_1 and A_2 (remember that we are literally comparing the quadratic trend at A_1 versus the trend at A_2), a possible error term would be given by the average of $MS_{B_{quad} \times S/A_1}$ and $MS_{B_{quad} \times S/A_2}$: $MS_{B_{quad} \times S/A} = (MS_{B_{quad} \times S/A_1} + MS_{B_{quad} \times S/A_2})/2$, which equals 1160.83 for our data. The general form of this F test is given by

$$F = SS_{A_{comp} \times B_{comp}}/MS_{B_{comp} \times S/A} \quad (29)$$

In our data, the F value equals $4687.5/1160.83 = 4.038$, with 1 and 18 degrees of freedom. The corresponding p value without any adjustment for multiple tests equals .0597, so this approach also fails to find significance at the .05 level.

Although using Equation 29 instead of Equation 27 results in fewer degrees of freedom, the advantage of Equation 29 is that it does not require a homogeneity assumption across the levels of B. As we have stated on several occasions, such an assumption fails to hold in many behavioral applications, so Equation 29 is generally preferred to Equation 27. However, Equation 29 is more consistent with the multivariate approach to repeated measures, so we will wait until Chapters 13 and 14 for a detailed discussion of the use of separate error terms for testing contrasts in within-subjects designs. Finally, we should mention that there are two possible versions of Equation 29. One approach uses all levels of the A factor to calculate $MS_{B_{comp} \times S/A}$, whereas the other uses only those levels of A that are explicitly involved in the interaction contrast. The former has more degrees of freedom than the latter but also requires homogeneity across levels of A. Notice that this choice is not an issue in our example because there are only two levels of the A factor, and both are naturally involved in the interaction contrast.

Finally, Figure 12.1 helps to clarify the nature of the age $\times$ angle interaction. There is some indication that the shape of younger subjects' mean reaction time might involve an inverted-U quadratic component, whereas the plot for older subjects suggests a U-shaped trend. That the test of the age by quadratic trend of angle interaction contrast was nonsignificant means that this difference cannot be regarded as conclusive, so another study might be conducted with a larger number of subjects to further investigate this issue. Also, the figure clearly shows the age main effect and the angle main effect. Also recall from Table 12.19 that the interaction is statistically significant. The plot of cell means suggests that the age groups

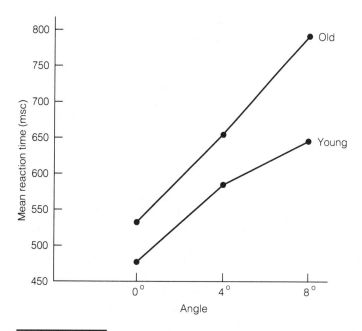

F I G U R E 12. 1 Plot of reaction times for old and young subjects as a function of angle.

differ most in the 8° angle condition. This issue could be pursued by testing an appropriate interaction contrast. Alternatively, the simple effect of age at each level of angle could be tested, although this would not address the specific question of whether the age difference is larger at 8° than at 0° or 4°.

Assumptions

As we have seen, the split-plot design is a combination of between-subjects and within-subjects designs. Not surprisingly, the statistical assumptions required in the split-plot design are also a combination of between- and within-subjects assumptions. We now discuss these assumptions for omnibus tests, as well as follow-up tests of simple effects and interaction contrasts.

We learned earlier that the F test of the between-subjects main effect (denoted A) in the split-plot design is identical to an F test that could be conducted as a one-way between-subjects test on the mean score for each subject, averaging over levels of the within-subjects factor. Thus, the assumptions are the same as those for a one-way between-subjects design, namely, normality, homogeneity of variance, and independence of observations (i.e., subjects). The practical importance of these assumptions for testing the A main effect in a split-plot design is exactly the same as their importance in a one-way between-subjects design, which we discussed back in Chapter 3. As usual, scores for different subjects should be independent of each other, or serious biases may result. Violations of normality typically have little impact on the F test, although in Chapter 15 we will see that more powerful tests may be available for nonnormal data. Finally, with equal n, the F test is generally robust to violations of homogeneity of variance. With unequal n, the test is not robust, and modifications to be discussed in Chapter 15 are generally preferable when heterogeneity of variance is suspected. Be certain you understand to what scores these assumptions apply. They are assumptions that refer to the mean score calculated for each subject, averaging over levels of the within-subjects factor. The assumptions do not necessarily have to hold for the original scores themselves, although if they do hold for the original scores, it can be shown that they must also hold for the mean scores as well.

The required statistical assumptions for testing the B and A $\times$ B effects are rather different from those required for testing the A effect. Notice that B and A $\times$ B are both within-subjects effects and that both use $MS_{B \times S/A}$ as the denominator of their F tests (see Equations 16 and 17). Besides the usual assumptions of normality and of independence of subjects, the mixed-model F tests of the B and A $\times$ B effects also require two other assumptions. First, it is assumed that within each level of A (the between-subjects factor), the levels of B display the homogeneity of treatment-difference variances property discussed in Chapter 11. Recall that the rationale for using $MS_{B \times S/A}$ as an error term was based partially on the fact that $MS_{B \times S/A_j}$ would be an appropriate error term for testing B effects at the jth level of A, if homogeneity is valid. Also, remember that this homogeneity assumption holds if and only if the population covariance matrix of the data possesses sphericity. The second required assumption is that these a covariance matrices, each of which is calculated at an individual level of A, must be identical to one another in the population.[17] It is important to realize that these two assumptions are logically separate from one another, in the sense that it is entirely possible for either to hold when the other is false. The most important practical aspect of these assumptions is that the B and A $\times$ B mixed-model tests are *not* robust to violations of the homogeneity of treatment-difference variances assumption. This should not be surprising because other within-subjects tests discussed earlier in this chapter and in Chapter 11 have also depended heavily on this assumption. The significance tests are robust to the second assumption, as long as sample sizes are equal. However, as sample sizes depart from equality, the tests become less robust. In general, however, the crucial assumption is that the covariance matrix corresponding to the B effect must exhibit sphericity. When the assumption is not met, there is a systematic tendency for the actual rate of Type I errors to exceed its nominal value. As we have said before, this assumption is likely to be violated in many behavioral applications. For this reason, it is often appropriate to consider either ε-adjusted tests, to be discussed momentarily, or a multivariate approach to analyzing split-plot data, to be discussed in Chapter 14.

As we have discussed throughout the chapter, the necessary assumptions required for follow-up tests depend strongly on the nature of the error term chosen for conducting these tests. Table 12.20 summarizes the available choices for each type of test and indicates which assumptions are required, as well as whether the test tends to be robust to violations of that assumption. As Table 12.20 shows, most of the within-subjects tests we have discussed in this chapter are sensitive to the

T A B L E **12. 20** Assumptions and Robustness Properties of Omnibus and Follow-Up Tests in Split-Plot Designs

Test	Error Term*	Assumptions			
		Equality of Levels of A		Spherical Covariance Matrix	
		Required?	Robust?	Required?	Robust?
A	$MS_{S/A}$ (15)	Yes[†]	Yes[‡]	No	—
A_{comp}	$MS_{S/A}$	Yes[†]	No	No	—
B	$MS_{B \times S/A}$ (16)	Yes[§]	Yes[‡]	Yes	No
B_{comp}	$MS_{B \times S/A}$ (20)	Yes[§]	Yes[‡]	Yes	No
	or				
	$MS_{B_{comp} \times S/A}$ (21)	Yes[§]	Yes[‡]	No	—
$A \times B$	$MS_{B \times S/A}$ (17)	Yes[§]	Yes[‡]	Yes	No
B at A_j	$MS_{B \times S/A}$	Yes[§]	Yes[‡]	Yes	No
	or				
	$MS_{B \times S/A_j}$ (23)	No	—	Yes	No
A at B_k	$MSWCELL$	Yes[‖]	Yes[‡]	Yes[#]	No
	or				
	$MS_{S/A}$ at B_k (24)	Yes[‖]	Yes[‡]	No	—
$A_{comp} \times B_{comp}$	$MS_{B \times S/A}$ (27)	Yes[§]	No	Yes	No
	or				
	$MS_{B_{comp} \times S/A}$ (29)	Yes[§]	No	No	—

*The numbers in parentheses after the error term show the equation number for testing this effect.
[†] The assumption is that mean scores averaged over levels of B must be equally variable.
[‡] Robust with equal *n*. With unequal *n*, not generally robust.
[§] The assumption is that the population covariance matrices must be identical at every level of A.
[‖] The assumption is that scores at this level of B must be equally variable for all levels of A.
[#] The assumption is that scores must be equally variable for all levels of B.

assumption that the covariance matrix of the repeated factor possesses sphericity. When this assumption is false, there are two alternatives to the mixed-model tests we have discussed: ε-adjusted tests and multivariate tests. We discuss ε-adjusted tests now and multivariate tests in Chapter 14.

Adjusted Univariate Tests

As in the other designs we have encountered, three adjusted univariate test procedures are available in split-plot designs: the Geisser–Greenhouse lower-bound correction, Box's $\hat{\varepsilon}$ adjustment (also called the Greenhouse–Geisser $\hat{\varepsilon}$ adjustment), and the Huynh–Feldt $\tilde{\varepsilon}$ adjustment. As before, each involves an adjustment of the numerator and denominator degrees of freedom of the critical value against which the observed value is judged. In all three procedures, the adjustment is applied only to the critical value, with no adjustment whatsoever of the observed value of the test statistic.

At the outset it is important to realize that there is no need to consider adjusted tests for effects involving only A, because these tests do not require sphericity (see Table 12.20). Thus, only within-subjects effects might be adjusted by one of these three approaches.

Although there are two omnibus within-subjects effects in the split-plot design (e.g., the B main effect and the A × B interaction), notice that both of these effects use $MS_{B \times S/A}$ as the error term. As a consequence, the $\hat{\varepsilon}$ value for B equals the $\hat{\varepsilon}$ value for A × B; the same equality holds for $\tilde{\varepsilon}$. Indeed, we will see in Chapters 13 and 14 that $\hat{\varepsilon}$ and $\tilde{\varepsilon}$ can be regarded as indices of the extent to which the individual $MS_{B_{comp} \times S/A}$ components of $MS_{B \times S/A}$ are providing independent (i.e., uncorrelated) estimates of a common population parameter. The important point for our purposes is that because B and A × B are both based on $MS_{B \times S/A}$, we do not need a different adjustment factor for each within-subjects effect, as we did with two within-subjects factors. To emphasize the distinction, remember that when A and B are both within-subjects factors, there were three different error terms: $MS_{A \times S}$ for testing A, $MS_{B \times S}$ for testing B, and $MS_{A \times B \times S}$ for testing A × B. Because there are three error terms, there are three values of $\hat{\varepsilon}$ and three values of $\tilde{\varepsilon}$. In the split-plot design with one within-subjects factor, there is one error term (i.e., $MS_{B \times S/A}$) and hence one value of $\hat{\varepsilon}$ and one value of $\tilde{\varepsilon}$. In addition, this single value of $\hat{\varepsilon}$ and the single value of $\tilde{\varepsilon}$ are also appropriate for testing simple effects of B at fixed levels of A and for testing interaction contrasts, if $MS_{B \times S/A}$ is used as the error term. Of course, if $MS_{B \times S/A_j}$ is used as the error term for testing B at A_j, we calculate $\hat{\varepsilon}$ and $\tilde{\varepsilon}$ values using only the data from the jth level of A. Similarly, if $MS_{B_{comp} \times S/A}$ is used as the error term for testing an interaction contrast, no $\hat{\varepsilon}$ or $\tilde{\varepsilon}$ adjustment is necessary because sphericity is not required for the F test to be valid with this separate error term.

Calculating $\hat{\varepsilon}$ or $\tilde{\varepsilon}$ by hand is again tedious. All three major mainframe statistical packages (e.g., BMDP, SAS, and SPSS-X) now calculate both $\hat{\varepsilon}$ and $\tilde{\varepsilon}$ for split-plot designs. For our numerical example, it turns out that $\hat{\varepsilon} = 0.94$ and $\tilde{\varepsilon} = 1.10$. Because $\tilde{\varepsilon}$ exceeds 1.00, it is shrunk back to 1.00. Because $\tilde{\varepsilon}$ in its shrunken form equals 1.00, using $\tilde{\varepsilon}$ here is literally equivalent to performing unadjusted tests. In addition, $\hat{\varepsilon}$ is so close to 1.00 that $\hat{\varepsilon}$-adjusted tests are for all practical purposes equivalent to unadjusted tests. However, as we have cautioned before, in many behavioral research studies, $\hat{\varepsilon}$ and $\tilde{\varepsilon}$ will be much lower than they are here, in which case their use may have a dramatic impact on the statistical significance of one's findings.

MORE COMPLEX DESIGNS

Designs with Additional Factors

In the real world of research, of course, designs are not necessarily restricted to two factors. Although the analysis of more complex designs is necessarily more complicated than what we have discussed in this chapter, the same logic applies. Thus, if you understand the principles we developed in Chapters 7 and 8 for between-subjects factorial designs and in this chapter for within-subjects factorial designs, you should be able to analyze more complex designs without a great deal of added difficulty.

Besides our abstract assurances, it might be helpful to explicate a few general rules. We assume that all factors except S (subjects) are regarded as fixed-effects factors.[18] In this case, any effect that involves only between-subjects factors can be analyzed using MS_W as the error term. As usual, MS_W would be calculated by averaging across the levels of all within-subjects factors, to obtain a single score for each subject. As we saw in Table 12.16, MS_W for the complex design would then equal MS_W from the resulting one-way between-subjects design multiplied by the number of scores on which the average for each subject was obtained (b in Table 12.16). Notice that there will be $N - a$ denominator degrees of freedom for the F statistic, where N is the total number of subjects and a is the total number of groups (i.e., truly distinct groups of subjects). Knowing the degrees of freedom provides at least a partial check of one's results, especially if they are obtained from a computer program. Of course, as Table 12.20 shows, a homogeneity assumption is required in order for MS_W to produce a test statistic whose distribution is exactly an F random variable; however, the test is robust with equal n (more on this in Chapter 15). As a second rule, tests involving only between-subjects effects at a fixed level of a within-subjects factor should generally use MS_W calculated just at the fixed level as an error term. Notice that this rule corresponds to using $MS_{S/A \text{ at } B_k}$ as the error term for testing A at B_k in a split-plot design with one between- and one within-subjects factor.

Naturally, tests involving a within-subjects factor require a different error term. As a third rule, tests of effects involving a within-subjects factor should use the mean square interaction of the effect itself by subjects within groups as the error term. Notice that this rule holds whether the effect to be tested also includes one or more between-subjects factors. Also notice that this rule is a straightforward generalization of Equation 5:

$$F = MS_{\text{effect}}/MS_{\text{effect} \times S} \qquad \text{(5, repeated)}$$

This third rule tells us that any effect involving a within-subjects factor can be tested as

$$F = MS_{\text{effect}}/MS_{\text{effect} \times S \text{ within groups}}$$

As a partial check of one's results, the denominator degrees of freedom here should equal $N - a$ times the numerator degrees of freedom (where N and a are as defined in the previous paragraph). Thus, significance tests in more complex designs really are straightforward generalizations of the tests we have developed. Readers who are interested in additional information should consult the excellent articles by Hertzog and Rovine (1985) and O'Brien and Kaiser (1985).

However, in more complex within-subjects designs—just as in the within-subjects designs we have discussed in detail—we must once again concern ourselves with the homogeneity of treatment-differences variances assumption. As in simpler designs, this assumption can equivalently be stated as a requirement that the covariance matrix for the effect to be tested must exhibit sphericity. When this assumption fails to hold, as it often will in many behavioral applications, the unadjusted mixed-model F test is not robust. As usual, there are two alternatives: ε-adjusted tests or a multivariate approach. The logic of the ε-adjusted tests is identical to what we have seen already in Chapter 11 and this chapter. The next two chapters consider the multivariate approach, beginning with a simple one-way within-subjects design and then moving to more complex designs.

Latin Square Designs

The design considerations we discussed in Chapter 11 are also pertinent in factorial within-subjects designs. In particular, when the repeated factor represents a treatment manipulation, order effects must again be considered. The general issues to be considered remain the same as in Chapter 11, so we will not repeat the discussion here. Instead, we want to return to our previous discussion of the Latin square design, which you may recall provides a method for controlling order effects.

Although we discussed design principles for Latin squares at some length, we did not discuss analysis in Chapter 11. The reason we postponed analysis considerations until now is that Latin square designs involve two within-subjects factors, and thus analysis builds on principles we have developed in this chapter. In general, the two within-subjects factors are treatment condition and trial (i.e., order of administration).

We approach the analysis of data from Latin square designs through an example we began in Chapter 11. Specifically, suppose that we are interested in comparing the effects of three drugs (A, B, and C) on aggressiveness in monkeys. To control for possible order effects, we use a Latin square design. Specifically, we suppose that six subjects are available (as we discussed in Chapter 11, a subject is actually a pair of monkeys in this design). Following the design principles outlined at the end of Chapter 11, we use a replicated Latin square design with two randomly constituted squares. Subjects are then randomly assigned to rows of the squares.

Table 12.21 presents hypothetical outcome data from this study. The dependent measure can be thought of as the number of aggressive behaviors engaged in during a fixed time period. Notice that each score is a function of three possible influences: subject, time period, and treatment condition (which here is drug, with three levels,

T A B L E **12. 21** Hypothetical Aggressiveness Scores
from Replicated Latin Square Design

		Time		
	Subject	*1*	*2*	*3*
	1	9 (B)	3 (C)	6 (A)
Square 1	2	18 (A)	6 (B)	12 (C)
	3	12 (C)	15 (A)	5 (B)
	4	14 (C)	11 (A)	8 (B)
Square 2	5	17 (A)	9 (B)	9 (C)
	6	7 (B)	7 (C)	7 (A)

either A, B, or C). Following this logic, a full model for the data can be written as

$$Y_{ijk} = \mu + \alpha_j + \beta_k + \pi_i + \varepsilon_{ijk} \tag{30}$$

where Y_{ijk} is the score on the dependent variable for the ith subject at the jth level of A (treatment) and kth level of B (time), μ is the grand mean parameter, α_j is the effect associated with the jth level of A (treatment), β_k is the effect associated with the kth level of B (time), π_i is the effect associated with the ith subject, and ε_{ijk} is the error term for the ith subject in the jth level of A and kth level of B. Notice that there are two within-subjects factors in the model, treatment condition, and time, in addition to the subjects factor. However, the full model for the Latin square design is a main-effects model, that is, a model with no interactions. In general, interactions cannot be estimated with this design, because all treatment orders may not be represented.

The null hypothesis to be tested is that the effects of all treatments are equal to each other. Symbolically, the null hypothesis can be written as

$$H_0 : \alpha_1 = \alpha_2 = \cdots = \alpha_a$$

As usual, a side restriction is imposed that the α_j parameters must sum to zero, that is, $\sum_{j=1}^{a} \alpha_j = 0$. However, this implies that when the null hypothesis is true, every α_j parameter equals zero. As a consequence, the null hypothesis leads to a restricted model of the form

$$Y_{ijk} = \mu + \beta_k + \pi_i + \varepsilon_{ijk} \tag{31}$$

As usual, the test of the treatment effect is obtained by using an F statistic to compare the full and restricted models:

$$F = \frac{(E_R - E_F)/(df_R - df_F)}{E_F/df_F}$$

As in previous designs, the sums of squared errors of the two models are given by

$$E_F = \sum_{k=1}^{a} \sum_{j=1}^{a} \sum_{i=1}^{n} [Y_{ijk} - \hat{Y}_{ijk}(F)]^2 \tag{32}$$

$$E_R = \sum_{k=1}^{a} \sum_{j=1}^{a} \sum_{i=1}^{n} [Y_{ijk} - \hat{Y}_{ijk}(R)]^2 \tag{33}$$

where for these models

$$\hat{Y}_{ijk}(F) = \hat{\mu} + \hat{\alpha}_j + \hat{\beta}_k + \hat{\pi}_i \tag{34}$$

$$\hat{Y}_{ijk}(R) = \hat{\mu} + \hat{\beta}_k + \hat{\pi}_i \tag{35}$$

Least squares parameter estimates in both models are obtained from the relevant marginal means:

$$\hat{\mu} = \sum_{k=1}^{a} \sum_{j=1}^{a} \sum_{i=1}^{n} Y_{ijk}/na^2$$

$$\hat{\alpha}_j = \bar{Y}_{.j.} - \bar{Y}_{...}$$

$$\hat{\beta}_k = \bar{Y}_{..k} - \bar{Y}_{...}$$

$$\hat{\pi}_i = \bar{Y}_{i..} - \bar{Y}_{...}$$

TABLE 12. 22 Marginal Means and Parameter
Estimates for Table 12.21 Data

	Marginal Means	Parameter Estimate
Subject		
1	$\bar{Y}_{1..} = 6.00$	$\hat{\pi}_1 = -3.72$
2	$\bar{Y}_{2..} = 12.00$	$\hat{\pi}_2 = 2.28$
3	$\bar{Y}_{3..} = 10.67$	$\hat{\pi}_3 = 0.94$
4	$\bar{Y}_{4..} = 11.00$	$\hat{\pi}_4 = 1.28$
5	$\bar{Y}_{5..} = 11.67$	$\hat{\pi}_5 = 1.94$
6	$\bar{Y}_{6..} = 7.00$	$\hat{\pi}_6 = -2.72$
Condition		
1 (A)	$\bar{Y}_{.1.} = 12.33$	$\hat{\alpha}_1 = 2.61$
2 (B)	$\bar{Y}_{.2.} = 7.33$	$\hat{\alpha}_2 = -2.39$
3 (C)	$\bar{Y}_{.3.} = 9.50$	$\hat{\alpha}_3 = -0.22$
Time		
1	$\bar{Y}_{..1} = 12.83$	$\hat{\beta}_1 = 3.11$
2	$\bar{Y}_{..2} = 8.50$	$\hat{\beta}_2 = -1.22$
3	$\bar{Y}_{..3} = 7.83$	$\hat{\beta}_3 = -1.89$
Grand Mean		
	$\bar{Y}_{...} = 9.72$	$\hat{\mu} = 9.72$

Let's now see how we can apply these formulas to our numerical example. Table 12.22 shows the marginal means and parameter estimates for the observed data. Notice that the treatment marginal means show that aggressiveness is highest for drug A and least for drug B. However, a significance test is needed to assess the generalizability of this pattern beyond the sample. Table 12.23 presents the predicted scores for the full model (from Equation 34) and for the restricted model (from Equation 35) for each observed score on the dependent variable. The sum of squared errors for the full model for these data is given by

$$E_F = \sum_{k=1}^{a} \sum_{j=1}^{a} \sum_{i=1}^{n} [Y_{ijk} - \hat{Y}_{ijk}(F)]^2 = 39.44$$

Similarly, the sum of squared errors for the restricted model equals[19]

$$E_R = \sum_{k=1}^{a} \sum_{j=1}^{a} \sum_{i=1}^{n} [Y_{ijk} - \hat{Y}_{ijk}(R)]^2 = 114.88$$

Thus, the sum of squares attributable to the treatment effect, $E_R - E_F$, equals 75.44. Alternatively, $E_R - E_F$ can be found directly from the formula

$$E_R - E_F = SS_{effect} = n \sum_{j=1}^{a} (\bar{Y}_{.j.} - \bar{Y}_{...})^2$$

TABLE 12.23 Predicted Scores and Errors for Full and Restricted Models

Subject	Treatment	Time	Y_{ijk}	$\hat{Y}_{ijk}(F)$	$Y_{ijk} - \hat{Y}_{ijk}(F)$	$\hat{Y}_{ijk}(R)$	$Y_{ijk} - \hat{Y}_{ijk}(R)$
1	2	1	9	6.72	2.28	9.11	-0.11
1	3	2	3	4.56	-1.56	4.78	-1.78
1	1	3	6	6.72	-0.72	4.11	1.89
2	1	1	18	17.72	0.28	15.11	2.89
2	2	2	6	8.39	-2.39	10.78	-4.78
2	3	3	12	9.89	2.11	10.11	1.89
3	3	1	12	13.56	-1.56	13.78	-1.78
3	1	2	15	12.06	2.94	9.44	5.56
3	2	3	5	6.39	-1.39	8.78	-3.78
4	3	1	14	13.89	0.11	14.11	-0.11
4	1	2	11	12.39	-1.39	9.78	1.22
4	2	3	8	6.72	1.28	9.11	-1.11
5	1	1	17	17.39	-0.39	14.78	2.22
5	2	2	9	8.06	0.94	10.44	-1.44
5	3	3	9	9.56	-0.56	9.78	-0.78
6	2	1	7	7.72	-0.72	10.11	-3.11
6	3	2	7	5.56	1.44	5.78	1.22
6	1	3	7	7.72	-0.72	5.11	1.89

Notice that the n term appears in the formula because each marginal mean $\bar{Y}_{.j.}$ is based on n observations. For our data, this formula yields

$$SS_{\text{effect}} = n \sum_{j=1}^{a} (\bar{Y}_{.j.} - \bar{Y}_{...})^2$$
$$= 6[(12.33 - 9.72)^2 + (7.33 - 9.72)^2 + (9.50 - 9.72)^2]$$
$$= 75.44$$

This value is the same (within rounding error) as our previous value.

The final step in obtaining an observed F value is to calculate the degrees of freedom for the two models. In both cases, the degrees of freedom equal the number of observations (i.e., scores) minus the number of independent parameters. The number of observations here is na, because each of the n subjects is observed in each of the a conditions. The full model has one μ parameter, $a - 1$ independent α parameters, $a - 1$ independent β parameters, and $n - 1$ independent π parameters. Thus, the degrees of freedom for the full model equals

$$df_{\text{F}} = na - (1 + a - 1 + a - 1 + n - 1)$$
$$= na - 2a - n + 2$$
$$= (n - 2)(a - 1) \tag{36}$$

The restricted model has one μ parameter, $a - 1$ independent β parameters, and $n - 1$ independent π parameters. Thus, its degrees of freedom are given by

$$df_{\text{R}} = na - (1 + a - 1 + n - 1)$$
$$= na - a - n + 1$$
$$= (n - 1)(a - 1) \tag{37}$$

The difference in the degrees of freedom of the two models equals

$$df_{\text{R}} - df_{\text{F}} = (n - 1)(a - 1) - (n - 2)(a - 1) = a - 1 \tag{38}$$

which is just the number of independent parameters that were restricted to equal zero according to the null hypothesis.

The form of the F statistic for testing treatment effects in a replicated Latin square design can be obtained by substituting degrees of freedom from Equations 36 and 38 into the general expression for the F statistic:

$$F = \frac{(E_{\text{R}} - E_{\text{F}})/(df_{\text{R}} - df_{\text{F}})}{E_{\text{F}}/df_{\text{F}}} = \frac{(E_{\text{R}} - E_{\text{F}})/(a - 1)}{E_{\text{F}}/(n - 2)(a - 1)}$$

For our numerical example, we know that $E_{\text{R}} - E_{\text{F}} = 75.44$ and $E_{\text{F}} = 39.44$. Substituting these values yields

$$F = \frac{75.44/(3 - 1)}{39.44/(6 - 2)(3 - 1)} = 7.65$$

With 2 numerator and 8 denominator degrees of freedom, the corresponding p value is .01. Thus, we can reject the null hypothesis that the three drugs have equal effects on aggressiveness.

We end our discussion of the Latin square design by reiterating a point we made in Chapter 11, namely, that the analysis should match the design. Many researchers who use Latin square designs fail to analyze their data accordingly and instead use the analysis procedures of Chapter 11. However, the resultant analysis is almost inevitably conservative and consequently not as powerful as it might be (see Exercise 20 for an illustration of this point). Thus, replicated Latin square designs should be analyzed using the procedures we have just developed in this chapter, which explicitly take into account the nature of the design itself.

EXERCISES

1. True or False: The denominator of the F statistic for testing a within-subjects effect can be conceptualized as an index of the extent to which the effect is inconsistent from subject to subject.

2. True or False: The primary difference between data analysis in factorial between-subjects designs and factorial within-subjects designs is that the meaning of a significant interaction is different.

3. True or False: The between-subjects main effect F test in the split-plot design is identical to the F test that would occur if each subject's mean score were used as the dependent variable in a purely between-subjects design.

4. True or False: The necessary statistical assumptions for testing between-subjects effects in a split-plot design are identical to those required for testing within-subjects effects in the design.

5. True or False: Using a separate error term for testing contrasts involving a within-subjects effect is more consistent with the mixed-model approach than with the multi-variate approach to repeated measures.

*6. Consider a design that employs two factors (in addition to subjects), factor A with three levels and factor B with four levels, both of which are manipulated within subjects. Eleven subjects participate in the study and serve in all conditions. You decide to take the univariate approach to analyzing this design. Specify the effects to be tested in this design, the associated error terms, and degrees of freedom for each. You are aware that in the univariate approach to repeated measures you need to perform adjusted tests of certain effects in order to account for possible violation of the assumption of sphericity. Thus, also indicate for each tested effect the lower bound of ε for that effect. Express your results in the form of the following table:

Testable Effects		Error Term		
Source	df	Source	df	Lower Bound of ε

7. What does it mean to say that the A main effect in a two-way A × B within-subjects design averages over levels of B? To address this question, consider the data shown in Table 12.1 for a 3 × 2 design, where angle has three levels and noise has two levels. In

what sense does the angle main effect average over levels of noise? Table 12.7 presents the mean reaction time for each subject for each level of the angle factor, averaging over the two levels of noise.

   a. Is there a statistically significant angle main effect for the data shown in Table 12.7?

   b. How does the F value you obtained in part a compare to the F value for the angle main effect in the 3 × 2 design (see Table 12.5)?

   c. Based on your answer to part b, what does it mean to say that the A main effect in a two-way A × B within-subjects design averages over levels of B?

*8. A psychologist has used a microcomputer statistical package to analyze data from a two-way 3 × 4 within-subjects design with 15 subjects (we call the factor with three levels A and the factor with four levels B). For each of the following effects, what should the value of the denominator degrees of freedom be, if the computer program has used a separate error term for testing contrasts?

   a. a comparison of the marginal means of A

   b. a comparison of the marginal means of B

   c. an interaction contrast

   d. a comparison of the first two levels of A within the third level of B

9. Kosslyn describes a program of research investigating processes involved in the formation of a visual image (Kosslyn, S. M. [1988] "Aspects of a cognitive neuroscience of mental imagery." *Science, 240,* 1621–1626). In one condition of one study, subjects were shown an uppercase letter superimposed on a grid. They were then shown a blank grid and a lowercase letter. Their task was to decide whether the corresponding upper-case letter would occupy one or two specific cells of the grid. In a second condition of this study, the task was the same, but the internal lines of the grid were eliminated and only the brackets at the four corners were presented. Perceptual theory suggests that when grid lines are present, subjects will use a categorical representation of how line segments in letters are connected. However, when only brackets are present, subjects will use a coordinate representation to arrange the parts of the stimulus letter. In both conditions, the stimulus was presented to the right visual field half of the time (and hence seen first in the left cerebral hemisphere) and to the left visual field on remaining trials (and hence seen first in the right cerebral hemisphere). The primary dependent variable of interest was response time (in milliseconds) averaged over a number of trials. The following hypothetical data assume that each of 10 subjects has been assessed in both the grids condition and the brackets condition:

	Grids Condition		**Brackets Condition**	
Subject	*Left Hemisphere*	*Right Hemisphere*	*Left Hemisphere*	*Right Hemisphere*
1	1600	1670	1690	1690
2	1420	1590	1580	1590
3	1670	1730	1790	1800
4	1430	1560	1550	1460
5	1550	1510	1570	1590
6	1520	1600	1680	1600
7	1610	1730	1780	1670
8	1600	1710	1670	1710
9	1680	1720	1800	1710
10	1570	1500	1610	1520

a. Perform a test of the condition main effect, the hemisphere main effect, and the condition × hemisphere interaction.

b. Based on your answers to part a, would it be appropriate to perform simple-effects tests here? If so, test effects of condition within hemisphere and hemisphere within condition.

c. Do your results support Kosslyn's contention that two different classes of processes are used to form mental images? In particular, do your results support the statement that some of the processes used to arrange parts of images are more efficient in the left hemisphere, whereas for other processes, the right hemisphere is more efficient?

d. Is the sphericity assumption required for your analyses here? Why or why not?

e. Should you consider using either the $\hat{\varepsilon}$ adjustment for the $\tilde{\varepsilon}$ adjustment here? Why or why not?

10. Suppose that a perceptual psychologist wants to compare younger and older adults on the perceptual tasks described in Chapter 12. As described in the chapter, angle is a within-subjects factor. Suppose that the experimenter obtains reaction times for all subjects first in the 0° angle condition, second in the 4° angle condition, and finally in the 8° angle condition. Further suppose that the resultant cell means have the same pattern as those shown in Table 12.18. Could the psychologist unambiguously assert on the basis of such results that age differences are larger for larger angles? If not, what alternate hypothesis might you propose to explain this pattern of results?

11. A psychologist has collected data for 15 females and 15 males on an eight-item Fear of Statistics Scale (FSS) in order to investigate whether a gender difference exists. Her data analysis consists of a t test for the two groups, using the sum over the eight items as the dependent variable for each subject. However, a colleague has argued that her analysis method throws away data and hence loses power. The colleague suggests that she use a split-plot design, with gender as a between-subjects factor and item as a within-subjects factor. (HINT: Items here can be thought of as levels of a fixed factor.)

a. Will the colleague's approach result in higher statistical power for assessing a gender difference on the FSS than the t test?

b. Explain (briefly) the reason for your answer in part a.

*12. Assume that you are a reader on a master's thesis committee. A student has carried out a study of the effects of mood on recall for different kinds of material. Each subject from a total sample of 40 was randomly assigned to either a depressed mood–induction condition or a neutral-mood condition. Following the mood induction, each subject was given a list of verbal tasks to solve, some of which were easy and some of which were difficult. The hypothesis motivating the study was that on a test of incidental recall of the verbal tasks the decrement in performance exhibited by the depressed subjects would be greater on the difficult items than on the easy items. The following source table was included in the thesis:

Source	SS	df	MS	F
Mood	360	1	360	7.2
Difficulty	160	1	160	3.2
Mood × difficulty	160	1	160	3.2
Within	3800	76	50	

a. What is wrong with this analysis?

b. If the analysis were to be done correctly, what sources, error terms, and degrees of freedom would be used?

  c. Can you determine the sum of squares for any of the effects in the correct analysis?

*13. What is the meaning of the main effect of the between-subjects factor in a split-plot design? To address this question, consider the data shown in Tables 12.7 and 12.15. Table 12.19 shows that the F value for the main effect of the between-subjects factor (age) for these data is 7.28.
  a. For each subject in Tables 12.7 and 12.15, calculate a mean reaction time score by averaging over the three levels of angle.
  b. Perform a one-way ANOVA on the mean scores you calculated in part a.
  c. How does the F value you obtained in part b compare to the F value for the age main effect in the split-plot design?
  d. Is your answer to part c consistent with the fact that according to Table 12.20 the test of the between-subjects main effect in a split-plot design does not require the sphericity assumption? Why or why not?

*14. According to Exercise 13, the main effect of the between-subjects factor in a split-plot design can be tested by simply collapsing over levels of the within-subjects factor and then performing a one-way between-subjects ANOVA. Does an analogous result apply for the main effect of the within-subjects factor? In particular, can the main effect of the within-subjects factor be tested by simply ignoring the between-subjects factor and then performing a one-way within-subjects ANOVA? To address this question, we once again consider the data shown in Tables 12.7 and 12.15.
  a. Suppose that you were to ignore the between-subjects factor of age. Then, these data could be regarded as coming from a one-way within-subjects design. Perform a one-way ANOVA on the data for these 20 subjects.
  b. How does the F value you obtained in part a compare to the F value reported in Table 12.19 for the within-subjects main effect (designated as B in the table)?
  c. To explore why the two F values you compared in part b are not identical, we will consider the numerator and the denominator of the F statistic separately. How does the sum of squares for the within-subjects main effect you calculated in part a compare to the value reported in Table 12.19?
  d. How does the error sum of squares you calculated in part a compare to the value reported in Table 12.19? Is the difference between these two values equal to any sum of squares shown in Table 12.19?
  e. Are the denominator degrees of freedom for the test you performed in part a the same as the denominator degrees of freedom for B × S/A, as shown in Table 12.19? Is the difference between these values equal to the degrees of freedom for any of the other sources shown in Table 12.19?
  f. Can the F value for the within-subjects main effect in a split-plot design be obtained by simply ignoring the between-subjects factor and then performing a one-way within-subjects ANOVA? If not, briefly explain why this approach fails to produce the same F value.

*15. For each of the following follow-up tests in a split-plot design, state whether the test requires an assumption of sphericity, if the designated error term is chosen as described below:
  a. Test of B_{comp}, using $MS_{B \times S/A}$ as the error term
  b. Test of B_{comp}, using $MS_{B_{comp} \times S/A}$ as the error term
  c. Test of B at A_j, using $MS_{B \times S/A_j}$ as the error term
  d. Test of $A_{comp} \times B_{comp}$, using $MS_{B_{comp} \times S/A}$ as the error term
  e. Test of $A_{comp} \times B_{comp}$, using $MS_{B \times S/A}$ as the error term
  f. Test of A_{comp}, using $MS_{S/A}$ as the error term

16. For each of the following follow-up tests in a split-plot design, state whether the designated error term is more consistent with the mixed-model or the multivariate approach to repeated measures:
    a. Test of B_{comp}, using $MS_{B \times S/A}$ as the error term
    b. Test of B_{comp}, using $MS_{B_{comp} \times S/A}$ as the error term
    c. Test of B at A_j, using $MS_{B \times S/A_j}$ as the error term
    d. Test of $A_{comp} \times B_{comp}$, using $MS_{B_{comp} \times S/A}$ as the error term
    e. Test of $A_{comp} \times B_{comp}$, using $MS_{B \times S/A}$ as the error term

17. Exercise 16 in Chapter 11 introduced hypothetical data obtained by a developmental psychologist interested in the role of the sound of a mother's heartbeat in the growth of newborn babies. This exercise uses the same data, but now we will assume that half of the infants were assigned to a control group. Specifically, seven babies were randomly assigned to a condition where they were exposed to a rhythmic heartbeat sound piped in over the PA system. The other seven babies were placed in an identical nursery, but without the heartbeat sound. Infants were weighed at the same time of day for four consecutive days, yielding the following data (weight is measured in ounces):

		Heartbeat Group		
Subject	Day 1	Day 2	Day 3	Day 4
1	96	98	103	104
2	116	116	118	119
3	102	102	101	101
4	112	115	116	118
5	108	110	112	115
6	92	95	96	98
7	120	121	121	123
		Control Group		
1	112	111	111	109
2	95	96	98	99
3	114	112	110	109
4	99	100	99	98
5	124	125	127	126
6	100	98	95	94
7	106	107	106	107

    a. Test the group main effect, the day main effect, and the group × day interaction.
    b. Write one or two sentences interpreting the meaning of the results you obtained in part a.
    c. (To be done by computer.) Repeat part a using the $\hat{\varepsilon}$ adjustment. To which effects is this adjustment applied?
    d. (To be done by computer.) Repeat part a using the $\tilde{\varepsilon}$ adjustment. To which effects is this adjustment applied?
    e. Explain why this two-group design is superior to the design described for these data in Chapter 11, where we assumed that all 14 infants were exposed to the heartbeat sound.
    f. Although the two-group design is a great improvement over the one-group design

described earlier for these data, might there still be some plausible threats to the validity of a conclusion that exposure to heartbeat sounds affects infants' growth?

18. DeCasper and Fifer conducted a study to investigate the extent to which newborn infants are able to discriminate their mother's voice from the voice of another woman, a process which could influence the formation of the mother–infant bond (DeCasper, A. J., & Fifer, W. P. [1980] "Of human bonding: Newborns prefer their mothers' voices." *Science*, 208, 1174–1176). The subjects were 10 newborns younger than three days of age. Baseline measures of each infant's sucking activity on a nonnutritive nipple were obtained for 5 minutes. Of particular interest was the median interburst interval (IBI), defined as the elapsed time between the end of one burst of sucking and the beginning of the next. A burst was defined as a series of individual sucks separated from one another by no more than two seconds. After baseline measures had been obtained, five infants were randomly assigned to a condition where IBIs greater than or equal to their individual baseline median would produce a tape recording of their own mother's voice. Bursts terminating intervals less than their baseline median produced a recording of the voice of one of the other nine mothers. The other five infants were assigned to a reversed condition. For them, bursts shorter than their median produced the mother's voice, and bursts longer than the median produced the nonmaternal voice. Two measures were obtained for each infant: median IBI during baseline and median IBI over a 20-minute period with differential vocal feedback. The following data (IBIs in seconds) approximate the actual data obtained in the study.

Group 1 (Larger IBI Produced Maternal Voice)

Subject	Baseline IBI	Feedback IBI
1	4.4	6.4
2	1.0	1.9
3	3.4	5.2
4	3.3	3.3
5	4.5	4.0

Group 2 (Smaller IBI Produced Maternal Voice)

Subject	Baseline IBI	Feedback IBI
1	5.8	1.8
2	4.3	1.9
3	3.7	2.5
4	3.4	1.7
5	3.8	3.0

a. Perform tests of the group main effect, the baseline versus feedback main effect, and the group $\times$ baseline versus feedback interaction.

b. Which of the three effects in part a is of the greatest theoretical importance? How would you interpret the results you obtained in part a for this effect?

c. Is the sphericity assumption necessary for any of the effects you tested in part a? Why or why not?

d. Might the pattern of results obtained here reflect the fact that shorter (or longer) IBIs were easier to produce after baseline, instead of infants' expressing a preference for their own mother's voice?

19. Jemmott, J. B., Borysenko, J. Z., Borysenko, M., McClelland, D. C., Chapman, R., Meyer, D., and Benson, H. (1983) report a study investigating the effect of academic stress on immune function ("Academic stress, power motivation, and decrease in secretion rate of salivary secretory immunoglobulin A." *The Lancet, 1,* 1400–1402). Immune function was measured five times during the academic year: an initial low-stress period, three high-stress periods coinciding with major exams, and a final low-stress period. Forty-seven first-year dental students served as subjects. Each subject was identified as belonging to one of three personality types on the basis of responses to the Thematic Apperception Test, which was administered prior to the assessment of immune function. The three groups were an inhibited power syndrome (IPS) group, a relaxed affiliative syndrome (RAS) group, and a residual or control (C) group, which consisted of subjects who failed to fit the criteria for either of the other two groups. The dependent measure was the rate of secretion of salivary secretory immunoglobulin A (s-IgA), obtained at each of the five time points. Higher values of s-IgA secretion rate (measured as mg s-IgA/min) reflect stronger functioning of the immune system. Consider the following hypothetical (but realistic) data:

		IPS Group			
Subject	*Sept.*	*Nov.*	*Apr.*	*June*	*July*
1	.21	.20	.21	.19	.16
2	.19	.20	.16	.14	.13
3	.25	.16	.16	.16	.13
4	.11	.09	.10	.10	.14
5	.19	.13	.15	.11	.11
6	.18	.16	.16	.17	.10
7	.21	.18	.15	.18	.08
8	.16	.12	.14	.11	.18
9	.20	.14	.11	.13	.11

		RAS Group			
Subject	*Sept.*	*Nov.*	*Apr.*	*June*	*July*
1	.28	.28	.25	.29	.29
2	.22	.18	.16	.21	.25
3	.30	.27	.26	.26	.29
4	.24	.23	.24	.23	.23
5	.26	.22	.23	.19	.17
6	.27	.22	.20	.22	.24
7	.32	.25	.24	.21	.23
8	.20	.19	.21	.27	.28
9	.21	.22	.20	.19	.20
10	.33	.28	.25	.28	.27
11	.23	.18	.19	.24	.28
12	.17	.12	.15	.14	.12
13	.20	.17	.14	.18	.19
14	.22	.23	.19	.24	.22
15	.24	.22	.22	.22	.21

(continued)

C Group

Subject	Sept.	Nov.	Apr.	June	July
1	.14	.12	.09	.17	.19
2	.25	.18	.15	.16	.26
3	.22	.21	.14	.16	.19
4	.17	.12	.10	.12	.15
5	.17	.15	.12	.12	.14
6	.14	.12	.11	.12	.20
7	.17	.12	.12	.09	.14
8	.20	.14	.16	.12	.15
9	.25	.24	.20	.13	.17
10	.15	.07	.05	.13	.15
11	.19	.12	.14	.15	.18
12	.23	.17	.20	.19	.27
13	.20	.19	.18	.16	.21
14	.20	.19	.19	.16	.24
15	.24	.16	.20	.20	.21
16	.15	.09	.12	.12	.20
17	.15	.16	.12	.09	.17
18	.18	.18	.17	.16	.21
19	.23	.22	.20	.15	.21
20	.22	.18	.14	.12	.18
21	.15	.15	.13	.17	.16
22	.22	.14	.16	.17	.24
23	.22	.14	.14	.16	.15

a. Test the statistical significance of the group main effect, the time main effect, and the group × time interaction. Use the unadjusted mixed-model approach.

b. (To be done by computer.) Repeat part a using the $\hat{\varepsilon}$ adjustment.

c. (To be done by computer.) Repeat part a using the $\tilde{\varepsilon}$ adjustment.

d. Test the group effect at each individual time point.

*20. Both Chapters 11 and 12 state that researchers often fail to analyze their data as a Latin square design, even when they have expended great efforts to create such a design. To better understand issues involved in analyzing such data, reconsider the data shown in Table 12.21. What if these data were analyzed ignoring the time factor? How would the results compare to the results reported in the chapter?

a. Perform a one-way within-subjects ANOVA on the subject × drug data shown in Table 12.21. Ignore the presence of the time factor. (HINT: Be certain to reorder the columns of the table, so that the columns correspond to the three drugs, instead of the three time points).

b. How does the F value you obtained in part a compare to the F value of 7.65 reported in the chapter?

c. How does the sum of squares for the drug effect you found in part a compare to the value of 75.44 reported in the chapter?

d. How does the denominator sum of squares you found in part a compare to the value of 39.44 reported in the chapter?

e. The sum of squares attributable to the time main effect for these data is 88.44. How is this relevant to the two values compared in part d?

f. How does the answer to part e help explain why it is often important to use a Latin square analysis to analyze data from Latin square designs?

21. A cognitive psychologist was interested in the effects of different difficulty manipulations on subjects' recall of brief text passages. Each of three different difficulty manipulations was believed to induce a different type of processing of the written material. The three difficulty manipulations of interest here were letter deletion, sentence scrambling, and a control condition (suggested by McDaniel, M. A., Einstein, G. O., Dunay, P. K., & Cobb, R. E. [1986]) "Encoding difficulty and memory: Toward a unifying theory." *Journal of Memory and Language, 25,* 645–656. We will suppose that a within-subjects design is chosen and that three different passages are to be used as stimuli. Each subject in the study reads all three passages. However, in one passage, letters have been deleted. In a second passage, sentences have been scrambled. The third passage serves as a control. The following design has been used for the 12 subjects in the study (LD indicates letter deletion, SS indicates sentence scrambling, and C indicates control).

Subject	Passage 1		Passage 2		Passage 3	
1	LD	(55)	SS	(38)	C	(54)
2	SS	(43)	C	(36)	LD	(39)
3	C	(49)	LD	(42)	SS	(39)
4	SS	(40)	C	(38)	LD	(42)
5	C	(61)	LD	(46)	SS	(45)
6	LD	(41)	SS	(26)	C	(40)
7	C	(53)	LD	(39)	SS	(43)
8	SS	(47)	C	(39)	LD	(41)
9	LD	(33)	SS	(36)	C	(36)
10	LD	(52)	SS	(36)	C	(51)
11	C	(53)	LD	(45)	SS	(42)
12	SS	(51)	C	(43)	LD	(47)

The numbers in parentheses represent recall scores for each subject in the designated condition.

a. What type of design has the cognitive psychologist used here?

b. Test whether the three difficulty manipulations have a differential effect on recall.

c. Suppose that the psychologist were to analyze these data without controlling for any differences between passages. Would a statistically significant difference among the difficulty manipulations be obtained?

d. Why are the F values in parts b and c different? Which approach provides a better test of the differences among the difficulty manipulations? Why?

13 One-Way Within-Subjects Designs: Multivariate Approach

CHAPTERS 11 AND 12 presented the mixed-model, or univariate, approach for analyzing data from within-subjects designs. Traditionally, this approach has been the most frequently used method for analyzing repeated measures data in psychology, but research during the 1970s and 1980s has pointed out the limitations of this approach. In particular, evidence has accumulated that the mixed-model approach is quite sensitive to violations of the sphericity assumption required by the co-variance matrix. Although the ε adjustments discussed in Chapters 11 and 12 provide one potential solution to this problem, our belief is that this solution is usually less useful than yet another solution, namely, the multivariate approach. We defer our justification for this statement until later in the chapter. Once we have explained the logic of the multivariate approach, we will be able to discuss why it is generally preferable to the ε-adjusted mixed-model approach. For the moment, however, we simply state that the multivariate approach requires no assumption of sphericity, can be substantially more powerful than the mixed-model approach (although under some circumstances, it can be also be substantially less powerful), is straightforward to use with statistical packages, and leads naturally to appropriate tests of specific individual comparisons.

Our general outline in this chapter parallels the development of the mixed-model approach in Chapter 11. First, we briefly review analysis of repeated-measures designs with two levels. Second, we consider designs with three levels. Third, we consider designs with more than three levels. Although we will see eventually that the basic formulas are the same in all three cases, the logic underlying these formulas is easiest to understand when the $a = 2$ and $a = 3$ cases are considered as special cases of the more general design.

A BRIEF REVIEW OF ANALYSIS FOR DESIGNS WITH TWO LEVELS

Recall that Chapter 11 began with a description of analysis procedures for repeated measures designs with two levels. Our intention here is to briefly review these procedures, to form the foundation for the multivariate approach with more than two levels. If you find our presentation here too succinct, you may want to return to the beginning of Chapter 11 for additional details.

You may be surprised that we recommend returning to the mixed-model approach of Chapter 11 for more detail because the multivariate approach of this chapter is a competitor of the mixed-model approach. The reason for our recommendation is that in the special case of designs with two levels, the mixed-model and multivariate approaches are exactly identical. Nevertheless, we believe that the

T A B L E **13. 1** Data for Two-Level Design

Subject	Time 1 (Y_1)	Time 2 (Y_2)	$D = Y_2 - Y_1$
1	2	3	1
2	4	7	3
3	6	8	2
4	8	9	1
5	10	13	3
Mean	6	8	2

transition to the multivariate approach with more than two levels is made easier by beginning our discussion in this chapter with a review of the two-level case. Once we have considered the more general multivariate approach, we will see why the two approaches are equivalent in this special case.

To motivate our discussion, consider the data in Table 13.1. As usual, in our hypothetical examples, the sample size has been kept small to facilitate your working through our calculations, to convince yourself that you understand the necessary computations.

The null hypothesis to be tested here is that the population means of time 1 and time 2 are equal to one another. Recall from Chapter 11 that in order to test this hypothesis we formed a difference score for each subject. The multivariate approach also requires that we form a difference score. The right-most column of Table 13.1 shows such a difference score, time 2 score minus time 1 score, for each subject. The full model for the difference score is given by

$$D_i = \mu + \varepsilon_i \tag{1}$$

where D_i is the difference score for the ith subject, μ represents the difference between the effects of time 2 and time 1, and ε represents error. The null hypothesis that the population means of time 1 and time 2 are equal is equivalent to the hypothesis that the difference scores have a population mean of zero. Thus, this hypothesis implies that μ in Equation 1 equals zero, which leads to a restricted model given by

$$D_i = 0 + \varepsilon_i \tag{2}$$

or just

$$D_i = \varepsilon_i \tag{3}$$

The error sum of squares for the full and restricted models are

$$E_F = \sum_{i=1}^{n} (D_i - \bar{D})^2 \tag{4}$$

$$E_R = \sum_{i=1}^{n} D_i^2 \tag{5}$$

Recall that the expression for the F-test statistic is in general given by

$$F = \frac{(E_R - E_F)/(df_R - df_F)}{E_F/df_F}$$

After substituting from Equations 4 and 5 and performing some simple algebra, the F statistic for comparing the full model of Equation 1 with the restricted model of Equation 3 equals

$$F = n\bar{D}^2/s_D^2 \tag{6}$$

For the data of Table 13.1, it can be shown that $\bar{D} = 2$ and $s_D^2 = 1$. Because $n = 5$, it follows that the observed value of the F statistic is 20. The observed F is compared to a critical F with 1 and $n - 1$ degrees of freedom. For $\alpha = .05$, the critical F with 1 and 4 degrees of freedom is 7.71 (see appendix Table A.2). Thus, we can reject the null hypothesis that μ equals zero at the .05 level because the observed F exceeds the critical F. In terms of models, a model restricting the mean score to be equal to zero fits the data significantly less well than a model that allows the mean to be freely estimated. Thus, we can conclude that the population means of time 1 and time 2 are not equal to one another.

MULTIVARIATE ANALYSIS OF WITHIN-SUBJECTS DESIGNS WITH THREE LEVELS

Next we consider designs with three levels. Although we could at this point consider the general case of three *or more* levels, we momentarily postpone the "or more" part because the formulas to be developed are simpler in the three-level case. Once we have developed this case, we will see that the formulas for more than three levels are straightforward generalizations of the formulas for three levels.

Table 13.2 presents hypothetical data for a three-level design. The null hypothesis to be tested is that the population means of scores at all three time points are

T A B L E **13. 2** Data for Three-Level Design

Subject	Time 1 (Y_1)	Time 2 (Y_2)	Time 3 (Y_3)
1	2	3	5
2	4	7	9
3	6	8	8
4	8	9	8
5	10	13	15
6	3	4	9
7	6	9	8
8	9	11	10
Mean	**6**	**8**	**9**

equal to each other. It is obvious from visual inspection of the data in Table 13.2 that scores tend to increase over time. However, we need to conduct a formal test to ascertain whether this apparent difference is statistically significant.

Need for Multiple D Variables

The logic behind the multivariate approach for three levels is based on the formation of D variables (i.e., difference scores), as in the two-level case. However, a single difference score cannot be used to explain all the possible patterns of mean differences that could occur among the three levels, as was possible in the two-level case. In other words, with only two levels, the only difference that can even potentially occur is that the two levels are simply different. This difference is completely captured by a single difference score contrasting the two levels. However, with three or more levels, an infinite pattern of mean differences could potentially occur. Although it is possible to formulate planned comparisons, it is highly unlikely that any single planned comparison by itself will completely explain the pattern of mean differences that occurs in the data.[1]

With three levels, we can completely explain any possible pattern of mean differences by forming two D variables, that is, two difference scores. As we saw in Chapter 4 for between-subjects designs, three levels implies 2 degrees of freedom, which corresponds to two independent comparisons. The particular difference scores we choose do not matter for testing the omnibus null hypothesis, as long as the two comparisons underlying the difference scores are linearly independent (see the discussion in Chapter 4 for more details on linear independence). We will have more to say about the irrelevance of the specific difference scores later in the chapter.

Returning to the data of Table 13.2, we need to form two difference scores to test the null hypothesis that all three time periods have the same population mean. Table 13.3 displays the scores for a particular pair of difference scores D_1 and D_2, where D_1 = time 2 − time 1, and D_2 = time 3 − time 2. The question now becomes how to test whether the population means of D_1 and D_2 both equal zero because both will equal zero if and only if all three time periods have equal means.

T A B L E **13. 3**   Difference Scores for Data of Table 13.2

Subject	$D_1 = Y_2 - Y_1$	$D_2 = Y_3 - Y_2$
1	1	2
2	3	2
3	2	0
4	1	−1
5	3	2
6	1	5
7	3	−1
8	2	−1
Mean	2	1

We now have a multivariate problem because we have two scores (D_1 and D_2) for each subject. Notice that in the two-level case, we were able to simplify our design to a univariate problem because there we could form a single D variable. However, in the three-level design, we have two D variables for each subject. In addition, it is quite possible that these two D variables will correlate with one another, both in the sample and in the population. As we will see later in the chapter, the multivariate approach is sensitive to such a possible correlation in a manner that a univariate approach is not.

Full and Restricted Models

The multivariate test that both D variables have population means of zero can be conceptualized in terms of model comparisons, very much like a univariate test. Specifically, we can write full and restricted models for both D_1 and D_2. The full model for D_1 is given by

$$D_{1i} = \mu_1 + \varepsilon_{1i} \tag{7}$$

where D_{1i} is the score of the ith subject on D_1, μ_1 is the population mean of D_1, and ε_{1i} reflects the error for the ith subject. Because, according to the null hypothesis, D_1 has a population mean of zero, the restricted model is obtained by restricting μ_1 of Equation 7 to equal zero, in which case the restricted model for D_1 is given by

$$D_{1i} = 0 + \varepsilon_{1i} \tag{8}$$

or simply

$$D_{1i} = \varepsilon_{1i} \tag{9}$$

By similar reasoning, the corresponding full and restricted models for D_2 are given by

$$D_{2i} = \mu_2 + \varepsilon_{2i} \tag{10}$$

$$D_{2i} = \varepsilon_{2i} \tag{11}$$

respectively. Least-squares estimates are readily obtained because each full model has only one parameter and each restricted model has none. In Equation 7, the least-squares estimate of μ_1 is $\bar{D}_1$, and in Equation 10, the least-squares estimate of μ_2 is $\bar{D}_2$. In each case, the error for a particular subject is that subject's score minus the predicted score, so in each full model an error for a subject will be that subject's deviation from the mean on a D variable. Notice that the restricted models of Equations 9 and 11 predict every subject's score to be zero, so here an error for a subject will simply be that subject's score on the D variable in question.

The notion of errors here can probably be conceptualized most easily by returning to the D variables of Table 13.3. Table 13.4 shows the corresponding errors for full and restricted models for both D_1 and D_2. The e_1 column shows errors for D_1, and the e_2 column shows errors for D_2. The e_1^2 and e_2^2 columns show squared errors, which not surprisingly play an important role here. The meaning of the $(e_1)(e_2)$ columns will be explained momentarily.

T A B L E **13. 4** Errors for Full and Restricted Models for D_1 and D_2 Variables of Table 13.3

	Full Model					Restricted Model				
Subject	e_1	e_2	e_1^2	e_2^2	$(e_1)(e_2)$	e_1	e_2	e_1^2	e_2^2	$(e_1)(e_2)$
1	-1	1	1	1	-1	1	2	1	4	2
2	1	1	1	1	1	3	2	9	4	6
3	0	-1	0	1	0	2	0	4	0	0
4	-1	-2	1	4	2	1	-1	1	1	-1
5	1	1	1	1	1	3	2	9	4	6
6	-1	4	1	16	-4	1	5	1	25	5
7	1	-2	1	4	-2	3	-1	9	1	-3
8	0	-2	0	4	0	2	-1	4	1	-2
Sum	**0**	**0**	**6**	**32**	**-3**	**16**	**8**	**38**	**40**	**13**

Just as in the univariate case, the sum of squared errors is important for judging the adequacy of a model. This sum of squared errors can be calculated for each variable individually (i.e., D_1 or D_2) simply by summing the e^2 scores across subjects for the individual variable and the specific model. Thus, for D_1, Table 13.4 shows that $E_F = 6$ and $E_R = 38$. For D_2, the figures are $E_F = 32$ and $E_R = 40$. The general expressions for these sums of squared errors are the same as in the univariate case with only a single D variable. Specifically, for the full model we have

$$E_F(D_1) = \sum_{i=1}^{n} (D_{1i} - \bar{D}_1)^2 = \sum_{i=1}^{n} e_{1i}^2(F) \tag{12}$$

for D_1, and

$$E_F(D_2) = \sum_{i=1}^{n} (D_{2i} - \bar{D}_2)^2 = \sum_{i=1}^{n} e_{2i}^2(F) \tag{13}$$

for D_2. For the restricted model, the corresponding expressions are

$$E_R(D_1) = \sum_{i=1}^{n} D_{1i}^2 = \sum_{i=1}^{n} e_{1i}^2(R) \tag{14}$$

$$E_R(D_2) = \sum_{i=1}^{n} D_{2i}^2 = \sum_{i=1}^{n} e_{2i}^2(R) \tag{15}$$

The Relationship Between D_1 and D_2

Although the usual F statistic for comparing models could be used to test the null hypothesis for either D_1 or D_2 individually, our goal is to test a null hypothesis that both D_1 and D_2 have population means of zero. The multivariate test that accomplishes this goal not only considers the sum of squared errors for D_1 and D_2 individually but also utilizes the relationship between D_1 and D_2. This relationship can be captured for a model by multiplying each subject's e_1 score times his or her

e_2 score for that model. At this point, we need to see how this multiplication process reflects the relationship between the variables, as well as find out how this term can be incorporated into a test statistic.

We first consider what meaning can be attached to the product of e_1 and e_2 for each subject. Specifically, we examine $\sum_{i=1}^{n} e_{1i}e_{2i}$ first for the full model and then for the restricted model. It turns out that $\sum_{i=1}^{n} e_{1i}(F)e_{2i}(F)$, which is called a *sum of cross-products* for the full model, is closely related to the correlation between D_1 and D_2. Recall that the formula for the correlation is of the form

$$r_{D_1 D_2} = \frac{\sum_{i=1}^{n} (D_{1i} - \bar{D}_1)(D_{2i} - \bar{D}_2)}{\sqrt{\sum_{i=1}^{n} (D_{1i} - \bar{D}_1)^2 \sum_{i=1}^{n} (D_{2i} - \bar{D}_2)^2}}$$

However, we can simplify this expression by realizing that

$$e_{1i}(F) = D_{1i} - \bar{D}_1 \quad \text{and} \quad e_{2i}(F) = D_{2i} - \bar{D}_2$$

Making these substitutions yields

$$r_{D_1 D_2} = \frac{\sum_{i=1}^{n} e_{1i}(F)e_{2i}(F)}{\sqrt{\sum_{i=1}^{n} e_{1i}^2(F) \sum_{i=1}^{n} e_{2i}^2(F)}}$$

This expression can be further simplified by substituting from Equations 12 and 13:

$$r_{D_1 D_2} = \frac{\sum_{i=1}^{n} e_{1i}(F)e_{2i}(F)}{\sqrt{E_F(D_1)E_F(D_2)}}$$

Rearranging terms we have

$$\sum_{i=1}^{n} e_{1i}(F)e_{2i}(F) = r_{D_1 D_2}\sqrt{E_F(D_1)E_F(D_2)} \tag{16}$$

The point of all of this algebra is that the cross-product term $\sum_{i=1}^{n} e_{1i}(F)e_{2i}(F)$ is a function of the correlation between D_1 and D_2 and the sum of squared errors for D_1 and D_2 in the full model. Thus, as stated earlier, the cross-product term provides information about the strength of relationship of D_1 and D_2. Table 13.4 shows that the sum of cross-products for D_1 and D_2 in the full model for our data equals -3. This corresponds to a correlation coefficient of -0.217, so D_1 and D_2 are slightly negatively related in our data.

What is the meaning of the restricted model sum of cross-products, represented by $\sum_{i=1}^{n} e_{1i}(R)e_{2i}(R)$? Recall that an error in the restricted model is simply the score on the D variable itself. Thus, the restricted model sum of cross-products is simply $\sum_{i=1}^{n} D_{1i}D_{2i}$, the sum of the products of the two D variables. After some straightforward algebra, it can be shown that

$$\sum_{i=1}^{n} D_{1i}D_{2i} = \sum_{i=1}^{n} (D_{1i} - \bar{D}_1)(D_{2i} - \bar{D}_2) + n\bar{D}_1\bar{D}_2$$

so that

$$\sum_{i=1}^{n} e_{1i}(R)e_{2i}(R) = \sum_{i=1}^{n} e_{1i}(F)e_{2i}(F) + n\bar{D}_1\bar{D}_2$$

This equation shows that the restricted model sum of cross-products equals the full model sum of cross-products plus the product of sample size times $\bar{D}_1$ times $\bar{D}_2$. Thus, the restricted model sum of cross-products also reflects the degree of relationship between D_1 and D_2 but does so in a manner that also reflects the means of $\bar{D}_1$ and $\bar{D}_2$.

Matrix Formulation and Determinants

Now that we have an indication that the sum of cross-products reflects the degree of relationship between the variables, we need to address the question of how this quantity can be incorporated into a test statistic. Notice that we have three indices for each model: two sum-of-squared-error terms (one for D_1 and one for D_2) and one sum-of-cross-products term. Multivariate analysis of variance (MANOVA) compares these three indices for the full model to the three indices for the restricted model through matrices. A *matrix* is simply a rectangular array of numbers. We will construct one matrix for the full model and a second matrix for the restricted model.

To simplify our notation, we will let $E_{11}(F)$ and $E_{22}(F)$ represent the sum of squared errors for the full model for D_1 and D_2, respectively. The sum of cross-products for the full model is written as $E_{12}(F)$. The same notation is used for the restricted model, except that the F in parentheses will be replaced by R.

Given this notation, the matrix for the full model is written as

$$\mathbf{E(F)} = \begin{bmatrix} E_{11}(F) & E_{12}(F) \\ E_{12}(F) & E_{22}(F) \end{bmatrix} \tag{17}$$

Similarly, the matrix for the restricted model is written as

$$\mathbf{E(R)} = \begin{bmatrix} E_{11}(R) & E_{12}(R) \\ E_{12}(R) & E_{22}(R) \end{bmatrix} \tag{18}$$

The task now is to somehow compare these two matrices. The concept of a *determinant* allows us to accomplish this task. The determinant of a matrix is an ordinary number, which distills the multivariate information in a matrix into a single piece of information. Determinants play an important role in multivariate statistics because the determinant can reflect the "generalized variance" of more than one variable. We will view the determinant as a useful tool, without dwelling on its mathematical foundation. Readers who are interested in learning more about determinants should consult such references as Green and Carroll (1976) or Namboodiri (1984).

Notice that $\mathbf{E(F)}$ and $\mathbf{E(R)}$, the matrices of Equations 17 and 18, have two rows and two columns. Such a matrix is referred to as a 2×2 matrix. The determinant in this case is defined as the difference between the product of the two numbers on the major diagonal of the matrix minus the product of the two numbers off the diagonal. To indicate the determinant of a matrix, vertical lines are placed on either side of the letter representing the matrix.[2] Thus, for the determinant of $\mathbf{E(F)}$ we have

$$|\mathbf{E(F)}| = E_{11}(\mathbf{F})E_{22}(\mathbf{F}) - [E_{12}(\mathbf{F})]^2$$

Similarly, the determinant of $\mathbf{E(R)}$ is given by

$$|\mathbf{E(R)}| = E_{11}(\mathbf{R})E_{22}(\mathbf{R}) - [E_{12}(\mathbf{R})]^2$$

Before seeing how these determinants can be incorporated into a significance test, it might be helpful to provide some intuitive meaning for the determinant. Notice that the determinant of the matrix for the full model is

$$|\mathbf{E(F)}| = E_{11}(\mathbf{F})E_{22}(\mathbf{F}) - [E_{12}(\mathbf{F})]^2$$

Substituting from Equation 16 for $E_{12}(\mathbf{F})$ yields

$$|\mathbf{E(F)}| = E_{11}(\mathbf{F})E_{22}(\mathbf{F}) - r_{D_1 D_2}^2 E_{11}(\mathbf{F})E_{22}(\mathbf{F})$$

Collecting terms, we have

$$|\mathbf{E(F)}| = E_{11}(\mathbf{F})E_{22}(\mathbf{F})(1 - r_{D_1 D_2}^2) \qquad (19)$$

For purposes of interpretation, we place brackets around the two right-most terms:

$$|\mathbf{E(F)}| = E_{11}(\mathbf{F})[E_{22}(\mathbf{F})(1 - r_{D_1 D_2}^2)]$$

The meaning of $E_{11}(\mathbf{F})$ should be clear. It equals the sum of squared errors in the full model for D_1, and hence reflects the extent to which the full model fails to completely explain scores on D_1. What about the term in brackets? It reflects the sum of squares in D_2 that neither the full model nor scores on D_1 can explain because $1 - r_{D_1 D_2}^2$ is the proportion of D_2 sum of squares left unexplained by D_1. Thus, the term in brackets reflects the sum of squares unique to D_2 (as opposed to shared with D_1) that the full model has not explained. In this manner, the determinant reflects simultaneously the extent to which the full model fails to explain scores on D_1 and D_2 together. A similar argument could be applied to the determinant for the restricted model.

That you understand what the determinant has accomplished here is important because we will continue to use determinants throughout this and the next chapter. Thus, we detour momentarily to present another perspective on the determinant. The Venn diagram in Figure 13.1 provides a conceptual picture of the full model sum of squared errors for two variables, D_1 and D_2. Specifically, the circle on the left represents $E_{11}(\mathbf{F})$, the sum of squared errors for the full model on D_1. Similarly, the circle on the right represents $E_{22}(\mathbf{F})$, the sum of squared errors for the full model on D_2. The determinant $|\mathbf{E(F)}|$ provides an index of how large the two circles taken together are. The specific way in which the determinant reflects such an index is shown by the horizontal and vertical stripes in Figure 13.1. The horizontal stripes depict the area that corresponds to $E_{11}(\mathbf{F})$. From Equation 19, the determinant equals the product of $E_{11}(\mathbf{F})$ and a term of the form $[E_{22}(\mathbf{F})(1 - r_{D_1 D_2}^2)]$. The vertical stripes represent this second term because they depict the portion of D_2 that is uncorrelated with D_1. In other words, the vertical stripes represent that portion

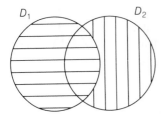

D_1 D_2

of $E_{22}(F)$ that is unique to D_2, in that the vertical stripes exclude the overlap between D_1 and D_2. However, the area of overlap has already been represented by $E_{11}(F)$. Notice that if we were simply to multiply $E_{11}(F)$ by $E_{22}(F)$, our index of error would count the area of overlap twice. However, the determinant avoids this problem by multiplying $E_{11}(F)$ by the portion of $E_{22}(F)$ that is unique to D_2, as represented by the vertical stripes in Figure 13.1.

Test Statistic

The determinants of the full and restricted models form an F-test statistic in the following manner:

$$F = \frac{(|E(R)| - |E(F)|)/(df_R - df_F)}{|E(F)|/df_F} \tag{20}$$

where df_R and df_F refer to the degrees of freedom for the restricted and full models, respectively. As usual, the degrees of freedom for a model equal the number of observations (sample size) minus the number of estimated parameters. When the within-subjects factor has three levels, there are two D variables, so there are two parameters estimated in the full model (μ_1 for D_1 and μ_2 for D_2). Thus, the degrees of freedom for the full model equals $n - 2$. There are no parameters to be estimated in the restricted model, so its degrees of freedom equals n. With a three-level factor, then, Equation 20 becomes

$$F = \frac{(|E(R)| - |E(F)|)/2}{|E(F)|/(n - 2)} \tag{21}$$

We will now see how this formula can be applied to our data. From Table 13.4 and Equations 17 and 18, the error matrices for the full and restricted models are given by

$$E(F) = \begin{bmatrix} 6 & -3 \\ -3 & 32 \end{bmatrix}$$

$$E(R) = \begin{bmatrix} 38 & 13 \\ 13 & 40 \end{bmatrix}$$

The determinant of $\mathbf{E}(\mathbf{F})$ equals

$$|\mathbf{E}(\mathbf{F})| = 6(32) - (-3)^2 = 183$$

Similarly, the determinant of $\mathbf{E}(\mathbf{R})$ is

$$|\mathbf{E}(\mathbf{R})| = 38(40) - (13)^2 = 1351$$

Substituting these values into Equation 21 yields

$$F = \frac{(1351 - 183)/2}{183/(8 - 2)} = 19.148$$

The *p* value associated with the *F* ratio is .0032; we can conclude that the population means of the three time periods are significantly different from each other at the .05 level.

MULTIVARIATE ANALYSIS OF WITHIN-SUBJECTS DESIGNS WITH *a* LEVELS

So far we have seen how to analyze data from within-subjects designs when the design consists of a single factor with either two or three levels. We will now see that the same logic can be used regardless of the number of levels—that is, for a factor with *a* levels, where *a* is any number greater than or equal to two.

Forming *D* Variables

In the general case of *a* levels of the repeated factor, it is necessary to form $a - 1$ *D* variables. The null hypothesis that all *a* levels of the repeated factor have equal population means is equivalent to a null hypothesis that all $a-1$ *D* variables have population means of zero. As in the case of two or three levels, this hypothesis can be tested by comparing full and restricted models. In general, there are $a - 1$ full models and $a - 1$ corresponding restricted models because there must be both a full and a restricted model for each of the $a-1$ *D* variables. Sums of squared errors are found for these models using least squares according to formulas shown in Equations 12–15. Because there are $a-1$ *D* variables, there are $a - 1$ sums of squared errors for full models and $a - 1$ corresponding sums of squared errors for restricted models.

Recall that when there are two *D* variables it is also necessary to compute a sum-of-cross-products term, once using the errors of the full model and then again using the errors of the restricted model. In the general case of $a-1$ *D* variables, comparable sums of cross-products must be calculated for every pair of *D* variables. For example, if $a = 4$, there are three *D* variables. Then sums of cross-products must be calculated for variables D_1 and D_2, D_1 and D_3, and D_2 and D_3, both for the errors of the full model and the errors of the restricted model. In general, then, it can be shown that it is necessary to calculate $(a - 1)(a - 2)/2$ sums of cross-products both for the full model and the restricted model.[3]

The sums of squared errors and sums of cross-products are once again represented in matrix form. With $a - 1$ D variables, the matrix has $a - 1$ rows and $a - 1$ columns. To show the form of this matrix, let $E_{ii}(F)$ and $E_{ii}(R)$ be the error sum of squares for D_i for the full and restricted models, respectively. Similarly, let $E_{ij}(F)$ and $E_{ij}(R)$ be the sum of cross-products of D_i and D_j for the full and restricted models, respectively. Then the general form of the matrix for the full model is

$$
\begin{bmatrix}
E_{11}(F) & E_{12}(F) & E_{13}(F) & \cdots & E_{1(a-1)}(F) \\
E_{12}(F) & E_{22}(F) & E_{23}(F) & \cdots & E_{2(a-1)}(F) \\
E_{13}(F) & E_{23}(F) & E_{33}(F) & \cdots & E_{3(a-1)}(F) \\
\vdots & \vdots & \vdots & & \vdots \\
E_{1(a-1)}(F) & E_{2(a-1)}(F) & E_{3(a-1)}(F) & & E_{(a-1)(a-1)}(F)
\end{bmatrix}
$$

Similarly, for the restricted model, the matrix is given by

$$
\begin{bmatrix}
E_{11}(R) & E_{12}(R) & E_{13}(R) & \cdots & E_{1(a-1)}(R) \\
E_{12}(R) & E_{22}(R) & E_{23}(R) & \cdots & E_{2(a-1)}(R) \\
E_{13}(R) & E_{23}(R) & E_{33}(R) & \cdots & E_{3(a-1)}(R) \\
\vdots & \vdots & \vdots & & \vdots \\
E_{1(a-1)}(R) & E_{2(a-1)}(R) & E_{3(a-1)}(R) & & E_{(a-1)(a-1)}(R)
\end{bmatrix}
$$

Once again, the determinants of these two matrices are used to form an F statistic. We will not attempt to describe how to find the determinant of an $(a - 1)$ by $(a - 1)$ matrix because we assume that such computations will be left to a computer program. What is important for our purposes is to realize that the conceptual meaning of the determinant in the $a - 1 \times a - 1$ case is the same as it was for a 2×2 matrix. Namely, the determinant once again reflects simultaneously the extent to which a model fails to explain scores on the set of D variables collectively. Readers interested in further details are referred to such books as Graybill (1969), Green and Carroll (1976), Namboodiri (1984), and Searle (1966).

Test Statistic

After the determinants of $\mathbf{E(F)}$ and $\mathbf{E(R)}$ have been calculated, the calculation of the F statistic is straightforward. Equation 20, which was presented for a three-level factor, also is appropriate when the factor has a levels:

$$
F = \frac{(|\mathbf{E(R)}| - |\mathbf{E(F)}|)/(df_R - df_F)}{|\mathbf{E(F)}|/df_F} \tag{20, repeated}
$$

This formula can be made more explicit by specifying df_R and df_F in the general case of a levels. As before, there are no parameters to be estimated in the restricted models, so $df_R = n$. Because there are $a - 1$ D variables, there are $a - 1$ parameters to be estimated in the full models (i.e., μ_1 for D_1, μ_2 for D_2, and so forth up to μ_{a-1} for D_{a-1}). Thus, $df_F = n - (a - 1) = n - a + 1$. The general form of the F statistic is given by

$$F = \frac{(|E(R)| - |E(F)|)/(a - 1)}{|E(F)|/(n - a + 1)} \tag{22}$$

This observed F value is compared to a critical F value with $a - 1$ and $n - a + 1$ degrees of freedom.

In case you may not have noticed, there is a remarkable similarity between Equation 20 and the equation for an F statistic in the univariate problems that we have discussed in Chapters 3–12. The form of the univariate F statistic we have seen repeatedly is given by

$$F = \frac{(E_R - E_F)/(df_R - df_F)}{E_F/df_F}$$

Equation 20 has exactly the same form, except that the univariate sum-of-squared-error terms are replaced by the corresponding determinant of the sum-of-squares and cross-products matrix:

$$F = \frac{(|E(R)| - |E(F)|)/(df_R - df_F)}{|E(F)|/df_F} \tag{20, repeated}$$

This similarity should convince you of the flexibility and power of approaching hypothesis tests through model comparisons. The same underlying logic applies to the multivariate tests here as it does to univariate tests.

Numerical Example

At this point, a numerical example involving more than two D variables may help solidify your understanding of the multivariate approach to repeated measures. Table 13.5 presents the hypothetical McCarthy IQ scores for 12 subjects that originally appeared as Table 11.5 in Chapter 11. Because $a = 4$ here (i.e., there are four levels of the repeated factor), it is necessary to define three D variables. Table 13.6 presents scores for the 12 subjects on the following three D variables: $D_1 = Y_2 - Y_1$, $D_2 = Y_3 - Y_2$, and $D_3 = Y_4 - Y_3$, where Y_1, Y_2, Y_3, and Y_4 represent IQ scores at 30, 36, 42, and 48 months, respectively. Table 13.7 presents the errors for the full model for D_1, D_2, and D_3. Recall that a subject's error for the full model is the subject's deviation from the mean of the D variable. Table 13.7 also shows the squared-errors and cross-products scores for the full model. Table 13.8 presents the comparable data for the restricted model. Recall that a subject's error for the restricted model is simply the subject's score on the D variable. The sums of squared errors and cross-products must be placed in matrix form. From Table 13.7, the matrix for the full model is

$$E(F) = \begin{bmatrix} 878 & -329 & -440 \\ -329 & 1004 & 399 \\ -440 & 399 & 658 \end{bmatrix}$$

TABLE **13. 5** Hypothetical McCarthy
Data for 12 Children

Subject	Age (Months)			
	30	36	42	48
1	108	96	110	122
2	103	117	127	133
3	96	107	106	107
4	84	85	92	99
5	118	125	125	116
6	110	107	96	91
7	129	128	123	128
8	90	84	101	113
9	84	104	100	88
10	96	100	103	105
11	105	114	105	112
12	113	117	132	130

TABLE **13. 6** Difference Scores for Data of Table 13.5

Subject	$D_1 = Y_2 - Y_1$	$D_2 = Y_3 - Y_2$	$D_3 = Y_4 - Y_3$
1	−12	14	12
2	14	10	6
3	11	−1	1
4	1	7	7
5	7	0	−9
6	−3	−11	−5
7	−1	−5	5
8	−6	17	12
9	20	−4	−12
10	4	3	2
11	9	−9	7
12	4	15	−2
Mean	4	3	2

From Table 13.8, the matrix for the restricted model is

$$\mathbf{E(R)} = \begin{vmatrix} 1070 & -185 & -344 \\ -185 & 1112 & 471 \\ -344 & 471 & 706 \end{vmatrix}$$

It can be shown that the determinant for the matrix of the full model equals
290,177,920 (i.e., two hundred ninety million, one hundred seventy-seven thousand,

T A B L E **13. 7** Errors for the Full Model for D_1, D_2, and D_3 Variables of Table 13.6

Subject	e_1	e_2	e_3	e_1^2	e_2^2	e_3^2	$(e_1)(e_2)$	$(e_1)(e_3)$	$(e_2)(e_3)$
1	−16	11	10	256	121	100	−176	−160	110
2	10	7	4	100	49	16	70	40	28
3	7	−4	−1	49	16	1	−28	−7	4
4	−3	4	5	9	16	25	−12	−15	20
5	3	−3	−11	9	9	121	−9	−33	33
6	−7	−14	−7	49	196	49	98	49	98
7	−5	−8	3	25	64	9	40	−15	−24
8	−10	14	10	100	196	100	−140	100	140
9	16	−7	−14	256	49	196	−112	−224	98
10	0	0	0	0	0	0	0	0	0
11	5	−12	5	25	144	25	−60	25	−60
12	0	12	−4	0	144	16	0	0	−48
Sum	**0**	**0**	**0**	**878**	**1004**	**658**	**−329**	**−440**	**399**

T A B L E **13. 8** Errors for the Restricted Model for D_1, D_2, and D_3 Variables of Table 13.6

Subject	e_1	e_2	e_3	e_1^2	e_2^2	e_3^2	$(e_1)(e_2)$	$(e_1)(e_3)$	$(e_2)(e_3)$
1	−12	14	12	144	196	144	−168	−144	168
2	14	10	6	196	100	36	140	84	60
3	11	−1	1	121	1	1	−11	11	−1
4	1	7	7	1	49	49	7	7	49
5	7	0	−9	49	0	81	0	−63	0
6	−3	−11	−5	9	121	25	33	15	55
7	−1	−5	5	1	25	25	5	−5	−25
8	−6	17	12	36	289	144	−102	−72	204
9	20	−4	−12	400	16	144	−80	−240	48
10	4	3	2	16	9	4	12	8	6
11	9	−9	7	81	81	49	−81	63	−63
12	4	15	−2	16	225	4	60	−8	−30
Sum	**48**	**36**	**24**	**1070**	**1112**	**706**	**−185**	**−344**	**471**

nine hundred and twenty), while the determinant for the restricted model equals 506,853,568 (five hundred and six million, eight hundred fifty-three thousand, five hundred and sixty-eight).[4] To find the value of the F statistic, we must also realize that $df_F = 9$ and $df_R = 12$. Substituting these values into the formula for the F statistic, we arrive at

$$F = \frac{(506,853,568 - 290,177,920)/(12 - 9)}{290,177,920/9}$$

which reduces to an F value of 2.2401. With 3 numerator and 9 denominator degrees of freedom, the associated p value is 0.1525. Thus, the mean differences are nonsignificant at the .05 level. Recall from Chapter 11 that this is the same conclusion we reached from the $\hat{\varepsilon}$- and $\tilde{\varepsilon}$-adjusted mixed-model tests, but that the unadjusted mixed-model test produced a significant result at the .05 level. A general comparison of the various approaches will be presented at the end of this chapter.

CHOOSING AN APPROPRIATE SAMPLE SIZE

Calculating statistical power and choosing an appropriate sample size is more complicated in within-subjects designs than in between-subjects designs. The additional complication is that effect size in repeated-measures designs depends not only on population means and population variances but also on population covariances. Although the mathematics necessary to calculate power is relatively straightforward, in practice it is difficult to specify accurate values of all parameters that influence power. Instead of attempting to provide a thorough theoretical presentation of power in within-subjects designs, we present some general guidelines for choosing an appropriate sample size to guarantee sufficient power when using the multivariate approach to analyze repeated-measures data.

Tables 13.9–13.11 present sample sizes to achieve a power of .50, .80, and .95, respectively, for $\alpha = .05$. As the tables show, the necessary sample size depends on the number of levels of the repeated factor, minimum degree of correlation between scores at these levels, and the anticipated effect size. We first illustrate how to use these tables. Then we discuss the underlying theory and practical implications to be drawn from the theory.

T A B L E **13.9** Minimum Sample Size Needed to Achieve Power of .50 with $\alpha = .05$

Number of Levels	Minimum Correlation	Design*	d					
			0.25	0.50	0.75	1.00	1.25	1.50
2	—	CRD	124	32	15	9	7	5
	0	RMD	125	33	16	10	7	6
	.1		113	30	15	9	7	6
	.2		101	27	13	9	7	5
	.3		88	24	12	8	6	5
	.4		76	21	11	7	6	5
	.5		64	18	9	6	5	4
	.6		52	15	8	6	5	4
	.7		39	12	7	5	4	4
	.8		27	9	5	4	4	3
	.9		15	6	4	3	3	3

T A B L E **13. 9** (Continued)

Number of Levels	Minimum Correlation	Design*	d					
			0.25	0.50	0.75	1.00	1.25	1.50
3	—	CRD	160	41	19	11	8	6
	0	RMD	162	43	21	14	10	8
	.1		146	39	19	13	9	8
	.2		130	35	18	12	9	7
	.3		115	31	16	11	8	7
	.4		99	27	14	10	8	6
	.5		83	23	12	9	7	6
	.6		67	19	11	8	6	6
	.7		51	16	9	7	6	5
	.8		35	12	7	6	5	5
	.9		19	8	6	5	4	4
4	—	CRD	186	48	22	13	9	7
	0	RMD	189	51	25	16	12	10
	.1		170	46	23	15	11	9
	.2		152	41	21	14	11	9
	.3		133	37	19	13	10	8
	.4		115	32	17	12	9	8
	.5		97	28	15	10	8	7
	.6		78	23	13	9	8	7
	.7		60	18	11	8	7	6
	.8		41	14	9	7	6	6
	.9		23	9	7	6	5	5
5	—	CRD	207	53	24	14	10	7
	0	RMD	211	57	28	18	14	11
	.1		190	52	26	17	13	11
	.2		170	46	24	16	12	10
	.3		149	41	21	15	11	10
	.4		129	36	19	13	11	9
	.5		108	31	17	12	10	9
	.6		87	26	15	11	9	8
	.7		67	21	12	10	8	7
	.8		46	16	10	8	7	7
	.9		26	11	8	7	7	6
6	—	CRD	225	57	26	15	10	8
	0	RMD	230	62	31	20	15	13
	.1		207	56	29	19	15	12
	.2		185	51	26	18	14	12
	.3		163	45	24	16	13	11
	.4		140	40	21	15	12	10
	.5		118	34	19	14	11	10
	.6		96	29	16	12	10	9
	.7		73	23	14	11	9	9
	.8		51	18	12	9	9	8
	.9		29	12	9	8	8	7

*CRD: completely randomized design; RMD: repeated-measures design.

T A B L E **13. 10** Minimum Sample Size Needed to
Achieve Power of .80 with $\alpha = .05$

Number of Levels	Minimum Correlation	Design*	d					
			0.25	0.50	0.75	1.00	1.25	1.50
2	—	CRD	253	64	29	17	12	9
	0	RMD	254	65	30	18	13	10
	.1		228	59	28	17	12	9
	.2		203	53	25	15	11	8
	.3		178	46	22	14	10	8
	.4		153	40	19	12	9	7
	.5		128	34	16	10	8	6
	.6		103	28	14	9	7	6
	.7		78	21	11	7	6	5
	.8		53	15	8	6	5	4
	.9		28	9	6	4	4	3
3	—	CRD	310	79	36	21	14	10
	0	RMD	312	81	38	23	16	12
	.1		281	73	34	21	15	11
	.2		250	65	31	19	14	11
	.3		219	58	28	17	12	10
	.4		188	50	24	15	11	9
	.5		158	42	21	13	10	8
	.6		127	34	17	11	9	7
	.7		96	27	14	10	8	6
	.8		65	19	11	8	6	6
	.9		34	11	7	6	5	5
4	—	CRD	350	89	40	23	15	11
	0	RMD	353	92	43	26	19	14
	.1		318	83	39	24	17	13
	.2		284	74	36	22	16	13
	.3		249	66	32	20	15	12
	.4		214	57	28	18	13	11
	.5		179	48	24	16	12	10
	.6		144	39	20	13	10	9
	.7		109	31	16	11	9	8
	.8		74	22	13	9	8	7
	.9		39	13	9	7	6	6
5	—	CRD	383	97	44	25	17	12
	0	RMD	387	101	48	29	21	16
	.1		349	91	44	27	19	15
	.2		311	82	39	25	18	14
	.3		273	72	35	22	16	13
	.4		234	63	31	20	15	12
	.5		196	53	27	18	13	11
	.6		158	44	23	15	12	10
	.7		120	34	18	13	10	9
	.8		82	25	14	11	9	8
	.9		44	15	10	8	8	7

T A B L E **13. 10**   (Continued)

Number of Levels	Minimum Correlation	Design*	d					
			0.25	0.50	0.75	1.00	1.25	1.50
6	—	CRD	412	104	47	27	18	13
	0	RMD	417	109	52	32	23	18
	.1		375	98	47	29	21	17
	.2		334	88	43	27	20	16
	.3		293	78	38	24	18	15
	.4		252	68	34	22	16	14
	.5		211	58	29	19	15	12
	.6		170	47	25	17	13	11
	.7		129	37	20	14	12	10
	.8		88	27	16	12	10	9
	.9		47	17	11	10	9	8

*CRD: completely randomized design; RMD: repeated-measures design.

T A B L E **13. 11**   Minimum Sample Size Needed to Achieve Power of .95 with $\alpha = .05$

Number of Levels	Minimum Correlation	Design*	d					
			0.25	0.50	0.75	1.00	1.25	1.50
2	—	CRD	417	105	48	27	18	13
	0	RMD	418	106	49	28	19	14
	.1		377	96	44	26	18	13
	.2		335	86	39	23	16	12
	.3		294	75	35	21	14	11
	.4		252	65	30	18	13	10
	.5		210	54	26	16	11	8
	.6		169	44	21	13	9	7
	.7		127	34	16	10	8	6
	.8		86	23	12	8	6	5
	.9		44	13	7	5	5	4
3	—	CRD	496	125	56	32	21	15
	0	RMD	498	127	58	35	23	17
	.1		448	115	53	31	21	16
	.2		399	102	48	28	20	15
	.3		349	90	42	25	18	13
	.4		300	78	37	22	16	12
	.5		251	65	31	19	14	11
	.6		201	53	26	16	12	9
	.7		152	41	20	13	10	8
	.8		102	28	15	10	8	7
	.9		53	16	9	7	6	5

T A B L E **13. 11** (Continued)

Number Levels	Minimum Correlation	Design*	d					
			0.25	0.50	0.75	1.00	1.25	1.50
4	—	CRD	551	139	63	36	23	17
	0	RMD	554	142	66	39	27	20
	.1		499	128	59	35	24	18
	.2		444	114	53	32	22	17
	.3		389	101	47	29	20	16
	.4		334	87	41	25	18	14
	.5		279	73	35	22	16	13
	.6		224	59	29	18	14	11
	.7		169	46	23	15	12	10
	.8		114	32	17	12	9	8
	.9		59	18	11	9	7	7
5	—	CRD	596	150	67	39	25	18
	0	RMD	600	154	71	43	29	22
	.1		540	139	65	39	27	21
	.2		481	124	58	35	25	19
	.3		421	109	52	32	22	17
	.4		362	94	45	28	20	16
	.5		302	80	38	24	18	14
	.6		243	65	32	21	15	13
	.7		184	50	25	17	13	11
	.8		124	35	19	13	11	9
	.9		65	21	13	10	9	8
6	—	CRD	634	160	72	41	27	19
	0	RMD	639	164	77	46	32	24
	.1		576	149	69	42	29	22
	.2		512	133	62	38	27	21
	.3		449	117	55	34	24	19
	.4		386	101	48	30	22	17
	.5		323	85	41	26	19	16
	.6		259	69	35	22	17	14
	.7		196	54	28	19	14	12
	.8		133	38	21	15	12	11
	.9		69	22	14	11	10	9

*CRD: completely randomized design; RMD: repeated-measures design.

Suppose that we are planning a four-group within-subjects study. We plan to use the multivariate approach to analyze our data and we use an α level of .05. How many subjects do we need? The answer depends on three factors: the power we desire, the anticipated effect size, and the correlation between scores at each level. Let's suppose for the moment that we are willing to have a power of .50. Given this choice, there is a 50 percent chance that we will detect a true effect of the anticipated magnitude. Table 13.9 provides sample sizes for a power value of .50. To use the table, we must next specify d, which is defined to be

$$d = \frac{\mu_{max} - \mu_{min}}{\sigma}$$

where it is assumed that every level of the factor has a common population standard deviation σ. Suppose that we want to detect a true effect if d is as large as 0.75, that is, if there is a three-quarters standard deviation difference between the largest and the smallest mean. Finally, we must specify the smallest correlation we anticipate among the levels of the factor. In other words, with four levels of the factor, there are six correlations to consider: $\rho_{12}, \rho_{13}, \rho_{14}, \rho_{23}, \rho_{24}$, and ρ_{34}. The smallest value among these six correlations must be specified. Suppose we decide that the minimum correlation is likely to be .4. From Table 13.9, with four levels of the factor, a d value of 0.75, and a minimum correlation of .4, 17 subjects are needed to obtain a power of .50.

If a power of .80 were desired for the same number of levels, d, and correlation, Table 13.10 shows that 28 subjects would be needed. Similarly, from Table 13.11, 41 subjects would be needed to achieve a power of .95. Thus, the number of subjects to include in the study depends greatly on the desired power. Comparing sample sizes across different values of d and across different values of the minimum correlation shows that the necessary sample size can also vary greatly as a function of these factors. Because the needed sample size depends on these three factors (desired power, d, and correlation) even for a fixed number of levels, it is impossible to state a general rule such as "20 subjects should be used in a four-level repeated-measures design." Instead, researchers should specify particular values for these three factors and pick a sample size accordingly. When it is difficult to anticipate precise values of d and minimum correlation in advance, it may be wise to specify a range of possible values. For example, with four levels, suppose that a power of .80 is desired, but d could be anywhere between 0.75 and 1.00 and the minimum correlation could be anywhere between .3 and .5. From Table 13.10, the necessary sample size ranges from 32 (for $d = 0.75$, correlation $= .3$) to 16 (for $d = 1.00$, correlation $= .5$). Thus, somewhere between 16 and 32 subjects should be included in the study. The exact number of subjects ultimately chosen should depend on factors such as the availability of subjects and the costs (in terms of time and effort, as well as money) of including additional subjects. In real-world research, there is no single "correct" value for the number of subjects needed in a study. However, Tables 13.9–13.11 provide researchers with guidelines for choosing reasonable sample sizes in repeated-measures designs.

The values in Tables 13.9–13.11 are based on mathematical results derived by Vonesh and Schork (1986). They show that the noncentrality parameter δ^2 of the F statistic in the multivariate approach to repeated measures is greater than or equal to $nd^2/2(1 - \rho_{min})$, where ρ_{min} is the minimum correlation. This formulation assumes that each level of the repeated factor has the same population variance, but population correlations are allowed to differ, as often is the case in repeated-measures designs. The values shown in Tables 13.9–13.11 were obtained by using a noncentrality parameter value of $\delta^2 = nd^2/2(1 - \rho_{min})$ in the noncentral F distribution. As Vonesh and Schork (1986) show, this value is a minimum value, so the actual power obtained from using the sample sizes shown in Tables 13.9–13.11 is at least as large as the stated power for the specific values of d and ρ_{min}. The actual power may be greater than the stated power for either of two reasons. First, the sample-size tables assume that the population means of all levels except μ_{max} and μ_{min} equal the grand mean. To the extent that this is false and other group means also differ from the grand mean, power will be increased. Second, the tables assume that ρ_{min} is the correlation between the levels represented by μ_{max} and μ_{min}. However, the actual power will be somewhat larger for other patterns of mean differences and correlations. The practical consequence of these two points is that Tables 13.9–13.11 provide a lower bound for the power that will be obtained for particular values of d and ρ_{min}. In other words, the sample sizes shown in Tables 13.9–13.11 guarantee that the resultant power will be a least as large as .50, .80, and .95, respectively.

Before leaving our discussion of these sample-size tables, we should draw your attention to some patterns in the tables. First, notice that the required number of subjects generally increases as the number of levels increases. Thus, it typically takes more subjects to compare a larger number of levels. Second, the number of subjects increases for corresponding entries as we move from Table 13.9 to Table 13.10 to Table 13.11. To increase power, all other things being equal, the number of subjects must be increased. Third, as d increases, the number of subjects decreases. Larger effects can be detected with fewer subjects. Fourth, as ρ_{min} increases, the number of subjects decreases. Higher correlations are indicative of greater consistency in subjects' relative scores across treatments; greater consistency makes effects easier to detect. Indeed, such consistency is the reason that the repeated-measures design is often more powerful than the between-subjects design, which leads to our final point.

Each CRD row in Tables 13.9–13.11 shows the number of subjects needed in a completely randomized design (hence, CRD), which is another term for a between-subjects design. Two important points must be made comparing the CRD sample-size values to the RMD (repeated-measures design) values. First, let's compare the CRD sample size to an RMD sample size for a fixed value of d, number of levels, and desired power. Typically, the sample size needed for the CRD is less than the sample size needed for the RMD when the correlation is zero because the CRD has larger denominator degrees of freedom. However, in most cases, if the correlation is even as large as .1 or .2, the RMD sample size is less than the CRD sample size. Second, it is important to realize that the CRD values shown here are the number of subjects per level. Because each subject appears in only one level (i.e., group), the total number of subjects needed for the study is the tabled value times the number of levels. In the RMD, on the other hand, every subject appears in every level, so the tabled value itself is the total number of subjects needed for the study. To ensure that this point is clear, consider this example. Suppose that we want a power of .80 in a four-level study. We anticipate an effect size of $d = 1.00$. In the RMD, the minimum correlation is expected to be .4. From Table 13.10, 18 subjects are needed for the RMD. The corresponding entry for the between-subjects design is 23, which means 23 subjects per group. Thus, the total number of subjects needed in the between-subjects design is 92 (4×23). Thus, a power of .8 can be obtained with 18 subjects in the RMD, but requires a total of 92 subjects in the between-subjects design. This illustration should provide some insight into the popularity of repeated-measures designs in the behavioral sciences, where subjects are often a precious commodity. Nevertheless, it would be a serious mistake to infer that repeated-measures designs are always preferable to between-subjects designs. As we discussed near the end of Chapter 11, certain types of questions can only be accurately addressed with between-subjects designs.

CHOICE OF *D* VARIABLES

We have now seen how to analyze data from a one-way repeated-measures design using the multivariate approach. At this point, we need to consider how we should choose the $a-1$ D variables from the original a variables. We will demonstrate empirically that the choice of D variables is irrelevant for testing the omnibus null hypothesis. Although we do not provide a mathematical proof, it can be shown that the only requirement is that the contrasts underlying the D variables must be linearly independent (again, see Chapter 4). Of course, strictly speaking, another requirement is that the sum of coefficients for each individual contrast must sum to zero.

To show that the particular choice of D variables is irrelevant, let's return to the three-level data of Table 13.2. (Although we can make the same point with the four-level data of Table 13.5, we will work with the smaller three-level data set for computational simplicity.) Recall that the way we analyzed these data was to form two D variables: $D_1 =$ time 2 $-$ time 1, and $D_2 =$ time 3 $-$ time 2. Using these two D variables, we obtained an observed F value of 19.148 ($p = .0032$); we concluded that the population means of the three time periods are not all equal.

What would have happened if we had chosen a different pair of D variables? For example, because the repeated factor here is time, which is quantitative in nature, we might have formed D variables to represent the linear and quadratic trends much as we discussed in Chapter 6 for between-subjects designs. When $a = 3$, the coefficients for these trends are $-1, 0, 1$ for linear and $-1, 2, -1$ for quadratic (see Appendix Table A.10). If we let Y_1, Y_2, and Y_3 represent the original variables for time 1, time 2, and time 3, respectively, we can write our new pair of D variables as $D_1 = Y_3 - Y_1$ and $D_2 = 2Y_2 - Y_1 - Y_3$. Table 13.12 shows the scores for our eight subjects on these two D variables. As usual, we now must calculate sum-of-squared-errors and sum-of-cross-product terms for the full and restricted models. As before, the full models are $D_{1i} = \mu_1 + \varepsilon_i$ and $D_{2i} = \mu_2 + \varepsilon_i$. Least-squares estimates are $\bar{D}_1$ for μ_1 and $\bar{D}_2$ for μ_2; thus, the error for a particular subject is the subject's deviation from the mean on the particular D variable. As before, the restricted models imply that μ_1 and μ_2 both equal zero, so the restricted models predict every subject's score on both D_1 and D_2 to be zero. Thus, the error for a subject is simply that subject's score on the particular D variable.

T A B L E **13. 12** Linear and Quadratic D Variables for Data of Table 13.2

Subject	D_1 = Linear	D_2 = Quadratic
1	3	-1
2	5	1
3	2	2
4	0	2
5	5	1
6	6	-4
7	2	4
8	1	3
Mean	**3**	**1**

T A B L E **13. 13** Errors for Full and Restricted Models for D_1 and D_2 Variables of Table 13.12

Subject	Full Model					Restricted Model				
	e_1	e_2	e_1^2	e_2^2	$(e_1)(e_2)$	e_1	e_2	e_1^2	e_2^2	$(e_1)(e_2)$
1	0	-2	0	4	0	3	-1	9	1	-3
2	2	0	4	0	0	5	1	25	1	5
3	-1	1	1	1	-1	2	2	4	4	4
4	-3	1	9	1	-3	0	2	0	4	0
5	2	0	4	0	0	5	1	25	1	5
6	3	-5	9	25	-15	6	-4	36	16	-24
7	-1	3	1	9	-3	2	4	4	16	8
8	-2	2	4	4	-4	1	3	1	9	3
Sum	**0**	**0**	**32**	**44**	**-26**	**24**	**8**	**104**	**52**	**-2**

Table 13.13 presents the errors for the full model and for the restricted model. From this table, the matrix of sum of squares and cross-products for the full model is

$$\mathbf{E(F)} = \begin{bmatrix} 32 & -26 \\ -26 & 44 \end{bmatrix}$$

The matrix for the restricted model is

$$\mathbf{E(R)} = \begin{bmatrix} 104 & -2 \\ -2 & 52 \end{bmatrix}$$

It follows that the two determinants are given by

$$|\mathbf{E(F)}| = 32(44) - (-26)^2 = 732$$

and

$$|\mathbf{E(R)}| = 104(52) - (-2)^2 = 5404$$

Equation 21 provides the formula for the F statistic with two D variables:

$$F = \frac{(|\mathbf{E(R)}| - |\mathbf{E(F)}|)/2}{|\mathbf{E(F)}|/(n-2)} \qquad \text{(21, repeated)}$$

Substituting the appropriate values into this equation yields

$$F = \frac{(5404 - 732)/2}{732/(8-2)} = 19.148$$

However, this is precisely the F value we obtained earlier with our other choice of D variables. Thus, as claimed, the same F value occurs regardless of the choice of coefficients used to define the D variables.

Although our empirical demonstration by no means carries the weight of a mathematical proof, such a proof is beyond the scope of this book. The interested reader is referred to Bock (1975), Harris (1985), Morrison (1976), or Timm (1975) for a more mathematical description. These books also provide a more technical presentation of "linear independence" than the intuitive "redundancy" explanation in Chapter 4.

TESTS OF INDIVIDUAL CONTRASTS

Although we have just seen that the particular choice of D variables is irrelevant for testing the omnibus null hypothesis, different D variables provide different information about which individual means differ from one another. As in between-subjects designs, a significant omnibus F value simply implies that a true difference exists somewhere among the means. To pinpoint the precise nature of this difference, it is necessary to test individual contrasts.

As we mentioned briefly in Chapters 11 and 12, there are two rather different approaches for testing contrasts in repeated-measures designs. Not surprisingly, one of these is based on the logic of the mixed-model approach to the omnibus test, whereas the other is based on the multivariate approach. Our presentation focuses on the multivariate-based approach. After providing a brief overview of the mixed-model approach as well, we will explain why we strongly prefer the multivariate approach.

Remember from our discussion of contrasts in between-subjects designs that testing a contrast involves two issues: calculating an observed value of the test statistic and determining an appropriate critical value. Calculating the observed value of the test statistic is simplified because it does not matter what other contrasts (if any) are also being tested. The protection required for performing multiple tests is obtained through the critical value. Thus, we can begin our consideration of testing contrasts in within-subjects designs by learning how to calculate the observed value of the test statistic. One we have accomplished this goal, we can consider the determination of an appropriate critical value.

To make calculation of the observed value of the test statistic more concrete, let's consider a specific problem. Suppose that we are interested in testing a null hypothesis that the linear trend is zero in the population for the data of Table 13.2. The first step in finding the value of the test statistic is to form the corresponding D variable. When $a = 3$, we have already seen that the coefficients of the linear trend are $-1, 0$, and 1, so the appropriate D variable is simply

$$D = Y_3 - Y_1$$

Table 13.12, which we used earlier to demonstrate the irrelevance of the choice of D variables for the omnibus null hypothesis, presents scores on the linear D variable for each of the eight subjects. The null hypothesis to be tested is that this D variable has a population mean of zero. This hypothesis can be tested by comparing a full model and a restricted model:

$$\text{Full:} \quad D_i = \mu + \varepsilon_i$$

$$\text{Restricted:} \quad D_i = 0 + \varepsilon_i$$

The least-squares estimate for μ will be $\bar{D}$, so errors for both models can be calculated very easily. In fact, we already calculated errors for both models when we performed the omnibus test. As shown in Table 13.13, we found that $E_F = 32$ and $E_R = 104$ for the linear variable. To determine whether this difference is statistically significant, we can use our usual formula

$$F = \frac{(E_R - E_F)/(df_R - df_F)}{E_F/df_F}$$

Notice that E_R and E_F are numbers instead of matrices because now our hypothesis pertains to only a single D variable. As a result, we are performing a univariate test. Also, notice that the restricted model has no parameters, so $df_R = n$. The full model has one parameter, so $df_F = n - 1$. Making these substitutions, the general expression for testing an individual contrast is given by

$$F = \frac{(E_R - E_F)/1}{E_F/(n - 1)} \tag{23}$$

which obviously simplifies to

$$F = \frac{E_R - E_F}{E_F/(n - 1)} \tag{24}$$

For our data, the F value then equals

$$F = \frac{104 - 32}{32/(8 - 1)} = 15.75$$

Before considering whether this value of 15.75 is statistically significant, we must make several additional points. First, when we performed the omnibus test for these data, we compared two matrices. The matrix for the full model was given by

$$\begin{bmatrix} 32 & -26 \\ -26 & 44 \end{bmatrix}$$

whereas the matrix for the restricted model was

$$\begin{bmatrix} 104 & -2 \\ -2 & 52 \end{bmatrix}$$

Notice that the numbers in the first row and first column of the two matrices are 32 and 104, which are the two sum of squared errors we compared to test the contrast. Thus, the test of the contrast makes use of part of the same data used in the multivariate test of the omnibus hypothesis. As stated previously, the omnibus hypothesis tests whether both D_1 and D_2 have means of zero, whereas the test of a contrast looks at a single variable individually. The test of the contrast is thus a univariate test of the specific D variable and for this reason is often labeled as a univariate test in computer printouts. Second, although we presented an example of how to find the value of the F statistic for testing a linear trend, the same approach is appropriate for testing any contrast. All that is required is to form the D variable whose coefficients correspond to the contrast of interest and calculate E_F and E_R for the resultant variable. Third, hand calculations can be simplified even further here because there is only a single D variable. As shown earlier in the chapter, for a single D variable, the formula for the F statistic simplifies to

$$F = n\bar{D}^2/s_D^2 \qquad\qquad \text{(6, repeated)}$$

Thus, this form of the F can also be used for testing individual contrasts.

OPTIONAL

Quantitative Repeated Factors

A fourth point is pertinent when the repeated factor is quantitative, such as time or dosage level. There is a special meaning that can be attached to a subject's linear D score because each subject's linear D score is proportional to the slope of that subject's least-squares regression line when the score is regressed on the quantitative predictor variable. To illustrate this point, we again consider the data of Table 13.2. Let's suppose that the three time periods represented here are 12 months, 24 months, and 36 months. What would happen if we performed a regression analysis of the three scores for subject 1? There are 3 X values: 12, 24, and 36. There are three corresponding Y values: 2, 3, and 5. The slope of a least-squares regression line is given by

$$b = \frac{\sum(X - \bar{X})(Y - \bar{Y})}{\sum(X - \bar{X})^2}$$

T A B L E **13. 14** Values of the Slope
of the Least-Squares Regression
Line and of the Linear D
Variable for Data of Table 13.2

Subject	Slope	Linear D
1	0.125	3
2	0.208	5
3	0.083	2
4	0.000	0
5	0.208	5
6	0.250	6
7	0.083	2
8	0.042	1

Substituting the three X and Y pairs into this formula results in a value of $b = 0.125$. Thus, the best-fitting regression line (in the sense of least squares) suggests that this subject's score increases by one-eighth of a point every month. Table 13.14 shows the slope of the least-squares regression line for each of the eight subjects, as well as the score on the linear D variable, reproduced from Table 13.12. There is a striking relationship between the numbers in the two columns of Table 13.14. Every subject's score on D is 24 times his or her slope.[5] In general, it can be shown that the slope for the ith subject, b_i, is related to the subject's D score, D_i, by the following formula:

$$b_i = D_i/h \sum_{j=1}^{a} c_j^2$$

The value of h expresses the relationship between the units of the time factor (expressed as deviations from the mean) and the values of the coefficients. Specifically, the two sets of numbers are necessarily proportional to one another, and h is the constant of proportionality. In our example, the units of the factor are 12, 24, and 36. Expressed as deviations from the mean, they become -12, 0, and 12 (because 24 is the mean of 12, 24, and 36). The coefficients for D are -1, 0, and 1. Thus, $h = 12$ because the units of the factor are uniformly 12 times larger than the coefficients. Notice also that the sum of squared coefficients ($\sum_{j=1}^{a} c_j^2$) equals 2, so we have

$$b_i = D_i/24$$

in agreement with Table 13.14. We have elaborated on this point because repeated-measures designs often involve time as a within-subjects factor. Our illustration, which holds for any value of a, shows an interesting way in which the test of a linear trend across time can be conceptualized. In effect, such a test asks whether the average (i.e., mean) subject has scores whose straight-line slope across time equals zero. There is sometimes also a practical advantage to viewing the test of the linear trend from this perspective. If data are missing (presumably at random) for some mixture of subjects at varying time points, it is still possible to calculate a regression slope for each subject (as long as at least two observations are available for the subject). These slopes can then be used as D variables in a repeated-measures analysis.[6]

═══════

MULTIPLE-COMPARISON PROCEDURES: DETERMINATION OF CRITICAL VALUES

We have now seen how to conduct the first step in testing a contrast, namely, the calculation of the observed value of the test statistic. We are now ready to discuss the second step, the determination of an appropriate critical value.

If it is deemed appropriate to employ a per-comparison alpha level, determining the appropriate critical value is trivial. Recall that the F statistic for testing an individual comparison is

$$F = \frac{(E_R - E_F)/1}{E_F/(n-1)} \qquad \text{(23, repeated)}$$

As this expression shows, the F statistic has 1 numerator and $n - 1$ denominator degrees of freedom. No adjustment is needed to use the desired per-comparison alpha level.

As an illustration, we discovered that the observed F value for a linear trend in the data of Table 13.2 equals 15.75. If we decide to use a per-comparison alpha level of .05, appendix Table A.2 of the F distribution shows that the critical F equals 5.59 for 1 numerator and 7 denominator degrees of freedom (remember that there were eight subjects in the data set). Thus, we can reject a null hypothesis of no linear trend at the .05 level. In other words, there is a statistically significant linear trend.

Planned Comparisons

If the familywise alpha level for a set of planned comparisons is to be maintained at .05, an adjustment in the critical value is necessary. As we discussed in Chapter 5 for the between-subjects design, the Bonferroni approach is again applicable. Instead of using a per-comparison alpha level of .05, a per-comparison level of $.05/C$ is used, where C is the total number of planned comparisons. Of course, .05 is used if it is the desired familywise alpha level, as it usually will be; otherwise, any other desired familywise level is divided by C. The easiest way to implement the Bonferroni approach is to obtain the p value for the individual contrast from a computer program. The resultant p value can then be compared to $.05/C$. For example, the p value associated with the F value of 15.75 for the linear trend in Table 13.2 is .0057. Suppose that we were testing both the linear and quadratic trends and wanted to maintain familywise alpha at .05. The linear trend is still statistically significant because the observed p value of .0057 is smaller than .025, which we use as the critical p value because it is .05/2. In summary, tests of planned comparisons in repeated-measures designs are based on the same logic and follow the same procedures as in the between-subjects design.

Pairwise Comparisons

In the between-subjects design, we advocated the use of Tukey's WSD to maintain familywise alpha at the desired level of testing all pairwise comparisons. However, our recommendation in the within-subjects design is to use the Bonferroni approach. This approach should be used regardless of whether the researcher planned to test all pairwise comparisons or only made this decision after examining the data.

The procedure for using the Bonferroni approach to test pairwise comparisons is the same as for the general case of planned comparisons. Namely, the observed p value is compared to .05/C, where .05 (or some other value, if desired) is the familywise alpha level and C is the number of contrasts potentially being tested. In the case of pairwise contrasts, $C = a(a - 1)/2$ because this is the formula for the number of distinct pairs with a levels.

It may seem odd that Tukey's WSD is not being recommended for testing pairwise comparisons in repeated-measures designs. The recommendation is based on Maxwell (1980), who showed that Tukey's approach here does not always successfully maintain α_{FW} at the desired level. In essence, the reason for this failure is that the homogeneity of variance assumption required by the WSD is violated unless the sphericity assumption required by the mixed-model repeated-measures approach is met. The Bonferroni procedure does not require this assumption and hence maintains α_{FW} at the desired level.

Post Hoc Complex Comparisons

As in the between-subjects design, occasions arise in within-subjects designs where the investigator decides after examining the data to test one or more complex comparisons. For example, consider the data in Table 13.2 again. Although it seems reasonable to test planned linear and quadratic trends for these data, suppose for the moment that the repeated factor were qualitative instead of quantitative. In this case, it might be decided post hoc to test the difference between the first level and the average of the other two, since levels 2 and 3 have similar means. The appropriate D variable would be

$$D = Y_1 - \tfrac{1}{2}(Y_2 + Y_3)$$

where Y_1, Y_2, and Y_3 refer to time 1, time 2, and time 3, respectively. Using either Equation 6 or 24, we would obtain an observed F value of 31.818. The appropriate critical value comes from a multivariate extension of Scheffé's method developed by Roy and Bose. The formula for the critical value (CV) is given by

$$CV = (n - 1)(a - 1)F_{\alpha_{FW};a-1,n-a+1}/(n - a + 1) \tag{25}$$

where α_{FW} is the familywise alpha level and $F_{\alpha_{FW};a-1,n-a+1}$ is the critical value for an F with $a-1$ numerator and $n-a+1$ denominator degrees of freedom. For our data, $a = 3$ and $n = 8$, so the CV of Equation 25 becomes CV = $(8-1)(3-1)(5.14)/(8-3+1) = 11.99$. Thus, the mean of D is significantly different from zero. Even after having looked at the data, we can conclude that the population mean of level 1 is different from the average of the means for levels 2 and 3.

The rationale for the Roy–Bose critical value in Equation 25 is exactly the same as in the between-subjects design. Specifically, recall that in the between-subjects design the omnibus F test is significant if and only if there exists some contrast that is significant using Scheffé's method. This same coherence also holds in the within-subjects design.

After observing the data, it is always possible to find a contrast whose observed F value will be $(n-1)(a-1)/(n-a+1)$ times larger than the observed omnibus F value. No other contrast can have a larger observed F value. For convenience, let's label the D variable associated with this largest observed F as D_{max}. We know that the observed F value for D_{max}, which we will label F_{max}, equals

$$F_{max} = (n-1)(a-1)F_{omnibus}/(n-a+1)$$

When will F_{max} exceed the Roy–Bose critical value of Equation 25? It will if and only if

$$(n-1)(a-1)F_{omnibus}/(n-a+1) > (n-1)(a-1)F_{\alpha_{FW};a-1,n-a+1}/(n-a+1)$$

However, this inequality obviously holds if and only if

$$F_{omnibus} > F_{\alpha_{FW};a-1,n-a+1}$$

which is equivalent to a rejection of the omnibus null hypothesis. Thus, it is possible to obtain significance for at least one contrast using the Roy–Bose critical value if and only if the omnibus test is significant.

OPTIONAL

Finding D_{max}

Finding the coefficients of the D_{max} variable is more difficult than in the between-subjects design. In the between-subjects design, the optimal coefficients depend only on the sample means; however, in the within-subjects design, the optimal coefficients depend not only on the sample means but also on the interrelationships among the variables. It is necessary to use matrix algebra to incorporate these interrelationships into the calculation of the optimal coefficients. For this reason, we provide only a brief overview.

Let's return to the D variables of Table 13.3, which were obtained from the data in Table 13.2. When a multivariate analysis is performed, it is possible to obtain *raw discriminant weights*, which convey information about the relative weights to be assigned to variables so as to maximize an effect. For our data, the weight for

D_1 is 1.08448, and the weight for D_2 is 0.19424. Thus, D_1 is more influential than D_2 in rejecting the null hypothesis. However, our real interest is to find weights for the original Y variables. We can accomplish this through matrix multiplication. The discriminant weights must be written as a column vector, which we will label $\mathbf{w}$. For our data, we have

$$\mathbf{w} = \begin{bmatrix} 1.08448 \\ 0.19424 \end{bmatrix}$$

Next the coefficients used to derive the D variables from the original Y variables must be written in matrix form; we will denote the matrix $\mathbf{T}$. Each column corresponds to a D variable and each row to a Y variable. Recall that D_1 in Table 13.3 was defined as $D_1 = Y_2 - Y_1$. This implies that the first column of $\mathbf{T}$ will have elements -1, 1, and 0. Similarly, D_2 was defined as $D_2 = Y_3 - Y_2$, so the second column of $\mathbf{T}$ will have elements 0, -1, and 1. Combining the two columns yields

$$\mathbf{T} = \begin{bmatrix} -1 & 0 \\ 1 & -1 \\ 0 & 1 \end{bmatrix}$$

The coefficients for the maximum contrast (or optimal subeffect, as it is sometimes called) are obtained by multiplying $\mathbf{T}$ by $\mathbf{w}$. Specifically, if we let $\mathbf{v}$ be the vector of optimal weights, then $\mathbf{v} = \mathbf{Tw}$. For our data,

$$\mathbf{v} = \begin{bmatrix} -1 & 0 \\ 1 & -1 \\ 0 & 1 \end{bmatrix} \begin{bmatrix} 1.08448 \\ 0.19424 \end{bmatrix}$$

which results in

$$\mathbf{v} = \begin{bmatrix} -1.08448 \\ 0.89024 \\ 0.19424 \end{bmatrix}$$

Thus, the optimal D variable is

$$D_{max} = -1.08448\, Y_1 + 0.89024\, Y_2 + 0.19424\, Y_3$$

Several points must be made here. First, notice that the sum of the coefficients for D_{max} equals zero, as it must if the contrast is to be meaningful. Second, it can be shown that the observed F value for testing a null hypothesis that the population mean of D_{max} is zero equals 44.678. Recall that the omnibus observed F value for these data was 19.148. Thus, within rounding error, it is the case that

$$F_{max} = (n - 1)(a - 1)F_{omnibus}/(n - a + 1)$$

because

$$44.678 = (8 - 1)(3 - 1)(19.148)/(8 - 3 + 1)$$

Third, notice that the optimal coefficients do not closely match the pattern of mean differences for Y_1, Y_2, and Y_3. As we saw in Table 13.2, the means of Y_1, Y_2, and Y_3 are 6, 8, and 9, respectively. Such a pattern would seem to suggest that the optimal contrast might weight the first and third levels most heavily. In fact, however, the optimal contrast is essentially a comparison of levels 1 and 2, with relatively little weight placed on the third level. The coefficients do not closely match the mean differences here because the optimal coefficients depend on the relationships among the variables and the standard deviations of the variables, as well as on the means. For our data, the correlation between Y_1 and Y_2 is much higher ($r = .966$) than either the correlation of Y_1 and Y_3 ($r = .719$) or Y_2 and Y_3 ($r = .772$). The standard deviations of the three variables are roughly the same. Because Y_1 and Y_2 are so highly correlated, the $Y_2 - Y_1$ difference score has a small variance. Another look at Equation 6 for testing a contrast shows that, all other things being equal, a small variance implies a large F value:

$$F = n\bar{D}^2/s_D^2 \qquad \text{(6, repeated)}$$

Thus, even though $Y_3 - Y_1$ has a larger mean than does $Y_2 - Y_1$, the F value for $Y_2 - Y_1$ is larger than the F value for $Y_3 - Y_1$ because the variance of $Y_2 - Y_1$ is so much smaller than the variance of $Y_3 - Y_1$.

We emphasize that rarely if ever would a researcher interpret the D_{max} variable itself. In our example, it is difficult to describe the psychological importance of $-1.08448Y_1 + 0.89024Y_2 + 0.19424Y_3$. However, the coefficients of D_{max} serve as a suggestion for more easily interpreted and hence more meaningful coefficients that might also prove to be significant. In our example, a natural choice would seem to be $D = Y_2 - Y_1$, which yields an F value of 37.3333 and hence easily exceeds the Roy–Bose critical value of 11.99.

All the methods for testing contrasts that we have presented in this chapter are based on the multivariate approach to repeated measures, in that the test of a contrast uses a portion of the information used by the multivariate approach. However, as we discussed in Chapters 11 and 12, it is also possible to test contrasts using a mixed-model approach. As we will see shortly, mixed-model tests of contrasts rely heavily on the sphericity assumption. Before we can see why this is true, we need to consider in more detail the relationship between the mixed-model approach and the multivariate approach.

THE RELATIONSHIP BETWEEN THE MULTIVARIATE APPROACH AND THE MIXED-MODEL APPROACH

Given our presentation to this point, the multivariate and mixed-model approaches to analyzing repeated-measures data probably seem entirely different. After all, in the multivariate approach, we calculate determinants of matrices obtained from D variables, whereas the mixed-model approach makes no use of determinants or even matrices. In the mixed-model approach, the F statistic is simply calculated as

$$F = MS_A/MS_{A \times S} \qquad \text{(11.28, repeated)}$$

On the surface, this bears little resemblance to the multivariate formula, except insofar as we have seen that both formulas come from comparing models using least squares.

Orthonormal Contrasts

The purpose of this section is to develop an explicit connection between the multivariate and mixed-model approaches. To accomplish this goal, it will be useful to work with *orthonormal contrasts*, which are contrasts that possess two properties. First, a set of orthonormal contrasts must be orthogonal. Second, the coefficients of each individual contrast must be normalized. This means that the sum-of-squared coefficients must equal 1.0.

We continue working with the data from Table 13.2 to make our theoretical points easier to follow. What would happen if we used orthonormal contrasts to create our two D variables? To answer this question, we need two orthonormal contrasts. We can simplify our task by realizing that the linear and quadratic D variables we formed earlier (see Table 13.12) were obtained from orthogonal contrasts. Recall that the D variables we used were

$$D_1 = Y_3 - Y_1 \qquad \text{and} \qquad D_2 = 2Y_2 - Y_1 - Y_3$$

To make the coefficients more explicit, the variables can be rewritten as:

$$D_1 = (-1)Y_1 + (0)Y_2 + (1)Y_3$$
$$D_2 = (-1)Y_1 + (2)Y_2 + (-1)Y_3$$

We can verify that the contrasts are indeed orthogonal because the sum of products of the coefficients equals zero:

$$(-1)(-1) + (0)(2) + (1)(-1) = 0$$

However, these contrasts are not yet normalized because the sum-of-squared coefficients is two for the linear trend and six for the quadratic trend. Normalizing the coefficients is quite simple. All we must do is to divide each nonnormalized coefficient by the square root of the sum-of-squared coefficients for that particular contrast. For example, because the sum-of-squared coefficients for the linear trend is two, we must divide each nonnormalized coefficient by $\sqrt{2}$. If we let D_1^* represent the resulting (normalized) variable, we have

$$D_1^* = (-0.70711)Y_1 + (0)Y_2 + (0.70711)Y_3$$

Notice that the coefficients for D^* are proportional to the coefficients for D, but the sum-of-squared coefficients for D^* equals 1.0 (within rounding error), so that D^* is a normalized contrast. Following the same logic for the quadratic trend yields

$$D_2^* = (-0.40825)\, Y_1 + (0.81650)\, Y_2 + (-0.40825)\, Y_3$$

Suppose that we performed a multivariate analysis of D_1^* and D_2^* instead of D_1 and D_2. Would the results be different? Although we could duplicate the procedures used to obtain Tables 13.12 and 13.13 to answer this question, we instead take a shortcut. It should be apparent that D_1^* and D_1 are closely related, as are D_2^* and D_2. In particular,

$$D_1^* = 0.70711 D_1 \qquad \text{and} \qquad D_2^* = 0.40825 D_2$$

As these equations show, D_1^* and D_2^* are really the same variables as D_1 and D_2—they are simply measured on a different metric. We can take advantage of this fact by realizing as a result that for any given subject

$$(D_{1i}^*)^2 = (0.70711 D_{1i})^2 = 0.5000 D_{1i}^2 \tag{26}$$

$$(D_{2i}^*)^2 = (0.40825 D_{2i})^2 = 0.1667 D_{2i}^2 \tag{27}$$

$$D_{1i}^* D_{2i}^* = (0.70711 D_{1i})(0.40825 D_{2i}) = 0.2887 D_{1i} D_{2i} \tag{28}$$

Because these equalities hold for each individual subject, they must also hold for the sums of squares and sums of cross-products, which are the numbers ultimately needed for performing a test. Recall that from Table 13.13 we had found error matrices for the full and restricted models:

$$\mathbf{E(F)} = \begin{bmatrix} 32 & -26 \\ -26 & 44 \end{bmatrix}$$

$$\mathbf{E(R)} = \begin{bmatrix} 104 & -2 \\ -2 & 52 \end{bmatrix}$$

We now need to realize (see Table 13.13) that 32 and 104 are sums of D_1^2 terms, 44 and 52 are sums of D_2^2 terms, and -26 and -2 are sums of $D_1 D_2$ terms. From Equation 26, the sum of the $(D_1^*)^2$ terms for the full model is related to the sum of the D_1^2 terms in the following manner:

$$\sum_{i=1}^{n} (D_{1i}^*)^2 = \sum_{i=1}^{n} (0.5000 D_{1i}^2) = 0.5000 \sum_{i=1}^{n} D_{1i}^2$$
$$= 0.5000(32) = 16$$

Thus, for the normalized linear trend, the sum of squared errors for the full model is 16. Similarly, the restricted model sum of squared errors for the normalized linear trend is

$$\sum_{i=1}^{n} (D_{1i}^*)^2 = 0.5000(104) = 52$$

The same logic holds for the sum of squared errors for the quadratic trend and for the sum of cross-products. Specifically, from Equation 27, the sums of $(D_2^*)^2$ terms must be 7.3333 and 8.6667, again for the full and restricted models. Finally, from Equation 28, the sum of $D_1^* D_2^*$ terms for the two models must be -7.5055 and -0.5774. Arranging these new numbers in matrix form and letting $\mathbf{E^*(F)}$ and $\mathbf{E^*(R)}$

represent the full and restricted matrices for the normalized D variables yields

$$\mathbf{E^*(F)} = \begin{bmatrix} 16.0000 & -7.5055 \\ -7.5055 & 7.3333 \end{bmatrix}$$

$$\mathbf{E^*(R)} = \begin{bmatrix} 52.0000 & -0.5774 \\ -0.5774 & 8.6667 \end{bmatrix}$$

The F statistic for the omnibus test is given by Equation 20:

$$F = \frac{(|\mathbf{E(R)}| - |\mathbf{E(F)}|)/(df_R - df_F)}{|\mathbf{E(F)}|/df_F} \qquad \text{(20, repeated)}$$

The determinant of $\mathbf{E(F)}$ is

$$|\mathbf{E(F)}| = (16)(7.3333) - (-7.5055)^2 = 61.0000$$

and the determinant of $\mathbf{E(R)}$ is

$$|\mathbf{E(R)}| = (52)(8.6667) - (-0.5774)^2 = 450.3333$$

Substituting these values into Equation 20 (along with $df_F = 6$ and $df_R = 8$) yields an observed F value of 19.148. Not surprisingly, this is exactly the same F value we obtained earlier for the omnibus test without normalizing the trend variables. As we stated then, the choice of D variables is irrelevant for the omnibus miltivariate test. However, the matrices that result from orthonormal variables have some special properties, which is why we have gone to all the trouble of normalizing the variables. It is to these properties that we now turn.

Comparison of the Two Approaches

To compare the $\mathbf{E^*(F)}$ and $\mathbf{E^*(R)}$ matrices of the multivariate approach to results from the mixed-model approach, we first need to see what the mixed-model results are for these data. Table 13.15 shows the ANOVA table that is produced by a mixed-model analysis of the data in Table 13.2. Although it is apparent that the mixed-model approach agrees with the multivariate approach that the null hypothesis should be rejected for these data, we want to focus our attention on another similarity between the two approaches.

From Table 13.15, the sum of squares for the subjects by time interaction is 23.3333. Recall from Chapter 11 that this interaction sum of squares is also the error sum of squares for the full model in the mixed-model approach. Does this value

T A B L E **13. 15** Mixed-Model Analysis of the Data in Table 13.2

Source	SS	df	MS	F	p
Time	37.3333	2	18.6667	11.2	.0015
Subjects × time	23.3333	14	1.6667		

have an analog in the multivariate approach? At first, the answer would seem to be No, because there is an entire matrix of errors for the full model in the multivariate approach. Before reaching this conclusion, however, let's look closely at the full matrix, for our data:

$$\mathbf{E^*(F)} = \begin{bmatrix} 16.0000 & -7.5055 \\ -7.5055 & 7.3333 \end{bmatrix}$$

You may have noticed that the sum of the two diagonal elements of $\mathbf{E^*(F)}$ (i.e., 16.0000 and 7.3333) equals the sum of squared errors (23.3333) for the full model in the mixed-model approach. Such an equality always holds when the D variables have been formed through orthonormal contrasts.[7] We discuss later why the mixed-model approach does not make use of information in the off-diagonal elements of the error matrix. Before pursuing this issue, however, we explore whether there is a similar equality for the restricted models of the two approaches.

From Table 13.15, the sum of squares for the time main effect is 37.3333. Recall from Chapter 11 that the main-effect sum of squares is the difference between the sum of squared errors of the full model and the restricted model in the mixed-model approach. Once again, this value can easily be reproduced from the multivariate approach. The matrix for the restricted model for our data is

$$\mathbf{E^*(R)} = \begin{bmatrix} 52.0000 & -0.5774 \\ -0.5774 & 8.6667 \end{bmatrix}$$

The sum of the diagonal elements (i.e., 52.0000 and 8.6667) is 60.6667. Subtracting the sum of the diagonal elements of $\mathbf{E^*(F)}$ from the sum of the diagonal elements of $\mathbf{E^*(R)}$ yields $60.6667 - 23.3333 = 37.3333$, which equals the sum of squares for the main effect in the mixed model.

This same relationship between the multivariate and the mixed models holds as long as the contrasts defining the D variables are orthonormal. To formalize the relationship, it is helpful to know that the sum of the diagonal elements of a square matrix is called the *trace* of the matrix. The expression $tr(\mathbf{A})$ is used to indicate the trace of a matrix $\mathbf{A}$. With this knowledge, the formula for the mixed-model F can be written in terms of the multivariate matrices as

$$F = \frac{\{tr(\mathbf{E^*(R)}) - tr(\mathbf{E^*(F)})\}/(a-1)}{tr(\mathbf{E^*(F)})/(n-1)(a-1)} \tag{29}$$

where the asterisk (*) is a reminder that the matrices must have been formed from orthonormal contrasts. Taking another look at the formula for the multivariate F shows that it differs from the mixed-model F in two respects:

$$F = \frac{(|\mathbf{E(R)}| - |\mathbf{E(F)}|)/(a-1)}{|\mathbf{E(F)}|/(n-a+1)} \tag{22, repeated}$$

First and most important, the multivariate approach is based on the determinants of matrices, whereas the mixed-model approach is based on traces of matrices. The practical implication of this difference is that the determinant is a function of all elements of the matrix, whereas the trace obviously depends only on the diagonal elements. As a result, the multivariate approach is sensitive to relationships among the D variables, whereas the mixed-model approach is not. Second, the mixed-model approach has larger denominator degrees of freedom than does the multivariate approach.

It is important to emphasize that Equation 29 produces the correct mixed-model F value only when the D variables are orthonormal. This requirement has not only theoretical but also practical implications. As of this writing, the SPSS-X MANOVA procedure can produce both the mixed-model F test and the multivariate F test in a single MANOVA statement. The mixed-model F is invoked by an AVERF command.[8] For the AVERF to be correct, MANOVA creates an orthonormal set of contrasts, even if the user has specified a set of nonorthogonal contrasts. In other words, in this situation, MANOVA does not use the D variables that the user has specified. As a result, the univariate tests printed out by the program are misleading because they do not correspond to the D variables that were input by the user. Because of this possible confusion, it is always wise to request that the statistical package print the relationship between the original Y variables and the new D variables. This is accomplished in SPSS-X MANOVA by specifying PRINT = TRANSFORM. Although neither SAS nor BMDP MANOVA programs suffer from this particular point of potential confusion, this example should serve as a warning to individuals who assume that they can obtain correct information from statistical packages without having to learn any statistical theory.

At this point, we are ready to consider why the mixed-model approach, unlike the multivariate approach, ignores the off-diagonal elements of the error matrices. The basic distinction between the two approaches is that the mixed-model approach requires an assumption of sphericity. Recall from Chapter 11 that sphericity is a property exhibited by certain specific forms of the covariance matrix for the Y variables. Huynh and Feldt (1970) and Rouanet and Lépine (1970) independently showed that the population covariance matrix of the Y variables possesses sphericity if and only if the population $\mathbf{E^*(F)}$ matrix of an orthonormal set of D variables possesses two properties: the off-diagonal elements all equal zero, and every diagonal element is the same. Because both of these properties are important, we discuss each in some detail.

If the mixed-model assumption of sphericity has been met, the population values of the off-diagonal elements of $\mathbf{E^*(F)}$ are all zero. Of course, sample values will differ somewhat from zero, but any such discrepancies reflect nothing more than sampling error if the sphericity assumption is satisfied. In this case, there is no reason whatsoever to incorporate information from the off-diagonal elements into a test statistic because there is literally no information in these values. They simply reflect random fluctuations around zero. On the other hand, if the sphericity assumption is not met, the off-diagonal population elements of $\mathbf{E^*(F)}$ are not generally zero. In this case, these elements do contain useful information. The multivariate approach makes use of this information, whereas the mixed-model approach ignores these values and thus implicitly assumes incorrectly that they reflect only random fluctuations. Thus, in summary, when sphericity holds, the multivariate test is suboptimal because it includes random, irrelevant information (i.e., noise) in its decision. On the other hand, when sphericity fails to hold, the mixed-model test is suboptimal because it fails to include relevant information in its decision. Although it may be overly simplistic, in a sense our general preference for the multivariate test is based on the belief that incorporating irrelevant information is a less serious error than failing to incorporate relevant information. As we will see shortly, this intuitive view translates into statistical considerations of Type I and Type II error rates that ultimately form the basis for our preference.

If the sphericity assumption holds, it is also the case that all diagonal elements of the population $E^*(F)$ matrix will be equal to each other. In essence, this is a homogeneity of variance assumption. That this is so can be seen by recalling that a diagonal element of $E^*(F)$ is simply a sum-of-squared deviations from the mean. If each element is divided by n (in the population) or $n-1$ (in the sample), the result is a variance. Thus, requiring equal diagonal elements of $E^*(F)$ is equivalent to requiring equality of variances of each D^* variable. In symbols, the assumption is that $\sigma^2_{D_1^*} = \sigma^2_{D_2^*} = \cdots = \sigma^2_{D_{a-1}^*}$. Of course, even if such an equality holds in the population, the corresponding sample variances (i.e., $s^2_{D_1^*}$, $s^2_{D_2^*}$, etc.) will differ at least slightly from each other due to sampling error.

OPTIONAL

Reconceptualization of ε in Terms of $E^*(F)$

We have seen in the previous section that one difference between the multivariate approach and the mixed-model approach is that the multivariate approach is based on all elements of the $E^*(F)$ matrix, whereas the mixed-model approach uses only the diagonal elements of $E^*(F)$. When homogeneity holds, only the diagonal elements are relevant; but when homogeneity does not hold, it is a mistake to ignore the off-diagonal elements of the $E^*(F)$ matrix.

One perspective on understanding how the ε-adjusted tests improve on the unadjusted mixed-model test is to realize that the ε-adjusted tests incorporate information about the off-diagonal elements of the $E^*(F)$ matrix into their calculation. Huynh (1978) showed that $\hat{\varepsilon}$ can be calculated from the elements of the $E^*(F)$ matrix in the following manner:

$$\hat{\varepsilon} = \frac{\left(\sum_{i=1}^{a-1} E_{ii}^*(F)\right)^2}{(a-1)\sum_{i=1}^{a-1}\sum_{j=1}^{a-1}(E_{ij}^*(F))^2} \tag{30}$$

where $E_{ij}^*(F)$ refers to the element in row i and column j of the $E^*(F)$ matrix. Before proceeding to discuss the theoretical implications of this formula, it may be helpful to demonstrate its use on the data from Table 13.2. We saw in the previous section that $E^*(F)$ for these data is given by

$$E^*(F) = \begin{bmatrix} 16.0000 & -7.5055 \\ -7.5055 & 7.3333 \end{bmatrix}$$

It then follows that the numerator of $\hat{\varepsilon}$ equals

$$\left(\sum_{i=1}^{a-1} E_{ii}^*(F)\right)^2 = (16.0000 + 7.3333)^2 = (23.3333)^2 = 544.4429$$

Similarly, the denominator of $\hat{\varepsilon}$ equals

$$(a-1)\sum_{i=1}^{a-1}\sum_{j=1}^{a-1} (E_{ij}^*(F))^2 = (3-1)[(16.0000)^2 + (-7.5055)^2 + (-7.5055)^2 + (7.3333)^2]$$

$$= 844.8847$$

Thus, the value of $\hat{\varepsilon}$ for these data is

$$\hat{\varepsilon} = \frac{544.4429}{844.8847} = 0.64444$$

If we wanted, we could now use Equation 11.34 to find the corresponding value of $\tilde{\varepsilon}$:

$$\tilde{\varepsilon} = \frac{n(a-1)\hat{\varepsilon} - 2}{(a-1)[n-1-(a-1)\hat{\varepsilon}]} \qquad \text{(11.34, repeated)}$$

which for our data yields $\tilde{\varepsilon} = 0.7276$.

What does Equation 30 for calculating $\hat{\varepsilon}$ from the $\mathbf{E}^*(F)$ matrix reveal about the nature of the $\hat{\varepsilon}$ adjustment? First, notice that the adjusted test, unlike the unadjusted mixed-model test, incorporates information about the off-diagonal elements of $\mathbf{E}^*(F)$ into the test. Because the off-diagonal elements are squared and appear only in the denominator of the expression for $\hat{\varepsilon}$ (see Equation 30), larger off-diagonal elements of $\mathbf{E}^*(F)$ (either positive or negative) lead to lower values of $\hat{\varepsilon}$. This should seem reasonable because, remember that when homogeneity holds, the off-diagonal elements deviate from zero only because of sampling error. In this case, the off-diagonal elements should have values close to zero, minimizing their influence in the denominator. On the other hand, when homogeneity is not met, the off-diagonal elements may be nonzero even in the population. In this case, the off-diagonal elements may deviate appreciably from zero, causing $\hat{\varepsilon}$ to be much less than 1.0. Thus, if homogeneity is violated, $\hat{\varepsilon}$ tends to compensate for the violation by reducing the degrees of freedom of the critical value.

Second, we saw in the previous section that if homogeneity holds, the diagonal elements of the population $\mathbf{E}^*(F)$ matrix are equal to each other. Although it may not be immediately obvious from Equation 30, $\hat{\varepsilon}$ is also sensitive to the degree of inequality of the diagonal elements of $\mathbf{E}^*(F)$. This point can be understood most easily by comparing two hypothetical $\mathbf{E}^*(F)$ matrices, both of which have off-diagonal elements of zero. Let's first consider such an $\mathbf{E}^*(F)$ matrix that also has equal diagonal elements. For example, $\mathbf{E}^*(F)$ might equal

$$\mathbf{E}^*(F) = \begin{bmatrix} 9 & 0 \\ 0 & 9 \end{bmatrix}$$

From Equation 30, $\hat{\varepsilon}$ for this matrix equals

$$\hat{\varepsilon} = \frac{(9 + 9)^2}{(3 - 1)(9^2 + 0^2 + 0^2 + 9^2)} = \frac{324}{2(81 + 81)} = 1.0$$

Of course, we would expect $\hat{\varepsilon}$ to equal 1.0 when the homogeneity assumption is perfectly satisfied, as it is here. Now, however, let's consider another $\mathbf{E^*(F)}$ matrix, which again has off-diagonal elements of zero, but this time has unequal diagonal elements. For example, $\mathbf{E^*(F)}$ might equal

$$\mathbf{E^*(F)} = \begin{bmatrix} 15 & 0 \\ 0 & 3 \end{bmatrix}$$

From Equation 30, $\hat{\varepsilon}$ for this matrix equals

$$\hat{\varepsilon} = \frac{(15 + 3)^2}{(3 - 1)(15^2 + 0^2 + 0^2 + 3^2)} = \frac{324}{468} = 0.6923$$

Thus, unequal diagonal elements of $\mathbf{E^*(F)}$ lower the value of $\hat{\varepsilon}$.

Using the $\hat{\varepsilon}$ adjustment (or $\tilde{\varepsilon}$) allows the mixed-model F test to be sensitive to the entire $\mathbf{E^*(F)}$ matrix, removing a typical inadequacy of the unadjusted mixed-model test. When homogeneity holds, off-diagonal elements of $\mathbf{E^*(F)}$ will be near zero, and the diagonal elements will be nearly equal to each other. As a result, $\hat{\varepsilon}$ (and $\tilde{\varepsilon}$) will be close to 1.0, and the degrees of freedom for the critical value of the adjusted test will be close to those of the unadjusted test. However, when homogeneity does not hold, off-diagonal elements of $\mathbf{E^*(F)}$ will be farther from zero, and/or the diagonal elements will vary from each other in value. As a result, $\hat{\varepsilon}$ (and $\tilde{\varepsilon}$) may be substantially less than 1.0, lowering the degrees of freedom for the critical value of the adjusted test. The corresponding increase in the critical value itself prevents the increase in Type I errors that would occur with the unadjusted mixed-model test.

MULTIVARIATE AND MIXED-MODEL APPROACHES FOR TESTING CONTRASTS

Although the homogeneity of variance of D^* variables is an assumption required for the mixed-model omnibus test, its validity is even more important for testing contrasts. Recall from our discussion of homogeneity of variance in between-subjects designs that the omnibus test there is rather robust to violations of this assumption (with equal n, which we have in the repeated-measures design) but that tests of contrasts are not robust. In the between-subjects design, when homogeneity fails, it is necessary to use an error term specific to each contrast. The same logic applies in the within-subjects design. Furthermore, the multivariate approach uses a specific error term, but the mixed-model approach does not.

We should state that throughout the remainder of this chapter, when we refer to the mixed-model approach for testing contrasts, we mean the use of a pooled error term. In the one-way within-subjects design, this is an error term of the form $MS_{A \times S}$, to be used for testing any contrast of interest. As we mentioned in Chapters 11 and 12, it is also possible to use a separate (or, specific) error term. In the one-way within-subjects design, this is an error term of the form $MS_{A_{comp} \times S}$, whose value changes depending on the particular comparison being tested.

Before comparing the use of pooled and separate error terms in detail, we need to explain why we are equating the use of a pooled error term with the mixed-model approach and the use of a separate error term with the multivariate approach. If planned comparisons are tested, using a pooled error term parallels the mixed-model approach for the omnibus test because both assume sphericity. The use of a separate error term parallels the multivariate approach for the omnibus test because neither assumes sphericity. In fact, the observed F value that is obtained using a separate error term is literally identical to the F value that is obtained from Equation 6 for testing a contrast with the multivariate approach.

When post hoc tests are conducted, there is an even stronger connection between the mixed-model approach and the pooled error term, and between the multivariate approach and the separate error term. The mixed-model omnibus test will be statistically significant if and only if a statistically significant comparison can be found using a pooled error term and a critical value (CV) of the form

$$CV = (a - 1)F_{.05;a-1,(a-1)(n-1)} \qquad \text{(11.37, repeated)}$$

On the other hand, the multivariate omnibus test will be statistically significant if and only if a statistically significant comparison can be found using a separate error term and a CV of the form

$$CV = (n - 1)(a - 1)F_{\alpha FW;a-1,n-a+1}/(n - a + 1) \qquad \text{(25, repeated)}$$

Thus, using a pooled error term is compatible with the mixed-model approach, and using a separate error term is compatible with the multivariate approach.

Despite this compatibility, testing the omnibus hypothesis with the mixed-model approach and testing comparisons using a separate error term is sometimes recommended. The problem with this combination is that inconsistencies may arise. For example, it is possible to obtain a statistically significant omnibus test, but then be able to find no significant contrasts, because none exists with a separate error term (when compared to the appropriate post hoc CV, as given in Equation 25). It is also possible for the omnibus test to be nonsignificant, yet a significant post hoc comparison could have been found using a separate error term. As a consequence, if a separate error term is to be used for testing contrasts, there is no purpose to performing a mixed-model omnibus test. However, the multivariate test would be useful because it informs us as to whether any significant contrasts exist, using a separate error term.

Thus, to reiterate, in our terminology, the mixed-model approach to testing a contrast refers to the use of a pooled error term, and the multivariate approach to testing a contrast refers to the use of a separate error term.

Numerical Example

To make the presentation of the multivariate and mixed-model approaches more concrete, let's reconsider the data of Table 13.2. How would the multivariate and mixed-model approaches differ in the way that the linear trend (for example) would be tested? To begin to answer the question, let's take another look at the $E^*(F)$ and $E^*(R)$ matrices for the normalized linear and quadratic trends for our data:

$$E^*(F) = \begin{bmatrix} 16.000 & -7.5055 \\ -7.5055 & 7.3333 \end{bmatrix}$$

$$E^*(R) = \begin{bmatrix} 52.0000 & -0.5774 \\ -0.5774 & 8.6667 \end{bmatrix}$$

For ease of discussion, we will again let $E_{ij}^*(F)$ and $E_{ij}^*(R)$ refer to the element in row i and column j of the full and restricted error matrices, respectively. We have already seen that the multivariate approach to testing an individual contrast consists simply of treating the relevant D variable as a single variable, at which point a univariate test is conducted. In terms of symbols,

$$\text{multi } F = \frac{E_{11}^*(R) - E_{11}^*(F)}{E_{11}^*(F)/(n-1)} \tag{31}$$

is the expression for testing D_1 in the multivariate approach. For our data, $E_{11}^*(F) = 16$ and $E_{11}^*(R) = 52$, so the F value is $(52 - 16)/[16/(8 - 1)] = 15.75$. The mixed-model approach uses the same numerator but a different denominator. The mixed-model approach assumes homogeneity of variance, which means that the two diagonal elements of $E^*(F)$ [i.e., $E_{11}^*(F)$ and $E_{22}^*(F)$] should be equal except for sampling error. Based on this assumption, the average of $E_{11}^*(F)$ and $E_{22}^*(F)$ will be a better estimate of the population variance than either term will be by itself. Thus, instead of using $E_{11}^*(F)$ in the denominator, the mixed-model approach uses $(E_{11}^*(F) + E_{22}^*(F))/2$. In general, there are $a - 1$ such terms, so we would have

$$(E_{11}^*(F) + E_{22}^*(F) + \cdots + E_{(a-1)(a-1)}^*(F))/(a-1)$$

We can simplify this expression by realizing that the sum of E^* elements here is simply the sum of the diagonal elements of $E^*(F)$, which is the trace of $E^*(F)$ and is written as $tr(E^*(F))$. Thus, the formula for the mixed-model F test of the D_1 contrast can be obtained by substituting $tr(E^*(F))/(a-1)$ for $E_{11}^*(F)$ in the denominator of the multivariate approach of Equation 31. The result of this substitution yields

$$\text{mixed } F = \frac{E_{11}^*(R) - E_{11}^*(F)}{tr(E^*(F))/(a-1)(n-1)} \tag{32}$$

For our data, $E_{11}^*(R) = 52$, $E_{11}^*(F) = 16$, and $tr(E^*(F)) = 23.3333$, so the observed mixed-model F for the linear trend is

$$F = \frac{52 - 16}{23.3333/(3 - 1)(8 - 1)} = 21.6$$

Notice that the mixed-model value of 21.6 is nearly 40 percent larger than the multivariate F value of 15.75. Before discussing whether this increase is a real improvement, it is useful to consider the F statistics of Equations 31 and 32 from another perspective.

The Difference in Error Terms

Recall that we showed that the trace of $\mathbf{E}^*(\mathbf{F})$ is equal to the mixed-model error sum of squares for its full model. However, this error sum of squares is also $SS_{A \times S}$, the sum of squares for the interaction of the factor (A) and subjects (S). Hence, Equation 32 can be rewritten as:

$$\text{mixed } F = \frac{E^*_{11}(R) - E^*_{11}(F)}{SS_{A \times S}/(a - 1)(n - 1)}$$

Because the term $(a - 1)(n - 1)$ represents the interaction degrees of freedom, the expression can be simplified to

$$\text{mixed } F = \frac{E^*_{11}(R) - E^*_{11}(F)}{MS_{A \times S}} \tag{33}$$

Thus, the mixed-model approach uses $MS_{A \times S}$, the same error term as used in the omnibus test, for testing all contrasts.

The multivariate approach, on the other hand, uses $E^*_{11}(F)/n - 1$ as the error term, that is, as the denominator of the F. Remember that $E^*_{11}(F)$ is simply the sum of squared deviations from the mean for D_1. Dividing this quantity by $n - 1$ results in a variance, namely $s^2_{D^*_1}$, the variance of the D^*_1 variable. Also, we saw earlier in the chapter that the difference in sum of squared errors of the restricted and full models—that is, $E^*_{11}(R) - E^*_{11}(F)$—equals $n(\bar{D}^*_1)^2$. Thus, Equation 31 for the multivariate approach to testing a contrast can be rewritten as

$$\text{multi } F = \frac{n(\bar{D}^*_1)^2}{s^2_{D^*_1}} \tag{34}$$

In fact, this formula (which is really the same as Equation 6) can be used regardless of whether the contrast coefficients for the D_1 variable are normalized. However, we have written the equation in its normalized form to facilitate comparison with the mixed-model equation. Following the same logic for the mixed-model approach, the trace of $\mathbf{E}^*(\mathbf{F})$ is the sum of $a - 1$ sums of squared deviations from their respective means. Dividing by $n - 1$ results in $a - 1$ variances, one for each D^* variable. Thus, Equation 32 can be written as

$$\text{mixed } F = \frac{n(\bar{D}^*_1)^2}{(s^2_{D^*_1} + s^2_{D^*_2} + \cdots + s^2_{D^*_{a-1}})/(a - 1)}$$

To simplify our notation, let's let $\bar{s}^2_{D^*}$ represent the mean variance of the $a - 1$ D^*

variables. Then the F statistic for the mixed-model approach to testing a contrast is

$$\text{mixed } F = \frac{n(\bar{D}_1^*)^2}{\bar{s}_{D^*}^2} \tag{35}$$

Comparing Equations 34 and 35 shows quite obviously that there is only one difference between the multivariate and the mixed-model approaches to testing a contrast. The multivariate approach uses an error term specific to the particular contrast being tested, whereas the mixed-model approach uses a pooled error term based on the average variance of the $a - 1$ orthonormal variables. Which approach is better? Intuition would suggest that the multivariate approach is better if the population variances are unequal, while the mixed-model approach is better if the population variances are equal. In this case, intuition is correct, which leads to three further questions. If the variances are equal, to what extent is the mixed-model approach superior to the multivariate approach? If they are unequal, to what extent is the multivariate approach better? Finally, how likely is it that population variances will be equal?

Which Error Term Is Better?

If the homogeneity of variance assumption is valid for the $a - 1$ orthonormal D variables, the mixed-model approach is superior to the multivariate approach for testing contrasts. As comparing Equations 34 and 35 shows, the mixed-model approach uses a pooled (i.e., average) variance in the denominator, whereas the multivariate approach does not. If homogeneity holds, the long-run expected values of the two denominators will be equal. As a result, the observed value of the F statistic for the two approaches will differ only due to sampling error. In the long run, both approaches will yield the same average observed F value.[9] However, in a particular sample, the mixed-model estimate of the population variance will likely be better than the estimate of the multivariate approach because the mixed-model estimate is based on additional data. This advantage is reflected in the denominator degrees of freedom, which equal $(n - 1)(a - 1)$ for the mixed-model approach but only $n - 1$ for the multivariate approach. As a consequence of the increased degrees of freedom, the mixed-model critical value will always be at least slightly less than the critical value of the multivariate approach, regardless of whether the comparison is planned or post hoc. For example, for the data of Table 13.2, where $n = 8$ and $a = 3$, an α_{PC} of .05 would imply a critical F value of 5.59 for the multivariate approach and 4.60 for the mixed-model approach. If the sample size were larger, the difference would be smaller. For example, if $n = 21$ and $a = 3$, an α_{PC} of .05 implies critical F values of 4.35 and 4.08 for the multivariate and mixed-model approaches, respectively. Of course, all other things being equal, a lower critical value is preferable because it implies greater statistical power. However, the difference in power is generally not very large, unless the sample size is quite small. For example, even when n is only 8, if we assume that $a = 3$, $\alpha_{PC} = .05$, and $\phi = 2.1$, the power of the multivariate approach is 0.72, whereas the power of the mixed-model approach is 0.79. As expected, for larger sample sizes, the difference in power is even smaller. In the preceding example, if n were 21 instead of 8, the power of the multivariate approach would be 0.81, whereas the power of the mixed-model approach would be 0.83. It should be realized that the relative power differences generally increase when α_{PC} is effectively lowered (either because of multiple planned comparisons or because of post hoc adjustments). Nevertheless, the power advantage of the mixed-model approach for testing contrasts is typically small even when the homogeneity of variance assumption is met.

If the homogeneity of variance assumption fails to hold for the $a - 1$ orthonormal D^* variables, the mixed-model approach to testing contrasts encounters serious difficulties. As in the between-subjects design, tests of some contrasts are overly conservative (implying lowered power), while tests of other contrasts are too liberal (i.e., too many Type I errors are made), if homogeneity fails. Boik (1981) has shown that departures from nominal values can be severe for some contrasts even when the ε value for the covariance matrix indicates only a slight departure from sphericity. Two examples from the data in Table 13.2 illustrate the extent of differences between the two approaches. First, consider a test of the linear trend. We found earlier that $E_{11}^*(R) - E_{11}^*(F) = 36$ for the linear trend and that $E_{11}^*(F) = 16$ for this variable individually. We applied Equations 31 and 32 to these data and discovered that the observed F value of the multivariate approach is 15.75 and that the F value of the mixed-model approach is 21.6. Although the larger F value might at first seem to be better because it will be more significant, further thought reveals that the F value can be larger for only one of two reasons. Either the F is larger due to random sampling error or the homogeneity assumption has been violated. The former explanation is not really an advantage because random error is obviously just as likely to produce a smaller F as it is a larger F. On the other hand, if the homogeneity assumption has been violated, the mixed-model approach uses an inappropriate error term. As a result of using an error term that is too small, the Type I error rate will exceed .05, perhaps even doubling or tripling it. Thus, in neither case is this larger observed F value an advantage. As a second example, consider testing the difference between the means of time 1 and time 2. This difference can be tested by constructing a D variable of the form $D = Y_2 - Y_1$, which we considered in Tables 13.3 and 13.4. In nonnormalized form, we found that $E_{11}(F) = 6$ and $E_{11}(R) = 38$. Although we could immediately write the F of the multivariate approach as

$$F = \frac{38 - 6}{6/(8 - 1)}$$

we instead consider the comparable sums of squared errors for the normalized D variable because these values are required by the mixed-model approach. Because the sum of squared coefficients for the D variable, as constructed above, equals two, the normalized sums of squares are one-half of the above values. Thus, $E_{11}^*(F) = 3$, and $E_{11}^*(R) = 19$. As a result, the F of the multivariate approach is given by

$$F = \frac{19 - 3}{3/(8 - 1)} = 37.3333$$

The mixed-model approach has the same numerator but uses $MS_{A \times S}$ as the denominator. As Table 13.15 shows, $MS_{A \times S} = 1.6667$ for the data. Thus, the F value of the mixed-model approach equals

$$F = \frac{19 - 3}{1.6667} = 9.6$$

Thus, the observed F of the mixed-model approach is only slightly more than one-quarter as large as the F of the multivariate approach. This calculation demonstrates vividly that the multivariate approach is not always conservative (in the sense of a lower F value) just because it does not take the gamble of assuming homogeneity. If homogeneity fails, there are by mathematical necessity some contrasts whose observed F value tends to be less with the mixed-model approach than with the multivariate approach. Tests of such contrasts are too conservative with the mixed-model approach, and power is lowered. On the other hand, there are also other contrasts for which the mixed-model approach yields too many rejections of the null hypothesis, that is, too many Type I errors. It should also be noted that ε adjustments employed for the omnibus mixed-model approach are of questionable benefit for testing contrasts. The effect of either an $\hat{\varepsilon}$ or an $\tilde{\varepsilon}$ adjustment is to increase the critical value for all contrasts because the denominator degrees of freedom are lowered from $(n - 1)(a - 1)$ to either $\hat{\varepsilon}(n - 1)(a - 1)$ or $\tilde{\varepsilon}(n - 1)(a - 1)$. However, the observed F value would be unchanged. In particular, the error term would still be $MS_{A \times S}$ for all contrasts. Although using the larger critical value that results from ε adjustment tends to prevent excessive Type I errors for some contrasts, it also makes tests of other contrasts even more conservative than they would have been without the adjustment. In essence, ε adjustments are of limited value for testing contrasts because they always lower the probability of a rejection, as compared to an unadjusted test using $MS_{A \times S}$ as the error term. However, as the multivariate approach shows, the problem with using $MS_{A \times S}$ as the error term for testing all contrasts is that it is sometimes too small and at other times too large. The multivariate approach solves this problem by sometimes using a denominator larger than $MS_{A \times S}$ and at other times using a denominator smaller than $MS_{A \times S}$. No such solution is available with the mixed-model approach, adjusted or unadjusted, because $MS_{A \times S}$ is still used as the error term for testing all contrasts. In summary, tests of contrasts conducted from the mixed-model formulas are not robust to violations of the homogeneity of variance assumption.

This lack of robustness leads to our third question: How likely is it that the assumption of equal population variances will be valid? The assumption of equal variances for $a - 1$ orthonormal D^* variables will be met if the covariance matrix of the a original variables possesses sphericity. As was discussed in Chapter 11, this assumption is equivalent to an assumption of homogeneity of treatment-difference variances. For all practical purposes, in a single-factor repeated-measures design, this assumption implies that all population correlations between the a original variables must be equal and all a original variables must have the same variance. Such a requirement is very restrictive and is unlikely to be satisfied in practice. For example, in many applications, the repeated factor will be time. Observations obtained closer in time will almost inevitably correlate more highly than those separated further in time. When this happens, the homogeneity assumption is violated. On the other hand, when the repeated factor represents some dimension other than time, it is more likely that the homogeneity assumption might be at least approximately true. Even so, as we have mentioned previously, Boik (1981) showed that even small departures from the assumption can drastically affect the Type I and Type II error rates for testing certain individual contrasts. Thus, the mixed-model approach for testing contrasts should be avoided, unless clear evidence is available to indicate that the homogeneity assumption has been met. As mentioned in Chapter 11, Mauchly's test is a procedure for testing the null hypothesis that the homogeneity condition holds in the population. However, as O'Brien and Kaiser (1985) pointed out, Mauchly's test is adversely affected by nonnormality, tending to accept the homogeneity assumption too often for short-tailed distributions and to reject too often for heavy-tailed distributions. As Huynh and Mandeville (1979) show, these tendencies become even more pronounced for larger sample sizes, so large n is no protection. Of course, with small n, the test might fail to reject the assumption simply because of low power resulting from an insufficient sample size. In summary, there are few circumstances where researchers can be even relatively certain that their data satisfy the homogeneity assumption required by the mixed-model approach. In the absence of such assurance, mixed-model tests of certain individual contrasts may be severely distorted. As a consequence, our recommendation is that contrasts in repeated-measures designs routinely be tested using the multivariate approach with a separate error term specific to each individual contrast.

A GENERAL COMPARISON OF THE MULTIVARIATE AND MIXED-MODEL APPROACHES

We have now presented in some detail two rather different approaches for analyzing data from repeated-measures designs: the multivariate approach and the mixed-model approach. Of course, in some respects the situation is even more complicated because there are several possible methods for adjusting degrees of freedom in the mixed-model approach. The purpose of this section is to summarize the advantages and disadvantages of each approach. As often happens in statistics, if we had enough prior knowledge about certain characteristics of the population, it would be immediately apparent which approach would be superior for our data. However, the amount and type of information required to make a choice that we would know to be optimal is rarely if ever available in the behavioral sciences. As a consequence, we have to consider the relative costs of using a less than optimal approach as well as the likelihood that requisite assumptions of the two approaches will be met.

Assumptions

A fundamental difference between the two approaches is that they require different statistical assumptions. As has been stressed repeatedly throughout our discussion, the basic difference in assumptions is that the mixed-model approach makes an assumption of homogeneity that is not required by the multivariate approach. We have seen that this assumption can be expressed in any of four equivalent ways. First, the assumption can be stated as a homogeneity of population treatment-difference variances; this form of the assumption was emphasized in Chapter 11. Second, an equivalent expression of the assumption is that the variables in a set of $a - 1$ orthonormal D^* contrast variables must be uncorrelated and have equal variances in the population. Third, in terms of matrices, the assumption requires that the error matrix for the full model for any set of $a - 1$ orthonormal D^* variables must have a certain restrictive form in the population. Specifically, the off-diagonal elements must equal zero (corresponding to a correlation coefficient of zero), and the diagonal elements must be a common value (corresponding to equal variances). The fourth form of the expression is not theoretically necessary for the mixed-model approach to be valid. However, in the single-factor repeated-measures design, the three forms of stating the assumption imply for all practical purposes that two conditions will both be true of the original Y variables. First, the population correlation between any pair of variables is a constant. Second, every variable has the same population variance. Stating the assumption in this form makes it clear that this assumption required by the mixed-model approach is unlikely to be met in most repeated-measures designs. Thus, the multivariate approach is preferable to the mixed-model approach in that the assumptions required by the mixed-model approach are more restrictive and less likely to be satisfied in practice.[10]

Although the multivariate approach is generally superior to the mixed-model approach with respect to assumptions, there are other dimensions that also need to be considered. In particular, we will compare the two approaches along three additional dimensions: tests of contrasts, Type I error rates for the omnibus tests, and Type II error rates for the omnibus tests.

Tests of Contrasts

The most persuasive argument for the multivariate approach is that it is "the natural generalization of the use of the specific type of error term for contrasts with 1 degree of freedom" (O'Brien & Kaiser, 1985, p. 319). The mixed-model approach, on the other hand, is consistent with the use of a pooled (average) error term. We have seen that the use of such an average error term can be extremely misleading in the absence of homogeneity. If contrasts are to be tested with a specific error term, as we think they should be, then it seems appropriate to adopt a consistent approach for the omnibus test. As we said earlier in the chapter, a significant contrast exists using a specific error term and an appropriate critical value (given by Equation 25) if and only if the omnibus test is significant with the multivariate approach. In general, there is no relationship between tests of contrasts with a specific error term and the omnibus test of the mixed-model approach, either adjusted or unadjusted. Consistency between the omnibus test and tests of contrasts, which only the multivariate approach provides, is the primary reason we recommend it as the better approach. The only exception occurs when n is very small relative to a, which is a problem we will discuss in terms of Type II error rates.

Type I Error Rates

Before we compare the approaches with respect to Type II error, we first consider Type I error. When the homogeneity assumption is not satisfied, the use of the unadjusted mixed-model approach cannot be recommended because its actual Type I error rate can reach double or triple the nominal α level. In other words, when α is set at .05, the mixed-model analysis may reject the null hypothesis 10 percent or even 15 percent of the time despite the fact that the null hypothesis is true. Two alternatives are available: an ε adjustment of the degrees of freedom in the mixed-model approach or the multivariate approach. There are theoretical reasons to prefer the multivariate alternative because when multivariate normality holds, its actual α level is guaranteed mathematically to be equal to the desired nominal α level. The ε-adjustment procedures, on the other hand, are only approximate. There is no guarantee that the actual α level will remain at the nominal value. Nevertheless, numerous empirical studies (see Maxwell & Arvey, 1982, for a review) have demonstrated that the ε-adjustment procedures (particularly $\hat{\varepsilon}$) maintain the actual α near the nominal value across a wide range of conditions. Thus, in theory, Type I error rate considerations favor the multivariate approach. However empirical evidence suggests that the ε-adjusted mixed-model approaches represent a viable alternative with respect to Type I error.

Type II Error Rates

The situation with respect to Type II error is extremely complicated. Before considering the complexities, we should remind you that the discussion of Type II error is also in reality a discussion of power because the statistical power of a test equals 1.0 minus the probability of a Type II error. If it were known that all assumptions of the mixed-model approach were met, it would provide the most powerful method of analysis for repeated-measures data. For this reason (and because the actual α level would equal the nominal α level), the mixed-model analysis would be superior to any other alternative. However, this superiority is limited in practice because the homogeneity assumption is unlikely to be satisfied. When the homogeneity assumption fails to hold, neither approach is uniformly more powerful than the other. Power comparisons are exceedingly complicated here because the relative power of the mixed-model and multivariate approaches depends on the population means, the population covariance matrix, and the relationship of mean differences to covariances. (Exercises 12 and 13 at the end of the chapter illustrate this point in some detail.) For some parameter values, the mixed-model approach is more powerful, but for other parameter values, the multivariate approach is more powerful. Anticipating these parameter values correctly is virtually impossible in practice; as a result, rarely is it possible to know which approach will be more powerful in a particular situation. Because this is such a complex topic, we must refer the interested reader to Davidson (1972) for details. However, we can state some of the general conclusions reached by Davidson and others who have investigated this issue.

One additional crucial factor influences the relative power of the mixed-model and multivariate approaches. Knowledge concerning this influence, unlike the population means and covariances, is available to the researcher and in fact is even at least partially under his or her control. This additional influence is sample size. Not surprisingly, larger samples tend to produce greater power for both the mixed-model and the multivariate approaches. What is less intuitive but more important for our purposes is that sample size also influences the relative power of the two approaches. All other things being equal, the multivariate test is relatively less powerful than the mixed-model test as n decreases. Notice that this statement does not stipulate which test is more powerful than the other. Instead, it implies that if the multivariate test has a power advantage for a certain pattern of population means and covariances, the magnitude of the advantage tends to decrease for smaller n and to increase for larger n. (In fact, for very small n, the power advantage of the multivariate approach may not just decrease, but may actually become a disadvantage, even when the pattern of means and covariances is otherwise favorable to the multivariate approach.) On the other hand, if the mixed-model test is more powerful for a particular pattern of population means and covariances, its advantage tends to be largest for small n. The practical implication of these results is that the multivariate test may lack power relative to the mixed-model test when n is small, especially if a is large. Unfortunately, there is no magical dividing line between "small" and "large," so it is impossible to state a precise rule for when n necessarily favors the mixed-model approach. In fact, such a rule is literally impossible because the power of both approaches depends not only on n but also the population means and covariances. It is theoretically possible for the multivariate test to be more powerful than the mixed-model test even for very small n, if the means and covariances happen to relate in a manner that strongly favors the multivariate approach. Nevertheless, the multivariate approach is inadvisable for small n. As a rough rule of thumb, we would suggest that the multivariate approach should probably not be used if n is less than $a + 10$. This rule is based on Davidson's finding that even when homogeneity holds, "the multivariate test is nearly as powerful as the univariate test when n exceeds k [the number of levels of the factor] by 20 or more" (1972, p. 448). We have chosen $a + 10$ rather than $a + 20$ for our admittedly arbitrary dividing line for two reasons. First, it is unlikely that the homogeneity assumption will be satisfied, in which case the multivariate test may actually be more powerful than the mixed-model test even for small n. Second, Davidson's findings were based on the unadjusted mixed-model approach, which is necessarily somewhat more powerful than the ε-adjusted approaches, which we think should be considered the viable alternatives to the multivariate approach.

Several related issues remain to be discussed. First, Tables 13.9–13.11 should be used as guidelines for choosing a sample size with the multivariate approach. However, circumstances beyond an investigator's control may preclude obtaining the recommended sample size. What if this sample size cannot be obtained, and at the same time, n is less than $a + 10$? Although one could proceed with the multivariate test and hope for the best, our advice would be to formulate a small number of planned comparisons, if at all possible. Although these tests may not be very powerful either for small n, they will likely be more powerful than either multivariate or mixed-model omnibus tests. It should also be recognized that one way to perform planned comparisons is to "plan" to test all pairwise comparisons. Although such an approach may be rather atheoretical, it nevertheless avoids some of the difficulties of the omnibus multivariate test. Where the researcher has no specific planned comparisons in mind, another alternative may be to reduce a by averaging scores over trials, for example, until the multivariate test is advisable. If neither of these options is feasible, the mixed-model test of the omnibus hypothesis can be performed. Second, why is the size of n relative to a so important for the multivariate approach? The answer to this question is contained in the denominator degrees of freedom. Recall that they equal $n - a + 1$ for the multivariate approach because $a - 1$ parameters have been estimated, one for each of the $a - 1$ D variables. As we have discussed previously, lower denominator degrees of freedom imply a higher critical F value and hence less power. If n is only slightly larger than a, the denominator degrees of freedom may be so small that power is quite low. In fact, it is important to note that the multivariate approach requires that n be at least as large as a. If n is less than a, the denominator degrees of freedom would be zero or negative, which is impossible. As a consequence, the multivariate approach is literally impossible mathematically if n is less than a.[11] For situations such as these, testing planned comparisons or using the mixed-model approach are the only alternatives. Third, it may seem puzzling that when homogeneity fails to hold the mixed-model approach commits too many Type I errors, yet may be less powerful than the multivariate approach.

Although this may seem to contradict the fact that Type I and Type II errors are inversely related, in reality there is no contradiction because the two tests are based on different test statistics. The technical explanation is that the multivariate test has a steeper power curve (or operating characteristic curve, as it is sometimes called) in some situations. In case the technical explanation is less than completely satisfactory, a more intuitive analogy may help. Suppose that we were to compare the multivariate approach to a rather strange approach to testing the null hypothesis that simply involves tossing a fair six-sided die. If we obtain a 1 on our toss, we will reject the null hypothesis; otherwise, we will not. You should be able to convince yourself that $\alpha = 1/6$ for this approach; thus, it commits too many Type I errors. Nevertheless, its power is only 1/6, no matter how false the null hypothesis is. Thus, the multivariate test will be more powerful than tossing the die, for reasonable alternative hypotheses. The test obtained by tossing a die has a higher Type I error rate but less power than the multivariate test. Because the test based on tossing a die fails to consider information in the data, its power curve is literally flat, making it insensitive to departures from the null hypothesis. We should immediately add that we are not implying that the mixed-model approach is analogous to tossing a die. It is a viable alternative that in some circumstances may be preferable to the multivariate approach. Our point is simply to show that it is possible for a test to make more Type I errors than another test and yet the first test can be less powerful than the second.

Summary

Power considerations do not uniformly favor either approach over the other. Our recommendation can best be summarized by quoting once more from Davidson (1972): "Provided that n exceeds k [the number of levels of the repeated factor] by a few, the modified univariate test ranges, with respect to power, from somewhat better to much worse than the multivariate test" (p. 451), and "among theoretically possible cases, the multivariate test is usually somewhat more powerful provided that n exceeds k by a few" (p. 452). Thus, our general recommendation based on power is that the multivariate approach should be used as long as n is not too small. At worst, when n is not too small, any disadvantage in power of the multivariate approach relative to an ε-adjusted test is likely to be small. At best, the multivariate test may be much more powerful than the mixed-model approach, either adjusted or unadjusted, for certain patterns of population means and covariances. Thus, considerations of both Type I and Type II error rates give a slight edge, in our opinion, to the multivariate approach over the ε-adjusted mixed-model approaches.

Table 13.16 summarizes the issues involved in choosing between the multivariate and mixed-model approaches. As we have said, our general preference is for the multivariate approach, although as the table shows, the choice involves a number of complex issues.

T A B L E 13. 16 Summary of Comparison Between the Multivariate and Mixed-Model Approaches

---

Assumptions

1. The mixed-model approach requires an assumption of homogeneity (or, sphericity), which is unlikely to be met in many behavioral studies.
2. The multivariate approach requires no such homogeneity assumption. It does assume multivariate normality, whereas the mixed-model approach assumes only univariate normality. However, violations of either normality assumption are generally regarded as less serious than violations of sphericity.

Tests of Contrasts

1. The multivariate approach is consistent with the use of specific error terms for testing contrasts.
2. The mixed-model approach is consistent with the use of a pooled (i.e., average) error term for testing contrasts. However, a pooled error term can lead to very misleading results when the homogeneity assumption is violated, even if the violation is slight.

Type I Error Rate

1. The Type I error rate of the multivariate approach is exact, assuming that its assumptions have been met.
2. When the homogeneity assumption is not satisfied, the Type I error rate of the unadjusted mixed-model test may be double or triple the nominal value. The ε-adjusted tests provide much better control, but they are only approximate, even when necessary assumptions have been met.

Type II Error Rate (Power)

1. When homogeneity holds, the mixed-model test is more powerful than the multivariate test.
2. When homogeneity fails to hold, neither test is uniformly more powerful than the other. For moderate sample sizes, the multivariate test ranges from somewhat less powerful to much more powerful than the mixed-model test. For small sample sizes, the multivariate test is inadvisable and may even be mathematically impossible.

There is yet one other reason to prefer the multivariate approach to the mixed-model approach. In many respects, the logic underlying the multivariate approach generalizes more easily to complex factorial designs than does the logic of the mixed-model approach. As we saw in Chapter 12, using the mixed-model approach in factorial designs sometimes involves complicated problems of choosing an appropriate error term or determining an appropriate ε adjustment of the degrees of freedom. As we will see in Chapter 14, neither of these complications arises in applying the multivariate approach to factorial designs.

EXERCISES

1. True or False: The multivariate approach to a one-way repeated measures design with a levels requires that $a - 1$ D variables be formed.

2. True or False: The determinant of a matrix is itself another matrix.

3. True or False: The denominator "degrees of freedom" of the omnibus F statistic in the multivariate approach to repeated measures will always be less than the corresponding degrees of freedom in the mixed-model approach.

4. True or False: A psychologist is planning a study with three levels of a repeated factor. Anticipated population parameters are $\mu_1 = 40$, $\mu_2 = 45$, $\mu_3 = 50$, $\sigma_1 = \sigma_2 = \sigma_3 = 10$, $p_{12} = .7$, $p_{13} = .5$, and $p_{23} = .7$. The multivariate approach with 13 subjects will guarantee statistical power of at least .80.

5. True or False: It is possible to obtain statistical significance for at least one contrast using a separate variance approach and the Roy-Bose critical value if and only if the omnibus test is significant with the multivariate approach.

6. True or False: Although a stringent homogeneity assumption is required for the mixed-model omnibus test in a repeated measures design, no such assumption is needed for testing contrasts with the mixed-model approach (i.e., using a pooled error term).

*7. (To be done by hand.) The following data represent level of EEG activity in four locations of the brain among five subjects who were engaged in a mental arithmetic task. The question of interest is whether there is differential level of EEG activity across the four locations.

		Location		
Subject	*1*	*2*	*3*	*4*
1	3	6	4	5
2	4	7	4	8
3	2	1	1	3
4	4	5	1	5
5	7	6	5	9

Although in actual practice, the multivariate approach would not be advisable with such a small sample size, this exercise uses the multivariate approach for pedagogical purposes.

a. Calculate three D variables for each subject: $D_1 =$ location 2 − location 1, $D_2 =$ location 3 − location 1, and $D_3 =$ location 4 − location 1.

b. Calculate the errors of the full model for each subject on each D variable in part a. (Also calculate squared errors and cross-product errors for each subject.)

c. Repeat part b for the restricted model.

d. From your results in parts b and c, calculate $|E(F)|$ and $|E(R)|$.

e. Should we reject a null hypothesis that the population means for the four locations are equal to each other? Show your work.

f. What meaning can be attached to the determinants you calculated in part d? To explore this question, let's first consider $|E(F)|$: How does $|E(F)|$ relate to the sums of squares for errors in the full model?

    (1) Find the sum of squared errors for e_1.

    (2) Find the unexplained (i.e., residual) sum of squares for e_2, when e_2 is predicted from e_1. (HINT: $r^2_{e_1,e_2} = .4$)

    (3) Find the unexplained (i.e., residual) sum of squares for e_3, where e_3 is predicted from both e_1 and e_2. (HINT: $R^2_{e_3 \cdot e_1, e_2} = .402778$)

    (4) How do the values in (1)–(3) relate to $|E(F)|$? What does this imply about how you might interpret $|E(F)|$?

    (5) The same type of relationship holds for $|E(R)|$, except that it is necessary to work with uncorrected sums of squares (i.e., regression equations without an intercept term). For our data, these uncorrected sums of squares have the following values: uncorrected SS for $e_1 = 21$; uncorrected residual SS for e_2 predicted from $e_1 = 14.57143$; uncorrected residual SS for e_3 predicted from e_1 and $e_2 = 9.09804$. Verify that the type of relationship you found for $|E(F)|$ also holds for $|E(R)|$.

g. Suppose that we had planned to test a single comparison involving locations 1 and 4. Would this contrast be statistically significant for our data? Show your work.

*8. (Can be done by calculator or computer.) The following $E(F)$ and $E(R)$ matrices have been obtained for 12 subjects:

$$E(F) = \begin{bmatrix} 1584 & 528 \\ 528 & 704 \end{bmatrix}$$

$$E(R) = \begin{bmatrix} 2784 & 1248 \\ 1248 & 1136 \end{bmatrix}$$

a. Should the omnibus null hypothesis be rejected using the multivariate approach?

b. Let's suppose that these matrices were obtained from a set of orthonormal contrasts. Can the omnibus null hypothesis be rejected using the unadjusted mixed-model approach?

c. Suppose that the D_1 variable in the above matrices represents a linear trend. Can the null hypothesis of no linear trend be rejected using an α_{PC} of .05?

9. (To be done by computer.)

a. Reanalyze the data in Table 13.5 by using the multivariate approach to perform a simultaneous test of the linear, quadratic, and cubic trends. How does your obtained F compare to the F value reported in the chapter?

b. Suppose that we had planned to test only the linear trend for these data. Would the trend be statistically significant?

c. Suppose that we had chosen to test the linear trend only after examining the data. Would the statistical significance of the trend remain the same as in part b?

   d. Explain how you could have used your answer to part a to answer part c without having to perform any further calculations after the omnibus test.

   e. The least-squares estimated slopes of a simple linear regression of IQ on age for the 12 subjects shown in Table 13.5 are as follows: 0.933, 1.667, 0.533, 0.867, -0.100, -1.133, -0.133, 1.433, 0.133, 0.500, 0.200, and 1.100. Test whether these scores come from a population with a nonzero mean. How does your result compare to your answer to part b?

   f. The mixed-model approach would use $MS_{A \times S}$ as the error term for testing the linear trend. How does the resultant F value compare to the F value you obtained using a separate error term? Which error term is better here? Why?

10. (To be done by computer.) Until the 1960s it was believed that infants had little or no pattern vision during the early weeks or even months of their lives. The following study is modeled after an experiment reported by Fantz, R. L. (1963) "Pattern vision in newborn infants." *Science, 140,* 294–297. Fourteen infants under 48 hours old were exposed to a series of targets, presented in a random sequence to each infant. Three of the targets contained black-and-white patterns: a schematic face, concentric circles, and a section of newspaper. The fourth target was an unpatterned white circle. A blue background was provided in all cases to contrast with the target. The dependent measure is the length of gaze (in seconds) of an infant at a particular target. The following (hypothetical) data were obtained:

Subject	Face	Circle	Newspaper	White
1	3.1	3.4	1.7	1.8
2	1.3	0.6	0.7	0.5
3	2.1	1.7	1.2	0.7
4	1.5	0.9	0.6	0.4
5	0.9	0.6	0.9	0.8
6	1.6	1.8	0.6	0.8
7	1.8	1.4	0.8	0.6
8	1.4	1.2	0.7	0.5
9	2.7	2.3	1.2	1.1
10	1.5	1.2	0.7	0.6
11	1.4	0.9	1.0	0.5
12	1.6	1.5	0.9	1.0
13	1.3	1.5	1.4	1.6
14	1.3	0.9	1.2	1.4

   a. Test the omnibus null hypothesis of no mean difference among the targets.

   b. (Optional.) Find the coefficient of D_{max} from your analysis in part a. How would you interpret this contrast?

   c. Suppose that instead of performing the omnibus test, you had decided to perform all pairwise comparisons. What would you find?

   d. As yet another alternative, formulate a theoretically meaningful set of three orthogonal contrasts. Test each contrast, maintaining your α_{FW} at .05.

11. (To be done by computer.) A developmental psychologist is interested in the role of the sound of a mother's heartbeat in the growth of newborn babies. Fourteen babies were

placed in a nursery where they were constantly exposed to a rhythmic heartbeat sound piped in over the PA system. Infants were weighed at the same time of day for four consecutive days, yielding the following data (weight is measured in ounces):

Subject	Day 1	Day 2	Day 3	Day 4
1	96	98	103	104
2	116	116	118	119
3	102	102	101	101
4	112	115	116	118
5	108	110	112	115
6	92	95	96	98
7	120	121	121	123
8	112	111	111	109
9	95	96	98	99
10	114	112	110	109
11	99	100	99	98
12	124	125	127	126
13	100	98	95	94
14	106	107	106	107

a. Test the omnibus null hypothesis that the population mean weight is the same for all four days.

b. Suppose that you had planned to test only the linear trend. What would your results show?

c. Suppose instead that you had planned to test differences from one day to the next (i.e., differences between adjacent days). Perform these tests, and maintain α_{FW} at .05.

d. Is this a good design for assessing the effects of a heartbeat sound on infants' growth? Why or why not? How could the internal validity of the design be strengthened?

*12. (To be done by computer.) Consider the following data obtained for 13 subjects.

Subject	Time 1	Time 2	Time 3
1	2	4	7
2	6	5	4
3	4	7	5
4	5	7	4
5	3	3	3
6	1	1	6
7	7	12	8
8	4	5	3
9	3	5	8
10	3	6	1
11	5	8	2
12	2	7	8
13	7	8	6

a. Test the omnibus null hypothesis using the multivariate approach.
b. Test the omnibus null hypothesis using the mixed-model approach. Although in actual practice, you might want to adjust the degrees of freedom, you need only consider the unadjusted test here.
c. How can you explain the results for parts a and b if the multivariate test is conservative and the mixed-model test is liberal? Is the multivariate test really conservative? Is the mixed-model test necessarily more powerful than the multivariate test?

13. (To be done by computer.) This exercise continues to use the data from Exercise 12 with the following changes:

> The time 3 scores of four subjects are different. Subject 1 has a score of 6, subject 10 has a score of 4, subject 11 has a score of 3, and subject 12 has a score of 5.
>
> A constant value of 0.4227 is to be added to each subject's time 1 score. (HINT: This is easy to do with most statistical packages. For example, in SPSS-X, use a COMPUTE statement; in SAS, use an assignment statement after an INPUT in the DATA step.)
>
> A constant value of 1.5773 is to be subtracted from each subject's time 2 score.
>
> A constant value of 1.1547 is to be added to each subject's time 3 score, after first altering the four scores as described above.

a. Test the omnibus null hypothesis using the multivariate approach.
b. Test the omnibus null hypothesis using the mixed-model approach.
c. Based on your answers to parts a and b, is it possible for the mixed-model approach, even after an appropriate adjustment (using $\hat{\varepsilon}$ or $\tilde{\varepsilon}$) and even when $n \geq a + 10$, to yield significance when the multivariate approach does not?

For further reading, Davidson (1972) discusses types of data for which the multivariate test is more powerful (as exemplified by Exercise 12) and other types of data for which the mixed-model test is more powerful (as exemplified by Exercise 13).

*14. (To be done by computer or by hand.) We saw in Exercise 12 that the multivariate test was statistically significant, but the mixed-model test was nonsignificant for these data. Does a contrast exist that would be significant if tested post hoc using a separate error term? It can be shown that D_{max} for these data is given by: $D_{max} = .56\text{time } 1 - .54\text{time } 2 - .02\text{time } 3$.
a. Test this contrast for significance using an appropriate post hoc critical value.
b. How would you interpret this contrast?
c. Is the mixed-model omnibus test necessarily a valid indicator of whether it is fruitless to search for a statistically significant post hoc contrast using a separate error term? Why or why not?

15. (To be done by computer or by hand.) We saw in Exercise 13 that the multivariate test is now nonsignificant while the mixed-model test is significant. Does a contrast exist that would be significant if tested post hoc using a separate error term? It can be shown that D_{max} for these data is given by $D_{max} = -.30\text{time } 1 - .10 \text{ time } 2 + .40\text{time } 3$.
a. Test this contrast for significance using an appropriate post hoc critical value.
b. Does a significant mixed-model omnibus test necessarily imply that a contrast can be found that will be significant if tested post hoc using a separate error term? Justify your answer.

16. A psychologist reports that she calculated a mixed-model F value of 5.73 for her repeated-measures data. With 1 numerator and 19 denominator degrees of freedom, the

result was significant at the .05 level. Should she have used the multivariate approach? Why or why not?

17. A psychologist has used the multivariate approach to analyze his repeated-measures data for 25 subjects. He reports an F value of 2.97, with 4 and 19 degrees of freedom. Should we trust his assertion that the null hypothesis should be rejected, or should we question his claim? Why?

18. Repeated-measures data with six levels have been collected for five subjects. Should the multivariate approach be used to analyze these data? Why or why not?

19. The chapter points out that some statistical packages create orthonormal D variables, even if the user has requested a nonorthogonal set. The following data will allow you to determine whether your favorite program allows you to test nonorthogonal contrasts within the multivariate approach. Consider the following data for five hypothetical subjects:

Subject	Condition 1	Condition 2	Condition 3
1	2	4	5
2	3	3	4
3	4	5	4
4	3	1	5
5	5	4	6
Mean	3.4	3.4	4.8

a. Ask the computer program to create the following 2 D variables: D_1 = condition 2 − condition 1, and D_2 = condition 3 − condition 2. Obtain univariate tests of D_1 and D_2 within the repeated-measures program.

b. Test D_1 in part a by hand.

c. Explain why you obtained the F value that resulted in part b.

d. Did the computer program yield the same answer as you obtained in part b? If so, the computer allows you to test nonorthogonal contrasts. If not, the program probably orthonormalizes its D variables. Remember that most programs will print the transformation matrix being used to obtain D variables. Of course, if your answer is different from the computer's, you may also want to check your arithmetic!

14 Higher-Order Designs with Within-Subjects Factors: Multivariate Approach

THIS CHAPTER EXTENDS THE multivariate methodology developed in Chapter 13 for one-way within-subjects designs to more complicated factorial designs. As such, the methods to be developed in this chapter are an alternative to the mixed-model approach to factorial within-subjects designs discussed in Chapter 12.

The general outline in this chapter parallels the development of the mixed-model approach in Chapter 12. First, we consider two-way factorial designs where both factors are within-subjects. Second, we consider two-way designs where one factor is between-subjects and the other is within-subjects. Third, we briefly compare the multivariate and mixed-model approaches for these two types of designs.

You should recall from Chapter 13 that the multivariate approach to the one-way within-subjects design requires the formation of $a-1$ D variables (where a is the number of levels of the repeated factor). We will see in this chapter that the same logic works as well in much more complicated designs. The only real complication turns out to be choosing the particular D variables to correspond to the hypotheses of interest. We begin with a design where both within-subjects factors have only two levels because it is easiest to comprehend the formation of D variables when each factor has only two levels. Once we have considered this special case in some detail, we consider the more general $a \times b$ design.

TWO WITHIN-SUBJECTS FACTORS, EACH WITH TWO LEVELS

To consider this design and analysis in detail, we orient our discussion around a specific study where a two-way within-subjects design might be used. The example and corresponding data to be used here are the same as we used in Chapter 12, except that for the moment we will only consider two levels of each factor. Nevertheless, we will once again describe the study in some detail because some readers may not have read Chapter 12 if they are focusing on the multivariate approach to repeated measures instead of the mixed-model approach. Readers who did read Chapter 12 may nevertheless benefit from a brief review of the perceptual study originally introduced in Chapter 12.

Suppose that a perceptual psychologist studying the visual system was interested in determining the extent to which interfering visual stimuli slow the ability to recognize letters. Subjects are brought into a laboratory and seated in front of a tachistoscope. Subjects are told that they will see either the letter T or the Letter I displayed on the screen. In some trials, the letter appears by itself, but in other trials the target letter is embedded in a group of other letters. This variation in the display constitutes the first factor, which is referred to as "noise." The noise factor has two

T A B L E **14. 1**   Hypothetical Reaction Time Data for a 2 × 2
Perceptual Experiment

Subject	Y_1	Y_2	Y_3	Y_4
	Noise Absent, 0° angle	*Noise Absent, 8° angle*	*Noise Present, 0° angle*	*Noise Present, 8° angle*
1	420	480	480	780
2	420	480	360	600
3	480	540	660	780
4	420	540	480	900
5	540	540	480	720
6	360	360	360	540
7	480	600	540	840
8	480	660	540	900
9	540	540	480	780
10	480	540	540	780
Mean	**462**	**528**	**492**	**762**

levels—absent and present. The other factor varied by the experimenter is where in the display the target letter appears. This factor, which is called "angle," also has two levels. The target letter is either shown at the center of the screen (where the subject has been told to fixate), or 8° off center (with the deviation from the center randomly varying between left and right). Table 14.1 presents hypothetical data for 10 subjects. As usual, the sample size is kept small to minimize the computational burden. The dependent measure is reaction time (or latency) measured in milliseconds. Each subject has four scores, one for each combination of the 2 × 2 design. In an actual perceptual experiment, each of these four scores would itself be the mean score for that subject across a number of trials in the particular condition.

The statistical questions to be addressed in this factorial design are precisely the same as those discussed in Chapter 7 for between-subjects factorial designs. In any two-way design, the questions typically of most interest are the significance of the two main effects and the interaction.[1] The effects to be tested are the same regardless of whether the factors are within- or between-subjects. Although the nature of the effects is the same, the way in which they are tested changes.

The three effects to be tested here are the main effect of angle (which we designate A), the main effect of noise (which we designate B), and the interaction of angle and noise. If we were interested in testing all three of these effects simultaneously, we could proceed along the lines of Chapter 13 by forming three D variables to be subjected to a multivariate test. However, because of our 2 × 2 design, we typically want a test of each effect considered separately. To conduct these tests, we still form D variables as in Chapter 13, but instead of testing all D variables simultaneously, we test each one individually. The only new aspect of the procedure is choosing how to form the D variables; in a sense, this is also not new because it follows the logic we developed in Chapter 7 for the meaning of main effects and interactions.

Formation of Main-Effect *D* Variables

To see how *D* variables are formed in a 2 × 2 within-subjects design, we first consider the angle main effect. As always, a main effect involves a comparison of marginal means, averaging over the other factor(s) in the design. As Table 14.2 shows, for our data the angle main effect compares the marginal mean of 477 (the average of 462 and 492) with the marginal mean of 645 (the average of 528 and 762). Of course, 477 and 645 are both averages of cell means. However, we could also average scores for each subject individually because the noise factor we need to average over is a within-subjects factor. For example, subject 1's average 0° score is 450, whereas his or her average 8° score is 630. This particular subject's reaction time averages 180 ms longer (630 versus 450) for the 8° angle condition than for the 0° angle condition. If the other 9 subjects' data show a similar pattern, we would infer that there is indeed a main effect due to angle. The first column of Table 14.3 (labeled D_1) shows these scores for all 10 subjects. Indeed, all 10 subjects have an average 8° reaction time that is slower than their average 0° reaction time. Such

T A B L E 14. 2 Cell Means and Marginal Means for Data in Table 14.1

		Angle		
		0°	8°	
Noise	Absent	462	528	495
	Present	492	762	627
		477	645	561

T A B L E 14. 3 Difference Scores for Data of Table 14.1

Subject	D_1	D_2	D_3
1	180	180	240
2	150	30	180
3	90	210	60
4	270	210	300
5	120	60	240
6	90	90	180
7	210	150	180
8	270	150	180
9	150	90	300
10	150	150	180
Mean	**168**	**132**	**204**

consistency strongly supports the existence of an angle main effect. Nevertheless, to develop formally the procedure for testing a main effect in the 2×2 design is important.

We will see that the basic logic of the hypothesis test in the two-way design is identical to the logic we used in Chapter 13 for the one-way design. The only new concept here is the creation of appropriate D variables. To understand how D variables are formed, let's consider how the D_1 scores in Table 14.3 were obtained. Recall that we averaged over the other factor (noise) and then found the difference between the average $8°$ score and the average $0°$ score for each individual subject. To represent this procedure in symbols, we will define the four original variables as follows:

$$Y_1 = \text{noise absent, } 0° \text{ angle reaction time}$$

$$Y_2 = \text{noise absent, } 8° \text{ angle reaction time}$$

$$Y_3 = \text{noise present, } 0° \text{ angle reaction time}$$

$$Y_4 = \text{noise present, } 8° \text{ angle reaction time}$$

Given this notation, D_{1i} is defined to be

$$D_{1i} = .5(Y_{2i} + Y_{4i}) - .5(Y_{1i} + Y_{3i}) \tag{1}$$

for the ith subject. Notice that D_{1i} is just the difference between the average $8°$ score and the average $0°$ score for subject i.

The null hypothesis for the angle main effect is that the population marginal means for the $0°$ and the $8°$ conditions are equal to one another. However, this is equivalent to stating that the difference in population marginal means equals zero. Thus, if the null hypothesis is true, the population mean of the D_1 variable will equal zero. As usual, we can test a null hypothesis that μ_1, the population mean of D_1, equals zero by comparing full and restricted models. The full model for the difference score allows μ_1 to be nonzero and is given by

$$D_{1i} = \mu_1 + \varepsilon_{1i} \tag{2}$$

The null hypothesis stipulates that $\mu_1 = 0$, which leads to a restricted model of the form

$$D_{1i} = 0 + \varepsilon_{1i} \tag{3}$$

or just

$$D_{1i} = \varepsilon_{1i} \tag{4}$$

As in the one-way design with two levels we considered at the beginning of Chapter 13, the error sums of squares for the full and restricted models are

$$E_F = \sum_{i=1}^{n} (D_{1i} - \bar{D}_1)^2 \tag{5}$$

$$E_R = \sum_{i=1}^{n} D_{1i}^2 \tag{6}$$

As usual, the general expression for the F statistic is given by

$$F = \frac{(E_R - E_F)/(df_R - df_F)}{E_F/df_F}$$

(7)

As we saw in Chapter 13, after substituting from Equations 5 and 6 and performing some simple algebra, the F statistic of Equation 7 can be simplified in this particular case to

$$F = n\bar{D}_1^2/s_{D_1}^2$$

(8)

From Table 14.3, $n = 10$, $\bar{D}_1 = 168$, and $s_{D_1}^2$ can be shown to equal 4240. The value of the F statistic then equals 66.57. The observed F is compared to a critical F with 1 and $n - 1$ degrees of freedom. For $\alpha = .05$, the critical F with 1 and 9 degrees of freedom is 5.12; thus, our observed F is easily significant at the .05 level, agreeing with our intuitive view of the D_1 scores in Table 14.3. Notice that, although we are taking the multivariate approach here, the test we performed is just a univariate test because the angle effect can be captured with a single D variable. We will consider the implications of the multivariate approach yielding a univariate test after we have considered the noise main effect and the angle × noise interaction.

The main effect for noise can be tested in exactly the same manner we tested the angle main effect. The only change is that the difference score we form now must reflect the noise effect instead of the angle effect. Specifically, we now want to average over the levels of angle and find the difference between the average score when noise is present and the average score when noise is absent. Thus, letting D_2 represent this noise effect, we have

$$D_{2i} = .5(Y_{3i} + Y_{4i}) - .5(Y_{1i} + Y_{2i})$$

(9)

Table 14.3 shows the D_{2i} scores for our 10 subjects. The test of significance is once again obtained by applying Equation 8 (using D_2 instead of D_1), which yields an F value of 45.37 for our data, which like the angle main effect is highly statistically significant.

Formation of Interaction D Variables

The final omnibus test is the angle × noise interaction. How can we obtain a D variable to represent the interaction? Recall that an interaction means that the effect of one factor (say, angle) is different at different levels of the other factor (here, noise). Thus, a measure of the magnitude of an interaction effect could be found by taking the difference between the angle effect when noise is present and the angle effect when noise is absent. To illustrate this idea, let's again consider the data for subject 1. We can see from Table 14.1 that when noise is present this subject responded 300 ms slower in the 8° condition than in the 0° condition. Thus, for this subject, the angle effect is 300 ms when noise is present. On the other hand, when noise is absent, this subject responded only 60 ms slower in the 8° condition than in the 0° condition. Thus, for this subject, the angle effect is 60 ms when Noise is absent. The difference between these two angle effects represents the magnitude of interaction. For this subject, the difference between the two angle effects is 240 (300 ms − 60 ms). At least for this subject, the angle effect is stronger when noise is present than when it is absent. The D_3 column of Table 14.3 shows these scores for all 10 subjects, and it is apparent that everyone in the sample shows a somewhat larger angle effect when noise is present than when noise is absent.

At this point, we need to consider more closely how D_3 scores were obtained. In symbols, D_3 can be written as

$$D_{3i} = (Y_{4i} - Y_{3i}) - (Y_{2i} - Y_{1i}) \tag{10}$$

Notice that $Y_{4i} - Y_{3i}$ is the angle effect (8° score minus 0° score) when noise is present. Similarly, $Y_{2i} - Y_{1i}$ is the angle effect (also 8° score minus 0° score) when noise is absent. Thus, D_{3i} is indeed the difference between the two angle effects. If the interaction null hypothesis is true, the population difference between the two angle effects equals zero. This hypothesis can be tested by once again applying Equation 8 (using D_3 instead of D_1), which yields an F value of 83.90 for our data, which again is highly statistically significant.

Two further points must be made regarding the D_3 variable. First, we defined D_3 as the difference between two angle effects, namely, the angle effect when noise is present minus the angle effect when noise is absent. However, our D_3 scores can also be conceptualized as the difference between two noise effects. To see why, notice from Equation 10 that D_3 can be rewritten as

$$D_{3i} = Y_{4i} - Y_{3i} - Y_{2i} + Y_{1i} \tag{11}$$

However, if we rearrange terms, the expression in Equation 11 is equivalent to

$$D_{3i} = (Y_{4i} - Y_{2i}) - (Y_{3i} - Y_{1i}).$$

But $Y_{4i} - Y_{2i}$ is the noise effect for the 8° angle condition, and $Y_{3i} - Y_{1i}$ is the noise effect for the 0° angle condition. Thus, D_3 can be thought of as either the difference between angle effects or the difference between noise effects. This equality follows from our initial discussion of the meaning of an interaction back in Chapter 7 on between-subjects factorial designs. Recall that we showed in Chapter 7 that an A × B interaction can be interpreted as implying that differences between levels of A vary at different levels of B, or equivalently that differences between levels of B vary at different levels of A. Second, seeing how the proper coefficients for D_3 can be obtained from the coefficients for D_1 and D_2 will be useful when either or both factors have more than two levels. Recall that D_{1i} was defined as

$$D_{1i} = .5(Y_{2i} + Y_{4i}) - .5(Y_{1i} + Y_{3i}) \tag{1, repeated}$$

It will be helpful to consider the coefficients for Y_{1i}, Y_{2i}, Y_{3i}, and Y_{4i} in that order, so we can rewrite D_{1i} as

$$D_{1i} = -.5Y_{1i} + .5Y_{2i} - .5Y_{3i} + .5Y_{4i}$$

To simplify our task a bit, we could replace all .5 values by 1.0 (in effect, doubling all the D_{1i} scores[2]) yielding

$$D_{1i} = -1Y_{1i} + 1Y_{2i} - 1Y_{3i} + 1Y_{4i} \tag{12}$$

Following the same procedure for D_{2i}, we can write D_{2i} as

$$D_{2i} = -1Y_{1i} - 1Y_{2i} + 1Y_{3i} + 1Y_{4i} \tag{13}$$

Finally, from Equation 11, we can write D_{3i} as

$$D_{3i} = \quad 1Y_{1i} - 1Y_{2i} - 1Y_{3i} + 1Y_{4i}$$

The coefficients for D_{3i}, the interaction difference score, are related to the coefficients of D_{1i} and D_{2i}, the two main-effect difference scores, by a simple rule. For example, to obtain the Y_{1i} coefficient for D_{3i}, we can multiply the Y_{1i} coefficient for D_{1i} (i.e., -1) times the Y_{1i} coefficient for D_{2i} (i.e., -1). Sure enough, -1 times -1 equals 1, the Y_{1i} coefficient for the D_{3i} variable. The same rule works for Y_{2i}, Y_{3i}, and Y_{4i}. Although the theory behind this principle is too advanced for our purposes (it involves something called Kronecker or direct products of matrices, which are described in such multivariate statistics textbooks as Bock, 1975, and Finn, 1974), the principle itself provides a handy rule for generating interaction difference variables from main-effect difference variables. As we said, we will see later that this rule is especially useful when one or both factors have more than two levels.

Relationship to Mixed-Model Approach

Although we could now consider simple-effects tests (the only potential follow-up tests in a 2 × 2 design—why?), we postpone consideration of all follow-up tests until we discuss the general $a \times b$ design. However, there is one further theoretical point that must be made, which applies only to the specific case of a 2 × 2 design. As we stated earlier, although by forming D variables we are following the principles of the multivariate approach to repeated measures, all our tests turn out to be univariate tests—that is, each of our three tests (angle main effect, noise main effect, and angle × noise interaction) turn out to involve a single D variable. The tests are all univariate because when both factors have only two levels, all three effects to be tested (A, B, and A × B) have only 1 numerator degree of freedom. The same F value that is produced by the multivariate approach is also produced by the mixed-model approach in a 2 × 2 design, provided that the mixed-model approach uses an error term of the form $MS_{effect \times S}$. The degrees of freedom are equivalent as well; thus, the multivariate and mixed-model approaches are literally identical to one another if all factors have only two levels. If this equivalence seems odd to you, remember from Chapter 12 that the sphericity assumption required in the mixed-model approach is necessarily satisfied for testing an effect with only 1 numerator degree of freedom. Thus, when all factors have only two levels, there is no need to debate the merits of the multivariate and mixed-model approaches. However, when some factors have more than two levels, the equivalence fails to hold, and relative merits must be considered. It is to the more general two-way within-subjects design that we now turn our attention.

MULTIVARIATE ANALYSIS OF TWO-WAY $a \times b$ WITHIN-SUBJECTS DESIGNS

Although the principles we have just developed for the 2×2 within-subjects design can also be applied to the more general $a \times b$ within-subjects design, the analysis of the $a \times b$ design is more complicated than the analysis of the 2×2, for two reasons. First, creation of appropriate D (difference) variables is slightly more complicated. As we will see, when a factor has more than two levels, not surprisingly more than one D variable must be formed. Second, because more than one D variable must be formed for each effect, the resulting tests are truly multivariate. As a consequence, we must once again concern ourselves with determinants of matrices, as we did in Chapter 13, for one-way designs.

To motivate our discussion of analyzing the $a \times b$ within-subjects design, we continue with the perceptual experiment example we have been considering. So far in this chapter, we have considered only a 2×2 version of this example because we omitted the $4°$ angle condition we originally included in Chapter 12. At this point, we reinstate this condition, so that we have a 2×3 design, just as we did in Chapter 12. Table 14.4 presents data for the 2×3 design. These data are identical to those presented in Table 12.1, to facilitate comparing results from the multivariate approach to those of the mixed-model approach.

Formation of Main-Effect D Variables

We assume that we are interested in testing the statistical significance of the two main effects and the interaction. As usual, the first step in the multivariate approach is to form D variables that correspond to the effects to be tested.

TABLE **14.4** Hypothetical Reaction Time Data for a 2×3 Perceptual Experiment

Subject	Noise Absent			Noise Present		
	$0°$ Angle	$4°$ Angle	$8°$ Angle	$0°$ Angle	$4°$ Angle	$8°$ Angle
1	420	420	480	480	600	780
2	420	480	480	360	480	600
3	480	480	540	660	780	780
4	420	540	540	480	780	900
5	540	660	540	480	660	720
6	360	420	360	360	480	540
7	480	480	600	540	720	840
8	480	600	660	540	720	900
9	540	600	540	480	720	780
10	480	420	540	540	660	780
Mean	462	510	528	492	660	762

We begin by considering the angle main effect. Because the angle factor has three levels, we have to form two D variables, just as we did in Chapter 13. Notice that the number of levels of the other factor (i.e., noise) has no effect on the number of D variables we need because each subject's angle-effect scores simply average across all levels of the noise factor. As usual, if we are only concerned with the omnibus main effect for angle, we can choose any two comparisons we want to represent the angle main effect.[3] However, because the angle factor is quantitative, we will form the two D variables to represent the linear and quadratic trends of angle, much as we did in Chapter 6 for between-subjects factors. With three levels, the coefficients for the linear trend are $-1, 0$, and 1, whereas those for the quadratic trend are $1, -2$, and 1 (see Appendix Table A.10). To apply these coefficients to our data in order to obtain scores on the linear and quadratic D variables, we must remember that because we are testing the angle main effect we have to average over the other factor in the design (i.e., noise). For example, the linear coefficients of -1, 0, and 1 need to be applied individually for each subject to that subject's average $0°$, $4°$, and $8°$ condition scores, respectively, where we have averaged over noise. Let's consider subject 1 (see Table 14.4). His or her average response time is 450 in the $0°$ condition, 510 in the $4°$ condition, and 630 in the $8°$ condition. Applying the coefficients of $-1, 0$, and 1 yields a value of 180 (notice that this value is simply the difference between the average $8°$ score and the average $0°$ score). It will be helpful to represent what we have done algebraically in symbols. We represent the six original scores as follows:

$$Y_1 = \text{noise absent, } 0° \text{ angle reaction time}$$

$$Y_2 = \text{noise absent, } 4° \text{ angle reaction time}$$

$$Y_3 = \text{noise absent, } 8° \text{ angle reaction time}$$

$$Y_4 = \text{noise present, } 0° \text{ angle reaction time}$$

$$Y_5 = \text{noise present, } 4° \text{ angle reaction time}$$

$$Y_6 = \text{noise present, } 8° \text{ angle reaction time}$$

Given this notation, we find subject 1's linear trend for angle by first averaging over levels of noise and then taking the difference between the $8°$ average score and the $0°$ average score. In terms of symbols, if we let D_{1i} represent the linear trend for angle, we have

$$D_{1i} = -1[.5(Y_{1i} + Y_{4i})] + 0[.5(Y_{2i} + Y_{5i})] + 1[.5(Y_{3i} + Y_{6i})] \qquad (14)$$

Notice that each term in brackets is an average reaction time for a particular level of the angle factor. For example, $.5(Y_{1i} + Y_{4i})$ is the average score for subject i in the $0°$ angle condition. Further notice that Equation 14 then applies the linear coefficients of $-1, 0$, and 1 to these average scores. Table 14.5 presents the D_1 scores for all 10 subjects. Following the same logic, if we let D_{2i} represent the quadratic trend for angle, we have

$$D_{2i} = 1[.5(Y_{1i} + Y_{4i})] - 2[.5(Y_{2i} + Y_{5i})] + 1[.5(Y_{3i} + Y_{6i})] \qquad (15)$$

T A B L E **14. 5** Difference Scores for Data of Table 14.4

Subject	D_1	D_2	D_3	D_4	D_5
1	180	60	180	240	0
2	150	−30	20	180	60
3	90	−30	240	60	−180
4	270	−150	220	300	−60
5	120	−180	40	240	120
6	90	−90	80	180	60
7	210	30	180	180	−180
8	270	−30	140	180	60
9	150	−150	100	300	−60
10	150	90	180	180	−180
Mean	**168**	**−48**	**138**	**204**	**−36**

Table 14.5 also presents the D_2 scores for all 10 subjects. To test the statistical significance of the angle main effect, we must test a null hypothesis that both D_1 and D_2 have population means of zero. We will see momentarily that this test is performed exactly as it was in Chapter 13. However, before considering this test, we will first finish our discussion of the formation of D variables.

The other main effect to be tested is the noise main effect. Not surprisingly, the way in which we form D variables for this main effect is exactly the same way in which we formed D variables for the angle main effect. Of course, now we average over angle, whereas before we averaged over noise. Notice that after we average over angle, we only have two scores for each subject—an average reaction time when noise is present and an average reaction time when noise is absent. The reason we have only two scores is because the noise factor has only two levels. As a result, we need to form only one D variable, which is simply defined as the difference between the average score when noise is present and the average score when noise is absent. In terms of symbols, if we let D_{3i} represent this difference score for the noise main effect, we have

$$D_{3i} = [\tfrac{1}{3}(Y_{4i} + Y_{5i} + Y_{6i})] - [\tfrac{1}{3}(Y_{1i} + Y_{2i} + Y_{3i})] \tag{16}$$

Notice that each term in brackets is an average score calculated over the levels of the angle factor. D_{3i} is simply the difference between the average score when noise is present (i.e., Y_{4i} through Y_{6i}) and the average score when noise is absent (Y_{1i} through Y_{3i}). Table 14.5 presents the D_3 scores for all 10 subjects.

Formation of Interaction D Variables

The final effect to be tested is the interaction of angle and noise. Although it would be fairly easy to develop the coefficients for the D variables intuitively in our rather simple 2×3 design, it is probably better to get some practice using the algorithm we developed in our discussion of the 2×2 design. Once we have obtained the coefficients, we will then develop an intuitive explanation of them.

Recall that to use the algorithm for generating interaction D variables, we must already have formed the main-effect D variables. In our case, we have three such D variables:

$$D_{1i} = -1[.5(Y_{1i} + Y_{4i})] + 0[.5(Y_{2i} + Y_{5i})] + 1[.5(Y_{3i} + Y_{6i})] \qquad \text{(14, repeated)}$$

$$D_{2i} = 1[.5(Y_{1i} + Y_{4i})] - 2[.5(Y_{2i} + Y_{5i})] + 1[.5(Y_{3i} + Y_{6i})] \qquad \text{(15, repeated)}$$

$$D_{3i} = [\tfrac{1}{3}(Y_{4i} + Y_{5i} + Y_{6i})] - [\tfrac{1}{3}(Y_{1i} + Y_{2i} + Y_{3i})] \qquad \text{(16, repeated)}$$

Remember that D_1 and D_2 represent the angle main effect, whereas D_3 represents the noise main effect. The algorithm is easier to use if we first rewrite the D variables so that the Y variables appear in order from Y_1 to Y_6 on the right-hand side of each equation. Reordering the Y variables and carrying out the appropriate multiplication in Equations 14–16 yields

$$D_{1i} = -.5Y_{1i} + 0Y_{2i} + .5Y_{3i} - .5Y_{4i} + 0Y_{5i} + .5Y_{6i} \qquad (17)$$

$$D_{2i} = .5Y_{1i} - 1Y_{2i} + .5Y_{3i} + .5Y_{4i} - 1Y_{5i} + .5Y_{6i} \qquad (18)$$

$$D_{3i} = -\tfrac{1}{3}Y_{1i} - \tfrac{1}{3}Y_{2i} - \tfrac{1}{3}Y_{3i} + \tfrac{1}{3}Y_{4i} + \tfrac{1}{3}Y_{5i} + \tfrac{1}{3}Y_{6i} \qquad (19)$$

Finally, we are less prone to mistakes if we express all coefficients for D_1, D_2, and D_3 as integers (i.e., whole numbers). We can accomplish this goal by multiplying the coefficients of D_1 by 2, D_2 by 2, and D_3 by 3, yielding:

$$D_{1i} = -1Y_{1i} + 0Y_{2i} + 1Y_{3i} - 1Y_{4i} + 0Y_{5i} + 1Y_{6i} \qquad (20)$$

$$D_{2i} = 1Y_{1i} - 2Y_{2i} + 1Y_{3i} + 1Y_{4i} - 2Y_{5i} + 1Y_{6i} \qquad (21)$$

$$D_{3i} = -1Y_{1i} - 1Y_{2i} - 1Y_{3i} + 1Y_{4i} + 1Y_{5i} + 1Y_{6i} \qquad (22)$$

Now that we have written the D variables in this form, creation of the interaction D variables will be easier. Recall that in the 2×2 design we obtained each coefficient of the interaction D variable by multiplying the corresponding coefficients of the two main-effect D variables. Our situation now is more complicated because we have more than two main-effect D variables. Instead we have a total of three: D_1 and D_2 for the angle effect and D_3 for the noise effect. In this situation, it turns out that we will create two interaction D variables. One comes from the product of D_1 and D_3 coefficients, and the other comes from the product of D_2 and D_3 coefficients. Carrying out this multiplication of coefficients of D_1 and D_3 yields

$$D_{4i} = 1Y_{1i} + 0Y_{2i} - 1Y_{3i} - 1Y_{4i} + 0Y_{5i} + 1Y_{6i} \qquad (23)$$

Similarly, multiplying the coefficients of D_2 and D_3 produces

$$D_{5i} = -1Y_{1i} + 2Y_{2i} - 1Y_{3i} + 1Y_{4i} - 2Y_{5i} + 1Y_{6i} \qquad (24)$$

Notice that in each case the sum of the coefficients equals zero; it can be shown that this must happen if the algorithm is applied correctly and is thus a useful check on one's arithmetic. The last two columns of Table 14.5 present scores on D_4 and D_5; do not worry if the numbers themselves do not mean much to you at this point.

As promised, we now develop an intuitive explanation of D_4 and D_5, beginning with D_4. Remember that D_4 was obtained by multiplying the coefficients of D_1, the linear angle variable, by the coefficients of D_3, the noise-effect variable. We can best understand the meaning of D_4 by rewriting Equation 23 in the following form:

$$D_{4i} = (-1Y_{4i} + 0Y_{5i} + 1Y_{6i}) - (-1Y_{1i} + 0Y_{2i} + 1Y_{3i}) \tag{25}$$

(You may want to convince yourself that Equation 25 is equivalent to Equation 23, by carrying out the subtraction in Equation 25.) The term in the first set of parentheses $(-1Y_{4i} + 0Y_{5i} + 1Y_{6i})$ is the linear trend for angle when noise is present. Similarly, the term in the second set of parentheses $(-1Y_{1i} + 0Y_{2i} + 1Y_{3i})$ is the linear trend for angle when noise is absent. Because the second set is subtracted from the first set, D_4 is the difference between the linear trend for angle when noise is present versus the linear trend when noise is absent. The fact that all 10 subjects have positive D_4 scores (see Table 14.5) implies that for every subject, the linear effect of angle is stronger when noise is present than when it is absent. Thus, D_4 represents one component (i.e., 1 degree of freedom) of the angle $\times$ noise interaction, namely, the interaction of noise with the linear trend for angle. Also, remember how we derived the coefficients for D_4. We multiplied the coefficients of D_1, the linear trend for the angle main effect, by the coefficients of D_3, the noise main effect. As we have just seen, the resultant coefficients produce a D variable that represents the interaction of D_1 and D_3, the two variables whose coefficients we multiplied. This correspondence turns out to be a general consequence of using our algorithm, which is one reason it proves to be so useful.

A similar meaning can be attached to D_5. We can rewrite Equation 24 as

$$D_{5i} = (1Y_{4i} - 2Y_{5i} + 1Y_{6i}) - (1Y_{1i} - 2Y_{2i} + 1Y_{3i}) \tag{26}$$

The term in the first set of parentheses is the quadratic trend for angle when noise is present, whereas the term in the second set of parentheses is the quadratic trend for angle when noise is absent. Because we are again taking the difference between the two sets, D_5 represents the interaction of noise with the quadratic trend for angle.

It is important to realize that D_4 and D_5 together collectively represent the interaction of angle and noise. In the general case of an $a \times b$ design, the interaction would have $(a - 1)(b - 1)$ degrees of freedom. In our example, $a = 3$ and $b = 2$, so the interaction has 2 degrees of freedom. The D_4 variable accounts for 1 degree of freedom and D_5 accounts for the other. Testing the two variables simultaneously in a multivariate test then constitutes a test of the interaction effect as a whole.

Before considering these multivariate tests, it is necessary to consider how the algorithm for constructing interaction D variables works when both factors have more than two levels. Recall that we originally illustrated the algorithm for a 2 $\times$ 2 design and then moved on to a 3 $\times$ 2 design. In each case, we multiplied the coefficients of variable(s) representing the A main effect by the coefficients of variable(s) representing the B main effect. In the general $a \times b$ design, there are $a - 1$ D variables for the A main effect and $b - 1$ D variables for the B main effect. The algorithm requires that the coefficients of each of the $a - 1$ variables be multiplied by the coefficients of each of the $b - 1$ variables, producing $(a - 1)(b - 1)$ D variables as a result. Not coincidentally, $(a - 1)(b - 1)$ is the number of degrees of freedom for the interaction. As in our examples, each individual interaction D variable accounts for 1 degree of freedom. The collection of $(a - 1)(b - 1)$ interaction D variables accounts for the omnibus A $\times$ B interaction.

Omnibus Tests—Multivariate Significance Tests

Now that we have learned how to form D variables in a two-way within-subjects design, we are in a position to see how these variables are used to perform F tests. Because we want to test three distinct hypotheses (viz., A main effect, B main effect, and A $\times$ B interaction), we must perform three F tests. Each test is based on the principles we developed in Chapter 13. In fact, each test is a straightforward application of Chapter 13 formulas with no modifications whatsoever. The only difference from Chapter 13 is that, instead of performing one simultaneous test of *all* our variables as we did in Chapter 13, we perform three tests here, each on a subset of our variables.

Let's begin by considering the A main effect. In general, we would have $a - 1$ D variables to represent this effect. The null hypothesis for the A main effect is equivalent to a null hypothesis that all $a - 1$ of these D variables have population means equal to zero. We can test this hypothesis just as we did in Chapter 13 by comparing a full model of the form

$$D_{vi} = \mu + \varepsilon_{vi}$$

to a restricted model of the form

$$D_{vi} = 0 + \varepsilon_{vi}$$

for each variable v. (NOTE: v is used here as an arbitrary placeholder to represent variable number v, reminding us that we will have as many pairs of full and restricted models as we have variables). Sums of squared errors and sums of cross-products are calculated just as they were in Chapter 13, once for the errors of the full model and once for the errors of the restricted model. As a result, we end up with two matrices: $E(F)$ for the full model and $E(R)$ for the restricted model. In general, each matrix is square, with $a - 1$ rows and $a - 1$ columns because we are testing the A main effect. The determinants of these two matrices can be used to compute an F statistic just as they were with Equation 13.20:

$$F = \frac{(|E(R)| - |E(F)|)/(df_R - df_F)}{|E(F)|/df_F} \tag{27}$$

For the A main effect, $a - 1$ parameters have been estimated in the full model; thus, $df_F = n - (a - 1) = n - a + 1$. No parameters have been estimated in the restricted model; thus, $df_R = n$. As a consequence, the F statistic for testing the A main effect is given by

$$F = \frac{(|E(R)| - |E(F)|)/(a - 1)}{|E(F)|/(n - a + 1)} \tag{28}$$

where $E(R)$ and $E(F)$ are the error matrices for the A main-effect D variables.

For the data in Table 14.4, we can compute $E(F)$ and $E(R)$ matrices for the D_1 and D_2 variables shown in Table 14.5. We will not go through the steps of these calculations because they are identical to the steps we showed in detail in Chapter 13. For this reason, we simply state that the error matrices for the full and restricted models for D_1 and D_2 are given by

$$E(F) = \begin{bmatrix} 38160 & 3240 \\ 3240 & 77760 \end{bmatrix}$$

$$E(R) = \begin{bmatrix} 320400 & -77400 \\ -77400 & 100800 \end{bmatrix}$$

The determinant of $E(F)$ equals 2,956,824,000, and the determinant of $E(R)$ equals 26,305,560,000. Substituting these values along with $n = 10$ and $a = 3$ into Equation 28 produces an F value of 31.59. With 2 and 8 degrees of freedom, the associated p value is .0002; thus, we can conclude that there is an angle main effect, using the .05 level of statistical significance.

Tests of the other two effects proceed in the same fashion. The only new wrinkle here is that because the noise factor has only two levels there is only one D variable (D_3) to represent the noise main effect. Nevertheless, Equation 27 can still be used because the determinant of a matrix with only one row and one column is defined to be equal to the single number that constitutes this matrix. For our data,

$$E(F) = [50760] \quad \text{and} \quad E(R) = [241200]$$

Substituting these values into Equation 27 produces an F value of 33.77, which implies a statistically significant noise main effect. In general, the F statistic for testing the B main effect would be given by

$$F = \frac{(|E(R)| - |E(F)|)/(b - 1)}{|E(F)|/(n - b + 1)} \tag{29}$$

where $E(R)$ and $E(F)$ are the error matrices for the B main-effect D variables.

The test of the interaction also follows the same logic and differs only in that matrices are formed for the interaction D variables (D_4 and D_5 in our data). In general, there are $(a - 1)(b - 1)$ such variables. The null hypothesis that there is no interaction is equivalent to a null hypothesis that all $(a - 1)(b - 1)$ of these D variables have population means equal to zero. This should seem reasonable because each individual interaction D variable accounts for 1 degree of freedom of the overall interaction. By testing all $(a - 1)(b - 1)$ interaction D variables simultaneously, we are therefore testing the overall A × B interaction. Once again, we use Equation 27 to perform this test. The specific form of the F statistic for testing the A × B interaction is given by

$$F = \frac{(|E(R)| - |E(F)|)/(a - 1)(b - 1)}{|E(F)|/n - [(a - 1)(b - 1)]} \tag{30}$$

where $E(R)$ and $E(F)$ are the error matrices for the interaction D variables. For our data, the value of the observed F equals 44.91, which with 2 and 8 degrees of freedom has an associated p value less than .001. Thus, the angle × noise interaction is significant at the .05 level, as were the angle main effect and the noise main effect.

Further Investigation of Main Effects

As usual, when statistically significant main effects are obtained, we may want to test comparisons of the marginal means. As we have discussed in earlier chapters, when the interaction is statistically significant, we should at the very least qualify our interpretation of the marginal means by making it explicit that they represent averages whose individual components are not different to the same extent across the other factor. We proceed with comparing marginal means in our numerical example primarily for pedagogical reasons; although depending on the precise purpose of the study, the marginal means might or might not truly be of interest, given the statistically significant interaction.

In our numerical example, statistically significant main effects were obtained both for noise and for angle. Because the noise factor has only two levels, no further tests are necessary for interpreting the nature of the noise main effect. On the other hand, the angle factor has three levels; thus, specific comparisons are likely to be useful for further understanding the angle effect.

As always, two things must be determined to test a comparison: an observed value and a critical value. The observed value of the test statistic for the multivariate approach to testing a main-effect comparison turns out to be extremely simple. All that must be done is to form a D variable whose coefficients correspond to the comparison to be tested. Then the significance test is a test of the null hypothesis that the population mean of this D variable equals zero. The formula for the observed value of the F statistic is just the same as it was in Chapter 13:

$$F = n\bar{D}^2/s_D^2 \qquad \text{(13.6, repeated)}$$

For example, suppose that we want to test the quadratic trend for the angle marginal means in our numerical example. The first step is to form an appropriate D variable. In fact, we have already performed this step because we earlier chose D_2 to represent the quadratic trend of angle. Recall that D_2 was defined as

$$D_2 = 1[.5(Y_{1i} + Y_{4i})] - 2[.5(Y_{2i} + Y_{5i})] + 1[.5(Y_{3i} + Y_{6i})] \quad \text{(15, repeated)}$$

Next, we must compute $\bar{D}_2$ and $s_{D_2}^2$ to use Equation 13.6. From Table 14.5, $\bar{D}_2 = -48$. Also from Table 14.5, we can show that $s_{D_2}^2 = 8640$. Substituting these values along with $n = 10$ into Equation 13.6 yields

$$F = 10(-48)^2/8640 = 2.67$$

as the observed F value for the quadratic trend of angle. It turns out that we have seen this observed F value before. We obtained an F of 2.67 for the quadratic angle trend in the mixed-model approach of Chapter 12 when we used a separate error term (Equation 12.7 instead of 12.6). We have more to say about how the multivariate and mixed-model approaches compare when we have finished our discussion of follow-up tests.

To judge the statistical significance of this observed F value, we must compare it to a critical value. The possible procedures are exactly the same here as they were in Chapter 13. The only difference is a possible change in notation. In Chapter 13, there was only one factor, with a levels. In this chapter, the a is replaced by b if we are testing comparisons of the B marginal means. No other changes are necessary because when we are comparing marginal means we have averaged over the other factor, effectively converting the two-way design into a one-way design for the purposes of the test.

The choice of an appropriate critical value depends on what other contrasts, if any, are being tested. One option is to set α_{PC} at a desired figure, in which case the critical F value is simply read from the F table with 1 numerator and $n-1$ denominator degrees of freedom. If a set of C planned comparisons is to be tested, α_{PC} for each contrast is adjusted to be equal to $.05/C$, using the Bonferroni technique. As we discussed in Chapter 13, the Bonferroni procedure is also appropriate for testing pairwise comparisons of marginal means in a two-way within-subjects design. Finally, for testing post hoc complex comparisons, the appropriate critical value comes from the multivariate extension of Scheffé's method developed by Roy and Bose. The formula is the same as that given in Equation 13.25, except that b replaces a when B marginal means are being compared. Thus, for tests involving comparisons of the A marginal means, the critical value is

$$CV = (n-1)(a-1)F_{\alpha_{FW};a-1,n-a+1}/(n-a+1) \qquad (31)$$

Similarly, for tests involving comparisons of the B marginal means, the CV is

$$CV = (n-1)(b-1)F_{\alpha_{FW};b-1,n-b+1}/(n-b+1) \qquad (32)$$

For our numerical example, the observed F value of 2.67 is nonsignificant, even using an α_{PC} of .05 because with 1 and 9 degrees of freedom the critical F at the .05 level equals 5.12. Of course, if additional contrasts were also being tested, the appropriate critical value would be even larger; thus, the quadratic trend for angle would remain nonsignificant.

Further Investigation of an Interaction—Simple Effects

As in other factorial designs, the most frequent approach for interpreting a statistically significant interaction in a two-way within-subjects design is to perform tests of simple effects. In our numerical example, we obtained a significant angle × noise interaction. A logical next step would be to test the angle effect at each noise level individually, as well as to test the noise effect at each individual level of angle.

As usual in the multivariate approach to repeated measures, the key to testing simple effects is to form appropriate D variables. To see how D variables are created, let's first consider the simple effect of noise at individual levels of angle. A D variable to test the effect of noise in the $0°$ angle condition would be given by $D_{6i} = Y_{4i} - Y_{1i}$, where Y_{4i} is a subject's reaction time when noise is present in the $0°$ angle condition and Y_{1i} is the same subject's reaction time when noise is absent in the $0°$ angle condition. We have labeled this simple-effect D variable D_6 because we have already formed five other D variables. (Be certain you understand that there is nothing special about the 6 designation here. We have used it simply to avoid confusion with the other five variables we have already formed.) Also notice that a single D variable suffices for testing the simple effect of noise in the $0°$ angle condition because noise has only two levels. As usual, an observed F can be computed from Equation 27:

$$F = \frac{(|\mathbf{E(R)}| - |\mathbf{E(F)}|)/(df_{\mathrm{R}} - df_{\mathrm{F}})}{|\mathbf{E(F)}|/df_{\mathrm{F}}} \qquad \text{(27, repeated)}$$

which simplifies to Equation 13.6 in the case of a single D variable:

$$F = n\bar{D}^2/s_D^2 \qquad \text{(13.6, repeated)}$$

Using either formula yields an F value of 1.55 for the noise effect in the $0°$ angle condition in our data. This F value is nonsignificant at the .05 level, even without a possible adjustment of the α level for any other simple-effects tests to be performed. Not suprisingly, this F value is precisely the same value that would be obtained if a one-way within-subjects analysis were performed using only the data from the $0°$ angle condition. Be certain to understand that in most situations we would also want to test the noise effect at the $4°$ and $8°$ angle conditions. Appropriate D variables for these two tests would be given by

$$D_{7i} = Y_{5i} - Y_{2i} \qquad \text{and} \qquad D_{8i} = Y_{6i} - Y_{3i}$$

respectively. For our data, both of these effects are considerably stronger than the noise effect in the $0°$ angle condition. The F values for noise at $4°$ and noise at $8°$ are 19.74 and 125.59, respectively. Thus, the data suggest that the effect of noise intensifies as the angle increases. We will see momentarily that interaction contrasts provide a more explicit method for testing this hypothesis.

Before we consider interaction contrasts, we should not forget that we would probably want to test the simple effect of angle at each noise level. The procedure is the same as we just saw for testing noise within levels of angle; the only difference is in the particular D variables we form. For example, let's consider the simple effect of angle when noise is absent. Because the angle factor has three levels, we must form two D variables to represent the angle effect. The particular choice of variables does not matter; thus, we continue to use linear and quadratic variables as our specific choice, just as we did earlier with D_1 and D_2. Indeed, the only change from D_1 and D_2 now that we are interested in simple effects is that we no longer want to average across levels of noise, as we did earlier (see Equations 14 and 15). Instead, we want to consider only one level of noise at a time. Thus, two appropriate D variables for testing the simple effect of angle when noise is absent are

$$D_{9i} = -1Y_{1i} + 0Y_{2i} + 1Y_{3i}$$
$$D_{10i} = 1Y_{1i} - 2Y_{2i} + 1Y_{3i}$$

Testing these two D variables simultaneously with Equation 27 provides a test of the simple effect of angle when noise is absent. For our data, the observed F value is 7.24, which with 2 and 8 degrees of freedom corresponds to a p value of .016.

Similarly, the simple effect of angle when noise is present can be tested by forming two other D variables:

$$D_{11i} = -1Y_{4i} + 0Y_{5i} + 1Y_{6i}$$
$$D_{12i} = 1Y_{4i} - 2Y_{5i} + 1Y_{6i}$$

Applying Equation 27 to these two D variables produces an observed F value of 45.07, which with 2 and 8 degrees of freedom corresponds to a p value of .001. As was the case for the simple effect of noise, these two F values for the simple effect of angle (7.24 and 45.07) are exactly the same values that would be obtained if one-way multivariate within-subjects analyses were performed using only the data from the relevant noise condition.

Yet one more set of tests would probably be conducted here because we obtained statistically significant simple effects for angle, which has three levels. All that we know so far is that angle has some kind of effect on reaction time, both when noise is absent and when it is present. To determine the nature of the angle effect, we need to test comparisons of individual cell means, within levels of the noise factor. Performing these tests is very straightforward with the multivariate approach. We begin by considering the angle effect when noise is absent. To test comparisons here, all we have to do is to test D_9 and D_{10} individually, instead of testing them simultaneously as we did to obtain our F value of 7.24. Because we are now testing D variables individually, Equation 27 again simplifies to Equation 13.6:

$$F = n\bar{D}^2/s_D^2 \qquad\qquad (13.6, \text{repeated})$$

For our data, the F value for D_9 is 12.24, whereas the F value for D_{10} is 0.53. Each has 1 and 9 (i.e., $n - 1$) degrees of freedom. Of course, we have to choose an appropriate critical value in accordance with whatever other contrasts we may also be testing. In particular, D_9 and D_{10} might not exhaust all contrasts of the angle factor we want to test, in which case more D variables would be formed and Equation 13.6 applied to them as well. A similar procedure would be used for probing the nature of the angle effect when noise is present.

Interaction Contrasts

As in other factorial designs, interaction contrasts provide an alternative to simple effects for investigating an interaction. As we pointed out in discussing the omnibus interaction test, in general there are $(a - 1)(b - 1)$ D variables that collectively represent the A × B interaction. Each individual D interaction variable represents a single degree of freedom of the A × B interaction and can be tested using Equation 13.6:

$$F = n\bar{D}^2/s_D^2 \qquad\qquad (13.6, \text{repeated})$$

Thus, the mechanics of the test are no different from the mechanics of other multivariate tests in repeated-measures designs. The only difference from other tests is the interpretation of the D variables.

This meaning can best be understood by returning to our numerical example. Recall from our earlier discussion of the omnibus interaction test that D_4 and D_5 collectively represent the omnibus interaction. The D_4 variable by itself represents the interaction of noise with the linear trend of angle. That is, D_4 represents the extent to which the linear trend for angle when noise is present is different from the linear trend for angle when noise is absent. The D_5 variable has a similar interpretation, except that it represents the interaction of noise with the quadratic trend for angle. Applying Equation 13.6 to our data yields an F value of 83.90 for D_4 and an F value of 1.00 for D_5. Each F has 1 numerator and 9 (i.e., $n-1$) denominator degrees of freedom.

As usual, the appropriate critical value against which to compare these observed F values depends on what other contrasts might be tested. At one extreme, we might use an α_{PC} of .05, in which case we would simply read the critical value from the F table. For our data, the critical value equals 5.12. Alternatively, if we planned to test C interaction contrasts, we would divide α_{FW} (typically .05) by C. Notice that C would often equal $(a-1)(b-1)$ because this is the number of degrees of freedom for the interaction; however, there is no reason that C must equal $(a-1)(b-1)$. Instead, C might be smaller than $(a-1)(b-1)$. For example, C would equal 1 if, before conducting the study, we could pinpoint a single interaction contrast to test. Of course, we would have to resist the possible temptation to test a few other "planned" contrasts after looking at the data. Alternatively, C could be larger than $(a-1)(b-1)$. Just as we might plan to test more than $a-1$ contrasts in a one-way design with a levels, we could also test more than $(a-1)(b-1)$ interaction contrasts. At some point, as C gets larger, the Bonferroni approach becomes less powerful than using a post hoc method. The appropriate critical value for post hoc tests of interaction contrasts again comes from the multivariate extension of Scheffé's method developed by Roy and Bose. This critical value for interaction contrasts is given by

$$CV = (n-1)(a-1)(b-1)F_{\alpha_{FW};(a-1)(b-1),n-[(a-1)(b-1)]}/(n-[(a-1)(b-1)]) \quad (33)$$

Notice that Equation 33 has the same general form as Equations 31 and 32. In fact, a more general expression of which all three equations (31, 32, and 33) are special cases is given by

$$CV = (n-1)(df_{\text{effect}})F_{\alpha_{FW};df_{\text{effect}},n-df_{\text{effect}}}/(n-df_{\text{effect}}) \quad (34)$$

Finally, we should state that for our data the test of D_4 is statistically significant even if tested post hoc, whereas the test of D_5 would be nonsignificant even if tested with an α_{PC} of .05. Thus, the noise by linear trend of angle variable appears to reflect an important component of the interaction. As Table 14.5 shows, the noise effect becomes stronger as the angle deviates from $0°$. In addition, the form of this strengthening appears to be linear.[4] In other words, the noise effect seems to grow stronger in direct proportion to the extent to which the level of the angle condition differs from $0°$.

The Relationship Between the Multivariate and the Mixed-Model Approaches

The multivariate and mixed-model approaches to analyzing data from two-way within-subjects designs relate to one another in a very similar manner to the way they are related for analyzing data from one-way designs, which we discussed in Chapter 13. To make the relationship between the two methods explicit, it is again necessary to work with orthonormal contrasts. Recall that orthonormal contrasts must be orthogonal and that the sum of squared coefficients for an orthonormalized contrast equals 1.0.

To develop the relationship between the two approaches, we again consider the data in Table 14.4. Recall that we formed five D variables to test the two main effects and the interaction. When we expressed the coefficients of these variables as integers, the equations for the five D variables were as follows:

$$D_{1i} = -1Y_{1i} + 0Y_{2i} + 1Y_{3i} - 1Y_{4i} + 0Y_{5i} + 1Y_{6i} \quad \text{(20, repeated)}$$

$$D_{2i} = 1Y_{1i} - 2Y_{2i} + 1Y_{3i} + 1Y_{4i} - 2Y_{5i} + 1Y_{6i} \quad \text{(21, repeated)}$$

$$D_{3i} = -1Y_{1i} - 1Y_{2i} - 1Y_{3i} + 1Y_{4i} + 1Y_{5i} + 1Y_{6i} \quad \text{(22, repeated)}$$

$$D_{4i} = 1Y_{1i} + 0Y_{2i} - 1Y_{3i} - 1Y_{4i} + 0Y_{5i} + 1Y_{6i} \quad \text{(23, repeated)}$$

$$D_{5i} = -1Y_{1i} + 2Y_{2i} - 1Y_{3i} + 1Y_{4i} - 2Y_{5i} + 1Y_{6i} \quad \text{(24, repeated)}$$

It can be shown that these contrasts are all orthogonal to each other—that is, they form an orthogonal set.[5] Thus, all that remains to be done is to normalize the coefficients of each contrast. As in Chapter 13, this is accomplished by dividing each nonnormalized coefficient by the square root of the sum of squared coefficients for that particular contrast. For example, because the sum of squared coefficients for D_1 is 4, we need to divide each nonnormalized coefficient by 2 (i.e., the square root of 4). Carrying out this process for all five D variables results in the following orthonormal set of D^* variables:

$$D_{1i}^* = -.5Y_{1i} + 0Y_{2i} + .5Y_{3i} - .5Y_{4i} + 0Y_{5i} + .5Y_{6i}$$

$$D_{2i}^* = .2887Y_{1i} - .5774Y_{2i} + .2887Y_{3i} + .2887Y_{4i} - .5774Y_{5i} + .2887Y_{6i}$$

$$D_{3i}^* = -.4082Y_{1i} - .4082Y_{2i} - .4082Y_{3i} + .4082Y_{4i} + .4082Y_{5i} + .4082Y_{6i}$$

$$D_{4i}^* = .5Y_{1i} + 0Y_{2i} - .5Y_{3i} - .5Y_{4i} + 0Y_{5i} + .5Y_{6i}$$

$$D_{5i}^* = -.2887Y_{1i} + .5774Y_{2i} - .2887Y_{3i} + .2887Y_{4i} - .5774Y_{5i} + .2887Y_{6i}$$

Remember that D_1^* and D_2^* represent the angle main effect, D_3^* represents the noise main effect, and D_4^* and D_5^* represent the interaction. For each test, there is a full matrix, denoted $\mathbf{E}^*(\mathbf{F})$, and a restricted matrix, denoted $\mathbf{E}^*(\mathbf{R})$. Computation of these matrices follows the same principles as were used in Chapter 13, so we do not bother with computational details here. Instead, we simply refer you to Table 14.6, which presents three $\mathbf{E}^*(\mathbf{F})$ and three $\mathbf{E}^*(\mathbf{R})$ matrices, one for each of the three effects being tested.

T A B L E **14. 6 E*(F)** and **E*(R)** Matrices for A Main Effect, B
Main Effect, and A × B Interaction

Effect	E*(F)	E*(R)
A	$\begin{bmatrix} 38{,}160.0 & -1{,}870.6 \\ -1{,}870.6 & 25{,}920.0 \end{bmatrix}$	$\begin{bmatrix} 320{,}400.0 & -44{,}686.9 \\ -44{,}686.9 & 33{,}600.0 \end{bmatrix}$
B	$[76{,}140]$	$[361{,}800]$
A × B	$\begin{bmatrix} 11{,}160.0 & 3{,}325.5 \\ 3{,}325.5 & 9{,}720.0 \end{bmatrix}$	$\begin{bmatrix} 115{,}200.0 & -7{,}274.6 \\ -7{,}274.6 & 10{,}800.0 \end{bmatrix}$

Comparing Table 14.6 to Table 12.5 shows that the same relationship holds here between the sum of the diagonal elements of an **E*** matrix in the multivariate approach and a sum-of-squares term in the mixed-model approach. For example, the sum of the two diagonal elements of **E*(F)** for the A main effect equals 64,080, which is equal to $SS_{A \times S}$ in the mixed-model approach. The sum of the two diagonal elements of **E*(R)** for the A main effect equals 354,000. Subtracting 64,080 from 354,000 yields 289,920, which is the value of SS_A in the mixed-model approach. The same type of equality holds for the B and the A × B effects. As a result, the mixed-model F for an effect can again be written in terms of the multivariate matrices as

$$F = \frac{\{tr(\mathbf{E^*(R)}) - tr(\mathbf{E^*(F)})\}/df_{\text{effect}}}{tr(\mathbf{E^*(F)})/(n-1)df_{\text{effect}}} \tag{35}$$

where $tr(\mathbf{E^*(R)})$ and $tr(\mathbf{E^*(F)})$ denote the trace (i.e., sum of diagonal elements) of the restricted and full matrices for the effect being tested. Notice that Equation 35 is a straightforward generalization of Equation 13.29, which we developed for a one-way within-subjects design:

$$F = \frac{(tr(\mathbf{E^*(R)}) - tr(\mathbf{E^*(F)}))/(a-1)}{tr(\mathbf{E^*(F)})/(n-1)(a-1)} \tag{13.29, repeated}$$

As in the one-way design, the mixed-model F test differs from the multivariate F test because the mixed-model F test is based on an assumption of sphericity. If the sphericity assumption is met, the population values of the off-diagonal elements of an **E*(F)** matrix are all zero. In addition, if sphericity holds, the population values of the diagonal elements of **E*(F)** are all equal to one another; thus, the sample mean of these values (i.e., $tr(\mathbf{E^*(F)})/df_{\text{effect}}$) is a good estimate of the single underlying population value. As we discussed in Chapter 12, sphericity may be met for some effects and yet fail for other effects, even in the same study. For example, the sphericity assumption is necessarily true for the B effect in our study because the B factor has only two levels. As a result, we only needed to form one D variable to capture the B main effect, and there are no off-diagonal elements in **E*(F)** for the

B main effect (see Table 14.6). Also, there is only one diagonal element of $\mathbf{E}^*(\mathbf{F})$; thus, equality of all diagonal elements need not be a concern. Not only is there no need to assume sphericity for the B effect here, but the mixed-model and multivariate approaches yielded exactly the same F value for the B main effect in our data. With both approaches, the F value was 33.77, with 1 and 9 degrees of freedom. Such an equality always occurs for all single degree of freedom effects, as long as $MS_{\text{effect} \times s}$ is used as the error term in the mixed-model approach.

It is also important to realize that the test of the B main effect in our example is valid even if compound symmetry fails to hold for the 6×6 matrix that would result from correlating scores in the six different conditions. Recall that compound symmetry requires that all correlations be equal to one another in the population. However, we have just argued that the sphericity assumption is always met for an effect with only 1 degree of freedom (as long as $MS_{\text{effect} \times s}$ is used as the error term), so sphericity and compound symmetry are different assumptions. It can be shown that compound symmetry implies sphericity—that is, if the compound symmetry assumption is met, the sphericity assumption is also met. However, the reverse is not always true because it is possible for sphericity to hold in the absence of compound symmetry.

Multivariate and Mixed-Model Approaches for Testing Contrasts

The relationship between the multivariate and mixed-model approaches for testing contrasts in the two-way within-subjects design is much the same as the relationship in the one-way design. For the same reasons as we discussed in Chapter 13, we recommend testing a contrast with an error term that corresponds specifically to that contrast. The formula for the F test of a contrast is given by

$$F = n\bar{D}^2/s_D^2 \qquad \text{(13.6, repeated)}$$

Notice that this formula for the F test is appropriate for testing both planned and post hoc comparisons.

The purpose of this section is to compare the mixed-model and multivariate approaches to testing contrasts in a two-way within-subjects design. As we discussed in Chapter 12, either of two error terms might be used for testing a within-subjects comparison. One approach uses a pooled error term (see, for example, Equations 12.6 and 12.10), whereas the second approach uses a separate error term (see, for example, Equations 12.7 and 12.11). As we have stated before, our preference is strongly in favor of the separate error term because it does not assume sphericity. The pooled error term, on the other hand, does assume sphericity, and F tests using the pooled error term are not robust to violations of sphericity.

If planned comparisons are tested, there is no need to perform an omnibus test. In this circumstance, it is not really meaningful to talk in terms of the multivariate or mixed-model approach because these are two approaches for conducting the omnibus test. Nevertheless, using a pooled error term for testing planned comparisons closely parallels the mixed-model approach to conducting the omnibus test because both assume sphericity. Using a separate error term, on the other hand, parallels the multivariate approach because neither assumes sphericity. When comparisons are tested in a post hoc fashion, there is an even stronger connection. The omnibus test is statistically significant with the mixed-model approach if and only if a statistically significant comparison can be found using a *pooled* error term and a critical value of the form

$$CV = (df_{effect})F_{\alpha_{FW}; df_{effect}, df_{effect \times S}}$$

where df_{effect} refers to the omnibus effect (for example, the A main effect). On the other hand, the omnibus test is statistically significant with the multivariate approach if and only if a statistically significant comparison can be found using a *separate* error term and a critical value of the form

$$CV = (n - 1)(df_{effect})F_{\alpha_{FW}; df_{effect}, n-df_{effect}}/(n - df_{effect}) \quad \text{(34, repeated)}$$

Thus, the use of a pooled error term is compatible with the mixed-model approach, and the use of a separate error term is compatible with the multivariate approach, just as was true in Chapter 13 for the one-way design. Once again, this is a major reason for preferring the multivariate approach to repeated measures.

Comparison of the Multivariate and Mixed-Model Approaches

The advantages and disadvantages of the multivariate and mixed-model approaches in the two-way within-subjects design are essentially the same as in the one-way design. Instead of repeating their relative merits here, we refer you to our earlier extended discussion of this issue at the end of Chapter 13. As before, our general recommendation is to use the multivariate approach unless sample sizes are very small. For a rough rule of thumb, for testing any within-subjects effect with the multivariate approach, n should probably exceed the degrees of freedom for the effect by at least 10.

ONE WITHIN-SUBJECTS FACTOR AND ONE BETWEEN-SUBJECTS FACTOR IN THE SAME DESIGN

A second type of factorial design with a within-subjects factor is the split-plot design, which contains a between-subjects factor as well as a within-subjects factor. Chapter 12 discussed several reasons for the importance of this design in the behavioral sciences.

We begin our discussion of this design by considering the same example that we analyzed in Chapter 12. Recall that in the example a perceptual psychologist is interested in age differences in reaction time on a perceptual task. As in Chapter 12, age is a between-subjects factor with two levels (young and old). The other factor in the design, angle, has three levels (0°, 4°, and 8°), which represent the position of the stimulus item in the subject's visual field. As in Chapter 12, angle is a within-subjects factor.

Split-Plot Design with Two Levels of the Repeated Factor

To simplify our initial consideration of the multivariate approach to split-plot designs, we begin with an example where the within-subjects factor has only two levels. The formulas we develop here serve primarily to illustrate the logic that can also be applied when the repeated factor has more than two levels. Table 14.7 presents the same data that we analyzed in Chapter 12 for 10 young subjects and 10 old subjects, except that for the moment we are only analyzing data from the 0° and 8° conditions of the angle factor.[6]

T A B L E **14. 7**   Reaction Time
Data for Young and Old Subjects
in the 0° and 8° Angle Conditions

Young Subjects	0°	8°
1	450	630
2	390	540
3	570	660
4	450	720
5	510	630
6	360	450
7	510	720
8	510	780
9	510	660
10	510	660
Mean	**477**	**645**
Old Subjects	**0°**	**8°**
1	420	690
2	600	810
3	450	690
4	630	780
5	420	780
6	600	870
7	630	870
8	480	720
9	690	900
10	510	810
Mean	**543**	**792**

In any two-factor design, the effects to be tested are typically the two main effects and the two-way interaction. In our example, then, we test the main effect of age (which we will designate as A), the main effect of angle (which we designate as B), and the interaction of age and angle.

Main Effect of Between-Subjects Factor. As usual, the multivariate approach to this within-subjects design requires that we create new transformed variables (e.g., D variables) to perform significance tests. To understand the nature of these variables in a split-plot design, we begin by considering the main effect of age, the between-subjects factor. As always, a main effect involves a comparison of marginal means, averaging over the other factor(s) in the design. For our data, we need to average over the angle factor. We can accomplish this quite easily for each subject, simply by averaging each subject's $0°$ score with his or her $8°$ score. To formalize this notion, we let

$Y_{1ij} = 0°$ angle reaction time   and $Y_{2ij} = 8°$ angle reaction time

for subject i in group j. Then, the average score for this subject is simply given by

$$M_{ij} = (Y_{1ij} + Y_{2ij})/2 \qquad (36)$$

The designation of M will be used here to remind us that we are computing a mean score for each subject. Notice that this M variable is similar to the D variables we have encountered previously in that both M and D are new, transformed variables that are linear combinations of the original Y variables. However, the M variable differs from these D variables in that D variables involve differences among the Ys, whereas M does not. Indeed, the coefficients assigned to the Ys have always summed to zero for all our D variables, but they obviously do not sum to zero for M. Whereas the D variables can be thought of as contrasts among the Y variables, the M variable is an average of all the Ys instead of a difference between them.

Table 14.8 presents the M scores for the 20 subjects whose Y scores were shown in Table 14.7. (Table 14.8 also shows D scores. Although you can probably guess how they were calculated, do not worry about them for the moment.) Now that we have calculated M scores for each subject, the test of the age main effect is straightforward. The sample marginal mean on M for the young subjects is 561 (see Table 14.8), which is simply the average reaction time for young subjects, where we have averaged over the $0°$ and $8°$ angle conditions. Notice that 561 is the average of 477 and 645, which were shown in Table 14.7 to be the mean reaction times for young subjects in the $0°$ and $8°$ angle conditions, respectively. Similarly, the value of the sample mean on M for the old subjects, 667.5, is the average of 543 and 792, the $0°$ and $8°$ angle means for old subjects. The test of the age main effect is simply a test of whether the two sample means on M are statistically significantly different from one another. We can answer this question by performing a one-way between-subjects ANOVA, using the M score for each subject as the dependent variable. Thus, this test is a straightforward application of the principles we developed in Chapter 3. Specifically, we can compare a full model to a restricted model, using the same models we used in Chapter 3. We write the full model as

$$M_{ij} = \mu + \alpha_j + \varepsilon_{ij} \qquad (37)$$

T A B L E **14. 8** M and D Scores for the Data in Table 14.7

Young Subjects	M	D
1	540	180
2	465	150
3	615	90
4	585	270
5	570	120
6	405	90
7	615	210
8	645	270
9	585	150
10	585	150
Mean	**561**	**168**
Old Subjects	**M**	**D**
1	555	270
2	705	210
3	570	240
4	705	150
5	600	360
6	735	270
7	750	240
8	600	240
9	795	210
10	660	300
Mean	**667.5**	**249**

where M_{ij} is the mean score on Y_1 and Y_2 for subject i in group j, μ is the grand mean parameter for M, α_j is the effect of the jth level of A (the between-subjects factor) on M, and ε_{ij} is the error associated with subject i in group j. As usual, the effect parameters α_j are defined so that $\alpha_j = \mu_j - \mu$, where μ_j is the population mean on the M variable for group j and μ is the grand mean, defined as $\mu = \sum \mu_j/a$. The null hypothesis to be tested for the A main effect implies that the α_j parameters all equal zero, leading to a restricted model given by

$$M_{ij} = \mu + \varepsilon_{ij} \tag{38}$$

The full and restricted models are compared using least-squares estimates of the parameters in each model, which yields our usual F test:

$$F = \frac{(E_R - E_F)/(df_R - df_F)}{E_F/df_F}$$

Because we are performing a 1-way between-subjects ANOVA with M as the dependent variable, we can simplify the expression for the F statistic just as we did in Chapter 3:

$$F = \frac{\sum_{j=1}^{a} n_j(\overline{M}_j - \overline{M})^2/(a - 1)}{\sum_{j=1}^{a} \sum_{i=1}^{n_j} (M_{ij} - \overline{M}_j)^2/(N - a)} \tag{39}$$

where $\overline{M}_j$ and $\overline{M}$ are the mean for the jth group and the grand mean, respectively, and N is the total number of subjects summed over the levels of the between-subjects factor. In our example, $N = 20$, because $n_1 = 10$ and $n_2 = 10$. We also have (see Table 14.8) $\overline{M}_1 = 561$, $\overline{M}_2 = 667.5$, $\overline{M} = 614.25$, and $\sum_{j=1}^{a} \sum_{i=1}^{n_j} (M_{ij} - \overline{M}_j)^2 = 110452.5$. Substituting these values into Equation 39 yields an F value of 9.24 with 1 and 18 degrees of freedom. The corresponding p value is .007; thus, the age main effect is statistically significant at the .05 level. We postpone a more general discussion of the between-subjects main effect until we consider a design with more than two levels of the within-subjects factor.

Within-Subjects Effects. Notice that the age main effect here is a between-subjects effect because it averages over the within-subjects factor. The other two effects yet to be tested, the angle main effect and the age × angle interaction, are within-subjects effects because both involve the difference between scores in the 0° angle condition and the 8° angle condition. Indeed, consistent with the multivariate approach to repeated measures, both of these effects are tested by forming D variables. Because in our example, angle has only two levels, a single D variable is sufficient to represent the angle effect:

$$D_{ij} = Y_{2ij} - Y_{1ij} \tag{40}$$

where Y_{2ij} is the 8° angle reaction time and Y_{1ij} is the 0° angle reaction time for subject i in group j. (We could just as easily have defined D_{ij} to be $Y_{1ij} - Y_{2ij}$. The F values would be identical either way.) The right-most column of Table 14.8 shows the D scores calculated from Table 14.7 for our 20 subjects.

Before proceeding with a formal test, let's pause momentarily to think intuitively about what the D scores in Table 14.8 mean. One striking characteristic of these D scores is that all 20 subjects have a positive D value. This is important because it means that every subject's reaction time was longer in the 8° angle condition than in the 0° angle condition, which strongly suggests the presence of an angle main effect. As always, the main effect averages over the other factor(s) in the design. Thus, the angle main effect should average over the two age groups instead of comparing them. The angle main-effects test should be a test of whether the average D score differs significantly from zero, when we average over both age groups. The other effect to be tested is the age × angle interaction. Unlike the angle main effect, the interaction does involve a comparison of the age groups because the interaction is a measure of whether the angle effect differs for the different age groups. It is important to realize that the D score we have calculated is a measure of the angle effect for each subject. To the extent that these D scores tend to be larger for some age groups than for others, an interaction is indicated. We can see from Table 14.8 that in our example the angle effect tends to be larger for old subjects than for young subjects. At this point, you should have some intuitive feeling that the D scores are useful for answering two questions. First, the average of all the D scores seems related to the angle main effect. Second, the difference between the D scores for old and young subjects seems related to the age × angle interaction. We now show how formal tests can be developed from these relationships.

Notice from Table 14.8 that we have a one-way between-subjects design for the D variable, just as we had for the M variable. As a result, we can again write a full model of the form

$$D_{ij} = \mu + \alpha_j + \varepsilon_{ij} \tag{41}$$

where D_{ij} is the difference between Y_2 and Y_1 for subject i in group j, μ is the grand mean parameter for D, α_j is the effect of the jth level of A (the between-subjects factor) on D, and ε_{ij} is the error associated with subject i in group j. It is extremely important to realize that the μ and α_j terms of Equation 41 generally have different values from the μ and α_j terms of Equation 37 because in one case the dependent variable is D, whereas in the other case it is M. In other words, the two equations have the same form because both are full models for one-way between-subjects designs; however, the numerical values of the parameters and the parameter estimates will generally differ in the two equations because the dependent variables are different. The parameters in Equation 41 are defined in the usual manner, so that $\alpha_j = \mu_j - \mu$, where μ_j is the population mean on the D variable for group j, and μ is the grand mean on the D variable. We define the grand mean μ to be $\mu = \sum_{j=1}^{a} \mu_j/a$. However, an alternate definition might be used with unequal n, where μ could be defined as $\mu = \sum_{j=1}^{a} n_j\mu_j/N$. The distinction is that the first definition yields an unweighted mean and the second yields a weighted mean. Of course, with equal n, the two definitions are equivalent.[7]

Test of the Interaction. Recall from our intuitive discussion that we need to perform two tests on the D variable. The angle main effect is a test of the average value of D, averaging over A. The age × angle interaction is a test of whether the average D value differs at different levels of A. We consider both of these tests, beginning with the interaction. If there is no interaction in the population, then the two age groups should show the same mean effect for angle. Recall that D represents the angle effect. Thus, if there is no interaction, the two age groups should show no mean difference on D. In other words, if the null hypothesis is true that there is no interaction, the α_j parameters all equal zero. An appropriate restricted model is given by

$$D_{ij} = \mu + \varepsilon_{ij} \tag{42}$$

The F test from Chapter 3 can be used to compare the full model of Equation 41 to the restricted model of Equation 42. Analogous to the F test on the M variable (Equation 39), the F test for the interaction is given by[8]

$$F = \frac{\sum_{j=1}^{a} n_j(\bar{D}_j - \bar{D})^2/(a-1)}{\sum_{j=1}^{a} \sum_{i=1}^{n_j} (D_{ij} - \bar{D}_j)^2/(N-a)} \tag{43}$$

Substituting the values from Table 14.8 along with $\bar{D} = 208.5$ and $\sum\sum(D_{ij} - \bar{D}_j)^2 = 67,050$ into Equation 43 yields an F value of 8.81, with 1 and 18 degrees of freedom. The corresponding p value is .008; thus, the age $\times$ angle interaction is statistically significant at the .05 level. From Table 14.8, we can see that the angle effect is stronger for old subjects ($\bar{D}_2 = 249$) than for young subjects ($\bar{D}_1 = 168$). We postpone a discussion of follow-up tests for the interaction until we consider a design with more than two levels of the within-subjects factor.

Within-Subjects Main Effect.   The one remaining omnibus effect to be tested is the within-subjects main effect, that is, the angle main effect in our example. We argued earlier that an angle main effect would be reflected in the average D score, averaging over age groups. Specifically, the grand mean of D should be statistically different from zero if there is an angle main effect. On the other hand, if there is no angle main effect in the population, then the population grand mean of D equals zero. The population grand mean of D is represented by μ in the full model of Equation 41. Thus, if the null hypothesis is true that there is no angle main effect, μ equals zero. An appropriate restricted model is given by

$$D_{ij} = \alpha_j + \varepsilon_{ij} \tag{44}$$

Our task at this point is to compare this restricted model of Equation 44 to the full model of Equation 41. We already know that the full model is equivalent to a cell means model; thus, the full model predicts each subject's score to be the mean score of that subject's group, that is, $\hat{D}_{ij}(F) = \bar{D}_j$. As a result, the sum of squared errors for the full model equals

$$E_F = \sum_{j=1}^{a} \sum_{i=1}^{n_j} [D_{ij} - \hat{D}_{ij}(F)]^2$$

$$= \sum_{j=1}^{a} \sum_{i=1}^{n_j} (D_{ij} - \bar{D}_j)^2 \tag{45}$$

We must now consider the sum of squared errors for the restricted model of Equation 44, which is a model unlike any other we have considered previously in this book because it has no grand mean term. For this reason, we consider the sum of squared errors for this model in considerable detail. It is crucial to remember that the α_j parameters are not independent of one another. Recall that α_j is defined as $\alpha_j = \mu_j - \mu$. As a result,

$$\sum_{j=1}^{a} \alpha_j = \sum_{j=1}^{a} (\mu_j - \mu) = \sum_{j=1}^{a} \mu_j - \sum_{j=1}^{a} \mu = \sum_{j=1}^{a} \mu_j - a\mu$$

However, $\mu = \sum_{j=1}^{a} \mu_j/a$, so

$$\sum_{j=1}^{a} \alpha_j = \sum_{j=1}^{a} \mu_j - a\left(\sum_{j=1}^{a} \mu_j/a\right)$$

$$= \sum_{j=1}^{a} \mu_j - \sum_{j=1}^{a} \mu_j = 0$$

Thus, the individual α_j values are constrained to sum to zero.[9] In the case of two levels of A such as in our example, it follows that $\alpha_2 = -\alpha_1$. In general, the implication is that we have only $a - 1$ independent α_j parameters. This is all relevant because we must find the least-squares estimates of the α_j parameters in Equation 44. Because the α_j parameters are constrained to sum to zero, it is necessary to use constrained least squares to obtain parameter estimates. Because this approach is too advanced for our level, we simply state without proof that the constrained least-squares estimator for α_j in Equation 44 turns out to be $\hat{\alpha}_j = \bar{D}_j - \bar{D}$.[10]

Notice that the sum of these parameter estimates—that is, $\sum_{j=1}^{a} \hat{\alpha}_j$—is guaranteed to obey the constraint of summing to zero. For example, in our data, we know that $\bar{D}_1 = 168$ and $\bar{D}_2 = 249$ from Table 14.8. Thus, $\bar{D} = 208.5$, and the values of the parameter estimates are

$$\hat{\alpha}_1 = 168 - 208.5 = -40.5$$

$$\hat{\alpha}_2 = 249 - 208.5 = 40.5$$

It can be shown that any other pair of values that sums to zero results in a larger sum of squares than the values of -40.5 and 40.5. In general, the restricted model of Equation 44 predicts each subject's score to be equal to $\hat{\alpha}_j$, that is,

$$\hat{D}_{ij}(\text{R}) = \hat{\alpha}_j = \bar{D}_j - \bar{D}$$

As a result, the sum of squared errors for the restricted model equals

$$E_R = \sum_{j=1}^{a} \sum_{i=1}^{n_j} [D_{ij} - \hat{D}_{ij}(\text{R})]^2$$

$$= \sum_{j=1}^{a} \sum_{i=1}^{n_j} [D_{ij} - (\bar{D}_j - \bar{D})]^2$$

To obtain a more workable form of E_R, it is helpful to rewrite E_R as

$$E_R = \sum_{j=1}^{a} \sum_{i=1}^{n_j} [(D_{ij} - \bar{D}_j) + \bar{D}]^2$$

Expanding the square of this expression, we get

$$E_R = \sum_{j=1}^{a} \sum_{i=1}^{n_j} (D_{ij} - \bar{D}_j)^2 + 2 \sum_{j=1}^{a} \sum_{i=1}^{n_j} (D_{ij} - \bar{D}_j)\bar{D} + \sum_{j=1}^{a} \sum_{i=1}^{n_j} \bar{D}^2$$

However, this expression can be simplified in two ways. First, the middle term equals zero because $\bar{D}$ is a constant and can be factored out. We are then left with each subject's deviation from the group mean, which equals zero within each group. Second, the far right term equals $N\bar{D}^2$, where N is total sample size. This follows because $\bar{D}^2$ is a constant for every subject. Thus, we can rewrite E_R as

$$E_R = \sum_{j=1}^{a} \sum_{i=1}^{n_j} (D_{ij} - \bar{D}_j)^2 + N\bar{D}^2$$

However, from Equation 45, we know that

$$\sum_{j=1}^{a} \sum_{i=1}^{n_j} (D_{ij} - \bar{D}_j)^2 = E_F$$

so that

$$E_R = E_F + N\bar{D}^2$$

which means that the difference in the error sums of squares of the restricted and full models is given by

$$E_R - E_F = N\bar{D}^2 \tag{46}$$

To be certain that you don't miss the forest because of the trees, what all of the preceding algebra has shown is that the sum of squares for the angle main effect equals $N\bar{D}^2$. For our data, $N = 20$ and $\bar{D} = 208.5$, so the sum of squares for the angle main effect equals 869,445. This expression for the sum of squares of the witnin-subjects main effect should seem reasonable to you even if you had trouble under-standing the algebraic derivation. Notice that $\bar{D}^2$ is large anytime $\bar{D}$ differs substan-tially from zero, either positively or negatively. However, we argued earlier that it is just such a departure of $\bar{D}$ from zero that indicates an angle main effect. The presence of N in the formula should also seem reasonable because $\bar{D}$, the difference in the marginal means of the within-subjects factor, is based on N subjects.

Now that we have found the expression for the difference in the sum of squared errors of the restricted and full models, we can easily write the expression for the F test of the angle main effect. Recall that the general form of the F statistic is given by

$$F = \frac{(E_R - E_F)/(df_R - df_F)}{E_F/df_F}$$

From Equation 46, we know that

$$E_R - E_F = N\bar{D}^2$$

From Equation 45, we know that

$$E_F = \sum_{j=1}^{a} \sum_{i=1}^{n_j} (D_{ij} - \bar{D}_j)^2$$

All that remains is to determine the degrees of freedom of the two models. As we showed earlier, in general the restricted model has $a - 1$ independent parameters, so its degrees of freedom equal $N - (a - 1)$, or $N - a + 1$. The full model has a parameters, so its degrees of freedom equal $N - a$. Of course, then, $df_R - df_F = 1$. This is logical because the restricted model has one fewer parameter (namely, μ) than the full model. Thus, the F statistic for the within-subjects main effect equals

$$F = \frac{N\bar{D}^2}{\sum_{j=1}^{a} \sum_{i=1}^{n_j} (D_{ij} - \bar{D}_j)^2/(N - a)} \tag{47}$$

with 1 and $N - a$ degrees of freedom.[11] For our data, the observed value of the F statistic equals 233.41, with 1 and 18 degrees of freedom, which is obviously highly statistically significant. As we suspected from a visual inspection of the D scores in Table 14.8, subjects responded significantly more slowly in the 8° angle condition than in the 0° angle condition. One final point will be helpful to us later when we consider split-plot designs with more than two levels of the within-subjects factor. Notice that the denominator terms of Equations 43 and 47 are identical. This means that the error term for the interaction test is identical to the error term for the within-subjects main-effects test. The reason for this equivalence is that both tests use the model shown in Equation 41 as the full model, and the full model comprises the denominator of the F test. As you may recall, this equivalence also parallels an equivalence of error terms in the mixed-model approach, where $MS_{B \times S/A}$ was used as the error term for testing both the B and A × B effects.

Summary. Thus, Equations 39, 43, and 47 provide F tests for the multivariate approach to the between-subjects main effect, the interaction, and the within-subjects main effect, respectively, in a split-plot design where the repeated factor has only two levels. Although these equations have some intrinsic merit, they are useful primarily as building blocks for split-plot designs where the repeated factor has more than two levels. The reasons these equations are not especially interesting in and of themselves is that when the repeated factor has only two levels, the F tests of the multivariate approach are equivalent to those of the mixed-model approach. Thus, when the repeated factor has only two levels, Equation 12.15 is equivalent to Equation 13.39, Equation 12.16 is equivalent to Equation 13.47, and Equation 12.17 is equivalent to Equation 13.43. The reason for this equivalence is that, as we have seen before, when the repeated factor has only two levels, the sphericity assumption is necessarily satisfied. However, when the repeated factor has three or more levels, sphericity may or may not hold. Whether it does or does not, the multivariate and mixed-model approaches are no longer equivalent. Although Equations 43 and 47 no longer apply when the repeated factor has three or more levels, the logic behind the comparison of models is still relevant. The only complication (admittedly, not a minor one) is that we need more than one D variable, requiring us again to formulate matrices in order to arrive at F tests.

General $a \times b$ Split-Plot Design

Although the principles developed in the previous section for the split-plot design with two levels of the repeated factor can also be applied when the repeated factor has more than two levels, the actual analysis is more complicated. We saw that when the repeated factor has two levels, we form two new variables. One of these variables, which we designate M, is a subject's mean score and is used to test the between-subjects main effect. The other variable, which we designate D, is the difference between the subject's two original scores and is used to test the two within-subjects effects (i.e., the within-subjects main effect and the two-way interaction). Although we have two variables (M and D), the multivariate approach can be carried out with univariate tests when there are only two levels of the repeated factor because we do not test M and D simultaneously. However, when the repeated factor has more than two levels, the within-subjects tests of the multivariate approach are truly multivariate. The reason is that it is necessary to form more than one D variable and these multiple D variables are tested simultaneously, much as we did in Chapter 13 and earlier in this chapter.

To make our discussion of analyzing the $a \times b$ split-plot design easier to follow, we continue with our perceptual experiment. So far in our discussion of the multivariate approach to the split-plot design, we have considered the data in Table 14.7, which omitted the 4° angle condition. At this point, we reinstate the 4° condition so that we have a 2 × 3 design, where it is the repeated factor that has three levels.

T A B L E 14. 9 Reaction Time Data for
Young and Old Subjects in Three Angle
Conditions

Young Subjects	0°	4°	8°
1	450	510	630
2	390	480	540
3	570	630	660
4	450	660	720
5	510	660	630
6	360	450	450
7	510	600	720
8	510	660	780
9	510	660	660
10	510	540	660
Mean	**477**	**585**	**645**
Old Subjects	**0°**	**4°**	**8°**
1	420	570	690
2	600	720	810
3	450	540	690
4	630	660	780
5	420	570	780
6	600	780	870
7	630	690	870
8	480	570	720
9	690	750	900
10	510	690	810
Mean	**543**	**654**	**792**

Table 14.9 presents data for the 2×3 design. These data are identical to those analyzed in Chapter 12 (see Tables 12.7 and 12.15) to facilitate comparisons of the multivariate approach and the mixed-model approach.

Between-Subjects Main Effect.   We will assume that we are interested in testing the two main effects and the interaction. As usual, the first step in the multivariate approach to the $a \times b$ split-plot design is to create new, transformed variables. As in the design we considered earlier with only two levels of the repeated factor, we begin by computing a variable to represent each subject's mean score across the levels of the within-subjects factor. We adopt the following notation:

$$Y_{1ij} = 0° \text{ angle reaction time}$$

$$Y_{2ij} = 4° \text{ angle reaction time}$$

$$Y_{3ij} = 8° \text{ angle reaction time}$$

for subject i in group j. For our data, each subject's mean score is simply calculated as

$$M_{ij} = (Y_{1ij} + Y_{2ij} + Y_{3ij})/3.$$

Regardless of the number of levels of the within-subjects factor or of the between-subjects factor, only one M variable is formed. With b levels of the within-subjects factor, the formula for M is

$$M_{ij} = \sum_{k=1}^{b} Y_{kij}/b \tag{48}$$

where Y_{kij} designates the score for subject i in group j at level k of the repeated factor. Indeed, only one M variable is formed even if there is more than one within-subjects factor and/or more than one between-subjects factor. After all, a subject's average score can always be represented by one number, namely, the mean of all of his or her scores. More technically, M is used to test between-subjects effects, which by their very nature average over *all* within-subjects factors. Thus, in any design with one or more between-subjects factors and one or more within-subjects factors, we always form one M variable, which represents each subject's mean score averaged over every score for that subject.[12]

Table 14.10 presents the M score for each of the 20 subjects whose Y scores were shown in Table 14.9. (Table 14.10 also presents scores on D_1 and D_2, to be discussed later.) We can test the age main effect by performing a one-way between-subjects ANOVA with M as the dependent variable. The equation for the observed F value is the same as it was when the repeated factor (i.e., angle) had only two levels:

$$F = \frac{\sum_{j=1}^{a} n_j(\overline{M}_j - \overline{M})^2/(a-1)}{\sum_{j=1}^{a} \sum_{i=1}^{n_j} (M_{ij} - \overline{M}_j)^2/(N-a)} \tag{39, repeated}$$

Substituting the values from Table 14.10 into Equation 39 yields an F value of 7.28 with 1 and 18 degrees of freedom. The corresponding p value is .0147; thus, the age main effect is statistically significant at the .05 level.

Before considering the other two effects to be tested, we want to compare the F value we obtained here with the F value we obtained in Chapter 12 using the mixed-model approach for these same data. Looking back at Table 12.19 shows that the mixed-model approach also yielded an F value of 7.28 with 1 and 18 degrees of freedom for the age main effect. The multivariate and mixed-model approaches are equivalent here because the age main effect is a between-subjects effect. To test this effect, we have averaged over the within-subjects factor, leaving us with a between-subjects design. The multivariate and mixed model approaches differ only in tests involving the within-subjects effect (i.e., tests involving angle). Notice that this equivalence is also consistent with our discussion of assumptions in Chapter 12 because we stated there that the sphericity assumption is not required for testing the between-subjects main effect. Thus, it is unnecessary to choose between the multivariate and mixed-model approaches for testing between-subjects effects in split-plot designs, because they always yield equivalent results for these effects.

TABLE **14. 10** M, D_1, and D_2 Scores for
the Data in Table 14.9

Young Subjects	M	D_1	D_2
1	530	180	60
2	470	150	−30
3	620	90	−30
4	610	270	−150
5	600	120	−180
6	420	90	−90
7	610	210	30
8	650	270	−30
9	610	150	−150
10	570	150	90
Mean	$\bar{M}_1 = 569$	$\bar{D}_{11} = 168$	$\bar{D}_{21} = -48$

Old Subjects	M	D_1	D_2
1	560	270	−30
2	710	210	−30
3	560	240	60
4	690	150	90
5	590	360	60
6	750	270	−90
7	730	240	120
8	590	240	60
9	780	210	90
10	670	300	−60
Mean	$\bar{M}_2 = 663$	$\bar{D}_{12} = 249$	$\bar{D}_{22} = 27$

Within-Subjects Effects.   Not surprisingly, the multivariate approach does not yield the same results as the mixed-model approach for testing the within-subjects main effect or the interaction when the repeated factor has more than two levels. To test within-subjects effects with the multivariate approach, it is necessary to form D variables. As usual, if the repeated factor has b levels, $b-1$ D variables must be created. In our example, angle has three levels, so we must form two D variables. The choice of the two variables does not matter for the omnibus test (you may recall our demonstration of this fact in Chapter 13). However, it is convenient to form D variables to represent specific comparisons we may wish to test of the repeated factor. Because the angle factor in our example is quantitative, we choose D_1 and D_2 to represent the linear and quadratic trends for angle, respectively. With three levels, from Appendix Table A.10, the coefficients of the linear trend are -1, 0, and 1, and those of the quadratic trend are 1, -2, and 1. Thus, in terms of our original Y variables, D_1 and D_2 are defined as

$$D_{1ij} = -1Y_{1ij} + 0Y_{2ij} + 1Y_{3ij}$$

$$D_{2ij} = 1Y_{1ij} - 2Y_{2ij} + 1Y_{3ij}$$

where Y_{1ij}, Y_{2ij}, and Y_{3ij} are the $0°$, $4°$, and $8°$ angle reaction times, respectively, for subject i in group j. Notice that D_{1ij} could be rewritten simply as the difference between the $8°$ and the $0°$ scores for each subject: $D_{1ij} = Y_{3ij} - Y_{1ij}$. Table 14.10 presents D_1 and D_2 scores for each of our 20 subjects.

The tests of the angle main effect and the age $\times$ angle interaction proceed much as they did when the angle factor had only two levels. The only difference is that we now have two D variables to be analyzed simultaneously, whereas before we had only one D variable. As a result, we must consider full and restricted matrices for our data, instead of just full and restricted sums of squared errors.

Recall that when we had only one D variable, we formed a full model of the form

$$D_{ij} = \mu + \alpha_j + \varepsilon_{ij} \qquad\qquad (41, \text{repeated})$$

With two D variables, we need one full model for D_1 and a second full model for D_2. These full models are given by

$$D_{1ij} = \mu_1 + \alpha_{1j} + \varepsilon_{1ij} \qquad\qquad (49)$$

$$D_{2ij} = \mu_2 + \alpha_{2j} + \varepsilon_{2ij} \qquad\qquad (50)$$

Notice that μ_1 is the grand mean parameter for D_1, and μ_2 is the grand mean parameter for D_2. Similarly, α_{1j} and α_{2j} are the between-subjects effect parameters for D_1 and D_2, respectively. Do not let the extra subscript 1 or 2 in Equation 49 and 50 (as compared to Equation 41) confuse you. For example, μ_1 has the same meaning for D_1 as μ had for D. We simply need the 1 subscript to distinguish the grand mean of D_1 from the grand mean of D_2. As when the repeated factor had two levels, we generally prefer to define μ_1 and μ_2 as unweighted means if sample sizes are unequal. Be certain to understand that if the repeated factor had b levels, we would have $b - 1$ full models, one for each of the $b-1$ D variables we would have formed.

Within-Subjects Main Effect. We need to consider two restricted models for D_1 and D_2, one that allows us to test the interaction and the other that allows us to test the within-subjects main effect. Let's consider the within-subjects main effect first. The null hypothesis for this effect states that the grand means of all the b original Y variables are equal to each other. However, this is equivalent to stating that the grand means of all the $b-1$ D variables equal zero. In our example, where $b = 3$, we have two restricted models, one for D_1 and another for D_2. The restricted models for testing this hypothesis are given by

$$D_{1ij} = \alpha_{1j} + \varepsilon_{1ij} \qquad\qquad (51)$$

$$D_{2ij} = \alpha_{2j} + \varepsilon_{2ij} \qquad\qquad (52)$$

The next step is to obtain least-squares estimates of parameters, both in the full models and in the restricted models. We can then calculate errors for D_1 and D_2 for each subject and compare the magnitude of errors for the full model to those of the restricted model. We present these steps in considerable detail to show that, although the nature of the models is different, the procedure for testing the within-subjects main effect follows the principles we have used throughout Chapter 13 and this chapter. That we have two variables for each subject has no effect on parameter estimation. In particular, the formulas we use here are identical to those we developed earlier for a single D variable (i.e., Equations 45 and 46), except that we must include a subscript to designate the particular D variable. As before, the predicted score for each subject from the full model is the mean score of that subject's group. This follows because the full models in Equations 49 and 50 are cell means models. As a result, we have

$$\hat{D}_{1ij}(\mathrm{F}) = \bar{D}_{1j}$$

$$\hat{D}_{2ij}(\mathrm{F}) = \bar{D}_{2j}$$

Thus, the errors for subject i in group j are given by the differences between the subject's actual scores (D_{1ij} and D_{2ij}) and the predicted scores:

$$e_{1ij}(\mathrm{F}) = D_{1ij} - \bar{D}_{1j}$$

$$e_{2ij}(\mathrm{F}) = D_{2ij} - \bar{D}_{2j}$$

Table 14.11 shows these errors for the full models for our 20 subjects. The table also includes columns for e_1^2, e_2^2, which are squared errors, and for $(e_1)(e_2)$, which is a cross-product of errors. As we have done previously in this chapter and in Chapter 13, we use the sums of e_1^2, e_2^2, and $(e_1)(e_2)$ to construct a matrix for the full model. Recall that we let $E_{11}(\mathrm{F})$ and $E_{22}(\mathrm{F})$ denote the sum of squared errors for the full model for D_1 and D_2, respectively. Similarly, we let $E_{12}(\mathrm{F})$ denote the sum of cross-products for the full model. In general, with two D variables, we would form a matrix for the full model of the form

$$\mathbf{E(F)} = \begin{bmatrix} E_{11}(\mathrm{F}) & E_{12}(\mathrm{F}) \\ E_{12}(\mathrm{F}) & E_{22}(\mathrm{F}) \end{bmatrix}$$

For our data, Table 14.11 shows that the matrix for the full model is given by

$$\mathbf{E(F)} = \begin{bmatrix} 67{,}050 & -9{,}090 \\ -9{,}090 & 125{,}370 \end{bmatrix}$$

We must also obtain least-squares estimates for the parameters in the restricted models of Equations 51 and 52. Once again, the formulas we use are identical to those we developed for a single D variable. The predicted scores from the restricted models are

$$\hat{D}_{1ij}(\mathrm{R}) = \bar{D}_{1j} - \bar{D}_1$$

$$\hat{D}_{2ij}(\mathrm{R}) = \bar{D}_{2j} - \bar{D}_2$$

The errors for subject i in group j are thus given by

$$e_{1ij}(\mathrm{R}) = D_{1ij} - (\bar{D}_{1j} - \bar{D}_1) = D_{1ij} - \bar{D}_{1j} + \bar{D}_1$$

$$e_{2ij}(\mathrm{R}) = D_{2ij} - (\bar{D}_{2j} - \bar{D}_2) = D_{2ij} - \bar{D}_{2j} + \bar{D}_2$$

T A B L E **14. 11**   Errors for Full Models for D_1 and D_2 Variables of Table 14.10

Young Subjects	e_1	e_2	e_1^2	e_2^2	$(e_1)(e_2)$
1	12	108	144	11,664	1,296
2	−18	18	324	324	−324
3	−78	18	6,084	324	−1,404
4	102	−102	10,404	10,404	−10,404
5	−48	−132	2,304	17,424	6,336
6	−78	−42	6,084	1,764	3,276
7	42	78	1,764	6,084	3,276
8	102	18	10,404	324	1,836
9	−18	−102	324	10,404	1,836
10	−18	138	324	19,044	−2,484
Old Subjects	e_1	e_2	e_1^2	e_2^2	$(e_1)(e_2)$
1	21	−57	441	3,249	−1,197
2	−39	−57	1,521	3,249	2,223
3	−9	33	81	1,089	−297
4	−19	63	9,801	3,969	−6,237
5	111	33	12,321	1,089	3,663
6	21	−117	441	13,689	−2,457
7	−9	93	81	8,649	−837
8	−9	33	81	1,089	−297
9	−39	63	1,521	3,969	−2,457
10	51	−87	2,601	7,569	−4,437
Sum for all 20 subjects	**0**	**0**	**67,050**	**125,370**	**−9,090**

Table 14.12 shows these errors for the restricted models for our 20 subjects. Notice from comparing Tables 14.11 and 14.12 that the $e_1(F)$ and $e_1(R)$ errors differ only in that every subject's $e_1(R)$ score is 208.5 ms larger than his or her $e_1(F)$ score. The e_2 scores show a similar pattern, except that the $e_2(R)$ scores are 10.5 ms less than the $e_2(F)$ scores. Not coincidentally, 208.5 is the sample grand mean of D_1, and −10.5 is the sample grand mean of D_2. The errors of the restricted models differ from the errors of the full model to the extent that the sample grand means of the D variables differ from zero. Thus, if the null hypothesis is true, the sample grand means differ from zero entirely due to sampling error, and the errors of the restricted model should be similar to those of the full model. On the other hand, if the null hypothesis is false, the errors of the restricted model are likely to be appreciably greater than those of the full model. Table 14.12 also includes columns for e_1^2, e_2^2, and $(e_1)(e_2)$, just as did Table 14.11. In general, with two D variables, we can form a matrix for the restricted model of the form

$$\mathbf{E(R)} = \begin{bmatrix} E_{11}(R) & E_{12}(R) \\ E_{12}(R) & E_{22}(R) \end{bmatrix}$$

T A B L E **14. 12** Errors for Restricted Model $\mu_1 = \mu_2 = 0$ for D_1 and D_2 Variables of Table 14.10

Young Subjects	e_1	e_2	e_1^2	e_2^2	$(e_1)(e_2)$
1	220.5	97.5	48,620.25	9,506.25	21,498.75
2	190.5	7.5	36,290.25	56.25	1,428.75
3	130.5	7.5	17,030.25	56.25	978.75
4	310.5	−112.5	96,410.25	12,656.25	−34,931.25
5	160.5	−142.5	25,760.25	20,306.25	−22,871.25
6	130.5	−52.5	17,030.25	2,756.25	−6,851.25
7	250.5	67.5	62,750.25	4,556.25	16,908.75
8	310.5	7.5	96,410.25	56.25	2,328.75
9	190.5	−112.5	36,290.25	12,656.25	−21,431.25
10	190.5	127.5	36,290.25	16,256.25	24,288.75

Old Subjects	e_1	e_2	e_1^2	e_2^2	$(e_1)(e_2)$
1	229.5	−67.5	52,670.25	4,556.25	−15,491.25
2	169.5	−67.5	28,730.25	4,556.25	−11,441.25
3	199.5	22.5	39,800.25	506.25	4,488.75
4	109.5	52.5	11,900.25	2,756.25	5,748.75
5	319.5	22.5	102,080.25	506.25	7,188.75
6	229.5	−127.5	52,670.25	16,256.25	−29,261.25
7	199.5	82.5	39,800.25	6,806.25	16,458.75
8	199.5	22.5	39,800.25	506.25	4,488.75
9	169.5	52.5	28,730.25	2,756.25	8,898.75
10	259.5	−97.5	67,340.25	9,506.25	−25,301.25

| Sum for all 20 subjects | 4170.0 | −210.0 | 936,495.00 | 127,575.00 | −52,875.00 |

For our data, Table 14.12 shows that the matrix for the restricted model is given by

$$\mathbf{E(R)} = \begin{bmatrix} 936,495 & -52,875 \\ -52,875 & 127,575 \end{bmatrix}$$

Before proceeding with a formal comparison of the $\mathbf{E(F)}$ and $\mathbf{E(R)}$ matrices to test the within-subjects main effect, it is useful to see how the individual elements of $\mathbf{E(R)}$ relate to the elements of $\mathbf{E(F)}$. You may recall that when we had a single D variable, we showed that

$$E_R = E_F + N\bar{D}^2$$

The same relationship holds here, so

$$E_{11}(R) = E_{11}(F) + N\bar{D}_1^2$$
$$E_{22}(R) = E_{22}(F) + N\bar{D}_2^2$$

Similarly, it turns out that

$$E_{12}(\mathbf{R}) = E_{12}(\mathbf{F}) + N\bar{D}_1\bar{D}_2$$

These relationships can be verified for our data by recalling that $\bar{D}_1 = 208.5$ and $\bar{D}_2 = -10.5$. Thus, as was true for the errors of individual subjects, the full and restricted matrices differ from one another to the extent that $\bar{D}_1$ and/or $\bar{D}_2$ differ from zero.

We are now in a position to consider how to compare the $\mathbf{E}(\mathbf{F})$ and $\mathbf{E}(\mathbf{R})$ matrices to arrive at an F test of the within-subjects main effect. As before, these matrices are compared by calculating the determinant of each matrix. In the general case of an $a \times b$ split-plot design, the test statistic is given by

$$F = \frac{(|\mathbf{E}(\mathbf{R})| - |\mathbf{E}(\mathbf{F})|)/(b-1)}{|\mathbf{E}(\mathbf{F})|/(N-a-b+2)} \tag{53}$$

This F statistic has $b - 1$ numerator and $N - a - b + 2$ denominator degrees of freedom, where N refers as usual to the total sample size, summed across all levels of the A factor.[13] The values of the determinants of the full and restricted matrices for our numerical example are rather imposing numbers because the individual elements of $\mathbf{E}(\mathbf{F})$ and $\mathbf{E}(\mathbf{R})$ are themselves large numbers. Nonetheless, with the help of a computer or a calculator that displays a large number of digits, it can be shown that the determinants for our data equal

$$|\mathbf{E}(\mathbf{F})| = 8,323,430,400$$

$$|\mathbf{E}(\mathbf{R})| = 116,677,584,000$$

Substituting these two values as well as $a = 2, b = 3$, and $N = 20$ into Equation 53 yields an F value of 110.65 with 2 and 17 degrees of freedom. The corresponding p value is less than .0001, so there is a highly statistically significant angle effect for our data.

Test of the Interaction. The remaining omnibus effect to be tested is the interaction. As always, this test involves a comparison of full and restricted models. Recall that the full models we used for testing the within-subjects main effect were given by

$$D_{1ij} = \mu_1 + \alpha_{1j} + \varepsilon_{1ij} \tag{49, repeated}$$

$$D_{2ij} = \mu_2 + \alpha_{2j} + \varepsilon_{2ij} \tag{50, repeated}$$

These same full models are also used for testing the interaction of the between- and within-subjects factors. We must now determine the restricted models that are implied by the interaction null hypothesis. The null hypothesis for the interaction states that the differences between the means of the levels of the within-subjects factor are a constant for every level of the between-subjects factor. In other words, if the null hypothesis is true, there are no group differences on the within-subjects differences. However, this absence of group differences implies that all α_j parameters equal zero. The appropriate restricted models are thus given by

$$D_{1ij} = \mu_1 + \varepsilon_{1ij} \tag{54}$$

$$D_{2ij} = \mu_2 + \varepsilon_{2ij} \tag{55}$$

The next step is to obtain least-squares estimates of parameters. Notice that we only have to perform this step for the restricted models because the full models for the interaction are identical to the full models for the within-subjects main effect. The least-squares estimates of the μ_1 and μ_2 parameters in Equations 54 and 55 are the sample grand means $\bar{D}_1$ and $\bar{D}_2$, respectively.[14] Thus, the restricted models simply predict each subject's score on a D variable to equal the grand mean of that variable:

$$\hat{D}_{1ij}(R) = \bar{D}_1 \quad \text{and} \quad \hat{D}_{2ij}(R) = \bar{D}_2$$

As a result, the errors for subject i in group j are given by

$$e_{1ij}(R) = D_{1ij} - \bar{D}_1 \quad \text{and} \quad e_{2ij}(R) = D_{2ij} - \bar{D}_2$$

Table 14.13 shows these errors for the restricted models for our 20 subjects. The table also includes columns for e_1^2, e_2^2, and $(e_1)(e_2)$, just as did Tables 14.11 and 14.12. In general, with two D variables, we would form a matrix for the restricted

T A B L E **14. 13** Errors for Interaction Restricted Model for D_1 and D_2 Variables of Table 14.10

Young Subjects	e_1	e_2	e_1^2	e_2^2	$(e_1)(e_2)$
1	−28.5	70.5	812.25	4,970.25	−2,009.25
2	−58.5	−19.5	3,422.25	380.25	1,140.75
3	−118.5	−19.5	14,042.25	380.25	2,310.75
4	61.5	−139.5	3,782.25	19,460.25	−8,579.25
5	−88.5	−169.5	7,832.25	28,730.25	15,000.75
6	−118.5	−79.5	14,042.25	6,320.25	9,420.75
7	1.5	40.5	2.25	1,640.25	60.75
8	61.5	−19.5	3,782.25	380.25	−1,199.25
9	−58.5	−139.5	3,422.25	19,460.25	8,160.75
10	−58.5	100.5	3,422.25	10,100.25	−5,879.25
Old Subjects	e_1	e_2	e_1^2	e_2^2	$(e_1)(e_2)$
1	61.5	−19.5	3,782.25	380.25	−1,199.25
2	1.5	−19.5	2.25	380.25	−29.25
3	31.5	70.5	992.25	4,970.25	2,220.75
4	−58.5	100.5	3,422.25	10,100.25	−5,879.25
5	151.5	70.5	22,952.25	4,970.25	10,680.75
6	61.5	−79.5	3,782.25	6,320.25	−4,889.25
7	31.5	130.5	992.25	17,030.25	4,110.75
8	31.5	70.5	992.25	4,970.25	2,220.75
9	1.5	100.5	2.25	10,100.25	150.75
10	91.5	−49.5	8,372.25	2,450.25	−4,529.25
Sum for all 20 subjects	**0.0**	**0.0**	**99,855.00**	**153,495.00**	**21,285.00**

model of the form

$$E(R) = \begin{bmatrix} E_{11}(R) & E_{12}(R) \\ E_{12}(R) & E_{22}(R) \end{bmatrix}$$

For our data, Table 14.13 shows that the matrix for the restricted model is given by

$$E(R) = \begin{bmatrix} 99,855 & 21,285 \\ 21,285 & 153,495 \end{bmatrix}$$

Before considering the formal test to compare $E(R)$ and $E(F)$, it may be instructive to see how the individual elements of the $E(R)$ and $E(F)$ matrices are related. When we compare the full and restricted models for D_1 (Equations 49 and 54, respectively), we are simply performing a one-way between-subjects ANOVA. We learned in Chapter 3 that the formula for the between-group sum of squares can be written as

$$SS_B = \sum_{j=1}^{a} n_j(\bar{Y_j} - \bar{Y})^2$$

where Y is the dependent variable. The same relationship holds here, so that

$$E_{11}(R) = E_{11}(F) + \sum_{j=1}^{a} n_j(\bar{D}_{1j} - \bar{D}_1)^2$$

Similarly,

$$E_{22}(R) = E_{22}(F) + \sum_{j=1}^{a} n_j(\bar{D}_{2j} - \bar{D}_2)^2$$

It can also be shown that

$$E_{12}(R) = E_{12}(F) + \sum_{j=1}^{a} n_j(\bar{D}_{1j} - \bar{D}_1)(\bar{D}_{2j} - \bar{D}_2)$$

These relationships can be verified for our data by recalling that $n_1 = n_2 = 10$, $\bar{D}_{11} = 168$, $\bar{D}_{12} = 249$, $\bar{D}_1 = 208.5$, $\bar{D}_{21} = -48$, $\bar{D}_{22} = 27$, and $\bar{D}_2 = -10.5$ (see Table 14.10 for these figures). Of course, the three formulas given above would save us a lot of work if we were computing quantities by hand because we would not have to compute errors for each subject individually for both the full and the restricted models. However, we typically rely on a computer to perform calculations, so our primary purpose for giving you these formulas is to show how the elements of the restricted matrix differ from the elements of the full matrix. Specifically, the elements differ to the extent that different groups have different sample means on the D variables. However, this is just an index of the extent to which there is an interaction in the sample, which is precisely what we want to test in the population.

We are now ready to consider how to compare the $E(F)$ and $E(R)$ matrices to arrive at an F test of the interaction. For reasons that are too advanced to discuss in this book, the procedure to be used is different when there are only two levels of the between-subjects factor (i.e., $a = 2$) than when there are more than two levels (i.e., $a > 2$).[15] We begin with the special case where $a = 2$, both because it is simpler and because $a = 2$ in our numerical example. Once we have presented the F test in this special case, we consider the more general case where $a \geq 2$.

In the special case of a $2 \times b$ split-plot design (i.e., two levels of the between-subjects factor and b levels of the within-subjects factor), we can proceed with an F test of the same general form that we used for testing the within-subjects main effect. With a $2 \times b$ split-plot design, the test statistic for the interaction is given by

$$F = \frac{(|\mathbf{E(R)}| - |\mathbf{E(F)}|)/(a - 1)(b - 1)}{|\mathbf{E(F)}|/(N - a - b + 2)} \tag{56}$$

Because this formula is applicable only when $a = 2$, it can be simplified to

$$F = \frac{(|\mathbf{E(R)}| - |\mathbf{E(F)}|)/(b - 1)}{|\mathbf{E(F)}|/(N - b)} \tag{57}$$

The F statistic for the interaction in the $2 \times b$ split-plot design has $b - 1$ numerator degrees of freedom and $N - b$ denominator degrees of freedom. For our data, we have already seen that $|\mathbf{E(F)}| = 8,323,430,400$ because the $\mathbf{E(F)}$ matrix for the interaction is identical to $\mathbf{E(F)}$ for the within-subjects main effect. The determinant of the restricted matrix for the interaction can be shown to be $|\mathbf{E(R)}| = 14,874,192,000$. Substituting these two values, as well as $b = 3$ and $N = 20$, into Equation 57 yields an F value of 6.69 with 2 and 17 degrees of freedom. The corresponding p value is .0072, so the age $\times$ angle interaction is statistically significant at the .05 level.

When the between-subjects factor has more than two levels, a different formula is needed for the F test. Notice that when this factor has only two levels, we have performed a multivariate extension of the t test. However, when the factor has more than two levels, neither a multivariate t test nor a univariate t test is applicable. In a sense, this is why Equations 56 and 57 are no longer applicable. In fact, however, there is a more technical explanation requiring knowledge of matrix algebra. Instead of attempting to explain the reason, we simply describe how the test must be modified.[16]

Even when $a > 2$, $\mathbf{E(F)}$ and $\mathbf{E(R)}$ matrices are formed in exactly the same manner as when $a = 2$. However, the way in which $\mathbf{E(F)}$ and $\mathbf{E(R)}$ are incorporated into a test statistic is somewhat different. In fact, when $a > 2$, four different multivariate test statistics are available. The test statistics are Wilks's lambda, the Pillai–Bartlett trace, Roy's greatest characteristic root, and the Hotelling–Lawley trace. Although for many data sets all four test statistics are likely to reach the same conclusion regarding statistical significance, such agreement is by no means guaranteed. In addition, without more theoretical information regarding the population than is usually available, it is generally impossible to state which test statistic is best. As a result, statisticians are not in complete agreement as to which test is best in practice. We will restrict our discussion to Wilks's lambda and the Pillai–Bartlett trace. Wilks's lambda is historically the most widely used of the four statistics and generalizes most easily from the foundation we have developed because it is the only statistic of the four that is based on determinants. We have chosen to present the Pillai–Bartlett trace because there is some evidence suggesting that it is the most robust of the four statistics.

Before we consider Wilks's lambda, it will be helpful to rewrite Equation 56 for the F test when $a = 2$. Recall that this equation was

$$F = \frac{(|\mathbf{E(R)}| - |\mathbf{E(F)}|)/(a - 1)(b - 1)}{|\mathbf{E(F)}|/(N - a - b + 2)} \qquad \text{(56, repeated)}$$

We can rewrite the portion of this equation involving the determinants of the $\mathbf{E(R)}$ and $\mathbf{E(F)}$ matrices (i.e., the part omitting degrees of freedom terms) as follows:

$$\frac{|\mathbf{E(R)}| - |\mathbf{E(F)}|}{|\mathbf{E(F)}|} = \frac{|\mathbf{E(R)}|}{|\mathbf{E(F)}|} - \frac{|\mathbf{E(F)}|}{|\mathbf{E(F)}|} = \frac{|\mathbf{E(R)}|}{|\mathbf{E(F)}|} - 1 \qquad (58)$$

Wilks's lambda, about which we discuss more momentarily, is denoted Λ and is defined as

$$\Lambda = \frac{|\mathbf{E(F)}|}{|\mathbf{E(R)}|} \qquad (59)$$

Notice then that $|\mathbf{E(R)}|$ divided by $|\mathbf{E(F)}|$ (as in Equation 58) is the reciprocal of Λ, that is,

$$\frac{|\mathbf{E(R)}|}{|\mathbf{E(F)}|} = \frac{1}{\Lambda}$$

Making this substitution into Equation 58 yields

$$\frac{|\mathbf{E(R)}| - |\mathbf{E(F)}|}{|\mathbf{E(F)}|} = \frac{1}{\Lambda} - 1$$

which can be rewritten as

$$\frac{|\mathbf{E(R)}| - |\mathbf{E(F)}|}{|\mathbf{E(F)}|} = \frac{1}{\Lambda} - 1$$

$$= \frac{1}{\Lambda} - \frac{\Lambda}{\Lambda}$$

$$= \frac{1 - \Lambda}{\Lambda}$$

Now, if we substitute this result into Equation 56, we have a new form for the F test when $a = 2$:

$$F = \frac{(1 - \Lambda)/(a - 1)(b - 1)}{\Lambda/(N - a - b + 2)} \qquad (60)$$

where Λ is defined as before, namely,

$$\Lambda = \frac{|\mathbf{E(F)}|}{|\mathbf{E(R)}|} \qquad \text{(59, repeated)}$$

Equation 60 is an entirely legitimate equation for testing the interaction when $a = 2$; indeed, we have just derived it algebraically from Equation 56, so the two equations produce identical F values when $a = 2$. Although for this reason Equation 60 is of no practical value when $a = 2$, it is nevertheless useful because it will make clearer the rationale for the form of the F test when $a > 2$.

When $a \geq 2$, the F test based on Wilks's lambda is given by

$$F = \frac{(1 - \sqrt[q]{\Lambda})/(a - 1)(b - 1)}{\sqrt[q]{\Lambda}/[mq - .5(a - 1)(b - 1) + 1]} \tag{61}$$

This F statistic has $(a - 1)(b - 1)$ numerator degrees of freedom and $mq - .5(a - 1)(b - 1) + 1$ denominator degrees of freedom (m and q are defined momentarily). Before explaining this admittedly ominous formula, we should hasten to tell you that most MANOVA computer packages calculate this F value for you. Nevertheless, it is useful to consider this F statistic piece by piece to better understand it.

First, notice that just like Equation 60, this F test is based on Λ, the ratio of $|\mathbf{E(F)}|$ to $|\mathbf{E(R)}|$. However, Equation 61, unlike Equation 60, requires that we calculate the qth root of Λ (as we said, q is defined momentarily). Nevertheless, the basic idea is the same. If the errors of the restricted model are similar in magnitude to those of the full model, $|\mathbf{E(R)}|$ will be only slightly larger than $|\mathbf{E(F)}|$. As a result, Λ (which remember equals $|\mathbf{E(F)}|$ divided by $|\mathbf{E(R)}|$) will be only slightly less than 1.0. Regardless of the value of q, $1 - \sqrt[q]{\Lambda}$ and $\sqrt[q]{\Lambda}$ will both be close to 1.0, so the F value will be relatively small. On the other hand, if the restricted model provides a much worse explanation of the data than does the full model, $|\mathbf{E(R)}|$ will be much larger than $|\mathbf{E(F)}|$. As a consequence, Λ will be much less than 1. However, as Λ decreases, the term $(1 - \sqrt[q]{\Lambda})/\sqrt[q]{\Lambda}$ increases, so the F value will be relatively large.

Second, it is necessary to define m and q in Equation 61. The respective formulas are

$$m = N - .5(a + b + 1)$$

$$q = \sqrt{\frac{(a - 1)^2(b - 1)^2 - 4}{(a - 1)^2 + (b - 1)^2 - 5}}$$

When $(a - 1)^2 + (b - 1)^2$ equals 5, q is defined to equal 1.

Third, this form of the multivariate F test is called Rao's approximation because it was developed by a statistician named Rao who proved that the sampling distribution of the statistic defined in Equation 61 approximates the F distribution. However, the statistic is distributed exactly as an F (provided the usual statistical assumptions are met) if $a = 2$ or $a = 3$ (regardless of the value of b), or if $b = 2$ or $b = 3$ (regardless of the value of a). The formulas given in Table 14.14 for $a = 2$ agree with Equation 57, which we developed earlier for the special case of $a = 2$. Also, the formulas in Table 14.14 for $b = 2$ can be shown to be equivalent to Equation 43, which we developed earlier for testing the interaction when $b = 2$. Thus, all other formulas we have developed for the multivariate test of the interaction in the split-plot design are special cases of Equation 61.

Fourth, we should point out a few facts regarding the degrees of freedom of this F test. First, notice that the numerator degrees of freedom always equal $(a - 1)(b - 1)$, which is exactly what we would expect for the interaction of two factors with a and b levels. Second, the denominator degrees of freedom are often different from what

T A B L E **14. 14**   Values of *a* and *b* for Which Wilks's Lambda Test of the Interaction Is Distributed Exactly as an *F* Ratio

			df	
a	*b*	**Formula for *F***	**Numerator**	**Denominator**
2	Any	$\dfrac{(1-\Lambda)/(b-1)}{\Lambda/(N-b)}$	$b-1$	$N-b$
3	Any	$\dfrac{(1-\sqrt{\Lambda})/(b-1)}{\sqrt{\Lambda}/(N-b-1)}$	$2(b-1)$	$2(N-b-1)$
Any	2	$\dfrac{(1-\Lambda)/(a-1)}{\Lambda/(N-a)}$	$a-1$	$N-a$
Any	3	$\dfrac{(1-\sqrt{\Lambda})/(a-1)}{\sqrt{\Lambda}/(N-a-1)}$	$2(a-1)$	$2(N-a-1)$

we have become accustomed to because of the way in which the test statistic in Equation 61 approximates the *F* distribution. For example, as Table 14.14 shows, the denominator degrees of freedom can exceed *N*, the total sample size. Also, in larger designs, the degrees of freedom for the denominator can be fractional (i.e., not a whole number). Because most computer programs provide *p* values, this poses no practical problems although it has been known to arouse suspicion in unsuspecting dissertation committee members and journal reviewers!

Keep in mind that the foregoing discussion has been restricted to one of four possible test criteria, namely, Wilks's lambda. We now present a brief introduction to the Pillai–Bartlett trace statistic. As we said earlier, the Pillai–Bartlett trace is also based on the **E(F)** and **E(R)** matrices. However, the information in these matrices is converted into an *F* test differently than Wilks's lambda. Once **E(F)** and **E(R)** matrices have been obtained, the next step in computing the Pillai–Bartlett trace is to subtract the **E(F)** matrix from the **E(R)** matrix. The resultant matrix, denoted **H**, is called the hypothesis sum of squares and cross-product matrix and is defined as **H = E(R) − E(F)**. The **E(R)** matrix is usually denoted **T** and is called the total sum of squares and cross-product matrix. The next step requires that the **H** matrix be multiplied by the inverse of **T**. If you are unfamiliar with matrix algebra, this operation is analogous to division with ordinary numbers. In a sense, then, we are dividing **H** by **T**; however, the result is a $(b-1) \times (b-1)$ matrix instead of a single number.[17] Instead of attempting to explain these matrix operations here, we simply state that the result of multiplying **H** by the inverse of **T** yields the following matrix for testing the interaction for the data in Table 14.9:

$$\begin{bmatrix} .2951 & .1570 \\ .2732 & .1453 \end{bmatrix}$$

The Pillai–Bartlett trace, usually denoted *V*, is simply the sum of the diagonal elements of this matrix (recall that the sum of diagonal elements is called the trace of a square matrix). For our data, then, $V = 0.4404$. An approximate F test based on V is obtained from the following equation:

$$F = \frac{(N - a - b + s + 1)V}{l(s - V)} \tag{62}$$

where s = the smaller of $a - 1$ and $b - 1$, and l = the larger of $a - 1$ and $b - 1$. The degrees of freedom for the F equal $(a - 1)(b - 1)$ for the numerator and $s(N - a - b + s + 1)$ for the denominator. Recall that in our numerical example, $a = 2$ and $b = 3$. Thus, $s = 1$ and $l = 2$, so that the F statistic for the Pillai–Bartlett trace for our data is given by

$$F = \frac{(20 - 2 - 3 + 1 + 1)(0.4404)}{2(1 - 0.4404)} = 6.69$$

with $(2 - 1)(3 - 1) = 2$ numerator degrees of freedom and $1(20 - 2 - 3 + 1 + 1) = 17$ denominator degrees of freedom.

You may have noticed that this F value of 6.69 with 2 and 17 degrees of freedom for the Pillai–Bartlett trace is identical to the F value we obtained using Equation 57, which is a special case of Wilks's lambda. Although the Pillai–Bartlett trace and Wilks's lambda tests are generally different from one another, it can be shown that they are equivalent in the special case where s, the smaller of $a - 1$ and $b - 1$, equals one. Thus, if $a = 2$ or if $b = 2$ (or both), then Wilks's lambda and the Pillai–Bartlett trace produce exactly the same results. Indeed, the reason we obtained the same F value and degrees of freedom with the two tests is because $a = 2$ in our example. It can also be shown that when $s = 1$, the other two tests we mentioned (Roy's greatest characteristic root and the Hotelling–Lawley trace) also yield exactly the same result as both Wilks's lambda and the Pillai–Bartlett trace. Thus, when $s = 1$, all four tests necessarily agree precisely; when $s > 1$, in general, all four tests disagree to some extent, although in practice the tests are often quite similar.[18]

At this point it is appropriate to explain why we did not raise the distinction among these four tests in Chapter 13 or in the first half of this chapter. Notice that in both these earlier sections of the book, we were testing effects that involved only within-subjects factors, whereas now we are considering the interaction of a within-subjects factor with a between-subjects factor. In all earlier cases, $s = 1$, so that all four tests produce identical results. Thus, we had no need to distinguish among the four tests, although many MANOVA computer programs nevertheless report all four F tests even when $s = 1$.

Remember that for the interaction in a split-plot design, we defined s as the smaller of $a - 1$ and $b - 1$. More generally, s = the smaller of df_{effect} and p, where p is the number of dependent variables. The df_{effect} term refers to the degrees of freedom per variable for the effect being tested. In other words, df_{effect} equals the difference in the number of parameters in the full and restricted models for a single variable. Until we considered the test of the interaction in a split-plot design, our tests of within-subjects effects could always be represented as a comparison of models of the form

$$D_i = \mu + \varepsilon_i \quad \text{(full model)}$$

$$D_i = \varepsilon_i \quad \text{(restricted model)}$$

The difference in the number of parameters equals one for each variable, so $df_{\text{effect}} = 1$. As a result, $s = 1$ regardless of the number of levels of the within-subjects factor. Hence, all four tests always yield identical F values for testing any purely within-subjects effect. Only effects that involve both between- and within-subjects factors ever yield different F values for the four different multivariate test statistics.

Further Investigation of Main Effects. As we discussed in Chapter 12, we do not need to introduce any new procedures for pursuing the meaning of a significant between-subjects main effect in a split-plot design. Comparisons of the marginal means of the between-subjects factor can be tested simply by averaging each subject's scores across the within-subjects factor and performing between-subjects contrasts of the resulting scores. As a result, the principles we developed in Chapters 4–6 can be directly applied to comparisons of between-subjects marginal means in a split-plot design.

Comparisons of within-subjects marginal means in a split-plot design are tested in much the same manner as in totally within-subjects designs. Specifically, a D variable is formed whose coefficients correspond to the comparison to be tested. As in other within-subjects designs, the null hypothesis is that the population mean of this D variable equals zero. However, the split-plot design is different from totally within-subjects designs because it includes a between-subjects factor whose effect must be taken into account. As we saw earlier in the chapter, an appropriate full model for a D variable in a split-plot design is given by

$$D_{ij} = \mu + \alpha_j + \varepsilon_{ij} \qquad \text{(41, repeated)}$$

The restricted model for testing that the grand mean of D equals zero in the population can be written as

$$D_{ij} = \alpha_j + \varepsilon_{ij} \qquad \text{(44, repeated)}$$

Earlier in the chapter, we derived the F statistic for comparing these two models:

$$F = \frac{N\bar{D}^2}{\sum\limits_{j=1}^{a} \sum\limits_{i=1}^{n_j} (D_{ij} - \bar{D}_j)^2/(N - a)} \qquad \text{(47, repeated)}$$

This F statistic has 1 numerator and $N - a$ denominator degrees of freedom.

If the particular D variable to be tested was one of the D variables formed to perform the multivariate test, the numerator and denominator values for the F statistic in Equation 47 are readily available from the appropriate diagonal elements of the $\mathbf{E(F)}$ and $\mathbf{E(R)}$ matrices. To illustrate this point, suppose that we want to test the statistical significance of the quadratic trend for the marginal means of the angle factor in our numerical example. Recall that our D_2 variable was chosen to represent this quadratic trend:

$$D_{2ij} = 1Y_{1ij} - 2Y_{2ij} + 1Y_{3ij}$$

Remember that the D_1 variable represents the linear trend for angle. When we considered D_1 and D_2 simultaneously, we calculated the following $\mathbf{E(F)}$ and $\mathbf{E(R)}$ matrices:

$$\mathbf{E(F)} = \begin{bmatrix} 67{,}050 & -9{,}090 \\ -9{,}090 & 125{,}370 \end{bmatrix}$$

$$\mathbf{E(R)} = \begin{bmatrix} 936{,}495 & -52{,}875 \\ -52{,}875 & 127{,}575 \end{bmatrix}$$

As usual, $\mathbf{E(F)}$ corresponds to the full model of Equation 41, and $\mathbf{E(R)}$ corresponds to the restricted model of Equation 44. We do not need to compare the entire matrices at this point because we are only interested in the D_2 variable. For this specific variable, the error sums of squares for the full and restricted models are given by the values in the second row and second column of the $\mathbf{E(F)}$ and $\mathbf{E(R)}$ matrices, respectively. Thus, in our example, $E_F = 125{,}370$, and $E_R = 127{,}575$ for the quadratic trend. We can substitute these values into Equation 47 by realizing that

$$E_F = \sum_{j=1}^{a} \sum_{i=1}^{n_j} (D_{ij} - \bar{D}_j)^2 \qquad \text{(45, repeated)}$$

$$E_R - E_F = N\bar{D}^2 \qquad \text{(46, repeated)}$$

For our data, we have

$$\sum_{j=1}^{a} \sum_{i=1}^{n_j} (D_{ij} - \bar{D}_j)^2 = 125{,}370$$

and

$$N\bar{D}^2 = 2205$$

Substituting these values along with $N = 20$ and $a = 2$ into Equation 47 yields an F value of 0.32 with 1 and 18 degrees of freedom. As in other cases we have seen, this F value is identical to the F value we obtained for the quadratic angle trend in the mixed-model approach of Chapter 12 when we used a separate error term (Equation 12.21 instead of 12.20). As we discuss in more detail later in the chapter, once again the multivariate approach is compatible with the use of a separate error term, whereas the mixed-model approach is compatible with the use of a pooled error term.

To judge the statistical significance of a contrast, we must, of course, compare the observed F value to an appropriate critical value. The choice of an appropriate critical value depends, as usual, on what other contrasts are being tested. One possibility is to set α_{PC} at a desired figure, in which case the critical F value is simply read from the F table with 1 numerator and $N - a$ denominator degrees of freedom. If a set of C planned comparisons is to be tested, α_{PC} for each contrast can be adjusted to equal .05/C, using the Bonferroni technique. As we discussed in Chapter 13, the Bonferroni method is also appropriate for testing pairwise comparisons of within-subjects marginal means in a split-plot design. Finally, for testing post hoc complex comparisons, the appropriate critical value comes from the multivariate extension of Scheffé's method developed by Roy and Bose. The formula follows from the same logic we used to arrive at Equation 13.25. Remembering that A denotes the between-subjects factor and B the within-subjects factor in a split-plot design, the appropriate critical value for testing complex contrasts among the levels of B is given by

$$CV = (N - a)(b - 1)F_{\alpha_{FW}; b-1, N-a-b+2}/(N - a - b + 2) \qquad (63)$$

For our numerical example, the observed F value of 0.32 is nonsignificant even using an α_{PC} of .05 because, with 1 and 18 degrees of freedom, the critical F at the .05 level equals 4.41. Of course, if additional contrasts were being tested, the appropriate critical value would be even larger, so the quadratic trend for angle would remain nonsignificant. For example, if the quadratic trend were tested as a post hoc complex comparison, the .05 critical value would be calculated from Equation 63 as follows:

$$CV = (20 - 2)(3 - 1)(3.59)/(20 - 2 - 3 + 2) = 7.60$$

a value which is appreciably larger than 4.41, the critical value for an α_{PC} of .05.

We should also point out that using a statistical package for performing the multivariate test of the within-subjects main effect also simplifies testing contrasts of the marginal means. The reason is that such programs typically report univariate as well as multivariate tests. These univariate tests are simply the tests of the individual D variables that collectively represent the omnibus effect, which is tested by the multivariate test. For the angle effect in our example, most multivariate computer programs (e.g., BMDP, SAS, and SPSS-X) report not only that the observed F for the multivariate test of the angle main effect equals 110.65 but also that the univariate F value for D_1 (the linear trend) equals 233.41 and the F value for D_2 (the quadratic trend) equals 0.32. Of course, D_1 and D_2 must be chosen to reflect the contrasts to be tested, and as we discussed in Chapter 13, this can be problematic with some computer programs if the D variables of interest are non-orthogonal. Also, be certain you understand that the univariate tests we are referring to here are different from the univariate F test of the mixed-model approach. Although the mixed-model approach does produce a univariate F test, it is still an omnibus test of the main effect. On the other hand, the univariate tests of individual D variables are tests of specific contrasts of the marginal means of the within-subjects factor.

Further Investigation of an Interaction—Simple Effects. As in most factorial designs, the most typical method of interpreting a statistically significant interaction in a split-plot design is to perform tests of simple effects. In our numerical example, we found a significant age × angle interaction, which we could pursue by testing the age effect within each level of angle, as well as the angle effect within each level of age. As we pointed out in Chapter 12, we need to consider how to perform both types of simple-effects tests because in one case (age within angle) we effectively have a one-way between-subjects design, whereas in the other case (angle within age) we effectively have a one-way within-subjects design.

Between-Subjects Effects at a Fixed Level of Within-Subjects Factor. We begin by considering the simple effect of age (the between-subjects factor) at a fixed level of angle (the within-subjects factor), which we would almost certainly be interested in testing in our example because it tells us whether young subjects differ significantly from old subjects at various specific levels of angle. It is important to notice that we no longer have a within-subjects factor in this design because we are considering only one level of the within-subjects factor. As a result, we are only interested in one score per subject, and we can simply perform a one-way between-subjects ANOVA on this variable. The analysis proceeds in exactly the same manner as we discussed in Chapter 12. Not surprisingly, then, the mixed-model and multivariate approaches are identical for testing the simple effect of A (the between-subjects factor) at a fixed level of B (the within-subjects factor). The two approaches are identical simply because (as we pointed out a moment ago) we effectively eliminate the within-subjects factor from the design when we focus our attention on a single level of the within-subjects factor.

Three further points need to be made here. First, recall from Chapter 12 that we discussed two possible error terms for simple-effects tests of A within levels of B. We stated a general preference in Chapter 12 for using $MS_{S/A \text{ at } B_k}$ as an error term instead of $MSWCELL$ (as defined in Equation 12.25) because the use of separate error terms of the form $MS_{S/A \text{ at } B_k}$ does not require sphericity. If a researcher is using the multivariate approach we are discussing in this chapter, it seems sensible to use $MS_{S/A \text{ at } B_k}$ as the error term for testing simple effects of A within B because neither the omnibus multivariate test nor the simple-effects test using this error term assumes sphericity. As we mentioned in Chapter 12, the major mainframe statistical packages (BMDP, SAS, and SPSS-X) all use $MS_{S/A \text{ at } B_k}$ as the error term instead of $MSWCELL$.

Second, notice that the test that results from using $MS_{S/A \text{ at } B_k}$ as the error term is literally identical to performing a one-way between-subjects univariate ANOVA on an individual Y variable. Is important not to confuse this univariate test with the univariate test we perform to test comparisons of the within-subjects marginal means. Remember that Y denotes one of our original variables. In this sense, a Y variable is very different from a D variable. Indeed, a D variable is a transformed variable that we create as some specific linear combination of the original Y variables. Thus, the simple effect of A at a particular level of B is tested by performing a one-way between-subjects univariate ANOVA on an original Y variable. Comparisons of within-subjects marginal means are univariate tests also, but they are performed on D variables instead of Y variables.

The third point is that when statistically significant simple effects of A are found at a fixed level of B, further tests are typically conducted to isolate the nature of the effect. Of course, such tests are unnecessary when A has only two levels, as it does in our example. However, when A has three or more levels, specific comparisons can be tested at a fixed level of B by regarding the data as a one-way between-subjects design. Thus, the principles we developed in Chapters 4–6 can be used to test comparisons among individual cell means within a fixed level of the within-subjects factor.

Within-Subjects Effects at a Fixed Level of Between-Subjects Factor. We frequently will also want to test the simple effect of the within-subjects factor at fixed levels of the between-subject factor. For example, we might want to test the significance of the angle effect separately for young subjects and for old subjects. To illustrate this procedure, we arbitrarily focus on the angle effect for young subjects (the test for old subjects would follow exactly the same logic). The question of interest here is, Are the sample means of 477, 585, and 645 (see Table 14.9) significantly different from each other? In effect, we have a one-way within-subjects design because we are no longer considering the older subjects whose previous inclusion was responsible for the between-subjects factor. Recall from our discussion of simple effects of B within A in Chapter 12 that either of two error terms might be used in the mixed-model approach. Two different error terms are also available in the multivariate approach, although they are not the same as the two terms in the mixed-model approach. In fact, the two "error terms" in the multivariate approach are really error matrices, unlike the mixed-model approach, where the choice was between two mean square terms.

We begin by considering the error matrix that results from performing a one-way within-subjects multivariate analysis of the data for young subjects, literally ignoring the data for old subjects. To conduct this test, we simply use the principles we developed in Chapter 13. Specifically, we begin by forming $b-1$ D variables. In our example, we would form two D variables because the angle factor has three levels. As usual, the particular choice of D variables does not matter for testing the simple effect. Nevertheless, it will be convenient to let D_1 be the linear trend and D_2 the quadratic trend for angle, because we may want to test these specific comparisons in a later analysis. As we discussed in detail in Chapter 13, full and restricted models are developed for D_1 and D_2, leading to an error score for each subject on each variable for each model. The full and restricted models are compared through a full matrix $\mathbf{E}(\mathbf{F})$ and a restricted matrix $\mathbf{E}(\mathbf{R})$. We do not go through the steps of these calculations because they are identical to the steps we showed in detail in Chapter 13. Instead, we simply state that the error matrices for the full and restricted models for D_1 and D_2 for young subjects are given by

$$\mathbf{E}(\mathbf{F})_1 = \begin{bmatrix} 38{,}160 & 3{,}240 \\ 3{,}240 & 77{,}760 \end{bmatrix}$$

$$\mathbf{E}(\mathbf{R})_1 = \begin{bmatrix} 320{,}400 & -77{,}400 \\ -77{,}400 & 100{,}800 \end{bmatrix}$$

The 1 subscript that appears in $\mathbf{E}(\mathbf{F})_1$ and $\mathbf{E}(\mathbf{R})_1$ is used as a reminder that these matrices are based on the data from A_1, that is, the first level of the A factor. In general, for testing the effect of B at A_j, we would represent these matrices as $\mathbf{E}(\mathbf{F})_j$ and $\mathbf{E}(\mathbf{R})_j$.

An F test is obtained by comparing the determinants of these two matrices. The equation we developed in Chapter 13 for the one-way design was

$$F = \frac{(|\mathbf{E}(\mathbf{R})| - |\mathbf{E}(\mathbf{F})|)/(a-1)}{|\mathbf{E}(\mathbf{F})|/(n-a+1)} \qquad \text{(13.22, repeated)}$$

where there was a single group of n subjects with a levels of the repeated factor. A corresponding equation for testing the simple effect of B at A_j in the split-plot design is given by

$$F = \frac{(|E(R)_j| - |E(F)_j|)/(b - 1)}{|E(F)_j|/(n_j - b + 1)} \tag{64}$$

where there are n_j subjects at level j of the A factor and there are b levels of the within-subjects factor. In our example, the determinant of $E(F)_j$ equals 2,956,824,000, and the determinant of $E(R)_j$ equals 26,305,560,000. Substituting these values along with $n_1 = 10$ and $b = 3$ into Equation 64 yields an F value of 31.59. In general, there would be $b - 1$ numerator and $n_j - b + 1$ denominator degrees of freedom associated with this F statistic. With 2 and 8 degrees of freedom, as in our example, the associated p value is .0002, so we can conclude that there is a statistically significant angle effect for young subjects, using the .05 level of significance.

An alternate error matrix might also be used to test the simple effect of B at a fixed level of A. The $E(F)$ matrix we used earlier in the chapter for testing both the angle main effect and the age × angle interaction was

$$E(F) = \begin{bmatrix} 67,050 & -9,090 \\ -9,090 & 125,370 \end{bmatrix}$$

This error matrix is the sum of $E(F)_1$ and $E(F)_2$, that is, the full model error matrices for young and old subjects separately. In other words, we could form a linear D_1 variable and a quadratic D_2 variable for old subjects, just as we have already done for young subjects. If we then fit a full model to the data for old subjects, completely disregarding the data for young subjects, the error matrix for the full model is

$$E(F)_2 = \begin{bmatrix} 28,890 & -12,330 \\ -12,330 & 47,610 \end{bmatrix}$$

where the 2 subscript designates the second level of A, that is, old subjects. The $E(F)$ matrix we found earlier relates to the $E(F)_1$ and $E(F)_2$ matrices in the following manner: Each element of $E(F)$ equals the sum of the corresponding elements of $E(F)_1$ and $E(F)_2$. For example, $67,050 = 38,160 + 28,890$, and the same form of equality holds for the other three elements as well. Matrix addition is performed by adding corresponding elements in just this fashion; thus, we can say that the sum of the $E(F)_1$ and $E(F)_2$ matrices equals $E(F)$.

When a homogeneity assumption (to be discussed momentarily) is met, a more powerful test of the angle effect for young subjects can be performed by basing the error term on the data from old subjects as well as young subjects. Specifically, we can use $E(F)$ as the error term for testing B within A_j, just as we used $E(F)$ for testing the B main effect and the A × B interaction. Recall that the degrees of freedom associated with $E(F)$ equal $N - a - b + 2$ (see Equation 53). The form of the F statistic is somewhat more complicated than what we have previously encountered because the error matrix for the full model is computed from all subjects, whereas the matrices reflecting the magnitude of the within-subjects simple effect are computed on only a subset of the subjects. As a result, the F statistic for testing the simple effect of B at A_j with an error term based on all subjects is given by

$$F = \frac{(|\mathbf{E(F)} + \mathbf{E(R)}_j - \mathbf{E(F)}_j| - |\mathbf{E(F)}|)/(b-1)}{|\mathbf{E(F)}|/(N-a-b+2)} \tag{65}$$

The somewhat unusual looking term $|\mathbf{E(F)} + \mathbf{E(R)}_j - \mathbf{E(F)}_j|$ requires that we find the determinant of the matrix that results from adding corresponding elements of $\mathbf{E(F)}$ and $\mathbf{E(R)}_j$ and then subtracting corresponding elements of $\mathbf{E(F)}_j$.[19] To compute this determinant for our data, it is helpful to recall that we have previously computed the following matrices:

$$\mathbf{E(F)} = \begin{bmatrix} 67{,}050 & -9{,}090 \\ -9{,}090 & 125{,}370 \end{bmatrix}$$

$$\mathbf{E(R)}_1 = \begin{bmatrix} 320{,}400 & -77{,}400 \\ -77{,}400 & 100{,}800 \end{bmatrix}$$

$$\mathbf{E(F)}_1 = \begin{bmatrix} 38{,}160 & 3{,}240 \\ 3{,}240 & 77{,}760 \end{bmatrix}$$

Adding corresponding elements of $\mathbf{E(F)}$ and $\mathbf{E(R)}_1$ produces a matrix given by

$$\begin{bmatrix} 387{,}450 & -86{,}490 \\ -86{,}490 & 226{,}170 \end{bmatrix}$$

We must now subtract corresponding elements of $\mathbf{E(F)}_1$, yielding

$$\begin{bmatrix} 349{,}290 & -89{,}730 \\ -89{,}730 & 148{,}410 \end{bmatrix}$$

The determinant of this matrix equals

$$|\mathbf{E(F)} + \mathbf{E(R)}_1 - \mathbf{E(F)}_1| = (349{,}290)(148{,}410) - (-89{,}730)^2 = 43{,}786{,}656{,}000$$

We previously found that $|\mathbf{E(F)}| = 8{,}323{,}430{,}400$. Substituting these values along with $N = 20$, $a = 2$, and $b = 3$ into Equation 65 yields an F value of 36.22. In general, there are $b - 1$ numerator and $N - a - b + 2$ denominator degrees of freedom associated with this F statistic. With 2 and 17 degrees of freedom, as in our example, the associated p value is .0001, so the F test using $\mathbf{E(F)}$ as an error term concurs with the F test using $\mathbf{E(F)}_j$ that there is a statistically significant angle effect for young subjects.

Choosing between $\mathbf{E(F)}$ and $\mathbf{E(F)}_j$ as an appropriate error term involves the usual considerations of choosing between a pooled and a separate error term. To see why, we need to examine the relationship between $\mathbf{E(F)}$ and the separate $\mathbf{E(F)}_j$ matrices more closely. When the A factor has a levels, $\mathbf{E(F)}$ is equal to the sum of all a $\mathbf{E(F)}_j$ matrices—that is,

$$\mathbf{E(F)} = \sum_{j=1}^{a} \mathbf{E(F)}_j$$

The meaning of this equality is clarified by realizing that each $E(F)_j$ sum of squares and cross-products matrix is itself equal to $(n_j - 1)$ times the covariance matrix for the D variables at level j of A. If we let S_j represent this sample covariance matrix, it follows that

$$E(F) = \sum_{j=1}^{a} (n_j - 1)S_j$$

Thus, $E(F)$ is a weighted sum of the separate covariance matrices. When the underlying population covariance matrices are identical to each other for each level of A, $E(F)$ provides a more stable measure of error than does any separate $E(F)_j$ matrix by itself. This advantage is reflected in the fact that the F statistic using $E(F)$ has more denominator degrees of freedom ($N - a - b + 2$) than does the F statistic using $E(F)_j$ (which has $n_j - b + 1$ denominator degrees of freedom). When the assumption is met, the critical value is less when $E(F)$ is used as the error term, so statistical power is increased. However, when the assumption is false, both Type I and Type II error rates may be distorted in either direction (i.e., either too liberal or too conservative). As we discussed in earlier chapters, the simple-effects F test based on a pooled error term is not robust to violations of homogeneity assumptions even with equal n.[20]

What should a researcher do in practice? As usual, the choice between a pooled and a separate error term is not always straightforward. In theory, one solution might be to perform a test of the assumption that the a covariance matrices for the D variables all equal each other in the population. Indeed, such a test is available, and it is called Box's M test. However, Box's M test depends very strongly on an assumption of normality and is not robust to violations of this assumption (Olson, 1974). Thus, Box's M test is generally of little practical value for choosing between pooled and separate error terms. When samples are sufficiently large (perhaps 40 or so, per level of A), a separate error term is preferable because the additional degrees of freedom afforded by the pooled error term will in all likelihood be inconsequential. However, when samples are small, the choice is more difficult and should probably be based on the researcher's theoretical beliefs as to whether different groups of subjects are likely to display different variances and covariances. We should add that as of this writing all three major mainframe statistical packages (e.g., BMDP, SAS, and SPSS-X) use a pooled error term by default. However, as we pointed out in Chapter 12, it is simple to perform tests using a separate error term. For example, in SAS these tests can be obtained by using PROC SORT and BY commands; in SPSS-X, the corresponding commands are SORT CASES and SPLIT FILE.

Cell Mean Comparisons. In our particular numerical example, the pooled and separate error terms yield very similar results. Because with either error term we obtained a significant angle effect for young subjects, we would probably want to conduct yet one more series of tests to ascertain the precise nature of the angle effect for young subjects. As usual, contrasts among the levels of the within-subjects factor are tested in the multivariate approach by forming an appropriate D variable. For example, suppose that we decide to test the quadratic trend for young subjects.

Because we are focusing our attention on one level of A, this test is essentially a straightforward application of principles we developed in Chapter 13 for testing contrasts in one-way within-subjects designs. The only reason we qualified the preceding sentence by stating the test is *essentially* a straightforward application is that there is again a choice of error terms. If we decide to test the simple effect using the $E(F)_j$ matrix, it then makes sense to use only the data from the jth level of A for testing contrasts at that level. If, on the other hand, we use the pooled $E(F)$ matrix for the simple-effects test, it is reasonable to continue using an error term that pools over the levels of A for testing contrasts of B at A_j. Because either approach may be preferable to the other, depending on the likely validity of the homogeneity assumption, we illustrate both approaches.

First, let's assume that we used the separate $E(F)_j$ matrix to test the simple effect of B at A_j. In this situation, the F statistic for testing a contrast among the levels of B at A_j follows directly from Chapter 13, except that we need to change the notation to reflect the fact that the test is being performed within a level of A. In Chapter 13, the F statistic for testing a contrast was given by

$$F = n\bar{D}^2/s_D^2 \qquad\qquad \text{(13.6, repeated)}$$

In a split-plot design, we simply need to add one subscript to represent the particular D variable to be tested and a second subscript to indicate that all calculations are performed at level j of the A factor. For example, the F statistic for testing D_2 can be written as

$$F = n_j\bar{D}_{2j}^2/s_{D_{2j}}^2 \qquad\qquad (66)$$

For our data, $n_1 = 10$, $\bar{D}_{21} = -48$ (see Table 14.10), and $s_{D_{21}}^2 = 8640$. Substituting these values into Equation 66 yields an F value of 2.67. This F statistic has 1 numerator and $n_j - 1$ denominator degrees of freedom (thus, 1 and 9 in our example); we postpone consideration of a critical value for the moment.

If the particular D variable to be tested was one of the D variables formed to perform the multivariate test, the numerator and denominator values for the F statistic in Equation 66 are readily available from the appropriate diagonal elements of the $E(F)_j$ and $E(R)_j$ matrices. For the quadratic angle trend for young subjects, the values of these diagonal elements are 77,760 for $E(F)_1$ and 100,800 for $E(R)_1$. The difference in these two values—that is, the diagonal element of $E(R)_j$ minus the diagonal element of $E(F)_j$—equals $n_j\bar{D}_{2j}^2$, the numerator of the F. The denominator of the F—that is, $s_{D_{2j}}^2$—is obtained by dividing the diagonal element of $E(F)_j$ by $n_j - 1$. For our data, the difference in values equals 23,040. The denominator equals 8640, producing an F value of 2.67, as we have already seen.

Second, we might have used the pooled $E(F)$ matrix to test the simple effect of B at A_j. To pool across levels of A for testing a contrast of B at A_j, we simply modify Equation 66 so that the denominator is the variance of D_2 averaged over the levels of A:

$$F = n_j\bar{D}_{2j}^2/s_{D_{2p}}^2 \qquad\qquad (67)$$

where the p subscript is a reminder that the variance estimate of D_2 has been pooled over levels of A. Recall that such a pooled variance is also referred to as a mean square for subjects within A, so that $s_{D_{2p}}^2$ is simply mean square within for the D_2

variable. For our data, $s^2_{D_{2_p}}$ is the (unweighted) average of $s^2_{D_{1_1}}$, which equals 8640, and $s^2_{D_{22}}$, which equals 5290.[21] Thus, the pooled estimate equals 6965. The resultant F value obtained from substituting this value along with $n_1 = 10$ and $\bar{D}_{21} = -48$ into Equation 67 is 3.31. In general, this F statistic has 1 numerator and $N - a$ denominator degrees of freedom.

Once again, if the particular D variable to be tested was one of the D variables formed to conduct the multivariate test, the numerator and denominator values for the F statistic in Equation 67 are readily available from the appropriate diagonal elements of the $\mathbf{E(F)}_j$, $\mathbf{E(R)}_j$, and $\mathbf{E(F)}$ matrices. In particular, because the numerator of Equation 67 is identical to the numerator of Equation 66, this quantity is again equal to the appropriate diagonal element of $\mathbf{E(R)}_j$ minus the corresponding diagonal element of $\mathbf{E(F)}_j$. The only difference between Equations 66 and 67 is that the denominator of Equation 66 was based on $\mathbf{E(F)}_j$, but the denominator of Equation 67 is based on $\mathbf{E(F)}$. Specifically, $s^2_{D_{2_p}}$ is obtained by dividing the appropriate diagonal element of $\mathbf{E(F)}$ by $N - a$. For the quadratic angle effect, the appropriate element of $\mathbf{E(F)}$ appears in the second row and second column and has a value of 125,370. Dividing 125,370 by 18 (i.e., $20 - 2$) produces a denominator equal to 6965, which as we saw earlier is indeed $s^2_{D_{2_p}}$.

The choice of an appropriate critical value against which to compare the observed F value of either Equation 66 or Equation 67 depends as always on what other contrasts, if any, are being tested. If a per-comparison alpha level is desired, the critical F value is simply read from the F table with 1 numerator and $n_j - 1$ denominator degrees of freedom for Equation 66 and with 1 numerator and $N - a$ denominator degrees of freedom for Equation 67. If a set of C planned comparisons is to be tested, α_{PC} for each contrast is simply adjusted to equal α_{FW}/C, using the Bonferroni procedure. The Bonferroni technique is also appropriate for testing pairwise comparisons. Finally, for testing complex comparisons, the appropriate critical value once again comes from the multivariate extension of Scheffé's method developed by Roy and Bose. When the separate error term $s^2_{D_{2_j}}$ of Equation 66 has been used, the appropriate critical value is given by

$$CV = (n_j - 1)(b - 1)F_{\alpha_{FW};b-1,n_j-b+1}/(n_j - b + 1) \tag{68}$$

When the pooled error term $s^2_{D_{2_p}}$ of Equation 67 has been used, the critical value equals

$$CV = (N - a)(b - 1)F_{\alpha_{FW};b-1,N-a-b+2}/(N - a - b + 2) \tag{69}$$

One final comment must be made here. As we discussed in Chapter 7, α_{FW} for the tests in the preceding paragraph could be set in either of two ways. First, we might consider each individual level of A to constitute a separate family, in which case we would typically set α_{FW} equal to .05. In our example, we might regard questions of the angle effect for young subjects as answering a distinct theoretical question from the angle effect for old subjects, justifying our treating each age group as a separate family. Second, we might regard the a separate levels of A collectively as representing a single family. In this case, α_{FW} in the preceding paragraph would typically equal $.05/a$, because we would want to keep the Type I error rate for all tests to be performed within a level of A at $.05/a$.

Interaction Contrasts. As usual, another approach for interpreting a statistically significant interaction is to test interaction contrasts. Because the omnibus interaction F statistic has $(a - 1)(b - 1)$ numerator degrees of freedom, it may be of interest to isolate one or more single degree of freedom interaction contrasts that are contributing to the omnibus interaction.

The procedure for testing an interaction contrast in a split-plot design follows rather directly from the procedure used to test the omnibus interaction. Recall that the omnibus interaction was tested by comparing the a levels of A on the $b-1$ D variables simultaneously through a multivariate test. An interaction contrast is tested similarly, but there are two differences. First, instead of an omnibus comparison of all of the levels of A, a specific contrast of the levels of A is chosen. Second, instead of testing for a group difference on all $b-1$ D variables, one D variable is selected to represent a contrast among the levels of B. Because there is only a single dependent variable in the test of an interaction contrast, the within-subjects factor is effectively eliminated, and there is no need for a multivariate test. Thus, the principles of Chapter 4 can be applied to test a specific between-group comparison on the particular D variable of interest. The sum of squares for the contrast equals

$$SS_\psi = (\hat\psi)^2 \left/ \sum_{j=1}^{a} (c_j^2/n_j) \right. \tag{70}$$

where $\hat\psi = \sum_{j=1}^{a} c_j \bar D_j$. An error term is provided by mean square within for the D variable, which we previously denoted $s_{D_p}^2$, but which we will now write as $MS_{S/A(D)}$, because of its greater similarity to the notation we used in Chapter 4. The F statistic for testing an interaction contrast is then given by

$$F = SS_\psi / MS_{S/A(D)} \tag{71}$$

We can rewrite this F statistic in another form by substituting from Equation 70 for SS_ψ, yielding

$$F = \frac{(\hat\psi)^2}{MS_{S/A(D)} \sum_{j=1}^{a} (c_j^2/n_j)}, \tag{72}$$

which (except for the notation of $MS_{S/A(D)}$) is identical to Equation 4.37. The reason for this equivalence is again that we are simply testing a specific between-group comparison, exactly as we did in Chapter 4. The only difference is that the dependent variable for this test is now a D variable, which we calculated as a contrast of the levels of the within-subjects factor.

To illustrate the procedure for testing an interaction contrast, suppose that we want to test whether the quadratic trend for young subjects is different from the quadratic trend for old subjects. From Table 14.10, we know that $\bar D_{21} = -48$ and $\bar D_{22} = 27$, where $\bar D_{21}$ is the mean quadratic score for young subjects and $\bar D_{22}$ is the mean quadratic score for old subjects. We can then define the interaction contrast as

$$\hat\psi = \bar D_{21} - \bar D_{22}$$
$$= -48 - 27 = -75$$

Earlier we found that mean square within for the quadratic D variable equals 6965 in our data, so $MS_{S/A(D)} = 6965$. Substituting these values along with $n_1 = n_2 = 10$, $c_1 = 1$, and $c_2 = -1$ into Equation 72 results in an observed F value of 4.04. In general, this F statistic has 1 numerator and $N - a$ denominator degrees of freedom. In our example, then, the degrees of freedom are 1 and 18, resulting in a p value of .0597 without any adjustment for the possibility of multiple tests. We should point out that these are exactly the same F and p values we obtained when we used a separate error term in Chapter 12 (as in Equation 12.29) for testing an interaction contrast. However, this approach is consistent with the multivariate omnibus interaction test instead of the mixed-model test because an appropriate critical value for post hoc tests is obtained from the multivariate approach.

As always, the choice of a critical value depends on what other contrasts are being tested. If a set of planned comparisons is tested, α_{PC} for each contrast can simply be adjusted to equal α_{FW}/C, using the Bonferroni method. For post hoc comparisons, an appropriate critical value comes from the multivariate extension of Scheffé's method developed by Roy and Bose. When A has only two levels (as in our example), this critical value is given by

$$CV = (N - a)(a - 1)(b - 1)F_{\alpha_{FW};(a-1)(b-1), N-a-b+2}/(N - a - b + 2) \quad (73)$$

Because Equation 73 is only appropriate for the situation where A has two levels, we can substitute $a = 2$ into Equation 73 to get

$$CV = (N - 2)(b - 1)F_{\alpha_{FW};b-1, N-b}/(N - b) \quad (74)$$

When a is greater than two, the critical value is more complicated because s is greater than one. Finding the value of the appropriate post hoc critical value then requires the use of tables of Roy's greatest characteristic root. Such tables are available in Harris (1985). See Harris (1985) or O'Brien and Kaiser (1985) for further details.

Notice that when $a = 2$ (as in our example), the test of an interaction contrast is identical to an ANOVA on an appropriately chosen D variable. Thus, in effect, we are comparing a full model of the form

$$D_{ij} = \mu + \alpha_j + \varepsilon_{ij}$$

to a restricted model of the form

$$D_{ij} = \mu + \varepsilon_{ij}$$

The distinction between an interaction contrast and a contrast of marginal means is sometimes difficult to grasp. For example, we tested an interaction contrast which examined whether the quadratic angle trend for old subjects differs from the quadratic angle trend for young subjects. Earlier in the chapter, we had tested the significance of a quadratic trend for the marginal means of the angle factor. The test of marginal means uses the same full model as the interaction contrast, namely, a model of the form

$$D_{ij} = \mu + \alpha_j + \varepsilon_{ij}$$

However, the restricted model is different. The restricted model for the test of marginal means is given by

$$D_{ij} = \alpha_j + \varepsilon_{ij}$$

Thus, the test of marginal means asks whether the D variable has a population mean of zero, averaging over groups. The interaction contrast, on the other hand, asks whether the two groups have different population means on D. Thus, the interaction contrast compares the two groups, whereas the test of marginal means averages over groups.

O P T I O N A L

THE RELATIONSHIP BETWEEN THE MULTIVARIATE AND THE MIXED-MODEL APPROACHES

The multivariate and mixed-model approaches for analyzing data from a split-plot design relate to one another as they do for other designs. As before, we do not provide a mathematical proof of this relationship but instead demonstrate it empirically for our data.

An appropriate reminder at this point is that the multivariate and mixed-model approaches yield identical results for testing between-subjects effects. In essence, if there is only one score per subject entered into a particular test of significance, the two approaches produce equivalent results. Thus, our comparison of the two approaches concerns itself with the main effect of the within-subjects factor and with the interaction between the two factors.

Recall that we formed two D variables in our example to perform the multivariate test. The first D variable represented the linear trend for angle and was defined as

$$D_{1ij} = -1Y_{1ij} + 0Y_{2ij} + 1Y_{3ij}$$

The second D variable, which represented the quadratic trend for angle, was defined as

$$D_{2ij} = 1Y_{1ij} - 2Y_{2ij} + 1Y_{3ij}$$

To compare the two approaches, we must normalize the coefficients of these contrast variables. Notice that the linear and quadratic trends are already orthogonal to one another, so we need not worry further about this requirement. As usual, each nonnormalized coefficient must be divided by the square root of the sum of squared coefficients for that particular contrast. Carrying out this process for the linear and quadratic trend variables yields

$$D^*_{1ij} = -.7071Y_{1ij} + 0Y_{2ij} + .7071Y_{3ij}$$

$$D^*_{2ij} = -.4082Y_{1ij} + .8164Y_{2ij} + .4082Y_{3ij}$$

We could now perform the multivariate test on D^*_1 and D^*_2 by calculating a full matrix $\mathbf{E^*(F)}$ and two restricted matrices $\mathbf{E^*(R)}$, one for the B main effect and one for the A × B interaction. Although such a procedure would produce the desired results, it is much simpler to work directly from the matrices we already calculated for the nonnormalized D_1 and D_2 variables. Earlier in the chapter, we found that the full and restricted matrices for D_1 and D_2 were given by

$$\mathbf{E(F)} = \begin{bmatrix} 67{,}050 & -9{,}090 \\ -9{,}090 & 125{,}370 \end{bmatrix}$$

$$\mathbf{E_B(R)} = \begin{bmatrix} 936{,}495 & -52{,}875 \\ -52{,}875 & 127{,}575 \end{bmatrix}$$

$$\mathbf{E_{A \times B}(R)} = \begin{bmatrix} 99{,}855 & 21{,}285 \\ 21{,}285 & 153{,}495 \end{bmatrix}$$

where $\mathbf{E_B(R)}$ is the restricted matrix for the B main effect and $\mathbf{E_{A \times B}(R)}$ is the restricted matrix for the A × B interaction. We can compute the $\mathbf{E^*}$ matrices for the normalized variables by realizing that for each subject

$$D^*_{1ij} = .7071 D_{1ij}$$

$$D^*_{2ij} = .4082 D_{2ij}$$

As a result,

$$(D^*_{1ij})^2 = .5(D_{1ij})^2$$

$$(D^*_{2ij})^2 = .1667(D_{2ij})^2$$

$$D^*_{1ij}D^*_{2ij} = .2887 D_{1ij}D_{2ij}$$

It then follows that the row 1, column 1 element of each $\mathbf{E^*}$ matrix equals .5 times the corresponding element of each $\mathbf{E}$ matrix. Similarly, the row 2, column 2 element of each $\mathbf{E^*}$ matrix equals .1667 times the corresponding element of each $\mathbf{E}$ matrix. Finally, the row 1, column 2 and row 2, column 1 elements of each $\mathbf{E^*}$ matrix equal .2887 times the corresponding elements of each $\mathbf{E}$ matrix. Carrying out the necessary multiplication results in the following $\mathbf{E^*}$ matrices:

$$\mathbf{E^*(F)} = \begin{bmatrix} 33{,}525.00 & -2{,}624.06 \\ -2{,}624.06 & 20{,}895.00 \end{bmatrix}$$

$$\mathbf{E^*_B(R)} = \begin{bmatrix} 468{,}247.50 & -15{,}263.70 \\ -15{,}263.70 & 21{,}262.50 \end{bmatrix}$$

$$\mathbf{E^*_{A \times B}(R)} = \begin{bmatrix} 49{,}927.50 & 6{,}144.45 \\ 6{,}144.45 & 25{,}582.50 \end{bmatrix}$$

We can now consider the relationship between these $\mathbf{E^*}$ matrices and three sums of squares in the mixed-model approach: $SS_{B \times S/A}$, SS_B, and $SS_{A \times B}$. The sum of the two diagonal elements of $\mathbf{E^*(F)}$ equals 54,420, which we saw in Chapter 12 is $SS_{B \times S/A}$ for our data. Remembering that the sum of the diagonal elements of a matrix is its trace, which is abbreviated tr, enables us to write

$$SS_{B \times S/A} = tr(\mathbf{E^*(F)})$$

The relationships involving SS_B and $SS_{A \times B}$ are similarly given by

$$SS_B = tr(\mathbf{E}_B^*(\mathbf{R})) - tr(\mathbf{E}^*(\mathbf{F}))$$

$$SS_{A \times B} = tr(\mathbf{E}_{A \times B}^*(\mathbf{R})) - tr(\mathbf{E}^*(\mathbf{F}))$$

As a result, the mixed-model F tests for B and A × B can be written as

$$F = \frac{\{tr(\mathbf{E}_B^*(\mathbf{R})) - tr(\mathbf{E}^*(\mathbf{F})\}/(b-1)}{tr(\mathbf{E}^*(\mathbf{F}))/(N-a)(b-1)} \tag{75}$$

for the B main effect, and

$$F = \frac{\{tr(\mathbf{E}_{A \times B}^*(\mathbf{R})) - tr(\mathbf{E}^*(\mathbf{F}))/(a-1)(b-1)}{tr(\mathbf{E}^*(\mathbf{F}))/(N-a)(b-1)} \tag{76}$$

for the A × B interaction.

The practical implication of Equations 75 and 76 is that once again the multivariate approach is sensitive to all elements of the $\mathbf{E}^*$ matrices, whereas the mixed-model approach ignores the off-diagonal elements. The reason, as before, is that if the sphericity assumption required by the mixed-model approach is met, the population values of the off-diagonal elements of the $\mathbf{E}^*(\mathbf{F})$ matrix are all zero. In addition, if sphericity holds, the population values of the diagonal elements of $\mathbf{E}^*(\mathbf{F})$ are all equal to one another so that the sample mean of these values—that is, $tr(\mathbf{E}^*(\mathbf{F}))/(b-1)$—is a good estimate of the single underlying population value. However, if sphericity fails to hold, the mixed-model approach suffers from an inflated Type I error rate, unless ε adjustments are applied to the degrees of freedom of the critical value.

Also notice that the trace of the $\mathbf{E}^*(\mathbf{F})$ matrix forms the denominator sum of squares for testing both the B main effect and the A × B interaction. For this reason, the sphericity assumption is either met for both effects or it fails for both. When there is only one within-subjects factor, there is only one matrix for which the sphericity assumption is an issue. If, however, there were a second within-subjects factor in the design, we would need to consider additional matrices, just as we did earlier in the chapter for factorial within-subjects designs.

ASSUMPTIONS OF THE MULTIVARIATE APPROACH

Although the multivariate approach does not require that the sphericity assumption of the mixed-model approach be valid, the multivariate approach nevertheless shares several assumptions in common with the mixed-model approach. For example, because these two approaches produce identical F tests for between-subjects effects, it follows that their assumptions are also identical. Recall that between-subjects effects are tested by performing a between-subjects ANOVA on an M variable, where M is simply a variable that averages over the levels of the within-subjects factor(s). As we discussed in Chapter 12, the necessary assumptions are thus the same as those for a between-subjects design, namely, normality, homogeneity of variance, and independence of the M scores. The detailed discussion of these assumptions in Chapter 3 is equally pertinent to the split-plot design.

The assumptions for testing the B and A $\times$ B effects are rather different from those required for testing the A main effect because B and A $\times$ B are both within-subjects effects. Before discussing the assumptions of the multivariate approach, it is helpful to recall the assumptions of the mixed-model approach. Besides the usual assumptions of normality and independence, the mixed-model approach requires two other assumptions, which together are called *multisample sphericity*. First, the mixed-model approach assumes sphericity of the population covariance matrix for each level of the A factor. Second, it assumes that the population covariance matrix at one level of A is identical to the population covariance matrix at every other level of A. As we have emphasized previously, the multivariate approach does not require the sphericity assumption. However, it shares the assumption with the mixed-model approach that all a population covariance matrices are identical to each other. The multivariate tests tend to be robust to this homogeneity of covariance matrix assumption, as long as sample sizes are equal. As we stated earlier in the chapter, there is some evidence (Olson, 1976) that the Pillai–Bartlett trace test statistic is the most robust of the four multivariate test statistics when $a > 2$. Of course, when $a = 2$, all four multivariate test statistics are equivalent. As usual, when sample sizes depart from equality, the tests become less robust. Finally, as we pointed out in Chapter 13, the multivariate approach also assumes multivariate normality and independence of observations.

MULTIVARIATE AND MIXED-MODEL APPROACHES FOR TESTING WITHIN-SUBJECTS CONTRASTS

We saw earlier in the chapter that the multivariate approach for testing within-subjects contrasts involves the formation of an appropriate D variable. When a univariate test is conducted on this variable, no assumption of sphericity is required. We also saw that the use of a separate error term, which was one of the methods we discussed in Chapter 12, produces identical results to the multivariate approach. The use of a pooled error term, which was the other method we discussed in Chapter 12, may yield very different results because this approach depends strongly on the validity of the sphericity assumption. For this reason, we recommend using a separate error term for each contrast. However, as in other designs, the use of a separate error term is more consistent with the multivariate approach than with the mixed-model approach for analyzing split-plot data.

If a separate error term is to be used and if an omnibus test is desired, it makes sense to use the multivariate approach for performing the omnibus test. This omnibus test is statistically significant with the multivariate approach if and only if a statistically significant contrast can be found using a separate error term and an appropriate critical value, such as those given by Equations 63, 68, 69, 73, and 74. Thus, if the multivariate test is statistically significant, specific contrasts are worth testing; if the multivariate test is not significant, there is no reason to test specific contrasts because none can be significant with a separate error term. What if the mixed-model approach were used instead to perform the omnibus test? It is entirely possible for the mixed-model approach to yield a nonsignificant omnibus F test, and yet a specific statistically significant contrast exists when tested with the separate error term, even using an appropriate post hoc critical value. The reverse can also happen. That is, the mixed-model omnibus test can be statistically significant, and yet no significant specific contrast exists when tested with a separate error term and an appropriate critical value. Thus, the mixed-model test fails to provide an unambiguous signal to the researcher as to whether post hoc tests should be conducted (unless we are willing to use a pooled error term). The multivariate approach, on the other hand, does provide this information, which is one reason we prefer it in general.[22]

Of course, another viable option is to test planned contrasts, using a separate error term for each contrast. With this approach, to perform an omnibus test is unnecessary, so the distinction between the mixed-model and multivariate approaches is largely irrelevant. Notice, however, that the choice of error term is still relevant for testing planned contrasts. Not surprisingly, we continue to recommend the use of a separate error term for each contrast.

Comparison of the Multivariate and Mixed-Model Approaches

The advantages and disadvantages of the multivariate and mixed-model approaches in the split-plot design are essentially the same as in completely within-subjects designs. For this reason, we refer you to our earlier extended discussion at the end of Chapter 13 for more information. As before, our general recommendation is to use the multivariate approach unless sample sizes are very small. A rough rule of thumb for a minimum sample size required with the multivariate approach can be stated in terms of the between-subjects and within-subjects degrees of freedom. The between-subjects degrees of freedom will equal the number of subjects on which the error matrix for the full model is based, minus the number of groups formed by these subjects. For example, if the error matrix for the full model is based on all subjects in a split-plot design, the between-subjects degrees of freedom will equal $N - a$. On the other hand, if only subjects at level j are used to form the error matrix for the full model, the between-subjects degrees of freedom will equal $n_j - 1$. The within-subjects degrees of freedom will equal the number of D variables involved in a particular test. The rough rule of thumb can now be stated: The between-subjects degrees of freedom should probably exceed the within-subjects degrees of freedom by at least 10, if the multivariate approach is to be used.

O P T I O N A L

MORE COMPLEX DESIGNS

We have focused our attention in this chapter on designs with two factors. However, both the logic and the procedural details we have developed generalize to higher-order designs. For example, the tests to be conducted in a three-way design with one or more repeated factors would be the same as those discussed in Chapter 8 for between-subjects designs. In particular, the flowchart shown in Figure 8.2 can still be used as a general guideline for choosing what effects to test. However, as in two-way repeated-measures designs, the form of the F test must take into account the lack of independence that arises from having more than one score per subject.

To illustrate how tests are conducted in higher-order repeated-measures designs, we consider a four-way $A \times B \times E \times F$ design. (We do not designate the design as $A \times B \times C \times D$ because D continues to designate a "difference" variable.) We assume that factors A and B are between-subjects factors and that E and F are within-subjects factors. As usual, the number of levels of the factors is designated as a, b, e, and f for A, B, E, and F, respectively. We further assume that all factors are completely crossed. This implies that data are obtained for $a \times b$ distinct groups of subjects, where each subject contributes $e \times f$ scores.

Table 8.21 shows that there are 15 omnibus effects to be tested in a four-way design: four main effects (viz., A, B, E, and F), six two-way interactions (viz., $A \times B$, $A \times E$, $A \times F$, $B \times E$, $B \times F$, and $E \times F$), four three-way interactions (viz., $A \times B \times E$, $A \times B \times F$, $A \times E \times F$, and $B \times E \times F$), and one four-way interaction (viz., $A \times B \times E \times F$). Interpretation of results would typically begin by considering the significance of the four-way interaction, then the three-way interactions, and so forth. We do not attempt to describe interpretations here because they are fundamentally the same in repeated-measures designs as in between-subjects designs. Instead, our focus is on what models to compare and what variables to form in order to test each effect of interest because these are the issues that change in a repeated-measures design.

We begin by considering the transformed variables that must be formed in the $A \times B \times E \times F$ design. After seeing how these variables are formed, we present full and restricted models to be compared. In the process, we will see that each of the 15 effects of interest can be tested by choosing an appropriate set of transformed variables (or, in some cases, a single transformed variable) and then comparing appropriate full and restricted models for this set of variables.

Each subject contributes $e \times f$ scores to the data because there are e levels of E and f levels of F, where E and F are the two repeated factors. We continue to refer to these original variables as Y variables. As in the designs we considered earlier in the chapter, the multivariate approach requires that these $e \times f$ original Y variables be transformed into a new set of variables. It is helpful to state at the outset that these new, transformed variables can be conceptualized best as constituting four types of variables. First, as in our earlier designs, a mean variable M can be calculated for each subject. Following the same logic as in the other designs of this chapter, a subject's score on M is literally the mean of the subject's scores on the original $e \times f$ Y variables.

The other three types of variables follow directly from the procedures we developed at the beginning of the chapter for designs with two repeated factors. In particular, transformed variables are formed for the $A \times B \times E \times F$ design just as they were at the beginning of the chapter when there were no between-subjects factors. The presence (or absence) of between-subjects factors has no effect on how transformed D variables are defined. Thus, the second type of variable is a set of $e - 1$ variables, each of which represents a contrast of the levels of E averaged over F. Each variable is a difference variable or a D variable in our abbreviated notation.

For clarity, we refer to this set of variables as the D_E set, where the E subscript serves as a reminder that these variables reflect differences among the levels of the E factor. Specifically, the set of $e-1$ D_E variables collectively represents average differences among the e levels of the E factor, where the average is computed over levels of F, the other within-subjects factor. Notice that scores on each of the $e-1$ D_E variables would be computed just as they were at the beginning of the chapter in the design that had two repeated factors but no between-subjects factors. Similarly, the third type of variable is a set of $f-1$ D variables, each of which represents a contrast of the levels of F averaged over E. We designate this set of variables as D_F. Finally, the fourth type of variable is a set of $(e-1)(f-1)$ D variables, each of which represents a component of the E × F interaction. This set is designated $D_{E \times F}$.

To summarize, the original $e \times f$ Y variables are transformed into four new sets of variables:

1. One M variable
2. $e - 1$ D_E variables
3. $f - 1$ D_F variables
4. $(e - 1)(f - 1)$ $D_{E \times F}$ variables

The total number of transformed variables equals $1+(e-1)+(f-1)+(e-1)(f-1)$. However, expanding the final term of this expression yields $1 + (e - 1) + (f - 1) + ef - f - e + 1$, which is equivalent to $ef + e - e + f - f + 1 - 1 - 1 + 1$, which reduces to ef. Thus, the total number of transformed variables equals the total number of original variables. A typical reaction to this statement might be, So why did we bother to transform the variables in the first place? The answer is that the sets of transformed variables explicitly contain information about the effects we want to test. Although the same information exists in the original variables, the form of the original variables does not permit us to test the effects of interest directly.

Transforming the original variables enables us to represent within-subjects effects. However, we also need a mechanism for incorporating between-subjects effects into our analyses. This is accomplished by forming a full model whose parameters correspond to the between-subjects effects in the design. For example, when we had only one between-subjects factor (and one within-subjects factor), we formed a full model of the form

$$M_{ij} = \mu + \alpha_j + \varepsilon_{ij} \qquad \text{(37, repeated)}$$

for the M variable and a model of the form

$$D_{ij} = \mu + \alpha_j + \varepsilon_{ij} \qquad \text{(41, repeated)}$$

for each of the D variable(s). The important point to notice here is that the full models have the same form for M and as for D. In both cases, the model corresponds to the between-subjects design, because there was one between-subjects factor. For this reason, the model has the same form as the models we introduced in Chapter 3.

Our current four-way A × B × E × F design has two between-subjects factors, so the appropriate full model now needs to include additional parameters to reflect the A main effect, the B main effect, and the A × B interaction. As a result, the full model has the same form as the full model we developed in Chapter 7 for two-way between-subjects designs. Specifically, in the four-way design, we will have a full model of the form

$$M_{ijk} = \mu + \alpha_j + \beta_k + (\alpha\beta)_{jk} + \varepsilon_{ijk}$$

for the M variable and a model of the form

$$D_{ijk} = \mu + \alpha_j + \beta_k + (\alpha\beta)_{jk} + \varepsilon_{ijk}$$

for each of the D variables. As in Chapter 7, μ is a grand mean parameter, α_j is an effect associated with the jth level of A, β_k is an effect associated with the kth level of B, and $\alpha\beta_{jk}$ is a parameter for the A $\times$ B interaction. When M is the dependent variable, the full model allows for A main effects, B main effects, and A $\times$ B interaction effects on each subject's mean score, averaged over levels of the repeated factors. Similarly, the full model for the dependent variable D allows for A, B, and A $\times$ B effects to exert themselves on differences among the levels of the repeated factors. The various combinations of restricted models and dependent variables together allow us to test the effects of interest.

Table 14.15 shows the type of dependent variable and the type of restriction to employ to test each omnibus effect in the A $\times$ B $\times$ E $\times$ F design. To ensure that the table is clear, we consider how to test a few specific effects. First, let's consider the A main effect. According to the table, this effect is tested using M as the dependent variable. Thus, the full model is

$$M_{ijk} = \mu + \alpha_j + \beta_k + (\alpha\beta)_{jk} + \varepsilon_{ijk}$$

The restriction imposed on this model is that all α_j parameters equal zero, which leads to a restricted model of the form

$$M_{ijk} = \mu + \beta_k + (\alpha\beta)_{jk} + \varepsilon_{ijk}$$

The F test comparing these models is conducted exactly as we described in Chapter 7. Although we hope that this brief description clarifies how to perform the test of the A main effect, even more important is to understand why such a procedure produces a test of the A main effect. The crucial point here is to remember that the M variable has averaged over the E and F factors. Thus, the model comparison we have performed effectively compares A marginal means, averaging over all other factors in the design, which is just the definition of a main effect.

Second, let's consider the A $\times$ E interaction. Table 14.15 shows that this effect is tested using the set of D_E variables as dependent variables. There are $e - 1$ variables in this set, necessitating a multivariate analysis whenever $e \geq 3$, that is, whenever the E factor has three or more levels. For each variable in the set, an appropriate full model is given by

$$D_{ijk} = \mu + \alpha_j + \beta_k + (\alpha\beta)_{jk} + \varepsilon_{ijk}$$

The restriction imposed on this model is that all α_j parameters equal zero, which leads to a restricted model of the form

$$D_{ijk} = \mu + \beta_k + (\alpha\beta)_{jk} + \varepsilon_{ijk}$$

T A B L E **14.15** Tests of Omnibus Effects in an A × B × E × F Design

Between-Subjects Effects—Full Model: $M_{ijk} = \mu + \alpha_j + \beta_k + (\alpha\beta)_{jk} + \varepsilon_{ijk}$

Effect	Type of Dependent Variable	Number of Dependent Variables	Restricted Parameters	df_{num}	df_{den}
A	M	1	$H_0: \alpha_j = 0$	$a-1$	$N-ab$
B	M	1	$H_0: \beta_k = 0$	$b-1$	$N-ab$
A × B	M	1	$H_0: \alpha\beta_{jk} = 0$	$(a-1)(b-1)$	$N-ab$

Within-Subjects Effects—Full Model: $D_{ijk} = \mu + \alpha_j + \beta_k + (\alpha\beta)_{jk} + \varepsilon_{ijk}$

Effect	Type of Dependent Variable	Number of Dependent Variables	Restricted Parameters	df_{num}	df_{den}
E	D_E	$e-1$	$H_0: \mu = 0$	$e-1$	$N-ab-e+2$
F	D_F	$f-1$	$H_0: \mu = 0$	$f-1$	$N-ab-f+2$
E × F	$D_{E \times F}$	$(e-1)(f-1)$	$H_0: \mu = 0$	$(e-1)(f-1)$	$N-ab-(e-1)(f-1)+1$
A × E	D_E	$e-1$	$H_0: \alpha_j = 0$	$(a-1)(e-1)$	Rao*
B × E	D_E	$e-1$	$H_0: \beta_k = 0$	$(b-1)(e-1)$	Rao*
A × B × E	D_E	$e-1$	$H_0: (\alpha\beta)_{jk} = 0$	$(a-1)(b-1)(e-1)$	Rao*
A × F	D_F	$f-1$	$H_0: \alpha_j = 0$	$(a-1)(f-1)$	Rao*
B × F	D_F	$f-1$	$H_0: \beta_k = 0$	$(b-1)(f-1)$	Rao*
A × B × F	D_F	$f-1$	$H_0: (\alpha\beta)_{jk} = 0$	$(a-1)(b-1)(f-1)$	Rao*
A × E × F	$D_{E \times F}$	$(e-1)(f-1)$	$H_0: \alpha_j = 0$	$(a-1)(e-1)(f-1)$	Rao*
B × E × F	$D_{E \times F}$	$(e-1)(f-1)$	$H_0: \beta_k = 0$	$(b-1)(e-1)(f-1)$	Rao*
A × B × E × F	$D_{E \times F}$	$(e-1)(f-1)$	$H_0: (\alpha\beta)_{jk} = 0$	$(a-1)(b-1)(e-1)(f-1)$	Rao*

* When Rao's F approximation is used, denominator degrees of freedom equal $df_{den} = mq - .5pd_H + 1$, where

$$m = N - ab + d_H - .5(p + d_H + 1)$$

$$q = \sqrt{\frac{(pd_H)^2 - 4}{p^2 + d_H^2 - 5}} \quad \text{where } q = 1 \text{ if } p^2 + d_H^2 = 5$$

p = number of dependent variables

d_H = number of independent restricted parameters (per dependent variable)

Errors for each subject must be calculated for both the full and restricted models. Sums of squared errors and sums of cross-products can then be put in matrix form, and an F statistic can be calculated. In general, as Table 14.15 shows, the numerator degrees of freedom equal $(a - 1)(e - 1)$, whereas the denominator degrees of freedom come from Rao's approximation (if Wilks's lambda is chosen as the test statistic). All of this discussion leads to what is in many respects the crucial question: Why does testing a null hypothesis that all α_j parameters equal zero test the A $\times$ E interaction? As in our discussion of the A main effect, the crucial point is to remember the nature of the dependent variable(s). The variables used to test the A $\times$ E interaction are the D_E difference variables, which collectively represent differences among levels of E, averaged over F. Testing whether the α_j parameters equal zero asks, Is there an A effect on the differences among levels of E? However, the presence of such an effect implies that the E differences vary at different levels of A, which means that A and E interact. Also notice that the other two factors in the design have been averaged over, as required for a two-way interaction in a four-way design. Specifically, F has been averaged over because the variables in the D_E set are defined to average over F. The B factor has also been averaged over because of the meaning of the α_j parameters in the full model. Thus, testing for an A effect on the set of D_E variables provides a test of the A $\times$ E interaction.

The other tests in Table 14.15 are based on the same underlying logic. In addition, follow-up tests could be performed by varying the nature of the models being compared and/or by varying the definitions of the transformed variables. Fortunately, if the logic is understood, the mechanics can be handled easily with available statistical packages.

We have now presented procedures for using the multivariate approach in a variety of repeated-measures designs. It may be helpful to summarize a general procedure that can be employed, for any combination of between-subjects and within-subjects factors. The general procedure can be conceptualized in terms of three steps:

1. Form an M variable and D variables that correspond to the within-subjects effects to be tested. Scores are calculated for every subject on each variable, irrespective of any between-subjects factors.

2. Form a full model whose parameters correspond to between-subjects effects, irrespective of any within-subjects factors.

3. Calculate an F statistic by comparing the full model of step 2 to an appropriate restricted model, using sets of variables from step 1 as dependent variables.

Table 14.16 provides general rules for calculating degrees of freedom for the multivariate approach to analyzing data from split-plot designs. Our purpose in presenting this table might be unclear because whatever computer program you are using will undoubtedly calculate degrees of freedom for you. However, calculating degrees of freedom by hand and checking them against the computer printout is frequently a good idea. Although it is unlikely that a "bug" in the computer program has caused it to calculate degrees of freedom incorrectly, it is not so unlikely that

T A B L E **14. 16** General Rules for Degrees of
Freedom in Split-Plot Designs

Type of Effect	df_{num}[†]	df_{den}[‡]
Between	d_H	$N - g$
Within*	p	$N - g - p + 1$
Between × within	pd_H	$mq - .5pd_H + 1$

* "Within" means any within-subjects effect that averages over levels of the between-subjects factor(s).
[†] d_H is the number of independent restricted parameters (per dependent variable). For a given variable, d_H equals $df_R - df_F$. p is the number of dependent variables.
[‡] N is total sample size. g is the number of groups (or between-subjects cells) in the design. m is defined as $m = N - g + d_H - .5(p + d_H + 1)$. q is defined as

$$q = \sqrt{\frac{(pd_H)^2 - 4}{p^2 + d_H^2 - 5}} \quad \text{where } q = 1 \text{ if } p^2 + d_H^2 = 5$$

the computer program may have provided the right answer to the wrong question. In other words, in complex designs, it is all too easy to think that a particular p value on the printout establishes the statistical significance of a certain effect, whereas in fact the instructions given to the program caused it to test an entirely different effect. While checking degrees of freedom does not guarantee accuracy, it does provide some additional assurance that the correct effect has been tested.

A few additional remarks may clarify some of the entries in Table 14.16. First, the numerator degrees of freedom for an effect are the same as in other designs. For example, the d_H entry for the numerator degrees of freedom of a between-subjects effect equals the number of independent restricted parameters, which is equivalent to $df_R - df_F$, as in earlier designs. This formula is appropriate regardless of the number of between-subjects factors in the model and applies to any type of between-subjects effect (e.g., main effect, interaction, simple effect, etc.). Similarly, the numerator degrees of freedom for any purely within-subjects effect (i.e., one which averages over levels of any between-subjects factors) equal the number of dependent variables. Finally, numerator degrees of freedom for effects involving between × within interactions equal the product of the respective degrees of freedom. Thus, for all types of effects, the numerator degrees of freedom in a split-plot design follow the same rules as in other designs.

Denominator degrees of freedom are straightforward, except for between × within interactions. For example, denominator degrees of freedom for between-subjects effects are the same as they would be if there were no within-subjects factors in the design. Denominator degrees of freedom for purely within-subjects effects are also easily calculated, as shown in Table 14.16. It is also worth pointing out that all four multivariate test statistics yield the same result for purely within-subjects effects. As the table shows, denominator degrees of freedom are considerably more complicated for effects involving between × within interactions. We should also add that the formula shown in the table is for Rao's approximation to Wilks's lambda. In general, the four multivariate test statistics differ at least slightly from each other for tests of between × within interactions. The only situation where the tests necessarily are identical is when $s = 1$. The s parameter equals the smaller of p and d_H, so unless $p = 1$ or $d_H = 1$, the four test statistics are not identical.

The analysis of data from higher-order repeated-measures designs can obviously become quite complicated. The technical complications should not cause you to lose sight of the underlying logic. Remember the three-step process that can be applied no matter how complicated the design:

1. Variables are transformed to represent within-subjects effects.

2. A full model whose parameters correspond to between-subjects effects is formed.

3. The full model of step 2 is compared to a restricted model, using sets of variables from step 1.

Understanding the logic behind these three steps should enable you to analyze and interpret data from higher-order repeated-measures designs. For readers interested in further specific details, several good sources are available. We particularly recommend Hand and Taylor (1987), Hertzog and Rovine (1985), and O'Brien and Kaiser (1985).

EXERCISES

1. True or False: Although the multivariate approach to repeated measures generally yields different results than the univariate (mixed-model) approach for testing omnibus effects, the two approaches are identical for testing contrasts.

2. True or False: The multivariate approach and the mixed-model approach to repeated measures in split-plot designs always yield identical F values for tests of between-subjects effects.

3. True or False: A major difference between data analysis in factorial between-subjects designs and split-plot designs is that the meaning of a significant interaction is different.

4. True or False: There are four different multivariate test statistics that can be used for testing an interaction in a split-plot design where both factors have more than two levels.

*5. A psychologist has conducted a study with a two-way 3 × 4 within-subjects design. We designate the three-level factor as A and the four-level factor as B.
   a. List the omnibus effects to be tested in this design.
   b. How many D variables will be needed to test each of the effects in part a?
   c. Assume that 20 subjects have been used in the study. Find the numerator and denominator degrees of freedom for each of the effects in part a.

6. Table 14.1 presents data for a two-way 2×2 within-subjects design. The F values obtained with the multivariate approach are 66.57 for the angle main effect, 45.37 for the noise main effect, and 83.90 for the angle $\times$ noise interaction. Analyze these same data using the mixed-model approach of Chapter 12. How do your results compare to those obtained with the multivariate approach? Why?

7. The chapter states that the difference variables D_4 of Equations 23 and 25 are equivalent to one another. The interaction contrast of Equation 23 was obtained by applying the algorithm for generating an interaction difference variable:

$$D_{4i} = 1Y_{1i} + 0Y_{2i} - 1Y_{3i} - 1Y_{4i} + 0Y_{5i} + 1Y_{6i} \tag{23}$$

Equation 25 was written as

$$D_{4i} = (-1Y_{4i} + 0Y_{5i} + 1Y_{6i}) - (-1Y_{1i} + 0Y_{2i} + 1Y_{3i}) \tag{25}$$

a. How would you interpret the effect represented by the D_4 variable of Equation 25?
b. Carry out the subtraction in Equation 25. Are the coefficients of Equation 25 equivalent to those of Equation 23?

*8. Suppose that 20 subjects have participated in a 3×4 two-way within-subjects design. We represent the factor with three levels as A and the factor with four levels as B.
a. Suppose that all pairwise comparisons of A marginal means are to be tested. Find the numerical value of the critical value (CV) that should be used to maintain α_{FW} at .05.
b. How would your answer to part a change if post hoc complex comparisons were also to be tested?
c. Suppose that an interaction contrast were to be tested post hoc. Find the numerical value of the critical value (CV) that should be used to maintain α_{FW} at .05.

*9. A graduate student has used a two-way 2×4 within-subjects design for his thesis. Fifteen individuals served as subjects. His most interesting result was a statistically significant A main effect. According to the computer program he used (which uses the mixed-model approach), the F value for this effect was 5.61 with 1 numerator and 98 denominator degrees of freedom. His thesis adviser has asked him to reanalyze his data using the multivariate approach. Will he necessarily obtain the same result once again for the A main effect? Explain your answer.

10. Kosslyn describes a program of research investigating processes involved in the formation of a visual image (Kosslyn, S. M. 1988. "Aspects of a cognitive neuroscience of mental imagery." *Science, 240*, 1621–1626). In one condition of one study, subjects were shown an uppercase letter superimposed on a grid. They were then shown a blank grid and a lowercase letter. Their task was to decide whether the corresponding uppercase letter would occupy one or two specific cells of the grid. In a second condition of this study, the task was the same, but the internal lines of the grid were eliminated and only the brackets at the four corners were presented. Perceptual theory suggests that when grid lines are present subjects use a categorical representation of how line segments in letters are connected. However, when only brackets are present, subjects use a coordinate representation to arrange the parts of the stimulus letter. In both conditions, the stimulus was presented to the right visual field half of the time (and hence seen first in the left cerebral hemisphere) and to the left visual field on remaining trials (and hence seen first in the right cerebral hemisphere). The primary dependent variable of interest was response time (in milliseconds) averaged over a number of trials. The following hypothetical data assume that each of 10 subjects has been assessed in both the grids condition and the brackets condition:

| | Grids Condition | | Brackets Condition | |
	Left Hemisphere	Right Hemisphere	Left Hemisphere	Right Hemisphere
Subject				
1	1600	1670	1690	1690
2	1420	1590	1580	1590
3	1670	1730	1790	1800
4	1430	1560	1550	1460
5	1550	1510	1570	1590
6	1520	1600	1680	1600
7	1610	1730	1780	1670
8	1600	1710	1670	1710
9	1680	1720	1800	1710
10	1570	1500	1610	1520

a. Perform a test of the condition main effect, the hemisphere main effect, and the condition × hemisphere interaction.

b. Based on your answers to part a, would it be appropriate to perform simple-effects tests here? If so, test effects of condition within hemisphere and hemisphere within condition.

c. Do your results support Kosslyn's contention that two different classes of processes are used to form mental images? In particular, do your results support the statement that some of the processes used to arrange parts of images are more efficient in the left hemisphere, whereas for other processes the right hemisphere is more efficient?

d. Is the sphericity assumption required for your analyses here? Why or why not?

*11. Under what conditions will the mixed-model and multivariate approaches necessarily yield the same results for testing the following effects in an A × B split-plot design (A is between, B is within)?

a. A main effect

b. B main effect

c. A × B interaction

12. Assume that the multivariate approach is being used to analyze a between × within design. The test of whether the grand means are zero for the transformed variables that represent contrasts among the levels of the within-subjects factor is a test of which omnibus effect?

*13. Consider the following cell means in a 3 × 2 split-plot design

		B	
		1	2
	1	10	12
A	2	16	20
	3	16	16

Twenty subjects were observed at each level of A, the between-subjects factor. Two transformed dependent variables were formed for each subject: $M_i = (Y_{1i} + Y_{2i})/2$ and $D_i = Y_{2i} - Y_{1i}$. The within-cell standard deviations for M were $s_1 = 4$, $s_2 = 6$, and $s_3 = 5$. The corresponding values for D were $s_1 = 6$, $s_2 = 4$, and $s_3 = 4$.
a. Test the statistical significance of the A main effect.
b. Test the statistical significance of the B main effect.
c. Test the statistical significance of the A × B interaction.

14. Exercise 18 at the end of Chapter 12 described a study that investigated the extent to which newborn infants are able to discriminate their mother's voice from the voice of another woman. Five infants in the first condition could produce a tape recording of their own mother's voice by increasing the interval between bursts of sucking on a nonnutritive nipple relative to their baseline rate of sucking; otherwise, they heard a recording of the voice of one of the other mothers whose infant was a subject in the study. Five other infants in the second condition could produce a tape recording of their own mother's voice by decreasing the interval between bursts of sucking; otherwise, they also heard a non-maternal voice. The following data (IBIs in seconds) approximate the actual data obtained in the study.

Group 1 (Larger IBI produced maternal voice)		
Subject	*Baseline IBI*	*Feedback IBI*
1	4.4	6.4
2	1.0	1.9
3	3.4	5.2
4	3.3	3.3
5	4.5	4.0

Group 2 (Smaller IBI produced maternal voice)		
1	5.8	1.8
2	4.3	1.9
3	3.7	2.5
4	3.4	1.7
5	3.8	3.0

a. Perform tests of the group main effect, the baseline versus feedback main effect, and the group × baseline versus feedback interaction.
b. A graduate student has reconceptualized these data. For each subject, she calculated a score reflecting that infant's preference for the maternal voice. Specifically, for group 1 subjects: maternal preference = feedback – baseline; and for group 2 subjects: maternal preference = baseline – feedback. Notice that with this definition, higher positive difference scores in both groups reflect greater preference for the mother's voice. Given this definition, the data from this study can be conceptualized as follows:

	Group 1
Subject	*Maternal Preference*
1	2.0
2	0.9
3	1.8
4	0.0
5	−0.5

	Group 2
1	4.0
2	2.4
3	1.2
4	1.7
5	0.8

A model for these data can be written as $Y_{ij} = \mu + \alpha_j + \varepsilon_{ij}$, where Y_{ij} is the maternal preference score for the ith subject in the jth group. Test a null hypothesis that the grand mean parameter equals zero for these data.

c. Is the F value you obtained in part b equal to any of the F values you obtained in part a? What is the meaning of the test you have conducted here?

d. Test a null hypothesis that the α_j parameters equal zero for the maternal preference scores.

e. Is the F value you obtained in part d equal to any of the F values you obtained in part a? What is the meaning of the test you have conducted here?

15. A graduate student has conducted a study using a 3 × 4 split-plot design. Which of the four multivariate test statistics would you recommend that he use for testing the within-subjects main effect? Why?

16. The student in Exercise 15 reports that he obtained an F value of 3.22 with 6 and 80 degrees of freedom for one of his effects. His adviser can't believe that he is so trusting of computer printouts. After all, he had only 15 subjects in each of his 3 groups; his adviser tells him that she certainly would have expected him to know that degrees of freedom cannot be larger than the number of subjects. He is uncertain what to do next and turns to you for assistance.

a. Is it possible that his computer printout is correct, that is, that he really has 6 and 80 degrees of freedom? Justify your answer.

b. If the printout is correct, which effect is being tested?

c. Which test statistic was used?

d. What would the degrees of freedom be for the Pillai–Bartlett test statistic?

e. From the available information, can you provide the observed F for the Pillai–Bartlett test? Why or why not?

*17. The same student in Exercises 15 and 16 has decided to test the following post hoc contrast: the average of levels 1 and 2 of B versus the average of levels 3 and 4 of B, within the first level of A where A is the between-subjects factor. Using a pooled error term (i.e., pooled across levels of A), he obtained an observed F value of 4.13 for this contrast. Is the contrast statistically significant, if he wants to maintain his α level at .05 for the family of all possible comparisons that could be conducted within the first level of A? Justify your answer.

18. A psychologist has used a $2 \times 3 \times 3$ design, where the first factor (A) is between-subjects and the other two factors (B and C) are within-subjects. The psychologist plans to use the multivariate approach to analyze her data.
    a. How many M variables will she need to define?
    b. How many D variables will she need to define?
    c. So far, she has defined the following four variables:

B_1C_1	B_1C_2	B_1C_3	B_2C_1	B_2C_2	B_2C_3	B_3C_1	B_3C_2	B_3C_3
1	-1	0	1	-1	0	1	-1	0
1	1	-2	1	1	-2	1	1	-2
1	1	1	-1	-1	-1	0	0	0
1	1	1	1	1	1	-2	-2	-2

What effect(s) can she test with the first pair of variables?
    d. What effect(s) can she test with the second pair of variables?
    e. Define additional variables that will enable her to test the remaining omnibus effects of interest.

*19. A researcher has conducted a study using a $3 \times 2 \times 4$ design. The first two factors are between-subjects, and the third factor is within-subjects. Ten subjects were obtained for each of the between-subjects cells. Wilks's lambda is chosen as the multivariate test statistic.
    a. How many dependent variables will be needed to test the three-way interaction?
    b. Write both the full model and the restricted model for one of the dependent variables used in part a to test the three-way interaction.
    c. How many numerator degrees of freedom are there for the F test of the three-way interaction?
    d. What will the value of the denominator degrees of freedom be equal to, for the three-way interaction?

20. Exercise 16 at the end of Chapter 11 introduced hypothetical data obtained by a developmental psychologist interested in the role of the sound of a mother's heartbeat in the growth of newborn babies. This exercise uses the same data, but now we assume that half of the infants were assigned to a control group. Specifically, seven babies were randomly assigned to a condition where they were exposed to a rhythmic heartbeat sound piped in over the PA system. The other seven babies were placed in an identical nursery, but without the heartbeat sound. Infants were weighed at the same time of day for four consecutive days, yielding the following data (weight is measured in ounces):

	Heartbeat Group			
Subject	*Day 1*	*Day 2*	*Day 3*	*Day 4*
1	96	98	103	104
2	116	116	118	119
3	102	102	101	101
4	112	115	116	118
5	108	110	112	115
6	92	95	96	98
7	120	121	121	123

		Control Group		
Subject	*Day 1*	*Day 2*	*Day 3*	*Day 4*
1	112	111	111	109
2	95	96	98	99
3	114	112	110	109
4	99	100	99	98
5	124	125	127	126
6	100	98	95	94
7	106	107	106	107

Despite the rather small sample size, use the multivariate approach throughout this problem to analyze these data.

a. Test the group main effect, the day main effect, and the group × day interaction.

b. Write one or two sentences interpreting the meaning of the results you obtained in part a. (HINT: A plot of the cell means may aid in your interpretation.)

c. Is the linear trend for days different in the heartbeat condition from the control condition? Treat this question as a single planned comparison.

d. Test the linear trend within each group for significance. Use an error term pooled over the two groups.

e. Another way to view these data might be to test the simple effect of condition at each day. Perform these tests, using an α level of .05 for each test. Do your results seem consistent with the results you obtained in parts c and d? How can you explain this pattern of results?

f. Yet another way to analyze these data might be to investigate the change across adjacent days. Suppose that we wanted to answer three questions:

   (1) Is there a group difference in the change from day 1 to day 2?
   (2) Is there a group difference in the change from day 2 to day 3?
   (3) Is there a group difference in the change from day 3 to day 4?

   Treat these questions as planned comparisons and perform tests of the three questions maintaining α_{FW} at .05.

g. Suppose that after looking at the data, a researcher decided to consider the following contrast of the time factor: -3(day 1) $- 1$(day 2) $+ 1$(day 3) $+ 3$(day 4). Would the two groups differ significantly on this contrast, maintaining α_{FW} at .05?

h. Explain why this two-group design is superior to the design described for these data in Chapter 11, where we assumed that all 14 infants were exposed to the heartbeat sound.

i. Although the two-group design is a great improvement over the one-group design described earlier for these data, might there still be some plausible threats to the validity of a conclusion that exposure to heartbeat sounds affects infants' growth?

21. Jemmott et al. report a study investigating the effect of academic stress on immune function (Jemmott, J. B., et al. 1983. "Academic stress, power, motivation, and decrease in secretion rate of salivary secretory immunoglobulin A," *The Lancet*, 1, 1400–1402). Immune function was measured five times during the academic year: an initial low-stress period, three high-stress periods coinciding with major exams, and a final low-stress period. Forty-seven first-year dental students served as subjects. Each subject was identified as belonging to one of three personality types on the basis of responses to the Thematic Apperception Test, which was administered prior to the assessment of immune function. The three groups were an inhibited power syndrome

(IPS) group, a relaxed affiliative syndrome (RAS) group, and a residual or control (C) group, which consisted of subjects who failed to fit the criteria for either of the other two groups. The dependent measure was the rate of secretion of salivary secretory immunoglobulin A (s-IgA), obtained at each of the five time points. Higher values of s-IgA secretion rate (measured as mg s-IgA/min) reflect stronger functioning of the immune system. Consider the following hypothetical (but realistic) data:

IPS Group

Subject	Sept.	Nov.	Apr.	June	July
1	.21	.20	.21	.19	.16
2	.19	.20	.16	.14	.13
3	.25	.16	.16	.16	.13
4	.11	.09	.10	.10	.14
5	.19	.13	.15	.11	.11
6	.18	.16	.16	.17	.10
7	.21	.18	.15	.18	.08
8	.16	.12	.14	.11	.18
9	.20	.14	.11	.13	.11

RAS Group

Subject	Sept.	Nov.	Apr.	June	July
1	.28	.28	.25	.29	.29
2	.22	.18	.16	.21	.25
3	.30	.27	.26	.26	.29
4	.24	.23	.24	.23	.23
5	.26	.22	.23	.19	.17
6	.27	.22	.20	.22	.24
7	.32	.25	.24	.21	.23
8	.20	.19	.21	.27	.28
9	.21	.22	.20	.19	.20
10	.33	.28	.25	.28	.27
11	.23	.18	.19	.24	.28
12	.17	.12	.15	.14	.12
13	.20	.17	.14	.18	.19
14	.22	.23	.19	.24	.22
15	.24	.22	.22	.22	.21

C Group

Subject	Sept.	Nov.	Apr.	June	July
1	.14	.12	.09	.17	.19
2	.25	.18	.15	.16	.26
3	.22	.21	.14	.16	.19
4	.17	.12	.10	.12	.15
5	.17	.15	.12	.12	.14
6	.14	.12	.11	.12	.20
7	.17	.12	.12	.09	.14
8	.20	.14	.16	.12	.15

Subject	Sept.	Nov.	Apr.	June	July
9	.25	.24	.20	.13	.17
10	.15	.07	.05	.13	.15
11	.19	.12	.14	.15	.18
12	.23	.17	.20	.19	.27
13	.20	.19	.18	.16	.21
14	.20	.19	.19	.16	.24
15	.24	.16	.20	.20	.21
16	.15	.09	.12	.12	.20
17	.15	.16	.12	.09	.17
18	.18	.18	.17	.16	.21
19	.23	.22	.20	.15	.21
20	.22	.18	.14	.12	.18
21	.15	.15	.13	.17	.16
22	.22	.14	.16	.17	.24
23	.22	.14	.14	.16	.15

a. Test the statistical significance of the group main effect, the time main effect, and the group × time interaction.

b. Test the group effect at each individual time point. Use an α level of .05 for each test.

c. Perform pairwise comparisons of the groups at each individual time point. Maintain α_{FW} at .05 for each time point.

d. September and July were perceived to be low-stress periods by these students; they perceived November, April, and June to be high-stress periods. Is the difference between the groups the same for the average of the low-stress periods as it is for the average of the high-stress periods? Use an alpha level of .05 for this test.

e. Perform pairwise comparisons of the groups to ascertain which specific groups are different from each other in part d. Maintain α_{FW} at .05.

f. Another question of potential interest concerns immune recovery from June to July. Do the groups change equally from June to July? Use an alpha level of .05 for this test.

g. Test the statistical significance of the change from June to July for each group individually, to determine which groups demonstrate a recovery of the immune system. With an α level of .05 for each group, how would you interpret your results?

Part Four

Alternative Analysis Strategies

We are now in the midst of a rapid retooling—a retooling that promises to extend to essentially all the techniques used in analyzing data. Initially we were very happy to have very high (preferably 100%) efficiency in only one situation—samples from a pure Gaussian distribution. Some call this the over-utopian situation. Later we went "nonparametric" and asked only for 5% to mean 5% in each of a very wide variety of situations, asking nothing explicit in the way of efficiency. Today we are trying to be reasonable (rather than puristic) and ask first for high efficiency in each of a rather wide variety of situations. An estimate which does this is called robust of efficiency. After reaching this behavior for the estimate, we go on to ask that, in significance or confidence, "5%" is either close to, or less than, 5% in a similarly wide variety of situations.

JOHN W. TUKEY, *THE COLLECTED WORKS OF JOHN W. TUKEY*

15   Robust ANOVA and ANCOVA

695

IN CHAPTER 3, WE stated that ANOVA is predicated on three assumptions: normality, homogeneity of variance, and independence of observations. When these conditions are met, ANOVA is a "uniformly most powerful" procedure. In essence, this means that the F test is the best possible test when one is interested uniformly (i.e., equally) in all possible alternatives to the null hypothesis. Thus, in the absence of planned comparisons, ANOVA is the optimal technique to use for hypothesis testing, whenever its assumptions hold. In practice, the three assumptions are often met at least closely enough so that the use of ANOVA is still optimal.

Recall from our Chapter 3 discussion that ANOVA is generally robust to violations of normality and homogeneity of variance, although robustness to the latter occurs only with equal n (more on this later). "Robustness" means that the actual rate of Type I errors committed is close to the nominal rate (typically .05) even when the assumptions fail to hold. In addition, ANOVA procedures generally appear to be robust with respect to Type II errors as well, although less research has been conducted on Type II error rate.

The general robustness of ANOVA was taken for granted by most behavioral researchers during the 1970s, based on findings documented in the excellent literature review by Glass, Peckham, and Sanders (1972). Because both Type I and Type II error rates were only very slightly affected by violations of normality or homogeneity (with equal n), there seemed to be little need to consider alternative methods of hypothesis testing.

However, the decade of the 1980s has seen a renewed interest in possible alternatives to ANOVA. Although part of the impetus behind this movement stems from further investigation of robustness with regard to Type I error rate, the major focus has been on Type II error rate, that is, on issues of power. As Blair (1981) points out, robustness implies that the power of ANOVA is relatively unaffected by violations of assumptions. However, the user of statistics is interested not in whether ANOVA power is unaffected but in whether ANOVA is the most powerful test available for a particular problem. Even when ANOVA is robust, it may not provide the most powerful test available when its assumptions have been violated.

Statisticians are currently developing possible alternatives to ANOVA. Our purpose in this chapter is to provide a brief introduction to a few of these possible alternatives. We should warn you that our coverage is far from exhaustive; we simply could not cover in a single chapter the wide range of possibilities already developed. Instead, our purpose is to make you aware that the field of statistics is dynamic and ever-changing, just like all other scientific fields of inquiry. Techniques (or theories) that are favored today may be in disfavor tomorrow, replaced by superior alternatives.

Another reason we make no attempt to be exhaustive here is that further research yet needs to be done, to compare the techniques of this chapter to usual ANOVA methods. At this time, it is unclear which, if any, of these methods will be judged most useful. Although we provide evaluative comments where possible, we should forewarn you that this area is full of complexity and controversy. The assumption that distributions are normal and variances are homogeneous simplifies the world enormously. A moment's reflection should convince you that "non-normal" and "heterogeneous" lack the precision of "normal" and "homogeneous." Data can be "nonnormal" in an infinite number of ways, rapidly making it very difficult for statisticians to find an optimal technique for analyzing "nonnormal" data. What's good for one form of nonnormality may be bad for another form. Also, what kinds of distributions occur in real data? A theoretical statistician may be interested in comparing data-analysis techniques for data from a specific nonnormal distribution but if that particular distribution never underlies behavioral data, the comparison may have no practical import to behavioral researchers. How far do actual data depart from normality and homogeneity? There is no simple answer, which partially explains why comparing alternatives to ANOVA is complicated and controversial.

The presentation of methods in this chapter generally parallels the structure of the earlier chapters in the book. The great majority of this chapter considers possible alternatives to ANOVA in the single-factor between-subjects design (Chapter 3) because most of the new methods have not been generalized to more complex designs. Where appropriate, we also mention extensions of these alternatives that can be applied to testing comparisons (Chapters 4–6). Next, we consider factorial designs (Chapters 7 and 8). Then, we briefly examine some competitors to ANCOVA (Chapter 9). Finally, we consider possible alternatives in repeated measures designs (Chapters 11–14). Designs with random factors (Chapter 10) are omitted because alternatives have not been developed (yet, anyway) for these designs.

ONE-WAY BETWEEN-SUBJECTS DESIGNS

Two possible types of alternatives to the usual ANOVA in between-subjects designs have received considerable attention in recent years. The first type is a parametric modification of the F test that does not assume homogeneity of variance. The second type is a nonparametric approach that does not assume normality. Because the third ANOVA assumption is independence, you might expect there to be a third type of alternative that does not assume independence. However, as we have stated earlier, independence is largely a matter of design, so modifications would likely involve changes in the design instead of changes in data analysis (see Kenny & Judd, 1986, which we initially recommended in Chapter 3). Besides these two broad types of alternatives, several other possible approaches are currently being investigated. We look at two of these after we examine the parametric modifications and the nonparametric approaches.

Parametric Modifications

As stated earlier, one assumption underlying the usual ANOVA F test is homogeneity of variance. Statisticians have known for many years that the F test can be either very conservative (too few Type I errors and hence decreased power) or very liberal (too many Type I errors) when variances are heterogeneous and sample sizes are unequal. In general, the F test is conservative when large sample sizes are paired with large variances. The F is liberal when large sample sizes are paired with small variances. The chapter extension shows why the nature of the pairing causes the F sometimes to be conservative and other times to be liberal. Obviously, either occurrence is problematic, especially because the population variances are unknown parameters. As a consequence, we can never know with complete certainty whether the assumption has been satisfied in the population. However, statistical tests of the assumption are available (see Chapter 3), so one strategy might be to use the standard F test to test mean differences only if the homogeneity of variance hypothesis cannot be rejected. However, this strategy seems to offer almost no advantage (Wilcox, Charlin, & Thompson, 1986). The failure of this strategy has led some statisticians (e.g., Tomarken & Serlin, 1986; Wilcox, Charlin, & Thompson, 1986) to recommend that the usual F test routinely be replaced by one of the more robust alternatives we will present, especially with unequal n.

Although these problems with unequal n have provided the primary motivation for developing alternatives, several recent studies have shown that the F test is not as robust as had previously been thought when sample sizes are equal. Clinch and Keselman (1982), Rogan and Keselman (1977), Tomarken and Serlin (1986) and Wilcox, Charlin, and Thompson (1986) show that the F test can become somewhat liberal with equal n when variances are heterogeneous. When variances are very different from each other, the actual Type I error rate may reach .10 or so (with a nominal rate of .05), even with equal n. Of course, when variances are less different, the actual error rate is closer to .05.[1] In summary, there seems to be sufficient motivation for considering alternatives to the F test when variances are heterogeneous, particularly when sample sizes are unequal.

We consider two alternatives: The first test statistic was developed by Brown and Forsythe (1974) and has a rather intuitive rationale. The second was developed by Welch (1951). Both are available in BMDP (procedure P7D), so we downplay computational details.[2]

The test statistic developed by Brown and Forsythe (1974) is based on the between-group sum of squares calculated in exactly the same manner as in the usual F test:

$$SS_B = \sum_{j=1}^{a} n_j (\bar{Y}_j - \bar{Y})^2 \tag{1}$$

where $\bar{Y} = \sum_{j=1}^{a} n_j \bar{Y}_j / N$. However, the denominator is calculated differently from the denominator of the usual F test. The Brown–Forsythe denominator is chosen to have the same expected value as the numerator if the null hypothesis is true, even if variances are heterogeneous. (Recall the rationale for finding a denominator with the same expected value as the numerator if the null hypothesis is true, from Chapter 10.) After some tedious algebra, it can be shown that the expected value of SS_B under the null hypothesis is given by

$$\mathcal{E}(SS_B) = \sum_{j=1}^{a} [1 - (n_j/N)]\sigma_j^2 \tag{2}$$

Notice that if we were willing to assume homogeneity of variance, Equation 2 would simplify to

$$\mathscr{E}(SS_B) = \sum_{j=1}^{a} [1 - (n_j/N)]\sigma^2 = \sigma^2 \left[a - \sum_{j=1}^{a} (n_j/N) \right] = (a-1)\sigma^2$$

where σ^2 denotes the common variance. With homogeneity, $\mathscr{E}(MS_W) = \sigma^2$, so the usual F is obtained by taking the ratio of MS_B (which is SS_B divided by $a-1$) and MS_W. Under homogeneity, MS_B and MS_W have the same expected value under the null hypothesis, so their ratio provides an appropriate test statistic.[3]

When we are unwilling to assume homogeneity, it is preferable to estimate the population variance of each group (i.e., σ_j^2) separately. This is easily accomplished by using s_j^2 as an unbiased estimate of σ_j^2. A suitable denominator can be obtained by substituting s_j^2 for σ_j^2 in Equation 2, yielding

$$\sum_{j=1}^{a} [1 - (n_j/N)]s_j^2 \tag{3}$$

The expected value of this expression equals the expected value of SS_B under the null hypothesis, even if homogeneity fails to hold. Thus, taking the ratio of SS_B and the expression in Equation 3 yields an appropriate test statistic:

$$F^* = \frac{\sum_{j=1}^{a} n_j(\bar{Y}_j - \bar{Y})^2}{\sum_{j=1}^{a} [1 - (n_j/N)]s_j^2} \tag{4}$$

The statistic is written as F^* instead of F because it does not have an exact F distribution. However, Brown and Forsythe show that the distribution of F^* can be approximated by an F distribution with $a-1$ numerator degrees of freedom and f denominator degrees of freedom. Unfortunately, the denominator degrees of freedom are tedious to calculate and are best left to a computer program. Nevertheless, we present the formula for denominator degrees of freedom as follows:

$$f = 1 \left/ \left[\sum_{j=1}^{a} g_j^2/(n_j - 1) \right] \right. \tag{5}$$

where

$$g_j = [1 - (n_j/N)]s_j^2 \left/ \left[\sum_{j=1}^{a} [1 - (n_j/N)]s_j^2 \right] \right.$$

It is important to realize that in general F^* differs from F in two ways. First, the denominator degrees of freedom for the two approaches are different. Second, the observed values of the test statistics are typically different as well. In particular, F^* may be either systematically smaller or larger than F. If large samples are paired with small variances, F^* tends to be smaller than F; however, this reflects an advantage for F^* because F tends to be liberal in this situation. On the other hand, if large samples are paired with large variances, F^* tends to be larger than F; once again, this reflects an advantage for F^* because F tends to be conservative in this situation. What if sample sizes are equal? With equal n, Equation 4 can be rewritten as

$$F^* = \frac{n \sum_{j=1}^{a} (\bar{Y}_j - \bar{Y})^2}{\sum_{j=1}^{a} [1 - (1/a)]s_j^2} = \frac{n \sum_{j=1}^{a} (\bar{Y}_j - \bar{Y})^2}{\sum_{j=1}^{a} [(a - 1)/a]s_j^2}$$

$$= \frac{n \sum_{j=1}^{a} (\bar{Y}_j - \bar{Y})^2}{(a - 1) \sum_{j=1}^{a} s_j^2 \Big/ a} = \frac{n \sum_{j=1}^{a} (\bar{Y}_j - \bar{Y})^2 \Big/ (a - 1)}{\sum_{j=1}^{a} s_j^2 \Big/ a}$$

$$= \frac{MS_B}{MS_W} = F$$

Thus, with equal n, the observed values of F^* and F are identical. However, the denominator degrees of freedom are still different. It can be shown that with equal n, Equation 5 for the denominator degrees of freedom associated with F^* becomes

$$f = \frac{(n - 1)\left(\sum_{j=1}^{a} s_j^2 \right)^2}{\sum_{j=1}^{a} (s_j^2)^2} \tag{6}$$

Although it may not be immediately apparent, f is an index of how different sample variances are from each other. If all sample variances were identical to each other, f would equal $a(n - 1)$, the denominator degrees of freedom for the usual F test. At the other extreme, as one variance becomes infinitely larger than all others, f approaches a value of $n - 1$. In general, then, f ranges from $n - 1$ to $a(n - 1)$ and attains higher values for more similar variances.

We can summarize the relationship between F^* and F with equal n as follows. To the extent that the sample variances are similar, F^* is similar to F; however, when sample variances are different from each other, F^* is more conservative than F because the lower denominator degrees of freedom for F^* imply a higher critical value for F^* than for F. As a consequence, with equal n, F^* rejects the null hypothesis less often than does F. If the homogeneity of variance assumption is valid, the implication is that F^* is less powerful than F. However, Monte Carlo studies by Clinch and Keselman (1982) and Tomarken and Serlin (1986) suggest that the power advantage of F over F^* rarely exceeds .03 with equal n.[4] On the other hand, if the homogeneity assumption is violated, F^* tends to maintain α at .05, whereas F becomes somewhat liberal. However, the usual F test tends to remain robust as long as the population variances are not widely different from each other. As a result, in practice any advantage that F^* might offer over F with equal n is typically slight, except when variances are extremely discrepant from each other.

However, with unequal n, F^* and F may be very different from one another. If it so happens that large samples are paired with small variances, F^* maintains α near .05 (assuming that .05 is the nominal value), while the actual α level for the F test can reach .15 or even .20 (Clinch & Keselman, 1982; Tomarken & Serlin, 1986), if population variances are substantially different from each other. On the other hand, if large samples happen to be paired with large variances, F^* provides a more powerful test than does the F test. The advantage for F^* can be as great as .15 or .20 (Tomarken & Serlin, 1986), depending on how different the population variances are and on how the variances are related to the sample sizes. Thus, F^* is not necessarily more conservative than F.

Welch (1951) also derived an alternative to the F test that does not require the homogeneity of variance assumption. Unlike the Brown and Forsythe alternative, which was based on the between-group sum of squares of the usual F test, Welch's test uses a different weighting of the sum of squares in the numerator. Welch's statistic is defined as:

$$W = \frac{\sum\limits_{j=1}^{a} w_j(\bar{Y}_j - \tilde{Y})^2 \Big/ (a-1)}{\left[1 + \frac{2}{3}(a-2)\Lambda\right]}$$

where

$$w_j = n_j/s_j^2$$

$$\tilde{Y} = \sum_{j=1}^{a} w_j \bar{Y}_j \Big/ \sum_{j=1}^{a} w_j$$

$$\Lambda = \frac{3 \sum\limits_{j=1}^{a} \left\{ \left[1 - \left(w_j \Big/ \sum\limits_{j=1}^{a} w_j\right)\right]^2 \Big/ (n_j - 1) \right\}}{a^2 - 1}$$

When the null hypothesis is true, W is approximately distributed as an F variable with $a - 1$ numerator and $1/\Lambda$ denominator degrees of freedom. (Notice that Λ was used to represent the value of Wilks's lambda in Chapter 14. Its meaning here is entirely different and reflects the unfortunate tradition among statisticians to use the same symbol for different expressions. In any event, the meaning here should be clear from the context.) It might alleviate some concern to remind you at this point that the BMDP program 7D calculates W as well as its degrees of freedom and associated p value.

The basic difference between the rationales behind F^* and W involves the weight associated with a group's deviation from the grand mean, that is, $\bar{Y}_j - \bar{Y}$. As Equation 1 shows, F^* weights each group according to its sample size. Larger groups receive more weight because their sample mean is likely to be a better estimate of their population mean. W, on the other hand, weights each group according to n_j/s_j^2, which is the reciprocal of the estimated variance of the mean. Less variable group means thus receive more weight, whether the lesser variability results from a larger sample size or a smaller variance. This difference in weighting causes W to be different from F^*, even though neither assumes homogeneity of variance. As an aside, also notice that the grand mean is defined differently in Welch's approach than for either F or F^*; although it is still a weighted average of the group means, the weights depend on the sample variances as well as the sample sizes.

Welch's W statistic compares to the usual F test in a generally similar manner as F^* compares to F. When large samples are paired with large variances, W is less conservative than F. When large samples are paired with small variances, W is less liberal than F. Interestingly, when sample sizes are equal, W differs more from F than does F^*. Whereas F and F^* have the same observed value with equal n, in general the observed value of W is different. The reason is that, as we saw earlier, W gives more weight to groups with smaller sample variances. When homogeneity holds in the population, this differential weighting is simply based on chance because sample variances differ from one another due only to sampling error in this situation. As a result, tests based on W are somewhat less powerful than tests based on F. Based on Tomarken and Serlin's (1986) findings, the difference in power is usually .03 or less and would rarely exceed .06 unless sample sizes are very small. However, when homogeneity fails to hold, W can be appreciably more powerful than the usual F test, even with equal n. The power advantage of W was often as large as .10 and even reached .34 in one condition in Tomarken and Serlin's simulations. This advantage stems from W giving more weight to the more stable sample means, which F does not do (nor does F^*). It must be added, however, that W can also have less power than F with equal n. If the group that differs most from the grand mean has a large population variance, W attaches a relatively small weight to the group because of its large variance. In this particular case, W tends to be less powerful than F because the most discrepant group receives the least weight. Nevertheless, Tomarken and Serlin found that W is generally more powerful than F for most patterns of means when heterogeneity occurs with equal n.

The choice between F^* and W when heterogeneity is suspected is difficult given the current state of knowledge. On the one hand, Tomarken and Serlin (1986) found that W is more powerful than F^* across most configurations of population means. On the other hand, Clinch and Keselman (1982) found that W becomes somewhat liberal when underlying population distributions are skewed instead of normal. They found that F^* generally maintains α close to a nominal value of .05 even for skewed distributions. In addition, Wilcox, Charlin, and Thompson (1986) found that W maintained an appropriate Type I error rate better than F^* when sample sizes are equal, but that F^* was better than W when unequal sample sizes are paired with equal variances. Choosing between F^* and W is obviously far from clear cut, given the complex nature of findings. Further research is needed to clarify their relative strengths. Although the choice between F^* and W is unsettled, it is clear that both are preferable to F when population variances are heterogeneous and sample sizes are unequal.

Table 15.1 summarizes the properties of F, F^*, and W as a function of population variances and sample sizes. Again, from a practical standpoint, the primary point of the table is that F^* or W should seriously be considered as a replacement for the usual F test when sample sizes are unequal and heterogeneity of variance is suspected.

Nonparametric Approaches

The parametric modifications of the previous section were developed for analyzing data with unequal population variances. The nonparametric approaches of this section were developed for analyzing data whose population distributions

TABLE 15.1 Properties of F, F^*, and W as a Function of Sample Sizes and Population Variances

	Test Statistic		
	F	F^*	W
Equal Sample Sizes			
Equal variances	Appropriate	Slightly conservative	Robust
Unequal variances	Robust, except can become liberal for very large differences in variances	Robust, except can become liberal for extremely large differences in variances	Robust
Unequal Sample Sizes			
Equal variances	Appropriate	Robust	Robust, except can become slightly liberal for very large differences in sample sizes
Large samples paired with large variances	Conservative	Robust, except can become slightly liberal when differences in sample sizes and in variances are both very large	Robust, except can become slightly liberal when differences in sample sizes and in variances are both very large
Large samples paired with small variances	Liberal	Robust, except can become slightly liberal when differences in sample sizes and in variances are both very large	Robust, except can become slightly liberal when differences in sample sizes and in variances are both very large

are nonnormal. As we discuss in some detail later, another motivating factor for the development of nonparametric techniques in the behavioral sciences has been the belief held by some researchers that they require less stringent measurement properties of the dependent variable. The organizational structure of this section consists of, first, presenting a particular nonparametric technique and, second, discussing its merits relative to parametric techniques.

There are several nonparametric alternatives to ANOVA for the single-factor between-subjects design. We present only one of these, the Kruskal–Wallis test, which is the most frequently used nonparametric test for this design. For information on other nonparametric methods, consult such nonparametric textbooks as Bradley (1968), Gibbons (1971), Marascuilo and McSweeney (1977), Noether (1976), or Siegel (1956).

The Kruskal–Wallis test is often called an "ANOVA by Ranks" because the basic distinction between the usual ANOVA and the Kruskal–Wallis test is that the original scores are replaced by their ranks in the Kruskal–Wallis test. Specifically, the first step in the test is to rank order all observations from low to high (actually high to low yields exactly the same result) in the entire set of N subjects. Be certain to notice that this ranking is performed across all a groups, independently of group membership. When scores are tied, each observation is assigned the average (i.e., mean) rank of the scores in the tied set. For example, if three scores are tied for sixth, seventh, and eighth place in order, all three scores are assigned to a rank of seven.

Once the scores have been ranked, the test statistic is given by

$$H = \frac{12}{N(N + 1)} \sum_{j=1}^{a} n_j \{\bar{R}_j - [(N + 1)/2]\}^2 \tag{7}$$

where $\bar{R}_j$ is the mean rank for group j. Although Equation 7 may look very different from the usual ANOVA F statistic, in fact there is an underlying similarity. For example, $(N + 1)/2$ is simply the grand mean of the ranks, which we know must have values of $1, 2, 3, \ldots, N$. Thus, the term $\sum_{j=1}^{a} n_j \{\bar{R}_j - [(N + 1)/2]\}^2$ is a weighted average of deviations from the grand mean, as in the parametric F test. It also proves to be unnecessary to estimate σ^2, the population error variance because the test statistic is based on a finite population of size N (cf. Marascuilo & McSweeney, 1977, for more on this point). The important point for our purposes is that the Kruskal–Wallis test is very much like an ANOVA on ranks.

When the null hypothesis is true, H is approximately distributed as a χ^2 with $a - 1$ degrees of freedom. The χ^2 approximation is accurate unless sample sizes within some groups are quite small, in which case tables of the exact distribution of H should be consulted in such sources as Siegel (1956) or Iman, Quade, and Alexander (1975). When ties occur in the data, a correction factor T should be applied:

$$T = 1 - \frac{\sum_{i=1}^{G} (t_i^3 - t_i)}{N^3 - N}$$

where t_i is the number of observations tied at a particular value, and G is the number of distinct values for which there are ties. A corrected test statistic H' is obtained by dividing H by T: $H' = H/T$. The correction has little effect (i.e., H' differs very little from H) unless sample sizes are very small or there are many ties in the data, relative to sample size. All three major statistical packages (BMDP, SAS, and SPSS-X) have a program for computing H (or H') and its associated p value. Also, it should be pointed out that when there are only two groups to be compared (i.e., $a = 2$), the Kruskal–Wallis test is equivalent to the Wilcoxon Rank Sum test, which is also equivalent to the Mann–Whitney U.

Choosing Between Parametric and Nonparametric Tests

Statisticians have debated the relative merits of parametric versus nonparametric tests ever since the inception of nonparametric approaches. As a consequence, all too often behavioral researchers are told either that parametric procedures should always be used (because they are robust and more powerful) or that nonparametric methods should always be used (because they make fewer assumptions). Not surprisingly, both of these extreme positions are oversimplifications. We provide a brief overview of the advantages each approach possesses in certain situations. Our discussion is limited to a comparison of the F, F^*, and W parametric tests and the Kruskal–Wallis nonparametric test.

Nevertheless, even with this limitation, do not expect our comparison of the methods to provide a definitive answer as to which approach is "best." The choice between approaches is too complicated for such a simple answer. We will see that there are certain occasions where parametric tests are preferable and others where nonparametric tests are better. A wise data analyst will carefully weigh the advantages in his or her situation and make an informed choice accordingly.

A primary reason the comparison of parametric and nonparametric approaches is so difficult is that they do not always test the same null hypothesis. To see why they do not, we need to consider the assumptions required by each approach. As stated earlier, we consider specifically the F test and Kruskal–Wallis test for one-way between-subjects designs.

As we saw in Chapter 3, the parametric ANOVA can be conceptualized in terms of a full model of the form

$$Y_{ij} = \mu + \alpha_j + \varepsilon_{ij}$$

ANOVA tests a null hypothesis

$$H_0 : \alpha_1 = \alpha_2 = \cdots = \alpha_a = 0$$

where it is assumed that population distributions are normal and have equal variances. In other words, under the null hypothesis, all a population distributions are identical normal distributions if ANOVA assumptions hold. If the null hypothesis is false, one or more distributions are *shifted* either to the left or to the right of the other distributions. Figure 15.1 illustrates such an occurrence for the case of three groups. The three distributions are identical except that $\mu_1 = 10$, $\mu_2 = 20$, and $\mu_3 = 35$. As long as the normality and homogeneity assumptions are met, the distributions still have the same shape, but they have different *locations*

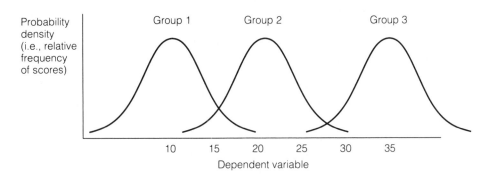

F I G U R E 15. 1 Shifted distributions under ANOVA assumptions.

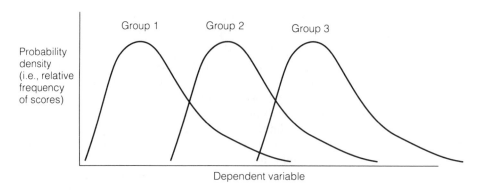

F I G U R E 15. 2 Shifted distributions under Kruskal–Wallis assumptions.

when the null hypothesis is false. For this reason, ANOVA is sometimes referred to as a test of location, or as testing a shift hypothesis.

The Kruskal–Wallis test can also be conceptualized as testing a shift hypothesis. Hollander and Wolfe (1973) show that the Kruskal–Wallis test can be thought of in terms of a full model of the form

$$Y_{ij} = \mu + \alpha_j + \varepsilon_{ij}$$

and that the null hypothesis being tested can be represented by

$$H_0 : \alpha_1 = \alpha_2 = \cdots = \alpha_a = 0$$

just as in the parametric ANOVA. The only difference concerns the assumptions involving the distribution of errors (ε_{ij}). Whereas the parametric ANOVA assumes both normality and homogeneity, the Kruskal–Wallis test assumes only that the population of error scores has an identical continuous distribution for every group. As a consequence, in the Kruskal–Wallis model, homogeneity of variance is still assumed but normality is not. The most important point for our purposes is that when the Kruskal–Wallis assumptions are met, it is testing a shift hypothesis, as is the parametric ANOVA, when its assumptions are met. Figure 15.2 illustrates such an occurrence for the case of three groups. As in Figure 15.1, the three distributions of Figure 15.2 are identical to each other except for their location on the x-axis. Notice, however, that the distributions in Figure 15.2 are skewed, unlike the distributions in Figure 15.1 that are required to be normal by the ANOVA model. Under these conditions, both approaches are testing the same null hypothesis, because the α_j parameters in the models are identical. For example, the difference $\alpha_2 - \alpha_1$ represents the extent to which the distribution of group 1 is shifted either to the right or to the left of group 2. Not only does $\alpha_2 - \alpha_1$ equal the difference between the population means, but as Figure 15.3 shows, it also equals the difference between the medians, the 5th percentile, the 75th percentile, or any other percentile. This is guaranteed to be true when requisite assumptions are met because then all distributions have the same shape. In this situation, the only difference between the two approaches is that the parametric ANOVA makes the additional assumption

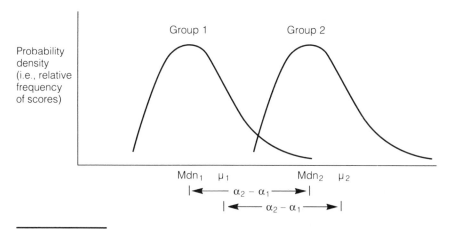

FIGURE 15.3 Meaning of $\alpha_2 - \alpha_1$ for two groups when shift hypothesis holds.

that this common shape is that of a normal distribution. Of course, this difference implies different properties for the tests, which we discuss momentarily. To summarize, when the assumptions of the Kruskal–Wallis test are met (namely, identical distributions for all a groups, except for a possible shift under the alternative hypothesis), it and the parametric ANOVA are testing the same null hypothesis. In this circumstance, it will be possible to compare the two approaches and state conditions under which each approach is advantageous.[5]

However, when the assumptions of the Kruskal–Wallis test are not met, it and the parametric ANOVA are not in general testing the same hypothesis. The parametric ANOVA can be regarded as a test of differences between population means, whereas the Kruskal–Wallis test can be regarded as a test of differences between population medians.[6] Of course, if all population distributions are symmetric, the mean will equal the median of each distribution, in which case the parametric and nonparametric methods are still testing the same hypothesis. However, when distributions have different asymmetric shapes, it is possible for the population means to all be equal and yet the population medians all be different, or vice versa. Thus, the parametric ANOVA may be testing a true null hypothesis, whereas the nonparametric approach is testing a false null hypothesis. In such a circumstance, the probabilities of rejecting the null hypothesis for the two approaches cannot be meaningfully compared because they are answering different questions.

In summary, when distributions have different shapes, the parametric and nonparametric approaches are generally testing different hypotheses. In such conditions, the basis for choosing between the approaches should probably involve consideration of whether the research question is best formulated in terms of population means or population medians. It should also be mentioned that heterogeneity of variance and floor and ceiling effects often lead to distributions with different shapes.

Suppose that in fact population distributions are identical—which approach is better, parametric or nonparametric? Although the question seems relatively straightforward, the answer is not. Under some conditions such as normal distributions, the parametric approach is better. However, under other conditions such as certain long-tailed distributions (where extreme scores are more likely than in the normal distribution), the nonparametric approach is better. As usual, the choice involves a consideration of Type I error rate and power.

If population distributions are identical and normal, both the F test and the Kruskal–Wallis test maintain the actual α level at the nominal value because the assumptions of both tests will have been met (assuming in addition, as we do throughout this discussion, that observations are independent of one another). On the other hand, if distributions are identical but nonnormal, only the assumptions of the Kruskal–Wallis test are met. Nevertheless, the extensive survey conducted by Glass and colleagues (1972) suggests that the F test is robust with respect to Type I errors to all but extreme violations of normality.[7] Thus, with regard to Type I error rates, there is little practical reason to prefer either test over the other if all population distributions have identical shapes.

While on the topic of Type I error rate, it is important to dispel a myth concerning nonparametric tests. Many researchers apparently believe that the Kruskal–Wallis test should be used instead of the F test when variances are unequal because the Kruskal–Wallis test does not assume homogeneity of variance. However, we can easily see that this belief is misguided because the Kruskal–Wallis test assumes that population distributions are identical under the null hypothesis. Identical distributions obviously have equal variances, so homogeneity of variance is in fact an assumption of the Kruskal–Wallis test. Further, the Kruskal–Wallis test is *not* robust to violations of this assumption with unequal n. Keselman, Rogan, and Feir-Walsh (1977) as well as Tomarken and Serlin (1986) found that the actual Type I error rate of the Kruskal–Wallis test could be as large as twice the nominal level when large samples are paired with small variances. It should be added that the usual F test was even less robust than the Kruskal–Wallis test. However, the important practical point is that neither test is robust. In contrast, Tomarken and Serlin (1986) found both F^* and W to maintain acceptable α levels even for various patterns of unequal sample sizes and unequal variances.[8] The important practical point is that F^* and W are better alternatives to the usual F test than is the Kruskal–Wallis test when heterogeneity of variance is suspected, especially with unequal n.

A second common myth surrounding nonparametric tests is that they are always less powerful than parametric tests. It is true that if the population distributions for all a groups are normal with equal variances, then the F test is more powerful than the Kruskal–Wallis test. The size of the difference in power varies as a function of the sample sizes and the means, so it is impossible to state a single number to represent how much more powerful the F test is. However, it is possible to determine mathematically that as sample sizes increase toward infinity, the efficiency of the Kruskal–Wallis test to the F test is 0.955 under normality.[9] In practical terms, this means that for large samples, the F test can achieve the same power as the Kruskal–Wallis test and yet require only 95.5 percent as many subjects as would the Kruskal–Wallis test. It can also be shown that for large samples, the

Kruskal–Wallis test is at least 86.4 percent as efficient as the F test, for distributions of *any* shape, as long as all a distributions have the same shape. Thus, at its absolute worst, for large samples, using the Kruskal–Wallis instead of the F test is analogous to failing to use 13.6 percent of the subjects one has observed. We must add, however, that the previous statement assumes that all population distributions are identical. If they are not, the Kruskal–Wallis test in some circumstances has little or no power for detecting true mean differences because it is a test of differences in medians.

So far, we have done little to dispel the myth that parametric tests are always more powerful than nonparametric tests. However, for certain nonnormal distributions, the Kruskal–Wallis test is in fact considerably more powerful than the parametric F test. Generally speaking, the Kruskal–Wallis test is more powerful than the F test when the underlying population distributions are symmetric but heavy-tailed, which means that extreme scores (i.e., outliers) are more frequent than in the normal distribution. The size of the power advantage of the Kruskal–Wallis test depends on the particular shape of the nonnormal distribution, sample sizes, and the magnitude of separation between the groups. However, the size of this advantage can easily be large enough to be of practical importance in some situations. It should also be added that the Kruskal–Wallis test is frequently more powerful than the F test when distributions are identical but skewed.

As mentioned earlier, another argument that has been made for using nonparametric procedures is that they require less stringent measurement properties of the data. In fact, there has been a heated controversy ever since Stevens (1946, 1951) introduced the concept of "levels of measurement" (i.e., nominal, ordinal, interval, and ratio scales) with his views of their implications for statistics. Stevens argues that the use of parametric statistics requires that the observed dependent variable be measured on an interval or ratio scale. However, many behavioral variables fail to meet this criterion, which has been taken by some psychologists to imply that most behavioral data should be analyzed with nonparametric techniques. Others (e.g., Gaito, 1980; Lord, 1953) argue that the use of parametric procedures is entirely appropriate for behavioral data.

We cannot possibly do justice in this chapter to the complexities of all viewpoints. Instead, we attempt to briefly describe a few themes and recommend additional reading. Gardner (1975) provides an excellent review of both sides of the controversy through the mid-1970s. Three points raised in his review deserve special mention here. First, parametric statistical tests do not make any statistical assumptions about level of measurement. As we stated in Chapter 3 and earlier in this chapter, the assumptions of the F test are normality, homogeneity of variance, and independence of observations. A correct numerical statement concerning population mean differences does not require interval measurement. Second, although a parametric test can be performed on ordinal data without violating any assumptions of the test, the meaning of the test could be damaged. In essence, this can be thought of as a potential construct validity problem (see Chapter 1). Although the test is correct as a statement of mean group differences on the observed variable, these differences might not reflect true differences on the underlying construct. Third, Gardner cites two empirical studies (Baker, Hardyck, & Petrinovich, 1966;

Labovitz, 1967) that showed that, although in theory construct validity might be problematic, in reality parametric tests produced meaningful results for constructs even when the level of measurement was only ordinal.

The 1980s have seen a number of demonstrations that the earlier empirical studies were correct as far as they went, but 15 or so years later, it became clear that the earlier studies were limited in an important way. In effect, the earlier studies assumed that the underlying population distributions on the construct not only had the same mean but were literally identical to each other. However, a number of later studies (Maxwell & Delaney, 1985; Spencer, 1983) show that, when the population distributions on the construct have the same mean but different variances, parametric techniques on ordinal data can result in very misleading conclusions. Thus, in some practical situations, nonparametric techniques may indeed be more appropriate than parametric approaches. Many interesting articles continue to be written on this topic. Recent articles deserving attention are Davison and Sharma (1988), Marcus-Roberts and Roberts (1987), Michell (1986), and Townsend and Ashby (1984).

In summary, the choice between a parametric test (F, F^*, or W) and the Kruskal–Wallis test involves consideration of a number of factors. First, the Kruskal–Wallis test does not always test the same hypothesis as the parametric tests. As a result, in general it is important to consider whether the research question of interest is most appropriately formulated in terms of medians or means. Second, neither the usual F test nor the Kruskal–Wallis test is robust to violations of homogeneity of variance with unequal n. Either F^* or W is preferable in this situation. Third, for some distributions, the F test is more powerful than the Kruskal–Wallis test; whereas for other distributions, the reverse is true. Thus, neither approach is always better than the other. Fourth, level of measurement continues to be controversial as a factor that might or might not influence the choice between parametric and nonparametric approaches.

O P T I O N A L

Two Other Approaches

As if the choice between parametric and nonparametric were not already complicated, there are yet other possible techniques for data analysis, even in the relatively simple one-way between-subjects design. As we stated at the beginning of the chapter, statisticians are constantly inventing new methods of data analysis. In this section, we take a brief glimpse at two methods that are still in the experimental stages of development. Because the advantages and disadvantages of these methods are largely unexplored, we would not recommend as of this writing that you use these approaches as your sole data-analysis technique without first seeking expert advice. Nevertheless, we believe that it is important to expose you to these methods because they represent the types of innovations currently being studied. As such, they may become preferred methods of data analysis during the careers of those of you who are reading this book as students.

The first innovation, called a *rank transformation* approach, has been described as a bridge between parametric and nonparametric statistics by its primary developers Conover and Iman (1981). The rank transformation approach simply consists of replacing the observed data with their ranks and then applying the usual parametric test. Conover and Iman (1981) discuss how this approach can be applied to such diverse problems as multiple regression, discriminant analysis, and cluster analysis. In the case of the one-way between-subjects design, the parametric F computed on ranks (denoted F_R) is closely related to the Kruskal–Wallis test. Conover and Iman show that F_R is related to the Kruskal–Wallis H by the formula:

$$F_R = [H/(a - 1)]/[(N - 1 - H)/(N - a)]$$

The rank transformation test compares F_R to a critical F value, whereas the Kruskal–Wallis test compares H to a critical χ^2 value. Both methods are large-sample approximations to the true critical value. Iman and Davenport (1976) found the F approximation to be superior to the χ^2 approximation in the majority of cases they investigated.

A second innovation involves a method of parameter estimation other than least squares. Least squares has formed the basis for comparing models in all parametric techniques we have discussed in this book. In one form or another, we have generally ended up finding a parameter estimate $\hat{\mu}$ to minimize an expression of the form $\sum (Y - \hat{\mu})^2$. Such an approach proves to be optimal when distributions are normal with equal variances. However, as we have seen, optimality is lost when these conditions do not hold. In particular, least squares tends to perform poorly in the presence of outliers (i.e., extreme scores) because the squaring function is very sensitive to extreme scores. For example, consider the following five scores: 5, 10, 15, 20, 75. If we regard these five observations as a random sample, we could use least squares to estimate the population mean. It is easily verified that $\hat{\mu} = 25$ minimizes $\sum (Y - \hat{\mu})^2$ for these data. As we know, the sample mean, which here equals 25, is the least-squares estimate. However, only one of the five scores is this large. The sample mean has been greatly influenced by the single extreme score of 75. If we are willing to assume that the population distribution is symmetric, we could also use the sample median as an unbiased estimator of the population mean.[10] It is obvious that the median of our sample is 15, but how does this relate to least squares? It can be shown that the median is the estimate that minimizes the sum of the absolute value of errors: $\sum |Y - \hat{\mu}|$. Thus, the sample mean minimizes the sum of squared errors, whereas the sample median minimizes the sum of absolute errors. The median is less sensitive than the mean to outliers—for some distributions, this is an advantage; but for others, it is a disadvantage. In particular, for heavy-tailed distributions, the median's insensitivity to outliers makes it superior to the mean. However, in a normal distribution, the median is a much less efficient estimator than is the mean. The fact that neither the median nor the mean is uniformly best has prompted the search for alternative estimators.

Statisticians have recently developed a class of estimators called M estimators that in many respects represent a compromise between the mean and the median. For example, one member of this class (the Huber M estimator) has been described as acting "like the mean for centrally located observations and like the median for observations far removed from the bulk of the data" (Wu, 1985, p. 339). As a consequence, these robust estimators represent another bridge between parametric and nonparametric approaches. These robust estimators are obtained once again by minimizing a term involving the sum of errors. However, M estimators constitute an entire class of estimators defined by minimizing the sum of some general function of the errors. The form of the function determines the specific estimator in the general class. For example, if the function is the square of the error, the specific estimation technique is least squares. Thus, least-squares estimators are members of the broad class of M estimators. The median is also a member of the class because it involves minimizing the sum of a function of the errors, the particular function being the absolute value function.

Although quite a few robust estimators have been developed, we describe only an estimator developed by Huber because of its relative simplicity.[11] Huber's estimator requires that a robust estimator of scale (i.e., dispersion, or variability) have been calculated prior to determining the robust estimate of location (i.e., population mean). Note that the scale estimate need not actually be based on a robust estimator; however, using a robust estimator of scale is sensible, if one believes that a robust estimator of location is needed in a particular situation. Although a number of robust estimators of scale are available, we present only one: the median absolute deviation from the median (MAD). MAD is defined as MAD = median $\{|Y - M|\}$, where M is the sample median. Although at first reading the definition of MAD may resemble doubletalk, its calculation is actually very straightforward. For example, consider again our hypothetical example of five scores: 5, 10, 15, 20, and 75. As we have seen, the median of these scores is 15, so we can write $M = 15$. Then the absolute deviations are given by $|5 - 15| = 10$, $|10 - 15| = 5$, $|15 - 15| = 0$, $|20 - 15| = 5$, and $|75 - 15| = 60$. MAD is defined to be the median of these five absolute deviations, which is five in our example.[12] MAD can be thought of as a robust type of standard deviation. However, the expected value of MAD is considerably less than σ for a normal distribution. For this reason, MAD is often divided by 0.6745, which puts it on the same scale as σ for a normal distribution. We let S denote this robust estimate of scale, so we have $S = \text{MAD}/0.6745$.

With this background, we can now consider Huber's M estimator of location. To simplify our notation, we define u_i to be $(Y_i - \hat{\mu})/S$, where S is the robust estimate of scale (hence we already know its value) and $\hat{\mu}$ is the robust estimate of location whose value we are seeking. Then, Huber's M estimator minimizes the sum of a function of the errors $\sum_{i=1}^{n} f(u_i)$ where the function f is defined as follows:

$$f(u_i) = \begin{cases} \dfrac{1}{2}u_i^2 & \text{if } |u_i| \leq 1 \\ |u_i| - \dfrac{1}{2} & \text{if } |u_i| > 1 \end{cases}$$

Notice that function f involves minimizing sums of squared errors for errors that are close to the center of the distribution but involves minimizing the sum of absolute errors for errors that are far from the center. Thus, as our earlier quote from Wu indicated, Huber's estimate really does behave like the mean for observations near the center of the distribution but like the median for those farther away. At this point you may be wondering how the $\hat{\mu}$ that minimizes the sum of Huber's function is determined. It turns out that the value must be determined through an iterative procedure. As a first step, a starting value for $\hat{\mu}$ is chosen; a simple choice for the starting value would be the sample median. We might denote this value $\hat{\mu}_0$, the zero subscript indicating that this value is the optimal value after zero iterations. Then, a new estimate is computed that minimizes the function $\sum_{i=1}^{n} f(u_i)$ where $u_i = (Y_i - \hat{\mu}_0)/S$. This yields a new estimate $\hat{\mu}_1$, where the one subscript indicates that one iteration has been completed. The process continues until it converges, meaning that further iterations would make no practical difference in the value.[13]

Not only does M estimation produce robust estimates, but it also provides a methodology for hypothesis testing. Schrader and Hettmansperger (1980) show how full and restricted models based on M estimates can be compared to arrive at an F test using the same basic logic that underlies the F test with least squares. Li (1985) and Wu (1985) describe how M estimation can be applied to robust tests in regression analysis.

In summary, we have seen two possible bridges between the parametric and nonparametric approaches. It remains to be seen whether either of these bridges will eventually separate the gap that has historically existed between proponents of parametrics and proponents of nonparametrics.

═══

Comparisons in Between-Subjects Designs

The previous section dealt with alternatives to the omnibus ANOVA F test when the assumptions of homogeneity of variance or normality are violated. This section provides an overview of alternative procedures for testing contrasts (i.e., comparisons) in the absence of homogeneity or normality.

Parametric Modifications.   As we discussed in Chapter 4, tests of comparisons are less robust than the omnibus test to violations of homogeneity of variance. Even with equal n, the use of MS_W as an error term can produce highly misleading results when population variances are unequal. Because a robust method for testing comparisons was presented in Chapter 4, only brief attention is paid to the topic here.

Suppose that we are interested in testing a null hypothesis $H_0 : \psi = 0$, where ψ is some linear combination of population means. If homogeneity of variance holds and distributions are normal, the appropriate test is given by $F = SS_\psi/MS_W$, where

$$SS_\psi = (\hat{\psi})^2 \bigg/ \sum_{j=1}^{a} (c_j^2/n_j) \qquad \text{(4.35, repeated)}$$

$$\hat{\psi} = \sum_{j=1}^{a} c_j \bar{Y}_j \qquad \text{(4.36, repeated)}$$

and c_j is the contrast coefficient for the jth group. This F test is robust to violations of homogeneity if all sample sizes are equal *and* all contrast coefficients are equal in absolute value. Notice that the requirement that all coefficients be equal in absolute value rules out the possibility that any coefficient equals zero. If the sample sizes are unequal *or* at least one of the coefficients differs from the others in absolute value, the F test is not robust.

A robust test of the contrast can be obtained by using an error term specific to the contrast instead of MS_W. As we showed in Chapter 4, an appropriate error term is given by

$$\sum_{j=1}^{a} (c_j^2 s_j^2/n_j) \bigg/ \sum_{j=1}^{a} (c_j^2/n_j) \qquad \text{(4.38, repeated)}$$

This expression is a weighted average of the individual group variances s_j^2, with weights proportional to c_j^2/n_j. In this manner, the weight a group receives in the denominator is analogous to the weight it receives in the numerator. For example, if a group is not involved in a specific contrast, so that its coefficient is zero, the group also does not contribute to the denominator. The approximate F statistic is obtained by dividing SS_ψ by the error term of Equation 4.38. The observed value is compared to a critical F whose numerator degrees of freedom equal one and whose denominator degrees of freedom are given by

$$df = \frac{\left(\sum_{j=1}^{a} c_j^2 s_j^2/n_j\right)^2}{\sum_{j=1}^{a} [(c_j^2 s_j^2/n_j)^2/(n_j - 1)]} \qquad \text{(4.39, repeated)}$$

When multiple comparisons are tested, it is necessary to adjust the critical value accordingly. For multiple planned comparisons, a Bonferroni adjustment is appropriate. Thus, any single contrast must achieve significance at a level of α_{FW}/C, where C is the total number of planned comparisons. As we discussed in Chapter 5, there are several possible modifications for testing all pairwise comparisons. The Games–Howell approach requires that the observed F be compared to a critical value equal to $q^2/2$, where q is the critical value of the studentized range statistic with degrees of freedom given by Equation 4.39. When complex comparisons are to be tested, Brown and Forsythe's (1974) modification of Scheffé's method can be used. The critical value is given by

$$(a - 1)F_{\alpha_{FW}; a-1, v}$$

where v (the denominator degrees of freedom) is calculated from Equation 4.39.

Nonparametric Comparisons.   Not surprisingly, several nonparametric methods are available for testing comparisons (cf. Miller, 1981). We present two approaches for testing all pairwise comparisons and one approach for testing complex comparisons. In all cases, the methods maintain α_{FW} at .05 (when assumptions have been met).

There are two different nonparametric approaches for testing all pairwise comparisons. In the first of these (called joint ranking), scores are ranked from 1 to

N for all a groups, independent of group membership. Then the mean ranks of any two groups are compared using an appropriate critical value. In the other approach (called pairwise ranking), the original scores are rank ordered only for the two groups being compared. Researchers in the past have sometimes failed to appreciate that these two approaches do not test the same hypothesis. That they differ can be seen by realizing that in the joint-ranking model, the test comparing any two groups is conditional on the location of the other $a - 2$ groups. Instead of attempting to resolve which approach is "better," we refer you to Zwick and Marascuilo (1984), who discuss advantages and disadvantages of the two approaches.

For joint ranking, Levy (1979) developed a procedure to test all pairwise contrasts. Two groups are significantly different from one another if the absolute value of the difference between their mean ranks exceeds a critical value of $\omega^* q_{\alpha_{FW}, a, \infty}$ where q is the critical value of the studentized range statistic (with infinite degrees of freedom) and ω^* is given by

$$\omega^* = \sqrt{\frac{N(N + 1)}{12n} - \frac{\sum_{i=1}^{G}(t_i^3 - t_i)}{12n(N - 1)}}$$

Recall from our discussion of the Kruskal–Wallis H' statistic that t_i is the number of observations tied at a specific value.

If a pairwise-ranking procedure is preferred, two-sample Wilcoxon Rank Sum tests should be performed. Recall that this test is equivalent to the Mann–Whitney U and is a special case of the Kruskal–Wallis test when $a = 2$. To maintain α_{FW} at the desired level, a Bonferroni approach is taken. Thus, α_{PC} equals α_{FW} divided by $a(a - 1)/2$ because this represents the number of pairwise contrasts.

Marascuilo and McSweeney (1977) describe a procedure for testing complex comparisons. To test a null hypothesis that the population value of a contrast ψ equals zero, it is first necessary to calculate $\hat{\psi}$, the sample value of the contrast. This value is given by

$$\hat{\psi} = \sum_{j=1}^{a} c_j \bar{R}_j$$

where $\bar{R}_j$ is the mean rank for group j and c_j is the contrast coefficient for that group. Marascuilo and McSweeney show that the variance of $\hat{\psi}$ equals $[N(N + 1)/12](\sum_{j=1}^{a} c_j^2/n_j)$. The contrast is statistically significant if

$$(\hat{\psi})^2/\text{Var}(\hat{\psi}) > \chi_{a-1}^2$$

where χ_{a-1}^2 is the appropriate critical value from the χ^2 distribution.

TWO-WAY BETWEEN-SUBJECTS DESIGNS

Both parametric modifications and nonparametric approaches have been extended to two-way factorial designs. Because many of these extensions are considerably more complex than their one-way counterparts, in most cases we simply provide a brief overview of the available alternatives. It will often be necessary to consult the original references for computational details.

Parametric Modifications

Both the Brown–Forsythe F^* and Welch W tests can be extended to two-way designs. In general, the calculations become quite complicated and are beyond the scope of this book. However, each simplifies substantially in a special case, which we present.

The Brown–Forsythe F^* test is relatively straightforward for an equal n (i.e., orthogonal) two-way design, regardless of the number of levels of either factor. With equal n, the three observed values of F^* (one for the row main effect, one for the column main effect, and one for the interaction) are unchanged from the usual F values. (Recall that F^* also equals F in the equal-n one-way design.) The only difference between F^* and F concerns the denominator degrees of freedom. Assuming homogeneity and equal n, the denominator degrees of freedom of all three F tests are given by $ab(n-1)$. However, the denominator degrees of freedom for the three F^* tests equal f, where f is defined as

$$f = (n-1) \left/ \sum_{k=1}^{b} \sum_{j=1}^{a} (s_{jk}^2 / \sum\sum s_{jk}^2)^2 \right.$$

Of course, there is reason to believe that the usual F tests are relatively robust to violations of homogeneity of variance with equal n. The F^* test can also be used with unequal n, but the procedure requires combining orthonormal contrasts. See Brown and Forsythe (1974) for details.

Welch's test turns out to have a relatively simple form for 2×2 designs, even with unequal n. Algina and Olejnik (1984) show that hypotheses involving unweighted marginal means (i.e., hypotheses based on Type III sums of squares) can be tested rather easily in the 2×2 design. In fact, tests based on either Type I or Type II sums of squares are also relatively straightforward for the 2×2 design because, as we saw in Chapter 6, all three tests in the 2×2 design can be performed by testing individual contrasts. Algina and Olejnik also show how matrix algebra can be used to obtain tests in larger designs than a 2×2.

Nonparametric Approaches

As Toothaker and Chang (1980) point out, few statistics textbooks present nonparametric approaches for two-way between-subjects designs. Although a variety of tests are once again available, they tend to be inefficient, and different procedures are typically required for testing main effects than for testing interactions. For these reasons, we only mention a few sources for additional reading. Books that present nonparametric methods for the two-way between-subjects design include Bradley (1968) and Marascuilo and McSweeney (1977). Marascuilo and McSweeney (1977, pp. 376–379) show how Friedman's test (to be discussed later for repeated-measures designs) can be used to test main effects in a two-way between-subjects design. They also describe how *aligned ranks* methods can be used to test for interaction.

ANALYSIS OF COVARIANCE

As for the other designs we have discussed, there are once again both parametric modifications and nonparametric approaches for the analysis of covariance (ANCOVA).

Parametric Modifications

Dretzke, Levin, and Serlin (1982) studied properties of a Welch-type F^* test for testing homogeneity of regression (i.e., parallelism of regression lines) when population variances are unequal. Their overall findings closely paralleled the pattern of results in similar ANOVA studies. Specifically, the F test maintained an appropriate Type I error rate with equal or approximately equal sample sizes, even when variances were different. Thus, with equal or almost equal n, there appears to be no particular need for F^*. However, when sample sizes were appreciably different, F^* performed much better than F. Dretzke and colleagues found that "whether the assumption was violated or not and whether or not equal sample sizes were used, the actual Type I error values associated with F^* were always in close agreement with the nominal values" (1982, p. 382). Not surprisingly, the usual F was overly conservative when the smaller sample size was paired with the smaller residual variance, but was overly liberal when the smaller sample size was paired with the larger residual variance. As a cautionary note, this study was limited to the two-group case, so generalizing these results to more than two groups is tenuous at present.

Nonparametric Approaches

As usual, several nonparametric variations of ANCOVA have been developed. Olejnik and Algina (1985) have written a comprehensive review of five nonparametric alternatives to parametric ANCOVA. The five techniques they consider are Quade's distribution-free test, Puri and Sen's approach, McSweeney and Porter's rank transformation, Burnett and Barr's rank difference scores, and Shirley's general linear model solution. All five approaches begin by ranking all scores on the dependent variable and the covariate separately across all groups. However, as Olejnik and Algina point out, the subsequent analyses are different in three ways. First, only McSweeney and Porter's and Shirley's methods are based on both within-group and total-sample relationships; the other three methods are based only on the total-sample relationship. Second, these other three methods are based on an analysis of residuals, which as we discussed in Chapter 9 can be problematic, particularly in nonequivalent group designs. Third, the techniques differ in the distribution that the observed test statistic is referred to; in other words, different critical values are used.

Olejnik and Algina's review suggests that these nonparametric ANCOVA approaches are rarely useful substitutes for parametric ANCOVA. They found that the nonparametric approaches maintained Type I error rates near the nominal value only for those situations where the parametric test is robust to violations of assumptions. In addition, nonparametric approaches provided a meaningful advantage in power only for situations where extreme violations of assumptions existed and the linear relationship between the dependent variable and the covariate was weak. Their final conclusion is that "because for most actual research studies, extreme violations of assumptions are unlikely and in general covariates are chosen because of their strong relationship with the dependent variable, there does not appear to be convincing evidence to support the recommendation for using distribution-free procedures rather than parametric analysis of covariance" (1985, p. 82). Readers with data where parametric ANCOVA assumptions have been seriously violated may also find Huitema's (1980) discussion of rank ANCOVA helpful in choosing an appropriate method of data analysis.

REPEATED-MEASURES DESIGNS

Parametric Modifications

To date there has been little research investigating possible parametric modifications in repeated-measures designs. One reason is that in a sense the multivariate approach described in Chapters 13 and 14 can itself be regarded as a robust modification of the mixed-model approach of Chapters 11 and 12. Although the multivariate approach makes a normality assumption, there is no requirement that the difference score variables (i.e., D variables) have equal variances. A second reason concerns the nature of tests performed in higher-order designs. Tests of between-subjects effects collapse over any within-subjects factors, so they are equivalent to between-subjects tests that would be performed on a dependent variable that averages across levels of the within-subjects factors. These tests could be modified, as described earlier in this chapter, because they are now just between-subjects tests. Thus, although it might be possible to develop other forms of modified tests, there are already methods available for between-subjects effects.

Within-subjects effects in the multivariate approach are tested by multivariate tests. Robust alternatives to multivariate tests are naturally more complex than robust univariate tests. Although a few robust multivariate tests have been developed, they are beyond the scope of this book. Useful overviews of the robustness of MANOVA are provided by Bray and Maxwell (1985), Harris (1985), and Stevens (1986).

Nonparametric Approaches

As usual, a number of nonparametric methods are available for testing hypotheses in repeated-measures designs. We focus primarily on the one-way within-subjects design. The nonparametric test that is generally most appropriate for this design is Friedman's test. The first step in performing Friedman's test is to rank order the scores for each subject individually. Thus, if there are a levels of the within-subjects factor, the ranks range from 1 to a for each subject. If we let $\bar{R}_j$ indicate the mean rank for level j of the factor and let $\bar{R}$ be the grand mean of the ranks, the Friedman test statistic is given by

$$S = [12n/a(a + 1)] \sum_{j=1}^{a} (\bar{R}_j - \bar{R})^2$$

which can be rewritten as

$$S = \left[\frac{12}{na(a + 1)} \sum_{j=1}^{a} R_j^2 \right] - 3n(a + 1)$$

where R_j is the *sum* of ranks for level j. This test statistic S is approximately distributed as a χ^2 with $a - 1$ degrees of freedom. Thus, the null hypothesis is rejected if and only if S exceeds the appropriate critical χ^2 value. It turns out that if an ANOVA were calculated on the rank scores, the sum of squares attributable to the factor (labeled SS_A) would be related to S as follows: $S = [12/a(a + 1)]SS_A$. Hollander and Wolfe (1973) provide a correction that should be used when some ranks are tied. As of this writing, both BMDP and SPSS-X have programs to perform Friedman's test, but SAS does not. However, the test can be performed easily with SAS as long as there are no ties, by using the PROC RANK (BY SUBJECTS) command and then calculating the sum of squares attributable to the factor.

In most respects, the Friedman test compares to the parametric F test for repeated-measures designs in much the same way that the Kruskal–Wallis test compares to the parametric F test in between-subjects designs. For example, in general Friedman's test does not test the same null hypothesis as tested by the parametric approach (either mixed-model or multivariate because their hypotheses are identical). A potential advantage of Friedman's test claimed by Marascuilo and McSweeney (1977) is that the test is not "sensitive to non-normality, unequal variances, and inequality of correlation coefficients" (p. 354). Their statement is certainly true when the assumptions of Friedman's test are met because it tests whether the assignment of ranks within each subject is random. If it is, then all correlation coefficients between ranks must equal a common value of $\rho = -1/(a-1)$ by mathematical necessity. However, when the Friedman test is used as an alternative to a parametric test, there is no assurance that a common value exists, either in the sample or the population. In other words, every level can have the same average rank and yet the variances and/or the correlations may be unequal. The effect of these influences on Friedman's test is unclear because apparently no studies have addressed this issue.

Consistent with findings in the between-subjects design, Friedman's test can either be less powerful or more powerful than a parametric test, even in the special case where they are testing the same null hypothesis. When all mixed-model F assumptions are met, the asymptotic efficiency (i.e., large-sample efficiency) of the Friedman test relative to the unadjusted mixed-model F equals $3a/\pi(a + 1)$, where $\pi = 3.14159\ldots$. So, for example, when $a = 2$, the asymptotic efficiency is 0.637; when $a = 3$, it is 0.716, when $a = 6$, it is 0.819. On the other hand, when distributions are nonnormal, there is reason to believe that Friedman's test may be more powerful than any of the parametric tests.

It is also possible to use a rank transformation approach in the one-way within-subjects design. One possibility would be to calculate the ranks as in Friedman's test but then calculate an F statistic using a parametric test on the ranks. An alternate approach, which seems to be preferable (Conover & Iman, 1981; Iman, Hora, & Conover, 1984), is to perform the parametric test on ranks obtained from all observations together. In other words, all na scores would be ranked from 1 to na, across subjects as well as levels of the factor. However, as a cautionary note, Blair and Higgins (1985) found this approach is generally inferior to Wilcoxon's signed ranks test, in a study restricted to repeated factors with only two levels.

Repeated-measures data are sometimes dichotomous. Cochran's Q statistic was developed specifically for this type of data. However, as Myers, DiCecco, White, and Borden (1982) show, this test is sensitive to violations of sphericity. These authors found that Type I error rate can be maintained at an appropriate level for moderate or large sample sizes ($n \geq 16$) by modifying the critical value of the Q test. They also found that an ε-adjusted F test performed well for samples as large as 16.

SUMMARY

A student in one of our classes read a preliminary draft of this chapter and concluded that it was not very important because all the techniques presented in the chapter were likely to be revised sometime in the future. Unfortunately, this student failed to realize that not only does the body of accumulated knowledge change over time but also the methods themselves used to obtain this knowledge evolve. Experimental design and data analysis are no different in this regard. One of the major lessons to be learned from this chapter is that statistics is not a static field of knowledge, but instead is a dynamic area full of active research.

Another major point of this chapter has been to combat the misconception that there is a single correct way to analyze one's data. All too often statistics is presented as a succession of meaningless formulas into which numbers are plugged. However, we believe that statistics should be thought of very differently. Statistics is a collection of techniques for extracting information from data. The maximum amount of information can be obtained only by understanding the logic and the concepts underlying statistics, a knowledge that enables an investigator to choose a technique appropriate to the scientific questions to be addressed as well as to the likely characteristics of the data. Such an approach yields the greatest promise of advancing scientific understanding.

EXERCISES

*1. True or False: Although the parametric modification F^* is more robust than the usual F test to violations of homogeneity of variance in between-subjects designs, the F^* test is always at least slightly less powerful than the F test.

2. True or False: The parametric test based on Welch's W statistic can either be more or less powerful than the usual F test in equal-n designs.

3. True or False: When sample sizes are unequal and heterogeneity of variance is suspected in one-way between-subjects designs, either F^* or W should seriously be considered as a replacement for the usual F test.

4. True or False: The Kruskal–Wallis test can be regarded as testing a "shift" hypothesis in location without requiring an assumption that scores are normally distributed with equal variances.

5. True or False: The nonparametric Kruskal–Wallis test and the parametric F test always test the same hypothesis, but they require different distributional assumptions.

6. True or False: Although the F test is more powerful than the Kruskal–Wallis test when the normality and homogeneity of variance assumptions are met, the Kruskal–Wallis test can be more powerful than the F test when these assumptions are not met.

*7. True or False: When sample sizes are unequal and heterogeneity of variance is suspected in one-way between-subjects designs, the nonparametric Kruskal–Wallis test should be considered seriously as a replacement for the usual F test.

*8. How do the values of F, F^*, and W compare to each other when samples are of different sizes and variances are considerably different from one another? Consider the following summary statistics:

Group 1	Group 2	Group 3
$n_1 = 20$	$n_2 = 20$	$n_3 = 50$
$\bar{Y}_1 = 10$	$\bar{Y}_2 = 12$	$\bar{Y}_3 = 14$
$s_1^2 = 10$	$s_2^2 = 10$	$s_3^2 = 50$

a. Calculate an observed F value for these data.
b. Calculate the F^* value for these data (however, you need not compute the denominator degrees of freedom).
c. Calculate the W value for these data.
d. Are your answers to parts a–c consistent with the assertion made in Table 15.1 that when large samples are paired with large variances the F is conservative, whereas F^* and W are more robust?

9. Suppose that, as in Exercise 8, samples are of different sizes and variances are considerably different from each other. Now, however, the large variance is paired with a small sample size:

Group 1	Group 2	Group 3
$n_1 = 20$	$n_2 = 20$	$n_3 = 50$
$\bar{Y}_1 = 10$	$\bar{Y}_2 = 12$	$\bar{Y}_3 = 14$
$s_1^2 = 50$	$s_2^2 = 10$	$s_3^2 = 10$

a. Calculate an observed F value for these data.
b. Calculate the F^* value for these data (however, you need not compute the denominator degrees of freedom).

c. Calculate the W value for these data (however, you need not compute the denominator degrees of freedom).

d. Are your answers to parts a–c consistent with the assertion made in Table 15.1 that when large samples are paired with small variances the F is liberal, whereas F^* and W are more robust?

e. Are the F, F^*, and W values of this exercise higher or lower than the corresponding F, F^*, and W values of Exercise 8? Is the direction of change consistent with Table 15.1?

*10. Exercise 15 at the end of Chapter 5 introduced the following data from a one-way between-subjects design:

Group 1	Group 2	Group 3
48	59	68
54	46	62
47	49	53
54	63	59
62	38	67
57	58	71

a. Perform a nonparametric test of the difference among these three groups.

b. Use a joint-ranking approach to perform all possible pairwise comparisons. Maintain α_{FW} at .05.

c. Use a pairwise-ranking approach to perform all possible pairwise comparisons. Maintain α_{FW} at .05.

d. From looking at the data, it would be interesting to test the difference between the average of the first two groups and the third group. Test this comparison and maintain α_{FW} at .05.

11. Exercise 17 at the end of Chapter 11 described a one-way within-subjects design that investigated the effect of perceived control on individuals' abilities to cope with stress. Each of 12 subjects was asked to perform a task for which their perceived coping self-efficacy was strong, one for which it was medium, and one for which it was weak. Higher scores on the dependent variable indicate greater stress.

Subject	Strong	Medium	Weak
1	.38	.25	.20
2	.36	.41	.37
3	.16	.49	.43
4	.22	.26	.18
5	.17	.27	.24
6	.41	.48	.40
7	.34	.39	.22
8	.19	.25	.34
9	.25	.35	.30
10	.36	.40	.32
11	.24	.33	.29
12	.30	.35	.27

a. Perform a nonparametric test of whether the three levels of self-efficacy are associated with different levels of stress.

b. How does your answer to part a compare to the answer you would obtain from using a parametric approach?

Extension   Why Does the Usual F Test Falter with Unequal ns When Population Variances Are Unequal?

Why is the F test conservative when large sample sizes are paired with large variances, yet liberal when large sample sizes are paired with small variances? The answer can be seen by comparing the expected values of MS_W and MS_B when the null hypothesis is true but variances are possibly unequal. In this situation, the expected values of both MS_B and MS_W are weighted averages of the a population variances. However, sample sizes play different roles in the two weighting schemes.

Specifically, it can be shown that if the null hypothesis is true, MS_B has an expected value given by

$$\mathscr{E}(MS_B) = \frac{\sum_{j=1}^{a} w_j \sigma_j^2}{\sum_{j=1}^{a} w_j} \tag{E.1}$$

where $w_j = N - n_j$. Thus, the weight a population variance receives in MS_B is inversely related to its sample size. Although this may seem counterintuitive, it helps to realize that MS_B is based on $\bar{Y}_j - \bar{Y}$, and larger groups contribute proportionally more to $\bar{Y}$.

Similarly, it can be shown that MS_W has an expected value equal to

$$\mathscr{E}(MS_W) = \frac{\sum_{j=1}^{a} w_j^* \sigma_j^2}{\sum_{j=1}^{a} w_j^*} \tag{E.2}$$

where $w_j^* = n_j - 1$. Thus, the weight a population variance receives in MS_W is directly related to its sample size.

What are the implications of Equations 15E.1 and 15E.2? Let's consider some special cases.

Case I. Homogeneity of Variance

If all σ_j^2 are equal to each other, Equations 15E.1 and 15E.2 simplify to $\mathscr{E}(MS_B) = \sigma^2$ and $\mathscr{E}(MS_W) = \sigma^2$ because the weights are irrelevant when all the numbers to be averaged are identical. In this case, the F ratio of MS_B to MS_W works appropriately, regardless of whether the sample sizes are equal or unequal.

Case II. Unequal Variances but Equal n

If all n_j are equal to each other, Equations 15E.1 and 15E.2 simplify to $\mathscr{E}(MS_B) = \sum_{j=1}^a \sigma_j^2/a$ and $\mathscr{E}(MS_W) = \sum_{j=1}^a \sigma_j^2/a$. Because the weights are equal to one another, in both cases the weighted averages become identical to simple unweighted averages. Thus, MS_B and MS_W are equal to one another in the long run. Although the ANOVA assumption has been violated, the F test is typically only slightly affected here.

Case III. Unequal Variances: Large Samples Paired with Small Variances

In this situation, we can see from Equation 15E.1 that $\mathscr{E}(MS_B)$ receives more weight from the smaller samples, which have larger variances. Thus, the weighted average used to calculate $\mathscr{E}(MS_B)$ is larger than the unweighted average of the σ_j^2 terms. On the other hand, $\mathscr{E}(MS_W)$ receives more weight from the larger samples, which have smaller variances. Thus, the weighted average used to calculate $\mathscr{E}(MS_W)$ is smaller than the unweighted average of the σ_j^2 terms. As a consequence, $\mathscr{E}(MS_B) > \mathscr{E}(MS_W)$, even when the null hypothesis is true. F values tend to be too large, resulting in too many rejections of the null hypothesis when it is true. Thus, the Type I error rate is too high.

Case IV. Unequal Variances: Large Samples Paired with Large Variances

This situation is just the opposite of Case III. Now, $\mathscr{E}(MS_B)$ gives more weight to the groups with small variances because they are smaller in size. In contrast, $\mathscr{E}(MS_W)$ gives more weight to the groups with large variances because they are larger in size. As a result, $\mathscr{E}(MS_B) < \mathscr{E}(MS_W)$ when the null hypothesis is true. The F test is conservative and rejects the null hypothesis too infrequently. Thus power suffers.

Appendix A Statistical Tables

T A B L E **A. 1** Critical Values of *t* Distribution

df α_1:	.05	.025	.0125	.0083	.00625	.005
α_2:	.10	.05	.025	.0167	.0125	.01
1	6.31	12.71	25.45	38.19	50.92	63.66
2	2.92	4.30	6.21	7.65	8.86	9.92
3	2.35	3.18	4.18	4.86	5.39	5.84
4	2.13	2.78	3.50	3.96	4.31	4.60
5	2.02	2.57	3.16	3.53	3.81	4.03
6	1.94	2.45	2.97	3.29	3.52	3.71
7	1.89	2.36	2.84	3.13	3.34	3.50
8	1.86	2.31	2.75	3.02	3.21	3.36
9	1.83	2.26	2.69	2.93	3.11	3.25
10	1.81	2.23	2.63	2.87	3.04	3.17
11	1.80	2.20	2.59	2.82	2.98	3.11
12	1.78	2.18	2.56	2.78	2.93	3.05
13	1.77	2.16	2.53	2.75	2.90	3.01
14	1.76	2.14	2.51	2.72	2.86	2.98
15	1.75	2.13	2.49	2.69	2.84	2.95
16	1.75	2.12	2.47	2.67	2.81	2.92
17	1.74	2.11	2.46	2.65	2.79	2.90
18	1.73	2.10	2.45	2.64	2.77	2.88
19	1.73	2.09	2.43	2.63	2.76	2.86
20	1.72	2.09	2.42	2.61	2.74	2.85
22	1.72	2.07	2.41	2.59	2.72	2.82
24	1.71	2.06	2.39	2.57	2.70	2.80
26	1.71	2.06	2.38	2.56	2.68	2.78
28	1.70	2.05	2.37	2.55	2.67	2.76
30	1.70	2.04	2.36	2.54	2.66	2.75
32	1.69	2.04	2.35	2.53	2.65	2.74
34	1.69	2.03	2.35	2.52	2.64	2.73
36	1.69	2.03	2.34	2.51	2.63	2.72
38	1.69	2.02	2.33	2.50	2.62	2.71
40	1.68	2.02	2.33	2.50	2.62	2.70
45	1.68	2.01	2.32	2.49	2.60	2.69
50	1.68	2.01	2.31	2.48	2.59	2.68
55	1.67	2.00	2.30	2.47	2.58	2.67
60	1.67	2.00	2.30	2.46	2.58	2.66
70	1.67	1.99	2.29	2.45	2.56	2.65
80	1.66	1.99	2.28	2.45	2.56	2.64
90	1.66	1.99	2.28	2.44	2.55	2.63
100	1.66	1.98	2.28	2.43	2.54	2.63
120	1.66	1.98	2.27	2.43	2.54	2.62
140	1.66	1.98	2.27	2.42	2.53	2.61
160	1.65	1.97	2.26	2.42	2.53	2.61
180	1.65	1.97	2.26	2.42	2.52	2.60
200	1.65	1.97	2.26	2.41	2.52	2.60
∞	1.645	1.96	2.24	2.39	2.50	2.58

NOTE: α_1 and α_2 represent alpha levels for one-tailed and two-tailed tests, respectively. These critical values were computed using the TINV function of SAS, except for the values corresponding to infinite degrees of freedom, which were computed using the CINV function of SAS.

T A B L E A. 2 Critical Values of *F* Distribution

df for Denom.	α	df for Numerator																	
		1	2	3	4	5	6	7	8	9	10	12	15	20	24	30	40	60	∞
1	.25	5.83	7.50	8.20	8.58	8.82	8.98	9.10	9.19	9.26	9.32	9.41	9.49	9.58	9.63	9.67	9.71	9.76	9.85
	.10	39.9	49.5	53.6	55.8	57.2	58.2	58.9	59.4	59.9	60.2	60.7	61.2	61.7	62.0	62.3	62.5	62.8	63.3
	.05	161	200	216	225	230	234	237	239	240	242	244	246	248	249	250	251	252	254
	.025	648	800	864	900	922	937	948	957	963	969	977	985	993	997	1001	1006	1010	1018
	.01	4052	5000	5403	5625	5764	5859	5928	5982	6022	6056	6106	6157	6209	6235	6261	6287	6313	6366
	.001	4053*	5000*	5404*	5625*	5764*	5859*	5929*	5981*	6023*	6056*	6107*	6158*	6209*	6235*	6261*	6287*	6313*	6366*
2	.25	2.57	3.00	3.15	3.23	3.28	3.31	3.34	3.35	3.37	3.38	3.39	3.41	3.43	3.43	3.44	3.45	3.46	3.48
	.10	8.53	9.00	9.16	9.24	9.29	9.33	9.35	9.37	9.38	9.39	9.41	9.42	9.44	9.45	9.46	9.47	9.47	9.49
	.05	18.5	19.0	19.2	19.3	19.3	19.3	19.4	19.4	19.4	19.4	19.4	19.4	19.5	19.5	19.5	19.5	19.5	19.5
	.025	38.5	39.0	39.2	39.3	39.3	39.3	39.4	39.4	39.4	39.4	39.4	39.4	39.5	39.5	39.5	39.5	39.5	39.5
	.01	98.5	99.0	99.2	99.3	99.3	99.3	99.4	99.4	99.4	99.4	99.4	99.4	99.5	99.5	99.5	99.5	99.5	99.5
	.001	999	999	999	999	999	999	999	999	999	999	999	999	999	1000	1000	1000	1000	1000
3	.25	2.02	2.28	2.36	2.39	2.41	2.42	2.43	2.44	2.44	2.44	2.45	2.46	2.46	2.46	2.47	2.47	2.47	2.47
	.10	5.54	5.46	5.39	5.34	5.31	5.28	5.27	5.25	5.24	5.23	5.22	5.20	5.18	5.18	5.17	5.16	5.15	5.13
	.05	10.1	9.55	9.28	9.12	9.01	8.94	8.89	8.85	8.81	8.79	8.74	8.70	8.66	8.64	8.62	8.59	8.57	8.53
	.025	17.4	16.0	15.4	15.1	14.9	14.7	14.6	14.5	14.5	14.4	14.3	14.2	14.2	14.1	14.1	14.0	14.0	13.9
	.01	34.1	30.8	29.5	28.7	28.2	27.9	27.7	27.5	27.4	27.2	27.0	26.9	26.7	26.6	26.5	26.4	26.3	26.1
	.001	167	148	141	137	135	133	132	131	130	129	128	127	126	126	125	125	124	124
4	.25	1.81	2.00	2.05	2.06	2.07	2.08	2.08	2.08	2.08	2.08	2.08	2.08	2.08	2.08	2.08	2.08	2.08	2.08
	.10	4.54	4.32	4.19	4.11	4.05	4.01	3.98	3.95	3.94	3.92	3.90	3.87	3.84	3.83	3.82	3.80	3.79	3.76
	.05	7.71	6.94	6.59	6.39	6.26	6.16	6.09	6.04	6.00	5.96	5.91	5.86	5.80	5.77	5.75	5.72	5.69	5.63
	.025	12.2	10.6	9.98	9.60	9.36	9.20	9.07	8.98	8.90	8.84	8.75	8.66	8.56	8.51	8.46	8.41	8.36	8.26
	.01	21.2	18.0	16.7	16.0	15.5	15.2	15.0	14.8	14.7	14.6	14.4	14.2	14.0	13.9	13.8	13.8	13.6	13.5
	.001	74.1	61.2	56.2	53.4	51.7	50.5	49.7	49.0	48.5	48.0	47.4	46.8	46.1	45.8	45.4	45.1	44.8	44.0

* These values must be multiplied by 100.

TABLE A.2 (Continued)

df for Numerator

df for Denom.	α	1	2	3	4	5	6	7	8	9	10	12	15	20	24	30	40	60	∞
5	.25	1.69	1.85	1.88	1.89	1.89	1.89	1.89	1.89	1.89	1.89	1.89	1.89	1.88	1.88	1.88	1.88	1.87	1.87
	.10	4.06	3.78	3.62	3.52	3.45	3.40	3.37	3.34	3.32	3.30	3.27	3.24	3.21	3.19	3.17	3.16	3.14	3.10
	.05	6.61	5.79	5.41	5.19	5.05	4.95	4.88	4.82	4.77	4.74	4.68	4.62	4.56	4.53	4.50	4.46	4.43	4.36
	.025	10.0	8.43	7.76	7.39	7.15	6.98	6.85	6.76	6.68	6.62	6.52	6.43	6.33	6.28	6.23	6.18	6.12	6.02
	.01	16.3	13.3	12.1	11.4	11.0	10.7	10.5	10.3	10.2	10.0	9.89	9.72	9.55	9.47	9.38	9.29	9.20	9.02
	.001	47.2	37.1	33.2	31.1	29.8	28.8	28.2	27.6	27.2	26.9	26.4	25.9	25.4	25.1	24.9	24.6	24.3	23.8
6	.25	1.62	1.76	1.78	1.79	1.79	1.78	1.78	1.78	1.77	1.77	1.77	1.76	1.76	1.75	1.75	1.75	1.74	1.74
	.10	3.78	3.46	3.29	3.18	3.11	3.05	3.01	2.98	2.96	2.94	2.90	2.87	2.84	2.82	2.80	2.78	2.76	2.72
	.05	5.99	5.14	4.76	4.53	4.39	4.28	4.21	4.15	4.10	4.06	4.00	3.94	3.87	3.84	3.81	3.77	3.74	3.67
	.025	8.81	7.26	6.60	6.23	5.99	5.82	5.70	5.60	5.52	5.46	5.37	5.27	5.17	5.12	5.07	5.01	4.96	4.85
	.01	13.8	10.9	9.78	9.15	8.75	8.47	8.26	8.10	7.98	7.87	7.72	7.56	7.40	7.31	7.23	7.14	7.06	6.88
	.001	35.5	27.0	23.7	21.9	20.8	20.0	19.5	19.0	18.7	18.4	18.0	17.6	17.1	16.9	16.7	16.4	16.2,	15.8
7	.25	1.57	1.70	1.72	1.72	1.71	1.71	1.70	1.70	1.69	1.69	1.68	1.68	1.67	1.67	1.66	1.66	1.65	1.65
	.10	3.59	3.26	3.07	2.96	2.88	2.83	2.78	2.75	2.72	2.70	2.67	2.63	2.59	2.58	2.56	2.54	2.51	2.47
	.05	5.59	4.74	4.35	4.12	3.97	3.87	3.79	3.73	3.68	3.64	3.57	3.51	3.44	3.41	3.38	3.34	3.30	3.23
	.025	8.07	6.54	5.89	5.52	5.29	5.12	4.99	4.90	4.82	4.76	4.67	4.57	4.47	4.42	4.36	4.31	4.25	4.14
	.01	12.2	9.55	8.45	7.85	7.46	7.19	6.99	6.84	6.72	6.62	6.47	6.31	6.16	6.07	5.99	5.91	5.82	5.65
	.001	29.2	21.7	18.8	17.2	16.2	15.5	15.0	14.6	14.3	14.1	13.7	13.3	12.9	12.7	12.5	12.3	12.1	11.7
8	.25	1.54	1.66	1.67	1.66	1.66	1.65	1.64	1.64	1.63	1.63	1.62	1.62	1.61	1.60	1.60	1.59	1.59	1.58
	.10	3.46	3.11	2.92	2.81	2.73	2.67	2.62	2.59	2.56	2.54	2.50	2.46	2.42	2.40	2.38	2.36	2.34	2.29
	.05	5.32	4.46	4.07	3.84	3.69	3.58	3.50	3.44	3.39	3.35	3.28	3.22	3.15	3.12	3.08	3.04	3.01	2.93
	.025	7.57	6.06	5.42	5.05	4.82	4.65	4.53	4.43	4.36	4.30	4.20	4.10	4.00	3.95	3.89	3.84	3.78	3.67
	.01	11.3	8.65	7.59	7.01	6.63	6.37	6.18	6.03	5.91	5.81	5.67	5.52	5.36	5.28	5.20	5.12	5.03	4.86
	.001	25.4	18.5	15.8	14.4	13.5	12.9	12.4	12.0	11.8	11.5	11.2	10.8	10.5	10.3	10.1	9.92	9.73	9.33

	α	1	2	3	4	5	6	7	8	9	10	12	15	20	24	30	40	60	∞
	.25	1.51	1.62	1.63	1.63	1.62	1.61	1.60	1.60	1.59	1.59	1.58	1.57	1.56	1.56	1.55	1.54	1.54	1.53
	.10	3.36	3.01	2.81	2.69	2.61	2.55	2.51	2.47	2.44	2.42	2.38	2.34	2.30	2.28	2.25	2.23	2.21	2.16
	.05	5.12	4.26	3.86	3.63	3.48	3.37	3.29	3.23	3.18	3.14	3.07	3.01	2.94	2.90	2.86	2.83	2.79	2.71
9	.025	7.21	5.71	5.08	4.72	4.48	4.32	4.20	4.10	4.03	3.96	3.87	3.77	3.67	3.61	3.56	3.51	3.45	3.33
	.01	10.6	8.02	6.99	6.42	6.06	5.80	5.61	5.47	5.35	5.26	5.11	4.96	4.81	4.73	4.65	4.57	4.48	4.31
	.001	22.9	16.4	13.9	12.6	11.7	11.1	10.7	10.4	10.1	9.89	9.57	9.24	8.90	8.72	8.55	8.37	8.19	7.81
	.25	1.49	1.60	1.60	1.59	1.59	1.58	1.57	1.56	1.56	1.55	1.54	1.53	1.52	1.52	1.51	1.51	1.50	1.48
	.10	3.29	2.92	2.73	2.61	2.52	2.46	2.41	2.38	2.35	2.32	2.28	2.24	2.20	2.18	2.16	2.13	2.11	2.06
	.05	4.96	4.10	3.71	3.48	3.33	3.22	3.14	3.07	3.02	2.98	2.91	2.85	2.77	2.74	2.70	2.66	2.62	2.54
10	.025	6.94	5.46	4.83	4.47	4.24	4.07	3.95	3.85	3.78	3.72	3.62	3.52	3.42	3.37	3.31	3.26	3.20	3.08
	.01	10.0	7.56	6.55	5.99	5.64	5.39	5.20	5.06	4.94	4.85	4.71	4.56	4.41	4.33	4.25	4.17	4.08	3.91
	.001	21.0	14.9	12.6	11.3	10.5	9.92	9.52	9.20	8.96	8.75	8.45	8.13	7.80	7.64	7.47	7.30	7.12	6.76
	.25	1.47	1.58	1.58	1.57	1.56	1.55	1.54	1.53	1.53	1.52	1.51	1.50	1.49	1.49	1.48	1.47	1.47	1.45
	.10	3.23	2.86	2.66	2.54	2.45	2.39	2.34	2.30	2.27	2.25	2.21	2.17	2.12	2.10	2.08	2.05	2.03	1.97
	.05	4.84	3.98	3.59	3.36	3.20	3.09	3.01	2.95	2.90	2.85	2.79	2.72	2.65	2.61	2.57	2.53	2.49	2.40
11	.025	6.72	5.26	4.63	4.28	4.04	3.88	3.76	3.66	3.59	3.53	3.43	3.33	3.23	3.17	3.12	3.06	3.00	2.88
	.01	9.65	7.21	6.22	5.67	5.32	5.07	4.89	4.74	4.63	4.54	4.40	4.25	4.10	4.02	3.94	3.86	3.78	3.60
	.001	19.7	13.8	11.6	10.4	9.58	9.05	8.66	8.35	8.12	7.92	7.63	7.32	7.01	6.85	6.68	6.52	6.35	6.00
	.25	1.46	1.56	1.56	1.55	1.54	1.53	1.52	1.51	1.51	1.50	1.49	1.48	1.47	1.46	1.45	1.45	1.44	1.42
	.10	3.18	2.81	2.61	2.48	2.39	2.33	2.28	2.24	2.21	2.19	2.15	2.10	2.06	2.04	2.01	1.99	1.96	1.90
	.05	4.75	3.89	3.49	3.26	3.11	3.00	2.91	2.85	2.80	2.75	2.69	2.62	2.54	2.51	2.47	2.43	2.38	2.30
12	.025	6.55	5.10	4.47	4.12	3.89	3.73	3.61	3.51	3.44	3.37	3.28	3.18	3.07	3.02	2.96	2.91	2.85	2.72
	.01	9.33	6.93	5.95	5.41	5.06	4.82	4.64	4.50	4.39	4.30	4.16	4.01	3.86	3.78	3.70	3.62	3.54	3.36
	.001	18.6	13.0	10.8	9.63	8.89	8.38	8.00	7.71	7.48	7.29	7.00	6.71	6.40	6.25	6.09	5.93	5.76	5.42
	.25	1.45	1.55	1.55	1.53	1.52	1.51	1.50	1.49	1.49	1.48	1.47	1.46	1.45	1.44	1.43	1.42	1.42	1.40
	.10	3.14	2.76	2.56	2.43	2.35	2.28	2.23	2.20	2.16	2.14	2.10	2.05	2.01	1.98	1.96	1.93	1.90	1.85
	.05	4.67	3.81	3.41	3.18	3.03	2.92	2.83	2.77	2.71	2.67	2.60	2.53	2.46	2.42	2.38	2.34	2.30	2.21
13	.025	6.41	4.97	4.35	4.00	3.77	3.60	3.48	3.39	3.31	3.25	3.15	3.05	2.95	2.89	2.84	2.78	2.72	2.60
	.01	9.07	6.70	5.74	5.21	4.86	4.62	4.44	4.30	4.19	4.10	3.96	3.82	3.66	3.59	3.51	3.43	3.34	3.17
	.001	17.8	12.3	10.2	9.07	8.35	7.86	7.49	7.21	6.98	6.80	6.52	6.23	5.93	5.78	5.63	5.47	5.30	4.97

TABLE A.2 (Continued)

df for Numerator

df for Denom.	α	1	2	3	4	5	6	7	8	9	10	12	15	20	24	30	40	60	∞
14	.25	1.44	1.53	1.53	1.52	1.51	1.50	1.49	1.48	1.47	1.46	1.45	1.44	1.43	1.42	1.41	1.41	1.40	1.38
	.10	3.10	2.73	2.52	2.39	2.31	2.24	2.19	2.15	2.12	2.10	2.05	2.01	1.96	1.94	1.91	1.89	1.86	1.80
	.05	4.60	3.74	3.34	3.11	2.96	2.85	2.76	2.70	2.65	2.60	2.53	2.46	2.39	2.35	2.31	2.27	2.22	2.13
	.025	6.30	4.86	4.24	3.89	3.66	3.50	3.38	3.29	3.21	3.15	3.05	2.95	2.84	2.79	2.73	2.67	2.61	2.49
	.01	8.86	6.51	5.56	5.04	4.69	4.46	4.28	4.14	4.03	3.94	3.80	3.66	3.51	3.43	3.35	3.27	3.18	3.00
	.001	17.1	11.8	9.73	8.62	7.92	7.43	7.08	6.80	6.58	6.40	6.13	5.85	5.56	5.41	5.25	5.10	4.94	4.60
15	.25	1.43	1.52	1.52	1.51	1.49	1.48	1.47	1.46	1.46	1.45	1.44	1.43	1.41	1.41	1.40	1.39	1.38	1.36
	.10	3.07	2.70	2.49	2.36	2.27	2.21	2.16	2.12	2.09	2.06	2.02	1.97	1.92	1.90	1.87	1.85	1.82	1.76
	.05	4.54	3.68	3.29	3.06	2.90	2.79	2.71	2.64	2.59	2.54	2.48	2.40	2.33	2.29	2.25	2.20	2.16	2.07
	.025	6.20	4.77	4.15	3.80	3.58	3.41	3.29	3.20	3.12	3.06	2.96	2.86	2.76	2.70	2.64	2.59	2.52	2.40
	.01	8.68	6.36	5.42	4.89	4.56	4.32	4.14	4.00	3.89	3.80	3.67	3.52	3.37	3.29	3.21	3.13	3.05	2.87
	.001	16.6	11.3	9.34	8.25	7.57	7.09	6.74	6.47	6.26	6.08	5.81	5.54	5.25	5.10	4.95	4.80	4.64	4.31
16	.25	1.42	1.51	1.51	1.50	1.48	1.47	1.46	1.45	1.44	1.44	1.43	1.41	1.40	1.39	1.38	1.37	1.36	1.34
	.10	3.05	2.67	2.46	2.33	2.24	2.18	2.13	2.09	2.06	2.03	1.99	1.94	1.89	1.87	1.84	1.81	1.78	1.72
	.05	4.49	3.63	3.24	3.01	2.85	2.74	2.66	2.59	2.54	2.49	2.42	2.35	2.28	2.24	2.19	2.15	2.11	2.01
	.025	6.12	4.69	4.08	3.73	3.50	3.34	3.22	3.12	3.05	2.99	2.89	2.79	2.68	2.63	2.57	2.51	2.45	2.32
	.01	8.53	6.23	5.29	4.77	4.44	4.20	4.03	3.89	3.78	3.69	3.55	3.41	3.26	3.18	3.10	3.02	2.93	2.75
	.001	16.1	11.0	9.00	7.94	7.27	6.81	6.46	6.19	5.98	5.81	5.55	5.27	4.99	4.85	4.70	4.54	4.39	4.06
17	.25	1.42	1.51	1.50	1.49	1.47	1.46	1.45	1.44	1.43	1.43	1.41	1.40	1.39	1.38	1.37	1.36	1.35	1.33
	.10	3.03	2.64	2.44	2.31	2.22	2.15	2.10	2.06	2.03	2.00	1.96	1.91	1.86	1.84	1.81	1.78	1.75	1.69
	.05	4.45	3.59	3.20	2.96	2.81	2.70	2.61	2.55	2.49	2.45	2.38	2.31	2.23	2.19	2.15	2.10	2.06	1.96
	.025	6.04	4.62	4.01	3.66	3.44	3.28	3.16	3.06	2.98	2.92	2.82	2.72	2.62	2.56	2.50	2.44	2.38	2.25
	.01	8.40	6.11	5.18	4.67	4.34	4.10	3.93	3.79	3.68	3.59	3.46	3.31	3.16	3.08	3.00	2.92	2.83	2.65
	.001	15.7	10.7	8.73	7.68	7.02	6.56	6.22	5.96	5.75	5.58	5.32	5.05	4.78	4.63	4.48	4.33	4.18	3.85

	α	1	2	3	4	5	6	7	8	9	10	12	15	20	24	30	40	60	∞
	.25	1.41	1.50	1.49	1.48	1.46	1.45	1.44	1.43	1.42	1.42	1.40	1.39	1.38	1.37	1.36	1.35	1.34	1.32
	.10	3.01	2.62	2.42	2.29	2.20	2.13	2.08	2.04	2.00	1.98	1.93	1.89	1.84	1.81	1.78	1.75	1.72	1.66
	.05	**4.41**	**3.55**	**3.16**	**2.93**	**2.77**	**2.66**	**2.58**	**2.51**	**2.46**	**2.41**	**2.34**	**2.27**	**2.19**	**2.15**	**2.11**	**2.06**	**2.02**	**1.92**
	.025	5.98	4.56	3.95	3.61	3.38	3.22	3.10	3.01	2.93	2.87	2.77	2.67	2.56	2.50	2.44	2.38	2.32	2.19
	.01	**8.29**	**6.01**	**5.09**	**4.58**	**4.25**	**4.01**	**3.84**	**3.71**	**3.60**	**3.51**	**3.37**	**3.23**	**3.08**	**3.00**	**2.92**	**2.84**	**2.75**	**2.57**
18	.001	15.4	10.4	8.49	7.46	6.81	6.35	6.02	5.76	5.56	5.39	5.13	4.87	4.59	4.45	4.30	4.15	4.00	3.67
	.25	1.41	1.49	1.49	1.47	1.46	1.44	1.43	1.42	1.41	1.41	1.40	1.38	1.37	1.36	1.35	1.34	1.33	1.30
	.10	2.99	2.61	2.40	2.27	2.18	2.11	2.06	2.02	1.98	1.96	1.91	1.86	1.81	1.79	1.76	1.73	1.70	1.63
	.05	**4.38**	**3.52**	**3.13**	**2.90**	**2.74**	**2.63**	**2.54**	**2.48**	**2.42**	**2.38**	**2.31**	**2.23**	**2.16**	**2.11**	**2.03**	**2.03**	**1.98**	**1.88**
	.025	5.92	4.51	3.90	3.56	3.33	3.17	3.05	2.96	2.88	2.82	2.72	2.62	2.51	2.45	2.39	2.33	2.27	2.13
	.01	**8.18**	**5.93**	**5.01**	**4.50**	**4.17**	**3.94**	**3.77**	**3.63**	**3.52**	**3.43**	**3.30**	**3.15**	**3.00**	**2.92**	**2.84**	**2.76**	**2.67**	**2.49**
19	.001	15.1	10.2	8.28	7.26	6.62	6.18	5.85	5.59	5.39	5.22	4.97	4.70	4.43	4.29	4.14	3.99	3.84	3.51
	.25	1.40	1.49	1.48	1.47	1.45	1.44	1.43	1.42	1.41	1.40	1.39	1.37	1.36	1.35	1.34	1.33	1.32	1.29
	.10	2.97	2.59	2.38	2.25	2.16	2.09	2.04	2.00	1.96	1.94	1.89	1.84	1.79	1.77	1.74	1.71	1.68	1.61
	.05	**4.35**	**3.49**	**3.10**	**2.87**	**2.71**	**2.60**	**2.51**	**2.45**	**2.39**	**2.35**	**2.28**	**2.20**	**2.12**	**2.08**	**2.04**	**1.99**	**1.95**	**1.84**
	.025	5.87	4.46	3.86	3.51	3.29	3.13	3.01	2.91	2.84	2.77	2.68	2.57	2.46	2.41	2.35	2.29	2.22	2.09
	.01	**8.10**	**5.85**	**4.94**	**4.43**	**4.10**	**3.87**	**3.70**	**3.56**	**3.46**	**3.37**	**3.23**	**3.09**	**2.94**	**2.86**	**2.78**	**2.69**	**2.61**	**2.42**
20	.001	14.8	9.95	8.10	7.10	6.46	6.02	5.69	5.44	5.24	5.08	4.82	4.56	4.29	4.15	4.00	3.86	3.70	3.38
	.25	1.40	1.48	1.47	1.45	1.44	1.42	1.41	1.40	1.39	1.39	1.37	1.36	1.34	1.33	1.32	1.31	1.30	1.28
	.10	2.95	2.56	2.35	2.22	2.13	2.06	2.01	1.97	1.93	1.90	1.86	1.81	1.76	1.73	1.70	1.67	1.64	1.57
	.05	**4.30**	**3.44**	**3.05**	**2.82**	**2.66**	**2.55**	**2.46**	**2.40**	**2.34**	**2.30**	**2.23**	**2.15**	**2.07**	**2.03**	**1.98**	**1.94**	**1.89**	**1.78**
	.025	5.79	4.38	3.78	3.44	3.22	3.05	2.93	2.84	2.76	2.70	2.60	2.50	2.39	2.33	2.27	2.21	2.14	2.00
	.01	**7.95**	**5.72**	**4.82**	**4.31**	**3.99**	**3.76**	**3.59**	**3.45**	**3.35**	**3.26**	**3.12**	**2.98**	**2.83**	**2.75**	**2.67**	**2.58**	**2.50**	**2.31**
22	.001	14.4	9.61	7.80	6.81	6.19	5.76	5.44	5.19	4.99	4.83	4.58	4.33	4.06	3.92	3.78	3.63	3.48	3.15
	.25	1.39	1.47	1.46	1.44	1.43	1.41	1.40	1.39	1.38	1.38	1.36	1.35	1.33	1.32	1.31	1.30	1.29	1.26
	.10	2.93	2.54	2.33	2.19	2.10	2.04	1.98	1.94	1.91	1.88	1.83	1.78	1.73	1.70	1.67	1.64	1.61	1.53
	.05	**4.26**	**3.40**	**3.01**	**2.78**	**2.62**	**2.51**	**2.42**	**2.36**	**2.30**	**2.25**	**2.18**	**2.11**	**2.03**	**1.98**	**1.94**	**1.89**	**1.84**	**1.73**
	.025	5.72	4.32	3.72	3.38	3.15	2.99	2.87	2.78	2.70	2.64	2.54	2.44	2.33	2.27	2.21	2.15	2.08	1.94
	.01	**7.82**	**5.61**	**4.72**	**4.22**	**3.90**	**3.67**	**3.50**	**3.36**	**3.26**	**3.17**	**3.03**	**2.89**	**2.74**	**2.66**	**2.58**	**2.49**	**2.40**	**2.21**
24	.001	14.0	9.34	7.55	6.59	5.98	5.55	5.23	4.99	4.80	4.64	4.39	4.14	3.87	3.74	3.59	3.45	3.29	2.97

TABLE A. 2 (Continued)

df for Denom.	α	\(df\) for Numerator																	
		1	2	3	4	5	6	7	8	9	10	12	15	20	24	30	40	60	∞
26	.25	1.38	1.46	1.45	1.44	1.42	1.41	1.39	1.38	1.37	1.37	1.35	1.34	1.32	1.31	1.30	1.29	1.28	1.25
	.10	2.91	2.52	2.31	2.17	2.08	2.01	1.96	1.92	1.88	1.86	1.81	1.76	1.71	1.68	1.65	1.61	1.58	1.50
	.05	4.23	3.37	2.98	2.74	2.59	2.47	2.39	2.32	2.27	2.22	2.15	2.07	1.99	1.95	1.90	1.85	1.80	1.69
	.025	5.66	4.27	3.67	3.33	3.10	2.94	2.82	2.73	2.65	2.59	2.49	2.39	2.28	2.22	2.16	2.09	2.03	1.88
	.01	7.72	5.53	4.64	4.14	3.82	3.59	3.42	3.29	3.18	3.09	2.96	2.81	2.66	2.58	2.50	2.42	2.33	2.13
	.001	13.7	9.12	7.36	6.41	5.80	5.38	5.07	4.83	4.64	4.48	4.24	3.99	3.72	3.59	3.44	3.30	3.15	2.82
28	.25	1.38	1.46	1.45	1.43	1.41	1.40	1.39	1.38	1.37	1.36	1.34	1.33	1.31	1.30	1.29	1.28	1.27	1.24
	.10	2.89	2.50	2.29	2.16	2.06	2.00	1.94	1.90	1.87	1.84	1.79	1.74	1.69	1.66	1.63	1.59	1.56	1.48
	.05	4.20	3.34	2.95	2.71	2.56	2.45	2.36	2.29	2.24	2.19	2.12	2.04	1.96	1.91	1.87	1.82	1.77	1.65
	.025	5.61	4.22	3.63	3.29	3.06	2.90	2.78	2.69	2.61	2.55	2.45	2.34	2.23	2.17	2.11	2.05	1.98	1.83
	.01	7.64	5.45	4.57	4.07	3.75	3.53	3.36	3.23	3.12	3.03	2.90	2.75	2.60	2.52	2.44	2.35	2.26	2.06
	.001	13.5	8.93	7.19	6.25	5.66	5.24	4.93	4.69	4.50	4.35	4.11	3.86	3.60	3.46	3.32	3.18	3.02	2.69
30	.25	1.38	1.45	1.44	1.42	1.41	1.39	1.38	1.37	1.36	1.35	1.34	1.32	1.30	1.29	1.28	1.27	1.26	1.23
	.10	2.88	2.49	2.28	2.14	2.05	1.98	1.93	1.88	1.85	1.82	1.77	1.72	1.67	1.64	1.61	1.57	1.54	1.46
	.05	4.17	3.32	2.92	2.69	2.53	2.42	2.33	2.27	2.21	2.16	2.09	2.01	1.93	1.89	1.84	1.79	1.74	1.62
	.025	5.57	4.18	3.59	3.25	3.03	2.87	2.75	2.65	2.57	2.51	2.41	2.31	2.20	2.14	2.07	2.01	1.94	1.79
	.01	7.56	5.39	4.51	4.02	3.70	3.47	3.30	3.17	3.07	2.98	2.84	2.70	2.55	2.47	2.39	2.30	2.21	2.01
	.001	13.3	8.77	7.05	6.12	5.53	5.12	4.82	4.58	4.39	4.24	4.00	3.75	3.49	3.36	3.22	3.07	2.92	2.59
40	.25	1.36	1.44	1.42	1.40	1.39	1.37	1.36	1.35	1.34	1.33	1.31	1.30	1.28	1.26	1.25	1.24	1.22	1.19
	.10	2.84	2.44	2.23	2.09	2.00	1.93	1.87	1.83	1.79	1.76	1.71	1.66	1.61	1.57	1.54	1.51	1.47	1.38
	.05	4.08	3.23	2.84	2.61	2.45	2.34	2.25	2.18	2.12	2.08	2.00	1.92	1.84	1.79	1.74	1.69	1.64	1.51
	.025	5.42	4.05	3.46	3.13	2.90	2.74	2.62	2.53	2.45	2.39	2.29	2.18	2.07	2.01	1.94	1.88	1.80	1.64
	.01	7.31	5.18	4.31	3.83	3.51	3.29	3.12	2.99	2.89	2.80	2.66	2.52	2.37	2.29	2.20	2.11	2.02	1.80
	.001	12.6	8.25	6.60	5.70	5.13	4.73	4.44	4.21	4.02	3.87	3.64	3.40	3.15	3.01	2.87	2.73	2.57	2.23

	α	1	2	3	4	5	6	7	8	9	10	12	15	20	24	30	40	60	∞
60	.25	1.35	1.42	1.41	1.38	1.37	1.35	1.33	1.32	1.31	1.30	1.29	1.27	1.25	1.24	1.22	1.21	1.19	1.15
	.10	2.79	2.39	2.18	2.04	1.95	1.87	1.82	1.77	1.74	1.71	1.66	1.60	1.54	1.51	1.48	1.44	1.40	1.29
	.05	**4.00**	**3.15**	**2.76**	**2.53**	**2.37**	**2.25**	**2.17**	**2.10**	**2.04**	**1.99**	**1.92**	**1.84**	**1.75**	**1.70**	**1.65**	**1.59**	**1.53**	**1.39**
	.025	5.29	3.93	3.34	3.01	2.79	2.63	2.51	2.41	2.33	2.27	2.17	2.06	1.94	1.88	1.82	1.74	1.67	1.48
	.01	**7.08**	**4.98**	**4.13**	**3.65**	**3.34**	**3.12**	**2.95**	**2.82**	**2.72**	**2.63**	**2.50**	**2.35**	**2.20**	**2.12**	**2.03**	**1.94**	**1.84**	**1.60**
	.001	12.0	7.76	6.17	5.31	4.76	4.37	4.09	3.87	3.69	3.54	3.31	3.08	2.83	2.69	2.55	2.41	2.25	1.89
120	.25	1.34	1.40	1.39	1.37	1.35	1.33	1.31	1.30	1.29	1.28	1.26	1.24	1.22	1.21	1.19	1.18	1.16	1.10
	.10	2.75	2.35	2.13	1.99	1.90	1.82	1.77	1.72	1.68	1.65	1.60	1.55	1.48	1.45	1.41	1.37	1.32	1.19
	.05	**3.92**	**3.07**	**2.68**	**2.45**	**2.29**	**2.17**	**2.09**	**2.02**	**1.96**	**1.91**	**1.83**	**1.75**	**1.66**	**1.61**	**1.55**	**1.50**	**1.43**	**1.25**
	.025	5.15	3.80	3.23	2.89	2.67	2.52	2.39	2.30	2.22	2.16	2.05	1.94	1.82	1.76	1.69	1.61	1.53	1.31
	.01	**6.85**	**4.79**	**3.95**	**3.48**	**3.17**	**2.96**	**2.79**	**2.66**	**2.56**	**2.47**	**2.34**	**2.19**	**2.03**	**1.95**	**1.86**	**1.76**	**1.66**	**1.38**
	.001	11.4	7.32	5.79	4.95	4.42	4.04	3.77	3.55	3.38	3.24	3.02	2.78	2.53	2.40	2.26	2.11	1.95	1.54
∞	.25	1.32	1.39	1.37	1.35	1.33	1.31	1.29	1.28	1.27	1.25	1.24	1.22	1.19	1.18	1.16	1.14	1.12	1.00
	.10	2.71	2.30	2.08	1.94	1.85	1.77	1.72	1.67	1.63	1.60	1.55	1.49	1.42	1.38	1.34	1.30	1.24	1.00
	.05	**3.84**	**3.00**	**2.60**	**2.37**	**2.21**	**2.10**	**2.01**	**1.94**	**1.88**	**1.83**	**1.75**	**1.67**	**1.57**	**1.52**	**1.46**	**1.39**	**1.32**	**1.00**
	.025	5.02	3.69	3.12	2.79	2.57	2.41	2.29	2.19	2.11	2.05	1.94	1.83	1.71	1.64	1.57	1.48	1.39	1.00
	.01	**6.63**	**4.61**	**3.78**	**3.32**	**3.02**	**2.80**	**2.64**	**2.51**	**2.41**	**2.32**	**2.18**	**2.04**	**1.88**	**1.79**	**1.70**	**1.59**	**1.47**	**1.00**
	.001	10.8	6.91	5.42	4.62	4.10	3.74	3.47	3.27	3.10	2.96	2.74	2.51	2.27	2.13	1.99	1.84	1.66	1.00

T A B L E A. 3   Critical Values of Bonferroni F Distribution with 1 Numerator Degree of Freedom and a Familywise
Alpha Level of .05

C = Number of Comparisons

Denominator df	1	2	3	4	5	6	7	8	9	10
1	161.45	647.79	1458.36	2593.16	4052.18	5835.43	7942.91	10374.62	13130.56	16210.72
2	18.51	38.51	58.50	78.50	98.50	118.50	138.50	158.50	178.50	198.50
3	10.13	17.44	23.59	29.07	34.12	38.83	43.29	47.54	51.62	55.55
4	7.71	12.22	15.69	18.62	21.20	23.53	25.68	27.68	29.56	31.33
5	6.61	10.01	12.49	14.52	16.26	17.80	19.20	20.48	21.67	22.78
6	5.99	8.81	10.81	12.40	13.75	14.92	15.98	16.93	17.82	18.63
7	5.59	8.07	9.78	11.12	12.25	13.22	14.08	14.86	15.58	16.24
8	5.32	7.57	9.09	10.28	11.26	12.10	12.85	13.52	14.13	14.69
9	5.12	7.21	8.60	9.68	10.56	11.32	11.98	12.58	13.12	13.61
10	4.96	6.94	8.24	9.23	10.04	10.74	11.34	11.89	12.38	12.83
11	4.84	6.72	7.95	8.89	9.65	10.29	10.86	11.36	11.81	12.23
12	4.75	6.55	7.73	8.61	9.33	9.94	10.47	10.94	11.37	11.75
13	4.67	6.41	7.54	8.39	9.07	9.65	10.16	10.60	11.01	11.37
14	4.60	6.30	7.39	8.20	8.86	9.42	9.90	10.33	10.71	11.06
15	4.54	6.20	7.26	8.05	8.68	9.22	9.68	10.09	10.46	10.80
16	4.49	6.12	7.15	7.91	8.53	9.05	9.50	9.90	10.25	10.58
17	4.45	6.04	7.05	7.80	8.40	8.90	9.34	9.73	10.07	10.38
18	4.41	5.98	6.97	7.70	8.29	8.78	9.20	9.58	9.91	10.22
19	4.38	5.92	6.89	7.61	8.18	8.67	9.08	9.45	9.78	10.07
20	4.35	5.87	6.83	7.53	8.10	8.57	8.97	9.33	9.65	9.94
22	4.30	5.79	6.71	7.40	7.95	8.40	8.79	9.14	9.45	9.73
24	4.26	5.72	6.62	7.29	7.82	8.27	8.65	8.98	9.28	9.55
26	4.23	5.66	6.55	7.20	7.72	8.15	8.53	8.85	9.14	9.41
28	4.20	5.61	6.48	7.13	7.64	8.06	8.42	8.74	9.03	9.28
30	4.17	5.57	6.43	7.06	7.56	7.98	8.34	8.65	8.93	9.18

C = Number of Comparisons

Denominator df	1	2	3	4	5	6	7	8	9	10
32	4.15	5.53	6.38	7.01	7.50	7.91	8.26	8.57	8.84	9.09
34	4.13	5.50	6.34	6.96	7.44	7.85	8.19	8.50	8.77	9.01
36	4.11	5.47	6.31	6.91	7.40	7.80	8.14	8.44	8.70	8.94
38	4.10	5.45	6.27	6.88	7.35	7.75	8.09	8.38	8.64	8.88
40	4.08	5.42	6.24	6.84	7.31	7.71	8.04	8.33	8.59	8.83
45	4.06	5.38	6.18	6.77	7.23	7.62	7.94	8.23	8.49	8.71
50	4.03	5.34	6.14	6.71	7.17	7.55	7.87	8.15	8.40	8.63
55	4.02	5.31	6.10	6.67	7.12	7.49	7.81	8.09	8.33	8.55
60	4.00	5.29	6.07	6.63	7.08	7.44	7.76	8.03	8.28	8.49
70	3.98	5.25	6.02	6.57	7.01	7.37	7.68	7.95	8.19	8.40
80	3.96	5.22	5.98	6.53	6.96	7.32	7.62	7.89	8.12	8.33
90	3.95	5.20	5.95	6.50	6.93	7.28	7.58	7.84	8.07	8.28
100	3.94	5.18	5.93	6.47	6.90	7.25	7.54	7.80	8.03	8.24
120	3.92	5.15	5.90	6.43	6.85	7.20	7.49	7.75	7.97	8.18
140	3.91	5.13	5.87	6.40	6.82	7.16	7.45	7.71	7.93	8.14
160	3.90	5.12	5.85	6.38	6.80	7.14	7.43	7.68	7.90	8.10
180	3.89	5.11	5.84	6.37	6.78	7.12	7.41	7.66	7.88	8.08
200	3.89	5.10	5.83	6.35	6.76	7.10	7.39	7.64	7.86	8.06
∞	3.84	5.02	5.73	6.24	6.63	6.96	7.24	7.48	7.69	7.88

NOTE: These critical values were computed using the FINV function of SAS, except for the values corresponding to infinite denominator degrees of freedom, which were computed using the CINV function of SAS.

TABLE A.4 Critical Values of Studentized Range Distribution

r = number of means (Tukey test) or number of steps between ordered means (Newman–Keuls test)

df_{error}	α_{FW}	2	3	4	5	6	7	8	9	10	11	12	13	14	15	16	17	18	19	20	α_{FW}	df_{error}
5	.05	3.64	4.60	5.22	5.67	6.03	6.33	6.58	6.80	6.99	7.17	7.32	7.47	7.60	7.72	7.83	7.93	8.03	8.12	8.21	.05	5
	.01	5.70	6.98	7.80	8.42	8.91	9.32	9.67	9.97	10.24	10.48	10.70	10.89	11.08	11.24	11.40	11.55	11.68	11.81	11.93	.01	
6	.05	3.46	4.34	4.90	5.30	5.63	5.90	6.12	6.32	6.49	6.65	6.79	6.92	7.03	7.14	7.24	7.34	7.43	7.51	7.59	.05	6
	.01	5.24	6.33	7.03	7.56	7.97	8.32	8.61	8.87	9.10	9.30	9.48	9.65	9.81	9.95	10.08	10.21	10.32	10.43	10.54	.01	
7	.05	3.34	4.16	4.68	5.06	5.36	5.61	5.82	6.00	6.16	6.30	6.43	6.55	6.66	6.76	6.85	6.94	7.02	7.10	7.17	.05	7
	.01	4.95	5.92	6.54	7.01	7.37	7.68	7.94	8.17	8.37	8.55	8.71	8.86	9.00	9.12	9.24	9.35	9.46	9.55	9.65	.01	
8	.05	3.26	4.04	4.53	4.89	5.17	5.40	5.60	5.77	5.92	6.05	6.18	6.29	6.39	6.48	6.57	6.65	6.73	6.80	6.87	.05	8
	.01	4.75	5.64	6.20	6.62	6.96	7.24	7.47	7.68	7.86	8.03	8.18	8.31	8.44	8.55	8.66	8.76	8.85	8.94	9.03	.01	
9	.05	3.20	3.95	4.41	4.76	5.02	5.24	5.43	5.59	5.74	5.87	5.98	6.09	6.19	6.28	6.36	6.44	6.51	6.58	6.64	.05	9
	.01	4.60	5.43	5.96	6.35	6.66	6.91	7.13	7.33	7.49	7.65	7.78	7.91	8.03	8.13	8.23	8.33	8.41	8.49	8.57	.01	
10	.05	3.15	3.88	4.33	4.65	4.91	5.12	5.30	5.46	5.60	5.72	5.83	5.93	6.03	6.11	6.19	6.27	6.34	6.40	6.47	.05	10
	.01	4.48	5.27	5.77	6.14	6.43	6.67	6.87	7.05	7.21	7.36	7.49	7.60	7.71	7.81	7.91	7.99	8.08	8.15	8.23	.01	
11	.05	3.11	3.82	4.26	4.57	4.82	5.03	5.20	5.35	5.49	5.61	5.71	5.81	5.90	5.98	6.06	6.13	6.20	6.27	6.33	.05	11
	.01	4.39	5.15	5.62	5.97	6.25	6.48	6.67	6.84	6.99	7.13	7.25	7.36	7.46	7.56	7.65	7.73	7.81	7.88	7.95	.01	
12	.05	3.08	3.77	4.20	4.51	4.75	4.95	5.12	5.27	5.39	5.51	5.61	5.71	5.80	5.88	5.95	6.02	6.09	6.15	6.21	.05	12
	.01	4.32	5.05	5.50	5.84	6.10	6.32	6.51	6.67	6.81	6.94	7.06	7.17	7.26	7.36	7.44	7.52	7.59	7.66	7.73	.01	
13	.05	3.06	3.73	4.15	4.45	4.69	4.88	5.05	5.19	5.32	5.43	5.53	5.63	5.71	5.79	5.86	5.93	5.99	6.05	6.11	.05	13
	.01	4.26	4.96	5.40	5.73	5.98	6.19	6.37	6.53	6.67	6.79	6.90	7.01	7.10	7.19	7.27	7.35	7.42	7.48	7.55	.01	
14	.05	3.03	3.70	4.11	4.41	4.64	4.83	4.99	5.13	5.25	5.36	5.46	5.55	5.64	5.71	5.79	5.85	5.91	5.97	6.03	.05	14
	.01	4.21	4.89	5.32	5.63	5.88	6.08	6.26	6.41	6.54	6.66	6.77	6.87	6.96	7.05	7.13	7.20	7.27	7.33	7.39	.01	
15	.05	3.01	3.67	4.08	4.37	4.59	4.78	4.94	5.08	5.20	5.31	5.40	5.49	5.57	5.65	5.72	5.78	5.85	5.90	5.96	.05	15
	.01	4.17	4.84	5.25	5.56	5.80	5.99	6.16	6.31	6.44	6.55	6.66	6.76	6.84	6.93	7.00	7.07	7.14	7.20	7.26	.01	
16	.05	3.00	3.65	4.05	4.33	4.56	4.74	4.90	5.03	5.15	5.26	5.35	5.44	5.52	5.59	5.66	5.73	5.79	5.84	5.90	.05	16
	.01	4.13	4.79	5.19	5.49	5.72	5.92	6.08	6.22	6.35	6.46	6.56	6.66	6.74	6.82	6.90	6.97	7.03	7.09	7.15	.01	

r = number of means (Tukey test) or number of steps between ordered means (Newman–Keuls test)

df_{error}	α_{FW}	2	3	4	5	6	7	8	9	10	11	12	13	14	15	16	17	18	19	20	α_{FW}	df_{error}
17	.05	2.98	3.63	4.02	4.30	4.52	4.70	4.86	4.99	5.11	5.21	5.31	5.39	5.47	5.54	5.61	5.67	5.73	5.79	5.84	.05	17
	.01	4.10	4.74	5.14	5.43	5.66	5.85	6.01	6.15	6.27	6.38	6.48	6.57	6.66	6.73	6.81	6.87	6.94	7.00	7.05	.01	17
18	.05	2.97	3.61	4.00	4.28	4.49	4.67	4.82	4.96	5.07	5.17	5.27	5.35	5.43	5.50	5.57	5.63	5.69	5.74	5.79	.05	18
	.01	4.07	4.70	5.09	5.38	5.60	5.79	5.94	6.08	6.20	6.31	6.41	6.50	6.58	6.65	6.73	6.79	6.85	6.91	6.97	.01	18
19	.05	2.96	3.59	3.98	4.25	4.47	4.65	4.79	4.92	5.04	5.14	5.23	5.31	5.39	5.46	5.53	5.59	5.65	5.70	5.75	.05	19
	.01	4.05	4.67	5.05	5.33	5.55	5.73	5.89	6.02	6.14	6.25	6.34	6.43	6.51	6.58	6.65	6.72	6.78	6.84	6.89	.01	19
20	.05	2.95	3.58	3.96	4.23	4.45	4.62	4.77	4.90	5.01	5.11	5.20	5.28	5.36	5.43	5.49	5.55	5.61	5.66	5.71	.05	20
	.01	4.02	4.64	5.02	5.29	5.51	5.69	5.84	5.97	6.09	6.19	6.28	6.37	6.45	6.52	6.59	6.65	6.71	6.77	6.82	.01	20
24	.05	2.92	3.53	3.90	4.17	4.37	4.54	4.68	4.81	4.92	5.01	5.10	5.18	5.25	5.32	5.38	5.44	5.49	5.55	5.59	.05	24
	.01	3.96	4.55	4.91	5.17	5.37	5.54	5.69	5.81	5.92	6.02	6.11	6.19	6.26	6.33	6.39	6.45	6.51	6.56	6.61	.01	24
30	.05	2.89	3.49	3.85	4.10	4.30	4.46	4.60	4.72	4.82	4.92	5.00	5.08	5.15	5.21	5.27	5.33	5.38	5.43	5.47	.05	30
	.01	3.89	4.45	4.80	5.05	5.24	5.40	5.54	5.65	5.76	5.85	5.93	6.01	6.08	6.14	6.20	6.26	6.31	6.36	6.41	.01	30
40	.05	2.86	3.44	3.79	4.04	4.23	4.39	4.52	4.63	4.73	4.82	4.90	4.98	5.04	5.11	5.16	5.22	5.27	5.31	5.36	.05	40
	.01	3.82	4.37	4.70	4.93	5.11	5.26	5.39	5.50	5.60	5.69	5.76	5.83	5.90	5.96	6.02	6.07	6.12	6.16	6.21	.01	40
60	.05	2.83	3.40	3.74	3.98	4.16	4.31	4.44	4.55	4.65	4.73	4.81	4.88	4.94	5.00	5.06	5.11	5.15	5.20	5.24	.05	60
	.01	3.76	4.28	4.59	4.82	4.99	5.13	5.25	5.36	5.45	5.53	5.60	5.67	5.73	5.78	5.84	5.89	5.93	5.97	6.01	.01	60
120	.05	2.80	3.36	3.68	3.92	4.10	4.24	4.36	4.47	4.56	4.64	4.71	4.78	4.84	4.90	4.95	5.00	5.04	5.09	5.13	.05	120
	.01	3.70	4.20	4.50	4.71	4.87	5.01	5.12	5.21	5.30	5.37	5.44	5.50	5.56	5.61	5.66	5.71	5.75	5.79	5.83	.01	120
∞	.05	2.77	3.31	3.63	3.86	4.03	4.17	4.29	4.39	4.47	4.55	4.62	4.68	4.74	4.80	4.85	4.89	4.93	4.97	5.01	.05	∞
	.01	3.64	4.12	4.40	4.60	4.76	4.88	4.99	5.08	5.16	5.23	5.29	5.35	5.40	5.45	5.49	5.54	5.57	5.61	5.65	.01	∞

T A B L E **A. 5** Critical Values of
Studentized Maximum Modulus Distribution

$\alpha = 0.10$

	Number of Groups			
df	3	4	5	6
2	4.38	5.30	5.96	6.45
3	3.37	4.01	4.47	4.82
4	2.98	3.51	3.89	4.18
5	2.77	3.24	3.58	3.84
6	2.64	3.07	3.38	3.62
7	2.56	2.96	3.25	3.48
8	2.49	2.88	3.16	3.37
9	2.45	2.82	3.09	3.29
10	2.41	2.77	3.03	3.23
11	2.38	2.73	2.98	3.18
12	2.36	2.70	2.95	3.14
13	2.34	2.67	2.91	3.10
14	2.32	2.65	2.89	3.07
15	2.31	2.63	2.87	3.04
16	2.29	2.62	2.85	3.02
17	2.28	2.60	2.83	3.00
18	2.27	2.59	2.81	2.99
19	2.26	2.58	2.80	2.97
20	2.26	2.57	2.79	2.96
21	2.25	2.56	2.78	2.94
22	2.24	2.55	2.77	2.93
23	2.24	2.54	2.76	2.92
24	2.23	2.53	2.75	2.91
25	2.23	2.53	2.74	2.90
26	2.22	2.52	2.73	2.89
27	2.22	2.52	2.73	2.89
28	2.21	2.51	2.72	2.88
29	2.21	2.51	2.71	2.87
30	2.21	2.50	2.71	2.87
35	2.19	2.48	2.69	2.84
40	2.18	2.47	2.67	2.82
45	2.18	2.46	2.66	2.81
50	2.17	2.45	2.65	2.80
60	2.16	2.44	2.63	2.78
80	2.15	2.42	2.61	2.76
100	2.14	2.41	2.60	2.75
120	2.14	2.41	2.60	2.74
200	2.13	2.40	2.58	2.72
∞	2.11	2.38	2.56	2.70

T A B L E **A. 5** (Continued)

		$\alpha = 0.05$		
		Number of Groups		
df	3	4	5	6
2	6.34	7.65	8.57	9.28
3	4.43	5.23	5.81	6.26
4	3.74	4.37	4.82	5.17
5	3.40	3.93	4.31	4.61
6	3.19	3.66	4.01	4.28
7	3.06	3.49	3.80	4.05
8	2.96	3.36	3.66	3.89
9	2.89	3.27	3.55	3.77
10	2.83	3.20	3.47	3.68
11	2.78	3.14	3.40	3.60
12	2.75	3.09	3.35	3.54
13	2.72	3.06	3.30	3.49
14	2.69	3.02	3.26	3.45
15	2.67	2.99	3.23	3.41
16	2.65	2.97	3.20	3.38
17	2.63	2.95	3.17	3.35
18	2.62	2.93	3.15	3.32
19	2.61	2.91	3.13	3.30
20	2.59	2.90	3.11	3.28
21	2.58	2.88	3.10	3.26
22	2.57	2.87	3.08	3.25
23	2.57	2.86	3.07	3.23
24	2.56	2.85	3.06	3.22
25	2.55	2.84	3.05	3.21
26	2.54	2.83	3.04	3.20
27	2.54	2.83	3.03	3.19
28	2.53	2.82	3.02	3.18
29	2.53	2.81	3.01	3.17
30	2.52	2.80	3.00	3.16
35	2.50	2.78	2.97	3.13
40	2.49	2.76	2.95	3.10
45	2.48	2.75	2.93	3.08
50	2.47	2.73	2.92	3.06
60	2.45	2.72	2.90	3.04
80	2.44	2.69	2.87	3.01
100	2.43	2.68	2.86	3.00
120	2.42	2.67	2.85	2.98
200	2.41	2.66	2.83	2.96
∞	2.39	2.63	2.80	2.93

	$\alpha = 0.01$			
	Number of Groups			
df	3	4	5	6
2	14.44	17.35	19.43	21.02
3	7.91	9.28	10.27	11.03
4	5.99	6.90	7.57	8.09
5	5.11	5.81	6.33	6.74
6	4.61	5.20	5.64	5.99
7	4.30	4.81	5.20	5.50
8	4.08	4.55	4.89	5.17
9	3.92	4.35	4.67	4.92
10	3.80	4.20	4.50	4.74
11	3.71	4.09	4.37	4.59
12	3.63	4.00	4.26	4.48
13	3.57	3.92	4.18	4.38
14	3.52	3.85	4.10	4.30
15	3.47	3.80	4.04	4.23
16	3.43	3.75	3.99	4.17
17	3.40	3.71	3.94	4.12
18	3.37	3.68	3.90	4.07
19	3.35	3.65	3.86	4.03
20	3.32	3.62	3.83	4.00
21	3.30	3.59	3.80	3.97
22	3.28	3.57	3.78	3.94
23	3.27	3.55	3.75	3.91
24	3.25	3.53	3.73	3.89
25	3.24	3.51	3.71	3.87
26	3.23	3.50	3.70	3.85
27	3.21	3.48	3.68	3.83
28	3.20	3.47	3.66	3.81
29	3.19	3.46	3.65	3.80
30	3.18	3.45	3.64	3.78
35	3.15	3.40	3.58	3.73
40	3.12	3.37	3.54	3.68
45	3.10	3.34	3.51	3.65
50	3.08	3.32	3.49	3.62
60	3.06	3.29	3.46	3.59
80	3.02	3.25	3.41	3.54
100	3.01	3.23	3.39	3.51
120	2.99	3.21	3.37	3.49
200	2.97	3.19	3.34	3.46
∞	2.93	3.14	3.29	3.40

Source: Computed by C. W. Dunnett. Abridged from Table 7 in Y. Hochberg and A. C. Tamhane, *Multiple Comparisons Procedures*. Used with permission of John Wiley & Sons, Inc.

T A B L E A. 6 Critical Values of Dunnett's Two-Tailed Test for Comparing Treatments to a Control

Error df	α	Number of Treatment Means, Including Control (a)								
		2	3	4	5	6	7	8	9	10
5	.05	2.57	3.03	3.29	3.48	3.62	3.73	3.82	3.90	3.97
	.01	4.03	4.63	4.98	5.22	5.41	5.56	5.69	5.80	5.89
6	.05	2.45	2.86	3.10	3.26	3.39	3.49	3.57	3.64	3.71
	.01	3.71	4.21	4.51	4.71	4.87	5.00	5.10	5.20	5.28
7	.05	2.36	2.75	2.97	3.12	3.24	3.33	3.41	3.47	3.53
	.01	3.50	3.95	4.21	4.39	4.53	4.64	4.74	4.82	4.89
8	.05	2.31	2.67	2.88	3.02	3.13	3.22	3.29	3.35	3.41
	.01	3.36	3.77	4.00	4.17	4.29	4.40	4.48	4.56	4.62
9	.05	2.26	2.61	2.81	2.95	3.05	3.14	3.20	3.26	3.32
	.01	3.25	3.63	3.85	4.01	4.12	4.22	4.30	4.37	4.43
10	.05	2.23	2.57	2.76	2.89	2.99	3.07	3.14	3.19	3.24
	.01	3.17	3.53	3.74	3.88	3.99	4.08	4.16	4.22	4.28
11	.05	2.20	2.53	2.72	2.84	2.94	3.02	3.08	3.14	3.19
	.01	3.11	3.45	3.65	3.79	3.89	3.98	4.05	4.11	4.16
12	.05	2.18	2.50	2.68	2.81	2.90	2.98	3.04	3.09	3.14
	.01	3.05	3.39	3.58	3.71	3.81	3.89	3.96	4.02	4.07
13	.05	2.16	2.48	2.65	2.78	2.87	2.94	3.00	3.06	3.10
	.01	3.01	3.33	3.52	3.65	3.74	3.82	3.89	3.94	3.99
14	.05	2.14	2.46	2.63	2.75	2.84	2.91	2.97	3.02	3.07
	.01	2.98	3.29	3.47	3.59	3.69	3.76	3.83	3.88	3.93
15	.05	2.13	2.44	2.61	2.73	2.82	2.89	2.95	3.00	3.04
	.01	2.95	3.25	3.43	3.55	3.64	3.71	3.78	3.83	3.88
16	.05	2.12	2.42	2.59	2.71	2.80	2.87	2.92	2.97	3.02
	.01	2.92	3.22	3.39	3.51	3.60	3.67	3.73	3.78	3.83
17	.05	2.11	2.41	2.58	2.69	2.78	2.85	2.90	2.95	3.00
	.01	2.90	3.19	3.36	3.47	3.56	3.63	3.69	3.74	3.79
18	.05	2.10	2.40	2.56	2.68	2.76	2.83	2.89	2.94	2.98
	.01	2.88	3.17	3.33	3.44	3.53	3.60	3.66	3.71	3.75
19	.05	2.09	2.39	2.55	2.66	2.75	2.81	2.87	2.92	2.96
	.01	2.86	3.15	3.31	3.42	3.50	3.57	3.63	3.68	3.72
20	.05	2.09	2.38	2.54	2.65	2.73	2.80	2.86	2.90	2.95
	.01	2.85	3.13	3.29	3.40	3.48	3.55	3.60	3.65	3.69
24	.05	2.06	2.35	2.51	2.61	2.70	2.76	2.81	2.86	2.90
	.01	2.80	3.07	3.22	3.32	3.40	3.47	3.52	3.57	3.61
30	.05	2.04	2.32	2.47	2.58	2.66	2.72	2.77	2.82	2.86
	.01	2.75	3.01	3.15	3.25	3.33	3.39	3.44	3.49	3.52
40	.05	2.02	2.29	2.44	2.54	2.62	2.68	2.73	2.77	2.81
	.01	2.70	2.95	3.09	3.19	3.26	3.32	3.37	3.41	3.44

T A B L E **A. 6** (Continued)

Error df	α	Number of Treatment Means, Including Control (a)								
		2	3	4	5	6	7	8	9	10
60	.05	2.00	2.27	2.41	2.51	2.58	2.64	2.69	2.73	2.77
	.01	2.66	2.90	3.03	3.12	3.19	3.25	3.29	3.33	3.37
120	.05	1.98	2.24	2.38	2.47	2.55	2.60	2.65	2.69	2.73
	.01	2.62	2.85	2.97	3.06	3.12	3.18	3.22	3.26	3.29
∞	.05	1.96	2.21	2.35	2.44	2.51	2.57	2.61	2.65	2.69
	.01	2.58	2.79	2.92	3.00	3.06	3.11	3.15	3.19	3.22

Table reproduced from New tables for multiple comparisons with a control, *Biometrics*, 1964, *20*, 482–491, with permission of the author, C. W. Dunnett, and the editor.

T A B L E **A. 7** Critical Values of Dunnett's One-Tailed Test for Comparing Treatments to a Control

Error df	α	Number of Treatment Means, Including Control (a)								
		2	3	4	5	6	7	8	9	10
5	.05	2.02	2.44	2.68	2.85	2.98	3.08	3.16	3.24	3.30
	.01	3.37	3.90	4.21	4.43	4.60	4.73	4.85	4.94	5.03
6	.05	1.94	2.34	2.56	2.71	2.83	2.92	3.00	3.07	3.12
	.01	3.14	3.61	3.88	4.07	4.21	4.33	4.43	4.51	4.59
7	.05	1.89	2.27	2.48	2.62	2.73	2.82	2.89	2.95	3.01
	.01	3.00	3.42	3.66	3.83	3.96	4.07	4.15	4.23	4.30
8	.05	1.86	2.22	2.42	2.55	2.66	2.74	2.81	2.87	2.92
	.01	2.90	3.29	3.51	3.67	3.79	3.88	3.96	4.03	4.09
9	.05	1.83	2.18	2.37	2.50	2.60	2.68	2.75	2.81	2.86
	.01	2.82	3.19	3.40	3.55	3.66	3.75	3.82	3.89	3.94
10	.05	1.81	2.15	2.34	2.47	2.56	2.64	2.70	2.76	2.81
	.01	2.76	3.11	3.31	3.45	3.56	3.64	3.71	3.78	3.83
11	.05	1.80	2.13	2.31	2.44	2.53	2.60	2.67	2.72	2.77
	.01	2.72	3.06	3.25	3.38	3.48	3.56	3.63	3.69	3.74
12	.05	1.78	2.11	2.29	2.41	2.50	2.58	2.64	2.69	2.74
	.01	2.68	3.01	3.19	3.32	3.42	3.50	3.56	3.62	3.67
13	.05	1.77	2.09	2.27	2.39	2.48	2.55	2.61	2.66	2.71
	.01	2.65	2.97	3.15	3.27	3.37	3.44	3.51	3.56	3.61
14	.05	1.76	2.08	2.25	2.37	2.46	2.53	2.59	2.64	2.69
	.01	2.62	2.94	3.11	3.23	3.32	3.40	3.46	3.51	3.56
15	.05	1.75	2.07	2.24	2.36	2.44	2.51	2.57	2.62	2.67
	.01	2.60	2.91	3.08	3.20	3.29	3.36	3.42	3.47	3.52

T A B L E **A. 7** (Continued)

Error df	α	Number of Treatment Means, Including Control (a)								
		2	*3*	*4*	*5*	*6*	*7*	*8*	*9*	*10*
16	.05	1.75	2.06	2.23	2.34	2.43	2.50	2.56	2.61	2.65
	.01	2.58	2.88	3.05	3.17	3.26	3.33	3.39	3.44	3.48
17	.05	1.74	2.05	2.22	2.33	2.42	2.49	2.54	2.59	2.64
	.01	2.57	2.86	3.03	3.14	3.23	3.30	3.36	3.41	3.45
18	.05	1.73	2.05	2.21	2.32	2.41	2.48	2.53	2.58	2.62
	.01	2.55	2.84	3.01	3.12	3.21	3.27	3.33	3.38	3.42
19	.05	1.73	2.03	2.20	2.31	2.40	2.47	2.52	2.57	2.61
	.01	2.54	2.83	2.99	3.10	3.18	3.25	3.31	3.36	3.40
20	.05	1.72	2.03	2.19	2.30	2.39	2.46	2.51	2.56	2.60
	.01	2.53	2.81	2.97	3.08	3.17	3.23	3.29	3.34	3.38
24	.05	1.71	2.01	2.17	2.28	2.36	2.43	2.48	2.53	2.57
	.01	2.49	2.77	2.92	3.03	3.11	3.17	3.22	3.27	3.31
30	.05	1.70	1.99	2.15	2.25	2.33	2.40	2.45	2.50	2.54
	.01	2.46	2.72	2.87	2.97	3.05	3.11	3.16	3.21	3.24
40	.05	1.68	1.97	2.13	2.23	2.31	2.37	2.42	2.47	2.51
	.01	2.42	2.68	2.82	2.92	2.99	3.05	3.10	3.14	3.18
60	.05	1.67	1.95	2.10	2.21	2.28	2.35	2.39	2.44	2.48
	.01	2.39	2.64	2.78	2.87	2.94	3.00	3.04	3.08	3.12
120	.05	1.66	1.93	2.08	2.18	2.26	2.32	2.37	2.41	2.45
	.01	2.36	2.60	2.73	2.82	2.89	2.94	2.99	3.03	3.06
∞	.05	1.64	1.92	2.06	2.16	2.23	2.29	2.34	2.38	2.42
	.01	2.33	2.56	2.68	2.77	2.84	2.89	2.93	2.97	3.00

Table reproduced from A multiple comparison procedure for comparing several treatments with a control, *Journal of the American Statistical Association*, 1955, *50*, 1096–1121, with permission of the author, C. W. Dunnett, and the editor.

T A B L E A. 8 Critical Values of Bryant–Paulson Generalized Studentized Range

Error df	Number of Covariates	α	Number of Means (a)										
			2	3	4	5	6	7	8	10	12	16	20
3	1	.05	5.42	7.18	8.32	9.17	9.84	10.39	10.86	11.62	12.22	13.14	13.83
		.01	10.28	13.32	15.32	16.80	17.98	18.95	19.77	21.12	22.19	23.82	25.05
	2	.05	6.21	8.27	9.60	10.59	11.37	12.01	12.56	13.44	14.15	15.22	16.02
		.01	11.97	15.56	17.91	19.66	21.05	22.19	23.16	24.75	26.01	27.93	29.38
	3	.05	6.92	9.23	10.73	11.84	12.72	13.44	14.06	15.05	15.84	17.05	17.95
		.01	13.45	17.51	20.17	22.15	23.72	25.01	26.11	27.90	29.32	31.50	33.13
4	1	.05	4.51	5.84	6.69	7.32	7.82	8.23	8.58	9.15	9.61	10.30	10.82
		.01	7.68	9.64	10.93	11.89	12.65	13.28	13.82	14.70	15.40	16.48	17.29
	2	.05	5.04	6.54	7.51	8.23	8.80	9.26	9.66	10.31	10.83	11.61	12.21
		.01	8.69	10.95	12.43	13.54	14.41	15.14	15.76	16.77	17.58	18.81	19.74
	3	.05	5.51	7.18	8.25	9.05	9.67	10.19	10.63	11.35	11.92	12.79	13.45
		.01	9.59	12.11	13.77	15.00	15.98	16.79	17.47	18.60	19.50	20.87	21.91
5	1	.05	4.06	5.17	5.88	6.40	6.82	7.16	7.45	7.93	8.30	8.88	9.32
		.01	6.49	7.99	8.97	9.70	10.28	10.76	11.17	11.84	12.38	13.20	13.83
	2	.05	4.45	5.68	6.48	7.06	7.52	7.90	8.23	8.76	9.18	9.83	10.31
		.01	7.20	8.89	9.99	10.81	11.47	12.01	12.47	13.23	13.84	14.77	15.47
	3	.05	4.81	6.16	7.02	7.66	8.17	8.58	8.94	9.52	9.98	10.69	11.22
		.01	7.83	9.70	10.92	11.82	12.54	13.14	13.65	14.48	15.15	16.17	16.95
6	1	.05	3.79	4.78	5.40	5.86	6.23	6.53	6.78	7.20	7.53	8.04	8.43
		.01	5.83	7.08	7.88	8.48	8.96	9.36	9.70	10.25	10.70	11.38	11.90
	2	.05	4.10	5.18	5.87	6.37	6.77	7.10	7.38	7.84	8.21	8.77	9.20
		.01	6.36	7.75	8.64	9.31	9.85	10.29	10.66	11.28	11.77	12.54	13.11
	3	.05	4.38	5.55	6.30	6.84	7.28	7.64	7.94	8.44	8.83	9.44	9.90
		.01	6.85	8.36	9.34	10.07	10.65	11.13	11.54	12.22	12.75	13.59	14.21

7	1	.05	3.62	4.52	5.09	5.51	5.84	6.11	6.34	6.72	7.03	7.49	7.84
	1	.01	5.41	6.50	7.20	7.72	8.14	8.48	8.77	9.26	9.64	10.24	10.69
	2	.05	3.87	4.85	5.47	5.92	6.28	6.58	6.83	7.24	7.57	8.08	8.46
	2	.01	5.84	7.03	7.80	8.37	8.83	9.21	9.53	10.06	10.49	11.14	11.64
	3	.05	4.11	5.16	5.82	6.31	6.70	7.01	7.29	7.73	8.08	8.63	9.03
	3	.01	6.23	7.52	8.36	8.98	9.47	9.88	10.23	10.80	11.26	11.97	12.51
8	1	.05	3.49	4.34	4.87	5.26	5.57	5.82	6.03	6.39	6.67	7.10	7.43
	1	.01	5.12	6.11	6.74	7.20	7.58	7.88	8.15	8.58	8.92	9.46	9.87
	2	.05	3.70	4.61	5.19	5.61	5.94	6.21	6.44	6.82	7.12	7.59	7.94
	2	.01	5.48	6.54	7.23	7.74	8.14	8.48	8.76	9.23	9.61	10.19	10.63
	3	.05	3.91	4.88	5.49	5.93	6.29	6.58	6.83	7.23	7.55	8.05	8.42
	3	.01	5.81	6.95	7.69	8.23	8.67	9.03	9.33	9.84	10.24	10.87	11.34
10	1	.05	3.32	4.10	4.58	4.93	5.21	5.43	5.63	5.94	6.19	6.58	6.87
	1	.01	4.76	5.61	6.15	6.55	6.86	7.13	7.35	7.72	8.01	8.47	8.82
	2	.05	3.49	4.31	4.82	5.19	5.49	5.73	5.93	6.27	6.54	6.95	7.26
	2	.01	5.02	5.93	6.51	6.93	7.27	7.55	7.79	8.19	8.50	8.99	9.36
	3	.05	3.65	4.51	5.05	5.44	5.75	6.01	6.22	6.58	6.86	7.29	7.62
	3	.01	5.27	6.23	6.84	7.30	7.66	7.96	8.21	8.63	8.96	9.48	9.88
12	1	.05	3.22	3.95	4.40	4.73	4.98	5.19	5.37	5.67	5.90	6.26	6.53
	1	.01	4.54	5.31	5.79	6.15	6.43	6.67	6.87	7.20	7.46	7.87	8.18
	2	.05	3.35	4.12	4.59	4.93	5.20	5.43	5.62	5.92	6.17	6.55	6.83
	2	.01	4.74	5.56	6.07	6.45	6.75	7.00	7.21	7.56	7.84	8.27	8.60
	3	.05	3.48	4.28	4.78	5.14	5.42	5.65	5.85	6.17	6.43	6.82	7.12
	3	.01	4.94	5.80	6.34	6.74	7.05	7.31	7.54	7.90	8.20	8.65	9.00
14	1	.05	3.15	3.85	4.28	4.59	4.83	5.03	5.20	5.48	5.70	6.03	6.29
	1	.01	4.39	5.11	5.56	5.89	6.15	6.36	6.55	6.85	7.09	7.47	7.75
	2	.05	3.26	3.99	4.44	4.76	5.01	5.22	5.40	5.69	5.92	6.27	6.54
	2	.01	4.56	5.31	5.78	6.13	6.40	6.63	6.82	7.14	7.40	7.79	8.09
	3	.05	3.37	4.13	4.59	4.93	5.19	5.41	5.59	5.89	6.13	6.50	6.78
	3	.01	4.72	5.51	6.00	6.36	6.65	6.89	7.09	7.42	7.69	8.10	8.41

TABLE A.8 (Continued)

Error df	Number of Covariates	α	Number of Means (a)										
			2	3	4	5	6	7	8	10	12	16	20
16	1	.05	3.10	3.77	4.19	4.49	4.72	4.91	5.07	5.34	5.55	5.87	6.12
		.01	4.28	4.96	5.39	5.70	5.95	6.15	6.32	6.60	6.83	7.18	7.45
	2	.05	3.19	3.90	4.32	4.63	4.88	5.07	5.24	5.52	5.74	6.07	6.33
		.01	4.42	5.14	5.58	5.90	6.16	6.37	6.55	6.85	7.08	7.45	7.73
	3	.05	3.29	4.01	4.46	4.78	5.03	5.23	5.41	5.69	5.92	6.27	6.53
		.01	4.56	5.30	5.76	6.10	6.37	6.59	6.77	7.08	7.33	7.71	8.00
18	1	.05	3.06	3.72	4.12	4.41	4.63	4.82	4.98	5.23	5.44	5.75	5.98
		.01	4.20	4.86	5.26	5.56	5.79	5.99	6.15	6.42	6.63	6.96	7.22
	2	.05	3.14	3.82	4.24	4.54	4.77	4.96	5.13	5.39	5.60	5.92	6.17
		.01	4.32	5.00	5.43	5.73	5.98	6.18	6.35	6.63	6.85	7.19	7.46
	3	.05	3.23	3.93	4.35	4.66	4.90	5.10	5.27	5.54	5.76	6.09	6.34
		.01	4.44	5.15	5.59	5.90	6.16	6.36	6.54	6.83	7.06	7.42	7.69
20	1	.05	3.03	3.67	4.07	4.35	4.57	4.75	4.90	5.15	5.35	5.65	5.88
		.01	4.14	4.77	5.17	5.45	5.68	5.86	6.02	6.27	6.48	6.80	7.04
	2	.05	3.10	3.77	4.17	4.46	4.69	4.88	5.03	5.29	5.49	5.81	6.04
		.01	4.25	4.90	5.31	5.60	5.84	6.03	6.19	6.46	6.67	7.00	7.25
	3	.05	3.18	3.86	4.28	4.57	4.81	5.00	5.16	5.42	5.63	5.96	6.20
		.01	4.35	5.03	5.45	5.75	5.99	6.19	6.36	6.63	6.85	7.19	7.45
24	1	.05	2.98	3.61	3.99	4.26	4.47	4.65	4.79	5.03	5.22	5.51	5.73
		.01	4.05	4.65	5.02	5.29	5.50	5.68	5.83	6.07	6.26	6.56	6.78
	2	.05	3.04	3.69	4.08	4.35	4.57	4.75	4.90	5.14	5.34	5.63	5.86
		.01	4.14	4.76	5.14	5.42	5.63	5.81	5.96	6.21	6.41	6.71	6.95
	3	.05	3.11	3.76	4.16	4.44	4.67	4.85	5.00	5.25	5.45	5.75	5.98
		.01	4.22	4.86	5.25	5.54	5.76	5.94	6.10	6.35	6.55	6.87	7.11

30	1	.05	2.94	3.55	3.91	4.18	4.38	4.54	4.69	4.91	5.09	5.37	5.58
		.01	3.96	4.54	4.89	5.14	5.34	5.50	5.64	5.87	6.05	6.32	6.53
	2	.05	2.99	3.61	3.98	4.25	4.46	4.62	4.77	5.00	5.18	5.46	5.68
		.01	4.03	4.62	4.98	5.24	5.44	5.61	5.75	5.98	6.16	6.44	6.66
	3	.05	3.04	3.67	4.05	4.32	4.53	4.70	4.85	5.08	5.27	5.56	5.78
		.01	4.10	4.70	5.06	5.33	5.54	5.71	5.85	6.08	6.27	6.56	6.78
40	1	.05	2.89	3.49	3.84	4.09	4.29	4.45	4.58	4.80	4.97	5.23	5.43
		.01	3.88	4.43	4.76	5.00	5.19	5.34	5.47	5.68	5.85	6.10	6.30
	2	.05	2.93	3.53	3.89	4.15	4.34	4.50	4.64	4.86	5.04	5.30	5.50
		.01	3.93	4.48	4.82	5.07	5.26	5.41	5.54	5.76	5.93	6.19	6.38
	3	.05	2.97	3.57	3.94	4.20	4.40	4.56	4.70	4.92	5.10	5.37	5.57
		.01	3.98	4.54	4.88	5.13	5.32	5.48	5.61	5.83	6.00	6.27	6.47
60	1	.05	2.85	3.43	3.77	4.01	4.20	4.35	4.48	4.69	4.85	5.10	5.29
		.01	3.79	4.32	4.64	4.86	5.04	5.18	5.30	5.50	5.65	5.89	6.07
	2	.05	2.88	3.46	3.80	4.05	4.24	4.39	4.52	4.73	4.89	5.14	5.33
		.01	3.83	4.36	4.68	4.90	5.08	5.22	5.35	5.54	5.70	5.94	6.12
	3	.05	2.90	3.49	3.83	4.08	4.27	4.43	4.56	4.77	4.93	5.19	5.38
		.01	3.86	4.39	4.72	4.95	5.12	5.27	5.39	5.59	5.75	6.00	6.18
120	1	.05	2.81	3.37	3.70	3.93	4.11	4.26	4.38	4.58	4.73	4.97	5.15
		.01	3.72	4.22	4.52	4.73	4.89	5.03	5.14	5.32	5.47	5.69	5.85
	2	.05	2.82	3.38	3.72	3.95	4.13	4.28	4.40	4.60	4.75	4.99	5.17
		.01	3.73	4.24	4.54	4.75	4.91	5.05	5.16	5.35	5.49	5.71	5.88
	3	.05	2.84	3.40	3.73	3.97	4.15	4.30	4.42	4.62	4.77	5.01	5.19
		.01	3.75	4.25	4.55	4.77	4.94	5.07	5.18	5.37	5.51	5.74	5.90

Table reproduced from An extension of Tukey's method of multiple comparisons to experimental designs with random concomitant variables. *Biometrika*, 1976, 63, 631–638, with permission of the editor.

T A B L E **A. 9** Critical Values of Chi-Square Distribution

df	.10	.05	.025	.01	.005	.001
1	2.71	3.84	5.02	6.63	7.88	10.83
2	4.61	5.99	7.38	9.21	10.60	13.82
3	6.25	7.81	9.35	11.34	12.84	16.27
4	7.78	9.49	11.14	13.28	14.86	18.47
5	9.24	11.07	12.83	15.09	16.75	20.51
6	10.64	12.59	14.45	16.81	18.55	22.46
7	12.02	14.07	16.01	18.48	20.28	24.32
8	13.36	15.51	17.53	20.09	21.95	26.12
9	14.68	16.92	19.02	21.67	23.59	27.88
10	15.99	18.31	20.48	23.21	25.19	29.59
11	17.28	19.68	21.92	24.72	26.76	31.26
12	18.55	21.03	23.34	26.22	28.30	32.91
13	19.81	22.36	24.74	27.69	29.82	34.53
14	21.06	23.68	26.12	29.14	31.32	36.12
15	22.31	25.00	27.49	30.58	32.80	37.70
16	23.54	26.30	28.85	32.00	34.27	39.25
17	24.77	27.59	30.19	33.41	35.72	40.79
18	25.99	28.87	31.53	34.81	37.16	42.31
19	27.20	30.14	32.85	36.19	38.58	43.82
20	28.41	31.41	34.17	37.57	40.00	45.31
21	29.62	32.67	35.48	38.93	41.40	46.80
22	30.81	33.92	36.78	40.29	42.80	48.27
23	32.01	35.17	38.08	41.64	44.18	49.73
24	33.20	36.42	39.36	42.98	45.56	51.18
25	34.38	37.65	40.65	44.31	46.93	52.62
26	35.56	38.89	41.92	45.64	48.29	54.05
27	36.74	40.11	43.19	46.96	49.64	55.48
28	37.92	41.34	44.46	48.28	50.99	56.89
29	39.09	42.56	45.72	49.59	52.34	58.30
30	40.26	43.77	46.98	50.89	53.67	59.70

NOTE: These critical values were computed using the CINV function of SAS.

TABLE A. 10 Coefficients of Orthogonal Polynomials

Number of Levels	Polynomial	Coefficients								$\sum(c_j)^2$
3	Linear	−1	0	1						2
	Quadratic	1	−2	1						6
4	Linear	−3	−1	1	3					20
	Quadratic	1	−1	−1	1					4
	Cubic	−1	3	−3	1					20
5	Linear	−2	−1	0	1	2				10
	Quadratic	2	−1	−2	−1	2				14
	Cubic	−1	2	0	−2	1				10
	Quartic	1	−4	6	−4	1				70
6	Linear	−5	−3	−1	1	3	5			70
	Quadratic	5	−1	−4	−4	−1	5			84
	Cubic	−5	7	4	−4	−7	5			180
	Quartic	1	−3	2	2	−3	1			28
	Quintic	−1	5	−10	10	−5	1			252
7	Linear	−3	−2	−1	0	1	2	3		28
	Quadratic	5	0	−3	−4	−3	0	5		84
	Cubic	−1	1	1	0	−1	−1	1		6
	Quartic	3	−7	1	6	1	−7	3		154
	Quintic	−1	4	−5	0	5	−4	1		84
8	Linear	−7	−5	−3	−1	1	3	5	7	168
	Quadratic	7	1	−3	−5	−5	−3	1	7	168
	Cubic	−7	5	7	3	−3	−7	−5	7	264
	Quartic	7	−13	−3	9	9	−3	−13	7	616
	Quintic	−7	23	−17	−15	15	17	−23	7	2,184

T A B L E A. 10 (Continued)

Number of Levels	Polynomial	Coefficients										$\sum(c_j)^2$
9	Linear	-4	-3	-2	-1	0	1	2	3	4		60
	Quadratic	28	7	-8	-17	-20	-17	-8	7	28		2,772
	Cubic	-14	7	13	9	0	-9	-13	-7	14		990
	Quartic	14	-21	-11	9	18	9	-11	-21	14		2,002
	Quintic	-4	11	-4	-9	0	9	4	-11	4		468
10	Linear	-9	-7	-5	-3	-1	1	3	5	7	9	330
	Quadratic	6	2	-1	-3	-4	-4	-3	-1	2	6	132
	Cubic	-42	14	35	31	12	-12	-31	-35	-14	42	8,580
	Quartic	18	-22	-17	3	18	18	3	-17	-22	18	2,860
	Quintic	-6	14	-1	-11	-6	6	11	1	-14	6	780

This table is abridged from Table 47 in E. S. Pearson and H. O. Hartley (Eds.), *Biometrika tables for statisticians* (3rd ed., Vol. 1), Cambridge University Press, New York, 1970, by permission of the *Biometrika Trustees*.

TABLE A.11 Pearson–Hartley Power Charts

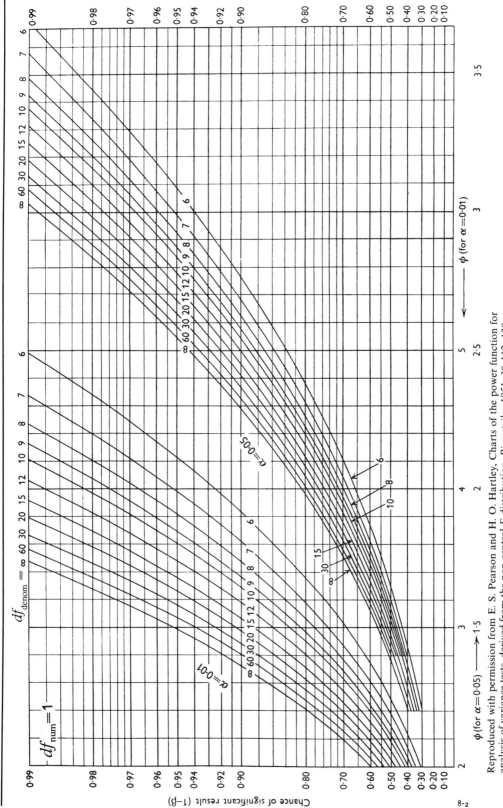

Reproduced with permission from E. S. Pearson and H. O. Hartley, Charts of the power function for analysis of variance tests, derived from the non-central F-distribution, *Biometrika*, 1951, 38, 112–130.

8-2

$df_{num} = 2$

$df_{denom} = \infty$

Chance of significant result $(1-\beta)$

ϕ (for $\alpha = 0.01$)

ϕ (for $\alpha = 0.05$)

$\alpha = 0.05$

$\alpha = 0.01$

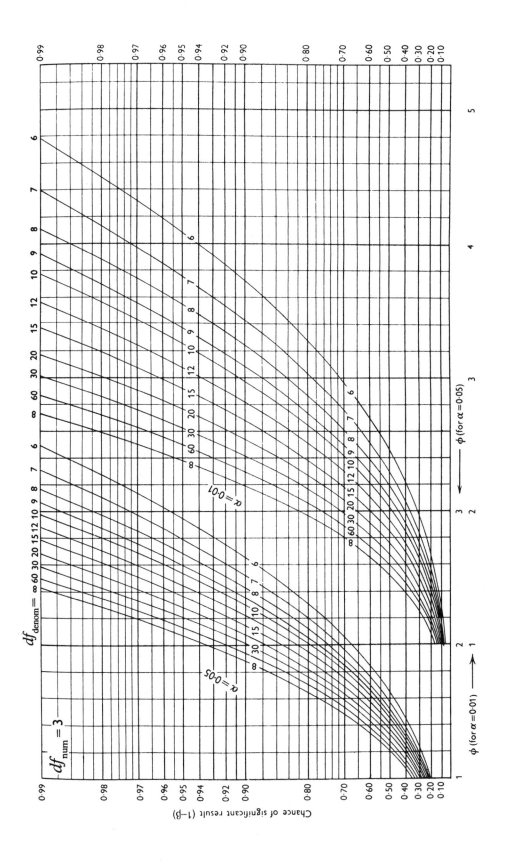

TABLE A.11 (Continued)

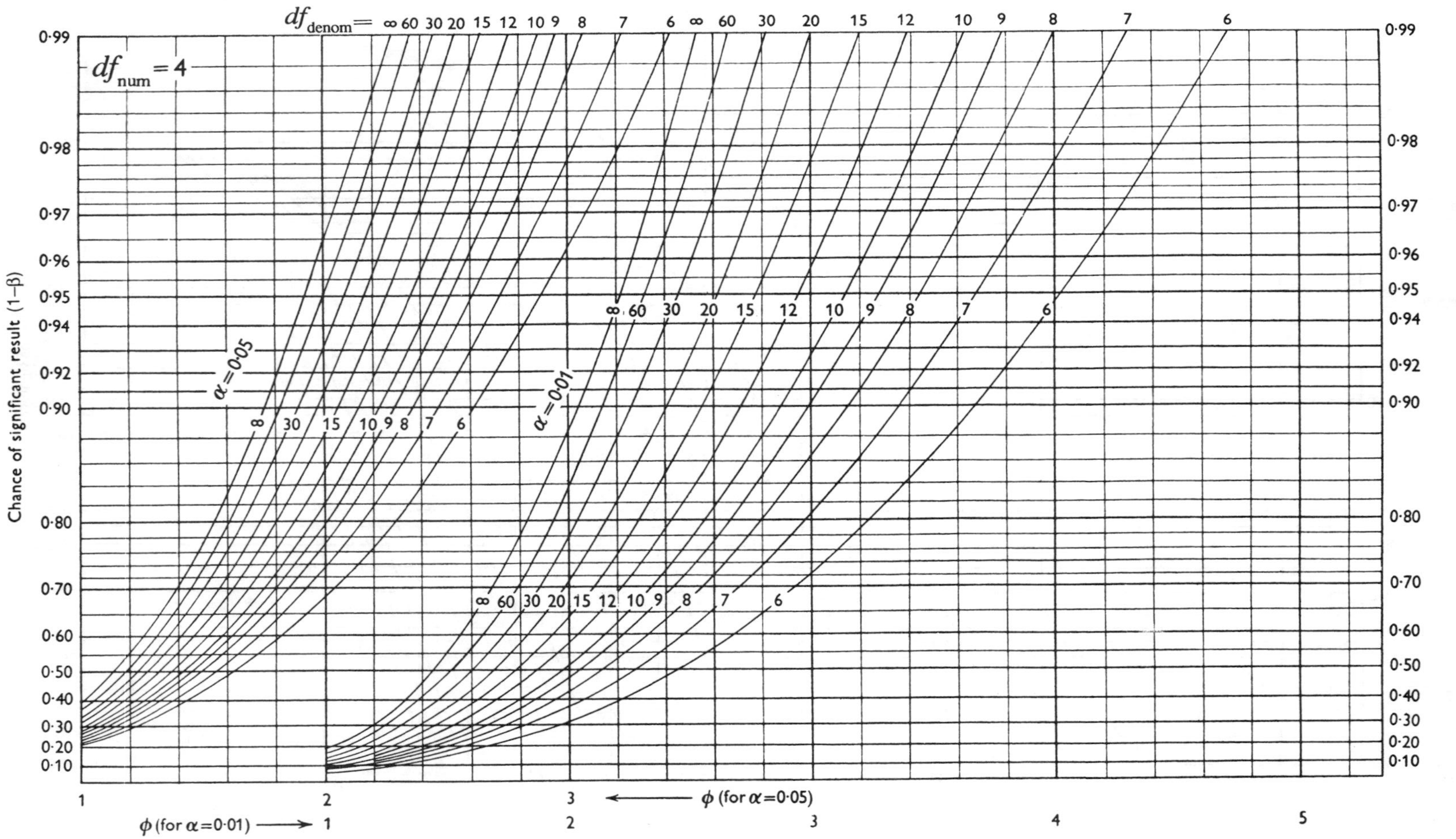

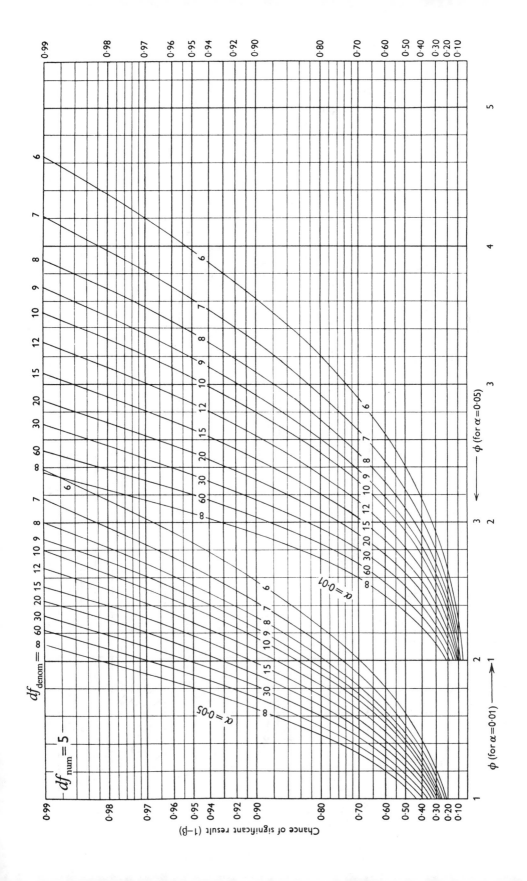

TABLE A.11 (Continued)

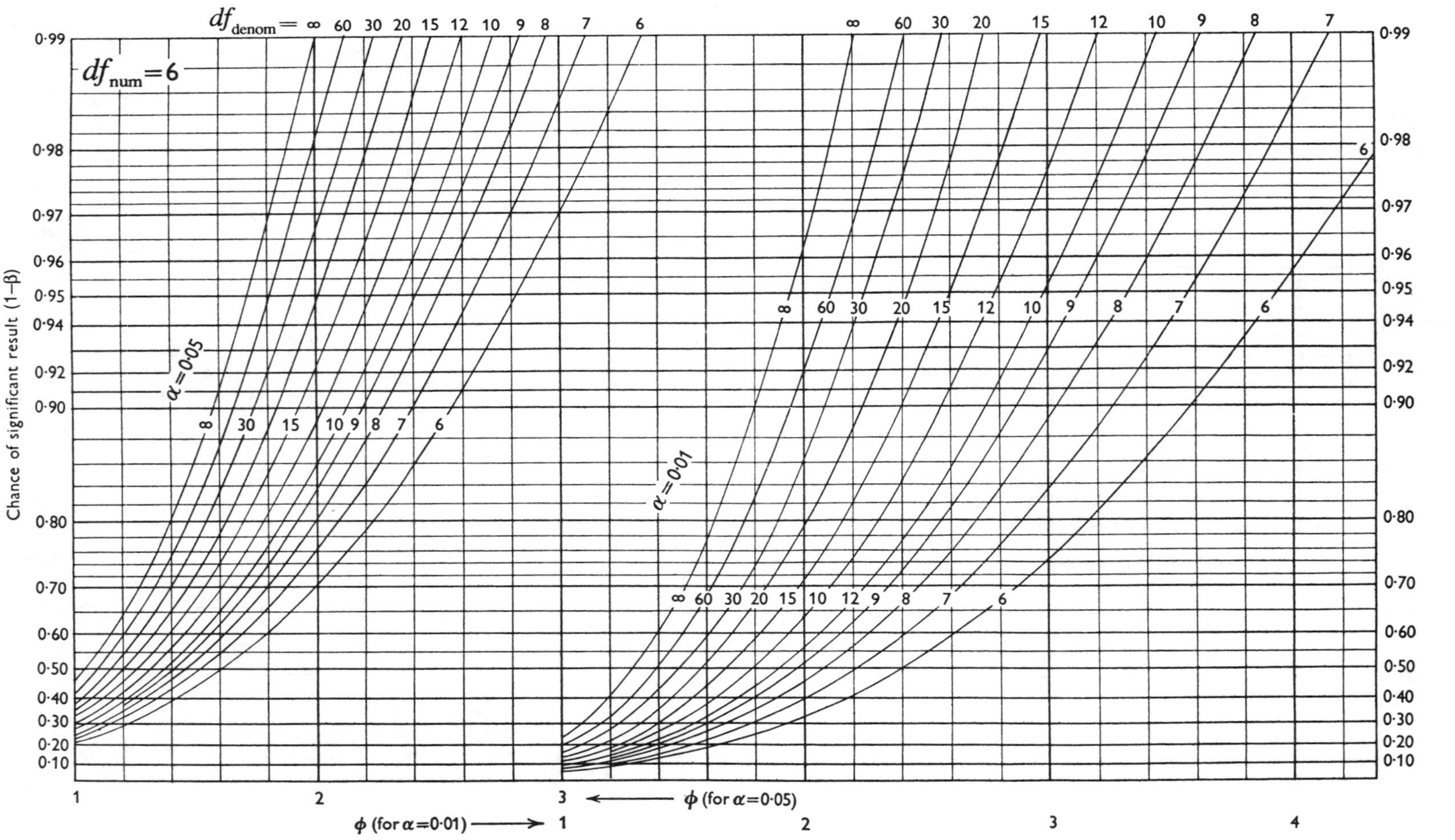

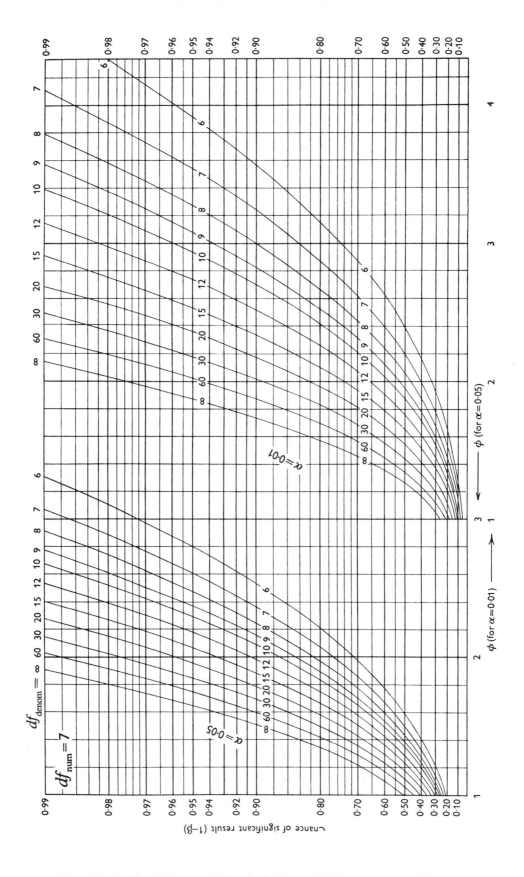

TABLE A. 11 (Continued)

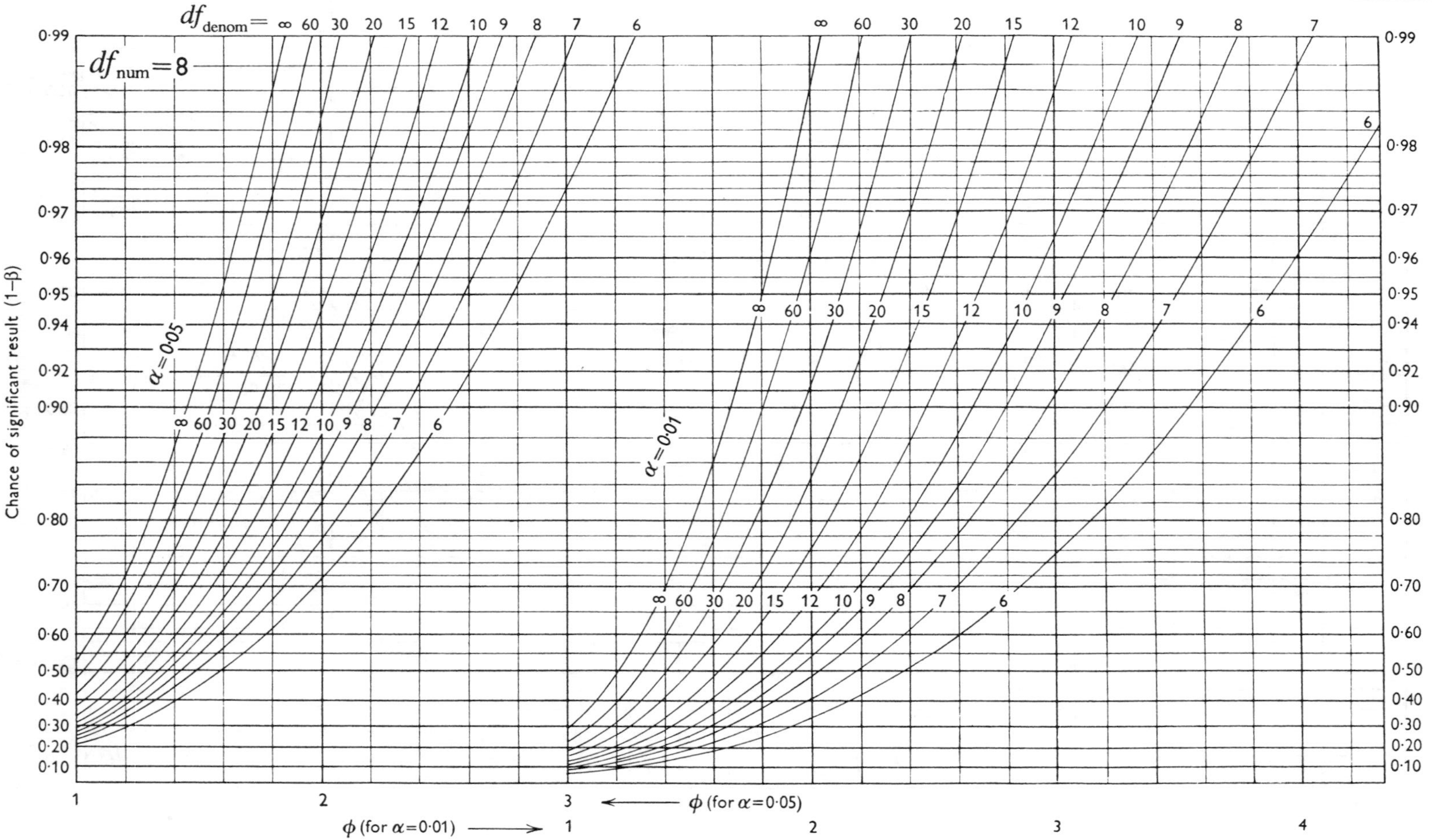

Appendix B Notes

Chapter 1

1. A more complete rendering of this statement in Einstein's own words is as follows:

    > The very fact that the totality of our sense experiences is such that by means of thinking (operations with concepts, and the creation and use of definite functional relations between them, and the coordination of sense experiences to these concepts) it can be put in order, this fact is one which leaves us in awe, but which we shall never understand. One may say "the eternal mystery of the world is its comprehensibility." It is one of the great realizations of Immanuel Kant that the setting up of a real external world would be senseless without this comprehensibility.
    >
    > In speaking here concerning "comprehensibility," the expression is used in its most modest sense. It implies: the production of some sort of order among sense impressions, this order being produced by the creation of general concepts, relations between these concepts, and by relations between these concepts and sense experience, these relations being determined in any possible manner. It is in this sense that the world of our sense experiences is comprehensible. The fact that it is comprehensible is a miracle (Einstein, 1936, p. 351).

2. A major distinction among experimental designs is whether the same individuals are assessed only once or repeatedly in a given study. This is the distinction between Parts II and III of this book. Perhaps not surprisingly given that psychologists, educators, and others tend to be concerned with change, most behavioral science studies involve repeated measurements of the same units.

3. Huck and Sandler (1979) have an excellent (and fun) book, which is organized somewhat like a series of mysteries, that is designed for practicing your skills at this.

Chapter 2

1. A discrete probability distribution is one with a countable (and typically a small finite) number of possible outcomes. An example would be the (flat) distribution of the probabilities of the six outcomes that can occur when you roll a (fair) die.

2. In attempting to formulate the probability of various outcomes, most students when

759

faced with the tea-tasting problem begin searching their memories for a familiar discrete probability distribution. Most graduate students in the behavioral sciences have studied the binomial distribution, and so it is frequently suggested as the method of analysis. Whether it is appropriate depends again on how the experiment was run. The binomial distribution arises from a series of independent trials. If the subject were told there were four of each kind of cups, the successive judgments would clearly not be independent because once four cups had been classified as being of one kind, the remaining ones would have to be put into the other category to have any hope of the set of judgments being correct. If the subject were *not* told there were four cups of each kind, in order to make use of a binomial with probability of success equal to .5, it would be necessary to hypothesize not only that the lady had no discrimination ability but also that she had no bias for responding in favor of one cup over another. Thus, it is not clear that the binomial would be appropriate if the number of cups of each kind were determined in advance, regardless of what the subject was told. If, on the other hand, the subject understood that you determined what kind of cup each successive cup would be by the toss of a fair coin, the binomial could be used. However, in this situation, both experimenter and subject should realize that it is possible that all eight cups might be of a single kind, thus potentially allowing no comparison across kinds of cups.

3. That is, a histogram showing the relative frequency of scores would be low in the middle range and high at either end; hence the distribution looks somewhat like a U. In the current data, there are more scores below 0 and more scores greater than 8 than there are between 0 and 8.

4. The corrected value of t is slightly smaller, 2.046, and in fact is exceeded by .038 of the t distribution.

5. Just how cumbersome may be surprising. For example, if a total of 30 observations are to be assigned in equal numbers to the groups in a study, with two groups over 150 million assignments are possible, and with three groups over 3 trillion assignments are possible. Although the number of calculations for a complete specification of the distribution of a test statistic is clearly prohibitive in general, interest in randomization methods is increasing because of recent developments making such tests more practical. These developments include the design of computational algorithms and computer programs that take random samples from the distribution (for example, Edgington, 1980, pp. 52–54, 71ff.; Green, 1977), algebraic simplifications (Gabriel & Hall, 1983), and approximations (Gabriel & Hsu, 1983). At the present writing, the computational methods are still being developed for various designs, and programs for even simple situations are not widely available. Thus, although the logic of randomization testing is important for what we are about, the specific procedures for more complex designs are not considered in subsequent chapters.

6. Students in the behavioral sciences are often familiar with the central limit theorem for explaining why *group means* can be expected to be normally distributed. However, here we are considering the application of the theorem in the way conceived by its originator, Laplace (Stigler, 1986, p. 143), and that is to view an individual observation or even the error in an individual observation as a composite or summation of the effects of a number of variables.

Chapter 3

1. You should note that although the values of ε_i are not known in advance, it is only the βs that are the parameters, or the basic descriptive summaries of the population of Y scores. The parameters are estimated and then the error scores can be determined

simply by seeing to what extent the combination of parameters specified by the model deviates from the observed value of the dependent variable. Thus, in one technical sense, the values of ε_i are not part of our model but serve to indicate to what extent our "real" model (consisting only of the weighted sum of parameters) fails to fit the data (see Finn, 1974, p. 6). However, for simplicity, we typically refer to the weighted parameters *together* with the associated error scores as our model. When used in this way, our model is a complete specification of the data values exactly, and competing models differ in how much of the variance in Y must be accounted for by the ε component of the model.

2. The steps in the derivation are as follows: Beginning with $\sum e_i^2 = \sum (Y_i - \mu_0)^2$, we add and subtract $\bar{Y}$ to each error, group terms, and expand:

$$\sum (Y_i - \mu_0)^2 = \sum (Y_i - \bar{Y} + \bar{Y} - \mu_0)^2$$
$$= \sum (Y_i - \bar{Y})^2 + \sum 2(\bar{Y} - \mu_0)(Y_i - \bar{Y}) + \sum (\bar{Y} - \mu_0)^2$$

The middle term again goes to zero, that is,

$$\sum 2(Y_i - \bar{Y})(\bar{Y} - \mu_0) = 2(\bar{Y} - \mu_0)\sum (Y_i - \bar{Y}) = 0$$

Thus, we have

$$\sum (Y_i - \mu_0)^2 = \sum (Y_i - \bar{Y})^2 + n(\bar{Y} - \mu_0)^2$$

3. The notion of sums of squared errors is pervasive in statistics. Most often these quantities are denoted SS, for sum of squares, or SSE, for sum of squared errors; the models to which these sums of squares correspond might be indicated parenthetically, for example, $SSE(F)$ and $SSE(R)$ for the sum of squared errors associated with the full and restricted models, respectively (cf. Neter, Wasserman, & Kutner, 1985, p. 95). Although we use SS notation for making connections with other approaches, it has been our experience that communication is facilitated, particularly for students in the behavioral sciences, by keeping the notation as simple as possible. Thus, we have chosen to denote sum of squared errors, the most commonly used term in our formulas, by a single capital E and indicate the model that generated the errors by a single capital letter subscript, either F for the full model or R for the restricted model. Because a lower case e is almost universally used to designate the error of prediction for an individual observation, it should be an easy transition to think of E as denoting a summary measure of these individual errors. We are attempting to minimize the "symbol shock" of beginning students by having it understood, rather than always explicit, that the way the individual errors are summarized is to square each one and sum the squared values over all individuals in the study.

4. Dividing the denominator of a fraction by $(n - 1)$ is equivalent to multiplying the fraction by $(n - 1)$. In fact, test statistics generally may be viewed as the product of (1) an index, like our PIE, of the size of the effect observed and (2) an index, like $(n - 1)$, of the size of the study. We discuss this perspective in greater detail near the end of the chapter when we consider alternative measures of effects.

5. Once again we make use of the technique of adding zero—that is, $-\bar{Y}_j + \bar{Y}_j$—to the terms used in computing E_R to simplify the numerator of the F statistic:

$$E_R = \sum_j \sum_i (Y_{ij} - \bar{Y})^2 = \sum_j \sum_i (Y_{ij} - \bar{Y}_j + \bar{Y}_j - \bar{Y})^2$$

Grouping terms and expanding, we obtain

$$E_R = \sum_j \sum_i [(Y_{ij} - \bar{Y}_j) + (\bar{Y}_j - \bar{Y})]^2$$
$$= \sum_j \sum_i (Y_{ij} - \bar{Y}_j)^2 + \sum_j \sum_i (\bar{Y}_j - \bar{Y})^2 + 2\sum_j \sum_i (Y_{ij} - \bar{Y}_j)(\bar{Y}_j - \bar{Y})$$

But because the sum of the deviations from the mean in any group equals zero [i.e., $\sum_i (Y_{ij} - \bar{Y}_j) = 0$], the last, cross-product term above always is zero and can be ignored, that is,

$$2 \sum_j \sum_i (Y_{ij} - \bar{Y}_j)(\bar{Y}_j - \bar{Y}) = 2 \sum_j (\bar{Y}_j - \bar{Y}) \sum_i (Y_{ij} - \bar{Y}_j)$$

$$= 2 \sum_j (\bar{Y}_j - \bar{Y}) \cdot 0 = 0$$

Thus, $E_R = \sum_j \sum_i (Y_{ij} - \bar{Y}_j)^2 + \sum_j \sum_i (\bar{Y}_j - \bar{Y})^2.$

6. The model-comparison perspective can be translated into SS_{Between} and SS_{Within}, but remember that it is more general than these concepts. One can impose other restrictions on the values of the population group means besides constraining all to be equal. In such a case, for example, E_R may no longer be equal to SS_{Total}. The appropriate model depends on the question of interest, and the theoretical background of a research project may dictate other models. Our general formulation in terms of E_R and E_F still applies although the traditional formulation would not. We consider such a situation in the next section.

7. Twenty subjects were run in each condition. To simplify the calculations for illustrative purposes here, only 10 scores are presented per group. The first 8 are the scores of the first 8 subjects run in each condition. The last two scores were selected from the remaining scores so that the mean of the subsample would equal the mean, rounded to the nearest integer, of all 20 subjects' scores.

8. The conventional grand mean, which is used as an estimate of μ in the restricted model, can be thought of as a weighted average of the group means, where the weights are the sizes of the groups. That is, because $\bar{Y}_j = (\sum_i Y_{ij})/n_j$, we have $\sum_i Y_{ij} = n_j \bar{Y}_j$, which when substituted in the definition of the grand mean $\bar{Y} = (\sum_j \sum_i Y_{ij})/(\sum_j n_j)$ yields $\bar{Y} = (\sum_j n_j \bar{Y}_j)/(\sum_j n_j)$. When the sample sizes are all equal—that is, all $n_j = n$—then this grand mean is seen to be the same as an unweighted average of the group means, that is, $\bar{Y} = (\sum_j n \bar{Y}_j)/(\sum_j n) = (n \sum_j \bar{Y}_j)/na = (\sum_j \bar{Y}_j)/a = \bar{Y}_u$. However, in the unequal-n case, the conventional grand mean will be "pulled" in the direction of the means from the larger groups. We consider the difference between weighted and unweighted means in much greater detail in the context of factorial designs in Chapter 7.

9. Two technical points can be made on the basis of his work. First, $\hat{d}$ is positively biased as an estimator of d—that is, the sample value of $\hat{d}$ tends to be somewhat larger than the true parameter. However, if df_F is greater than 10, the expected value of $\hat{d}$ will be less than 10 percent larger than d (Hedges, 1981, p. 113). Second, error of measurement in the dependent variable tends to make S larger than it should be and thus, when present, tends to make $\hat{d}$ smaller. However, if the reliability is greater than .80, error of measurement tends to deflate the expected value of $\hat{d}$ by less than 10 percent (Hedges, 1981, p. 120). Because these two effects are in most situations small and tend to offset each other, $\hat{d}$ may for practical purposes generally be regarded as an essentially unbiased estimator of d.

Chapter 4

1. For later developments in the chapter, it is helpful to note that because

$$\frac{n_1 n_2}{n_1 + n_2} = \frac{1}{\left(\dfrac{1}{n_1} + \dfrac{1}{n_2} \right)}$$

an equivalent form of Equation 23 is

$$F = \frac{(\bar{Y}_1 - \bar{Y}_2)^2}{MS_W \left(\dfrac{1}{n_1} + \dfrac{1}{n_2} \right)}$$

This makes sense because we know that each mean $\bar{Y}_j$ has a sampling variance of σ^2/n_j and that the variance of the difference of two independent random variables is equal to the sum of their individual variances.

2. Of course, the model can be written explicitly. It is just cumbersome (and somewhat confusing) in such a case. The interested reader can demonstrate that the null hypothesis model could be expressed here as

$$Y_{i1} = \mu_1 + \varepsilon_{i1}$$
$$Y_{i2} = \mu_2 + \varepsilon_{i2}$$
$$Y_{i3} = \mu_3 + \varepsilon_{i3}$$
$$Y_{i4} = \tfrac{1}{3}\mu_1 + \tfrac{1}{3}\mu_2 + \tfrac{1}{3}\mu_3 + \varepsilon_{i4}$$

However, if one persists in this approach, one must remember that because each μ_j appears in the model expression for more than one group, the estimate of μ_j here does *not* depend solely on the observations in the jth group. Thus, for reasons of clarity, the approach taken in the text is preferred here.

3. Strictly speaking, the mathematics also allows hypotheses of the form $H_0 : \psi = k$ to be tested, where k is any constant. In other words, k need not equal zero. However, in actual applications, behavioral scientists rarely if ever test a hypothesis other than that ψ equals zero.

4. Lunneborg and Abbott (1983, p. 197) show that a matrix expression for constrained least-squares estimates $_c\mathbf{b}$ is given by

$$_c\mathbf{b} = \mathbf{b} - (\mathbf{X}'\mathbf{X})^{-1}\mathbf{C}[\mathbf{C}'(\mathbf{X}'\mathbf{X})^{-1}\mathbf{C}]^{-1}\mathbf{C}'\mathbf{b}$$

After some tedious algebra, this expression reduces to the form given in the text.

5. The pooled variance approach also provides an unbiased estimate if sample sizes are equal, and the contrast coefficients for all a groups equal either 1 or -1. In this case, the weights for both approaches simplify to $w_j = 1/a$, so that each group receives an equal weight in deriving a variance estimate.

6. Note that linearly independent does *not* mean statistically independent. This is in contrast to the terminology used in describing variables where it is conventional to say that one variable can have varying degrees of dependence on another, but statistical independence is an absolute property, not a matter of degree. In the present context, linearly dependent is the absolute characteristic meaning one contrast is totally redundant with one or more others, whereas two contrasts can be linearly independent and yet have some degree of relationship. This variation in usage of *dependent* and *independent* is perhaps unfortunate but is standard in the statistical literature. With contrasts, the concept of orthogonality, to be introduced shortly, is used to define contrasts that are unrelated. A more detailed exposition of these concepts can be found in Rodgers, Nicewander, and Toothaker (1984).

7. Strictly speaking, for $\hat{\psi}_1$ and $\hat{\psi}_2$ to be statistically independent, the normality assumption must be met. Otherwise, it can only be said that $\hat{\psi}_1$ and $\hat{\psi}_2$ are uncorrelated. Further discussion of the relationship between correlation and independence can be found in Hays (1981, pp. 463–464).

Chapter 5

1. Tukey actually developed several multiple-comparisons procedures, which at times has resulted in confusing labels for the various techniques. The particular method we describe is referred to as Tukey's WSD (for Wholly Significant Difference), Tukey's HSD (for Honestly Significant Difference), or Tukey's T Procedure. As we will see later, the "wholly" and "honestly" terms serve to distinguish Tukey's method from Fisher's LSD (Least Significant Difference), which does not always properly control the α_{EW} level. Also, when we discuss within-subject designs (i.e., repeated measures designs) in Chapters 11–14, we will see that the Bonferroni approach is better than Tukey's technique for testing pairwise comparisons of within-subject means.

2. Tukey originally developed a more general formula that allowed for tests of complex comparisons and pairwise comparisons, but Scheffé's procedure is more powerful for testing complex comparisons.

3. For our purposes, it suffices to state that the studentized maximum modulus distribution is similar in concept to the studentized range distribution. Readers seeking a more mathematical treatment are referred to Dunnett (1980) and to Hochberg and Tamhane (1987).

4. In most published tables of the studentized maximum modulus distribution, the columns refer to the number of comparisons being tested. We have chosen to present the columns in terms of the number of groups because we only discuss the distribution in the context of performing all pairwise comparisons.

5. In other words, the parameters of Model III are a subset of the parameters of Model II.

6. Suppose that we define a contrast to have coefficients given by $c_j = n_j(\bar{Y}_j - \bar{Y})$. The sum of squares for this contrast will equal

$$SS_\psi = (\hat{\psi})^2 \bigg/ \sum_{j=1}^{a} c_j^2/n_j$$

However, $\hat{\psi}$ is defined to be

$$\hat{\psi} = \sum_{j=1}^{a} c_j \bar{Y}_j = \sum_{j=1}^{a} n_j(\bar{Y}_j - \bar{Y})\bar{Y}_j$$

Substituting for $\hat{\psi}$ and c_j in the expression for SS_ψ yields

$$SS_\psi = \left[\sum_{j=1}^{a} n_j(\bar{Y}_j - \bar{Y})\bar{Y}_j \right]^2 \bigg/ \left[\sum_{j=1}^{a} n_j^2(\bar{Y}_j - \bar{Y})^2/n_j \right]$$

which immediately reduces to

$$SS_\psi = \left[\sum_{j=1}^{a} n_j(\bar{Y}_j - \bar{Y})\bar{Y}_j \right]^2 \bigg/ \sum_{j=1}^{a} n_j(\bar{Y}_j - \bar{Y})^2$$

It can be shown through some simple algebra that

$$\sum_{j=1}^{a} n_j(\bar{Y}_j - \bar{Y})\bar{Y}_j = \sum_{j=1}^{a} n_j(\bar{Y}_j - \bar{Y})^2$$

Making this substitution into the numerator of SS_ψ, we have

$$SS_\psi = \left[\sum_{j=1}^{a} n_j(\bar{Y}_j - \bar{Y})^2 \right]^2 \bigg/ \sum_{j=1}^{a} n_j(\bar{Y}_j - \bar{Y})^2$$

$$= \sum_{j=1}^{a} n_j(\bar{Y}_j - \bar{Y})^2$$

$$= SS_B$$

7. See Hochberg and Tamhane (1987) for a review of these studies. However, Kaiser and Bowden (1983) found that the Brown–Forsythe procedure can in some situations produce too many Type I errors. They propose multiplying the Brown–Forsythe critical value by the term $(1 + (a - 2)/df)$, where df is the denominator degrees of freedom from Equation 10.

Chapter 6

1. To see that $\sum_{j=1}^{a} c_j \sum_{i=1}^{n_j} (Y_{ij} - \bar{Y})$ can be reduced to $\sum_{j=1}^{a} c_j n_j \bar{Y}_j$, notice that the term $\sum_{i=1}^{n_j} (Y_{ij} - \bar{Y})$ can be simplified as follows:

$$\sum_{i=1}^{n_j} (Y_{ij} - \bar{Y}) = \sum_{i=1}^{n_j} Y_{ij} - \sum_{i=1}^{n_j} \bar{Y}$$
$$= n_j \bar{Y}_j - n_j \bar{Y}$$

Substituting this expression into the numerator of $\hat{\beta}_1$ results in the following new expression for the numerator:

$$\sum_{j=1}^{a} c_j \sum_{i=1}^{n_j} (Y_{ij} - \bar{Y}) = \sum_{j=1}^{a} c_j (n_j \bar{Y}_j - n_j \bar{Y})$$
$$= \sum_{j=1}^{a} c_j n_j \bar{Y}_j - \sum_{j=1}^{a} c_j n_j \bar{Y}$$
$$= \sum_{j=1}^{a} c_j n_j \bar{Y}_j - \left(\bar{Y} \sum_{j=1}^{a} c_j n_j \right)$$

However, $\sum_{j=1}^{a} c_j n_j = 0$ because c_j is defined to be $X_j - \bar{X}$ and

$$\sum_{j=1}^{a} n_j (X_j - \bar{X}) = 0.$$

2. See Morrison (1983, p. 10).

3. The least-squares estimate of 2.3 is simply a weighted average of the sample differences of 4, 2, and 1. In other words, the logic behind the estimated slope here suggests that the slope of the "best" straight line is just an average of the slopes of the individual line segments. For example, with equal n and equal spacing of one unit on X and with four levels of the quantitative factor, the estimated slope is given by

$$\hat{\beta}_1 = -.3\bar{Y}_1 - .1\bar{Y}_2 + .1\bar{Y}_3 + .3\bar{Y}_4.$$

If we let $d_1 = \bar{Y}_2 - \bar{Y}_1$, $d_2 = \bar{Y}_3 - \bar{Y}_2$, and $d_3 = \bar{Y}_4 - \bar{Y}_3$ represent the differences between mean scores on adjacent levels of the factor, the estimated slope turns out to be

$$\hat{\beta}_1 = .3d_1 + .4d_2 + .3d_3$$

which is just a weighted average of the three d terms. This conceptualization is also helpful for understanding the meaning of the estimated value of the slope in the presence of significant nonlinear trends. From this perspective, the slope estimate is a weighted average of the individual slopes between adjacent levels of the factor.

4. We could multiply all coefficients by -1, which would not change the meaning of the contrast but would produce an inverted U shape, instead of a U-shaped curve.

5. This approach must be distinguished from an "unweighted means" analysis, where the sum of squares attributable to a contrast is based on the harmonic mean of sample sizes. The use of the harmonic mean to calculate sum of squares here is not recommended.

Chapter 7

1. It might seem that mathematical rather than substantive considerations are dictating how we analyze these data. This would be unfortunate because in general it is preferable to formulate substantive hypotheses, which can be translated into statistical hypotheses. Only then does data analysis become a consideration (although as we stated in Chapter 2, all these steps, including how the data will eventually be analyzed, should be thought through prior to executing the study). However, for pedagogical purposes, it is helpful here to begin with the mathematics in order to develop an appreciation of the meaning behind the "missing" sum of squares.

2. We briefly discuss the importance of the distinction between disordinal and ordinal interactions later in the chapter. For further reading, see Cronbach and Snow (1977, p. 93), Lubin (1962), and Wilcox (1987b, pp. 208, 220–224).

3. In fact, there are some mathematical advantages to the form of the model shown in Equation 5. However, matrix algebra is required to take advantage of this formulation. Because we generally want to avoid matrix algebra in our presentation if at all possible, the model formulation of Equation 6 will be useful to us. Advanced readers are advised to consult Timm and Carlson (1975) for an exposition of ANOVA based on cell means models, such as the one shown in Equation 5.

4. For example, we could represent the interaction as γ_{jk}, in which case Equation 6 would be written as

    $$Y_{ijk} = \mu + \alpha_j + \beta_k + \gamma_{jk} + \varepsilon_{ijk}$$

    This form of the model would be perfectly acceptable, but we might have difficulty reminding ourselves that γ_{jk} represented the A × B interaction. The confusion would likely increase in three-way designs (to be covered in Chapter 8), where we have to distinguish four interactions from one another: A × B, A × C, B × C, and A × B × C. As we will see in Chapter 8, the $(\alpha\beta)_{jk}$ form of notation provides mnemonic labels for the various interactions in this design.

5. As stated, these effects are obviously average effects across columns. The effect of row j may or may not be the same within each column, depending on whether the factors do not or do interact. The interpretation of marginal means in the presence of an interaction is sometimes problematic. We will discuss this issue later in the chapter.

6. For technical reasons that are beyond the scope of this book, it is actually preferable to regard the constraint that $\sum_{j=1}^{a} \alpha_j = 0$ as the reason α_j equals the difference $\mu_j - \mu$. In other words, the constraint results in the meaning, instead of the meaning leading to the constraint, as we have presented it.

7. We do not prove that these estimates are least-squares estimates. Instead, we simply provide an intuitive justification by reminding you that the sample mean is a least-squares estimator of a population mean.

8. As discussed in Chapter 5, the definition of a family is somewhat arbitrary, just as is the decision to set α at .05 in the first place. However, it generally seems reasonable to perform three tests with an α of .05 for each test in the factorial design because of the logical structure created by crossing two factors with one another. Of course, we could reduce Type I errors by choosing α_{EW} instead of α_{FW} to equal .05. However, in doing so, we would inevitably reduce the power to detect true effects. As we said in Chapter 5, ultimately these issues boil down to a trade-off between Type I and Type II errors.

9. As discussed in Chapter 5, we would typically want to use Tukey's WSD to control

α_{FW} if we are testing all pairwise comparisons or if we decided to test this particular pairwise comparison after having examined the data.

10. The marginal means are particularly misleading when the interaction is disordinal but can also be regarded as misleading even for an ordinal interaction. For example, consider the following cell means in a 2 × 2 design: $\bar{Y}_{11} = 50$, $\bar{Y}_{12} = 66$, $\bar{Y}_{21} = 80$, and $\bar{Y}_{22} = 74$, where as usual the first subscript refers to levels of A and the second subscript refers to levels of B. The marginal means for A are $\bar{Y}_{1.} = 58$ and $\bar{Y}_{2.} = 77$, implying that A_2 is 19 points "better" (on the average) than A_1. For these data, it is true that A_2 is better than A_1 regardless of the level of B, but the difference is 30 points at B_1 and only 8 points at B_2. When A_2 is consistently better (or worse) than A_1 regardless of B, the interaction is ordinal for the A factor. In this situation, the marginal means at least maintain the correct rank ordering of cell means. However, even here, it may be misleading to say that A_2 is 19 points better than A_1. What happens if we consider the marginal means for B? They are $\bar{Y}_{.1} = 65$ and $\bar{Y}_{.2} = 70$, so B_2 is 5 points better (on the average) than B_1. However, at the second level of A, B_2 is actually 6 points *worse* than B_1. The average value of 5 comes from the average of -6 and $+16$. This inconsistency in the sign of the simple effects of B at specific levels of A implies a disordinal interaction for the B factor. The marginal mean difference of $+5$ in favor of B_2 is especially misleading here, even though $+5$ is the *average* advantage of B_2 over B_1, just as $+19$ was the *average* advantage of A_2 over A_1.

11. Notice, however, that the questions being addressed are not literally the same. For example, Dr. Multiple's test of biofeedback effects averages over the three types of drugs. Dr. Single's test is more likely to assess the biofeedback effect in the presence of a single drug because the one-factor design by definition does not include type of drug as a factor.

12. Some individuals would argue that a significance test is not needed here because we are studying the entire population. In other words, the sample *is* the population, so we do not need a significance test to tell us whether there is a "true" difference. However, as Beaton (1978), Freedman and Lane (1983), and McCabe (1980) argue, a randomization test could be used in this type of situation to assess how unusual the observed salary difference is, if in fact salaries have been randomly assigned without regard to an employee's gender. As discussed in Chapter 2, ANOVA significance levels usually closely approximate significance levels from randomization tests. Thus, the ANOVA may be quite useful to help us decide whether a particular pay disparity simply reflects natural variation or is truly gender-related.

13. Another method for taking educational attainment into account is analysis of covariance. As we will see in Chapter 9, analysis of covariance is most appropriate when the variable to be taken into account is continuous rather than discrete.

14. The harmonic mean can be thought of as an "effective" sample size. This concept can be illustrated most easily in the case of two groups, whose means (i.e., arithmetic means) are to be compared. For example, suppose we have a sample of 10 observations in group 1 and 40 observations in group 2. The variance of the difference in sample means $\bar{Y}_1 - \bar{Y}_2$ is given by

$$\text{Var}(\bar{Y}_1 - \bar{Y}_2) = \frac{\sigma_1^2}{n_1} + \frac{\sigma_2^2}{n_2}$$

With homogeneity of variance, this expression becomes

$$\text{Var}(\bar{Y}_1 - \bar{Y}_2) = \sigma^2 \left(\frac{1}{n_1} + \frac{1}{n_2} \right)$$

Substituting $n_1 = 10$ and $n_2 = 40$, we find that

$$\text{Var}(\bar{Y}_1 - \bar{Y}_2) = \sigma^2 \left(\frac{1}{10} + \frac{1}{40} \right) = 0.125\,\sigma^2.$$

Are samples of sizes 10 and 40 as good as two samples each of size 25? After all, 25 is the "average" (i.e., arithmetic mean) of 10 and 40. However, the variance of $\bar{Y}_1 - \bar{Y}_2$ for $n_1 = n_2 = 25$ equals

$$\text{Var}(\bar{Y}_1 - \bar{Y}_2) = \sigma^2 \left(\frac{1}{25} + \frac{1}{25} \right) = 0.080\,\sigma^2$$

so two samples of size 25 provide a more precise estimate of $\bar{Y}_1 - \bar{Y}_2$ than do samples of sizes 10 and 40. Thus, the "effective" n of $n_1 = 10$ and $n_2 = 40$ is something less than 25. To find out how much less, we can use the harmonic mean of 10 and 40:

$$\tilde{n} = 2/(1/10 + 1/40) = 16$$

Now, the variance of $\bar{Y}_1 - \bar{Y}_2$ for $n_1 = n_2 = 16$ equals

$$\text{Var}(\bar{Y}_1 - \bar{Y}_2) = \sigma^2 \left(\frac{1}{16} + \frac{1}{16} \right) = 0.125\,\sigma^2,$$

which equals the variance of $\bar{Y}_1 - \bar{Y}_2$ for samples of 10 and 40. Thus, two samples of size 10 and 40 provide the same precision as equal size samples of 16. In this sense, the harmonic mean of sample sizes can be thought of as an "effective" sample size.

15. We could just as easily have used coefficients of 1, 1, -1, and -1, instead of .5, .5, $-.5$, and $-.5$. As we saw in Chapter 4, multiplying each coefficient by a constant does not change the sum of squares for the contrast. We have chosen to use coefficients of .5 and $-.5$ here because the value of this contrast equals the difference in the row marginal means:

$$\psi = .5\mu_{11} + .5\mu_{12} - .5\mu_{21} - .5\mu_{22}$$
$$= .5(\mu_{11} + \mu_{12}) - .5(\mu_{21} + \mu_{22})$$
$$= \mu_{1.} - \mu_{2.}$$

Thus, this choice of coefficients makes the numerical value of the contrast easy to interpret.

16. In reality, Type I sums of squares are calculated in a hierarchical (i.e., sequential) manner, whereby effects are added to the model one at a time. We are assuming here that the A main effect is the first term to be entered into the model.

17. There is also a Type IV sum of squares, but it is identical to Type III, unless one or more cells in the design are missing, that is, unless there are no observations in one or more cells.

18. The reason for these peculiar looking weights is actually very straightforward. The weight for $\bar{Y}_{11} - \bar{Y}_{21}$, namely $n_{11}n_{21}/n_{+1}$, is twice the harmonic mean of n_{11} and n_{21}. Similarly, the weight for $\bar{Y}_{12} - \bar{Y}_{22}$, namely $n_{12}n_{22}/n_{+2}$, is twice the harmonic mean of n_{12} and n_{22}. Thus, the columns are weighted in proportion to the harmonic mean of the sample sizes in the columns, which implies that each column is being weighted by its "effective" sample size (see Note 14). In this manner, the most precise estimates receive the most weight.

19. Alternatively, models can be formulated in terms of multiple regression. Dummy variables can be created to represent group membership. The regression model for the full model of Equation 42 has $ab - 1$ predictor variables, while the restricted model

has $a + b - 2$ predictors (excluding the intercept, in both cases). The difference in error sums of squares then equals

$$E_R - E_F = SS_{total}(R^2_{Full} - R^2_{Restricted}),$$

where R^2_{Full} and $R^2_{Restricted}$ are the squared multiple correlations for the full and restricted models, respectively. For additional details, see Cohen and Cohen (1983, pp. 335–345); Kirk (1982, pp. 401–422); Kleinbaum, Kupper, and Muller (1988, pp. 457–473); and Pedhazur (1982, pp. 371–387).

20. This statement is true for the Type I sum of squares when the interaction term is the last term to enter the model in the hierarchical sequence, as it usually is.

21. Searle (1987, p. 90) actually writes $E_R - E_F$ as

$$SS_A = \sum_i w_i \left(\bar{Y}_{i.(U)} - \sum_i w_i \bar{Y}_{i.(U)} \bigg/ \sum_i w_i \right)^2$$

where

$$1/w_i = (1/b^2) \sum_j (1/n_{ij})$$

However, simple algebra shows that this expression is equivalent to our Equation 44.

22. Remember that a "Type II error" is failing to reject a null hypothesis when it is false. Thus, the meaning of "Type II" here is unrelated to the meaning of "Type II" as applied to sums of squares. Instead, remember that Type II error is related to power. Specifically, power equals 1.0 minus the probability of a Type II error. Thus, the problem here can be thought of as failing to detect the interaction because of insufficient power.

23. However, there is almost always an even greater advantage to forming the blocks prior to assigning subjects to treatments. Both forms of blocking are discussed in greater detail in Chapter 9.

24. For example, "Type II" marginal means can be found easily using PROC GLM in SAS. The MODEL statement should include both main effects, but not the interaction term. The MODEL statement is then followed by an LSMEANS statement that also includes only the main effects.

Chapter 8

1. As in the two-way design of Chapter 7, there are also abc independent parameters in the full model of the form given by Equation 2. Although the total number of parameters in this form of the model exceeds abc, they are not all independent of each other. It can be demonstrated just as we did in Chapter 7 that certain constraints must apply to these parameters, reducing the number of independent parameters to abc.

2. Strictly speaking, although this is a logical inference to apply to the population, tests of simple interaction effects of biofeedback × drug within each level of the diet factor could be nonsignificant, both for diet absent and for diet present. Such an occurrence is analogous to finding omnibus significance in a one-way design, yet failing to detect any pairwise differences between groups. For further discussion of this general point, see Levin and Marascuilo (1972).

3. In reality, we might want to test either the effect of biofeedback at each level of the drug factor *or* the drug effect at each level of biofeedback. In some situations, only one of these two effects will be of theoretical interest, and only it should be tested. However, because

the biofeedback and drug factors have been found to interact here, it is important to realize that we would generally want to interpret simple effects instead of main effects, regardless of whether we decide to test both of the effects or only one effect.

4. In fact, as discussed in Chapter 5, if we were interested solely in pairwise comparisons, it would be unnecessary to perform the omnibus test of drug differences first. Instead, we could simply use Tukey's WSD to control the α_{FW} level and skip the omnibus test entirely.

5. These estimates are calculated in the following manner:

$$\widehat{(\alpha\beta)}_{11} = \bar{Y}_{11.} - \bar{Y}_{1..} - \bar{Y}_{.1.} + \bar{Y}_{...}$$
$$= 168.50 - 179.17 - 174.50 + 184.50$$
$$= -0.67$$

$$\widehat{(\alpha\gamma)}_{12} = \bar{Y}_{1.2} - \bar{Y}_{1..} - \bar{Y}_{..2} + \bar{Y}_{...}$$
$$= 171.33 - 179.17 - 176.00 + 184.50$$
$$= 0.67$$

$$\widehat{(\beta\gamma)}_{12} = \bar{Y}_{.12} - \bar{Y}_{.1.} - \bar{Y}_{..2} + \bar{Y}_{...}$$
$$= 171.00 - 174.50 - 176.00 + 184.50$$
$$= 5.00$$

$$\widehat{(\alpha\beta\gamma)}_{112} = \bar{Y}_{112} - \bar{Y}_{11.} - \bar{Y}_{1.2} - \bar{Y}_{.12} + \bar{Y}_{1..} + \bar{Y}_{.1.} + \bar{Y}_{..2} - \bar{Y}_{...}$$
$$= 169.00 - 168.50 - 171.33 - 171.00 + 179.17 + 174.50 + 176.00 - 184.50$$
$$= 3.33$$

6. It might also be assumed that *all* higher-order effects are zero, whether or not they involve A. In this example, then, the B × C interaction might also be omitted from both the full and the restricted models. For further discussion of what effects to omit from both models, see Appelbaum and Cramer (1974).

Chapter 9

1. The question is sometimes raised if one can make different variables commensurate by transforming them to z scores. Doing so would result in both variables being in standard deviation units, and so the new variables would be commensurate by our definition. However, if your interest is in determining if a group of subjects is at the same level on the two measures, as in a matched-pairs t test, transforming to z scores is pointless because you can know in advance that the mean z score must be zero (for both variables). What is useful in some situations is to express two variables in terms of standard deviations away from the mean of a normative group. For example, in a study of brain-damaged patients, one might express their performance on two different measures—for example, finger tapping and grip strength—in terms of z-score units away from the mean of normal adults, and then do a matched-pairs t to determine on which test the extent of impairment is greater.

2. Most texts use deviation scores on the covariate $X_{ij} - \bar{X}$, rather than X_{ij}, in their models. The principal results in ANCOVA in terms of significance tests and the estimates of α_j and β are identical whether raw or deviation score forms of X are used. Using deviation scores has the advantage of resulting in μ being the grand mean on the dependent variable, as in the other models we have treated, instead of the intercept

of a regression line (in the restricted model) or the mean of the intercepts of the regression lines (in the full model). However, we prefer to use the raw-score form of X to underscore that ANCOVA and its extensions involve the comparison of regression lines and that an estimate of performance under a particular treatment can be made at any point on the X dimension. This becomes more important when we generalize the model to allow for heterogeneous regressions (see the chapter extension).

3. This is clearly a smaller data set than you would want to use ANCOVA on in practice. However, because the computations are somewhat more involved than previous techniques we have considered, we use a miniscule data set with simple numerical solutions so that the logic of the procedure will not be obscured by messy arithmetic.

4. We are rather guarded about what you can conclude from an ANCOVA in such a quasi-experimental situation because of the implicit causal model underlying the conditional assertion you would be tempted to make—for example, "if the SES of Headstart children were increased, then their reading achievement will increase." It may be that the causal variable related to SES is the number of books in the home and parental attitude toward reading. If one were to increase SES without affecting these other variables, then reading achievement might not change. See the illuminating discussion of this problem by Meehl (1971) and also our other cautions below, for example, "Lack of Independence of the Treatment and Covariate."

5. Although the conclusion that $\beta_Q = 0$ does not necessarily eliminate all possibility of nonlinearity (because higher-order trends could be present even though a quadratic trend is not), for most practical purposes such a test suffices.

6. A reviewer notes that these rather contrived data suggest an unrealistically consistent deterioration of motor control with age. (We readily agree that people, particularly professors, do not pass on so predictably!) However, such data allow us to illustrate the *statistical* loss of sensitivity associated with blocking. Admittedly this effect may be somewhat less pronounced when blocking is used with more realistic data.

Chapter 9: Extension

1. Both E_R and E_F can be viewed as binomials of the form $(p - q)^2$. When these are expanded the p^2 terms are the same for E_R and E_F and so drop out. The cross-product terms, which are of the form $-2pq$, as frequently is the case in expressions for sums of squares, can be rewritten and shown to be a multiple of the final term, that is, $-2pq = -2q^2$. Thus, the difference between E_R and E_F can be expressed as the difference between the q^2 terms, and Equation E.7 is one way of writing this difference.

2. The proof makes use of the fact that both $\bar{Y}$ and b can be expressed as linear combinations of the Y_i and that the covariance of $\bar{Y}$ and b can be shown to be zero.

3. This is a legitimate rewriting of the definitional formula for the slope because $\sum(X_i - \bar{X})(Y_i - \bar{Y}) = \sum(X_i - \bar{X})Y_i$. This in turn is true because $\sum(X_i - \bar{X})(Y_i - \bar{Y}) = \sum(X_i - \bar{X})Y_i - \sum(X_i - \bar{X})\bar{Y}$, but $\sum(X_i - \bar{X})\bar{Y} = \bar{Y}\sum(X_i - \bar{X}) = 0$ because the sum of the deviations from the mean must equal zero. Thus, we have

$$b = \frac{\sum(X_i - \bar{X})Y_i}{\sum(X_i - \bar{X})^2}$$

which may be rewritten

$$b = \sum \frac{X_i - \bar{X}}{\sum(X_i - \bar{X})^2} Y_i$$

Chapter 10

1. The only difference in the one-way case with unequal n is that the multiplier of σ_α^2 will be somewhat less than the mean of the n_js. In general, in a one-way random-effects design, $\mathscr{E}(MS_\alpha) = \mathscr{E}[(E_R - E_F)/(df_R - df_F)] = \sigma_\varepsilon^2 + n'\sigma_\alpha^2$, where $n' = [1/(a-1)][\sum n_i - (\sum n_i^2/\sum n_i)]$. If all $n_j = n$, then $n' = n$, else $0 < n' < \bar{n}$.

Chapter 11

1. Even with only six subjects, the sample correlation of 0.96 is statistically significant at the .005 level (two-tailed). Thus, we have strong evidence that the errors are correlated in the population.

2. The models may appear to be slightly different, but in fact the difference is really just notational. In Chapter 7, the full model for a two-way factorial design was written as

$$Y_{ijk} = \mu + \alpha_j + \beta_k + (\alpha\beta)_{jk} + \varepsilon_{ijk}$$

In the repeated measures design, we have

$$Y_{ij} = \mu + \alpha_j + \pi_i + (\pi\alpha)_{ij} + \varepsilon_{ij}$$

Notice that π_i (the subject effect) is analogous to β_k in the earlier model, because "subject" is now the second factor in the design. Also, we only need two subscripts now instead of three because with only one observation per cell, there is no need to allow for variation within a cell.

3. An equivalent approach would be to obtain the sum of squares for the condition effect from the difference between the sum of squared errors of the models in Equations 20 and 21:

$$Y_{ij} = \mu + \alpha_j + \pi_i + (\pi\alpha)_{ij} + \varepsilon_{ij} \tag{20}$$

$$Y_{ij} = \mu + \pi_i + (\pi\alpha)_{ij} + \varepsilon_{ij} \tag{21}$$

Then, from Chapter 10, the denominator sum of squares would be the difference between the sum of squared errors of the models in Equations 20 and 22:

$$Y_{ij} = \mu + \alpha_j + \pi_i + (\pi\alpha)_{ij} + \varepsilon_{ij} \tag{20}$$

$$Y_{ij} = \mu + \alpha_j + \pi_i + \varepsilon_{ij} \tag{22}$$

However, the resultant F value would be identical to the value obtained more simply by directly comparing the models of Equations 22 and 23 as shown in the text.

4. Consistent with the discussion in Chapter 1, the validity of this study might be strengthened if there were a second group of children with whom we were comparing this group. We will discuss analysis of data from such a design in Chapters 12 and 14.

5. In fact, the within-groups assumption is in an important sense identical to the between-groups assumption. If we rewrite Equation 22 as $Y_{ij} - \pi_i = \mu + \alpha_j + \varepsilon_{ij}$, the right-hand side of the model is the same as that for a one-way between-subjects design. Indeed, McNemar (1969) has shown that the mixed-model ANOVA produces the same results as would a between-subjects ANOVA on $Y_{ij} - \bar{Y}_{i.}$. Notice that this between-subjects ANOVA uses an adjusted score as the dependent variable. Specifically, the adjustment results from subtracting out the person (i.e., subject) effect represented by $\bar{Y}_{i.}$. However, a between-subjects ANOVA requires homogeneous variances across the treatment levels for the dependent variable. Within treatment level j, the variance of the adjusted dependent variable is given by $\operatorname{Var}(Y_{ij} - \bar{Y}_{i.}) = \sigma_{\varepsilon_j}^2 + \sigma_\pi^2 - (2/a)\sum_l \operatorname{Cov}(Y_{ij}, Y_{il})$.

Comparison of this formula with Equation 29 of the text shows that they both involve variances and covariances. Indeed, it turns out that the treatment-difference variance of Equation 29 is equal for every pair of groups if and only if the above variance is a constant for every group. Thus, the homogeneity of treatment-difference variance assumption is equivalent to the between-subjects assumption of homogeneity of variance for the adjusted scores $Y_{ij} - \bar{Y}_{i.}$.

6. In fact, it is possible to perform a statistical test to assess the presence of differential carryover. Differential carryover is indicated when the sum of each subject's two scores in one group is different from the sum in the other group. Notice that in our example (Table 11.13), the mean sum in group 1 is only 30, whereas in group 2 it is 40. However, Brown (1980) shows that the test of differential carryover frequently lacks power, so that differential carryover may go undetected even when it exists in the population. When differential carryover does exist, an unbiased estimate of treatment effects can still be obtained by comparing scores at time 1. On this basis, we stated that our best guess is that the true treatment effect here equals 10. Although this capability offers some solace, notice that when we use only time 1 scores, we effectively have a between-subjects design, so any possible advantages of the within-subjects design have been lost.

7. The digram-balanced Latin square design provides unbiased estimates of treatment effects even in the presence of differential carryover, if carryover effects persist only into the next time point (Fleiss, 1986, p. 281). However, in much behavioral research, it is likely that carryover effects are more persistent, in which case estimates of treatment effects are again biased.

Chapter 12

1. Although it is usually true that analysis of two-way designs begins with tests of the main effects and interaction, an important alternative in some situations is to perform tests of planned comparisons. When the research hypotheses are sufficiently explicit, power can potentially be increased by focusing tests on these questions instead of testing more global main effects or interactions.

2. We acknowledge that even the expressions shown in Table 12.2 are laborious to calculate by hand; although we assume that most actual calculations will be left to the computer, we nevertheless believe that the expressions shown in Table 12.2 enhance understanding of the meaning of each effect in the model. It may be instructive to compare the "General Expression for SS" column in Table 12.2 to the same column in Table 8.11. The expression for each effect is the same in the two tables, except that S in Table 12.2 has replaced C in Table 8.11, and there are only three levels of summation in Table 12.2 because there is only one score per cell.

3. As in the between-subjects factorial design, we might want to qualify our interpretation of the main effects here because of the statistically significant interaction. Nevertheless, the main-effect tests are still correct tests of *average* differences. As in the between-subjects design, the question is, Are these averages directly interpretable when we know that the individual simple effects are different? For the current numerical example, we proceed under the assumption that marginal means are still of interest despite the significant interaction.

4. Notice that Equation 9 is of the same basic form as Equation 8. However, the b term that was included in Equation 8 does not appear in Equation 9. The reason is that the contrast in Equation 8 compares marginal means, each of which is based on nb scores, whereas the contrast in Equation 9 compares cell means, each of which is based on n

scores. If the contrast in Equation 8 were rewritten in terms of individual cell means, it would be identical to Equation 9.

5. Note that although the F values are the same, the sums of the squares are not. The sums of squares computed from the data in Table 12.7 are one-half those shown in Table 12.5 because the one-way analysis for Table 12.7 does not take into account the fact that these scores are themselves means, averaged over the two levels of B. However, the same F value is obtained because the ratio of MS_A to $MS_{A \times S}$ is still the same in both cases.

6. Huynh (1978) presents a very general procedure for calculating $\hat{\varepsilon}$ and $\tilde{\varepsilon}$ in complex designs, with any combination of between-subjects and within-subjects factors. However, the procedure requires the use of matrix algebra, so we do not describe it here.

7. In fact, sequence might interact with condition, in which case a between-subjects design might be preferred. However, we continue to discuss the example as a within-subjects design.

8. Another question that may be of interest here is the extent to which scores are generalizable across raters. In other words, while the quasi-F allows for the raters factor to be random, it does not address the question of generalizability, which may be of interest in its own right. Readers interested in learning more about generalizability theory should consult Brennan (1983) and Shavelson, Webb, and Burstein (1986).

9. Of course, these two groups might differ on other variables in addition to age, in which case the Chapter 9 discussion on comparing nonequivalent groups becomes relevant.

10. Greenwald (1976) provides an interesting comparison of the ecological validity of context effects in between- and within-subjects designs. Either may be more valid than the other, depending on the nature of the factors. Readers who are faced with a choice between the two types of designs are urged to read Greenwald's article.

11. We might want to qualify our interpretation of the angle main effect because the interaction of angle and age is statistically significant. However, as we stated in Note 3, tests of comparisons of angle are still correct tests of *average* angle differences, where the average is calculated over the two age groups. The issue here is whether we should be describing average angle differences or angle differences within each age group (i.e., simple effects). In our opinion, the answer depends on the specific goals of the study. For the purposes of our example, we assume that average angle differences are of interest despite the statistically significant interaction.

12. A more efficient way to use $MS_{B \times S/A_j}$ is to use PROC SORT and BY commands in SAS or to use SORT CASES and SPLIT FILE in SPSS-X.

13. Two points are relevant here. First, it is interesting to notice that Equation 26 follows from an equality among the sums of squares:

$$\sum_{k=1}^{b} SS_{S/A \text{ at } B_k} = SS_{S/A} + SS_{B \times S/A}$$

The sum of squares for the b simple-effects tests of S/A at each level of B equals the sum of squares for the main effect of S/A plus the sum of squares for the interaction of S/A with B. Second, $MSWCELL$ can be regarded as a weighted average of $MS_{S/A}$ and $MS_{B \times S/A}$:

$$MSWCELL = \frac{(N-a)MS_{S/A} + (b-1)(N-a)MS_{B \times S/A}}{(N-a) + (b-1)(N-a)}$$

14. This statement assumes that the SAS analysis is conducted using the REPEATED statement in PROC GLM and that the SPSS-X analysis is conducted using the WSFACTORS statement in MANOVA.

15. Of course, as always, we cannot affirm the null hypothesis. That is to say, we would not want to conclude here that we have shown that there is absolutely no age difference in the angle quadratic trend. Such a conclusion would be especially misguided in our example, where the power for detecting a difference whose magnitude is of theoretical importance may be low because of the rather small sample sizes.

16. If there were an unequal number of subjects at the different levels of A, $MS_{B \times S/A}$ would be a weighted average of these four components. The weight for a component at level A_j would be equal to $(n_j - 1)/(N - a)$, where N represents the total number of subjects.

17. As we will see in Chapter 14, technically if there are b levels of the B factor, the covariance matrices that must be identical to one another have $b - 1$ rows and $b - 1$ columns, each corresponding to a degree of freedom of the B effect.

18. When one or more additional factors are random, error terms must be chosen differently to account for these additional sources of variance.

19. In fact, summing the squared errors shown in Table 12.23 produces a value of 114.97 instead of 114.88. The discrepancy is due to rounding error and could be reduced by retaining more digits in the predicted values.

Chapter 13

1. As in the between-subjects design, it is generally impossible prior to examining the data to formulate a single comparison that can completely account for all mean differences when there are more than 2 groups. Recall that with a means, there are $a - 1$ degrees of freedom, and hence $a - 1$ independent ways in which means may differ. However, as in the between-subjects design, it is possible after examining the data to formulate a post hoc comparison that will completely account for all mean differences. As we will see later in the chapter, however, in the within-subjects design, the coefficients of this optimal comparison are determined not just by the sample means but also by the sample covariance matrix as well.

2. This symbol is identical to the symbol that is used to represent the absolute value of a number. Hence, it must be kept in mind whether the term inside the vertical lines is a number or a matrix. The meaning should be clear from the context and the boldface type used to represent a matrix.

3. The quantity $(a - 1)(a - 2)/2$ is the number of pairs that exist among $a - 1$ D variables. For example, when $a = 4$, there are three D variables, and $(4 - 1)(4 - 2)/2 = 3$ pairs: D_1 and D_2, D_1 and D_3, and D_2 and D_3. On the other hand, if $a = 5$, four D variables are required, and there are $(5 - 1)(5 - 2)/2 = 6$ pairs: D_1 and D_2, D_1 and D_3, D_1 and D_4, D_2 and D_3, D_2 and D_4, and D_3 and D_4.

4. The determinant of a 3×3 matrix of the form

$$\begin{vmatrix} a & d & e \\ d & b & f \\ e & f & c \end{vmatrix} = a(bc - f^2) + d(ef - cd) + e(df - be)$$

5. Because of rounding error, multiplying a number in column 1 of Table 13.14 by 24 may not exactly reproduce the corresponding number in column 2. However, any

discrepancy is due to the presentation of only three decimal places for the slope values. If enough decimal places were shown, the relationship would be exact.

6. The approach we used here of calculating a regression slope for each subject and then performing an analysis on the slopes has received considerable attention in the last few years as a general methodology for handling complex problems in analyzing longitudinal data. The interested reader is urged to consult Bryk and Raudenbush (1987), Goldstein (1987), and Rogosa (1988) for more information.

7. Notice that this equality requires that the contrasts be orthonormal. When nonnormalized linear and quadratic trend variables were used, the full matrix we found had diagonal values of 32 and 44, which obviously fail to sum to 23.3333. Not only must the contrasts be normalized, but they must also form an orthogonal set for this equality to hold.

8. AVERF is an abbreviation for average F. Notice that the numerator of the mixed-model F is an average of the two diagonal elements of $\mathbf{E^*(R)} - \mathbf{E^*(F)}$. Similarly, the denominator is an average of the diagonal elements of $\mathbf{E^*(F)}$ divided by $n - 1$. The mixed-model F is also an average of the F values for the individual orthonormal F values, if a pooled error term is used (we discuss the use of a pooled error term shortly).

9. For technical reasons, this statement is only approximately true. Although the numerators of the F statistics in Equations 33 and 34 are identical and the denominators have the same expected value under sphericity, the mean F values will not be literally identical, because the expected value of a ratio does not necessarily equal the ratio of the expected values. Under the null hypothesis, the expected value of an F statistic is $df_{denom}/(df_{denom} - 2)$. Thus, the expected value of the F statistic will be slightly larger for the multivariate approach than for the mixed-model approach.

10. As a technical point, it should be acknowledged that the multivariate approach requires a normality assumption that is theoretically more restrictive than the normality assumption of the mixed-model approach. Specifically, the multivariate approach assumes not only that each individual variable has a normal distribution but also that the joint distribution of the variables is multivariate normal. However, this additional assumption is unlikely to be of practical importance, both because univariate normality typically implies multivariate normality in practice and because the Type I error rate is robust to the degree of nonnormality that usually occurs in practice (see Bray & Maxwell, 1985, for a review of the robustness literature).

11. When n is less than a, the $\mathbf{E^*(F)}$ matrix for the full model is necessarily singular. As a result, its determinant equals zero; because the determinant appears in the denominator of the F statistic, the F is undefined in this situation.

Chapter 14

1. Although it is usually true that analysis of two-way designs begins with tests of the main effects and interaction, an important alternative in some situations is to perform tests of planned comparisons. When the research hypotheses are sufficiently explicit, power may be increased by focusing tests on these questions instead of testing more global main effects or interactions.

2. Although all scores are doubled, the F value is unchanged, because $s^2_{D_1}$ (in the denominator of the F) is quadrupled, exactly offsetting the quadrupling of $\bar{D}_1^2$. Thus, using coefficients of ± 1 is functionally equivalent to using coefficients of $\pm.5$.

3. As always, these comparisons must be linearly independent.

4. Of course, we must be careful not to literally accept the null hypothesis. Although the test of the noise by quadratic trend of angle component was nonsignificant, we should not conclude that this component is exactly zero in the population.

5. You should be able to convince yourself that these contrasts are indeed orthogonal, by applying the test for orthogonality that was presented in Chapter 4.

6. The data for this example were originally presented in Tables 12.7 and 12.15.

7. With unequal n, these two different definitions result in different tests of the within-subjects main effect. The general issue here is whether to perform tests of unweighted or weighted marginal means, which you may recall was an issue we discussed in considerable detail in Chapter 7. Our general preference is for tests of unweighted means; as of this writing, all three major mainframe statistical packages (BMDP, SAS, and SPSS-X) produce a test of the unweighted marginal mean by default in the split-plot design. However, as we discussed in Chapter 7, there may be occasions where a test of the weighted marginal means is more appropriate. We will see later that the only difference in the tests concerns whether the sample grand mean $\bar{D}$ is calculated as an unweighted or as a weighted mean across the levels of A, the between-subjects factor.

8. Notice that with unequal n, $\bar{D}$ of Equation 43 is the weighted sample mean because the weighted sample mean is the least-squares estimator of μ in the restricted model of Equation 42.

9. With unequal n, either $\sum_{j=1}^{a} \alpha_j$ or $\sum_{j=1}^{a} n_j \alpha_j$ can be constrained to equal zero. The former occurs when μ is unweighted, and the latter occurs when μ is weighted. In addition, with either equal or unequal n, for technical reasons it may be preferable to regard the constraint that the α_j parameters sum to zero as leading to the definition that α_j equals $\mu_j - \mu$, instead of the definition leading to the constraint.

10. The estimator $\hat{\alpha}_j = \bar{D}_j - \bar{D}$ is identical to the estimator we obtained in the full model containing μ (Equation 41) because the constraint that $\sum_{j=1}^{a} \alpha_j = 0$ was also imposed in that model. Were it not for this constraint, however, we could estimate α_j with $\bar{D}_j$ in the restricted model, in which case the errors of the full and restricted models would be identical, so the comparison of models would not be meaningful. Thus, the constraint we have imposed makes it possible to compare the models meaningfully because the constrained α_j parameters have the same meaning in both models. Lunneborg and Abbott (1983, pp. 196–197) provide details of constrained least-squares estimation.

11. If an experimenter decides to test the weighted mean, then $\bar{D}$ in the numerator of Equation 47 is the sample weighted mean. Otherwise, $\bar{D}$ is the unweighted mean. As usual, with equal n, the weighted and unweighted means are identical.

12. The only exception to this statement is when the design is "doubly multivariate," meaning that more than one dependent variable exists at each and every level of the repeated factor. For example, in the perceptual study, we might have two variables, number of errors and reaction time, for each subject in all three angle conditions. We would then form one M variable for number of errors and a second M variable for reaction time. See Hertzog and Rovine (1985) for more information.

13. Although the numerator degrees of freedom are exactly what we would expect based on df_F and df_R, the denominator degrees of freedom are different. As we will see in more detail later in the chapter, denominator degrees of freedom in the multivariate approach do not always follow rules developed in the univariate case.

14. If we had unequal n, the least-squares estimates of μ_1 and μ_2 would be the weighted grand means $\bar{D}_1$ and $\bar{D}_2$. Notice that each weighted grand mean is simply the mean for that D variable averaged over all N subjects, irrespective of group membership.

15. The technical reason is that when $a = 2$, the magnitude of the interaction can be measured with a single eigenvalue. When $a > 2$, more than one eigenvalue exists, and a different form of the test statistic must be used.

16. The reason involves the matrix that results from subtracting the $E(F)$ matrix from the $E(R)$ matrix. When $a = 2$, this matrix has a rank equal to 1 (regardless of the value of b), so the matrix has only one nonzero eigenvalue. When $a > 2$ (and $b > 2$), the rank of the matrix exceeds 1, and there is more than one nonzero eigenvalue. A different form of the F test is necessary to account for these multiple nonzero eigenvalues.

17. Most multivariate statistics textbooks provide an introduction to matrix algebra, which includes coverage of matrix multiplication and the inverse of a matrix. Some examples of such books are Green (1978), Harris (1985), Marascuilo and Levin (1983), Stevens (1986), Tabachnick and Fidell (1983), and Tatsuoka (1988). For our purposes, it suffices to state that multiplying H by the inverse of T is analogous to division of ordinary numbers. The result is similar to $SS_{\text{effect}}/SS_{\text{total}}$, but the multiplication process for the two matrices is affected by the correlations among the variables. It turns out (cf. Bray & Maxwell, 1985) that the Pillai–Bartlett trace V equals the sum of the ratios $SS_{\text{effect}}/SS_{\text{total}}$ for the s discriminant variates that can be formed. As a result, V ranges between 0 and s because we are summing s ratios, each of which is between 0 and 1. Larger values of V are associated with larger effects.

18. A complete theoretical explanation of the parameter s is beyond the scope of this book. However, s turns out to be equal to the rank of the H matrix (where $H = E(R) - E(F)$), so s is the number of nonzero eigenvalues of the H matrix. All four multivariate test statistics are based on these eigenvalues. However, they differ in how they combine these eigenvalues; so when $s > 1$, the four test statistics are generally somewhat different. On the other hand, when $s = 1$, there is no need to combine multiple eigenvalues, and all four test statistics agree.

19. At first glance, this process of adding and subtracting matrices seems very different from what we have done before, where the error term was based on all subjects. However, in fact, the underlying logic is identical. To demonstrate this equivalence, let's compare Equations 64 and 65. One difference is that each place where $E(F)_j$ appears in Equation 64, $E(F)$ takes its place in Equation 65. As a consequence, denominator degrees of freedom increase from $n_j - b + 1$ to $N - a - b + 2$. In addition, there is an apparent departure from previous logic because $E(R)_j$ in Equation 64 has been replaced by $E(F) + E(R)_j - E(F)_j$ in Equation 65. To understand why the logic is in fact the same, we must understand the origin of the $E(R)_j$ term in Equation 64. In fact, a more general equation can be written in terms of the H and E matrices that we discussed in connection with the Pillai–Bartlett trace statistic. For example, a general expression for an F statistic to test the effect of B at A_j could be written as

$$F = \frac{(|E + H| - |E|)/(b - 1)}{|E|/df_E}$$

where E is an appropriately chosen error matrix. H is the hypothesis matrix, so for testing B at A_j, H would be given by $H = E(R)_j - E(F)_j$. We have discussed two choices for E. First, suppose we decide to use $E(F)_j$ as our error matrix. Then, the above expression for the F statistic can be written as

$$F = \frac{(|E(F)_j + E(R)_j - E(F)_j| - |E(F)_j|)/(b - 1)}{|E(F)_j|/(n_j - b + 1)}$$

However, $E(F)_j + E(R)_j - E(F)_j$ simply equals $E(R)_j$, so we can simplify this F

statistic as

$$F = \frac{(|\mathbf{E(R)}_j| - |\mathbf{E(F)}_j|)/(b - 1)}{|\mathbf{E(F)}_j|/(n_j - b + 1)}$$

which is identical to Equation 64. Second, suppose that we decide to use $\mathbf{E(F)}$ as our error term. Then, the general expression for the F statistic can be written as

$$F = \frac{(|\mathbf{E(F)} + \mathbf{E(R)}_j - \mathbf{E(F)}_j|) - |\mathbf{E(F)}|/(b - 1)}{|\mathbf{E(F)}|/(N - a - b + 2)}$$

No further simplification is possible, because $\mathbf{E(F)}$ and $\mathbf{E(F)}_j$ do not cancel out, unlike $\mathbf{E(F)}_j$ and $\mathbf{E(F)}_j$ when $\mathbf{E(F)}_j$ is the error matrix. As a result, we are left with the more complex expression of Equation 65. However, in fact both Equations 64 and 65 follow the same logic, and both are based on the more general expression given here in this note. For the sake of caution, we should add that even this more general expression is appropriate only when $s = 1$.

20. We should emphasize that simple-effects tests conducted with a pooled error term are not robust to violations of the homogeneity assumption regardless of which of the four multivariate test statistics is used. Indeed, because the simple-effects test is effectively performed for a one-way within-subjects design, all four test statistics yield exactly the same F value. Although there is some evidence to suggest that the Pillai–Bartlett trace statistic is generally more robust to violations of homogeneity than are the other three statistics, this finding applies only to omnibus tests, such as the A × B interaction.

21. Recall that, in general, mean square within is a weighted average of the individual $s_{D_{2j}}^2$ terms, where the weight for level j of the A factor equals $(n_j - 1)/(N - a)$.

22. For technical reasons, if $s > 1$ (as it might be for testing an interaction contrast), this statement is only true if the Roy–Bose greatest characteristic root is used as the test statistic. See Bird and Hadzi-Pavlovic (1983) for further information.

Chapter 15

1. Wilcox, Charlin, and Thompson's (1986) results suggest that Type I error rates are more likely to be excessive as the number of groups increases. For example, with equal ns as small as 11, the Type I error rate of the t test remains close to .05, even when the population standard deviations have a 4:1 ratio. However, the Type I error rate for a four-group ANOVA with equal ns of 11 was .109 when the population standard deviation of one group was four times larger than the standard deviation of the other groups. Even for equal ns of 50, the Type I error rate for ANOVA was .088 in this situation. Thus, for more than two groups, wide disparities in population standard deviations can make the usual ANOVA excessively liberal, even with equal n.

2. As of this writing, neither SAS nor SPSS-X provides the Brown–Forsythe or the Welch test for more than two groups.

3. Strictly speaking, MS_B and MS_W are both unbiased estimators of the same population variance if homogeneity holds and the null hypothesis is true. The further assumptions of normality and independence guarantee that the ratio of MS_B and MS_W follows an F distribution.

4. Monte Carlo studies by necessity investigate power differences only under a limited set of conditions. Nevertheless, the value of .03 would seem to be a reasonable figure for most practical situations. The single exception is likely to be where n is very small, in which case F might enjoy a larger advantage over F^*.

5. Cleveland (1985, pp. 135–143) presents two graphical techniques that are especially appropriate for judging whether the data conform to a shift hypothesis when comparing the distributions of two groups. The *percentile comparison graph* is obtained by plotting the percentiles of one distribution against the corresponding percentiles of the other distribution. If a shift of location describes the difference between the groups, the resultant plot should resemble a straight line. The *Tukey sum–difference graph* plots sums of corresponding percentiles against differences of corresponding percentiles and should resemble a flat straight line when the shift hypothesis holds. Cleveland argues that comparing means may be misleading when the percentile comparison graph is curved (or the Tukey sum–difference graph is not flat). Indeed, in such a situation, any single value (e.g., mean or median) may hide important characteristics of the difference between the two distributions. Darlington's (1973) ordinal dominance curve methodology provides an interesting alternative in this situation.

6. When population distributions have different shapes, alternative methods have been developed for testing differences between population medians. For further information, see Fligner and Rust (1982) or Wilcox and Charlin (1986).

7. Although the general consensus among statisticians is that the F test is robust to violations of nonnormality, there are some dissenters to this view. For an example, the interested reader should consult Bradley (1978), who provides a very readable set of arguments for why he believes that the robustness of parametric tests has been oversold.

8. As stated earlier, Tomarken and Serlin only sampled from normal populations. Clinch and Keselman (1982) found F^* to be somewhat more robust than W when sampling from nonnormal populations.

9. Relative efficiency as sample sizes approach infinity is referred to as *asymptotic relative efficiency*, which is often abbreviated ARE. Although ARE is a useful concept, the relative efficiency of two tests in small samples may differ considerably from the ARE. In particular, one limitation of the Kruskal–Wallis test is that it is typically impossible to establish a critical value that will set $\alpha = .05$, even when all assumptions have been met. Especially with small sample sizes, α may have to be set considerably below .05, which inevitably results in a loss of power. In such a situation, the relative efficiency of the nonparametric test suffers relative to the parametric test.

10. The sample median is always a median-unbiased estimator of the population median for random sampling. When the population distribution is symmetric, its mean and median are identical. Although the sample mean and sample median are generally different, both are unbiased estimators of the population mean of a symmetric distribution.

11. To simplify even further, we show Huber's estimator with a fixed *tuning constant* set equal to 1.0. See Hoaglin, Mosteller, and Tukey (1983), Huber (1981), or Wu (1985) for more details.

12. The median can be defined in more than one way when some scores are tied. We have chosen the simplest definition here, which simply ignores the presence of ties, and defines the median to equal the value of the middle observation.

13. Hoaglin, Mosteller, and Tukey (1983) show that M estimators can be thought of as weighted averages of the observations. Specific members of the class differ in terms of how they weight the observations. For example, the mean weights each observation equally, whereas Huber's M estimator weights observation near the center of the data more heavily than observations at the extremes.

Appendix C References

ABELSON, R. P. (1985). A variance explanation paradox: When a little is a lot. *Psychological Bulletin, 97,* 129–133.

ALGINA, J., and OLEJNIK, S. F. (1984). Implementing the Welch-James procedure with factorial designs. *Educational and Psychological Measurement, 44,* 39–48.

APPELBAUM, M. I., and CRAMER, E. M. (1974). Some problems in the nonorthogonal analysis of variance. *Psychological Bulletin, 81,* 335–343.

BACON, F. (1928a). Novum organum. In M. T. McClure (ed.), *Bacon: Selections* (pp. 269–432). New York: Charles Scribner's. (Original work published 1620).

BACON, F. (1928b). The great instauration. In M. T. McClure (ed.), *Bacon: Selections* (pp. 1–33). New York: Charles Scribner's. (Original work published 1620.)

BAILEY, D. F. (1971). *Probability and statistics: Models for research.* New York: John Wiley.

BAKAN, D. (1966). The test of significance in psychological research. *Psychological Bulletin, 66,* 423–437.

BAKER, B. O., HARDYCK, C. D., and PETRINOVICH, L. F. (1966). Weak measurements vs. strong statistics: An empirical critique of S. S. Stevens' proscriptions on statistics. *Educational and Psychological Measurement, 26,* 291–309.

BEATON, A. E. (1978). Salvaging experiments: Interpreting least squares in non-random samples. *1978 Proceedings of Computer Science and Statistics, 10,* 137–145.

BENNETT, E. L., DIAMOND, M. C., KRECH, D., and ROSENZWEIG, M. R. (1964). Chemical and anatomical plasticity of the brain. *Science, 146,* 610–619.

BERNHARDSON, C. S. (1975). Type I error rates when multiple comparison procedures follow a significant F test of ANOVA. *Biometrics, 31,* 229–232.

BHASKAR, R. (1975). *A realist theory of science.* Bristol, England: Western Printing Services.

BHASKAR, R. (1982). Emergence, explanation and emancipation. In P. F. Secord (ed.), *Explaining social behavior: Consciousness, behavior and social structure* (pp. 275–309). Beverly Hills, CA: Sage.

BIRD, K. D., and HADZI-PAVLOVIC, D. (1983). Simultaneous test procedures and the choice of a test statistic in MANOVA. *Psychological Bulletin, 93*, 167–178.

BISHOP, Y. M. M., FIENBERG, S. E., and HOLLAND, P. W. (1975). *Discrete multivariate analysis: Theory and practice.* Cambridge: MIT Press.

BLAIR, R. C. (1981). A reaction to "Consequences of failure to meet assumptions underlying the fixed effects analysis of variance and covariance." *Review of Educational Research, 51*, 499–507.

BLAIR, R. C., and HIGGINS, J. J. (1985). A comparison of the power of the paired samples rank transform statistic to that of Wilcoxon's signed ranks statistic. *Journal of Educational Statistics, 10*, 368–383.

BOCK, R. D. (1975). *Multivariate statistical methods in behavioral research.* New York: McGraw-Hill.

BOIK, R. J. (1979). Interactions, partial interactions, and interaction contrasts in the analysis of variance. *Psychological Bulletin, 86*, 1084–1089.

BOIK, R. J. (1981). A priori tests in repeated measures designs: Effects of nonsphericity. *Psychometrika, 46*, 241–255.

BORING, E. G. (1950). *A history of experimental psychology.* New York: Appleton-Century-Crofts.

BOX, G. E. P. (1954). Some theorems on quadratic forms applied in the study of analysis of variance problems: II. Effects of inequality of variance and of correlation between errors in the two-way classification. *Annals of Mathematical Statistics, 25*, 484–498.

BRADLEY, J. V. (1968). *Distribution-free statistical tests.* Englewood Cliffs, NJ: Prentice-Hall.

BRADLEY, J. V. (1978). Robustness? *British Journal of Mathematical and Statistical Psychology, 31*, 144–152.

BRATCHER, T. L., MORAN, M. A., and ZIMMER, W. J. (1970). Tables of sample sizes in the analysis of variance. *Journal of Quality Technology, 2*, 391–401.

BRAY, J. H., and MAXWELL, S. E. (1985). *Multivariate analysis of variance.* Beverly Hills, CA: Sage.

BRENNAN, R. L. (1983). *Elements of generalizability theory.* Iowa City, IA: American College Testing Program.

BRIDGMAN, P. W. (1927). *The logic of modern physics.* New York: Macmillan.

BRIDGMAN, P. W. (1945). Some general principles of operational analysis. *Psychological Review, 52*, 246–249.

BROAD, W., and WADE, N. (1982). *Betrayers of the truth: Fraud and deceit in the halls of science.* New York: Simon & Schuster.

BROWN, B. W. (1980). The crossover experiment for clinical trials. *Biometrics, 36*, 69–79.

BROWN, H. I. (1977). *Perception, theory and commitment: The new philosophy of science.* Chicago: Precedent Publishing.

BROWN, M. B., and FORSYTHE, A. B. (1974). The ANOVA and multiple comparisons for data with heterogeneous variances. *Biometrics, 30*, 719–724.

BRYANT, J. L., and PAULSON, A. S. (1976). An extension of Tukey's method of multiple comparisons to experimental designs with random concomitant variables. *Biometrika, 63*, 631–638.

BRYK, A. S., and RAUDENBUSH, S. W. (1987). Application of hierarchical linear models to assessing change. *Psychological Bulletin, 101*, 147–158.

BUSEMEYER, J. R. (1980). Importance of measurement theory, error theory, and experimental design for testing the significance of interactions. *Psychological Bulletin, 88,* 237–244.

CAMPBELL, D. T. (1969). Prospective: Artifact and control. In R. Rosenthal and R. L. Rosnow (eds.), *Artifact in behavioral research* (pp. 351–382). New York: Academic Press.

CAMPBELL, D. T. (1986). Relabeling internal and external validity for applied social scientists. In W. M. K. Trochim (ed.), *Advances in quasi-experimental design and analysis* (pp. 67–77). San Francisco: Jossey-Bass.

CAMPBELL, D. T., and FISKE, D. W. (1959). Convergent and discriminant validation by the multitrait-multimethod matrix. *Psychological Bulletin, 56,* 81–105.

CAMPBELL, D. T., and STANLEY, J. C. (1963). *Experimental and quasi-experimental designs for research.* Chicago: Rand McNally.

CHAMBERS, J. M., CLEVELAND, W. S., KLEINER, B., and TUKEY, P. A. (1983). *Graphical methods for data analysis.* Belmont, CA: Wadsworth.

CHOW, S. L. (1988). Significance test or effect size? *Psychological Bulletin, 103,* 105–110.

CLARK, H. H. (1973). The language-as-fixed-effect fallacy: A critique of language statistics in psychological research. *Journal of Verbal Learning and Verbal Behavior, 12,* 335–359.

CLEVELAND, W. S. (1985). *The elements of graphing data.* Belmont, CA: Wadsworth.

CLINCH, J. J., and KESELMAN, H. J. (1982). Parametric alternatives to the analysis of variance. *Journal of Educational Statistics, 7,* 207–214.

COCHRAN, W. G. (1957). Analysis of covariance: Its nature and uses. *Biometrics, 13,* 261–281.

COCHRAN, W. G. (1967). Footnote to an appreciation of R. A. Fisher. *Science, 156,* 1460–1462.

COCHRAN, W. G., and COX, G. M. (1957). *Experimental designs.* New York: John Wiley.

COHEN, J. (1977). *Statistical power analysis for the behavioral sciences* (rev. ed.). New York: Academic Press.

COHEN, J., and COHEN, P. (1983). *Applied multiple regression/correlation analysis for the behavioral sciences* (2d ed.). Hillsdale, NJ: Lawrence Erlbaum Associates.

COLLIER, R. O., JR., BAKER, F. B., MANDEVILLE, G. K., and HAYES, T. F. (1967). Estimates of test size for several test procedures based on conventional variance ratios in the repeated measures design. *Psychometrika, 32,* 339–353.

COLLINGWOOD, R. G. (1940). *An essay on metaphysics.* Oxford, England: Clarendon Press.

CONOVER, W. J., and IMAN, R. L. (1981). Rank transformations as a bridge between parametric and nonparametric statistics. *The American Statistician, 35,* 124–129.

COOK, T. D., and CAMPBELL, D. T. (1979). *Quasi-experimentation: Design and analysis issues for field settings.* Chicago: Rand McNally.

COOMBS, C. H. (1967). Thurstone's measurement of social values revisited forty years later. *Journal of Abnormal and Social Psychology, 6,* 85–91.

CRAMER, E. M., and APPELBAUM, M. I. (1980). Nonorthogonal analysis of variance—Once again. *Psychological Bulletin, 87,* 51–57.

CRONBACH, L. J. (1982). *Designing evaluations of educational and social programs.* San Francisco: Jossey-Bass.

CRONBACH, L. J., and MEEHL, P. E. (1955). Construct validity in psychological tests. *Psychological Bulletin, 52,* 281–302.

CRONBACH, L. J., and SNOW, R. E. (1977). *Aptitudes and instructional methods: A handbook for research on interactions.* New York: Irvington.

DALLAL, G. E. (1988). Statistical microcomputing—Like it is. *The American Statistician, 42,* 212–216.

DAR, R. (1987). Another look at Meehl, Lakatos, and the scientific practices of psychologists. *American Psychologist, 42,* 145–151.

DARLINGTON, R. B. (1973). Comparing two groups by simple graphs. *Psychological Bulletin, 79,* 110–116.

DAVIDSON, M. L. (1972). Univariate versus multivariate tests in repeated measures experiments. *Psychological Bulletin, 77,* 446–452.

DAVISON, M. L., and SHARMA, A. R. (1988). Parametric statistics and levels of measurement. *Psychological Bulletin, 104,* 137–144.

DAWES, R. M. (1975). The mind, the model, and the task. In F. Restle, R. M. Shiffrin, N. J. Castellan, H. R. Lindman, and D. B. Pisoni (eds.), *Cognitive theory: Volume I* (pp. 119–129). Hillsdale, NJ: Lawrence Erlbaum Associates.

DEWEY, J. (1916). *Essays in experimental logic.* Chicago: University of Chicago Press.

DRETZKE, B. J., LEVIN, J. R., and SERLIN, R. C. (1982). Testing for regression homogeneity under variance heterogeneity. *Psychological Bulletin, 91,* 376–383.

DUNN, O. J. (1961). Multiple comparisons among means. *Journal of the American Statistical Association, 56,* 52–64.

DUNNETT, C. W. (1955). A multiple comparison procedure for comparing several treatments with a control. *Journal of the American Statistical Association, 50,* 1096–1121.

DUNNETT, C. W. (1980). Pairwise multiple comparisons in the unequal variance case. *Journal of the American Statistical Association, 75,* 796–800.

DURANT, W., and DURANT, A. (1961). *The story of civilization: VII The age of reason begins.* New York: Simon & Schuster.

EACKER, J. N. (1972). On some elementary philosophical problems of psychology. *American Psychologist, 27,* 553–565.

EDGINGTON, E. S. (1966). Statistical inference and nonrandom samples. *Psychological Bulletin, 66,* 485–487.

EDGINGTON, E. S. (1980). *Randomization tests.* New York: Marcel Dekker.

EINSTEIN, A. (1936). Physics and reality. *Journal of the Franklin Institute, 221,* 349–382.

EINSTEIN, A. (1944). Remarks on Bertrand Russell's theory of knowledge. In P. A. Schilpp (ed.), *The philosophy of Bertrand Russell.* Chicago: Northwestern University.

EINSTEIN, A. (1950). *Out of my later years.* New York: Philosophical Library.

EMERSON, J. D., and STOTO, M. A. (1983). Transforming data. In D. C. Hoaglin, F. Mosteller, and J. W. Tukey (eds.), *Understanding robust and exploratory data analysis* (pp. 97–128). New York: John Wiley.

FENSTAD, G. U. (1983). A comparison between the U and V tests in the Behrens-Fisher problem. *Biometrika, 70,* 300–302.

FESSARD, A. (1926). Les temps de réaction et leur variabilité, étude statistique. *Annale de Psychologie, 27,* 215–224.

FINE, A. (1987). And not anti-realism either. In J. A. Kourany (ed.), *Scientific knowledge: Basic issues in the philosophy of science* (pp. 359–368). Belmont, CA: Wadsworth.

FINN, J. D. (1974). *A general model for multivariate analysis.* New York: Holt, Rinehart & Winston.

FISHER, A. C., and WALLENSTEIN, S. (1981). Crossover designs in medical research. In C. R. Buncher and J. Y. Tsay (eds.), *Statistics in the pharmaceutical industry* (pp. 139–156). New York: Marcel Dekker.

FISHER, R. A. (1971). *Design of experiments*. New York: Hafner Press. (Originally published 1935.)

FLEISS, J. L. (1986). *The design and analysis of clinical experiments*. New York: John Wiley.

FLIGNER, M. A., and RUST, S. W. (1982). A modification of Mood's median test for the generalized Behrens-Fisher problem. *Biometrika, 69*, 221–226.

FORSTER, K. I., and DICKINSON, R. G. (1976). More on the language-as-fixed-effect fallacy: Monte Carlo estimates of error rates for F_1, F_2, F', and $min\ F'$. *Journal of Verbal Learning and Verbal Behavior, 15*, 135–142.

FREEDMAN, D. A., and LANE, D. (1983). Significance testing in a nonstochastic setting. In P. J. Bickel, K. A. Doksum, and J. L. Hodges (eds.), *A Festschrift for Erich L. Lehmann in honor of his sixty-fifth birthday*. Belmont, CA: Wadsworth.

FREEDMAN, D., PISANI, R., and PURVES, R. (1978). *Statistics*. New York: W. W. Norton.

FREUND, J. E., and WALPOLE, R. F. (1980). *Mathematical statistics* (3d ed.). Englewood Cliffs, NJ: Prentice-Hall.

GABRIEL, K. R., and HALL, W. J. (1983). Rerandomization inferences on regression and shift effects: Computationally feasible methods. *Journal of the American Statistical Association, 78*, 827–836.

GABRIEL, K. R., and HSU, C. F. (1983). Evaluation of the power of rerandomization tests, with applications to weather modification experiments. *Journal of the American Statistical Association, 78*, 766–775.

GAITO, J. (1961). Repeated measurements designs and counterbalancing. *Psychological Bulletin, 58*, 46–54.

GAITO, J. (1980). Measurement scales and statistics: Resurgence of an old misconception. *Psychological Bulletin, 87*, 564–567.

GAMES, P. A. (1973). Type IV errors revisited. *Psychological Bulletin, 80*, 304–307.

GAMES, P. A. (1983). Curvilinear transformation of the dependent variable. *Psychological Bulletin, 93*, 382–387.

GAMES, P. A. (1984). Data transformations, power, and skew: A rebuttal to Levine and Dunlap. *Psychological Bulletin, 95*, 345–347.

GAMES, P. A., & HOWELL, J. F. (1976). Pairwise multiple comparison procedures with unequal N's and/or variances: A Monte Carlo study. *Journal of Educational Statistics, 1*, 113–125.

GAMES, P. A., KESELMAN, H. J., and ROGAN, J. C. (1981). Simultaneous pairwise multiple comparison procedures for means when sample sizes are unequal. *Psychological Bulletin, 90*, 594–598.

GARDNER, M. (1979). *Mathematical circus*. New York: Alfred A. Knopf.

GARDNER, M. R. (1987). Realism and instrumentalism in pre-Newtonian astronomy. In J. A. Kourany (ed.), *Scientific knowledge: Basic issues in the philosophy of science* (pp. 369–387). Belmont, CA: Wadsworth.

GARDNER, P. L. (1975). Scales and statistics. *Review of Educational Research, 45*, 43–57.

GASTORF, J. W. (1980). Time urgency of the Type A behavior pattern. *Journal of Consulting and Clinical Psychology, 48*, 299.

GEISSER, S., and GREENHOUSE, S. W. (1958). An extension of Box's results on the use of the *F* distribution in multivariate analysis. *Annals of Mathematical Statistics, 29,* 885–891.

GHOLSON, B., and BARKER, P. (1985). Kuhn, Lakatos, and Lauden: Applications in the history of physics and psychology. *American Psychologist, 40,* 755–769.

GIBBONS, J. D. (1971). *Nonparametric statistical inference.* New York: McGraw-Hill.

GINGERICH, O. (1973). From Copernicus to Kepler: Heliocentrism as model and as reality. *Proceedings of the American Philosophical Society, 117,* 513–522.

GLASS, G. V. (1976). Primary, secondary, and meta-analysis of research. *Educational Researcher, 5,* 3–8.

GLASS, G. V., and HAKSTIAN, A. R. (1969). Measures of association in comparative experiments: Their development and interpretation. *American Educational Research Journal, 6,* 401–414.

GLASS, G. V., PECKHAM, P. D., and SANDERS, J. R. (1972). Consequences of failure to meet assumptions underlying the analysis of variance and covariance. *Review of Educational Research, 42,* 237–288.

GLASS, G. V., and STANLEY, J. C. (1970). *Statistical methods in education and psychology.* Englewood Cliffs, NJ: Prentice-Hall.

GOLDSTEIN, H. (1987). *Multilevel models in educational and social research.* New York: Oxford University Press.

GRAYBILL, F. A. (1969). *Introduction to matrices with applications in statistics.* Belmont, CA: Wadsworth.

GRAYBILL, F. A. (1976). *Theory and application of the linear model.* North Scituate, MA: Duxbury Press.

GREEN, B. F. (1977). A practical interactive program for randomization tests of location. *The American Statistician, 31,* 39–47.

GREEN, P. E. (1978). *Analyzing multivariate data.* Hinsdale, IL: Dryden Press.

GREEN, P. E., and CARROLL, J. D. (1976). *Mathematical tools for applied multivariate analysis.* New York: Academic Press.

GREENWALD, A. G. (1975). Consequences of prejudice against the null hypothesis. *Psychological Bulletin, 82,* 1–20.

GREENWALD, A. G. (1976). Within-subjects designs: To use or not to use? *Psychological Bulletin, 83,* 314–320.

GRICE, G. R. (1966). Dependence of empirical laws upon the source of experimental variation. *Psychological Bulletin, 66,* 488–499.

GUTTING, G. (ed.) (1980). *Paradigms and revolutions: Appraisals and applications of Thomas Kuhn's philosophy of science.* Notre Dame, IN: University of Notre Dame Press.

HALE, G. A. (1977). On use of ANOVA in developmental research. *Child Development, 48,* 1101–1106.

HAMILTON, B. L. (1976). A Monte Carlo test of the robustness of parametric and nonparametric analysis of covariance against unequal regression slopes. *Journal of the American Statistical Association, 71,* 864–869.

HAMILTON, B. L. (1977). An empirical investigation of the effects of heterogeneous regression slopes in analysis of covariance. *Educational and Psychological Measurement, 37,* 701–712.

HAND, D. J., and TAYLOR, C. C. (1987). *Multivariate analysis of variance and repeated measures: A practical approach for behavioural scientists.* New York: Chapman and Hall.

HARRÉ, R., and MADDEN, E. H. (1975). *Causal powers: A theory of natural necessity*. Oxford, England: Basil Blackwell.

HARRIS, R. J. (1985). *A primer of multivariate statistics* (2d ed.). Orlando, FL: Academic Press.

HATHAWAY, S. R., and McKINLEY, J. C. (1940). A multiphasic personality schedule (Minnesota): I. Construction of the schedule. *Journal of Psychology, 10*, 249–254.

HAYS, W. L. (1981). *Statistics* (3d ed.). New York: Holt, Rinehart & Winston.

HEDGES, L. V. (1981). Distribution theory for Glass's estimator of effect size and related estimators. *Journal of Educational Statistics, 6*, 107–128.

HEDGES, L. V. (1982). Estimation of effect size from a series of independent experiments. *Psychological Bulletin, 92*, 490–499.

HEDGES, L. V. (1983). A random effects model for effect sizes. *Psychological Bulletin, 93*, 388–395.

HEMPEL, C. G. (1945). Studies in the logic of confirmation. *Mind, 54*, 1–26, 97–121.

HERR, D. G., and GAEBELEIN, J. (1978). Nonorthogonal two-way analysis of variance. *Psychological Bulletin, 85*, 207–216.

HERTZOG, C., and ROVINE, M. (1985). Repeated-measures analysis of variance in developmental research: Selected issues. *Child Development, 56*, 787–809.

HOAGLIN, D. C., MOSTELLER, F., and TUKEY, J. W. (1983). Introduction to more refined estimators. In D. C. Hoaglin, F. Mosteller, and J. W. Tukey (eds.), *Understanding robust and exploratory data analysis* (pp. 283–296). New York: John Wiley.

HOCHBERG, Y., and TAMHANE, A. C. (1987). *Multiple comparison procedures*. New York: John Wiley.

HOGG, R. V., and CRAIG, A. T. (1978). *Introduction to mathematical statistics* (4th ed.). New York: Macmillan.

HOLLAND, B. S., and COPENHAVER, M. D. (1988). Improved Bonferroni-type multiple testing procedures. *Psychological Bulletin, 104*, 145–149.

HOLLANDER, M., and WOLFE, D. A. (1973). *Nonparametric statistical methods*. New York: John Wiley.

HOWARD, G. S., and CONWAY, C. G. (1986). Can there be an empirical science of volitional action? *American Psychologist, 41*, 1241–1251.

HOWELL, D. C., and McCONAUGHY, S. H. (1982). Nonorthogonal analysis of variance: Putting the question before the answer. *Educational and Psychological Measurement, 42*, 9–24.

HUBER, P. J. (1981). *Robust statistics*. New York: John Wiley.

HUBERTY, C. J. (1987). On statistical testing. *Educational Researcher, 16*, 4–9.

HUCK, S. W., and SANDLER, H. M. (1979). *Rival hypotheses: Alternative interpretations of data based conclusions*. New York: Harper & Row.

HUITEMA, B. E. (1980). *The analysis of covariance and alternatives*. New York: John Wiley.

HUYNH, H. (1978). Some approximate tests for repeated measurement designs. *Psychometrika, 43*, 161–175.

HUYNH, H., and FELDT, L. S. (1970). Conditions under which mean square ratios in repeated measurements designs have exact *F*-distributions. *Journal of the American Statistical Association, 65*, 1582–1589.

HUYNH, H., and FELDT, L. S. (1976). Estimation of the Box correction for degrees of freedom from sample data in randomized block and split-plot designs. *Journal of Educational Statistics, 1,* 69–82.

HUYNH, H., and MANDEVILLE, G. K. (1979). Validity conditions in repeated measures designs. *Psychological Bulletin, 86,* 964–973.

IMAN, R. L., and CONOVER, W. J. (1983). *A modern approach to statistics.* New York: John Wiley.

IMAN, R. L., and DAVENPORT, J. M. (1976). New approximations to the exact distribution of the Kruskal-Wallis test statistic. *Communications in Statistics, Series A, 5,* 1335–1348.

IMAN, R. L., HORA, S. C., and CONOVER, W. J. (1984). Comparison of asymptotically distribution-free procedures for the analysis of complete blocks. *Journal of the American Statistical Association, 79,* 674–685.

IMAN, R. L., QUADE, D., and ALEXANDER, D. (1975). Exact probability levels for the Kruskal-Wallis test. In H. L. Harter and D. B. Owen (eds.), *Selected tables in mathematical statistics.* Providence, RI: American Mathematical Society.

JENNINGS, J. R. (1987). Editorial policy on analysis of variance with repeated measures. *Psychophysiology, 24,* 474–475.

JENSEN, A. R. (1980). *Bias in mental testing.* New York: Free Press.

JUDD, C. M., and KENNY, D. A. (1981). *Estimating the effects of social interventions.* Cambridge, England: Cambridge University Press.

KAISER, L., and BOWDEN, D. (1983). Simultaneous confidence intervals for all linear contrasts of means with heterogeneous variances. *Communications in Statistics—Theory and Methods, 12,* 73–88.

KAZDIN, A. E. (1980). *Research design in clinical psychology.* New York: Harper & Row.

KEMPTHORNE, O. (1952). *The design and analysis of experiments.* New York: John Wiley.

KENNY, D. A., and JUDD, C. M. (1986). Consequences of violating the independence assumption in the analysis of variance. *Psychological Bulletin, 99,* 422–431.

KEPLER, J. (1984). *A defense of Tycho against Ursus.* In N. Jardine (trans. and ed.), *The birth of history and philosophy of science: Kepler's defense of Tycho against Ursus, with essays on its provenance and significance.* New York: Cambridge University Press. (Original work published 1601.)

KEPPEL, G. (1982). *Design and analysis: A researcher's handbook* (2d ed.). Englewood Cliffs, NJ: Prentice-Hall.

KESELMAN, H. J., and ROGAN, J. C. (1980). Repeated measures *F* tests and psychophysiological research: Controlling the number of false positives. *Psychophysiology, 17,* 499–503.

KESELMAN, H. J., ROGAN, J. C., and FEIR-WALSH, B. J. (1977). An evaluation of some nonparametric and parametric tests for location equality. *British Journal of Mathematical and Statistical Psychology, 30,* 213–221.

KESELMAN, H. J., ROGAN, J. C., MENDOZA, J. L., and BREEN, L. J. (1980). Testing the validity conditions of repeated measures *F* tests. *Psychological Bulletin, 87,* 479–481.

KIRK, R. E. (1982). *Experimental design: Procedures for the behavioral sciences* (2d ed.). Monterey, CA: Brooks/Cole.

KLEINBAUM, D. G., KUPPER, L. L., and MULLER, K. E. (1988). *Applied regression analysis and other multivariable methods* (2d ed.). Boston: PWS-Kent.

KOCH, S. (1981). The nature and limits of psychological knowledge: Lessons of a century qua "science." *American Psychologist, 36,* 257–269.

KRAMER, C. Y. (1956). Extension of multiple range test to group means with unequal numbers of replications. *Biometrics, 12*, 307–310.

KRATHWOHL, D. R. (1985). *Social and behavioral science research: A new framework for conceptualizing, implementing, and evaluating research studies.* San Francisco: Jossey-Bass.

KUHN, T. S. (1970). *The structure of scientific revolutions* (2d ed.). Chicago: University of Chicago Press.

LABOVITZ, S. (1967). Some observations on measurement and statistics. *Social Forces, 46*, 151–160.

LAKATOS, I. (1978). Falsification and the methodology of scientific research programs. In J. Worrall and G. Currie (eds.), *The methodology of scientific research programs: Imre Lakatos philosophical papers* (Volume 1, pp. 8–101). Cambridge, England; Cambridge University Press.

LEVIN, J. R., and MARASCUILO, L. A. (1972). Type IV errors and interactions. *Psychological Bulletin, 78*, 368–374.

LEVINE, D. W., and DUNLAP, W. P. (1982). Power of the *F* test with skewed data: Should one transform or not? *Psychological Bulletin, 92*, 272–280.

LEVINE, D. W., and DUNLAP, W. P. (1983). Data transformation, power, and skew: A rejoinder to Games. *Psychological Bulletin, 93*, 596–599.

LEVY, K. J. (1979). Nonparametric large-sample pairwise comparisons. *Psychological Bulletin, 86*, 371–375.

LEWIS, D. (1960). *Quantitative methods in psychology.* New York: McGraw-Hill.

LI, G. (1985). Robust regression. In D. C. Hoaglin, F. Mosteller, and J. W. Tukey (eds.), *Exploring data tables, trends, and shapes* (pp. 281–343). New York: John Wiley.

LORD, F. M. (1953). On the statistical treatment of football numbers. *American Psychologist, 8*, 750–751.

LORD, F. M. (1967). A paradox in the interpretation of group comparisons. *Psychological Bulletin, 68*, 304–305.

LUBIN, A. (1962). The interpretation of significant interaction. *Educational and Psychological Measurement, 21*, 807–817.

LUNNEBORG, C. E., and ABBOTT, R. D. (1983). *Elementary multivariate analysis for the behavioral sciences: Applications of basic structure.* New York: Elsevier.

MANICAS, P. T., and SECORD, P. F. (1983). Implications for psychology of the new philosophy of science. *American Psychologist, 38*, 339–413.

MARASCUILO, L. A., and LEVIN, J. R. (1976). The simultaneous investigation of interaction and nested hypotheses in two-factor analysis of variance designs. *American Educational Research Journal, 13*, 61–65.

MARASCUILO, L. A., and LEVIN, J. R. (1983). *Multivariate statistics in the social sciences: A researcher's guide.* Monterey, CA: Brooks/Cole.

MARASCUILO, L. A., and MCSWEENEY, M. (1977). *Nonparametric and distribution-free methods for the social sciences.* Monterey, CA: Brooks/Cole.

MARCUS-ROBERTS, H. M., and ROBERTS, F. S. (1987). Meaningless statistics. *Journal of Educational Statistics, 12*, 383–394.

MARK, M. M. (1986). Validity typologies and the logic and practice of quasi-experimentation. In W. M. K. Trochim (ed.), *Advances in quasi-experimental design and analysis* (pp. 47–66). San Francisco: Jossey-Bass.

MAXWELL, S. E. (1980). Pairwise multiple comparisons in repeated measures designs. *Journal of Educational Statistics, 5,* 269–287.

MAXWELL, S. E., and ARVEY, R. D. (1982). Small sample profile analysis with many variables. *Psychological Bulletin, 92,* 778–785.

MAXWELL, S. E., CAMP, C. J., and ARVEY, R. D. (1981). Measures of strength of association. *Journal of Applied Psychology, 66,* 525–534.

MAXWELL, S. E., and DELANEY, H. D. (1985). Measurement and statistics: An examination of construct validity. *Psychological Bulletin, 97,* 85–93.

MAXWELL, S. E., DELANEY, H. D., and DILL, C. A. (1984). Another look at ANCOVA versus blocking. *Psychological Bulletin, 95,* 136–147.

MAXWELL, S. E., DELANEY, H. D., and MANHEIMER, J. M. (1985). ANOVA of residuals and ANCOVA: Correcting an illusion by using model comparisons and graphs. *Journal of Educational Statistics, 10,* 197–209.

MCCABE, G. P., JR. (1980). The interpretation of regression analysis results in sex and race discrimination problems. *The American Statistician, 34,* 212–215.

MCCALL, R. B., and APPELBAUM, M. I. (1973). Bias in the analysis of repeated-measures designs: Some alternative approaches. *Child Development, 44,* 401–415.

MCGILL, W. J. (1963). Stochastic latency mechanisms. In R. D. Luce, R. R. Bush, and E. Galanter (eds.), *Handbook of mathematical psychology* (Vol. 1, pp. 309–360). New York: John Wiley.

MCKINLEY, J. C., and HATHAWAY, S. R. (1956). Scale 1 (Hypochondrias). In G. S. Welsh and W. G. Dahlstrom (eds.), *Basic readings on the MMPI in psychology and medicine* (pp. 64–72). Minneapolis: University of Minnesota Press.

MCNEMAR, Q. (1969). *Psychological statistics* (4th ed.). New York: John Wiley.

MEEHL, P. E. (1967). Theory-testing in psychology and physics: A methodological paradox. *Philosophy of Science, 34,* 103–115.

MEEHL, P. E. (1970a). Nuisance variables and the ex-post-facto design. In M. Radner and S. Winokur (eds.), *Minnesota studies in the philosophy of science. Volume IV: Analyses of theories and methods of physics and psychology* (pp. 373–402). Minneapolis: University of Minnesota Press.

MEEHL, P. E. (1970b). Psychological determinism and human rationality: A psychologist's reactions to Professor Karl Popper's "Of clouds and clocks." In M. Radner and S. Winokur (eds.), *Minnesota studies in the philosophy of science. Volume IV: Analyses of theories and methods of physics and psychology* (pp. 310–372). Minneapolis: University of Minnesota Press.

MEEHL, P. E. (1971). High school yearbooks: A reply to Schwarz. *Journal of Abnormal Psychology, 77,* 143–148.

MEEHL, P. E. (1978). Theoretical risks and tabular asterisks: Sir Karl, Sir Ronald, and the slow progress of soft psychology. *Journal of Consulting and Clinical Psychology, 46,* 806–834.

MEEHL, P. E. (1986). What social scientists don't understand. In D. W. Fiske and R. A. Shweder (eds.), *Metatheory in social science* (pp. 315–338). Chicago: University of Chicago Press.

MICHELL, J. (1986). Measurement scales and statistics: A clash of paradigms. *Psychological Bulletin, 100,* 398–407.

MILLER, R. G. (1981). *Simultaneous statistical inference* (2d ed.). New York: Springer-Verlag.

MILLIGAN, G. W., WONG, D. S., and THOMPSON, P. A. (1987). Robustness properties of nonorthogonal analysis of variance. *Psychological Bulletin, 101*, 464–470.

MOOD, A. M., GRAYBILL, F. A., and BOES, D. C. (1974). *Introduction to the theory of statistics* (3d ed.). New York: McGraw-Hill.

MORLEY, J. (1955). Auguste Comte. In *Encyclopedia Britannica*, Volume 6 (pp. 190–195). Chicago: Encyclopedia Britannica.

MORRISON, D. E., and HENKEL, R. E. (eds.) (1970). *The significance test controversy: A reader.* Chicago: Aldine.

MORRISON, D. F. (1976). *Multivariate statistical methods* (2d ed.). New York: McGraw-Hill.

MORRISON, D. F. (1983). *Applied linear statistical methods.* Englewood Cliffs, NJ: Prentice-Hall.

MYERS, J. L. (1979). *Fundamentals of experimental design* (3d ed.). Boston: Allyn & Bacon.

MYERS, J. L., DiCECCO, J. V., WHITE, J. B., and BORDEN, V. M. (1982). Repeated measurements on dichotomous variables: Q and F tests. *Psychological Bulletin, 92*, 517–525.

NAMBOODIRI, K. (1972). Experimental designs in which each subject is used repeatedly. *Psychological Bulletin, 77*, 54–64.

NAMBOODIRI, K. (1984). *Matrix algebra: An introduction.* Beverly Hills, CA: Sage.

NETER, J., WASSERMAN, W., and KUTNER, M. H. (1985). *Applied linear statistical models: Regression, analysis of variance, and experimental designs.* Homewood, IL: Richard D. Irwin.

NEWTON-SMITH, W. H. (1981). *The rationality of science.* London: Routledge & Kegan Paul.

NICEWANDER, W. A., and PRICE, J. M. (1983). Reliability of measurement and the power of statistical tests. *Psychological Bulletin, 94*, 524–533.

NOETHER, G. E. (1976). *Introduction to statistics: A nonparametric approach.* Boston: Houghton Mifflin.

NUNNALLY, J. C. (1978). *Psychometric theory* (2d ed.). New York: McGraw-Hill.

O'BRIEN, R. G. (1981). A simple test for variance effects in experimental designs. *Psychological Bulletin, 89*, 570–574.

O'BRIEN, R. G., and KAISER, M. K. (1985). MANOVA method for analyzing repeated measures designs: An extensive primer. *Psychological Bulletin, 97*, 316–333.

O'GRADY, K. E. (1982). Measures of explained variance: Cautions and limitations. *Psychological Bulletin, 92*, 766–777.

OLEJNIK, S. F., and ALGINA, J. (1985). A review of nonparametric alternatives to analysis of covariance. *Evaluation Review, 9*, 51–83.

OLLER, J. W., Jr. (ed.) (1989). *Language and experience: Classic pragmatism.* Lanham, MD: University Press of America.

OLSON, C. L. (1974). Comparative robustness of six tests in multivariate analysis of variance. *Journal of the American Statistical Association, 69*, 894–908.

OLSON, C. L. (1976). On choosing a test statistic in multivariate analysis of variance. *Psychological Bulletin, 83*, 579–586.

OVERALL, J. E., SPIEGEL, D. K., and COHEN, J. (1975). Equivalence of orthogonal and non-orthogonal analysis of variance. *Psychological Bulletin, 82*, 182–186.

OVERALL, J. E., and WOODWARD, J. A. (1977). Nonrandom assignment and the analysis of covariance. *Psychological Bulletin, 84*, 588–594.

PEDHAZUR, E. J. (1982). *Multiple regression in behavioral research: Explanation and prediction* (2d ed.). New York: Holt, Rinehart & Winston.

PEIRCE, C. S. (1878). Illustrations of the logic of science: Second paper—How to make our ideas clear. *Popular Science Monthly, 12,* 286–302.

PITMAN, E. J. G. (1937). Significance tests which may be applied to samples from any population: III. The analysis of variance test. *Biometrika, 29,* 322–335.

POPPER, K. R. (1968). *The logic of scientific discovery.* London: Hutchinson.

POPPER, K. R. (1972). *Objective knowledge: An evolutionary approach.* Oxford, England: Clarendon Press.

POPPER, K. R. (1976). A note on verisimilitude. *British Journal for the Philosophy of Science, 27,* 147–195.

POTTHOFF, R. F. (1964). On the Johnson-Neyman technique and some extensions thereof. *Psychometrika, 29,* 241–256.

POULTON, E. C. (1975). Range effects in experiments on people. *American Journal of Psychology, 88,* 3–32.

PRUITT, S. D. (1988). Multimodal assessment of experimentally manipulated affect: An investigation of mood induction with critical controls. Master's thesis, University of New Mexico, Albuquerque, NM.

RATZSCH, D. (1986). *Philosophy of science.* Downers Grove, IL: InterVarsity Press.

REICHARDT, C. S. (1979). The statistical analysis of data from nonequivalent group designs. In T. D. Cook and D. T. Campbell (eds.), *Quasi-experimentation: Design and analysis issues for field settings* (pp. 147–205). Chicago: Rand McNally.

RIMLAND, B. (1979). Death knell for psychotherapy? *American Psychologist, 31,* 192.

ROBINSON, D. N. (1981). *An intellectual history of psychology.* New York: Macmillan.

RODGERS, J. L., NICEWANDER, W. A., and TOOTHAKER, L. (1984). Linearly independent, orthogonal, and uncorrelated variables. *The American Statistician, 38,* 133–134.

ROETHLISBERGER, F. S., and DICKSON, W. J. (1939). *Management and the worker.* Cambridge, MA: Harvard University Press.

ROGAN, J. C., and KESELMAN, H. J. (1977). Is the ANOVA *F*-test robust to variance heterogeneity when sample sizes are equal? An investigation via a coefficient of variation. *American Educational Research Journal, 14,* 493–498.

ROGOSA, D. R. (1980). Comparing non-parallel regression lines. *Psychological Bulletin, 88,* 307–321.

ROGOSA, D. R. (1981). On the relationship between the Johnson-Neyman region of significance and statistical tests of parallel within-group regressions. *Educational and Psychological Measurement, 41,* 73–84.

ROGOSA, D. (1988). Myths about longitudinal research. In K. W. Schaie, R. T. Campbell, W. Meredith, and S. C. Rawlings (eds.), *Methodological issues in aging research.* New York: Springer-Verlag.

ROSEN, E. (ed. and trans.) (1959). *Three Copernican treatises.* New York: Dover.

ROSENTHAL, R. (1976). *Experimenter effects in behavioral research* (enlarged ed.). New York: Irvington.

ROSENTHAL, R. (1987). *Judgment studies: Design, analysis, and meta-analysis.* Cambridge, England: Cambridge University Press.

ROSENTHAL, R., and RUBIN, D. B. (1978). Interpersonal expectancy effects: The first 345 studies. *The Behavioral and Brain Sciences, 3,* 410–415.

Rosenthal, R., and Rubin, D. B. (1982). A simple, general purpose display of magnitude of experimental effect. *Journal of Educational Psychology, 74,* 166–169.

Rosenthal, R., and Rubin, D. B. (1985). Statistical analysis: Summarizing evidence versus establishing facts. *Psychological Bulletin, 97,* 527–529.

Rothstein, L. D. (1974). Reply to Poulton. *Psychological Bulletin, 81,* 199–200.

Rouanet, H., and Lépine, D. (1970). Comparison between treatments in a repeated-measures design: ANOVA and multivariate methods. *British Journal of Mathematical and Statistical Psychology, 23,* 147–163.

Rozeboom. W. W. (1979). Ridge regression: Bonanza or beguilement? *Psychological Bulletin, 86,* 242–249.

Rubin, D. B. (1977). Assignment to treatment group on the basis of a covariate. *Journal of Educational Statistics, 2,* 1–26.

Russell, B. (1914). *Our knowledge of the external world as a field for scientific method in philosophy.* London: George Allen & Unwin.

Russell, B. (1919a). *Introduction to mathematical philosophy.* London: George Allen & Unwin.

Russell, B. (1919b). On propositions. What they are and how they mean. *Aristotelian Society Proceedings, 2,* 1–43.

Russell, B. (1937). *Principles of mathematics.* New York: W. W. Norton.

Russell, B. (1950). *Human knowledge: Its scope and limits.* New York: Simon & Schuster.

Salmon, W. (1973). Confirmation. *Scientific American, 228,* 75–83.

Santa, J. L., Miller, J. J., and Shaw, M. L. (1979). Using quasi F to prevent alpha inflation due to stimulus variation. *Psychological Bulletin, 86,* 37–46.

Satterthwaite, F. E. (1946). An approximate distribution of estimates of variance components. *Biometrics Bulletin, 2,* 110–114.

Scheffé, H. (1959). *The analysis of variance.* New York: John Wiley.

Schrader, R. M., and Hettmansperger, T. P. (1980). Robust analysis of variance based upon a likelihood ratio criterion. *Biometrika, 67,* 93–101.

Searle, S. R. (1966). *Matrix algebra for the biological sciences (including applications in statistics).* New York: John Wiley.

Searle, S. R. (1987). *Linear models for unbalanced data.* New York: John Wiley.

Serlin, R. C., and Lapsley, D. K. (1985). Rationality in psychological research: The good-enough principle. *American Psychologist, 40,* 73–83.

Shavelson, R. J., Webb, N. M., and Burstein, L. (1986). Measurement of teaching. In M. C. Wittrock (ed.), *Handbook of research on teaching: A project of the American Educational Research Association* (3d ed.). New York: Macmillan.

Siegel, S. (1956). *Nonparametric statistics for the behavioral sciences.* New York: McGraw-Hill.

Smith, M. L., and Glass, G. V. (1977). Meta-analysis of psychotherapy outcome studies. *American Psychologist, 32,* 752–760.

Spencer, B. D. (1983). Test scores as social statistics: Comparing distributions. *Journal of Educational Statistics, 8,* 249–269.

Stevens, J. (1986). *Applied multivariate statistics for the social sciences.* Hillsdale, NJ: Lawrence Erlbaum Associates.

Stevens, S. S. (1946). On the theory of scales of measurement. *Science, 103,* 667–680.

STEVENS, S. S. (1951). Mathematics, measurement and psychophysics. In S. S. Stevens (ed.), *Handbook of experimental psychology* (pp. 1–49). New York: John Wiley.

STIGLER, S. M. (1986). *The history of statistics: The measurement of uncertainty before 1900.* Cambridge, MA: Belknap Press.

STRAHAN, R. F. (1981). Time urgency, Type A behavior, and effect strength. *Journal of Consulting and Clinical Psychology, 49,* 134.

SUPPE, F. (1977). *The structure of scientific theories* (2d ed.). Urbana, IL: University of Illinois Press.

TABACHNICK, B. G., and FIDELL, L. S. (1983). *Using multivariate statistics.* New York: Harper & Row.

TATSUOKA, M. M. (1988). *Multivariate analysis: Techniques for educational and psychological research* (2d ed.). New York: Macmillan.

TIMM, N. H. (1975). *Multivariate analysis with applications in education and psychology.* Monterey, CA: Brooks/Cole.

TIMM, N. H., & CARLSON, J. E. (1975). Analysis of variance through full rank models. *Multivariate Behavioral Research Monographs,* No. 75-1.

TITUS, H. H. (1964).. *Living issues in philosophy.* New York: American Book Company.

TOMARKEN, A. J., and SERLIN, R. C. (1986). Comparison of ANOVA alternatives under variance heterogeneity and specific noncentrality structures. *Psychological Bulletin, 99,* 90–99.

TOOTHAKER, L. E., and CHANG, H. (1980). On "The analysis of ranked data derived from completely randomized factorial designs." *Journal of Educational Statistics, 5,* 169–176.

TOWNSEND, J. T., and ASHBY, F. G. (1984). Measurement scales and statistics: The misconception misconceived. *Psychological Bulletin, 96,* 394–401.

TUKEY, J. W. (1953). *The problem of multiple comparisons.* Mimeographed monograph.

TUKEY, J. W. (1977). *Exploratory data analysis.* Reading, MA: Addison-Wesley.

UNDERWOOD B. J. (1957). *Psychological research.* New York: Appleton-Century-Crofts.

VASEY, M. W., & THAYER, J. F. (1987). The continuing problem of false positives in repeated measures ANOVA in psychophysiology: A multivariate solution. *Psychophysiology, 24,* 479–486.

VONESH, E. F. (1983). Efficiency of repeated measure designs versus completely randomized designs based on multiple comparisons. *Communications in Statistics—Theory and Methods, 12,* 289–302.

VONESH, E. F., and SCHORK, M. A. (1986). Sample sizes in the multivariate analysis of repeated measurements. *Biometrics, 42,* 601–610.

WAGENAAR, W. A. (1969). A note on the construction of digram-balanced Latin squares. *Psychological Bulletin, 72,* 384–386.

WALD, A., and WOLFOWITZ, J. (1944). Statistical tests based on permutations of the observations. *Annals of Mathematical Statistics, 15,* 358–372.

WEISBERG, H. I. (1979). Statistical adjustments and uncontrolled studies. *Psychological Bulletin, 86,* 1149–1164.

WELCH, B. L. (1938). The significance of the difference between two means when the population variances are unequal. *Biometrika, 29,* 350–362.

WELCH, B. L. (1951). On the comparison of several mean values: An alternative approach. *Biometrika, 38,* 330–336.

WHERRY, R. J. (1931). A new formula for predicting the shrinkage of the coefficient of multiple correlation. *Annals of Mathematical Statistics, 2*, 440–457.

WHITEHEAD, A. N. (1957). *The concept of nature.* Ann Arbor, MI: University of Michigan Press.

WIKE, E., and CHURCH, J. (1976). Comments on Clark's "The language-as-fixed-effect fallacy." *Journal of Verbal Learning and Verbal Behavior, 15*, 249–255.

WILCOX, R. R. (1985). On comparing treatment effects to a standard when the variances are unknown and unequal. *Journal of Educational Statistics, 10*, 45–54.

WILCOX, R. R. (1987a). New designs in analysis of variance. *Annual Review of Psychology, 38*, 29–60.

WILCOX, R. R. (1987b). *New statistical procedures for the social sciences: Modern solutions to basic problems.* Hillsdale, NJ: Lawrence Erlbaum Associates.

WILCOX, R. R., and CHARLIN, V. (1986). Comparing medians: A Monte Carlo study. *Journal of Educational Statistics, 11*, 263–274.

WILCOX, R. R., CHARLIN, V. L., and THOMPSON, K. L. (1986). New Monte Carlo results on the robustness of the ANOVA F, W, and F^* statistics. *Communications in Statistics— Simulation and Computation, 15*, 933–943.

WOODWORTH, R. S., and SCHLOSBERG, H. (1954). *Experimental Psychology.* New York: Holt, Rinehart & Winston.

WU, L. L. (1985). Robust m-estimation of location and regression. In N. B. Tuma (ed.), *Sociological Methodology 1985* (pp. 316–388). San Francisco: Jossey-Bass.

YEATON, W. H., and SECHREST, L. (1981). Meaningful measures of effect. *Journal of Consulting and Clinical Psychology, 49*, 766–767.

ZWICK. R., and MARASCUILO, L. A. (1984). Selection of pairwise multiple comparison procedures for parametric and nonparametric analysis of variance models. *Psychological Bulletin, 95*, 148–155.

Appendix D Solutions to Selected Exercises

Chapter 1

1. As discussed in the text, the Baconian view that the whole process of science can be purely objective and empirical is flawed with regard to:
   a. *Data collection*—Preexisting ideas of what is interesting and relevant necessarily influence the scientist's decisions about what to study.
   b. *Data analysis*—Selecting the most appropriate means for summarizing the collected data involves the judgment of the scientist, and although precise rules can be stated for certain steps of the process once a procedure has been decided upon, critical preliminary decisions, such as what statistical hypotheses should be tested and how, are certainly debatable.
   c. *Data interpretation*—The task of discovering theoretical mechanisms appropriate for explaining any particular phenomenon is not accomplished by following a specified set of logical rules.

3. The logical problem in the suggestion that a materialist monism is necessitated by empirical findings can be stated succinctly: one does not prove the nonexistence of nonempirical entities by empirical methods. To suggest that a materialistic monist position is necessitated by empirical findings is to fall into the logical error of begging the question, that is, of using as a premise of an argument the conclusion the argument is trying to prove. In the present case, the erroneous argument takes the following form as a solution to the problem of determining what exists:
   1. One can use empirical observation of material entities to determine what exists.
   2. With these methods, one observes only material entities.
   3. Therefore, all that exists is material.
   The argument rests on the premise stated in the first proposition, which is valid only if the conclusion stated in the third proposition is correct. Examples of this kind of argument in the history of psychology are given by Robinson (1981, Chapter 9).

   For our purposes, the general methodological lesson to be learned concerns the relationship between assumptions and conclusions. One must presuppose certain principles—for example, regarding the uniformity of nature—in order to do science; the validity of the conclusions one draws from data will rest on the validity of those presuppositions, but one's findings will not ensure or necessitate the validity of those presuppositions. Similarly, within statistics, conclusions reached are valid *under certain assumptions*. For example, under the assumption of homogeneity of within-group variances across groups, a statistical test may suggest that the means of two groups are different, but the test of means will say nothing about the validity of the homogeneity of variance assumption. As another example, and to anticipate developments in Chapter 2, the probability value associated with a test statistic assumes that a particular hypothesis is true, but it does not inform you of the probability that the hypothesis presupposed is true (cf. Exercise 5 at the end of Chapter 2).

9. The contrapositive of an assertion, in general, is that the negation of the conclusion of the assertion implies the negation of the antecedent condition assumed in the assertion. Thus, the contrapositive of the learning theorist's assertion is, "If partially reinforced animals do *not* persist longer in responding during extinction than continuously reinforced animals, then frustration theory is *not* correct."

10. Because students in the U.S. are not randomly assigned to public vs. Catholic high schools, you should not conclude from a difference between means on a mathematics achievement test that it is the education provided by the Catholic high schools that caused the scores of the Catholic students to be higher. One would be concerned as to whether there was a selection bias operating. The attribution of the cause of the difference to the nature of the high school education would be made more compelling if other information were to be presented showing that public and Catholic students were comparable on other background variables that could reasonably be viewed as contributing causes of mathematics achievement. In fact, it turns out, as Wolfle (1987) reports, that there are large pre-existing differences between the two groups of students on variables that would predict higher mathematics achievement for the Catholic students even if the mathematics instruction they received was the same as that received by the public school students. For example, the mothers and fathers of the Catholic students had higher levels of education and socioeconomic status, on the average, than the parents of the public school students. Within each group of students, these variables were related to students' achievement, and fathers' educational level in particular was predictive of higher mathematics achievement. This kind of information about selection factors operating makes the effectiveness of the high school education per se less compelling an explanation of the 3-point difference in mathematics achievement scores.

Chapter 2

5. False. The *p* value is the probability of the observed (or more extreme) results, given that you assume that the results are due to chance. The question, on the other hand, asserts that the *p* value is the probability that "chance," or the null hypothesis, is the correct explanation of the results. The distinction is an important one.

    The point can be underscored by using conditional probability notation. The *p* value is a probability of the form: Pr (data | null hypothesis), that is, the probability that data having particular characteristics will occur, assuming that the null hypothesis is true. However, *p* values are frequently misunderstood as indicating Pr (null hypothesis | data), that is, the probability that the null hypothesis is true, given the data (see Bakan, 1966). Arriving at such a probability requires far more knowledge than is typically available in a scientific investigation—for example, what are the alternative hypotheses that are possible, and for each, what is the prior probability that it is true and the probability of obtaining the data if it were true? Thus, although one may wish that the probability of the truth of a particular hypothesis could be determined on the basis of the results of a study, that is not the information yielded by a Fisherian hypothesis test.

7. Decisions about whether the staff member's performance is significantly different from chance can be made by carrying out Fisher's exact test. To this end it is convenient to summarize the obtained results as a 2 × 2 table, where the columns correspond to the actual categories of patients and the rows indicate the staff member's judgments about who was released early. Thus, "5 out of 6 correct" would be indicated by the following table:

		Actual		
		Released	*Not Released*	
Judged	*Released*	5	1	6
	Not Released	1	5	6
		6	6	12

Following the logic used in the tea-tasting example, there are $_6C_5 \cdot {}_6C_1$ ways of choosing 5 out of the 6 actually "released" patients and 1 out of the 6 actually "not released" patients, or $6 \cdot 6 = 36$ ways of correctly identifying 5 out of 6 early-release patients. This number must be considered relative to the $_{12}C_6 = (12 \cdot 11 \cdot 10 \cdot 9 \cdot 8 \cdot 7)/(6 \cdot 5 \cdot 4 \cdot 3 \cdot 2 \cdot 1) = 924$ different ways of selecting 6 patients out of the total group of 12. Thus, given that the staff member knew 6 patients were released, the probability that he would identify 5 of those 6 correctly just by guessing is

$$Pr(5 \text{ of } 6 \text{ correct}) = \frac{_6C_5 \cdot {}_6C_1}{_{12}C_6} = \frac{36}{924} = .039$$

Notice that, with the table arrayed as above with the actual categories corresponding to the columns, the combinations involved in the probability are the number of ways of choosing the number indicated in the first row out of the column total. Thus, the denominator of the probability is the number of ways of choosing the number of patients judged to have been released, that is, the marginal total for the first row or 6, out of the total for the table, 12. Similarly, the numerator involves the product of the number of combinations of ways of choosing the number indicated in the first row cells from the corresponding column totals. Notice also that the numbers chosen (5 and 1) and the sizes of the subgroups from which they are chosen (6 and 6) in the numerator must sum to, respectively, the number chosen (6) and the total sample size (12) in the denominator.

To determine a significance level, one needs to compute the probability not only of the obtained results but also of every other outcome that provides as much or more evidence of association (cf. Hays, 1981, p. 553). Clearly, getting all 6 correct would be stronger evidence of an association between the actual categories and the staff member's judgments than that obtained. The probability of this occurring would be computed similarly:

$$Pr(6 \text{ of } 6 \text{ correct}) = \frac{_6C_6 \cdot {}_6C_0}{_{12}C_6} = \frac{1 \cdot 1}{924} = \frac{1}{924} = .001$$

The problem also requests that a *two-tailed* test be performed. To carry out a two-tailed test, one needs to consider the possibility of judgments that are predominantly incorrect but that are as strongly indicative of an association between the actual and judged classifications (albeit in the opposite direction) as the obtained results. (In actual practice, neither the staff member nor you might be persuaded that you owe him money if his judgments were surprisingly worse than would be expected by chance. Nonetheless, carrying out two-tailed tests here allows an important pedagogical point to be made about when the two tails of the distribution used in Fisher's exact test will be symmetrical.) It turns out that, when either the column totals are equal to each other or the row totals are equal to each other, the problem is perfectly symmetrical. For example, the probability of getting 5 of 6 incorrect is the same as the probability of getting 5 of 6 correct. Thus, the probability of results as good as or better than those obtained can be doubled to obtain a final answer that may be interpreted as having a two-tailed significance. To illustrate this and to summarize the answer for the current example, we have

$$Pr(\text{results as extreme as or more extreme than those obtained})$$

$$= Pr(5 \text{ of } 6 \text{ or } 6 \text{ of } 6 \text{ correct}) + Pr(1 \text{ of } 6 \text{ or } 0 \text{ of } 6 \text{ correct})$$

$$= \left(\frac{36}{924} + \frac{1}{924}\right) + \left(\frac{36}{924} + \frac{1}{924}\right) = .04 + .04 = .08$$

Because the significance level of .08 is greater than the specified alpha level of .05, you conclude the results are not significant. You do not owe the staff member any money.

If the staff member had identified 5 of 6 early-release patients out of a total set of 15, the computed probability would of course be different. The obtained results in such a case could be summarized as follows:

		Actual		
		Released	Not Released	
Judged	Released	5	1	6
	Not Released	1	8	9
		6	9	15

The probability of these results is

$$Pr(5 \text{ of } 6 \text{ correct, out of } 15) = \frac{{}_6C_5 \cdot {}_9C_1}{{}_{15}C_6} = \frac{6 \cdot 9}{5005} = \frac{54}{5005} = .0108$$

The one outcome that would be better would be to classify all 6 correctly:

$$Pr(6 \text{ of } 6 \text{ correct, out of } 15) = \frac{{}_6C_6 \cdot {}_9C_0}{{}_{15}C_6} = \frac{1}{5005} = .0002$$

Thus, the probability of results as good as or better than those obtained is

$$Pr(5 \text{ of } 6 \text{ or } 6 \text{ of } 6, \text{ out of } 15) = \frac{54 + 1}{5005} = .0110$$

Now, since both row totals are unequal and column totals are unequal, one cannot simply double probabilities to get a significance level but must examine probabilities of predominantly incorrect classifications to see if they are as extreme as the probabilities of these predominantly correct classifications. Again treating the marginal totals as fixed, we might first consider the likelihood of getting 5 out of 6 incorrect, as we did before. The corresponding table would be

		Actual		
		Released	*Not Released*	
Judged	*Released*	1	5	6
	Not Released	5	4	9
		6	9	15

The probability of these results is

$$Pr(1 \text{ of } 6 \text{ correct, out of } 15) = \frac{{}_6C_1 \cdot {}_9C_5}{{}_{15}C_6} = \frac{6 \cdot 126}{5005} = \frac{756}{5005} = .1510$$

This value is considerably larger than the .0108 probability of classifying 5 of 6 *correctly*. In effect, increasing the number of patients who were not released results in there being many more ways of being wrong, making this a more probable outcome. Because the probability of 5 of 6 incorrect is less extreme, we do not need to consider it in determining the significance level of the outcome.

We also need to consider the possibility of being totally incorrect by chance alone; perhaps that outcome would be as improbable as what was observed. Being totally incorrect would mean choosing 0 of the 6 actual early-release patients and instead selecting all 6 from the 9 who were not released. The probability of this outcome is

$$Pr(0 \text{ of } 6 \text{ correct, out of } 15) = \frac{{}_6C_0 \cdot {}_9C_6}{{}_{15}C_6} = \frac{1 \cdot 84}{5005} = \frac{84}{5005} = .0168$$

Thus the probability of missing them all is also a more likely outcome in this situation than getting 5 of 6 correct by chance alone.

This means that the only other chance outcome that is as extremely unlikely as or more extremely unlikely than the observed outcome is correctly identifying all the early-release patients. Thus, in this case the two-tailed probability associated with the observed results turns out to be the same as the one-tailed probability, namely .0110. We would conclude that 5 of 6 correct identifications out of a set of 15 is compelling evidence for the staff member's claim. In this case, he could collect on his bet.

9. a. The observed sum of differences is 372, that is, $22 + 34 + 38 + 38 + 12 + 3 + 55 + 29 + 76 + 23 - 17 + 39 = 372$.

   b. 2^{12} or 4096 assignments of signs to differences are possible.

   c. (1) When all 12 differences are assigned positive values, the largest possible sum of 406 results; e.g., $372 - (-17) + 17 = 406$.

      (2) If either or both of the absolute differences that are less than 17 were negative, one would obtain a sum in between the maximal sum of 406 and the observed sum of 372. There are three such sums—one when 3 has the only negative sign, one when 12 has the only negative sign, and one when both 3 and 12 are negative:

Case	Sum
"3" negative	$406 - 3 - 3 = 400$
"12" negative	$406 - 12 - 12 = 382$
"3" and "12" negative	$406 - 3 - 12 - 3 - 12 = 376$

(3) We have enumerated the 5 assignments of signs that result in sums greater than or equal to the observed sum of 372. If all 12 signs were reversed in each of these 5 assignments, the 5 most extremely negative sums possible would be obtained, namely, $-372, -406, -400, -382$, and -376. Thus, 10 of the 4096 possible assignments of signs to the obtained differences result in sums at least as large in absolute value as the obtained sum.

Since the probability of obtaining a sum at least as extreme as that observed is only 10/4096 or .0024, one would reject the null hypothesis that it was equally likely that sums would be preceded by negative as by positive signs. Thus, it appears on the basis of this experiment that the enriched environment caused an increase in the size of the cortex.

10. a. Several issues regarding Darwin's design may be commented on and related to the four kinds of validity discussed in Chapter 1. The most important relate to his basic design strategy, which was to attempt to achieve an unbiased and precise experiment by comparing each cross-fertilized plant against a matched self-fertilized plant under conditions controlled to be as equal as possible. As Darwin was well aware, many factors, besides the independent variable encapsulated in the two seeds for a pair, would influence the height the plants ultimately achieved. Thus he attempted to achieve a valid experiment by trying to ensure that the plants experienced equal soil fertility, illumination, and watering. That he would be unable to achieve exact equality in such conditions, even within a pair of plants, is evident not only logically but in the data we have to analyze, as we shall see.

One can think of the environmental conditions for each potential plant site as being predetermined. Certainly Darwin was aware of some of the relevant factors, such as amount of watering, and just as certainly there were factors he could not assess, such as air currents around the plants. The internal validity of the experiment would have been ensured had Darwin, once the plots were divided into 15 pairs of locations where environmental conditions were thought to be similar within a pair of locations, randomly assigned the cross-fertilized plant to one location and the matched self-fertilized plant to the other paired location. As it was, the internal validity of the experiment has to rest on the presumption that Darwin knew enough not to bias conditions in favor of the cross-fertilized plants by the particular set of sites to which he assigned them. Lack of perfect knowledge of the relevant causes virtually ensures some inadvertent biasing of the true difference between the plant types.

Less critical concerns relate to external and construct validity. That Darwin attempted to equalize conditions not only within pairs of plants but across pairs as well results in diminished external validity. The fact that the precision of a matched-pairs experiment is much more closely tied to the similarity of conditions within a pair than across pairs seemed not to be appreciated. Allowing differences among pairs of sites would have permitted greater statistical generalization to a wider variety of conditions. In terms of construct validity, presumably the height of the plant was an indicant of the strength or hardiness or productivity of the plant, and other measures of the plant may have been more appropriate for specific purposes of interest.

b. (1) As shown in the table of data in the answer to part (b)(2), 13 of the 15 differences in columns II and III favor the cross-fertilized plant. If cross-fertilization had no effect, each of the 15 differences would have a .5 probability of being positive, and one would expect .5(15) = 7.5 differences on the average to favor cross-fertilization. One can determine if the observed number of differences favoring cross-fertilization is significantly different from this expected number by using the binomial probability formula, namely,

$$Pr(r \text{ successes}) = {}_nC_r p^r (1 - p)^{n-r}$$

where r is the required number of successes, n is the number of trials, and p is the probability of success. Here a success is defined as a difference favoring cross-fertilization, and each difference constitutes a trial or an opportunity for a success. The statistical significance here is determined by the "sign test" which simply computes the binomial probability of results at least as extreme as those observed. The probability of 13 or more differences favoring cross-fertilization is

$Pr(13 \text{ or more successes})$

$$= {}_{15}C_{13}(\tfrac{1}{2})^{13}(1 - \tfrac{1}{2})^2 + {}_{15}C_{14}(\tfrac{1}{2})^{14}(1 - \tfrac{1}{2})^1 + {}_{15}C_{15}(\tfrac{1}{2})^{15}(1 - \tfrac{1}{2})^0$$

$$= \left[\frac{15!}{13!2!} + \frac{15!}{14!1!} + \frac{15!}{15!0!} \right] (\tfrac{1}{2})^{15}$$

$$= [105 + 15 + 1]\frac{1}{32{,}768} = \frac{121}{32{,}768} = .00369$$

Given the symmetry of the distribution under the null hypothesis that $p = .5$, the probability of 2 or fewer successes is also .00369. Thus, the significance of the observed number of differences equals the probability of the observed or more extreme results:

$$Pr(2 \text{ or fewer successes, or 13 or more successes}) = .00369 + .00369$$

$$= .00738.$$

Since this is considerably less than .05, we would reject the null hypothesis that the probability of a difference favoring cross-fertilization is .5.

(2) The simplest possible parametric test appropriate for these data is a matched-pairs t test. The test is carried out as a one-sample t test on the differences shown next.

Crossed	Self-fertilized	Difference
$23\frac{4}{8}$	$17\frac{3}{8}$	$6\frac{1}{8}$
12	$20\frac{3}{8}$	$-8\frac{3}{8}$
21	20	1
22	20	2
$19\frac{1}{8}$	$18\frac{3}{8}$	$\frac{6}{8}$
$21\frac{4}{8}$	$18\frac{5}{8}$	$2\frac{7}{8}$
$22\frac{1}{8}$	$18\frac{5}{8}$	$3\frac{4}{8}$
$20\frac{3}{8}$	$15\frac{2}{8}$	$5\frac{1}{8}$
$18\frac{2}{8}$	$16\frac{4}{8}$	$1\frac{6}{8}$
$21\frac{5}{8}$	18	$3\frac{5}{8}$
$23\frac{2}{8}$	$16\frac{2}{8}$	7
21	18	3
$22\frac{1}{8}$	$12\frac{6}{8}$	$9\frac{3}{8}$
23	$15\frac{4}{8}$	$7\frac{4}{8}$
12	18	-6
Mean difference, $\bar{D}$		**2.617**
Standard deviation, s_D		**4.718**

We wish to test the null hypothesis that the population mean difference μ_D is 0. We can do so by using the test statistic (see Hays, 1981, p. 297)

$$t = \frac{\bar{D} - \mu_D}{s_{\bar{D}}}$$

where $\bar{D}$ is the mean difference score, and $s_{\bar{D}}$ is the estimated standard error of the mean and is defined as

$$s_{\bar{D}} = \frac{s_D}{\sqrt{n}}$$

Here we have

$$s_{\bar{D}} = \frac{4.718}{\sqrt{15}} = \frac{4.718}{3.873} = 1.218$$

and

$$t = \frac{\bar{D} - \mu_D}{s_{\bar{D}}} = \frac{2.617 - 0}{1.218} = 2.148$$

which just exceeds the critical t value of 2.145 for a two-tailed test with 14 degrees of freedom and α of .05. In particular, the p value associated with an observed t of 2.148 is .0497. The p value for the parametric t test is in this case considerably less extreme than the p value for the nonparametric sign test of part (b) (1). This will not in general be the case. The sign test ignores the magnitude of the differences and thus in effect treats them all as equal. The t test of course uses a mean that reflects all the differences, and in these data the two negative differences happen to be two of the largest differences in the set and thus bring down the mean more than they would if they were only average in absolute value. So, since the two negative differences are large ones, the evidence in favor of cross-fertilization is less compelling when appraised using a procedure that considers the magnitude of the disconfirming evidence in these two cases. In a sense, the sign test makes the evidence appear stronger than it really is by not taking into account the fact that the differences that do favor self-fertilization in these data are large ones.

(3) The assumption required for the sign test is only that the trials or replications or pairs of plants included in the experiment are independent of each other. In the case of the t test, one not only assumes that the differences are independent of each other but also that, over replications of the study, the differences would be distributed as a normally distributed random variable.

(4) Carrying out a randomization test for these data requires consideration of the mean difference resulting from each of the 32,768 possible assignments of signs to the 15 observed differences. The significance level for a two-tailed randomization test is simply twice the proportion of these mean differences that are equal to or greater than the observed mean of 2.617. Although only two of the observed differences were negative, because these were large scores, there are many combinations of signs (including some with as many as six negative signs being assigned to small differences) that result in mean differences larger than 2.617. Enumeration of these is very tedious, but Fisher (1935/1971, p. 46) reports that 863 of the 32,768 mean differences are at least this large and positive, and so the significance level of the randomization test is $2(863/32,768) = 2(.02634) = .0527$.

The only assumptions required by the randomization test are that the differences are independent of each other and that not only their signs but their magnitudes are meaningful. Notice that all three of the tests make the assumption of independence, and we are not assured by Darwin's procedures that this was achieved. Because of the lack of random assignment, it is conceivable that some factor was inadvertently confounded with the type of fertilization. Any causal factor that Darwin's procedures made systematically different across levels of the independent variable would thus invalidate all three tests. To take a blatant example, if all the cross-fertilized plants were given a more southerly exposure than the self-fertilized member of the pair, and if southerly exposure is good for plant growth, then the difference scores would not be independent.

The hypothesis tested by the randomization test is that the observed set of signed differences arose by a process of assigning a $+$ or $-$ sign with equal likelihood to each of the absolute differences observed. Because of the lack of random assignment, we cannot be assured that this test or the others are valid. However, assuming the test's validity, we have only marginal evidence for the difference between the two kinds of fertilization, since the results fail to reach the conventional .05 level. These data would need to be combined with other similar results to make the case compelling.

c. Although the mean of Galton's differences in column VIII is necessarily the same as the mean of the differences between the original pairs of plants in columns II and III, the mean difference is made to appear far too reliable by the re-pairing of the data. In essence, the differences in column VIII make it look as though Darwin had far greater control over his experimental material than he did. In particular, the data as arranged in columns VI and VII imply that Darwin knew enough to control the factors affecting the height of plants to such an extent that, if one member of a pair were the tallest of its type, the other member of the pair would also be the tallest in *its* series. Despite his best efforts to achieve homogeneous pairs of plants, Darwin in fact was not able to approach this degree of control. Rather than the correlation approaching $+1$ as implied by columns VI and VII, the correlation of the heights of the original pairs was actually negative, $r = -.338$. Perhaps because of competition for resources between plants planted close together, all of Darwin's efforts to achieve homogeneous plants within pairs were not sufficient in that the taller one member of a pair in his data, the shorter the other member is expected to be.

Carrying out the computations for a matched-pairs t test on the rearranged data, we find that the standard deviation s_D of the differences in column VIII is only 1.9597. This yields a standard error of 0.5060 and a t value as follows:

$$t = \frac{2.617}{0.516} = 5.171$$

The probability of a result this large occurring, given that the null hypothesis is true, is less than 2 in 10,000 or .0002. Similarly, when a randomization test is performed on the differences in column VIII, the significance level is extreme, with only 46 of the 32,678 mean differences being as large as or larger in absolute value than the one obtained, implying $p = .0014$.

Thus, the mean difference by Galton's approach is made to appear so reliable that it would occur only on the order of 10 times in 10,000 replications if there were no effect of cross-fertilization. In fact, results as extreme as those obtained would occur 5 times in 100 by chance alone, or on the order of 500 times in 10,000 replications. Galton's rearrangement in effect makes the evidence appear 50 times more compelling than it really is.

Chapter 3

5. False. MS_B is an estimate of the variance of the individual scores in the population. It is, however, based on the variability among the sample means. In particular, in an equal-n design, MS_B is n times the variance of the sample means, or n times the quantity that estimates the variance of the sampling distribution of sample means.

7. False. Although in one-way designs it is most often the case that E_R will equal SS_{Total}, this will not always be the case. E_R equals SS_{Total} when the restriction being tested is that the means of all groups are equal. In other cases E_R could be either larger or smaller than SS_{Total}, depending on the restriction of interest.

8. The loss function used to solve estimation problems in this book is to summarize the errors by squaring each one and summing them over all observations. Parameters are estimated so as to minimize such losses, that is, to satisfy the least squares criterion.

10. a. Although 24 animals were used in Experiment 2, because they represent 12 pairs of litter mates whose cortex weights are expected to be positively correlated, there are only 12 independent observations. The information from each pair can be summarized as a difference score that we may denote D_i, as shown below. (The error scores on the right are used in the answer to part (d).)

Experiment #2

Exp.	Con.	D_i	$e_{i_F} = D_i - \bar{D}$	$e_{i_F}^2$	$e_{i_R}^2 = D_i^2$
707	669	38	−7	49	1444
740	650	90	45	2025	8100
745	651	94	49	2401	8836
652	627	25	−20	400	625
649	656	−7	−52	2704	49
676	642	34	−11	121	1156
699	698	1	−44	1936	1
696	648	48	3	9	2304
712	676	36	−9	81	1296
708	657	51	6	36	2601
749	692	57	12	144	3249
691	618	73	28	784	5329
				10,690	34,990

b. The full model for the 12 difference scores might be written

$$D_i = \mu_D + \varepsilon_i$$

c. Here we want to test the null hypothesis (restriction) that the mean difference score μ_D is zero. The restricted model incorporating this constraint is

$$D_i = 0 + \varepsilon_i$$

d. The estimated parameter value for the full model is the sample mean of the difference scores $\bar{D}$, which here is 45. Subtracting this from the observed differences, we obtain the error scores e_{i_F} for the full model shown in the preceding data table. Squaring these errors and summing yields $E_F = 10,690$, as shown. Alternatively, if one were computing E_F using a hand calculator having a single-key standard deviation function, one could compute E_F as $(n - 1)s_D^2$. Here $n = 12$, and $s_D = 31.374$, and consequently

$$E_F = (12 - 1)(31.174)^2 = 11(971.818) = 10,690$$

Since there are no parameters to estimate in the restricted model, the errors are the differences between the observed difference scores and 0, or simply the observed difference scores themselves. Thus, the values of $e_{i_R}^2$ are as shown in the rightmost column of the table part (a) and sum to 34,990. Alternatively, one could obtain $E_R - E_F$ as the sum over all observations of the squared differences of the predictions of the two models (see Equation 3.64), that is

$$E_R - E_F = \sum_{\text{all obs}} (\hat{Y}_F - \hat{Y}_R)^2 = \sum_i (\bar{D} - 0)^2 = n\bar{D}^2 = 12 \cdot 45^2 = 12 \cdot 2025 = 24,300$$

and so

$$E_R = E_F + 24,300 = 10,690 + 24,300 = 34,970$$

e. The full model requires estimation of one parameter, and the restricted model none, so $df_F = n - 1 = 12 - 1 = 11$ and $df_R = n = 12$. Thus we have

$$F = \frac{(E_R - E_F)/(df_R - df_F)}{E_F/df_F} = \frac{(34,990 - 10,690)/(12 - 11)}{10,690/11} = \frac{24,300/1}{971.818} = 25.005$$

which exceeds the critical value of 19.7 from Table A-2 for an F with 1 and 11 degrees of freedom at $\alpha = .001$.

f. On the basis of the test in part (e), we reject the restricted model. That is, we conclude that it is not reasonable to presume that the population mean cortex weight is the same for experimental as for control animals. Or stated positively, we conclude that being raised in an enriched (as opposed to a deprived) environment results in rats that have heavier cortexes.

g. The data from the three experiments can again be summarized by using difference scores. We will use these differences to compare the following two models:

$$\text{Full model:} \quad D_{ij} = \mu_j + \varepsilon_{ij_F}$$

$$\text{Restricted model:} \quad D_{ij} = \mu + \varepsilon_{ij_R}$$

The parameter estimates for the full model are the mean difference scores for the three experiments, $\bar{D}_1 = 26$, $\bar{D}_2 = 45$, and $\bar{D}_3 = 31$. Subtracting these from the observed differences yields the errors and squared errors shown next.

Experiment 1			Experiment 2			Experiment 3		
D_{i1}	e_{i1}	e_{i1}^2	D_{i2}	e_{i2}	e_{i2}^2	D_{i3}	e_{i3}	e_{i3}^2
33	7	49	38	−7	49	22	−9	81
32	6	36	90	45	2025	34	3	9
16	−10	100	94	49	2401	38	7	49
6	−20	400	25	−20	400	58	27	729
24	−2	4	−7	−52	2704	12	−19	361
17	−9	81	34	−11	121	3	−28	784
64	38	1444	1	−44	1936	55	24	576
7	−19	361	48	3	9	29	−2	4
89	63	3969	36	−9	81	76	45	2025

	Experiment 1			Experiment 2			Experiment 3	
	−2	−28	784	51	6	36	23	−8	64
	11	−15	225	57	12	144	−17	−48	2304
	15	−11	121	73	28	784	39	8	64
$\sum$	312		7574	540		10,690	372		7050
$\bar{D}_j$	26			45			31		
s_j	26.240			31.174			25.316		

Thus, the sum of squared errors for the full model is

$$E_F = \sum_j \sum_i e_{ij}^2 = 7574 + 10{,}690 + 7050 = 25{,}314$$

Equivalently we could use the standard deviations (see Equation 62) as follows:

$$E_F = (n-1)\sum_j s_j^2 = (12-1)(26.240^2 + 31.174^2 + 25.316^2)$$

$$= 11(688.546 + 971.818 + 640.909)$$

$$= 7574.006 + 10{,}689.998 + 7049.999$$

$$= 25{,}314.003$$

This would enable us to obtain the same result within rounding errors.

The numerator sum of squares for our test statistic may be obtained by taking n times the sum of squared deviations of group means around the grand mean (see Equation 3.58). Because the grand mean $\bar{D}$, the estimate of the restricted model's population mean, is here $(26 + 45 + 31)/3 = 34$, we have

$$E_R - E_F = n \sum_{j=1}^{a} (\bar{D}_j - \bar{D})^2$$

$$= 12[(26-34)^2 + (45-34)^2 + (31-34)^2]$$

$$= 12[(-8)^2 + (11)^2 + (-3)^2]$$

$$= 12 \cdot [64 + 121 + 9] = 12 \cdot 194 = 2328$$

The full model with its 3 parameters has $N - a = 36 - 3 = 33$ degrees of freedom. The restricted model requires estimation of only one mean, so $df_R = N - 1 = 36 - 1 = 35$. Thus, our test statistic may be computed as

$$F = \frac{(E_R - E_F)/(df_R - df_F)}{E_F/df_F} = \frac{2328/(35-33)}{25{,}314/33} = \frac{2328/2}{767.09} = \frac{1164}{767.09} = 1.517.$$

Since this is smaller than the critical value of $F(2, 33)$ = approximately 3.3 (either rounding the denominator degrees of freedom down to 30, or interpolating between the table values of 3.32 and 3.23 for 30 and 40 denominator degrees of freedom, respectively), we cannot reject the restricted model. The time of year when the experiments were run did not seem to affect the magnitude of the effect of the environment on the cortex weights.

11. a. Designating the experimental group as group 1 and the control group as group 2, we wish to test the restriction $\mu_1 = \mu_2$ by comparing the following models:

$$\text{Full model:} \quad Y_{ij} = \mu_j + \varepsilon_{ij_F}$$

$$\text{Restricted model:} \quad Y_{ij} = \mu + \varepsilon_{ij_R}$$

The parameter estimates for the full model are the group sample means, that is, $\hat{\mu}_1 = \bar{Y}_1 = 702$ and $\hat{\mu}_2 = \bar{Y}_2 = 657$, whereas for the restricted model the single population mean is estimated by the grand mean, that is, $\hat{\mu} = \bar{Y} = 679.5$. The errors for the full model are as follows:

	Experimental Group			Control Group		
	Y_{i1}	e_{i1}	e_{i1}^2	Y_2	e_{i2}	e_{i2}^2
	707	5	25	669	12	144
	740	38	1444	650	−7	49
	745	43	1849	651	−6	36
	652	−50	2500	627	−30	900
	649	−53	2809	656	−1	1
	676	−26	676	642	−15	225
	699	−3	9	698	41	1681
	696	−6	36	648	−9	81
	712	10	100	676	19	361
	708	6	36	657	0	0
	749	47	2209	692	35	1225
	691	−11	121	618	−39	1521
$\sum$			11,814			6224
$\bar{Y}_j$	702			657		
s_j	32.772			23.787		

Thus,

$$E_F = \sum_j \sum_i e_{ij}^2 = 11{,}814 + 6224 = 18{,}038$$

and

$$E_R - E_F = n\sum_j (\bar{Y}_j - \bar{Y})^2 = 12[(702 - 679.5)^2 + (657 - 679.5)^2]$$
$$= 12[(22.5)^2 + (-22.5)^2] = 12[506.25 + 506.25]$$
$$= 12{,}150$$

which means $E_R = E_F + 12{,}150 = 18{,}038 + 12{,}150 = 30{,}188$. Because at the moment we are acting as if the observations within a pair are independent, we have $df_F = n - a = 24 - 2 = 22$ and $df_R = N - 1 = 24 - 1 = 23$. Thus, our test statistic is

$$F = \frac{(E_R - E_F)/(df_R - df_F)}{E_F/df_F} = \frac{12{,}150/(23 - 22)}{18{,}038/22} = \frac{12{,}150}{819.909} = 14.819$$

which just exceeds the critical F of 14.4 for 1 and 22 degrees of freedom at $\alpha = .001$.
b. Certainly, we have strong evidence ($p < .001$) against the null hypothesis in both the independent groups analysis conducted for the current problem and the matched pairs analysis conducted in parts (a)–(f) of the previous problem. However, closer inspection reveals that there is slightly less evidence against the restricted model here. If p values were computed by a statistical computer program, we would see that,

in the current analysis, we have $p = .0009$ associated with $F(1, 22) = 14.819$ here, whereas $p = .0004$ for $F(1, 11) = 25.005$ in Exercise 10(e). There are two main differences in the analyses that are relevant. The more important difference is in the magnitude of E_F, which appears in the denominator of our test statistic. E_F in the independent groups analysis is 68.7% larger than E_F in the matched pairs analysis (18,038 vs. 10,690) and is responsible for the F being 68.7% larger in the matched pairs analysis than in the independent groups analysis. This sum of squared errors will be smaller (and hence the F larger) in the matched pairs analysis whenever the pairs of scores are positively correlated, which they are here, $r = .4285$. This within-pair predictability of scores allows us to reduce our errors and results in more sensitive tests, as we discuss extensively in Part III of the text.

A secondary difference in the analysis is in the denominator degrees of freedom, which determine the particular F distribution used to determine the significance of the observed F. As df_F increases, the critical value required to declare a result significant at a given p value decreases. While for larger values of n this decrease is trivial, for relatively small n the difference in critical F's is noticeable, particularly for very small p values. For example, for $p = .05$, the critical F of 4.84 for 1 and 11 degrees of freedom is 13% larger than the critical F of 4.30 for 1 and 22 degrees of freedom, but for $p = .001$, the critical F is 37% larger in the matched pairs case (19.7 vs. 14.4). Even so, the matched pairs analysis is more compelling here because the cost of having fewer degrees of freedom is more than outweighed by the benefit of reduced error variability.

12. a. To standardize the observed difference between means of $702 - 657 = 45$ milligrams, we need to determine an estimate of the within-group standard deviation as indicated in Equations 3.83 through 3.86. The corresponding pooled estimate of the within-group variance was determined in the answer to the preceding question to be 819.909. Thus, the estimated standard deviation is

$$S = \sqrt{E_F/df_F} = \sqrt{819.909} = 28.634$$

This implies that the difference in mean cortex weights is more than one and a half standard deviations:

$$\hat{d} = \frac{\bar{Y}_1 - \bar{Y}_2}{S} = \frac{45}{28.634} = 1.572$$

b. The proportion of the total sum of squares accounted for by the between-group differences is, from Equation 3.90 and the results of the preceding problem,

$$R^2 = \frac{E_R - E_F}{E_F} = \frac{12,150}{30,188} = .4025$$

A corrected estimate of the proportion of variability in the population accounted for by group membership is provided by $\hat{\omega}^2$ as defined in Equation 91:

$$\hat{\omega}^2 = \frac{(E_R - E_F) - (a - 1)(E_F/df_F)}{E_R + (E_F/df_F)} \tag{3.91}$$

$$= \frac{12,150 - (1)(819.909)}{30,188 + 819.909} = \frac{11,330.091}{31,007.909} = .3654$$

14. Given $\mu_1 = 21$, $\mu_2 = 24$, $\mu_3 = 30$, $\mu_4 = 45$, and $\sigma_\varepsilon = 20$, we need to compute σ_m and f, as indicated in Equations 3.88 and 3.89; where $\mu = (\sum \mu_j)/a = (21 + 24 + 30 + 45)/4 = 120/4 = 30$:

$$\sigma_m = \sqrt{\frac{\sum_j (\mu_j - \mu)^2}{a}}$$

$$= \sqrt{\frac{(21 - 30)^2 + (24 - 30)^2 + (30 - 30)^2 + (45 - 30)^2}{4}}$$

$$= \sqrt{\frac{81 + 36 + 0 + 225}{4}} = \sqrt{\frac{342}{4}} \doteq \sqrt{85.5} = 9.2466$$

$$f = \frac{\sigma_m}{\sigma_e} = \frac{9.2466}{20} = .4623$$

From this, we may obtain ϕ for trial values of n, using Equation 3.100, and determine the resulting power from Table A-11. With $n = 9$ per group, we would have

$$\phi = f\sqrt{n} = .4623\sqrt{9} = .4623(3) = 1.3869,$$

which would result in $df_F = 4(9 - 1) = 4 \cdot 8 = 32$. However, the vertical line above a ϕ of 1.4 for the chart with 3 numerator degrees of freedom intersects the power curve for 30 denominator degrees of freedom at a height corresponding to just less than a power of .60. Thus, we need to try a larger value for n. If we were to increase n to 16, we would have

$$\phi = f\sqrt{n} - .4623\sqrt{16} = .4623(4) = 1.8492$$

which for $df_F = 4(16 - 1) = 60$ would result in a power of over .86. Because this is more than the required power, we would decrease n. A computation with $n = 14$ yields

$$\phi = .4623\sqrt{14} = .4623(3.7417) = 1.7298$$

$$df_F = 4(14 - 1) = 52$$

and a power of approximately .80.

Chapter 4

1. a. $c_1 = 1, c_2 = -1, c_3 = 0, c_4 = 0$
   b. $c_1 = 1, c_2 = -.5, c_3 = -.5, c_4 = 0$
   c. $c_1 = 0, c_2 = 1, c_3 = 0, c_4 = -1$
   d. $c_1 = -\frac{1}{3}, c_2 = -\frac{1}{3}, c_3 = -\frac{1}{3}, c_4 = 1$

3. a. Testing the contrast for statistical significance involves a four-step process. First, $\hat{\psi}$ must be found from Equation 36:

$$\hat{\psi} = \sum_{j=1}^{a} c_j \bar{Y}_j \qquad (4.36)$$

$$= .5(12) + .5(10) - 1(6)$$

$$= 5$$

Second, the sum of squares associated with the contrast is determined from Equation 35:

$$E_R - E_F = (\hat{\psi})^2 \bigg/ \sum_{j=1}^{a} (c_j^2/n_j) \qquad (4.35)$$

$$= (5)^2 \bigg/ \left[\frac{(.5)^2}{10} + \frac{(.5)^2}{10} + \frac{(-1)^2}{10} \right]$$

$$= 25/(.025 + .025 + .100)$$

$$= 166.67$$

Third, the F value for the contrast can be determined from Equation 37:

$$F = \frac{(\hat{\psi})^2}{MS_W \sum\limits_{j=1}^{a} (c_j^2/n_j)}$$

From the second step above, we know that

$$(\hat{\psi})^2 \bigg/ \sum\limits_{j=1}^{a} (c_j^2/n_j) = 166.67$$

We are told that $MS_W = 25$, so the F value for the contrast is given by

$$F = \frac{166.67}{25}$$

$$= 6.67$$

Fourth, this F value must be compared to a critical F value. The critical F here has 1 numerator and 27 (i.e., $30 - 3$) denominator degrees of freedom. Appendix Table A.2 shows the critical F for 1 and 26 degrees of freedom or for 1 and 28 degrees of freedom, but not for 1 and 27 degrees of freedom. To be slightly conservative, we will choose the value for 1 and 26 degrees of freedom, which is 4.23. The observed value of 6.67 exceeds the critical value, so the null hypothesis is rejected. Thus, there is a statistically significant difference between the group 3 mean and the average of the group 1 and 2 means.

b. Once again, the same four steps as in part (a) provide a test of the contrast. First, from Equation 36:

$$\hat{\psi} = \sum\limits_{j=1}^{a} c_j \bar{Y}_j \tag{4.36}$$

$$= 1(12) + 1(10) - 2(6)$$

$$= 10$$

Second, from Equation 35:

$$E_R - E_F = (\hat{\psi})^2 \bigg/ \sum\limits_{j=1}^{a} (c_j^2/n_j) \tag{4.35}$$

$$= (10)^2 \bigg/ \left[\frac{(1)^2}{10} + \frac{(1)^2}{10} + \frac{(-2)^2}{10} \right]$$

$$= 100/(.1 + .1 + .4)$$

$$= 166.67$$

Third, from Equation 37:

$$F = \frac{(\hat{\psi})^2}{MS_W \sum\limits_{j=1}^{a} (c_j^2/n_j)} \tag{4.37}$$

$$= \frac{166.67}{25}$$

$$= 6.67$$

Fourth, as in part (a), the critical F value is 4.23. Thus, the null hypothesis is rejected.

c. In part (a), $(\hat{\psi})^2 = 25$. In part (b), $(\hat{\psi})^2 = 100$. Thus, $(\hat{\psi})^2$ is four times larger in part (b) than in part (a). Similarly, in part (a),

$$\sum_{j=1}^{a} c_j^2 = (.5)^2 + (.5)^2 + (-1)^2$$

$$= .25 + .25 + 1.00$$

$$= 1.50.$$

In part (b),

$$\sum_{j=1}^{a} c_j^2 = (1)^2 + (1)^2 + (-2)^2$$

$$= 1 + 1 + 4$$

$$= 6$$

Thus, $\sum_{j=1}^{a} c_j^2$ is four times larger in part (b) than in part (a). The inclusion of the $\sum_{j=1}^{a} c_j^2$ term in Equation 37 guarantees that the F test of a contrast will not be affected by the absolute magnitude of the contrast coefficients. As our result for part (b) shows, all of the contrast coefficients can be multiplied by 2 (or any other constant), without changing the F value for the contrast.

7. a. Because this is a pairwise comparison, Equation 23 provides the simplest expression for the F value for the contrast:

$$F = \frac{n_1 n_2 (\bar{Y}_1 - \bar{Y}_2)^2}{(n_1 + n_2) MS_W} \qquad (4.23)$$

We know that $n_1 = 20$, $n_2 = 20$, $\bar{Y}_1 = 6.0$, and $\bar{Y}_2 = 4.0$. To find MS_W, recall that, during the discussion of pooled and separate error terms, it was stated that

$$MS_W = \sum_{j=1}^{a} (n_j - 1)s_j^2 \Big/ \sum_{j=1}^{a} (n_j - 1)$$

$$= \frac{(20-1)(3.2)^2 + (20-1)(2.9)^2 + (10-1)(3.3)^2}{(20-1) + (20-1) + (10-1)}$$

$$= \frac{194.56 + 159.79 + 98.01}{19 + 19 + 19}$$

$$= 9.62$$

Making the appropriate substitutions,

$$F = \frac{(20)(20)(6.0 - 4.0)^2}{(20 + 20)(9.62)}$$

$$= 4.16$$

The critical F here has 1 numerator and 47 (i.e., $50 - 3$) denominator degrees of freedom. Appendix Table A.2 shows the critical F for 1 and 40 degrees of freedom or for 1 and 60 degrees of freedom, but not for 1 and 47 degrees of freedom. To be slightly conservative, we will choose the value for 1 and 40 degrees of freedom, which is 4.08. The observed F value of 4.16 exceeds the critical value, so the null hypothesis is rejected. Thus, there is a statistically significant difference between the means of the cognitive and the behavioral groups.

b. Once again, this is a pairwise comparison, so Equation 23 can be used:

$$F = \frac{n_1 n_2 (\bar{Y}_1 - \bar{Y}_2)^2}{(n_1 + n_2) MS_W} \qquad (4.23)$$

where the "1" subscript refers to the cognitive group, and the "2" subscript refers to the control group. Substituting into the formula for F yields

$$F = \frac{(20)(10)(6.0 - 3.8)^2}{(20 + 10)(9.62)}$$

$$= 3.35$$

As in part (a), the critical F value is 4.08. The observed F value is less than the critical value, so the null hypothesis cannot be rejected. The difference between the means of the cognitive and the control groups is not statistically significant.

c. The mean difference between the cognitive and behavioral groups is 2.0; the mean difference between the cognitive and control groups is 2.2. However, the smaller mean difference is statistically significant, while the larger mean difference is not. The reason for this discrepancy is that the smaller mean difference is based on larger samples (viz., samples of 20 and 20, instead of 20 and 10). As a result, the mean difference of 2.0 is based on a more precise estimate than the mean difference of 2.2.

10. a. *Using* MS_W:

$$\hat{\psi} = \bar{Y}_3 - \bar{Y}_4$$

$$= -2$$

$$E_R - E_F = (\hat{\psi})^2 \Big/ \sum_{j=1}^{a} (c_j^2/n_j)$$

$$= (-2)^2 \Big/ \left(\frac{(0)^2}{5} + \frac{(0)^2}{5} + \frac{(1)^2}{5} + \frac{(-1)^2}{5}\right)$$

$$= 10.00$$

$$MS_W = \frac{\sum_{j=1}^{a} s_j^2}{a} \qquad \text{(with equal } n \text{, from Equation 3.63)}$$

$$= \frac{(1 + 1 + 9 + 9)}{4}$$

$$= 5.00$$

Thus,

$$F = \frac{(\hat{\psi})^2}{MS_W \sum_{j=1}^{a} (c_j^2/n_j)}$$

$$= \frac{10.00}{5.00}$$

$$= 2.00$$

From Appendix Table A.2, the critical F value for 1 numerator and 16 denominator degrees of freedom is 4.49. Thus, the null hypothesis cannot be rejected.
Using a Separate Error Term:
The F statistic is now given by

$$F = \frac{(\hat{\psi})^2}{\sum_{j=1}^{a} (c_j^2/n_j)s_j^2}$$

$$= \frac{(-2)^2}{\dfrac{(0)^2}{5}(1) + \dfrac{(0)^2}{5}(1) + \dfrac{(1)^2}{5}(9) + \dfrac{(-1)^2}{5}(9)}$$

$$= \frac{4.00}{3.60}$$

$$= 1.11$$

The denominator degrees of freedom of the critical value are given by Equation 39:

$$df = \frac{\left(\sum\limits_{j=1}^{a} c_j^2 s_j^2 / n_j\right)^2}{\sum\limits_{j=1}^{a} [(c_j^2 s_j^2 / n_j)^2 / (n_j - 1)]} \tag{4.39}$$

$$= \frac{\left(\dfrac{(0)^2(1)}{5} + \dfrac{(0)^2(1)}{5} + \dfrac{(1)^2(9)}{5} + \dfrac{(-1)^2(9)}{5}\right)^2}{\dfrac{\left(\dfrac{(0)^2(1)}{5}\right)^2}{5-1} + \dfrac{\left(\dfrac{(0)^2(1)}{5}\right)^2}{5-1} + \dfrac{\left(\dfrac{(1)^2(9)}{5}\right)^2}{5-1} + \dfrac{\left(\dfrac{(-1)^2(9)}{5}\right)^2}{5-1}}$$

$$= \frac{(3.60)^2}{0 + 0 + .81 + .81}$$

$$= 8.00$$

The corresponding critical value is 5.32. Thus, the separate error term approach here produces an appreciably smaller observed F and a somewhat larger critical F.

b. *Using* MS_W:

$$\hat{\psi} = \bar{Y}_1 - \bar{Y}_2$$

$$= -2$$

$$E_R - E_F = (\hat{\psi})^2 \bigg/ \sum_{j=1}^{a} (c_j^2 / n_j)$$

$$= (-2)^2 \bigg/ \left[\frac{(1)^2}{5} + \frac{(-1)^2}{5} + \frac{(0)^2}{5} + \frac{(0)^2}{5}\right]$$

$$= 10.00$$

$$MS_W = \frac{\sum\limits_{j=1}^{a} s_j^2}{a}$$

$$= \frac{1 + 1 + 9 + 9}{4}$$

$$= 5.00$$

Thus,

$$F = \frac{(\hat{\psi})^2}{MS_W \sum\limits_{j=1}^{a} (c_j^2 / n_j)}$$

$$= \frac{10.00}{5.00}$$

$$= 2.00$$

As in part (a), the critical F value is 4.49, so the null hypothesis cannot be rejected.
Using a Separate Error Term:
The F statistic is now given by

$$F = \frac{(\hat{\psi})^2}{\sum_{j=1}^{a}(c_j^2/n_j)s_j^2}$$

$$= \frac{(-2)^2}{\frac{(1)^2}{5}(1) + \frac{(-1)^2}{5}(1) + \frac{(0)^2}{5}(9) + \frac{(0)^2}{5}(9)}$$

$$= \frac{4.00}{.40}$$

$$= 10.00$$

The denominator degrees of freedom of the critical value are given by Equation 39:

$$df = \frac{\left(\sum_{j=1}^{a} c_j^2 s_j^2/n_j\right)^2}{\sum_{j=1}^{a}[(c_j^2 s_j^2/n_j)^2/(n_j-1)]} \qquad (4.39)$$

$$= \frac{\left(\frac{(1)^2(1)}{5} + \frac{(-1)^2(1)}{5} + \frac{(0)^2(9)}{5} + \frac{(0)^2(9)}{5}\right)^2}{\frac{\left(\frac{(1)^2(-1)}{5}\right)^2}{5-1} + \frac{\left(\frac{(1)^2(-1)}{5}\right)^2}{5-1} + \frac{\left(\frac{(0)^2(9)}{5}\right)^2}{5-1} + \frac{\left(\frac{(0)^2(9)}{5}\right)^2}{5-1}}$$

$$= \frac{(.40)^2}{.01 + .01 + .00 + .00}$$

$$= 8.00$$

The corresponding critical value is 5.32, so the null hypothesis is rejected.
Unlike part (a), the separate error term approach in part (b) produced a substantially larger F value than was obtained using MS_W. The reason is that the separate error term approach takes into account that, in these data, the $\bar{Y}_1$ and $\bar{Y}_2$ estimates are much more precise than are $\bar{Y}_3$ and $\bar{Y}_4$, because of the large differences in within-group variances. Although the separate error term approach necessarily has a larger critical value than does the pooled error term approach, in these data the much larger F value associated with the separate error term approach overrides the slight increase in critical value.

c. *Using MS_W*:

$$\hat{\psi} = \bar{Y}_1 + \bar{Y}_2 - \bar{Y}_3 - \bar{Y}_4$$

(*Note*: Coefficients of ± 1 instead of ± 0.5 are used to simplify calculations.)

$$\hat{\psi} = 4 + 6 - 6 - 8$$

$$= -4$$

$$E_R - E_F = (\hat{\psi})^2 \Big/ \sum_{j=1}^{a}(c_j^2/n_j)$$

$$= (-4)^2 \Big/ \left(\frac{(1)^2}{5} + \frac{(1)^2}{5} + \frac{(-1)^2}{5} + \frac{(-1)^2}{5}\right)$$

$$= 20.00$$

$$MS_W = \frac{\sum\limits_{j=1}^{a} s_j^2}{a}$$

$$= \frac{(1 + 1 + 9 + 9)}{4}$$

$$= 5.00.$$

Thus,

$$F = \frac{(\hat{\psi})^2}{MS_W \sum\limits_{j=1}^{a} (c_j^2/n_j)}$$

$$= \frac{20.00}{5.00}$$

$$= 4.00$$

As in parts (a) and (b), the critical F value is 4.49, so the null hypothesis cannot be rejected.

Using a Separate Error Term:
The F statistic is now given by

$$F = \frac{(\hat{\psi})^2}{\sum\limits_{j=1}^{a} (c_j^2/n_j)s_j^2}$$

$$= \frac{(-4)^2}{\left[\frac{(1)^2}{5}(1)\right] + \left[\frac{(1)^2}{5}(1)\right] + \left[\frac{(-1)^2}{5}(9)\right] + \left[\frac{(-1)^2}{5}(9)\right]}$$

$$= \frac{16.00}{4.00}$$

$$= 4.00$$

The denominator degrees of freedom of the critical value are given by Equation 39:

$$df = \frac{\left(\sum\limits_{j=1}^{a} c_j^2 s_j^2/n_j\right)^2}{\sum\limits_{j=1}^{a} [(c_j^2 s_j^2/n_j)^2/(n_j - 1)]} \tag{4.39}$$

$$= \frac{\left(\frac{(1)^2(1)}{5} + \frac{(1)^2(1)}{5} + \frac{(-1)^2(9)}{5} + \frac{(-1)^2(9)}{5}\right)^2}{\frac{\left(\frac{(1)^2(1)}{5}\right)^2}{5-1} + \frac{\left(\frac{(1)^2(1)}{5}\right)^2}{5-1} + \frac{\left(\frac{(-1)^2(9)}{5}\right)^2}{5-1} + \frac{\left(\frac{(-1)^2(9)}{5}\right)^2}{5-1}}$$

$$= \frac{(4.00)^2}{.01 + .01 + .81 + .81}$$

$$= 9.76$$

The critical value for 1 numerator and 9 denominator degrees of freedom is 5.12, so the null hypothesis cannot be rejected. Notice that the only difference between the two approaches here is that the critical value is larger for the separate error term approach. In particular, the observed F values are identical for the two approaches. Such equivalence will occur whenever sample sizes are equal and all contrast coefficients are either 1 or -1.

Chapter 5

2. a. The Bonferroni procedure should be used because all comparisons are planned, but not every possible pairwise comparison will be tested (see Figure 5.1). In addition, from Table 5.5, it is clear that the Bonferroni critical value is less than the Scheffé critical value, since the number of contrasts to be tested is less than 8.
    b. With 13 subjects per group, the denominator degrees of freedom equal 60 (i.e., $65 - 5$). From Appendix Table A.3, we find that the critical Bonferroni F value for testing 3 comparisons at an experimentwise alpha level of .05 with 60 denominator degrees of freedom is 6.07.
    c. Because the comparison of μ_3 versus μ_4 has been chosen post hoc, but all comparisons to be tested are still pairwise, Tukey's method must be used to maintain the experimentwise alpha level (see Figure 5.1).
    d. From Appendix Table A.4, we find that the critical q value for 5 groups, 60 denominator degrees of freedom, and $\alpha_{EW} = .05$ equals 3.98. The corresponding critical F value is $(3.98)^2/2$, which equals 7.92.
    e. The Bonferroni critical value for testing 3 planned comparisons is substantially lower than the Tukey critical value for testing all pairwise comparisons. Thus, the price to be paid for revising planned comparisons after having examined the data is an increase in the critical value, which will lead to a decrease in power for each individual comparison.

3. a. With equal n, the F statistic for this pairwise comparison is given by

$$F = \frac{n(\bar{Y}_2 - \bar{Y}_4)^2}{2MS_W} \tag{4.24}$$

Further, with equal n, MS_W is the unweighted average of the within-group variances:

$$MS_W = \frac{\sum_{j=1}^{a} s_j^2}{a} \tag{3.63}$$

$$= \frac{96 + 112 + 94 + 98}{4}$$

$$= 100$$

Substituting $n = 25$, $\bar{Y}_2 = 46$, $\bar{Y}_4 = 54$, and $MS_W = 100$ into Equation 4.24 yields

$$F = \frac{25(46 - 54)^2}{2(100)}$$

$$= 8.00$$

The Scheffé critical value is given by

$$(a - 1)F_{.05;a-1,N-a} \tag{5.24}$$

which for this design implies a critical value of

$$(4 - 1)F_{.05;4-1,100-4}$$

From Appendix Table A.2, we find that

$$F_{.05;3,60} = 2.76$$

so the Scheffé critical F value is

$$3(2.76) = 8.28$$

Thus, the experimenter is correct that the mean difference is nonsignificant by Scheffé's method.

b. Tukey's WSD can be used to maintain α_{EW} at .05, since the post hoc contrast is pairwise. The value of the observed F is still 8.00, but the Tukey critical F value is given by

$$(q_{.05;a,N-a})^2/2 \qquad \text{(Table 5.7)}$$

For these data, from Appendix Table A.4, the Tukey critical value equals $(3.74)^2/2$, or 6.99. The observed F exceeds the critical F, so the mean difference can be declared statistically significant with Tukey's method. This exercise illustrates the fact that Tukey's method is more powerful than Scheffé's method for testing pairwise comparisons.

5. a. *Using MS_W*:
We saw in Chapter 4 that the observed F equals 2.00 for this comparison (see the answer to problem 10(a) in Chapter 4). Also, using a pooled error term, there are 16 denominator degrees of freedom. The critical value for testing all pairwise comparisons is given by

$$(q_{.05;a,N-a})^2/2 \qquad \text{(Table 5.7)}$$

For these data, from Appendix Table A.4, $q_{.05;4,16} = 4.05$, so the appropriate Tukey critical value is $(4.05)^2/2 = 8.20$. Because the observed F value is less than the critical F, the contrast is nonsignificant.
Using a Separate Error Term:
We saw in the Chapter 4 answers that the observed F now equals 1.11, and there are now only 8 denominator degrees of freedom. The critical value is now given by

$$(q_{.05;4,8})^2/2 = (4.53)^2/2$$
$$= 10.26$$

The observed F value is now lower than it was with MS_W as the error term, and the critical value is now higher. Thus, the contrast is also nonsignificant using a separate error term.

b. *Using MS_W*:
We saw in the Chapter 4 answers that the observed F value for this contrast is 2.00. Again there are 16 denominator degrees of freedom, so the Tukey critical value is 8.20, and this contrast is also nonsignificant.
Using a Separate Error Term:
We saw in the Chapter 4 answers that the observed F value is now 10.00. With 8 denominator degrees of freedom, the Tukey critical value is again 10.26, so the contrast just misses being statistically significant.

c. The separate error term seems more appropriate, given the wide disparity in sample values. In particular, there is more evidence that μ_1 and μ_2 are different from one another than that μ_3 and μ_4 are. The separate error term reflects this fact, unlike the pooled error term, which regards these two differences as equally significant.

7. a. It is possible to perform the test of the omnibus null hypothesis. Because this set of contrasts is orthogonal, the sums of squares attributable to the three contrasts are

additive. As a result, the between-group sum of squares is given by

$$SS_B = SS_{\psi 1} + SS_{\psi 2} + SS_{\psi 3}$$
$$= 75 + 175 + 125$$
$$= 375$$

The observed value of the F statistic then equals

$$F = \frac{SS_B/(a-1)}{MS_W}$$
$$= \frac{375/3}{25}$$
$$= 5.00$$

From Appendix Table A.2, we find that the critical F with 3 and 40 degrees of freedom is 2.84. Thus, the group means are significantly different from one another at the .05 level.

b. From Equation 4.37, the observed F for a contrast is

$$F = \frac{(\hat{\psi})^2}{MS_W \sum\limits_{j=1}^{a} (c_j^2/n_j)} \tag{4.37}$$

However, we know from Equation 4.35 that the term

$$\frac{(\hat{\psi})^2}{\sum\limits_{j=1}^{a} (c_j^2/n_j)}$$

is simply the sum of squares for the contrast. Thus,

$$F = \frac{SS_\psi}{MS_W}$$

For the data of this problem, we have

$$\psi_1: \quad F = \frac{75}{25} = 3.0$$

$$\psi_2: \quad F = \frac{175}{25} = 7.0$$

$$\psi_3: \quad F = \frac{125}{25} = 5.0$$

The appropriate procedure for maintaining α_{EW} at .05 here is the Bonferroni approach (see Figure 5.1 and Table 5.5). From Appendix Table A.3, we find that the Bonferroni F critical value for testing three contrasts (at $\alpha_{EW} = .05$) with 40 denominator degrees of freedom is 6.24. Thus, only the second contrast can be declared statistically significant, using an experimentwise alpha level of .05.

c. The omnibus observed F value of part (a) equaled 5.00. The three observed F values of part (b) equaled 3.00, 7.00, and 5.00. Thus, the omnibus F value equals the average (i.e., the mean) of the F values for the three contrasts. In general, the omnibus F value can be conceptualized as an average F value, averaging over a set of $a-1$ orthogonal contrasts. That this is true can be seen from the following algebraic equivalence:

$$F_{omnibus} = \frac{MS_B}{MS_W}$$

$$= \frac{SS_B/(a-1)}{MS_W}$$

$$= \frac{\sum_{j=1}^{a-1} SS_{\psi j}/(a-1)}{MS_W} \quad \text{(where the contrasts are orthogonal)}$$

$$= \left(\sum_{j=1}^{a-1} \frac{SS_{\psi j}}{MS_W} \right) \Big/ (a-1)$$

$$= \sum_{j=1}^{a-1} F_{\psi j} \Big/ (a-1)$$

For a related perspective, see Exercise 9 at the end of Chapter 3.

11. a. In general, the value of the observed F is

$$F = \frac{(E_R - E_F)/(df_R - df_F)}{E_F/df_F}$$

Substituting from Equations 3.58 and 3.63 yields

$$F = \frac{n \sum_{j=1}^{a} (\bar{Y}_j - \bar{Y})^2 \Big/ (a-1)}{\sum_{j=1}^{a} s_j^2 / a}$$

For these data, $n = 11$, $\bar{Y}_1 = 10$, $\bar{Y}_2 = 10$, $\bar{Y}_3 = 22$, $\bar{Y} = 14$, $a = 3$, $s_1^2 = 100$, $s_2^2 = 196$, and $s_3^2 = 154$. Substituting these values into the expression for the F statistic yields

$$F = \frac{11(16 + 16 + 64)/2}{150}$$

$$= \frac{528}{150}$$

$$= 3.52$$

From Appendix Table A.2, we find that the critical F value for 2 numerator and 30 denominator degrees of freedom at the .05 level is 3.32. Thus, the professor is correct that the null hypothesis can be rejected.

b. With equal n, Equation 4.24 can be used to test pairwise comparisons. For example, the F statistic for comparing the means of groups 1 and 3 is given by

$$F = \frac{n(\bar{Y}_1 - \bar{Y}_3)^2}{2MS_W}$$

For these data, $n = 11$, $\bar{Y}_1 = 10$, $\bar{Y}_3 = 22$, and $MS_W = 150$ (from part (a)). Thus, the observed F equals

$$F = \frac{11(10 - 22)^2}{2(150)}$$

$$= 5.28$$

From Appendix Table A.4, we find that the critical value for 3 groups, 30 denominator degrees of freedom, and $\alpha_{EW} = .05$ is 3.49. The corresponding critical F value is $(3.49)^2/2$, or 6.09. Thus, the means of groups 1 and 3 are not significantly different from one another. The exact same conclusion applies to a comparison of groups 2 and 3, and the difference between groups 1 and 2 is obviously non-significant. Thus, the professor is correct that none of the pairwise differences are significant.

c. As we pointed out in the chapter, a statistically significant omnibus test result does not necessarily imply that a significant pairwise difference can be found. Instead, a significant omnibus result implies that there is at least one comparison that will be declared significant with Scheffé's method. However, that comparison need not be pairwise. Indeed, using a pooled error term, in this numerical example, the contrast that produces $F_{maximum}$ is a complex comparison with coefficients of 1, 1, and -2. This comparison is statistically significant, even using Scheffé's method to maintain $\alpha_{EW} = .05$ for all possible contrasts.

Chapter 6

2. a. With equal n,

$$SS_{linear} = E_R - E_F = n(\hat{\psi}_{linear})^2 \bigg/ \sum_{j=1}^{a} c_j^2 \qquad (6.11)$$

The linear contrast coefficients are $c_1 = -3$, $c_2 = -1$, $c_3 = 1$, and $c_4 = 3$ (see Appendix Table A.10). Thus,

$$\hat{\psi}_{linear} = -3(10) - 1(20) + 1(30) + 3(40)$$
$$= 100$$

and

$$\sum_{j=1}^{a} c_j^2 = (-3)^2 + (-1)^2 + (1)^2 + (3)^2$$
$$= 20$$

Thus,

$$SS_{linear} = 10(100)^2/20$$
$$= 5000$$

b.

$$SS_{quadratic} = n(\hat{\psi}_{quadratic})^2 \bigg/ \sum_{j=1}^{a} c_j^2$$

From Appendix Table A.10, the quadratic contrast coefficients are $c_1 = 1$, $c_2 = -1$, $c_3 = -1$, and $c_4 = 1$.
Thus,

$$\hat{\psi}_{quadratic} = 1(10) - 1(20) - 1(30) + 1(40)$$
$$= 0$$

and

$$\sum_{j=1}^{a} c_j^2 = (1)^2 + (-1)^2 + (-1)^2 + (1)^2$$
$$= 4$$

Thus,

$$SS_{quadratic} = 10(0)^2/4$$
$$= 0$$

c.

$$SS_{cubic} = n(\hat{\psi}_{cubic})^2 \bigg/ \sum_{j=1}^{a} c_j^2$$

From Appendix Table A.10, the cubic contrast coefficients are $c_1 = -1$, $c_2 = 3$, $c_3 = -3$, and $c_4 = 1$. Thus,

$$\hat{\psi}_{cubic} = -1(10) + 3(20) - 3(30) + 1(40)$$
$$= 0$$

and

$$\sum_{j=1}^{a} c_j^2 = (-1)^2 + (3)^2 + (-3)^2 + (1)^2$$
$$= 20$$

Thus,

$$SS_{cubic} = 10(0)^2/20$$
$$= 0$$

d. Yes, Figure 6.3(a) reflects a pure linear trend, because SS_{linear} is nonzero but $SS_{quadratic}$ and SS_{cubic} are both zero (that is, all the other $a - 1$ trends are zero).

5. a.

$$F = \frac{SS_{linear}}{MS_W}$$

We are told that $MS_W = 150$, but we need to calculate SS_{linear}, which we can do from

$$SS_{linear} = n(\hat{\psi}_{linear})^2 \bigg/ \sum_{j=1}^{a} c_j^2$$

For 5 groups, the linear contrast coefficients are $c_1 = -2$, $c_2 = -1$, $c_3 = 0$, $c_4 = 1$, and $c_5 = 2$ (see Appendix Table A.10). Thus,

$$\hat{\psi}_{linear} = -2(80) - 1(83) + 0(87) + 1(89) + 2(91)$$
$$= 28$$

and

$$\sum_{j=1}^{a} c_j^2 = (-2)^2 + (-1)^2 + (0)^2 + (1)^2 + (2)^2$$
$$= 10$$

Thus,

$$SS_{linear} = 15(28)^2/10$$
$$= 1176$$

The value of the F test statistic for the linear trend then equals

$$F = \frac{SS_{linear}}{MS_W}$$
$$= \frac{1176}{150}$$
$$= 7.84$$

The critical F value has 1 and 70 degrees of freedom. From Appendix Table A.2, we find that the critical F with 1 and 60 degrees of freedom (rounding downward) is 4.00 at the .05 level. Thus, the linear trend is statistically significant at the .05 level.

b. To test the omnibus null hypothesis, we must calculate an observed F of the form

$$F = \frac{MS_B}{MS_W}$$

We are told that $MS_W = 150$, but we must find MS_B, which is given by

$MS_B = SS_B/(a-1)$

$$= n \sum_{j=1}^{a} (\bar{Y}_j - \bar{Y})^2/(a-1)$$

$$= 15[(80-86)^2 + (83-86)^2 + (87-86)^2 + (89-86)^2 + (91-86)^2]/4$$

$$= 1200/4$$

$$= 300$$

As a result, the observed F is

$$F = \frac{MS_B}{MS_W}$$

$$= \frac{300}{150}$$

$$= 2.00$$

The critical F value has 4 and 70 degrees of freedom. From Appendix Table A.2, we find that the critical F with 4 and 60 degrees of freedom (rounding downward) is 2.53 at the .05 level. Thus, the omnibus null hypothesis cannot be rejected.

c. The F statistic for the linear trend is

$$F = \frac{SS_{linear}}{MS_W}$$

while the F statistic for the omnibus test is

$$F = \frac{SS_{between}/4}{MS_W}$$

For these data, the linear trend accounts for 98% of the between-group sum of squares (that is, 1176 out of 1200), so that SS_{linear} is almost as large as $SS_{between}$. However, the linear trend is based on 1 degree of freedom, whereas the omnibus test is based on 4 degrees of freedom. In other words, with one parameter, the linear trend model decreases the sum of squared errors by 1176 relative to a restricted model of the form

$$Y_{ij} = \mu + \varepsilon_{ij}$$

On the other hand, the "cell means" model (that is, the full model of the omnibus test) decreases the sum of squared errors by 1200 relative to the same restricted model, but requires three more parameters than does the restricted model to accomplish this reduction. As a consequence, although SS_{linear} is slightly smaller than $SS_{between}$, MS_{linear} is almost four times larger than $MS_{between}$. The same ratio applies to the observed F values.

d. If in fact the true difference in population means is entirely linear, the observed F value for the linear trend will likely be appreciably larger than the omnibus F

value. Thus, statistical power is substantially increased in this situation by planning to test the linear trend. Of course, if the true trend is nonlinear, the planned test of the linear trend may be sorely lacking in power. This same effect may occur for any planned comparison—not just for a linear trend.

e. Yes, because the omnibus test need not even be performed when planned comparisons have been formulated.

8. The estimated slope of 2.35 is not accurate. Using Equation 8 to calculate the slope requires that linear trend coefficients be defined as

$$c_j = X_j - \bar{X}, \tag{6.8}$$

which in this problem implies that the coefficients should be

$$c_1 = \ 4 - 7 = -3$$
$$c_2 = \ 7 - 7 = 0$$
$$c_3 = 10 - 7 = 3$$

The values of -1, 0, and 1 from Appendix Table A.10 are proportional to the proper values, but in general they cannot be used to calculate an estimated slope, although they can be used to test the statistical significance of the linear trend. Substituting $c_1 = -3, c_2 = 0, c_3 = 3, \bar{Y}_1 = 5.5, \bar{Y}_2 = 7.7$, and $\bar{Y}_3 = 10.2$ into Equations 6 and 7 yields

$$\hat{\psi}_{linear} = \sum_{j=1}^{a} c_j \bar{Y}_j \tag{6.6}$$
$$= -3(5.5) + 0(7.7) + 3(10.2)$$
$$= 14.10$$

$$\hat{\beta}_1 = \hat{\psi}_{linear} \bigg/ \sum_{j=1}^{a} c_j^2 \tag{6.7}$$
$$= 14.10/[(-3)^2 + (0)^2 + (3)^2]$$
$$= .78$$

Thus, the correct estimated slope is .78, which is one-third (within rounding error) of the claimed value of 2.35. Now, with a slope of .78, we would expect 10-year-olds to outperform 4-year-olds by approximately 4.68 units, which is virtually identical to the observed difference of 4.70 units.

10. a. The linear trend coefficients shown in Appendix Table A.10 for testing a linear trend with 4 groups are $-3, -1, 1$, and 3. However, Equation 8 requires that the contrast coefficients be defined as

$$c_j = X_j - \bar{X}$$

which for our data implies that

$$c_1 = 1 - 2.5 = -1.5$$
$$c_2 = 2 - 2.5 = -0.5$$
$$c_3 = 3 - 2.5 = 0.5$$
$$c_4 = 4 - 2.5 = 1.5$$

The estimated slope $\hat{\beta}_1$ is calculated from Equation 7 as follows:

$$\hat{\beta}_1 = \hat{\psi}_{linear} \bigg/ \sum_{j=1}^{a} c_j^2 \tag{6.7}$$

The $\hat{\psi}_{linear}$ term can be calculated from Equation 6:

$$\hat{\psi}_{linear} = \sum_{j=1}^{a} c_j \bar{Y}_j \qquad (6.6)$$

$$= -1.5(6.16) - .5(4.44) + .5(3.44) + 1.5(4.76)$$

$$= -2.60$$

Also,

$$\sum_{j=1}^{a} c_j^2 = (-1.5)^2 + (-.5)^2 + (.5)^2 + (1.5)^2$$

$$= 5.00$$

Substituting the values of -2.60 and 5.00 into Equation 7 yields

$$\hat{\beta}_1 = -2.60/5.00$$

$$= -.52$$

b. The observed F is given by

$$F = \frac{SS_{linear}}{MS_W}$$

where

$$SS_{linear} = n(\hat{\psi}_{linear})^2 \bigg/ \sum_{j=1}^{a} c_j^2 \qquad (\text{see } 6.11)$$

$$= 5(-2.60)^2/5.00$$

$$= 6.760$$

and

$$MS_W = \sum_{j=1}^{a} s_j^2/a \qquad (3.63)$$

$$= (.688 + .228 + .068 + .148)/4$$

$$= .283$$

Therefore,

$$F = \frac{SS_{linear}}{MS_W}$$

$$= \frac{6.760}{.283}$$

$$= 23.89$$

From Appendix Table A.2, the critical F value with 1 and 16 degrees of freedom is 4.49, so the linear trend is statistically significant at the .05 level.

c. The least squares estimate of the slope parameter is $\hat{\beta}_1 = -.52$, which is identical to the value obtained in part (a).

d. The F value of 7.28 (which is the square of $t = -2.698$) is considerably less than the F value of 23.89 obtained in part (b).

e. Yes, in both cases, the sum of squares attributable to the linear trend equals 6.760. Thus, the value of $E_R - E_F$ is the same in the two analyses.

f. The denominator of the F statistic for testing the linear contrast in part (b) was MS_W, which has a value of 0.283 for these data. Because $df_F = 16$ for this analysis, the corresponding error sum of squares is 4.528 (16 × .283). However, the error sum of squares for the regression approach is 16.720, obviously a much larger value.

The associated degrees of freedom equal 18, so the denominator of the F statistic using this approach is .929 ($16.720 \div 18$). The larger denominator of the regression approach (relative to testing the contrast, as in part (b)) produces a lower F value.

g. As stated in the text, the "cell means" model is mathematically equivalent to a model that includes all $a - 1$ trends, such as

$$Y_{ij} = \beta_0 + \beta_1 X_{ij} + \beta_2 X_{ij}^2 + \beta_3 X_{ij}^3 + \varepsilon_{ij}$$

when $a = 4$. However, the full model of the regression approach excludes the quadratic and cubic terms. As a result, any quadratic and cubic effects contribute to the error of this model. Specifically,

$$E_{F(regression)} = E_{F(cell\ means)} + SS_{quadratic} + SS_{cubic}$$

It turns out that, for these data,

$$SS_{quadratic} = 11.552$$
$$SS_{cubic} = .640$$

Thus,

$$E_{F\ (regression)} = 4.528 + 11.552 + .640$$
$$= 16.72$$

in agreement with our earlier finding.

h. To the extent that nonlinear trends are nonzero, testing the linear trend using procedures for testing a contrast will yield a larger F value than will the regression approach. Thus, in this situation, using MS_W as the error term increases the test's power. If, on the other hand, the nonlinear trends are truly zero, the regression approach gains an additional $a - 2$ degrees of freedom for the error term. As a result, the critical F value is somewhat lower, and power is somewhat higher. However, this potential advantage is likely to be very small unless a is large relative to N. Thus, unless there are very few subjects at each level of the factor, the use of MS_W as the error term is generally preferable to the use of the error term based on the regression model with X as the single predictor variable. This problem is not unique to trend analysis, nor to differences between ANOVA and regression. Instead, the general point is that, if one fails to include relevant variables in a model, estimates of error variability calculated from that model can seriously overestimate the magnitude of true error.

Chapter 7

1. a. (1) From Equation 10, α_j is defined to be

$$\alpha_j = \mu_{j.} - \mu_{..} \qquad (7.10)$$

For these data, the marginal mean for row 1 is

$$\mu_{1.} = \sum_{k=1}^{b} \mu_{1k}/b \qquad \text{(see 7.7)}$$

$$= \sum_{k=1}^{3} \mu_{1k}/3$$

$$= (\mu_{11} + \mu_{12} + \mu_{13})/3$$

$$= (10 + 10 + 10)/3$$

$$= 10$$

Similarly,

$$\mu_{2.} = (12 + 12 + 12)/3$$
$$= 12$$

and

$$\mu_{3.} = (17 + 17 + 17)/3$$
$$= 17$$

In addition, the population grand mean is defined to be

$$\mu_{..} = \sum_{k=1}^{b} \sum_{j=1}^{a} \mu_{jk}/ab \qquad\qquad (7.9)$$
$$= \sum_{k=1}^{3} \sum_{j=1}^{3} \mu_{jk}/9$$
$$= (10 + 12 + 17 + 10 + 12 + 17 + 10 + 12 + 17)/9$$
$$= 13$$

Substituting the values for $\mu_{j.}$ and $\mu_{..}$ into Equation 10 yields

$$\alpha_1 = \mu_{1.} - \mu_{..}$$
$$= 10 - 13$$
$$= -3$$
$$\alpha_2 = \mu_{2.} - \mu_{..}$$
$$= 12 - 13$$
$$= -1$$
$$\alpha_3 = \mu_{3.} - \mu_{..}$$
$$= 17 - 13$$
$$= 4$$

(2) The β parameters are obtained in a similar manner, except that now we must focus on column marginal means, instead of row marginal means:

$$\mu_{.1} = (10 + 12 + 17)/3 \qquad\qquad \text{(see 7.8)}$$
$$= 13$$
$$\mu_{.2} = (10 + 12 + 17)/3$$
$$= 13$$
$$\mu_{.3} = (10 + 12 + 17)/3$$
$$= 13$$

Thus, the values of the column main effect β parameters are given by

$$\beta_1 = \mu_{.1} - \mu_{..}$$
$$= 13 - 13$$
$$= 0$$
$$\beta_2 = \mu_{.2} - \mu_{..}$$
$$= 13 - 13$$
$$= 0$$

$$\beta_3 = 13 - 13$$
$$= 0$$

(3) The interaction parameters are defined in terms of the cell means and the other effect parameters:

$$(\alpha\beta)_{jk} = \mu_{jk} - (\mu_{..} + \alpha_j + \beta_k). \tag{7.12}$$

For example,

$$(\alpha\beta)_{11} = \mu_{11} - (\mu_{..} + \alpha_1 + \beta_1)$$
$$= 10 - (13 + (-3) + 0)$$
$$= 10 - 10$$
$$= 0$$

For these data, all 9 interaction parameters have a value of zero.

(4) Only the A main effect is nonzero in the population. For these data, simple visual inspection of the cell means shows that the rows differ from one another but the columns do not. In addition, the row differences are identical in each column. The α_j, β_k, and $(\alpha\beta)_{jk}$ parameter values confirm that the B main effect and AB interactions are null in the population.

c. (1) From Equation 10, α_j is defined to be

$$\alpha_j = \mu_{j.} - \mu_{..} \tag{7.10}$$

For these data, the marginal mean for row 1 is

$$\mu_{1.} = \sum_{k=1}^{b} \mu_{1k}/b \tag{see 7.7}$$

$$= \sum_{k=1}^{3} \mu_{1k}/3$$

$$= (\mu_{11} + \mu_{12} + \mu_{13})/3$$

$$= (26 + 22 + 21)/3$$

$$= 23.$$

Similarly,

$$\mu_{2.} = (23 + 19 + 18)/3$$
$$= 20$$

and

$$\mu_{3.} = (17 + 13 + 12)/3$$
$$= 14$$

In addition, the population grand mean is defined to be

$$\mu_{..} = \sum_{k=1}^{b} \sum_{j=1}^{a} \mu_{jk}/ab$$

$$= \sum_{k=1}^{3} \sum_{j=1}^{3} \mu_{jk}/9$$

$$= (26 + 22 + 21 + 23 + 19 + 18 + 17 + 13 + 12)/9$$

$$= 19$$

Substituting the values for $\mu_{j.}$ and $\mu_{..}$ into Equation 10 yields

$$\alpha_1 = \mu_{1.} - \mu_{..}$$
$$= 23 - 19$$
$$= 4$$
$$\alpha_2 = \mu_{2.} - \mu_{..}$$
$$= 20 - 19$$
$$= 1$$
$$\alpha_3 = \mu_{3.} - \mu_{..}$$
$$= 14 - 19$$
$$= -5$$

(2) The β parameters are obtained in a similar manner, except that now we must focus on column marginal means, instead of row marginal means:

$$\mu_{.1} = (26 + 23 + 17)/3$$
$$= 22$$
$$\mu_{.2} = (22 + 19 + 13)/3$$
$$= 18$$
$$\mu_{.3} = (21 + 18 + 12)/3$$
$$= 17$$

Thus, the values of the column main effect β parameters are given by

$$\beta_1 = \mu_{.1} - \mu_{..}$$
$$= 22 - 19$$
$$= 3$$
$$\beta_2 = \mu_{.2} - \mu_{..}$$
$$= 18 - 19$$
$$= -1$$
$$\beta_3 = \mu_{.3} - \mu_{..}$$
$$= 17 - 19$$
$$= -2$$

(3) The interaction parameters are defined in terms of the cell means and the other effect parameters:

$$(\alpha\beta)_{jk} = \mu_{jk} - (\mu_{..} + \alpha_j + \beta_k). \tag{7.12}$$

For example,

$$(\alpha\beta)_{11} = \mu_{11} - (\mu_{..} + \alpha_1 + \beta_1)$$
$$= 26 - (19 + 4 + 3)$$
$$= 26 - 26$$
$$= 0$$

For these data, it turns out that all 9 interaction parameters have a value of zero.

(4) The A main effect and the B main effect are nonzero in the population. The nonzero α_j and β_k parameters corroborate the visual impression that rows differ from one another, and so do columns. However, the row differences are the same in all 3 columns (or, conversely, the column differences are the same in all 3 rows), which is why the interaction is null in the population.

4. a. From Equation 16, the general form of an estimated row main effect parameter is

$$\hat{\alpha}_j = \bar{Y}_{j.} - \bar{Y}_{..} \qquad (7.16)$$

For these data,

$\hat{\alpha}_1 = [(8 + 10 + 15)/3] - [(8 + 10 + 15 + 9 + 14 + 10 + 13 + 9 + 11)/9]$

$\qquad = 11 - 11$

$\qquad = 0$

$\hat{\alpha}_2 = [(9 + 14 + 10)/3] - 11$

$\qquad = 11 - 11$

$\qquad = 0$

$\hat{\alpha}_3 = [(13 + 9 + 11)/3] - 11$

$\qquad = 11 - 11$

$\qquad = 0$

b.
$$SS_A = \sum_{all\,obs} \hat{\alpha}_j^2$$

Notice that with equal n, a total of $n\,b$ subjects have an $\hat{\alpha}_j$ value of $\hat{\alpha}_1$, another $n\,b$ subjects have an $\hat{\alpha}_j$ value of $\hat{\alpha}_2$, and so forth. For these data, then, 24 subjects have an $\hat{\alpha}_j$ value of $\hat{\alpha}_1$, 24 have $\hat{\alpha}_2$, and 24 have $\hat{\alpha}_3$. Thus,

$$SS_A = 24\hat{\alpha}_1^2 + 24\hat{\alpha}_2^2 + 24\hat{\alpha}_3^2$$
$$= 24(0)^2 + 24(0)^2 + 24(0)^2$$
$$= 0.$$

c. From Equation 17, the general form of an estimated column main effect parameter is

$$\hat{\beta}_k = \bar{Y}_{.k} - \bar{Y}_{..} \qquad (7.17)$$

For these data,

$\hat{\beta}_1 = [(8 + 9 + 13)/3] - 11$

$\qquad = 10 - 11$

$\qquad = -1$

$\hat{\beta}_2 = [(10 + 14 + 9)/3] - 11$

$\qquad = 11 - 11$

$\qquad = 0$

$\hat{\beta}_3 = [(15 + 10 + 11)/3] - 11$

$\qquad = 12 - 11$

$\qquad = 1.$

d.
$$SS_B = \sum_{all\,obs} \hat{\beta}_k^2$$

As in part (b), 24 subjects have a $\hat{\beta}_k$ value of $\hat{\beta}_1$, 24 have $\hat{\beta}_2$, and 24 have $\hat{\beta}_3$. Thus,

$$SS_B = 24\hat{\beta}_1^2 + 24\hat{\beta}_2^2 + 24\hat{\beta}_3^2$$
$$= 24(-1)^2 + 24(0)^2 + 24(1)^2$$
$$= 48$$

e. From Equation 18, the general form of an estimated interaction parameter is

$$\widehat{\alpha\beta}_{jk} = \bar{Y}_{jk} - (\bar{Y}_{j.} + \bar{Y}_{.k} - \bar{Y}_{..}) \tag{7.18}$$

For these data,

$$\widehat{\alpha\beta}_{11} = 8 - (11 + 10 - 11)$$
$$= -2$$

$$\widehat{\alpha\beta}_{12} = 10 - (11 + 11 - 11)$$
$$= -1$$

$$\widehat{\alpha\beta}_{13} = 15 - (11 + 12 - 11)$$
$$= 3$$

$$\widehat{\alpha\beta}_{21} = 9 - (11 + 10 - 11)$$
$$= -1$$

$$\widehat{\alpha\beta}_{22} = 14 - (11 + 11 - 11)$$
$$= 3$$

$$\widehat{\alpha\beta}_{23} = 10 - (11 + 12 - 11)$$
$$= -2$$

$$\widehat{\alpha\beta}_{31} = 13 - (11 + 10 - 11)$$
$$= 3$$

$$\widehat{\alpha\beta}_{32} = 9 - (11 + 11 - 11)$$
$$= -2$$

$$\widehat{\alpha\beta}_{33} = 11 - (11 + 12 - 11)$$
$$= -1.$$

f.
$$SS_{AB} = \sum_{all\,obs} (\alpha\beta_{jk})^2$$

In general, with equal n, a total of n subjects will have an $\widehat{\alpha\beta}_{jk}$ value of $\widehat{\alpha\beta}_{11}$, n will have a value of $\widehat{\alpha\beta}_{12}$, and so forth. Thus,

$$SS_{AB} = 8[(-2)^2 + (-1)^2 + (3)^2 + (-1)^2 + (3)^2 + (-2)^2 + (3)^2 + (-2)^2 + (-1)^2]$$
$$= 336$$

5. a.
$$SS_A = E_R - E_F = nb \sum_{j=1}^{a} (\bar{Y}_{j.} - \bar{Y}_{..})^2 \tag{7.25}$$
$$= 5(3)[(187 - 193)^2 + (199 - 193)^2]$$
$$= 1080$$

b.
$$SS_A = E_R - E_F = n \sum_{j=1}^{a} (\bar{Y}_j - \bar{Y})^2 \tag{7.26}$$
$$= 15[(187 - 193)^2 + (199 - 193)^2]$$
$$= 1080$$

c. The answers to parts (a) and (b) are the same. This equivalence provides an empirical demonstration of the assertion in Chapter 7 that, in equal n designs, the sum of squares for the A main effect in a factorial design equals the sum of squares due to A in a single factor design when the data are analyzed as if the B factor never existed.

8. a. We need to calculate ϕ from the formula given in the problem:

$$\phi = .40\sqrt{n}.$$

Assuming $n = 10$,

$$\phi = .40\sqrt{10}$$
$$= 1.26$$

The chart for $df_{numerator} = 1$ must be consulted. Also, notice that $df_{denominator} = 18$. With $\alpha = .05$, the power appears to be approximately .40.

b. With 5 groups and $n = 10$, ϕ again equals 1.26. Now, however, the chart for $df_{numerator} = 4$ must be consulted with $df_{denominator} = 45$. With $\alpha = .05$, the power appears to be approximately .53.

c. In the factorial design, ϕ is calculated from

$$\phi = .40\sqrt{\frac{df_{denominator}}{df_{effect} + 1} + 1}$$

For a main effect in a 2×2 design with $n = 10$,

$$df_{effect} = 1 \qquad \text{(see 7.28)}$$
$$df_{denominator} = (2)(2)(10 - 1) = 36 \qquad \text{(see 7.27)}$$

so

$$\phi = .40\sqrt{\frac{36}{2} + 1}$$
$$= 1.74$$

The chart for $df_{numerator} = 1$ must be consulted with $df_{denominator} = 36$. With $\alpha = .05$, the power appears to be approximately .67.

d. The power will be the same as in part (c), because $df_{effect} = 1$ for the interaction effect in a 2×2 design (see Equation 7.34).

e. Once again, ϕ is calculated from

$$\phi = .40\sqrt{\frac{df_{denominator}}{df_{effect}} + 1}$$

For a main effect in a 3×3 design with $n = 10$,

$$df_{effect} = 2 \qquad \text{(see 7.28)}$$
$$df_{denominator} = (3)(3)(10 - 1) = 81 \qquad \text{(see 7.27)}$$

so

$$\phi = .40\sqrt{\frac{81}{2 + 1} + 1}$$
$$= 2.12$$

The chart for $df_{numerator} = 2$ must be consulted with $df_{denominator} = 81$. With $\alpha = .05$, the power appears to be approximately .91.

f. Yet again, ϕ is calculated from

$$\phi = .40 \sqrt{\frac{df_{denominator}}{df_{effect} + 1} + 1}$$

For an interaction effect in a 3×3 design with $n = 10$,

$$df_{effect} = 4 \qquad\qquad\qquad\text{(see 7.34)}$$

$$df_{denominator} = (3)(3)(10 - 1) = 81 \qquad\qquad\text{(see 7.27)}$$

so

$$\phi = .40 \sqrt{\frac{81}{4 + 1} + 1}$$

$$= 1.66$$

The chart for $df_{numerator} = 4$ must be consulted with $df_{denominator} = 81$. With $\alpha = .05$, the power appears to be approximately .85.

g. Only 2 of the 6 effects in parts (a) through (f) would have a power as high as .8 for detecting a large effect with 10 subjects per cell.

h. Two comments are pertinent here. First, the power of a test is a function not only of the sample size and the effect size (that is, small, medium, or large), but also of the type of design and the type of effect to be tested in that design. Thus, $n = 10$ may be sufficient for some effects in some designs, but not for others. Second, in many cases, $n = 10$ per cell may be too few subjects to have a power of .8 to detect even a large effect, much less a medium or small effect.

11. a. Notice that this student has performed tests of the simple effect of therapy for females and males separately. In each case the sum of squares for therapy can be found from

$$SS_{effect} = n \sum_{j=1}^{a} (\bar{Y}_j - \bar{Y})^2 \qquad\qquad\qquad (7.39)$$

where the sample means refer to the means for the specific individuals under consideration. For females, $\bar{Y}_1 = 60$, $\bar{Y}_2 = 80$, and $n = 10$. Thus, for females,

$$SS_{therapy} = 10[(60 - 70)^2 + (80 - 70)^2]$$

$$= 2000$$

The observed F value is given by

$$F = \frac{SS_{effect}/df_{effect}}{MS_W}$$

$$= \frac{2000/1}{800}$$

$$= 2.50$$

The critical F value with 1 and 36 degrees of freedom is approximately 4.17 (see Appendix Table A.2), so the difference between the therapies is nonsignificant at the .05 level for the females. For males, $\bar{Y}_1 = 40$, $\bar{Y}_2 = 60$, and $n = 10$, so

$$SS_{therapy} = 10[(40 - 50)^2 + (60 - 50)^2)$$

$$= 2000$$

The observed F is 2.50, so the difference between the therapies is also nonsignificant for the males.

b. The only difference from part (a) will involve the critical F value, which now equals

4.41, because there are now only 18 denominator degrees of freedom. However, as in part (a), the difference between the therapies is nonsignificant for females and males considered separately.

c. The sum of squares for the therapy main effect is

$$SS_{therapy} = (10)(2)[(50 - 60)^2 + (70 - 60)^2] \qquad \text{(see 7.25)}$$
$$= 4000$$

As a result,

$$F = \frac{SS_{therapy}/df_{therapy}}{MS_W}$$
$$= \frac{4000/1}{800}$$
$$= 5.00$$

As in part (a), the critical F with 1 and 36 degrees of freedom is approximately 4.17. Now, however, the difference between the therapies is statistically significant at the .05 level. Incidentally, for later parts of this problem, it is helpful to note that the interaction sum of squares for these data is exactly zero.

d. As we saw in Chapter 3, the t-test can be regarded as a comparison of models of the form

$$\text{Full:} \quad Y_{ij} = \mu_j + \varepsilon_{ij}$$
$$\text{Restricted:} \quad Y_{ij} = \mu + \varepsilon_{ij}$$

Group membership is solely a function of form of therapy, so any effects due to sex appear in the error term of both models. An F test to compare these models would be

$$F = \frac{(E_R - E_F)/(df_R - df_F)}{E_F/df_F}$$

In this situation,

$$df_F = N - a$$
$$= 40 - 2$$
$$= 38$$

and

$$df_R - df_F = 1$$

Further,

$$E_R - E_F = n \sum_{j=1}^{a} (\bar{Y}_j - \bar{Y})^2$$
$$= 20[(50 - 60)^2 + (70 - 60)^2]$$
$$= 4000$$

To calculate the observed F, we must find the sum of squared errors of the full model. However, the errors of this model will include the within-cell errors of the 2×2 factorial design, as well as any effects due to sex. Specifically,

$$E_F = SS_{within} + SS_{sex} + SS_{sex\,by\,therapy}$$

For these data,

$$SS_{within} = df_{within} MS_W$$
$$= 36(800)$$
$$= 28,800$$
$$SS_{sex} = (10)(2)[(70-60)^2 + (50-60)^2]$$
$$= 4000$$
$$SS_{sex\ by\ therapy} = 0$$

Thus,

$$E_F = 28,800 + 4000 + 0$$
$$= 32,800$$

The observed F is then

$$F = \frac{4000/1}{32,800/38}$$
$$= 4.63$$

The critical F value with 1 and 38 degrees of freedom is approximately 4.17 (see Appendix Table A.2), so the difference between the therapies is significant at the .05 level. Alternatively, as a t-test, the observed t value of 2.15 exceeds the critical t of approximately 2.04.

e. Testing the therapy main effect in the 2×2 design produced the largest F value for these data, reflecting the fact that this approach will often provide the most powerful test of the difference between the therapies. Tests of simple effects are less powerful than the test of the main effect when there is no interaction, so, generally speaking, main effects should be tested instead of simple effects when the interaction is nonsignificant (see Figure 7.2). In general, it is true that

$$SS_{A\ within\ B1} + SS_{A\ within\ B2} = SS_A + SS_{AB}$$

In our example,

$$SS_{therapy\ for\ females} + SS_{therapy\ for\ males} = SS_{therapy} + SS_{therapy\ by\ sex}$$

Specifically,

$$2000 + 2000 = 4000 + 0$$

Because there is no interaction here, the sum of squares for each simple effect is only one-half as large as the sum of squares for the main effect. The same ratio occurs for the F values, making the main effect test considerably more powerful than the simple effects tests. It should also be noted that the t-test of part (d) will be less powerful than the main effect test to the extent that the other factor (in this case, sex) has any effect on the dependent variable. This tendency is illustrated in these data, where the observed F value for the therapy main effect is 5.00, but the observed F corresponding to the t-test approach is 4.63.

16. a. Unweighted marginal means would reflect personality type effects for individuals at a particular stress level. The unweighted row marginal means for these data are

$$\bar{Y}_{1.(U)} = \sum_{k=1}^{b} \bar{Y}_{1k} / b$$
$$= (170 + 150)/2$$
$$= 160$$

$$\bar{Y}_{2.(U)} = \sum_{k=1}^{b} \bar{Y}_{2k} \Big/ b$$

$$= (140 + 120)/2$$

$$= 130$$

b. If the effect of stress is not taken into account, personality type effects are reflected in weighted marginal means. The weighted row marginal means for these data are

$$\bar{Y}_{1.(W)} = \sum_{k=1}^{b} n_{1k} \bar{Y}_{1k} \Big/ \sum_{k=1}^{b} n_{1k}$$

$$= [14(170) + 6(150)]/(14 + 6)$$

$$= 164$$

$$\bar{Y}_{2.(W)} = \sum_{k=1}^{b} n_{2k} \bar{Y}_{2k} \Big/ \sum_{k=1}^{b} n_{2k}$$

$$= [6(140) + 14(120)]/(6 + 14)$$

$$= 126$$

Thus, the estimated magnitude of the mean blood pressure difference between personality types, ignoring level of stress, is 38 units. We saw in part (a) that the comparable difference when the effect of stress is taken into account is 30 units. Thus, taking the effect of stress into account lowers the estimated difference between personality types. The reason is that Type A individuals are predominantly found in high-stress environments, while Type B's are more likely to be in low-stress environments, so some of the 38-unit difference found overall between A's and B's may reflect differences in their environments.

19. a. Table 5.8 (in Chapter 5) provides formulas for forming a confidence interval for a contrast. We can conceptualize the current problem as one of planning to test a single contrast, so that $C = 1$. In this situation, Table 5.8 shows that a 95% confidence interval for ψ has the form

$$\hat{\psi} \pm \sqrt{F_{.05;1,N-a}} \sqrt{MS_W \sum_{j=1}^{a} (c_j^2/n_j)}$$

For the Type III sum of squares, ψ is given by

$$\psi = .5\mu_{11} + .5\mu_{12} - .5\mu_{21} - .5\mu_{22}$$

Then,

$$\hat{\psi} = .5\bar{Y}_{11} + .5\bar{Y}_{12} - .5\bar{Y}_{21} - .5\bar{Y}_{22}$$

$$= .5(52) + .5(46) - .5(48) - .5(42)$$

$$= 4.00$$

$$F_{.05;1,N-a} = F_{.05;1,19}$$

$$= 4.38$$

$$\sum_{j=1}^{a} (c_j^2/n_j) = \frac{(.5)^2}{6} + \frac{(.5)^2}{4} + \frac{(-.5)^2}{8} + \frac{(-.5)^2}{5}$$

$$= .1854$$

Substituting these values, along with $MS_W = 19$ (which we were given in the problem), into the formula for the confidence interval yields

$$4.00 \pm \sqrt{4.38} \sqrt{19(.1854)}$$

which reduces to

$$4.00 \pm 3.93$$

Equivalently, we can be 95% confident that the population difference in unweighted marginal means is between .07 and 7.93. Given an equal number of females and males, we are 95% confident that CBT is between .07 and 7.93 points better than CCT.

b. We can use the same formula as in part (a), but the contrast coefficients are now defined to be

$$c_1 = \frac{n_{11}n_{21}/n_{+1}}{n_{11}n_{21}/n_{+1} + n_{12}n_{22}/n_{+2}}$$

$$= \frac{(6)(8)/14}{(6)(8)/14 + (4)(5)/9}$$

$$= .61$$

$$c_2 = \frac{n_{12}n_{22}/n_{+2}}{n_{11}n_{21}/n_{+1} + n_{12}n_{22}/n_{+2}}$$

$$= \frac{(4)(5)/9}{(6)(8)/14 + (4)(5)/9}$$

$$= .39$$

$$c_3 = -\frac{n_{11}n_{21}/n_{+1}}{n_{11}n_{21}/n_{+1} + n_{12}n_{22}/n_{+2}}$$

$$= -\frac{(6)(8)/14}{(6)(8)/14 + (4)(5)/9}$$

$$= -.61$$

$$c_4 = -\frac{n_{12}n_{22}/n_{+2}}{n_{11}n_{21}/n_{+1} + n_{12}n_{22}/n_{+2}}$$

$$= -\frac{(4)(5)/9}{(6)(8)/14 + (4)(5)/9}$$

$$= -.39$$

for μ_{11}, μ_{12}, μ_{21}, and μ_{22}, respectively. Thus,

$$\hat{\psi} = .61\bar{Y}_{11} + .39\bar{Y}_{12} - .61\bar{Y}_{21} - .39\bar{Y}_{22}$$

$$= .61(52) + .39(46) - .61(48) - .39(42)$$

$$= .61(52 - 48) + .39(46 - 42)$$

$$= 4.00$$

$$F_{.05;1,N-a} = F_{.05;1,19}$$

$$= 4.38$$

$$\sum_{j=1}^{a}(c_j^2/n_j) = \frac{(.61)^2}{6} + \frac{(.39)^2}{4} + \frac{(-.61)^2}{8} + \frac{(-.39)^2}{5}$$

$$= .1770$$

Substituting these values along with $MS_W = 19$ into the formula for the confidence interval yields

$$4.00 \pm \sqrt{4.38} \sqrt{19(.1770)}$$

which reduces to

$$4.00 \pm 3.84$$

We can be 95% confident that CBT is between .16 and 7.84 points better than CCT in the population, if we are willing to assume that the difference is the same for females as for males.

c. The contrast corresponding to the Type II sum of squares can be estimated slightly more precisely than the contrast corresponding to the Type III sum of squares. This advantage is the reason the Type II sum of squares is preferable to Type III if there is known to be no interaction in the population.

d. Once again, the confidence interval has the form

$$\hat{\psi} \pm \sqrt{F_{.05;1,N-a}} \sqrt{MS_W \sum_{j=1}^{a} (c_j^2/n_j)}$$

$\hat{\psi}$ is given by

$$\hat{\psi} = .5\bar{Y}_{11} + .5\bar{Y}_{12} - .5\bar{Y}_{21} - .5\bar{Y}_{22}$$
$$= .5(52) + .5(46) - .5(48) - .5(42)$$
$$= 4.00$$

$$F_{.05;1,N-a} = F_{.05;1,16}$$
$$= 4.75$$

$$\sum_{j=1}^{a} (c_j^2/n_j) = \frac{(.5)^2}{4} + \frac{(.5)^2}{4} + \frac{(-.5)^2}{4} + \frac{(-.5)^2}{4}$$
$$= .2500$$

Substituting these values, along with $MS_W = 19$, into the formula for the confidence interval yields

$$4.00 \pm \sqrt{4.75} \sqrt{19(.2500)}$$
$$4.00 \pm 4.75$$

Thus, we can be 95% confident that CBT is between .75 units worse and 8.75 units better than CCT.

e. The interval computed in part (d) is considerably wider than the intervals we found in parts (a) and (b). In particular, based on the equal n approach, we could not confidently rule out the possibility that CBT is worse than CCT, as we could with the two nonorthogonal approaches. Randomly deleting observations decreases precision and hence lowers the power to detect a true effect.

Chapter 8

3. The marginal mean for the Drug Present condition is

$$\mu_{.1.} = \sum_{l=1}^{c} \sum_{j=1}^{a} \mu_{j1l}/ac$$
$$= (180 + 205 + 170 + 190)/4$$
$$= 186.25$$

Similarly, the marginal mean for the Drug Absent condition is

$$\mu_{.2.} = \sum_{l=1}^{c} \sum_{j=1}^{a} \mu_{j2l}/ac$$

$$= (200 + 210 + 185 + 190)/4$$

$$= 196.25$$

There is a Drug main effect in the population, since mean blood pressure is lower when the Drug is present than when it is absent.

8. The correct answer is (c). Notice that the contrast coefficients for ψ represent an AB interaction, because the A effect at B_1 is compared to the A effect at B_2 (see Equation 7.1 for a reminder). Specifically, ψ equals the difference between A_1 and A_2 at B_1 minus the difference between A_1 and A_2 at B_2. Thus, the fact that the estimated value of ψ at C_1 is -8 implies that A_1 minus A_2 is smaller at B_1 than at B_2, for the first level of C. However, because the estimated value of ψ at C_2 is $+8$, A_1 minus A_2 is larger at B_1 than at B_2, for the second level of C. As a result, the AB interaction at C_1 differs from the AB interaction at C_2, suggesting the possibility of a three-way ABC interaction (see Table 8.8). In contrast, the AB interaction would average ψ at C_1 and ψ at C_2 (see Table 8.8), resulting in a value of 0. Thus, there is no evidence here for an AB interaction. Finally, it is impossible to tell whether the simple two-way interactions of A and B at the two levels of C would be significant, without knowing the sample size and MS_W.

10. a. From Table 8.9,

$$\alpha_j = \mu_{j..} - \mu$$

so

$$\hat{\alpha}_j = \bar{Y}_{j..} - \bar{Y}_{...}$$

For these data,

$$\hat{\alpha}_1 = (45 + 55 + 65 + 40 + 40 + 70)/6 - (45 + 55 + 65 + 40 + 40 + 70 + 55$$

$$+ 75 + 65 + 20 + 30 + 40)/12$$

$$= 52.5 - 50.0$$

$$= 2.5$$

$$\hat{\alpha}_2 = (55 + 75 + 65 + 20 + 30 + 40)/6 - 50.0$$

$$= 47.5 - 50.0$$

$$= -2.5$$

Similarly, for the B main effect,

$$\beta_k = \mu_{.k.} - \mu \qquad\qquad \text{(see Table 8.9)}$$

so

$$\hat{\beta}_k = \bar{Y}_{.k.} - \bar{Y}_{...}$$

For these data,

$$\hat{\beta}_1 = (45 + 55 + 40 + 20)/4 - 50.0$$

$$= 40.0 - 50.0$$

$$= -10.0$$

$$\hat{\beta}_2 = (55 + 75 + 40 + 30)/4 - 50.0$$

$$= 50.0 - 50.0$$

$$= 0$$

$$\hat{\beta}_3 = (65 + 65 + 70 + 40)/4 - 50.0$$
$$= 60.0 - 50.0$$
$$= 10.0$$

b. The observed F value for the A main effect is given by

$$F = \frac{SS_A/(a-1)}{MS_W}$$

From Table 8.11,

$$SS_A = \sum_{j=1}^{a}\sum_{k=1}^{b}\sum_{l=1}^{c}\sum_{i=1}^{n} \hat{\alpha}_j^2$$

$$= bcn \sum_{j=1}^{a} \hat{\alpha}_j^2$$

$$= (3)(2)(10)[(2.5)^2 + (-2.5)^2]$$

$$= 750.0$$

We know that $a = 2$, so $a - 1 = 1$, and

$$MS_W = \frac{SS_W}{N-a}$$

$$= \frac{86,400}{120-12}$$

$$= 800$$

Thus, the F value for the A main effect is

$$F = \frac{750/1}{800}$$

$$= 0.94$$

The critical F with 1 and 108 degrees of freedom is approximately 4.00 (see Appendix Table A.2), so the A main effect is nonsignificant at the .05 level. The observed F value for the B main effect is given by

$$F = \frac{SS_B/(b-1)}{MS_W}$$

From Table 8.11,

$$SS_B = \sum_{j=1}^{a}\sum_{k=1}^{b}\sum_{l=1}^{c}\sum_{i=1}^{n} \hat{\beta}_k^2$$

$$= acn \sum_{k=1}^{b} \hat{\beta}_k^2$$

$$= (2)(2)(10)[(-10.0)^2 + (0.0)^2 + (10.0)^2]$$

$$= 8000.0$$

We know that $b = 3$, so $b - 1 = 2$, and we found that $MS_W = 800$. Thus, the F value for the B main effect is

$$F = \frac{8000/2}{800}$$

$$= 5.00$$

The critical F with 2 and 108 degrees of freedom is approximately 3.15 (see Appendix Table A.2), so the B main effect is statistically significant at the .05 level.

c. The following plot is probably the clearest way to picture the three-way interaction:

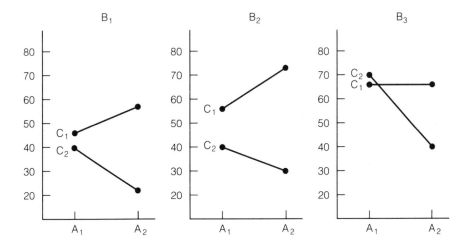

This plot reveals that the AC interaction is the same at every level of B, so there is no evidence of a three-way interaction. To see this explicitly, we will consider the magnitude of the AC interaction at each level of B. Specifically, the following table shows the magnitude of the C_1 mean minus the C_2 mean for both A_1 and A_2, separately for each level of B:

Level of B	$C_1 - C_2$ at A_1	$C_1 - C_2$ at A_2	Difference Between $C_1 - C_2$ at A_1 and $C_1 - C_2$ at A_2
B_1	5	35	-30
B_2	15	45	-30
B_3	-5	25	-30

As the rightmost column shows, the AC interaction is the same at each level of B, so there is no three-way interaction.

11. a.
$$\psi_{C1} = \mu_{111} - \mu_{121} - \mu_{211} + \mu_{221}$$
$$\psi_{C2} = \mu_{112} - \mu_{122} - \mu_{212} + \mu_{222}$$

The contrast for the three-way interaction is

$$\psi_{C1} - \psi_{C2} = \mu_{111} - \mu_{121} - \mu_{211} + \mu_{221} - \mu_{112} + \mu_{122} + \mu_{212} - \mu_{222}$$

b.
$$\psi_{B1} = \mu_{111} - \mu_{112} - \mu_{211} + \mu_{212}$$
$$\psi_{B2} = \mu_{121} - \mu_{122} - \mu_{221} + \mu_{222}$$

The contrast for the three-way interaction is

$$\psi_{B1} - \psi_{B2} = \mu_{111} - \mu_{112} - \mu_{211} + \mu_{212} - \mu_{121} + \mu_{122} + \mu_{221} - \mu_{222}$$

which can be rewritten as

$$\mu_{111} - \mu_{121} - \mu_{211} + \mu_{221} - \mu_{112} + \mu_{122} + \mu_{212} - \mu_{222}$$

c.
$$\psi_{A1} = \mu_{111} - \mu_{112} - \mu_{121} + \mu_{122}$$
$$\psi_{A2} = \mu_{211} - \mu_{212} - \mu_{221} + \mu_{222}$$

The contrast for the three-way interaction is

$$\psi_{A1} - \psi_{A2} = \mu_{111} - \mu_{112} - \mu_{121} + \mu_{122} - \mu_{211} + \mu_{212} + \mu_{221} - \mu_{222}$$

which can be rewritten as

$$\mu_{111} - \mu_{121} - \mu_{211} + \mu_{221} - \mu_{112} + \mu_{122} + \mu_{212} - \mu_{222}$$

d. The contrast coefficients of parts (a), (b), and (c) are identical to one another. This implies that the three interpretations of a three-way interaction are indeed equivalent to one another.

12. a. To find interaction contrasts, corresponding coefficients must be multiplied times one another.

   AB:

1	1	0	0	−1	−1	−1	−1	0	0	1	1
0	0	1	1	−1	−1	0	0	−1	−1	1	1

   AC:

1	−1	1	−1	1	−1	−1	1	−1	1	−1	1

   BC:

1	−1	0	0	−1	1	1	−1	0	0	−1	1
0	0	1	−1	−1	1	0	0	1	−1	−1	1

   The three-way interaction contrasts can be found in any of several equivalent ways. For example, the AB contrast coefficients can be multiplied by the C contrast coefficients.

   ABC:

1	−1	0	0	−1	1	−1	1	0	0	1	−1
0	0	1	−1	−1	1	0	0	−1	1	1	−1

b. (1) **AB at C₁:**

1	0	0	0	−1	0	−1	0	0	0	1	0
0	0	1	0	−1	0	0	0	−1	0	1	0

   AB at C₂:

0	1	0	0	0	−1	0	−1	0	0	0	1
0	0	0	1	0	−1	0	0	0	−1	0	1

   (2) It can be shown that

   $$SS_{AB \, at \, C1} + SS_{AB \, at \, C2} = SS_{AB} + SS_{ABC}$$

   Thus, the 4 contrasts for AB at C_1 and AB at C_2 would replace the 4 contrasts for AB and ABC.

Chapter 9

2. The primary considerations are (1) that the covariate correlate with the dependent variable, and (2) that the covariate be independent of the treatment factor(s). The first consideration is critical inasmuch as the covariate is being used to reduce within-cell variability and the strength of the correlation determines the extent of error reduction. The second consideration is important for facilitating interpretation. With the covariate and treatment factor independent, one is assured that the estimate of the treatment effect in a randomized study is unbiased. When the treatment and covariate happen to be correlated, one cannot generally know if the extent of the adjustment for differences on the covariate is too large, too small, or just right.

      Two other, secondary considerations that make a covariate desirable are (1) the covariate can be obtained easily and economically, and (2) the process of obtaining the covariate scores does not affect the scores on the dependent variable. The latter possible effect of "testing," if it occurs, can limit the external validity of the study but does not threaten the internal validity of the research.

4. a. As indicated in Equations 9.1 and 9.2, the models being compared are

$$\text{Full:} \quad Y_{ij} = \mu + \alpha_j + \beta X_{ij} + \varepsilon_{ij}$$

$$\text{Restricted:} \quad Y_{ij} = \mu + \beta X_{ij} + \varepsilon_{ij}$$

b.

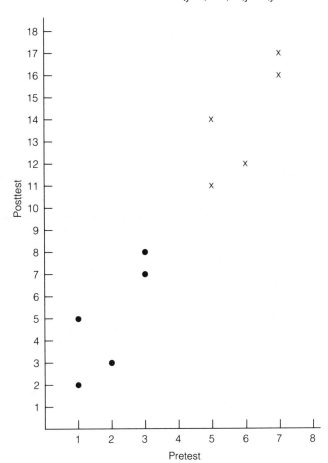

As shown in the preceding plot, there is a very strong positive relationship between the pretest and posttest within each of the two groups. Further, the group with the higher mean on the pretest also has the higher mean on the posttest. Thus, the data follow the pattern discussed in the text (see Figure 9.5(a)) where an apparent treatment effect is due primarily to preexisting differences. It appears in fact that a single regression line would fit all the data nearly as well as separate regression lines for the two groups. Because group membership does not add much to the pretest as a predictor of posttest scores, it appears that the ANCOVA test of the treatment effect would not be significant.

c. Designating groups C and T as groups 1 and 2, and the pretest and posttest as variables X and Y, respectively, we may determine the slope for a group by using Equation 9.11. That is, for each group, we compute the ratio of the sum of cross-products of deviations from the variables' means to the sum of squared deviations on the pretest.

Group C

X_{i1}	$X_{i1} - \bar{X}_1$	Y_{i1}	$Y_{i1} - \bar{Y}_1$	$(X_{i1} - \bar{X}_1)(Y_{i1} - \bar{Y}_1)$	$(X_{i1} - \bar{X}_1)^2$
1	-1	5	0	0	1
3	1	8	3	3	1
3	1	7	2	2	1
1	-1	2	-3	3	1
2	0	3	-2	0	0
$\bar{X}_1 = 2$		$\bar{Y}_1 = 5$		$\sum = 8$	$\sum = 4$

$$b_1 = \frac{\sum_i (X_{i1} - \bar{X}_1)(Y_{i1} - \bar{Y}_1)}{\sum (X_{i1} - \bar{X}_1)^2} = \frac{8}{4} = 2.$$

The computations for group T are carried out similarly:

Group T

X_{i2}	$X_{i2} - \bar{X}_2$	Y_{i2}	$Y_{i2} - \bar{Y}_2$	$(X_{i2} - \bar{X}_2)(Y_{i2} - \bar{Y}_2)$	$(X_{i2} - \bar{X}_2)^2$
5	-1	14	0	0	1
7	1	17	3	3	1
7	1	16	2	2	1
5	-1	11	-3	3	1
6	0	12	-2	0	0
$\bar{X}_2 = 6$		$\bar{Y}_2 = 14$		$\sum = 8$	$\sum = 4$

Since the deviations from the mean in group T are identical here to those in group C, the slopes necessarily are the same:

$$b_2 = \frac{\sum_i (X_{i2} - \bar{X}_2)(Y_{i2} - \bar{Y}_2)}{\sum (X_{i2} - \bar{X}_2)^2} = \frac{8}{4} = 2$$

Although normally these slopes would differ, in this particular example, because $b_1 = b_2 = 2$, it follows that their weighted average b_W must also be 2 (see Equation 9.12). Thus, the intercept for each group's regression line in this case will be the same as the intercept computed using the common within-group slope, that is,

$$a_1 = \bar{Y}_1 - b_1 \bar{X}_1 = \bar{Y}_1 - b_W \bar{X}_1 = 5 - 2(2) = 5 - 4 = 1$$
$$a_2 = \bar{Y}_2 - b_2 \bar{X}_2 = \bar{Y}_2 - b_W \bar{X}_2 = 14 - 2(6) = 14 - 12 = 2$$

The pooled within-group slope we have computed is the estimate of the population slope β in the full model, and the intercepts are the estimates of the combination of parameters $\mu + \alpha_j$ for that group (see Equation 9.18), that is,

$$\hat{\beta} = b_W = 2$$
$$\hat{\mu} + \hat{\alpha}_1 = a_1 = 1$$
$$\hat{\mu} + \hat{\alpha}_2 = a_2 = 2$$

Note here that μ is the mean of the intercepts, so $\hat{\mu} = (1 + 2)/2 = 1.5$, and that α_j is the effect of the treatment as indicated by the vertical displacement of the regression line. Here, group 1 results in the regression line's intercept being .5 units lower than the average of the intercepts, and group 2 results in its regression line's intercept being .5 units above the average of the intercepts, that is, $\hat{\alpha}_1 = -.5$ and $\hat{\alpha}_2 = +.5$.

d. We can use our parameter estimates to form the prediction equation for our full model:

$$\hat{Y}_j = a_j + b_W X_{ij} \tag{9.25}$$

That is,

$$\hat{Y}_1 = \alpha_1 + b_W X_{ij} = 1 + 2X_{ij}$$
$$\hat{Y}_2 = \alpha_2 + b_W X_{ij} = 2 + 2X_{ij}$$

Substituting the observed values of X, we obtain the following predictions and errors of prediction, $e_{ij} = Y_{ij} - \hat{Y}_{ij}$:

X	Y	$\hat{Y}$	e	e^2
1	5	3	2	4
3	8	7	1	1
3	7	7	0	0
1	2	3	−1	1
2	3	5	−2	4
5	14	12	2	4
7	17	16	1	1
7	16	16	0	0
5	11	12	−1	1
6	12	14	−2	4
			$\sum = 20 = E_F$	

e. As indicated in Equation 3, the predictions of the restricted model are just a linear transformation of the X scores:

$$\hat{Y}_{ij} = \hat{\mu} + \hat{\beta} X_{ij} \tag{9.3}$$

Thus, the overall correlation between Y_{ij} and X_{ij} will be identical to the correlation between Y_{ij} and the prediction of the restricted model. Thus, the proportion of variance accounted for by the restricted model is

$$R_R^2 = r_{XY}^2 = (.95905)^2 = .91978$$

Recall from the Chapter 3 Extension that the sum of squared errors for a model can be expressed simply as the proportion of variance not accounted for by that model times the total sum of squares (see discussion of Equation 3E.13). Thus we have

$$E_R = (1 - R_R^2)SS_{Total} = (1 - .91978)254.5 = (.08022)254.5 = 20.416.$$

f. We can readily perform the ANCOVA test of treatment effects, using these results for the errors of our models and $df_R = N - 2 = 10 - 2 = 8$ and $df_F = N - (a + 1) = 10 - 3 = 7$. Thus our test statistic is

$$F = \frac{(E_R - E_F)/(df_R - df_F)}{E_F/df_F} = \frac{(20.416 - 20)/(8 - 7)}{20/7} = \frac{.416/1}{2.857} = 0.146$$

Clearly, this is nonsignificant, and we conclude we cannot reject the null hypothesis of no treatment effect here, once we take the pretest scores into account.

9. Power is of course related to the absolute magnitude of the effect you are trying to detect, and this in turn is indicated by the standard deviation of the population means (the numerator of the formula for ϕ given in the problem). Given the population group means provided, the population grand mean is 20, and we have the following standard deviation of means σ_m:

$$\sigma_m = \sqrt{\sum \alpha_j^2/a} = \sqrt{\sum(\mu_j - \mu)^2/a}$$
$$= \sqrt{[(10 - 20)^2 + (20 - 20)^2 + (30 - 20)^2]/3}$$
$$= \sqrt{(100 + 0 + 100)/3} = \sqrt{200/3} = \sqrt{66.667}$$
$$= 8.165$$

This fixed characteristic of the population will be the same regardless of the method used to analyze the data. In addition, the degrees of freedom are practically the same for the three approaches. The numerator degrees of freedom are $a - 1 = 3 - 1 = 2$ in each case. The denominator degrees of freedom are $N - a = 30 - 3 = 27$ for the posttest only and gain score analyses, and $N - a - 1 = 26$ for ANCOVA, which requires estimation of a slope parameter as well as a parameter for each of the a groups.

What can vary across the analyses, depending on the correlation between the pretest and the posttest, is the error variance, as indicated in the problem. The error variance in the posttest only analysis, $\sigma_\varepsilon^2 = 20^2 = 400$, is unaffected by this correlation, since information about the pretest is ignored. However, the error variance in the other approaches can be quite different from that in the posttest only approach and in some cases can in fact be larger. For example, when $\rho = 0$, as in part (a), the error variance in the gain score analysis is

$$\sigma_{\varepsilon(gains)}^2 = \sigma_\varepsilon^2 2(1 - \rho) = \sigma_\varepsilon^2 2(1 - 0) = 2(20)^2 = 800$$

On the other hand, the error variance in ANCOVA will be no larger than that in the posttest only analysis and will generally be smaller. For example, when $\rho = .7$, the error variance in ANCOVA is

$$\sigma_{\varepsilon(ANCOVA)}^2 = \sigma_\varepsilon^2(1 - \rho^2) = (20)^2(1 - .7^2) = 400(1 - .49) = 400(.51) = 204$$

Carrying out these calculations for the error variances for the various analyses and values of the pretest-posttest correlation yields the following values.

Error Variance, σ_ε^2

ρ	Posttest Only	ANCOVA	Gains
0	400	400	800
.3	400	364	560
.5	400	300	400
.7	400	204	240

Given these error variances, we can readily calculate the values of ϕ that we need to determine power using the Pearson-Hartley chart in Table A-11 for $df_{num} = 2$. For example, for the posttest only design we have

$$\phi = \frac{\sqrt{\sum \alpha_j^2 / a}}{\sigma_\varepsilon / \sqrt{n}} = \frac{8.165}{\sqrt{400} / \sqrt{10}} = \frac{8.165}{20/3.162} = (.408)(3.162) = 1.291$$

Going up vertically from the point on the horizontal axis corresponding to $\phi = 1.291$ for $\alpha = .05$ in the chart, we see that the lines for $df_{denom} = 20$ and $df_{denom} = 30$ are around a height of .45 for this ϕ. Thus, power is .45 in the posttest only design for $\rho = 0$; and because σ_ε^2 is not affected by ρ for this analysis, this is the power for all values of ρ.

In the gain score analysis for $\rho = 0$, the inflated error variance results in a smaller ϕ and hence in less power. Specifically,

$$\phi = \frac{\sqrt{\sum \alpha_j^2 / a}}{\sigma_\varepsilon / \sqrt{n}} = \frac{8.165}{\sqrt{800} / \sqrt{10}} = \frac{8.165}{28.284/3.162} = \frac{8.165}{8.944} = .913$$

This value of ϕ is so small that it does not appear on the Pearson-Hartley charts for $\alpha = .05$. However, at the smallest value that does appear of $\phi = 1.0$, the power for 30 denominator degrees of freedom is only barely above .30. Thus the power to detect a smaller effect with 27 degrees of freedom would be even less, although projecting the power curve out to $\phi = .9$ indicates that the power is still only a little below .3.

At the other extreme, when the correlation is .7 and an ANCOVA approach to analysis is used, the relatively small value of σ_ε^2 translates into a large ϕ value and high power:

$$\phi = \frac{\sqrt{\sum \alpha_j^2 / a}}{\sigma_\varepsilon / \sqrt{n}} = \frac{8.165}{\sqrt{204} / \sqrt{10}} = \frac{8.165}{14.283/3.162} = \frac{8.165}{4.517} = 1.808$$

Visually interpolating between the curves for 20 and 30 degrees of freedom results in an estimate of .75 power for $df = 26$.

Using these same methods for the other values of ρ yields the following values of ϕ and corresponding estimates of power.

Approach

	Posttest Only		ANCOVA		Gains	
	ϕ	Power	ϕ	Power	ϕ	Power
(a) $\rho = 0$	1.291	.45	1.291	.45	.913	.30
(b) $\rho = .3$	1.291	.45	1.353	.50	1.091	.32
(c) $\rho = .5$	1.291	.45	1.491	.58	1.291	.45
(d) $\rho = .7$	1.291	.45	1.808	.75	1.667	.68

e. There are two principal conclusions suggested by these power results. First, the power of the ANCOVA approach is in general larger than that of the posttest only approach, with the extent of the power advantage increasing with the pretest-posttest correlation. Second, the gain score analysis is in general less powerful than the ANCOVA approach and requires a pretest-posttest correlation of .5 to be as powerful as a procedure that ignores the pretest entirely. As the correlation increases beyond +.5, the power of the gain score analysis exceeds that of the posttest only approach and approaches that of the ANCOVA approach.

Though not suggested by these results, there are two extreme cases where minor exceptions to these general principles arise. First, if there is no pretest-posttest correlation, the posttest only approach is slightly more powerful than the ANCOVA approach, as a result of having one more degree of freedom. Second, if the pretest-posttest correlation is approximately +1.0, the gain score analysis can be slightly more powerful than ANCOVA, again by virtue of having an additional degree of freedom for error.

Chapter 10

7. a. (1) The design may be diagrammed as follows, where C designates cleaning and F filling.

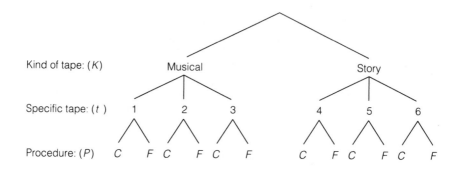

The factor of dental procedure (P) is crossed with the random factor of the specific tape (t), which in turn is nested within levels of the factor of kind of tape (K). "Subjects" of course constitutes a random factor that is nested within combinations of levels of all the other factors. Thus, the basic structure of the design may be labeled as $P \times t/K$.

(2) With three factors, if the factors were completely crossed, there would be 7 effects that could be tested (three main effects, three two-way interactions, and one three-way interaction). However, because here t is nested within K, the t main effect and the tK and PtK interactions cannot be tested. Instead, we can examine the simple effects of factor t within levels of K (that is, t/K) and the simple interactions of factors P and t within levels of K (that is, Pt/K). Thus the testable effects are

Testable Effect	Verbal Label	Status
P	Procedure main effect	Fixed
K	Kind of tape main effect	Fixed
PK	Procedure × Kind of tape interaction	Fixed
t/K	Simple effects of specific tape within Kinds of tape	Random
Pt/K	Simple interactions of Procedure × specific tape within Kinds of tape	Random

The degrees of freedom associated with the main effects of the crossed factors are as usual one less than the number of levels of each factor, and the degrees of freedom for their interaction is equal to the product of the degrees of freedom for the main effects of the factors involved in the interaction. Thus, if P and K are crossed factors with p levels of factor P and k levels of factor K, the main effect of P would have $p - 1$ degrees of freedom, the main effect of K would have $k - 1$ degrees of freedom, and the PK interaction would have $(p - 1)(k - 1)$ degrees of freedom. The tests of the nested factor are carried out as pooled tests of simple effects. For example, carrying out the test of the simple main effects of a factor having t levels nested within each of the k levels of factor K is like carrying out k one-way ANOVAs, each of which would have $t - 1$ degrees of freedom. Thus the pooled test of the simple main effects of factor t within each level of factor K, or the test of the t/K effect, has $k(t - 1)$ degrees of freedom. Similarly, in considering the Pt/K effect, one is pooling k simple interaction effects each of which has $(p - 1)(t - 1)$ degrees of freedom, and so the Pt/K effect has $k(p - 1)(t - 1)$ degrees of freedom.

The error terms for testing these effects can be determined by reference to the preceding diagram and the flowchart in Figure 10.7. Considering first the P main effect, there are no random factors nested under levels of P; but since P is crossed with t, there is an interaction of factor P with the random factor t within each level of K. There is only one such effect, so Pt/K suffices as the error term for testing P. For the main effect of kind of tape, factor K, there is a random factor nested within its levels at the next lowest level of the hierarchy, and thus t/K is selected as the error term. In considering the KP interaction, as explained in the discussion in the main text of the Figure 10.7 flowchart's rule (i), Pt/K is considered to be an interaction of the effect to be tested with a random factor and thus is selected as the error term. Both effects t/K and Pt/K involve all the random factors and so the flowchart implies MS_W is the correct error term. MS_W in a design of this structure is the average of the ptk within-group variances, each of which is based on $n - 1$ degrees of freedom, and so has $ptk(n - 1)$ degrees of freedom.

Thus, the summary of effects, error terms, and degrees of freedom is as follows:

Effect	df_{Effect}	Denominator Error Term	df_{Error}
P	$p-1=2-1=1$	Pt/K	$k(p-1)(t-1)=2(2-1)(3-1)=4$
K	$k-1=2-1=1$	t/K	$k(t-1)=2(3-1)=4$
PK	$(p-1)(k-1)=1\cdot 1=1$	Pt/K	$k(p-1)(t-1)=2(2-1)(3-1)=4$
t/K	$k(t-1)=2(3-1)=4$	MS_W	$ptk(n-1)=2\cdot 3\cdot 2(t-1)=12\cdot 4=48$
Pt/K	$k(p-1)(t-1)=2\cdot 1\cdot 2$ $\quad =4$	MS_W	$ptk(n-1)=2\cdot 3\cdot 2(t-1)=12\cdot 4=48$

b. Although usually increasing the number of subjects will increase df for the denominator, that is not the case for testing the effect of the kind of tape here. The denominator term for testing the main effect of factor K is t/K and its df depends solely on the number of levels of factors t and K. To increase df for testing the effect of kind of tape, one would need to increase the number of specific tapes of each kind, not the number of subjects. However, increasing n will result in more precise estimates of the means of the levels of K and will thus cause power to increase, even though the critical F value is not affected.

9. a. The type of feedback (factor F), immediate or delayed, is a fixed factor crossed with the other factors in the design. The type of concept (factor C), either disjunctive or conjunctive, is also a fixed factor and is crossed with factor F. The specific problem (factor p) is a random factor nested within levels of factor C but crossed with factor F. That is, each problem appears together with only one type of concept but each problem appears together with all types of feedback. Thus, the basic structure of the design may be labeled $F \times p/C$.

b. Following the same logic as was explained in the answer to problem 7, we arrive at the following 5 testable effects in this design, and the logic of the flowchart of Figure 10.7 leads to the error terms indicated.

Effect	Verbal Label of Effect	Denominator Error Term
F	Feedback main effect	Fp/C
C	Concept main effect	p/C
FC	Feedback $\times$ Concept interaction	Fp/C
p/C	Simple effects of problems within concepts	MS_W
Fp/C	Simple interactions of feedback and problems within concepts	MS_W

c. Let us designate specific levels of the factor of feedback by $j = 1, 2$, specific levels of the concept factor by $k = 1, 2$, and the specific problems within a type of concept by $l = 1, 2, 3, 4$. Thus, we would have the following table of cell and marginal means:

Concept:	**Disjunctive** $(k = 1)$				**Conjunctive** $(k = 2)$		
Feedback:	*Immed.* $(j = 1)$	*Delayed* $(j = 2)$			*Immed.* $(j = 1)$	*Delayed* $(j = 2)$	
Problem 1 $(l = 1)$	3	3	3	Problem 5 $(l = 1)$	1	2	1.5
Problem 2 $(l = 2)$	3	5	4	Problem 6 $(l = 2)$	1	1	1.0
Problem 3 $(l = 3)$	2	6	4	Problem 7 $(l = 3)$	4	5	4.5
Problem 4 $(l = 4)$	4	6	5	Problem 8 $(l = 4)$	0	2	1.0
	3	5	4.0		1.5	2.5	2.0

The effects of the completely crossed factors of feedback and concept can be handled by estimating effect parameters as discussed in Chapters 7 and 8, squaring them, and summing over all observations. To apply this logic to the effects involving the nested factor of problems would require estimating a different set of effects for each of the levels of the concept factor within which it is nested. For example, if α_j, β_k, and $(\alpha\beta)_{jk}$ refer to the main effects of feedback, concept, and their interaction, respectively, one might refer to the simple effect of problems within the kth level of concepts by $\gamma_{l(k)}$ and the simple interaction of problems by feedback within the kth level of concepts by $\alpha\gamma_{jl(k)}$. Because such notation in the subscripts is rather cumbersome, it may be easier to approach the analysis as we did in the text (see discussion of Table 10.5), by thinking in terms of the differences in the predictions of two competing models for the various cells of the design.

Let us begin with the most complex testable effect, that is, the simple interactions of feedback and problems within concepts, Fp/C. The null hypothesis is that, for each of the two kinds of concepts, the difference between immediate and delayed feedback is the same for all problems under investigation. In terms of models, this corresponds to a comparison between a full model of the form

$$\text{Full:} \quad Y_{ijkl} = \mu_{jkl} + \varepsilon_{ijkl}$$

with one incorporating the restrictions that, when $k = 1$, the $\mu_{111} - \mu_{211}$ differences are the same for all four values of l, and when $k = 2$, the $\mu_{121} - \mu_{221}$ differences are also equal to each other across the four values of l. Although, as we discussed in Chapter 4, it is difficult to write out such restricted models, the predictions of models, with and without interactions, can be described simply. In particular, the predictions of the full model above would just be the cell means:

$$\hat{Y}_{jkl_F} = \bar{Y}_{jkl}$$

Numerically, the predictions of the full model are thus the values given in the preceding table. For the restricted model, at each level of the concept factor, we allow for problem and feedback main effects to cause differences from the average level for that concept, but we do not allow for problem × feedback interactions. That is,

$$\hat{Y}_{jkl_R} = \bar{Y}_{.k.} + (\bar{Y}_{jk.} - \bar{Y}_{.k.}) + (\bar{Y}_{.kl} - \bar{Y}_{.k.}) = \bar{Y}_{jk.} + \bar{Y}_{.kl} - \bar{Y}_{.k.}$$

For example, if problem and feedback do not interact for disjunctive concepts, our best guess of the population mean for subjects learning a disjunctive concept under immediate feedback for problem 1 is

$$\hat{Y}_{111_R} = \bar{Y}_{11.} + \bar{Y}_{.11} - \bar{Y}_{.1.} = 3 + 3 - 4 = 2.$$

Or again, for subjects learning a disjunctive concept under immediate feedback for problem 4, the prediction is

$$\hat{Y}_{114_R} = \bar{Y}_{11.} + \bar{Y}_{.14} - \bar{Y}_{.1.} = 3 + 5 - 4 = 4.$$

Carrying out these calculations for all the cells yields the following set of predictions for the model incorporating the restriction of no Fp/C interactions:

$$\hat{Y}_{jkl_R} = \bar{Y}_{jk.} + \bar{Y}_{.kl} - \bar{Y}_{.k.}.$$

Concept:	**Disjunctive** $(k = 1)$				**Conjunctive** $(k = 2)$		
Feedback:	*Immed.* $(j = 1)$	*Delayed* $(j = 2)$			*Immed.* $(j = 1)$	*Delayed* $(j = 2)$	
Problem 1 $(l = 1)$	2	4	3	Problem 5 $(l = 1)$	1	2	1.5
Problem 2 $(l = 2)$	3	5	4	Problem 6 $(l = 2)$	.5	1.5	1.0
Problem 3 $(l = 3)$	3	5	4	Problem 7 $(l = 3)$	4	5	4.5
Problem 4 $(l = 4)$	4	6	5	Problem 8 $(l = 4)$	.5	1.5	1.0
	3	5	4.0		1.5	2.5	2.0

Note that, in conformity to the restriction that there be no simple interactions of problems and feedback, the differences across feedback conditions are equal to 2 for all disjunctive problems and are equal to 1 for all 4 conjunctive problems.

Thus, the difference in sum of squared errors for these models is the sum over all observations of the differences in predictions:

$$E_R - E_F = \sum_{\text{all obs}} (\hat{Y}_{jkl_F} - \hat{Y}_{jkl_R})^2 = \sum_l \sum_k \sum_j \sum_i [\bar{Y}_{jkl} - (\bar{Y}_{jk.} + \bar{Y}_{.kl} - \bar{Y}_{.k.})]^2$$

(The differences in brackets on the right above are, in fact, the estimates of $\alpha\gamma_{jl(k)}$.) Numerically, taking the differences between the predictions for the various cells of the design, in an order highlighting the simple interactions at the two levels of the concept factor, we have

$$E_R - E_F = \sum_l \sum_k \sum_j \sum_{i=1}^{2} [\bar{Y}_{jkl} - (\bar{Y}_{jk.} + \bar{Y}_{.kl} - \bar{Y}_{.k.})]^2$$

$$= \sum_k \left\{ s \sum_l \sum_j [\bar{Y}_{jkl} - (\bar{Y}_{jk.} + \bar{Y}_{.kl} - \bar{Y}_{.k.})]^2 \right\}$$

$$= 2[(3 - 2)^2 + (3 - 4)^2 + (3 - 3)^2 + (5 - 5)^2 + (2 - 3)^2 + (6 - 5)^2$$
$$+ (4 - 4)^2 + (6 - 6)^2] + 2[(1 - 1)^2 + (2 - 2)^2 + (1 - .5)^2$$
$$+ (1 - 1.5)^2 + (4 - 4)^2 + (5 - 5)^2 + (0 - .5)^2 + (2 - 1.5)^2]$$

$$= 2[1 + 1 + 0 + 0 + 1 + 1 + 0 + 0] + 2[0 + 0 + .25 + .25 + 0 + 0$$
$$+ .25 + .25]$$
$$= 2(4) + 2(1) = 8 + 2 = SS_{Fp \ at \ c_1} + SS_{Fp \ at \ c_2} = 10 = SS_{Fp/C}$$

The sum of squares for the simple effects of problems within concepts can be obtained similarly. There we could compare the models:

$$\text{Full:} \quad Y_{ijkl} = \mu_{.kl} + \varepsilon_{ijkl}$$
$$\text{Restricted:} \quad Y_{ijkl} = \mu_{.k.} + \varepsilon_{ijkl}$$

That is, the sum of squares is computed as in a one-way ANOVA of problems at each of the two levels of concepts, and these sums are then combined. (Note again that the differences in predictions could be denoted $\hat{\gamma}_{l(k)}$.) Numerically, we have

$$E_R - E_F = \sum_l \sum_k \sum_{j=1}^{2} \sum_{i=1}^{2} (\hat{Y}_{jkl_F} - \hat{Y}_{jkl_R})^2$$

$$= \sum_k [2 \cdot 2 \sum_l (\bar{Y}_{.kl} - \bar{Y}_{.k.})^2]$$

$$= 4[(3 - 4)^2 + (4 - 4)^2 + (4 - 4)^2 + (5 - 4)^2]$$
$$+ 4[(1.5 - 2.0)^2 + (1.0 - 2.0)^2 + (4.5 - 2)^2 + (1.0 - 2.0)^2]$$

$$= 4[1 + 0 + 0 + 1] + 4[.25 + 1 + 6.25 + 1]$$

$$= 4 \cdot 2 + 4 \cdot 8.5 = 8 + 34 = SS_{p \ at \ c_1} + SS_{p \ at \ c_2} = 42 = SS_{p/C}$$

The sums of squares for the remaining, completely crossed effects can be obtained very easily from the following summary table of marginal means for the feedback and concept factors.

		Concept			
		Disjunctive $(k = 1)$	Conjunctive $(k = 2)$	$\bar{Y}_{j..}$	$\hat{\alpha}_j$
Feedback	*Immed.* $(j = 1)$	3	1.5	2.25	$-.75$
	Delayed $(j = 2)$	5	2.5	3.75	$+.75$
	$\bar{Y}_{.k.}$	4	2.0		
	$\hat{\beta}_k$	$+1$	-1.0		

$$SS_F = \sum_l \sum_k \sum_j \sum_i \hat{\alpha}_j^2 = 4 \cdot 2 \cdot 2 \sum_j \hat{\alpha}_j^2 = 16[(-.75)^2 + .75^2] = 16(1.125) = 18$$

$$SS_C = \sum_l \sum_k \sum_j \sum_i \hat{\beta}_k^2 = 4 \cdot 2 \cdot 2 \sum_k \hat{\beta}_k^2 = 16[1^2 + (-1)^2] = 32$$

Interaction effects are estimated as usual, that is,

$$(\widehat{\alpha\beta})_{jk} = \bar{Y}_{jk.} - (\hat{\mu} + \hat{\alpha}_j + \hat{\beta}_k)$$

For example $(\widehat{\alpha\beta})_{11} = 3 - (3 - .75 + 1) = 3 - 3.25 = -.25$. Thus, we have

$$SS_{FC} = \sum_l \sum_k \sum_j \sum_i (\widehat{\alpha\beta})_{jk}^2 = 4 \cdot 2 \sum_k \sum_j (\widehat{\alpha\beta})_{jk}^2 = 8[(-.25)^2 + .25^2 + .25^2 + (-.25)^2]$$

$$= 8 \cdot .25 = 2$$

To carry out the tests against the error terms outlined in part (b), we only need to determine the degrees of freedom for the various effects. Using lower-case letters to designate the number of levels of a factor, we have the following values:

Source	df
F	$(f-1) = (2-1) = 1$
C	$(c-1) = (2-1) = 1$
FC	$(f-1)(c-1) = (2-1)(2-1) = 1$
p/C	$c(p-1) = 2(4-1) = 2 \cdot 3 = 6$
Fp/C	$c(f-1)(p-1) = 2(2-1)(4-1) = 2 \cdot 1 \cdot 3 = 6$
MS_W	$fcp(n-1) = 2 \cdot 2 \cdot 4(2-1) = 16(1) = 16.$

Thus, we have the following test statistics and critical values at $\alpha = .05$ for our 5 testable effects:

$$F_F = \frac{SS_F/df_F}{SS_{Fp/C}/df_{Fp/C}} = \frac{18/1}{10/6} = 10.8; \quad F_{crit} = F_{1,6} = 5.99; p < .05$$

$$F_C = \frac{SS_C/df_C}{SS_{p/C}/df_{p/C}} = \frac{32/1}{42/6} = \frac{32}{7} = 4.57; \quad F_{crit} = F_{1,6} = 5.99; \, n.s.$$

$$F_{FC} = \frac{SS_{FC}/df_{FC}}{SS_{Fp/C}/df_{Fp/C}} = \frac{2/1}{10/6} = 1.2; \quad F_{crit} = F_{1,6} = 5.99; \, n.s.$$

$$F_{p/C} = \frac{SS_{p/C}/df_{p/C}}{MS_W} = \frac{42/6}{5} = \frac{7}{5} = 1.4; \quad F_{crit} = F_{6,16} = 2.74; \, n.s.$$

$$F_{Fp/C} = \frac{SS_{Fp/C}/df_{Fp/C}}{MS_W} = \frac{10/6}{5} = .33; \quad F_{crit} = F_{6,16} = 2.74; \, n.s.$$

It follows that the only effect for which we have grounds for rejecting the null hypothesis is the main effect of feedback. Delayed feedback results in more errors being required to reach the criterion performance than immediate feedback.

10. a. Combining the 15 scores for each therapy method into one group, we obtain the following means, standard deviations, and sums of squared deviations from group means.

Method	$\bar{Y}_j$	s_j	$\sum_i (Y_{ij} - \bar{Y}_j)^2$
RET	40	3.3166	154
CCT	42	3.1396	138
BMOD	44	3.0938	134

Thus, the grand mean $\bar{Y}$ is 42, and the sum of squares for the method (A) effect here is

$$SS_A = \sum_j \sum_{i=1}^{15} (\bar{Y}_j - \bar{Y})^2 = 15 \sum_j (\bar{Y}_j - \bar{Y})^2 = 15[(-2)^2 + 0^2 + 2^2] = 15[4+4] = 120$$

The degrees of freedom for the method effect is $a - 1 = 3 - 1 = 2$. The sum of squares within (or error of the full model) is here

$$SS_W = \sum_j \sum_i (Y_{ij} - \bar{Y}_j)^2 = 154 + 138 + 134 = 426$$

and is based on $a(n-1) = 3(15-1) = 3 \cdot 14 = 42$ degrees of freedom. Thus, the F for the method effect, analyzed as a one-way design, is

$$F = \frac{SS_A/df_A}{SS_W/df_W} = \frac{120/2}{426/42} = \frac{60}{10.1429} = 5.9155$$

Comparing against the critical F for $\alpha = .01$, $F(2, 42) = 5.16$, the results are declared significant.

b. Approaching the data as a two-way, fixed-effects design, we have the following cell means, standard deviations, and sums of squared deviations from cell means.

Summary Statistics for Two-Way Design

Method	Formula	Therapist			
		1	*2*	*3*	$\bar{Y}_{j.}$
	$\bar{Y}_{jk}$	38	42	40	40
RET	s_{jk}	2.9155	2.9155	3.3912	
	$\sum_i (Y_{ijk} - \bar{Y}_{jk})^2$	34	34	46	
	$\bar{Y}_{jk}$	41	44	41	42
CCT	s_{jk}	2.4495	3.3912	3.0822	
	$\sum_i (Y_{ijk} - \bar{Y}_{jk})^2$	24	46	38	
	$\bar{Y}_{jk}$	46	44	42	44
BMOD	s_{jk}	2.3452	3.5355	2.3452	
	$\sum_i (Y_{ijk} - \bar{Y}_{jk})^2$	22	50	22	
	$\bar{Y}_{.k}$	41.6667	43.3333	41.0000	

Thus, the method effect is evaluated using

$$SS_A = \sum_j bn(\bar{Y}_{j.} - \bar{Y})^2 = 3 \cdot 5[(-2)^2 + 0^2 + 2^2] = 15 \cdot 8 = 120$$

$$df_A = a - 1 = 3 - 1 = 2$$

$$SS_W = \sum_i \sum_j \sum_k (Y_{ijk} - \bar{Y}_{jk})^2 = 34 + 34 + 46 + 24 + 46 + 38 + 22 + 50 + 22 = 316$$

$$df_W = ab(n-1) = 3 \cdot 3(5-1) = 9 \cdot 4 = 36$$

Combining these values to compute the F for the method effect, we have

$$F_A = \frac{SS_A/df_A}{SS_W/df_W} = \frac{120/2}{316/36} = \frac{60}{8.7778} = 6.8354$$

We compare this against a critical F for $\alpha = .01$, $F(2, 36) = 5.26$ and again would declare the result statistically significant.

c. Treating the therapist factor as random would imply that the method effect should be compared with a denominator error term corresponding to the method $\times$ therapist interaction. The method $\times$ therapist interaction sum of squares may be computed from the effect parameters calculated as

$$(\widehat{\alpha\beta})_{jk} = \bar{Y}_{jk} - \bar{Y}_{j.} - \bar{Y}_{.k} + \bar{Y}_{..}$$

For example, $(\widehat{\alpha\beta})_{11} = 38 - 40 - 41.6667 + 42 = -1.6667$. The sum of squares for the method $\times$ therapist effect is then

$$SS_{AB} = \sum_{i}\sum_{j}\sum_{k}(\widehat{\alpha\beta})_{jk}^2 = n\sum_{j}\sum_{k}(\bar{Y}_{jk} - \bar{Y}_{j.} - \bar{Y}_{.k} + \bar{Y}_{..})^2$$

$$= 5[(-1.6667)^2 + (0.6667)^2 + 1^2 + (-0.6667)^2 + (0.6667)^2 + 0^2$$

$$+ (2.3333)^2 + (-1.3333)^2 + (-1)^2]$$

$$= 5(13.3333) = 66.6666$$

This is based on $(a - 1)(b - 1) = (3 - 1)(3 - 1) = 4$ degrees of freedom. Thus the test of the method effect, analyzing the data as a two-factor mixed design, yields

$$F = \frac{SS_A/df_A}{SS_{AB}/df_{AB}} = \frac{120/2}{66.6666/4} = \frac{60}{16.6667} = 3.60$$

However, this is now compared against a critical F with only 2 and 4 degrees of freedom. For $\alpha = .05$, the critical F is 6.94; for .01, it would be 18.00. Thus, treating therapists as a random factor, the method effect does not approach significance.

d. The sum of squares for the method effect was 120 in each of the three analyses.

e. The denominator mean square error terms were 10.1429 for the one-way approach, 8.7778 for the two-way fixed effects approach, and 16.6667 for the two-way mixed effects approach. The sum of squares within for the two-way approach removes from the sum of squares within for the one-way approach any variability that can be attributed to B or AB effects. In fact it is the case that

$$Mean \; square \; error \; term \; in \; (a) = \frac{SS_B + SS_{AB} + SS_{W(part\; b)}}{2 + 4 + 36}$$

$$= \frac{43.3316 + 66.6666 + 316}{42} = \frac{425.9982}{42} = 10.1428$$

The error term for the random effects approach uses the mean square for the AB interaction, which here happens to be larger than either MS_W value.

f. It is reasonable that Kurtosis obtained different results than Skewed. Kurtosis obtained a smaller F for the method effect yet had to compare it against a larger critical F value since she had fewer degrees of freedom for her error term. In addition, the rationale for evaluating the Method effect is quite different in the mixed effects case than in the fixed effect case. In the mixed effects case the question is, Is the effect of methods large relative to the variability that we would expect to result from randomly selecting therapists for whom the methods effects differ? Because the magnitude of the Method effect varies somewhat over therapists (from an 8-point mean difference for therapist 1 to a 2-point mean difference for therapist 3), it is reasonable to conclude that the variability among the marginal means for methods may just be the result of which therapists happened to be used in the study. However, it is the case (as Skewed found) that, if outcomes with these three therapists are the only ones to which we want to generalize, we can conclude that the three methods would result in different mean outcomes for the population of possible subjects.

Chapter 11

3. a. From Equation 24, predicted scores for the full model are of the form

$$\hat{Y}_{ij} = \bar{Y}_{.j} + \bar{Y}_{i.} - \bar{Y}_{..} \qquad (11.24)$$

For example,

$$\hat{Y}_{11} = (3 + 4 + 2 + 4 + 7)/5 + (3 + 6 + 4 + 5)/4 - 4.5$$
$$= 4 + 4.5 - 4.5$$
$$= 4$$
$$\hat{Y}_{12} = (6 + 7 + 1 + 5 + 6)/5 + (3 + 6 + 4 + 5)/4 - 4.5$$
$$= 5 + 4.5 - 4.5$$
$$= 5$$
$$\hat{Y}_{21} = (3 + 4 + 2 + 4 + 7)/5 + (4 + 7 + 4 + 8)/4 - 4.5$$
$$= 4 + 5.75 - 4.5$$
$$= 5.25$$

and so forth. Completing similar calculations for all other rows and columns, we find that the predicted scores for the full model are as follows.

	Location			
Subject	*1*	*2*	*3*	*4*
1	4.00	5.00	3.00	6.00
2	5.25	6.25	4.25	7.25
3	1.25	2.25	0.25	3.25
4	3.25	4.25	2.25	5.25
5	6.25	7.25	5.25	8.25

b. Discrepancies between actual scores and predicted scores are follows.

	Location			
Subject	*1*	*2*	*3*	*4*
1	−1.00	1.00	1.00	−1.00
2	−1.25	.75	−.25	.75
3	.75	−1.25	.75	−.25
4	.75	.75	−1.25	−.25
5	.75	−1.25	−.25	.75

c. From Equation 25, predicted scores for the restricted model are of the form

$$\hat{Y}_{ij} = \hat{Y}_{i.} \qquad (11.25)$$

For example,

$$\hat{Y}_{11} = \bar{Y}_{1.}$$
$$= (3 + 6 + 4 + 5)/4$$
$$= 4.50$$
$$\hat{Y}_{12} = \bar{Y}_{1.}$$
$$= (3 + 6 + 4 + 5)/4$$
$$= 4.50$$
$$\hat{Y}_{21} = \bar{Y}_{2.}$$
$$= (4 + 7 + 4 + 8)/4$$
$$= 5.75$$

and so forth. Completing similar calculations for all other rows and columns, we find that the predicted scores for the restricted model are as follows.

	Location			
Subject	*1*	*2*	*3*	*4*
1	4.50	4.50	4.50	4.50
2	5.75	5.75	5.75	5.75
3	1.75	1.75	1.75	1.75
4	3.75	3.75	3.75	3.75
5	6.75	6.75	6.75	6.75

d. Discrepancies between actual scores and predicted scores are as follows.

	Location			
Subject	*1*	*2*	*3*	*4*
1	−1.50	1.50	−.50	.50
2	−1.75	1.25	−1.75	2.25
3	.25	−.75	−.75	1.25
4	.25	1.25	−2.75	1.25
5	.25	−.75	−1.75	2.25

e. The observed F value is

$$F = \frac{(E_R - E_F)/(df_R - df_F)}{E_F/df_F}$$

First, notice that

$$df_R - df_F = a - 1$$
$$= 4 - 1$$
$$= 3$$

$$df_F = (n - 1)(a - 1)$$
$$= (5 - 1)(4 - 1)$$
$$= 12$$

In addition,

$$E_R = (-1.50)^2 + (-1.75)^2 + (.25)^2 + \cdots + (1.25)^2 + (2.25)^2$$
$$= 5.50 + 6.50 + 14.50 + 13.50$$
$$= 40.00$$
$$E_F = (-1.00)^2 + (-1.25)^2 + (.75)^2 + \cdots + (-.25)^2 + (.75)^2$$
$$= 4.25 + 5.25 + 3.25 + 2.25$$
$$= 15.00$$

Thus, the observed F is

$$F = \frac{(40.00 - 15.00)/3}{15.00/12}$$
$$= 6.67$$

For the unadjusted test, there are 3 numerator and 12 denominator degrees of freedom. The critical value at $\alpha = .05$ is 3.49 (see Appendix Table A.2), so there is a statistically significant difference among the locations.

f. The degrees of freedom for the Geisser-Greenhouse lower bound correction are

$$df_{num} = 1 \tag{11.32}$$
$$df_{den} = n - 1 \tag{11.33}$$
$$= 5 - 1$$
$$= 4$$

The critical F value for 1 numerator and 4 denominator degrees of freedom is 7.71 at the .05 level. Thus, the difference among locations is nonsignificant with the Geisser-Greenhouse lower bound correction.

g. Obviously the simplest way to obtain the value of $\hat{\varepsilon}$ is to rely on a computer program. Nevertheless, we will illustrate its calculation here. The first step is to calculate the covariance matrix for the data. If we let Y_{ij} represent the score of subject i in condition j (i.e., the score in row i and column j of the original data matrix), the element in row j and column k of the covariance matrix is given by

$$E_{jk} = \sum_{i=1}^{n} (Y_{ij} - \bar{Y}_{.j})(Y_{ik} - \bar{Y}_{.k})/n$$

Performing this calculation for our data yields the following matrix:

$$\begin{bmatrix} 2.8 & 2.0 & 1.8 & 3.2 \\ 2.0 & 4.4 & 2.6 & 3.6 \\ 1.8 & 2.6 & 2.8 & 3.0 \\ 3.2 & 3.6 & 3.0 & 4.8 \end{bmatrix}$$

The value of $\hat{\varepsilon}$ then is

$$\hat{\varepsilon} = \frac{a^2(\bar{E}_{jj} - \bar{E}_{..})^2}{(a - 1)[(\sum\sum E_{jk}^2) - (2a\sum \bar{E}_{j.}^2) + (a^2 \bar{E}_{..}^2)]}$$

where

$$a = 4$$

$$\bar{E}_{jj} = (2.8 + 4.4 + 2.8 + 4.8)/4 = 3.70$$

$$\bar{E}_{..} = (2.8 + 2.0 + 1.8 + 3.2 + 2.0 + 4.4 + \cdots + 3.0 + 4.8)/16 = 2.95$$

$$\sum\sum E_{jk}^2 = (2.8)^2 + (2.0)^2 + (1.8)^2 + \cdots + (3.0)^2 + (4.8)^2 = 150.48$$

$$\sum \bar{E}_{j.}^2 = (2.45)^2 + (3.15)^2 + (2.55)^2 + (3.65)^2 = 35.75$$

so that

$$\hat{\varepsilon} = \frac{(4)^2(3.70 - 2.95)^2}{(4 - 1)[(150.48) - (2)(4)(35.75) + (4)^2(2.95)^2]}$$

$$= \frac{9.00}{11.16}$$

$$= .81$$

The adjusted degrees of freedom are

$$df_{num} = \hat{\varepsilon}(a - 1)$$

$$= .81(4 - 1)$$

$$= 2.43$$

$$df_{den} = \hat{\varepsilon}(a - 1)(n - 1)$$

$$= .81(4 - 1)(5 - 1)$$

$$= 9.72$$

Rounding down (to be conservative), the critical F value with 2 and 9 degrees of freedom is 4.26 at the .05 level. Thus, the difference among locations is statistically significant at the .05 level with the $\hat{\varepsilon}$-adjusted test, just as it was with the unadjusted test. Using either SAS or BMDP, we can find that the p-value for the $\hat{\varepsilon}$-adjusted test is .0125, corroborating the statistical significance at the .05 level.

h. Now that we have calculated $\hat{\varepsilon}$, the value of $\tilde{\varepsilon}$ follows easily from Equation 34:

$$\tilde{\varepsilon} = \frac{n(a - 1)\hat{\varepsilon} - 2}{(a - 1)[n - 1 - (a - 1)\hat{\varepsilon}]} \qquad (11.34)$$

$$= \frac{5(4 - 1)(.81) - 2}{(4 - 1)[5 - 1 - (4 - 1)(.81)]}$$

$$= \frac{10.15}{4.71}$$

$$= 2.15$$

Because $\tilde{\varepsilon}$ exceeds 1.00 for these data, it is shrunk back to 1.00. As a consequence, the use of the $\tilde{\varepsilon}$ adjustment simply duplicates the unadjusted test for these data.

4. To calculate SS_A and $SS_{A \times S}$, it is helpful to represent the data as in Table 11.3, adding row and column marginal means, in which case we have the following values.

Subject	Condition 1	Condition 2	Marginal Mean
1	8	10	9.00
2	3	6	4.50
3	12	13	12.50
4	5	9	7.00
5	7	8	7.50
6	13	14	13.50
Marginal Mean	**8.00**	**10.00**	**9.00**

Now, the sum of squares for the condition main effect is

$$SS_A = \sum_{j=1}^{a} n(\bar{Y}_{.j} - \bar{Y}_{..})^2$$

$$= 6[(8 - 9)^2 + (10 - 9)^2]$$

$$= 12.00$$

The interaction sum of squares is

$$SS_{A \times S} = \sum_{i=1}^{n} \sum_{j=1}^{a} (Y_{ij} - \bar{Y}_{.j} - \bar{Y}_{i.} + \bar{Y}_{..})^2$$

$$= (8 - 8.00 - 9.00 + 9.00)^2 + (10 - 10.00 - 9.00 + 9.00)^2$$
$$+ (3 - 8.00 - 4.50 + 9.00)^2 + (6 - 10.00 - 4.50 + 9.00)^2$$
$$+ (12 - 8.00 - 12.50 + 9.00)^2 + (13 - 10.00 - 12.50 + 9.00)^2$$
$$+ (5 - 8.00 - 7.00 + 9.00)^2 + (9 - 10.00 - 7.00 + 9.00)^2$$
$$+ (7 - 8.00 - 7.50 + 9.00)^2 + (8 - 10.00 - 7.50 + 9.00)^2$$
$$+ (13 - 8.00 - 13.50 + 9.00)^2 + (14 - 10.00 - 13.50 + 9.00)^2$$
$$= (0)^2 + (0)^2 + (-.50)^2 + (.50)^2 + (.50)^2 + (-.50)^2 + (-1.00)^2 + (1.00)^2$$
$$+ (.50)^2 + (-.50)^2 + (.50)^2 + (-.50)^2$$
$$= 4.00.$$

b. The observed F value is

$$F = \frac{SS_A/(a - 1)}{SS_{A \times S}/(n - 1)(a - 1)}$$

$$= \frac{12/1}{4/(5)(1)}$$

$$= 15.00$$

c. The F values are identical.
d. Yes, since they yield the same F value.

5. a. To calculate the sums of squares, it is helpful to include row and column marginal means, in which case the original data can be written as follows.

Subject	1	2	3	Marginal Mean
1	10	12	14	12
2	2	5	5	4
3	5	6	10	7
4	12	15	18	15
5	16	17	18	17
Marginal Mean	**9**	**11**	**13**	**11**

Now, the sum of squares for the condition main effect is

$$SS_A = \sum_{j=1}^{a} n(\bar{Y}_{.j} - \bar{Y}_{..})^2$$
$$= 5[(9 - 11)^2 + (11 - 11)^2 + (13 - 11)^2]$$
$$= 40$$

The sum of squares for the subject main effect is

$$SS_S = \sum_{i=1}^{n} a(\bar{Y}_{i.} - \bar{Y}_{..})^2$$
$$= 3[(12 - 11)^2 + (4 - 11)^2 + (7 - 11)^2 + (15 - 11)^2 + (17 - 11)^2]$$
$$= 354$$

Finally, the interaction sum of squares is

$$SS_{A \times S} = \sum_{i=1}^{n} \sum_{j=1}^{a} (Y_{ij} - \bar{Y}_{.j} - \bar{Y}_{i.} + \bar{Y}_{..})^2$$
$$= (10 - 9 - 12 + 11)^2 + (12 - 11 - 12 + 11)^2 + (14 - 13 - 12 + 11)^2$$
$$+ (2 - 9 - 4 + 11)^2 + \cdots + (17 - 11 - 17 + 11)^2$$
$$+ (18 - 13 - 17 + 11)^2$$
$$= (0)^2 + (0)^2 + (0)^2 + (0)^2 + (1)^2 + (-1)^2 + (0)^2 + (-1)^2 + (1)^2 + (-1)^2$$
$$+ (0)^2 + (1)^2 + (1)^2 + (0)^2 + (-1)^2$$
$$= 8$$

b. The observed F value is

$$F = \frac{SS_A/(a - 1)}{SS_{A \times S}/(n - 1)(a - 1)}$$
$$= \frac{40/2}{8/(4)(2)}$$
$$= 20.00$$

The critical F value at $\alpha = .05$ with 2 numerator and 8 denominator degrees of freedom is 4.46. Thus, the null hypothesis can be rejected.

c. If these data came from a between-subject design, the between-group sum of squares would be calculated as

$$SS_A = n \sum_{j=1}^{a} (\bar{Y}_j - \bar{Y})^2 \qquad\qquad (3.58)$$

$$= 5[(9-11)^2 + (11-11)^2 + (13-11)^2]$$

$$= 40$$

$$SS_W = \sum_{j=1}^{a} \sum_{i=1}^{n} (\bar{Y}_{ij} - \bar{Y}_j)^2 \qquad\qquad (3.65)$$

$$= (10-9)^2 + (2-9)^2 + (5-9)^2 + (12-9)^2 + (16-9)^2 + (12-11)^2$$

$$+ (5-11)^2 + (6-11)^2 + (15-11)^2 + (17-11)^2 + (14-13)^2$$

$$+ (5-13)^2 + (10-13)^2 + (18-13)^2 + (18-13)^2$$

$$= 362$$

First, notice that the main effect sum of squares SS_A is the same whether the data come from a within-subjects design or from a between-subjects design. However, the within-group sum of squares SS_W in the between-subjects design equals the sum of SS_S and $SS_{A \times S}$ in the within-subjects design. In general, it is true that

$$SS_W = SS_S + SS_{A \times S}$$

For these data,

$$362 = 354 + 8$$

d. The observed F value would be

$$F = \frac{SS_A/(a-1)}{SS_W/(N-a)}$$

$$= \frac{40/2}{362/12}$$

$$= .66$$

The critical F value would be 3.89 (see Appendix Table A.2, for 2 numerator degrees of freedom, 12 denominator degrees of freedom, and $\alpha = .05$), so the null hypothesis could not be rejected.

e. The consistent individual differences among subjects are captured by SS_S in the within-subjects design. This source of variance does not contribute to the error term, as it would in a between-subjects design. As a result, the within-subjects design provides appreciably greater power than the between-subjects design, when large individual differences exist. Notice that, in this numerical example, the observed F value of 20.00 in the within-subjects design was drastically reduced to a mere .66 in the between-subjects design.

6. a. The new scores on the adjusted dependent variable $Y_{ij} - \bar{Y}_{i.}$ are as follows.

30	36	42	48
−1	−13	1	13
−17	−3	7	13
−8	3	2	3
−6	−5	2	9

	30	36	42	48
	−3	4	4	−5
	9	6	−5	−10
	2	1	−4	1
	−7	−13	4	16
	−10	10	6	−6
	−5	−1	2	4
	−4	5	−4	3
	−10	−6	9	7
Mean ($\bar{Y}_j$)	**−5.00**	**−1.00**	**2.00**	**4.00**
$\sum_{i=1}^{n} (Y_{ij} - \bar{Y}_j)^2$	**474.00**	**584.00**	**220.00**	**728.00**

The observed F value for a one-way between-subjects ANOVA on these data would be

$$F = \frac{(E_R - E_F)/(df_R - df_F)}{E_F/df_F}$$

In this design,

$$E_R - E_F = n \sum_{j=1}^{a} (\bar{Y}_j - \bar{Y})^2 \tag{3.58}$$
$$= 12[(-5 - 0)^2 + (-1 - 0)^2 + (2 - 0)^2 + (4 - 0)^2]$$
$$= 552$$

$$E_F = \sum_{j=1}^{a} \sum_{i=1}^{n} (Y_{ij} - \bar{Y}_j)^2$$
$$= 474 + 584 + 220 + 728$$
$$= 2006$$

If these data really came from a between-subjects design,

$$df_R = N - 1$$
$$df_F = N - a$$

so

$$df_R - df_F = a - 1$$

For these data, then,

$$df_F = 48 - 4$$
$$= 44$$
$$df_R - df_F = 4 - 1$$
$$= 3$$

Thus, the observed F would be

$$F = \frac{552/3}{2006/44}$$

$$= 4.04$$

With 3 numerator and 44 denominator degrees of freedom, the critical F value at $\alpha = .05$ would be approximately 2.84 (see Appendix Table A.2), so the null hypothesis would be rejected.

b. The F value of 4.04 in part (a) is larger than the F value of 3.03 obtained from Equation 28 in the text. However, notice from Tables 11.8 and 11.9 that, when we regarded these data as coming from a within-subjects design, the error sums of squares were

$$E_R = 2558 \qquad \text{(see Table 11.9)}$$

$$E_F = 2006 \qquad \text{(see Table 11.8)}$$

so

$$E_R - E_F = 552$$

Thus, E_F and $E_R - E_F$ as calculated in the within-subjects design are identical to the value obtained in part (a). However, in the within-subjects design, the degrees of freedom for the restricted and full models are

$$df_R = n(a - 1)$$
$$= 12(4 - 1)$$
$$= 36$$
$$df_F = (n - 1)(a - 1)$$
$$= (12 - 1)(4 - 1)$$
$$= 33$$

Thus, $df_F - df_F = 3$ in both approaches, but $df_F = 33$ for the within-subjects design, whereas $df_F = 44$ in part (a). We can resolve this apparent inconsistency by realizing that the first step in part (a) was to subtract each subject's row marginal mean from each original score. In effect, we have calculated a new dependent variable of the form

$$Y_{ij} - \bar{Y}_{i.}$$

which equals

$$Y_{ij} - \hat{\pi}_i$$

However, there are $n - 1$ independent π_i parameters, so we must increase the number of estimated parameters by $n - 1$. In part (a), we had said

$$df_R = N - 1$$
$$df_F = N - a$$

However, if we count the $n - 1$ additional independent π_i parameters we estimated, the new degrees of freedom become

$$df_R = N - 1 - (n - 1)$$
$$= N - n$$
$$= an - n$$
$$= n(a - 1)$$

$$df_F = N - a - (n - 1)$$
$$= N - a - n + 1$$
$$= an - a - n + 1$$
$$= (a - 1)(n - 1)$$

For our data, then,

$$df_R = n(a - 1)$$
$$= 12(4 - 1)$$
$$= 36$$
$$df_F = (a - 1)(n - 1)$$
$$= (4 - 1)(12 - 1)$$
$$= 33$$

As a result, $df_R - df_F = 3$ and $df_F = 33$. Applying these adjusted degrees of freedom in part (a) would have given us

$$F = \frac{552/3}{2006/33}$$
$$= 3.03$$

in agreement with the F value calculated in the within-subjects design. Thus, the within-subjects ANOVA is identical to a between-subjects ANOVA on $Y_{ij} - \bar{Y}_{i.}$, once we make the proper adjustment in degrees of freedom.

c. The answers to parts (a) and (b) show that the within-subjects ANOVA can be duplicated by performing a between-subjects ANOVA on $Y_{ij} - \bar{Y}_{i.}$. However, by subtracting $\bar{Y}_{i.}$ from each score, the new scores treat each subject's average score as a baseline. Each new score reflects a subject's performance at level j compared to his or her average performance. In this sense, each subject serves as his or her own control.

9. a. The theoretical minimum value of ε is $1/(a - 1)$. For $a = 3$, this minimum value is .50.

  b. *Minimum* $\varepsilon = 1/(a - 1)$
  $$= 1/(4 - 1)$$
  $$= .33$$

  c. *Minimum* $\varepsilon = 1/(a - 1)$
  $$= 1/(5 - 1)$$
  $$= .25$$

  d. *Minimum* $\varepsilon = 1/(a - 1)$
  $$= 1/(2 - 1)$$
  $$= 1.00$$

11.   **Unadjusted**   **Adjusted** (see 11.32 and 11.33)

  a. $F_{.05;2,28} = 3.34$ $F_{.05;1,14} = 4.60$
  b. $F_{.05;3,33} = 2.92$ (for $df_{den} = 30$) $F_{.05;1,11} = 4.84$
  c. $F_{.05;4,60} = 2.53$ $F_{.05;1,15} = 4.54$
  d. $F_{.05;1,9} = 5.12$ $F_{.05;1,9} = 5.12$

Chapter 12

6.

Testable Effects		Error Term		
Source	*df*	*Source*	*df*	*Lower Bound of* ε
A	2	$A \times S$	20	.50
B	3	$B \times S$	30	.33
$A \times B$	6	$A \times B \times S$	60	.17

Notice that all three of the error terms have the general form $MS_{effect \times S}$ (see Equation 12.5, as well as 12.2, 12.3, and 12.4). The degrees of freedom for the three effects are $a - 1$ for A, $b - 1$ for B, and $(a - 1)(b - 1)$ for $A \times B$. The degrees of freedom for each error term equal $n - 1$ times the degrees of freedom of the effect to be tested. In general, the minimum theoretical value of ε for an effect is

$$Minimum\ \varepsilon = 1/df_{effect}$$

Thus, in the 2-way design, the theoretical minimum values are

$$Minimum\ \varepsilon = 1/(a - 1) \text{ for the } A \text{ main effect}$$
$$Minimum\ \varepsilon = 1/(b - 1) \text{ for the } B \text{ main effect}$$
$$Minimum\ \varepsilon = 1/(a - 1)(b - 1) \text{ for the } A \times B \text{ interaction.}$$

These theoretical minimum values follow from the dimensions of the covariance matrices used to test these different effects (for example, see Tables 12.8, 12.10, and 12.12).

8. Tests of comparisons using a separate error term always have $n - 1$ denominator degrees of freedom, whether the comparison involves marginal means, cell means, or an interaction contrast (see Equations 12.7 and 12.11, and the subsequent discussion of statistical packages). Thus, with 15 subjects, the denominator degrees of freedom for testing a contrast with a separate error term will equal 14. Thus, the correct answers here are as follows.
    a. 14
    b. 14
    c. 14
    d. 14

12. a. This source table would be appropriate for a 2×2 design with 80 subjects, where both factors were between-subjects. The actual design, however, is a "split-plot" design, where 40 subjects have each been tested twice.
    b. The proper sources, error terms, and degrees of freedom should be as follows (see Tables 12.16 and 12.19).

Source	df
Between-Subjects	
Mood (A)	1
S/A	38
Within-Subjects	
Difficulty (B)	1
Mood × Difficulty	1
B × S/A	38

Notice that $a = 2$, $b = 2$, and $N = 40$ (see Table 12.16). Thus, the total degrees of freedom sum to 79, as shown in the student's table, but the student's "Within" term fails to distinguish S/A from $B \times S/A$. In addition, $MS_{S/A}$ is the proper error term for testing the A main effect, while $MS_{B \times S/A}$ is the proper error term for testing the B main effect and the $A \times B$ interaction.

c. The sums of squares for the effects shared in common by the two designs will be the same. Thus, the sums of squares for Mood, Difficulty, and Mood × Difficulty are all correct (presuming, of course, that they were calculated correctly in the between-subjects design). Further, it is true that SS_{within} as calculated by the student equals the sum of $SS_{S/A}$ and $SS_{B \times S/A}$:

$$SS_{within} = SS_{S/A} + SS_{B \times S/A}$$

However, it is impossible to tell from the student's analysis the magnitude of either $SS_{S/A}$ or $SS_{B \times S/A}$ individually. Thus, F values cannot be calculated for any of the effects.

13. a. Mean reaction time scores are as follows.

Younger Subjects	Older Subjects
530	560
470	710
620	560
610	690
600	590
420	750
610	730
650	590
610	780
570	670

b. The F statistic for testing the difference between the mean of the younger subjects and the mean of the older subjects is

$$F = \frac{SS_{between}/(a-1)}{MS_W}.$$

To calculate this F value, we first find

$$SS_{between} = n \sum_{j=1}^{a} (\bar{Y}_j - \bar{Y})^2 \qquad \text{(see 3.58)}$$

$$= 10[(569 - 616)^2 + (663 - 616)^2]$$

$$= 44{,}180$$

$$MS_W = \frac{\sum_{j=1}^{a} s_j^2}{a} \qquad \text{(see 3.63)}$$

$$= \frac{5410.00 + 6734.44}{2}$$

$$= 6072.22$$

Finally, notice that $a - 1 = 1$, because $a = 2$.
Thus,

$$F = \frac{44,180/1}{6072.22}$$

$$= 7.28$$

The critical value with 1 numerator and 18 denominator degrees of freedom is
4.41 (see Appendix Table A.2), so the Age difference is significant at the .05 level.
   c. The two F values are identical (see Table 12.19).
   d. Yes. The test of the between-subjects main effect in a "split-plot" design is equivalent
   to a between-subjects ANOVA on mean scores (averaged over levels of the within-
   subjects factor). No sphericity assumption need be made in purely between-subjects
   designs, so the F test here does not assume sphericity.
14. a. The source table that results from this analysis is as follows.

Source	SS	df	MS	F
Subjects	460,440	19	24,233.68	
Angle	435,090	2	217,545.00	109.48
Angle × Subjects	75,510	38	1987.11	

Of course, the observed F of 109.48 for the Angle main effect is statistically
significant at the .05 level.
   b. The F value in part (a), although still large, is only about three-fourths as large as
   the F value reported in Table 12.19 for the within-subjects main effect.
   c. Both numerator sums of squares equal 435,090.
   d. The error sum of squares in part (a) equals 75,510. The value reported in Table
   12.19 is 54,420. The difference in these two values is 21,090, which equals the sum
   of squares for the Age by Angle interaction.
   e. No. The degrees of freedom for the Angle by Subjects interaction is 38, whereas the
   degrees of freedom for Angle by Subjects within Age is 36. The difference equals the
   degrees of freedom for the Age by Angle interaction. (It also equals the degrees of
   freedom for the Angle main effect here, because there are only two levels of Age.)
   f. No. The F value for the within-subjects main effect in a "split-plot" design cannot
   be obtained by simply ignoring the between-subjects factor and then performing a
   one-way within-subjects ANOVA. This latter approach does yield the proper
   numerator sum of squares for the main effect. However, the denominator sum of
   squares is not properly calculated with this approach. The reason is that the
   denominator sum of squares in the "split-plot" design represents the inconsistency
   of subjects across treatments *within each group*. Ignoring the between-subjects factor,
   $SS_{A \times S}$ represents inconsistencies across treatments of subjects within groups and
   between the groups. As we saw in part (d),

$$SS_{A \times S} = SS_{B \times S/A} + S_{A \times B}$$

To the extent that the between-subjects and the within-subjects factors interact,
$SS_{A \times S}$ of the one-way repeated measures design will overestimate the proper
measure of inconsistency for assessing the main effect of the within-subjects factor.
Instead, the $B \times S/A$ effect of the "split-plot" design will generally provide the
proper error term.

15. The following answers can be found in Table 12.20.
    a. Yes, sphericity is assumed.
    b. No, sphericity is not assumed.
    c. Yes, sphericity is assumed.
    d. No, sphericity is not assumed.
    e. Yes, sphericity is assumed.
    f. No, sphericity is not assumed.

20. a. The data are as follows.

Subject	Drug A	Drug B	Drug C	Marginal Mean
1	6	9	3	6.00
2	18	6	12	12.00
3	15	5	12	10.67
4	11	8	14	11.00
5	17	9	9	11.67
6	7	7	7	7.00
Marginal Mean	12.33	7.33	9.50	9.72

The observed F value for these data is

$$F = \frac{SS_A/(a-1)}{SS_{A \times S}/(n-1)(a-1)}$$

where

$$SS_A = \sum_{j=1}^{a} n(\bar{Y}_{\cdot j} - \bar{Y}_{\cdot\cdot})^2$$

$$= 6[(12.33 - 9.72)^2 + (7.33 - 9.72)^2 + (9.50 - 9.72)^2]$$

$$= 75.44$$

$$SS_{A \times S} = \sum_{i=1}^{n} \sum_{j=1}^{a} (\bar{Y}_{ij} - \bar{Y}_{\cdot j} - \bar{Y}_{i\cdot} + \bar{Y}_{\cdot\cdot})^2$$

$$= (6 - 12.33 - 6.00 + 9.72)^2 + (9 - 7.33 - 6.00 + 9.72)^2 + \cdots$$

$$+ (7 - 9.50 - 7.00 + 9.72)^2$$

$$= (-2.61)^2 + (5.39)^2 + (-2.78)^2 + (3.39)^2 + (-3.61)^2 + (0.22)^2$$

$$+ (1.72)^2 + (-3.28)^2 + (1.55)^2 + (-2.61)^2 + (-0.61)^2 + (3.22)^2$$

$$+ (2.72)^2 + (-0.28)^2 + (-2.45)^2 + (-2.61)^2 + (2.39)^2 + (0.22)^2$$

$$= 127.89$$

In addition, $a = 3$ and $n = 6$, so the observed F is

$$F = \frac{75.44/2}{127.89/(5)(2)}$$

$$= 2.95$$

The critical F value with 2 numerator and 10 denominator degrees of freedom is 4.10 (see Appendix Table A.2), so the null hypothesis cannot be rejected at the .05 level.

b. The F value in part (a) is considerably smaller than the F value of 7.65 reported in the chapter.

c. These values are identical.

d. The denominator sum of squares in part (a) equals 127.89, as compared to a value of only 39.44 in the Latin square analysis.

e. The two denominator sums of squares in part (d) differ by 88.45, which is the same (except for rounding error) as the sum of squares for the time main effect:

$$SS_{A \times S} = SS_{Latin\ square\ error} + SS_{Time}$$

or, equivalently,

$$SS_{Latin\ square\ error} = SS_{A \times S} - SS_{Time}$$

f. As the last equation for part (e) shows, the sum of squared errors for the Latin square analysis will be smaller than the sum of squared errors for the ordinary repeated measures design to the extent that Time (that is, sequence) has an effect on subjects' scores. Indeed, the general purpose of a Latin square design and analysis is to control for such effects of time. In the numerical example, the increased statistical power of the Latin square analysis produces a statistically significant treatment effect that would have gone undetected in an ordinary repeated measures analysis.

Chapter 13

7. a.

Subject	D_1	D_2	D_3
1	3	1	2
2	3	0	4
3	-1	-1	1
4	1	-3	1
5	-1	-2	2

b. In the full model, the predicted score for each subject on a D variable is the mean of that variable.

Thus, here we have

$$\hat{D}_{1i} = \bar{D}_1 = 1$$
$$\hat{D}_{2i} = \bar{D}_2 = -1$$
$$\hat{D}_{3i} = \bar{D}_3 = 2.$$

Errors then equal

$$e_{1i}(F) = D_{1i} - \bar{D}_1$$
$$e_{2i}(F) = D_{2i} - \bar{D}_2$$
$$e_{3i}(F) = D_{3i} - \bar{D}_3$$

The following table presents the errors, squared errors, and cross products for each subject.

Subject	e_1	e_2	e_3	e_1^2	e_2^2	e_3^2	e_1e_2	e_1e_3	e_2e_3
1	2	2	0	4	4	0	4	0	0
2	2	1	2	4	1	4	2	4	2
3	−2	0	−1	4	0	1	0	2	0
4	0	−2	−1	0	4	1	0	0	2
5	−2	−1	0	4	1	0	2	0	0
Sum	0	0	0	16	10	6	8	6	4

c. In the restricted model, the predicted score for each subject on a D variable is zero. Thus, the error for a variable is just the score itself:

$$e_{1i}(R) = D_{1i}$$
$$e_{2i}(R) = D_{2i}$$
$$e_{3i}(R) = D_{3i}.$$

The following table presents the errors, squared errors, and cross products for each subject.

Subject	e_1	e_2	e_3	e_1^2	e_2^2	e_3^2	e_1e_2	e_1e_3	e_2e_3
1	3	1	2	9	1	4	3	6	2
2	3	0	4	9	0	16	0	12	0
3	−1	−1	1	1	1	1	1	−1	−1
4	1	−3	1	1	9	1	−3	1	−3
5	−1	−2	2	1	4	4	2	−2	−4
Sum	5	−5	10	21	15	26	3	16	−6

d. To find the determinant of $E(F)$, we first write $E(F)$ in the form of a matrix:

$$E(F) = \begin{bmatrix} 16 & 8 & 6 \\ 8 & 10 & 4 \\ 6 & 4 & 6 \end{bmatrix}$$

Then, from Footnote 4, the determinant of $E(F)$ is given by

$$|E(F)| = 16[(10)(6) - (4)^2] + 8[(6)(4) - (6)(8)] + 6[(8)(4) - (10)(6)]$$
$$= 704 - 192 - 168$$
$$= 344.$$

Similarly, for the restricted model,

$$E(R) = \begin{bmatrix} 21 & 3 & 16 \\ 3 & 15 & -6 \\ 16 & -6 & 26 \end{bmatrix}$$

so

$$|E(R)| = 21[(15)(26) - (-6)^2] + 3[(16)(-6) - (26)(3)] + 16[(3)(-6) - (15)(16)]$$

$$= 7434 - 522 - 4128$$

$$= 2784$$

e. From Equation 22, the observed F value equals

$$F = \frac{(|E(R)| - |E(F)|)/(a - 1)}{|E(F)|/(n - a + 1)} \tag{13.22}$$

$$= \frac{(2784 - 344)/(4 - 1)}{344/(5 - 4 + 1)}$$

$$= 4.73$$

The critical F value with 3 numerator and 2 denominator degrees of freedom is 19.2 (see Appendix Table A.2), so the null hypothesis cannot be rejected at the .05 level.

f. (1) From part (b),

$$\sum_{i=1}^{n} e_{1i}^2 = 16.$$

(2) The unexplained sum of squares for e_2 equals

$$(1 - r_{e_1 e_2}^2) \sum_{i=1}^{n} e_{i2}^2 = (1.00 - .40)(10)$$

$$= 6$$

(3) The unexplained sum of squares for e_3 equals

$$(1 - R_{e_3 . e_1, e_2}^2) \sum_{i=1}^{n} e_{i3}^2 = (1 - .402778)(6)$$

$$= 3.58333$$

(4) The value of the determinant $|E(F)|$ equals (except for rounding error) the product of the three values computed in (i), (ii), and (iii):

$$|E(F)| = 344$$

$$= (16)(6)(3.58333)$$

$$= \left[\sum_{i=1}^{n} e_{1i}^2 \right] \left[(1 - r_{e_1 e_2}^2) \left(\sum_{i=1}^{n} e_{i2}^2 \right) \right] \left[(1 - R_{e_3 . e_1, e_2}^2) \left(\sum_{i=1}^{n} e_{i3}^2 \right) \right]$$

The determinant reflects simultaneously the extent to which the full model fails to explain scores on D_1, D_2, and D_3. Specifically, the determinant equals the product of three sum of squared error terms:

(a) The sum of squared errors for D_1

(b) The unexplained sum of squared errors for D_2 predicted from D_1

(c) The unexplained sum of squared errors for D_3 predicted from D_1 and D_2

In this way, the determinant takes into account the correlations among D_1, D_2, and D_3, and avoids overcounting areas of overlap (see Figure 13.1), in arriving at an index of error for the model.

(5) The value of the determinant $|E(R)|$ equals (except for rounding error) the product of uncorrected residual sums of squares:

$$|E(R)| = 2784$$

$$= (21)(14.57143)(9.09804)$$

Thus, the same type of relationship holds for the restricted model as for the full model. As a result, the determinant serves the same purpose for representing the overall magnitude of error in the restricted model as it does in the full model.

g. Equation 6 provides an appropriate test statistic for testing a comparison:

$$F = n\bar{D}^2/s_D^2 \tag{13.6}$$

The D_3 variable we formed earlier compares locations 1 and 4. From the table we constructed in part (a), we can see that $\bar{D}_3 = 2$ and $s_D^2 = 1.5$. Thus, the observed F value is

$$F = (5)(2)^2/1.5$$

$$= 13.33$$

If this is the only planned comparison to be tested, an appropriate critical F value can be found in Appendix Table A.2. With 1 numerator and 4 denominator degrees of freedom, the critical F value is 7.71, so the mean difference between EEG activity at Locations 1 and 4 is statistically significant at the .05 level.

8. a. From Equation 22, the test statistic for the omnibus null hypothesis is

$$F = \frac{(|E(R)| - |E(F)|)/(a - 1)}{|E(F)|/(n - a + 1)} \tag{13.22}$$

We are told that $n = 12$. The fact that the $E(F)$ and $E(R)$ matrices have 2 rows and columns implies that $a - 1 = 2$, that is, $a = 3$. Thus, the determinants of $|E(F)|$ and $|E(R)|$ are

$$|E(F)| = (1584)(704) - (528)^2$$

$$= 836,352$$

$$|E(R)| = (2784)(1136) - (1248)^2$$

$$= 1,605,120.$$

Substituting these values into the formula for the F statistic yields

$$F = \frac{(1,605,120 - 836,352)/2}{836,352/(12 - 3 + 1)}$$

$$= 4.60$$

The critical F value with 2 numerator and 10 denominator degrees of freedom is 4.10 (see Appendix Table A.2), so the null hypothesis can be rejected at the .05 level.

b. Given orthonormal contrasts, the mixed-model F can be written as

$$F = \frac{(\text{tr}(E^*(R)) - \text{tr}(E^*(F)))/(a - 1)}{\text{tr}(E^*(F))/(n - 1)(a - 1)} \tag{13.29}$$

For these data,

$$\text{tr}(E^*(R)) = 2784 + 1136$$

$$= 3920$$

$$\text{tr}(E^*(F)) = 1584 + 704$$

$$= 2288$$

Substituting these values, along with $a = 3$ and $n = 12$, into Equation 29 yields

$$F = \frac{(3920 - 2288)/2}{2288/(11)(2)}$$

$$= 7.85$$

The critical F value for 2 numerator and 22 denominator degrees of freedom is 3.44, so the null hypothesis is rejected at the .05 level, using the mixed-model approach.

c. The test statistic for testing a single D variable is given by

$$F = \frac{(E_R - E_F)/(df_R - df_F)}{E_F/df_F}$$

In the one-way within-subjects design,

$$df_R = n$$
$$df_F = n - 1$$

so

$$df_R - df_F = 1$$

Further, E_R and E_F are the entries in row 1 and column 1 of the $\mathbf{E(R)}$ and $\mathbf{E(F)}$ matrices, respectively. For these data,

$$F = \frac{(2784 - 1584)/1}{1584/11}$$

$$= 8.33$$

The critical F value for $\alpha_{PC} = .05$ with 1 numerator and 11 denominator degrees of freedom is 4.84, so the null hypothesis can be rejected.

12. a. The observed F value using the multivariate approach is 7.19. The associated p-value is .010, so the null hypothesis is rejected at the .05 level.
    b. The observed F value using the mixed-model approach is 3.23. The associated p-value is .057, so the null hypothesis cannot be rejected at the .05 level.
    c. As discussed at the end of the chapter, the multivariate approach may be more powerful than the mixed-model approach when the homogeneity assumption is violated. It is possible for the mixed-model test to be liberal if the null hypothesis is true, and yet the mixed-model test can be less powerful than the multivariate test when the null hypothesis is false.

14. a. Equation 6 provides the test statistic for testing this contrast:

$$F = n\bar{D}^2/s_D^2 \tag{13.6}$$

To work this problem by hand, it is necessary to calculate a D score for each subject. For example, D for subject 1 is

$$D = .56(2) - .54(4) - .02(7)$$

$$= -1.18$$

Using the same formula for all 13 subjects yields the following scores:

$$-1.18, .58, -1.64, -1.06, 0, -.10, -2.72, -.52, -1.18, -1.58, -1.56, -2.82, -.52.$$

The mean of these 13 scores is $\bar{D} = -1.10$, and the estimated population variance is $s_D^2 = 1.003$. Thus, the observed F value is

$$F = (13)(-1.10)^2/1.003$$

$$= 15.68$$

An appropriate critical value for this post hoc complex comparison is

$$CV = (n - 1)(a - 1)F_{\alpha FW; a-1, n-a+1}/(n - a + 1) \qquad (13.25)$$

$$= (13 - 1)(3 - 1)F_{.05; 2, 11}/(13 - 3 + 1)$$

$$= (12)(2)(3.98)/11$$

$$= 8.68$$

Thus, the null hypothesis can be rejected for this contrast, as we know it should, since this is the maximum contrast, and the omnibus null hypothesis was rejected with the multivariate approach.

b. This contrast is essentially a comparison of Time 1 versus Time 2. In fact, we might want to test a contrast with coefficients of 1, -1, and 0, to enhance interpretability.

c. No. We saw in Problem 12 that the mixed-model omnibus test is nonsignificant for these data. This result would seem to suggest that it would be fruitless to search for a post hoc contrast to test. In fact, however, we saw in part (a) that it is possible to find a statistically significant post hoc contrast by using a separate error term. Thus, we cannot necessarily trust the mixed-model test to inform us as to whether we should pursue tests of post hoc contrasts, if we use a separate error term. However, the multivariate test will be statistically significant if and only if a significant contrast exists when we use a separate error term (remember from Problem 12 that the multivariate test was significant for these data). This agreement (or "coherence") between the multivariate test and the use of a separate error term is a major reason for preferring the multivariate approach to the mixed-model approach.

Chapter 14

5. a. The omnibus effects are the A main effect, the B main effect, and the $A \times B$ interaction.

b. A main effect requires $a - 1$ D variables, or 2 D variables in this particular design. B main effect requires $b - 1$ D variables, or 3 D variables in this particular design. $A \times B$ interaction requires $(a - 1)(b - 1)$ D variables, or 6 D variables in this particular design.

c.

	General Form of Degrees of Freedom		**Degrees of Freedom in This Design**	
Effect	Num	Denom	Num	Denom
A	$a - 1$	$n - a + 1$	2	18
B	$b - 1$	$n - b + 1$	3	17
$A \times B$	$(a - 1)(b - 1)$	$n - [(a - 1)(b - 1)]$	6	14

8. a. The appropriate multiple comparison procedure for testing all pairwise comparisons of a within-subjects factor is the Bonferroni method. With 3 levels of A, there are 3 pairwise comparisons of the marginal means, so $C = 3$. The denominator degrees of freedom equal $n - 1$, or 19. From Appendix Table A.3, the value of the critical Bonferroni F is 6.89.

b. If post hoc complex comparisons were also to be tested, the Roy-Bose procedure would be used, in which case the critical value would be

$$CV = (n-1)(a-1)F_{\alpha FW;a-1,n-a+1}/(n-a+1) \qquad (14.31)$$
$$= (20-1)(3-1)F_{.05;3-1,20-3+1}/(20-3+1)$$
$$= (19)(2)(3.55)/18$$
$$= 7.49$$

Notice that the larger critical value here than for the Bonferroni procedure in part (a) reflects the greater protection needed for testing complex comparisons.

c. Equation 33 provides the appropriate critical value for testing a post hoc interaction contrast:

$$CV = (n-1)(a-1)(b-1)F_{\alpha FW;(a-1)(b-1),n-[(a-1)(b-1)]}/(n-[(a-1)(b-1)]) \qquad (14.33)$$
$$= (20-1)(3-1)(4-1)F_{.05;(3-1)(4-1),20-[(3-1)(4-1)]}/(20-[(3-1)(4-1)])$$
$$= (19)(2)(3)F_{.05;6,14}/14$$
$$= (19)(2)(3)(2.85)/14$$
$$= 23.21$$

9. a. At first glance, the answer might seem to be "yes," because the multivariate and mixed-model approaches can yield the same answer for tests involving 1 numerator degree of freedom. However, this agreement occurs only when the error term of the mixed-model approach is $MS_{effect \times S}$. In this problem, the use of this error term would lead to 14 denominator degrees of freedom (that is, $(2-1)$ times $(15-1)$), the same as the multivariate approach. However, the F value reported by the computer program has 98 denominator degrees of freedom. In all likelihood, the computer has used an error term of the form

$$MS_{error} = \frac{SS_{A \times S} + SS_{B \times S} + SS_{A \times B \times S}}{df_{A \times S} + df_{B \times S} + df_{A \times B \times S}}$$

which indeed leads to 98 denominator degrees of freedom. However, this form of error term is not generally recommended, because it requires a stringent sphericity assumption, even for single degree of freedom tests (see the discussion of Equation 12 in Chapter 12 for further information). The important practical point here is that the multivariate test will give a somewhat different result from the reported result, and the multivariate test is generally to be preferred. In general, then, the mixed-model test will differ from the multivariate test unless the numerator degrees of freedom equal 1 *and* the denominator degrees of freedom equal $n-1$.

11. a. They will always be the same, since the A main effect is a between-subjects effect.
    b. They will necessarily be the same only when $b=2$, because then there is a single D variable, so the multivariate approach yields a univariate test.
    c. The answer here is the same as for part (b). Once again, when $b=2$, the multivariate approach yields a univariate test, and the two approaches yield identical answers.

13. a. The test statistic for the A main effect is given by Equation 39:

$$F = \frac{\sum\limits_{j=1}^{a} n_j(\overline{M}_j - \overline{M})^2/(a-1)}{\sum\limits_{j=1}^{a}\sum\limits_{i=1}^{n_j} (M_{ij} - \overline{M}_j)^2/(N-a)} \qquad (14.39)$$

For these data, we know that $a=3$ and $n_1 = n_2 = n_3 = 20$. Further, the group means on the M variable are

$$\overline{M}_1 = (10 + 12)/2$$
$$= 11$$
$$\overline{M}_2 = (16 + 20)/2$$
$$= 18$$
$$\overline{M}_3 = (16 + 16)/2$$
$$= 16,$$

so

$$\overline{M} = (11 + 18 + 16)/3$$
$$= 15$$

In addition, with equal n,

$$\sum_{j=1}^{a} \sum_{i=1}^{n} (M_{ij} - \overline{M}_j)^2/(N - a) = \frac{\sum_{j=1}^{a} s_j^2}{a} \qquad \text{(see 3.63)}$$

$$= \frac{(4)^2 + (6)^2 + (5)^2}{3}$$

$$= 25.67$$

Making the appropriate substitutions into the formula for the F statistic yields

$$F = \frac{20[(11 - 15)^2 + (18 - 15)^2 + (16 - 15)^2]/(3 - 1)}{25.67}$$

$$= 10.13$$

The critical F value with 2 numerator and 57 denominator degrees of freedom is approximately 3.23 (see Appendix Table A.2), so the A main effect is significant at the .05 level.

b. The test statistic for the B main effect is given by Equation 47:

$$F = \frac{N\overline{D}^2}{\sum_{j=1}^{a} \sum_{i=1}^{n_j} (D_{ij} - \overline{D}_j)^2/(N - a)} \qquad (14.47)$$

For these data,

$$N = \sum_{j=1}^{a} n_j$$
$$= 20 + 20 + 20$$
$$= 60$$

Further, the grand mean of D can be found as follows:

$$\overline{D} = \frac{\overline{D}_1 + \overline{D}_2 + \overline{D}_3}{3}$$

$$= \frac{(12 - 10) + (20 - 16) + (16 - 16)}{3}$$

$$= 2.00$$

In addition, with equal n,

$$\sum_{j=1}^{a}\sum_{i=1}^{n}(D_{ij}-\bar{D}_j)^2/(N-a) = \frac{\sum_{j=1}^{a}s_j^2}{a} \qquad \text{(see 3.63)}$$

$$= \frac{(6)^2+(4)^2+(4)^2}{3}$$

$$= 22.67$$

Substituting these values, along with $a = 3$, into Equation 47 yields

$$F = \frac{60(2.00)^2}{22.67}$$

$$= 10.59$$

The critical F value with 1 numerator and 57 denominator degrees of freedom is approximately 4.08 (see Appendix Table A.2), so the B main effect is significant at the .05 level.

c. The test statistic for the $A \times B$ interaction is given by

$$F = \frac{\sum_{j=1}^{a}n_j(\bar{D}_j-\bar{D})^2/(a-1)}{\sum_{j=1}^{a}\sum_{i=1}^{n_j}(D_{ij}-\bar{D}_j)^2/(N-a)}$$

For these data, we know that $a = 3$ and that $n_1 = n_2 = n_3 = 20$. Further, as we saw in part (b),

$$\bar{D}_1 = 12 - 10$$

$$= 2$$

$$\bar{D}_2 = 20 - 16$$

$$= 4$$

$$\bar{D}_3 = 16 - 16$$

$$= 0$$

so

$$\bar{D} = (2+4+0)/3$$

$$= 2$$

In addition, as in part (b), with equal n,

$$\sum_{j=1}^{a}\sum_{i=1}^{n}(D_{ij}-\bar{D}_j)^2/(N-a) = \frac{\sum_{j=1}^{a}s_j^2}{a} \qquad \text{(see 3.63)}$$

$$= \frac{(6)^2+(4)^2+(4)^2}{3}$$

$$= 22.67$$

Substituting these values into the formula for the F statistic yields

$$F = \frac{20[(2-2)^2+(4-2)^2+(0-2)^2]/(3-1)}{22.67}$$

$$= 3.53$$

The critical F value with 2 numerator and 57 denominator degrees of freedom is approximately 3.23 (see Appendix Table A.2), so the $A \times B$ interaction is significant at the .05 level.

17. It is necessary to realize several facts in order to arrive at the proper critical value. First, this contrast is a within-subjects comparison of cell means. As such, the error term can either be based on those particular cells (see Equation 66), or pooled over levels of the between-subjects factor (see Equation 67). The student decided to pool over levels of the between-subjects factor, so Equation 67 was used to calculate an observed F value. Second, the appropriate critical value to accompany Equation 67 is given by Equation 69:

$$CV = (N - a)(b - 1)F_{\alpha FW; b-1, N-a-b+2}/(N - a - b + 2) \qquad (14.69)$$

From Problem 16, we know that $N = 45$, since the student had 15 subjects in each of his 3 groups. We also know that $a = 3$ and $b = 4$. Finally, we know that $\alpha_{FW} = .05$ here, since he wants to maintain his alpha level at .05 within this level of A. Making these substitutions into Equation 69 yields

$$CV = (45 - 3)(4 - 1)F_{.05; 4-1, 45-3-4+2}/(45 - 3 - 4 + 2)$$
$$= (42)(3)F_{.05; 3, 40}/40$$
$$= (42)(3)(2.84)/40$$
$$= 8.95$$

Because the observed F value of 4.13 is less than the critical value of 8.95, the contrast is nonsignificant.

19. a. The three-way interaction requires the formation of difference variables for the within-subjects factor. With 4 levels of the within-subjects factor, there will be 3 such D (that is, difference) variables.

b. Suppose that we label the first D variable as D_1 and that we represent the score for subject i at level j of the first between-subjects factor and level k of the second between-subjects factor as D_{1ijk}. Then the full model can be written as

$$D_{1ijk} = \mu_1 + \alpha_{1j} + \beta_{1k} + (\alpha\beta)_{1jk} + \varepsilon_{1ijk}$$

The three-way interaction is tested by restricting the two-way $(\alpha\beta)_{1jk}$ parameters for each within-subjects difference variable to be equal to zero. As a consequence, the restricted model for D_1 is given by

$$D_{1ijk} = \mu_1 + \alpha_{1j} + \beta_{1k} + \varepsilon_{1ijk}$$

c. From Table 14.16, the numerator degrees of freedom will equal pd_H, where p is the number of dependent variables, and d_H is the number of independent restricted parameters per dependent variable. From part (a), we know that there are 3 dependent variables, so $p = 3$. From part (b), the restricted model omitted the $(\alpha\beta)_{1jk}$ parameters. With 3 levels of one factor and 2 levels of the other, the number of independent restricted interaction parameters is $(3 - 1)(2 - 1)$, or 2. Thus, $d_H = 2$. The numerator degrees of freedom equal $(3)(2)$, or 6. Notice that this is the same value we would obtain if all three factors were between-subjects, or if all three were within-subjects, or any other combination. Although the denominator degrees of freedom will depend on the particular design (that is, the specific combination of between- and within-subjects factors), the numerator degrees of freedom will be the same regardless of which factors are between-subjects and which are within-subjects.

d. From Table 14.16, we find that the denominator degrees of freedom for the three-way interaction will equal

$$df_{den} = mq - .5pd_H + 1$$

where m is defined as

$$m = N - g + d_H - .5(p + d_H + 1)$$

and q is defined as

$$q = \sqrt{\frac{(pd_H)^2 - 4}{p^2 + d_H^2 - 5}}$$

We know that $p = 3$ and $d_H = 2$ (from part (c)), the total number of subjects is $N = 60$ (that is, 10 subjects for each of the 3×2 cells), and the number of distinct groups of subjects is $g = 6$ (that is, 3×2). Making the appropriate substitutions yields

$$m = N - g + d_H - .5(p + d_H + 1)$$
$$= 60 - 6 + 2 - .5(3 + 2 + 1)$$
$$= 53$$

$$q = \sqrt{\frac{(pd_H)^2 - 4}{p^2 + d_H^2 - 5}}$$
$$= \sqrt{\frac{[(3)(2)]^2 - 4}{(3)^2 + (2)^2 - 5}}$$
$$= \sqrt{\frac{32}{8}}$$
$$= 2$$

Thus, the denominator degrees of freedom equal

$$df_{den} = mq - .5pd_H + 1$$
$$= (53)(2) - .5(3)(2) + 1$$
$$= 104$$

Chapter 15

1. False. F^* can be more powerful than F when sample sizes are unequal and population variances are also unequal.

7. False. Simulation studies have shown that the Kruskal-Wallis test is sensitive to heterogeneity of variance when sample sizes are unequal. F^* and W are usually better alternatives in this situation.

8. a.

$$F = \frac{\sum_{j=1}^{a} n_j(\bar{Y}_j - \bar{Y})^2/(a - 1)}{\sum_{j=1}^{a} (n_j - 1)s_j^2/(N - a)}$$

For these data,

$$\bar{Y} = \frac{(20)(10) + (20)(12) + (50)(14)}{20 + 20 + 50}$$

$$= 12.6667$$

so

$$\sum_{j=1}^{a} n_j(\bar{Y}_j - \bar{Y})^2 = 20[(10 - 12.6667)^2] + 20[(12 - 12.6667)^2]$$

$$+ 50[(14 - 12.6667)^2]$$

$$= 240.00$$

In addition,

$$\sum_{j=1}^{a} (n_j - 1)s_j^2/(N - a) = \frac{19(10) + 19(10) + 49(50)}{87}$$

$$= 32.5287$$

Thus,

$$F = \frac{240.00/2}{32.5287}$$

$$= 3.69$$

b.

$$F^* = \frac{\displaystyle\sum_{j=1}^{a} n_j(\bar{Y}_j - \bar{Y})^2}{\displaystyle\sum_{j=1}^{a} (1 - (n_j/N))s_j^2}$$

We discovered in part (a) that

$$\sum_{j=1}^{a} n_j(\bar{Y}_j - \bar{Y})^2 = 240.00$$

The denominator of F^* equals

$$\sum_{j=1}^{a} (1 - (n_j/N))s_j^2 = \left(1 - \frac{20}{90}\right)(10) + \left(1 - \frac{20}{90}\right)(10) + \left(1 - \frac{50}{90}\right)(50)$$

$$= 7.7778 + 7.7778 + 22.2222$$

$$= 37.7778$$

Thus,

$$F^* = \frac{240.00}{37.7778}$$

$$= 6.35$$

c.

$$W = \frac{\displaystyle\sum_{j=1}^{a} w_j(\bar{Y}_j - \tilde{Y})^2/(a - 1)}{[1 + \frac{2}{3}(a - 2)\Lambda]}$$

where

$$w_j = n_j/s_j^2$$

$$\tilde{Y} = \sum_{j=1}^{a} w_j \bar{Y}_j \bigg/ \sum_{j=1}^{a} w_j$$

$$\Lambda = \frac{3 \sum_{j=1}^{a} \left[\left(1 - \left(w_j \bigg/ \sum_{j=1}^{a} w_j \right) \right)^2 \bigg/ (n_j - 1) \right]}{a^2 - 1}$$

For these data,

$$w_1 = 20/10 = 2$$
$$w_2 = 20/10 = 2$$
$$w_3 = 50/50 = 1$$

Further,

$$\tilde{Y} = \frac{2(10) + 2(12) + 1(14)}{2 + 2 + 1}$$

$$= 11.6$$

and

$$\Lambda = \frac{3[((1 - \frac{2}{5})^2/19) + ((1 - \frac{2}{5})^2/19) + (1 - \frac{1}{5})^2/49)]}{(3)^2 - 1}$$

$$= \frac{3(.01895 + .01895 + .01306)}{8}$$

$$= .01911$$

Thus,

$$W = \frac{2(10 - 11.6)^2 + 2(12 - 11.6)^2 + 1(14 - 11.6)^2/2}{1 + (2/3)(1)(.01911)}$$

$$= \frac{(5.12 + .32 + 5.76)/2}{1.01274}$$

$$= 5.53$$

d. Yes, the F value obtained in part (a) is substantially lower than either F^* from part (b) or W from part (c). When large samples are paired with large sample variances, as in this example, F will be smaller than F^* or W. When this pattern holds for population variances, F will tend to be conservative, while F^* and W will tend to be robust.

10. a. The Kruskal-Wallis test provides a nonparametric analysis of these data. The first step in applying the test is to rank order all observations in the entire set of N subjects. Replacing each score with its rank (where 1 = lowest and 18 = highest) for these data yields the following values.

	Group 1	Group 2	Group 3
	4	11.5	17
	7.5	2	13.5
	3	5	6
	7.5	15	11.5
	13.5	1	16
	9	10	18
Mean Rank	**7.4167**	**7.4167**	**13.6667**

The Kruskal-Wallis test statistic is given by Equation 7:

$$H = \frac{12}{N(N+1)} \sum_{j=1}^{a} n_j (\bar{R}_j - ((N+1)/2))^2 \tag{15.7}$$

$$= \frac{12}{18(19)} [6(7.4167 - 9.5000)^2 + 6(7.4167 - 9.5000)^2 + 6(13.6667 - 9.5000)^2]$$

$$= (.03509)(26.0408 + 26.0408 + 104.1683)$$

$$= 5.48$$

Because there are tied observations the correction factor T should be applied, where

$$T = 1 - \frac{\sum_{i=1}^{G} (t_i^3 - t_i)}{N^3 - N}$$

There are 3 sets of tied scores (at 7.5, 11.5, and 13.5), so $G = 3$.

In each case, there are 2 observations tied at the value, so $t_1 = 2, t_2 = 2$, and $t_3 = 2$. Thus, the correction factor for these data is

$$T = 1 - \frac{(2^3 - 2) + (2^3 - 2) + (2^3 - 2)}{(18)^3 - 18}$$

$$= 1 - \frac{6 + 6 + 6}{5814}$$

$$= .9969$$

The corrected test statistic H' equals

$$H' = H/T$$

$$= 5.48/.9969$$

$$= 5.50$$

The critical value is a chi-square with $a - 1$, or 2, degrees of freedom. At the .05 level, the critical value is 5.99 (see Appendix Table A.9), so the null hypothesis cannot be rejected.

b. The joint ranking approach uses the same ranks that were computed in part (a). Two groups are significantly different from one another if the absolute value of the difference between their mean ranks exceeds a critical value of $\omega^* q_{\alpha_{FW}, a, \infty}$. For these data,

$$\omega^* = [(N(N+1)/12n) - \sum_{i=1}^{G} (t_i^3 - t_i)/12n(N-1)]^{1/2}$$

$$= \sqrt{[18(19)/12(6)] - \frac{(2^3 - 2) + (2^3 - 2) + (2^3 - 2)}{12(6)(17)}}$$

$$= \sqrt{4.75 - .01}$$

$$= 2.18$$

and

$$q_{.05;3,\infty} = 3.31$$

Thus, the critical mean difference is 7.21 (that is, 2.18 times 3.31). However, the largest mean difference in ranks in these data is only 6.25 (that is, 13.6667 minus 7.4167), so none of the pairwise comparisons is significant.

c. The pairwise ranking approach requires that scores be ranked for each particular pair of groups. In these data, we have:

	Groups 1 and 2		Groups 1 and 3		Groups 2 and 3	
	1	*2*	*1*	*3*	*2*	*3*
	4	10	2	11	6.5	11
	6.5	2	4.5	8.5	2	8
	3	5	1	3	3	4
	6.5	12	4.5	7	9	6.5
	11	1	8.5	10	1	10
	8	9	6	12	5	12
Mean Rank	**6.5**	6.5	4.4167	8.5833	4.4167	8.5833

For these particular data, Groups 1 and 2 are obviously not significantly different. In addition, the comparison of Groups 1 and 3 is identical to the comparison of Groups 2 and 3, except that the latter has one fewer set of ties. Thus, the value of the test statistic H is the same for both comparisons, for these data:

$$H = \frac{12}{N(N+1)} \sum_{j=1}^{a} n_j(\bar{R}_j - ((N+1)/2))^2 \qquad (15.7)$$

$$= \frac{12}{12(13)} [6(4.4167 - 6.5000)^2 + 6(8.5833 - 6.5000)^2]$$

$$= 4.01$$

For comparing Groups 1 and 3,

$$T = 1 - \frac{\sum_{i=1}^{G} (t_i^3 - t_i)}{N^3 - N}$$

$$= 1 - \frac{(2^3 - 2) + (2^3 - 2)}{12^3 - 12}$$

$$= .9930$$

so

$$H' = H/T$$

$$= 4.04$$

For comparing Groups 2 and 3,

$$T = 1 - \frac{(2^3 - 2)}{12^3 - 12}$$

$$= .9965$$

so

$$H' = H/T$$

$$= 4.02$$

To maintain the familywise alpha level at .05, the Bonferroni method should be used. The critical value comes from the chi-square distribution with 1 degree of freedom, and $\alpha = .05/3$. Because the chi-square with 1 degree of freedom is the square of a standard normal variable, tables of the standard normal distribution can be used here. For $\alpha = .05/3$, the critical z is 2.39, so the critical chi-square is 5.71. None of the observed chi-square values exceeds the critical value, so none of the pairwise differences is significant at $\alpha_{FW} = .05$.

d. To test a complex comparison, it is necessary to use the joint rankings of parts (a) and (b):

$$\bar{R}_1 = 7.4167$$
$$\bar{R}_2 = 7.4167$$
$$\bar{R}_3 = 13.6667$$

The coefficients for this contrast can be written as

$$c_1 = 1$$
$$c_2 = 1$$
$$c_3 = -2$$

The contrast is statistically significant if

$$(\hat{\psi})^2/\text{Var}(\hat{\psi}) > X^2_{a-1}$$

where

$$\hat{\psi} = \sum_{j=1}^{a} c_j \bar{R}_j$$
$$= 1(7.4167) + 1(7.4167) - 2(13.6667)$$
$$= -12.50$$

and

$$\text{Var}(\hat{\psi}) = (N(N+1)/12)\left(\sum_{j=1}^{a} c_j^2/n_j\right)$$
$$= (18(19)/12)(\tfrac{1}{6} + \tfrac{1}{6} + \tfrac{4}{6})$$
$$= 28.50$$

Thus,

$$(\hat{\psi})^2/\text{Var}(\hat{\psi}) = (-12.50)^2/28.50$$
$$= 5.48$$

The critical chi-square with 2 degrees of freedom is 5.99 (see Appendix Table A.9), so the contrast is not statistically significant at $\alpha_{FW} = .05$. As an aside, notice that the value of

$$(\hat{\psi})^2/\text{Var}(\hat{\psi})$$

for this contrast equals the H value we calculated in part (a) for the omnibus test, because the coefficients of 1, 1, and -2 reflect the maximum contrast for these data.

Name Index

Subject Index